FROMMER'S

COMPREHENSIVE TRAVEL GUIDE

ENGLAND & SCOTLAND '91

by Darwin Porter
Assisted by Danforth Prince

PRENTICE
HALL
PRESS

NEW YORK • LONDON • TORONTO • SYDNEY • TOKYO • SINGAPORE

FROMMER BOOKS

Published by Prentice Hall Press
A division of Simon & Schuster Inc.
15 Columbus Circle
New York, NY 10023

ISBN 0-13-326844-6
ISSN 1044-2359

**PRENTICE
HALL
PRESS**

Manufactured in the United States of America

CONTENTS

Introduction ENGLAND & SCOTLAND   1
1. Orientation   1
2. Using This Guide   3

I. GETTING THERE, GETTING AROUND   5
1. Plane Economics   5
2. Traveling by Ship   9
3. Traveling Within Britain   10
4. Alternative and Special-Interest Travel   15
5. Fast Facts for Britain   21

PART ONE

ENGLAND

II. INTRODUCING ENGLAND   31
1. The English   34
2. The Culture   37
3. Food and Drink   41

III. SETTLING INTO LONDON   44
1. Orientation   45
2. Mayfair   58
3. St. James's   62
4. Piccadilly   64
5. The Strand and Covent Garden   66
6. Holborn   69
7. Westminster   69
8. Victoria   70
9. Belgravia   71
10. Knightsbridge   72
11. Chelsea   77
12. Chelsea Harbour   79
13. Earl's Court   80
14. Kensington   81
15. South Kensington   82
16. Notting Hill Gate   86
17. Holland Park   87
18. Lancaster Gate   87
19. Paddington/Bayswater   88
20. St. Marylebone   89

21. Bloomsbury 92
22. Other Locales 93
23. Airport Hotels 96

IV. LONDON'S RESTAURANTS AND PUBS   99
1. The West End 100
2. Other Locales 123
3. Specialty Dining 127
4. Pubs of London 129
5. Wine Bars 136

V. WHAT TO SEE AND DO IN LONDON   141
1. Seeing the Sights 141
2. Kids' London 166
3. Taking the Tours 170
4. Shopping for Value 172
5. Evening Entertainment 188
6. One-Day Trips from London 202

VI. WINDSOR, OXFORD, AND THE HOME
COUNTIES   209
1. Windsor 210
2. Ascot 217
3. Henley-on-Thames 218
4. Inns Along the Thames 219
5. Oxford 220
6. Woodstock (Blenheim Palace) 230
7. Hertfordshire 231
8. Buckinghamshire 234
9. Bedfordshire (Woburn Abbey) 239

VII. KENT, SURREY, AND SUSSEX   243
1. Kent's Country Houses, Castles, and Gardens 246
2. Canterbury 250
3. Dover 254
4. Royal Tunbridge Wells 255
5. Richmond 258
6. Haslemere 259
7. Guildford 260
8. Dorking 261
9. Rye and Winchelsea 263
10. Hastings and St. Leonards 266
11. Battle 268
12. Alfriston and Lewes 269
13. Brighton and Hove 271
14. Arundel 277
15. Chichester 279

VIII. HAMPSHIRE AND DORSET   283
1. Portsmouth and Southsea   284
2. Southampton   289
3. The New Forest   291
4. Isle of Wight   294
5. Winchester   297
6. Bournemouth   300
7. Shaftesbury   303
8. Wareham   304
9. Dorchester   304
10. Bridport   305
11. Chideock   306
12. Charmouth   307
13. Lyme Regis   307
14. Chedington   308
15. Sherborne   309

IX. DEVON   311
1. Exeter   312
2. Dartmoor   318
3. Chagford   320
4. Torquay   322
5. Totnes   324
6. Dartmouth   325
7. Plymouth   327
8. Milton Damerel   329
9. Clovelly   330
10. Lynton-Lynmouth   331
11. The Taw Valley   332

X. CORNWALL   333
1. Looe   334
2. Polperro   336
3. Fowey   337
4. Truro   338
5. Portloe   339
6. St. Mawes   340
7. Falmouth   341
8. Penzance   343
9. The Isles of Scilly   345
10. Newlyn, Mousehole, and Land's End   348
11. St. Just-in-Penwith   350
12. St. Ives   350
13. Port Isaac   352
14. Tintagel   353
15. Bolventor   354

XI. WILTSHIRE, SOMERSET, AND AVON   355
1. Salisbury   356
2. Castle Combe   363
3. Lacock   364
4. Exmoor National Park   365
5. Dunster   366
6. Taunton   367
7. Glastonbury   368
8. Wells   369
9. The Caves of Mendip   371
10. Bath   372
11. Bristol   379
12. Thornbury   381

XII. THE COTSWOLDS   383
1. Tetbury   384
2. Malmesbury   385
3. Cirencester   386
4. Painswick   387
5. Cheltenham   388
6. Royal Sudeley Castle   390
7. Bibury   391
8. Clanfield   392
9. Burford and Minster Lovell   392
10. Shipton-under-Wychwood   394
11. Chipping Norton   394
12. Bourton-on-the-Water   395
13. Stow-on-the-Wold   396
14. Lower Swell   398
15. The Slaughters   398
16. Moreton-in-Marsh   399
17. Broadway   400
18. Chipping Campden   402

XIII. STRATFORD AND THE HEART OF ENGLAND   404
1. Stratford-upon-Avon   404
2. Warwick   416
3. Kenilworth Castle   419
4. Coventry   420
5. Hereford and Worcester   422
6. Shropshire   428
7. Staffordshire   430

XIV. CAMBRIDGE AND EAST ANGLIA   435
1. Cambridge   436
2. Ely   444

    3. Thaxted 446
    4. Saffron Walden 447
    5. Dedham 448
    6. Newmarket 450
    7. Clare 451
    8. Long Melford 452
    9. Lavenham 453
  10. Woodbridge 454
  11. Aldeburgh 455
  12. East Bergholt 456
  13. Norwich 456
  14. Shipdham 460
  15. North Norfolk 460

XV. EAST MIDLANDS   464
    1. Northamptonshire 464
    2. Leicestershire 467
    3. Derbyshire 470
    4. Nottinghamshire 476
    5. Lincolnshire 480

XVI. CHESHIRE, LIVERPOOL, AND THE LAKES   486
    1. Chester 487
    2. Nantwich 490
    3. Liverpool 491
    4. Cartmel 495
    5. Kendal 496
    6. Windermere 498
    7. Ambleside 499
    8. Rydal 501
    9. Grasmere 501
  10. Hawkshead and Coniston 503
  11. Keswick 505
  12. Borrowdale 506
  13. Bassenthwaite 507
  14. Ullswater 507
  15. Brampton 508

XVII. YORKSHIRE AND NORTHUMBRIA   509
    1. York 510
    2. North Yorkshire 516
    3. West Yorkshire 523
    4. Durham 525
    5. Tyne and Wear 528
    6. Northumberland 530

PART TWO

SCOTLAND

XVIII. INTRODUCING SCOTLAND   539
1. The Country   540
2. Flying to Scotland   544
3. Getting Around Scotland   546
4. Fast Facts for Scotland   548

XIX. SOUTHERN SCOTLAND   554
1. The Border Country   554
2. Burns Country   559
3. Dumfries and Galloway   564

XX. EDINBURGH, GLASGOW, AND CENTRAL SCOTLAND   577
1. Edinburgh   577
2. Day Trips from Edinburgh   601
3. The Kingdom of Fife   608
4. Glasgow and the Clyde   614
5. The Trossachs and Loch Lomond   629

XXI. NORTHEAST SCOTLAND   633
1. Exploring Tayside   633
2. The Grampian Region   647

XXII. HIGHLANDS AND ISLANDS   656
1. Speyside   656
2. Inverness and Loch Ness   666
3. Fort William and Lochaber   672
4. Kyle of Lochalsh and Skye   677
5. Oban and District   682
6. The Inner Hebrides   687
7. Kintyre, Arran, and Islay   693

Index   699

MAPS

England   33
Where to Go from London   35
London   48–49
London Underground   53
Piccadilly   65
Covent Garden   67
Chelsea/Knightsbridge   74–75
Kensington   83
Regent's Park and St. Marylebone   91
Bloomsbury and Russell Square   95
The West End   103
Tottenham Court Road/Charing Cross/Soho   121
The City   155
Oxford   221
Kent, Surrey, and Sussex   245
Southwestern Counties   287
Cornwall and Devon   313
Salisbury   359
Gloucester, Worcester, and Warwick   407
Cambridge   439
East Anglia   449
Yorkshire/Derbyshire/Lincolnshire/Lancaster   474–75
The Lake District   497
Durham and Northumberland   527
Scotland   542–43
Edinburgh   579
Glasgow   617
Highlands and Islands   658
The Whisky Trail   665

A Disclaimer

Readers are advised that prices fluctuate in the course of time and travel information changes under the impact of the varied and volatile factors that affect the travel industry. The authors and publisher cannot be held responsible for the experiences of the reader while traveling. Readers are invited to write the publisher with ideas, comments and suggestions for future editions.

Readers should also note that the establishments described under Readers' Selections or Suggestions have not in all cases been inspected by the authors and that opinions expressed there are those of the individual reader(s) only and do not in any way represent the opinions of the publisher or author(s) of this guide.

Inflation Alert

It is hardly a secret that inflation has affected the countries of northern Europe, and Britain also has been hit. The author of this book has spent laborious hours researching to try and ensure the accuracy of prices appearing in this guide. As we go to press, I believe we have obtained the most reliable data possible. However, I cannot offer guarantees for tariffs quoted.

Britain's VAT

Great Britain has a standard Value Added Tax (called VAT for short) of 15%. Most European Community countries already have a tax similar to VAT (France, for example, has a paralyzing one of 23%). This extra VAT charge will show up on your bill unless otherwise stated. It is in addition to the service charge. Should the service charge in a restaurant by 15%, you will, in effect, by paying 30% higher than the prices quoted. The service charges, if included as part of the bill, are also taxable.

As part of an energy-saving scheme, the British government has also added a special 25% tax on gasoline (petrol).

ENGLAND AND SCOTLAND

1. ORIENTATION
2. USING THIS GUIDE

England, and Scotland too, sent her children across the waves to settle North America, Australia, New Zealand, and a host of other lands. Today the offspring of those children are returning to visit their mother lands at a rate that is practically an invasion.

What's the big attraction?

1. Orientation

England, as in Restoration days, has thrown out the Puritan and is experimenting in all sorts of imaginative, creative ways. Vigorous and exciting changes are taking place, and England today is, in a word, fun. The island may be small, but, like Mighty Mouse, it packs a powerful punch.

On the other hand, Scotland fulfills romantic myths—a land of shimmering lochs, pepper-pot towers and moated castles, clans with bagpipes, and balladeers. Scotland is very different from England. When English people go to Scotland, they are, in effect, "going abroad."

I have set for myself the formidable task of seeking out the best of England and Scotland and condensing it between the covers of a guide. The best includes not only descriptions of hotels, restaurants, pubs, and nightspots, but descriptions of cities, towns, and sightseeing attractions. Part of the philosophy of this book is based on the fact that the best need not be the most expensive. Hence, my ultimate aim— beyond that of familiarizing you with the life of merrie old England and romantic Scotland—is to stretch your dollar power, to show you that you need not always pay scalper's prices for charm, top-grade comfort, and food.

In this guide, I'll devote a great deal of attention to the tourist meccas of London, Edinburgh, Stratford-upon-Avon, and Oxford. But these ancient cities and towns are not the full "reason why" of the book. Important as they are, they simply do not fully reflect the complexity and diversity of both countries. Unlike most nations of Europe, England and Scotland defy a clear, logical, coherent plan of sightseeing. Both lands are a patchwork quilt of treasures, with many of the most scenic items tucked away in remote corners—an Elizabethan country estate in Devon, a half-timbered thatched cottage by the sea in Cornwall, a Regency manor in the Lake District, an old whitewashed coaching inn at Loch Ness.

Meeting the English and the Scots is perhaps the most important reason for making the trip. If possible, try to arrive with few preconceptions. For example, generalizing about the character of the English in a land filled with "soopah" dukes, cockney porters, Rudyard Kipling adventurers, and Miss Marple–type ladies is fraught with hazards. Suffice it to say, they'll surprise you—particularly if you think of the English as a cold, snobbish, withdrawn people. A few visits to the haunts of Soho, or to a local pub for a "lager and lime," or even a look at the racy London tabloids, will cure you of stereotypes.

A TRAVELER'S ADVISORY

You should take the figures quoted in this guide only as an indication of the regular charges of a hotel or other establishment. Almost all hotels have special offers at various times of year, and some, such as the Priory in Bath, may offer as much as a 40% discount for a two-night stay.

The standard of **cooking**, the use of high-quality products, and the current wave of chefs born, bred, and trained in England and Scotland has led to the appearance, during the last few years, of a number of pleasant small hotels where the main attractions for guests are the cooking and the comfort. These hotels are generally in attractive buildings on the outskirts of interesting towns. "Very Professional Amateurs" is how one food writer described the chef-proprietors of these new-wave restaurants and inns, dozens of which I have included in this edition. *A word of warning*, however: Don't be misled by prominently displayed plaques denoting awards for the culinary arts. If you wish to use such an award as a quick guide, ask if the chef who won it is still in charge of the kitchens. I have found on occasion that the hotel/restaurant claims the award, while the chef who actually earned it has already moved on.

Also, many of these places do not permit smoking in the dining room or anywhere near it, so check this out before you light up.

The historic buildings for which the country is famous are well worth a visit, although many top places, such as Woburn Abbey, find it uneconomical to remain open during the winter, except on Saturday and Sunday. Security staffing costs are astronomical, I am told. Also, many of the fine houses looked after by the National Trust close at the end of October and do not reopen until the following Easter. However, there are still many places to see for the winter visitor who seeks history and a taste of the real Britain.

Traveling in Britain is becoming easier, as many destinations are now served by economical express buses, which are equipped with aircraft-type reclining seats, toilets, TV, and a host who serves light refreshments. Train service continues to improve, and although porters are often hard to find, the railways are becoming highly competitive with airlines for internal travel. Some services even have telephones now. Improved night-sleeper accommodations enable you to enjoy dinner and the theater in London, catch the train, and be awakened for coffee and cookies before you arrive for breakfast in Scotland. Airlines offer all sorts of special tickets.

If you are writing for information to one of the organizations or individuals mentioned in this book, it is important that you include an **International Reply Coupon,** obtainable from your local post office. It won't cover the full cost of reply postage, but it helps. Remember that yours is probably only one of many inquiries.

Many visitors wonder what **VAT (Value Added Tax)** is. This is a Common Market tax, set in 1979 at 15% for Britain, which is lower than in some other Common Market countries. Basically, the tax is added to your hotel or restaurant bill, unless otherwise stated. Restaurants must include the tax in menu prices displayed outside their premises. In most stores and shops, it is included in the price of the item you purchase. If in doubt, ask if VAT is included or must be added to the cost of accommodation, food, or goods. If you wish to export an item on which the tax is charged, you can avoid paying it, provided certain requirements are fulfilled, but you must arrange this at the time of purchase and complete the appropriate forms.

---

2. Using This Guide

This guidebook gives specific, practical details (including prices) about the hotels, restaurants, pubs, sightseeing attractions, and nightlife of England and Scotland. First-class to budget establishments have been documented and described, from the elegant Park Lane Hotel in London to a bed-and-breakfast house in an old fishing village in Scotland. Each establishment has been judged by the strict yardstick of value.

The major focus of the book is on the average voyager who'd like to patronize the almost wholly undocumented establishments of England and Scotland—that is, the second-class hotels and some of the better, although less-heralded, restaurants where you can often get a superb dinner.

The sights of England and Scotland have been set forth in what I believe is a human, personal, and practical style. In both England and Scotland, the bewildered visitor is faced with a staggering number of attractions from the most catholic collection of art and artifacts in the world (the British Museum), to George Washington's ancestral home (Sulgrave Manor), to Anne Hathaway's Cottage at Stratford-upon-Avon, to some of the Scottish castles where Mary Queen of Scots lived during her brief, tragic reign.

Frommer guides attempt to lead readers through the maze of important sights, such as the Tower of London and Edinburgh Castle, then introduce them to a number of lesser-known locales, such as the little hamlets, flint churches, and historic houses of East Anglia, or perhaps the mellow old towns of the Scottish "Borders." The hours and prices of admission to these attractions have been detailed.

SOME DISCLAIMERS

No restaurant, inn, hotel, guesthouse, or shop paid to be mentioned in this book. What you read are personal recommendations—in many cases, proprietors never knew their establishments were being investigated.

A word of warning: Unfortunately, prices change, and they rarely go downward, at least not in Britain. The government does not control hotel prices, as is customary in Spain and Italy. Always inquire about the price—and agree on it—when checking into a hotel or reserving a room. This policy can save much embarrassment and disappointment when it comes time to settle the tab. In no circumstances can you invariably demand to be charged the price quoted in this book, although every effort has been made to state the accurate tariff as much as it was foreseeable when this guide was published.

This guide is revised every year, yet even in a book that appears fresh annually it may happen that that cozy little family dining room changes colors, blossoming out with cut-velvet walls and dining tabs that include the decorator's fee and the owner's new Bentley. It may be that some of the people, animals, and settings I've described are no longer there or have been changed beyond recognition.

AN INVITATION TO READERS

Like all the Frommer books, Frommer's *England and Scotland* hopes to maintain a continuing dialogue between its author and its readers. All of us share a common aim—to travel as widely and as well as possible, at the best value for our money. And in achieving that goal, your comments and suggestions can be of tremendous help. Therefore, if you come across a particularly appealing hotel, restaurant, store, even sightseeing attraction, please don't keep it to yourself. The solicitation for letters applies not only to new establishments, but to hotels or restaurants already recommended in this guide. The fact that a listing appears in this edition doesn't give it squatter's rights in future publications. If its services have deteriorated, its chef grown stale, its prices risen unfairly, whatever, these failings should be known. Even if you enjoyed every place and found every description accurate—that, too, can cheer many a gray day. Send your comments to Darwin Porter, c/o Prentice Hall Press, 15 Columbus Circle, New York, NY 10023.

TIME OUT FOR A COMMERCIAL

Even a book as fat as this one does not pretend to have covered fully the budget accommodations of Great Britain. Frommer's *England and Scotland* is a wide-ranging survey of accommodations, mainly hotels, as well as restaurants and other attractions. However, if you'd like to economize seriously but still maintain a good standard of living, you may want to go what is known as the "B&B route." B&B, of course, means "bed-and-breakfast," and the British invented the term.

A companion guide to this one, Frommer's *England on $50 a Day,* documents hundreds of budget accommodations, most often guesthouses, as well as low-cost restaurants serving good food at very reasonable prices, and dozens and dozens of pubs throughout the land.

Many budget travelers will want to venture beyond the borders of England and discover Scotland to the north and Wales to the west. With those people in mind, we offer a separate guide, Frommer's *Scotland and Wales on $50 a Day,* which covers the two countries sharing the same island with England. How close they are geographically, but how different they are culturally.

Like its older sister guide to England, the book on Scotland and Wales is written in the same theme, describing hundreds of budget hotels and inns, B&B houses, restaurants, tearooms, and pubs—usually offbeat favorites that offer the most authentic and enriching travel experience. In addition, budget-conscious travelers will find the information they need on low-cost transportation, shopping bargains, and inexpensive nightlife. Because of space limitations, this guide contains only the highlights of Scotland, whereas the book devoted to Scotland presents a full survey, including chapters on the more remote provinces and all the famous Hebridean islands, as well as the Shetlands and Orkneys. Even the Isle of Man, lonely and isolated in the Irish Sea, is included.

Frommer's Dollarwise Travel Club—How To Save Money On All Your Travels

In this book we'll be looking at how to get your money's worth in England and Scotland, but there is a "device" for saving money and determining value on all your trips. It's the popular, international Frommer's Dollarwise Travel Club, now in its 31st successful year of operation. The club was formed at the urging of numerous readers of the $-A-Day and Frommer Guides, who felt that such an organization could provide continuing travel information and a sense of community to value-minded travelers in all parts of the world. And so it does!

The club publishes a quarterly newspaper, **The Dollarwise® Traveler,** that keeps you up to date on fastbreaking developments in low-cost travel in all parts of the world, and brings you not only the latest money-saving information but also new ideas for travel with a difference as well as all the new information about your favorite, familiar places. For details about the Dollarwise Travel Club, turn to the last pages of this book.

I

GETTING THERE, GETTING AROUND

1. PLANE ECONOMICS

2. TRAVELING BY SHIP

3. TRAVELING WITHIN BRITAIN

4. ALTERNATIVE AND SPECIAL-INTEREST TRAVEL

5. FAST FACTS FOR BRITAIN

The deregulation of the airline industry made world headlines in 1979, and since that time any vestiges of uniformity in price structures for transatlantic flights have disappeared. Airlines compete fiercely with one another, offering a confusing barrage of pricing systems and package deals, each straining the capacities of anyone trying to sort the system into a coherent whole. Travel agents refer to the masses of documentation they receive daily as "chaos." However, that can mean beneficial to the alert traveler willing to study and consider all the options available.

1. Plane Economics

The best strategy for securing the least expensive airfare is to shop around and, above all, remain as flexible as possible. Keep calling the airlines or your travel agent. Sometimes you can purchase a ticket that is lower in price at the last minute. If the flight is not fully booked, an airline might discount ticket prices in an attempt to achieve a full passenger load.

Most airlines charge different fares according to the season. For the pricing of flights to Europe, midsummer months are the peak travel times when fares are the most expensive. Basic season, which falls (with just a few exceptions) in the winter months, offers the least expensive fares. Travel during Christmas and Easter weeks is usually more expensive than in the weeks just before or after those holidays. The periods between basic and peak seasons are termed "shoulder."

Even within the various seasons, airlines offer a variety of seating arrangements, ranging from first class through business and economy classes. Most airlines also offer heavily discounted promotional fares available erratically according to last-minute market plans. But, be warned: the less expensive your ticket is, the more stringent the restrictions. These restrictions will most often include advance purchase, a minimum stay abroad, and cancellation or alteration penalties. The most common and frequently used such fare is the APEX or advance purchase excursion.

Also note that prices tend to be higher in many classes on weekends, which, depending on the airline, is usually defined as Friday, Saturday, and Sunday.

THE AIRLINES

Several airlines fly the enormously popular routes from North America to Great Britain. In fact, you have a greater choice of flights to Britain than you do to any other country outside of North America in the world. Some of these airlines include the company with more flights into London than any other, British Airways, as well as American Airlines, Delta, Pam Am, TWA, and such smaller carriers as Virgin Atlantic.

Many passengers prefer to fly the national carrier of the nation they intend to visit as an advance preview into its manners and methods. **British Airways** (BA) is the premier airline and national carrier of the United Kingdom, and, since its partial privatization several years ago, a model of the newly energized face of British business. It offers flights to London from at least 19 different U.S. cities, a fact that makes time-consuming transfers through New York unnecessary for visitors coming from such cities as Boston, Washington, D.C., Atlanta, Denver, Hartford, and many others. It also flies to London from Bermuda and San Juan, Puerto Rico. BA offers five daily nonstop flights to Britain from the New York area, including one to Manchester from JFK Airport, three to Heathrow Airpot from JFK, and a recent addition of one to Heathrow from Newark.

At New York's JFK, British Airways is the only non–U.S. based carrier to have its own terminal. BA is one of the two airlines offering seats on the most sophisticated commercial aircraft in the world, the supersonic Concorde. Its terminal 4 at London's Heathrow and its North Terminal at Gatwick Airport (on the periphery of London) are considered among the most up-to-date and best-designed in the world. For reservations and information, call toll free at 800/247-9297.

The competition, however, is stiff in the transatlantic wars between airlines for consumer business, and many passengers have strong individual preferences in their choice of airlines.

American Airlines offers daily service to Gatwick from Dallas. It also features daily service from Chicago's O'Hare Airport to both Manchester and Glasgow. Call toll free 800/433-7300.

Delta, depending on the season, makes either one or two nonstop flights every day between its headquarters in Atlanta and Gatwick. Seasonal discounts often apply, so residents of America's Southeast are well advised to research carefully the current schedules of this carrier. Delta's toll free number for its international routes is 800/241-4141.

Northwest Airlines flies from both Minneapolis and Boston, usually nonstop, to Gatwick. It has good connections from Detroit to Gatwick through Boston. Call toll free 800/225-2525.

Pam Am makes nonstop runs from JFK to Heathrow three times a day. Pan Am also makes daily nonstop service from Detroit, Miami, San Francisco, and Washington, D.C. (Dulles). It flies five times a week to London from Los Angeles and three times a week from Seattle. Call toll free 800/221-1600.

Air Canada flies to Heathrow nonstop from Calgary (four times a week), from Toronto and from Montréal's Mirabel Airport (daily), from Edmonton (three times a week), and from Vancouver once a week. (Other flights from Vancouver to London are funneled through Edmonton or Toronto.) Call toll free 800/422-6232.

TWA flies from both St. Louis and Chicago to Heathrow daily, and to Heathrow from JFK three times daily. It also flies to Gatwick Airport from St. Louis once a day nonstop, and to London from Los Angeles, Boston, and Baltimore. Call toll free 800/221-2000.

Long considered a no-frills alternative to Western Europe's larger airlines, **Virgin Atlantic Airways** now offers services and amenities comparable to those of most major carriers. Owned by the same people who spin Virgin Atlantic Records and several of London's more unusual nightclubs, the airline offers competitive prices for its flights to London from JFK, Newark, Miami, and Los Angeles. Depending on their origin, flights leave between four and seven times a week. Call toll free 800/862-8621.

TYPES OF FARES

Generally, your cheapest option on a regular airline is to book an APEX fare. This is the most heavily used fare to London from North America on any airline, although its exact definition can vary widely even within the same airline. British Airways, for example, offers two types of APEX fares. The least expensive is a non-refundable 30-day advance purchase that requires a 7- to 21-day stopover before using the return ticket. Depending on the season, midweek (Monday through Thursday) round-trip fares range from $438 to $659, weekend (Friday through Sunday) round-trip fares range from $490 to $712. (All round-trip fares are subject to a $16 government tax.) A slightly more expensive, but much more flexible, APEX fare requires a 21-day advance booking, a minimum stay of between 7 days and 6 months, and allows cancellations or changes of flight dates for a $75 fee. For passage from New York to Heathrow, these tickets range in price from $575 to $828 for midweek passage, and from $627 to $880, plus tax, for weekend travel, depending on the season. Occasional promotional fares from Chicago to London cost the same or slightly less than the fares from New York to London.

British Airways is always introducing promotional fares. Available at presstime (and probably in a somewhat altered form by the time of your flight) was a Special Seat Fare of $399 round-trip, from New York to London, available from early May till mid-June, perhaps in honor of flowering season in English gardens. A very appealing option was a Late Saver Fare, for last-minute passages to London from any of British Airways' departure points in North America. This fare could be booked only 48 hours before departure, required full payment at the time of booking (through a travel agent), a stopover of at least one Saturday night in London, a maximum stopover of 14 days, and the ironclad designation of a return date at the time of booking. The price of this ticket from New York to London in midsummer was a cost-conscious $439 (plus $16 tax).

These fares come and go, and you must always check with the airline or a reputable travel agent. Whatever happens, be assured that the terrific fare that disappears today will reappear in a slightly altered form tomorrow. Also remember that the price of a ticket is less dependent on the anticipated distance than it is on competitive market forces.

Senior citizens (in this case, anyone older than 60) receive special 10% discounts at BA through its much-appreciated "Privileged Traveler" program. They also qualify for less stringent restrictions on cancellation policies of APEX tickets. The discounts are granted to BA's inventory of tours, and intra-Britain air tickets as well. For information on joining this program (it requires mailing a $10 fee to BA and waiting for a membership card), contact one of the company's reservations staff. The $10 fee almost immediately pays for itself with the savings and added incentives. BA also offers youth fares to anyone ages 12 to 24.

Predictably, the other airlines follow suit. At presstime, Pam Am and Delta both offered the same Late Saver Fare as British Airways, with roughly the same restrictions, for $514 round-trip between New York and Heathrow (on Pam Am) or between Atlanta and Gatwick (on Delta). Delta offered a youth fare (for ages 12 to 24) with a liberal open-ended return ticket priced between $500 and $849, depending on the day of the week and the season. The Atlanta to Gatwick ticket could be purchased no more than 72 hours before departure. But once in Britain, the passenger had the freedom to declare his or her intended return date (space available) at any Delta office within 72 hours of the return flight.

TWA offered a $424 round-trip flight from New York to London, requiring that travel be completed before June 30, with several unbreakable restrictions. These fares are cited only to give you an idea of what is available. They will surely change in even the short lifetime of this edition, but others will come to take their places.

BUCKET SHOPS

The name originated in the 1960s in Britain, where mainstream airlines gave that (then pejorative) name to resalers of blocks of unsold tickets consigned to them by major transatlantic carriers. "Bucket shop" has stuck as a label, but it might be more polite to refer to them as "consolidators." They exist in many shapes and forms. In their purest sense, bucket shops act as clearing houses for blocks of tickets that airlines discount and consign during normally slow periods of air travel. Charter operators (see below) and bucket shops use to perform separate functions, but their offerings in many cases have been blurred in recent times. Many outfits perform both functions.

Tickets are sometimes—but not always—priced at up to 35% below the full fare. Perhaps your reduced fare will be no more than 20% off the regular fare. Terms of payment can vary—say, from anywhere from 45 days prior to departure to last-minute sales offered in a final attempt by an airline to fill a disturbingly empty craft.

Bucket shops abound from coast to coast, but just to get you started, here are some recommendations:

Maharaja Travel, 518 Fifth Ave., New York, NY 10036 (tel. 212/391-0122, or toll free 800/223-6862), has been around for some 20 years, offering tickets to 400 destinations worldwide, including London.

Access International, 101 W. 31st St., Suite 1104, New York, NY 10001 (tel. 212/333-7280, or call toll free at 800/827-3633), just may be the country's biggest consolidator. It specializes in thousands of discounted tickets to the capitals of Europe, including London.

CHARTER FLIGHTS

Strictly for reasons of economy (and never for convenience), some travelers are willing to accept the possible uncertainties of a charter flight to England. In a strict sense, a charter flight occurs on an aircraft reserved months in advance for a one-time-only transit to some predetermined point. Before paying for a charter, check carefully the restrictions on your ticket or contract. You may be asked to purchase a tour package and pay far in advance. You'll pay a stiff penalty (or forfeit the ticket entirely) if you cancel. Charters are sometimes cancelled when the plane doesn't fill up. In some cases, the charter ticket seller will offer you an insurance policy for your own legitimate cancellation (hospital certificate, death in the family, whatever).

There is no way to predict if a proposed flight to London will cost less on a charter or less in a bucket shop. You have to investigate at the time of your trip.

Among charter flight operators is a name possibly remembered from one's younger days, the **Council on International Educational Exchange** (Council Charters), 205 E. 42nd St., New York, NY 10017 (tel. 212/661-0311, or toll free 800/223-7402). This outfit can arrange "charter seats on regularly scheduled aircraft."

A word of warning: Some charter companies have proven unreliable in the past.

STANDBY FARES

A favorite of spontaneous travelers with absolutely no scheduled demands on their time, a standby fare leaves your departure to the whims of fortune, and the hopes that a seat will remain open for your last-minute claim on it. Standby fares seem to be somewhat of an embarrassment to airlines. Experience has taught that would-be passengers are not good losers when the security gates close on them and they didn't get aboard a particular flight.

This type of discounted fare might be available at times on Virgin Atlantic Airways (tel. toll free 800/862-8621). The airline offers "day-of-departure" discounted fares, or else promotional fares whereby you can be assured of a confirmed seat a day prior to your departure. It's worth checking into.

2. Traveling by Ship

Traveling by air sometimes brings cultures jarringly close to one another, allowing only a few hours to elapse before total immersion in a different lifestyle. Because of that, you might find sea travel in either direction a distinctive and restful way to collect your thoughts and feelings before or after the onslaught of your British experience. Travel can be on a luxury liner with resort-level facilities or on a more relaxed, time-consuming freighter.

Here is a description of the major services offered from the Atlantic seaboard to various ports in England (most often Southampton, where you'll pay a small debarkation fee):

THE PREMIER CRUISE LINE

Cunard Line, 555 Fifth Ave., New York, NY 10017 (tel. 212/880-7500), boasts the *Queen Elizabeth 2* as its flagship—self-styled, quite accurately, as "the most advanced ship of the age." It is the only ocean liner providing regular transatlantic service—18 sailings a year from July to December—between New York; Boston; Philadelphia; Cherbourg, France; Cork, Ireland; and Southampton, England. Built along the Clyde River near Glasgow in the late 1960s, the *QE2* was radically modernized in 1987 at a cost of $152 million. Designed for extended cruises, the *QE2* is reaching the younger market once leery of the traditional liner-type crossing. Hence, you'll find four swimming pools, a sauna, nightclubs, a balconied theater, cinema, chic boutiques (including the world's first seagoing branch of Harrods), as well as four restaurants, paddle-tennis courts, and a children's playroom staffed with English nannies.

The tempting lifestyle on the ship also includes access to an on-board branch of California's "Golden Door Spa at Sea," a computer learning center with 12 IBM personal computers, seminars by trained professionals on astrology, cooking, art, fitness, and health, and a Festival of Life series that introduces you to such personalities as Larry Hagman or Meryl Streep.

Fares are extremely complicated, based on the desirability of the cabin and the season of sailing. I suggest that you call your travel agent or a Cunard representative (tel. toll free 800/221-4770; in New York City 212/661-7777).

One of the most popular packages offered is the air/sea trip: You cross in one direction by air, the other by ship. Round-trip fares for this air/sea passage depend on time of year and the size and opulence of your cabin. BA serves some 60 gateways in North America through which you can start or end your trip; however, conditions strictly state that the amount of time spent abroad cannot exceed 20 days for transatlantic-class passengers and 40 days for first-class passengers—including the time spent on board ship.

A series of maneuvers as to scheduling is possible, but in thrift/superthrift seasons—roughly defined as late autumn—sailings usually cost a minimum of $1,410 in transatlantic class and around $2,615 in first class. Prices go up from there and can reach a maximum of $8,925 per person. For a supplement of less than $1,000, you can fly the Concorde on one leg of your trip. All passengers pay a $100 port tax, regardless of the options chosen.

The Cunard Line divides its sailing year into superthrift, thrift, value, and regular season. The prices quoted by Cunard are per person, based on double occupancy.

THE FREIGHTERS

For an offbeat alternative, if you have time and an adventurous spirit, you can try to secure a cabin aboard a freighter. Passage on a freighter tends to be less expensive than on a passenger ship, but this requires a little comparison shopping. For example, a budget accommodation aboard the *QE2* can cost less money and require less time than passage on a freighter. For legal reasons, no freighter can carry more than 12 passengers (more than that would require a full-time ship's doctor). Your cabin might be adequate, but there is little organized activity.

Most freighters dock at Le Havre, Rotterdam, or Bremerhaven, but a limited number make stops at such unlikely British ports as Felixstowe. The voyage takes from 7 days to 12 days. Sometimes the final port will change during crossing, throwing prearranged itineraries into confusion.

In summer, cabins tend to be fully booked for as much as a year in advance. Space is more likely to be available in winter. For more information on freighter travel, write Fords Freighter Travel Guide, 19448 Londelius St., Northridge CA 91324 (tel. 818/701-7414).

One freighter service is operated by **Lykes Brothers Steamship Co.**, Lykes Center, 300 Poydras St., New Orleans, LA 70130 (tel. toll free 800/535-1861). Owned and operated by a Florida-based family, this American-registered company runs four freighters, plying goods every six days between New Orleans and Rotterdam and Bremerhaven. On the way back west from Bremerhaven, vessels stop at Felixstowe, England, and at Le Havre, France, going on to Norfolk Virginia, and Galveston, Texas, before returning to New Orleans. No more than 12 passengers are accommodated at one time. Passengers dine in the saloon with the officers and crew, mingling in the alcohol-free lounge. There is no entertainment of any kind, and six double cabins are available on each of these vessels.

---

3. Traveling Within Britain

BY AIR

Although Britain enjoys one of the world's best maintained network of motorways, many visitors prefer to commute from their arrival point in London to other cities by air. **British Airways** (tel. toll free 800/247-9297) maintains routes to more than 20 other destinations within the United Kingdom. Several flights a day leave London for such cities as Manchester (the heart of the Midlands), Glasgow, and Edinburgh. British Airways telephone representatives within North America are well qualified to give price and schedule information and to make reservations. Ask about the British Airways Supper Shuttle Saver fares. If granted one of these fares to certain key British cities you may find your ticket cost reduced by 50%. Of course, trips must be reserved and ticketed two weeks in advance and you can fly only during off-peak times (weekends or daily 10am to 3:30pm and after 7pm).

The best deal is the **UK Airpass,** which allows travel to a minimum of 3 cities and a maximum of 12 cities on BA's domestic services. The cost is only $49 to $66 per flight (subject to change). The pass is available for travel from either London, Birmingham, or Manchester, and all journeys must end in the originating city. The UK Airpass must be booked and paid for at least 7 days prior to your departure from the U.S. Check with BA for full details and restrictions.

BY TRAIN

You should, of course, be warned that *your Eurailpass is not valid on trains in Great Britain.* But the cost of rail travel in England, Scotland, Northern Ireland, and Wales can be quite low—particularly if you take advantage of certain cost-saving travel plans, some of which can only be purchased in North America, before leaving for Great Britain.

Great Britain is said to be a country "made for the train." The British Rail network is among the best in the world, with more than 15,000 trains a day leaving for more than 2,400 destinations. Trains are usually on time, and stations are most often located in the center of a town. Travel time is surprisingly short, because the country is so compact. Reservations are not normally necessary, especially at times other than the peak morning and evening hours.

BritRail Pass

This pass gives unlimited rail travel in England, Scotland, and Wales, and is valid on all British Rail routes. It is not valid on ships between Great Britain and the continent, the Channel Islands, or Ireland. Gold (first-class) and silver (economy-class) passes are sold for travel periods of varying lengths. An 8-day gold pass costs $285; a silver ticket goes for $189. For 15 days, a gold pass costs $409; silver, $285. For 22 days, gold costs $499; silver, $359. For one month gold is $589; silver, $415. Children up to 5 travel free. Those 5 to 15 pay $143 gold and $95 silver for the 8-day pass, or $205 gold and $143 silver for the 15-day pass.

Youth passes, all silver, are $169 for 8 days, $239 for 15 days. The youth passes are available for persons 16 through 25 years of age, but they must pay the full adult fare if they choose to go first class.

BritRail also offers a Senior Citizen gold pass to those age 60 and more, costing less than the regular gold pass. Prices are $235 for 8 days, $345 for 15 days, $435 for 22 days, and $505 for one month.

Prices for BritRail Passes are higher for Canadian travelers.

BritRail Passes cannot be obtained in Britain, but should be secured before leaving North America either through travel agents or by writing or visiting BritRail Travel International, 1500 Broadway, New York, NY 10036. Canadians can write to 94 Cumberland St., Toronto M5R 1A3, ON; or 409 Granville St., Vancouver, V6C 1T2, BC.

BritRail Passes do not have to be predated. Validate your pass at any British Rail station when you start your first rail journey.

BritRail Flexipass

The Flexipass allows the traveler the same unlimited access to the British Rail network as the regular BritRail pass at a lower cost with certain restrictions. The Flexipass is available only for either 8 days or for 15 days. The 8-day Flexipass can be used for any four (nonconsecutive) days. The 15-day Flexipass can be used for any eight (nonconsecutive) days of travel out of 15. The 8-day pass costs $229 in first class, $159 in economy. Children 5 to 15 are charged $115 first class, $80 economy. Seniors pay $199 (first class), and youths 16 through 25 pay $139 to travel economy class. The 15-day Flexipass costs $329 first class; $229 economy. For children, the charges are $165 first class, $115 economy. First class for seniors is $279, and economy class for youths is $199.

Remember, you cannot purchase your Flexipass in Great Britain. You must secure it from either your travel agent or from BritRail Travel International in the U.S.

Capital Travel Pak

The Capital Travel Pak is a package offered by BritRail for purchase before you leave home to let you see all the best of London and take easy rail trips to many nearby attractions for four days or a full week. The package combines a 4- or 7-day rail pass with a 4- or 7-day London Visitor Travelcard (see "Transportation in Greater London" in Chapter III). The 4-day Travel Pak costs $99 for adults, $50 for children 5 to 15. The price of a 7-day package is $139 for adults, $70 for children. The passes and Travelcards are for consecutive days from the day of validation. Gatwick or Heathrow Airport transfers are included.

The Britainshrinkers

This is a bonanza for travelers who want to make several quickie trips into the heart of England without having to check out of their hotel rooms in London. From early April to the end of October, scheduled full-day tours are operated by British Rail. You're whisked out of London by train to your destination, where you hop on a waiting bus to visit the various sights during the day. You have a light lunch in a local pub, and there is also free time to shop or explore. A guide accompanies the tour from London and back. Except for overnight trips to Scotland or Wales, your return is in time for dinner or the theater. Included in the rates are entrance fees and VAT.

The Britainshrinkers offer excellent value for the money. If you use a valid BritRail Pass or Flexipass, you can save up to 60% of the cost of each tour you take. By far, this is the best value. For example, passholders can go to Bath and Stonehenge in one day for $55, Stratford-upon-Avon for $58, or Oxford and the Cotswolds for $50. Regular tour fares are $86 to Bath and Stonehenge, $83 to Stratford-upon-Avon, and $75 to Oxford and the Cotswolds.

Special Bargain Fares

British Rail from time to time offers special round-trip fares for optional travel and weekend travel that may only be purchased in Great Britain. Because of the changing nature of these fares and facilities, it is not possible to give information about them to travelers from abroad. Information may be obtained from travel agents and British Rail stations in Great Britain.

If you're in London and want more information on transportation rates, schedules, or facilities, go to the **British Travel Centre,** Rex House, 4-12 Lower Regent St., S.W.1 (tel. 071/730-3400), only a few minutes' walk from Piccadilly Circus. This office deals only with inquiries made in person. Don't try to telephone for information. The office is open from 9am to 6:30pm Mon. to Fri., and from 10am to 4pm Sat. and Sun. You can also make reservations and purchase rail tickets there and at the British Travel Centres at Victoria Station, the Strand, King William Street, Heathrow Airport, and the main London stations—Waterloo, King's Cross, Euston, Victoria, and Paddington—where each deals mainly with its own region. For general information, call the appropriate station. All numbers are listed in the telephone directory.

CAR RENTALS

Once you get over the initial awkwardness of driving on the left-hand side of the road, you will quickly discover that the best way to see the real Britain is to have a car while you're there. There is, quite simply, no substitute for the freedom and flexibility that only your own vehicle can provide.

Partly because of the huge number of visitors to the United Kingdom, the car-rental market is among the most competitive in all of Europe, with many different companies bidding avidly for the U.S.-based business.

Many companies will grant discounts to clients who reserve their cars in advance, usually 48 business hours, through the toll-free reservations offices in a renter's home country. When renting, be certain to ask in advance whether the 15% VAT, much-needed extra insurance, and Collision Damage Waiver (CDW) are included. This can make a big difference in your bottom-line costs.

Budget-Rent-a-Car has 13 offices throughout London, including at all the major London Airports and Victoria railway station. Their most central London office is near Marble Arch, 89 Wigmore St., London W.1 (tel. 071/723-8038). The cheapest car at Budget is a two-door, hatchback Fiat Uno, renting for £19.95 ($32.90) per day, inclusive of VAT and CDW. If you keep it for 6 days, you get the 7th day free. An Uno is very small, and many renters prefer a larger car. A Ford Fiesta is priced at £33 ($54.45) per day, with VAT and CDW included.

Hertz, 35 Edgware Rd., Marble Arch, W.2 (tel. 071/402-4242) is also quite reliable. If you reserve a car from outside the U.K. more than 48 business hours in advance of its pickup, it will cost £105 ($173.25) for a seven-day rental, plus 15% for VAT plus £7 ($11.55) for CDW. (If you don't buy the CDW, you'll be responsible for the first £2,000 ($3,300) of damage to the car in the event of an accident.) This price applies to Hertz's least expensive car, a Ford Fiesta. All this math works out to very good value at around £24 ($39.60) per day. Most renters, however, will probably walk in off the street without making plans long in advance. If this is your case, and if you agree to return the car to the location of its original pickup, the same car will cost £34 ($56.10) per day, with VAT and all insurance already included in the price.

Avis Rent-a-Car maintains offices at Heathrow (tel. 081/897-9321), at Gatwick, and at all other major airports within the United Kingdom. If you're phoning from within Britain, their number for reservations throughout the U.K. is 071/848-8733. Their all-inclusive rate for a Ford Fiesta, their cheapest car, is £189.57 ($312.80) per week, with VAT and full insurance included. If you plan to keep the car for 21 days or more, the all-inclusive rate goes down to £165.85 ($273.65) per week.

Driving Requirements

To drive a car in Britain, your passport and your own driver's license must be presented with your deposit; no special British license is needed. The prudent driver will secure a copy of the *British Highway Code,* available from almost any stationer or news agent.

Although not mandatory, a membership in one of the two major auto clubs in England can be helpful: the **Automobile Association** and the **Royal Automobile Club.** The headquarters of the AA are at Fanum House, Basingstoke, Hampshire RG21 2EA (tel. 0256/20123). The RAC address is P.O. Box 700, Spectrum, Bond St., Bristol, Avon BS99 1RB (tel. 0272/232340). Membership in one of these clubs is usually handled by the agent from whom you rent your car. Upon joining, you'll be given a key to the many telephone boxes you see along the road, so that you can phone for help in an emergency.

A word of warning: Pedestrian crossings are marked by striped lines (zebra crossings) on the road. Also, flashing lights near the curb indicate that drivers *must* stop and yield the right of way if a pedestrian has stepped out into the zebra zone to cross the street.

Wearing seatbelts is mandatory in the British Isles.

Fuel

Gasoline, called petrol by the British, is usually sold by the liter, with 4.5 liters making their imperial gallon. Most pumps show a list of prices and measures. The prices, incidentally, will be much higher than you are used to paying. You'll probably have to serve yourself at the petrol station. In some remote areas, especially in Scotland, stations are few and far between, and many all over the country are closed on Sunday.

BUSES (COACHES) IN BRITAIN

For the traveler who wants to see the country as even a train cannot reveal it, but who can't afford to rent a car, the old, reliable, and inexpensive (at least half the cost of railway fares) bus offers a fine form of transportation. While the trains do go everywhere, passing through towns and villages, they rarely bring you into contact with country life, and they almost never carry you across the high (main) streets of the villages, as the buses do. Moreover, distances between towns in England are usually short. Every remote village is reachable by bus. The term "coach" is usually used for long-distance or touring buses; the term "bus" is reserved for local transportation.

The express motorcoach networks, operated by **National and Scottish Citylink Coaches,** covers the greater part of Britain. They link many villages and most towns and cities with frequent schedules, convenient timetables, and efficient operation in all seasons. Most places off the main route can be easily reached by stopping and switching to a local bus. Fares are relatively cheap, often half that of an equivalent journey by rail, making travel on the express motorcoach network economical. It is nearly always cheaper to purchase a return ticket than to pay for two one-way fares.

The departure point from London for most of the bus lines is **Victoria Coach Station,** Buckingham Palace Rd. (tel. 071/730-0202), a block up from Victoria Station (railroad). It is the hub of Britain's largest coach operators, National Express and Caledonian Express, whose long-distance coach network covers England, Wales, and Scotland. Services also operate to Ireland and to the rest of Europe. Tickets should be bought in advance if possible, and reservations can be made for any journey.

National Express Rapides are luxurious coaches operating on most of the long-distance runs with hostesses, light refreshments, reclining seats, toilets, and no-smoking areas. Details of all coach services can be obtained from 071/730-0202 from 8am to 10pm daily. The National Express ticket office at Victoria Coach Station is open from 6am to midnight daily. The ticket bureau for Ireland and Europe is open daily from 7:30am to 10:30pm. You can arrange coach excursions here, as well as sightseeing tours, rail and ferry travel tickets, and even hotel accommodations.

The **Credit Card Sales Department of Victoria Coach Station** (tel. 071/730-3499) can make reservations and precharge tickets to anywhere within Britain on either National Express bus lines or the Scottish Citylink bus lines. Pick up your tickets at the counter as late as 30 minutes before your departure. Phone reservations and purchases are taken daily from 8am to 9pm, and only MasterCard and Visa are accepted.

For journeys within a roughly 35-mile radius of London, including such major attractions as Windsor, Hampton Court, Chartwell, and Hatfield House, try the **Green Line** bus service. Personal callers should go to the Green Line Enquiry office at Eccleston Bridge, Victoria, S.W.1 (off Buckingham Palace Road), or else phone 071/668-7261 for more information.

Golden Rover tickets cost £4.99 ($8.25) per person, and are available for one day's travel on most London Country and Green Line routes, but not on their Jetlink and Flightline buses connecting London and the airports. It is possible to cover quite a large area around London and into the country for a small cost. For more precise information on routes, fares, and schedules, write to Green Line Country Bus Lines, Lesbourne Rd., Reigate, Surrey RH2 7LE (tel. 081/668-7261). The Country Bus Lines ring the heart of London. They never go to the center of the capital, although they hook up with the routes of the red buses and the Green Line coaches that do.

Britexpress Card and Tourist Trail

This offers one third off all adult tickets purchased on Britain's Express Coach network operated by National Express and Caledonian Express. The card is valid for any 30-day period throughout the year. You can travel when and where you like with a choice of around 1,500 destinations in England, Scotland, and Wales. The card costs £10 ($16.50). A Tourist Trail Card offers unlimited travel for £50 ($82.50) for 5 days going up to £145 ($239.25) for 30 days. Both cards are available from your U.S. travel agent or on arrival in London at 13 Regent St., W.1, near Piccadilly Circus. Here are some examples of one-way fares and travel times: London to Edinburgh (Rapide service) £14.50 ($23.95), 7 hours 45 minutes; London to Stratford-upon-Avon, £10.50 ($17.35), 3 hours; London to York (Rapide service) £19.50 ($32.20), 4 hours; London to Cambridge, £7.40 ($12.20), 1 hour 50 minutes. In Britain, coach tickets should be bought in advance from 3,000 agents nationwide.

BARGAIN SIGHTSEEING TIP

English Heritage is an organization set up by the government (but independent of it) to be responsible for preservation and maintenance of ancient monuments and historic buildings in England most of which are open to the public, including Stonehenge, Dover Castle, and Osbourne House (Queen Victoria's Isle of Wight retreat). English Heritage membership gives you an annual season ticket for free entrance to any of its 400 sites, together with a map and regular up-to-the-minute information on activities and innovations. Even if you don't plan to tour the country, membership will provide information and free entrance to a number of attractions in and around the London area, including Kensington Palace, Hampton Court, and the Tower of London. Membership is £12.50 ($20.65) for adults. You can also purchase a family ticket covering both parents and all children under 16 for £25 ($41.25) per year. Join when you are in England at an English Heritage property or write to English Heritage, Membership Department, P.O. Box 1BB, London W1A 1BB England (tel. 071/973-3000).

The **National Trust** specializes in historic and stately homes. They offer a year-long membership in the Royal Oak Foundation for £19 ($31.35). This can be purchased at the National Trust, 36 Queen Anne's Gate, London, S.W.1 (tel. 071/222-9251). Hours are Mon. to Fri. from 9:30am to 5:30pm. Tube: St. James's Park.

If you plan to do extensive sightseeing in Britain, consider the **Great Britain Heritage Pass.** Information about it can be obtained by calling 071/846-9000. The pass grants you entrance to 600 properties within the country, including Edinburgh Castle, Churchill's Chartwell, Woburn Abbey, Hampton Court Palace, and Windsor Castle. The ticket covers all properties in care of the National Trust and those run by the Department of the Environment. It is estimated that anyone visiting as many as five of these sightseeing attractions will get back the initial outlay of £23.50 ($38.78) for a 15-day pass and £36 ($59.40) for a 1-month pass. In the United States you can purchase this pass at any branch office of British Airways or its specially appointed travel agents. In Great Britain, it can be purchased at any of the major tourist offices in the country.

TOURS

Many questions arise for persons planning their first trip to the British Isles as well as to other European destinations. Sometimes a prospective traveler isn't sure what he or she really wants to see in England, aside, of course, from the Tower of London and Big Ben. How do you plan the trip to be sure of seeing the most outstanding sights of the country? How much of a problem will you have in trying to get from place to place, complete with luggage?

My answer to all these questions, indeed, my advice to many people going to England and/or other European countries for the first time is simply this: Go on a good tour where you and your needs will be looked after from your arrival in England to your departure en route back to the United States. Choose a tour suited to the time you have for your trip, the money you can spend, and the places you want to go. Check with your travel agent for the latest and most appealing offers.

The best and most imaginative tours are offered by **British Airways** (tel. toll free 800/AIRWAYS for complete details). The airline offers an almost bewildering choice of options in both London and Great Britain and Ireland for the traveler. For the visitor in a real rush, they cater to the need with a Quick Look at Britain, all in 3 nights and 4 days. Other excursions include Scottish Interlude, Heart of England and Stately Homes, Scottish Highlands and Skye, and many, many others. If you're an independent traveler (who's also interested in doing Britain on the cheap), BA offers a Bed and Breakfast Fly/Drive Holiday. That way, you can tour Britain at your own pace, but you're assured of a prepaid stopover at a B&B every night. These options are available across England, Scotland, and Wales. You can also take the same independent tour staying at major hotels in Britain.

---

4. Alternative and Special-Interest Travel

Mass tourism of the kind that has transported vast numbers of North Americans to the most obscure corners of the map has been a by-product of the affluence, technology, and democratization that only the last half of the 20th century was able to produce.

With the advent of the 1990s some of America's most respected travel visionaries have perceived a change in the needs of many experienced (and sometimes jaded) travelers. A demand has emerged for specialized travel experiences whose goals and objectives are clearly defined well in advance of an actual departure. There is also an increased demand for organizations that can provide like-minded companions to share and participate in often esoteric travel plans.

Caveat: Under no circumstances is the inclusion of an organization in the following pages to be interpreted as a guarantee either of its credit-worthiness or its competency. Information is presented only as a preview, to be followed by your own investigation should you be interested.

INTERNATIONAL UNDERSTANDING

About the only thing the following organizations have in common is reflected by the headline. These organizations not only promote trips to increase international understanding, but they often encourage and advocate what might be called "intelligent travel."

The Friendship Force 575 South Tower, 1 CNN Center, Atlanta, GA 30303 (tel. 404/522-9490). Founded in Atlanta, Georgia, under the leadership of former President Jimmy Carter during his tenure as governor, this nonprofit organization exists for the sole purpose of fostering and encouraging friendship among disparate peoples around the world.

Dozens of branch offices throughout North America meet regularly and appoint volunteer directors whose responsibility it is to recruit new members and cultivate potential destinations for en masse visits, that usually occur once a year. Because of group bookings by the Friendship Force, air fare to the host country is usually less than an individual APEX ticket. Each participant is required to spend two weeks in the host country (primarily in Europe, but also throughout the world). One stringent requirement is that a participant must spend one full week in the home of a family as a guest, supposedly to further the potential for meaningful friendships between the host family and the participants. Most volunteers spend the second week traveling in the host country.

It should be noted that no particular study regime or work program is expected of participants, but only a decorum and interest level that speaks well of America and its residents. Again, the goal and aim of this group is to further friendship in a nonpolitical, nonreligious context of cooperation and good will.

People to People International, 501 E. Armour Blvd., Kansas City, MO 64109 (tel. 816/531-4701). Defining its purpose as the promotion of international understanding among individuals through educational and cultural exchanges, this philanthropic, nonprofit organization was established by President Dwight D. Eisenhower in the late 1950s. People to People organizes 3- to 4-week, adult, counterpart professional exchanges around the world in a wide array of specialized careers. There is also a summer, 4-week high school educational program. A collegiate summer study abroad program offers courses by an American professor for credit. People to People chapters are located throughout the United States and abroad to provide homestay possibilities for members. Privileges include access to membership travel opportunities, newsletters, and a magazine. Costs are $25 annually for families, $15 for individuals, and $10 for students.

World Wide Christian Tours, P.O. Box 506, Elizabethtown, KY 42702 (tel. 502/769-5900 or toll free 800/732-7920), focuses on Christian travel. These trips include ecumenical tours of England and golf-related tours of Scotland. This organization will tailor-make tours for special-interest and church groups of from 2 to more than 200. World Wide Christian Tours is bonded and approved by ARC and IATA and also has a bus brokerage license.

Servas, 11 John St., New York, NY 10038 (tel. 212/267-0252). Founded in 1948 by an American-born conscientious objector living in Denmark, this organization grew slowly from a collection of index cards kept in a friend's kitchen to one of the most prominent goodwill organizations in the world. Servas (translated from the Esperanto, it means "to serve") is a nonprofit, nongovernmental, international, interfaith network of travelers and hosts whose goal is to help build world peace, goodwill, and understanding. Servas travelers are invited to share living space within a community, normally staying without charge for visits lasting a maximum of two days. Day visits as well as a single shared meal can also be arranged. Visitors pay a $45 annual fee, fill out an application, and are interviewed for suitability. They then receive a Servas directory listing the names and addresses of Servas hosts on six continents who welcome visitors into their homes. What's amazing is that with all

MILEAGE BETWEEN MAJOR CITIES
(Distance in Miles)

	Southampton	Plymouth	Oxford	Oban	Nottingham	Norwich	Newcastle	LONDON	Liverpool	Inverness	Glasgow	Edinburgh	Coventry	Cambridge	Brighton	Aberdeen
Aberdeen	583	641	509	180	432	527	235	558	368	107	150	130	461	500	616	
Ayr	434	492	360	127	282	377	150	409	219	207	35	81	311	351	467	196
Brighton	81	222	105	574	193	170	349	53	277	642	474	475	158	117		616
Bristol	79	124	73	484	149	225	297	121	187	552	384	385	96	166	157	526
Cambridge	128	287	100	458	88	61	230	55	208	526	358	335	88		117	500
Coventry	118	211	54	419	52	149	208	100	121	487	318	319		88	158	461
Dover	152	320	146	595	214	173	354	78	186	663	459	458	179	199	84	637
Dumfries	375	433	301	179	223	318	91	350	160	247	79	80	252	292	408	231
Dundee	516	574	442	116	365	460	168	491	301	134	83	63	394	433	594	67
Edinburgh	442	500	368	123	266	361	105	417	227	156	46		319	335	475	130
Glasgow	411	499	367	93	289	384	157	416	226	172		46	318	358	474	150
Inverness	609	667	535	118	458	553	261	584	394		172	156	487	526	642	107
Leicester	166	236	70	428	26	117	188	107	130	496	327	293	24	74	165	470
Liverpool	244	302	170	326	130	235	170	219		394	226	227	121	208	277	368
LONDON	87	242	59	516	135	109	276		219	584	416	417	100	55	53	558
Manchester	277	285	153	321	72	190	139	202	35	389	221	222	105	163	260	363
Newcastle	350	412	254	258	161	256		276	170	261	157	105	208	230	349	235
Norwich	188	346	160	485	120		256	109	235	553	384	361	149	61	170	527
Nottingham	194	264	98	390		120	161	135	130	458	289	266	52	88	193	432
Oban	541	599	467		390	485	258	516	326	118	93	123	419	458	574	180
Oxford	64	194		467	98	160	254	59	170	535	367	368	54	100	105	509
Plymouth	161		194	599	264	346	412	242	302	667	499	500	211	287	222	641
Portsmouth	21	182	85	562	199	192	354	78	265	630	441	463	139	133	48	604
Southampton		161	64	541	194	188	350	87	244	609	411	442	118	128	81	583
Stoke-on-Trent	187	187	113	355	50	177	190	182	58	423	255	256	85	133	220	397

the potential problems that an organization this diverse might have, there seem to be surprisingly few trouble zones.

International Visitors Information Service, 733 15th St. NW, Suite 300, Washington, DC 20005 (tel. 202/783-6540). For $5, this organization will mail anyone a booklet listing opportunities someone might use for contact with local residents in foreign countries. Europe is heavily featured. Checks should be made out to Meridian House/IVIS.

Staying with a British Family

An ideal way to find out about the British way of life is provided by a number of hosts operating under a code of conduct set up by the British Tourist Authority. For information on this program, a booklet is available published by the BTA listing dozens of agencies and services offering help in finding the place where you might like to stay for a happy British holiday.

In the U.S. write to any of the following British Tourist Authority offices: Third Floor, 40 W. 57th St., New York, NY 10019; World Trade Center, 350 South Figueroa St., Los Angeles, CA 90071; 625 N. Michigan Ave., Suite 1510, Chicago, IL 60611-1977.

ADVENTURE/WILDERNESS TRAVEL

Whether by bicycle or on foot, the following organizations offer tours for the athletic who want to explore "the wilds," or at least country roads, before they disappear forever.

Outward Bound, 383 Field Point Rd., Greenwich, CT 06830 (tel. 203/661-0797, or toll free 800/243-8520 outside Conn.) is considered the oldest and largest outdoor experimental education organization in America. Founded in 1941 by a German-English educator, Kurt Hahn, Outward Bound's goal is to help people "go beyond their self-imposed limits, to use the wilderness as a metaphor for personal growth and self-discovery." Courses last from three days to three months. A three-month course will sometimes be accepted for college credit toward a degree. The location of these courses is usually a wilderness setting near the sea or high in the mountains. Outward Bound maintains 48 different schools and centers throughout the world.

Wilderness Travel, Inc., 801 Allston Way, Berkeley, CA 94710 (tel. 415/548-0420, or toll free 800/247-6700 outside Calif.), specializes in mountain tours and bicycle tours, but also offers walking tours of Cornwall and the Cotswolds. The system is to combine vehicular transport with strategic walking sessions of no more than three hours at a time. One feature is called England from the North Sea to the Irish Sea, covering the English coast. Another walking tour takes in Scotland on a Highlands and Islands Tour. Call or write for more information.

Country Cycling Tours, 140 W. 83d St., New York, NY 10024 (tel. 212/874-5151). One of New York's largest tour operators for bicyclists, this company has tours of the back roads of England and Ireland. Tours (costing from $1,699 to $1,899) include overnight accommodations in three-star hotels, breakfast, and most dinners, and last 10 to 13 days. Luggage precedes you in a van. Cyclists can bring their own bicycles or rent them on site.

The American company referred to as "the granddaddy of cycle tour operators" is **Vermont Bicycle Touring,** P.O. Box 711, Bristol, VT 05443 (tel. 802/453-4811). Tours range from 25 to 40 miles a day, and a van transports luggage. The tours allow flexibility for individual levels of cycling experience, but additional guidance, assistance, and services are always available. Most of this group's tours are in England.

For hiking, walking, and sightseeing tours, get in touch with **Outdoor Bound,** 1A, 18 Stuyvesant Oval, New York, NY 10009 (tel. 212/505-1020). Founded by Seth Steiner, this company specializes in hiking and walking tours, and also offers separate sightseeing tours through the Lake District of England. Tours are one to two weeks, and the hiking trips are designed for the average active person. Accommodations and gourmet meals are in a charming 17th-century country inn near Ambleside and Windermere. A minibus takes hikers and sightseers daily to trails and sightseeing points throughout the region. Experts lecture on the culture, nature, and history of the area. Depending on the tour and options, charges are $1,000 to $1,800 per person.

INLAND WATERWAYS

For a completely new angle on travel in the British Isles, visitors can take boat trips on the network of inland waterways threading through the country. You can choose between a skipper-yourself boat, equipped with food, comprehensive instructions, and suggested routes, or else a hotel boat, where you get good food, a helpful crew, and the companionship of fellow passengers. Waterways holidays make sightseeing easy, allowing you to leave your luggage aboard as you spend the days exploring. Some places allow you to take your boat right into the center of a city, as at Chester, Stratford-upon-Avon, Norwich, Cambridge, York, and Windsor.

Cruising areas include canals, the River Thames, Scottish and Irish lochs, and the fascinating Cambridgeshire rivers: Ouse, Cam, and Nene. For information and reservations, contact **UK Waterway Holidays Ltd.,** Welton Hythe, Daventry, Northamptonshire NN11 5LG (tel. 0327/843773).

SENIOR CITIZEN VACATIONS

One of the most dynamic organizations in the world of postretirement studies for senior citizens is **Elderhostel,** 80 Boylston St., Boston, MA 02116 (tel. 617/426-7788). Established in 1975 by Martin Knowlton, a retired engineer and professor of political science, Elderhostel maintains a dazzling array of university-based summer educational programs for senior citizens throughout the world, including England, Scotland, and all major countries on the continent. Most courses last around three weeks, representing remarkable value, considering that air fare, hotel accommodations in student dormitories or modest inns, all meals, and tuition are included. Currently, three weeks with all of these included cost a surprisingly low $1,992 for a program in England, for example. Courses involve no homework, are ungraded, and are especially focused on the liberal arts. Even field trips are related to the academic discipline being studied in the classroom.

In no way is this to be considered a luxury vacation, but rather an adventure in academic fulfillment for senior citizens. Participants must be more than 60 years of age. However, if a pair of members goes as a couple, only one member needs to be older than 60. Meals are the kind of solid, no-frills fare typical of educational institutions worldwide. A frequently unpublicized side benefit of this program is the safety in which many older single women can travel. Some 70% of the participants are women, who understandably prefer to travel with a goal, an orientation, amid likeminded individuals waiting for them at the end of their transatlantic airplane ride.

Anyone interested in participating in one of Elderhostel's programs should write for their free newsletter and a list of upcoming courses and destinations.

One company that has made a reputation exclusively because of its quality tours for senior citizens is **Saga International Holidays,** established in the 1950s as a sensitive and highly appealing outlet for tour participants at least 60 years of age or older. Insurance and air fare are included in the net price of all of their tours, which encompass dozens of locations in Europe and usually last for an average of 17 nights. For $5, you get a three-year membership. For more information, get in touch with Saga International Holidays, 120 Boylston St., Boston, MA 02116 (tel. 617/451-6808, or toll free 800/343-0273 outside Mass.).

EDUCATIONAL AND STUDY TRAVEL

University vacations, or **UNIVAC,** offers study opportunities at Oxford and Cambridge, where participants find themselves surrounded by history in a rich atmosphere of culture and academic excellence spanning more than 700 years. These cultural vacations combine relaxation with the stimulus of an academic purpose; you can explore history, literature, and the arts through lectures, excursions, and guided walking tours, without the pressures of exams or preparing papers. There are no formal academic requirements for participation in UNIVAC—all adults over 18 are invited to share in the programs, living in one of the colleges, eating in an elaborate dining hall or intimate fellows' dining rooms.

Programs, lasting 7 to 12 days, include university architecture, history, art, and literature, among other English treasures. North American headquarters for UNIVAC is the International Building, 9602 N.W. 13th St., Miami, FL 33172 (tel. 305/591-1736, or toll free 800/792-0100). In the United Kingdom, its headquarters is at 8 Beaufort Pl., Cambridge, England CB5 8AG; in summer, Brasenose College, Oxford, England OX1 4AJ, or Corpus Christi College, Cambridge, England CN2 1RH.

British Universities Summer Schools, University of Oxford, Department for External Studies, Rewley House, Wellington Square, Oxford OX1 2JA, England, offers academic programs in literature and history related to the cultural resources of the universities of Birmingham (at its Stratford-upon-Avon center), London, and Oxford. These programs are designed for graduates, particularly teachers, for graduating seniors, and some undergraduates.

The **Institute of International Education,** the largest U.S. organization in the field of international higher education, administers a variety of postsecondary academic, training, and grant programs. It is best known for administering the USIA predoctoral and collaborative Fulbright grants. For information on IIE-administered programs for U.S. citizens, contact the U.S. Student Programs Division of IIE, 809 United Nations Plaza, New York, NY 10017 (tel. 212/984-5330). College students, teachers, university faculty, adults, and professionals looking for study opportunities abroad can visit the IIE Information Center at 809 United Nations Plaza (First Avenue at 45th Street).

If you're interested in participating in scientific discoveries in Europe, you might look into **Earthwatch,** P.O. Box 403N, Watertown, MA 02172 (tel. 617/926-8200). A nonprofit organization, it organizes scientific projects throughout the world, including 12 in Europe. Most expeditions are organized into 2-week work teams. Participants interested in a "hands on study project" contribute to the cost of that project. Examples include surveys of glaciers in Switzerland, excavating Bronze Age villages in Spain, studying Europe's last virgin forest in Poland, or identifying birds and mammals in Majorca's wetlands.

University professors from around the world apply to have the paying volunteers assigned to their research projects; about a fourth of these applications are accepted on the basis of the research merits of the projects. Payments that volunteers make are considered tax-deductible contributions to a scientific project. A work project with Earthwatch offers a "chance to pursue for a brief while the path not taken." It has also been defined as a "short term scientific Peace Corps." Volunteer tasks include everything from weighing a wolf pup to measuring turtle eggs to examining genealogical records. The organization publishes a magazine six times a year, listing more than 100 unusual opportunities.

HEALTH AND FITNESS FACILITIES

A wide range of health and fitness facilities is offered at a number of hotels in England and Scotland, together with sporting amenities, such as golf, riding, and fishing at some places. Included in the hotels' offerings are saunas, solariums, gymnasiums, whirlpools, steam cabinets, massage facilities, slimming and beauty treatments, jogging tracks, squash and tennis courts, and indoor or outdoor heated swimming pools. Health farms and hydros are also available, with a selection of therapies, such as Swedish, gyratory, and underwater massages, and other treatments.

For information on locations and offerings, write to the **British Tourist Authority,** 40 W. 57th St., New York, NY 10019 (tel. 212/581-4700).

OPERA TOURS

On a cultural note, **Dailey-Thorp,** 315 W. 57th St., New York, NY 10019 (tel. 212/307-1555), is probably the best-regarded organizer of music and opera tours in America. Because of its "favored" relation with European box offices, it's often able to purchase blocks of otherwise unavailable tickets to such events as the Salzburg Festival, the Vienna, Milan, Paris, and London operas, or the Bayreuth Festival in Germany. Tours range from 7 to 21 days, including first-class or deluxe accommodations and meals in top-rated European restaurants. Dailey-Thorp also offers visits to operas in Eastern Europe and the regional operas of Italy.

A TRAVEL COMPANION

A recent American census showed that 77 million Americans more than 15 years of age are single; unfortunately, the travel industry is far better geared for double occupancy of hotel rooms. One company that has made heroic efforts to match single travelers with like-minded companions is headed by Jens Jurgen, who charges between $36 and $66 for a 6-month listing in his well-publicized records. New applicants desiring travel companions fill out forms stating their preferences and needs. They then receive a mini-listing of potential travel partners. Companions of the same or opposite sex can be requested. Because of the large number of listings, success is often a reality.

For an application and more information, get in touch with Jens Jurgen, **Travel Companion,** P.O. Box P-833, Amityville, NY 11701 (tel. 516/454-0880).

---

5. Fast Facts for Britain

The aim of this "grab bag" section—dealing with the minutiae of your stay— is to make your adjustment to the British way of life easier. It is maddening to have your trip marred by an incident that could have been avoided had you been tipped off earlier. To prevent this from happening, I'll try to anticipate the addresses, data, and information that might come in handy on all manner of occasions.

For more specific information on two particular areas, refer to "Fast Facts" under the Orientation section on London, Chapter III, and on Edinburgh in Chapter XX.

BABYSITTERS: These are hard to find, and the safest way is to get your hotel to recommend someone—possibly a staff member. Expect to pay the cost of travel to and from your hotel by taxi. There are a number of organizations advertised in the Yellow Pages of the telephone directory that provide sitters, usually registered nurses and carefully checked mothers, as well as trained nannies.

CIGARETTES: Most U.S. brands are available in major towns. *Warning:* Smoking is banned at an increasing number of places. Make sure you enter a "smoker" on the train or Underground, and only smoke on the upper decks of buses or in the smoking area of single-deckers, theaters, and other public places. Some restaurants restrict smoking, as do many bed-and-breakfast houses.

CLIMATE: British temperatures can range from 30° to 110° Fahrenheit. The British Isles, however, have a temperate climate with no real extremes, and even in summer evenings are cool. No Britisher will ever really advise you about the weather —it is far too uncertain. If you come here from a hot area, bring some warm clothes. If you're from cooler climes, you should be all right.

CURRENCY: At the time of writing this book, the pound (£) was worth $1.65. Each pound breaks down into 100 pence (p). There are £1 coins as well as coins of 20p, 10p, 2p, and 1p.

CUSTOMS: Visitors from overseas may bring in 400 cigarettes and one quart of liquor. If you come from the European Economic Community (EEC, or Common Market) area, you are allowed to bring in 300 cigarettes and one quart of liquor, provided you bought them and paid tax on them in that EEC country. If you have obtained your allowance on a ship or plane, then you may import only 200 cigarettes and one liter of liquor. There is no limit on money, film, or other items for your own use, except that all drugs other than medical supplies are illegal. Obviously, commercial goods such as video films and nonpersonal items will require payment of a bond and will take a number of hours to clear Customs. Do not try to import live birds or animals. You may be subject to heavy fines if you try to sneak one through, and the pet will be destroyed.

Upon leaving Britain, citizens of the United States who have been outside the country for 48 hours or more are allowed to bring back to their home country $400 worth of merchandise duty free—that is, if they haven't claimed such an exemption within the past 30 days. Beyond that free allowance, you'll be charged a flat rate of 10% duty on the next $1,000 worth of purchases. If you make purchases in Britain, it is most important to keep your receipts. On gifts, the duty-free limit has been increased to $50.

DENTISTS: Outside London, ask the nearest sympathetic local resident—perhaps your hotelier—for information.

DOCTORS: Hotels have their own lists of local practitioners for whom you'll have to pay. Outside London, dial 100 and ask the operator for the local police, who will give you the name, address, and telephone number of a doctor in your area. Emergency treatment is free, but if you visit a doctor at his or her surgery (office) or if he or she makes a "house call" to your hotel, you will have to pay. It's wise to take out adequate medical/accident insurance coverage before you leave home.

DOCUMENTS FOR ENTRY: U.S. citizens, Canadians, Australians, New Zealanders, and South Africans all fall under the same category for entry into the United Kingdom. A passport is definitely required, but no visa is necessary. Immigration officers prefer to see a passport with two months' remaining validity. Much depends on the criteria and observations of Immigration officers. The one checking you through will want to be satisfied that you have the means to return to your original destination (usually a round-trip ticket) and visible means of support while you're in Britain. If you are planning to fly from, say, the U.S. to the U.K. and then on to a country that requires a visa (India, for example), it's wise to secure the Indian visa before your arrival in Britain.

DRUGSTORES: In Britain, they are called chemist shops. Every police station in the country has a list of emergency chemists. Dial "0" (zero) and ask the operator for the local police, who will give you information as to a druggist you can reach.

ELECTRICAL APPLIANCES: British current is 240 volts, AC cycle, roughly twice the voltage of North American current, which is 115-120 volts, AC cycle. Because of their deliberately different sizes, you will probably not be able to plug the flat pins of your appliance's plugs into the holes of British wall outlets. Under no circumstances should you try without suitable converters or adapters. Some (but definitely not all) hotels will supply them for guests. Experienced travelers bring their own converters with them. An electrical supply shop will have what you need. Be warned that you will destroy the inner workings of your appliance (and possibly start a fire as well) if you plug an American appliance directly into a European electrical outlet without a converter.

EMBASSIES AND HIGH COMMISSIONS: Passports, visas, whatever your problem, London has representatives in offices from nearly all the countries of the world.

The **U.S. Embassy,** 24 Grosvenor Sq., W.1 (tel. 071/499-9000). Hours in the passport office are Mon. to Fri. from 8:30am to 1pm. Tube: Bone Street.

The **Canada High Commission** is at Canada House, Trafalgar Sq., W.1 (tel. 071/629-9492), open Mon. to Fri. from 9am to 5:30pm. Tube: Charing Cross.
The **Australian High Commission** is at Australia House, The Strand, W.C.2 (tel. 071/397-4334), open Mon. to Fri. from 9am to 5:30pm. Tube: Charing Cross, Aldwych.
The **New Zealand High Commission** is at New Zealand House, the Haymarket at Pall Mall, S.W.1 (tel. 071/930-8422). Tube: Charing Cross.

EMERGENCY: For police, fire, or ambulance, dial 999. Give your name and address, plus the telephone number, and state the nature of the emergency. Misuse of the 999 service will result in a heavy fine. Cardiac arrest, yes. Sprained ankle, no. Accident injury, yes. Dented fender, no.

ETIQUETTE: Be normal, be quiet. The British do not like hearing other people's conversations. In pubs you are not expected to buy a round of drinks unless someone has bought you a drink. Don't talk politics or religion in pubs.

FILM: All types are available, especially in large cities. Processing takes about 24 hours although many places, particularly in London, will do it almost while you wait. There are few restrictions on the use of your camera, except where notices are posted, as in churches, theaters, and certain museums. If in doubt, ask.

HAIRDRESSING: Ask at your hotel. It may even have its own salon. Hairdressing services are available in most department stores. For men, barbershops are to be found at the main railway stations in London. Hairdressers and barbers get 10%.

HITCHHIKING: It is not illegal and is normally safe and practical. However, getting into a car with any stranger anywhere in the world can be extremely dangerous, especially for solo travelers. That smiling face opening the car door might be a 1990s Jack the Ripper, so exercise caution always. In Great Britain, it is illegal for pedestrians to attempt hitchhiking on motorways. The cleaner and tidier you look, the better your chances for getting a ride. Have a board with your destination written on it to hold up for drivers to see.

HOLIDAYS AND FESTIVALS: Christmas Day, Boxing Day (December 26), New Year's Day, Good Friday, Easter Monday, May Day, and spring and summer bank holidays (the last Monday in May and August respectively) are observed. Scotland also takes January 2 as a holiday but does not recognize the summer bank holiday, taking the first Monday in August instead of the last for a holiday. Scotland does not observe Easter Monday as a bank holiday.

LAUNDRY AND DRY CLEANING: Most places take two days to complete the job and most hotels require the same length of time. London and most provincial towns have launderettes where you can wash and dry your own clothes, but there are no facilities for ironing. Many launderettes also have dry-cleaning machines. Otherwise, there are establishments that will do dry-cleaning for you with one-day service.

LIBRARIES: Every town has a public library, and as a visitor you can use the reference sections. The borrowing of volumes, however, is restricted to local citizens.

LIQUOR LAWS: No alcohol is served to anyone under the age of 18. Children under 16 aren't allowed in pubs, except in certain rooms, and then only when accompanied by a parent or guardian. Don't drink and drive. Penalties are stiff and inconvenient (or worse), even if you are an overseas visitor.
  In England, pubs can open from 11am to 11pm Mon. to Sat. and from noon to 3pm and 7 to 10:30 or 11pm Sun. Likewise, restaurants are allowed to serve liquor during these hours; however, only people who are eating a meal on the premises can

be served a drink. The law allows 30 minutes for "drinking-up time." A meal, incidentally, is defined as "substantial refreshment." And, you have to eat and drink sitting down. In hotels, liquor may be served from 11am to 11pm to both residents and nonresidents; after 11pm, only residents, according to the law, may be served.

LITERATURE: If you're really dedicated in your exploring, I suggest Churchill's *History of the English Speaking Peoples* (four volumes) and Trevelyan's *History of England.* These tomes will help you to understand a lot more about what you'll be seeing. Otherwise, just read this guidebook, and use a good map if you are touring. I recommend the Collins *Road Atlas of Britain,* which makes a good souvenir.

LOST PROPERTY: For help in finding items lost in London, see "London Fast Facts," Chapter III. Wherever you are in England, report your loss to the nearest police station.

NEWSPAPERS: *The Times* is the top, then the *Telegraph,* the *Daily Mail,* and the *Guardian,* but all papers carry the latest news. Others have some news but rely on gimmicks to sell. The *International Herald-Tribune,* published in Paris, and an international edition of *USA Today* are available daily.

OFFICE HOURS: Business hours with many, many exceptions are Mon. to Fri. from 9am to 5pm. The lunch break lasts an hour, but most offices stay open all day.

PETS: See "Customs." It is illegal to bring in pets, except with veterinary documents. Most are subject to six months in quarantine. Hotels have their own rules, but usually dogs are not allowed in restaurants or public rooms, and often not in bedrooms.

POLICE: The best source of help and advice in emergencies is the police. Stop a "bobby" in the street, or dial 999 if the matter is serious. If the local force cannot help, they will know the address of the person who can. Losses, theft, and other criminal matters should be reported to the police immediately.

POSTAL SERVICE: Letters and parcels to be called for may, as a rule, be addressed to you at any post office except a town sub-office. The words "To Be Called For" or "Poste Restante" must appear in the address. When claiming your mail, always carry some sort of identification. Letters generally take seven to ten days to arrive from the U.S. Post Restante service is provided solely for the convenience of travelers, and it may not be used in the same town for more than three months. It can be redirected, upon request, for a one-month period, unless you specify a longer time, not to exceed three months, on the application form you will be asked to fill out. Post offices and sub-post offices are centrally located and open from 9am to 5:30pm Mon. to Fri., 9:30am to noon on Sat.; closed Sun.

RADIO AND TELEVISION: There are 24-hour radio channels operating throughout the United Kingdom, with mostly pop music and chat shows during the night. TV starts around 6am with breakfast TV and educational programs. Lighter entertainment begins around 4 or 5pm, after the children's programs, and continues until around midnight. There are now four television channels—two commercial and two BBC without commercials.

RELIGIOUS SERVICES: Times of services are posted outside the various places of worship. Almost every creed is catered to in London and other large cities, but in the smaller towns and villages you are likely to find only Anglican (Episcopalian), Roman Catholic, Baptist, and Nonconformist forms of worship. Scotland is mainly a Protestant country, its Church of Scotland being the leading faith.

REST ROOMS: These are usually found at signs saying "Public Toilets." Expect to put 5p (8¢) in the slot to enter a stall if you're a woman. Men usually go free. Hotel facilities can be used, but they discourage nonresidents. Garages (filling stations) also have facilities for the use of customers only, and the key is often kept by the cash register. There's no need to tip except in hotels where there is an attendant.

SAFETY: Whenever you're traveling in an unfamiliar city or country, stay alert. Be aware of your immediate surroundings. Don't sling your camera or purse over your shoulder; wear the strap diagonally across your body. Always lock your car and protect your valuables. Stay in well-lit areas and out of questionable neighborhoods. This will minimize the possibility of becoming a victim of crime. While Britain is a fairly safe country, every society has its criminals. It's your responsibility to be aware and alert even in the most heavily touristed areas, especially in London and other large cities.

SENIOR DISCOUNTS: These are only available to holders of British Pension books.

SHOE REPAIRS: Many of the large department stores in Britain have "Shoe Bars" where repairs are done while you wait.

STORE HOURS: In general, stores are open from 9am to 5:30pm Mon. to Sat. In country towns, there is usually an early-closing day when the shops shut down at 1pm. The day varies from town to town.

TAXES: As part of an energy-saving program, the British government has added a special 25% tax on gasoline (petrol). There is no local sales tax in cities and towns, but 15% Value Added Tax (VAT) is added to all hotel and restaurant bills. VAT is also included in the cost of many of the items you purchase to take home with you.

At shops that participate in the Retail Export Scheme, it is possible to get a refund sent to you at home for the amount of the VAT tax on your purchases. However, you must have your passport with you when you make your purchase to be eligible. Ask the salesperson for a Retail Export Scheme form (Form VAT 407) and a stamped, preaddressed envelope to return it in. Save the VAT form along with your sales receipt to show at Customs. You may also have to show the actual purchases to Customs officials at airports or other ports of departure. After the form has been stamped by Customs, mail it back to the shop in the envelope provided.

Here are three organizing tips to help you through the Customs procedures: Keep your VAT forms with your passport as Customs is often located near passport control; pack your purchases in a carry-on bag so you will have them handy after you've checked your other luggage; and allow yourself enough time at your departure point to find a mailbox.

TELEPHONES: British TeleCom is carrying out a massive improvement program of its public pay-phone service. During the transitional period, you could encounter four types of pay phones. The old style (gray) pay phone is being phased out, but there are a lot still in use. You will need 10p (17¢) coins to operate such phones, but you should not use this type for overseas calls. Its replacement is a blue-and-silver push button model that accepts coins of any denomination. The other two types of phones require cards instead of coins to operate. The Cardphone takes distinctive green cards especially designed for it. They are available in five values—£1 ($1.65), £2 ($3.30), £4 ($6.60), £10 ($16.50), and £20 ($33)—and they are reusable until the total value has expired. Cards can be purchased from news agencies and post offices. Finally, the Creditcall pay phone operates on credit cards—Access (MasterCard), Visa, American Express, and Diners—and is most common at airports and large railway stations.

Phone numbers in Britain outside of the major cities consist of an exchange name (like the U.S. area code) plus telephone number. In order to dial the number, you will need the code of the exchange being called. Information sheets on call box walls give the codes in most instances. If your code is not there, however, call the operator by dialing 100. In major cities phone numbers consist of the exchange code and number. These local digits are all you need to dial if you are calling from within the same city. If you are calling from elsewhere, you will need to prefix them with the dialing code for the city. Again, you will find these codes on the call box information sheets. If you do not have the telephone number of the person you want to call, dial 192 or 142 for either London or elsewhere in the country. Give the operator the name of the town and then the person's name and address.

Here is a brief guide to telephone costs: A 3-minute call from London to, say, Reading, costs the most from 9am to 1pm (peak rate), a total of 80p ($1.30). The same 3-minute call costs only 60p (99¢) if made from 8am to 9am and 1 to 6pm (standard rate). The tariff is cut in half if you call Sat. or Sun. from 6pm to 8am. At that time, the cost is only 30p (50¢). The charges quoted are for pay phones. You will have to pay far more if you use a hotel operator at any time.

TELEX AND FAX: Telexes and Faxes are very common in offices and hotels. If your hotel has a telex or a Fax, the staff will send it for you for a fee. Refer to the Yellow Pages for telex bureaux or dial 100 and ask for Freefone Intelpost for information on Fax.

TIME: England and Scotland are based on Greenwich Mean Time, five hours ahead of the U.S. East Coast, with British Summer Time (GMT + 1 hour) during the summer, roughly from the end of March to the end of October.

TIPPING: In restaurants, service charges in the 15% to 20% range are usually added to the bill. Sometimes this is clearly marked; at other times it isn't. When in doubt, always ask. If service is not included, it is customary to add 15% to the bill. Sommeliers (wine stewards) get about £1 ($1.65) per bottle of wine served. Tipping in pubs is not common, although in cocktail bars the waiter or barmaid usually gets about 75p ($1.25) per round of drinks.

Like restaurants, hotels often add a service charge of 10% to 15% to most bills. In smaller B&Bs, the tip is not likely to be included. Therefore, tip for special services, such as the waiter who serves you breakfast. If several persons have served you in a B&B, many guests ask that 10% to 15% be added to the bill and divided among the staff. Otherwise, room attendants get about 75p ($1.25) per day or about £4 ($6.60) per week. The hall porter is tipped only for specific services rendered. Tip porters about 75p ($1.25) per piece of luggage. It's standard to tip taxi drivers 10% to 15% of the fare (never less than 20p or 35¢, however). Theater ushers are not tipped.

TOURIST INFORMATION: Before you go, you can obtain information about Great Britain from offices in the United States and Canada.

In the United States, the main office for the **British Tourist Authority** is 40 W. 57th St., New York, NY 10019 (tel. 212/582-4700). Other offices are 625 N. Michigan Ave., Suite 1510, Chicago, IL 60611-1977 (tel. 312/787-0490); World Trade Center, 350 S. Figueroa St., Suite 450, Los Angeles, CA 90071 (tel. 213/628-3525), and Cedar Maple Plaza, 2305 Cedar Springs Rd., Suite 210, Dallas, TX 75201 (tel. 214/720-4040).

In Canada, information is available at 94 Cumberland St., Suite 600, Toronto, ON, M5R 3N3 (tel. 416/925-6326).

In England the British Tourist Authority has a **British Travel Centre** at Rex House, 4-12 Lower Regent St., London S.W.1 (tel. 071/730-3400). This center offers a full information service on all parts of Britain, a British Rail ticket office, a travel agency, a theater ticket agency, hotel-booking service, a bookshop, and a souvenir shop, all under one roof. Hours are 9am to 6:30pm Mon. to Fri. and 10am to 4pm on Sat. and Sun., with extended hours on Sat. in June, July, August, and September. Telephone information is available Mon. to Sat.

Detailed information on various areas of the British Isles is available in London from the following agencies: the Wales Tourist Board, 34 Piccadilly S.W.1 (tel. 071/409-0969); the Scottish Tourist Board, 19 Cockspur St., S.W.1 (tel. 071/930-8661); and the Northern Ireland Tourist Board, 11 Berkeley St., W.1 (tel. 071/493-0601).

For various sources of information on London itself, see Section 1 of Chapter III.

WEATHER: For London, telephone 071/246-8091; for Devon and Cornwall, 0392/8091; for the Midlands, 021/8091; for the Scottish Highlands, 0224/8091; and for Edinburgh and Lothian, 031/8091.

WEIGHTS AND MEASURES: England and Scotland use the metric system. Follow the formula instructions to convert.

Length

1 millimeter = 0.04 inches (*or* less than 1/16 inch)
1 centimeter = 0.39 inches (*or* just under 1/2 inch)
1 meter   = 1.09 yards (*or* about 39 inches)
1 kilometer = 0.62 mile (*or* about 2/3 mile)

To convert kilometers to miles, take the number of kilometers and multiply by .62 (for example, 25 km × .62 = 15.5 miles).

To convert miles to kilometers, take the number of miles and multiply by 1.61 (for example, 50 miles × 1.61 = 80.5 km).

Capacity

1 liter = 33.92 ounces
        = 1.06 quarts
        = 0.26 gallons

To convert liters to gallons, take the number of liters and multiply by .26 (for example, 50 l × .26 = 13 gal).

To convert gallons to liters, take the number of gallons and multiply by 3.79 (for example, 10 gal × 3.79 = 37.9 l).

Weight

1 gram   = 0.04 ounce (*or* about a paperclip's weight)
1 kilogram = 2.2 pounds

To convert kilograms to pounds, take the number of kilos and multiply by 2.2 (for example, 75 kg × 2.2 = 165 lbs).

To convert pounds to kilograms, take the number of pounds and multiply by .45 (for example, 90 lb × .45 = 40.5 kg).

Area

1 hectare (100m^2) = 2.47 acres

To convert hectares to acres, take the number of hectares and multiply by 2.47 (for example, 20 ha × 2.47 = 49.4 acres).

To convert acres to hectares, take the number of acres and multiply by .41 (for example, 40 acres × .41 = 16.4 ha).

Temperature

To convert degrees C to degrees F, multiply degrees C by 9, divide by 5, then add 32 (for example, $9/5 × 20°C + 32 = 68°F$).

To convert degrees F to degrees C, subtract 32 from degrees F, then multiply by 5, and divide by 9 (for example, $85°F - 32 × 5/9 = 29°C$).

ENGLAND

II

INTRODUCING ENGLAND

1. THE ENGLISH
2. THE CULTURE
3. FOOD AND DRINK

Why go to England? This question inspires a variety of answers, many by the greatest writers of the world who have placed this little country at or near the top of the list of places to savor and explore in a lifetime. I must speak of my own deeply felt enthusiasm. I have ancestral roots in England—as do many readers of this book—but my affection and interest are also colored by other "roots." Many of the world's greatest Anglophiles have no ancestral link to England at all, but they are inspired and ensnared by its cultural, historical, and spiritual heritage.

The people of this little land, relying largely on their wits—perhaps their most important resource—have played a dynamic role in world history, shaping the character, customs, and even major languages in many countries besides their own.

To travel in England is like experiencing a living, illustrated history book. You can ponder over the ancient mystery of Stonehenge, relive the days of Roman Britain when you walk through an excavated villa, and hear the linguistic influence of Celtic, Norse, and Norman as well as Anglo-Saxon in words and place names.

The very smallness of the landmass of England makes it possible to see a lot in a comparatively short time. You can stand in the inner courtyard of the Tower of London where Lady Jane Grey was beheaded, walk through Westminster Abbey on the stone grave markers of such figures as Disraeli, Newton, Darwin, Chaucer, and Kipling, or visit the homes where Samuel Johnson, Charles Dickens, and Emily Brontë lived and worked and where Shakespeare wooed Anne Hathaway. Courts of law, great colleges at Oxford and Cambridge, and many other monuments all are here to illustrate the richness of the English heritage. There are innumerable museums, and libraries hold vast treasures: early Bibles, the Magna Carta, and countless priceless musical, literary, political, and historical documents.

Unlike travel in the huge area of the United States, a trip through England takes you through much diversity in a short time. Move from the mountainous Lake District, through the rolling hills of the Cotswolds, past the Holland-like canals of Lincoln and the fens of the Norfolk Broads, to moody Lorna Doone country in North Devon with rugged hills and coastline.

From imposing and romantic moated castles to splendid country manor houses, half-timbered Tudor dwellings, thatched-roof houses, their gardens riotous with bright flowers, and humble cottages—the habitations in England reflect the lifestyle of the people of history and today. The architecture of England is a reflection of the inner spirit, shown in churches and cathedrals with soaring Gothic arches and stained-glass windows to be seen in nearly every city.

Whatever your major interest, you'll probably find an occasion for its pursuit in the English calendar of events. Attend one of the Bard's plays at Stratford-upon-Avon, go through the Midlands on a canal or houseboat, or spend time at a West Country farm riding over hill and moor on horseback. Watch boat races at Henley-on-Thames or walk through the Yorkshire Dales. You can sample true English "fayre" at ancient pubs and inns, visit spectacular gardens at stately homes and parks, even swim in a hidden cove off Cornwall.

London's theater is stimulating and refreshing, and there are concerts, festivals, country fairs, ballet, and opera at many places throughout the country, not just in the capital. Visitors are often fascinated with the English enthusiasm for their sports—cricket, football (soccer), rugby, tennis, skating, sailing, field hockey, hiking, and mountaineering.

Best of all is getting to know the English people, who are usually warm and gracious. Of course, just like everywhere else in the world, England has its share of cranks, but the average man or woman is a helpful host to better acquaint you with the country.

Certainly you won't be able to do everything and go everyplace in just one trip. You'll most definitely want to come back for a second visit—and then for a third, and more.

WHERE TO GO

It takes weeks to tour England thoroughly, and many readers do just that, either by car, train, or bus. However, others are much more rushed and will need to direct their limited sightseeing time carefully. London is targeted at the top of every first-time visitor's list. Even those on the most rushed of schedules generally fit in Windsor Castle, lying about an hour's train ride from central London. For many, that's it. Then they're off to Paris or other places on the continent.

However, those with more time will want to go to the south of England, the cradle of English history, centering their exploration around the cathedral city of Canterbury, some 65 miles southeast of London. It can be done on a rushed day trip. I'd suggest two nights there, however: one day for Canterbury; another day for exploring some of the historic homes of Kent, including Knole, a showplace of England, lying in the village of Sevenoaks, about 25 miles from central London; and Churchill's home, Chartwell, 1½ miles south of Westerham. Those with yet a third night to spend in the south can go to Rye, the old Cinque port near the English Channel, 65 miles south of London.

The second most popular jaunt is to Stratford-upon-Avon and the university city of Oxford. At minimum, this should take two nights. The first night can be spent at Oxford, 57 miles northwest of London, and the second night at Stratford-upon-Avon, 40 miles northwest from Oxford, a total distance of 92 miles from London. Those with one or two more nights to spend in Stratford-upon-Avon can use it as a base for day trips to Warwick Castle, Kenilworth Castle, Sulgrave Manor (ancestral home of George Washington), and Coventry Cathedral.

My favorite tour—and perhaps yours too—might be to the fabled West Country of England, taking in Winchester, Salisbury, the New Forest, and the old spa at Bath. Bath is considered by many to be the most outstanding place to visit in the west of England. Your first night can be spent in Salisbury, which is a base for exploring the prehistoric ruins of Stonehenge on the Salisbury Plain. Salisbury is an 83-mile drive from London. From Salisbury, you can head north to Bath, that Georgian city on a bend of the River Avon, a distance of some 115 miles from London.

After that, those with three or four days remaining can either head southwest of Bath, taking in Devon and Cornwall, perhaps the two most charming shires of England, or can head north to the Cotswolds, the rolling hills and old wool towns that always seem to enchant. I've left out the Lake District, Cambridge, East Anglia, the

cathedral city of York, and many, many more places. But there's a great deal here to take in. As I said, it will take weeks.

---

1. The English

The British Isles have been a melting pot of races since prehistoric times, as attested by artifacts and traces of settlements from many centuries.

HISTORY

Until about 6,000 years before Christ, Britain was probably part of the continent of Europe. It was split off by the continental drift and other natural forces, but even after the split people on the mainland could look across to what was now a big island. Pressed by marauders from the east or simply seeking living room for their increasing tribes, some brave souls made their way across the often wild waters of the channel. Some came simply seeking plunder.

The earliest inhabitants of the British Isles archeologists believe were the small, dark people known as Iberians (connected to the early people of Spain, Portugal, and Sicily), also called pre-Celts. These are the people believed to have been the creators of Stonehenge before 500 B.C., when the early Celts, blond, often blue-eyed immigrants poured in from along the continental coastal areas of Europe from Denmark to northern Italy. The little, dark Iberians who survived the bloody assaults of these invaders fled to the Scottish Highlands and the mountains of Wales, where some of their descendants of almost pure stock can be seen today. Of course, there was interbreeding among the races in those early centuries, producing the type of people living in the country when it was invaded by Julius Caesar in 54 B.C.

The land the Romans came to was heavily wooded, from the south of what is today England to the north coast of Scotland, with treeless areas around marshes and on hills and moors. But it was not this asset that drew the Roman leaders to the land. It was the reports of precious metals that spurred the dispatch of scouts to the unknown island across the channel. The Britons, as the people of the land were known, resisted the onslaught of Roman troops but lacked the leadership and war experience to prevent the takeover. The Romans took all of the southern part of the island, from the Cheviot Hills in Scotland to the English Channel, and added it to the Roman Empire by A.D. 43. During almost four centuries of occupation, they built roads, villas, towns, walls, and fortresses, farmed the land, and introduced first their pagan religions and then Christianity. Agriculture and trade flourished, and the lives of the people were permanently influenced.

After the withdrawal of Roman legions around A.D. 410, waves of Jutes, Angles, and Saxons flocked in, establishing themselves in small "kingdoms" throughout the formerly Roman colony. From the 8th through the 11th centuries, they contended with Danish raiders for control of the land.

In 1066 William the Conqueror invaded from Normandy and defeated and slew Harold, the last Anglo-Saxon king, at the Battle of Hastings. The Norman rulers were on the throne from 1066 to 1154, when the first of the Plantagenets, Henry II (that "friend" of Thomas à Becket), was crowned. That line held power until 1399. A notable date here is 1215, when King John was forced by his nobles to sign the Magna Carta at Runnymede, guaranteeing certain rights to his nobles and the rule of law, beginning a process that led eventually to the development of the parliamentary system.

In 1399 the Lancastrians took the throne; their reign was marked by defeat in the Hundred Years' War and loss of their claims to lands in France. Opposing the Lancastrians were the Yorkists, with ambitions to regain the crown they had lost. The dissension led to the Wars of the Roses, the red rose representing Lancaster and the white rose York. By 1461 the house of York seized power, but the war continued. It was during this time that the death of the boy king, Edward V, and his younger brother in the Tower of London was laid at the door of their uncle, Richard III, an

accusation only recently questioned. Richard III was slain at the Battle of Bosworth Field in 1485, ending the Wars of the Roses and placing the Tudors on the throne.

The first Tudor king, Henry VII, curbed the powers of the barons, reformed the legal system, gave more importance to the landed gentry, and improved England's economic situation. His son, Henry VIII, is notorious for his six wives: two beheaded, two set aside, one who died in childbirth, and one who survived him. Henry VIII split with the Roman Catholic Church and established the Church of England. The Dissolution of the Monasteries that followed left an indelible mark on the nation; the riches of the abbots and bishops poured into the coffers of Henry and his associates, and the large properties formerly owned by the church were placed in lay ownership. There followed the brief reign of Henry's eldest daughter, Mary, whose attempts to turn back the clock and reinstate Roman Catholicism earned her the epithet of "Bloody Mary."

Under Elizabeth I, England flourished. Elizabeth managed successfully to walk a risky line between Catholic and Protestant factions. Under Elizabeth, England became a major naval power, defeating the Spanish Armada. The first colonies were founded in the New World, and a vigorous trade was established with Asia and Europe. In this period, England experienced a flowering of literature.

Elizabeth's reign ended the Tudor dynasty, and England and Scotland were united under James I of England (James VI of Scotland), son of Elizabeth's rival for the English throne, Mary Queen of Scots. The Stuarts came to power in 1603 and held it until 1649, when Charles I was beheaded. During this period, the *Mayflower* sailed for the New World. Dissatisfaction with the established Church of England as well as with what many saw as Papist leanings by the monarchs created a time of great stress in England. Parliament and the Stuart kings came into conflict, resulting in a bloody Civil War between Parliamentarian troops, led by Oliver Cromwell, and Royalists who were on the side of King Charles. The Royalists lost the war, the king lost his head, and in 1649 the Puritan Commonwealth was established, with Cromwell as Lord Protector, a situation that lasted until 1660.

With the restoration of the monarchy in 1660, Charles II, a Stuart, came to the throne, but troubles still beset the country. The Great Plague wiped out thousands of lives in 1665–1666, and the Great Fire destroyed large portions of London in 1666.

Then in 1688—after what was called the "Glorious Revolution," which removed Catholic King James II from the throne and crowned in his place William of Orange and his wife, James's daughter, Mary—a Bill of Rights was signed by the monarchs, settling once and for all the question that had been at the very root of the Civil War: The king was king by will of Parliament, not by divine right from God.

The Hanoverian dynasty, which began its 110-year reign in 1727, had many ups and downs. Canada was won from the French, the British Indian Empire was firmly entrenched through the redoubtable Clive of India, the Boston Tea Party marked the start of the American Revolution, Captain Cook claimed Australia and New Zealand for England, and the British became embroiled in the Napoleonic Wars in France and Spain—a time of glory for two of the country's great leaders, Admiral Lord Horatio Nelson at Trafalgar, and the Duke of Wellington at Waterloo.

Perhaps the single most important development in this period was the Industrial Revolution, which forever changed the lives of the laboring class, created a wealthy middle class, and changed England from a rural, agricultural to an urban, industrial economy.

The reign of Queen Victoria, which began in 1837, was also a time of great changes. Trade unions were formed, a universal public school system was developed, industrialization and urbanization steadily spread, and railroads were extended to almost every section of the British Isles. The glories of empire dazzled the nation; Parliament, under the auspices of Benjamin Disraeli, declared Victoria empress of India. When Edward VII succeeded to the throne in 1901, the country entered the 20th century with the advent of the telephone and the motorcar, which again changed everybody's lifestyle and thinking.

Edward's son, George V, ascended the throne in 1910, and led the nation

THE CULTURE □ 37

through World War I. During this conflict, he patriotically dropped his German titles and changed the name of the royal house to Windsor. His oldest son, Edward VIII, abdicated before his coronation to marry the American divorcée, Wallis Simpson (he became the Duke of Windsor). George VI became king.

Then, in 1939, came World War II. The Blitz, the Dunkirk evacuation in 1941, and the successful D-Day operation that placed the Allies firmly on the road to victory over Hitler have all been kept alive through documentaries, movies, and memories of those who participated. Winston Churchill had his finest hour as prime minister in those perilous times.

After World War II, Labor came into power and the welfare state was set up. At present, under Conservative Margaret Thatcher, England is undergoing a reaction against those measures.

Queen Elizabeth II came to the throne on the death of her father in 1952. Since then, Britain has joined the NATO alliance and the Common Market—and Big Ben still chimes the hours outside the Houses of Parliament.

GOVERNMENT

The United Kingdom of Great Britain and Northern Ireland comprises England, Wales, Scotland, and Northern Ireland. It is governed by a constitutional monarchy, the present head of state being Queen Elizabeth II. The head of government, however, is the prime minister, selected by the majority party in Parliament and then requested by the queen to form a government, in other words, to take charge and name cabinet members to head the various branches of government.

Parliament is technically three separate entities: the sovereign, the House of Lords, and the House of Commons. The "government" consists of the prime minister and the cabinet members (who must be members of Parliament). The sovereign's function is chiefly ceremonial.

There are two main political parties, Conservative and Labour. The Conservatives, currently led by England's first woman prime minister, Margaret Thatcher, believe in free enterprise, private ownership, and membership in the European community. Labour believes in public ownership of important industries, with a maximum support structure for the individual. The Liberals and the Social Democrat party have joined in an uneasy alliance to form the Social Democratic and Liberal party, which is beginning to have some impact.

---

2. The Culture

The English are friendly people, happy to share their music, art, literature, and other cultural benefits with people who come from what was, after all, once a colonial possession of Great Britain (and Canada still is a member of the Commonwealth). With no language barrier—except for a dialect here and there—this is an opportunity for English speaking visitors to easily enjoy a great cultural experience.

LITERATURE

The most outstanding figure of all in England's literary tapestry is—who dare say me nay?—William Shakespeare (1564–1616). But if England had had no Shakespeare, that tapestry would still be a rich and glowing panoply of artists with words—oral, written, sung, in poetry, in prose, in drama. From the Old English epic poem, *Beowulf,* almost surely the result of centuries of verse recited through the ages by tribal bards, to the works of the post–World War II "angry young men," English literature is much too vast to approach in a limited space.

Old English poetry and historical prose (the *Anglo-Saxon Chronicle* of Alfred the Great and other works) yielded to the language called Middle English, in which the culture and tongue of the Normans enriched the speaking and writing of the Anglo-Saxon language. Middle English was used by philosophers, historians, and romance writers from the 13th and 14th centuries. Greatest of the writers of this period was Geoffrey Chaucer, whose *Canterbury Tales* are masterfully told. The literary highlight of the 15th century was *Le Morte d'Arthur,* Sir Thomas Malory's freehanded story about the legend of King Arthur and his court. Ballads were also popular storytelling devices in that century, a sort of continuation of the bardic epic tradition.

During the Tudor (and Elizabethan) era, stars in the literary sky were Sir Thomas More (*Utopia*), Edmund Spenser (*The Faerie Queen*), and Christopher Marlowe (*The Tragical History of Dr. Faustus*). In this era the sonnet form was adopted from an Italian verse model, attracting as users a number of poets, such as Sir Philip Sidney and the greatest of them all, Shakespeare (remember "Shall I compare thee to a summer's day"?).

The Jacobean period (early 17th century) saw the best work of "rare Ben Jonson," author of satirical comedies and leader of the poets who met at the Mermaid Tavern in London, and the writings of John Donne (". . . never send to know for whom the bell tolls . . ."). The translation of the Bible, known as the King James Version, was undertaken at this time under the auspices of James I, and assumed its immortal place in literature.

By the mid-17th century, writers, like all English people, began to be divided in allegiance between the king and Parliament. The Cavalier poets, of whom Robert Herrick heads the list, wrote lyrical verse and backed the king. The literary giant of the mid-17th century was John Milton, a pro-Parliamentarian and author of *Paradise Lost,* considered even in his lifetime to be one of the country's top geniuses. John Bunyan, a Baptist lay-preacher caught up in the Puritan cause, was sent to prison after the restoration of the monarchy, where he wrote *Pilgrim's Progress,* whose powerful imagery transcended theological differences. After Charles II regained the throne, theaters closed by Cromwell reopened, and literature took on a lighter, lively tone, reflected in the plays of Sheridan and the diary of Samuel Pepys.

Throughout the 18th century the literary world of England was crowded with the output of geniuses and near-geniuses from the rising middle class. Among these were Defoe (*Robinson Crusoe* and *Moll Flanders*), Alexander Pope (*An Essay on Man*), Fielding (*Tom Jones*), and a host of essayists and novelists. Most memorable in this period, however, is Samuel Johnson, whose *Dictionary of the English Language* made him the premier lexicographer and man of letters. His association with James Boswell from Scotland resulted in Johnson's becoming a major figure in literary annals, albeit through Boswell's writings.

To enter into a dissertation on the early 19th-century literary scene in England and try to expound on the stars in that galaxy in limited space would be to bog down utterly. So I'll just mention several names known to everyone who has ever studied literature in school: William Blake, William Wordsworth, Samuel Taylor Coleridge, Lord Byron, John Keats, Percy Bysshe Shelley, Jane Austen, and Charles Lamb— but there are oh! so many more. As you travel through the country, you will see birthplaces, familiar haunts, habitations, and burial places of many such writers.

Now to the years that challenge a student of literature—the mid- and late-1800s. These encompass the Victorian Age when storytellers developed emotional themes and reflected the stresses of their times, and poets created both romantic and humorous works. In this letters-rich age, readers devoured the works of Charles Dickens, William Thackeray, the Brontë sisters, Alfred Lord Tennyson, the Brownings, Lewis Carroll, George Eliot, George Meredith, Matthew Arnold, Thomas Hardy, A. C. Swinburne, and Oscar Wilde, with a little heavier reading from John Ruskin thrown in. The great middle class had learned to read, printing was flourishing, and the union of these forces produced a literary thrust that took the country at a gallop into the 20th century.

Straddling the turn of the century but usually considered literary figures of modern times—from the early 1900s, it's true—are such notables as Rudyard Kipling, H. G. Wells, Galsworthy, Maugham, Walter de la Mare, and Sir Arthur Conan Doyle. Writers of the 20th century include Robert Graves, Stephen Spender, W. H. Auden, Virginia Woolf, D. H. Lawrence, Aldous Huxley, Kingsley Amis, Graham

Greene, George Orwell, E. M. Forster, Antonia Fraser, Ted Hughes, William Golding, Muriel Spark, and—not to be forgotten—Winston Churchill.

In the category of "good reads" are some of the best mystery and suspense novels to be found. From these, you can learn about life in England from cottages to castles, in the cities and in the remote country, in the past and in the present, and a lot about the police and the crime scene from before the Bow Street Runners to to-day's New Scotland Yard. The tradition began with Sherlock Holmes; Dorothy Sayers places you in the fen country in the 1920s, Agatha Christie brings to life vil-lage atmosphere in St. Mary Mead, and today Ellis Peters makes you feel at home at Shrewsbury in the 12th century. There are many other writers of this ilk whose stor-ies, whether you're a mystery fan or not, can enrich your visit to England by giving you a personal "word tour" of all the country.

I could go on and on and on—and I still might well leave out your favorite English writer. In fact, I'm sure someone will ask, "But what about Jonathan Swift? Oliver Goldsmith? George Bernard Shaw? Sir Walter Scott? Robert Burns? Robert Louis Stevenson? Joseph Conrad? Dylan Thomas? Doris Lessing?" Indeed, these writers made their mark in English literature. But to keep this list within manageable limits, I've left out those who were not born in England. The British Isles are rich in literary greats, and I've only reminded you of *some* of them.

MUSIC

From the time the English monks' choirs surpassed those of Germany and France in singing the Gregorian chant (brought to this country in 597 by St. Augus-tine of Canterbury, Pope Gregory's missionary), and were judged second only to the choirs of Rome, music has been heard throughout England. Polyphonic music developed after the simple chant, and sacred vocal music was early accompanied by the organ. The first organ at Winchester was installed in the 10th century. One of the earliest written compositions was the polyphonic piece (a round), *Summer is icumen in,* with six parts.

Instruments commonly used in the Middle Ages, besides the organ found only in churches, were the fiddle, the lute, and the rebec, used in court circles for the en-tertainment of royalty and courtiers. Kings had musicians at court, and Henry VIII, in particular, was known as a composer. He wrote sonnets for his ladyloves and set them to music. The British Museum contains some 34 manuscripts of Henry's compositions. So flourishing was music in England in the 16th century that Erasmus of Rotterdam reported, after one of his visits: "They are so much occupied with music here that even the monks don't do anything else."

Music among the common people of the time may have been less polished but no less enthusiastic, as ditties and rounds were composed and heard in taverns and fields, the richness of the tunes compensating for the frequent vulgarity of the words. Some of the songs Shakespeare had his characters sing attest to the coarseness of the lyrics.

During the Tudor dynasty English cathedral music came into full flower. Dur-ing these years, too, the forerunners of the opera and operetta came into being as spectacles called masques. These combined instrumental and vocal music, dancing, satire, recitations, and elaborate scenic effects—the beginning of stage design.

Musicians were persecuted in the 1600s under the Commonwealth, but they came back into glory with the restoration of the Stuart monarchy: Henry Purcell wrote the first English opera, *Dido and Aeneas,* in 1689. In the 18th century Italian opera became the rage, even as Sir John Gay satirized such productions in *The Beg-gars' Opera* in 1728. Handel, who became an English subject, composed many operas and oratorios here, including *Messiah,* and other musicians followed (some-times haltingly) in his train.

The 19th century's outstanding contribution was the uniquely English operet-tas of Gilbert and Sullivan.

Many great names in the 20th century music world are English: Sir Edward Elgar, Ralph Vaughan Williams, Sir William Walton, Benjamin Britten, to name just a few.

Paul McCartney and John Lennon of the Beatles began what has been called in America "the British invasion." Since the 1960s, English rock musicians have often dominated the American music scene. Individual vocalists such as Phil Collins, David Bowie, and Sting, and guitarists such as Eric Clapton have been leading forces in popular music. But the biggest musical influence from England has been the rock bands: The Rolling Stones, The Who, Pink Floyd, Genesis, The Sex Pistols, and XTC. British rock's influence on Western popular music and culture has been and is still tremendous.

ART

From the first carved and jewel-bedecked baubles, utensils, and even weapons of prehistoric man, the craze for ornamentation continued and grew. Intricately wrought crosses, religious statuary, and illuminated manuscripts led the way to stained-glass windows, ecclesiastical paintings, and other art forms connected first with the abbeys and cathedrals that came into being over the centuries and throughout the country. Soon these were followed by decorative glorification and expansion of the homes of royal and noble personages, and then by the gentry and whoever could afford to have their persons and structures beautified.

Ornate tombs with sculptured effigies of the dead marked the resting places of the nobility and the princes in the church of the Middle Ages, and the cathedrals became art galleries of awesome beauty. Medieval painting consisted mostly of illumination of manuscripts by monks who took as models work done in European monasteries. Other art by the 13th century was in the embroidering of tapestries, metalwork, and carving, with panel painting, stained glass, and frescoes among the media of expression.

Art, and even beauty, were considered the work of the devil during the religious upheavals of the 16th and 17th centuries, but when peace of a sort returned, sculpture came into vogue again, and painting reached an enviable grandeur. The name of Grinling Gibbons looms large for his baroque carvings in the late 17th and early 18th centuries, but it was not really until the 20th century that sculpture became a serious competitor to painting in England. Names such as Henry Moore, Barbara Hepworth, Sir Jacob Epstein, and Kenneth Armitage are only a few of the greats connected with English sculpture of today.

In painting in England, portraiture was the early favorite. Everybody who was anybody had themselves depicted—alone, with family, with pets, whatever. The early leader in this field was Hans Holbein the Younger, a Swiss-born artist who became painter to Henry VIII. Among the outstanding painters of the Tudor and Stuart periods, neither Van Dyck nor Lely were English-born.

However, native English painters came into their own by the 18th century, during the same era that landscape and animal painting and social satire began to vie with portraiture as recognized art forms. A roll call of the greats of that time resounds even today: Constable, Gainsborough, Hogarth, Reynolds, Romney, Turner, and many more. It was in that era that the Royal Academy of Arts was formed (1768), which you can visit in Piccadilly. (The academy is considered old hat by many artists and art critics today.)

Painters of the 19th and 20th centuries whose supremacy is recognized include Sir Edward Burne-Jones, Dante Gabriel Rossetti, W. Holman Hunt, Ben Nicholson, Augustus John, Francis Bacon, Graham Sutherland, to name a few. Some of these, it is true, are felt to be too romantic or too iconoclastically avant-garde for all tastes, but each has earned a place in art history.

Whatever your preferences may be—old masters or 20th-century artists—you can find something to please you (and probably something to complain about) in the hundreds of galleries large and small throughout England.

ARCHITECTURE

From ancient human-made ceremonial sites such as Stonehenge, through the great minsters and cathedrals of the Middle Ages, on up to the modern places of worship at Coventry and Liverpool, art has ever sought to bring a functional shape to sites where a higher power is invoked, as well as to places of human habitation.

Architecture in England has moved through many periods; examples can be seen today in preserved, restored, and reconstructed form. These periods embrace the Anglo-Saxon, 6th to mid-11th centuries; the Norman, 11th and 12th centuries; Gothic (actually comprising four phases: Early English, Decorated, Perpendicular, and Tudor), 12th to 16th centuries; Renaissance (including Elizabethan, Jacobean, Palladian, and Byzantine), mid-16th to early 18th centuries; Georgian, early 18th to 19th; Regency, early 19th; Victorian, mid-19th to early 20th; and the architecture of the present century, which has taken many forms.

Many examples exist of work from all these periods since the Norman, so that the interested visitor has little difficulty in finding them among the sights of England. Many of the names of the architects responsible for these lasting monuments to humanity's genius have not survived, but enough are known to make a formidable roster of greatness. From the monk, Gandulf, a stonemason credited with construction of the White Tower, the list reads through Inigo Jones, Sir Christopher Wren, Nicholas Hawksmoor, Sir John Vanbrugh, James Gibbs, John Nash, Sir Edwin Lutyens, and countless others. (Robert Adam, whose name is synonymous with handsome interiors and some exterior work, was a Scotsman, but much of his work can be seen in England.)

Not a builder of houses but a landscape architect was Lancelot ("Capability") Brown, whose work also lives on, framing the beauty of many palaces and manor houses.

The rich legacy of a millennium of builders is an integral part of the visitor's enjoyment of England.

---

3. Food and Drink

Understanding British traditional dishes will help you enjoy your visit even more. The following comments will explain a few; other "surprises" you must seek out for yourself. Many good old-fashioned dishes are available in restaurants, wine bars, and pubs—sometimes called inns or taverns, names going back to the Middle Ages.

The most common pub meal is based on the food a farm worker took with him to work, a **ploughman's lunch.** Originally a good chunk of local cheese, a hunk of homemade crusty brown bread, some butter, and a pickled onion or two, it was washed down with ale. You will now find such variations as pâté and chutney replacing the onions and cheese. **Cheese** is still, however, the most common ingredient.

English **cheese** comes in many regional variations, the best known being Cheddar, a good, solid, mature cheese, as is Cheshire. Another is the semismooth-textured Caerphilly from Wales, and Stilton, a softer tangy cheese, popular with a glass of port.

Dishes with names so perplexing you have no hint of their ingredients are found on the little tea shoppe menu or in pubs and the like. Perhaps the most popular is **shepherd's pie,** a deep dish of chopped cooked beef mixed with onions and seasoning and covered with a layer of mashed potatoes and served hot. Another version is **cottage pie,** which is minced beef covered with potatoes and also served hot.

Traveling in the southeast part of England around Colchester, you will find a most prized British dish, the **oyster** for which, it is suggested, Julius Caesar really invaded Britain in 54 B.C.

As you move about England, you will come across dishes that were developed to fulfill a particular need. The **Cornish pasty** was made from the remains of the family's Sunday dinner in Cornish fishing villages: minced meat, chopped potato, carrot, onion, and seasoning mixed together and put into a pastry envelope, ready to be taken to sea by the fisherman on Monday for his lunch. In Grasmere you can buy

gingerbread cookies made from a recipe more than 125 years old, coming in the same alphabet shapes used to teach children to read in the 19th century. A *"flitting dumpling,"* northern in origin, is made of dates, walnuts, and syrup mixed with other ingredients into a pudding. It was cut into slices and could feed a family when "flitting" from one area to another. It is said that "hurry pudding" or **hasty pudding** in some areas was invented by those avoiding the bailiff. This dish from Newcastle uses up stale bread (some dried fruit and milk were added before it was put into the oven). In the northwest you'll come across **Lancashire hotpot,** a stew of mutton, potatoes, kidneys, and onions (sometimes carrots). This concoction was originally put into a deep dish and set on the edge of the stove to cook slowly while the family went to work in a local mill.

Among the most known and traditional of English dishes is **roast beef and Yorkshire pudding.** The pudding is made with a flour base and cooked under the joint, allowing the fat from the meat to drop onto it. The beef could easily be a large "sirloin" (rolled loin), which, so the story goes, was named by King James I (not Henry VIII as some claim) when he was a guest at Hoghton Tower, Lancashire. "Arise, Sir Loin," he cried, as he knighted the joint with his dagger.

Meat left over would be eaten the next day in **"bubble and squeak"** fried together with chopped cabbage and potatoes. Another dish that makes use of a batter similar to Yorkshire pudding is **"toad-in-the-hole,"** in which sausages are cooked in batter.

On the west coast you'll find a delicacy not to be missed, the Morecambe Bay shrimp. Of course, the whole coast of Britain provides a feast of **fish dishes,** the champions being cod, haddock, herring, plaice, and the aristocrat of flat fish, Dover sole. Cod and haddock are the most popular fish used in the making of that British tradition, **"fish and chips"** (chips, of course, are fried potatoes or french fries). The true Briton covers this dish with salt and vinegar. In the past the wrapping was newspaper, but now the demands of hygiene have removed the added—some say, indispensable—taste of newsprint from the dish.

Kipper, a smoked herring, is a popular breakfast dish. The finest are from the Isle of Man, Whitby, or Loch Fyne in Scotland. Herrings are split open and placed over oak chips and smoked slowly to produce a nice pale-brown smoked fish. The British eat large breakfasts, or at least many of them do. "Ham and eggs" is said to have originated in Britain.

High tea, almost unknown in the south, is common in the north of England and in Scotland. It is a meal that is a mix of hot and cold foods, giving the worker on his return home a combination of tea and supper. In the north the word *dinner* describes the midday meal (lunch), while in the south it means the evening meal. Supper, by tradition, is a meal taken late at night, usually after the theater.

Incidentally, real English **mustard** is simply the finely ground seed mixed with water, nothing else.

The East End of London has quite a few interesting old dishes, among them tripe and onions. Dr. Johnson's favorite tavern, the Cheshire Cheese on Fleet Street, still offers a **beefsteak, kidney, mushroom, and game pudding** in a suet case in winter and a pastry case in summer. The East Ender will be seen on Sunday at the jellied eel stall by Petticoat Lane, eating eel or perhaps cockles, mussels, whelks, and winkles, all small shellfish eaten with a touch of vinegar. The eel-pie-and-mash shop can still be found in London. The name, **eel pie,** however, is misleading, because it is really a minced-beef pie topped with flaky pastry and served with mashed potatoes and accompanied by a portion of jellied eel.

It is a misconception to believe that "everything" stops for tea. People in Britain drink an average of four cups of **tea** a day, mainly at work. The real delight is to visit the little country tea shops where you can enjoy a pot of tea, some toasted tea cake (currant bun), or a crumpet (sometimes confused with the rarely found muffin), scones, bread and butter, or sandwiches, and good homemade cakes, all enjoyed while listening to the conversation at the next table. In recent years, coffee has grown more popular in England, especially for morning breaks.

A word about the **wine** of the country: Britain does not produce much real

FOOD AND DRINK □ 43

wine. It does produce some very pleasant white wine on the medium-sweet side and quite fruity in taste. The real "wines" are cider and beer, both of which go well with the traditional dishes mentioned earlier.

Beer is served in all pubs. Draft beer is traditionally served at cellar temperature; the British like to taste their beer so they prefer it on the warm side of cold. Most bottled beer, however, is similar to light lager beers and is served cold. Draft beer comes in several different tastes, the most common being called "bitter," which is light in color and taste, not really bitter. A half pint is the equivalent in strength to a single measure of scotch. Others are mild ale, which is full flavored, and brown ale, which is dark and flavorsome. Stout is a strong, rich dark beer, often mixed with champagne to make "black velvet." The most famous stout is from Ireland, called Guinness, and it is strong tasting and very dark with a good white head (froth). **Cider,** made from apples and fermented, can be stronger than expected.

However, after saying all the above, I can still assure you that the food and drink (including French and Italian wines) served in most restaurants will be international in scope, with some traditional British dishes. The reputation that Britain had for years for its soggy cabbage and tasteless dishes is no longer deserved. If you pick and choose carefully, and use this guide to help you seek out the finer dining rooms, you can enjoy some of the finest food in Europe while touring the British Isles.

III

SETTLING INTO LONDON

1. ORIENTATION

2. MAYFAIR

3. ST. JAMES'S

4. PICCADILLY

5. THE STRAND AND COVENT GARDEN

6. HOLBORN

7. WESTMINSTER

8. VICTORIA

9. BELGRAVIA

10. KNIGHTSBRIDGE

11. CHELSEA

12. CHELSEA HARBOUR

13. EARL'S COURT

14. KENSINGTON

15. SOUTH KENSINGTON

16. NOTTING HILL GATE

17. HOLLAND PARK

18. LANCASTER GATE

19. PADDINGTON/BAYSWATER

20. ST. MARYLEBONE

21. BLOOMSBURY

22. OTHER LOCALES

23. AIRPORT HOTELS

London is a hybrid, a gathering place for people from the far corners of a once-great empire. People from country villages and provincial towns visit London in the mood of going abroad. But British and foreign visitors alike come to admire its magnificent synthesis of historic city and contemporary life.

The true Londoner, usually from the East End, is called a cockney, the name for a person born within the sound of the Bow Bells, the chimes of a church in Cheapside. But the city is also the home of the well-bred English lady who has had to sell her family estate of 400 years and take meager lodgings in Earl's Court; of the expatriate Hollywood actress living in elegance in a Georgian town house; of the islander from Jamaica who comes seeking a new life and ends up collecting fares on one of London's red double-decker buses; of the young playwright from Liverpool whose art reflects the outlook of the working class.

Cosmopolitan or not, Europe's largest city is still like a great wheel, with Piccadilly Circus at the hub and dozens of communities branching out from it. Since London is such a conglomeration of sections—each having its own life (hotels, restaurants, pubs)—the first-time visitor may be intimidated until he or she gets the hang of it. In this chapter, I'll concentrate on the so-called West End, although nobody has been able to come up with a satisfactory explanation as to what that entails. For the most part, a visitor will live and eat in the West End, except when he or she ventures into the old and historic part of London known as "The City," or goes on a tour to the Tower of London, or seeks lodgings in the remote villages such as Hampstead Heath.

1. Orientation

London is a city that has never quite made up its mind about its own size. The "City of London" proper is merely one square mile of (very expensive) real estate around the Bank of England. All the gargantuan rest is made up of separate cities, towns, boroughs, and corporations, called Westminster, Chelsea, Hampstead, Kensington, Camden Town, and so forth, each with its own mayor and administration and ready to fight for its independent status at the drop of an ordinance. These were once separate villages entirely, but through the centuries, the growth of Greater London has filled in the fields and woods that once separated them. Together, they add up to a mammoth metropolis—once the largest city on the globe, now dropped to 16th in a United Nations survey of population.

The millions of people loosely governed by the Greater London Council live spread out over 609 square miles. Luckily, only a minute fraction of this territory need concern us. The rest is simply suburbs, stretching endlessly to the horizon, red-roofed and bristling with TV antennas. But the heart, the brick and mortar core of this giant, is perhaps the most fascinating area on earth. For about a century, one quarter of the world was ruled from there, and with every step you take, you'll come across some sign of the tremendous influence this city has exerted over our thoughts and past actions—and still wields today.

HISTORY

London is a very old city, even by European standards. The Roman conquerors of Britain founded Londinium on the site of a British village in A.D. 43 by settling and fortifying two small hills on the north bank of the River Thames and linking them via a military network of roads with the rest of the island.

More than a thousand years later, another conqueror turned the city into his capital. This was William II, Duke of Normandy, who defeated the last Saxon ruler of England, Harold Godwin, in 1066. There isn't much remaining of the Roman period, but William the Conqueror left his imprint on London for all time to come. For a start, he had himself crowned in Westminster Abbey. Every British monarch since has been crowned there, right up to the present Queen Elizabeth II. William also built the White Tower, which today forms part of the Tower of London, and did even more to transform London (or rather, the area known as Westminster) into a royal capital. He and his nobles superimposed their Norman French on the country's original Anglo-Saxon language. Both the richness and the maddening illogicality of the English we speak today are direct results of that transplant.

The Normans weren't exactly gentle rulers, but the nation they created did pretty well. No one, for instance, has ever successfully invaded Britain since William's time—unless you count Americans, Canadians, Australians, Japanese, and other tourists from around the world.

Royal but Democratic

London is a mass of contradictions, some of them dating far back in her history. On one hand, she's decidedly a royal city, studded with palaces, court gardens, coats-of-arms, and other royal paraphernalia. Yet she is also the home of the second-oldest parliamentary assembly (Iceland has the oldest). When rash King Charles I tried to defy its representatives, he found himself swept off his throne and into the hands of the headsman (1649) long before the French got around to dealing likewise with their anointed monarch.

The huge gray building that houses the "Mother of Parliaments," with its famous clock, Big Ben, is more truly symbolic of London than is Buckingham Palace. It was there that Prime Minister William Pitt intoned, "You cannot make peace with dictators—you have to defeat them," at a time when England stood alone against the might of Napoleon. It was there, too, that Sir Winston Churchill repeated these sentiments in even better phrases when England—alone again—stood up against Hitler. It was also in Parliament that "His Majesty's Loyal Opposition" stood up to give a rousing cheer for Gen. George Washington's army, which had just whipped His Majesty's Hessian mercenaries—whom the English detested every ounce as much as did the American colonists.

Nevertheless, London itself was largely shaped by the monarchs who ruled her —imposingly by the tough Tudors, beautifully by the wicked Georges, clumsily by the worthy Victoria.

Bouncing Back from Disasters

Much of London is also the result of disasters, both accidental and premeditated. The first was the Great Fire of 1666, which swept away most of the old wooden Tudor houses and resulted in a new city built of brick. The cause of the fire remains forever unknown, but considering the fire hazards of those tightly packed, timbered dwellings, the remarkable thing is that the town didn't burn down annually. As it was, the blaze gutted three-quarters of London—about 13,300 homes, churches, and public buildings. But it also gave England's greatest architect, Christopher Wren, the chance to design St. Paul's Cathedral as it stands today, as well as 51 other superb churches, plus the magnificent Royal Hospitals in Chelsea and Greenwich.

The blitz Hitler unleashed on the city during 1940–1941 also had one beneficial result. Along with wiping out beautiful structures, the rain of incendiary bombs demolished vast patches of the pestilential slum areas around Whitechapel in the East End. The region—made equally famous by Charles Dickens and Jack the Ripper—had been London's festering sore, boasting possibly the worst housing conditions in the Western world. With slum clearance, courtesy of the Luftwaffe, the London County Council rebuilt most of the area into rather drab but infinitely superior apartment blocks.

There was something else the blitz gave London: a world image as the embattled fortress of freedom, caught unforgettably by the wartime news photo showing the white dome of St. Paul's silhouetted against the black smoke of a dozen simultaneous fires.

The postwar building boom may have made London a little less "quaint," but it also made her a very much healthier, happier place to live in, and it provided the overture of her present phase, which is that of a lively, cosmopolitan city.

A BIT OF GEOGRAPHY

There is, fortunately, an immense difference between the sprawling vastness of Greater London and the pocket-size chunk that might be called "Tourist Country."

For a start, practically all of the latter is north of the River Thames, but make no mistake—this is still a hefty portion of land to cover and a really thorough exploration of it would take a couple of years. But it has the advantage of being flat and eminently walkable, besides boasting one of the best transport systems ever devised.

The local but not the geographical center of our "Tourist Country" is **Trafalgar Square,** which we'll therefore take as our orientation point. The huge, thronged, fountain-splashed square was named for the battle in which Nelson destroyed the combined French and Spanish fleets and lost his own life. His statue tops the towering pillar in the center, and local residents maintain that the reason he's been up there all these years is that nobody has told him the lions at the base are made of stone. If you stand in the square facing the imposing **National Gallery,** you're looking northwest. That is the direction of **Piccadilly Circus,** which is the real core of tourist London, as well as the maze of streets that make up **Soho.** Farther north runs **Oxford Street,** London's gift to moderately priced shopping, and still farther northwest lies **Regent's Park** with its zoo.

At your back—that is, south—runs **Whitehall,** which houses or skirts nearly every British government building, from the Ministry of Defence to the official residence of the prime minister at 10 **Downing Street.** In the same direction, a bit farther south, stand the **Houses of Parliament** and **Westminster Abbey.**

Flowing southwest from Trafalgar Square is the table-smooth **Mall,** flanked by magnificent parks and mansions and leading to **Buckingham Palace,** residence of the queen. Farther in the same direction lie **Belgravia** and **Knightsbridge,** the city's poshest residential areas, and south of them **Chelsea,** with its chic flavor, plus **Kings Road,** the boutique-filled shopping drag.

Due west from where you're standing stretches the superb and distinctly high-priced shopping area bordered by **Regent Street** and **Piccadilly** (the street, not the Circus). Farther west lie the equally elegant shops and even more elegant homes of **Mayfair.** Then come **Park Lane** and on the other side **Hyde Park,** the biggest park in London and one of the largest in the world.

Running north from Trafalgar Square is **Charing Cross Road,** past **Leicester Square** and intersecting with **Shaftesbury Avenue.** This is London's theaterland, boasting an astonishing number of live shows as well as first-run movie houses. A bit farther along, Charing Cross Road turns into a browser's paradise, lined with bookshops selling both new and secondhand books. Finally, it funnels into **St. Giles Circus.** This is where you enter **Bloomsbury,** site of the University of London, the awesome **British Museum,** and erstwhile stamping ground of the famed "Bloomsbury Group," led by Virginia Woolf. Northeast of your position lies **Covent Garden,** known for its **Royal Opera House.**

Follow **the Strand** eastward from Trafalgar Square, and you'll come into **Fleet Street.** Beginning in the 19th century, this corner of London became the most concentrated newspaper district in the world. But over the decades, the newspapers folded or moved away. The last newspaper edition was published on Fleet Street in 1989. At the end of Fleet Street lies **Ludgate Circus**—and only there do you enter the actual City of London. This was the original walled settlement and is today what the locals mean when they refer to **"The City."** Its focal point and shrine is the Bank of England on **Threadneedle Street** with the Stock Exchange next door and the Royal Exchange across the road.

The City is unique in that it retains its own separate police force (distinguished by a crest on their helmets) and its own Lord Mayor. Its 677 acres are an ant heap of jammed cars and rushing clerks during the week and totally deserted on Sunday, because hardly a soul lives within its boundaries. Its streets are winding, narrow, and fairly devoid of charm. But it has more bankers and stockbrokers per square inch during business hours than any other place on the globe. In the midst of all the hustle rises **St. Paul's Cathedral,** a monument to beauty and tranquility. At the far eastern fringe of The City looms the **Tower of London,** shrouded in legend, blood, and history. It is permanently besieged by battalions of visitors.

Designed to Confuse

I'd like to tell you that London's thoroughfares follow a recognizable pattern in which, with a little intelligence, even a stranger can find his or her way around. Unfortunately, they don't and you can't. London's streets follow no pattern whatsoever, and both their naming and house numbering seem to have been perpetrated by a bunch of xenophobes with an equal grudge against postal carriers and foreigners.

Be warned that the use of logic and common sense will get you nowhere. Don't think, for instance, that Southampton Row is anywhere near Southampton Street and that either of these places has any connection with Southampton Road. This is only a mild example. London is checkered with innumerable squares, mews, closes, and terraces, which jut into or cross or overlap or interrupt whatever street you're trying to follow, usually without the slightest warning. You may be walking along ruler-straight Albany Street and suddenly find that you are on Colosseum Terrace, according to the signs (with a different numbering system). Just keep on walking and after a couple of blocks you're right back on Albany Street (and the original system of house numbers), without having encountered the faintest reason for the sudden change in labels.

House numbers run in odds or evens, clockwise or counterclockwise as the wind blows—that is, when they exist at all, and frequently they don't. Every so often you'll come upon a square that is called a square on the south side, a road on the north, a park on the east, and possibly a something-or-other close on the west side. Your only chance is to consult a map or ask your way along. Most of the time, you'll probably end up doing both.

But there are a couple of consoling factors. One is the legibility of the street signs. The other is the extraordinary helpfulness of the locals, who sometimes pass you from guide to guide like a bucket in a fire chain.

LONDON'S AIRPORTS

There are three airports serving London: Heathrow, where most international flights come in; the smaller Gatwick, where many charter and some scheduled flights arrive; and London City Airport, used mainly for STOL (short takeoff and landing) and commuter-type flights to and from the continent. Each airport has several kinds of land transportation connecting it with London proper.

Heathrow Airport, in Houndslow, Middlesex, is one of the busiest airports in the world, with flights arriving from all parts of Great Britain and all over the globe. It is divided into four terminals. Terminal 4, the longhaul hub operation of British Airways, has been called the most modern air terminal in the world. It is also home to BA's Super Shuttle, linking London with Edinburgh, Glasgow, Belfast, and Manchester. Most flights from North America, including those of Pan American and Trans World Airlines, arrive at Terminals 1 and 2. Terminal 3 is home to intra-European flights.

It takes 50 minutes by **Underground** to make the 15-mile trip from Heathrow Central to the center of London and costs £1.90 ($3.15) for adults and 70p ($1.15) for children aged 5 to 15. You can also take an **airbus,** which gets you into central London in about an hour and costs £4 ($6.60) for adults and £2 ($3.30) for children. A **taxi** to central London is likely to cost more than £20 ($33).

For **flight information,** call Heathrow at 081/759-4321.

Gatwick Airport lies 30 miles from London. **Trains** leave from there for London every 15 minutes until midnight, and every hour after midnight. There is also an **express bus** from Gatwick to Victoria Station every half hour from 6:30am to 8pm and every hour from 8 to 11pm. This Flightline Bus 777 costs £5.50 ($9.10) per person. A **taxi** from Gatwick to central London usually costs £35 ($57.75). However, you must negotiate a fare with the driver before you get in the cab as the meter does not apply (Gatwick is outside the Metropolitan Police District).

For **flight information,** call Gatwick at 0293/31299.

Yet a third airport, **London City Airport,** lies about six miles east of The City in the Royal Docklands. It's used mainly by business people from Common Market countries. There are no direct Underground or rail links connecting this airport to the center of London (it's still too new). You can take a short **taxi** ride to the Plaistow station of the Underground's District line, but most business passengers take a taxi into town at fares that run about £10 ($16.50) and up. However, it would be a lot cheaper to go by **riverbus.** The riverbus landing pier is just a short walk from the airline's terminal. Leaving every hour on the hour from 7:30am to 6:30pm Mon. to Fri., these boats stop at Swan Lane Pier (close to the financial district) and, finally, at Charing Cross Pier. The cost of a one-way ticket to Swan Lane is £5 ($8.25) and from Charing Cross £6 ($9.90).

Among the STOL and commuter airlines that use this terminal are Air France's link to Brymon Airlines, with routes to Lille, Strasbourg, and Nantes in France; Flex Air's flights to Rotterdam; London City Airways' (linked to Sabena) routes to Brussels; and UTA's flights to Paris.

For **flight information,** call London City Airport at 081/474-5555.

TRANSPORTATION IN GREATER LONDON

If you know the ropes, transportation within London can be unusually easy and inexpensive. Both the Underground (subway) and bus systems are operated by **London Regional Transport,** with Travel Information Centers in the Underground stations at King's Cross, Oxford Circus, and Piccadilly Circus, and also in the British Rail stations at Euston and Victoria and each of the terminals at Heathrow Airport.

Travelcards, for use on bus, Underground, and British Rail services and available in a number of combinations of adjacent zones, are offered by the London Regional Transport. Travelcards can be purchased for a minimum of seven days or any period (including odd days) from a month to a year. For example, a Travelcard allowing travel in two zones for one week costs adults £9.10 ($15) and children £2.80 ($4.60).

To purchase a Travelcard, you must present a Photocard. For persons 16 years old or older, the Photocard is easy to get. Just take a passport-type picture of yourself with you when you buy your Travelcard, and the Photocard will be issued free. Child-rate Photocards are only issued at main post offices in the London area, and in addition to a passport-type photograph, proof of age is required (for example, a passport or a birth certificate). Travelcards are not issued at child rates unless supported by a Photocard. Older children (14 or 15) are charged adult fares on all services unless in possession of one of the cards. A child-rate Photocard is not, however, required for tours.

For shorter stays in London, you may want to consider the **One-Day Off-Peak Travelcard.** This ticket can be used on most bus, Underground, and British Rail services throughout Greater London after 9:30am Mon. to Fri. and at any time on bank holidays. The ticket is available from Underground ticket offices, bus garages, Travel Information Centers, and some newsstands. It costs £2.60 ($4.30) for adults, 90p ($1.50) for youths 14 or 15. For four zones, the cost is £2.30 ($3.80) for adults, 80p ($1.30) for children.

The London Transport Information Centres provide information on a wide range of facilities and places of interest in addition to data on most bus and Underground services. They take reservations for London Transport's guided tours and have free Underground and bus maps and other information leaflets. A 24-hour telephone information service is available (tel. 071/222-1234).

In addition to the information obtainable from any of the Travel Information Centres, information is also available by writing London Regional Transport, Travel Information Service, 55 Broadway, London SW1H OBD.

The Underground

Londoners usually refer to the Underground as the "tube." Stations are identified by a distinctive sign, a red circle with blue crossbar, and the words "London Underground." If you ask for a "subway," you risk ending up in a tunnel for pedestrians running beneath the road. Destinations are listed on ticket machines. Maps showing the Underground network are displayed in every station, on each platform, and in Underground train cars.

If you have British coins, you can get your ticket at one of the vending machines that make change. Otherwise you buy it at the ticket office. You can transfer as many times as you like so long as you stay in the Underground.

The electric subways are, to begin with, comfortable—the trains have cushioned seats, no less. The flat fare for one journey within the central zone is 70p ($1.15). Trips from the central zone to destinations in the suburbs range from 60p ($1) to £2.10 ($3.45) in most cases. Be sure to keep your ticket; it must be presented when you get off. If you owe extra, you'll be billed by the attendant.

Note: If you're out on the town and are dependent on the Underground, watch your time carefully. Many of the trains stop running at midnight (11:30pm on Sun.).

The line serving Heathrow Airport to central London has trains with additional luggage space, as well as moving walkways from the airport terminals to the Underground station.

Buses

The comparably priced bus system is almost as good as the Underground—and you have a better view. To find out about current routes, pick up a free bus map at one of the London Transport Travel Information Centres listed previously. (They are not available by mail.)

After you've queued up for the **red double-decker bus** and selected a seat downstairs or on the upper deck (the best seats are on top, where you'll see more of the city), a conductor will come by to whom you'll tell your destination. He or she then collects the fare and gives you a ticket. As with the Underground, the fare varies according to the distance you travel. If you want to be warned when to get off, simply ask the conductor.

Victoria Coach Station, Buckingham Palace Rd., S.W.1 (tel. 071/750-0202), is the main bus terminal. Tube: Victoria. Other bus stations are at King's Cross Coach Station and at Gloucester Road beside the Forum Hotel. The **green single-decker buses** you see on London streets link the center with outlying towns and villages.

Taxis

You can pick up a cab in London either by heading for a cab rank or by hailing one in the street (the taxi is available if the light on the hood is on). Or else you can phone 071/253-5000, 071/272-0271, or 071/272-3030 for a radio cab. The minimum fare is £1 ($1.65) for the first 1,152 yards or three minutes and 49.5 seconds, with increments of 20p (35¢) thereafter, based on a distance or time. Each additional passenger is charged 20p (35¢). From 8pm to midnight Mon. to Fri. and from 6am to 8pm on Sat., after the £1 ($1.65) minimum, increments are 40p (65¢). From midnight to 6am Mon. to Fri. and between 8pm on the day before until 6am on the day after Sun. and public holidays, the meter clicks over at 60p ($1.05). From 8pm on December 24 to 6am on December 27 and from 8pm on December 31 to 6am on January 1, the flag still drops at £1 ($1.65) but increments are £2 ($3.30). Passengers are charged 10p (17¢) for each piece of luggage in the driver's compartment and any other item more than two feet long. All these tariffs include VAT. It's recommended that you tip 10% to 12% of the fare.

Warning: If you phone for a cab, the meter starts running when the taxi receives instructions from the dispatcher. So you could find £1 ($1.65) or more on the meter when you get inside the taxi.

If you have a complaint about the taxi service you get, or if you leave something in a cab, phone the **Public Carriage Office,** 15 Penton St., N.1 (tel. 071/278-1744). If it's about a complaint, you must have the cab number, which is displayed in the passenger compartment.

Cab sharing is now permitted in London, as British law allows cabbies to offer

THE LONDON UNDERGROUND

shared rides for two to five passengers. The taxis accepting ride-sharing display a notice of yellow plastic with the words "Shared Taxi." These shared rides are mainly available at Heathrow Airport, main train stations, and the some 200 taxi stands in London. The savings per person is as follows: Each of two riders sharing is charged 65% of the fare a lone passenger would be charged. Three persons pay 55% each, four are charged 45% each, and five (the seating capacity of all new London cabs) pay 40% of the single-passenger fare.

Bicycles

This is the cheapest transportation apart from what you walk on. You can rent bikes by the day or by the week from a number of outfits.

One of the most popular places to rent a bike is **On Your Bike,** 22 Dukes' Street Hill, London Bridge, S.E.1 (tel. 071/378-6669; Tube: London Bridge). It is open Mon. to Fri. from 9am to 6pm and on Sat. from 9:30am to 4:30pm. The staff there has an inventory of around 50 bikes for both men and women that they rent by the day or week. The 10-speed sports bikes are the most preferred, with a high seat and low-slung handlebars. These cost £6 ($9.90) per day or £25 ($41.25) a week, requiring a £40 ($66) deposit. Also popular are the 18-gear "mountain bikes" which have straight handlebars and oversized gears. Designed for rough terrain, they are preferred by many clients for their maneuverability on the roads of "backstreet London." These cost £10 ($16.50) a day or £55 ($90.75) per week, requiring a deposit of £200 ($330). Deposits are payable by MasterCard or Visa.

LONDON FAST FACTS

Besides the general information on England and Scotland given in "Fast Facts of Britain," Chapter I, some facts pertaining mainly to London may help make your visit here better.

AMERICAN EXPRESS: The main office is 6 Haymarket, S.W.1 (tel. 071/930-4411; Tube: Piccadilly Circus). Full services are available from 9am to 5pm Mon. to Fri. and from 9am to noon on Sat. At other times—Sat. from noon to 6pm and Sun. from 10am to 4pm—only the foreign exchange desk and the travel desk (for the purchase of tours, rail, and air tickets) are open. The American Express office at the British Travel Center is open from 9am to 6:30pm Mon. to Fri. and from 10am to 4pm Sat. and Sun. The location of the British Travel Centre is 4-12 Lower Regent St., S.W.1 (tel. 071/839-2682); Tube: Piccadilly Circus. There are nine other London locations.

AREA CODES: London has two area codes—071 and 081. The 071 area code is good for Central London within a 4-mile radius of Charing Cross (including The City of London, Knightsbridge, and Oxford Street, and as far south as Brixton), and 081 works for outer London (including Heathrow Airport, Wimbledon, and Greenwich). Within London, you will need to dial the area code when calling from one of these sections of the city to the other, but not within a section.

BABYSITTERS: These are hard to find, but sometimes you can get your hotel to recommend someone, possibly a staff member. Expect to pay the cost of travel to and from your hotel by taxi. There are, as well, a number of organizations advertised in the Yellow Pages of the telephone directory that provide sitters using registered nurses and carefully checked mothers, as well as trained nannies.

One such company is **Childminders,** 67A Marylebone High St., W.1 (tel. 071/935-9763). Established in 1967, this is London's leading babysitting service, covering all of London, the suburbs, even some country areas. You pay £25 ($41.25), plus VAT, for a membership, then £3.50 ($5.80) per hour in the daytime, £2.30 ($3.80) per hour at night, depending on the day of the week. The membership fee is paid to the agency, while pay for the job goes to the employee, together with reasonable transportation costs. Tube: Regent's Park.

Universal Aunts, 250 King's Rd., S.W.3 (tel. 071/352-5767), established in

1921, provides personal services such as child care, mother's help, proxy parents, and nannies. Its location is opposite Chelsea Town Hall. Tube: Sloane Square.

BANKS: Hours generally are 9:30am to 3:30pm Mon. to Fri., although some banks in the suburbs are open on Saturday from 9:30am to 12:30pm. There are also Bureaux de Change, which charge high fees for cashing traveler's checks or personal (United Kingdom) checks and for changing foreign currency into pounds sterling. Bureaux are often open seven days a week, at least 12 hours or more a day. There are branches of the main banks at London's airports. You'll always get the best rates at banks.

CHURCH SERVICES: The interdenominational **American Church in London** is at 79 Tottenham Court Rd., W.1 (tel. 071/580-2791). Two services are usually held on Sun., one at 9:45am, another at 11:45am. Tube: Goodge Street.

DENTISTS: For dental emergencies, call **Emergency Dental Service** (tel. 071/752-0133). The staff there can match dental emergencies with dentists located not only in London, but in different parts of Britain as far north (but not beyond) Durham and Liverpool. The service is available 24 hours a day.

DOCTORS: In an emergency, contact **Doctor's Call** at 071/351-5312. The staff there handles calls relating to illnesses or emergency needs, and they match the call with an available doctor in your vicinity. Some hotels also have doctors on call. Ask at the reception desk.

DRUGSTORES: In Britain, they're called "chemist shops." Every police station in the country has a list of emergency chemists. Dial "0" (zero) and ask the operator for the local police. One of the most centrally located chemists in London, keeping long hours, is **Bliss the Chemist,** 5 Marble Arch, W.1 (tel. 071/723-6116). It is open daily from 9am to midnight. Tube: Marble Arch.

EMERGENCIES: To call for police, fire, or ambulance, dial 999.

EYEGLASSES: Lost or broken? Try **Imperial Optical of Selfridges,** a branch of the well-known Canadian optical company, at Selfridges Department Store, 400 Oxford St., W.1 (tel. 071/629-1234, ext. 3889). An eye exam costs £15 ($24.75), and the least expensive pair of eyeglasses with an uncomplicated prescription costs an additional £50 ($82.50). Contact lenses are also available within the same day in most cases. Multifocal lenses sometimes take two to three working days to complete, but simple prescriptions may be filled in two to three hours. You will pay more for designer frames. It's always wise to take a copy of your glasses prescription with you when you travel. Tube: Bond Street.

HAIRDRESSERS: Hairdressers and hairstylists crop up on most major street corners of London (a slight exaggeration), and range from the grandly imperial refuges of English dowagers to punk-rock citadels of purple hair and chartreuse mascara. One of the most visible—and one of the best—is a branch of **Vidal Sassoon,** 11 Floral St., W.C.2 (tel. 071/240-6635), in Covent Garden. Unlike some other Sassoon outlets, this caters to both men and women. A cut and finish by a stylist costs from £22.50 ($37.15) for men and £29.50 ($48.70) for women. The shop is open Mon. to Fri. from 10am to 7:30pm and on Sat. from 9:30am to 5pm. Tube: Covent Garden.

HOSPITALS: The following offer emergency care in London 24 hours a day, and the first treatment is free under the National Health Service. These include **Royal Free Hospital,** Pond St., N.W.3 (tel. 071/794-0500; Tube: Belsize Park), and the **University College Hospital,** Gower Street, W.C.1 (tel. 071/387-9300; Tube: Euston Square). Many other London hospitals also have accident and emergency departments. (See also "Dentists," "Doctors," and "Medical Services" elsewhere in this section.)

INFORMATION: Tourist information is available from the London Tourist Board's facilities. The **Tourist Information Centre,** Victoria Station Forecourt, S.W.1 (tube: Victoria Station), can and will help you with almost anything of interest to a tourist in the U.K. capital. The center deals chiefly with accommodations in all size and price categories, from single travelers, family groups, and students to large-scale conventions. They also arrange for tour ticket sales and theater reservations and operate a bookshop. Hours are 9am to 8:30pm daily from early April to the end of October; 9am to 7pm Mon. to Sat. and 9am to 5pm on Sun. from November to April. The bookshop is open from 9am to 6:30pm Mon. to Sat. and 9am to 4pm on Sun., and these hours are extended in July and August. For most types of service, you must apply in person.

The center also has offices at the following locations:

Harrods, Knightsbridge, S.W.3, in the basement. Open during store hours. Tube: Knightsbridge.

Selfridges, Oxford Street, W.1, basement services area, Duke Street entrance. Open during store hours. Tube: Bond Street.

The Tower of London, West Gate, E.C.3. Open early April to the end of October from 10am to 6pm daily. Tube: Tower Hill Station.

Heathrow Airport Terminals 1, 2, and 3, Underground Concourse, open from 9am to 6pm; and Terminal 2, Arrivals Concourse, open from 9am to 7pm daily.

Telephone inquiries may be made to the bureau by calling 071/730-3488 Mon. to Fri. from 9am to 6pm. Written inquiries should be addressed to the Correspondence Assistant, Distribution Department, **London Tourist Board and Convention Bureau,** 26 Grosvenor Gardens, London SW1W ODU.

For **riverboat information,** phone 071/730-4812.

LAUNDERETTES AND DRY CLEANING: If you want to have your clothes done for you (and avoid expensive hotel charges, assuming your hotel has such a service), go to **Danish Express Laundry,** 16 Hinde St., W.1 (tel. 071/935-6306), open Mon. to Fri. from 8:30am to 5:30pm and on Sat. from 9:30am to 12:30pm. This outfit will clean, repair, or alter your clothes, even repair shoes. It's one of the best places in London for such service. Tube: Marble Arch.

Even cheaper is to go to one of the launderettes in London which are plentiful. If you're staying in one of the B&B houses in the Bayswater area, try **Lancaster Laundromat,** 28 Craven Terrace, W.2 (tel. 071/723-5724). Hours are Mon. to Fri. from 8am to 9pm; Sat., 8am to 8pm; and Sun., 9am to 8pm. Tube: Lancaster Gate.

Or, in the vicinity of the Bloomsbury B&Bs, patronize **Red and White Laundries,** 78 Marchmont St., W.C.1 (tel. 071/387-3667), open daily from 7am to 9pm. Tube: Russell Square.

LOST PROPERTY: To find property lost in London on the tube or in a taxi—or elsewhere—report the loss to the police first, and they will advise you where to apply for its return. Taxi drivers are required to deliver property left in their vehicles to the nearest police station. London Transport's Lost Property Office will try to assist personal callers only at their office at the Baker Underground station. For items lost on British Rail, report the loss as soon as possible to any station on the line where the loss occurred. For lost passports, credit cards, or money, report the loss and circumstances immediately to the nearest police station. For lost passports, you should then go directly to your embassy or high commission. The address will be in the telephone book, or see "Embassies and High Commissions" in Chapter I's "Fast Facts for Britain." For lost credit cards, report to the appropriate organization; the same holds true for lost traveler's checks.

LUGGAGE SHIPPED: Airlines charge a lot for excess luggage. It's cheaper to have it shipped independently. Try **London Baggage Company,** 115 Buckingham

Palace Rd., Desk 18, S.W.1 (tel. 071/834-9411, ext. 41). Tube: Victoria Station. Their main office is at Gatwick Village, Gatwick Airport, West Sussex (tel. 0293/50-2197).

MEDICAL SERVICES: Consult **Medical Express,** Chapel Place, W.1 (tel. 071/ 499-1991), just off Oxford Street, almost equidistant from the Oxford Circus and Bond Street Underground stations. It's a medical center where you can have a consultation and full medical/clinical examinations, such as a blood-pressure test, an ECG, and X-rays. This is a small, select, private health clinic, associated with more than 20 different specialists, each of whom has a private practice; the facility is not part of the free British medical establishment. Medical Express is an excellent place to go if you suspect something is wrong with your health. An initial consultation fee is £50 ($82.50). Filling the British equivalent of a U.S. prescription costs £20 ($33). Open Mon. to Fri. from 9am to 7pm and Sat. from 10am to 5pm. (See also "Dentists," "Doctors," and "Hospitals" elsewhere in this section.)

POST OFFICES: Hours for the **Chief Post Office** in London at King Edward St., EC1A 1AA, near St. Paul's Cathedral, are from 8:30am to 6:30pm Mon. to Fri., closed Sat. and Sun. Tube: St. Paul's. The Trafalgar Square Post Office, 24-28 William IV St., London WC2N 4DL, operates as three separate businesses: inland and international postal services and banking, open from 8am to 8pm Mon. to Sat.; philatelic sales, open from 10am to 7pm Mon. to Fri. and 10am to 4:30pm Sat.; and greeting card and stationery sales, open from 9am to 6:30pm Mon. to Fri. and 9:30am to 5pm Sat. Tube: Charing Cross. Other post offices and sub-post offices are open from 9am to 5:30pm Mon. to Fri. and 9am to 12:30pm Sat. Many sub-post offices and some main post offices close for an hour at lunchtime.

SAFETY: See "Fast Facts for Britain" in Chapter I.

TELEX AND FAX: These are mostly restricted to business premises and hotels. If your hotel has a telex or Fax, they will send a message for you and you may have to arrange in advance for the receipt of a message back. Otherwise, go to **Chesham Executive Centre,** 150 Regent St., W.1 (tel. 071/439-6288); Tube: Piccadilly Circus. They rent offices by the hour and have secretarial and stenographical services. They also accept walk-in business and will send Fax messages, too. The cost of sending a one-page Fax from London to New York, for example, is £2.50 ($4.15), plus VAT and the cost of the phone call. That works out, in the case of a single page to New York, at around £5 ($8.25). Hours are 9am to 6pm Mon. to Fri. and 9am to noon on Sat.

WEATHER: For information on London weather, call 071/246-8091.

London's Average Daytime Temperature and Rainfall

	Jan	Feb	Mar	Apr	May	June	July	Aug	Sept	Oct	Nov	Dec
Temp. ° F	40	40	44	49	55	61	64	64	59	52	46	42
Rainfall"	2.1	1.6	1.5	1.5	1.8	1.8	2.2	2.3	1.9	2.2	2.5	1.9

THE HOTEL OUTLOOK

The hotel picture has changed drastically since the 19th century, when the Hotel Victoria had only four bathrooms for its 500 guests. London now offers accommodations to satisfy all purposes, tastes, and pocketbooks—ranging from the deluxe suites to army cots that rent to students in hostels.

New hotels sprout up every year, and others are on the drawing boards. For too long London hotels seemed lost in the days of Victoria (many still are). Now, increased pressure from overseas has brought about a discernible upgrading. Of course, in the name of progress Edwardian architectural features have often given way to the worst and most impersonal of modern, and showers (even bedrooms) are placed in broom closets best left to serve their original functions. Nevertheless, a hotel revolution is in the air.

Warning: July and August are the vacation months in England, when nearly two-thirds of the population strikes out for a long-awaited holiday. Many head for the capital, further exacerbating what has become a crowded hotel situation at all price levels. That doesn't mean you won't get a room if you should arrive at this peak time. There are so many hotels nowadays you can almost always find a room, but perhaps it won't be in the price bracket you want.

When the summer vacations are over, the "season" in London begins, lasting through October. Therefore, in September and October, as in June, low-budget hotels are tight—although nothing like they are in the peak summer months. It is recommended that you nail down a reservation before arriving in London. If you don't like to book a blind date, then by all means arrive early to begin your search for a room. Many of the West End hotels have vacancies, even in peak season, between 9 and 11am, but by noon they are often packed solidly again with fresh arrivals.

Hotels in Four Price Ranges

All hotels, motels, inns, and guesthouses in Britain with four bedrooms or more (including self-catering accommodations) are required to display notices showing minimum and maximum overnight charges. The notice must be displayed in a prominent position in the reception area or at the entrance. The prices shown *must* include any service charge and *may* include VAT. If VAT is not included, then it must be shown separately. If meals are provided with the accommodation, this must be made clear too.

The hotels of London we have selected are listed here according to districts, such as Mayfair, Belgravia, Bloomsbury. I have further broken them down into categories, beginning with the deluxe and following with the expensive hotels, the latter with first-class amenities. Next, I will provide a listing of the best of London's moderately priced hotels with or without private baths. Finally, for those who want to keep travel costs bone-trimmed, I'll list budget hotels wherever possible. Establishments in this category are most often converted town houses.

But I should issue a strong warning. What is considered "moderate" in price in London may not be moderate to you in terms of your hometown rates. The prices are "moderate" in London terms, and London is one of the most expensive cities on earth. Likewise, actual "budget" choices are few. You can be almost assured that any really good budget hotel in London is likely to be full 12 months a year, because the demand is so great for low-priced rooms.

First-class hotels in London have generally abandoned the time-honored English tradition of serving you a full English breakfast (bacon and eggs) for the price of the room. The hotels in the medium-priced range are a toss-up—the majority still maintain this custom, although many establishments rely on skimpy continental fare instead of the works, while some serve an in-between meal they call a London breakfast.

Some budget hotels in London still provide a full English breakfast for the price of the room. Because the policy of charging extra for breakfast is so erratic, always inquire when making a reservation or before checking in.

---

2. Mayfair

Mayfair, W.1, bounded by Piccadilly, Hyde Park, and Oxford and Regent streets, is an elegant section of London. Luxury hotels exist side by side with Georgian town houses and swank shops. Here are the parks, names, and streets that have snob appeal the world over, including Grosvenor Square (pronounced Grohv-nor) and Berkeley Square (pronounced Barkley).

DELUXE HOTELS

An outstanding place to stay, **Claridge's,** Brook Street, London W1A 2JO (tel. 071/639-8860), in Mayfair, dates from the mid-Victorian age. It has cocooned royal visitors in an ambience of discreet elegance since the time of the Battle of Waterloo. Queen Victoria visited the Empress Eugénie of France here, and thereafter, Claridge's lent respectability to the idea of ladies dining out in public. During World War II, Claridge's came to be known as "the annex of Buckingham Palace," from the royalty and heads of state staying there. Today such figures still appear, as well as top-echelon members of the financial, diplomatic, business, and cultural worlds.

Furnished with antiques as well as television sets, the 109 bedrooms (53 are suites) are spacious, many having generously sized bathrooms complete with dressing rooms and numerous amenities. Suites can be separated by private foyers from the main corridors, providing large self-contained units suitable for a sultan and his entourage. Tariffs, including VAT and service, are £175 ($288.75) to £200 ($330) daily in a single, £225 ($371.25) to £260 ($429) in a double (twin-bedded). It's necessary to reserve a room at Claridge's far in advance.

Excellent food is stylishly served in the intimacy of the Causerie, renowned for its lunchtime smörgåsbord and pre-theater suppers, and in the more formal restaurant offering English and French specialties. From the restaurant, the strains of the Hungarian Quartet, a Claridge's institution since 1902, can be heard from the adjacent foyer during luncheon and dinner. Both the Causerie and the restaurant are open from noon to 3pm. The Causerie serves evening meals from 5:30 to 11pm, and dinner is offered in the restaurant from 7:30 to 11pm. Tube: Bond Street.

The Dorchester, Park Lane, London W1Y 3DH (tel. 071/629-8888), was completely restored and reopened in 1990. A series of prominent buildings had stood on the site for as long as anyone could remember, but in 1929, with an increased demand for hotel space in the expensive Park Lane district, a famous mansion—whose inhabitants had been known for everything from great debauchery to great aesthetic tastes—was torn down. In its place was erected the finest hotel London had seen in many years. Breaking from the neoclassical tradition, which contemporary critics felt had hidebound the city into one homogenized unit, the most ambitious architects of the era designed a building of reinforced concrete clothed with terrazzo slabs. One way designers muffled noise from the street (indeed, the rooms today are almost soundless) was with the compression of layers of seaweed between slabs of concrete. Today, the fully air-conditioned hotel also has double- and triple-glazed windows.

The facade facing Hyde Park rises into a graceful concave art deco sweep. An array of uniformed doormen greet newcomers with courtesy, and visitors register at an imposingly beautiful reception desk.

Throughout the hotel, you find a 1930s interpretation of Regency motifs. The elegant, flower-adorned main hall seems appropriate for a diplomatic reception, yet it possesses a kind of sophisticated comfort which guests from all over the world find appealing. All this production is presided over and skillfully managed by one of London's most deservedly famous hoteliers, Ricci Obertelli.

The Dorchester contains 252 rooms, including 55 opulently furnished and spacious suites, which have sheltered everyone from Elizabeth Taylor to Stephanie Powers, from Jack Nicholson to assorted magnates of the world's social, political, and financial hierarchy. Linen sheets are a standard feature, as well as all the electronic gadgetry you'd expect from a world-class hotel. The famous Grill Room and Terrace restaurants are considered among the finest dining establishments in London, and the Dorchester Bar is a legend. In addition, the hotel also operates an Oriental Restaurant, combining the cuisines of various Far East countries. Other facilities include one of the best outfitted health clubs in London and an exclusive private membership night club, as well as a business center. Prices (approximate) are £198 ($328.35) daily in a single, £250 ($412.50) in a double or twin, and from £325 ($536.25) to £1,200 ($1,980) for two in a suite. Owned by the Sultan of Brunei, the hotel is a member of the Steigenberger Reservations System. Tube: Hyde Park Corner.

Inn on the Park, Hamilton Place, Park Lane, London W1A 1AZ (tel. 071/499-0888), has captured the imagination of the glamour-mongers of the world ever since it was inaugurated by Princess Alexandra in 1970. Bordered with a smallish triangular-shaped garden and ringed by one of the most expensive neighborhoods in the world, it sits behind a tastefully modern facade. The hotel's acres of superbly crafted paneling and opulently conservative decor create the impression that the building is far older than it is. Piano music accompanies afternoon tea, served on excellent copies of Chippendale and Queen Anne furniture. A pair of alluring restaurants includes the highly starred Four Seasons, which is both elegant and stylish, with views opening onto Park Lane. The finest wines and continental specialties dazzle guests either at lunch or at dinner, which is served until 11pm. The alternative dining choice is the less expensive Lanes Restaurant where many members of London's business community, come to partake of the hors d'oeuvres table. Open from 6pm to midnight daily, it offers pre- and post-theater suppers.

The hotel's 228 rooms are large and beautifully fitted with well-chosen chintz patterns, reproduction antiques, and plush upholstery, along with dozens of well-concealed electronic extras. On the second floor of the inn, the owners have created 16 unique rooms, each with its own private glass conservatory. Singles cost £160 ($264) to £180 ($297) daily, and doubles begin at £200 ($330), plus VAT. Tube: Hyde Park Corner.

The Connaught, Carlos Place, London W1Y 6AL (tel. 071/499-7070), perhaps more than any other hotel in London, captures an elegant old English atmosphere. Located in the center of Mayfair, two short blocks from both Berkeley and Grosvenor squares, it ranks at the top with Claridge's for prestige and character. The Connaught is a 19th-century architectural treasure house. It's a brick structure, with a formal entrance, and its tall French windows overlook two curved, tree-lined streets. Throughout the hotel are antiques, such as in the drawing room with its formal fireplace, soft lustrous draperies at high windows, and bowls of fresh flowers. Singles cost from £150 ($247.50) daily, doubles, £179 ($295.35) to £195 ($321.75), inclusive of VAT. All meals are extra, and the service charge is 15%. The 114 bedrooms vary in size, but all are furnished with well-selected antiques and tasteful reproductions. It is imperative to reserve well in advance.

The paneled bar-lounge is old-school-tie conservative; the fashionable (with everybody from movie stars to bestselling novelists) restaurant is also mahogany paneled, but it glitters with mirrors and crystal. The chef, having perfected the English cuisine and a selection of French dishes, prepares superb food. Attentive waiters and fresh flowers set the proper mood. Guests can also dine in the Grill Room, which is smaller and open only Mon. to Fri. The same menu is served in both the restaurant and grill, except that charges in the restaurant are based on three courses while, in the grill, prices are à la carte with a minimum charge. Reservations are essential for nonresidents of the hotel. Tube: Bond Street.

The Park Lane Hotel, Piccadilly, London, W1Y 8BX (tel. 071/499-6321), is one of the long established Park Lane deluxe hotels, having its own loyal clients and winning new converts all the time. It was begun in 1913 and advanced engineering techniques were used to construct the foundations and the intricately detailed iron skeleton. When its creator was killed in World War I, local gossips mockingly referred to the echoing and empty shell as "the bird cage." Completed in 1924, the Park Lane became one of the leading hotels of Europe.

Today you'll enter an intensely English hotel which sits behind a discreet stone-block facade. One of its gateways, the Silver Entrance, is considered such an art deco marvel that its soaring columns have been used in many films, including *Brideshead Revisited, The Winds of War,* and *Shanghai Surprise.* The hotel's restaurant, Bracewells, is recommended separately.

This is the last of the Park Lane deluxe hotels to be privately owned by an English family. Designed in a U shape, with a view overlooking Green Park, it has more than 321 luxurious and comfortable accommodations, which are among the least expensive of any of the other major Park Lane competitors. Each contains a private bath, color TV, radio, mini-bar, phone, and double glazing for interior peace and quiet. Many of the suites offer marble fireplaces and the original marble-sheathed bathrooms. Depending on the season and the accommodation, singles cost £150 ($247.50) to £160 ($264) daily; doubles or twins, £180 ($297) to £190 ($313.50). For an afternoon tea, you can enter the beautifully decorated yellow-and-white lobby, capped by a glass ceiling and filled with palms evoking the Edwardian era. Tube: Hyde Park Corner.

Grosvenor House, Park Lane, London W1A 3AA (tel. 071/499-6363), the flagship of Trusthouse Forte, is an art deco palace, a bastion of tradition and elegance. It was named after the famous residence of the duke and duchess of Westminster, which around the turn of the century occupied this frontage along Hyde Park. In the late 1920s, the famous architect, Sir Edwin Lutyens, spearheaded the construction of the Grosvenor House, and today it is practically a miniature city unto itself, with 160 apartments (contained within a separate tower) and 468 bedrooms and suites. Along the hallways lie many spacious accommodations, each different from its neighbor, filled with English chintz, inlaid headboards, and traditional furnishings. Accommodations contain large tile or marble baths, color TVs, radios, trouser presses, mini-bars, and phones. Singles rent for £205 ($338.25) to £225 ($371.25) daily and doubles or twins £225 ($371.25) to £245 ($404.25).

The hotel has an array of dining and drinking facilities for any occasion, plus a modern health club in its basement with a 65-foot swimming pool, sauna, steambath, and exercise and aerobics room. Tube: Marble Arch.

EXPENSIVE HOTELS

The tallest building along Park Lane, and indeed one of the tallest structures in London, **London Hilton on Park Lane,** Park Lane, London W1A 2HH (tel. 071/493-8000), created an uproar when it was constructed in 1963. Persistent allegations accused residents of its uppermost floors of being able to spy into the boudoirs of faraway Buckingham Palace.

There's a roof-top restaurant on the 28th floor, with sweeping views over London. Facilities at the hotel include a sauna and a massage service. Graced with large picture windows overlooking London and Hyde Park, the 448 bedrooms are decorated in tastefully restful colors, with fine copies of Georgian furniture. Each has a color TV, mini-bar, marble-sheathed bath, and other amenities. Rooms on floors 22 through 27 tend to be at the more expensive end of the price scale, offering extra facilities such as complimentary continental breakfast and drinks throughout the day. Depending on the accommodation, singles rent from £155 ($255.75) to £205 ($338.25) daily, with doubles going for £170 ($280.50) to £230 ($379.50). VAT and breakfast are extra. Tube: Hyde Park Corner.

London Marriott, Grosvenor Square, London W1A 4AW (tel. 071/493-1232). Built in a grander era as the conservative Hotel Europa, Marriott has poured millions of dollars into its refurbishment, retaining only the very best elements and, of course, much of the tradition. It sits proudly behind a redbrick and stone Georgian facade on Grosvenor Square. The American Embassy is just a few doors away.

Throughout the hotel's interior, the same colors are consistently used in combinations of pink, peach, ivory, and virgin green. The breakfast room is delightful with chintz and Chippendale antiques. Rolling silver trolleys serve elegant meals in the adjacent Diplomat Restaurant. The hotel's 223 accommodations are plushly Georgian in design, and contain all the electronic extras you'd expect. Singles cost £175 ($288.75) to £195 ($321.75) daily, and doubles go for £195 ($321.75) to £220 ($363). Tube: Green Park.

Brown's Hotel, Dover St. and Albemarle St., London W1A 4SW (tel. 071/493-6020), is recommended for those who want a fine hotel among the top traditional choices. This prestigious establishment was created by James Brown, a former manservant of Lord Byron. He and his wife, Sarah, who had been Lady Byron's personal maid, wanted to go into business for themselves. Brown knew the tastes of gentlemen of breeding and wanted to open a dignified, club-like place for them, his dream culminating in the opening of the hotel in a town house at 23 Dover St. in 1837, the year Queen Victoria ascended the throne of England. Today Brown's Hotel occupies some 14 historic houses on two streets, in an appropriate location—in Mayfair, just off Berkeley Square. To this day, old-fashioned comfort is dispensed with courtesy. The lounges on the street floor are inviting, including the Roosevelt Room, the Rudyard Kipling Room (the writer was a frequent visitor here), and the paneled St. George's Bar. A good, old-fashioned English tea is served in the Albemarle Room. Men are required to wear jackets and ties for tea and for dining in the dining room.

The 133 bedrooms vary considerably in size and are a tangible record of England's past. Even the wash basins are antiques. The rooms show restrained taste in decoration and appointments, with good soft beds and phones. The rate for a single room is £150 ($247.50) daily, a double renting for £190 ($313.50) to £245 ($404.25). All rates include VAT and service. Tube: Green Park.

MODERATELY PRICED HOTELS

Something of a discovery, **Green Park Hotel,** Half Moon Street, London, W1Y 8BP (tel. 071/629-7522), lies on one of the narrow, almost hidden streets of Mayfair, yet the location is just off busy Piccadilly, near Park Lane. In this ideal location, Green Park was created from a series of period houses and converted into one of the most select of London's moderate range hotels. Designer decorated and furnished throughout, it offers 160 tasteful, often stylish, bedrooms that come in a variety of sizes and layouts, ranging from singles, doubles (also twins) to triple rooms ideal for families. The most expensive are a series of deluxe rooms and individually designed suites. All accommodations have direct-dial phones, trouser presses, private baths, color TVs, and 24-hour room service. Singles range from £85 ($140.25) daily, with doubles or twins costing up to £160 ($264). The traditionally designed Claudes Restaurant offers a first-rate cuisine inspired by recipes from the French Riviera. Tube: Green Park.

The Londoner, 57-59 Welbeck St., London W1M 8HS (tel. 071/935-4442), has retained its traditional facade but completely modernized its interior. The contrast, the moment you walk in, is delightful. Tucked away in Mayfair, off Wigmore Street (near Cavenish Square and Wigmore Hall), the hotel is an excellent remake of an older building.

All of its 144 comfortably furnished bedrooms contain private baths, phones, radios, and TVs. There's also 24-hour room service. Singles rent for £109.25 ($180.25) to £126.50 ($208.75) daily, and doubles or twins cost from £132.25 ($218.20) to £143.75 ($237.20), inclusive of VAT. Oliver's Restaurant is comfortably traditional and welcoming, serving British fare at breakfast, lunch, and dinner. The Londoner Cocktail Bar offers a range of spirits and beer. Tube: Bond Street.

Flemings Hotel, 7-12 Half Moon St., London W1Y 7RA (tel. 071/499-2964), is a traditional-style hotel set in a quiet street off Piccadilly. The reception area and spacious lounge have an air of peaceful charm and elegance with elaborate chandeliers and period furniture. The restaurant and bar offer a wide choice from à la carte and table d'hôte menus served in a warm and relaxing atmosphere. There are 135 charmingly decorated rooms, all with private baths, color TVs with in-house movies, radios, direct-dial phones, and hairdryers. Singles rent for £90 ($148.50) daily, with a twin or double costing £115 ($189.75). Executive rooms rent for £125 ($206.25) for two persons, and a family room—suitable for three—costs £145 ($239.25). Tariffs include service and VAT. Tube: Green Park.

3. St. James's

This section, the beginning of Royal London, starts at Piccadilly Circus and moves southwest. It's frightfully convenient, as the English say, enclosing a number of important locations such as American Express on Haymarket, many of the leading stores (Burberry of raincoat wear), and Buckingham Palace.

It basks in its associations with royalty—it was the "merrie monarch" himself, Charles II, the famous skirt chaser (Nell Gwynne the favorite), who founded St. James's Park. And it was in St. James's Palace that his father, Charles I, spent his last troubled night, awaiting his beheading the following morning. At one time the palace was a hunting lodge of Henry VIII and his wife of the moment, Anne Boleyn.

For the traditionalist in particular, living in the heart of aristocratic London has many advantages—none more important than its well-run and discriminating hotels themselves. Their number is limited, but their addresses are most fashionable, just as they were in the society heyday of the 18th century.

A DELUXE HOTEL

Along with its namesake on the Place Vendôme in Paris, the **Ritz Hotel,** Piccadilly, London W1V 9DG (tel. 071/493-8181), made the word "ritzy" synonymous in the English vernacular with luxury. Of the Ritz in the "other city," a French writer once said, "It isn't a hotel, it isn't even a big hotel, it's a monument." Much the same can be said of the London Ritz. The Ritz world is one of crystal, gilt, Italian marble, all that epitomizes the frivolous comfort of Edwardian high life.

Through extensive renovation, Cunard Leisure has restored the lovely hotel to much of its original elegance, the way César Ritz wanted it back in 1906. The hotel has had a long and colorful history since then, memorialized by Noël Coward's lyrics to "Children of the Ritz." Pavlova danced here for the amusement of the Prince of Wales. In 1931 Mahatma Gandhi, wearing his familiar loincloth, was greeted by the Aga Khan, and years later, De Gaulle, Churchill, and Eisenhower met in the Marie Antoinette Suite. The public places are spacious. The Palm Court is like a stage setting: oval shaped, with its centerpiece the sculptured fountain in exhellon marble, adorned by the gilt figure *La Source.* The restaurant has a paneled wall lining of melting marbles and a handpainted ceiling depicting skies with billowing clouds. The sumptuous chandeliers are linked to each other around the room by a chain of gilt bronze garlands, so that the dining area appears to be permanently *en fête.*

Decidely for those who enjoy "Putting on the Ritz," the 130 bedrooms and suites are traditionally decorated in pastel shades with some of the original Victorian brass beds, Carrara marble fireplaces, and crystal lighting fixtures, giving them the look of a stately English home. They are also provided with private baths, color TVs, radios, in-house films, and 24-hour room service. Staying here costs from £175 ($288.77) daily in a single, and from £205 ($338.25) to £245 ($404.25) in a double or twin, VAT and service included. Tube: Green Park.

EXPENSIVE HOTELS

Dukes Hotel, 35 St. James's Place, London SW1A 1NY (tel. 071/491-4840), provides elegance without consideration. A hotel since 1908, it stands in a quiet courtyard off St. James's Street with its turn-of-the-century gas lamps. From the hotel it's possible to walk to Buckingham Palace, St. James's Palace, and the Houses of Parliament. Shoppers will be near Bond Street and Piccadilly, and literature buffs will be interested in knowing that Oscar Wilde lived and wrote for a period at St. James's Place. Each of the well-furnished bedrooms, 36 in all, plus 26 suites, is decorated in the style of a particular period.

There is central heating throughout, and every bedroom has its own private bath and direct-dial phone. A total renovation has made rooms brighter and more spacious than ever. A single rents for £165 ($272.25) daily, and a double or twin goes for £195 ($321.75), including service charge and VAT. Suites are priced from £380 ($627). Room service is available 24 hours a day. Main meals are served daily in Dukes Restaurant from 12:30 to 2:30pm and 6 to 10:30pm. Tube: Piccadilly Circus.

Stafford Hotel, 16-18 St. James's Place, London SW1A 1NJ (tel. 071/493-0111), a hostelry dating from Edwardian days, lies in a cul-de-sac off St. James's Street and Green Park. It can be entered via St. James's Place, or through the Blue

Ball Yard when the hotel's cocktail bar is open. Built in the 19th century as a private home, the Stafford has retained a home-like, country-house atmosphere, which has made it a favorite London address for visitors looking for something elegant and comfortable, with modern amenities yet without the cold anonymity of big, chain hotels (although it is owned by the Cunard group). Comfort is the keynote in the tastefully decorated public rooms. The dining room, lighted by a chandelier and wall sconces, plus candles on the tables, gleams with silver. Here you can lunch or dine on classic dishes prepared with fresh, select ingredients and practiced know-how. The bar of the hotel is a cozy attraction.

The 62 bedrooms, including 7 suites, are individually decorated and of varying shapes, in keeping with the private-home background of the structure. Rates are £170 ($280.50) daily in a single, £185 ($305.25) to £205 ($338.25) in a double, including VAT and service. The Stafford is often used by those who need a place of tranquility in the heart of London, to be near court and the embassy and political life of the city. There's easy access to good shopping and to the theaters. Tube: Green Park.

A MODERATELY PRICED HOTEL

Dating from 1910, the **Goring Hotel,** 15 Beeston Place, Grosvenor Gardens, London SW1W 0JW (tel. 071/834-8211), achieves the seemingly impossible: It provides the charm of traditional, dignified English living and at the same time offers all modern comforts. Hotelier Goring built the establishment in 1910 with "revolutionary ideas"—that is, that every room should have a private bath, foyer, and central heating. His grandson, George Goring, continues to provide top service. The 90 rooms (here they are called apartments) rent for £105 ($173.25) daily in a single, £155 ($255.75) in a double or twin. Rates include color TV, service, and VAT. You can have a three-course table d'hôte luncheon for £18 ($29.70), and dinner from £21 ($34.65). Afternoon teas are served by waiters from a trolley in the large, paneled Garden Lounge, where you can sit and view the garden. The dining room reflects the charm and elegance of an English country hotel. The Goring's situation is choice, close to Victoria Station, and a ten-minute walk from Buckingham Palace, Westminster Abbey, and the Houses of Parliament. Tube: Victoria Station.

4. Piccadilly

If you want to be in the middle of the West End, right at Piccadilly Circus and Leicester Square, then the following recommendations will appeal to you. Most of London's theaters, Soho, Regent Street, and many famous restaurants and pubs will be at your doorstep.

A DELUXE HOTEL

First built in 1908, **Le Meridién,** 21 Piccadilly, London W1V 0BH (tel. 071/734-8000), is now happily enjoying its reincarnation. At the time of its original opening, the Ionic arcade capping the arched neoclassical facade was considered the height of Edwardian extravagance. It was instantly pronounced the grandest hotel in London, but its huge expense bankrupted its creator. New owners continued to make the hotel one of the most stylish in the world, receiving such luminaries as Mary Pickford accompanied by Douglas Fairbanks, and much earlier, Edward VII. After World War II the hotel sank into a kind of musty obscurity until its lavish refurbishment during the revitalization of the Piccadilly theater district. Today, after the expenditure of some $30 million, the hotel is considered the European flagship of the French-owned Meridien chain. It has enough elaborately detailed plasterwork, stained glass, and burnished oak paneling to make any Francophile feel at home, yet offers enough old-world service and style to satisfy even the most discerning Briton.

The hotel offers a formal and very elegant restaurant, the Oak Room (more about this later), and the less formal Terrace Room, a sun-flooded aerie under the greenhouse walls of the facade's massive Ionic portico. There is, as well, a very British bar sheathed in hardwoods and featuring a pianist. The hotel is also proud of Champney's, one of the most exotic health clubs in London. Graced with a pool almost 50 feet long, whose tilework looks like something from the grand art deco days of Budapest, it features saunas, steambaths, aerobic workshops, squash courts, billiard tables, and a private membership clientele. Each of the nearly 284 handsome bedrooms (30 are suites) contains an ample amount of space, private bath, TV, radio, phone, and a mini-bar, plus an array of fine and conservatively tasteful furniture. Singles rent for £175 ($288.75) daily and doubles or twins for £195 ($321.75). Tube: Piccadilly Circus.

AN EXPENSIVE HOTEL

Cavendish Hotel, 81 Jermyn St., London SW1Y 6JF (tel. 071/930-2111), has an old name but a newer body with a lively spirit. It was built in 1966 on the site of the old Cavendish, the subject of numerous stories about the days of Edward VII, when it thronged with theatrical and royal personages. The hotel grew to fame under its colorful proprietor, Rosa Lewis, known as "The Duchess of Jermyn Street" in a biography written about her. In the St. James's district (Royal London), just off Piccadilly and a five-minute walk from Pall Mall, this former landmark has been transformed into a contemporary hotel. On the ground floor are a business center and the Sub-Rosa bar. Up a flight of stairs are two restaurants and the lounge area. The 253-bedroom tower is set back, rising above it.

The rooms are bright and airy, decorated in pastels, with wall-to-wall curtains, sitting areas, mini-bars, videos, and TVs. Double-thickness windows keep out traffic noises. All rooms have private baths. Singles rent from £110 ($181.50), and doubles cost from £145 ($239.25), with VAT and service included in the rates. Tube: Green Park.

MODERATELY PRICED HOTELS

The **Regent Palace Hotel,** Piccadilly Circus, London W1A 4BZ (tel. 071/734-7000), one of the largest hotels in Europe, has 996 bedrooms, hot-beverage facilities, radios, and color TVs. Standing in the center of London, with theaterland around the corner and Oxford Circus a five-minute walk away, it charges £47.50 ($78.40) in a single, £63 ($103.95) in a twin- or double-bedded room. Rates include an English breakfast, VAT, and service. The hotel's carvery is a good place to dine, and Sherwood's coffeeshop is open for pre-theater meals. Drinks are served in the Half Sovereign and the Planters bars. The Palace has a wide range of services you can learn about at the hall porter's desk. Tube: Piccadilly Circus.

---

5. The Strand and Covent Garden

Beginning at Trafalgar Square, the Strand runs east into Fleet Street. Londoners used to be able to walk along the Strand and see the Thames, and in the 17th century the wealthy built their homes on the Strand, their gardens stretching to the Thames. But the river has receded and today the Strand is less grand—flanked as it is with theaters, shops, hotels, and restaurants.

Lanes jut off from the Strand, leading to the Victoria Embankment Gardens along the river. Opposite the gardens is Cleopatra's Needle, an ancient Egyptian obelisk, now London's oldest monument. You might want to stroll along the river if weather permits. You may also want to book a hotel along the Strand.

DELUXE HOTELS

A landmark hotel, **The Savoy,** the Strand, London WC2R 0EU (tel. 071/836-4343), with eight stories behind a facade of light, glazed terra-cotta tiles, stands ma-

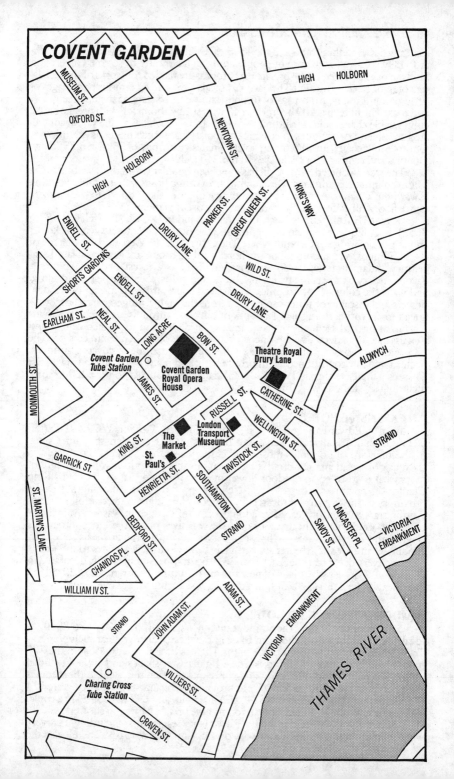

jestically between the Strand and the Thames. Opened in 1889, it was built by Richard D'Oyly Carte for the use of people going to his theater to see the Gilbert and Sullivan operas. Seven of the private party rooms are named for works of those masters of light opera. Through The Savoy's portals have walked famous personages of yesterday and today, from royalty to political leaders to stars of stage, screen, TV, and rock. The hotel has 200 bedrooms, 48 with sitting rooms, all with private baths, comfortable chairs, solid furniture, and large closets. Each has a different decor created by a blend of antiques in eclectic combinations of such pieces as gilt mirrors, Queen Anne chairs, and Victorian sofas. Singles cost from £155 ($255.75) daily. Doubles and twins go for £180 ($297) to £240 ($396).

The wood-paneled Savoy Grill has long been popular with a theatrical clientele. The even more elegant Savoy Restaurant is in a prime position, with tables looking toward the Thames. A quartet plays in the evening for those drawn to the intimate dance floor. Tube: Temple, Embankment, or Covent Garden.

Howard Hotel, Temple Place, the Strand, London WC2R 2PR (tel. 071/836-3555), is a unique luxury hotel overlooking the Embankment between Blackfriars and Waterloo bridges, at a point where The City meets the West End. The facade of the building is very modern, but the hotel's public rooms are authentic late-18th-century, Adam-style fantasies. So what you'll see is a forest of Ionic columns, Savonnerie-style carpets in vivid pinks, blues, and golds, elaborate plaster detailing, and walls the color of cotton candy. A terraced courtyard with masses of seasonal flowers and cascades of water can be seen from the high-ceilinged bar, whose walls are adorned with a spun-sugar lacework of pink and turquoise. There's an elegant restaurant in the basement, the acclaimed Quai d'Or, with its domed ceiling and Renaissance-style decor, which offers a classic menu of French haute cuisine. The 135 semi-rococo bedrooms are filled with copies of marquetry-covered antiques. Each room is air conditioned, with private bath, and many open onto a view of the Thames. Singles rent for £195 ($321.75) daily, and doubles go for £220 ($363), including service and VAT. Tube: Temple.

AN EXPENSIVE HOTEL

Born in Edwardian days, **The Waldorf,** Aldwych, London WC2B 4DD (tel. 071/836-2400), is alive and well today. Its art nouveau tea garden, the Palm Court, has become one of London's most sought-after places for a "cuppa," consumed to the music of a resident orchestra. The glass canopy that covers its marble floor illuminates what used to be an outdoor flower market. It is said that in the 1600s King Charles II's favorite mistress, "sweet Nell Gwynn," used to sell oranges here. Its proximity to the five largest theaters in London almost guaranteed a full roster of visiting stars and celebrities. After a long period of tattiness it was renovated, and today the vaudevillian theatricality of yesteryear lives on in the old photographs ringing the reception area. A brasserie serves informal French meals in a belle époque setting for after-theater suppers. The Palm Court reverberates to the strains of music every day at teatime. Each of the 310 bedrooms is comfortably decorated in chintz and a conservative blend of new and old furniture. They rent for £120 ($198) daily in a single, £150 ($247.50) in a double, VAT included. Tube: Aldwych.

A MODERATELY PRICED HOTEL

Strand Palace Hotel, the Strand, London WC2R 0JJ (tel. 071/836-8080), is ideally situated for those who want to be in the theater district, near such points as Trafalgar Square, yet within a block of the Thames Embankment. Most of the 777 rooms have been recently refurbished in light pastel shades and have direct-dial phones, color TVs, radios, and tea-and-coffee making facilities. Behind the scenes is a staff of more than 400 standing by to provide personalized service. Rates are £74 ($122.10) daily in a single, £89 ($146.85) in a twin, and £97 ($160.05) in a triple. VAT and service are included, and all rooms have private baths and showers.

One of the assets of the Strand Palace is its restaurants, including a carvery where you can gorge yourself every day on England's finest roasts. There's also the

Café at the Strand, which attracts show people. The intimate Mask Bar is another favorite. To complete the dining possibilities, there is the Italian Connection, where you can select from an à la carte menu. Tube: Embankment, Charing Cross, or Covent Garden.

6. Holborn

The old borough of Holborn, W.C.2, includes the heart of legal London. Drinking and dining selections and several sightseeing attractions will be reviewed later. It is normally not thought of as a hotel district. However, there is one recommendable hotel on the edge of Holborn near the Covent Garden district.

AN EXPENSIVE HOTEL

A concrete-and-glass structure, **Drury Lane Moat House,** 10 Drury Lane, High Holborn, London WC2B 5RE (tel. 071/836-6666), was originally built in 1978 as an office building. Once you're inside its confines, however, the atmosphere is subdued, suggesting neither a chain hotel nor one of such severe modernity as the facade might indicate. Built with terraced gardens and its own plaza, the hotel is a self-contained entity. All of its 153 spacious bedrooms have good views and are furnished in a harmonious fashion, with many luxurious touches, such as individually controlled central heating, color TVs, even 24-hour room service. Singles range from £104 ($171.60) to £113 ($186.45) daily and doubles from £132.50 ($218.65) to £146 ($240.90). Tariffs include VAT and service. Maudie's Restaurant is named after Sir Osbert Lancaster's famous arbiter-of-chic cartoon character Maudie Littlehampton, and offers a French cuisine. Maudie's Bar makes a good post-theater rendezvous. Tube: High Holborn.

7. Westminster

This area has been the seat of British government since the days of Edward the Confessor. Dominated by the Houses of Parliament and Westminster Abbey, Parliament Square symbolizes the soul of England. Westminster, a large borough of London, includes Whitehall, headquarters of many government offices.

EXPENSIVE HOTELS

One of London's most stylish hotels, **St. James Court Hotel,** Buckingham Gate, London SW1 6AF (tel. 071/824-6655), was carved from a complex of Edwardian apartment buildings near the Houses of Parliament. Its 390 accommodations wrap themselves around the fountain in a central courtyard adorned with caryatids, emerald-green tiles, and neo-Gothic stonework. You enter a lobby adorned with travertine, burnished walnut, 18th-century oil portraits, and a Georgian-era sedan chair.

Although no two rooms are exactly alike, each has a color TV, mini-bar, radio, phone, and full bath. Most fall into two types—"transitional modern" and reproduction Georgian. More expensive units are air conditioned. Singles cost £130 ($214.50) to £150 ($247.50) daily, and twins and doubles go for £150 ($247.50) to £170 ($280.50). Among its attractions, the hotel has a business center and a health and fitness center for the use of its guests. Its restaurant, L'Auberge de Provence, offers Provençal cuisine prepared by an all-French staff. My favorite spot, however, is the hotel's elegantly formal Chinese restaurant, Inn of Happiness, whose walls are covered with hand-painted murals in motifs of ferns and flowers. Le Café Mediterranée is open all day. Tube: St. James's Park.

In a turn-of-the-century, red-brick building, **Stakis St. Ermins Hotel,** 2 Caxton St., London SW1H 0QW (tel. 071/222-7888), stands in the heart of Westminster, halfway between Victoria Station and Big Ben, and only a few minutes' walk from Buckingham Palace, the Houses of Parliament, Westminster Abbey, and New Scotland Yard. Its 296 bedrooms all have private baths, radios, TVs, and individually controlled central heating, with 24-hour room service. The hotel has two restaurants: the Caxton Grill offers an à la carte menu, while the Carving Table has a set price for lunch and dinner, serving a selection of roast meats. The lounge bar offers an alternative, serving light snacks 24 hours a day. The rates at the hotel are £108 ($178.20) to £133 ($219.45) daily in a single, rising to £137 ($226.05) to £163 ($268.95) for a twin-bedded room. These rates include VAT. Tube: St. James's Park.

A MODERATELY PRICED HOTEL

One of the largest block of flats (apartments) in all of Europe, **Dolphin Square,** Dolphin Square, London SW1 V3LX (tel. 071/834-3800), while not a traditional hotel, offers one of the best values in the city. It rents 152 bedrooms, some with fully equipped kitchens and others with two bedrooms. The location, if not prestigious, is interesting—set back from the Thames-bordering Grosvenor Road, between Chelsea and the Tate Gallery. Dolphin Square, an "instant home in London," has a vast inner courtyard and lots of gardens and lawns. Apartments, all with color TVs, come in a wide range of sizes. Single studios cost £70.15 ($115.75) to £80.50 ($132.85) daily, and double studios go for £80.50 ($132.85) to £96.60 ($159.40). One-bedroom suites, single or double occupancy, cost £102.35 ($168.90) to £118.45 ($195.45), and two- and three-bedroom suites, suitable for three to six persons, range from £125 ($206.25) to £197.80 ($326.35).

Besides the apartments, guest rooms are also rented at £29 ($47.85) daily in a single, £41 ($67.65) in a double, plus VAT. Early-morning tea and biscuits are served to persons staying in these facilities. The Dolphin Square Restaurant overlooks the heated swimming pool. In addition, there is a health club, plus eight squash courts and a sauna. The complex stands in 3 acres of gardens. It's best reached by taxi. Tube: Pimlico Station.

8. Victoria

Directly south of Buckingham Palace in Belgravia, just west of Westminster and Pimlico is a section often referred to as "Victoria," with its namesake—sprawling, bustling Victoria Station—as its center. Known as "the Gateway to the Continent," Victoria Station is where you get boat trains to Dover and Folkestone for that trip across the Channel to France.

The area also has many other advantages from the standpoint of location, as the British Airways Terminal, the Green Line Coach Station, and the Victoria Coach Station are all just five minutes from Victoria Station. From the bus stations, you can board many a Green Line coach for the suburbs. And an inexpensive bus tour of London departs from a point on Buckingham Palace Road, just behind Victoria Station. From Grosvenor Gardens, you can get a bus direct to Heathrow Airport, and from Victoria Station, trains to Gatwick Airport.

Your best bet in this area is to walk about Ebury Street, which lies directly to the east of Victoria Station and Buckingham Palace Road. There you'll find some of the best reasonably priced lodgings in central London.

BUDGET HOTELS

Created out of a group of five townhouses, **Ebury Court,** 26 Ebury St., London SW1W 0LU (tel. 071/730-8147), has a country-house flavor; it's brightly painted (turquoise and white), with railings to match and flower-filled windowboxes. The little reception rooms are informal and decorated with flowery chintz and good antiques. Best of all, it has a cordial and informal staff. Terms quoted include an English breakfast and VAT. A single with no bath costs £45 ($74.25) nightly, rising to £48 ($79.20) in a room with a shower but no toilet. Double and twin-bedded rooms without bath rent for £75 ($123.75), rising to £90 ($148.50) with a private bath. Each of the 40 rooms has hot and cold running water as well as color TV, phone, and radio. In the small restaurant, you can order either a lunch or dinner. A special feature of this establishment is the bar, which caters only to guests and to members of the Ebury Court Club, a group of local people who enjoy their drinks in a congenial atmosphere. A night porter is on duty to look after late arrivals.

The A1 bus, which goes to Heathrow every 20 minutes, leaves from Grosvenor Gardens, approximately a 1½ minute walk from the Ebury Court. Porters from the hotel will help visitors transport their luggage on a trolley if required. Tube: Victoria Station.

Elizabeth Hotel, 37 Eccleston Square, London SW1V 1PB (tel. 071/828-6812), is an intimate, privately owned establishment overlooking the gardens of Eccleston Square, which was built by Thomas Cubitt, Queen Victoria's favorite builder. It is an excellent place to stay, convenient to Belgravia and Westminster, and not far from Buckingham Palace. The hotel rents 24 bedrooms, 14 suitable as doubles or family rooms and the rest singles. Only one contains a complete private bath, although six offer a private shower. Singles rent for £28 ($46.20) per day, with doubles or twins costing from £43 ($70.95) to £61 ($100.65). Three persons are charged from £54 ($89.10) to £70 ($115.50), and four persons pay from £60 ($99) to £77 ($127.05). Prices include tax and a full English breakfast. Each accommodation is individually decorated, and a Victorian atmosphere has been carefully preserved, as reflected in the furnishings, framed prints, and wallpaper. Tube: Victoria Station.

Collin House, 104 Ebury St., London SW1W 9QD (tel. 071/730-8031), provides a good, clean B&B under the watchful eye of its resident proprietors, Mr. and Mrs. D. L. Thomas. Everything is well maintained in this mid-Victorian townhouse, and all 13 bedrooms, the majority with private showers and toilets, have wall-to-wall carpets, hot and cold running water, built-in wardrobes, and comfortable divan beds. Single rooms with private bath/shower and toilet cost £32 ($52.80), with doubles renting for £40 ($66) without bath, £45 ($74.25) with bath. All rates are inclusive of a full English breakfast, VAT, and the use of showers and toilets for those who don't have private facilities. There are a number of family rooms here. The main bus, rail, and Underground terminals are about a five-minute walk from the hotel. Tube: Victoria Station.

Lewis House Hotel, 111 Ebury St., London SW1W 9QU (tel. 071/730-2094), is a townhouse that was the home of playwright Sir Noël Coward from 1917 to 1930. It was his parents who opened this place to paying guests. During World War II, military leaders were housed here, each with a direct phone link to the Admiralty and the War Office. Today, this family-run hotel is managed by John Evans and offers 12 bedrooms, one with shower and toilet and five with shower but no toilet. Bathless singles rent for £30 ($49.50) per night. The price of twins and doubles is £40 ($66) to £45 ($74.25), depending on the plumbing. Triples with shower are offered for £95 ($156.75). Charges include VAT and a full English breakfast. Tube: Victoria Station.

---

9. Belgravia

Belgravia, south of Hyde Park, is the aristocratic quarter of London, challenging Mayfair for grandness. It reigned in glory along with Queen Victoria, but today's aristocrats are likely to be the top echelon in foreign embassies, along with a rising new-money class of actors and models.

Near Buckingham Palace Gardens and Brompton Road, its center is Belgrave Square, one of the more attractive plazas in London. A few town houses once occupied by eminent Edwardians have been discreetly turned into hotels (others were built specifically for that purpose). For those who prefer a residential address, Belgravia is choice real estate.

AN EXPENSIVE HOTEL

An elegant place to stay is the **Berkeley Hotel,** Wilton Place, London SW1X 7RL (tel. 071/235-6000). The original hotel, so beloved by Noël Coward, was moved, along with the loyalty of its well-heeled clients, to a travertine-faced building near Hyde Park in 1972. Its French-inspired facade conceals a world of impeccable service, flickering fireplaces, and richly textured oak paneling, as well as a news-service telex machine set between the Ionic marble columns of the lobby, formally dressed receptionists, a penthouse swimming pool designed like a modernized Roman bath, and a lot of hideaway corners for drinks and conversations. "The Restaurant," as it is called, serves a superb French cuisine in a decor of bleached paneling, masses of flowers, gracious proportions, and English chintz. The Buttery and Perroquet Bar provides a reasonable buffet and à la carte luncheon. In the evening an à la carte Italian menu is provided. The bar, newly decorated in tones of terra-cotta, is the latest venue in town for drinks and late-night entertainment from Mon. to Sat. All the 133 accommodations are comfortable, but the hotel is perhaps best known for its 27 opulent suites, many of which contain exquisite paneling and luxurious bathrooms. With VAT and service included, singles cost £140 ($231) or £200 ($330) daily, while doubles go from £200 ($330) to £250 ($412.50). Tube: Knightsbridge.

A MODERATELY PRICED HOTEL

For best all around value, the **Diplomat Hotel,** 2 Chesham St., London SW1X 8DT (tel. 071/235-1544), is a leader in its field. Part of its multiple allure lies in its status as a small, reasonably priced family-operated hotel in an otherwise prohibitively expensive neighborhood filled with privately owned Victorian homes and high-rise, first-class hotels. You register at a desk framed by the sweep of a partially gilded circular staircase beneath the benign gaze of cherubs set in the borders of a Regency-era chandelier.

The 28 comfortable bedrooms have modern baths, color TVs, phones, high ceilings, and well-chosen wallpaper in vibrant Victorian-inspired colors, as well as such extra touches as a hairdryers and morning newspapers. Each is named after one of the famous streets in this posh district. Singles rent for £49.95 ($82.40) daily and doubles or twins for £74.95 ($123.65) plus VAT. A sumptuous English buffet breakfast is served in a private dining room. Tube: Sloane Square.

---

10. Knightsbridge

Adjoining Belgravia is Knightsbridge, another top residential and shopping district of London. Just south of Hyde Park, Knightsbridge is close in character to Belgravia, although much of this section to the west of Sloane Street is older— dating back in architecture and layout to the 18th century. Several of the major department stores, such as Harrods, are here (take the Piccadilly Underground line to Knightsbridge). Since Knightsbridge is not principally a hotel district, my recommendations are limited.

EXPENSIVE HOTELS

Rising like a concrete cylinder, the **Sheraton Park Tower,** 101 Knightsbridge, London SW1X 7RN (tel. 071/235-8050), is not only one of the most convenient

hotels in London, virtually at the doorstep of Harrods, but one of the best. Its unusual circular architecture provides a stark but interesting contrast to the well-
heeled, 19th-century neighborhood around it. From its windows, guests have a
magnificent view of Hyde Park. The front door is unexpectedly and discreetly placed
in the rear of the building, where taxis can deposit guests more conveniently. Managed by the Sheraton group as the flagship for their European enterprises, they have
tried to make it, in the words of one spokesperson, "a modern version of the Connaught."

Designers have decorated each of the rooms in a tastefully international kind of
plushness. Each of the accommodations, 295 in all, contains air conditioning, central heating, soundproof windows, in-house movies, radio, and phone. Room
service and babysitting are also available. Singles range from £180 ($247) to £215
($354.75) daily, and doubles or twins go for £200 ($330) to £215 ($354.75), plus
VAT.

Its travertine-covered lobby bustles with scores of international clients (the
French Embassy is across the street) who congregate on the well-upholstered sofas or
in the Edwardian comfort of the hideaway bar. In the rotunda, near the ground-floor
kiosks, you can be served afternoon tea. The champagne bar offers you a choice of
either a glass or a silver tankard filled with bubbly, along with oysters, dollops of
caviar, and iced vodka. "The Restaurant" is open daily from 7am to midnight, ideal
for an after-theater supper. There you can dine on such dishes as English crab, medallions of venison, and Scottish lamb. The restaurant has its own entrance on
Knightsbridge. Tube: Knightsbridge.

One of the most personalized hotels in the West End is **The Capital,** 22 Basil
St., London SW3 1AT (tel. 071/589-5171), a member of *Relais & Châteaux*.
Small and modern, it's a stone's throw from Harrods. It has a warm townhouse ambience, a result of an extensive refurbishment program. The elegant *fin de siècle*
decoration is matched by the courtesy and professionalism of the staff. From the
lobby, an elevator takes guests to each floor, where the corridors and staircase are all
treated as an art gallery. Each of its 48 rooms has air conditioning, direct-dial phone,
radio, TV, and twin or king-size beds. Singles rent for £160 ($264) daily and dou-
bles for £185 ($305.25) to £200 ($330). The Capital Restaurant is among the finest
in London. Tube: Knightsbridge.

MODERATELY PRICED HOTELS

One of London's most charming small hotels, **The Beaufort,** 33 Beaufort Gardens, London SW3 1PP (tel. 071/584-5252), sits behind two Victorian porticos.
Each of the 29 air-conditioned bedrooms contains at least one painting by an art
student, a modern color scheme, and plush carpeting. Amenities include a private
bath, color TV, earphone radio, and phone. With a continental breakfast and VAT
included, singles cost from £150 ($247.50) daily, and doubles or twins go for £160
($264) to £200 ($330). Suites are more expensive. One added advantage of this
place is the pleasant staff and the inspired direction of its owner, Diana Wallis, a television producer. She did everything she could to create the feeling of a private house
in the heart of London. Tube: Knightsbridge.

Parkes Hotel, 41-43 Beaufort Gardens, London SW3 1PW (tel. 071/581-
9944), is a classy Edwardian style townhouse in one of the most desirable locations
in London, close to Harrods. Fronting a quiet and stately square, this is very much
an individual, private houselike hotel, with charm and style. Period furnishings are
used throughout, in a predominantly blue and buttercup yellow color scheme. The
staff does much to make guests feel at home. The hotel offers 33 accommodations,
ranging from regular rooms to studios and suites, the latter with equipped kitchens.
Two persons, depending on the room assignment, are charged from £85 ($140.25)
to £123.35 ($203.55) daily, depending on the accommodation. Four guests are
housed from £144.50 ($238.45) to £229.50 ($378.70), the latter for a two-
bedroom, two-bath suite. VAT is extra. Rooms are equipped with hairdryers, color
TVs, hospitality trays, and direct-dial phones. Tube: Knightsbridge.

Basil Hotel, 8 Basil St., London SW3 1AH (tel. 071/581-3311), has long been

a favorite little hotel of discerning British, who make an annual pilgrimage to London to shop at Harrods and perhaps attend the Chelsea Flower Show. This Edwardian charmer is totally unmarred by pseudo-modernization, and guests who can appreciate this individualistic hotel are preferred. The open mahogany staircase seems ideal as a setting for the entrance line of a drawing room play: "You're just in time for tea, Braddie." There are several spacious and comfortable lounges, appropriately furnished with 18th- and 19th-century decorative accessories. Off the many rambling corridors are smaller sitting rooms and comfortable lounges, appropriately furnished with 18th- and 19th-century decorative accessories. The hotel offers 92 pleasantly furnished bedrooms with private baths, costing £94 ($155.10) daily in a single, rising to £121 ($199.65) in a double. A three-course table d'hôte luncheon is served in the dining room for £12.50 ($20.65), and dinner is à la carte. Candlelight and piano music re-create the atmosphere of a bygone era. The upstairs restaurant serves lighter meals and snacks, and the downstairs wine bar offers an excellent selection of wines and inexpensive food. Tube: Knightsbridge.

L'Hotel, 28 Basil St., London SW3 1AT (tel. 071/589-6286), has been converted by David and Margaret Levin, owners of the nearby Capital Hotel on Basil Street, into a 12-room inn with countrified bedrooms and modern baths. Downstairs is the Metro, a café/wine bar where breakfast is served, with dishes of the day offered later. You can rent a room, either single or double occupancy, for £110 ($181.50) per night, which includes a continental breakfast. If you'd like an excellent gourmet meal, try the Capital Hotel's well-known restaurant, just down the street. Tube: Knightsbridge.

BUDGET HOTELS

The Executive Hotel, 57 Pont St., London SW1X 0BD (tel. 071/581-2424), was built in 1870 as a private house behind an ornate, neo-Romanesque facade of red brick. After costly restoration, it is now one of the most appealing and convenient small hotels in the district. Part of its charm lies in its Adam-style frieze, which ascends and curves around the high ceilings and graceful stairway of the main entrance. From the front you see only a discreet metal plaque announcing the establishment's status as a hotel. But once inside, you find 29 comfortable, modernized, high-ceilinged bedrooms. Each of these contains built-in furniture, radio, color TV, phone, private bath, in-house movies, hospitality tray, ironing center/trouser press, and central heating. An elevator services the five upstairs floors and a cozy modern lounge occupies one of the rooms off the lobby. Its location, near the attractions of Knightsbridge, makes the Executive a convenient lodging. With a full English breakfast included, singles cost £49.95 ($82.40), and doubles or twins rent for £74.95 ($123.65), plus VAT. Tube: Knightsbridge.

Claverley House Hotel, 13-14 Beaufort Gardens, London SW3 1PS (tel. 071/589-8541), an award-winning hotel lying just a few blocks from Harrods, is a small cozy place with Georgian-era accessories. The lounge is one of the hotel's most interesting features, containing 19th-century oil portraits, a Regency fireplace, and a collection of antiques and leather-covered sofas much like an ensemble you'd find in a private country house. Of the 32 bedrooms, all but six have private baths and several have balconies overlooking the rear end of Harrods. Decorated with frilly Victorian wallpaper and wall-to-wall carpeting, they all have comfortable armchairs, direct-dial phones, color TVs, and in-house movies. With VAT and a full English breakfast, singles cost £70 ($115.50) daily, and doubles or twins rent for £85 ($140.25). Tube: Knightsbridge.

Knightsbridge Hotel, 10 Beaufort Gardens, London SW3 1PT (tel. 071/598-9271), sandwiched between the restaurants and fashionable boutiques of Beauchamp Place and Harrods, still retains the feeling of a traditional British hotel. On a tranquil, tree-lined square, free from traffic, it has a subdued Victorian charm.

The place is small—only 20 bedrooms—and personally run. Units have phones, radios, and central heating, and there's a lounge with a color "telly" and a bar on the premises. Most expensive are rooms with private baths or showers, costing £38.50 ($63.55) to £46 ($75.90) in a single, from £55 ($90.75) to £75 ($123.75) in a twin. The best for the budget are the bathless specials, from £32.50 ($53.65) in a single and from £49 ($80.85) in a twin. All tariffs include a continental breakfast, VAT, and service charge. Tube: Knightsbridge.

Knightsbridge Green Hotel, 159 Knightsbridge, London SW1X 7PD (tel. 071/584-6274). This unusual establishment was constructed a block from Harrods in the 1890s. In 1966, when it was converted into a hotel, the developers were careful to retain the wide baseboards, cove molding, high ceilings, and spacious proportions of the dignified old structure.

None of the 22 accommodations contains a kitchen, but the result comes close to apartment-style living. Many of the doubles or twins are suites, each well furnished with access to the second-floor "club room" where coffee and pastries are available throughout the day. Each of the units contains a private bath, phone, and TV. Singles rent for £70 ($115.50) a night, doubles or twins for £85 ($140.25), and suites for £105 ($173.25), including VAT and service charge. Tube: Knightsbridge.

---

11. Chelsea

This stylish district stretches along the Thames, south of Hyde Park and South Kensington. Beginning at Sloane Square, it runs westward toward the periphery of Earl's Court and Brompton. Its spinal cord: King's Road, center for boutique hopping. The little streets and squares on either side of King's Road have hundreds of tiny cottages used formerly by the toiling underprivileged of the 18th and 19th centuries (although Carlyle lived there—see "Homes of Famous Writers" in Chapter V). Now, except for Belgravia and Mayfair, Chelsea couldn't be more chic.

DELUXE HOTELS

One of the most plushly decorated and best-maintained hotels in London is the **Hyatt Carlton Tower,** 2 Cadogan Place, London SW1X 9PY (tel. 071/235-5411). Its location and its height made this luxurious hotel a landmark even before Hyatt transformed it into their European flagship. It overlooks one of the most civilized gardens in London, whose Regency-era townhouses were originally built as part of an 18th-century plan. Its marble-floored lobby, with a resident harpist, looks a lot like the private salon of an 18th-century merchant, complete with the lacquered and enameled treasures he might have brought back from the Far East. A massive bouquet of flowers almost, but not quite, dominates the clusters of Chippendale-style chairs and sideboards, creating a haven for breakfast, light lunches, afternoon tea, and nightcaps. In fact, after the publicity it generated once as "Britain's Tea Place of the Year," the hotel has been considered one of the capital's most fashionable corners in which to enjoy a midafternoon pick-me-up. The hotel contains a few hideaway bars, the Rib Room for relatively informal meals in a warmly atmospheric setting, and the Chelsea Room, considered one of the great restaurants of London (both covered in the dining chapter).

The 224 bedrooms are opulently outfitted, the beneficiary of the more than $30 million that Hyatt spent. Each contains all the modern comforts you'd expect, as well as a marble-lined bathroom, artwork, air conditioning, and in-house movies. For either single or double occupancy, the charges range from £190 ($313.50) to £210 ($346.50) nightly. Suites are more expensive, of course. A family plan allows children under 18 sharing a room with their parents to stay free. Of particular note is a chic health club, whose two stories of shimmering glass overlook a panorama of the old trees of Cadogan Place. On its upper floor, a neo-Grecian bar serves health-conscious light meals, and it's also preferred as an early rendezvous place for its breakfast buffet. Tube: Knightsbridge.

Durley House, 115 Sloane St., London SW1X 9PJ (tel. 071/235-5537), on a fashionable street, is a coveted place to stay in London. Here in one of 11 elegantly furnished one- and two-bedroom apartments (some with grand pianos), discerning and well-heeled clients from around the world are nestled in English country house charm and comfort. It's a "home away from home"—providing that your home is a decorator showcase with conveniences literally appearing out of walls and with a staff always there to do your bidding. Kit and Tim Kemp created these distinctive lodgings, along with their other two small but posh hotels, Pelham Hotel and Dorset Square. Nearly all the services you'd find at a five-star luxury hotel are provided at Durley House, except that the guest list is small—small and pampered, that is. The hotel is filled with flowers, antiques, oil paintings, and a duet of fireplaces bringing cheer to the cozy visitors lounge and a bar operated on the honor system. There is no restaurant on the premises, but room service provides a quality cuisine, including breakfast, and each suite has a well-stocked kitchen in case you wish to dash in for an impromptu lunch or a pre-theater snack. Guests are even allowed to use the private tennis courts in the park opposite the house.

Durley House has been called "the perfect place to stay if you don't like hotels." Suites with one bedroom, single or double occupancy, cost £230 ($379.50) a night, rising to £250 ($412.50) with two bedrooms, suitable for four. Services include a valet, concierge, and 24-hour room service. If you're in London on business, full secretarial and office facilities are also available. Tube: Sloane Square.

EXPENSIVE HOTELS

Draycott, 24-26 Cadogan Gardens, London SW3 2RP (tel. 071/730-6466), near Sloane Square in the heart of Chelsea, is a "secret address" known to fanciers of elegant but small hotels around the world. Here you might rest comfortably in a four-poster bed on fresh, crisp linen, as your champagne cools in a silver bucket. Opened in 1988, it draws a prestigious crowd, so check in with your most impressive luggage. Out back the view opens onto a well-tended English garden, but inside the tone is set by chintz and a warming fire. Staying here is like being a guest in a stately British home. There's even a bowl of apples set out so you can help yourself.

The hotel's cozy bar is a gem, but the allure of the place is in its 25 beautifully furnished bedrooms with private baths. In your room you are likely to find a copy of *An Innkeeper's Diary,* by John Fothergill, but the Draycott doesn't take all his advice seriously—that is, his belief that boring clients should pay a higher tariff. Instead, the Draycott bases its rates on its room size. Singles begin at only £65 ($107.25) daily, but these accommodations are unusually small. The more expensive singles cost £125 ($206.25), and the larger doubles range from £165 ($272.25) to £185 ($305.25). You can also rent junior suites for two at £225 ($271.25). Prices include VAT, but breakfast is extra. All double units have gas fires. The Draycott doesn't have a restaurant, but offers room service, including perfectly cooked and served breakfasts. Tube: Sloane Square.

The elegant 75-room **Cadogan Thistle Hotel,** 75 Sloane St., London SW1X 9SG (tel. 071/235-7141), dates back to the middle of the 19th century. Although recently refurbished, the Edwardian style of the interior has been retained and is complemented by well-chosen antiques. The oak-paneled drawing room leads through to Langtry's Restaurant, which is open from noon to 10pm daily. Bedrooms are comfortable, well furnished, and modernized. Guests can stay in Lillie Langtry's suite or the room lived in by Oscar Wilde, writer and wit, who was a frequent guest at the hotel until he was arrested in these same quarters. Rates are from £124 ($204.60) to £150 ($247.50) daily for a single and from £145 ($239.25) to £170 ($280.50) for a twin room, inclusive of VAT and service. Tube: Sloane Square or Knightsbridge.

Chic and welcoming, the **Fenja,** 69 Cadogan Gardens, London SW3 2RB (tel. 071/589-7333), is one of the most luxurious, upscale B&Bs in London. It stands in a highly desirable location, close to the Peter Jones Department Store and the boutiques of King's Road. Only 13 bedrooms are offered in this restored Victorian townhouse. Each is decorated tastefully in traditional English styling and furnished in part with antiques. Each accommodation, which contains a modern bath with all the amenities, honors a writer or painter, everybody from Jane Austen to Henry James. Prices are from £90 ($148.50) to £120 ($198) daily in a single, rising to £180 ($297) in a double. Drinks can be ordered in a small drawing room; otherwise, meals are served in your room. Tube: Sloane Square.

BUDGET HOTELS

A 19th-century townhouse opening onto gardens, **The Willett,** 32 Sloane Gardens, Sloane Square, London SW1W 8DJ (tel. 071/824-8415), is one of the choice nuggets of Chelsea. It has many architectural curiosities, including a Dutch roof and bay windows. While retaining its traditional charm, the hotel has been fully renovated with new furnishings in all the well-equipped bedrooms and in the public lounge areas. The breakfast room is especially inviting, with plush red velvet chairs. In fact, the hotel has rapidly become a favorite address with many discriminating English who like a townhouse address and who prefer being close to the restaurants, attractions, and good shops of Chelsea. Singles rent for £49.95 ($82.40) to £54.95 ($90.65) daily, and doubles or twins for £49.95 ($82.40) to £64.95 ($107.15). An extra single bed in a family room costs an additional £19.95 ($32.90). A 15% tax is added. VAT is added to all tariffs. Most of the 18 accommodations contain private baths. Tube: Sloane Square.

The **Wilbraham Hotel,** Wilbraham Place, off Sloane Street, London SW1X 9AE (tel. 071/730-8296), is as dyed-in-the-wool British as you can get. On a quiet little street, just a few hundred yards from busy Sloane Square, three Victorian townhouses have been joined together as one hotel. It has an intimate sitting room and an attractively old-fashioned bar/lounge where you can have a simple lunch or dinner. There are 52 rooms in all, plus 42 baths, and prices range according to plumbing. Singles go for £36.50 ($60.25) to £51.50 ($85) daily, and twins or doubles for £62 ($102.30) to £85 ($140.25), the latter for a deluxe chamber. VAT is added. Tube: Sloane Square.

The **Blair House Hotel,** 34 Draycott Place, London, SW3 2SA (tel. 071/581-2323), is a good, budget choice for those who'd like to anchor deep in the heart of Chelsea. An old-fashioned, 17-room building of architectural interest, it has been modified and completely refurnished. Rooms are comfortable and contain such conveniences as direct-dial phones, radios, and facilities for making tea or coffee, along with TVs. Most rooms have a private bath or shower. Singles range in price daily from £35 ($57.75) without bath to £52 ($85.80) with bath. A bathless twin goes for £50 ($82.50), a twin with complete bath costs £65 ($107.25), including continental breakfast and VAT. Tube: Sloane Square.

Annandale House, 39 Sloane Gardens, London SW1W 8EB (tel. 071/730-6291), has a highly desirable address in Chelsea—in fact, some members of Parliament have used it as their London home. The facade of the building, and everything around it, is in a style known as "Pont Street Dutch," dating from the days (around 1860) when they were constructed by the same builder. The furnishings in the 12 bedrooms are traditional, and all but three contain private baths. Most of the accommodations, each with phone and TV, are fairly large. Singles cost from £30 ($49.50) to £55 ($90.75) daily, with doubles priced from £57 ($94.05) to £62 ($102.30) with VAT and breakfast included. An extra person sharing a double (up to a maximum of four, preferably in the same family) pays from £10 ($16.50) per night. Mrs. Morris, the capable owner, is known for her meatless English breakfasts—also called English dairy breakfasts—which are different every day. Food items might include kippers, Welsh rarebit, and scrambled eggs. Tube: Sloane Square.

---

12. Chelsea Harbour

To the west of Chelsea, Chelsea Harbour is a new "village" for London, a marina-like complex of boutiques and restaurants opening onto the Thames. It also contains an array of some of the most desirable apartments in London.

A DELUXE HOTEL

Hotel Conrad, Chelsea Harbour, London SW10 0XG (tel. 071/823-3000), is one of London's newest five-star deluxe hotels and perhaps the first all-suite hotel in Europe built expressly for this purpose. A stunning modern architectural achievement, it has style, grace, and sophistication, along with an elegant decor, compliments of the famous designer, David Hicks. The hotel rents 160 suites ranging from standard to deluxe. There are seven penthouse suites with extensive security if you happen to be a movie star or a visiting president. Each of these has its own beautifully decorated bedroom, living room, and bath (with a separate shower), along with executive desks. A host of modern facilities ensure comfort and convenience, including air conditioning, electronic safety locks, Fax machines, a full line of toiletries, personal computers, non-allergenic pillows, hairdryers, color satellite TVs, three phones with two-line capability, and well stocked mini-bars, to cite only a few. Rates range from £215 ($354.75) to £300 ($495) daily, single or double occupancy, plus VAT. The hotel also offers an array of special services, including babysitting, message service, and luggage storage. It also has a health club, a heated swimming pool, saunas, and the staff will even set you on a jogging route.

Its dining and entertainment facilities are excellent, including Compass Rose, one of the premier dining rooms of London (see separate recommendation in Chapter IV). At its Broadwood Lounge, you can enjoy a breakfast, a light snack, or afternoon tea, climaxed by a glass of champagne in the evening to the accompaniment of piano music. Drakes Bar is stylish and dramatic, with a view of the marina. Chelsea Harbour Hoppa buses run to Chelsea Harbour from Earl's Court and Kensington High Street (take bus C3), Mon. to Sat., or else you can take a riverbus from Charing Cross Mon. to Fri.

---

13. Earl's Court

This is one of the most popular hotel and rooming house districts in London, lying below Kensington and bordering the western half of Chelsea. Before the mid-1970s, it was virtually "occupied" by Australians, but nowadays everybody goes here. The area is convenient to both the West End Air Terminal and the exhibition halls. It is considered one of the most reasonable places for lodgings in London.

BUDGET HOTELS

The Barkston Hotel, 34-44 Barkston Gardens, London SW5 0EW (tel. 071/373-7851), is convenient to the Earl's Court tube stop with its direct link to Heathrow. It is also within easy access of the M4 motorway, going along Cromwell Road. On a historical note, it offered B&B at 5p (10¢) back in 1905. Nowadays, it comprises six different buildings that are harmoniously connected. Each of its 80 bedrooms is well maintained, with a private bath or shower, direct-dial phone, color TV, coffee-making equipment, and hairdryer. Some rooms are large family accommodations. Singles rent for £54 ($89.10) daily, with doubles costing £72 ($118.80) and triples £85 ($140.25). Prices include VAT, but breakfast is extra. The hotel also has its own restaurant. Tube: Earl's Court.

Swiss House Hotel, 171 Old Brompton Rd., London SW5 0AN (tel. 071/373-2769), is one of the more desirable B&Bs in the Earl's Court area. The hotel lies within a white-fronted Victorian row house festooned with flowers and vines. The rear windows overlook someone else's charming garden, but at least you can enjoy the view. Like its neighbors, Swiss House has a front porch portico. Its 16 country-inspired bedrooms, 11 with full baths, are individually designed and contain color TVs and phones. Some also have working fireplaces. With VAT and a continental breakfast included, singles range from £25 ($41.25) to £36 ($59.40) daily, with doubles costing from £38 ($62.70) to £45 ($74.25). Family rooms, which have baths, rent for a supplement of £7 ($11.55) extra for each additional guest. There's a snack menu, including hot dishes, which can be served in the bedrooms. Traffic is heavy outside, but windows are double glazed. Tube: Gloucester Road.

Hotel 167, 167 Old Brompton Rd., London SW5 0AN (tel. 071/373-0672), is one of the more fashionable guesthouses in the area, sheltered in a Victorian era, once-private townhouse, which, including the basement, has four floors of living space. Some of the bedrooms are in the basement, but, in spite of that, they are illuminated by big windows. The hotel rents 19 individually furnished bedrooms, all but two (the smallest singles) equipped with private baths. Singles range from £46 ($75.90) to £55 ($90.75) daily, with doubles costing £58 ($95.70) to £64 ($105.60), depending on the plumbing. VAT and a continental breakfast are included. Breakfast is consumed on marble-topped tables adjacent to the reception area. The decor is quite stylish, with such statements as metallic and chrome, all pinewood, Scandinavian modern, even Japanese in style. Windows have venetian blinds, not curtains, and each accommodation contains a color TV, phone, and coffee machine. Tube: Gloucester Road.

14. Kensington

Although the Royal Borough draws its greatest number of visitors from shoppers (Kensington High Street), it also attracts with a number of fine hotels, for the most part on Kensington Gardens. In Victoria's day the rows of houses along Kensington Palace Gardens were inhabited by millionaires (although Thackeray also lived there). Today the houses are occupied largely by ambassadors.

EXPENSIVE HOTELS

A deluxe Kensington hostelry, **Royal Garden Hotel,** 2-24 Kensington High St., London W8 4PT (tel. 071/937-8000), is well known for its stylish accommodations and supper club, the Royal Roof (see Chapter V). A large modern building, the Royal Garden towers over the fringe of Kensington Gardens next to Kensington Palace, where the prince and princess of Wales live. It also fronts one of London's most fashionable shopping streets. The hotel has 398 large bedrooms and suites, two restaurants, and three bars. The Garden Café offers all-day dining with an international flavor and is adjacent to the Garden Bar, a sunken area with settees. In the Royal Roof, the cuisine is French and is served with well-chosen wines in traditional English surroundings. The bedrooms are modern, with decor in warm colors and facilities that include radios, color TVs, in-house films, direct-dial phones, air conditioning, electronic message systems, refrigerated bars, hairdryers, sitting room areas, dressing rooms, and private baths or showers. Singles are £127.50 ($210.40) to £155 ($255.75) daily, increasing to £162.50 ($268.15) to £175 ($288.75) for a twin. These rates include tax. The Reserve Club wing on the 10th floor has spacious rooms patronized by businesspeople and other guests seeking extra amenities. Tube: High Street Kensington.

A 1970s hotel, **Hilton Kensington International,** 179 Holland Park Ave., London W11 4UL (tel. 071/603-3355), is less expensive than its more famous Park Lane relative. The reason for the price difference has nothing to do with comfort: Simply, it boasts fewer restaurants, bars, lounges, and other peripherals. One of its restaurants, Hiroko of Kensington, features a Japanese cuisine, while the Market Restaurant dispenses English and international dishes and on Sun. offers one of the best brunch values in town. The hotel's 606 bedrooms strike a balance between eye-pleasing decor and practical gadgetry. Singles start at £102 ($168.30) daily, with doubles going for £145 ($239.25). Tube: Holland Park.

A MODERATELY PRICED HOTEL

Observatory House, 37 Hornton St., London W8 7NS (tel. 071/937-1577), on the corner of Observatory Gardens, was once owned by Count Dangerville of

France, and over the years the house entertained many royal figures, including the deposed king of Yugoslavia. Converted into a 23-room hotel in 1988, it stands in the most desirable part of Kensington. One of a row of red-brick-fronted, Victorian terrace houses, it has been beguilingly restored and converted, with many original embellishments retained. Rooms, for the most part, are large, and all of them are comfortable, with TVs and phones and many thoughtful extras such as hairdryers and trouser presses. Only breakfast is served. Including VAT, the price of a single is £57.40 ($94.70) a night, with doubles costing £80 ($132) and triples £103.40 ($170.60). It's also possible to rent a family room (quad) for £118.40 ($195.35). Tube: Kensington High Street.

---

15. South Kensington

South Kensington, south of Kensington Gardens and Hyde Park, is essentially a residential area, not as elegant as that bordering Belgravia and Knightsbridge. However, the section is rich in museums, and it has a number of colleges.

Staying in South Kensington has much to recommend it. Besides its proximity to the Kensington museums, such as the Victoria and Albert, the area encompasses Albert Hall, and is within walking distance of Kensington Gardens and Harrods department store. At the South Kensington Station, you can catch trains for Kew Gardens and the Thames River town of Richmond.

EXPENSIVE HOTELS

The **Pelham Hotel,** 15 Cromwell Place, London, SW7 2LA (tel. 071/589-8288), has charm, style, and class all tied up with a Victorian bow. Privately owned by Kit and Tim Kemp, and small (only 37 bedrooms), it is one of the gems of London, suitable for everyone from a visiting movie star to an individualistic and discerning traveler. Personal service is the hallmark here. One of the most stunningly decorated hotels of London, it is formed from part of a row of early 19th-century terrace houses with white porticoed facades. Inside, high ceilings and fine moldings create a backdrop for a luxurious decor, including richly draped fabrics, linens, and silks, and a collection of antiques, Victorian oil paintings, even 18th-century paneling from a bank in Suffolk (now lining the drawing room, which is like that of an elegant London private townhouse). Mrs. Kemp, an inveterate collector, was the hotel decorator, filling Pelham with, among other fine trappings, needlepoint, rugs, and cushions for a homelike warmth.

All the individually decorated bedrooms and suites offer sumptuous and comfortable beds, and bathrooms designed in granite and mahogany. This fully air-conditioned hotel, in spite of its size, tries to provide all the services of a major hotel, such as a "solve-everything" concierge, room service when you want it, theater ticket arrangements, whatever. Doubles or twins range from £130 ($214.50) to £155 ($255.75) per night, with suites for two costing from £250 ($412.50). The hotel's Pelham Restaurant is one of the finest in South Kensington. Tube: South Kensington.

Blakes, 33 Roland Gardens, London SW7 3PF (tel. 071/370-6701), is one of the best small hotels in London, certainly the most sophisticated. It was created by joining four former Victorian townhouses together and painting them a uniform shade of bottle green. The neighborhood may be staunchly middle class, but Blakes is strictly an upper-class bastion of privilege. London's parade of the young and stylish, including "rag trade" types, photographers, and actors, dine downstairs in what is one of the best-reputed restaurants in town. It's so glamorous, in fact, that guests might see Princess Margaret dining among them. You enter a richly appointed lobby furnished with Victorian-era campaign furniture, probably brought back by some empire-builder from a sojourn in India. Near an ornate wire birdcage (a miniature version of a mogul's palace in itself), a receptionist quotes singles beginning at £130

KENSINGTON

($214.50) daily and doubles or twins from £165 ($272.25). The 55 rooms tend to be smallish, yet impeccably outfitted with unusual accessories and furniture, some of it antique. Tube: South Kensington (but a taxi's better).

MODERATELY PRICED HOTELS

The Regency Hotel, 100 Queen's Gate, SW7 5AG (tel. 071/370-4595), takes its name from the Prince Regent, later George IV. The hotel used this leading figure to set the style for its gracious living close to museums, Kensington, and Knightsbridge. Five Victorian terrace houses were converted into one 200-room stylish hotel which offers exceptional value for London. In the warmly decorated interior, a Chippendale fireplace, flanked with wing chairs, greets guests near the polished hardwood of the reception area. One of the building's main stairwells contains a most unusual chandelier, consisting of five Empire chandeliers suspended vertically, one on top of the other. Another attraction is a basement-level Elysium Health Spa, with a steamroom, a sauna, and a sensory-deprivation "deprogramming" tank.

Each of the hotel's bedrooms contains mahogany trim, direct-dial phone, hairdryer, color TV, and private bath. Five of the accommodations are duplex suites, added to the roof structures of the original houses. An executive single room rents for £94 ($155.10), with a twin or double costing £109 ($179.85). Some luxury suites for two persons are priced from £180 ($297). The hotel's Pavilion Restaurant is recommended separately. Tube: Gloucester Road or South Kensington.

When it was built in the 1880s, **Bailey's Hotel,** 140 Gloucester Rd., London SW7 4QH (tel. 071/373-6000), to quote the management, was a "firm favorite with the squirearchy," but now caters to average visitors, both foreign and domestic, along with budding executives. This brick corner establishment in South Kensington, with its formal arched entrance and mansard roof, was one of those first revolutionary hotels to install an "ascending room"—that is, an elevator. The ground floor bar and lounge is paneled in limed oak. All 162 bedrooms have private baths/showers, color TVs, radios, and direct-dial phones. Many amenities, such as automatic elevators and a restaurant, were added during an extensive upgrading. Singles cost £90 ($148.50) to £95 ($156.75) daily, and twins rent for £105 ($173.25) to £150 ($247.50). All prices include VAT and service. Tube: Gloucester Road.

Gore Hotel, 189 Queen's Gate, London SW7 5EX (tel. 071/584-6601). This elegantly detailed neoclassical townhouse was built in 1870 as the private home of a relative of the marquess of Queensberry. (The latter's fame resides in his formalizing the rules of boxing as well as a lawsuit that helped to destroy Oscar Wilde.) Transformed into a private hotel in 1908, today banks of potted shrubs shelter its Corinthian-style half-columns from the wide boulevard of the residential neighborhood where it sits. There's an informal brasserie in what used to be the high-ceilinged parlor, a cluster of 19th-century oil paintings in the lobby, and 54 pleasantly furnished bedrooms, each with a remote-control TV, radio, phone, hairdryer, and tile bathroom. A comfortable bar, lined with paintings, gilt mirrors, and potted palms, is often the haunt of English journalists. Several of the bedrooms are more opulent than the others, each designed with a name such as Tudor, Venus, the Crown, or the Consort Room. With VAT included, singles cost £76 ($125.40) to £87 ($143.55) daily, and doubles go for £93 ($153.45) to £116 ($191.40), depending on the accommodation. Tube: Gloucester Road.

Alexander Hotel, 9 Sumner Place, London SW7 3EE (tel. 071/581-1591), is among the most expensive on the street, but it is also the best. The four properties, built as a sumptuous private hotel in 1842, are still elegant today thanks to the extensive refurbishment program. Part of the Alexander has such a large array of artwork, both modern and antique, that it seems more like a gallery than a hotel. English hunting scenes alternate with original theater posters of Mistinguette to create an ambience that made S. J. Perelman, the American humorist, return again and again. The 39 rooms contain private baths/showers, color TVs, videos, direct-dial phones, and artworks. Singles cost £75 ($123.75) daily, and doubles go for £85 ($140.25) to £105 ($173.25). Rooms with four posters cost £110 ($181.50) to £140 ($231) for two. A cottage, with a garden entrance suitable for four to five guests, costs £175 ($288.75). Prices include breakfast and VAT. Tube: South Kensington.

Number Sixteen, 16 Sumner Place, London SW7 3EG (tel. 071/589-5232), is an elegant luxury pension, made up of four early Victorian townhouses linked together into a dramatically organized whole, with an elevator. As each house was added, the front and rear gardens expanded, and now their flowering shrubs and tulips create one of the most idyllic spots on the street. The 33 rooms contain an eclectic mixture of English antiques and modern paintings. There's an honor-system self-service bar in one of the elegantly formal sitting rooms, where a blazing fire is lit to take off the cold-weather chill. Extensive refurbishments took place in 1990. Prices are from £60 ($99) to £95 ($156.75) daily in a single, £125 ($206.25) to £140 ($231) in a double. Tube: South Kensington.

One Cranley Place, 1 Cranley Place, London SW7 3AB (tel. 071/589-7704), is one of the little gems of London, a "secret address." Lying on a little mews behind a Regency-style Victorian row house, this well-accessorized hotel offers only ten bedrooms, but each is tastefully furnished, evoking the aura of an elegant country home filled with summertime colors. A front parlor, for example, is embellished with Turkish kilim weavings, Chinese vases, and a scattering of antiques. A fireplace is lit in the reception, and a stairway takes you to the gallery-windowed alcoves, carpeted hallways, and the bedrooms. Doubles range from £90 ($148.50) to £140 ($231) daily. Breakfast is served in a blue-and-white, skylit, country-style kitchen with views of a well-maintained garden. Tube: South Kensington.

BUDGET HOTELS

Aston's Budget Studios, Designer Studios, and **Luxury Apartments,** 39 Rosary Gardens, London SW7 4NQ (tel. 071/370-0737), offering 60 studios and apartments, combine the elegance of a Victorian home with the convenience and economy of self-catering under the personal management of Shelagh King.

Each of the Aston's Budget Studios has a fresh colorful decor, a compact, complete kitchenette, and each of the immaculate bathrooms is shared by only a few guests. The studios range in size from singles to large family units. Prices quoted on a per week basis are £160 ($264) for one person, £130 ($214.50) per person for two, £110 ($181.50) per person for three, and £105 ($173.25) per person for four.

Aston's Designer Studios combine a sophisticated decor with high tech accessories, fine amenities, and service. These studios are £225 ($371.25) to £260 ($429) per person daily for two and offer air conditioning, private phones with remote answering machine, private Fax lines, marble showers, maid service, and much more.

Shelagh King also rents spacious one-bedroom apartments for £650 ($1,072.50) to £800 ($1,320) per week. Tube: Gloucester Road.

Prince Hotel, 6 Sumner Place, London SW7 3AB (tel. 071/589-6488), has been successfully converted from an early Victorian terrace house constructed around 1850. Decorated and restored in a classic English style, it opens onto a conservatory in the rear with a garden. Each of the 20 individually decorated bedrooms has a private bath or shower, direct-dial telephone, and color TV. Singles rent for £45 ($74.25) daily, with doubles or twins costing £65 ($107.25) to £80 ($132). A family room, suitable for four persons, costs £100 ($165). Rates include a full English breakfast and tax. Tube: South Kensington.

5 Sumner Place, 5 Sumner Place, London SW7 3EE (tel. 071/584-7586), stands next door to the Prince (listed previously), and is another carefully restored Victorian terrace house (circa 1850). It is classical and traditional in decor and furnishings. Each of its 14 bedrooms contains a private bath or shower, radio, and color TV (some have a small refrigerator as well). Guests are charged £65 ($107.25) daily in a single, £90 ($148.50) in a double, and £95 ($156.75) in a triple, with breakfast and VAT included. The hotel is served by an elevator, which delivers guests down to a lovely Victorian-style conservatory in the rear where breakfast is served. Tube: South Kensington.

Eden Plaza, 68-69 Queensgate, London SW7 5TJ (tel. 071/370-6111), stands on a broad, tree-lined boulevard and offers well-run and modernized services. Windows are double glazed to cut down on the traffic noise, and the hotel charges reasonable prices for the neighborhood. It offers 67 bedrooms, compact in size but equipped with all the necessary amenities, including private baths or showers, hairdryers, direct-dial phones, color TVs, and radios. Prices are £59 ($97.35) in a single, £72 ($118.80) to £79 ($130.35) in a double, and £89 ($146.85) in a triple, including VAT and an English breakfast. An elevator services all floors. The cocktail bar makes a cozy rendezvous point, and a good restaurant on the premises serves full English breakfasts along with dinner nightly from 6:30 to 9, offering a selection of British and continental dishes. Tube: Gloucester Road.

Number Eight Hotel, 8 Emperor's Gate, South Kensington, London SW7 4HH (tel. 071/370-7516), is a hotel in a cul-de-sac of the museum district of London, offering warmth and elegance in a stately Victorian building. Bedrooms in this small hotel are individually decorated, each one named after a county of England. Most of the 15 units have baths or showers and all have direct-dial phones, color TVs, radios, hairdryers, and other modern amenities. A generous English buffet breakfast is served. There is a bar vending machine and room service. Depending on the plumbing singles range from £50 ($82.50) to £55.95 ($92.30) daily, with doubles or twins costing from £60 ($99) to £65 ($107.25), plus 15% VAT. Personal service of a high standard is the keynote of Number Eight. The hotel is convenient for Knightsbridge and Kensington High Street shops, Earl's Court, and Olympia Exhibitions Centres. Tube: Gloucester Road.

Aster House, 3 Sumner Place, London SW7 3EE (tel. 071/581-5888). The smallest hotel on this unusual street of hotels, the Aster has an early Victorian facade. It is, in the view of many, "the best B&B in London." Rachel and Peter Carapiet are the owners, and their guests come from around the world, looking for the discreet no. 3, as there is no hotel sign. Peter, an architect, has built L'Orangerie, over the adjacent garage, adding a Machin Conservatory which doubles as a breakfast room and lounge. All 12 of the hotel's individually decorated rooms have private baths, color TVs, mini-bars, direct-dial phones, and central heating. Two of the attractive units are on the ground floor, one with a fireplace and a curtained four-poster. Singles cost £50 ($82.50) daily, and doubles and twins go for £70 ($115.50) to £85 ($140.25), the higher price for a four-poster room. You can begin your day with a walk in the garden, strictly "London in bloom." Tube: South Kensington.

16. Notting Hill Gate

Increasingly gaining in fashion and frequented by such personages as the princess of Wales, Notting Hill Gate is bounded on the south by Bayswater Road and on the east by Gloucester Terrace. It is hemmed in on the north by West Way and on the west by the Shepherds Bush ramp leading to the M40. It has many turn-of-the-century mansions and small houses that sit on quiet, leafy streets.

MODERATELY PRICED HOTELS

It refers to itself as a "Bed and Breakfast Hotel," but **Abbey Court,** 20 Pembridge Gardens, London, W2 4DU (tel. 071/221-7518), is more luxurious than the name suggests; its furnishings and decor are strictly up-scale. Contained within a white-fronted, mid-Victorian townhouse, it has a flowery patio in front and a small garden in back. Breakfast served in the 22 bedrooms is included in the price of £75 ($123.75) daily in a single, £105 ($173.25) in a double or twin, and £145 ($239.25) for a larger than usual four-poster bed suitable for two. Each accommodation offers carefully coordinated fabrics, fine furniture, a full bath with Jacuzzi jets, heated towel racks, and a bath lined with beige Italian marble. Light snacks and drinks are available 24 hours a day. Kensington Gardens is a short walk away, as are the antique stores along Portobello Road. Tube: Notting Hill Gate.

The **Pembridge Court Hotel,** 34 Pembridge Gardens, London W2 4DX (tel.

071/229-9977), presents a neoclassically elegant, cream-colored facade to a residential neighborhood that is making gains toward a rapid gentrification. The building was constructed in 1852 as a private house. In its brick-lined restaurant, Caps, full meals with wine costing from £15 ($24.75) are popular with the owners of neighboring townhouses. Most of the 25 comfortably outfitted bedrooms contain at least one antique, as well as 19th-century engravings and plenty of warmly patterned fabrics. Each has its own bath, color TV, direct-dial phone, and hairdryer. The largest and most stylish rooms are on the top floor with bathrooms tiled in Italian marble. A full English breakfast is included in the price of £55 ($90.75) to £75 ($123.75) daily in a single, £70 ($115.50) to £95 ($156.75) in a double. VAT is extra. Tube: Notting Hill Gate.

17. Holland Park

About a ten-minute taxi ride from the heart of the West End, Holland Park was once meadowland belonging to Lady Holland. The park grew up around a 1606 Jacobean structure, Holland House, which was a beehive of social and political activity at the dawn of the 19th century when the area became a favored address for the upper classes. In the closing years of the Victorian era it was the scene of some of the most fashionable garden parties and masquerade balls in London. Although heavily bombed during the Luftwaffe attacks on London in the early 1940s, the formally laid-out gardens have been restored, and in summer this is a rendezvous for concerts and open-air plays.

AN EXPENSIVE HOTEL
Called "by far the grandest of London's small hotels," the **Halcyon Hotel,** 81 Holland Park, London W11 3RZ (tel. 071/727-7288), was formed from a pair of Victorian mansions originally built in 1860 by upper-class Londoners wanting to live on former meadowland owned by Lady Holland. Today their successful union contains a hotel of charm, class, fashion, urban sophistication, and much comfort. Since it opened in 1985, its clientele has included a bevy of international film and recording stars who like the privacy and anonymity provided by this place, where maids, dressed in black with starched white pinafores, glide silently through the corridors. More than half the 44 accommodations are classified as suites, and each unit is lavishly outfitted with the kinds of furnishings and textiles you might find in an Edwardian country house. Several accommodations are filled with such whimsical touches as tented ceilings, and each contains all the modern luxuries you'd expect in a hotel of this caliber. Rates in a single range from £155 ($255.75) to £175 ($288.75) daily; in a double or twin, £215 ($354.75) to £235 ($387.75); and in a suite, £265 ($437.25) to £500 ($825).

The public rooms are inviting oases, with trompe-l'oeil paintings against backgrounds of turquoise. A complimentary limousine service takes clients to and from the West End, and there are a host of extras, including 24-hour rooms service, one-hour pressing of clothes, and a message-paging system that extends 20 miles from the hotel. The hotel's restaurant, Kingfisher, is recommended in the next chapter. Tube: Holland Park.

18. Lancaster Gate

North of Kensington Gardens and Hyde Park stands Lancaster Gate, a highly desirable section of London south of Paddington Station. It grew into prominence when residential development at Marble Arch pushed westward at the beginning of the 1800s. In time this area grew seedy, but with much restoration it has come back.

AN EXPENSIVE HOTEL

A classic townhouse hotel right in the center of London, **Whites Hotel,** Lancaster Gate, London W2 3NR (tel. 071/262-2711), is a home for the discerning. A trio of French Renaissance style terraced private residences were joined together to form this engaging hotel. The entrance, through a courtyard with limited parking, leads into a series of beautifully decorated public rooms, with an elegant connecting bar and restaurant. Overlooking Kensington Gardens, the 54 bedrooms are designed in exquisite English taste, with swagged moiré draperies and soft muted colors, along with marble baths imported from Italy. Such luxury commands a price tag, with singles renting for £130 ($214.50) daily, and doubles climbing the scale from £170 ($280.50) to £225 ($371.25) at this five-star winner. The restaurant offers a setting of gleaming silver place settings and crystal chandeliers where you can enjoy a carefully chosen English cuisine, with traditional grills and flambé dishes, along with such seasonal produce as grilled saddle of Highland venison in its own juices laced with Scotch malt whisky. Tube: Lancaster Gate.

19. Paddington/Bayswater

A popular hotel area, particularly for budget travelers, is the Paddington section, around Paddington Station, just to the northwest of Kensington Gardens and Hyde Park. Here you'll be within walking distance of the great Marble Arch, the entrance to Hyde Park. The main Paddington avenue, Sussex Gardens, has been known for years to pence-shy travelers who seek out its bed-and-breakfast houses. But as more and more townhouses are being razed on Sussex Gardens to make way for expensive flats, Norfolk Square is gaining importance as the area in which to shop for budget hotels. Allowed to deteriorate after World War II, the square was formerly one of the most prestigious squares of London, especially in the reign of Victoria when the eminent built large, beautiful townhouses ideal for big families, maids, and nannies.

Lying just north of Bayswater Road and Kensington Gardens, slightly to the west of Hyde Park, Bayswater is an unofficial district with a number of decently priced lodgings. Many former townhouses—converted into guest houses or private hotels—date back to the days when Bayswater spelled the good life to a prosperous upper middle class. Some of these houses, often lined up in rows, open onto pleasant squares.

Tube stops serving the Bayswater and Paddington areas are Paddington, Bayswater, Queensway, Notting Hill Gate, and Ladbroke.

MODERATELY PRICED HOTELS

For those seeking a moderately priced accommodation overlooking Kensington Gardens, **The Coburg Hotel,** 129 Bayswater Rd., London W2 4RJ (tel. 071/823-7020), is an ideal choice. With that view, you feel almost as if you are in the country. Yet a walk around the corner will put you on one of the most popular restaurant streets of London, Queensway, and the nearby Underground will whisk you into the heart of the West End in minutes. The hotel, a famous landmark on the Bayswater skyline, has been massively renovated. Its motto is delivering "value for money," and in that it succeeds admirably, as evidenced by its many repeat customers.

A wide number of accommodations are offered, 140 bedrooms in all, including some family rooms. Many bedrooms are quite spacious, and others, such as singles, are snugly cozy with all the necessary amenities. All the rooms have color TVs, radios, phones, private baths, and electric trouser presses. Those at front, overlooking busy Bayswater Road, have double-glazed windows for tranquility's sake. The most sumptuous accommodation is the Duke's Suite in the dome. You can see the whole of Hyde Park from there. Singles range from £69.50 ($114.70) daily, with doubles costing £94.50 ($155.95), plus VAT. The hotel also has one of the leading Indian restaurants of Bayswater, Spice Merchant (see separate recommendation in Chapter IV) on its ground floor. Tube: Queensway or Bayswater.

In a residential area, **Colonnade Hotel,** 2 Warrington Crescent, London W9 1ER (tel. 071/286-1052), is an imposing townhouse built in 1853 as two private homes, just a block from the Warwick Avenue tube station in a section of London known as "Little Venice." This was the first home in England of Sigmund Freud. The 50 bedrooms are spacious (some with balconies) and are equipped with private baths/showers. All have TVs, videos, radios, phones, hairdryers, and trouser presses. There are 16 special rooms with four-poster beds. Some are air conditioned and some have Jacuzzis. The rates are from £55 ($90.75) daily in a single and from £66 ($108.90) to £88 ($145.20) in a double. Tariffs depend on the plumbing. A full English breakfast and VAT are included. The hotel has a restaurant and a cocktail piano bar called Cascades. Tube: Warwick Avenue.

Mornington Hotel, 12 Lancaster Gate, London W2 3LG (tel. 071/262-7361), brings a touch of Swedish hospitality to the center of London. Just north of Hyde Park and Kensington Gardens, the hotel has been completely redecorated with a Scandinavian-designed interior. The bedrooms, 68 in all, are not only tastefully conceived and most comfortable, but each unit is complete with private bath and shower, color TV, phone, and radio. Rates are £64 ($105.60) daily in a single, rising to £75 ($123.75) to £84 ($138.60) in a double or twin. If you're traveling with a child, the Swedish-speaking staff will place an extra bed in your room for an additional charge. Tariffs include a Scandinavian buffet breakfast, service, and VAT. Naturally, there's a genuine Finnish sauna, but you'll also find a well-stocked bar where you can order snacks and, if you're in time, afternoon tea. Tube: Lancaster Gate.

---

20. St. Marylebone

Below Regent's Park, northwest of Piccadilly Circus, is the district of St. Marylebone (pronounced Mar-li-bone), primarily a residential section that faces Mayfair to the south and extends north of Marble Arch. A number of gracious townhouses in this section have been converted into private hotels.

EXPENSIVE HOTELS

A grand English country house, the **Dorset Square Hotel,** 39-40 Dorset Square, London NW1 6QN (tel. 071/723-7874), is made up of four Georgian Regency townhouses similar to their neighbors on the small square near Regent's Park. Hotelier Tim Kemp and his wife, Kit, have transformed the former dwellings into a hotel with 37 bedrooms and 12 suites, with an interior so designed that the public rooms, bedrooms, and baths still give the impression of being in an elegant private home. The bedrooms are decorated in chintz or print materials that complement the furniture, a mix of antiques and reproductions. Rates are £70 ($115.50) daily in a single, from £85 ($140.25) to £140 ($231) in a double. The handsome restaurant, Country Manners, is graced by a mural showing Dorset Square when it was the home of the Marylebone Cricket Club. The menu, featuring the best of English cuisine, changes daily, offering such dishes as Stilton soup, venison (in season), and poached Scottish salmon with hollandaise sauce. Tube: Baker Street or Marylebone.

Hotel Montcalm, 33 Great Cumberland Place, London W1A 2LG (tel. 071/402-4288). Set near Marble Arch, along the inner curve of a Georgian-era crescent of identical townhouses, this hotel is a favorite of visiting rock stars and international celebrities, who can often be seen in the hotel restaurant, Les Celebrites. The guests who have registered at the lobby's vintage Louis XVI writing table have included everyone from Michael Jackson to Duran Duran to Stevie Wonder. This is the first

Nikko Hotel (fully owned by Japan Air Lines) in London, but the decor includes only a hint of eastern flavor. The public rooms are plushly decorated with brown carpeting and brown leather sofas whose modern lines are attractively compatible with an overall flavor of 18th-century opulence. The polite staff is formally dressed, sometimes in amusing contrast to the blue jeans and sneakers of the musical artists who make this place a favorite. Because the Georgian lines of the building's facade couldn't be altered, some of the biggest accommodations are duplexes, connected upstairs and down by circular metal staircases. Each of the 116 accommodations contains air conditioning, security locks, color TV, in-house movies, and dozens of extra touches. Singles cost £149 ($245.85) daily, and doubles go for £169 ($278.85) to £195 ($321.75), with service and VAT included. Tube: Marble Arch.

A MODERATELY PRICED HOTEL

A 200-year-old, 96-room hostelry, 26-32 **Durrants Hotel,** George St., London W1H 6BJ (tel. 071/935-8131), has a sprawling Georgian facade of brown brick incorporating several neighboring houses. A walk through the pine- and mahogany-paneled public rooms is like a tour through another century. Its restaurant serves full afternoon teas and satisfying meals in one of the most beautiful Georgian decors in the neighborhood. The less formal breakfast room is ringed with 19th-century political cartoons by the noted Victorian artist, Spy. The 18th-century niceties include a letter-writing room sheathed with old paneling, plus a popular neighborhood pub with Windsor chairs, an open fireplace, and a decor that probably hasn't changed much in 200 years. The establishment's oldest bedrooms face the front and have slightly higher ceilings than the newer ones. Even the most recent accommodations, however, have elaborate cove moldings, comfortable furnishings, and a solid feeling. Each has color TV, phone, radio, and private bath. Singles cost £48 ($79.20) to £65 ($107.25) daily, and doubles rent for £72 ($118.80) to £122 ($201.30). Tube: Bond Street.

BUDGET HOTELS

A well-preserved building, **Hart House Hotel,** 51 Gloucester Place, Portman Square, London W1H 3PE (tel. 071/935-2288), is part of a group of Georgian mansions occupied by the French nobility during the French Revolution. The hotel is in the heart of the West End and is convenient for shopping, theaters, and sightseeing. Hart House is centrally heated, and all 15 bedrooms have hot and cold running water, color TVs, radios, and phones. Prices, which include an English breakfast, are £30 ($49.50) daily for a single, £45 ($74.25) in a twin or double, and £65 ($107.25) in a triple, the rate depending on the plumbing. Tube: Marble Arch or Baker Street.

Bryanston Court Hotel, 56-60 Great Cumberland Place, London W1H 8DD (tel. 071/262-3141), is composed of three individual houses, each around 190 years old, which were joined together. Owned by the Theodore family, today it is one of the better hotels on the street, with a gas fireplace in the Chesterfield-style bar, plus a stairway leading up to the 54 bedrooms. Each of these contains a private bath, color TV, phone, and radio. Singles cost £65 ($107.25) daily, and doubles or twins go for £80 ($132). VAT and a continental breakfast are included in the prices. The opulent red dining room, the Brunswick Restaurant, is furnished in an early 19th-century style, with antiques and oil paintings. Tube: Marble Arch.

Hotel La Place, 17 Nottingham Place, London W1M 3FB (tel. 071/486-232), is a refurbished B&B hotel, one of the finest in the area. A Victorian building with a red-brick facade, similar to many other buildings on its street, it rents 24 bedrooms. Each of these (most are painted pink) contains a private bath, TV, phone, and radio. Singles range from £50 ($82.50) to £55 ($90.75) daily, with doubles costing from £65 ($107.25) to £70 ($115.50). You can also rent a triple at £75 ($123.75) and a quad at £90 ($148.50). Rates include VAT and an English breakfast. The basement of the little hotel contains the Greenery Restaurant which serves lunch and dinner daily. Tube: Baker Street.

INNER CIRCLE

Queen
Mary's
Gardens

PARK RD.

OUTER CIRCLE

Regents
Park

Bedford
College

ROSSMORE RD.

GLOUCESTER PL.

BALCOMBE ST.

Madame
Tussaud's

LISSON GROVE

HARROWOOD AVE.

Marylebone

Dorset Sq.

to Royal Academy of Music

BROADLEY ST.

Baker Street

CHILTERN ST.

PADDINGTON ST.

BELL ST.

UPPER MONTAGU ST.

MARYLEBONE RD.

CHAPEL ST.

YORK ST.

CRAWFORD ST.

DORSET ST.

MANCHESTER ST.

BAKER ST.

CRAWFORD PL.

MONTAGU PL.

Montagu Sq.

BLANDFORD ST.

HARROWBY ST.

BRYANSTON SQ.

SEYMOUR PL.

Wallace
Collection

EDGWARE RD.

GEORGE ST.

Cambridge
Sq.

Portman Sq.

ORCHARD ST.

Oxford Sq.

KENDAL ST.

UPPER BERKELEY ST.

GREAT CUMBERLAND PL.

SEYMOUR ST.

CONNAUGHT ST.

OXFORD ST.

HYDE PARK ST.

ALBION ST.

GREEN ST.

Marble Arch Marble
Arch

BAYSWATER RD.

PARK ST.

THE RING.

Speaker's
Corner

Hyde
Park

REGENTS PARK
AND ST. MARYLEBONE

Blandford Hotel, 80 Chiltern St., London W1M 1PS (tel. 071/486-3103), is somewhat of a find and definitely one of London's better B&Bs for the price. The 33 bedrooms are well proportioned, and all have direct-dial phones, color TVs, hairdryers, coffee-making equipment, and private baths with showers. Singles rent for £56 ($92.40) daily, with doubles costing £70 ($115.50). The charge for a triple is £87 ($143.55). Rates include VAT and a large English breakfast, but service is left to the client. A car park is situated next door to the hotel. Tube: Baker Street.

Hotel Concorde, 50 Great Cumberland Place, London W9 1ER (tel. 071/402-6316), is a small hotel with style. The reception desk, nearby chairs, and part of the tiny bar area were at one time part of a London church. A display case in the lobby contains an array of reproduction English silver, each piece of which is for sale. This establishment was built as a private house and later converted into a hotel.

Each of the 50 accommodations is pleasantly decorated with flowered wallpaper and has a color TV, direct-dial phone, and a private bath. Owned by the Theodore family, the hotel is now run by the third generation. Breakfast is the only meal served. Singles rent for £50 ($82.50) daily, while doubles or twins cost £65 ($107.25) to £85 ($140.25). A continental breakfast is included in the rates. Tube: Marble Arch.

Edward Lear Hotel, 28-30 Seymour St., London W1H 5WD (tel. 071/402-5401), is a popular hotel, made all the more desirable by the bouquets of fresh flowers set up around the public rooms. It's one city block from Marble Arch in a pair of brick townhouses, both of which date from 1780. The western house was the London home of the 19th-century artist and poet Edward Lear, whose illustrated limericks and original lithographs adorn the walls of one of the sitting rooms. Steep stairs lead to the 30 bedrooms, 11 of which contain private baths. The cozy units are fairly small but have all the usual amenities, including color TVs, radios, phones, and hot beverage facilities. Singles cost from £34.75 ($57.35) to £48.50 ($80.05) daily, doubles and twins from £47.75 ($78.80) to £57.50 ($94.95). Tariffs include VAT and a large English breakfast. The owner, Peter Evans, is helpful to guests. Tube: Marble Arch.

Hallam Hotel, 12 Hallam St., Portland Place, London W1N 5LJ (tel. 071/580-1166), is a heavily ornamented stone-and-brick Victorian house, one of the few on the street to escape bombing in World War II. Today it's the property of Earl Baker and his sons, Grant and David, who maintain it well. The bright breakfast room overlooks a pleasant patio. There is also a bar for residents. An elevator leads to the 23 simple but comfortable bedrooms, each with TV, phone, radio, and 24-hour room service. VAT and a light English breakfast are included in the price of the rooms, which cost £50 ($82.50) in a single and £70 ($115.50) in a double. Tube: Oxford Circus.

21. Bloomsbury

To the northeast of Piccadilly Circus, beyond Soho, is Bloomsbury, a world unto itself. It is, among other things, the academic heart of London, where you'll find the University of London, several other colleges, the British Museum, and many bookstores. Despite its student overtones, the section is fairly staid and quiet. Its reputation has been fanned by such writers as Virginia Woolf (it figures in her novel *Jacob's Room*). She and her husband, Leonard, were once the unofficial leaders of a coterie of artists and writers known as the Bloomsbury Group, nicknamed Bloomsberries.

The exact heart of Bloomsbury is difficult to pinpoint. There are those who say it is Russell Square, with its university buildings, private homes, and hotels. Others feel it is the nearby British Museum. Still others are convinced it's the sprawling University of London, which also contains the Royal Academy of Dramatic Art on Gower Street. In any case there are at least four other old tree-filled squares—Bloomsbury, Bedford, Gordon, and Tavistock—each one an oasis of green in the midst of some of London's finest buildings. The unquestioned northern border is Euston Road, with its three railway stations—St. Pancras, King's Cross, and Euston —and its southern border is New Oxford Street.

A MODERATELY PRICED HOTEL

Hotel Russell, Russell Square, London WC1B 5BE (tel. 071/837-6470), is a late Victorian hotel facing the gardens of this famous square and within easy reach of theaters and shopping. It is run by Trusthouse Forte and offers 326 rooms, all with private baths and showers and 24-hour room service. Rates for a single are from £99 ($163.35) to £110 ($181.50) daily, rising to £120 ($198) to £130 ($214.50) in a twin. The public rooms have been refurbished and include an excellent carvery restaurant and a brasserie. The Kings Bar serves cocktails in the atmosphere of a London club, and you can enjoy draft beer in the country-pub ambience of the Trade Winds Bar. A theater-ticket agency, secretarial services, and car rental are available. Tube: Russell Square.

BUDGET HOTELS

One of a row of similar buildings, the **Morgan Hotel,** 24 Bloomsbury St., London WC1B 3QJ (tel. 071/636-3735), is distinguished by its gold-tipped iron fence railings. Several of the 14 rooms overlook the British Museum, and the whole establishment is very much part of the international scholastic scene of Bloomsbury. The lobby is a bit cramped, the stairs rather steep, but the rooms are pleasant and the atmosphere congenial; consequently, the hotel is heavily booked. The bedrooms in this completely refurbished hotel are well carpeted and have private showers and toilets, big beds (by British standards), dressing tables with mirrors, and ample wardrobe space, as well as central heating. Singles cost £35 ($57.75) daily, and doubles go for £50 ($82.50). Prices include a full English breakfast and VAT. Tubes: Russell Square and Tottenham Court Road.

Academy Hotel, 17-21 Gower St., London, WC1E 6HG (tel. 071/634-4115), is a joining of three 1776 Georgian row houses that retain many of the original architectural details. Substantially modernized and stylishly refurbished in 1987, the 34-room hotel is different from the standard chain hotel and a good choice for travelers tired of paying four-star prices for two-star comforts (if that). It is conveniently located within walking distance of the theater district, Covent Garden, and other points of interest in the West End. Facilities include an elegant bar, library room, and a secluded patio garden. The hotel offers 24-hour room service, and each accommodation is not only well furnished but contains color TV, radio, direct-dial phone, and beverage-making equipment. Most rooms have private showers and toilets, but the public facilities are adequate. Singles rent for £68 ($112.20) daily, with doubles going for £92.50 ($152.65), including tax and a continental breakfast. Tube: Tottenham Court Road and Goodge Street.

22. Other Locales

EAST OF THE TOWER

Carefully developed and thoughtfully restored, St. Katharine's Dock is immediately east of the Tower of London and Tower Bridge. In the once-dilapidated section are boutiques, pubs, walkways, and bridges surrounding the docks where yachts from many ports tie up. Many visitors prefer to stay in this area, too.

An Expensive Hotel

With a sweeping view, the **Tower Thistle Hotel,** St. Katharine's Way, London E1 9LD (tel. 071/488-4134), stands tall, with the Tower and its bridge on one side, the dock on another, and the Thames on yet another. A modern building with 826 bedrooms, the hotel has its own parking facility, a bonus in crowded London. The units are air conditioned and have private baths and TVs with in-house video, in addition to the views from all angles. Singles rent for £99 ($163.35) to £132 ($217.80) daily, and doubles go for £112 ($184.80) to £145 ($239.25), with VAT and service included. The hotel offers a choice of three restaurants, the Princes Room, the Carvery, and the Which Way West Café. The Thames Bar and the Lounge both have relaxing ambiences in which to enjoy drinks with sweeping views of the river. For late-night entertainment, the hotel has its own nightclub. Tube: Tower Hill.

HAMPSTEAD

The old village of Hampstead, sitting high on a hill, is the most desirable residential suburb of London. The village borders a wild heathland, which contains sprawling acres of wooded dells and fields of heather. Yet the Northern Line of the Underground reaches the edges of the heath, making it possible for Londoners to enjoy isolated countryside while living only 20 minutes from city center. These advantages have caused many young artists to discover what Keats could have told them years ago—Hampstead is the place to live. The little Georgian houses have never received so much attention and love as they do now.

A Budget Hotel

Standing on a residential street, **Sandringham (Igar) Hotel,** 3 Holford Rd., London NW3 1AD (tel. 071/435-1569), is in one of the best parts of London. Coming out of the Hampstead tube station, you'll be on Heath Street. Turn right and walk up toward the hill, past interesting shops, restaurants, and pubs. On the fourth turning to the right, you enter Hampstead Square, which leads to Holford Road. If you have a car, you can park in the hotel's driveway. Comfortable rooms often house professional people who want to be near the center of London while retaining the feel of rural life. From the upper rooms, you will have a view over Hampstead Heath and the heart of London. The 19-room hotel has a comfortable lounge with a color TV. The B&B charge in rooms without bath are £30 ($49.50) to £40 ($66) daily in a single, £50 ($82.50) in a double, and £68 ($112.20) for a four-bedded room. A double with a private bath or shower costs £56 ($92.40), rising to £65 ($107.25) in a triple and £75 ($123.75) in a four-bedded room. VAT is included. Breakfast is served in a pretty room that has view of the well-kept garden.

SWISS COTTAGE

A moderately priced hotel on a tree-lined residential street in north London is named for the district in which it stands. The **Swiss Cottage Hotel,** 4 Adamson Rd., London NW3 3HP (tel. 071/722-2281), consists of four late-Victorian houses that were joined to create the intriguing accommodations. The result is a maze of halls and staircases, with varying floor levels and bedrooms of different sizes and decor. Throughout, however, you'll find paintings and antique furniture, Persian rugs, chandeliers, wood inlay writing desks or bureaus, and patterned wallpaper. The glass-fronted reception desk contains a fine collection of porcelain figures. There is a quiet bar, a dining room where à la carte meals are served, and 24-hour room service. Behind the hotel is a small formal town garden, plus the Tea House area. This is the honeymoon suite, but you need not be on honeymoon to rent it. Bedrooms in the main hotel are comfortable and, except for some singles, have modern showers or bathrooms. All have TVs and phones. Singles without bath cost £40 ($66) daily. The most expensive singles go for £72 ($118.80) to £85 ($140.25) for a large deluxe unit with private bath. Doubles or twins range from £86 ($141.90) to £115 ($189.75). Tariffs include a continental breakfast and VAT. Tube: Swiss Cottage on the Jubilee Line, 10 minutes from the West End.

WIMBLEDON

Wimbledon, in South London, has been linked with the history of the British capital for centuries, particularly in High Street at the top of Wimbledon Hill, but

little is left from the days of yore. Today it's known for its international tennis championships, as the world's premier tennis competition is held here over a two-week period each summer. Also famous is the 1,000-acre Wimbledon Common, one of the largest green areas in the London environs.

An Expensive Hotel

Providing Georgian country-house elegance, **Cannizaro House,** West Side Wimbledon Common, London SW19 4UF (tel. 081/897-1464), is an oasis of tranquility only a short distance from the center of London. Built in the 1720s, the house took its name from the duke of Cannizaro, a Sicilian nobleman whose wife sponsored musical recitals here in the 1830s, establishing a lasting tradition. The 46-room house has housed the rich and famous as residents and guests since its construction. The structure, with stone walls, painted ceilings, and mansard roof, is set in parkland overlooking the common. Individually furnished bedrooms offer luxury accommodations with a decor reflecting the colors and scents of gardens. Singles rent for £85 ($140.25) to £105 ($173.25) daily, and doubles or twins go for £99 ($163.35) to £140 ($231). Two persons pay £170 ($280.50) to £200 ($330) daily for suites and four-poster bedrooms. The restaurant looks out on lawns, a sunken garden, and woodlands. Tube: Wimbledon.

---

23. Airport Hotels

As one of the major gateways to Europe (not to mention England), London's two major airports are among the busiest in the world. Many readers have expressed a desire to be near their point of departure, spending the night in ease before "taking off."

AT OR NEAR GATWICK

The airport's most convenient resting place is the **Gatwick Hilton International-al,** Gatwick Airport, Horley, Surrey RH6 0LL (tel. 0293/518080), a deluxe, five-floor hotel of the Hilton chain. A covered footbridge links the hotel and air terminal with a five-minute walk. You can also obtain porterage to the airport, and there are trolleys and electric cars if you can't cope with the walk. In the first-floor lobby, a glass-covered portico rises through four floors, containing a full-scale replica of the de Havilland Gypsy Moth airplane, *Jason,* used by Amy Johnson on her solo flight from England to Australia in 1930. The reception desk is close by, an area of greenery, trees, and flowering shrubs. There is a health club with sauna, massage room, Jacuzzi, large gymnasium, and heated indoor swimming pool. On the ground floor is a restaurant serving both English and continental dishes. The Jockey bar serves snacks, and there is also a cozy lounge bar, where refreshments are available 24 hours a day.

Rooms have full air conditioning, double-glazed windows, phones, radios, color TVs with a full-length feature film shown daily, and a mini-bar. Laundry and dry cleaning are returned within the day if collected at 9am. The 552 bedrooms, each with private bath and shower, cost from £92.50 ($152.65) daily in a single and from £103 ($169.95) in a double. Up-to-date flight information is flashed on the TV screen.

Gravetye Manor, Vowels Lane, near East Grinstead, West Sussex RH19 4LJ (tel. 0342/810567), is a 16th-century Elizabethan manor just 12 miles from Gatwick, part of an estate set in the hills, standing in its own 30 acres of woods, orchards, and a trout lake. It's approached by a mile-long winding driveway leading into an entrance courtyard. Later, you can discover the restored formal gardens, the lifetime creation of one of England's leading horticulturists, William Robinson, pioneer of the English natural garden. The spacious drawing room has tasteful furnishings, oak-paneled walls, and many antiques. Guests and area residents gather in the sitting room, warmed by a large fireplace, for aperitifs before dinner. All the 14 bedchambers are different, named after trees on the estate: Ash, Bay, Beech, whatever. My favorite is the Willow, an elegant, comfortable double with Tudor windows in both bedroom and bath from which you have a panorama of the gardens. The former master bedroom has a massive, carved four-poster and, over the fireplace, wood-carved portraits of the original owners (Richard and Katherine Infield in 1598). Doubles or twin-bedded rooms range in price from £90 ($148.50) to £165 ($272.25) daily. The rates in a single with private bath are from £75 ($123.75). Service is included, but breakfast isn't, and VAT is added to the entire account. Write well in advance for reservations in high season.

Dinner here is to be savored, not rushed. The restaurant has the best wine cellar in England, with some 500 listings. In addition, they smoke their own salmon and venison in a smokehouse on the estate. Expect to spend from £35 ($57.75) for a complete meal, excluding wine and bar. Luncheon is served daily from 12:30 to 2pm and dinner from 7:30 to 9:30pm.

Effingham Park Hotel, West Park Road, Copthorne, West Sussex, RH10 3EU (tel. 0342/714994), is set within 40 acres of beautiful parkland and gardens in the heart of the Sussex countryside, near the Surrey border. Opened in 1988, it's only minutes from the Gatwick Airport and the M23/M25 motorways. The location is 30 minutes by train from central London. The land was first mentioned in the *Domesday Book* (1086), and today it's ideal for a country weekend retreat, even if you don't have a plane to catch. The hotel emphasizes maximum comfort in its 122 well-appointed bedrooms, each with private bath. Singles range from £65 ($107.25) to £75 ($123.75), and doubles from £80 ($132.60) to £90 ($148.50). Tariffs include VAT. The hotel operates the Wellingtonia à la carte restaurant (named after the Wellingtonia trees lining the drive), the McLaren Restaurant (bearing the name of the world champion racing driver, Bruce McLaren), and the Circuit, the McLaren's buffet and carvery. PJ's Leisure Club is extensively equipped, and there's a large indoor swimming pool. The grounds embrace a 2,000 yard, 9-hole executive golf course.

Cisswood House Hotel, Sandygate Lane, Lower Beeding, near Horsham, West Sussex RH13 6NF (tel. 0403/891216), was called "Harrods in the country" by the locals when it was built in the late 1920s for Sir Woodman Burbidge, chairman of Harrods store. Craftspeople from the Harrods workshops were employed to create the wood and plasterwork and give the house its character, even if it is mock country Tudor. It is surrounded by traditional gardens with shrubs and flowering creepers, herbaceous borders, and well-kept lawns, with dovecotes and trees.

Othmar and Elizabeth Illes, who have owned Cisswood since 1979, have built a reputation for their high-quality cooking and the comfort of their 32 rooms, which have color TVs, mini-bars, and coffee-making equipment. The dining room is beamed, and there is a cheerful bar. The bedrooms are all individually designed and have flower prints, potted plants, modern baths, and direct-dial phones. Four have four-poster beds. Prices range from £56 ($92.40) daily in a single and £75 ($123.75) to £85 ($140.25) in a double. The hotel also has an indoor swimming pool and exercise equipment. Cisswood lies about 12 minutes from Gatwick Airport, and you can order a taxi for an early departure if necessary.

Gatwick Copthorne Hotel, Copthorne, near Crawley, West Sussex RH10 3PG (tel. 0342/714971), a four-star hotel centered around a 16th-century farmhouse, is set in 100 acres of gardens and woodlands. A garden room overlooks the central patio with its fountains and weeping willows. The bar and many of the bedrooms in the old part of the house have ancient beams. Floral bedspreads and chintz curtains add to the ambience. Bathrooms are modern, but most singles have showers only. The restaurant is dark, with a low, beamed ceiling and wooden balustrades. Meals include mainly French dishes, such as onion soup and bouillabaisse. The ingredients are fresh, and you have a good choice of desserts from the trolley. A set dinner costs £12.95 ($21.35), with an à la carte meal going for about £30 ($49.50) for three courses. As befits an airport hotel, food is available daily from 6:30am to 10:45pm. A single bedroom with a shower rents for £88 ($145.20) to £105 ($173.25) daily, while doubles go for £98 ($161.70) to £105 ($173.25). There are some ground-floor rooms suitable for the disabled. The hotel has buses and mini-vans (one of them antique) shuttling to the airport every 20 or 30 minutes.

Langshott Manor, Horley, Surrey RH6 9LN (tel. 0293/786680), may lie only minutes from the modernity of Gatwick Airport, but it is a manor house whose Elizabethan core was originally constructed in 1580. It was successively enlarged in 1684 and again in the 18th century. In the small market town of Horley, the location is about half an hour from the heart of London on the Gatwick-Victoria Express. Geoffrey and Rish Noble took over this manor, standing on a 2½-acre estate, and have painstakingly restored it. They rent six individually decorated bedrooms, with porcelains, print wallpaper and fabrics from old designs, and antiques. The bedrooms have adjoining bathrooms luxuriously appointed with extra amenities such as bubble bath in an apothecary jar. Charges for overnight stays range from £80 ($132) daily in a single to £100 ($165) in a double. The Nobles provide traditional English cuisine with a three-course dinner costing from £17.50 ($28.90). They also cheerfully provide transportation to Gatwick Airport.

AT OR NEAR HEATHROW

If you've got an overnight wait between planes, you might consider **Sheraton Skyline,** Bath Road, (A4), Hayes, Middlesex UB3 5BP (tel. 081/759-2535), a leading airport hotel, which operates on an international schedule, with travelers from around the world checking in around the clock. The hotel, which opened in 1971, offers 352 well-furnished bedrooms. Charges are from £115 ($189.75) daily in a single and from £130 ($214.50) in a double plus VAT. Facilities include an indoor swimming pool and a tropical patio. The Colony Room Restaurant offers gourmet cuisine. A wild west cabaret show and dinner are presented at Diamond Lil's.

Heathrow Penta Hotel, Bath Road, Hounslow, Middlesex, TW6 2AQ (tel. 081/897-6363), is within the perimeter of the airport. Many of the rooms have a view of Concorde and jumbo jet takeoffs, with double glazing protecting your ears from the sound. The 607 air-conditioned bedrooms and suites have up-to-date amenities including hot beverage facilities, mini-bars, satellite TVs, and in-house movies. All bedrooms contain private baths and showers, and there is an indoor swimming pool and leisure center, plus a hairdresser and 24-hour laundry service. Singles are £89 ($146.85) daily, twins and doubles cost £100 ($165) including VAT and service. Besides the 24-hour coffeeshop and room service, the hotel has a restaurant, London Chop House, as well as the Flying Machine Bar.

Another convenient choice for a first or last night near Heathrow Airport is the **Post House Hotel,** Sipson Road, West Drayton, Middlesex UB7 0JU (tel. 081/759-2323). This modern 10-story building is conveniently situated just off the M4 Motorway, only minutes from the airport. The hotel has its own private car park and also offers frequent coach services to and from all airport terminals. The Post House has 569 bedrooms, with 159 on the two Executive Club floors, offering club guests the use of the sauna, solaria, Jacuzzi, pool room, and fitness room. All the bedrooms have remote-control TVs, radios, direct-dial phones, mini-bars, private baths, hot beverage facilities, and are fully air conditioned. The prices are £80 ($132) daily for a standard single and £90 ($148.50) for an executive single. Doubles and twins cost £90 ($148.50) in a standard room and £100 ($165) in executive quarters. The hotel has two bars as well as a choice of restaurants.

IV

LONDON'S RESTAURANTS AND PUBS

1. THE WEST END
2. OTHER LOCALES
3. SPECIALTY DINING
4. PUBS OF LONDON
5. WINE BARS

With the pressure of tourism and the influx of foreign chefs, the reputation of English cuisine has risen considerably. Now there is also a wave of English-born and -trained chefs who have set a superb standard of cookery, using high-quality ingredients. One food writer called this new breed "the very professional amateur."

In the snackeries of suburbia the vegetables may still taste as if they had a grudge against you and the soup may remain reminiscent of flavored tapwater. But in the central sections of London—where you'll probably do your eating—the fare has improved immeasurably. This is largely because of intense competition from foreign establishments, plus the introduction of espresso machines, which make English coffee now resemble—well, coffee.

In the upper brackets, London has always boasted magnificent restaurants, several of which have achieved world renown. But these were the preserve of the middling wealthy, who have had their palates polished by travel abroad. Those less fortunate enjoyed a diet akin to parboiled blotting paper. There are some dishes, however—mostly connected with breakfast—at which the English have always excelled. The traditional morning repast of eggs and bacon (imported from Denmark) or kippers (smoked herring, of Scottish origin) is a tasty starter for the day, and locally brewed tea beats any American bag concoction. It's with the other meals that you have to use a little caution. If you want to splurge in a big way, you have the London "greats" at your disposal. But if these eateries are too expensive, you'll find dozens of good, moderately priced restaurants as well as budget establishments that charge even less for a three-courser.

What may astonish you is the profusion of international restaurants. London offers an array of Italian, Indian, Chinese, French, German, Swiss, Greek, Russian, Jewish, and Middle Eastern dineries, which probably outnumber the native establishments. You'll find them heavily represented on my list.

If you're a vegetarian, as more and more people are these days, you will find it no longer necessary to seek out a specific vegetarian restaurant as many restaurants now provide vegetarian dishes. In fact, the health-conscious individual can find something good to eat in almost any place he or she selects.

The prevailing mealtimes are much the same as in the U.S. You can get lunch from about midday onward and dinner until about 11pm—midnight in the Soho area. The difference is that fewer Londoners go in for the "business lunch." They'll either make do with sandwiches or take lunch in a pub. The once-hallowed custom of afternoon tea became for many years the preserve of matrons unworried about their waistlines. However, in the past few years it is having a renaissance. Viewed as a civilized pause in the day's activities, it's particularly appealing to those who didn't have time for lunch or plan an early theater engagement.

Most establishments—but not all—add a 10% to 15% service charge to your bill. You'll have to look at your check to make sure about that. If nothing has been added, leave a 12% to 15% tip.

All restaurants and cafés in Britain are required to display the prices of the food and drink they offer in a place where the customer can see them before entering the eating area. An establishment with an extensive à la carte menu must display prices of a representative selection of food and drink and the table d'hôte menu, if one is offered. Charges for service and any minimum or cover charge must also be made clear. The prices shown must be inclusive of VAT.

Finally, there's the matter of location. Once upon a time, London had two traditional dining areas: Soho for Italian and Chinese fare, Mayfair and Belgravia for French cuisine. Today you're likely to find any type of eatery anywhere from Chelsea to Hampstead. The majority of my selections are in the West End region, but only because this happens to be the handiest for visitors.

Note: If you wish to phone ahead from out of town for reservations at the more popular restaurants, remember the area code for central London is 071.

1. The West End

I'll begin the pleasant task of exploring the cuisine in the major districts of the West End.

MAYFAIR
Stick a few extra "quid" in your pocket and join the swells for a memorable meal in chic, high-priced Mayfair.

Expensive Restaurants
Le Gavroche, 43 Upper Brook St., W.1 (tel. 071/408-0881), has long stood for the finest quality French cuisine in Great Britain. It's the creation of two Burgundy-born brothers, Michel and Albert Roux. Service is faultless; the ambience chic and formal, but not stuffy. The menu changes constantly, depending on the availability of the freshest produce of the season, but more important, on the inspiration of the Roux brothers, who began modestly in London at another location and have gone on to fame in the culinary world.

Their wine cellar is among the most interesting in London, with many quality burgundies and bordeaux. Try, if featured, their stuffed smoked salmon and their mousseline of lobster. Most main courses are served on a silver tray covered with a silver dome. The lid is lifted off with great flourish, and the platters, like a stage play, are artistically arranged. You can enjoy an aperitif upstairs while perusing the menu and enjoying the delectable canapés. A set luncheon is offered at a relatively modest price of £22.50 ($37.15), with a table d'hôte dinner costing £50 ($82.50). To order à la carte in the evening will cost from £60 ($99) per person. Open from noon to 2pm and from 7 to 10:30pm Mon. to Fri. To be assured of a table, reserve well in advance. Tube: Bond Street or Marble Arch.

The Oak Room, Le Meridien, 21 Piccadilly, W.1 (tel. 071/734-8000), is one of the finest restaurants in London, recipient of many culinary awards. The setting alone—said to be the most beautiful dining room in the center of London—would be worth the trip. But it is the refined cuisine that is the draw. Lavish in its appointments, this splendid period room where the greats of the world have dined (then and now) has been restored to all its gilded splendor, including the ceiling and the original oak paneling. The menu is the creation of French Consultant Chef Michel Lorain and resident Executive Chef David Chambers.

You can select from "Cuisine Creative" or "Cuisine Traditionelle," enjoying such dishes as sea bass lightly smoked and served in a cream and caviar sauce on a bed of celeriac and mangetout. The set business lunch at £19.50 ($32.20) is acclaimed as one of the food bargains of London, considering the quality of the ingredients that go into it. A set seven-course "menu gourmand" at £42 ($69.30) is also presented in the evening. Reservations are vital and service is from noon to 2:30pm and 7 to 10:30pm Mon. to Fri.; closed Sat. lunch and all day Sun. Tube: Piccadilly Circus.

Bracewell's, Park Lane Hotel, Piccadilly, W.1 (tel. 071/499-3621). Bracewell's is one of chic London's better-kept secrets. The cuisine prepared by English-born chef David Ryan is among the best in the capital, and the decor and the five-star service are worthy of its distinguished clientele. You might begin with a drink among the gilded torchères and comfortable armchairs of Bracewell's Bar. Later you will be ushered into an intimately illuminated room whose deeply grained Louis XVI paneling, once part of the London home of the American banker and philanthropist Pierpont Morgan, was installed at the Park Lane in the 1920s.

The specialties are based on the freshest ingredients in any seasons, using only British dishes and the best of British produce. The menu throughout the year features such dishes as Colchester oysters, Cornish lobsters, Dover sole, Aberdeen Angus rib of beef, Morayshire venison, and English lamb. Mr. Ryan pays careful attention to his vegetables and salads. The vegetables are carved like little works of art and served al dente, and salads are crisp and fresh. Look for the corner of the menu spotlighting the chef's selected dishes. These might include a nest of quail eggs— fresh pasta molded in a nest shape and filled with quail eggs cooked with Parmesan cheese, ham, and truffle, and glazed with a hollandaise sauce. The desserts are delectable, and a trolley is wheeled to your table so you can make a selection. Or else a medley of exotic tropical fruit will be flambéed at your table.

On the three-course table d'hôte menu at £17.50 ($28.90), there are such long-standing British favorites as Lancashire hot pot, oxtail, and roast beef and Yorkshire pudding. In the evening a four-course menu gastronomique is priced at £27.50 ($45.40), or else you can order three courses for £24.50 ($40.45). A la carte meals can cost £45 ($74.25) per person. Open 12:30 to 2:30pm and 7 to 10:30pm; closed Sat. lunch and all day Sun. Tube: Hyde Park Corner.

Expensive Seafood

Bentley's, 11 Swallow St., W.1 (tel. 071/734-4756), in business since 1916, lies just off Piccadilly Circus in the heart of London. There used to be a certain type of English person who emerged only in the early evening, headed for Bentley's, and then downed a daily quota of oysters. If such creatures still exist, English to the core, Bentley's is there to serve them. The oysters here, in fact, are considered among the best in London. You can also order such fare as home-smoked eel, sole Bentley, and salmon fishcakes. On the ground floor is a marble-topped oyster bar (the elegant restaurant is upstairs). Meals cost from £28 ($46.20) and are served from noon to 3pm and 5:30 to 10:30pm; closed Sun. Tube: Piccadilly Circus.

Scotts, 20 Mount St., W.1 (tel. 071/629-5248), is considered the most noted restaurant in the world for oysters, lobster, and caviar. It is one of the most expensive fish restaurants in London. In addition to its regular spacious restaurant and cocktail bar, it has a special caviar bar and an oyster bar. Its origins are humble, going back to a fishmonger in 1851 in Coventry Street. However, its fame rests on its heyday at Piccadilly Circus when it often entertained Edward VII and his guests in private dining rooms. It has been at its present reincarnation since 1967, enjoying a chic address near the swank Connaught Hotel and Berkeley Square. Its decor, with its terra-cotta walls, has been called "Assyrian Monumental," the wall panels hung with English primitive pictures.

The restaurant's longtime chef, John Bertram, believes in British produce, and he handles the kitchen with consummate skill and authority. You get top-notch quality and ingredients: Lobster, crab, oysters, and perhaps smoked Ellingham eel are featured. The eel comes from Suffolk where it is "swum" (that is, kept alive) until it's ready for smoking. Dover sole is prepared "any way." The English prefer it "on the bone," considering filet fish for sissies. A favorite appetizer is salad chlóe, and more down-to-earth dishes, such as fish cakes, appear regularly or at least weekly on the luncheon menu. The price will be around £50 ($82.50) per person. Open daily from 12:30 to 3pm and 6 to 10:45pm. On Sun. only dinner is offered, from 7 to 10pm. Tube: Green Park.

Moderately Priced Restaurants

Langan's Brasserie, Stratton Street, W.1 (tel. 071/491-8822), is a relaxed, café-style restaurant modeled after a Parisian brasserie. The food is both traditional English and French. Langan's was the brainchild of the late restaurateur Peter Langan, in partnership with actor Michael Caine and the chef de cuisine, Richard Shepherd. It has been a chic spot since its opening in 1976. The potted palms and overhead fans create a faded '30s atmosphere; you expect the evening instrumentalists to break into "As Time Goes By" at any moment.

Complete dinners, including wine, VAT, and service, come to about £30 ($49.50) per person. Upstairs is a more intimate dining room with silver service, although the same prices are charged. Open 12:30 to 3pm and 7pm to midnight Mon. to Fri., 8pm to 12:45am Sat.; closed Sun. Tube: Green Park.

Al Hamra, 31 Shepherd Market, W.1 (tel. 071/493-1954), is the premier Lebanese restaurant in London. You get good value, impeccable service, and food that delights the palate. As for the staff, Beirut's loss was London's gain. Nostalgic refugees—those who managed to get out with their money—come here for a taste of the old country, and they rarely leave disappointed. To begin with, you are faced with a dazzling selection of *mezes* (appetizers). There are at least five dozen, both hot and cold, ranging from the inevitable hummus (chick peas) to such delights as shinklish (cheese salad of Lebanon). A salad of fresh vegetables is placed on each table for you to help yourself. For a main course, you can select from such dishes as grilled quail in garlic sauce and succulent grilled meats on a skewer. Bread, baked on the premises, is an important part of the dining ritual here. Likewise, the Lebanese who frequent the place like the honeyed sweets, but a member of the staff assured me that these desserts are "adjusted" for English diners—that is, prepared with less sugar than is customary. The cost is £20 ($33) per head, which is reasonable, considering the quality of the fresh ingredients and the time-consuming preparation they take. Open noon to midnight daily. Sometimes it's very difficult to get a table, so call early for a reservation. Tube: Green Park.

The Veeraswamy, 99-101 Regent St., W.1 (tel. 071/734-1401), is London's oldest and most famous Indian restaurant, having opened in 1927. It was founded by Edward Palmer, a spice merchant born in India in 1860. Now beautifully restored in muted tones, it is still a leading choice for Indian regional and tribal dishes. In the kitchen each chef is a specialist in his particular region of the subcontinent. In the past, kings and show-business personalities have flocked here, learning a lesson in gastronomic geography. From Gujarat to Goa (try the fiery coconut-flavored chicken), the cuisine is often mouth tingling. Vegetarians will delight in the thalis and home-baked breads. The best bargain, popular with the Regent Street business crowd, is the all-you-can-eat luncheon buffet at £12.50 ($20.65), a price rising to £20 ($33) and up for an à la carte dinner. A set dinner costs £18 ($29.70). Open daily from noon to 2:30pm and 6 to 11:30pm. Tube: Piccadilly Circus.

Coconut Grove, 3-5 Barrett St., W.1 (tel. 071/486-5269), in Mayfair, along St. Christopher's Street, is just off Oxford Street. Bright and lively, the restaurant has an art deco mood with subtle pastel shades enhancing the ambience. A dozen or so salads are offered, including avocado and bacon, spinach, and chicken and walnut.

Vegetarian dishes are an important part of the menu. You might like the Coconut Grove fresh pasta. A specialty is a seafood orgy for £32 ($52.80) for two. The cost of a dinner is from £15 ($24.75). An American Sunday brunch is also served from noon to 4pm costing from £9 ($14.85). Open daily from noon to 1am. Adjoining the restaurant is the Polo Bar, serving superb cocktails. In summer, tables are placed outside the bar on the pavement overlooking St. Christopher's Place walkway. Tube: Bond Street.

Budget Restaurants

Gaylord Mayfair, 16 Albemarle St., W.1 (tel. 071/629-9802), has established an enviable reputation among local connoisseurs of Indian cuisine. An elegant Asian atmosphere pervades the restaurant. So many regional dishes are available that one hardly knows where to begin. The restaurant features three different types of cooking: Tandoori centers on the tandoor, an oven of Indian clay that is used for cooking foods while retaining the flavor and natural moisture; Mughlai cooking dates from the Moghul period of Indian history in which exotic dishes were prepared with rich combinations of spices; and Kashmiri specialties frequently include combinations of lamb and yogurt. A set meal of tandoori mix or other meat costs £14.50 ($23.95), and a vegetarian fixed-price menu goes for £11.50 ($19). Open daily noon to 3pm and 6 to 11:30pm (to 11pm on Sun.). Tube: Green Park.

The Brasserie on The Park, Park Lane Hotel, Piccadilly, W.1 (tel. 071/499-6321), opened in 1986, may be a part of a deluxe hotel, but it offers good food and excellent wines, all for a moderate price. Its subtle pink and gray decor was specially designed to blend with the Hollywood-style, art deco ballroom of the hotel. Its special lure is its £12.75 ($21.05) table d'hôte, which changes weekly and includes a bottle of wine, service, and VAT, a remarkable value. Typical dishes include grilled anglerfish on a bed of spinach, magret of duck, and mussels marinara. You can also order à la carte, with meals costing around £15 ($24.75). Hours are noon to 3pm and 6 to 11:30pm Mon. to Fri., noon to 11:30pm Sat. and Sun. Tube: Hyde Park Corner.

CHELSEA

This area is comparable to the Left Bank of Paris or the more elegant parts of Greenwich Village. Here diplomats, the wealthy-chic, stars of stage and screen, and successful sculptors and painters long ago replaced struggling artists. In the Mauve Decade, Chelsea became popular with artists and writers. Oscar Wilde found refuge here, as did Henry James, James Whistler, and many others.

King's Road (named after Charles II) is the main street of Chelsea, and activity is lively both day and night. On Saturday morning, Chelsea boutiques blossom with London's flamboyantly attired. What were once stables and garages (mews), built for the townhouses nearby, have been converted and practically rebuilt, so that you see little alleyways with two-story houses, all brightly painted. The best-known and most interesting part of the Chelsea Embankment, an esplanade along the Thames, is the Cheyne Walk (pronounced Chain-y). With its Georgian townhouses, it's a good place for a stroll around dusk.

The district boasts some of the city's finest restaurants. To reach the area take the Circle or District Line to Sloane Square.

Expensive Restaurants

La Tante Claire, 68 Royal Hospital Rd., S.W.3 (tel. 071/352-6045). The quality of its cuisine is so legendary that this "Aunt Claire" has become one of the grande dames of the capital's gaggle of French restaurants. The waiting list for an available table continues to make a meal here one of the more sought-after status symbols of London. A discreet doorbell, set into the Aegean-blue and white of the facade, prompts an employee to usher you politely inside. There, birchwood and chrome trim, bouquets of flowers, and a modernized, vaguely Hellenistic decor complement an array of paintings that might have been inspired by Jean Cocteau. Pierre Koffman, the celebrated chef, creates such specialties as galette de foie gras, turbot served with a cinnamon and lemon sauce, and pistachio-nut soufflé with pistachio ice cream. Every gastronome in London talks about his pigs' trotters stuffed with morels and the exquisite sauces that complement many of his dishes. A set luncheon is good value at £19.50 ($32.30). However, in the evening, expect to pay around £60 ($99) per person for dinner, from 12:30 to 2pm and 7 to 11pm; closed Sat., Sun., and for three weeks in August. You have a better chance of getting a table if you dine very early or very late. Tube: Sloane Square.

Chelsea Room, Hyatt Carlton Tower, 2 Cadogan Place, S.W.1 (tel. 071/235-5411), is a superb restaurant in the Hyatt (recommended in the previous chapter). The combination of haute cuisine, stylish clientele, and elegant decor make it a much-sought-after place for lunch or dinner. The location is one floor above lobby level of the hotel, at the end of a paneled hallway. Artwork, from contemporary Asian watercolors to original 18th-century oils, was chosen with taste and an eye to beauty, and everywhere you look are fresh flowers and plants. The dining room is run by a winning team: maître cuisinier de France, Bernard Gaume, and the long-standing maître d'hôtel, Jean Quero. Original offerings, time-tested classics, and very fresh ingredients are the chef's forte. The menu will change by the time of your visit, but to give you an idea, you are likely to be served baked sea bass in a light sauce with leeks and a garnish of salmon and Russian caviar, roast partridge served on a bed of savoy cabbage, or small filets of venison in a game sauce with port and a medley of multicolored peppercorns with juniper berries. His desserts require a separate menu. Wedgwood plates with the restaurant's cockerel motif adorn each place setting. The average lunch costs from £22 ($36.30); dinners, from £55 ($90.75). Open daily from 12:30 to 2:45pm and 7 to 11:15pm (to 10:45pm on Sun.). Tube: Sloane Square.

Moderately Priced Restaurants

Rib Room, Hyatt Carlton Tower, 2 Cadogan Place, S.W.1 (tel. 071/235-5411). Many of the residents of the well-heeled neighborhood surrounding this five-star hotel drop in just for drinks. On the ground floor of Hyatt's premier European hotel, its glass windows allow light to stream in from Cadogan Place. The place is richly textured with rust-colored marble, deeply grained hardwoods, subtle lighting, and brass trim. The food includes the very finest of Scottish beef along with fresh fish; both preparation and service are excellent. You might ask for one of the seafood trays, including the "Billingsgate," containing two kinds of oysters, clams, shrimp, and crab. Traditional specialties include roast prime rib of Aberdeen Angus, New York sirloin, roast rack of English lamb with rosemary, and a special mixed grill. A la carte dinners cost from £42 ($69.30), with a set lunch going for £22.50 ($37.15). Open 12:30 to 2:45pm and 7 to 11:15pm Mon. to Sat. (to 10:30pm Sun.). Tube: Sloane Square.

The English House, 3 Milner St., S.W.3 (tel. 071/584-3002), is a tiny restaurant in the heart of Chelsea, where dining is like being a guest in an elegant private house. Its decor provides both spectacle and atmosphere. The walls are clad in a printed cotton with a traditional English design of autumn leaves and black currants. The fireplace and collection of beautiful furniture adds to the background. The food is British with such succulent offerings as oak-smoked pigeon breast, Old English steak pie with pickled walnuts, and Welsh rarebit made by a new recipe based on the time-honored ingredients: beer, mustard, cheese, and egg yolks. The chef's daily choices are included in a special luncheon menu at £10.50 ($17.35) for two courses and coffee. A la carte dinners average £26 ($42.90), all prices inclusive of VAT and service. Open daily 12:30 to 2:30pm (to 2pm Sun.), and 7:30 to 11:30pm (to 10:30pm Sun.). Tube: Sloane Square.

The English Garden, 10 Lincoln St., S.W.3 (tel. 071/584-7272), is pretty and lighthearted. The Garden Room on the ground floor is whitewashed brick with panels of large stylish flowers and stark white curtains. With the domed conservatory roofs and banks of plants, the atmosphere lives up to its namesake. The menu is extensive and includes plenty of salads and fish. Interesting dishes are a checkerboard of freshwater fish (an intricately patterned mousse of salmon, carp, and pike), collops of beef with plum brandy, and lemon flummery, a deceptively rich confection of lemon and eggs, adapted from an 18th-century recipe, served with ratafia biscuits. The chef's daily choices are included in a special luncheon menu at £14.50 ($23.95) for three courses and coffee. A la carte dinners average £28 ($46.20), and all prices include VAT and service. A comprehensive wine list is available, with an excellent French house wine always available. Open daily for lunch from 12:30 to 2:30pm (to 2pm Sun.) and for dinner from 7:30 to 10pm. Tube: Sloane Square.

Gavvers, 61-63 Lower Sloane St., S.W.1 (tel. 071/730-5983), was the setting for the original Le Gavroche (now the premier restaurant of London). But Le Gavroche moved to Mayfair in 1981, and the owners, the Roux brothers, turned their former premises into this winning choice for dining on truly French food in an informal atmosphere. It is said that members of the young staff of this charming restaurant are "in training" for Le Gavroche. Chic and sophisticated, with a soft, inviting atmosphere, the restaurant is likely to be crowded, so reservations are important. Considering the quality of the food, this is one of the best value-for-money dining choices among the French restaurants in London. For £27 ($44.55) you get a glass of Kir as you are seated, followed by three courses with half a bottle of the Roux label wine, which is excellent. Menus change daily but are likely to include such main dishes as chicken stuffed with "treasures of the woods," or an eggplant cake with a tomato essence, preceded perhaps by a scallop mousse. Open noon to 2:30pm and 7 to 11pm Mon. to Fri.; dinner only Sat. Tube: Sloane Square.

Les Trois Plats, 4 Sydney St., S.W.3 (tel. 071/352-3433), in the heart of Chelsea, is smart and sophisticated, opened by the Roux brothers in 1988. At their Chelsea home, they have a chic small café at street level, with enough tables for 30 diners, who enjoy the British and French Provençal–type dishes at moderate tabs. Here you can order grilled entrecôte, a tasty omelet, and a fresh salad. Café meals are served from noon to 11pm Mon. to Fri., 6 to 11pm on Sat., averaging £15 ($24.75) for lunch and £19 ($29.70) for dinner.

The basement level of this Georgian townhouse just off Brompton Road has been turned into an air-conditioned dining room, plush in style and trappings, with paneling, tiles, and fabric-covered walls. As you're seated, you're offered Kir, then you can peruse "the surprise of the evening," a £28.50 ($47.05) table d'hôte menu of three courses, including half a bottle of Roux label wine and coffee. Service and VAT are also included. You're given a choice of three appetizers and three main dishes on the menu, which is changed weekly but might include such dishes as fish layered in puff pastry, followed by a warm chocolate soufflé for dessert. Reservations are vital. Open from 7 to 11pm (closed Mon.), seating 50 nearly always satisfied diners. Tube: South Kensington.

VICTORIA
This area, popularly known as "Victoria," is in Westminster, near Belgravia.

Moderately Priced Restaurants
Ken Lo's Memories of China, 67-69 Ebury St., S.W.1 (tel. 071/730-7734), is considered the finest Chinese restaurant in London by many food critics. The restaurant was founded by Ken Lo, whose grandfather was the Chinese ambassador to the Court of St. James (he was knighted by Queen Victoria in 1880). Mr. Lo has written more than 30 cookbooks and once had his own TV cooking show. His "Memories" in Belgravia has been called "a gastronomic bridge between London and China." Against a modern minimalist decor, such dishes are served as Cantonese quick-fried beef in oyster sauce, lobster with handmade noodles, pomegranate prawn balls, and "bang bang chicken" (a Szechuan dish). Set menus range in price from £20 ($33) to £24.50 ($40.45), with à la carte costing from £25 ($41.25) per person. Service is from noon to 2:30pm and 7 to 10:45pm; closed Sun. Reservations are necessary. Tube: Victoria Station.

Eatons Restaurant, 49 Elizabeth St., S.W.1 (tel. 071/730-0074). Finding a reasonably priced restaurant serving good food in expensive Belgravia is a bit of a trick. Long a reliable choice, Eatons is near Victoria Station. Guests enter a narrow room with a clublike ambience, where the service is first rate. The cuisine has been called "enlightened English" with French overtones. Translated, that means you are likely to be served such dishes as grilled Scottish beef with herb butter, chicken suprême, or roast English lamb with rosemary. Meals cost from £21 ($34.65) and up and are served from noon to 2pm and 7 to 11:15pm; closed Sat. and Sun. Tube: Sloane Square or Victoria.

Very Simply Nico, 48A Rochester Row, S.W.1 (tel. 071/630-8061), was created in a moment of whimsy by Nico Ladenis, considered by many as the finest chef in London. His grander and more expensive restaurant is at 35 Great Portland St., Fitzrovia (but more about that later). Run by his sous chef, Very Simply Nico, is in the words of Nico, "cheap and cheerful." Nevertheless, you can expect to spend from £22 ($36.30) per person. The food is often simply prepared and invariably French inspired, with fresh ingredients handled deftly. The menu changes frequently. Open from noon to 2pm and 6 to 11:15pm Mon. to Fri.; dinner only Sat.; closed Sun. Tube: Victoria.

ST. JAMES'S

Already described and previewed as a hotel district (see the previous chapter), elegant, aristocratic St. James's has for decades been known as a center of gastronomy.

Expensive Restaurants

Wiltons, 55 Jermyn St., S.W.1 (tel. 071/629-9955), is one of the leading exponents of cookery called "as British as a nanny." In spite of its move into new quarters, its developers re-created the ambience of the original premises. The thoroughly British menu of this restaurant is known for its fish and game. You might begin with an oyster cocktail and follow with Dover sole, plaice, salmon, or lobster, prepared in any number of ways. In season you can enjoy such delights as roast partridge, roast pheasant, or roast grouse properly hung. The chef might ask you if you want them "blue" or "black," a reference to roasting times. If, after a dessert of, say, a sherry trifle or syllabub, you wish to be truly British, you may order a savory such as Welsh rarebit or soft roes, even anchovies. Dinners cost from £50 ($82.50) and reservations are vital. Lunch hours are 12:30 to 2:15pm Mon. to Fri.; dinner, 6:30 to 10:30pm Mon. to Sat. Wiltons closes the last week in July and two weeks in August. Tube: Green Park or Piccadilly Circus.

Suntory, 71 St. James's St., S.W.1 (tel. 071/409-0201), is the best, most elite, and most expensive Japanese restaurant in London. Owned and operated by the Japanese distillers and brewers, it offers a choice of dining rooms. First-time visitors seem to prefer the Teppan-Yaki dining room downstairs, where iron grills are set in each table and you share the masterful skills of the high-hatted chef, who is frighteningly familiar with a knife. You can also dine in other rooms on fare such as sukiyaki and tempura, perhaps selecting sushi, especially the fresh raw tuna fish delicately sliced. You can also reserve one of the traditional Japanese dining rooms where waitresses in Japanese dress serve you with all the highly refined rituals of a Japanese meal, including the presentation of hot towels. You may prefer a salad of shellfish and seaweed or a superb squid. Appetizers are artful and delicate, and even the tea is superior. Japanese businesspeople on expense accounts like the hushed tone of the place, and the elegant decor, which is said to evoke the ambience of a Japanese manor house. The least expensive way to eat here is to order the £18 ($29.70) set lunch. Dinners begin at £27 ($44.55). Open from noon to 1:30pm and 7 to 9:30pm Mon. to Sat. Tube: Green Park.

LEICESTER SQUARE

Named for the Earl of Leicester, and once the site of the home of Sir Joshua Reynolds, Leicester Square has since become the movie center of London. The 19th-century square is a congested area of stores, theaters, movie houses, even churches. It also has some moderately priced restaurants and pubs (popular with West End actors) in its little offshot lanes and alleyways.

Moderately Priced Restaurants

Chez Solange, 35 Cranbourne St., W.C.2 (tel. 071/836-0542), is crowded and cozy, and has a loyal following. It is located near the Wyndham Theatre, and its kitchen still specializes in traditional bourgeois French cuisine, such as cassoulet Toulousain and blanquette de veau. Try the breast of chicken stuffed with mushrooms and baked in puff pastry, with truffles and a sherry sauce. The best value is its pre-theater menu, costing £13.50 ($22.30) per person, but watch those supplements. The average à la carte meal will cost £25 ($41.25). Open from noon to 12:15am; closed Sun. Piano entertainment is provided in the evening, and it's vital to reserve if you're dining after the theater, as Chez Solange is most popular then. Tube: Leicester Square.

J. Sheekey Ltd., 28-32 St. Martin's Court, W.C.2 (tel. 071/240-2565), is an 1896 restaurant and an art nouveau oyster bar that over the years has been a gathering place for show people (autographed celebrity photos on the wall). Trying to get a table may make you feel like a salmon going upstream, but it's worth it. Sheekey serves a pre- and post-theater meal. For a beginning, I suggest native oysters. Most fish dishes are either grilled or poached. The fish cakes are now classic, and if you want to know how the British used to dine, ask for the "stewed eels and mash." A complete meal will cost £24 ($39.60) to £30 ($49.50), more if you order lobster. Open 12:30 to 3pm and 5:30 to 11:30pm Mon. to Sat. It faces the stage doors of the Albury and Wyndham theaters and is around the corner from the English National Opera. Tube: Leicester Square.

ON THE STRAND

In another major geographic and tourist center, the Strand, you can sample "English fayre" or else have a nostalgic taste of American food.

Moderately Priced Restaurants

Simpson's-in-the-Strand, 100 the Strand, W.C.2 (tel. 071/836-9112), is more of an institution than a restaurant. Next to the Savoy Hotel, it has been doing business since 1828. All this very Victorian place needs is an empire. It has everything else: Adam paneling, crystal, and an army of grandly formal waiters hovering about. On many first-time visitors' lists, there is the notation, "See the changing of the guard, then lunch at Simpson's." It's that popular, so make a reservation. Diners usually agree that Simpson's serves the best roasts (joints) in London. One food critic wrote that "nouvelle cuisine here means anything after Henry VIII." Huge roasts are trolleyed to your table and you can have slabs of beef carved for you and served with traditional Yorkshire pudding. The classic dishes are roast sirloin of beef, roast saddle of mutton with red currant jelly, roast Aylesbury duckling, and steak, kidney, and mushroom pie. Remember to tip the tail-coated carver. For dessert, you might order the treacle roll and custard, or else Stilton with a vintage port. Meals cost £18 ($29.70) to £25 ($41.25). Service is from noon to 2:45pm and 6 to 9:45pm Mon. to Sat. Tube: Covent Garden.

Joe Allen's, 13 Exeter St., W.C.2 (tel. 071/836-0651), is a fashionable American restaurant attracting theater people. It lies north of the Strand in the vicinity of the Savoy Hotel. The restaurant, serving an American and international cuisine, is a sister to other branches in Paris, Los Angeles, Toronto, and New York. The decor is inspired by the New York branch, with theater posters, gingham tablecloths in red-and-white check, and a menu offering such specialties as black-bean soup, barbecued ribs with blackeyed peas, Cajun chicken breast, a bowl of chili, and carrot cake. A simple meal will begin at £16 ($26.40), although you can spend far more, of course, perhaps £20 ($33), depending on how much you order to drink. Open from noon to 1am Mon. to Sat., till midnight Sun. Tube: Covent Garden or Embankment.

COVENT GARDEN

In 1970 London's flower, fruit, and veg market celebrated its 300th anniversary. But "Auld Lang Syne" should have been the theme song that day, as the historic, congested market was transferred in 1974 to a 64-acre site at Nine Elms, in the suburb of Vauxhall.

Covent Garden was originally designed in the 1630s by Inigo Jones, using the Florentine style he imported to England. The Covent Garden Market was established in 1671 by Charles II on the site of the abbot of Westminster's convent garden (hence its name). The king's mistress, Nell Gwynne, once peddled oranges on the market's Drury Lane (and later appeared on the stage of the Drury Lane Theatre).

All that remains of the original buildings is the church of **St. Paul's Covent Garden,** where the actress Dame Ellen Terry is buried. In fact, St. Paul's eastern face looks down on the market where Professor Higgins from Shaw's *Pygmalion* met his "squashed cabbage leaf," Eliza Doolittle. On the wall of St. Paul's Church is a carving commemorating the first performance in England of Punch's Puppet Show, witnessed in 1662 by Samuel Pepys. Nowadays there are often guitarists, flautists, and violinists playing in the area. Nearby is the **Royal Opera House** on Bow Street, home of the Royal Opera and the Royal Ballet. On nearby Russell Street, Samuel Johnson met his admirer, James Boswell, and coffeehouses in the district were once patronized by Addison and Steele.

Covent Garden has now been turned into a district complete with restaurants, hotels, and a convention center. Wine bars and boutiques now fill the old market buildings. An old cabbage warehouse was reopened as the Jubilee Market.

The area also, appropriately, attracts art galleries. In the 18th century it was a beehive of artists, including Lely and Kneller (famous portrait painters; the latter is buried at St. Paul's Church, around the corner). Others who lived here were Thornhill, Richard Wilson, Fuseli, Daniel Mytens, the sculptor Roubiliac, Zoffany, and Flaxman. The American painter Benjamin West also lived here after he got out of jail for trying to study in London during the American Revolution.

An Expensive Restaurant

Boulestin, 1A Henrietta St., W.C.2 (tel. 071/836-7061). This famous old restaurant was founded by Marcel Boulestin, the first Fleet Street restaurant critic, more than half a century ago. It's reached by a side door that leads down into the basement beneath a bank. Kevin Kennedy, who is both the manager and the chef, is one of the new British-bred cuisine experts who has style, flair, and imagination in the kitchen. The chandeliers are still there, and the menu still has many of the old Boulestin dishes, including crab with artichoke, coquilles St-Jacques, and magret de canard. You might also try the tulipe de sorbets maison. But Mr. Kennedy is also free to experiment—much to the pleasure of his guests. He offers a set lunch for £18 ($29.70), but dinner could run higher than £45 ($74.25) per person, including some wine. Open from 12:30 to 2:30pm and 7:30 to 11:15pm; closed for lunch Sat., all day Sun., on bank holidays and the last three weeks of August. Tube: Covent Garden.

Moderately Priced Restaurants

Poons of Covent Garden, 41 King St., W.C.2 (tel. 071/240-1743), is one of the best Chinese restaurants in London. The place is run by Bill and Cecilia Poon. Mr. Poon's great-great-grandfather cooked for the Chinese emperors, and succeeding generations of the family have all interested themselves in traditional Chinese cookery. The decor is reminiscent of *The World of Suzie Wong*. Tables surround an island, see-through kitchen. Two of the most recommendable courses include Poons special crispy duck and Poons special wind-dried meat, including sausage, which is quite different in flavor from smoked. If you're a serious and dedicated gourmet of Cantonese cuisine, Mr. and Mrs. Poon will arrange special menus for parties of 10 or more, featuring dishes not on the à la carte menu, if given at least 24 hours' notice. An à la carte meals averages £20 ($33) including VAT and service. A table d'hôte lunch goes for £11.50 ($19), and set dinners cost £20.25 ($33.40) to £25.25 ($41.65). Open daily from noon to midnight. Tube: Covent Garden.

Rules, 35 Maiden Lane, off the Strand, W.C.2 (tel. 071/836-5314), dates from 1798 when it made its debut as an oyster bar. As such, it lays claim to being the oldest restaurant in London still operating on the original premises. Over its long and legendary history, it has been the steady haunt of actors and actresses, newspaper columnists, barristers, and such literary giants as William Thackeray, John Galsworthy, H.G. Wells, and Graham Greene. In the Gay '90s the prince of Wales (later Edward VII) was its most famous patron, accompanied, as always, by the Jersey Lillie. The prince dined on the second floor, now the Edward VII Room. Pictures of Lillie hang in the alcove where they used to sit. Another alcove honors Charles Dickens, who used to dine and do some of his writing at Rules. The walls are hung with cartoons George Whitelaw did in the '20s and '30s.

Rules has both a summer and a winter menu. You can order such dishes as Rossmore Irish oysters; steak, kidney, and mushroom pudding; roe deer with shallots and baked pear; and wild boar with an onion confit. Depending on the season you might have game fish, such as wild Scottish salmon and wild sea trout, or game birds, perhaps grouse, snipe, partridge, pheasant, and woodcock. You can also order those unusual British savories, such as angels on horseback (oysters wrapped in bacon on toast). Meals begin at £20 ($33) per person, plus the cost of your drink. Open from noon to midnight Mon. to Sat.; closed Sun. Reservations are important. Tube: Covent Garden.

A Budget Restaurant

Porter's English Restaurant, 17 Henrietta St., W.C.2 (tel. 071/836-6466), owned by the earl of Bradford, who is a frequent visitor, has an informal and lively atmosphere in comfortable surroundings. Known as a "pie and pudding" restaurant, it specializes in classic English pies, including steak and kidney, lamb and apricot, chicken and asparagus, and steak, oyster, and clam. The traditional roast beef with Yorkshire pudding is served on weekends. With whipped cream or custard, the "puddings" come hot or cold, including bread-and-butter pudding and a steamed syrup sponge. Count on a bill of around £12 ($19.80). The bar does quite a few exotic cocktails, and you can also order Westons Farmhouse Draught cider by the half pint, even traditional English mead. Open noon to 3pm and 5:30 to 11:30pm Mon. to Fri., noon to 11:30pm Sat., and noon to 10:30pm Sun. Tube: Covent Garden.

BLOOMSBURY

In the academic heart of London, you may wish to stop for a meal after spending time at the British Museum or browsing through the many bookstores.

For a very special meal in truly British surroundings, try **Winstons Restaurant and Wine Bar,** 24 Coptic St., W.C.1 (tel. 071/580-3422), named in honor of Winston Spencer Churchill. Winstons offers good food and wine in a traditional but informal way. The fully air-conditioned restaurant is set in an original 18th-century Bloomsbury house full of Churchill mementos, whose first-floor dining room is decorated in Edwardian club style. Your meal might begin with a Stilton or Brie wrapped in pastry and deep-fried, served with fresh cranberries, followed by Scottish salmon, steak, or filet of beef Wellington. Desserts include the old favorite English apple pie. The average price for a meal, including wine, is £22 ($36.30). Open for lunch from 11am to 3pm Mon. to Fri. and for dinner from 5:30 to 11pm Mon. to Sat.; closed Sun. On the ground floor, the wine bar offers a unique Churchillian meeting place with an extensive wine list. Tube: Tottenham Court Road.

WESTMINSTER

Our dining expedition to Westminster will take us to the Tate Gallery among other places.

Moderately Priced Restaurants

Pomegranates, 94 Grosvenor Rd., S.W.1 (tel. 071/828-6560). The owner of this basement restaurant, Patrick Gwynn-Jones, has traveled far and collected dishes from throughout the world. Asian and Indonesian delicacies vie for a place on the menu with European and North American dishes: Tijuana Caesar salad, escargot and mushroom pie, Welsh salt duck with a white onion sauce, or Creole-Cajun jambalaya. The decor is purely European, with mirrors and well-laid tables. Set lunches cost from £12.50 ($19.80), with a set dinner going for £15.75 ($26). A la carte dinners cost from £30 ($49.50). House wines are reasonable in price, and there is in addition a good wine list. Open for lunch from 12:30 to 2:15pm Mon. to Fri., and for dinner from 7:30 to 11:15pm Mon. to Sat.; closed Sun. It's best reached by taxi.

The Tate Gallery Restaurant, Millbank, S.W.1 (tel. 071/834-6754), in the Tate Gallery, is better than ever. Even if it weren't, it would still be a viable choice as the Whistler Room contains the famous murals by Rex Whistler. The menu undergoes seasonal changes, but you can count on good, wholesome food in the British tradition. Some recipes, I suspect, were in use in Victoria's time, and the lamb chops, for example, are likely to be named after Lord Nelson. The wine list is extensive, and the restaurant is widely praised for its moderate tabs on some excellent vintages. It's essential to reserve a table (many in-the-know locals call ahead and even order their wine so that it can be at the right temperature upon their arrival). Costing from £16 ($26.40), lunches in this highly unusual setting are served from noon to 3pm Mon. to Sat. Tube: Pimlico. Bus: 88.

BELGRAVIA

Belgravia after dark used to be a gastronomic wilderness. Happily, that situation changed long ago.

Moderately Priced Restaurants

Ciboure, 21 Eccleston St., S.W.1 (tel. 071/730-2505). The artfully simple decor mingles elements of hi-tech with clear colors, unusual flowers, and imaginative lighting. Even the menu is abbreviated and enlightened, offering flavorful combinations of food whose ingredients are impeccably fresh. The vegetables, too often neglected in England, are perfectly cooked. It lies on the periphery of Belgravia. A set lunch is offered for £14.50 ($23.95), and à la carte dinners go for around £30 ($49.50). An after-the-theater, fixed-price menu is priced at £14.50 ($23.95). Specialties include a papillote of barbue aux légumes fondants, spring lamb with a duxelle of mushrooms, and filets of red snapper with a rosemary-cream sauce. Open from noon to 2:30pm and 7 to 11:30pm Mon. to Fri. Reservations are necessary. Tube: Victoria Station.

Drones, 1 Pont St., S.W.1. (tel. 071/235-9638), was labeled by one newspaper columnist as "the unofficial club for bright people at least half of whom seem to know each other." The late David Niven and friends launched this two-floor restaurant some years ago, and its reputation for charm and chic has spread. Reservations are imperative, preferably a day in advance. The decor is that of an Edwardian conservatory, with hanging baskets and patchwork quilts on the walls. There is no elaborate menu, no fancy sauces, just simple but good food. At lunch have the Droneburger or salmon fish cakes and parsley sauce. For dinner, the calves' liver with bacon is superb (have it cooked pink if you prefer it). As an appetizer, the mousse de saumon (salmon) fumée au caviar is worthy, as is the salad sasha. Main dish specialties are veal pojarsky, palace duck with orange, poached turbot sauce hollandaise, and a fresh crab salad. Chocolate mousse and soufflé au Grand Marnier vie for your attention in the dessert department. The menu is wisely limited and seldom changes, although plats du jour are featured. A meal, not including your wine selection, costs from £18 ($29.70). If you're lingering at the bar while waiting for a table (a likely possibility), take a look at the collection of baby pictures of famous movie stars. Open daily from 12:30 to 3pm and 7:30pm to midnight. Tube: Sloane Square.

KNIGHTSBRIDGE/BROMPTON ROAD

After splurging at the high-priced shops of Knightsbridge, these choices will make you feel better.

Expensive Restaurants

Waltons of Walton Street, 121 Walton St., S.W.3 (tel. 071/584-0204), is elegant and intimate, serving some of the best food in London. A rendezvous of the posh, it offers the best quality fresh produce from local and European markets served with flair in surroundings of silk walls and floral decorations. Its chefs prepare a refined international cuisine, featuring such British dishes as roast breast of Norfolk duckling or roast filet of Welsh lamb with crab. Specialties include terrine of truffled foie gras, whole roast lobster with coriander and ginger, and orange mousse in a white chocolate sauce. Waltons, long a favorite with the Harrods' shoppers' crowd, has a reputation for being expensive. However, its "Simply Waltons" lunch at £13 ($21.45) offers three courses and is considered one of London's best dining values. For theater-goers and late eaters, a late-night supper, available from 10pm, goes for £19.50 ($32.20). Sunday lunch is only £15 ($24.75) for three courses and offers the traditional Sunday roast. Otherwise, à la carte orders can range from £45 ($74.25) per person. The wine list, which features the best champagne list in London, is wide ranging, from Australia to California. Open daily from 12:30 to 2:30pm (to 2pm Sun.) and 7:30 to 11pm (to 10:30pm Sun.). Tube: Knightsbridge.

Turner's, 87 Walton St., S.W.3 (071/584-6711), is named for Brian J. Turner, one of the most accomplished chefs of London, who gained fame at a number of establishments he didn't own. As one critic aptly put it, his food comes not only fresh from the market that day but "from the heart." He has early roots in Yorkshire, but surely he didn't learn his refined cuisine working in his father's transport "caff" in Leeds. His cooking has been called "cuisine à la Brian Turner," meaning he doesn't seem to imitate anyone but sets his own standards. Try, for example, his marinated raw scallops with shredded gherkins, sea bass with fresh tomato-and-basil dressing, or a roast rack of lamb with a herb crust. He seems to view cooking as a performance, and sometimes he'll make an appearance in the dining room, asking about the appearance and taste of his food. A four-course menu is offered for £22.50 ($37.15), but you will more likely spend from £35 ($57.75). A table d'hôte lunch is a superb bargain at £14.50 ($23.95). Lunch is served from 12:30 to 2:45pm Mon. to Fri. and Sun. Dinner is offered daily from 7:30 to 11pm. Tube: Knightsbridge.

St. Quentin, 243 Brompton Rd., S.W.3 (tel. 071/581-5131), founded in 1980, is probably the most authentic looking French brasserie in London. Modeled on the famous La Coupole in Paris (with its memories of "The Lost Generation"), St. Quentin attracts a lot of the French community in London (a good sign). The decor of mirrors and crystal chandeliers has been aptly described as "glitzy," a word that might refer to the clientele as well. You can spend £18 ($29.70) at lunch ordering à la carte and at least £30 ($49.50) or more at dinner. However, the chef more democratically offers a four-course lunch at £11.90 ($19.65) and a set dinner for £14.90 ($24.60), which are both remarkable in value considering their high quality. Try such dishes as rack of lamb perfectly roasted and served very pink in the French style, roast quail with truffle and a foie gras sauce, or potted duck with a mustard sauce. Look also for the plats du jour. For an hors d'oeuvres, you might ask for a mixed salad with grilled goat's cheese, perhaps raw salmon marinated in lime and olive oil. Lunch is served from noon to 3pm Mon. to Fri.; from noon to 4pm on Sat. and Sun. Dinner hours are 7pm to midnight Mon. to Sat.; from 7 to 11:30pm Sun. Reservations are essential. Tube: Knightsbridge or South Kensington.

Moderately Priced Restaurants

San Lorenzo, 22 Beauchamp Place, S.W.3 (tel. 071/584-1074). This is fashionable, young, modern place that has a two-level dining room capped with a glass canopy that is pulled back on sunny days. Reliability is the hallmark of the cuisine, that and good-quality produce, often seasoned with fresh herbs. Nearly everything you order seems delectable, from the homemade fettuccine with salmon to the carpaccio, and certainly the risotto with fresh asparagus. Meals, costing from £22 ($36.30), are served from 12:30 to 3pm and 7:30 to 11:30pm Mon. to Sat.

Always make a reservation, and even then, it may be hard to get a table when you show up. Tube: Knightsbridge.

Shezan, 16-22 Cheval Place, off Montpelier Street, S.W.7 (tel. 071/589-7918), is a leading Indian/Pakistani restaurant a five-minute walk from Harrods. This brick-and-tile establishment in Kensington turns out zesty dishes from its clay tandoor ovens. Murgh tikki lahori (marinated tandoori chicken) is usually served slightly pink. Another specialty is bhuna gosht (lamb cooked with tomatoes and spices). Tandoori charcoal barbecues and grills are always featured as are kebabs. The tandoori breads are excellent, especially roti, a dark wholewheat bread. Expect to spend from £20 ($33) for a complete dinner. However, a set lunch costs only £10.50 ($17.35). Open from noon to 2:30pm and 7 to 11:30pm; closed Sun. Tube: Knightsbridge.

A Budget Restaurant

Harvey's at the Top, the rooftop restaurant above Harvey Nichols's store, 109 Knightsbridge, S.W.1 (tel. 071/235-5000, ext 2149, for table reservations), is a light, airy place among the rooftops of Knightsbridge. In summer you can eat in the open air, but there is also a large restaurant inside. The day starts with a continental breakfast at 10am, costing £2.60 ($4.30). The staff serves morning coffee, luncheon, then afternoon tea until 5:30pm, although the store remains open until 7pm. The restaurant is closed Sun. There is a selection of appetizers, main courses, desserts, cheese, and coffee, or you can help yourself from the cold buffet. The average cost is around £12 ($19.80). They also do a real old-fashioned cream tea, with homemade scones, strawberry jam, and clotted Devon cream to revive the flagging shopper. Tube: Knightsbridge.

KENSINGTON

If Princess Di didn't ask you to stay to dinner at Kensington Palace, you'll be just as happy with the range of restaurants available here.

An Expensive Restaurant

Launceston Place Restaurant, 1A Launceston Place, W.8 (tel. 071/937-6912), is in an affluent, almost village-like neighborhood. The restaurant is a series of uncluttered Victorian parlors illuminated in the rear by a skylight at lunch. Lying off Gloucester Road, it stands next to Lady Eden's School, known for training what used to be called—and still is around here—debutantes. Since its opening in 1986 Launceston Place has been known for its food. You get a classic British cuisine, including such dishes as steamed mussels in cider with spring onions, liver with red onion marmalade and "bubble and squeak," and a casserole of pheasant with wild mushrooms. A set menu, served from 12:30 to 2:30pm and 7 to 8pm, costs £12.75 ($21.05). A Sunday lunch costs £12.75 ($21.05). A la carte dinners cost from £28 ($46.20). Hours are from 12:30 to 2:30pm and 7 to 11:30pm; closed for lunch Sat. and for dinner Sun. Tube: Gloucester Road.

Moderately Priced Restaurants

Clarke's, 124 Kensington Church St., W.8 (tel. 071/221-9225), is named after English chef Sally Clarke, who is considered one of the finest in London, and hers is one of the hottest restaurants here. She trained in California at Michaels in Santa Monica and the River Café in Venice (California, that is). Sally Clarke is justifiably proud of this excellent Anglo-French restaurant. Everything is bright and modern, with wood floors, discreet lighting, and additional tables in the basement. Here you get a set menu with a very limited choice, but the food is so well prepared "in the new style" that diners rarely object. You might begin with appetizers such as a hot cream soup of roasted red peppers with parmesan and rosemary breadsticks, then follow with charcoal-grilled lamb sausage with chile mayonnaise. Desserts are likely to include a strawberry and vanilla ice cream trifle. A set two-course lunch costs £14 ($23.10); a table d'hôte dinner, £25 ($41.25). Lunch is from 12:30 to 2pm and dinner from 7:30 to 11pm Mon. to Fri.; closed Sat. and Sun. Tube: Notting Hill Gate or High Street Kensington.

Boyd's Glass Garden, 135 Kensington Church St., W.8 (tel. 071/727-5452), is one of the stellar lights along this street of antique shops, which is also becoming known for its outstanding English restaurants. Small, cozy, and intimate, Boyd's is named for its chef and owner, Boyd Gilmour, who has stylishly decorated the place with the look of a Victorian conservatory. The menu he conceives is always one of the most imaginative on the street—light-hearted fare prepared with fresh, carefully chosen ingredients. Try, for example, char-grilled salmon marinated in balsamic vinegar. A set luncheon is offered for £14.75 ($24.35), but an à la carte dinner is likely to cost from £25 ($41.25). Hours are 12:30 to 2:30pm and 7:30 to 10:30pm Mon. to Fri. Tube: Notting Hill Gate.

A Budget Restaurant

Although Middle Eastern establishments of every breed have been flourishing in London for years, the **Persepolis,** 39 Kensington High St., W.8 (tel. 071/937-3555), is one of the few Persian restaurants. And if this is a representative sample of Iranian cooking, let's have more of it.

The Persepolis is sleek and modern, minus even the slightest touch of Asian "kitsch." A small, subtly lit place, it features dark-wood tables and chairs and picture windows viewing the street. The only distinctive Persian features are bas relief friezes on the walls showing winged lions and spade-bearded ancient kings illuminated by colored lanterns. You get two menus: one in flowery Persian script, the other in English.

Appetizers include homemade creamy yogurt with either chopped, mint-flavored cucumber or chopped spinach flavored with fried onions. For a main dish, you might choose chicken with grated walnuts and pomegranate puree served over rice, or perhaps chopped lamb and beans cooked with leeks and parsley. Baklava and halva shekari (a sesame-seed concoction) are among the desserts. Most specials cost £9 ($14.85) to £14 ($23.10), including VAT. Open from noon to 11pm; closed Sunday evening. Tube: High Street Kensington.

SOUTH KENSINGTON

When you're exhausted from touring South Kensington's museums, try a feast at any of the spots listed below.

Expensive Restaurants

Bibendum, Michelin House, 81 Fulham Rd., S.W.3 (tel. 071/581-5817), is a fashionable restaurant in a whimsical art nouveau style. On the ground level is a more affordable Oyster Bar, and upstairs is an elegant restaurant attracting the glitterati, everybody from Fergie to Dustin Hoffman. At the Oyster Bar you can order wine by the glass along with oysters from Colchester in East Anglia or West Cork in Ireland, plus an array of seafood. A meal here just begins at £12 ($19.80) but could easily run two or three times that. No reservations are accepted: you just show up and hope for a seat. Upstairs, reservations (as far in advance as possible) are mandatory if you wish to taste the viands prepared by Simon Hopkinson, one of the most outstanding chefs on the London scene. Hearty regional French cooking is all the rage here, some critics calling the fare *cuisine bourgeoise.* A set lunch goes for £19.50 ($32.20), with à la carte dinners costing from £38 ($62.70) per person. Open 12:30 to 2:30pm Mon. to Fri., 12:30 to 3pm Sat. and Sun., and 7 to 11pm nightly. Tube: South Kensington.

Pelham Restaurant, Pelham Hotel, 15 Cromwell Place, S.W.7 (tel. 071/589-8288), is one of the dining "secrets" of London. In this previously recommended, elegant little hotel, filled with charm and comfort, one of London's finest restaurants is found on the ground floor. The restaurant has a subtle racing theme. (The hotel takes its name from nearby Pelham Place and Pelham Street and also from the Pelham horse "bit.") The restaurant is accented with sophisticated lighting, cove moldings, a blue-and-white decor, and a large mahogany bar. It provides uniformed and impeccable French service at its limited number of well-attended tables, which often are filled with London luminaries.

Fashion aside, it is the food that attracts diners. Seasonal menus glean the "pick of the market," as the English say. Dishes are expertly prepared, and represent a marvelous interpretation of modern French cuisine. Making for very exciting eating are such selections as tartlet of sautéed sweetbreads and foie gras, terrine of escargot, or perhaps a leek quiche with essence of tomatoes. For your main course, your selection might be fricassee of chicken breast with grapes and a basil-flavored sauce (the pure essence, with no starchy thickener) or a blanquette of lamb. Desserts are sumptuous, often presented like portrait miniatures, including a dark chocolate mousse on a mint sauce or a gratin of exotic fruits. A set lunch costs only £12.50 ($20.65), rising to £14.50 ($23.95) on Sunday. A la carte meals cost from £25 ($41.25). Open 12:30 to 2:30pm and 6:30 to 10:30pm; closed Sat. Reservations are essential. Tube: South Kensington.

Moderately Priced Restaurants

Bombay Brasserie, Courtfield Close, S.W.7 (tel. 071/370-4040), is the finest, most popular, and most talked-about Indian restaurant in London. Established in 1982, with a cavernous trio of rooms, it is staffed by one of the capital's most accommodating teams of Indian-born waiters, each of whom is willing to advise you on the spice-laden delicacies that thousands of years of Indian culinary tradition have developed. Lattices cover the windows, dhurrie rugs the floors, and sepia photographs of imperial Britain at its Asian height adorn the walls. You might order a drink amid the wicker chairs of the pink-and-white bar before heading into dinner. The atmosphere there has often been compared to Singapore's Raffles. One of the two dining rooms curves like a half moon beneath a glass-covered ceiling to create an Edwardian conservatory. One look at the menu, and you're launched on "A Passage to India," a grand culinary tour of the subcontinent: every dish from tandoori scallops to chicken tikki (a dish from the Hindukush mountains). Whole meals for vegetarians are also served. One corner of the menu is reserved for the cookery of Goa. A buffet lunch costs £11.50 ($19) and, considering its quality, is one of the best food values in London. It's served daily from 12:30 to 3pm and is especially popular on Sunday, so reservations are important. A la carte meals, costing from £22 ($36.30) each, are served nightly from 7:30pm to midnight. Tube: Gloucester Road.

Hilaire, 68 Old Brompton Rd., S.W.7 (tel. 071/584-8993), is a jovially cramped restaurant, housed in what was originally built as a Victorian storefront. Ceiling fans, apple-green walls, fresh flowers, and twin Corinthian columns form the framework for elegant French specialties. There is no à la carte menu here, since both lunch at £15.50 ($25.60) and dinner at £24.50 ($40.45) are offered at a fixed price. Bryan Webb prepares a mixture of classical French and cuisine moderne that has made this one of the most stylish restaurants in London. Menu items include oysters au gratin, roast end of lamb with eggplant and pesto, and such game dishes as grouse, partridge, pheasant, and venison, followed by a choice of luscious desserts. Reservations are absolutely necessary. Open 12:30 to 2:30pm and 7:30 to 11pm; closed Sat. at lunch and all day Sun. Tube: South Kensington.

Pavilion Restaurant, Regency Hotel, 100 Queen's Gate, S.W.7 (tel. 071/370-4595), is a glamorous but reasonably priced choice if you're staying at one of the many hotels in South Kensington and would like to come here for meals and drinks. Diners look forward to an enjoyable choice of modern dishes based on prime seasonal produce. For example, lamb is roasted to pink perfection with a flavor of rosemary, and prime beef is brought to your table, cut into strips, flavored with spices, and sizzled in butter before a finish with a brandy flambé. Seabass, grilled in butter, is served on a bed of seaweed with lemon on the side. Sole can be grilled or pan-fried to your request, and you can always order tender steaks from the charcoal grill. Vegetarian dishes are available. Care and attention also go into the appetizers, which offer some unusual "New Wave" surprises, including the chef's favorite salad (mango, avocado, and lobster), or perhaps you'd prefer the smoked goose breast with papaya mousse. A la carte meals cost from £15 ($24.75). The restaurant also offers a three-course carvery menu for £14.50 ($23.95). You can make a selection of roast joints of the day carved by a chef (or a selection from the main course of the day). Open daily from 12:30 to 2:30pm and 5:30 to 11:30pm. Tube: Gloucester Road or South Kensington.

Eleven Park Walk, 11 Park Walk, S.W.10 (tel. 071/352-3449), is a high-key, smart little restaurant drawing a bevy of chic Londoners, including many from the art, fashion, and photography worlds. Modern and beautiful, it has big mirrors and three skylights. In addition to being seen, you can also order some good food. The restaurant's owners serve mainly northern Italian dishes, beginning with minestrone primavera, and a number of good pasta dishes, principally ravioli with ricotta and fettuccine with salmon. Fish specialties include calamari fritti and sea bass with herbs. Main meat courses include bollito misto with green sauce. A three-course meal, including half a liter of wine, costs from £25 ($41.25) per person. Hours are 12:30 to 3pm and 7pm to midnight daily. Tube: South Kensington or Gloucester Road. Bus: 14.

Phoenicia, 11 Abingdon Rd., W.8 (tel. 071/937-0120), is highly regarded, both for the quality of its Lebanese cuisine and its moderate prices. The food is outstanding in its presentation and freshness. For the best value, go for lunch when you can enjoy a buffet of more than a dozen *mezze* (appetizers), which are presented in little pottery dishes. Many Lebanese patrons begin their meal with the aperitif *arak,* which some have compared to ouzo. You can select as an appetizer such classic Middle Eastern dishes as hummus or stuffed grape leaves. Fatayer, the "Lebanese pizza," is coated with onion, pine nuts, and spinach. Various charcoal-grilled dishes are also offered. Minced lamb, spicy and well flavored, is the eternal favorite. The buffet lunch costs £8.95 ($14.75). Each day at lunch the chef prepares two or three home-cooked dishes to tempt your tastebuds, including, as for example, chicken in garlic sauce or stuffed lamb with vegetables. At night, prices go up, of course, with meals averaging £15 ($24.75) or more, but you still get good value. Open noon to 11:45pm daily. Tube: South Kensington.

WEST BROMPTON AND FULHAM

South of Earl's Court and Kensington, in the general vicinity of the Earl's Court Exhibition Hall, is an increasingly fashionable area sometimes called West Brompton. Once the best cuisine you could hope to find around here was "bangers and mash." But today some of the most fashionable members of young London gravitate here, drawn by the exclusive, costly shops here. Many are attracted to this area's restaurants and pubs in the evening also. To the southwest of West Brompton is a section known as Fulham, which is beginning to distinguish itself for restaurants.

Moderately Priced Restaurants

Brinkley's, 47 Hollywood Rd., S.W.10 (tel. 071/351-1683), in West Brompton, is rumored to be a favorite of the princess of Wales. It has a small garden terrace in back, although London's gray skies usually encourage diners to head for the lower dining room instead. The cuisine has been described as "modern European." The menu is wisely limited, but dishes are well prepared, based on fresh ingredients. You might select a crispy bacon, Stilton, and watercress salad to begin with, followed by cold wild salmon with new potatoes, or perhaps roast breast of duck with plum marmalade. A loin of lamb flavored with sage and wrapped in parsley is also good, and vegetables, which cost extra, are served *al dente*. Reservations are essential, and meals, costing from £22 ($36.30), are served from 7:30 to 11:30pm; closed Sun. Tube: West Brompton.

La Croisette, 168 Ifield Rd., S.W.10 (tel. 071/373-3694), lies in an unlikely neighborhood in southwest London. Yet because of its French decor you might believe you're in the south of France. You enter a turn-of-the-century aperitif bar, then descend a wrap-around iron staircase into an intimate dining room inspired by Cannes. The £25 ($41.25) set menu offers a wide choice of seafood. For example, your first course might include one of five different kinds of oysters. Most visitors opt for the plateau des fruits de mer, where all the bounty of the sea's shellfish is served from a cork platter dripping with garlands of seaweed and fresh crustaceans. Open 12:30 to 2:30pm and 7 to 11:30pm; closed Mon.; closed Tue. lunch. Tube: Earl's Court.

Blue Elephant, 4-5 Fulham Broadway, S.W.6 (tel. 071/385-6595), is the sister of the famous l'Eléphant Bleu in Brussels. In a converted factory building, London's Blue Elephant has been all the rage since it opened in 1986. It is the leading Thai restaurant of London, where the competition is growing. In an almost magical garden setting of tropical foilage, Londoners and foreign visitors alike are treated to an array of ancient and modern Thai food. You can begin with a "floating market" (shellfish in clear broth flavored with chile paste and lemon grass), and then go on to a splendid and varied selection of main courses, for which many of the ingredients were flown in from Thailand. For a main course, you might try roasted duck curry served in a clay cooking pot. The average price for dinner is from £30 ($49.50), and hours are noon to 2:30pm and 7 to 11:30pm; closed Sat. lunch. It is important to reserve a table. Tube: Fulham Broadway.

Tiger Lee, 251 Old Brompton Rd., S.W.5 (tel. 071/370-2323), is one of the best as well as most expensive Chinese restaurants of London, but the dining is well worth the cost. Many discerning diners make pilgrimages from all parts of the city to enjoy the Hong Kong cuisine of this establishment, which has a tank swimming with fish at the entrance. The decor is in a soothing blue, and service is polite and attentive. The kitchen is known for its "fried yam basket," which might be filled with various kinds of Chinese mushrooms, vegetables, and shredded duck. The yam basket also comes with scallops and roasted pine kernels. Many versions of shark's fin are presented, including one with crab. You might also try crispy shredded eel, called "the popcorn of the sea." The roast squab, which diners prefer "crackling crisp," is sent in from Tiger Lee's own farm outside London. The restaurant is also known for raising warm-water fish in tropical conditions, thereby avoiding the all too common frozen fish. Frankly, you can spend a little or a whole lot here, depending on how exotic your tastes are; meals, however, average £30 ($49.50). Open daily from 6 to 11pm. Tube: Earl's Court.

Tall Orders, 676 Fulham Rd., S.W.6 (tel. 071/371-9673). The decor consists of a central bar, minimalist trappings in dark blue and beige, and an eye-catching mural covering the expanse of one entire wall, showing the crumbs and dregs of a completed and satisfying banquet table. The cuisine is distinctively Mediterranean-inspired, and is deliberately designed to make it difficult to differentiate between an appetizer and a main course. Food is served stacked into dim-sum steamers, piled high (thus "tall orders") on top of one another. Tables are tiny, making a balancing act a bit of a necessary skill. Dishes include roasted free-range chicken with rosemary and aïoli, spinach torte with smoked salmon, pan-fried eggplant with mint-and-cucumber flavored yogurt, rice-shaped pasta with tomato sauce, and parsely prawns roasted in their shells with coriander, ginger, and garlic.

Three set menus are priced at £12.90 ($21.30) each, and each consists of five different courses. These include a varied assortment called "multi-story." The Emerald Tower is all vegetarian, and the Pudding Tower is all desserts. Open daily from noon to 11:45pm. Tube: Parson's Green.

ST. MARYLEBONE

In Mar-li-bone you're in for a treat when you visit these two selections.

Moderately Priced Restaurants

Odin's, 27 Devonshire St., W.1 (tel. 071/935-7296). Amid an eclectic decor of gilt-touched walls, art deco armchairs, Japanese screens, ceiling fans, and evocative paintings and prints, you can enjoy the well-prepared specialties of the chef Christopher German at this restaurant owned by actor Michael Caine and Richard Shepherd. The menu offers an excellent wine list and selections from many culinary traditions. Dishes change every day, depending on the shopping and the availability of fresh ingredients. You might begin your meal with pigeon breast in puff pastry. Main courses include a filet of turbot with prawns from Dublin Bay and a Scottish sirloin with garlic and breadcrumbs. Meals cost from £35 ($57.75). Open 12:30 to 2:30pm and 7 to 11:30pm; closed Sat. for lunch and all day Sun. Tube: Baker Street.

Langan's Bistro, 26 Devonshire St., W.1 (tel. 071/935-4531), has been a busy fixture on the London restaurant scene since the mid-1960s. The actor Michael Caine is one of the owners. Set next to Odin's Restaurant (recommended previously), the bistro is less expensive than the better-known Langan's Brasserie in Mayfair. You'll find it behind a storefront in a residential neighborhood. Inside, almost every square inch of the high ceiling is covered with fanciful clusters of Japanese parasols. Rococo mirrors accent the black walls, setting off surrealistic paintings and old photos. The French-inspired menu changes frequently, and only the best and freshest seasonal ingredients are used in the specialties. These include roast guinea fowl, veal with Pommery mustard and tarragon, and pork with a honey-flavored ginger sauce. The dessert extravaganza is known as "Langan's chocolate pudding." Full meals cost from £25 ($41.25). Open 12:30 to 2:30pm and 7 to 11:30pm; closed Sat. for lunch and all day Sun. Tube: Regent's Park.

BAYSWATER

Along Queensway in Bayswater, the children of a once far-flung empire have come back to the mother country to open restaurants, or so it would seem. As you wander up and down this street, you'll think you are in Hong Kong perhaps. The street is filled with restaurants of many nationalities, not all offering a reliable cuisine. However, there are exceptions.

Budget Restaurants

Spice Merchant, Coburg Hotel, 129 Bayswater Rd., W.2 (tel. 071/823-7020), is one of London's finest Indian restaurants, having made its debut in 1990. It's part of this previously recommended hotel and is decorated with artifacts of India. What makes this restaurant different from the hundreds of Indian restaurants that pepper London is its emphasis on very fresh ingredients. Dishes are individually prepared, and each thing is cooked in its own juice. The chef barbecues to perfection using subtle spices. Many dishes seem to have originated in East Africa; these are known for robust flavors and spices. The buffet lunch is one of London's noonday bargains at £13 ($21.45). In the evening, ordering à la carte, you can spend from £20 ($33) or more. Open daily from noon to 2:30pm and 6:30pm to midnight. Tube: Queensway.

Mandarin Kitchen, 14 Queensway, W.2 (tel. 071/727-9012), serves some of the best Chinese-style fish dishes in London. Sometimes rather elegantly dressed members of the Mayfair crowd journey out to Queensway to sample the kettle of fish simmering in this mandarin's kitchen. You can also feast on seabass, Dover sole, monkfish, Chinese pomfret, and yellow croaker, prepared, it would seem, in an infinite number of ways. Barbecued Peking duck is another specialty. It'll take a good half hour to make it through the menu, as you carefully study items such as mussels in a black bean and chile sauce, trying to make up your mind for that final order. The restaurant is rather large, and reservations are rarely needed. The average meal costs £15 ($24.75). Open daily noon to 11:30pm. Tube: Queensway.

NOTTING HILL GATE

For a gourmet treat in an increasingly fashionable area, this neighborhood offers some excellent choices.

An Expensive Restaurant

Leiths, 92 Kensington Park Rd., W.11 (tel. 071/229-4481). Prudence Leith long ago brought her culinary talents from South Africa to the unlikely Notting Hill Gate district of London, a few blocks from the Portobello Road Market and near the Portobello Hotel. Prue studied at the Cordon Bleu in Paris and also at the Cordon Bleu in London. At Leiths, you dine with French silver, Darlington crystal, and beautiful English crockery, along with luxurious furnishings. Special features are the first-course, dessert, and cheese trolleys, the latter bearing a variety of both traditional and new British cheeses. There are four seasonal menus, from which guests are free to select two courses if they wish. One menu is vegetarian. Prices are based on the number of courses: two go for £26 ($42.90), three for £32.50 ($53.65), and four for £36 ($59.40), including coffee, petits fours, service, and VAT. One recent autumn menu included seared brill filet with beetroot-butter sauce, smoked breast of chicken with a chive-and-cream sauce, and saddle of venison. Some of the produce is grown on a farm in the Cotswolds. To end your meal, you might select a ginger syllabub from the dessert trolley. An ambitious wine list offers vintages from all over the world. Open daily from 7:30pm to midnight. Tube: Notting Hill Gate.

A Moderately Priced Restaurant

L'Artiste Assoiffe, 122 Kensington Park Rd., W.11 (tel. 071/727-4714), is housed in a handsome Georgian building in Kensington Park, near Portobello Road. Charles Dickens used to stop here to pick up his prescriptions when this was a drugstore, but there's no hint of that use of the location in the charming restaurant of today. Paintings and murals by Liz Reber (whose art also decorates the menus), statues, carousel horses, old washing equipment, and parrots create a pleasing ambience in which diners can relax and enjoy their meals and drinks. As the name of the place leads you to expect, the cuisine is mainly French, but with interesting additions. The menu is geared to what was the freshest at the market on any given day. You might begin with an assortment of plump snails prepared with garlic butter and follow with duck in a cream and green pepper sauce. If you're not tempted by one of the luscious desserts, you might choose from the cheeses brought from France on a weekly basis. Dinner costs £25 ($41.25) and up. Hours are 7:30 to 11pm Mon. to Fri., noon to 3pm Sat.; closed Sun. Tube: Notting Hill Gate.

HOLLAND PARK

This park grew up around Holland House, a Jacobean building from 1606. Once fashionable, it's becoming so again.

An Expensive Restaurant

Kingfisher, Halcyon Hotel, 81 Holland Park, W.11 (tel. 071/727-7288), in this previously recommended hotel, is an exciting dining possibility and worth the ten-minute taxi ride from the heart of the West End. To reach the dining room, you pass a medley of trompe-l'oeil murals with color and whimsy. You might enjoy an apéritif in the pink-tinted bar before heading for a meal in the tasteful, uncluttered restaurant. Lattices and views of a garden create an image of springtime even in winter.

The menu is sophisticated and highly individual. One food critic wrote that the menu "reads like a United Nations of cuisine." Based on the inspiration of the chef and the shopping, only the freshest ingredients are used. You might begin with a crab, coriander, and ricotta ravioli before going on to roast breast of guinea fowl with noodles, prunes, and leek, or salmon baked in pastry with pesto. Desserts are worth saving room for, as reflected by a ginger parfait with mango coulis. A three-course set luncheon costs £17 ($28.05), dinner is from £29 ($47.85), and à la carte, £35 ($57.75). Hours are daily from 12:30 to 2:30pm and 7:30 to 11:30pm. Reservations are necessary. Tube: Holland Park.

SOHO

This section of narrow lanes and crooked streets, once the main foreign quarter of London, has some of the city's best international restaurants. European and Asian life echoes through Soho. One writer wrote of Gerrard Street: "The smell of pickled ginger and roast duckling seeps from restaurant doors. The men scurry into stores from afternoon games of fan-tan and mah-jongg. A lilting twang of Chinese rock'n'roll envelops the downtown street." Gerrard Street has succeeded in becoming London's Chinatown. Strip shows and honky-tonk clubs have given way to Chinese restaurants and bookstores keeping you informed of the latest developments in Hong Kong.

Soho starts at Piccadilly Circus, spreading out like a peacock and ending at Oxford Street. From Piccadilly Circus, walk northeast and you'll come to Soho, to the left of the theater center on Shaftesbury Avenue. This jumbled section can also be approached from the Tottenham Court Road tube station. Walk south along Charing Cross Road and Soho will be to your right.

Expensive Restaurants

The Lindsay House, 21 Romilly St., W.1 (tel. 071/439-0450). This upstairs restaurant bases many of its dishes on 18th-century English recipes. Other platters have been called Tudor, still others cuisine moderne. Everyone from royalty to film stars, from diplomats to ordinary people shows up here. The owners, Roger Wren and Malcolm Livingston, who already run several other fashionable restaurants, selected a 19th-century house in the heart of Soho and converted it tastefully and dramatically, with rich colors and fabrics—a medley of greens and reds. For what is called "first dishes," you might begin with Hannah Glasse's stewed "scollops" with oranges, based on an old recipe. To follow, you might try roast rack of Southdown lamb or a traditional fish pie with cubes of halibut, salmon, scallops, and quail eggs in a creamy sauce. Summer puddings are often featured—packed with such traditional fruits as strawberries, red currants, and raspberries, all served with a raspberry "cullis" with Devonshire clotted cream. A set lunch costs £13.75 ($22.70), and dinner may go as high as £35 ($57.75) per person. Open 12:30 to 2:30pm and 6pm to midnight Mon. to Sat.; 12:30 to 2pm and 7 to 10pm Sun. Tube: Leicester Square or Tottenham Court Road.

Burts, 42 Dean St., W.1 (tel. 071/439-0972), is the most fashionable vegetarian restaurant in London, lying deep in the heart of Soho. It also serves fresh fish. It's named for Burt Shevelove, the New Jersey–born writer best known for the 1962 hit musical, *A Funny Thing Happened on the Way to the Forum*. This is hardly your typical "veg caff," as it offers such classy dishes as toasted onion brioche with baked goat's cheese and walnut oil, artichoke tortellini with a pistou sauce, and wild rice risotto. Assorted fish come with a hot potato salad and a mustard vinaigrette, or perhaps you'd prefer the seafood cassoulet sometimes featured as a daily special. Luncheon menus begin at £16.70 ($27.55); dinner menus from £17.80 ($29.40). Otherwise, count on spending from £30 ($49.50) à la carte. This restaurant doesn't cater to the old-fashioned concept of what was considered a "vegetarian." Rather, it attracts hip, often media-employed people who like to eat healthy food, take care of their bodies, and dine out in sophisticated trappings that are elegant but not overpowering. Of course, absolute freshness of its high quality ingredients is the rule in the kitchen. The wine list is wisely chosen, with an emphasis on French vintages. Service is from 12:15 to 2:30pm and 5:30 to 11:30pm; on Sat. dinner only is served; closed Sun. Tube: Tottenham Court Road.

Moderately Priced and Budget Restaurants

Gay Hussar, 2 Greek St., W.1 (tel. 071/437-0973), is called the "last of the great Soho restaurants." The cuisine of Central Europe is served in this intimate, cozy rendezvous where diners can begin with the chilled wild-cherry soup or perhaps a hot, spicy red-fish soup in the style of Szeged in Hungary's southern Great Plain. Main courses may include stuffed cabbage or roast saddle of carp. A set lunch costs £12 ($19.80), and dinner goes for £18 ($29.70). Open 12:30 to 2:30pm and 5:30 to 11pm; closed Sun. Tube: Tottenham Court Road.

Au Jardin des Gourmets, 5 Greek St., W.1 (tel. 071/437-1816), is an "Ile de France" off Soho Square where devotees of Gallic cuisine gather to enjoy traditional

specialties. Today, Soho Square and Greek Street have been largely rebuilt and are back in fashion again. The Jardin itself has climbed to a level never previously attained, with new kitchens and wine cellars, toilets that can be reached without climbing two floors, and—most important of all—an air-conditioned restaurant that separates smokers and nonsmokers. There is an à la carte menu with a comprehensive selection. Among several specialties are feuillete of braised lamb's tongue, sauté of fresh foie gras Aigre-Doux, noisettes of lamb with sauce Riches, and breast of pigeon roasted with cloves of garlic. A masterful selection of vintage bordeaux and burgundies are expertly served. The average price of a meal, including half a bottle of house wine, is £25 ($41.25) per person. There is a set lunch or dinner offered for just £16.50 ($27.25). Open 12:30 to 2:15pm and 6:30 to 11:30pm; closed Sat. lunch and all day Sun. Tube: Tottenham Court Road.

Jamdani, 34 Charlotte St., W.1 (tel. 071/636-1178), brings a fresh, healthy approach to Indian cuisine. Operated by the same people who run Red Fort (one of the finest Indian restaurants in London), Jamdani was inspired by the fine muslin of that name, woven in Bangladesh and described as "woven air" because of its quality and delicacy. That delicacy is also apparent in the food. Featuring the cookery of rural India, most specifically that of Bangladesh, among the dishes offered here are tandoori specialties from the north, fisk tikka, even cashew rolls in a date sauce. Lentils (called *dal*) are used in many dishes, and vegetables are fresh and expertly handled. In effect, this is a lighter, more enjoyable cuisine than that served in your typical street corner Indian restaurant that hasn't varied any recipes in 30 years. The setting for such delectable dishes as eggplant flavored with yogurt and spices or fish amritsari with coriander and mint is modern and stylized, with unpainted wood and rough plaster in abundance. The restaurant is air conditioned, with meals averaging £25 ($41.25) à la carte. However, a set lunch and dinner are offered for £12 ($19.80). Open daily noon to 3pm and 6 to 11:30pm (to 11pm on Sun.). Call for a reservation. Tube: Goodge Street.

Chuen Cheng Ku, 17 Wardour St., W.1 (tel. 071/437-1398), is one of the best eateries in Soho's "New China." A large restaurant seating 400 on several floors, Chuen Cheng Ku is noted for its Cantonese food and is said to have the longest and most interesting menu in London. Specialties are paper-wrapped prawns, steamed spareribs in black-bean sauce, and shredded pork with cashew nuts, all served in generous portions. Dim sum is served from 11am to 6pm. The Singapore noodles, reflecting one of the Chinese-Malaysian inspirations, are thin rice noodles, sometimes mixed with curry and pork or else shrimp with red and green peppers. A set lunch or dinner costs from £14 ($23.10) per person. The average à la carte meal costs from £12 ($19.80) per person. Open daily from 11am to 11:45pm. Tube: Leicester Square or Piccadilly Circus.

FITZROVIA

North of Soho is a section of London called Fitzrovia, where some of the most discerning diners in the world head for what is considered by many to be the best restaurant in London.

An Expensive Restaurant

Chez Nico, 35 Great Portland St., W.1 (tel. 071/436-8846), is the domain of Nico Ladenis, who is firmly entrenched as one of the great chefs of Britain. A former oil company executive, a trained economist, and a self-taught cook, he was reared by Greek and French parents in East Africa. His restaurant is very expensive, very chic, and very Nico, with a decor of pastels and art deco touches. It is stylish, yet understated. Meals are profoundly satisfying and often memorable in the very best gastronomic tradition of cuisine moderne. The menu changes frequently, according to the imagination of Mr. Ladenis, so some patrons leave the menu choice entirely up to him. For example, you might begin with hot foie gras with beans, truffle oil, and caramelized oranges, followed by a pair of tournedos Rossini. Reservations are absolutely vital because he could easily fill this restaurant three times or more every night. Lunch, at £25 ($41.25), has been called "surely London's greatest lunchtime bargain," considering that this is a two-star restaurant. At dinner there is a two-course meal for £34 ($56.10). However, the average tab for a not-average meal will be around £60 ($99) per person. Hours are 12:30 to 2pm and 7:30 to 11pm Mon. to Fri. only. Tube: Oxford Circus.

CHELSEA HARBOUR

Compass Rose, Hotel Conrad, Chelsea Harbour, S.W.10 (tel. 071/823-3000), is the premier restaurant at one of London's newest developments, the plush Chelsea Harbour created on the water in a marina complex of expensive apartments, restaurants, and boutiques. An international cuisine is prepared with fresh English produce and top quality ingredients. The saucing is subtle and distinct, and each dish arrives at your table perfectly cooked. Your meal might begin with a memorable salad of artichoke bottoms and delicate green beans in a walnut oil–flavored vinaigrette, or perhaps a country terrine of hare and hazelnuts. Bouillabaisse Provençale appears on the menu, as does Dover sole and filet of turbot soufflé with a chive butter sauce. Among meat dishes, try medallions of veal with a lavender honey-vinegar sauce, or Norfolk squab braised with forest mushrooms. A choice of sumptuous desserts comes on a trolley. Meals cost from £20 ($33). Open daily from noon to 2:30pm and 6:30 to 10:30pm. Chelsea Harbour Hoppa buses run to Chelsea Harbour from Earl's Court and Kensington High Street (bus C3) Mon. to Sat., or take a riverbus from Charing Cross Mon. to Fri.

Ken Lo's Memories of China, Harbour Yard, Chelsea Harbour, S.W.10 (tel. 071/352-4953), is the far-flung branch of Ken Lo's (described previously). Ken Lo did much to launch the Chinese cuisine in Britain, which is now an invasion of major dimensions; Mr. Lo chose a riverside site for his second restaurant, perhaps recalling his childhood in Foochow on the banks of the Ming River. The restaurant is decorated in blue and gold, the colors of the Ming Dynasty. The cuisine wanders from region to region of China, with an emphasis on fish and seafood. Specialties include steamed sea bass, Mongolian barbecued lamb, and chicken in a hot black-bean sauce. Set menus cost from £22.50 ($37.15) to £26 ($42.90) with à la carte orders averaging £25 ($41.25) and up. Open noon to 2:15pm and 7 to 10:45pm Mon. to Sat.; Sun. brunch is noon to 2:30pm. Ken Lo's also operates a dim sum bar noon to 2:30pm Mon. to Fri. when a selection of dim sum costs £3.50 ($5.80). To reach the restaurant, board a Chelsea Harbour Hoppa bus at Earl's Court or Kensington High Street (C3), Mon. to Sat., or take a riverbus from Charing Cross Mon. to Fri.

Deals Restaurant and Diner, Harbour Yard, Chelsea Harbour, S.W.10 (tel. 071/376-3232). Once the Queen Mother arrived on a barge here to order a "Deals burger," the success of this place was assured. Deals is co-owned by Princess Margaret's son, Viscount Linley, and his friend, Lord Litchfield. It's like an early 1900s Singapore trading post (fantasy version only) of colonial days, with ceiling fans and bentwood banquettes. Some critics have characterized the food as American-diner style, yet there are Asian variations such as teriyaki burgers. You might try prawn curry, spareribs, or even a vegetarian dish, perhaps finishing with New England apple pie. An average meal costs from £12 ($19.80). Open 11am to 11pm Mon. to Sat., noon to 10pm Sun. To reach the restaurant, board a Chelsea Harbour Hoppa bus at Earl's Court or Kensington High Street (C3), Mon. to Sat., or take a riverbus from Charing Cross Mon. to Fri.

2. Other Locales

THE CITY

When the English talk about The City, they don't mean London. The City is the British version of Wall Street. Not only is it an important square mile of finance and business, but it contains many sights. Here are the buildings known the world over: the **Bank of England** on Threadneedle Street (entrance hall open to the public); the **Stock Exchange,** where you can watch transactions from a special gallery; **Lloyd's of London,** on Leadenhall, one of the world's great insurance centers. Lloyd's will insure anything from a stamp collection to a giraffe's neck.

Typical English food—shepherd's pie, mixed grills, roast beef—is dished up in dozens of the old pubs of The City. Here you can eat expensively or inexpensively along with the English.

Expensive Restaurants
Le Poulbot, 45 Cheapside, E.C.2 (tel. 071/236-4379), is a French restaurant par excellence. Founded by the Roux brothers of Le Gavroche fame, it was launched in 1969 and ever since has been an attraction for the movers and shakers of the high-profile business world of The City. Only lunch is served, a table d'hôte costing £28.50 ($47.05), whereas à la carte lunches range from £30 ($49.50) for one person. Reservations are vital. The menu is seasonally adjusted, depending on what is best at the market. While ensconced on a high-backed banquette, you can peruse a menu of sheer delight, selecting your favorites among light, new-style continental dishes or longtime favorites. Perhaps you'll be offered such dishes as a turbot fricassee or lamb cooked in its own juice and flavored with mint. Open noon to 3pm Mon. to Fri.

Upstairs, Le Poulbot offers what the French call a *casse-croûte* bar, which enjoys great renown among City workers less well heeled than those who patronize the expensive basement restaurant. Here you can order from a limited menu, or else enjoy French snacks, with light meals costing from £10 ($16.50). You can also drink without eating if that is your choice. The pub or brasserie upstairs is open from 7:30am to 3pm Mon. to Fri., and might be an ideal choice for breakfast if you're beginning your sightseeing tour of The City early. Tube: South St. Paul's.

Le Gamin, 32 Old Bailey, E.C.4 (tel. 071/236-7931), is another City dining room established by the Roux brothers to feed hungry businesspeople at lunch during the work week. Meaning "urchin" in French, Le Gamin opened in 1971 and has been full ever since. It has a pronounced French decor, with French food and impeccable French service even when it's rushed, which seems to be all of the time. Sometimes clients return two or three times in one week, so advance reservations as far in advance as possible are highly recommended. For a set price of £25.50 ($42.10), you are given a Kir upon being seated, presented with three delectable courses, including half a bottle of wine, and finished by a coffee. You might, for example, begin with gazpacho and gravad lax, then follow with boeuf à la bourguignonne. But the menu changes daily. The house wines are excellent. Open noon to 2:30pm Mon. to Fri. On the same premises, and for those watching their wallets, Le Gamin operates a popular snack bar, serving breakfasts, take-away lunches, sandwiches, and Roux pastries from 7am to 2:30pm Mon. to Fri. Tube: St. Paul's or Blackfriars.

Budget Restaurants
Barbican Centre, Silk Street, E.C.2 (tel. 071/638-4141), offers a choice of eating and drinking establishments in several price ranges. On Level 5, the Waterside Cafeteria is self-service, offering a range of hot meals, salads, sandwiches, pastries, tea, and coffee, along with wine and beer. Hot meals include roast chicken with bacon, or you may prefer to make a selection from the salad bar, with meals costing from £6.50 ($10.75). Open daily from 11am to 8pm. It offers views over the lake, and in summer, there are seats on the terrace. On Level 7, the Cut Above is a first-class restaurant that features English and continental dishes. Meals cost from £15 ($24.75), plus VAT and service. Open daily from noon to 3pm and 6pm until the last orders are taken half an hour after the last performance at the Barbican Hall Theatre. On Level 6, you might also want to patronize Wine on Six, which has an extensive list of bottled and draft wines and beers, accompanied by a variety of cold meats, fish, and salads, along with specialty breads and cheese. Light meals with drinks cost from £6.50 ($10.75). Open daily from noon to 2:30pm and from 5:30

to 8pm. There are bars, along with coffee and snack bars, in the foyers of the Barbican Hall Theatre and Cinema One. Tube: Moorgate.

George & Vulture, 3 Castle Court, Cornhill, E.C.3 (tel. 071/626-9710), an olde Pickwickian hostelrie, is for the Dickens enthusiast. This chophouse, founded in 1660, claims that it is "probably" the world's oldest tavern, and refers to an inn on this spot in 1175. The George & Vulture no longer puts up overnight guests (although Dickens used to bed down here), but its three floors are still used for serving English meals. The Pickwick Club now meets here, by the way. Reservations are accepted only if you agree to arrive by 12:30pm. Besides the daily specials, the George & Vulture features a mixed grill, a "loin chop, chump chop," and fried filets of Dover sole with tartar sauce. Potatoes and buttered cabbage are the standard vegetables. The apple tart is always reliable. The average meal will cost from £12 ($19.80) for three courses. The system is to arrive and give your name, then retire to the Jamaica pub opposite for a drink. You are then "fetched" when your table is ready. After lunch, explore the intricate nearby passageways, and discover the maze of shops, wine houses, pubs, and old buildings surrounding the tavern. Open noon to 2:30pm Mon. to Fri. Tube: Bank.

FLEET STREET

The gateway to The City, Fleet Street was known as the "street of ink." In the 19th century, it was the center of London's newspaper and publishing world. Nowadays, the big newspapers are printed elsewhere, but Fleet Street still retains some of its old charm.

A Budget Restaurant

Cheshire Cheese, Wine Office Court, 145 Fleet St., E.C.4 (tel. 071/353-6170), is one of the greatest of the old city chophouses, running since 1667. It claims to be the place where Samuel Johnson dined with his friends and entertained them with his acerbic wit. This is quite possible, as the good doctor's house was practically within shouting distance of the Cheese. The two specialties of the house are "ye famous pudding"—(steak, kidney, mushroom, and game)—and Scottish roast beef, with Yorkshire pudding and horseradish sauce. The hot plate holds a giant joint of the roast beef. For dessert, try "ye famous pancake." A meal costs from £12 ($19.80). Open 11:30am to 11pm; closed Sun. night. Tube: St. Paul's.

BATTERSEA

Cavaliers, 129 Queenstown Rd., S.W.8 (071/720-6960), has a reputation based on its superb food. In increasingly fashionable Battersea, it was founded by the famous chef Nico Landenis and served as his home base before he moved. The restaurant was then purchased by David and Susan Cavalier, who moved from their much-praised Pebbles Restaurant in Aylesbury.

In an L-shaped dining room ringed with natural pine and pastel shades of *café au lait* and pink, you can enjoy such specialties as a pot roast of baby guinea fowl and breast of Bombay duck in red wine sauce, with an orange salad. A three-course dinner is offered for £31.50 ($52), and a special lunch menu goes for £16.50 ($27.25). Open 12:15 to 2pm and 7:15 to 10:30pm Tues. to Sat. Because of the location, this establishment is best reached by taxi.

HAMPSTEAD

In the footsteps of Keats, you can head for a dining adventure in the north of London. Try **Le Cellier du Midi,** 28 Church Row, N.W.3 (tel. 071/435-9998), something of a paradox—a basement French bistro that's crisp, light, and comfortable—off Hampstead Heath Street. It's decorated with Victorian knick-knacks and its rough wooden tables are covered with red cloths. The kitchen offers classic French cooking with the day's specialties shown on the blackboard. For £17.75 ($29.30), you're given a four-course meal, which may also seem paradoxical—a fixed-price repast ordered à la carte. You get your choice of appetizer, perhaps choosing escargots de Bourgogne. Main courses include beef filet, lamb, duck, veal, chicken, or fish, served with vegetables or salad, and then comes a selection of desserts. Coffee and wine are extra, of course, but VAT and the cover charge are included in the price. Open daily from 7 to 11:30pm. It is wise to reserve, particularly on Sat. and Sun. Tube: Hampstead.

Keats, 3-4 Downshire Hill, Hampstead, N.W.3 (tel. 071/435-1499), is called "a small serious restaurant for committed gourmets." Not more than a stone's throw from Keats's house in Hampstead, it is the finest dining choice you can uncover in that residential suburb. The owners take pride that only the finest ingredients go into their dishes; some items are actually flown in. The large and varied menu lists a classic French cuisine strong on meat and fish. The wine cellar is perhaps the finest in Hampstead, especially the bordeaux selection. Expect to pay about £28 ($46.20) for dinner. A set lunch is £16 ($26.40). Open noon to 2:30pm and 7 to 10pm Mon. to Fri., 7 to 10pm Sat.; closed Sun. Reservations are a must. Tube: Belsize Park.

ISLINGTON

This is the area for the antique hunter, so you may find yourself there with time to enjoy a meal at **Frederick's Restaurant,** Camden Passage, N.1 (tel. 071/359-2888). Originally, in 1789, the building was a pub called the Gun. Then in 1834 it was rebuilt and renamed "The Duke of Sussex" in honor of George III's sixth son, Prince Augustus Frederick. So when the restaurant opened in 1970, what more natural than to name it after the prince? You can eat in the Garden Room, designed like a Victorian conservatory with a domed ceiling, as well as at the tables inside. Glass doors lead to a terrace and the large garden. The French cuisine changes every fortnight. The menu has six main-dish selections—fish, poultry, meat, specialties (noisettes d'agneau au strudel, for instance), vegetarian, game in season—and sometimes a cuisine minceur selection. Desserts are all homemade, and there is a good cheese board. A three-course meal with coffee will cost from £26 ($42.90), including VAT. Wine is extra. There is a long, excellent wine list and a palatable house wine. If you are in the area on Sat., they do a set luncheon for £9.95 ($16.40), offering a choice of three appetizers, two main dishes with vegetables, and a trio of desserts. VAT and service are included. Hours are noon to 2:30pm and 7 to 11:30pm Mon. to Sat. Tube: Angel.

WATERLOO

RSJ, 13A Coin St., S.E.1 (tel. 071/928-4554). Set on the traditionally unglamorous south bank of the Thames, this restaurant has clients so loyal that they arrive from many different parts of London to reach it. Others dine here after seeing a program at the South Bank Cultural Center. Named after a type of construction material (rolled structural joists), used during its restoration, the restaurant occupies the 250-year-old premises of what was originally built as a stable for the duke of Cornwall. You'll enter from a nondescript street, perhaps order a drink from the stand-up aperitif bar, and be led upstairs to a table in a room that used to be the hayloft for the horses downstairs. Nigel Wilkenson is the sophisticated owner of this place, personally selecting the vast array of excellent French (especially Loire Valley) wines which fills his impressive and reasonably priced wine list.

Food is prepared in the tradition of modern British cuisine, and includes such specialties as a bavarois of salmon, a brace of quails stuffed with smoked ham and sweetbreads, filet of Scottish beef with a fricassee of pink mushrooms, tortellini of shellfish, and French duck marinated in sherry vinegar. Fixed price meals cost £12.75 ($21.05) for two courses and £14.25 ($23.50) for three courses. A la carte orders go for £28 ($46.20) per person. Open noon to 2pm and 6 to 11pm Mon. to Fri., 6 to 11pm Sat.; closed Sun. Reservations are necessary. Tube: Waterloo.

THE EAST END

Bloom's, 90 Whitechapel High St., E.1 (tel. 071/247-6001), London's best-known kosher restaurant, is worth the cross-over to the wrong side of the tracks. Although the place tends to get overcrowded, the manager sees to it you get quick service, and Bloom's continues to tempt with kosher delights. Sunday lunch, however, is extremely busy, so try to schedule your visit at some other time. Feast on a chicken blintz, followed by cabbage borscht. The main dishes are reasonably priced, with specialties such as sauerbraten and salt beef (corned). For dessert, you can order apple strudel. An average meal will cost £15 ($24.75). Open 11am to 10pm Sun. to Thurs., 11am to 3pm Fri. (last orders at 2:30pm); closed Sat. and on all Jewish holidays. Tube: Aldgate East.

---

3. Specialty Dining

For a memorable experience, take a taxi, tube, or bus to Aldgate East and spend a hectic hour or so at **Petticoat Lane.** That's the street market where, on Sunday, even if you don't want to buy the goods, you can see the full wit and expertise of the cockney street vendors. Look for the one who sells tea services, buy a toffee apple or a hot dog, and then go around the corner to **Club Row,** a street market for animals and birds.

A short walk will bring you down to the Tower of London and, right beside it, just below Tower Bridge, **St. Katharine's Dock.** After you've had a look around, you may be interested in dining or just having a snack to tide you over. Some places you'll see are overpriced and have become careless about the quality of their cuisine, while others still provide good food and good value.

Tower Thistle Hotel, St. Katharine's Way, E.1 (tel. 071/481-2575). At the Carvery Restaurant in this modern hotel built overlooking the Thames, you can enjoy all you want of some of the most tempting roasts in the Commonwealth. For example, you can select (rare, medium, or well done) from a standing rib of prime beef with Yorkshire pudding, horseradish sauce, and the juice; or from tender roast pork with crackling accompanied by a spiced bread dressing and apple sauce; or perhaps the roast spring Southdown lamb with mint sauce. Then you help yourself to the vegetables. Perhaps you'll prefer a selection of cold meats and salads from the buffet table. No one counts—even if you go back for seconds or thirds. Before going to the carving table, you will be served either a shrimp cocktail, a bowl of soup, or a cold slice of melon. Afterward, you can end the meal with a selection from the dessert trolley (especially recommended is the fresh fruit salad, ladled out with thick country cream poured over). You also receive a large cup of American-style coffee. Lunch costs £13.25 ($21.85), going up to £14.25 ($23.50) at dinner. Hours are daily from 12:15 to 2:30pm and 6 to 10pm.

Before or after dinner you might want to visit the Thames Bar, which has a nautical theme and a full panoramic view of its namesake, along with Tower Bridge and the river traffic. There is a small balcony outside for drinks in summer. Tube: Tower Hill.

Dickens Inn by the Tower, St. Katharine's Way, E.1 (tel. 071/488-9936), is a carefully reconstructed 19th-century warehouse. Incorporating the original redwood beams, stock bricks, and ironworks, it is a balconied pub/restaurant on three levels. I prefer it for its bar snacks. On the ground level is the Tavern Room, where you can order cockles, smoked mackerel, or a ploughman's lunch, among other offerings. In the restaurant, the choice is seafood or traditional English meat dishes. Price begin at £2.50 ($4.15) for one of the snacks, around £4 ($6.60) for the hot dish of the day accompanied by a vegetable. A three-course meal in the restaurant begins at around £15 ($24.75). Open daily 11am to 11pm. Tube: Tower Hill.

CRUISE AND DINE

You can explore the waterways of London while you dine and cruise along historic Regent's Canal aboard *My Fair Lady,* 250 Camden High St., N.W.1 (tel. 071/485-4433). You go all the way to Robert Browning's island at Little Venice before returning. A three-course meal, freshly cooked in the galley, is served, and you also have a well-stocked open bar during the cruise. The dinner cruise boards Tues. to Sat. at 7:30pm, sailing at 8 with a return at 11. The price is £18 ($29.70) including tax. It's also possible to take a Sun. lunch cruise, with a boarding at 12:30pm. Leaving at 1, the cruise takes 2½ hours, costing £14 ($23.10) for a menu of traditional English food. Tube: Camden Town.

R.S. Hispaniola, Victoria Embankment, Charing Cross, W.C.2 (tel. 071/839-3011), is a large, luxurious, air-conditioned restaurant ship (hence, R.S.) offering a splendid view of the heart of London from Big Ben to St. Paul's, armchair comfort at the tables, and two cocktail bars for other brands of comfort. Meals are served on both the upper and lower decks, and at night the sparkling lights along the banks turn the entire area into a romantic scene. The menu offers many meat and vegetarian dishes, and the cost without service is £15.50 ($25.60) for lunch, £19 ($31.35) for dinner. Open daily noon to 2pm (except Sat.) and 7pm to midnight (to 10pm only Sun. and Mon.). Tube: Embankment.

TIME OUT FOR TEA

During the 18th century the English from every class became enamored of a caffeine-rich brew finding its way into London from far-away colonies. Tea-drinking became the rage. The great craftsmen of England designed furniture, porcelain, and silver services for the elaborate ritual, and the schedules of aristocrats became increasingly centered around teatime as a mandatory obligation. Alexander Pope found it expedient to satirize teatime as something uniquely English.

The most dramatic way to enjoy this custom is to experience tea at the **Ritz Palm Court,** Ritz Hotel, Piccadilly, W.1 (tel. 071/493-8181). The gold and white, sound stage–like Palm Court has daily afternoon tea dances, where gentlemen are requested to wear jackets and ties and ladies are encouraged to wear hats—those little ones with veils. Jeans and running shoes are not acceptable. The cost is £11 ($18.15) per person. Tea is served at 3pm and 4:30pm. You are advised to book a table at least one week in advance. Tube: Green Park.

Oak Room Lounge, Le Méridien, 21 Piccadilly, W.1 (tel. 071/734-8000), which has been restored to its former Edwardian glory and is situated on the ground floor of the hotel, welcomes non-residents daily for the very British tradition of tea. Afternoon tea as served in the soothing elegance of this oak-paneled room is accompanied by the resident harpist, comfortable armchairs, and formal, but unstuffy service. A complete tea, which includes a selection of sandwiches and tarts, costs from £8.25 ($13.60) per person. The menu lists a tempting array of more exotic teas, some of which you may never have tried before. Open daily 3 to 6pm. Tube: Piccadilly Circus and Green Park.

Palm Court Lounge, Park Lane Hotel, Piccadilly, W.1 (tel. 071/499-6321), is one of the great favorites of London for tea, with an atmosphere straight from 1927. It was refurbished by John Siddeley, one of the world's leading interior designers, right before his death. The lounge has a domed yellow and white glass ceiling, torchères and palms in Compton stoneware jardinières. A delightful afternoon tea, with three scones, Devonshire cream and thick jam, sandwiches, and a selection of cakes, is served daily from 3 to 6pm. A full tea, costing £7.75 ($12.80) per person, is highly recommended for theater-goers who won't be able to eat until much later. Many guests come here after the theater for a sandwich and a drink, as food is served 24 hours a day. A club sandwich costs £3.50 ($5.80), for example. Tube: Hyde Park Corner.

The Palm Court, Waldorf Hotel, Aldwych, W.C.2 (tel. 071/836-2400), combines afternoon tea with afternoon dancing, such as the fox-trot, the quickstep, and the waltz. The Palm Court is aptly compared to a 1920s movie set, which is in fact what it's been several times in its long life. It's hard for an art director to duplicate a natural set like this place. You can order tea on a terrace or in a skylighted pavilion the size of a ballroom. The orchestra leader will conduct such favorites as "Ain't She Sweet" and "Yes, Sir, That's My Baby," as a butler in a cutaway inquires if you want a cucumber sandwich. Tea is served from 3:30 to 6:30pm daily. On Mon. to Thur. from 4pm, a pianist entertains as you enjoy your Earl Grey. However, Fri. to Sun. is tea-dance time. Of course, men must wear a jacket and tie. Reservations are needed. Tube: Covent Garden.

Fortnum & Mason's **The Fountain Restaurant,** 181 Piccadilly, W.1 (tel. 071/734-8040), has long been the most famous place in London for afternoon tea, served from 2:30 to 6pm Mon. to Sat., costing from £3.50 ($5.80). In London's most famous grocery store, you can enjoy sizeable pots of tea served with wafer-thin cucumber sandwiches or, if you prefer, filled with caviar, along with French pastries. For some tea aficionados, a visit here is part of the ritual of living in London. Of course, some people, instead of taking tea, prefer the sundaes, frappés, and sorbets. These have been called "forbidden delights." Reservations are not accepted for tea. Tube: Piccadilly Circus.

OUTSIDE OF LONDON

In a redbrick early-Victorian vicarage near Reading, in Berkshire, sits one of the finest dining rooms in the London environs. It's **L'Ortolan,** The Old Vicarage, Church Lane, Shinfield (tel. 0734/883783), which is worth the effort to get there. This once was an out-of-the-way hamlet: Now the world comes to the door of this restaurant, named for a game bird. It seems to breathe both material warmth and a seriousness about gastronomy, which implies almost at once that this is one of the culinary citadels of England. You might be offered a table in an alcove: the glass-enclosed conservatory. The cuisine is self-styled as "contemporary classic." The menu changes constantly, based on seasonal produce and inspirations of the chef. A set lunch costs £22 ($36.30), and a set dinner goes for £38.50 ($63.55), but you are likely to spend far more, of course. Hours are from 12:15 to 2:15pm and 7:15 to 10:30pm; closed Sun. evening, all day Monday, and for the last two weeks of February and August. Reservations are essential.

---

4. Pubs of London

No activity is more typically British than to head for that venerated institution, the public house, affectionately known as pub. Many are dreary Victorian monstrosities, patronized by men and women in the neighborhood. Others, particularly those in the West End, have glamour, basking in associations real (Charles Dickens, Samuel Johnson) or imagined (Sherlock Holmes). Pub crawling is a real part of your English experience. Many North American visitors who don't usually go to bars at home become enthusiasts of the English pub. And most single women feel comfortable in them.

The most noticeable change in English pubs, especially those in the West End, is in the improved standard of food served. However, many pubs still rely on snacks, which are typically drab. Others serve superb sandwiches (fresh salmon stuffed between healthy slices of brown bread), even hot dishes, such as shepherd's pie. Some London pubs offer a fine cuisine in separate dining rooms on their premises—the fare ranging from lobster soup to river trout grilled in butter to roast Aylesbury duckling in orange sauce.

My pub recommendations in the major tourist centers of the West End follow, with the emphasis on those having historic interest (The Prospect of Whitby, Ye Olde Cock Tavern) or else those catering to special-interest groups, such as theater buffs and actors (Salisbury).

ST. JAMES'S

A short walk from Piccadilly Circus is the **Red Lion,** 2 Duke of York St., St. James's Square, S.W.1 (tel. 071/930-2030). Ian Nairn compared its spirit to that of Edouard Manet's painting, *A Bar at the Folies-Bergère* (see the collection at the Courtauld Institute Galleries). The food is pub grub: chips, pork sausages, cheese and onion pie, Cornish pasties, and chicken pies. It is prepared in upstairs kitchens, sent down in a century-old dumbwaiter, and placed at the bar. A simple meal costs £3.50 ($5.80) and up. Everything is washed down with Ind Coope's fine ales in this little Victorian pub with its post turn-of-the-century decorations—patterned glass, deep-mahogany curlicues—that recapture the gin-palace atmosphere. Hours are from 11am to 11pm Mon. to Sat. Try to avoid peak hours. Tube: Piccadilly Circus.

LEICESTER SQUARE

One of the most famous Victorian pubs of London is the **Salisbury, 90** St. Martin's Lane, W.C.2 (tel. 071/836-5863). Its glittering cut-glass mirrors reflect the faces of English stage stars (and would-be stars) sitting around the curved, buffet-style bar. If you want a less prominent place to sit, choose the old-fashioned wall banquette with its copper-topped tables and art nouveau decor. The light fixtures, veiled bronze women in flowing togas holding up clusters of electric lights concealed in bronze roses, are appropriate. In the saloon, you'll see and hear the Oliviers of yesterday and tomorrow. Open 11am to 11pm Mon. to Sat., noon to 3pm and 7 to 10:30pm Sun. Tube: Leicester Square.

A perennial favorite is the **Sherlock Holmes, 10** Northumberland St., W.C.1 (tel. 071/930-2644), the old gathering spot for the "Baker Street Irregulars," a once mighty clan of mystery lovers who met here to honor the genius of Sir Arthur Conan Doyle's most famous fictional character. Upstairs you'll find a re-creation of the living room at 221B Baker St. and such Holmesiana as the cobra of *The Speckled Band* and the head of *The Hound of the Baskervilles*. The downstairs is mainly for drinking, but upstairs you can order complete meals with wine. Main dishes are reliable, including roast beef and Yorkshire pudding and chicken Sherlock Holmes with red wine and mushroom sauce. You select a dessert from the trolley. Meals begin at £12 ($19.80). There's also a good snack bar downstairs, with cold meats, salads, cheese, and wine sold by the glass. Here, snacks cost from £2 ($3.30) to £3.50 ($5.80). Hours are 11:30am to 11pm Mon. to Sat., noon to 3pm and 7 to 10:30pm Sun. Tube: Charing Cross.

COVENT GARDEN

Nag's Head, 10 James St., W.C.2 (tel. 071/836-4678), is one of the most famous Edwardian pubs of London. In days of yore, patrons had to make their way through lorries of fruit and flowers for a drink here. Elegantly dressed operagoers in the evening used to mix with cockney cauliflower peddlers at the bar. But 300 years of British tradition happily faded away, and with the moving of the market, the pub is now patronized mainly by young people who seem to fill up the tables every evening, including drinking space around the bar counter. Lunches are served daily from 11:30am to 2:30pm, with meals costing from £3.85 ($6.35). Try a draft Guinness for a change of pace. Hours are 11am to 11pm daily. Tube: Covent Garden.

Lamb & Flag, 33 Rose St. (off Garrick St.), W.C.2 (tel. 071/836-4108), dates back three centuries and was once known as "The Bucket of Blood." Bare-fisted fights were held in a room upstairs in front of drunken revelers urging the fighters on to more violence. If you go here, you'll be following in the footsteps of Charles Dickens, who used to be a patron, rubbing elbows with solicitors from Middle Temple. It is said that Dryden was roughed up here once because he'd satirized Louise, then the mistress of Charles II. Today, all that history forms part of the legend and lore of this tiny, paneled pub, which lies in a cul-de-sac, perhaps the smallest street in Covent Garden (you'll need a very detailed map to find it). Lager costs from £1.40 ($2.30) and, in good weather, it's often taken outside because there's no room to stand in the little pub. The upstairs room, now called the Dryden Room, also absorbs the overflow. Come here for lunch and feast on one of several pâtés with French bread (washed down with real ale) or perhaps shepherd's pie, chili con carne, or one of the curry dishes. Hot plates of food cost from £2 ($3.30) and are quite filling. Only lunch is served (Mon. to Sat.), but on every night except Friday you can order bar snacks. Hours are daily from 11am to 11pm. Tube: Covent Garden.

SOHO

Old Coffee House, 49 Beak St., W.1 (tel. 071/437-2196), once honored as Soho pub of the year, takes its name from the coffeehouse heyday of 18th-century

London. Coffee was called "the devil's brew" back then. But when most establishments switched to serving lager, or "demon drink," names were changed. This place holds on to an old tradition. The pub is heavily decorated with bric-a-brac, including such items as old musical instruments and World War I recruiting posters. Have your drink at a long narrow bar, with a lager costing from £1.40 ($2.30), or else retreat to the restaurant upstairs where you can enjoy good pub food, including such typically English dishes as steak and kidney pie. Meals and snacks, costing from £4 ($6.60), are served only at lunch, although the pub is open daily from 11am to 11pm. Tube: Oxford Circus or Piccadilly Circus.

CHELSEA

In a fashionable residential district of London, **King's Head and Eight Bells,** 50 Cheyne Walk, S.W.3 (tel. 071/353-1820), is a historic Thamesside pub. It's popular with stage and TV personalities as well as writers. Many distinguished personalities once lived in this area. A short stroll in the neighborhood will take you to the former homes of such personages as Thomas Carlyle, Algernon Thomas Swinburne, and George Eliot. Press gangs used to roam these parts of Chelsea seeking lone travelers, who were abducted for a life at sea. The snack bar has been upgraded to Cordon Bleu standards at pub prices. The best English beers are served here, as well as a goodly selection of wines and liquors. A refrigerated display case holds cold dishes and salads, and there is also a modern hot table. For a main course and a "sweet" (dessert), you'll pay around £6 ($9.90) for a pub-style meal. At night, however, there is table service and à la carte dining, with meals costing from £9 ($14.85) per person. Main platters are usually seafood, including filet of plaice with prawns, tuna steak, or swordfish steak with mussels. Open daily 11am to 11pm. Tube: Sloane Square.

Front Page, Old Church Street, S.W.3 (tel. 071/352-2908), is favored by Chelsea yuppies who like its mellow atmosphere, with wood paneling, wooden tables, and pews and benches. In one section an open fire burns on cold nights. The pub stands in an expensive residential section of Chelsea, and is a good, safe place to go for a drink, with lager costing from £1.40 ($2.30). You can also order bottled Budweiser. Look at the blackboard for a listing of the daily specials, which might include ratatouille au gratin or lamb curry, perhaps even mackerel with a kumquat sauce. You might begin with a homemade soup du jour. Main dishes cost from £3.50 ($5.80). Open 11am to 3pm and 5:30 to 11pm Sun. to Fri., 11am to 11pm Sat. Tube: South Kensington.

CHELSEA HARBOUR

Boaters Wine Bar, Harbour Yard, Chelsea Harbour, S.W.10 (tel. 071/352-3687), occupies premises in one of London's new "villages," Chelsea Harbour. Well-heeled local flat dwellers who own the soaringly expensive apartments in the complex often come here to drink champagne by the bottle, while munching from the bowls of popcorn left on the long wooden bar. Visitors from all over the world pour in here as well, ordering, if not champagne, then wine and lager. No hard spirits are sold.

You can enjoy jazz on Thursday night, and reasonably priced food all week. Cold food is served in the evening, but you can order hot food at lunch. Most main dishes cost £5 ($8.25) and include such fare as Brie salad, chili con carne, and whole trout with almonds. An impressive wine list offers wine by the glass, costing from £1.95 ($3.20) for the house version up to £3.25 ($5.35) for a Cru Beaujolais. Hours are 11am to 11pm Mon. to Fri., 7pm to midnight Sat., and noon to 3pm Sun. In summer, however, the pub extends its weekend hours: from 11am to 11pm on Sat. and from noon to 7pm on Sun. To reach the pub, take a riverbus from Charing Cross Mon. to Fri. or else board a Chelsea Harbour Hoppa bus (C3) at either Earl's Court or Kensington High Street.

Ferret & Firkin in the Balloon up the Creek, 114 Lots Rd., S.W.10 (tel. 071/352-4645), stands near Chelsea Harbour and is not the lowly pub it first appears to be. Michael Caine, who owns an apartment at nearby Chelsea Harbour, might occasionally drop in for a drink, and the pub has been visited by Princess Margaret's son, Viscount Linley, who owns the nearby restaurant, Deals. Guests come here to enjoy beer such as Stoat or Ferret Ale, perhaps Dogbolter, which one pub critic declared as aptly named. Another called it "notoriously strong." Some guests, often seen standing on the bare floorboards at the long bar, enjoy a mug of cider (more potent than you'd think). Lagers cost from £1.40 ($2.30), and you can also enjoy pub food here during the day, not only the traditional ploughman's lunch but salads and such fare as chili con carne and barbecued ribs. Open daily from 11am to 11pm, the pub offers evening entertainment such as a guitarist or a pianist. To reach the pub, take a riverbus from Charing Cross Mon. to Fri. You can also board a Chelsea Harbour Hoppa bus (C3) at Earl's Court and Kensington High Street, Mon. to Sat.

BELGRAVIA

Protected from the noise of traffic, **The Grenadier,** Wilton Row, S.W.1 (tel. 071/235-3074), is an old-time pub on a cobblestone street, sheltered by higher buildings. The Grenadier is one of the special pubs of London—associated with the Iron Duke (Wellington). But today it's filled with a sophisticated crowd of Belgravia flatmates and chic mews-dwellers. At the entrance to Wilton Row (in the vicinity of Belgrave Square), a special guard ("good evening, guv'nor") was once stationed to raise and lower a barrier for those arriving by carriage. The guard's booth is still there. A gentle ghost is said to haunt the premises, that of a Grenadier guard who was caught cheating at cards and died of the flogging given as punishment. Pub enthusiasts are fanatic about The Grenadier.

You can lunch or dine as well as drink here. English meals are served in front of fireplaces in two of the small rooms behind the front bar. A soup of the day might be followed by baked Virginia ham, steak, kidney, and mushroom pie, guinea fowl, or, in honor of the former patron, beef Wellington. Meals range from £15 ($24.75) to £18 ($29.70). Bar snacks are available during the same hours the restaurant serves. Lunch is available daily from noon to 2:30pm and dinner from 6 to 9:45pm Mon. to Sat., from 7 to 9:45pm Sun. The bar is open daily from 11am to 3pm and 5:30 to 11pm. The Grenadier is known for its Bloody Marys, with a Bloody Mary bar operating during lunch Sat. and Sun. The pub is closed only on Christmas Day. Tube: Hyde Park Corner.

The Antelope, 22 Eaton Terrace, S.W.1 (tel. 071/730-7781), is on the fringe of Belgravia, at the gateway to Chelsea. This eatery caters to a hodgepodge of clients, aptly described by one employee as "people of all classes, colours, and creeds who repair for interesting discussion on a whole gamut of subjects, ranging from port to medieval, mid-European wickerwork, bedbug traps, and for both mental and physical refreshment." It is also a base for English rugby aficionados (not to be confused with those who follow football, or soccer). Rugby is a game not unlike American football, but it is played continuously for 80 minutes, and the players wear no bodily protection. The trappings here have long since mellowed as The Antelope goes back to about 1800. You can take a lunch in a ground-floor bar that provides hot and cold pub food. On the floor above (British first floor), food is served at a wine bar both morning and evening. The ground floor is devoted at night to drinks only. The food is principally English, with steak and kidney pie and jugged hare among the specialties. Steaks are also served. Meals are offered from 11am to 3pm Mon. to Sat., costing from £10 ($16.50). Pub hours are from 11am to 11pm Mon. to Sat., noon to 3pm and 7:30 to 10:30pm Sun. Tube: Sloane Square.

Star Tavern, 6 Belgrave Mews W., S.W.1 (tel. 071/235-3019), is famous. Set in a Georgian mews, it is one of the most colorful pubs in the West End, lying behind a picture-postcard facade. In winter it's one of the coziest havens around, with two fireplaces going. Groups of office workers descend after work, staking out their territories. The place is attractive inside, with olive-green Victorian walls and banquettes beneath the 19th-century Victorian moldings. You can order plates of food for £4.90 ($8.10), including such dishes as baby spring chicken, sirloin steak, or perhaps a vegetable quiche. Food is served 11:30am to 3pm and 6:30 to 8:45pm Mon. to Fri. Pub hours are 11:30am to 3pm and 5 to 11pm Mon. to Thurs.,

11:30am to 11pm Fri., 11:30am to 3pm and 6:30 to 11pm Sat., and noon to 3pm and 7 to 10:30pm Sun. Tube: Knightsbridge.

KNIGHTSBRIDGE

Nag's Head, 53 Kinnerston St., S.W.1 (tel. 071/235-1135), is snuggled on a "back street" in Knightsbridge, a short walk from the deluxe Berkeley Hotel. Dating from 1780, it is said to be the smallest pub in London, although others claim that distinction. The pub is housed in what was previously a jail. In 1921, it was sold for £12 and 6p ($19.90) in what might be called a steal. Take your drink up front or wander to a tiny little bar in the rear. The pub is warm and cozy, with a welcoming staff. Here, in the midst of a cosmopolitan clientele, you might enjoy "real ale sausage" (made with pork and ale), or perhaps shepherd's pie, steak and mushroom pie, even quiche of the day. Hot plates of food cost from £2.75 ($4.55). Lager costs from £1.40 ($2.30). The pub is patronized by newspaper people, musicians, and what one columnist called "mechanics and gay young things." Hours are daily from 11am to 3pm and 5:30 to 11pm. Tube: Knightsbridge.

SHEPHERD MARKET

Considered the pub of Mayfair, **Shepherds Tavern,** 50 Hertford St., W.1 (tel. 071/499-3017), is a nugget, attracting a congenial mixture of patrons. There are many luxurious touches, including a collection of antique furniture. Chief among these is a sedan chair that once belonged to the son of George III, the duke of Cumberland. Many of the local habitués recall the tavern's association with the pilots of the Battle of Britain. Bar snacks and hot dishes include shepherd's pie or fish pie with vegetables. Upstairs, the owners operate a cozy restaurant, Georgian in style with cedar paneling. There they serve staunchly British food, with a three-course fixed meal costing from £14.95 ($24.60). You can also order à la carte. Meals are served noon to 2:30pm and 6 to 10:30pm Mon. to Sat., 7 to 10:30pm Sun. The street-level pub is open 11am to 11pm Mon. to Fri., noon to 3pm and 5:30 to 11pm Sat., and noon to 3pm and 7 to 10:30pm Sun. Tube: Green Park.

BLOOMSBURY

Opposite the British Museum, **Museum Tavern,** 49 Great Russell St., W.C.1 (tel. 071/242-8987), is a turn-of-the-century pub, with all the trappings: velvet, oak paneling, and cut glass. It's right in the center of the University of London area and popular with writers and publishers. Very crowded at lunchtime, it is also popular with researchers from the museum. It is said that Karl Marx wrote in the pub over a meal. Traditional English food is served, with steak and kidney pie, beef-in-ale casserole, sausages cooked in English cider, and chef's specials on the hot-food menu. Cold food includes turkey and ham pie, ploughman's lunches, cheeses, salads, and quiches. A hot-food meal costs from £5 ($8.25), a menu of cold food going for £3.50 ($5.80) and up. There are several different real English ales, cold lagers, cider, Guinness, wines, and spirits. Open 11am to 11pm Mon. to Sat., to 10:30pm Sun. Food and coffee are served all day. Tube: Holborn or Tottenham Court Road.

THE CITY

Dating back to 1549, **Ye Olde Cock Tavern,** 22 Fleet St., E.C.4 (tel. 071/353-3454), boasts a long line of ghostly literary patrons, such as Charles Dickens, who have favored this ancient pub. Samuel Pepys mentioned the pub in one of his diary entries, and Lord Tennyson referred to it in one of his poems, a copy of which is framed and proudly displayed near the front entrance. It is one of the few buildings in London to have survived the Great Fire. Downstairs, you can order a pint as well as snack-bar food. You can also order steak and kidney pie or a cold chicken-and-beef plate with salad. Light meals cost from £4 ($6.60). At the carvery upstairs, a meal costs from £12 ($19.80) and includes a choice of appetizers, followed by all the roasts you can carve—beef, lamb, pork, or turkey. The carvery serves only lunch, from noon to 3pm, and the street-level pub's hours are 11:30am to 2:30pm and 5 to 9:30pm. Closed Sat. and Sun. Tube: Temple or Chancery Lane.

Associated with Sir Christopher Wren, **Ye Olde Watling,** 29 Watling St., E.C.4 (tel. 071/248-6252), was built after the Great Fire of London in 1666. On the ground level is a mellow pub, with an intimate restaurant upstairs. Under oak beams and at trestle tables you can have a good choice of English food. The menu varies daily by including the choice of four hot dishes, such as beef and ale pie, steak and kidney pie, seafood Mornay, lasagne, chili con carne, and usually a vegetarian dish. All are served with two vegetables or a salad, rice, or potatoes. You'll be charged around £4.50 ($7.45) for a meal. The restaurant serves lunch only noon to 2pm Mon. to Fri. Tube: Mansion House.

NEAR CLERKENWELL

Once frequented by Dr. Samuel Johnson, **Ye Olde Mitre** is hidden in Ely Court, E.C.1 (tel. 071/405-4751), a narrow little entryway linking Ely Place, which leads off Charterhouse Street at Holborn Circus, and Hatton Garden, home of London's diamond trade. Another entrance is beside 8 Hatton Garden. This tavern was first built in 1546 by the Bishop of Ely for his palace servants. The sign hanging outside the present building bears a drawing of a bishop's mitre, and the sign above the door bears the date. The carefully rebuilt pub consists of small rooms with dark oak paneling, ancient settles, and jugs hanging from the low beams. In good weather, you may be lucky enough to find a seat in the tiny courtyard between the pub and the Church of St. Etheldreda. Interesting relics in the pub include a preserved chunk of a cherry tree around which Queen Elizabeth I is said to have danced the maypole when the tree marked the dividing line between the part of the garden belonging to Sir Christopher Hatton and that which was the property of the bishop. A metal bar at the entrance of Ely Court was placed there to prevent horsemen from riding into this tiny space. Light bar meals are available in the tavern for £2.50 ($4.15) and up. Hours are 11am to 11pm; closed Sat. and Sun. Tube: Farringdon.

HOLBORN

Cittie of Yorke, 22-23 High Holborn, W.C.1 (tel. 071/242-7670), stands near the Holborn Bars, the historic entrance to London marked by dragons holding the coat of arms of the city between their paws. Persons entering and leaving London were checked and paid tolls here. A pub has stood on this site since 1430. The present pub is named the Cittie of Yorke after a 16th-century hostelry, later called the Staple Inn (now across on the other side of High Holborn). Its principal hall, said to have the longest bar in England, has handsome screenwork, comfortable little compartments, a long row of huge vats, and a high trussed roof. The place is popular with barristers and judges. Lunch is a bar snack type of thing, not formal in any way. You get a choice of four different hot platters, priced from £3.50 ($5.75) each. Other fare includes burgers, goulash, and casseroles. Dinner is slightly more formal. Full dinners cost from £5 ($8.25) to £10 ($16.50) each, and entrées include ham steak, fresh fish, lasagne, or rumpsteak. Lager costs from £1.40 ($2.30). Hours are 11am to 11pm Mon. to Fri., noon to 3pm and 5:30 to 11pm on Sat.; closed Sun. Tube: Holborn or Chancery Lane.

ALONG THE THAMES

One of London's oldest riverside pubs, the **Prospect of Whitby,** 57 Wapping Wall, E.1 (tel. 071/481-1095), was founded originally in the days of the Tudors, taking its name from a coal barge that made weekly trips from Yorkshire to London. In a traditionally pubby atmosphere, the Prospect has a balcony overlooking the Thames, where "hanging judge" Jeffries used to enjoy his ale in the 18th century as he watched the hangman string up men he'd judged. The pub was visited by Dickens, Whistler, and Turner searching for local color. Come here for a tot, a noggin, or whatever it is you drink. Downstairs you can enjoy beer and snacks.

Or you can go upstairs to the Pepys Rooms, which honors the diarist, who may —just may—have visited the Prospect in rowdier days, when the seamy side of London dock life held sway here. You can enjoy such foods as lemon chicken and homemade fish pies (with scallops, scampi, salmon, cod, and prawns). Meals are priced from £15 ($24.75) per person. The hours of the upstairs restaurant are from noon to 2pm and 7 to 10pm; closed Sat. for lunch and Sun. for dinner. The pub is open 11:30am to 3pm and 5:30 to 11pm Mon. to Sat., noon to 3pm and 7 to 10:30pm Sun.

To get there, take the Metropolitan Line to Wapping station. When you emerge onto Wapping High Street, turn right and head down the road along the river. Wapping Wall will be on your right, running parallel to the Thames. It's about a five-minute walk.

City Barge, 17 Strand-on-the-Green, Chiswick, W.4 (tel. 071/994-2148). Londoners head west for an outing and an evening pint of ale on a summer night. A little country pub, a nostalgic link with the past—it can be reached in 45 minutes from the center of London. Take the tube to Hammersmith, then change to bus 27 and get off at the beginning of Kew Bridge (during the day this can be combined with a visit to Kew Gardens). Then walk down a townpath (about a five-minute jaunt), past moored boats and a row of little Regency, Queen Anne, Georgian, and Dutch houses, till you reach the pub. Or you can go by boat from Westminster Pier to Kew Gardens, then visit the City Barge, and return to London by train. Regulars often bypass the little tables set outside (in summer) so as to have their pint while sitting on the embankment wall under a willow tree and enjoying the boats chugging or gliding by. The kitchen makes good sandwiches and also offers hot dishes such as moussaka or steak and kidney pie, with meals costing from £4 ($6.60). Open daily 11am to 3pm and 5:30 to 11pm, 11am to 11pm Sat.

The Anchor, 1 Bankside, Southwark, S.E.1 (tel. 071/407-1577), is steeped in atmosphere, standing near what used to be the infamous debtors' prison, The Clink (hence, the expression—"thrown in the clink"). The original Anchor burned down in 1676 but was rebuilt and survived the bombs of World War II. Much of the present tavern, however, is aptly described by the management as "Elizabeth II." After getting off at the tube stop, you pass by Southwark Cathedral through a warehouse district that looks at night like Jack the Ripper country till you reach the riverside tavern. There's a viewing platform—especially popular during the day—right on the Thames. You'll find a number of bars named after the historical associations of the inn (Thrale Room, Dr. Johnson's Room, the Globe Bar, the Clink Bar, and the Boswell Bar). In addition, you can dine either upstairs or down in such "parlours" as the Chart Rooms or the Georgian, pine-paneled Shakespeare Room. The food is good, and meals begin at £15 ($24.75) in the Chart Rooms. Sunday lunch costs £11.95 ($18.70). From May to October, there is an outdoor barbecue area. Open noon to 2pm and 7 to 10pm Mon. to Sat., noon to 2pm and 7 to 9pm Sun. Tube: London Bridge.

ELEPHANT & CASTLE

South of the Thames, the following pub is easily reached by Underground to Elephant & Castle. From the station where you get off, it's a five-minute walk.

Goose and Firkin, 47 Borough Rd., S.E.1 (tel. 071/403-3590), is a pub that brews its own beer; moreover, there are three special strengths: Goose at £1.06 ($1.75) for a pint; Borough Bitter at £1.20 ($2) a pint; and Dogbolter, £1.32 ($2.15) a pint. For special occasions, the pub produces a variety of strong ales with names such as Earthstopper, Kneetrambler, Gobstopper, and for Christmas, Slay Belles, all costing £1.80 ($2.95) a pint. Be warned: these latter brews are extremely potent. Food is also available in this lovely old London pub. Each day, there is a different hot dish. You can also order extra large baps (bread buns) filled with your choice of meat and salad. A meal will cost from £2.50 ($4.15). A pianist plays all the old numbers in good old "knees up" style Tue. to Sat. Hours are 11am to 3pm and 5 to 11pm Mon. to Fri., noon to 3pm and 6 to 11pm Sat., and 7 to 10:30pm Sun.

ST. JOHN'S WOOD

The Clifton, 96 Clifton Hill, N.W.8 (tel. 071/624-5233), one of the most charming pubs in London, stands in northern London in an expensive residential area. The Clifton is like a country pub in many ways with tables placed outside in summer. Built in 1837, it was a hotel renowned for its fine ports and other vintages. Edward VII discovered it and used it as a hideaway, a place of retreat with his mistress, Lillie Langtry. Restored in 1984, it is better than ever, attracting a lively crowd with its roaring fireplace and mellow atmosphere. The pub is handsomely decorated with many more Victorian and Edwardian touches. There are tables in the rear. Look for the daily specials, such as beef and Guinness stew with dumplings, or else order a steak sandwich, perhaps preceded by smoked mackerel pâté. Hot plates of food cost from £4.50 ($7.45). Open daily 11am to 3pm and 5 to 11pm. However, meals and snacks are served only from 11am to 3pm and 6:30 to 10:30pm. Tube: St. John's Wood or Maida Vale.

HAMPSTEAD

This residential suburb of London, beloved by Keats and Hogarth, is a favorite excursion spot for Londoners on the weekend.

Spaniards Inn, Spaniards Lane, N.W.3 (tel. 071/455-3276), is a Hampstead Heath landmark, opposite the old tollhouse, a bottleneck in the road where people had to pay a toll to enter the country park of the bishop of London. The pub, built in 1630, still contains some antique benches, open fireplaces, and cozy nooks in the rooms with their low, beamed ceilings and oak paneling. Old muskets on the walls are mute survivors of the time of the Gordon Riots of 1780, when a mob stopped in for drinks on their way to burn nearby Kenwood House, property of Lord Mansfield. The innkeeper set up so many free drinks that when the Horse Guards arrived, they found many of the rioters *hors de combat* from too much libation and relieved them of their weapons. A few years later, Byron, Shelley, Dickens, and Galsworthy patronized the pub. Even Keats may have quaffed a glass here. These days, in summer, customers can sit at slat tables on a garden terrace beside a flower-bordered lawn with an aviary.

The pub serves traditional but above-average food. A light repast begins at £2.95 ($4.85). Food is served from 11:30am to 9:30pm except on Sun., when hours are from noon to 3pm and 7 to 9:30pm. Pub hours are 11am to 11pm Mon. to Sat., noon to 3pm and 7 to 10:30pm Sun. Tube: Northern Line to Hampstead Heath.

Jack Straw's Castle, North End Way, N.W.3 (tel. 071/435-8374). This weather-board pub is on the summit of the heath, about 443 feet above sea level. The nearby Whitestone Pond was used in the war as an emergency water tank, and previously Shelley used to sail paper boats there. The pub was rebuilt and enlarged in the 1960s on the site of the original. Jack Straw was one of the leaders of the peasants who revolted along with Wat Tyler in 1381 against what was, basically, a wage freeze, while prices were allowed to rise.

The pub was created in Jack's old home, now a bustling place with a large L-shaped bar and quick-snack counter where there are cold salads, meats, and pies, plus three hot dishes with vegetables served every day. You can eat in the bar or on the large patio overlooking part of the heath.

The Carving Room offers a main course and dessert for £8.45 ($13.95), and serves from noon to 2pm and 6 to 10pm Mon. to Sat., 7 to 9:30pm only Sun. Pub hours are 11am to 3pm and 5:30 to 11pm Mon. to Fri., 11am to 11pm Sat., and noon to 2pm and 7 to 10:30pm Sun. The pub is a five-minute walk from the tube station, up the hill, where you can enjoy the good fresh air. Tube: Northern Line to Hampstead Heath.

---

5. Wine Bars

For years, the stark, atmospheric, and ancient wine cellars of the old City had been patronized by businessmen in bowlers and were almost a well-kept secret—you never ran into a tourist or a woman there. However, that changed long ago.

Wine bars are the fashion, and the pub no longer dominates the drinking scene in the English capital.

With the coming of the newer wine bars, London's drinking habits have undergone significant change. Wine bars are not only places at which to drink, but also to meet friends and enjoy good food. A few of the older established ones still offer only wine, but in today's terms a wine bar is likely to mean anything, including a disco.

The English taste for wine has increased, hence the number of wine bars springing up in all parts of the city. Nearly all the establishments recommended below sell wine by the glass, although if you're traveling in a party you may want to order by the bottle and share as it's less expensive that way.

I'll lead off with the most interesting collection of wine bars that still lie in The City and are best visited Monday to Friday for lunch. In the other sections of town you can go for both lunch and dinner.

THE CITY

Dating from 1663, the **Olde Wine Shades,** 6 Martin Lane, off Cannon Street, E.C.4 (tel. 071/626-6876), is the oldest wine house in The City. It was the only City tavern to survive the Great Fire of 1666, not to mention the Blitz of 1940. Only 100 yards from the Monument, the Olde Wine Shades used to attract Charles Dickens, who enjoyed its fine wines. In the smoking room the old oil paintings have darkened with age, and the 19th-century satirical political cartoons remain enigmatic to most of today's generation. Some of the fine wines of Europe are served here, and port and sherry are drawn directly from an array of casks behind the counter. A candlewick bar and restaurant are found downstairs, but upstairs, along with your wine, you can order French bread with ham off the bone. Breton pâté, sandwiches, jacket potatoes filled with cheese, venison pie with salad garnish, and a large beef salad. Meals range from £9 ($14.85). Jackets, collars, and ties are required for men. Hours are 11:30am to 3pm and 5 to 8pm; closed Sat., Sun., and bank holidays. Tube: Monument or Cannon.

Bow Wine Vaults, 10 Bow Churchyard, E.C.4 (tel. 071/248-1121), existed since long before the current wine bar fad that began in the 1970s and now is a firmly entrenched institution on the London scene. One of the most famous wine bars of London, it attracts cost-conscious diners and drinkers who head below ground to its steel and vaulted cellars. There, a glass of wine costs from £1.60 ($2.65) and a two-course meal goes for £10.25 ($16.90). Menu choices in the cellar grill include such traditional fare as deep-fried camembert, chicken Kiev, and a mixed grill, along with fish. Hours are from 11:30am to 3pm Mon. to Fri.

More elegant meals are served in the street-level dining room, The Restaurant, which charges from £25 ($41.25) per person for a meal with wine included. A more elegant and always English-inspired menu is offered here, including, perhaps, mussels in cider sauce, English wild mushrooms in puff pastry, and individual servings of beef Wellington. Try the steak with brown butter sauce. Meals are served 11am to 3pm Mon. to Fri. Adjacent to the restaurant is a cocktail bar, popular with City employees after work. It's open from 11am to 8pm Mon. to Fri. Tube: Bank or St. Paul's.

Jamaica Wine House, St. Michael's Alley, off Cornhill, E.C.3 (tel. 071/626-9496), lies in a tangle of City alleyways, and if you do manage to find it, you'll be at one of the first coffeehouses to be opened in England. In fact, the Jamaica Wine House is reputed to be the first coffeehouse in the Western world. Pepys used to visit it and mentioned the event in his *Diary*. The coffeehouse was destroyed in the Great Fire of 1666, rebuilt in 1674, and has remained, more or less, in its present form ever since. For years London merchants and daring sea captains came here to lace deals with rum and coffee. Nowadays, the two-level house dispenses beer, ale, lager, and fine wines, among them a variety of ports, to appreciative drinkers. The oak-paneled bar at street level is for the money-makers, the jacket-and-tie investment banker crowd, whereas the rowdier basement bar is patronized by The City's messengers and service personnel. The basement bar's beer is on draft, cheaper and less prestige-conscious than the imported, bottled beer served upstairs. You can order a glass of wine from £1.20 ($2), along with light snacks such as port pie, stuffed baked potatoes with various fillings, and toasted sandwiches. Light meals cost from £3.50 ($5.75). Open 11:30am to 8pm Mon. to Fri. The Bank of England is only a stone's throw away. Tube: Bank.

NEAR PICCADILLY

Among the many wine bars in London, **Greens Restaurant and Oyster Bar,** 36 Duke St., S.W.1 (tel. 071/930-4566), is a good choice for the excellence of its menu, the charm of its staff, and its central location. A busy place, it has a cluttered entrance leading to a crowded bar. There you can stand at what the English call "rat-catcher counters" if the tables are full, sip fine wines, and, from September to May, enjoy oysters. Other foods to encourage the consumption of the wines are quail's eggs, king prawns, smoked Scottish salmon, crab, and baby lobsters. If you choose to go on into the dining room, you can select from a long menu, with a number of fish dishes or such grilled foods as calves' liver and bacon, kedgeree, and Green's fish cakes with parsley sauce. Desserts include Duke of Cambridge tart, black-currant sorbet, and banana fritters. Meals cost from £20 ($33). Open 12:30 to 2:45pm and 6:30 to 10:30pm, 11:30am to 3:30pm only Sun. It's best to reserve a table if you're not planning to arrive early in the evening. Tube: Piccadilly Circus or Green Park.

Daniel's Wine Bar (Café Royal), 68 Regent St., W.1 (tel. 071/437-9090 ext. 277), is the consciously unpretentious annex to the chillingly expensive Café Royal Grill, which dates from 1865. Both are accessible from the marble-floored lobby of a watering hole where the literary greats of 19th-century England have trod. Designed in an opulent motif of art nouveau moldings, oaken half-paneling, and lots of framed cartoons and illustrations, the bar has a resident pianist whose melodies seem to make the wine ever-so-more drinkable.

Platters of food such as beef Stroganoff are served only from noon to 2:30pm Mon. to Fri. A platter (with perhaps a glass of wine) is a full meal, and costs £4.45 ($7.35). The rest of the day, until late into the night, only wine and drinks are served. A glass of wine costs from £1.30 ($2.15) to £1.60 ($2.65), a bottle of wine from £6.25 ($10.30). Open noon to 3pm and 5:30 to 11pm Mon. to Fri. Tube: Piccadilly Circus.

NEAR LEICESTER SQUARE

In the theater district, **Cork and Bottle Wine Bar,** 44-46 Cranbourn St., W.C.2 (tel. 071/734-7807), is just off Leicester Square. Don Hewitson, the owner, has revitalized the food, with a wide range of hot dishes, so that it is not a typical "glass of wine and slice of pâté" type of bistro. The most successful dish is a raised cheese-and-ham pie. It has a cream-cheesy filling, and the well-buttered pastry is crisp—not your typical quiche. (In just one week the bar sold 500 portions of this alone.) Don also offers a mâchon lyonnaise, a traditional worker's lunch in Lyon. He imports his own saucisson from a charcuterie in Lyon, serving it hot with warm potato salad, a mixed green salad, spicy Dijon mustard, and French bread. You can also order an "American gourmet salad," consisting of lettuce, tomato, avocado, green beans, and croutons, in a spicy red Stilton dressing. Meals cost from £12 ($19.80). The expanded wine list features an excellent selection of Cru Beaujolais and wines from Alsace, as well as some 30 selections from "down under." The carte lists some 30 champagnes and a good selection of California labels. Open 11am to 3pm and 5:30 to 11pm Mon. to Sat., noon to 2pm and 7 to 10:30pm Sun. Tube: Leicester Square.

MAYFAIR

Near the American Embassy, **Bubbles,** 41 North Audley St., W.1 (tel. 071/491-3237), is an interesting wine bar lying between Upper Brook Street and Oxford Street (in the vicinity of Selfridges). The owners attach equal importance to their food and to their impressive wine list. Some selections of wine are sold by the glass, beginning at £1.50 ($2.50). On the ground floor guests find not only fine wines but also draft beer and liquor, along with a limited but well-chosen selection of bar food, including such dishes as mussels marinière. Meals there begin at £3.75 ($6.20). You can also order meat and fish salads, including one made with honey-roast ham. Downstairs is an à la carte restaurant serving both English and continental dishes, including a selection appealing to vegetarians. Start, for example, with French onion soup, followed by roast rack of English lamb or perhaps roast duckling with a lemon and tarragon sauce. Meals downstairs cost from £12 ($19.80). Hours are 11am to 3pm and 5 to 11pm Mon. to Fri., 11am to 3pm Sat. Tube: Marble Arch.

Shampers, 4 Kingly St., W.1 (tel. 071/437-1692), is a venture of New Zealander Don Hewitson of Cork and Bottle Wine Bar near Leicester Square, who has perked up the wine bar movement with his excellent selection of wines and the imaginatively prepared food. You have a choice of seats either upstairs or down. Or perhaps you'll elect to perch on a stool alongside the bar. I prefer the cozy ambience of the downstairs.

A meal for one person with wine comes to about £12 ($19.80). Salads are a star, and look for the hot dish of the day, possibly including grilled marinated rabbit with mustard sauce. The sources of wines range from California to Germany to Australia. This might make Shampers an especially good place to stop if you're shopping in the area. Hours are 11am to 3pm and 5:30 to 11pm Mon. to Fri. The bar also serves lunch on Saturday. Tube: Oxford Circus.

NEAR VICTORIA STATION

On one of London's most popular streets for budget hotels, **Ebury Wine Bar,** 139 Ebury St., S.W.1 (tel. 071/730-5447), is convenient for dining or drinking. This wine bar and bistro attracts a youthful clientele to its often crowded but always atmospheric precincts. Wine is sold either by the glass or bottle. You can always get an enticing plat du jour, such as traditional beef Wellington or perhaps one of the grilled filet steaks. All the food is prepared fresh daily, with meals costing from £15 ($24.75). Open 11am to 3pm and 5:30 to 11pm Mon. to Sat., noon to 2:45pm and 6 to 10:30pm Sun. Tube: Victoria Station or Sloane Square.

Methuselah's, 29 Victoria St., S.W.1 (tel. 071/222-1750), is the latest venture of the wine-bar maven, Don Hewitson. Located opposite New Scotland Yard, it is popular with MPs from the House of Commons for its excellent wine cellar, sophisticated menu, and attractive surroundings. Hewitson calls his food "bourgeois," and it shows a devotion to Provence and Lyon. The day's specialties are written on the blackboard. There is a ground-floor bar, along with two cellar buffet and wine bars, plus a more formal dining room, the Burgundy Room, on the mezzanine. Meals cost from £12 ($19.80) and are served from 11:30am to 3pm and 5:30 to 11pm Mon. to Fri. Tube: Victoria.

KNIGHTSBRIDGE

Said by some people who know about such matters to be the finest wine bar in London, **Le Métro Wine Bar,** 28 Basil St., S.W.3 (tel. 071/589-6286), around the corner from Harrods Department Store, draws a fashionable crowd to its precincts in the basement. You can order special wines by the glass instead of by the bottle, thanks to a cruover machine that stands in a position of honor behind the bar. This machine keeps the wine in perfect condition even after it is opened. As the wine is drawn, the vacuum is replaced by an inert gas that prevents oxidization. The food served at Le Métro is good, solid, and reliable, and it's also prepared with flair. The dishes might include fried chicken livers with salad, a lamb Dijonnaise, mussels in white-wine sauce, and roast preserved duck. You might begin with a pâté of smoked mackerel. Meals cost from £12 ($19.80). Reservations for tables, if you plan to eat, are a good idea, as these same tables might be occupied by customers who are here just to order a glass of wine. Open 7:30am to 11pm Mon. to Fri., 7:30am to 4pm Sat. Tube: Knightsbridge.

Bill Bentley's, 31 Beauchamp Place, S.W.3 (tel. 071/589-5080), stands on this restaurant- and boutique-lined street near Harrods. A small Georgian house, it offers many ground-floor rooms and a little sun-filled patio in back. Cozy and atmospheric, it presents a varied list of reasonably priced wines, including a fine selection of bordeaux. If you're in the neighborhood, you can enjoy a pub-style lunch, such as ham and salad. Hot main dishes are likely to include Bill Bentley's fish cakes and grilled sirloin steak. The oysters are the special treat here. Menus change frequently. Meals cost from £15 ($24.75). It's open from 11am to 11pm Mon. to Sat.; closed Sun. and bank holidays. Tube: Knightsbridge.

CHELSEA

A face-lift has put **Blushes Café,** 52 King's Rd., S.W.3 (tel. 071/589-6640), in the pink through the efforts of proprietors Geoffrey Thorpe and Stephen Lynn. They bring a continental flavor to one of the leading wine bars of Chelsea, which is also a basement cocktail bar, café, et al. Food from Italy to France to Mexico to Asia is offered, with meals costing from £10 ($16.50) to £15 ($24.75). Open daily 8:30am to midnight. A full English breakfast, costing £4.95 ($8.15), is offered from 8:30 to 11am Mon. to Sat. and until 1pm on Sun. Tube: Sloane Square.

V

WHAT TO SEE AND DO IN LONDON

1. SEEING THE SIGHTS

2. KIDS' LONDON

3. TAKING THE TOURS

4. SHOPPING FOR VALUE

5. EVENING ENTERTAINMENT

6. ONE-DAY TRIPS FROM LONDON

Dr. Johnson said: "When a man is tired of London, he is tired of life, for there is in London all that life can afford." And that holds true today.

Come along with me as we survey only a fraction of that life: ancient monuments, debates in Parliament, art galleries, Soho dives, museums, theaters, flea markets, and castles. Some of what we're about to see was known to Johnson and Boswell, even to Shakespeare, but much of it is new.

1. Seeing the Sights

London is not a city to visit hurriedly. It is so vast, so stocked with treasures, that, on a cursory visit, a person will not only miss many of the highlights but also fail to grasp the spirit of London and to absorb fully its unique flavor. Still, faced with an infinite number of important places to visit and a time clock running out, the visitor will have to concentrate on a manageable group.

THE TOP TEN SIGHTS

Here is a list of the top ten sights of London. Try to see them even if you have to skip all the rest, saving them for "next time."

(1) The Tower of London

This ancient fortress on the north bank of the Thames continues to pack 'em in because of its macabre associations with the legendary figures who were either imprisoned or executed here, or both. James Street once wrote, "there are more spooks to the square foot than in any other building in the whole of haunted Britain. Headless bodies, bodiless heads, phantom soldiers, icy blasts, clanking chains—you name them, the Tower's got them."

Back in the days of the executioner, London was "swinging" long before *Time* magazine discovered that fact in the 1960s. Ranking in interest are the colorful attending Yeoman Warders, the so-called Beefeaters, in Tudor dress, who look as if they are on the payroll for gin advertisements (but don't like to be reminded of it).

Many visitors consider a visit to the Tower to be the highlight of their sightseeing in London—so schedule plenty of time for it. You don't have to stay as long as Sir Walter Ralegh (released after some 13 years), but give it an afternoon.

Don't expect to find only one tower. The fortress is actually a compound, in which the oldest and finest structure is the White Tower, begun by William the Conqueror. Here you can view the Armouries, the present collection dating back to the reign of Henry VIII. A display of instruments of torture and execution will recall some of the more ghastly moments in the history of the Tower. In the Bloody Tower, the Little Princes (Edward V and the Duke of York) were allegedly murdered by their uncle, Richard III.

The hospitality today far excels that of years ago, when many of the visitors left their cells only to walk to the headsman's block on Tower Hill. Through Traitors' Gate passed such ill-fated, but romantic, figures as Robert Devereux, a favorite of Elizabeth I, known as the second earl of Essex. Elizabeth herself, when a princess, was once imprisoned briefly in Bell Tower. At Tower Green, Anne Boleyn and Katharine Howard, two wives of Henry VIII, lost their lives. The 9-day queen, Lady Jane Grey, and her husband, Dudley, also were executed, along with such figures as Sir Thomas More.

According to legend, the disappearance of the well-protected ravens at the Tower will presage the collapse of the British Empire (seen any around lately?).

To see the **Jewel House,** where the Crown Jewels are kept, go early in the day during summer, as long lines usually form by late morning. Get a Beefeater to tell you how Colonel Blood almost made off with the crown and regalia in the late 17th century. Of the three English crowns, the Imperial State Crown is the most important—in fact, it's probably the most famous crown on earth. Made for Victoria for her coronation in 1838, it is worn today by Queen Elizabeth II when she opens Parliament. Studded with some 3,000 jewels (principally diamonds), it contains the Black Prince's Ruby, worn by Henry V at Agincourt, the 1415 battle when the English defeated the French. Don't miss the 530-carat Star of Africa, a cut diamond on the Royal Sceptre with Cross.

The Tower of London has an evening ceremony called the **Ceremony of the Keys.** It is, in fact, the ceremonial locking up of the Tower for yet another day in its 900 years. Nothing stops the ceremony. During World War II, a bomb fell within the castle walls during the ceremony and nobody flinched—but the Tower was locked up two minutes late. Rumor has it that the guard that night was censured for tardiness, the pilot of the plane that dropped the bomb blamed as the culprit. The Beefeater will explain to guests the significance of the ceremony. For free tickets, write to the Yeoman Clerk, Tower of London, London EC3N 4AB, requesting a specific date but also giving alternative dates you'd like to attend. At least six weeks' notice is required. All requests must be accompanied by a stamped, self-addressed envelope (*British stamps only*) or two International Reply Coupons. With ticket in hand, you'll be admitted by a Yeoman Warder around 9:35pm.

The Tower and all its buildings are closed on New Year's Day, Good Friday, the Christmas holidays, and on Sun. from November through February. The gates open at 9:30am Mon. to Sat. all year and at 2pm on Sun. from March to the end of October (closed Sun. the remainder of the year). The last tickets are sold at 5pm from March to the end of October and at 4pm from November to the end of February, with actual closing at 5:45pm in summer, 4:30pm in winter. The Tower Wharf, entered by the East or West Gate, is open daily except Christmas Day from 7am Mon. to Sat., from 10am on Sun. Closing times vary depending on the season but never earlier than 6:30pm.

Tours of approximately an hour in length are given by the Yeoman Warders at about 30-minute intervals, starting from the Middle Tower near the main entrance. The tours include the Chapel Royal of St. Peter ad Vincula. The last guided walk starts about 3:30pm in summer, 2:30pm in winter. For further information about opening times and visiting privileges, telephone 071/709-0765, ext. 235.

Admission to the Tower, including the Jewel House, is £5.50 ($9.10) for adults, £3 ($4.95) for children, except for the last three weeks in January and the first week in February, when the Jewel House is closed for the annual cleaning and maintenance, and prices are reduced to £3.80 ($6.25) for adults, £1.50 ($2.50) for children. Those under 5 are admitted free. Take either the Circle or District Line to reach the Tower (the site is only a short walk from the station). Or on a sunny day, why not take a boat instead, leaving from Westminster Pier? Tube: Tower Hill.

(2) Westminster Abbey

No less an illustrious figure than St. Peter is supposed to have left his calling card at the abbey. If it's true, I wouldn't be surprised—for nearly everybody else, at least nearly everybody in English history, has left his or her mark. But what is known for certain is that in 1065 the Saxon king Edward the Confessor rebuilt the old minster church on this spot, overlooking Parliament Square, and founded the Benedictine abbey.

The first English king crowned in the abbey was Harold in 1066, who was killed at the Battle of Hastings that same year. The man who defeated him, Edward's cousin, William the Conqueror, was also crowned at the abbey; the coronation tradition has continued to the present day, broken only twice (Edward V and Edward VIII). The essentially Early English Gothic structure existing today owes more to Henry III's plans than to any other sovereign, although many architects, including Wren, have contributed to the abbey.

Built on the site of the ancient Lady Chapel in the early 16th century, the Henry VII Chapel is one of the loveliest in Europe, with its fan vaulting, Knights of Bath banners, and Torrigiani-designed tomb of the king himself over which is placed a 15th-century Vivarini painting, *Madonna and Child*. The chapel represents the flowering of the Perpendicular Gothic style. Also buried here are Elizabeth I and Mary Tudor ("Bloody Mary"). The effigy of Elizabeth I that lies on top of her tomb has been fitted with a gilded collar and pendant, a modern copy from a painting now at Hatfield House. The originals were stolen by souvenir hunters in the early 18th century. Her orb and sceptre were added earlier. In one end of the chapel you can stand on Cromwell's memorial stone and view the R.A.F. chapel containing the Battle of Britain memorial stained-glass window, unveiled in 1947 to honor the R.A.F.

You can also visit the most hallowed spot in the abbey, the shrine of Edward the Confessor (canonized in the 12th century). In the saint's chapel is the Coronation Chair, made at the command of Edward I in 1300 to contain the Stone of Scone. Scottish kings were once crowned on this stone (in 1950 the Scots took it back, but it was later reacquired for the abbey).

Another noted spot in the abbey is Poets' Corner, to the right of the entrance to the Royal Chapel, with its monuments to everybody from Chaucer on down—Shakespeare, "O Rare Ben Johnson" (his name misspelled), Samuel Johnson, the Brontë sisters, Thackeray, Dickens, Tennyson, Kipling, even the American Longfellow. The most stylized and controversial monument is Sir Jacob Epstein's sculptured bust of William Blake. One of the more recent tablets commemorates the poet Dylan Thomas.

Statesmen and men of science—such as Disraeli, Newton, Charles Darwin—are also either interred in the abbey or honored by monuments. Near the west door is the 1965 memorial to Sir Winston Churchill. In the vicinity of this memorial is the tomb of the Unknown Soldier, symbol of British dead in World War I. Surprisingly, some of the most totally obscure personages are buried in the abbey, including an abbey plumber.

Many visitors overlook such sights as the 13th-century Chapter House, where Parliament used to meet. The Chapter House in the Great Cloister is open March to September from 9:30am till 6pm (closed on Sun.). It shuts down at 3:30pm off-season.

Even more fascinating are the treasures in the museum in the Norman undercroft (crypt), part of the monastic buildings erected between 1066 and 1100. The collection includes effigies—figures in wax, such as that of Nelson, and woodcarvings of early English royalty. Along with the wax figures—the abbey's answer to Madame Tussaud—are ancient documents, seals, replicas of coronation regalia, old religious vestments (such as the cope worn at the coronation of Charles II), the sword of Henry V, and the famous Essex Ring that Elizabeth I is supposed to have given to her favorite earl. The museum is open daily from 10am to 4pm. Admission is £1.60 ($2.65) for adults, 40p (65¢) for children. This also provides a visit to the Chapter House and the Pyx Chamber (containing a treasury).

Adults pay £2.20 ($3.65) and children 50p (85¢) to visit the Royal Chapels, the Royal Tombs, the Coronation Chair, and the Henry VII Chapel. Hours are 9:20am to 4pm Mon. to Fri. and 9:20am to 2pm and 3:45 to 5pm Sat.; Wed. from 6 to 7:45pm with free admission. This is the only time photography is allowed in the abbey. On Sun. the Royal Chapels are closed, but the rest of the church, at Broad Sanctuary, S.W.1, is open between services.

For tours of the abbey with an expert guide, the cost is £6 ($9.90) per person. These tours operate 10am to 3pm Mon. to Fri. On Sat., the hours are 10am, 11am and 12:30pm. Inquire at the West Door for the meeting point. Up to six super-tours of the abbey are conducted by the verger Mon. to Fri., beginning at 10am. For information and reservations for these super-tours, phone 071/222-7110. For times of services and other information, phone the Chapter Office (tel. 071/222-5152).

Off the Cloisters, **College Garden** is the oldest garden in England, under cultivation for more than 900 years. Surrounded by high walls, flowering trees dot the lawns, and park benches provide comfort where you can hardly hear the roar of passing traffic. It is open on Thurs. throughout the year, from 10am to 4pm in winter, to 6pm in summer. In August and September, band concerts are held at lunchtime from 12:30 to 2pm. Admission is free. Tube: Westminster.

(3) Houses of Parliament

These are the spiritual opposite of the Tower, the stronghold of Britain's democracy, the assemblies that effectively trimmed the sails of royal power.

Although I can't assure you of the oratory of a Charles James Fox or a William Pitt the Elder, the debates are often lively and controversial in the House of Commons (seats are at a premium during crises). The chances of getting into the House of Lords when it's in session are generally better than they are in the more popular House of Commons, where even the Queen isn't allowed. Moreover, the old guard of the palace informs me that the peerage speak their minds more freely and are less likely to adhere to party line than their counterparts in the Commons.

The present Houses of Parliament was built in 1840, on the site of the former Palace of Westminster, residence of the English kings until the time of Henry VIII. The Commons chamber was bombed and destroyed by the Luftwaffe in 1941. The 320-foot tower that houses Big Ben, however, remained standing and the "symbol of London" continued to strike its chimes—the signature tune of Britain's wartime news broadcasts. "Big Ben," incidentally, was named after Sir Benjamin Hall, a cabinet minister distinguished only by his long-windedness.

The general public is admitted to the Strangers' Gallery in the House of Commons on "sitting days"—normally from about 4:15pm Mon. to Thurs. and from about 9:30am on Fri. You have to join a public queue outside the St. Stephen's entrance on the day in question. Often there is considerable delay before the head of the public queue is admitted. You might speed matters up somewhat by applying at the American Embassy or the Canadian High Commission for a special pass, but this is too cumbersome for many people. Besides, the embassy has only four tickets for daily distribution, so probably you might as well stand in line. It is usually easier to get in after 6pm Mon. to Thurs. or after 9:30am on Fri. The head of the queue is normally admitted to the Strangers' Gallery of the House of Lords after 2:40pm Mon. to Wed. (often at 3pm on Thurs.).

Except for the Strangers' Galleries, the Houses of Parliament are presently closed to tourists.

Further information about the work of the House of Commons is available by phoning 071/219-4272; House of Lords, 071/219-3107; or on the British Telecom Prestel Viewdata system, frame 5,000. In a fast-changing world, these details should be confirmed before planning a visit. Tube: Westminster.

(4) The British Museum

Within its imposing citadel on Great Russell Street, W.C.1, in Bloomsbury (tel. 071/636-1555), the British Museum shelters one of the most catholic collections of art and artifacts in the world, containing countless treasures of ancient and modern civilizations. To storm this bastion in a day is a formidable task, but there are riches to see even on a cursory first visit. Among them the Oriental collections: the finest assembly of Islamic pottery outside the Islamic world, the finest collection of Chinese porcelain in Europe, the best holdings of Indian sculpture outside India and Pakistan; and the Prehistoric and Romano-British collections, as well as many others. Basically, the overall storehouse splits into the national collections of antiquities; prints and drawings; coins, medals, and banknotes; and ethnography.

As you enter the front hall, you may want to head first to the Assyrian Transept on the ground floor, where you'll find the winged and human-headed bulls and lions that once guarded the gateways to the palaces of Assyrian kings. Nearby is the Black Obelisk of Shalmaneser III (858–824 B.C.), tribute from Jehu, King of Israel. From here you can continue into the angular hall of Egyptian sculpture to see the Rosetta Stone, whose discovery led to the deciphering of the mysterious hieroglyphs, explained in a wall display behind the stone.

Also on the ground floor is the Duveen Gallery, housing the Elgin Marbles, consisting chiefly of sculptures from the Parthenon. The frieze shows a ceremonial procession that took place in Athens every 4 years. Of the 92 metopes from the Parthenon, 15 are housed today in the British Museum. These depict the to-the-death struggle between the handsome Lapiths and the grotesque, drunken Centaurs. The head of the horse from the chariot of Selene, goddess of the moon, is one of the pediment sculptures.

The classical sculpture galleries also hold a caryatid from the Erechtheum, a temple started in 421 B.C. and dedicated to Athena and Poseidon. Displayed here, too, are sculptures from the Mausoleum at Halicarnassus (one of the Seven Wonders of the Ancient World), built for Maussollos, ruler of Caria, who died around 350 B.C. Look also for the blue-and-white Portland Vase, considered the finest example of ancient cameo carving, made in the 1st century B.C. or A.D.

The Department of Medieval and Later Antiquities has its galleries on the first floor (second floor to Americans), reached by the main staircase. Of its exhibitions, the Sutton Hoo Anglo-Saxon ship burial, discovered in Suffolk, is, in the words of an expert, "the richest treasure ever dug from English soil," containing gold jewelry, armor, weapons, bronze bowls and cauldrons, silverware, and the inevitable drinking horn of the Norse culture. No body was found, although the tomb is believed to be that of a king of East Anglia who died in the 7th century A.D. You'll also see the bulging-eyed Lewis chessmen, Romanesque carvings in Scandinavian style of the 12th century, and the Ilbert collection of clocks and watches.

The featured attractions of the upper floor are the Egyptian Galleries, especially the mummies. Egyptian room 63 is extraordinary, looking like the props for *Cleopatra,* with its cosmetics, domestic utensils, toys, tools, and other work. Some items of Sumerian art, unearthed from the Royal Cemetary at Ur (southern Iraq), lie in a room beyond: a queen's bull-headed harp (oldest ever discovered); a queen's sledge (oldest known example of a land vehicle); and a figure of a he-goat on its hind legs, crafted about 2500 B.C. In the Iranian room rests "The Treasure of the Oxus," a hoard of riches, perhaps a temple deposit, ranging in date from the 6th to the 3rd century B.C., containing a unique collection of goldsmith work, such as a nude youth, signet rings, a fish-shaped vase, and votive plaques.

If your visit to the museum makes you want to know more about this treasure trove, I recommend a book by M. L. Caygill of the museum director's office, *Treasures of the British Museum,* which gives detailed account of the major treasures and summaries of departmental collections.

The museum is open from 10am to 5pm Mon. to Sat. and from 2:30 to 6pm

Sun. (The galleries start to close ten minutes earlier.) It is closed Good Friday, December 24–26, New Year's Day, and the first Mon. in May. Admission to the entire museum is free. Tube: Holborn or Tottenham Court Road.

THE BRITISH LIBRARY Some of the treasures from the collections of the British Library (tel. 071/636-1544), one of the world's greatest libraries, are on display in the exhibition galleries in the east wing of the British Museum building. In the Grenville Library are displayed western illuminated manuscripts. Notable exhibits are the Benedictional (in Latin) of St. Ethelwold, Bishop of Winchester (963–984), the Luttrell Psalter, and the Harley Golden Gospels of about 800.

In the Manuscript Saloon are manuscripts of historical and literary interest. Items include two of the four surviving copies of King John's Magna Carta (1215) and the Lindisfarne Gospels (an outstanding example of the work of Northumbrian artists in the earliest period of English Christianity, written and illustrated about 698). Almost every major literary figure, such as Jane Austen, Charlotte Brontë, Charles Dickens, W. B. Yeats, is represented in the English literature section. Also on display are historical autographs, including Nelson's last letter to Lady Hamilton and the journals of Captain Cook.

In the King's Library, so called because this is where the library of King George III is housed, the history of the book is illustrated by notable specimens of early printing, including the Diamond Sutra of 868, the first dated example of printing, as well as the Gutenberg Bible, the first book ever printed from movable type, 1455.

In the center of the gallery is an exhibition of fine bookbindings dating from the 16th century. Beneath Roubiliac's 1758 statue of Shakespeare is a case of documents relating to the Bard, including a mortgage bearing his signature and a copy of the First Folio of 1623. The library's unrivaled collection of philatelic items, including the 1840 Great British Penny Black and the rare 1847 post office issues of Mauritius, are also to be seen.

The library regularly mounts special temporary exhibitions, usually in the Crawford Room off the Manuscript Saloon. The opening times of the British Library's exhibition galleries are the same as those of the museum. Admission is free.

MUSEUM OF MANKIND At Burlington Gardens, W.1 (tel. 071/437-2224), this museum houses the Ethnography Department of the British Museum, showing the art and material culture of the indigenous peoples of many parts of the world. Hours are the same as at the main museum. (The Café de Colombia within the Museum of Mankind closes half an hour before the museum itself closes.) There is no charge for admission. Tube: Piccadilly.

(5) Madame Tussaud's and the London Planetarium

In 1770 an exhibition of life-size wax figures was opened in Paris by Dr. Curtius. He was soon joined by his niece, Strasbourg-born Marie Tussaud, who learned the secret of making lifelike replicas of the famous and the infamous. During the French Revolution, the head of almost every distinguished victim of the guillotine was molded by Madame Tussaud or her uncle.

After the death of Curtius, Madame Tussaud inherited the exhibition, and in 1802 she left France for England. For 33 years she toured the United Kingdom with her exhibition, and in 1835 she settled on Baker Street. The exhibition was such a success that it practically immortalized her in her day; she continued to make portraits until she was 81 (she died in 1850).

While some of the figures still on display today come from molds taken by the imcomparable Madame Tussaud, the exhibition also introduces new images of whoever is *au courant*. An enlarged Grand Hall continues to house years of royalty and old favorites such as Winston Churchill, as well as many of today's heads of state and political leaders. In the Chamber of Horrors you can have the vicarious thrill of meeting such types as Dr. Crippen, and walking through a Victorian London street where special effects include the shadow terror of Jack the Ripper. The instruments and victims of death penalties contrast with the portraits of contemporary criminals nowadays confined to prison.

You are invited to mingle with the more current entertainment stars in the garden party, "meeting" Dudley Moore and Jane Seymour. "Super Stars" offers the latest technologies in sound, light, and special effects, celebrating the success of new figures in the fields of film and sports. A popular attraction—200 years of Tussaud's treasures—opened in 1990.

Madame Tussaud's, air-conditioned throughout, is open 364 days a year (closed on Christmas Day only). Hours are 10am to 5:30pm Mon. to Fri. and 9:30am to 5:30pm Sat. and Sun. Doors open earlier throughout the summer season. Admission for adults is £5.20 ($8.60) and £3.45 ($5.70) for children under 16.

The **London Planetarium** is right next door, costing £2.95 ($4.85) for adults and £1.90 ($3.15) for children. A combined ticket costing £6.65 ($11) for adults and £4.25 ($7) for children, for both the London Planetarium and Madame Tussaud's, will save you money. For information on scheduled shows, phone 071/ 935-6861. The entrance to Madame Tussaud's is on Marylebone Road, N.W.1. Tube: Baker Street.

(6) Tate Gallery

This building beside the Thames on Millbank, S.W.1 (tel. 071/821-1313), houses British paintings from the 16th century on, as well as England's finest collection of modern art: the works of British artists born after 1860 and European art from the impressionists onward. The number of paintings is staggering. If time permits, try to schedule at least two visits—the first to see the classic English works, the second to take in the modern collection. Since only a portion of the collection can be shown simultaneously, the works on display vary from time to time. However, the most time-pressed individual may not want to miss the following, which are almost invariably on view:

The first giant among English painters, William Hogarth (1697–1764), is well represented, particularly by his satirical *O the Roast Beef of Old England* (known as *Calais Gate*), with its caricatured figures, such as the gluttonous monk. The ruby-eyed *Satan, Sin, and Death* remains one of his most imaginative works.

Two other famous British painters of the 18th century are Sir Joshua Reynolds (1723–1792) and Thomas Gainsborough (1727–1788). Reynolds, the portrait painter, shines brightest when he's painting himself (three self-portraits hang side by side). Two other portraits, of Francis and Suzanna Beckford, are typical of his early work. His rival, Gainsborough, is noted for his portraits and also for his landscapes ("my real love"). His landscapes with gypsies are subdued, mysterious; *Wooded Landscape with Peasant Resting* is more representative. One of Gainsborough's most celebrated portraits is *Edward Richard Gardiner,* a handsome boy in blue (the more famous *Blue Boy* is in California). Two extremely fine Gainsborough portraits have recently been acquired: *Sir Benjamin Truman,* the notable brewer, and *Giovanna Baccelli* (1782), who was well known both as a dancer and as the mistress of the third earl of Dorset.

In the art of J. M. W. Turner (1775–1851), the Tate possesses its greatest collection of the works of a single artist. Most of the paintings and watercolors exhibited here were willed to the nation by Turner. His studio at the time held 282 oils and more than 19,000 drawings, watercolors, and sketches. In 1987, a new wing at the Tate, called Clore Gallery, was opened so that the entire bequest could be seen. Of his paintings of stormy seas, none is more horrifying than *Shipwreck* (1805). In the Petworth series he broke from realism (see his *Interior at Petworth*). His delicate impressionism is best conveyed in his sunset and sunrise pictures, with their vivid reds and yellows. Turner's vortex paintings, inspired by color theories of Goethe, are *Light and Color—the Morning After the Deluge* and *Shade and Darkness —the Evening of the Deluge.*

The drawings of William Blake (1757–1827) are outstanding and not to be missed. Blake, of course, was the incomparable mystical poet and illustrator of such works as *The Book of Job, The Divine Comedy,* and *Paradise Lost.* In a nation of landscape painters, John Constable (1776–1837) stands out. Some of his finest works include *Flatford Mill,* a scene from his native East Anglia, and in a different mood, the stormy sketch for *Hadleigh Castle.*

The Tate owns some of the finest works of the Pre-Raphaelite period of the mid-19th century. One of the best of the English artists of the 20th century, Sir Stanley Spencer (1891–1959) is best represented by his two versions of *Resurrection* and three remarkable self-portraits.

The Tate has many major paintings from both the 19th and 20th centuries, including Wyndham Lewis's portraits of Edith Sitwell and of Ezra Pound, and Paul Nash's *Voyages of the Moon.*

In the modern collections, the Tate contains Matisse's *L'Escargot* and *The Inattentive Reader,* along with works by Dali, Chagall, Modigliani, Munch, Ben Nicholson (large collection of his works), and Dubuffet. The different periods of Picasso bloom in *Woman in a Chemise* (1905), *Three Dancers* (1925), *Nude Woman in a Red Armchair* (1932), *Goat's Skull, Bottle, and Candle* (1952), and *Reclining Nude* (1968).

Truly remarkable is the room devoted to several enormous, somber, but rich abstract canvases by Mark Rothko, the group of paintings by Giacometti and sculptures by Giacometti (1901–1966), and the paintings of three of England's best-known modern artists: Francis Bacon (*Three Studies for Figures at the Base of a Crucifixion*), Graham Sutherland (his portrait of W. Somerset Maugham), and David Hockney.

Rodin's *The Kiss,* a world-famous piece of sculpture, is on show. Some of the bronzes of American-born Sir Jacob Epstein are displayed. In addition, there are sculptures by Henry Moore and Barbara Hepworth.

Downstairs is the internationally renowned restaurant (see Chapter IV), with murals by Rex Whistler, as well as a coffeeshop.

Open 10am to 5:50pm Mon. to Sat., 2 to 5:50pm Sun. Tube: Pimlico. Bus 88 or 77A.

(7) National Gallery

On the north side of Trafalgar Square, W.C.2, in an impressive neoclassic building, the National Gallery (tel. 071/839-3321) houses one of the most comprehensive collections of European paintings, representing all the major schools from the 13th to the early 20th century. The largest part of the collection is devoted to the Italians, including the Sienese, Venetian, and Florentine masters.

Of the early Gothic works, the *Wilton Diptych* (French school, late 14th century) is the rarest treasure. It depicts Richard II being introduced to the Madonna and Child by such good contacts as John the Baptist and the Saxon king, Edward the Confessor.

A Florentine gem, the Virgin and grape-eating Bambino, by Masaccio (one of the founders of Renaissance painting) is displayed, as are notable works by Piero della Francesca, particularly his linear *The Baptism.*

Matter and spirit meet in the haunting nether world of the *Virgin of the Rocks,* by Leonardo da Vinci. Also shown are two other giants of the Renaissance—Michelangelo (represented by an unfinished painting, *The Entombment*), and Raphael (*The Ansidei Madonna,* among others).

A number of satellite rooms are filled with works by major Italian masters of the 15th century—artists such as Andrea Mantegna of Padua (*Agony in the Garden*); his brother-in-law, Giovanni Bellini (his portrait of the Venetian doge, Leonardo Loredano, provided a change of pace from his many interpretations of madonnas); and finally, Botticelli, represented by *Mars and Venus, Adoration of the Magi,* and *Portrait of a Young Man.*

Among the Venetian masters of the 16th century, to whom color was paramount, the most notable works include a rare *Adoration of the Kings* by Giorgione; *Bacchus and Ariadne* by Titian; *The Origin of the Milky Way* by Tintoretto (a lush galaxy, with milk streaming from Juno's breasts); and *The Family of Darius Before Alexander* by Veronese (one of the best paintings at the National).

The painters of northern Europe are well represented. For example, there is Jan van Eyck's portrait of G. Arnolfini and his bride, plus Pieter Brueghel the Elder's Bosch-influenced *Adoration*, with its unkingly kings and ghoul-like onlookers. The 17th-century pauper, Vermeer, is rich on canvas in a *Young Woman at a Virginal*, a favorite theme of his. Fellow Delftite Pieter de Hooch comes on sublimely in a *Patio in a House in Delft*.

One of the drawing cards of the National is its collection of Rembrandts. Rembrandt, son of a miller, became the greatest painter in the Netherlands in the 17th century. His *Self-Portrait at the Age of 34* shows him at the pinnacle of his life; his *Self-Portrait at the Age of 63* is deeply moving and revealing. For another Rembrandt study in old age, see his *Portrait of Margaretha Trip*. *The Woman Taken in Adultery* shows the artist's human sympathy. Rembrandt's portrait of his mistress, Hendrickje Stoffels, is also displayed. The picture is signed and dates from 1659.

Part of the prolific output of Peter Paul Rubens is to be seen, notably his *Peace and War*, the *Rape of the Sabine Women*, and *Samson and Delilah*.

Five of the greatest of the homegrown artists—Constable, Turner, Reynolds, Gainsborough, and Hogarth—have masterpieces here. Constable's *Cornfield* is another scene of East Anglia, along with *Haywain*, a harmony of light and atmosphere. Completely different from Constable is the work of Turner, including his dreamy *Fighting Téméraire* and *Rain, Steam, and Speed*. You can see several works by Sir Joshua Reynolds, along with a Gainsborough masterpiece, *The Morning Walk*, an idealistic blending of portraiture with landscape. Finally, in a completely different brush stroke, Hogarth's *Marriage à la Mode* caricatures an 18th century marriage of convenience between a bankrupt young nobleman and a rich young woman of the bourgeoisie.

The three giants of Spanish painting are represented by Velázquez's portrait of sunken-faced Philip IV, El Greco's *Christ Driving the Traders from the Temple*, and Goya's portrait of the duke of Wellington (once stolen) and his mantilla-wearing *Doña Isabel de Porcel*.

Other rooms are devoted to early 19th-century French painters such as Delacroix and Ingres; late 19th-century French impressionists such as Manet, Monet, Renoir, and Degas; and post-impressionists such as Cézanne, Seurat, and Van Gogh.

The National Gallery is open from 10am to 6pm Mon. to Sat., from 2 to 6pm Sun.; closed January 1, Good Friday, the 3-day Christmas holiday, and May 1. Admission is free. Tube: Charing Cross or Leicester Square.

(8) Kensington Palace

Home of the State Apartments, some of which were used by Queen Victoria, this is another major attraction at the western end of Kensington Gardens. The palace was acquired by asthma-suffering William III (William of Orange) in 1689, and was remodeled by Sir Christopher Wren. George II, who died in 1760, was the last king to use it as a royal residence.

The most interesting chamber is Queen Victoria's bedroom. In this room, on the morning of June 20, 1837, she was aroused from her sleep with the news that she had ascended the throne, following the death of her uncle, William IV. Thus the woman who was to become the symbol of the British Empire and Empress of India began the longest reign in the history of England. In the anteroom are memorabilia from Victoria's childhood—a dollhouse and a collection of her toys.

A special attraction is the Court Dress Collection, which shows restored rooms from the 19th century, including Queen Victoria's birthroom and a series of room settings with the appropriate court dress of the day, from 1760 to 1950. However, a more modern dress captures the attention of most visitors—the wedding dress worn by the princess of Wales on July 29, 1981.

As you wander through the apartments, you can admire many fine paintings from the Royal Collection. The State Apartments are open from 9am to 5pm Mon. to Sat., from 1 to 5pm Sun. Adults pay admission of £3.50 ($5.80) and children £2.30 ($3.80). You enter from the Broad Walk, and you reach the building by taking the tube either to Queensway or Bayswater on the north side of the gardens, or High Street Kensington on the south side. You'll have to walk a bit from there, however. For more information, telephone 071/937-9561.

The palace gardens, originally the private park of royalty, are also open to the public for daily strolls around Round Pond, near the heart of Kensington Gardens. The gardens adjoin Hyde Park. Also in Kensington Gardens is the Albert Memorial, honoring Queen Victoria's consort. Facing Royal Albert Hall, the statue reflects the ostentation of the Victorian era.

(9) St. Paul's Cathedral

During World War II, newsreel footage reaching America showed the dome of St. Paul's Cathedral, St. Paul's Churchyard, E.C.4 (tel. 071/248-2705), lit by fires burning all around it. That it survived at all is miraculous, as it was hit badly twice. But St. Paul's is accustomed to calamity, having been burned down three times and destroyed once by invading Norsemen. It was in the Great Fire of 1666 that the old St. Paul's was razed, making way for a new Renaissance structure designed (after many mishaps and rejections) by Sir Christopher Wren.

The masterpiece of this great architect was erected between 1675 and 1710. Its classical dome dominates The City's square mile. Inside, the cathedral is laid out like a Latin cross, containing few art treasures (Grinling Gibbons's choir stalls are an exception) but many monuments, including one to the "Iron Duke" and a memorial chapel to American service personnel who lost their lives in World War II while stationed in the United Kingdom. Encircling the dome is the Whispering Gallery, where discretion in speech is advised. In the crypt lie not only Wren but the Duke of Wellington and Lord Nelson. A fascinating Diocesan Treasury was opened in 1981.

The cathedral is open daily from 8am to 6pm. The crypt and galleries, including the Whispering Gallery, are open only from 10am to 4:15pm Mon. to Fri., from 11am on Sat. Guided tours, lasting 1½ hours, and including the crypt and parts of St. Paul's not normally open to the public, take place at 11 and 11:30am and 2 and 2:30pm when the cathedral is open (except Sun.), costing £4 ($6.60) for adults, £1.80 ($2.95) for children.

St. Paul's is an Anglican cathedral with daily services held at 8am and 5pm. On Sunday, services are at 10:30 and 11:30am and 3:15pm. In addition, you can climb to the very top of the dome for a spectacular 360° view of all of London, costing £2 ($3.30) per person. Tube: St. Paul's.

(10) Victoria and Albert Museum

When Queen Victoria asked that this museum be named after herself and her consort, she could not have selected a more fitting memorial. The Victoria and Albert is one of the finest museums in the world, devoted to fine and applied art of many nations and periods, including Asia. In many respects, it's one of the most difficult for viewing, as many of the most important exhibits are so small they can easily be overlooked.

I have space only to suggest some of its finest art. The medieval holdings include many treasures, such as the Eltenberg Reliquary (Rhenish, second half of the 12th century). In the shape of a domed, copper-gilt church, it is enriched with champlevé enamel and set with walrus-ivory carvings of Christ and the Apostles. Other exhibits in this same salon include the Early English Gloucester Candlestick, the Byzantine Veroli Casket, with its ivory panels based on Greek plays, and the Syon Cope, made in the early 14th century, an example of the highly valued embroidery produced in England at that time. The Gothic tapestries, including the Devonshire ones depicting hunting scenes, are displayed in another gallery. An area devoted to Islamic art contains the Ardabil carpet from 16th-century Persia (320 knots per square inch).

Renaissance art in Italy includes such works as a Donatello marble relief, *The*

Ascension; a small terra-cotta statue of the Madonna and Child by Antonio Rossellino; a marble group, *Samson and a Philistine,* by Giovanni Bologna; and a wax model of a slave by Michelangelo. The highlight of 16th-century art from the continent is the marble group *Neptune with Triton,* by Bernini.

The cartoons by Raphael, which are owned by the Queen, can be seen here. These cartoons—conceived as designs for tapestries for the Sistine Chapel—include scenes such as *The Sacrifice of Lystra* and *Paul Preaching at Athens.*

A most unusual, huge, and impressive exhibit is the Cast Courts, with life-size plaster models of ancient and medieval statuary and architecture, made from molds formed over the originals.

Of the rooms devoted to English furniture and decorative art during the period from the 16th to the mid-18th century, the most outstanding exhibit is the Bed of Ware, big enough for eight. In the galleries of portrait miniatures, two of the rarest ones are by Hans Holbein the Younger (one of Anne of Cleves, another of a Mrs. Pemberton). In the painting galleries are many works by Constable. His *Flatford Mill* represents a well-known scene from his native East Anglia. All paintings, prints, drawings, and photographs are in the new Henry Cole wing.

The museum is on Cromwell Road, S.W.7 (tel. 071/938-8500). Open Mon. to Sat. from 10am to 5:50pm, on Sun. from 2:30 to 5:50pm. No admission is charged, but they suggest a donation of £2 ($3.30) for adults, 50p (85¢) for children under 12. Tube: South Kensington.

A restaurant serving wholesome traditional English snacks and meals is open from 10am to 5pm Mon. to Sat., from 2:30 to 5pm on Sun. Two museum shops, with gifts, posters, cards, and books, are open from 10am to 5:30pm Mon. to Sat. and 2:30 to 5:30pm on Sun.

THE BEST OF THE REST

Now, for those with more time to get acquainted with London, we'll continue our exploration of this sight-filled city.

Royal London

From Trafalgar Square, you can stroll down the wide, tree-flanked avenue known as the Mall. It leads to **Buckingham Palace,** the heart of Royal London (English kings and queens have lived here since the days of Victoria). Three parks—St. James's, Green, and Buckingham Palace Gardens (private)—converge at the center of this area, where you'll find a memorial honoring Victoria.

You can tell if Her Majesty is at home by whether the royal standard is flown at the masthead. You can't, of course, drop in for a visit (and getting an official invite isn't easy, even for ambassadors), but you can do what thousands of others do . . . peep through the railing into the front yard.

The palace was built as a red-brick country house for the notoriously rakish duke of Buckingham. In 1762 it was bought by King George III, who—if nothing else—was prolific. He needed room for his 15 children. From then on the building was expanded, remodeled, faced with Portland stone, and twice bombed (during the Blitz). Today it stands 360 feet long in a 40-acre garden and contains 600 rooms.

London's most popular daily pageant, particularly with North American tourists, is the changing of the Queen's Guard in the forecourt of Buckingham Palace. This ceremony is perhaps the finest example of military pageantry extant.

The troops are from the Guards Division, Britain's elite equivalent of the United States Marines. They wear their traditional black bearskins and scarlet tunics, the different regiments distinguished by the plumes worn on the headdress: white for the Grenadiers, red for the Coldstreams, blue for the Irish, green and white for the Welsh. The Scots wear no plumes. The drill movements are immensely intricate and performed with a robot precision that makes the ceremony seem like a kind of martial ballet, set to rousing music.

But don't get the idea that these are toy soldiers. The Guards date back to 1642, and since then they have fought on every battlefield Britain ever disputed, an endless gory chain stretching from Scotland in 1650 to Korea three centuries later. And those scarlet tunics were originally designed to hide bloodstains on their wearers. Tube: St. James's Park or Green Park.

You can't visit the palace, of course, without an invitation, but you can inspect **The Queen's Gallery,** S.W.1 (entrance on Buckingham Palace Road; tel. 071/930-4832). As is known, all the royal families of Europe have art collections— some including acquisitions from centuries ago. The English sovereign has one of the finest, and has consented to share it with the public. I can't predict what exhibition you're likely to see, as they are changed yearly at the gallery. You may find a selection of incomparable works by old masters, and sometimes furniture and objets d'art. The queen's collection contains an unsurpassed range of royal portraits, from the well-known profile of Henry V, through the late Plantagenets, the companion portraits of Elizabeth I as a girl and her brother, Edward VI, and four fine Georgian pictures by Zoffany, to recent works including two portraits of Queen Alexandria from Sandringham and paintings of Queen Elizabeth II and other members of the royal family. The picture gallery may be visited from 10:30am to 5pm Tues. to Sat. and bank holidays, and from 2 to 5pm Sun.; closed Mon., except bank holidays. Admission is £1.50 ($2.50) for adults, £1 ($1.65) for children. Tube: Green Park or St. James's.

You can get a close look at Queen Elizabeth's coronation carriage at the **Royal Mews,** on Buckingham Palace Road, S.W.1 (tel. 071/930-4832). Her Majesty's State Coach, built in 1761 to the designs of Sir William Chambers, contains emblematic and other paintings on the panels. Its doors were executed by Cipriani. It was formerly used by sovereigns when they traveled to open Parliament in person and on other state occasions. Queen Elizabeth used it upon her coronation in 1953 and in 1977 for her Silver Jubilee Procession. It was traditionally drawn by eight gray horses. Many other official carriages are housed here as well, including the new Australian coach, Glass coach, and Scottish and Irish state coaches. The queen's carriage horses are also housed here. The mews is open to the public 2 to 4pm Wed. and Thurs. and charges an admission of £1 ($1.65) for adults, 50p (85¢) for children. It is closed during Ascot week in June and at some other times as announced. Tube: Green Park or St. James's.

Official London

Whitehall, S.W.1, the seat of the British government, grew up on the grounds of Whitehall Palace and was turned into a royal residence by Henry VIII, who snatched it from its former occupant, Cardinal Wolsey. Beginning at Trafalgar Square, Whitehall extends southward to Parliament Square (Houses of Parliament and Westminster Abbey, described earlier). Along it you'll find the Home Office, the Old Admiralty Building, and the Ministry of Defense.

Visitors today can see the Cabinet War Rooms, the bomb-proof bunker suite of rooms large and small, just as they were left by Winston Churchill and the British government at the end of World War II. During the war, many of the objects were removed only for dusting, and the Imperial War Museum studied photographs to replace everything exactly as it had been, including notepads, files, and typewriters —right down to pencils, pins, and clips. You can see the Map Room with its huge wall maps, the Atlantic map a mass of pinholes. Each hole represents at least one convoy. Next door is Churchill's bedroom-cum-office, reinforced with stout wood beams. It has a very basic bed and a desk with two BBC microphones on it for his broadcasts of those famous speeches that stirred the nation.

The entrance to the Cabinet War Rooms is by Clive Steps at the end of King Charles Street, S.W.1, off Whitehall near Big Ben (take the tube to Westminster). It is open daily from 10am to 6pm (last admission at 5:25pm); closed on New Year's Day, Christmas holidays, and on short notice on state occasions. Visitors to the Cabinet War Rooms receive a cassette-recorded guided tour. Charges are £3.50 ($5.80) for adults and £1.75 ($2.90) for children. For more information, telephone 071/930-6961.

At the **Cenotaph** (honoring the dead in two world wars), turn down unpretentious Downing Street to the modest little townhouse at **No. 10,** flanked by two bobbies. Walpole was the first prime minister to live here: Churchill the most famous.

Nearby is the **Horse Guards Building,** Whitehall, S.W.1 (tel. 071/930-4466, ext. 2396), which is now the headquarters, Household Division and London District. There has been a guard change here since 1649 when the site was the entrance to the old Palace of Whitehall. You can watch the Queen's Lifeguards in the mounted guard change ceremony at 11am (at 10am on Sun.) when 12 mounted troopers arrive from Knightsbridge Barracks. Photographers can get a good view of the London traffic halted for this troop to cross out of Hyde Park, past the Wellington Arch. They proceed down Constitution Hill and the Mall. If you are at Hyde Park Corner at 10:30am, you can follow them. You can also see the smaller change of the guard hourly when mounted troopers are changed. At 4pm you can watch the evening inspection when 10 unmounted troopers and 2 mounted troopers assemble in the courtyard. Tube: Westminster.

Across the street is Inigo Jones's **Banqueting House,** Palace of Whitehall, S.W.1 (tel. 071/930-4179), site of the execution of Charles I. William and Mary accepted the crown of England here, but they preferred to live at Kensington Palace. The Banqueting House was part of Whitehall Palace, which burned to the ground in 1698. The ceremonial hall escaped razing. Its most notable feature today is an allegorical ceiling painted by Peter Paul Rubens. The Banqueting House may be visited from 10am to 5pm Tues. to Sat. and from 2 to 5pm Sun. The admission fee is £1.60 ($2.65) for adults and 80p ($1.30) for children. Tube: Westminster.

Finally, you may want to stroll to Parliament Square for a view of **Big Ben,** the world's most famous timepiece, the very symbol of the heart and soul of England. Big Ben is actually the name of the deepest and loudest bell, although it's also the common name for the clock tower on the Houses of Parliament. Opposite, in the gardens of Parliament Square, stands the statue of Churchill by Oscar Nemon. Tube: Westminster.

Financial London

The **Stock Exchange,** in terms of the number of stocks and shares listed, is the largest in the world. From the Visitors' Gallery, you can watch the dealers on the trading floor below you, and guides are in attendance to give talks and to explain the functions and operations of the stock market. After each talk, there is a film in the adjoining cinema, which gives an insight into the financial world. The Visitors' Gallery entrance is on Old Broad Street, E.C.2. For the film, reservations are necessary; contact the publicity department (tel. 071/588-2355). Tube: Bank.

The historic headquarters of the worldwide insurers, **Lloyd's of London,** 1 Lime St., E.C.3 (tel. 071/623-7100), opened its doors to visitors in 1986, and already thousands of people have come to see the workings of the world's biggest insurance market. A visitors' exhibition on the fifth floor is entered via the portico of an original 17th-century coffeehouse, similar to the establishment owned by Edward Lloyd. Guides explain how risks are placed and about the worldwide intelligence service operated for Lloyd's. A gallery lets you look down into an atrium to the underwriting room below in which is centered the rostrum bearing the famous Lutine Bell, sounded when a ship disaster occurred at sea. The Visitors' Gallery is open 10am to 2:30pm Mon. to Fri. Admission is free. There is a coffeehouse where light refreshments are served, as well as a gift shop. Tube: Bank, Monument, or Aldgate.

Legal London

The smallest borough in London, bustling **Holborn** (pronounced Hoburn) is often referred to as Legal London, the home of the city's barristers, solicitors, and law clerks. It also embraces the university district of Bloomsbury. Holburn, which houses the ancient Inns of Court—Gray's Inn, Lincoln's Inn, Middle Temple, and

Inner Temple—was severely damaged in World War II bombing raids. The razed buildings were replaced with modern offices housing insurance brokers, realtors, whatever. But the borough still retains quadrangled pockets of its former days.

Going from the Victoria Embankment, Middle Temple Lane leads between Middle and Inner Temple Gardens in the area known as **The Temple,** E.C.4 (tel. 071/353-4355; tube: Temple), named after the medieval order of the Knights Templar (originally formed by the Crusaders in Jerusalem in the 12th century). It was in Temple Gardens that Henry VI's barons are supposed to have picked the blooms of red and white roses and started the Wars of the Roses in 1430. Today only members of the Temples and their guests are allowed to enter the Inner Temple Gardens. The Middle Temple contains a Tudor hall completed in 1570 with a double hammerbeam roof. It is believed that Shakespeare's troupe played *Twelfth Night* here in 1602. A table on view is said to have come from timber from Sir Francis Drake's *The Golden Hind.* The hall may be visited from 10am to noon and 3 to 4pm Mon. to Fri.

Within the precincts of the Inner Temple, E.C.4 (tube: Temple), is the **Temple Church,** one of three Norman "round churches" left in England. First completed in the 12th century, it has been restored. Look for the knightly effigies and the Norman door any time from 10am to 4pm Mon. to Fri. Take note of the circle of grotesque portrait heads, including a goat in a mortar board. Continue north on Middle Temple Lane to about where the Strand becomes Fleet Street going east. Look for the memorial pillar called Temple Bar, marking the boundary of The City.

North across the Strand stand the **Royal Courts of Justice,** W.C.2 (tel. 071/405-7641, ext. 3439; tube: Temple), which are open from 10am to 4pm Mon. to Fri. You can go through its main doorway on the Strand and on through the building, which was completed in 1882 but designed in the style of the 13th century. This is the home of such courts as admiralty, divorce, probate, chancery, appeals, and Queen's Bench. Leave the Royal Courts building by the rear door and you'll be on Carey Street, not far from New Square. From there, you're in the near vicinity of **Lincoln's Inn,** W.C.2 (tube: Holborn), another of the famous Inns of Court, and **Lincoln's Inn Fields.** Lincoln's Inn, founded in the 14th century, evokes colleges at Cambridge or Oxford. This ancient inn forms an important link in the architectural maze of London. Its chapel and gardens are open to the public between noon and 2:30pm, and they're well worth seeing. The chapel was rebuilt around 1620 by Inigo Jones. Cromwell lived here at one time. To the west of the inn lies the late 17th-century square, one of the few such London areas still complete, called Lincoln's Inn Fields. Near the south of the fields on Kingsway is the **Old Curiosity Shop,** immortalized by Charles Dickens.

If you proceed north on Chancery Lane to High Holborn, W.C.1, heading toward **Gray's Inn,** the fourth of the ancient Inns of Court still in operation, take a look at the old **Staple Inn,** near the Chancery Lane tube stop. This half-timbered edifice and eight other former Inns of Chancery are no longer in use in the legal world. Now lined with shops, it was built and rebuilt many times, originally having come into existence between 1545 and 1589. Dr. Johnson moved here in 1759, the year *Rasselas* was published.

Gray's Inn, on Gray's Inn Road north of High Holborn, is entered from Theobald's Road. As you enter, you'll see a late-Georgian terrace lined with buildings that, like many of the other houses in the inns, are combined residences and offices. Gray's has been restored after being heavily damaged by World War II bombings. Sir Francis Bacon, scientist and philosopher (1561–1626), was the most eminent tenant who resided here in other days. The inn contains a rebuilt Tudor Hall, but its greatest attraction is the plane tree–shaded lawn and handsome gardens, considered the best in the inns. The 17th-century atmosphere exists today only in the square.

When Horace Rumpole, known to readers and TV audiences as *Rumpole of the Bailey,* leaves his chambers in one of the Temple Inns of Court to go to court, he usually heads not for the Royal Courts of Justice mentioned above, which are involved with civil cases, but to the **Central Criminal Court,** better known as **Old**

Bailey, on the corner of Old Bailey and Newgate Street, E.C.4. To reach it, go east on Fleet Street, which along the way becomes Ludgate Hill. Cross Ludgate Circus and turn left to the Old Bailey, a domed structure with the figure of Justice standing atop it. The courthouse replaced the infamous Newgate Prison, once the scene of public hangings and other forms of public "entertainment." The public is permitted to enter from 10:20am to 1pm and 1:50 to 4pm Mon. to Fri. Entry is strictly on a first-arrival basis. Guests queue up outside (where, incidentally, the final public execution took place in the 1860s). Courts 1 to 4, 17, and 18 are entered from Newgate Street, and the balance from Old Bailey (the street). No one under 14 is admitted, and teenagers from 14 to 17 must be accompanied by a responsible adult. No cameras or tape recorders are allowed. Tube: Temple, Chancery Lane, or St. Paul's.

Still further afield, the present **guildhall,** King Street in Cheapside, The City, E.C.2 (tel. 071/606-3030), was built in 1411. But the Civic Hall of the Corporation of London has had a rough time, notably in the Great Fire of 1666 and the 1940 Blitz. The most famous tenants of the rebuilt guildhall are *Gog* and *Magog,* two giants standing over 9 feet high. The original effigies, burned in the London fire, were rebuilt only to be destroyed again in 1940. The present giants are third generation. Restoration has returned the Gothic grandeur to the hall, which is replete with a medieval porch entranceway; monuments to Wellington, Churchill, and Nelson; stained glass commemorating lord mayors and mayors; the standards of length; and shields honoring fishmongers, haberdashers, merchant tailors, ironmongers, and skinners—some of the major Livery Companies. The guildhall may be visited from 2 to 4pm Mon. to Sat. Admission is free. Tube: Bank.

Leading Museums

Sir John Soane's Museum, 13 Lincoln's Inn Fields, W.C.2 (tel. 071/405-2107), is the former home of an architect who lived from 1753 to 1837. Sir John, who rebuilt the Bank of England (not the present structure, however), was a "space-man" in a different era. With his multilevels, fool-the-eye mirrors, flying arches, and domes, Soane was a master of perspective, a genius of interior space (his picture gallery, for example, is filled with three times the number of paintings a room of similar dimensions would be likely to hold). That he could do all this—and still not prove a demon to claustrophobia victims—was proof of his remarkable talent. Even if you don't like Soane (he was reportedly a cranky fellow), you may still want to visit this museum to see William Hogarth's satirical series, *The Rake's Progress,* containing his much reproduced *Orgy,* and the satire on politics in the mid-18th century, *The Election.* Soane also filled his house with paintings (Watteau's *Les Noces,* Canaletto's large *Venetian Scene*) and classical sculpture. Finally, be sure to see the sarcophagus of Pharaoh Seti I found in a burial chamber in Egypt's Valley of the Kings. The museum is open from 10am to 5pm Tues. to Sat. A guided tour is given at 2:30pm on Sat. Admission is free. Tube: Chancery Lane or Holborn.

Just across the Thames on Lambeth Road, S.E.1 is the **Imperial War Museum** (tel. 071/735-8922). Built around 1815, this large domed building, the former Bethlehem Royal Hospital for the Insane, or Bedlam, houses the museum's collections relating to the two world wars and other military operations involving the British and the Commonwealth since 1914.

The museum, reopened by the Queen, offers four floors of exhibitions, including the Large Exhibits Gallery, a vast area showing historical displays, two floors of art galleries, and a dramatic re-creation of London at war during the Blitz. You can see a Battle of Britain Spitfire, the rifle carried by Lawrence of Arabia, Hitler's political testament, as well as models, decorations, uniforms, photographs, and paintings.

The museum is open daily from 10am to 6pm. Admission is £2.50 ($4.15) for adults, £1.25 ($2.05) for children. Tube: Lambeth North or Elephant & Castle.

National Army Museum, Royal Hospital Road, S.W.3 (tel. 071/730-0717), in Chelsea, traces the history of the British land forces from 1485 to 1982, as well as the Indian Army, and colonial land forces. The museum backers agreed to begin the collection at the year 1485, because that was the date of the formation of the Yeomen of the Guard. The saga of the forces of the East India Company is also traced, beginning in 1602 and going up to Indian independence in 1947. The gory and the glory —it's all here, everything from Florence Nightingale's lamp to the French Eagle captured in a cavalry charge at Waterloo, even the staff cloak wrapped around the dying Wolfe at Québec. Naturally, there are the "cases of the heroes," mementos of such outstanding men as the dukes of Marlborough and Wellington. But the field soldier isn't neglected either. The Flanders to the Falklands gallery tells the soldier's story from the 1914–1918 war through World War II and on to the conflict in the Falklands in 1982. The admission-free museum is open from 10am to 5:30pm Mon. to Sat., from 2 to 5:30pm Sun. It is closed on New Year's Day, Good Friday, from December 24 to 26, and on the May bank holiday. Tube: Sloane Square.

Apsley House, The Wellington Museum, 149 Piccadilly, Hyde Park Corner, W.1 (tel. 071/499-5676), takes us into the former townhouse of the Iron Duke, the British general (1769–1852) who defeated Napoleon at the Battle of Waterloo. Designed by Robert Adam and built in the late 18th century, Wellington's London residence was opened as a public museum in 1952. Once Wellington had to retreat behind the walls of Apsley House—even securing it in fear of a possible attack from citizens outraged by his autocratic opposition as prime minister to reform. In the vestibule you'll find a colossal statue in marble of Napoleon by Canova—ironic, to say the least. Completely idealized, it was presented to the duke by King George IV. In addition to the famous *Waterseller of Seville* by Velázquez, the Wellington collection includes Correggio's *Agony in the Garden,* Jan Steen's *The Egg Dance,* and Pieter de Hooch's *A Musical Party.* You can see the gallery where Wellington used to invite his officers for the annual Waterloo banquet. The house also contains a large porcelain and china collection, including a magnificent Sèvres porcelain Egyptian service, made originally for Empress Josephine and given by Louis XVIII to Wellington. In addition, superb English silver and the extraordinary Portuguese centerpiece, a present from a grateful Portugal to its liberator, are exhibited. The house is open from 11am to 5pm Tues. to Sun.; closed Mon., May Day, Christmas holidays, and New Year's Day. Admission is £2 ($3.30) for adults, £1 ($1.65) for children. Tube: Hyde Park Corner.

In London's Barbican district near St. Paul's Cathedral, the **Museum of London** at 150 London Wall, E.C.2 (tel. 071/600-3699), allows visitors to trace the history of London from prehistoric times to the present—through relics, costumes, household effects, maps, and models. Exhibits are arranged so that visitors can begin and end their chronological stroll through 250,000 years at the main entrance to the museum. You can see the death mask of Oliver Cromwell, but the pièce de résistance is the Lord Mayor's coach, built in 1757 and weighing in at three tons. Still used each November in the Lord Mayor's Procession, this gilt-and-red, horse-drawn vehicle is like a fairy-tale coach. Visitors can also see the Great Fire of London in living color and sound; reconstructed Roman dining rooms with the kitchen and utensils; cell doors from Newgate Prison made famous by Charles Dickens; and most amazing of all, a shop counter with pre–World War II prices on the items.

The museum, opened in 1976, overlooks London's Roman and medieval walls and, in all, has something from every era before and after—including little Victorian shops and re-creations of what life was like during the Iron Age in what is now the London area. Anglo-Saxons, Vikings, Normans—they're all there, arranged on two floors around a central courtyard. With quick labels for museum sprinters, more extensive ones for those who want to study, and still deeper details for scholars, this museum, built at a cost of some $18 million, is an enriching experience.

At least an hour should be allowed for a full (but still quick) visit to the museum. Free lectures on London's past are given during lunch hours. These aren't given daily, but it's worth inquiring at the entrance hall. You can reach the museum by going up to the elevated pedestrian precinct at the corner of London Wall and Aldersgate, 5 minutes from St. Paul's. Admission free, the museum is open from 10am to 6pm Tues. to Sat., from 2 to 6pm Sun.; closed Mon. A restaurant overlooks a garden. Tube: St. Paul's, Barbican, or Moorgate.

London Transport Museum, Covent Gardens, W.C.2 (tel. 071/379-6344), is in a splendidly restored Victorian building that formerly housed the flower market. Horse buses, motorbuses, trams, trolley buses, railway vehicles, models, maps, posters, photographs, and audio-visual displays illustrate the fascinating story of the evolution of London's transport systems and how this has affected the growth of London. There are also a number of unique working displays. You can put yourself in the driving seat of a tube train, a tram, and a bus, and also operate full-size signaling equipment. The exhibits include a reconstruction of George Shillibeer's omnibus of 1829, a steam locomotive that ran on the world's first underground railway, and a coach from the first deep-level electric railway. The museum is open every day of the year except December 24, 25, and 26, from 10am to 6pm (last admission at 5:15pm). Admission charges are £2.60 ($4.30) for adults, £1.20 ($2) for children. A family ticket for two adults and two children is £6 ($9.90). The museum sells a variety of souvenirs of London Transport, (see shopping section under "Posters"). Tube: Covent Garden, Leicester Square, or Charing Cross.

National Postal Museum, King Edward Building, King Edward Street, E.C.1 (tel. 071/239-5420), attracts philatelists from all over the world—and even vaguely kindred spirits. Actually part of the post office, it features permanent exhibitions of the stamps of Great Britain and the world and special displays of stamps and postal history, changing every few months, according to certain themes. The museum is open from 10am to 4:30pm Mon. to Thurs. and to 4pm on Fri. Admission is free. Tube: St. Paul's or Barbican.

Royal Air Force Museum, Grahame Park Way, Hendon, N.W.9 (tel. 081/205-2266). The Royal Air Force Museum, Britains national museum of aviation, contains one of the world's finest collections of historic aircraft, telling the story of flight through the display of more than 60 aircraft. The museum stands on 15 acres of the former airfield at Hendon in North London, and its main aircraft hall occupies two large hangars dating from World War I. The complex also includes the Bomber Command Hall, which houses a collection of famous bomber aircraft, including the Lancaster, Wellington, B17 Flying Fortress, Mosquito, and Vulcan.

In 1990, to celebrate the 50th anniversary of the Battle of Britain, the museum launched a major exhibition, the Battle of Britain Experience. Aircraft on display include the Spitfire, Hurricane, Gladiator, Blenheim, and Messerschmitt BF109. Features include cassette tape tour guides and a flight simulator that allows visitors to experience flying an RAF Tornado. It is open daily from 10am to 6pm (closed December 24–26, and January 1). Admission to the entire complex is £3.60 ($5.95) for adults, £1.80 ($2.95) for children. The nearest British Rail station is Mill Hill Broadway, and access by road is via the A41, the A1, and the M2 junction 4. Tube: Colindale.

The **Science Museum,** Exhibition Rd., S.W.7 (tel. 071/938-8000), on the corner of Imperial Road, traces the development of both science and industry and their influences in everyday life. The collections are among the largest, most comprehensive, and most significant anywhere. On display is Stephenson's original *Rocket,* the tiny locomotive that won a race against all competitors in the Rainhill Trials and became the world's prototype railroad engine. You can also see Whittle's original jet engine and the Gloster aircraft, the first jet-powered British plane. A cavalcade of antique cars from the Stanley steam car to a yellow Rolls-Royce can be seen, side by side with carriages and vintage bicycles and motorcycles. To aid the visitor's understanding of many scientific and technological principles, working models and video displays are here, including a hands-on gallery called Launch Pad where you can take part in experiments and demonstrations. The recently designed East Hall welcomes visitors with an audio-visual slide show and the soothing sound of a huge Lancashire Hill engine of 1903, running on steam. A shopping concourse provides the opportunity of taking home a souvenir. The museum is open from 10am to 6pm Mon. to Sat., from 11am to 6pm Sun. Admission is £2.50 ($4.15) for adults, £1 ($1.65) for children 5 to 15. Tube: South Kensington. Bus 14.

You can step back into the days of Queen Victoria when you visit the **Linley Sambourne House,** 18 Stafford Terrace, W.8 (tel. 071/994-1019), which has remained unchanged for more than a century. The house, part of a terrace built between 1868 and 1874, is a five-story, Suffolk brick structure to which Linley

Sambourne brought his bride. Sambourne was a draftsman who later became a cartoonist for *Punch*. The Sambourne family owned and occupied the house until 1980, when it was purchased by the Greater London Council and leased to the Victorian Society. From the moment you step into the entrance hall, you see a mixture of styles and clutter that typified Victorian decor, with a plush portière, a fireplace valance, stained glass in the backdoor depicting an orange tree in a blue-and-white bowl, and a large set of antlers vying for attention. The drawing room alone contains an incredible number of items. Admission to the house, which is open March 1 to October 31 from 10am to 4pm Wed. and from 2 to 5pm Sun., is £2 ($3.30). Tube: High Street Kensington.

Woburn House, Tavistock Square, W.C.1, near Euston Station is London's main Jewish center. In these precincts you'll also come upon the hard-to-find **Jewish Museum** (tel. 071/388-4525), tucked away on a lovely square. Walk along Euston Road, and turn right onto Upper Woburn Place. When you reach Tavistock Square, turn right again, and there's the entrance. After entering, you're invited to sign a guest book, then you're guided up to the museum, a large salon filled with antiques relating to the history of the Jews. You'll come across many artifacts used in Jewish rituals and other exhibits of interest to those concerned with Anglo-Judaica. It is open from 10am to 4pm Sun. and Tues. to Thurs. as well as Fri. in summer. In winter, Fri. hours are from 10am to 12:45pm. It is closed Mon., Sat., public holidays, and Jewish holidays. No admission is charged. Tube: Euston.

London Design Museum, Butler's Wharf, E.1 (tel. 071/403-6933), is the first museum in the world devoted to industrial design. A three-story museum, the building also is home to a lecture theater, restaurant, bar, and library. Designs show the evolution of various items, such as the telephone, ranging from one that might have been familiar to Alexander Graham Bell to a black Bakelite phone of the '30s and '40s. The museum constantly stages changing exhibitions. Computers allow you to access biographies of famous designers, such as Finnish designer Alvar Aalto. As you study the exhibits on each floor, you can enjoy a river view from the windows, including Tower Bridge and the Tower of London. The museum is open from 11:30am to 6:30pm Tues. to Sun. Admission is £2 ($3.30). To reach the museum, you can take the Design Museum boat, leaving Tower Wharf (adjacent to the Tower of London), heading for Butler's Wharf. The ride takes only three minutes.

Other Galleries

National Portrait Gallery, St. Martin's Place, W.C.2 (tel. 071/306-0055, entrance around the corner from the National Gallery on Trafalgar Square), gives you a chance to outstare the stiff-necked greats and not-so-greats of English history. In a gallery of remarkable and unremarkable portraits, a few paintings tower over the rest, including Sir Joshua Reynolds's first portrait of Samuel Johnson ("a man of most dreadful appearance"). Among the best are Nicholas Hilliard's miniature of a handsome Sir Walter Raleigh and a full-length Elizabeth I (painted to commemorate her visit to Sir Henry Lee at Ditchley in 1592), along with the Holbein cartoon of Henry VIII (sketched for a family portrait that hung, before it was burned, in the Privy Chamber in Whitehall Palace). You'll also see a portrait of William Shakespeare (with gold earring, no less) which is claimed to be the most "authentic contemporary likeness" of its subject of any work yet known. The John Hayls portrait of Samuel Pepys adorns one wall. Whistler could not only paint a portrait, but also be the subject of one, as shown here. One of the most unusual pictures in the gallery—a group of the three Brontë sisters (Charlotte, Emily, Anne)—was painted by their brother, Branwell. An idealized portrait of Lord Byron by Thomas Phillips is pleased with itself, and you can treat yourself to the likeness of the incomparable Aubrey Beardsley. For a finale, Princess Diana is on the Royal Landing. The gallery is open from 10am to 5pm Mon. to Fri., to 6pm on Sat., and from 2 to 6pm on Sun. Admission is free except for special exhibitions held at the gallery throughout the year. Tube: Charing Cross or Leicester Square.

Wallace Collection, Manchester Square, W.1 (tel. 071/935-0687), off Wigmore Street, has an outstanding collection of works of art of all kinds bequeathed to the nation by Lady Wallace in 1897 and still displayed in the house of its founders. There are important pictures by artists of all European schools, including Titian, Rubens, Van Dyck, Rembrandt, Hals, Velázquez, Murillo, Reynolds, Gainsborough, and Delacroix. Representing the art of France in the 18th century are paintings by Watteau, Boucher, and Fragonard, and sculpture, furniture, goldsmiths' work, and Sèvres porcelain. Also found are valuable collections of majolica and European and Oriental arms and armor. Frans Hals's *Laughing Cavalier* is the most celebrated painting in the collection, but Pieter de Hooch's *A Boy Bringing Pomegranates* and Watteau's *The Music Party* are also well known. Other notable works include Canaletto's views of Venice (especially *Bacino di San Marco*), Rembrandt's *Titus*, and Gainsborough's *Mrs. Robinson (Perdita)*. Boucher's portrait of the marquise de Pompadour is also worthy. The Wallace Collection may be viewed daily from 10am to 5pm (from 2pm on Sun.); closed Christmas Eve, Christmas Day, Boxing Day, New Year's Day, Good Friday, and the first Monday in May. Admission free. Tube: Bond Street.

Courtauld Institute Galleries, Somerset House, the Strand, W.C.2 (tel. 071/580-1015), is the home of the art collection of the University of London—noted chiefly for its superb impressionist and post-impressionist works. It has eight works by Cézanne alone, including his *A Man with a Pipe.* Other notable art includes Seurat's *La Poudreuse,* Van Gogh's self-portrait (with ear bandaged), a nude by Modigliani, Gauguin's *Day-Dreaming,* Monet's *Fall at Argenteuil,* Toulouse-Lautrec's delicious *Tête-à-Tête,* and Manet's *Bar at the Folies Bergère.* The galleries also feature classical works, including *Virgin and Child* by Bernardino Luini, a Botticelli, a Giovanni Bellini, a Veronese, a triptych by the Master of Flémalle, works by Pieter Brueghel, Massys, Parmigianino, 32 oils by Rubens, oil sketches by Tiepolo, three landscapes by Kokoschka, and wonderful old master drawings (especially Michelangelo and Rembrandt). The artworks may be viewed from 10am to 5pm Mon. to Sat. and from 2 to 5pm Sun. Admission is £1.50 ($2.50) for adults, 50p (85¢) for children. Tube: Charing Cross.

Hayward Gallery, South Bank Centre, S.E.1 (tel. 071/928-3144), presents a changing program of major exhibitions organized by the South Bank Centre. The gallery forms part of the South Banks Arts Centre, which also includes the Royal Festival Hall, the Queen Elizabeth Hall, the Purcell Room, the National Film Theatre, and the National Theatre. Depending on the exhibitions, the admission charge is variable, usually from £2 ($3.30) to £4 ($6.60). When it has a presentation, the gallery is open daily from 10am to 6pm (on Tues. and Wed. until 8pm); 10am to 2pm Sun. Tube: Waterloo Station.

Royal Academy of Arts, Piccadilly, W.1 (tel. 071/439-7438; 071/439-4996 for recorded information), founded in 1768, is the oldest established society in Great Britain devoted solely to the fine arts. The academy is made up of a self-supporting, self-governing body of artists, who conduct art schools, hold exhibitions of the work of living artists, and organize loan exhibits of the arts of past and present. A summer exhibition, which has been held annually for an unbroken 222 years, presents contemporary paintings, drawings, engravings, sculpture, and architecture.

Occupying old Burlington House, which was built in Piccadilly in the 1600s, the academy has exhibitions that display pieces of art from many countries; admission charges vary. The Royal Academy Shop and a restaurant are open during exhibition hours, usually 10am to 6pm daily, and the framing workshop can be visited from 10am to 5pm Mon. to Fri. Burlington House is opposite Fortnum and Mason. Tube: Piccadilly Circus or Green Park. Buses 9, 14, 19, 22, and 38 stop outside.

Homes of Famous Writers

Samuel Johnson's House: The Queen Anne house of the famed lexicographer, essayist, poet, and fiction writer is at 17 Gough Square (tel. 071/353-3745). It'll cost you £1.50 ($2.50), and it's well worth it. Children pay £1 ($1.65). It was there that Dr. Johnson and his copyists compiled his famous dictionary. The 17th-century building has been painstakingly restored (surely "Dear Tetty," if not Boswell, would approve). Although Johnson lived at Staple Inn in Holborn and at a number of other houses, the Gough Square house is the only one of his residences remaining in London. He occupied it from 1748 to 1759. It is open May to September from 11am to 5:30pm Mon. through Sat., closing half an hour earlier off-season. From the tube station, walk up New Bridge Street, turning left onto Fleet. Gough Square is a tiny, hidden square, north of Fleet. Tube: Blackfriars.

Thomas Carlyle's House: 24 Cheyne Row, S.W.3 (tel. 071/352-7087), in Chelsea, along King's Road. For nearly half a century, from 1834 to 1881, the author of *Sartor Resartus, The French Revolution,* and other works, along with his letter-writing wife, took up abode in this modest 1708 terraced house, about three-quarters of a block from the Thames, near the Chelsea Embankment. Still standing and furnished essentially as it was in Carlyle's day, the house was described by his wife as being "of most antique physiognomy, quite to our humour; all wainscotted, carved and queer-looking, roomy, substantial, commodious, with closets to satisfy any Bluebeard." Now who could improve on that? The second floor contains the drawing room of Mrs. Carlyle. But the most interesting chamber is the not-so-soundproof "soundproof" study in the skylit attic. Filled with Carlyle memorabilia — his books, a letter from Disraeli, a writing chair, even his death mask — this is the cell where the author labored over his *Frederick the Great* manuscript. The Cheyne (pronounced chainey) Row house is open Easter Sat. to the end of October from 11am to 5pm; closed Mon. and Tues. Admission is £2 ($3.30) for adults and half price for accompanied children. The nearest tube, Sloane Square, is a long way off. Bus 11, 19, 22, or 39.

Charles Dickens's House: 48 Doughty St., W.C.1 (tel. 071/405-2127). In Bloomsbury stands the house of the great novelist accused in his time of "supping on the horrors" of Victorian England. Born in 1812 in what is now Portsmouth, Dickens is known to have lived here from 1837 to 1839. Unlike some of the London townhouses of famous men (Wellington, Soane), the Bloomsbury house is simple, the embodiment of middle-class restraint. The house contains an extensive library of Dickensiana, including manuscripts and letters. Dickens's drawing room on the first floor has been reconstructed, as have the still room, wash house, and wine cellar in the basement. The house is open from 10am to 5pm; closed Sun. and bank holidays. Admission is £1.50 ($2.50) for adults, 75p ($1.25) for children, and £3 ($4.95) for families.

Hampstead and Highgate

Hampstead Heath is hundreds of acres of wild and unfenced royal parkland about 4 miles north from the center of London, so elevated that on a clear day you can see St. Paul's Cathedral and even the hills of Kent south of the Thames. It is the scene of big one-day fairs in good weather, and it has for years drawn Londoners on such weekend pursuits as kite-flying, sunning, fishing in the ponds, swimming, and picnicking, and it is a favorite place for joggers. It was the common of Hampstead Manor in the time of King Charles II, a good ride out from London. Tube: Hampstead Heath.

Hampstead Village developed from a village to a fashionable spa town during the 18th century, and the changes gave picturesque names such as "Well Walk" to parts of the growing town. With the coming of the Underground in 1907, its attractions as a place to live, just 20 minutes by tube from Piccadilly Circus, became widely known, and writers, artists, architects, musicians, and scientists came to join earlier residents. Among the many eminent figures in the literary world who have lived in Hampstead are John Keats, D. H. Lawrence, Rabindranath Tagore, Percy Bysshe Shelley, and Robert Louis Stevenson, and some (such as Kingsley Amis, and John Le Carré) still do. History-rich pubs, toy shops, and chic boutiques, are seen along Flask Walk, a pedestrian mall. The original village, on the side of a hill, still has pleasing features such as the old lanes, alleys, steps, rises, courts, and groves to be strolled through.

John Keats's House: The darling of romantics, Keats lived for only 2 years at Wentworth Place, Keats Grove, Hampstead, N.W.3 (tel. 071/435-2062). But for the poet, that was something like two-fifths of his creative life, as he began writing poetry at the age of 18 and died in Rome of tuberculosis at the age of 25 (1821). In

Hampstead, Keats wrote some of his most celebrated *Odes*—in praise of a Grecian urn and to a nightingale. In the garden stands an ancient mulberry tree that the poet must have known. His Regency house is well preserved, and contains the manuscripts of his last sonnet ("Bright star, would I were steadfast as thou art"), a final letter to the mother of Fanny Brawne (his correspondence to his Hampstead neighbor, who nursed him while he was ill, forms part of his legend), and a portrait of him on his death bed in a house near the Spanish Steps in Rome. The admission-free house is open April to October from 2 to 6pm Mon. to Fri., from 10am to 1pm and 2 to 5pm Sat., and from 2 to 5pm Sun. From November to March, hours are 1 to 5pm Mon. to Fri., 10am to 2pm Sat., and 2 to 5pm Sun. Tube: Belsize Park or Hampstead. Bus 24.

Kenwood (the Iveagh Bequest), Hampstead Lane, N.W.3 (tel. 071/348-1286), handsome with its columned portico, was built as a gentleman's country home around the start of the 18th century. It became the seat of Lord Mansfield in 1754 and was enlarged and decorated by the famous Scottish architect, Robert Adam from 1764. In 1927 it was given to the nation by Lord Iveagh, together with his collection of pictures. The Adam stamp is strongest in the restored oval library, painted in rose, blue, white, and gold. The rooms contain some fine neoclassical furniture, but the main attractions are the old masters and the work of British artists. You can see paintings by Rembrandt *(Self-Portrait in Old Age)*, Vermeer, Turner, Hals, Cuyp, Crome, Gainsborough, Reynolds, Romney, Raeburn, Guardi, and Angelica Kauffmann, plus a portrait of the earl of Mansfield, Lord Chief Justice, who made Kenwood such an important home. In the coach house, where there is a cafeteria, stands a 19th-century family coach that carried 15 people comfortably. The house is open daily from Easter Sat. to September 30 10am to 6pm, October 1 to Maundy Thursday. 10am to 4pm; closed Christmas Eve, Christmas Day, and Good Friday. Tube: Hampstead.

Fenton House, Windmill Hill, N.W.3 (tel. 071/435-3471), a National Trust property, is in a village area on the west side of Hampstead Grove, just a short distance north of Hampstead Village. You pass through beautiful wrought-iron gates to reach the redbrick house in a fine walled garden. Built in 1693, it is one of the earliest, largest, and finest houses in the Hampstead section. The south front is striking, with a central pediment and seven bays. The original main staircase, some door frames, and chimney pieces remain of the early construction. Paneled rooms contain furniture; pictures; English, German, and French porcelain from the 18th century; and the outstanding Benton-Fletcher collection of early keyboard musical instruments. Exhibits of these date from 1540 to 1805, including a 17th-century Flemish harpsichord on loan from the Queen Mother. On the second floor you'll see harpsichords, spinets, square pianos, clavichords, and also a virginal. There are also some fine needlework pictures on the walls. The house is open in March from 2 to 6pm Sat. and Sun., April to October from 2 to 6pm Sat. to Wed. Last admission is at 5pm. It's closed on Good Friday. Admission is £2.50 ($4.15). Occasional concerts are held at the house. Tube: Hampstead.

Freud Museum, 30 Maresfield Gardens, N.W. 3 (tel. 071/435-2002), is a spacious, three-story, redbrick house in northern London. Sigmund Freud, the founder of psychoanalysis, lived, worked, and died here after he and his family left Nazi-occupied Vienna as refugees. On view are rooms containing original furniture, letters, photographs, paintings, and personal effects of Freud and his daughter, Anna. A focal point of the museum is the study and library where you can see the famous couch and Freud's large collection of Egyptian, Roman and Asian antiquities. This domestic and working environment offers a unique perspective on the contribution that Freud made to the understanding of the human mind. Temporary exhibitions and archive film programs are also on view. The museum is developing as a research archive, educational resource, and cultural center. Open noon to 5pm Wed. to Sun. Admission is £2 ($3.30). Tube: Finchley Road.

Burgh House, New End Square, N.W.3 (tel. 071/431-0144), is a Queen Anne structure built in 1703 in the middle of the village, the home of professional men and later the residence of the daughter and son-in-law of Rudyard Kipling, who often visited here. It is now used for local art exhibits, concerts, recitals, talks, and public meetings on many subjects. The house is also the home of several local societies, including the Hampstead Music Club and the Hampstead Scientific Society, and it houses the Hampstead Museum, which displays the local history of the area. It has an art collection, including a room devoted to the great artist, John Constable, who lived nearby for many years and was buried in the local parish church. There is also a bookstall, well stocked with souvenirs and postcards, plus a licensed buttery (tel. 071/431-2516), popular for lunch or tea (its prices are the lowest in Hampstead). The buttery is open from 11am to 5:30pm Wed. to Sun. Tube: Hampstead. Just ask one of the mums pushing her pram or a passing villager walking a dog to direct you to the place.

Highgate Village, a stone's throw east of Hampstead Heath, has a number of mansions from the 16th and 17th centuries, as well as small cottages lining three sides of the now pondless Pond Square. Its most outstanding feature, however, is **Highgate Cemetery,** which is entered from Swain's Lane, N.6. This cemetery is the ideal setting for a collection of Victorian sculpture. Described as everything from "walled romantic rubble" to "an anthology of horror," the 37-acre burial ground attracts tombstone fanciers. Highgate's most famous grave is that of Karl Marx who died in Hampstead in 1883. On the tomb is a huge bust of Marx, inscribed with the unsurprising quotation, "Workers of the world, unite." For further information, phone 071/348-0808. Tube: Hamstead Heath.

The Parks of London

London's parklands easily rate as the greatest, most wonderful system of "green lungs" of any large city on the globe. Not as rigidly artificial as the parks of Paris, those in London are maintained with a loving care and lavish artistry that puts their American equivalents to shame. Above all, they've been kept safe from land-hungry building firms and city councils, and still offer patches of real countryside right in the heart of the metropolis. Maybe there's something to be said for inviolate "royal" property, after all. Because that's what most of London's parks are.

Largest of them—and one of the biggest in the world—is **Hyde Park,** W.2. With the adjoining Kensington Gardens, it covers 636 acres of central London with velvety lawns interspersed with ponds, flowerbeds, and trees. Hyde Park was once a favorite deer-hunting ground of Henry VIII. Running through the width is a 41-acre lake known as the Serpentine. Rotten Row, a 1½-mile sand track, is reserved for horseback riding and on Sun. attracts some skilled equestrians.

Kensington Gardens, W.2, blending with Hyde Park, border on the grounds of Kensington Palace. Kensington Gardens also contain the celebrated statue of Peter Pan, with the bronze rabbits that toddlers are always trying to kidnap. The Albert Memorial, that previously mentioned Victorian extravaganza, is also here.

East of Hyde Park, across Piccadilly, stretch **Green Park** and **St. James's Park,** W.1, forming an almost unbroken chain of landscaped beauty. This is an ideal area for picnics, and you'll find it hard to believe that this was once a festering piece of swamp near the leper hospital. There is a romantic lake, stocked with a variety of ducks and pelicans, descendants of the pair that the Russian ambassador presented to Charles II in 1662.

Regent's Park, N.W.1, covers most of the district by that name, north of Baker Street and Marylebone Road. Designed by the 18th-century genius John Nash to surround a palace of the prince regent that never materialized, this is the most classically beautiful of London's parks. The core is a rose garden planted around a small lake alive with waterfowl and spanned by humped Japanese bridges. In early summer, the rose perfume in the air is as heady as wine.

Regent's Park also contains the Open-Air Theatre and the London Zoo. Also— as in all the local parks—there are hundreds of deck chairs on the lawns in which to sunbathe. The deck chair attendants, who collect a small fee, are mostly college students on vacation.

SPEAKERS CORNER At the northwest extremity of Mayfair, head for **Marble Arch,** an enormous *faux pas* that the English didn't try to hide but turned into a monument. Originally it was built by John Nash as the entrance to Buckingham Palace, until it was discovered that it was too small for carriages to pass through. If you see a crowd of people nearby who look as if they are plotting revolution, you might be right. In this part of Hyde Park is **Speakers Corner,** where you will see English free speech in action. Comedians, anarchists, religious fanatics, and would-be politicians mount the soapbox to speak his or her mind. The speeches reach their most violent pitch on Sun., the best day to visit Marble Arch. Tube: Marble Arch.

Landmark Churches

St. Martin-in-the-Fields, overlooking Trafalgar Square, W.C.2 (tel. 071/839-4342), is the Royal Parish Church. The present classically inspired church, with its famous steeple, dates back to 1726. James Gibbs, a pupil of Wren's, is listed as its architect. The origins of the church go back to the 11th century. Among the congregation in years past was George I, who was actually a churchwarden, unique for an English sovereign. From St. Martin's vantage position in the theater district, it has drawn many actors to its door—none more notable than Nell Gwynne, the mistress of Charles II. On her death in 1687, she was buried in the crypt. Throughout the war, many Londoners rode out an uneasy night in the crypt, while Blitz bombs rained down overhead. The crypt contains a pleasant restaurant, a bookshop, and a gallery. Tube: Charing Cross.

St. Etheldreda's, Britain's oldest Roman Catholic church, lies on Ely Place, Clerkenwell, E.C.1 (tel. 071/405-1061), leading off Charterhouse Street at Holborn Circus. Built in 1251, it was mentioned by the Bard in both *Richard II* and *Richard III.* One of the survivors of the Great Fire of 1666, the church was built by and was the property of the Diocese of Ely in the days when many bishops had their episcopal houses in London rather than in the actual cathedral cities in which they held their sees. Until this century, the landlord of Ye Olde Mitre public house near Ely Place where the church stands had to obtain his license from the Justices of Cambridgeshire rather than in London, and even today the place is still a private road, with impressive iron gates and a lodge for the gate-keeper, all administered by six commissioners who are elected. St. Etheldreda, whose name is sometimes shortened to St. Audrey, was a 7th-century king's daughter who left her husband and turned to religion, establishing an abbey on the Isle of Ely. The name St. Audrey is the source of the word *tawdry,* from cheap trinkets sold at the annual fair honoring the saint. St. Etheldreda's is made up of a crypt and an upper church, catering to working people and visitors who come to pray. It has a distinguished musical tradition, with the 11am mass on Sun. sung in Latin. Other mass times are 9am and 6pm on Sun. and at 8am and 1pm Mon. to Fri. Lunches are served from noon to 2pm Mon. to Fri. in the pantry, with a varied choice of hot and cold dishes. Tube: Farringdon.

Along the Thames

There is a row of fascinating attractions lying on, across, and alongside the River Thames. All of London's history and development is linked with this winding ribbon of water. The Thames connects the city with the sea, from which it drew its wealth and its power. For centuries the river was London's highway and main street.

Some of the bridges that span the Thames are household words. London Bridge, which, contrary to the nursery rhyme, has never "fallen down," but was dismantled and shipped to the United States, ran from the Monument (a tall pillar commemorating the Great Fire of 1666) to Southwark Cathedral, parts of which date back to 1207.

Its neighbor to the east is the still-standing **Tower Bridge,** E.1 (tel. 071/407-0922), one of the city's most celebrated landmarks and possibly the most photographed and painted bridge on earth. Tower Bridge was built during 1886–1894 with two towers 200 feet apart, joined by footbridges that provide glass-covered walkways for the public who can enter the north tower, take the elevator to the walkway, cross the river to the south tower, and return to street level. It's a photographer's dream, with interesting views of St. Paul's, the Tower of London, and in the distance, a part of the Houses of Parliament. You can also visit the main engine room with its Victorian boilers and steam-pumping engines, which used to raise and lower the roadway across the river.

There are models showing how the 1,000-ton arms of the bridge can be raised in 1½ minutes to allow ships passage upstream, among the exhibitions that trace the history and operation of this unique bridge. Nowadays, electric power is used to raise the bridge, an occurrence that usually happens on an average of once a day, more often in summer. You'll know if it is going to open, however, as a bell sounds throughout the bridge and road traffic is stopped. Admission to exhibits is £2.50 ($4.15), £1 ($1.65) for children. It is open daily in summer from 10am to 6:30pm (to 4:45pm in winter). Tube: Tower Hill.

The piece of river between the site of the old London Bridge and the Tower Bridge marks the city end of the immense row of docks stretching 26 miles to the coast. Although most of them are no longer in use, they have long been known as the Port of London.

Particular note should be taken of the striking removal of pollution from the Thames in the past decades. The river, so polluted in the 1950s that no marine life could exist in it, can now lay claim to being "the cleanest metropolitan estuary in the world," with many varieties of fish, even salmon, back as happy denizens of these waters.

The Thames Flood Barrier

Since its official opening in 1984, the engineering spectacle known as the Thames Flood Barrier has drawn increasing crowds to the site, at a point in the river known as Woolwich Reach in east London, where the Thames is a straight stretch about a third of a mile in width. For centuries the Thames estuary has from time to time brought tidal surges that have on occasion caused disastrous flooding at Woolwich, Hammersmith, Whitehall, and Westminster, and elsewhere within the river's flood reaches. The flooding peril has increased during this century due to a number of natural causes, including the unstoppable rise of tide levels in the Thames, surge tides from the Atlantic, and the down-tilt of the country by some 12 inches a century.

All this led to the construction, beginning in 1975, of a great barrier with huge piers linking mammoth rising sector gates, smaller rising sector gates, and falling radial gates, all of which when in use make a solid steel wall about the height of a five-story building, which completely dams the waters of the Thames, keeping the surge tides from passage up the estuary. The gates are operated every month to remove river silt and be sure they work smoothly.

London Launches offers trips to the barrier, operating from Westminster Pier. Passengers can get off at the barrier pier and visit the Barrier Centre. An audio-visual show depicting the need for the barrier and its operation is presented at the center, where there are also a souvenir shop, a snack bar, and a cafeteria. London Launches (tel. 071/930-3373) leave five times daily from Westminster Pier, with returns from Barrier Pier. Adults pay £4.50 ($7.45) round-trip or £2.80 ($4.60) one-way. Children under 14 are charged £2.50 ($4.15) round-trip or £1.50 ($2.50) one-way. It's also possible to go by boat, then return by underground. After viewing the barrier, walk to the nearby tube of Charleton Station. Trains there depart for central London every 30 minutes, the ride taking only 15 minutes.

The **Thames Barrier Visitors' Centre,** Unity Way, Woolwich, S.E.11 (tel. 081/854-1373), is open 10:30am to 5pm Mon. to Fri. and 10:30am to 5:30pm Sat. and Sun. Admission is £2 ($3.30) for adults and £1.20 ($2) for children.

A Floating Museum

H.M.S. *Belfast,* Morgan's Lane, Tooley Street, S.E.1 (tel. 071/407-6434), Europe's largest historic warship, is permanently moored on the Thames, opposite the Tower of London. This World War II veteran was among the first to open fire against German fortifications on D-Day. She also served with distinction during the

Korean War, where she earned the name, "that straight-shooting ship," from the United States Navy. By exploring the ship from the bridge right down to her engine and boiler rooms, seven decks below, you can discover how Royal Navy sailors lived and fought during the past 50 years. Among the many areas to be visited aboard are the bridge, operations room, 6-inch gun turrets, living quarters, galley, and the D-Day exhibition. H.M.S. *Belfast* is open daily from 10am to 5:30pm in summer and from 11am to 4pm in winter. Last boardings are 30 minutes before closing. Admission is £3.50 ($5.80) for adults, £1.75 ($2.90) for children. A ferry runs daily from Tower Pier (Tower of London) directly to the ship. It operates only on Sat. and Sun. in winter. Tube: London Bridge or Tower Hill.

London Docklands

What was a dilapidated 8 square miles of property surrounded by water—some 55 miles of waterfront acreage within a sailor's cry of London's major attractions—has been reclaimed and restored until now London Docklands is coming into its own as a leisure, residential, and commercial lure.

Included in this complex are Wapping, the Isle of Dogs, the Surrey and Royal Docks, and more, all with Limehouse at its heart. The former urban wasteland of deserted warehouses and derelict wharves and the many facilities already completed can be visited by taking the **Docklands Light Railway** that links the Isle of Dogs and London Underground's Tower Hill station, via several new local stations. To see the whole complex, take the railway at the Tower Gateway near Tower Bridge for a short journey through Wapping and the Isle of Dogs. You can get off at Island Gardens and then cross through the 100-year-old Greenwich Tunnel under the Thames to see the attractions at Greenwich described in Section 5 of this chapter, "One-Day Trips from London." A regular water-bus service connects Greenwich with Charing Cross, a river voyage of about half an hour, and other tunnels are planned to link the Docklands with port points and motorways.

A visit to the **Exhibition Centre** on the Isle of Dogs offers an opportunity to see what the Docklands past, present, and future include. Already the area has provided space for overflow from the City of London's square mile, and it looks as though the growth and development is more than promising. A shopping Village at Tobacco Dock, a new home at Shadwell Basin for the Academy of St. Martin-in-the-Fields Orchestra, and the London Arena (largest artificial sport and leisure complex in the country) at the tip of the Isle of Dogs are being joined by luxury condominiums, offices, hotels, museums, and theaters; these and all the other amenities aimed at making the East End of London a shining star have been or soon will be completed.

---

2. Kids' London

It's almost impossible to draw a clear distinguishing line between junior and senior brands of entertainment in London. The British Museum, for example, is definitely rated as an adult attraction. Yet I've watched group after group of kids stand absolutely spellbound in front of the Egyptian mummies, still completely absorbed long after their parents were champing at the bit to trot along.

The attractions to follow are not meant specifically for children. They are general and universal fun places to which you can take youngsters without having to worry about either their physical or moral safety. There's nothing to stop you from going to any of them minus a juvenile escort. It is even possible that you'll enjoy them more thoroughly than any kid around. Many of the interesting sights, such as the Royal Mews, where you can see the queen's horses and royal and state coaches, are described earlier in this chapter.

THE LONDON DUNGEON

The premises at 34 Tooley St., S.E.1 (tel. 071/403-0606), simulate a ghoulish atmosphere designed deliberately to chill the blood while reproducing faithfully the conditions that existed in the Middle Ages. Set under the arches of London Bridge Station, the dungeon is a series of tableaux, more grizzly than Madame Tussaud's, depicting life in medieval London. The rumble of trains overhead adds to the spine-chilling horror of the place. Bells toll, and there is constant melancholy chanting in the background. Dripping water and live rats (caged) make for even more atmosphere. The heads of executed criminals were stuck on spikes for onlookers to observe through glasses hired for the occasion. The murder of Thomas à Becket in Canterbury Cathedral is also depicted. Naturally, there's a burning at the stake, as well as a torture chamber with racking, branding, and fingernail extraction. The Great Fire of London is brought to crackling life by a computer-controlled spectacular that recreates Pudding Lane where the fire started. Wonderfully done, the exhibit is not for the faint-hearted.

If you survive, there is a souvenir shop selling certificates to testify that you have been through the works. The dungeon is open daily from April to September 10am to 5:30pm, to 4:30pm October to March. Admission is £4.50 ($7.45) for adults, £2.50 ($4.15) for children under 14. Tube: London Bridge.

BATTERSEA PARK
The park, S.W.11 (tel. 071/871-7530), is a vast patch of woodland, lakes, and lawns on the south bank of the Thames, opposite Chelsea Embankment between Albert Bridge and Chelsea Bridge. It boasts just about everything that makes for happiness on a dry day. Formerly known as Battersea Fields, the present park was laid out in 1852–58 on an old dueling ground. The most famous duel here was fought between Lord Winchelsea and the Duke of Wellington in 1829. The park has a lake for boating, a deer field with fenced-in deer and wild birds, and fields for tennis and football (soccer). There's even a children's zoo, open from Easter to late September daily from 11am to 5pm, charging an entrance of 50p (85¢). The park measures ¾ of a mile on each of its four sides. Its architectural highlight is a stone and wood Peace Pagoda, built by Japanese craftspeople in 1986 in cooperation with British architects, who ensured that it would fit gracefully into its English surroundings. It was donated to the now-defunct Council of Greater London by an order of Japanese monks. The park can be visited daily from 7:30am to dusk. It's not well serviced by public transportation. The nearest tube is in Chelsea on the Right Bank (Sloane Square). From there it is a brisk 15-minute walk. If you prefer to ride the bus, take no. 137 from the Sloane Square station, exiting at the first stop after the bus crosses the Thames.

Theaters for Kids
The Arts Theatre, Great Newport Street, W.C.2, is situated in the heart of London's "Theatreland." The **Unicorn** is the only theater just for children. Founded in 1947 and going stronger than ever, Unicorn presents a season of plays for 4 to 12 year olds from September to June each year. A program includes specially commissioned plays, adaptations of old favorites, and entertainment of the highest quality. Adult actors play to an audience of children. Performances are at 2:30pm Sat., Sun. and school holidays. Tickets cost £3 ($4.95), £4 ($6.60), and £5 ($8.25) plus 10p (15¢) temporary membership just for the show. You can also become a temporary member while you are in London and join in an exciting program of workshops every weekend. For further information about what's on, telephone 071/379-3280. To book tickets, ring the box office at 071/836-3334. Tube: Leicester Square.

Little Angel Marionette Theatre, 14 Dagmar Passage, Cross St., N.1 (tel. 071/226-1787), is especially constructed for and devoted to presentation of puppetry in all its forms. It is open to the general public, and 200 to 300 performances are given each year. The theater is the focal point of a loosely formed group of some 20 professional puppeteers who work here as occasion demands, presenting their own shows or helping with performances of the resident company. In the current repertory, there are 25 programs. These vary in style and content from *The Soldier's Tale,* using 8-foot-high figures, to *Wonder Island* and *Lancelot the Lion,* written especially for the humble glove puppet. Many of the plays, such as Hans Christian Andersen's *The Little Mermaid*, are performed with marionettes (string puppets), but whatever is being presented, you'll be enthralled with the exquisite lighting and the skill with which the puppets are handled.

The theater is beautifully decorated and well equipped. There is a coffee bar in the foyer and a workshop adjacent where the settings and costumes, as well as the puppets, are made. To find out what's playing and to reserve your seats, call the number above. Performances are at 11am on Sat., when the seats are £2 ($3.30) for children, £3 ($4.95) for adults, and at 3pm on Sat. and Sun., when the cost is £2.50 ($4.15) for children, £3.50 ($5.80) for adults. Take the tube to Angel Station, then walk up Upper Street to St. Mary's Church and down the footpath to the left of the church. You can go by car or taxi to Essex Road and then up to Dagmar Terrace to Dagmar Passage.

LONDON ZOO

One of the greatest zoos in the world, the London Zoo is more than a century and a half old. Run by the Zoological Society of London, Regent's Park, N.W.1 (tel. 071/722-3333), with an equal measure of showbiz style and scholarly know-how, this 36-acre garden houses some 8,000 animals, including some of the rarest species on earth. One of the most fascinating exhibits is the Snowdon Aviary. Separate houses are reserved for some species: the insect house (incredible bird-eating spiders, a cross-sectioned ant colony), the reptile house (huge dragon-like monitor lizards and a fantastic 15-foot python), and other additions, such as the Sobell Pavilion for Apes and Monkeys and the Lion Terraces.

Designed for the largest collection of small mammals in the world, the Clore Pavilion has a basement called the Moonlight World, where special lighting effects simulate night for the nocturnal beasties, while rendering them clearly visible to onlookers. You can see all the night rovers in action—leaping bush babies, rare kiwis, a fierce Tasmanian devil, and giant Indian fruit bats with heads like prehistoric dogs.

Many families budget almost an entire day to spend with the animals, watching the sea lions being fed, enjoying an animal ride in summer, and meeting the baby elephants on their walks. The zoo is open daily from 9am in summer and from 10am in winter, until 6pm or dusk, whichever is earlier. Last entrance is half an hour before closing. Admission is £4.70 ($7.75) for adults, £2.90 ($4.80) for children 4 to 15 (under 4 free). On the grounds are two fully licensed restaurants, one self-service and the other with servers. Take the tube to Baker Street or Camden Town, then take bus 74 (Camden Town is nearer and an easy ten-minute walk).

NATURAL HISTORY MUSEUM

This museum, on Cromwell Road, S.W.7 (tel. 071/589-6323), is the home of the national collections of living and fossil plants, animals, minerals, rocks, and meteorites, with lots of magnificent specimens on display. Exciting exhibitions designed to encourage people of all ages to enjoy learning about modern natural history include "Human Biology—An Exhibition of Ourselves," "Dinosaurs and Their Living Relatives," "Man's Place in Evolution," "British Natural History," and "Discovering Mammals." Admission is £2.50 ($4.15) for adults and £1.25 ($2.05) for children. The museum is open from 10am to 6pm Mon. to Sat., from 1 to 6pm Sun. Tube: South Kensington.

BETHNAL GREEN MUSEUM OF CHILDHOOD

On Cambridge Heath Road, E.2 (tel. 071/980-2415), this establishment displays toys from the past century. The variety of dolls alone is staggering, some of them dressed in period costumes of such elaborateness that you don't even want to think of the price tags they must have carried. With the dolls go dollhouses, from simple cottages to miniature mansions, complete with fireplaces and grand pianos, plus carriages, furniture, kitchen utensils, and household pets. It might be wise to explain to your children beforehand that none of them is for sale. In addition, the museum displays optical toys, toy theaters, marionettes, puppets, and a considerable exhibit of soldiers and battle toys of both world wars. There is also a display of children's clothing and furniture related to childhood. The museum is open from 10am to 6pm Mon. to Thur. and Sat., from 2:30 to 6pm Sun. Admission is free. Tube: Bethnal Green.

THE LONDON TOY AND MODEL MUSEUM

Two restored Victorian houses at 21-23 Craven Hill, W.2 (tel. 071/262-7905), off Bayswater Road, shelter one of the finest collections of commercially made toys and models on public display in Europe, with items by all the major toy and model manufacturers. The model and toy train collection is particularly comprehensive, tracing the development of the miniature train from the inception of railways in the early 19th century. There are several garden railway systems, including a child's ride-on train. The permanent collection details the rise of toys with the Industrial Revolution. There is a fine display of dolls, teddy bears, and a quarter-scale child's model of a Cadillac sports roadster made in 1916. A children's activity area within the museum also is an attraction. The museum has a café and a large recreational garden area. It's open 10am to 5:30pm Tues. to Sat., 11am to 5:30pm Sun. and bank holidays. Admission is £2.20 ($3.65) for adults, 80p ($1.30) for children (free for children under 5 years of age). Tube: Lancaster Gate.

FUN ON HAMPSTEAD HEATH

This is the traditional playground of the Londoner, the 'Appy 'Ampstead of cockney legend, the place dedicated "to the use of the public forever" by a special act of Parliament in 1872. Londoners might just possibly tolerate the conversion of, say, Hyde Park into housing estates or supermarkets, but they would certainly mount the barricades if Hampstead Heath were imperiled. This 800-acre expanse of high heath entirely surrounded by London is a chain of continuous park, wood, and grassland, bearing different names in different portions. It contains just about every known form of outdoor amusement, with the exceptions of deep-sea fishing and big-game hunting. There's something here for children and grownups alike, with activities to include the entire family. There are natural lakes for swimmers (who don't mind goosebumps), bridle paths for horseback riders, athletic tracks, hills for kite flying, and a special pond for model yachting.

At the shore of Kenwood Lake, in the northern section, is a concert platform devoted to symphony performances on summer evenings. In the northeast corner, in Waterlow Park, ballets, operas, and comedies are staged at the Grass Theatre in June and July.

History-minded youngsters and adults should stand for a moment on top of Parliament Hill on the south side. It was from that vantage point that the ancient British (Iceni tribe) Queen Boadicea and her daughters watched the burning of the Roman camp of Londinium, which her tribe put to the torch in A.D. 61. Tube: Hampstead or Belsize Park.

Rock Circus

Run by the Tussaud's Group of Madame Tussaud's waxworks, Rock Circus, London Pavilion, 1 Piccadilly Circus, W.1 (tel. 071/734-7203), tells the story of rock and pop music from the 1950s through the present day, using a combination of wax and moving bionic likenesses of all the big names in rock from the past four decades, with soundtracks of their hits. Very young children might not understand it, but pre-teens and teenagers will love it. The highlight of the Rock Circus is a show using Audio Animatronic techniques, in which the Beatles, Elvis Presley, Madonna, Bruce Springsteen, and others perform "live." Hours are daily from 10am to 10pm. Admission is £4.80 ($7.90) for adults and £3.45 ($5.70) for children. Tube: Piccadilly Circus.

SHOPPING FOR CHILDREN

The best place to go for children's books is the **Children's Book Centre**, 237 Kensington High St., W.8 (tel. 071/937-7497). It has thousands of titles. A feature of the bookshop is that fiction, both hardback and paperback, is arranged according to age, including the young adult reader in the 14 to 16 age group. Open from 9:30am to 6pm Mon. to Sat. Tube: High Street Kensington.

Hamleys of Regent Street, 188-196 Regent St., W.1 (tel. 071/734-3161), is an Ali Baba's cave of toys and games, ranging from electronic games and Star Wars robots on the ground floor to different toys for all age groups on each of the other floors: table and card games, teddy bears, nursery animals, dolls, and outdoor games. Hours are 10am to 6pm Mon. to Wed. and Fri. and Sat. and 10am to 8pm Thurs. Tube: Oxford Circus.

---

3. Taking the Tours

In addition to the sights you can see in London by foot, or by using the tubes, there are numerous attractions that can be reached via several coach tours. As an added bonus, there are dozens of fascinating trips that can be made on the Thames.

EASIEST WAY TO SEE LONDON

For the first-timer, the quickest and most economical way to bring the big city into focus is to take a 2-hour, 20-mile circular tour of the West End and The City, the guided **Original London Sightseeing Tour,** which passes virtually all the major places of interest in central London. Operated by London Transport Tours, part of the city's official bus company, the journeys leave at frequent intervals daily from Victoria, Piccadilly Circus, Marble Arch, and Baker Street. Tickets cost £7 ($11.55) for adults and £4 ($6.60) for children under 16 and are available from the driver. Tickets can also be purchased from London Regional Transport Travel Information Centres, where you can get a discount of £1 ($1.65) off each ticket. Locations of the travel centers are given under "Transportation," Chapter III.

LONDON'S WEST END AND THE CITY

If you prefer a more detailed look at the city's sights, then London Transport offers two highly regarded conducted coach tours.

For a look at the West End, a 3-hour tour is offered, passing Westminster Abbey (guided tour), Houses of Parliament, Horse Guards, Trafalgar Square, and Piccadilly Circus, including the changing of the guard. The tour starts at 10am Mon. to Sun.

London Transport's other popular three-hour tour is of The City, and includes guided trips to the Tower of London and St. Paul's Cathedral. The fare for the Westminster and Changing of the Queen's Guard tour is £11.50 ($19) for adults and £9 ($14.85) for children under 14. For The City and Tower tour, the cost is £16 ($26.40) for adults, £13 ($21.45) for children under 14. The City tour leaves at 2pm Mon. through Sat. from March to October. For about three months during the summer the tour also runs on Sun.

These two tours are also combined to form the London Day tour, which costs £31.50 ($52) for adults and £28 ($46.20) for children under 14, including lunch.

The tours begin at London Transport's own Wilton Road coach station, alongside Victoria train station. To reserve seats or for information, phone 071/227-3456, or go to a London Transport Travel Information Centre.

LONDON PRIDE SIGHTSEEING TOUR

A 90-minute panoramic **Grand Tour of London** aboard double-decker buses (open top in summer) is offered by London Pride, taking in all the sights, and with a commentary. Buses run at least every 30 minutes daily beginning at 10am, and run until late, so this is a good way to see London at night when many of the buildings are floodlit. Buses leave from near Piccadilly Circus, outside the Trocadero on Coventry Street. Just show up and jump on. Tickets costs £6 ($9.90) for adults, £2 ($3.30) for children. For information, call 0708/865656 day or night. London Pride tours are operated by Ensign Bus Services Ltd. in Essex.

HARRODS SIGHTSEEING BUS

A double-decker bus in the discreet green-and-gold livery of Harrods, the luxury observation coach, takes sightseeing tours around London's attractions. Mon. to Sat., the first departure from door 8 of Harrods in Brompton Road is at 10am, and there are also tours at 1 and 4pm. Tea, coffee, and orange juice are served on board. The tour costs £14 ($23.10) for adults, £7 ($11.55) for children under 12. All-day excursion tours to Bath, Windsor, Stratford-upon-Avon, and around all of London are available. You can purchase tickets at Harrods, Sightseeing Department, lower ground floor, or you can obtain information by telephoning Harrods at 071/730-1234.

BOAT TRIPS

Touring boats operate on the Thames all year, taking you various places within Greater London. Main embarkation points are Westminster Pier, Charing Cross Pier, and Tower Pier—a system that enables you, for instance, to take a "water taxi" from the Tower of London to Westminster Abbey. Not only are the boats energy saving, bringing you painlessly to your destination, but they permit you to sit back in comfort as you see London from the river.

Pleasure boats operate down the Thames from Westminster Pier to the Tower of London and Greenwich and the Thames Barrier all year, departing daily every 20 minutes in summer, from 10am to 4pm, and every 30 minutes in winter. It takes 20 minutes to reach the Tower and 40 minutes to arrive at Greenwich. In the summer, services operate upriver to Kew, Richmond, and Hampton Court from Westminster Pier. There are departures every 30 minutes from 10:30am to 4pm for the 1½-hour journey to Kew and three departures daily for the 2½-hour Richmond trip as well as to Hampton Court, a 3- to 5-hour trip each way.

The multitude of small companies operating boat services from Westminster Pier have organized themselves into the **Westminster Passenger Service Association,** Westminster Pier, Victoria Embankment (tel. 071/930-4097). Boats leave the pier for cruises of varying lengths throughout the day and evening.

A CANAL BOAT IN LITTLE VENICE

When you get tired of fighting the London traffic, you might want to come here and take a peaceful trip (1½ hours) aboard the traditionally painted Narrow Boat *Jason* and her butty boat *Serpens.* Come for lunch along the most colorful part of Regent's Canal in the heart of London. The boat is moored in Blomfield Road, just off Edgware Road in Maida Vale. Little Venice is the junction of two canals and was given its name by Lord Byron.

To inquire about bookings, including the Boatman's Basket Luncheon Trip, get in touch with **Jason's Trip,** just opposite 60 Blomfield Rd., Little Venice, W.9 (tel. 071/286-3428). Advance booking is essential during high season. If you come by tube, take the Bakerloo Line to Warwick Avenue. Face the church, turn left, and walk up Clifton Villas to the end and turn right (about 2 minutes). If you arrive early, you can browse around the shop, which sells many brightly colored traditionally painted canal wares.

On the trip you'll pass through the long Maida Hill tunnel under Edgware Road, through Regent's Park, the mosque, the zoo, Lord Snowdon's Aviary, past the Pirate's Castle to Camden Lock and return to Little Venice. The season begins Good Friday and lasts through September. During April and May, the boats run daily at 12:30 and 2:30pm. In June, July, August, and September, there are additional trips at 10:30am to 4:30pm daily. Always telephone first. Refreshments are served on all trips: prebooked lunches on the 12:30 and 2:30pm cruises, and a cream tea on the 4:30pm voyage. The fare is £3.25 ($5.35) for adults, £2 ($3.30) for children.

ORGANIZED LONDON WALKS

Hunt for ghosts or walk in the steps of Jack the Ripper, the infamous East End murderer of prostitutes in the 1880s. Retrace the history of The City from the Romans to the Blitz. Visit glamorous Chelsea or elegant Mayfair. Investigate the London of Shakespeare, Dickens, and Sherlock Holmes, or taste the delights of an evening's drinking in four historic pubs. These and many other walks are included in the program of unusual and historical walks organized by **London Walks,** 10 Greenbrook Ave., Hadley Wood, Hertfordshire EN4 OLS (tel. 081/441-8906). Walks take place on Sat. and Sun. throughout the year and also during the week from April to October. The cost is £4 ($6.60); £3 ($4.95) for students with ID cards; children under 14 are free. No reservation is required. If you want to write for information from abroad send an International Reply Coupon for their answer.

Another small and enthusiastic company, a husband-and-wife team, offering a vast variety of London walks, is **Discovering London.** It's operated by a Scot, Alex Cobban, a historian of some note whose guides are professionals. Mainly on Sat. and Sun., but during the week as well, scheduled walks are planned, starting at easily found Underground stations, to Dickens's London, Roman London, Ghosts of the City, the Inns of Court–Lawyers' London, and Jack the Ripper's London. Mr. Cobban's knowledge of Sherlock Holmes is immense. No advance booking is necessary, and the walks cost £3 ($4.95) for adults; children under 16 go free, and students with ID cards are charged £2.15 ($3.55). Each walk takes about 1½ to 2 hours. Write, enclosing an International Reply Coupon, for a detailed schedule of the walks available during your stay in London. The address is Discovering London, 11 Pennyfields, Warley, Brentwood, Essex CM14 5JP (tel. 0277/213704).

John Wittich, of **J. W. Travel,** 66 St. Michael's St., W.2 (tel. 071/262-9572), started walking tours of London in 1960. He is a Freeman of the City of London and a member of two of the ancient guilds of London. He also has written several books on London walks. There is no better way to search out the unusual, the beautiful, and the historic than to take a walking tour. The company concentrates on personal walking tours for families and groups who have booked in advance. John Wittich conducts all tours. The cost for 1½-hour walks is £10 ($16.50) minimum for one or two adults. Call for information.

---

4. Shopping for Value

In London, this "nation of shopkeepers" displays an enormous variety of wares. You can pick up bargains ranging from a still-functioning hurdy-gurdy to a replica of the crown jewels. For the best buys, search out new styles in clothing, as well as traditional and well-tailored men's and women's suits, small antiques and curios, woolens, tweeds, tartans, rare books, Liberty silks, Burberrys, English china, silver, even arms and armor, to name just a few.

London stores keep fairly uniform hours. They are open from 9am to 5:30pm Mon. to Sat., with late shopping on Wed. or Thurs. until about 7 or 8pm. Most central shops close around 1pm on Sat. In the East End, around Aldgate and Whitechapel, many shops are open Sun. from 9am to 2pm. There are a few all-night stores, mostly in the Bayswater section.

As for bargains—that magic word in every traveler's dictionary—they are everywhere, but likely to be limited by the U.S. Customs regulations.

According to the latest rules, you—and everyone traveling with you—are entitled to bring back $400 worth of foreign-made merchandise without paying U.S. duty. This applies only to goods actually accompanying you. You can quite legitimately stretch that amount by mailing unsolicited gifts back from abroad. No gift, however, can be worth more than $50, and you are not permitted to send more than one present per day to the same address.

Many London shops will help you beat the whopping purchase tax levied on much of England's merchandise. By presenting your passport, you can frequently purchase goods tax-free, but only on the following conditions: You must have your purchase sent directly to your home address, or have it delivered to the plane you're taking back.

The huge purchase taxes imposed on so-called luxury goods are responsible for the extremely high cost of items such as wines, spirits, tobacco, cigarettes, and gasoline.

SHOPPING DISTRICTS

London's retail stores tend to cluster in certain areas, a hangover from the times when each guild or craft had its own street. This is what gives a London shopping spree its special flavor: You head in a certain direction to find a certain style of merchandise. In English shops, you'll usually meet with tact, courtesy, and patience, coupled—in some of the smaller establishments—with an almost courtly sense of pride.

Herewith, I present a very rough outline of the main shopping districts (not including the "Special Shopping Districts," which I will detail below):

Regent Street

Curving down elegantly from Oxford Circus to Piccadilly Circus, this stylish thoroughfare is crammed with fashionable stores, selling everything from silks to silverware. It has both department stores and boutiques, but the accent is on the medium-size establishment in the upper-medium price range.

Oxford Street

The main shopping drag of the metropolis, it runs from St. Giles Circus to Marble Arch, an endless, faceless, totally uninspiring but utility-crammed band of stores, stores, and yet more stores. It contains six of London's major department stores, apart from just about every kind of retailing establishment under the sun.

Piccadilly

Unlike the circus, the street Piccadilly is distinctly in the upper bracket, specializing in mouthwatering automobile showrooms, travel offices, art galleries, plus London's poshest grocery store, Fortnum & Mason.

Bond Street

Divided into new and old, Bond Street connects Piccadilly and Oxford Street and is synonymous with the luxury trade. Here are found the very finest—and most expensive—tailors, hatters, milliners, cobblers, as well as stores for sporting goods, antiques, and much more.

Knightsbridge

Together with Kensington and Brompton roads, this forms an extremely svelte shopping district south of Hyde Park. It's patronized for furniture, antiques, jewelry, and Harrods department store.

The Strand

Stately, broad, and dignified, the Strand runs from Trafalgar Square into Fleet Street. It's lined with hotels and theaters, and a selection of specialty stores you could spend a whole day peeking into.

Kensington High Street

This has been called "the Oxford Street of West London." Stretching for about a mile and a half, it includes many famous shops, such as the House of Fraser. (Kensington incidentally, was the name of a Saxon village found in the *Domesday Book*.) Many shops are on side streets, including Earl's Court Road and Abingdon Road. Thackeray Street and Victoria Street retain some of the old village atmosphere. From Kensington High Street, you can walk up Kensington Church Street, which, like Portobello Road, is one of the city's main shopping avenues, selling everything from antique furniture to impressionist paintings.

SPECIAL SHOPPING STREETS AND AREAS

If London has unique department stores, it also has unique streets. The first one achieved such legendary fame abroad that you owe yourself a visit.

King's Road

The formerly villagelike main street of Chelsea starts at Sloane Square with Peter Jones's classy department store, and meanders on for a mile before losing its personality and dissolving into what used to be called World's End. Nowadays a walk to World's End will put you at the doorstep of a swank new shop-filled complex, Chelsea Harbour.

Up until the year 1830, King's Road was actually a king's private road, running from the palaces at Whitehall or St. James's to the country places at Hampton Court, Richmond, and Chelsea. (Queen Victoria ended that when she became the first sovereign to live in Buckingham Palace in 1837.)

King's Road in our lifetimes will forever remain a symbol of London in the sixties. The leap of King's Road to the "mod" throne came with the advent of designer Mary Quant (whose popularity seems to flourish mainly in Japan these days). But, back in the late sixties, she scored a bull's eye in the English fashion world with her then (and still) daring designs. Fashion boutiques, including the famous "Granny Takes a Trip" (it had half a motor car crashing through its window), once lined the boulevard. Today, the street is still full of young people, but perhaps the Mohawk haircuts, "Bovver boots," and Edwardian ballgowns are worn less frequently than before.

More and more in the 1990s, King's Road is a lineup of markets and "multistores," large or small conglomerations of in- and outdoor stands, stalls, and booths fulfilling all sorts of functions within one building or enclosure. They spring up so fast that it's impossible to keep them tabulated, but few thorough shopping strolls in London can afford to miss King's Road. Tube: Sloane Square.

Carnaby Street

Just off Regent, Carnaby is a legend, and legends take time to build. Often, by the time they are entrenched, fickle fashion has moved on elsewhere. Alas, Carnaby Street no longer dominates the world of pacesetting fashion as it did in the 1960s. But it is still visited by the young people, and some of its shops display lots of claptrap and quick-quid merchandise. For value, style, and imagination in design, the Chelsea (King's Road) and Kensington boutiques have left Carnaby far behind.

Mary Quant has returned to London with the **Mary Quant Colour Shop,** 21 Carnaby St., W.1 (tel. 071/494-3277). Her shop sells cosmetics and accessories along with some clothing, especially provocative swimwear. Hours are from 10am to 7pm Mon. to Sat. Tube: Oxford Circus.

Saint Christopher's Place

One of London's most interesting and little-known (to the foreign visitor) shopping streets is Saint Christopher's Place, W.1. It lies just off Oxford Street—walk down Oxford from Selfridges toward Oxford Circus, ducking north along Gees Court across Barrett Street. There you will be surrounded by antique markets and good shops for women's clothing and accessories. Tube: Bond Street.

Beauchamp Place

This is one of London's top shopping streets. Beauchamp Place (pronounced Beecham) is a block off Brompton Road, near Harrods Department Store. The *In-*

ternational Herald-Tribune called it "a higgledy-piggledy of old-fashioned and trendy, quaint and with-it, expensive and cheap. It is deliciously unspecialized." Whatever you're looking for—from a pâté de marcassin to a carved pine mantelpiece—you are likely to find it here. Reject china, crystal, and pottery; secondhand silver; old alligator bags; collages; custom-tailored men's shirts— whatever. It's pure fun even if you don't buy anything. Tube: Knightsbridge.

Princes Arcade

If you like one-stop shopping, you may be drawn to the Princes Arcade, which was opened by Edward VII in 1883, when he was prince of Wales. Between Jermyn Street and Piccadilly, in the heart of London, it has been restored. Wrought-iron lamps light your way as you search through some 20 bow-fronted shops, looking for that special curio (say, a 16th-century nightcap) or a pair of shoes made by people who have been satisfying royal tastes since 1847. A small sign hanging from a metal rod indicates what kind of merchandise a particular store sells. Tube: Piccadilly Circus.

BURLINGTON ARCADE

Next door to the Royal Academy of Arts is the **Burlington Arcade,** W.1 (tel. 071/427-3568), which is more than 150 years old. It was built in 1819 by Lord George Cavendish. The bawdy Londoners of those days threw rubbish over his garden wall, particularly oyster shells, so he built the arcade as a deterrent, history's most expensive antigarbage campaign. The arcade is now an ancient monument protected by Her Majesty. You can wander at leisure through this holdover from Regency London, checking out each of its 38 shops for some antique or bric-a-brac. It's a concentrated bit of luxury. Who knows what might happen? Mary Ann Evans —alias George Eliot, author of *Silas Marner, The Mill on the Floss,* and *Middlemarch* —met the journalist George Lewes in Jeff's Bookshop and they were lovers until he died in 1866. Even Charles Dickens commented on the arcade and its double row of shops, "like a Parisian passage," in his 1879 guide to London.

Pomp and ceremony may be departing, but if you linger in the arcade until 5:30 in the afternoon, you can watch the beadles, in their black-and-yellow livery and top hats, ceremoniously put in place the iron grills that block off the arcade until 9 the next morning, when they just as ceremoniously remove them, marking the start of a new business day. Also at 5:30pm, a hand bell called the Burlington Bell is sounded, signaling the end of trading. It's rung by one of the beadles, the last of London's top-hatted policemen and Britain's oldest police force. There are only three of these constables remaining. Tube: Piccadilly Circus.

COVENT GARDEN ENTERPRISES

In the Central Market Building an impressive array of shops, pubs, and other attractions can be found. For the shops listed below, take the tube, of course, to Covent Garden.

Jubilee Market, Covent Garden Piazza, W.C.2, is a small general market operating from 9am to 5pm Mon. to Sat. Antiques are sold on Mon., crafts on Sat., and various other items on other days. Tube: Covent Garden.

Apple Market, Covent Garden Piazza, W.C.2, almost qualifies as street entertainment. A fun, bustling place, the Apple Market is filled with traders selling . . . well, everything. Much is what the English call "collectible nostalgia." Some items are generally worthless (of the type you capriciously give "to someone who has everything"), and other pieces are genuinely worthy, such as brass door knockers. Wander through the market and keep your sales resistance up. Some of the vendors are mighty persuasive. On Mon. the antique market overflows into the Jubilee Market, Jubilee Hall, the Piazza, W.C.2. Antiques are sold from 7am to 5pm (go early). The general market operates daily from 9am to 5pm Tues. to Fri. Crafts take over from 9am to 5pm on Sat. and Sun. This everchanging market has a wide array of merchandise, so among the inevitable junk are some real prizes, ranging from perfumes to household goods.

Contemporary Applied Arts, 43 Earlham St., W.C.2 (tel. 071/836-6993), is an association of craftspeople that is pioneering in its energetic encouragement of contemporary artwork, both traditional and progressive. The galleries at the center house a diverse retail display of members' work that includes glass, rugs, lights, ceramics for both use and decoration, fabric, clothing, paper, metalwork, and jewelry —all selected from the work of the most outstanding artisans currently producing in the country. There is also a program of special exhibitions that focus on innovations in the crafts. These are lone or small-group shows from the membership. Many of Britain's best-established makers are represented, as well as promising, lesser-known ones. The center is open from 10am to 5:30pm Mon. to Sat.

The General Store, 111 Long Acre, W.C.2 (tel. 071/240-0331), offers thousands of ideas for gifts and souvenirs with prices of a few pence to several pounds. It is ideally situated in Covent Garden, and because of the entertainment nature of the area, the store offers extended trading hours: from 10am to 11:30pm Mon. to Sat. and 11am to 7pm on Sun. The store also features the Covent Garden General Store Restaurant, serving salads from a salad bar, jacket potatoes, chili con carne, and macaroni and cheese, among other items. The restaurant is found downstairs, and is open from 10:30am to 10pm Mon. to Sat. and from noon to 6pm Sun.

At 21 Neal St., W.C.2 (tel. 071/836-5254), the **Natural Shoe Store** sells all manner of comfort and quality footwear from Birkenstock to the best of the British classics. It carries shoes for both men and women, and it will also repair shoes. Hours are 10am to 6pm Mon., Tues., and Sat.; 10am to 7pm Wed. to Fri.

The Tea House, 15A Neal St., W.C.2 (tel. 071/240-7539), is a shop devoted to tea and "tea-phernalia," which includes anything associated with tea, tea drinking, and tea time. It boasts 69 different teas and more than 250 teapots. It is open from 10am to 7pm Mon. to Sat.

The Glasshouse, 65 Long Acre, W.C.2 (tel. 071/836-9785), sells beautiful glass. Visitors can watch the craftspeople producing glass works of art in the workshop. It is open 10am to 6pm Mon. to Fri. and 11am to 4:30pm Sat.

Penhaligon's, 41 Wellington St., W.C.2 (tel. 071/836-2150), is a Victorian perfumery established in 1870, holding royal warrants to the duke of Edinburgh and the prince of Wales. It offers a large selection of perfumes, aftershaves, soaps, and bath oils for women and men. Perfect gifts include scented books and antique, silver scent bottles. It is open 10am to 6pm Mon. to Fri. and 10am to 5:30pm Sat.

Neal Street East, 5 Neal St., W.C.2 (tel. 071/240-0135), is a vast shop devoted to Asian or Asian-inspired merchandise. Here you can find dried and silk flowers, pottery, baskets, chinoiserie, and toys, as well as calligraphy, modern and antique clothing, textiles, and ethnic jewelry. There is also an extensive cookware department and bookshop. Open 10am to 7pm Mon. to Sat.

Naturally British, 13 New Row (by Covent Garden), W.C.2 (tel. 071/240-0551), specializes in items handmade in Britain and displayed on excellent antique furniture of oak, pine, yew, and fruitwood. Naturally British aims to present the best of contemporary craftworks from many fields: pottery; jewelry; glass; clothes from Ireland, Wales, and Scotland; cosmetics; rocking horses; games; puzzles; painted firescreens; and iron works; as well as soft toys. There is a wide range of prices. Open from 10:30am to 6:45pm Mon. to Sat., Sun. in summer.

The Royal School of Needlework, 5 King St., W.C.2 (tel. 071/240-3186), offers in kit form many of the great number of almost classic tapestry designs bequeathed to them by such designers as Burne-Jones and William Morris. Classes and courses are available either full- or part-time, covering all aspects of embroidery and related textile skills, art and design, the history of textiles and textile techniques, textile conservation and restoration, and youth training in needle skills. The school is open from 10am to 5:30pm Mon. to Fri. Numerous books on the subject of needlework as well as materials are for sale through the mail-order service.

Behind the warehouse off Neal Street runs a narrow road leading to **Neal's Yard,** a mews of warehouses that seem to retain some of the old London atmosphere. The open warehouses display such goods as vegetables, health foods, fresh-baked breads, cakes, sandwiches, and, in an immaculate dairy, the largest variety of flavored cream cheeses you are likely to encounter.

SHOPPING A TO Z

Antiques Markets

Sheltered in a rambling old building, the **Chelsea Antiques Market,** 245-253 King's Rd., S.W.3 (tel. 071/352-1720), is a gold mine where you can pan for some hidden little treasure. It offers endless browsing possibilities for the curio addict. In this ever-changing display you're likely to run across Staffordshire dogs, shaving mugs, Edwardian buckles and clasps, ivory-handled razors, old velours and lace gowns, wooden tea caddies, antique pocket watches, wormy Tudoresque chests, silver snuff boxes, grandfather clocks, and jewelry of all periods. It is open from 10am to 6pm Mon. to Sat.; closed Sun. Tube: Sloane Square.

Grays and Grays in the Mews Antique Markets, 58 Davies St., and 1-7 Davies Mews, W.1 (tel. 071/629-7034), just south of Oxford Street are in a triangle formed by Davies Street, South Molton Lane, and Davies Mews. The two old buildings have been converted into walk-in stands with independent dealers. The term "antique" here covers items from oil paintings to, say, the 1894 edition of the *Encyclopaedia Britannica.* Also sold here are exquisite antique jewelry; silver and gold; maps and prints; bronzes and ivories; arms and armor; Victorian and Edwardian toys; furniture; art nouveau and art deco items; antique luggage; antique lace; scientific instruments; crafting tools; and Chinese, Persian, and Islamic pottery, porcelain, miniatures, and antiquities. There is also a whole floor of repair workshops, an engraver, and a bureau de change. Tube: Bond Street.

Alfies Antique Market, 13-25 Church St., N.W.8 (tel. 071/723-6066), is the biggest and one of the cheapest covered markets in London, and it's where many dealers come to buy. Alfies is named after the father of Bennie Gray, the owner of Grays and Grays in the Mews Antique Markets and former owner of the Antique Hypermarket Kensington and Antiquarius. The market contains more than 370 stalls, showrooms, and workshops on 35,000 square feet of floor, plus an enormous, 70-unit basement area. Hours are 10am to 6pm Tues. to Sat. Tube: Edgware Road.

Antiquarius, 131-141 King's Rd., S.W.3 (tel. 071/351-5353), echoes the artistic diversity of the street on which it is located. More than 150 stallholders offer specialized merchandise, usually of the small, domestic variety. Such items used to gather dust on top of Victorian consoles, but now they can be packed and taken home with you. In the main, merchandise tends to run to period clothing, porcelain, silver, antique books, boxes, clocks, prints, and paintings, with an occasional piece of antique furniture. You'll also find a lot of items circa 1950. It is open from 10am to 6pm Mon. to Sat. Tube: Sloane Square.

Chenil Galleries, 181-183 King's Rd., S.W.3 (tel. 071/351-5353), seem to specialize in art nouveau and art deco objects along with lots of jewelry. A permanent exhibition of an Epstein statue reflects the long association of the galleries with the arts. The various galleries have a wide range of merchandise, including Asian carpets, collectors' dolls, and teddy bears, as well as prints and maps, fine porcelain, chess sets, some period furniture, and 17th- and 18th-century paintings. Tube: Sloane Square.

Mall Antiques Arcade at Camden Passage, Islington, N.1, contains one of Britain's greatest concentrations of antique businesses. Here you will find some 35 dealers, specializing in fine furniture, porcelain, and silver, and housed in individual shop units. Go from 7:30am to 5pm Wed. or from 9am to 6pm Sat. The center is also open from 10am to 5pm Tues., Thur., and Fri. Tube: Angel.

Arts and Crafts

On a Sunday morning along **Bayswater Road,** for more than a mile, pictures, collages, and craft items are hung on the railings along the edge of Hyde Park and Kensington Gardens. If the weather is right, start at Marble Arch and walk and walk, shopping or just sightseeing as you go along. Along Piccadilly, you'll see much of the same thing by walking along the railings of **Green Park** on a Saturday afternoon.

Crafts Council, 12 Waterloo Place, S.W.1 (tel. 071/930-4811), is a public body that exists to promote crafts in England and Wales. It has galleries that offer a broad program of changing crafts exhibitions from British domestic pottery to American traditional patchwork. Most exhibitions are free; concessions are available. Other facilities include a lively information center, which can direct you to crafts events throughout Britain, a slide library, and a bookstall. (*Note:* Crafts Council runs a quality craft shop at the Victoria and Albert Museum, South Kensington.) The galleries and information center are open from 10am to 5pm Tues. to Sat. and from 2 to 5pm Sun. Tube: Piccadilly Circus.

Books

Claiming to be the world's largest bookstore, **W. & G. Foyle Ltd.,** 113-119 Charing Cross Rd., W.C.2 (tel. 071/439-8501), has an impressive array of hardcovers and paperbacks, including travel maps. The shop includes records, videotapes, and sheet music. Tube: Leicester Square.

Hatchards Ltd., 187-188 Piccadilly, W.1 (tel. 071/439-9921), is an old-fashioned looking place on the south side of Piccadilly stuffed with books ranging from popular fiction and specialist reference books to paperbacks. There are shelves of guidebooks, atlases, cookbooks, and books of puzzles to occupy you on train and plane trips. Hours are 9am to 6pm Mon. to Fri., 9am to 5pm Sat. Tube: Piccadilly Circus.

For history buffs, **History Bookshop,** 2 The Broadway, N.11 (tel. 071/368-8568), stands at the corner of Friern Barnet Road and MacDonald Road. Behind its 1890s facade, this is one of the largest repositories of secondhand books in London, containing some 80,000 volumes scattered over three floors. It specializes in military history. Catalogs are issued at regular intervals. Hours are 9:30am to 5:30pm Wed. to Sat. Tube: Arnos Grove.

Stanfords, 12-14 Long Acre, W.C.2 (tel. 071/836-1321), the world's largest map shop, was established in 1852. It's also the best travel book store in London. A large selection of travel literature, along with worldwide touring and survey maps, are sold here in this well-stocked store. Hours are 10am to 6pm Mon. to Sat.; 9am to 6pm Tues., Wed., and Fri.; and 9am to 7pm Thurs. Tube: Leicester Square.

Brass Rubbing

London Brass Rubbing Centre is at St. Martin-in-the-Fields Church, Trafalgar Square, W.C.2 (tel. 071/437-6023), in the big, brick-vaulted, 1730s crypt, alongside a brasserie restaurant, a bookshop, and a craft market. The center has 85 exact copies of bronze portraits ready for use. Paper, rubbing materials, and instructions on how to begin are furnished. The charges range from 50p (85¢) for a small copy to £10.50 ($17.35) for the largest, a life-size Crusader knight. The center is open all year except Christmas Day and from 10am to 6pm Mon. to Sat., noon to 6pm on Sun. A gift area is open, selling brass-rubbing kits for children, budget-priced readymade rubbings, plaques, a wide variety of books, souvenirs with a heritage theme, posters, and postcards. For those who wish to make brass rubbings in the countryside churches, the center offers instructions and sells guidebooks and the necessary materials. Tube: Charing Cross.

The same company operates a brass-rubbing center at **All Hallows Church by the Tower,** Byward Street, E.C.3 (tel. 071/481-2928), where material and instruction are supplied. It is open on the same schedule and prices are the same as the St. Martin-in-the-Field center. Next door to the Tower, this center is a quiet place to relax. The church is a fascinating place with a crypt museum, Roman artifacts, and traces of early London, including a Saxon wall pre-dating the Tower. Samuel Pepys, famed diarist, climbed to the spire of this church to watch the raging fire of London in 1666. The center has a bookshop and restaurant that is open from noon to 2pm Mon. to Fri. Tube: Tower Hill.

British Design

Exhibitions in **The Design Centre,** 28 Haymarket, S.W.1 (tel. 071/839-8000), deal with topical design subjects of all kinds. There is an innovation center that provides a showcase for new ideas and prototypes to attract potential manufacturers and a related materials information center offering advice and information. The Design Council Bookshop stocks a wide range of publications related to design, architecture, and crafts. In 1989, the Young Designers' Centre opened, providing the first permanent year-round national exhibition area dedicated to the work of design students and graduates. The Design Centre is open from 10am to 6pm Mon. and Tues., from 10am to 8pm Wed. to Sat., and from 1 to 6pm Sun. Tube: Piccadilly Circus.

China

A wide range of English bone china, as well as crystal and giftware, is sold at **Lawleys,** 154 Regent St., W.1 (tel. 071/734-3184). The firm specializes in Royal Doulton, Minton, Royal Crown Derby, Wedgwood, and Aynsley china; Royal Doulton, Stuart, Waterford, Brierley, Swarovski, and Edinburgh crystal; Lladro figures; David Winter Cottages; Border Fine Arts; and other famous giftware ranges. They also sell cutlery. Hours are 9:30am to 6pm Mon. to Sat. (to 7pm on Thurs.). Tube: Piccadilly Circus or Oxford Circus.

Waterford-Wedgwood has a large shop at 249 Oxford St., W.1 (tel. 071/734-5656), at the corner of Regent Street. The staff there will explain their export plan to save you money on your souvenir buying. Besides selling tableware and glassware, the store offers inexpensive ashtrays in the traditional blue-and-white or sage-green-and-white. In any case, the store is like a miniature museum and well worth a visit. It also carries a collection of china, jewelry, pendants, earrings, and brooches. Hours are 9am to 6pm Mon. to Sat. (until 7pm on Thurs.). Tube: Oxford Circus. There are also Waterford-Wedgwood shops at 158 Regent St., and 173 Piccadilly. Tube: Piccadilly.

Thomas Goode, 19 S. Audley St., Grosvenor Square, W.1 (tel. 071/499-2823), was established in 1827, 10 years before Queen Victoria came to the throne. It is perhaps the most famous china and glass shop in the world, with three Royal Warrants, and has Minton majolica elephants gracing its front windows. The main entrance, with its famous mechanical doors, gives access to the china, glass, and silverware displayed in 14 showrooms. You can choose a small gift or purchase a unique dinner service with cresting and a monogram. A Thomas Goode catalog is available. Hours are 9am to 5pm Mon., Wed., Thurs., and Fri.; 9:30am to 5pm Tues., and 9:30am to 1pm Sat. Tube: Hyde Park Corner.

Chocolates

What may be the finest chocolates in the world are made by **Charbonnel et Walker Ltd.,** 1 Royal Arcade, 28 Old Bond St., W.1 (tel. 071/491-0939). They will send messages of thanks or love, spelled out on the chocolates themselves. The staff of this bow-fronted shop on the corner of the Royal Arcade off Old Bond Street will help you choose from the variety of centers. A box will be priced by weight. They have ready-made presentation boxes as well. Hours are 9:30am to 5:30pm Mon. to Fri. and 10am to 4pm Sat. Tube: Green Park.

Prestat, 14 Princes Arcade, S.W.1 (tel. 071/629-4838), is chocolate maker "to Her Majesty the Queen by appointment." Why not impress your friends by taking home a box of assorted Napoleon truffles? Brandy cherries may also tempt you. All boxes are gift wrapped with an extra touch of elegance. Hours are 10am to 6pm Mon. to Fri. and 9:30am to 5:30pm Sat. Tube: Bond Street.

Clocks

In the heart of the Camden Passage Antiques Village in Islington, **Strike One Limited,** 51 Camden Passage, N.1 (tel. 071/226-9709), sells clocks and barometers. Strike One clearly dates and prices each old clock, and every clock is guaranteed worldwide for a year against faulty construction. A wide selection of clocks is displayed, ranging from Victorian dial clocks to early English, long-cast timepieces. Strike One specializes in Act of Parliament clocks. They issue an illustrated catalog, which is mailed internationally to all serious clock collectors. They also undertake to find any clock a customer might request, if they do not have a suitable example in stock. The shop is open from 9am to 5pm (at other times by appointments); closed Sun. Tube: Angel.

Contemporary Art

Originally established as a branch office of Christie's specializing in modern art, **CCA Galleries,** 8 Dover St., W.1 (tel. 071/499-6701), in 1987 broke away from its illustrious parent. Today it offers some etchings, lithographs, and screenprints by up-and-coming artists, priced from £35 ($57.75) to £200 ($330). It also offers major works by such world masters as Henry Moore, which cost small fortunes. The gallery is considered innovative and creative even within the competitive world of London galleries. Hours are 9:30am to 5:30pm Mon. to Fri. and 10am to 4pm Sat. Tube: Green Park.

Department Stores

The department store to end all department stores is **Harrods,** Brompton Road, at Knightsbridge, S.W.1 (tel. 071/730-1234). As firmly entrenched in English life as Buckingham Palace and the Ascot Races, it is an elaborate emporium, at times as fascinating as a museum. In a magazine article about Harrods, a salesperson was quoted as saying: "It's more of a sort of way of life than a shop, really." The store underwent refurbishment to restore it to the elegance and luxury of the '20s and '30s. Aside from the fashion department (including high-level tailoring and a "Way In" section for young people), you'll find such incongruous sections as a cathedral-ceilinged and arcaded meat market, even a funeral service. Harrods has everything: men's custom-tailored suits, tweed overcoats, cashmere or lambswool sweaters for both men and women, hand-stiched traveling bags, raincoats, mohair jackets, patterned ski sweaters, scarves of hand-woven Irish wool, pewter reproductions, a perfumery department, "lifetime" leather suitcases, pianos. There's also a men's grooming hall, the first in-store one in Europe. Harrods is open 9am to 6pm Mon. to Sat. (9:30am to 7pm Thurs.). There is a choice of 10 restaurants and bars in the store. Tube: Knightsbridge.

Much more economical than Harrods, however, is **Selfridges,** 400 Oxford St., W.1 (tel. 071/629-1234), one of the biggest department stores in Europe, with more than 300 divisions, selling everything from artificial flowers to groceries. The specialty shops are particularly enticing, with good buys in Irish linen, Wedgwood, leather goods, silver-painted goblets, and cashmere and woolen scarves. There's also the Miss Selfridge Boutique for the young. To help you travel light, the export bureau will air freight your purchases to anywhere in the world, completely tax free. In the basement services arcade, the London Tourist Board will help you find your way around London's sights with plenty of maps, tips, and advice. Selfridges is open 9:30am to 6pm Mon. to Sat., 10am to 8pm Thurs. Tube: Bond Street or Marble Arch.

Liberty & Company Limited, 210 Regent St., W.1 (tel. 071/734-1234), is renowned worldwide for selling high-quality, stylish merchandise in charming surroundings. Its flagship store on Regent Street houses six floors of fashion, fabrics, china, and home furnishings, plus the Oriental department in the basement. As well as the famous Liberty Print fashion fabrics, furnishing fabrics, scarves, ties, luggage, and gifts, the shop sells well-designed, high-quality merchandise from all over the world. Liberty offers a personal "corner shop" service with helpful and informed assistants selling its stylish and often unique merchandise. Hours are 9:30am to 6pm Mon. to Sat. (to 7:30pm Thurs.). Tube: Oxford Street. The company has outlets in Bath, Cambridge, Canterbury, Edinburgh, Glasgow, Manchester, Norwich, York, and Oxford. Tube: Oxford Circus.

Marks & Spencer has several branches in London, attracting the thrifty Britisher, who gets fine buys, especially in woolen goods. The main department store is at 458 Oxford St., W.1 (tel. 071/935-7954), three short blocks from Marble Arch. However, there are a number of branches in London as well as in most towns of any size in Britain. This chain has built a reputation for quality and value, and now clothes some 70% of British workers—wholly or partially. It is said that 25% of the socks worn by men in Britain come from M&S. The prices are competitive even when you go as far as cashmere sweaters for women. Hours are 9am to 8pm Mon. to Fri. and 8:30am to 6pm Sat. Tube: Marble Arch.

Simpson's, 203 Piccadilly, W.1 (tel. 071/734-2002), opened in 1936 as the home of DAKS clothing, and it's been going strong ever since. It is known not only for men's wear but also for women's fashions, perfume, jewelry, and lingerie. The clothes are the highest quality and exude elegance and style, from casual weekend wear to a wide selection of evening dress. The store also has a good restaurant serving traditional English food. It is open for breakfast, at around £7.50 ($12.40), from 9 to 11:30am; for lunch, £15 ($24.75), from noon to 2:30pm; and it's also a good choice for afternoon tea, £5 ($8.25), from 3:30 to 5:15pm. The store is open from 9am to 5:30pm Mon. to Sat. (to 7pm Thurs.). Tube: Piccadilly Circus.

Peter Jones, Sloane Square, S.W.1 (tel. 071/730-34340, is one of the finest department stores in Europe. It has an impressive array of home furnishings, kitchenware, household goods, china and glass, even antiques, and it's especially known for its linens. Its Irish linens represent real value. The classy store also carries an array of perfumes, fashions with accessories for both men and women, and has, in addition, two restaurants and a coffee shop. Many women come here just for its hairdressing salon. Open from 9am to 5:30pm Mon. to Sat. (from 9:30am to 7pm Wed.). Tube: Sloane Square.

Designer Clothing (Secondhand)

A London institution since it was first established in the 1940s, **Pandora,** 16-22 Cheval Place, S.W.7 (tel. 071/589-5289), stands in fashionable Knightsbridge, a stone's throw from Harrods. It features dozens of hand-me-down designer dresses, and it is generally acknowledged that this store carries the finest such merchandise in London. Several times a week, chauffeurs will drive up with bundles packed by the anonymous gentry of England. These are likely to include dresses, jackets, suits, and gowns that the ladies wish to sell. Entire generations of London women have clothed themselves at this store. One woman, voted best dressed at Ascot several years ago, was wearing a secondhand dress acquired at Pandora's. Identities of the owners are strictly guarded. But many buyers are titillated at the thought they might be wearing a hand-me-down from a royal person, perhaps Princess Di. Prices are generally one third to one half of their retail value. Chanel, Yves St. Laurent, and Valentino are among the designers represented. Hours are 10am to 5pm Mon. to Sat. Tube: Knightsbridge.

Groceries with Elegance

Down the street from the Ritz, **Fortnum and Mason Ltd.,** 181 Piccadilly, W.1 (tel. 071/734-8040), draws the carriage trade, the well-heeled dowager from Mayfair or Belgravia who comes seeking such tinned treasures as pâté de foie gras or a boar's head. She would never set foot in a regular grocery store, but Fortnum and Mason, with its swallow-tailed attendants, is no mere grocery store—it's a British tradition dating back to 1707. In fact, the establishment likes to think that Mr. Fortnum and Mr. Mason "created a union surpassed in its importance to the human race only by the meeting of Adam and Eve." Today this store exemplifies the elegance and style one would expect from an establishment with two royal warrants. Enter the doors and be transported to another world of deep-red carpets, crystal chandeliers, spiraling wooden staircases, and unobtrusive, tail-coated assistants.

The grocery department is renowned for its impressive selection of the finest foods from around the world—the best champagne, the most scrumptious Belgian chocolates, and succulent Scottish smoked salmon. You might choose one of their wicker baskets of exclusive foods to have shipped home, perhaps through their telephone and mail order service. You can wander through the other four floors and consider the purchase of bone china and crystal cut glass, perhaps find the perfect present in the leather or stationery departments, or reflect on the changing history of furniture, paintings, and ornaments in the antiques department. Dining choices include Patio & Buttery, St. James's Restaurant, and the Fountain Restaurant. Hours are 9:30am to 5:30pm Mon. to Sat. Tube: Piccadilly Circus or Green Park.

Irish Wares

Northern Ireland and the Republic of Ireland are united at the **Irish Shop,** 11 Duke St., W.1 (tel. 071/935-1366), by stocking so much stuff in such a small area. Directed by Gerard Collet, it is a useful place for those who missed buying souvenirs in Ireland. All products are genuine. Prices are reportedly as close as possible to those you'd pay in Ireland. Merchandise ranges from Donegal tweed caps and hats to china, from tea-cozies to Celtic-design jewelry sets with precious stones. Waterford and Galway crystal comes in all styles and types. Belleek china and Gaelic coffee glasses, single or in a set, are also featured. You can purchase handwoven tweed and Irish linen by the yard. Irish linen tablecloths range from plain to damask. Hand crocheted women's handkerchiefs cost £10.50 ($17.35) for two. As the Aran and jerseys are all handknitted, you have to rummage to find the exact one to suit your particular shape and size. Also offered are Donegal tweed jackets for men and skirts for women. Duke Street is off Wigmore, a street running alongside Selfridges from Oxford Street. Tube: Bond Street or Marble Arch.

Jewelry

A family firm, **Sanford Brothers Ltd.,** 3 Holborn Bars, Old Elizabethan Houses, E.C.1 (tel. 071/405-2352), has been in business since 1923. They sell anything in jewelry, both modern and Victorian, silver of all kinds, and a fine selection of clocks and watches. The Elizabethan buildings are one of the sights of old London. Hours are 10am to 4:30pm Mon. to Fri. Tube: Chancery Lane.

London Diamond Centre, 10 Hanover St., W.1 (tel. 071/629-5511), offers organized tours of a permanent exhibition showing how diamonds are mined, cut, polished, and made into exclusive jewelry, as well as a visit to the showroom where unmounted diamonds, ready-to-wear diamond jewelry, and other gem jewelry from costly to inexpensive can be purchased or ordered to your requirements. Hours are from 9:30am to 5:30pm Mon. to Fri., from 9:30am to 1:30pm Sat. Admission is £3.45 ($5.70) per person, the fee including a souvenir, brillant-cut zirconium (not a diamond), which you can have mounted in a 9-karat gold setting of your choice at modest cost. Tube: Oxford Circus.

Maps and Engravings

An ideal place to find an offbeat souvenir of your visit to London is **The Map House,** 54 Beauchamp Place, S.W.3 (tel. 071/589-4325), selling antique maps and engravings. The shop also has a vast selection of old prints of London and England, both in the original and in reproduction. An original engraving, guaranteed more than 100 years old, can cost from as little as £1 ($1.65) to as much as £10,000 ($16,500). The Map House is open from 9:45am to 5:45pm Mon. to Fri., and from 10:30am to 5pm on Sat. Tube: Knightsbridge.

The **Greater London Record Office and History Library,** 40 Northampton Rd., E.C.1 (tel. 071/633-6851), has archives, maps, books, and photographs on the history of London. Reproductions of old maps and prints of London are available for sale. It is open 9:30am to 7:30pm Tues., 9:30am to 4:45pm Wed. to Fri. Tube: Farringdon or Angel.

Men's Clothing

The selection in England is perhaps the finest in the world, ranging from Savile Row (at celestial prices) to bargain-basement wear. Your best buys are in ready-to-wear, rather than the super-expensive, tailored ("bespoke") clothing, which is perhaps suitable for successful bankers.

Offering both British and international designers, **Austin Reed,** 113 Regent St., W.1 (tel. 071/734-6789), has long stood for quality clothing for both men and women. The suits of Chester Barre, for example, are said to fit like bespoke models. The polite employees are usually honest about telling you what looks good on you. The store always stocks top-notch but expensive cashmere jackets, along with well-made conventional clothes. Men can outfit themselves from dressing gowns to overcoats. An entire floor, the third, is devoted to the clothing needs of women, with carefully selected suits, separates, coats, shirts, knitwear, and accessories offered. It is open from 9am to 5:30pm Mon., Wed., Fri., Sat.; 9:30am to 5:30pm Tues. and from 9am to 7pm Thurs. Tube: Piccadilly Circus.

The popular magazine *Time Out* said it all about **Aquascutum,** 100 Regent St., W.1 (tel. 071/734-6090). It is "about as quintessentially British as you'll get this side of Savile Row, and it's a popular stop-off for American tourists wanting to look more British than the Brits." On a trio of floors, this classic shop serves only high-quality British and imported clothing for men desiring "the classic look." It is open from 9am to 6pm Mon. to Sat. (to 7pm on Thurs.). Tube: Piccadilly Circus.

Gieves & Hawkes, 1 Savile Row, W.1 (tel. 071/434-2001), has a prestigious address on Savile Row, and a list of clients that includes the prince of Wales, yet its prices are not the lethal tariffs of other stores along this street. It's expensive but you get good quality here, as befits its reputation as a supplier to the British Royal Navy since the days of Lord Nelson. Cotton shirts, silk ties, Shetland jumpers, and exceptional suits—both ready-to-wear and "bespoke"— are sold. Hours are 9am to 5:30pm Mon. to Sat. Tube: Piccadilly Circus.

Harrods, Knightsbridge, S.W.1 (tel. 071/730-1234), is a worthy choice for just about everything (see separate recommendation under "Department Stores"). But do not overlook its men's store with a huge array of high quality, ready-to-wear suits, and all the accessories, ranging from shoes, knitwear, socks, shirts, and pajamas for that elegant look. Tube: Knightsbridge.

Since tailor-made British suits tend to be beyond the wallets of most men, a much cheaper alternative is to go to one of the **Burton** stores found all over Britain. There are 66 branches in the Greater London area alone. The main store is at 311 Oxford St., W.1 (tel. 071/491-0032). Ready-made suits, where a man selects first his jacket, then the trousers to match in his size, range from £95 ($158.75) to £150 ($247.50). Hours are 9am to 6pm Mon., Tues., and Sat.; 9:30am to 7pm Wed. and Fri.; and 9:30am to 8pm Thurs. Tube: Oxford Circus.

SHIRTS AND TIES Perhaps the finest name in men's shirts is **Hilditch & Key,** 87 Jermyn St., S.W.1 (tel. 071/930-4126), in business since 1899. There are three shops on this street, with no. 37 specializing in women's wear and no. 73 offering men's clothing in the main. But at no. 87 they sell "bespoke shirt service" as well as shoes for men. Hilditch also has an outstanding tie collection. Hours are 9:30am to 6pm Mon., Tues., Wed., and Fri.; 9:30am to 7pm Thurs.; and 9:30am to 5:30pm Sat. Tube: Green Park or Piccadilly Circus.

But Hilditch & Key is too expensive for the average budget. In that case, head for **Thomas Pink,** 16 Cullum St., E.C.3 (tel. 071/929-1405), where cotton shirts of excellent quality begin at £32 ($52.80). They also sell shirts for women beginning at approximately the same price. The store became famous for its twofold poplin shirts. A small square of pine cotton is sewn at the bottom edge, and this trademark tells all who see that your shirt came from Thomas Pink, a prestige symbol for "gents of The City." Hours are 10am to 6pm Mon. to Fri. Tube: Tower Hill.

Military Miniatures

A bewildering array of military miniatures, perfect in every detail, is sold at **Tradition,** 5A Shepherd St., W.1 (tel. 071/439-7452). You name it, Tradition makes it. It has a vast stock of French cavalry figures, all sorts of British soldiers from the Napoleonic Wars, U.S. cavalrymen from the War of 1812 and the Civil War, to name but a few. What more fitting souvenir of London than a British Grenadier, a Beefeater, or a Chelsea Pensioner? The range is enormous, and the shop will sell you figures painted or unpainted, marching, running, firing, kneeling, even dying. Hours are 9:30am to 5:30pm Mon. to Fri., 9:30am to 3pm Sat. Tube: Green Park.

Notions

A variety of toilet articles and fragrances is found at **Floris,** 89 Jermyn St., S.W.1 (tel. 071/930-2885). The floor-to-ceiling mahogany cabinets that line its walls are considered architectural curiosities in their own right. They were installed relatively late in the establishment's history (that is, 1851), long after the shop had received its royal warrants as supplier of toilet articles to the king and queen. The business was established in 1730 by a Minorcan entrepreneur, Juan Floris, who brought from his Mediterranean home a technique for extracting fragrances from local flowers. Fashionable residents of St. James's flocked to his shop, purchasing his soaps, perfumes, and grooming aids. Today you can buy essences of flowers grown in English gardens, including stephanotis, rose geranium, lily-of-the-valley, violet, white jasmine, and carnation. Open from 9:30am to 5:30pm Mon. to Fri., 9:30am to 4pm Sat. Tube: Piccadilly Circus.

Philately

The **National Postal Museum,** King Edward Building, King Edward St., E.C.1 (tel. 071/239-5420), houses a magnificent collection of postage stamps and allied material. It also sells postcards illustrating the collection and has a distinctive Maltese Cross postmark first used on the Penny Black. Open 9:30am to 4:30pm Mon. to Thurs. (to 4pm Fri.). Tube: St. Paul's.

A letter mailed from Heathrow Airport is franked at Hounslow with an attractive Concorde cancellation. In country areas, the post office provides a postbus service between many remote and otherwise isolated villages. Often passenger tickets are cancelled with a special stamp of collector interest, and postcards depicting places of interest along the routes are issued and mailed from these buses. More specialized, many of the narrow-gauge and privately owned railroads in the country issue and cancel their own stamps. Among these are the Ravenglass and Eskdale, the Keighley and Worth Valley Light Railway, and the Bluebell Railway, along with the Romney, Hythe, and Dymchurch Railway.

Posters

For a fine souvenir of your visit to London, try the **London Transport Museum Shop,** Covent Garden, W.C.2 (tel. 071/379-6344). This unique shop carries a fine selection of a wide range of posters. The London Underground maps can be purchased here, as well as massive pictorial posters as seen at tube stations (size 40 inches by 60 inches). The shop also carries books, cards, T-shirts, and other souvenir items. Open daily 10am to 5:45pm; closed Christmas Day and Boxing Day. Tube: Covent Garden.

Raincoats

Where else but **Burberry,** 18 Haymarket, S.W.1 (tel. 071/930-3343), near the London offices of American Express. The word Burberry has been synonymous with raincoats ever since King Edward VII publicly ordered his valet to "bring my Burberry" when the skies threatened rain. Its circa-1912 Haymarket store connects three lavishly stocked floors to an oak-lined staircase upon which have trod some of the biggest names in politics, the stage, and screen. An impeccably trained staff sells the famous raincoat, along with a collection of excellent men's shirts, sportswear, knitwear, and accessories. Raincoats are available in women's sizes and styles as well as men's. Don't think you'll get anything cheap from such a world-famous retailer. You get prestige and quality. Hours are 9am to 5:30pm Mon. to Sat. (to 7pm Thurs.). Tube: Piccadilly Circus.

Shoes

London is called the footwear capital of the world, and somewhere in this city you can find your shoe fantasy.

See the recommendation of **Natural Shoe Store** under "Covent Garden" if you like your shoes wholesome—that is, made from natural materials. They stock shoes for both men and women.

Charles Jourdan, 39-43 Brompton Rd., S.W.1 (tel. 071/581-3333), carries one of the largest ranges of women's shoes in London, including a variety of styles. Imelda Marcos could run wild here, especially if she saw those peep-toe, diamente-studded, satin flatties. Hours are 10am to 6:30pm Mon. to Sat. and to 7pm Wed. Tube: Knightsbridge.

Lilley & Skinners, 360 Oxford St., W.1 (tel. 071/629-6381), is the biggest shoe store in the world, displaying its merchandise across four floors. It markets shoes both under its own label as well as designer creations. All sizes of feet are fitted here, including extra small. Prices, likewise, are wide ranging. Hours are 9:30am to 6:30pm Mon. to Wed. and on Fri., 9:30am to 8pm on Thurs., and 9am to 6pm on Sat. Tube: Bond Street.

Top quality shoes have been turned out by the famous shoemakers, **Church's,** 143 Brompton Rd., S.W.3 (tel. 071/589-9136), since 1873 when the company was founded at Northampton. A trio of brothers (Alfred, Thomas, and William) started what has become a tradition among well-outfitted English gents who stamp around London in their shoes from Church's. Of course, the company, always a bastion of English tradition, has changed with the tides of style, and now offers more modish selections along with their traditional footwear. There is also a fashionable selection of shoes for women. The shop is open from 9am to 5:30pm Mon. to Fri. (9am to 5pm Sat.). Tube: Knightsbridge.

Silver

Established in Victoria's day (1882), the **London Silver Vaults,** Chancery Lane, W.C.2 (tel. 071/242-3844), soon became the largest silver vaults in the world. You can actually go shopping in vault after vault for that special treasure. The vaults are open from 9am to 5:30pm Mon. to Fri., 9am to 12:30pm Sat. Tube: Chancery Lane.

A very special place is **Stanley Leslie,** 15 Beauchamp Place, S.W.3 (tel. 071/589-2333). Behind a cramped and black-painted, big-windowed storefront lies a staggering array of Georgian, Victorian, and early 20th-century silver. It's just the place to spend hours ferreting around for a special present. The quality is very high. Hours are 9am to 5pm Mon. to Fri., 9am to 1pm Sat. Tube: Knightsbridge.

Souvenirs

Charles Dickens enthusiasts can go to the **Old Curiosity Shop,** 13-14 Portsmouth St., off Lincoln's Inn Fields, W.C.2 (tel. 071/405-9891), used by Dickens as the abode of Little Nell. One of the original Tudor buildings still remaining in London (built in 1567), the shop crams every nook and cranny with general knickknackery, whatnots, and souvenirs, including Dickens first editions. A popular item is an unframed silhouette of a Dickens character. Horse brasses are also sold, as are Old Curiosity Shop bookmarks and ashtrays with Dickensian engravings. Upstairs is an exhibition relating the story of the Old Curiosity Shop. Also on view is a series of letters from Charles Dickens, and other artifacts. Admission to the shop is free, but it costs £1.50 ($2.50) to view the exhibit. The shop is open April to October from 9am to 5:30pm Mon. to Fri., 9:30am to 5pm Sat. and Sun., and November to March from 9:30am to 5pm Mon. to Fri., 9:30am to 4:30pm Sat. and Sun. Tube: Holborn.

Sports Goods

Britain's biggest sports store, **Lillywhites Ltd.,** Piccadilly Circus, S.W.1 (tel. 071/930-3181), has floor after floor of sports clothing, equipment, and footwear. Established in 1863 and Europe's most renowned sports store, Lillywhites offers everything connected with sport, together with new and exciting ranges of stylish and fashionable leisure-wear for both men and women. Lillywhites special orders and international departments offer a worldwide service. Hours are 9:30am to 6pm Mon. to Sat., to 7pm Thurs. Tube: Piccadilly Circus.

Street Markets

Street markets have played an important role in the life of London. They are recommended not only for bric-a-brac but as a low-cost adventure. In fact, you don't have to buy a thing. But be warned—some of the stallkeepers are quite persuasive.

PORTOBELLO ROAD MARKET A magnet for collectors of virtually everything, Portobello Market, Portobello Road, W.11, is mainly a Sat. happening from 8am to 5pm (it's best to go early). The name came from Admiral Vernon's capture of a Caribbean city, Puerto Bello, in 1739. A farm once stood here, but by the 1860s a market had grown up. Once known mainly for fruit and vegetables (still sold, incidentally, throughout the week), in the past four decades Portobello has become synonymous with antiques. But don't take the stallholder's word for it that the mildewed fiddle he's holding is a genuine Stradivarius left to him in the will of his Italian great-uncle. It might just as well have been "nicked" from an East End pawn shop. You can browse around for jewelry, weapons (modern and antique), toys, kitchenware, scientific instruments, china, books, old cigarette cards, movie posters, magazines long defunct, watches, pens, music boxes, whatever.

The market is divided among three major sections, including the most crowded, the southern antiques section running between Colville Road and Chepstow Villas. The greatest concentration of pickpockets are in this area, so be duly warned. The second sector (and the oldest part) is the "fruit and veg" market, lying between Westway and Colville Road. In the third and final section, Londoners operate a flea market here, selling bric-a-brac and lots of secondhand goods they didn't really want in the first place. But it still makes interesting fun for a look-around.

In addition to stalls, many permanent shops are found both on and off Portobello Road, and these can be visited throughout the week. The majority of these are located between Westway and Colville Road. Many art galleries also operate in and around the area. Dealers scout these daring galleries looking for tomorrow's Francis Bacon. Search for these galleries on Kensington Park Road, Blenheim Crescent, and the fruit and veg section of Portobello Road. Many food stalls also operate during market day on Portobello Road. Tube: Ladbroke Grove or Notting Hill Gate.

NEW CALEDONIAN MARKET Commonly known as the **Bermondsey Market** because of its location, it's at Bermondsey Square, S.E.1, at the corner of Long Land and Bermondsey Street. At its extreme east end, it begins at Tower Bridge Road. This is one of Europe's outstanding street markets in size and quality of goods offered. The stalls are well known, and many dealers come into London from the country. The market gets under way on Fri. at 7am. The most serious bargain hunters are the early birds. Antiques and other items are generally lower in price here than at Portobello Road and the other street markets, but bargains are gone by 9am. The market closes at noon. It's best reached by taking the Underground to Elephant and Castle, then bus 1 or 188.

PETTICOAT LANE On Sun. between 9am and 2pm (go before noon), throngs of shoppers join the crowds on Petticoat Lane (also known as Middlesex Street, E.1). It is surrounded by a maze of lanes that begin at the Liverpool Street station on the Bishopsgate side where you can buy clothing, food, antiques, and plenty of junk. Tube: Liverpool Street, Aldgate, or Aldgate East.

LEATHER LANE At this lively market, you'll find a good variety of items for sale: fruit from carts, vegetables, books, men's shirts and sweaters, and women's clothing. There are no try-ons at this outdoor market, so make sure of the size clothing you want before buying. Open 11am to 3pm Mon. to Sat. Tube: Chancery Lane.

BERWICK STREET MARKET This may be the only street market in the world that is flanked by two rows of strip clubs, porno stores, and adult movie dens. Don't let that put you off, however. Humming six days a week in the scarlet heart of Soho, this array of stalls and booths sells probably the best and cheapest fruit and vegetables in town. It also sells ancient records that may turn out to be collectors' items, tapes, books, and old magazines. Open 8am to 5pm Mon. through Sat. Tube: Oxford Circus or Tottenham Court Road.

Travel Center

British Airways First, 156 Regent St., W.1 (tel. 071/434-4700), is the retail flagship of British Airways, housed on three floors. It offers not only worldwide travel and ticketing, but also a wide range of services and shops. These even include a travel clinic for immunization and a pharmacy selling first-aid kits and travel medication. There's also a bureau de change, plus a passport and visa service, as well as a theater-booking desk. The ground floor offers such quality goods as fashion, luggage, glass and porcelain, jewelry, silver, and fragrances. A coffee shop serves teas, coffee, and pastries. Hand-baggage only passengers may check in for a BA flight here. Other services include a change machine, photobooth, phones, toilets, public Fax, and photocopying facilities. Hours are from 8am to 7pm Mon. to Fri., from 9am to 6pm Sat. Tube: Piccadilly Circus.

Women's Clothing

Austin Reed, which offers an excellent selection of styles for both women and men, is described under "Men's Clothing." For raincoats, refer under that heading to **Burberry's,** which has a selection of raincoats and other coats for women, along with scarves and handbags. For sporting wear, refer to **Lillywhites** under "Sports Goods." That famous store has running shoes, ski wear, and all sorts of well-made items for the active woman. Under "Department Stores," check out **Simpson,** which used to be exclusively a men's store, but now offers a variety of "fashionable fashions" for women, showcasing its DAKS clothing. Also under that heading, women will want to take a preview of the fashions at the world's most famous department store, **Harrods.**

In addition to these emporiums, London is filled with stores and specialty boutiques catering to women. Just to get you going on your search, I'll make only a few suggestions, but know that there are hundreds more in all parts of town.

Laura Ashley, 7-9 Harriet St., S.W.1 (tel. 071/235-9796), will outfit you with flowerprint Victorian dresses, everything very feminine with pinafores. Women seem to like its white cotton nightgowns. Ms. Ashley's son, Nick, is in charge of the empire today, and many changes have been made. Hours are 9:30am to 6pm Mon., Tues. Thurs., and Fri.; 9:30am to 7pm Wed.; and 9am to 6pm Sat. Tube: Knightsbridge.

Changing Room, 10A Gees Court, W.1 (tel. 071/408-1596), is a small shop, but it displays the clothing of at least a dozen British designers at one time. The special feature of this shop is that it affords an opportunity to "mix and match" the clothing and accessories of various designers. Hours are 10:30am to 6:30pm Mon. to Wed. and Fri. to Sat., 10:30am to 7:30pm Thurs. Tube: Bond Street.

English Eccentrics, 155 Fulham Rd., S.W.3 (tel. 071/589-7154), known for its prints, offers daring clothing for women (also men). It's definitely for the extrovert. You never know until you get there what the latest stock will turn out to be. Hours are 10am to 6pm Mon. to Sat. Tube: South Kensington.

Hyper-Hyper, 26-40 Kensington High St., W.8 (tel. 071/937-6964), has been showcasing young and talented British fashion designers since 1983. The work of nearly 75 designers is on display at all times. From sportswear to eveningwear, with plenty of accessories thrown in, including shoes, Hyper-Hyper will thrill and intrigue. Menswear is also sold here. Hours are 10am to 6pm Mon. to Sat. Tube: Kensington High Street.

Fenwick of Bond Street, 63 New Bond St., W.1 (tel. 071/629-9160), is a small department store that offers an excellent collection of womenswear, ranging from moderately priced ready-to-wear to designer fashions. A wide range of lingerie (in all price ranges) is also sold here. The store dates from 1891, and no clerk will talk to you until you speak first. That's their policy. It is open 9:30am to 6pm Mon. to Wed. and Fri. to Sat., 9:30am to 7:30pm Thurs. Tube: Bond Street.

Bradley's, 85 Knightsbridge, S.W.1 (tel. 071/235-2902), is the best known lingerie specialty store in London. Even some members of the royal family shop here. Bradley's fits "all sizes" in silk, cotton, lace, polycotton, whatever. You'll love its fluffy slippers. Its satin or silk nightgowns will make you feel like Myrna Loy on the late show, enticing William Powell. Hours are 9:30am to 6pm Mon., Tues., and Thurs. to Sat.; 9:30am to 7pm Wed. Tube: Knightsbridge.

Woolens

For top-quality woolen fabric and garments, go to the **Scotch House,** 84 Regent St., S.W.1 (tel. 071/734-5966), renowned worldwide for its comprehensive selection of cashmere and wool knitwear for both men and women. Also available is a wide range of tartan garments and accessories, as well as Scottish tweed classics. The children's collection covers ages 2 to 13 and also offers excellent value and quality. Hours are 9am to 6pm Mon. to Sat. (to 7pm Thurs.). Tube: Piccadilly Circus. The Scotch House also has stores at 191 Regent St., W.1; 2 Brompton Rd., S.W.1; and 187 Oxford St., W.1.

Westaway & Westaway, opposite the British Museum at 62-65 Great Russell St., W.C.1 (tel. 071/405-4479), is a substitute for a shopping trip to Scotland. They stock an enormous range of kilts, scarves, waistcoats, capes, dressing gowns, and rugs in authentic clan tartans. What's more, they are knowledgeable on the subject of these minutely intricate clan symbols. They also sell superb—and untartaned —cashmere, camel-hair, and Shetland knitwear, along with Harris tweed jackets, Burberry raincoats, and cashmere overcoats for men. Hours are 9am to 5:30pm Mon. to Sat. Tube: Tottenham Court Road. Another branch is at 92-93 Great Russell St., W.C.1.

Berk, 46 Burlington Arcade, W.1 (tel. 071/493-0028), the cashmere specialist, is one of those irresistible "fancy shops" for which London is famous. To shelter your precious cashmere from the elements, Berk also carries Burberry's raincoats, golf jackets and caps, and rain hats. And all this is displayed in the 150-year-old Burlington Arcade, an attraction in its own right. Hours are 9am to 5:30pm Mon. to Fri., 9am to 5pm Sat. Tube: Piccadilly Circus.

5. Evening Entertainment

London is crammed with nighttime entertainment. You'll have a wide choice of action—from the dives of Soho to elegant clubs. So much depends on your taste, pocketbook, and even the time of year. Nowhere else will you find such a panorama of legitimate theaters, operas, concerts, gambling clubs, discos, vaudeville at Victorian music halls, striptease joints, jazz clubs, folk music cafés, nightclubs, and ballrooms. For information about any of these events, ask a newsstand dealer for a copy of *Time Out* or *What's On in London* containing listings of restaurants, theaters, and nightclubs.

The following is a quick-reference list of major performance spaces in London, with box office telephone numbers. Details are provided in the listings below.

Barbican Centre	(tel. 071/638-8891)
London Coliseum	(tel. 071/836-3161, or 240-5258)

National Theatre   (tel. 071/928-2252)
Royal Albert Hall   (tel. 071/589-8212)
Royal Court Theatre   (tel. 071/730-1745)
Royal Opera House   (tel. 071/240-1066)
South Bank Centre
(including Royal
Festival Hall)   (tel. 071/928-8800)

LONDON'S THEATERS

The fame of the English theater has spread far and wide. In London, you'll have a chance to see it on its home ground. You may want to spend a classical evening with the Royal Shakespeare Company or the National Theatre Company, or you may settle for a new play. You might even want to catch up on that Broadway musical you missed in New York, or be an advance talent scout for next year's big stateside hit.

You can either purchase your ticket from the theater's box office (recommended method), or from a ticket agent, such as the one at the reservations desk of American Express (with agent's fee charges, however). Many theaters will accept bookings by telephone if you give your name and credit card number when you call. Then all you have to do is go along before the performance to collect your tickets, which will be sold at the theater price. Once confirmed, the booking will be charged to your account even if you don't use the tickets. Only cardholders can collect the tickets charged to their accounts.

Remember, if you are calling ahead from out of town, the area code for central London is 071. In a few theaters, you can reserve your spot in the gallery, the cheapest seats of all, but in some cases the inexpensive seats are sold only on the day of performance. This means that you'll have to buy your ticket earlier in the day, and—because you don't get a reserved seat—return about an hour before the performance and queue up for the best gallery seats.

For full details on West End productions, pick up a free biweekly *London Theatre Guide* at the Leicester Square booth or at any West End theater, tourist or travel information center, hotel, or library on your arrival in London.

Discount Theater Tickets and Reservations

London theater prices are—by U.S. standards—quite reasonable. Matinees are on Wednesday (or Thursday at some theaters) and on Saturday. Prices for London shows can vary widely—usually from £6 ($9.90) to £22 ($36.36), depending on the seat.

The **Leicester Square Half-Price Ticket Booth,** Leicester Square, W.C.2, sells theater tickets on the day of performance for half price (cash only) plus up to a £1.25 ($2.05) service charge. It's open Mon. to Sat. noon to 2pm for matinee performances and 2:30 to 6:30pm for evening performances. The staff there has a wide range of seats available. Obviously, tickets for "hits" are not available often. There is a long queue, but it moves quickly, and it's well worth the savings if you want to take in a lot of theater when you're in London. The shows for which tickets are available are displayed at the booth, so you can make up your mind on what to see as you wait in the queue. The booth is operated by the Society of West End Theatre.

If you want to see specific shows, particularly hit ones, you'll have to reserve in advance through one of the many London ticket agencies, including **Keith Prowse** (tel. 071/741-9999). If you want to attend a hit show that is likely to be sold out by the time you visit London, it's possible to reserve seats long before you go. Keith Prowse has an office in the United States that will reserve seats weeks or even months in advance. Contact Keith Prowse, 234 W. 44th St., Suite 902, New York, NY 10036 (tel. 212/398-1430, or call toll free 800/223-4466).

British Airways operates one of the most sure-fire ticket-ordering agencies in Europe. Its box office service permits the telephone purchase of the best seats available for theater and musical productions in London, Stratford-upon-Avon, and the Edinburgh Festival. Many theater lovers, without the help of BA's enormous buying power behind them, would find it impossible to locate or reserve tickets.

If a passenger holds tickets on BA, a phone call to the airline's telephone reservations service will pre-book and reserve tickets for the desirable theater seats. These may be charged to a credit card if they are reserved more than 7 days in advance. BA will issue a voucher to be exchanged in London for the actual tickets (seats preassigned). Many passengers—especially those who consider several evenings at the London theater an essential part of their trips to Britain—have found the service invaluable. For reservations and information, call BA toll-free 800/AIRWAYS.

Traveler's Advisory: Beware of "scalpers" who hang out in front of hit shows at London theaters. If their tickets are valid, they charge lethal prices. But there are many reports of their selling forged tickets.

Note: London theaters generally start and finish earlier than their American cousins. Evening performances are between 7:30 and 8:30, midweek matinees at 2:30 and 3pm, Sat. at 5:45pm.

There are two weekly publications giving full entertainment listings, *Time Out* and *What's On in London.*

Theaters

Since it is quite impossible to describe all of London's live theaters in this space, I'll just pick out a few for your benefit. Don't forget, these are merely gleanings from a treasure trove.

The **National Theatre,** South Bank, S.E.1 (tel. 071/928-2252), is London's premier repertory company, housed in a three-theater complex that stands as a landmark beside the Waterloo Bridge on the south bank of the Thames. A national theater building was first suggested in 1848, and it took Parliament 101 years to pass a bill vowing government support. Flaring out like a fan, the most thrilling theater in this complex is the **Olivier,** named after Lord Laurence Olivier, its first director when the company was born in 1962. The Olivier Theatre bears a resemblance in miniature to an ancient Greek theater: it's an open-stage, 1,160-seat house. The **Cottesloe** is a simple box theater for 400 people. Finally, the 890-seat **Lyttelton** is a traditional proscenium-arch house that doesn't have one bad seat. In the foyers there are three bookshops, eight bars, two restaurants, and five self-service buffets (some open all day except Sun.), and many outside terraces with river views. For everyone, with or without tickets for a play, there is live foyer music, free, before evening performances and Sat. matinees, and free exhibitions. The foyers are open from 10am to 11pm Mon. to Sat.; closed Sun.

Tickets usually range fron £7 ($11.55) to £20 ($33), but midweek matinees are cheaper. You can have a meal in the National Theatre Restaurant for around £12 ($19.80), or at one of the coffee bars. A snack will cost around £3.50 ($5.80). Tube: Waterloo Station.

The **Old Vic,** a 170-year-old theater on Waterloo Road, S.E.1 (tel. 071/928-2651, or the box office at 071/928-7616), underwent a mammoth facelift and modernization. The facade and much of the interior were restored in their original early 19th-century style, and most of the modernization was behind the scenes. The proscenium arch was moved back, and the stage trebled in size, and more seats and stage boxes added. It is air-conditioned and contains five bars. There are short seasons of varied plays, and several subscription offers have been introduced with reductions of up to £7 ($11.55) a seat if you purchase six tickets for different shows at once. Otherwise, top prices vary, with the best stalls or dress circle going for about £16 ($26.40) a ticket. Tube: Waterloo Station.

Royal Shakespeare Company, one of the world's finest theater companies, is based in Stratford-upon-Avon and at the Barbican Centre, Barbican, E.C.2 (tel. 071/638-8891). The central core of the company's work remains the plays of William Shakespeare, but it also presents a wide-ranging program of three different productions each week in the Barbican Theatre, the 1,200-seat main auditorium, which has excellent sightlines throughout, thanks to a raked orchestra. You can also attend productions at the Pit, the small studio space where the company's new playwrights are showcased.

In recent years, the RSC has had great success in transferring its hit shows, such as *Les Misérables* and *Les Liaisons Dangereuses* (the basis of the film *Dangerous Liaisons*) to West End theaters, while continuing its diverse repertoire both in London and Stratford. Tube: Barbican or Moorgate.

Those wanting to experience Shakespeare on his home territory can take the Shakespeare Connection, a road/rail link from Euston Station to Stratford-upon-Avon (bookings in advance at the station or tel. 0789/294466), which runs every day of the week; or the Shakespeare Stopover, a meal/theater-ticket/accommodation package (bookings tel. 0789/414999). In Stratford, the RSC plays in the 1,500-seat Royal Shakespeare Theatre and the 400-seat Swan Theatre; for bookings, phone 0789/295623. Seat prices range from £7 ($11.55) to £17.50 ($28.90) in the Barbican Theatre, £7.50 ($12.40) to £11 ($18.15) at the Swan, but you should check before booking as a ticket price rise is due in the future.

London Palladium, Argyle Street, W.1 (tel. 071/437-7373), is a show business legend. It's hard to encapsulate the prestige of this variety theater in a paragraph. Performers from Britain, Europe, and America consider that they have "arrived" when they've appeared here. Highlight of the season is the "Royal Command Performance" held before the queen, which includes an introduction of the artists to Her Majesty. It's amazing to watch hardboiled showbiz champions moved close to tears after receiving the royal handshake.

In days of yore the Palladium has starred aces such as Frank Sinatra, Shirley MacLaine, Andy Williams, Perry Como, Julie Andrews, Tom Jones, Sammy Davis, Jr., and so on; it's the Milky Way of showbiz. Second-line program attractions are likely to include, say, "Los Paraguayos" and the Ukrainian Cossack Ensemble. Today it may offer a production of *The Pirates of Penzance*. Ticket prices, usually in the £8 ($13.20) to £20 ($33) range, and showtimes vary. The Palladium is usually closed on Sunday. Tube: Oxford Circus.

Royal Court Theatre, Sloane Square, S.W.1 (tel. 071/730-1745). The English Stage Company has operated this theater for more than 30 years. The emphasis is on new playwrights (John Osborne got his start here with the 1956 production of *Look Back in Anger*). Also on the premises is the Theatre Upstairs, a studio theater devoted to the work of even newer or experimental playwrights. Shows are at 8pm Mon. to Fri., 4 and 8pm Sat.; for the Theatre Upstairs, 7:30pm Mon. to Fri., 3:30 and 7:30pm Sat. Seats are in the £4 ($6.60) to £15 ($24.75) range. Tube: Sloane Square.

The Young Vic, 66 The Cut, Waterloo, S.E.1 (tel. 071/928-6363), aims primarily at the 15 to 25 age group, but many other age groups use the theater as well. The Young Vic's repertoire includes such authors as Shakespeare, Ben Jonson, Arthur Miller, and Harold Pinter, plus specially written new plays. Performances normally begin at 7:30pm. Seats cost £8 ($13.20), reduced to £4 ($6.60) for students and children. Tube: Waterloo Station.

Sadler's Wells, Rosebery Avenue, E.C.1 (tel. 071/278-8916). A theater has stood here since 1683, on the site of a well which was once known for the healing powers of its waters. Today the theater is a showcase for British and foreign ballet and modern dance companies, and international opera. Seat prices range from £4 ($6.60) to £16 ($26.40). Performances usually begin at 7:30pm. The Lilian Baylis Theatre, a small studio theater, opened in 1988 behind Sadler's Wells. It offers a wide range of theater and events. Its Café Bar is open from 10am to 11pm Mon. to Sat. De Valois restaurant is open for pre- and post-performance suppers. Tube: Angel.

Whitehall Theatre, at the top of Whitehall, S.W.1 (tel. 071/867-1119), just off Trafalgar Square, has been restored to its original 1930s art deco glory. To the splendid auditorium has been added continental seating (620 seats) to allow greater comfort and more legroom for the audience. Air conditioning has been installed, and the bar areas considerably enlarged. Tube: Charing Cross.

The **Drury Lane, Theatre Royal,** Covent Garden, W.C.2 (tel. 071/836-8101), is one of the oldest and most prestigious establishments in town, crammed with traditions, not all of them venerable. This is the fourth theater on this site, dating from 1812. The first was built in 1663. Nell Gwynne, cockney wench who became King Charles's mistress, used to sell oranges under the long colonnade in front. Nearly every star of the London stage has played here at some time. It has a wide-open repertoire but leans toward musicals including long-running hits. Shows are at 7:45pm Mon. to Sat., with matinees at 3pm on Wed. and Sat. Guided tours of this historic theater may be arranged through George Hoare, the theater historian for Stoll Moss theaters. Tube: Covent Garden.

OPERA AND BALLET

You may be getting a little tired of superlatives, but in this particular chapter they're unavoidable. Britain's innovative Royal Opera and English National Opera are among the world's leading companies, as is the Royal Ballet.

The **Royal Opera House** is a classical building on Bow Street, W.C.2 (actually the northeast corner of Covent Garden), which was London's first square, laid out by Inigo Jones as a residential piazza. Until a few years ago the whole area was a thriving fruit and vegetable market. In the 16th century the section became fashionable to live in and was soon to become one of the centers of London nightlife. The first theater was built on the present site in 1732. The existing opera house, one of the most beautiful theaters in Europe, was built in 1858 and is now the home of the Royal Opera and Royal Ballet.

The Opera House advance box office, at 48 Floral St., W.C.2 (tel. 071/240-1066), is open from 10am to 8pm Mon. to Sat. Seat prices range from £1 ($1.65) to £41 ($67.65) for ballet, from £2.50 ($4.15) to £98 ($161.70) for opera. Tube: Covent Garden.

English National Opera, London Coliseum, St. Martin's Lane, W.C.2 (tel. 071/836-3161 for reservations or 071/240-5258 for inquiries and credit card bookings). The London Coliseum, built in 1904 as a variety theater and converted into an opera house in 1968, is London's largest and most splendid theater. The English National Opera performs a wide range of works, from the classics to modern experimental works to the operettas of Gilbert and Sullivan, and every performance is in English. A repertory of 18 to 20 productions is presented 5 or 6 nights a week for 11 months of the year. Balcony tickets are available for as little as £2.50 ($4.15), but many visitors prefer the Upper Circle or Dress Circle at about £12.50 ($20.65) to £14 ($23.10). During the opera season, usually from August to June, about 100 cheap seats in the balcony are held for sale on the day of the performance, from 10am. Tube: Charing Cross or Leicester Square.

Opera, ballet, and modern dance are also presented at the Sadler's Wells Theatre (see "Theaters" above).

CONCERTS

In recent years, the musical focal point in London has shifted to a superbly specialized complex of buildings on the South Bank side of Waterloo Bridge, called the **South Bank Centre**, at South Bank, S.E.1. It includes the Hayward Gallery and houses three of the most stylish, comfortable, and acoustically perfect concert structures in the world: the **Royal Festival Hall,** the **Queen Elizabeth Hall,** and the **Purcell Room.** Here, more than 1,200 performances a year are presented, and it's not all classical music: included are ballet, jazz, popular classics, pop, and folk. The Royal Festival Hall is open from 10am every day and offers an extensive range of things to see and do. There are free exhibitions in the foyers and free lunch music from 12:30 to 2pm, plus guided tours of the building, and book, record, and gift shops. The Festival Buffet has a wide selection of food at reasonable prices, and there are a number of bars throughout the foyers. The office that prebooks with credit cards is open daily from 10am to 9pm (tel. 071/928-8800). Tickets range from £4 ($6.60) to £20 ($33). Tube: Waterloo Station.

Barbican Centre, the Barbican, E.C.2, is considered the largest art and exhibition center in Western Europe. It was created to make a perfect setting in which to enjoy good music and theater from comfortable, roomy seating and has already been discussed under "Theaters." The Concert Hall is the permanent home of the London Symphony Orchestra and host to visiting orchestras and performers. Hall seat prices range from £4.50 ($7.45) to £20 ($33). Theater prices go from £6 ($9.90) to

£17.50 ($28.90). You can call the box office for seats for concerts and theaters at 071/638-8891.

Royal Albert Hall, Kensington Gore, S.W.7 (tel. 071/589-8212), opened in 1871, dedicated to the memory of Queen Victoria's consort, Prince Albert. The building encircles one of the world's largest auditoriums with a seating capacity of 5,500. Home since 1941 to the BBC Promenade Concerts, the famous 8-week annual festival of classical music, it is also a popular venue for music by stars such as Frank Sinatra and Johnny Mathis plus the latest in rock and pop. Sport and pageantry figure strongly. Boxing events are held here as well as covered-court lawn tennis, with the Masters Doubles Championship being played here a month after the annual Royal British Legion Festival of Remembrance. Guided tours of the building are conducted from June to September. Tube: South Kensington, High Street Kensington, or Knightsbridge.

Wigmore Hall, 36 Wigmore St., W.1 (tel. 071/935-2141). At this intimate auditorium, you'll hear excellent recitals and chamber concerts. There are regular series, master concerts by chamber music groups and instrumentalists, song recital series, and concerts featuring special composers or themes throughout the year. There are nightly performances plus Sunday Morning Coffee Concerts and also concerts on Sun. at 4 and 7pm. Many good seats are in the £4 ($6.60) range. A free list of the month's program is available from the hall. Tube: Bond Street or Oxford Circus.

MOVIES

The films shown in London are much like those you'd see in any large American city, but with a stronger international flavor. Screenings, however, are not continuous, so you'd better consult a newspaper for exact showtimes. Prices vary according to seats, all of them considerably cheaper than at home. And don't forget that movie theaters are called cinemas.

London has a dozen or so real movie palaces in the old meaning of the term, gigantic citadels with plush loges, grand buffets, and triple curtains. But its prime piece is the kind of ultra-modern movie mansion you might expect to find in Hollywood, but won't.

Cannon Cinema is a streamlined, black-and-white block on Panton Street, off Leicester Square, S.W.1 (tel. 071/930-0631), housing four superb theaters under one roof. They share one sleekly plush lobby, but each runs a separate program, always including at least one European film. Tube: Leicester Square.

Another major London cinema is **Odeon Leicester Square,** Leicester Square, S.W.1 (tel. 071/936-6111), with one large screen. Tube: Leicester Square.

You may also be interested in the activities of the **National Film Theatre,** S.E.1 (tel. 071/928-3232), in the South Bank complex. More than 2,000 films a year from all over the world and all periods are shown here, including features, shorts, animation, and documentaries. A visitor can obtain daily membership at 40p (66¢). If booked in advance, tickets cost £3.25 ($5.35). Tube: Waterloo Station.

MOMI, the Museum of the Moving Image, underneath Waterloo Bridge, S.E.1 (tel. 071/401-2636), is also part of the South Bank complex. Tracing the history of the development of cinema and television, MOMI takes the visitor on an incredible journey from cinema's earliest experiments to modern animation, from Charlie Chaplin to the operation of a TV studio. There are artifacts to handle, buttons to push, and a cast of actors to tell visitors more. Admission is £3.95 ($6.50) for adults and £2.75 ($4.55) for children. There is also a £12 ($19.80) family ticket. The museum is open from 10am to 8pm Tues. to Sat., to 6pm Sun. From June to September, Sun. hours extend to 8pm; closed Monday. Allow two hours for a visit. Tube: Waterloo Station.

GILBERT AND SULLIVAN EVENINGS

The English Heritage Singers present Gilbert and Sullivan programs at the **Mansion House at Grim's Dyke,** Old Redding, Harrow Weald, Middlesex HA3 6SH (tel. 081/954-4227), every other Sun. in winter and every Sun. the rest of the year. This is a dinner event, costing £29.50 ($48.70) per person. You arrive for cock-tails in the Library Bar of the house, where Sir William Gilbert once lived and where he and Sir Arthur Sullivan worked on their charming operettas—when they were at peace with each other. A full Edwardian-style dinner is served at 8pm, with cos-tumed performances of the most beloved of Gilbert and Sullivan songs both during and after the meal. You can request favorite melodies from the Gilbert and Sullivan works. The singers know them all.

OPEN-AIR THEATER

As the name indicates, **Regent's Park,** N.W.1 (tel. 071/486-2431), is an out-door theater, right in the center of Regent's Park. The setting is idyllic, and the longest theater bar in London provides both drink and food. Performances are given in June, July, August, and the first half of September, evenings at 7:45, matinees on Wed., Thurs., and Sat. at 2:30pm. Presentations are mainly Shakespeare, usually in period costume. Both seating and acoustics are excellent. If it rains, you're given tickets for another performance. Prices are £5 ($8.25) to £12 ($19.80). Tube: Baker Street.

MUSIC HALLS

Rheingold Club thrives in a century-old wine cellar at Sedley Place, just off 361 Oxford St., W.1 (tel. 071/629-5343), and has a restaurant, two bars, and a good-size dance floor. The main attraction is a top-class band playing from 9:30pm to about 2am Mon. to Sat., except on bank holidays. There is also an occasional cabaret, usually with big-time guest stars, but most of the entertainment is created by the patrons themselves. The Rheingold, founded in 1959, is the oldest and most suc-cessful "singles club" in London, existing long before the term had been coined. It is a safe place for men to take their wives or girlfriends, and single women are wel-come and comfortable here. The temporary membership you purchase at the club's reception desk includes admission for the first visit and costs £4 ($8.25) per person. The club is open from 8pm to 1:30am Mon. and Tues.; to 2am on Wed., Thurs., and cabaret nights; and to 2:30am on Fri. and Sat. Take the tube to Bond Street station, use the main exit to Oxford Street, turn right and turn right again to Sedley Place. It's only 40 yards from the station.

A CABARET RIVER CRUISE

Romance of London, a cabaret river cruise, complete with commentary, takes you all the way through the heart of London to the Thames Barrier. A superior four-course meal is served with wine shortly after boarding, while you are entertained at your table. Live cabaret and dancing are also featured. Romance of London cruises are available every Sun. evening from May to September. They depart from West-minster Pier, Victoria Embankment, S.W.1 at 7pm, returning at 10:30pm. The price is £28.75 ($47.45) per person. For information and reservations call 071/620-0474. Tube: Westminster.

NIGHTCLUBS

There are several kinds of nightclubs where you can eat or drink, be entertained, dance—even gamble. Most often these clubs are private—but don't turn away yet. The private club came into existence to avoid the unpopular early closing hour of 11pm for licensed public establishments, and may stay open till 3 or 4am. In most cases the clubs welcome overseas visitors showing passports, granting them a tem-porary membership. The cost of a temporary membership may even be deducted from the price of dinner; however, there is no hard-and-fast rule. Many clubs offer dinner, a show, and dancing. No visitor to London should be afraid to ask about membership in a private club. After all, most of the clubs are in business to make money and welcome foreign patronage.

Comedy Store, 28A Leicester Sq., W.C.2 (tel. 071/839-6665, but ring 0426/914433 for reservations), is London's most visible showcase of rising and emerging comedic talent. Set in the heart of the city's nighttime district, it announces by means of a prerecorded telephone message the various comedians and musicians who are scheduled to appear during the upcoming week. Even if the names of the performers are unfamiliar to you (highly likely), you will still enjoy the spontaneity of live comedy performed before a live British audience. Visitors must be more than 18. If under 25, clients might be asked for identification with proof of age. There is no particular dress code at this place, and many clients wear jeans. No reservations are accepted, and the club opens one hour before each show. Depending on the night, the entrance fee ranges from £6 ($9.90) to £7 ($11.55). Shows are Wed. at 8:30pm, Thurs. at 9pm, Fri. and Sat. at 8pm and midnight, and Sun. at 8:30pm. Tube: Leicester Square.

Tiddy Dols, 55 Shepherd Market, Mayfair, W.1 (tel. 071/499-2357), in nine small, atmospheric Georgian houses, circa 1741, is named for the famous gingerbread baker and eccentric. Guests come to Tiddy Dols to enjoy such dishes as jugged hare, game soup, plum pudding, and the original gingerbread of Tiddy Dol. While dining they are entertained with madrigals, Noël Coward songs, Gilbert and Sullivan songs, music hall songs, and a town crier. In the summer there is a large pavement café with parasols and a view of the "village" of Shepherd Market. During winter there are open fires and throughout December there is a choice of a normal à la carte dinner or a traditional Christmas gala. Dinner, costing £27.50 ($45.40), is served nightly, from 6pm to 1am (11:30pm last arrivals). Dancing is restricted to special evenings. Tube: Green Park.

Eve, 189 Regent St., W.1 (tel. 071/734-0557), is London's longest established late-night club. Doyen of London's nightlife, owner Jimmy O'Brien launched it in 1953. International variety cabaret entertainment (at 1am) has replaced the floor shows previously presented. Dancing is to disco, alternating with live music of a high standard. Eve is open from 10pm to 3:30am Mon. to Fri. Admittance is by membership only. There is an annual subscription of £8 ($13.20), but a special temporary membership for overseas visitors, valid for one night only, is granted for £2 ($3.30). Only one person in a party need be a member, and overseas visitors may be admitted on application without waiting the customary 48 hours. There is an entrance fee or cover charge of £8 ($13.20) for a member and each guest. An à la carte menu is offered throughout the night. All prices include VAT. Female escorts, many of whom speak more than one language, are available as dining or dancing partners for unaccompanied men. Tube: Oxford Circus.

Royal Roof Restaurant, Royal Garden Hotel, Kensington High Street, W.8 (tel. 071/937-8000), on the top floor of the hotel, is elegant and refined, and overlooks Kensington Gardens and Hyde Park. From your table you will see the lights of Kensington and Knightsbridge, with a view of London's West End skyline. In a romantic candlelit aura, you can enjoy a three-course dinner costing £40 ($66). The restaurant is open from 7pm to 1am Mon. to Sat. (last orders taken at 11:30pm). A band plays for dancing. Reservations are necessary. Tube: High Street Kensington.

L'Hirondelle, Swallow Street, off Regent Street, W.1 (tel. 071/734-6666), stands in the heart of the West End. L'Hirondelle puts on some of the most lavish, gorgeous floor shows in town. What's more, it lets you dine, drink, and dance from 8:30pm in the evening till 3:30am without the ceremonial "Temporary Memberships." Neither does it charge an entrance fee. The shows are really fullscale revues and go on at 10:45pm and 1am. It is closed on Sun. Dancing to one of the few bands in London is from 9:30pm. Dancing-dining partners are available. There is a cover charge of £12.50 ($20.65) for non-diners, but the club offers a three-course dinner for £25.50 ($42.10) per person, including VAT and service charges, or you can choose from their very large à la carte menu. A bottle of wine costs from £23 ($37.95). Tube: Piccadilly Circus.

Henry's, 9 Young St., W.8 (tel. 071/937-9493), lying off Kensington High Street, is a good place to go for a widely varied repertoire of music. The patrons come from many different countries and backgrounds and span a wide age spectrum as well. The club is open from 10pm to 2am Tues., Wed., and Thurs., and from

10pm to 3am Fri. and Sat.; closed Sun. and Mon. Admission ranges from £3 ($4.95) to £6 ($9.90) depending on the night of the week. Tube: Kensington High.

Bouzouki

The Elysée, 13 Percy St., W.1 (tel. 071/636-4804), is for *Never on Sunday* devotees who like the reverberations of bouzouki, dancing, and the smashing of plates. The domain of the Karegeorgis brothers—Michael, Ulysses, and the incomparable George—it offers hearty fun at moderate tabs. At two different intervals (last one at 1am) a cabaret is provided, highlighted by brother George's altogether amusing act of balancing wine glasses (I'd hate to pay his breakage bill). You can book a table on either the ground floor or the second floor, but the Roof Garden is a magnet in summer. The food is good too, including the house specialty, the classic moussaka, and the kebabs from the charcoal grill. Expect to pay about £25 ($41.25) each for a complete meal, including a bottle of wine. Dinner is served from 7pm to 2:45am (the music stops at 3am), Mon. to Sat. There's a £3 ($4.95) cover charge. Tube: Goodge Street or Tottenham Court Road.

A THEATER RESTAURANT

A unique theater restaurant in a unique setting, that's **The Talk of London** (tel. 071/408-1001), in the New London Theatre, an entertainment complex at Parker Street, off Drury Lane, W.C.2, the heart and soul of the city's theaterland. The restaurant is ingeniously designed so that every guest gets "the best seat in the house." By using a circular layout and varying floor levels, every seat has been given an uninterrupted view of the show. The Talk of London offers a complete evening's entertainment from 8pm to 1am: a four-course dinner of your choice, dancing to an orchestra, a top show band, and an international cabaret at 10:30pm. All this and coffee, service, and VAT are included in the price of £26 ($42.90) Sun. to Fri., £28 ($46.20) on Sat. Drinks are extra. Phone for reservations, which are essential. Tube: Covent Garden or Holborn.

MEDIEVAL "FEESTES"

Beefeater Club by the Tower of London, St. Katharine's Yacht Marina, E.1 (tel. 071/408-1001), offers traditional feasting and continuous entertainment at the "Court of Henry VIII" in the historic vaults of Ivory House, surrounded on three sides by the Thames. British pageantry is re-created here, complete with jesters, knights, wenches, and royal entertainers. Traditional honeyed wine is served at 8 nightly, with dancing until 11:30pm. During a five-course medieval feast, guests are given unlimited wines and ale. The cost is £28 ($46.20) per person Sun. to Fri., rising to £30 ($49.50) per person on Sat. night. Tube: Tower Hill.

STRIP SHOWS

Once upon a time, Britain's film censors were kept busy snipping the bare patches out of those "daring" French movies, and London's stage regulations permitted braless belles only on condition that they didn't move a limb while thus exposed. All this might just as well have happened in the last century for all the relevance it has today. Sheer acreage of undress currently on view in London outshows anything in Paris, New York, San Francisco, or Hamburg. Only Tokyo must be on a par.

The big, plush establishments, of course, have regular and highly paid casts, the most spectacular is the **Raymond Revuebar,** Walker's Court, Brewer St., W.1 (tel. 071/734-1593), which dates from 1958. Proprietor Paul Raymond is considered the doyen of strip society and his young, beautiful, carefully selected women are among the best in Europe. The stage show is a festival of erotica. This strip theater occupies the much restored premises of a Victorian dance hall, with a decor of flaming red velvet. There are two bars, which allow clients to take their drinks to their seats. The entrance charge is £15 ($24.75) per person, and whisky costs £2.50 ($4.15) for a large measure. The club presents "titillating" shows at 8 and 10pm Mon. to Sat. Tube: Piccadilly Circus.

Stork Club, 99 Regent St., W.1 (tel. 071/734-3686), near the corner of Swallow Street, in the heart of Mayfair, is a first-class nightclub, offering cabaret acts and a line-up of women who don't believe in overdressing. Two cabaret shows are staged nightly, one at 11pm, another at 1am. Foreign visitors don't have to go through the tedium of obtaining membership. You can order a table d'hôte menu for £22 ($36.30), plus a 15% service charge. The club is open nightly from 8:30pm to 3:30am. (however, the last food orders go in at 2:45am). If you don't want to order dinner, you can see the show from the cocktail bar. Tube: Piccadilly Circus.

DISCOS

Disco life still holds forth. Many clubs open, enjoy a quick but fast-fading popularity, then close. I list some possible favorites that might be going at the time of your visit.

Stringfellows, 16 Upper St. Martins Lane, W.C.1 (tel. 071/240-5534), is one of London's most elegant night-time rendezvous spots. It is said to have £1 ($165) million worth of velvet and hi-tech gloss and glitter. In theory, it's a members-only club, but—and only at the discretion of management—nonmembers may be admitted. It offers two lively bars and a first-class restaurant. Its disco has a stunning glass dance floor and a dazzling sound-and-light system. It's been called "an exquisite oasis of elegance," and its nightclub food "the best in London," (for a nightclub, that is). Dancing starts at 11pm, dinner at 8, and the fun continues until 3am. Prices start at £8 ($13.20) for entrance Mon. to Thurs. and £12.50 ($20.65) on Fri. and Sat.; closed Sun. Tube: Leicester Square.

In the **Hippodrome,** at the corner of Charing Cross Road and Leicester Square, W.C.2 (tel. 071/437-4311), you will find one of London's greatest discos, an enormous place where light and sound beam in on you from all directions. Revolving speakers even descend from the roof to deafen you in patches, and you can watch yourself on closed-circuit video. Golden Scan lights are a spectacular treat. There are six bars, together with a balcony restaurant. Lasers and a hydraulically controlled stage for visiting international performers are only part of the attraction of this place. Depending on the night of the week, admission prices at the door range from £6 ($9.90) to £12 ($19.80) per person. The Hippodrome is open from 9am to 3:30am Mon. to Sat. Tube: Leicester Square.

Limelight, 136 Shaftesbury Ave., W.1 (tel. 071/434-1761), was originally built in the 1880s by the Welsh Presbyterian Church. It was deconsecrated and subsequently sold in the early 1980s, reopening as a disco in 1986. You can dance beneath the soaring dome of the interior, or sip iced vodka or champagne in the circular gallery high above the spectacle. The average age of the clients in this unusual place is 20. Entrance fees range from £5 ($8.25) to £10 ($16.50), depending on the night of the week. The music covers a broad range of electronically impulsed styles. There is an upstairs wine bar open nightly from 5:30 to 10pm, whereas the disco is open from 10:30pm to 3:30am nightly.

Camden Palace, 1A Camden High St., N.1 (tel. 071/387-0428), is housed inside what was originally a theater. It draws an over-18 crowd who flock in various costumes and energy levels according to the night of the week. It offers rotating styles of music, so it's best to phone in advance to see if that evening's musical genre appeals to your taste. Styles range from rhythm and blues to what young rock experts call "boilerhouse," garage music, "acid funk," "hip-hop," and "twist and shout." A band performs only on Tues. Hours are 9pm to 2:30am Mon. to Sat., 8pm to 2:30am Fri.; closed Sun. Admission costs between £4 ($6.60) and £5 ($8.25) Mon. to Thurs., from £8 ($13.20) to £10 ($16.50) on Fri., and from £6 ($9.90) to £7 ($11.55) on Sat. The cheaper admission on Fri. and Sat. is before 9pm. Once inside, a pint of lager goes for £2 ($3.30). There's also a restaurant if you get the munchies. Tube: Camden Town or Mornington Crescent.

Barbarella 2, 43 Thurloe St., S.W.7 (tel. 071/584-2000), combines a first-class Italian restaurant with a carefully controlled disco. So that diners can converse in normal tones, the flashing lights and electronic music of the disco are separated from the dining area by thick sheets of glass. Full meals, costing from £20 ($33), include an array of Neopolitan-inspired dishes. Only clients of the restaurant are allowed into the disco, which prevents hordes of late-night revelers from cramming into the place when the regular pubs close. It is open from 7:30pm to 3am Mon. to Sat., with the last food orders going in at 12:45am. Tube: South Kensington.

DANCING TO LIVE MUSIC

A legendary setting is the **Café de Paris,** 3 Coventry St., off Piccadilly Circus, W.1 (tel. 071/437-2036). Once Robert Graves considered it a worthy subject for a book, and the duke of Windsor went here to see Noël Coward perform. But those days are long gone. The place is almost unique in London in that it draws slightly more mature patrons who like to dance the way they did in the 50s to live bands and records. They get to do so on a superb maple floor to continuous music. The floor is bathed in changing mood lights and surrounded by gilded balustrades. Tea dances are Wed., Thurs., Sat., and Sun., with admission prices ranging from £2.50 ($4.15) to £3 ($4.95). No liquor is served at tea dances—only tea, coffee, and cakes. Tea dances last from 3 to 5:45pm. The café is open at 7:30pm Mon. and Thurs. to Sun., closing between midnight and 3am, depending on business and the night of the week. Admission prices range from £4 ($6.60) to £7 ($11.55). They serve simple platters of food such as steaks. Tube: Leicester Square.

Empire, Leicester Square, W.C.1 (tel. 071/437-1446), was originally built in the 1880s, and it's been revamped and rebuilt so many times since then, going in and out of style, that today it is considered a virtual cultural monument. The bandstand is a leaping, revolving, and ever-changing spectrum of light. In the heart of London's entertainment district, the Empire features top caliber bands along with music by DJs. Hours are 8:30pm to 2am Mon. to Thurs., 8:30pm to 3:30am Fri. and Sat. Admission cost ranges from £6 ($9.90) to £7 ($11.55) Mon. to Thurs. and from £7 ($11.55) to £11 ($18.15) on Fri. and Sat. Tube: Leicester Square.

ROCK AND SOUL

Gulliver's, 15 Ganton St., W.1 (tel. 071/499-0760), was established in 1971 at another location as one of the first purpose-built discos in London. Most other places were converted from other types of buildings. Lying on a small street off Carnaby, it specializes in American soul music, which in London means far more that Otis Redding and the Supremes. In addition to American imports, you might also enjoy Caribbean calypso, soca music, reggae, and rap. Large enough for 250 patrons, Gulliver's is owned by a longtime nightlife entrepreneur, Graham Davies. At the long expanse of bar, set against one wall of the place, you can order a Budweiser for £2 ($3.30). The club is open from 10pm to 3:30am Wed. to Sat. Admission ranges from £6 ($9.90) to £9 ($14.85). Tube: Oxford Circus.

The place where new bands are launched, **Rock Garden Restaurant & Rock Music Venue,** 6-7 the Piazza, Covent Garden, W.C.2 (tel. 071/240-3961), is where such renowned groups as Dire Straits, The Police, U2, and The Stanglers all played before becoming famous. The restaurant is open from noon to midnight Sun. to Thurs. to 1am on Fri. and Sat. In summer there is outside seating in the heart of Covent Garden. The cover charge in the Venue ranges from £5 ($8.25) to £7 ($11.55), depending on the performance. A wide range of meals is offered, costing from £8 ($13.20). The Venue is open from 7:30pm to 3am Mon. to Sat., to midnight on Sun. Both the restaurant and the Venue have licensed bars. Tube: Covent Garden; night buses from neighboring Trafalgar Square.

The Marquee, 105 Charing Cross Rd., W.C.2 (tel. 071/437-6603), is considered one of the best-known centers for rock in Europe. Its reputation goes back to the 1950s and another location, but it remains forever young, in touch with the sounds of the future. Famous groups such as the Rolling Stones played at the Marquee long before their names spread beyond the shores of England. Fortunately, you don't have to be a member—you just pay at the door. If you have a student I.D. card from any country, it will cost you less to enter. The entrance fees vary, but usually fall in the £3.50 ($5.80) to £6 ($9.90) range, depending on who is appearing.

There's a coffee and a soda bar for light snacks; those 18 or older can order hard drinks. Many well-known musicians frequent the place regularly on their nights off. The club occupies a building that was once a cinema. Hours are 7pm to 1am nightly. Tube: Leicester Square or Tottenham Court Road.

JAZZ

Mention the word "jazz" in London and people immediately think of **Ronnie Scott's,** 47 Frith St., W.1 (tel. 071/439-0747), long the citadel of modern jazz in Europe where the best English and American groups are booked. Featured on almost every bill is an American band, often with a top-notch singer. It's in the heart of Soho, a 10-minute walk from Piccadilly Circus via Shaftesbury Avenue, and worth an entire evening. You can not only saturate yourself in the best of jazz, but also get reasonably priced drinks and dinners. There are three separate areas: the main room, the upstairs room, and the downstairs bar. You don't have to be a member, although you can join if you wish. The nightly entrance fee is about £12 ($19.80), depending on who is appearing. If you have a student ID you are granted considerable reductions on entrance fees. The main room is open from 8:30pm to 3am Mon. to Sat. You can either stand at the bar to watch the show or sit at a table, where you can order dinner. The downstairs bar is more intimate, a quiet rendezvous where you can meet and talk with the regulars, usually some of the world's most talented musicians. The upstairs room is separate. It has a disco called the Tango and is open from 8:30pm to 2am Mon. to Thurs., from 8:30pm to 3am Fri. and Sat. Tube: Tottenham Court Road or Leicester Square.

Although considerably less plush and less expensive, the **100 Club** is considered a serious rival of Ronnie Scott's among many dedicated jazz gourmets. At 100 Oxford St., W.1 (tel. 071/636-0933), the 100 Club sprinkles disco-dance among its cavalcade of bands, which include the best British jazz musicians, as well as many touring Americans. The club has sessions from 8:30pm to 3am Fri., when all tickets cost £6 ($9.90). On Sat., from 7:30pm to 1am, tickets cost £5 ($8.25) for members and £7 ($11.55) for non-members. On Sun., from 7:30 to 11:30pm, members pay £4 ($6.60) and non-members are charged £5 ($8.25). Tube: Tottenham Court Road or Oxford Circus.

Bull's Head, 373 Lonsdale Rd., Barnes, S.W.13 (tel. 071/876-5241), has presented live modern jazz concerts every night of the week for more than 30 years. One of the oldest hostelries in the area, it was a staging post in the mid-19th century where travelers on their way to Hampton Court and beyond could eat, drink, and rest while the coach horses were changed. The place is known today for its jazz, performed by musicians from all over the world. It's said by many to be the best in town. Jazz concerts are presented from noon to 2:30pm and 8:30 to 10:30pm on Sun. You can hear music from 8:30 to 11pm Mon. to Sat. Admission ranges from £2.50 ($4.15) to £6 ($9.90) per person. You can order good food at the carvery in the Saloon Bar daily and dine in the 17th-century Stable Restaurant. The restaurant, in the original, restored stables, specializes in steaks, fish, and other traditional fare. It is open from 6pm to midnight Mon. to Sat. and from noon to 4pm Sun. Meals cost £5 ($8.25) and up. To get there, take the tube to Hammersmith, then bus 9 the rest of the way.

FAMOUS BARS

For those who like bars instead of pubs, **Jules,** 85 Jermyn St., S.W.1 (tel. 071/930-4700), is the best-known watering hole in St. James's. It was constructed originally as the Waterloo Hotel in 1830. After Jules Ribstein bought it in 1903, he turned it into a ground-floor restaurant, and in time it became a rendezvous for the "bucks and blades." Today it serves many purposes. It will even serve you lunch from 11am to 3pm Mon. to Sat. But it's known mainly for cocktails, some 50 in all, ranging from those made with champagne to a Hawaiian Dream. Godfather is scotch and amaretto; Godmother, vodka and amaretto. Cocktails cost from £2.90 ($4.80). At the restaurant in back you can order such treats as smoked salmon, salmon and sole "as you like it," or perhaps one of a variety of steaks, with meals costing from £18 ($29.70). Evening hours are 5:30 to 11pm Mon. to Sat. Tube: Piccadilly Circus or Green Park.

Bracewell's Bar, Park Lane Hotel, Piccadilly, W.1 (tel. 071/499-6321), is a chic rendezvous point. Its stylish decor is in Cinebar Chinese red lacquer and includes painted bamboo bucket chairs, deep comfortable sofas, and soft lighting. Mixed cocktails range from £4 ($6.60) to £5 ($8.25) (a martini and a zombie, respectively). Whisky, depending on its rarity, costs from £3.20 ($5.30) to £3.50 ($5.80), the latter price for a single malt. The bar adjoins Bracewell's (see separate recommendation), one of the finest hotel restaurants in London. Hours are from 11am to 3pm and 5:30 to 11pm Mon. to Sat.; from noon to 2:30pm and 7 to 10:30pm Sun. Tube: Hyde Park Corner.

American Bar, Savoy Hotel, the Strand, W.C.2 (tel. 071/836-4343), is, in the words of one London nighttime commentator, a "survivor of the age when cocktails were the province of the rich social set." It still, after all these decades, remains one of the most sophisticated places at which to order a drink in London. The barman is known for such special concoctions as Royal Silver and Savoy 90. Dare you try Moonwalk? From Mon. to Sat. evenings, a pianist and singer entertain. The après-theater crowd flocks here (it's near many West End theaters) and listens to show tunes. Men should wear a jacket and tie. Many people enjoy the fruity champagne cocktails. Drinks cost from £4 ($6.60). Hours are 11am to 11pm Mon. to Sat., noon to 3pm and 7 to 10:30pm Sun. Tube: Aldwych.

The Cocktail Bar, Café Royal, 68 Regent St., W.1 (tel. 071/437-9090), in business since 1865, was once patronized by Oscar Wilde and James Whistler. Decorated in a 19th-century rococo style, it is one of the more glamorous places in London at which to drink, as Aubrey Beardsley, one of its former patrons, might agree if he were still around. Café Royal cocktails, including Golden Cadillac and Royal Romance, begin at £3.95 ($6.50). Non-alcoholic drinks are also served. You can also order wine by the glass from the superb wine cellars of the café. Prices begin at £1.75 ($2.90). It's also possible to come here from 3 to 5pm for a traditional English tea, costing £7.50 ($12.40). Hours are noon to 11:30pm Mon. to Sat., noon to 10:30pm Sun. Tube: Piccadilly Circus.

Lillie Langtry Bar, Cadogan Hotel, Sloane Street, S.W.1 (tel. 071/235-7141), epitomizes some of the charm and elegance of the Edwardian era. Lillie Langtry, actress and society beauty at the turn of the century (notorious as the mistress of Edward VII), used to live here. She became known as "Jersey Lily." The bar, next to Langtry's Restaurant, exudes a 1920s aura. The most dubious event that ever occurred here was the arrest of Oscar Wilde on charges of sodomy. But that unfortunate event is long forgotten, and the great playwright is honored on the drink menu with Hock and Selzer, his favorite drink at the Cadogan, according to Sir John Betjeman's poem, "The Arrest of Oscar Wilde at the Cadogan Hotel." We'd call it a white wine spritzer today. One drink, a Green Carnation, honors the Cecil Graham character in Wilde's *Lady Windermere's Fan*. Still another drink—champagne, cognac, and strawberry liqueur—honors Queen Victoria. Cocktails begin at £3.50 ($5.75), and are served from 11am to 11pm daily. Tube: Sloane Square.

GAY AND LESBIAN NIGHTLIFE

The most reliable source of information on gay clubs and activities is the **Gay Switchboard** (tel. 071/837-7324). The staff there runs a 24-hour service of information on places and activities catering to homosexual men and women.

London Lesbian & Gay Centre, 67-69 Cowcross St., E.C.1 (tel. 071/608-1471), is the best place to meet and talk with like-minded individuals. It's especially recommended for both men and women who are tired of the bar and disco scene. It always seems to stage some event of interest to the lesbian and gay community, and does so in a relaxed, friendly atmosphere. Activities include cabarets, benefit discos, art exhibitions, comedy revues, and even counseling and gay legal advice. Annual membership in the club costs £15 ($24.75) or else you can join for a day at 40p (65¢). Hours are 5:30 to 11pm Mon. to Thurs., noon to 2am Fri. and Sat., and noon to 10:30pm Sun. On Fri. nights, there are mixed theme discos and on Sat. nights a women-only disco. Entry fee for these discos is £3 ($4.95). On the first floor is a women-only bar, the Orchid, with good drinks and bar snacks. Special entertainment evenings are featured here. Tube: Farringdon.

Here are some other suggestions; some are membership clubs that, nevertheless, welcome overseas visitors.

Napoleon Club, 2-6 Lancashire Ct., 123 New Bond St., W.1 (tel. 071/493-3075), is the most exclusive club for gay men in London, charging a membership fee of £10 ($16.50). It's been called a "gay Annabel's," a reference to the most exclusive straight disco in London. Decorated in a stylish, vaguely Napoleonic style, the club attracts a sophisticated theatrical crowd, with its four bars and basement disco. The piano bar is a regular feature, as are disco and cabaret acts. Sun. is leather night. Cover charges range from £1 ($1.65) to £4 ($6.60). Hours are 10pm to 2am Tues. to Wed., 10pm to 3am Thurs. to Sat., and 9pm to 3am Fri. and Sat. Tube; Bond Street.

Roy's, 206 Fulham Rd., S.W.10 (tel. 071/352-6828), is the leading gay restaurant of London. People come here not only for the good food, but the entertaining and relaxing ambience. The set menu of freshly prepared ingredients is only £12.50 ($20.65) at this basement restaurant. Meals are served from 7:30 to 11:30pm Mon. to Sat., from 1:30 to 3pm and 8 to 11:30pm Sun. Tube: Earl's Court or South Kensington.

Steph's, 39 Dean St., W.1 (tel. 071/734-5976), looking like a stage set for *Pink Flamingos,* is one of the most charming restaurants of Soho, near the exclusive Groucho Club. Its owner is blond-haired Stephanie Cooke, born in the north of England, a well-traveled former schoolteacher who is today the sophisticated hostess of this little well-run restaurant. A theatrical clientele, among others, is attracted to the place. Bring your boy friend, your girl friend (or one of each). The place is straight, gay, bi, or "no labels at all."

You conceivably could go here just to have fun, but the food is worthy in its own right. Everything is cooked fresh, so sit back, relax and enjoy some of Steph's specialties such as Snuffy's chicken, beef and oyster pie, leek and pecan pancakes, or else selections from the charcoal grill including lime chicken breast. Steph might even suggest her own "diet"—a plate of wild Scottish smoked salmon and a bottle of champagne. The ubiquitous burger also appears on the menu, as do salads and even a vegetarian club sandwich (how fashionable can you get?). Meals cost from £15 ($24.75). Hours are noon to 3pm and 5:30 to 11:30pm Mon. to Fri. On Fri. and Sat., the restaurant is open until midnight. Tube: Piccadilly Circus.

Madame Jo Jo's, 8 Brewer St., W.1 (tel. 071/734-2473), is set side by side with some of Soho's most explicit strip shows. Madame Jo Jo also presents "girls," but they are in drag. This is London's most popular transvestite show, with revues staged at 12:15am and 1:15am. The club, with its popular piano bar, is open from 10pm to 3am Mon. to Sat. Entrance ranges from £6 ($9.90) to £8 ($13.20) per person, depending on the night of the week. Tube: Piccadilly Circus.

Brief Encounter, 41 St. Martin's Lane, W.C.2 (tel. 071/240-2221), is aptly named. Standing across from the Duke of York's Theatre, it is in the very heart of West End theaterland. In fact, it's the most frequented West End gay pub. Bars are on two levels, but even so it's hard to find room to stand up, much less drink. Nevertheless, the place is packed nightly, with a mixed bag. Some men are in jeans, leather, whatever, whereas others are dressed in business suits from their stockbroker jobs in The City. The Brief Encounter is where you "begin" a gay evening in London, perhaps fanning out later to some of the private clubs. Lager costs from £1.50 ($2.50). The club is open from 11am to 11pm Mon. to Sat., from 7 to 10:30pm Sun. Tube: Leicester Square or Charing Cross.

Heaven, the Arches, Craven Street, W.C.2 (tel. 071/839-3852), is not only the biggest gay venue in Great Britain, but perhaps in Europe. It also has the most sophisticated sound and laser system of any gay club in Europe. Heaven is a London landmark, set within vaulted cellars of Charing Cross Railway Station and painted a universal black inside. It is divided into at least four distinctly different areas, each of these connected by a labyrinth of catwalks, stairs, and hallways, allowing different activities to happen within the club at the same time. The dance floor, with a viewing gallery, is cavernous. Heaven has different club theme nights. For example, Wed. is Lesbian/Gay mixed night, going under the name of "Pussies Galore." Sat. is men only. However, Thurs. (at least partially) is straight night. The tabloid, the *Evening Standard*, pronounced straight night at Heaven as "among the five most fun nights out in London." On any night, cost of entrance ranges from £4 ($6.60) to £7 ($11.55) per person. Hours are 10:30pm to 3:30am Tues. to Sat. Tube: Charing Cross/Embankment.

Young gay men in leather or denim often make their way to the well-established **Coleherne**, 261 Old Brompton Rd., S.W.5 (tel. 071/373-8356), which must have been featured in every guide to the gay scene in Europe ever written. The place is often jammed with cruising customers. Lunch and afternoon tea are served upstairs, and if you stand at the bar long enough you'll invariably hear a discussion turning to "safe sex." A lager costs from £1.50 ($2.50), and it can be enjoyed from 11am to 11pm Mon. to Sat., from noon to 3pm and 7 to 10:30pm Sun. Tube: Earl's Court.

GAMBLING

London was a gambling metropolis long before anyone had ever heard of Monte Carlo and when Las Vegas was an anonymous sandpile in the desert. From the Regency period until halfway into the 19th century, Britain was more or less governed by gamblers. Lord Sandwich invented the snack named after him so he wouldn't have to leave the card table for a meal. Prime Minister Fox was so addicted that he frequently went to a cabinet meeting straight from the green baize table.

Queen Victoria's reign changed all that, as usual, by jumping to the other extreme. For more than a century games of chance were so rigorously outlawed that no barmaid dared to keep a dice cup on the counter. The pendulum swung again in 1960 when the present queen gave her royal assent to the new "Betting and Gambling Act." According to this legislation, gambling was again permitted in "bona fide clubs" by members and their guests.

Since London's definition of a "club" is as loose as a rusty screw in a cardboard wall, this immediately gave rise to the current situation, which continues to startle, amaze, and bewilder foreign visitors. For the fact is that you come across gambling devices in the most unlikely spots, such as discos, social clubs, and cabaret restaurants. All of which may, by the haziest definition, qualify as "clubs." The legitimate gambling clubs offer pleasant trimmings in the shape of bars and restaurants, but their central theme is unequivocally the flirtation with Lady Luck. There are at least 25 of them in the West End alone, with many scattered through the suburbs. Contrasts between them are much sharper than you find in the Nevada casinos.

Owing to a new law, casinos are not allowed to advertise, and if they do, they are likely to lose their licenses. Their appearance in a travel guide is still considered "advertising"—hence, I cannot recommend specific clubs. However, most hall porters can tell you where you can gamble in London. It's not illegal to gamble, just to advertise it. You'll be required to become a member of your chosen club, and must wait 24 hours before you can play the tables, then strictly for cash. The most common games are roulette, blackjack, punto banco, and baccarat.

---

6. One-Day Trips from London

It would be sad to leave England without ever having ventured into the countryside, at least for a day. The English are the greatest excursion travelers in the world, forever dipping into their own rural areas to discover ancient abbeys, 17th-century village lanes, shady woods for picnic lunches, and stately mansions. From London, it's possible to take advantage of countless tours—either by conducted coach, boat, or via a do-it-yourself method on bus or train. On many trips, you can combine two or more methods of transportation; for example, you can go to Windsor by boat and return by coach or train.

Highly recommended are the previously described Green Line Coaches, operated by London Country Bus Services Ltd. (see Chapter I, section 3, "Traveling Within Britain").

For longer tours, say, to Stratford-upon-Avon, you will find the trains much more convenient. Often you can take advantage of the many bargain tickets outlined in Chapter I. For further information about trains to a specific location, go to the British Rail offices on Lower Regent Street.

London Regional Transport system conducts tours of places of interest in and around London. For example, a day tour (in summer) visits Windsor and Hampton Court Palace Mon. to Sat., departing Wilton Road Coach Station at 9:15am. The return to Victoria Station is at 5:15pm. Adults pay £28 ($46.20) and children are charged £22 ($36.30). Operating all year, an afternoon tour visits Windsor and goes on a river cruise to Runnymede. Departures are from Wilton Road Coach Station on Tues., Wed., and Fri. to Sun. at 1pm, with a return to Victoria Station at 6:15pm. The price is £16 ($26.40) for adults and £13 ($21.45) for children. For details on the transport system's information and ticket centers, see "Transportation in Greater London" in section 1 of Chapter III.

HAMPTON COURT PALACE

On the north side of the Thames, 13 miles west of London in East Molesey, Surrey (tel. 081/977-8441), this 16th-century palace of Cardinal Wolsey can teach us a lesson. Don't try to outdo your boss—particularly if he happens to be Henry VIII. The rich cardinal did just that. But the king had a lean and hungry eye. Wolsey, who eventually lost his fortune, power, and prestige, ended up giving his lavish palace to the Tudor monarch, who out-Wolseyed the Wolsey embellishments. The Tudor additions included the Anne Boleyn gateway, with its 16th-century astronomical clock that even tells the high-water mark at London Bridge. From Clock Court, you can see one of Henry's major contributions, the great hall, with its hammer-beam ceiling. Also added by Henry were the tiltyard, a tennis court, and kitchen.

To judge from the movie *A Man for All Seasons,* Hampton Court had quite a retinue to feed. Cooking was done in the great kitchens. Henry cavorted through the various apartments with his wives of the moment—everybody from Anne Boleyn to Catherine Parr (the latter reversed things and lived to bury her erstwhile spouse). Charles I was imprisoned here at one time, and temporarily managed to escape his jailers.

Although the palace enjoyed prestige and pomp in Elizabethan days, it owes much of its present look to William and Mary—or rather to Sir Christopher Wren, who designed and had built the Northern or Lion Gates, intended to be the main entrance to the new parts of the palace. The fine wrought-iron screen at the south end of the south gardens was made by Jean Tijou around 1694 for William and Mary. You can parade through the apartments today, filled as they are with porcelain, furniture, paintings, and tapestries. The King's Dressing Room is graced with some of the best art. In Queen Mary's closet, you'll find Pieter Brueghel the Elder's macabre *Massacre of the Innocents.* Tintoretto and Titian deck the halls of the King's Drawing Room. Finally, be sure to inspect the royal chapel (Wolsey wouldn't recognize it). To confound yourself totally, you may want to get lost in the serpentine shrubbery maze in the garden, also the work of Sir Christopher Wren.

The cloisters, courtyards, state apartments, great kitchens, cellars, Hampton Court exhibition, Montegna paintings gallery, and maze are open from mid-March to mid-October daily 9:30am to 6pm, and from mid-October to mid-March daily 9:30am to 4:30pm. The Tudor tennis court and banqueting house are open the same hours as the above, but only from mid-March to mid-October. Admission to all these attractions is £3.80 ($6.25) for adults, £2 ($3.30) for children (children under 5 free).

The maze is open daily the same times as the palace. A maze only ticket costs £1 ($1.65) for adults, 50p (85¢) for children.

You can go to Hampton Court by bus, train, boat, or car. London Regional

Transport buses 111, 131, 216, 267, and 461 make the trip, as do Green Line Coaches (ask at the nearest London Country Bus office) for routes 715, 716, 718, and 726. Frequent trains from Waterloo Station (Network Southeast) go to Hampton Court Station. Boat service is offered to and from Kingston, Richmond, and Westminster.

Where to Dine

After visiting the palace, lunch at **Bastians,** Hampton Court Road, in East Molesey, Surrey (tel. 081/977-6074), an attractive old building with a large, stone-floored hall, roaring log fire, and comfortable chairs. Here you order an aperitif and select your meal. Then you go into the simple dining room or, in summer, into the tiny garden to eat al fresco.

The French menu includes such appetizers as an enormous platter of moules marinières in season, or salmon mousse. Main dishes include filet steak and lamb cutlets in a light mustard sauce. These courses are served with a variety of sauces and well-cooked vegetables, depending on the season and availability. A carafe of house wine is always available. Expect to spend from £18 ($29.70) to £25 ($41.25), plus wine. Prices include VAT but not the 12½% service charge. The restaurant is open from 12:30 to 2:30pm Mon. to Fri. for lunch, from 7:30 to 10:30pm Mon. to Sat. for dinner.

KEW

Nine miles southwest of central London at Kew, near Richmond, are the **Royal Botanic Gardens,** better known as **Kew Gardens** (tel. 081/940-1171), among the best known in Europe, containing thousands of varieties of plants. But Kew is no mere pleasure garden—it is essentially a vast scientific research center that happens to be beautiful. A pagoda, erected in 1761–1762, represents the "flowering" of chinoiserie. One of the oddities of Kew is a Douglas-fir flagstaff, more than 220 feet high. The classical Orangery, near the main gate on Kew Green, houses an exhibit telling the story of Kew, as well as a bookshop where guides to the garden are available.

The gardens cover a 300-acre site encompassing lakes, greenhouses, walks, garden pavilions, and museums, together with fine examples of the architecture of Sir William Chambers. At whatever season you visit Kew, there's always something to see: in spring, the daffodils and bluebells, through to the coldest months when the heath garden is at its best. Among the 50,000 plant species are notable collections of arum lilies, ferns, orchids, aquatic plants, cacti, mountain plants, palms, and tropical water lilies. The gardens are open daily except Christmas and New Year's Day from 9:30am to no later than 4 to 6:30pm (8pm on Sun. and public holidays), depending on the season. The entrance fee has gone above the traditional "one penny" in effect for a couple of centuries and is now £1 ($1.65).

Much interest focuses on the redbrick **Kew Palace** (dubbed the Dutch House), a former residence of King George III and Queen Charlotte. It is reached by walking to the northern tip of the Broad Walk. Now a museum, it was built in 1631 and contains memorabilia of the reign of George III, along with a royal collection of furniture and paintings. It is open only April to September from 11am to 5:30pm daily. Admission is £1 ($1.65) for adults, 50p (85¢) for children.

At the gardens, **Queen Charlotte's Cottage** has been restored to its original spendor. Built in 1771, it is half-timbered and thatched. George III is believed to have been the architect. The house has been restored in great detail, including the original Hogarth prints that hung on the downstairs walls. The cottage is open April to September on Sat. and Sun. and bank holidays.

The least expensive and most convenient way to visit the gardens is to take the Underground, District Lake line, to Kew Gardens on the south bank of the Thames. The most romantic way to come in summer is via a steamer from Westminster Bridge to Kew Pier. Admission is 50p (85¢) for adults, 30p (50¢) for children.

Kew Bridge Steam Museum, Green Dragon Lane, Brentford, Middlesex (tel. 081/568-4757), houses what is probably the world's largest collection of steam-powered beam engines. These were used in the Victorian era and up to the 1940s to pump London's water, and one engine has a capacity of 700 gallons per stroke. There are six restored engines that are steamed on weekends, plus other unrestored engines, a steam railway, and a working forge. The museum has a tea room, plus free parking for cars. It's open and in steam from 11am to 5pm Sat., Sun., and Mon. when it falls on a holiday. From Mon. to Fri., you can see it as a static exhibition during the same time period. Admission on steam days is £1.80 ($2.95) for adults, 90p ($1.49) for children, with a family price of £5 ($8.25). On other days, adults are charged £1 ($1.65) and children 50p (85¢), with the family rate being £2.75 ($4.55). The museum is north of Kew Bridge, under the tower, a 10-minute walk from Kew Gardens. You can reach it by a Southern Region British Rail train from Waterloo Station to Kew Bridge Station; by buses 27, 65, 237, or 267 (7 on Sun.); or by Gunnersbury or South Ealing tube and then by bus.

GREENWICH

Greenwich Mean Time, of course, is the basis of standard time throughout most of the world, the zero point used in the reckoning of terrestrial longitudes since 1884. Greenwich is also home of the Royal Naval College, the National Maritime Museum, and the Old Royal Observatory. In drydock at Greenwich Pier is the clipper ship *Cutty Sark,* as well as Sir Francis Chichester's *Gipsy Moth IV.*

About 4 miles from The City, Greenwich is reached by a number of methods, and part of the fun of making the jaunt is getting there. Ideally, you'll arrive by boat, as Henry VIII preferred to do on one of his hunting expeditions. In summer, launches leave at regular intervals from either the pier at Charing Cross, Tower Bridge, or Westminster. The boats leave daily for Greenwich about every half hour from 10am to 7pm (times are approximate, depending on the tides). Bus 1 runs from Trafalgar Square to Greenwich; bus 188 goes from Euston through Waterloo to Greenwich. From Charing Cross station, the British Rail train takes 15 minutes to reach Greenwich, and there is now the new Docklands Light Railway, running from Tower Gateway to Island Gardens on the Isle of Dogs. A short walk under the Thames through a foot tunnel brings you out in Greenwich opposite the *Cutty Sark.*

Unquestionably, the *Cutty Sark*—last of the great clippers—holds the most interest, having been seen by millions. At the spot where the vessel is now berthed stood the Ship Inn of the 19th century (Victorians came here for whitebait dinners, as they did to the Trafalgar Tavern). Ordered built by Capt. Jock Willis ("Old White Hat"), the clipper was launched in 1869 to sail the China tea trade route. It was named after the Witch Nannie in Robert Burns's *Tam o' Shanter* (note the figurehead). Yielding to the more efficient steamers, the *Cutty Sark* later was converted to a wool-carrying clipper, plying the route between Australia and England. Before her retirement she knew many owners, even different names, eventually coming to drydock at Cutty Sark Gardens, Greenwich Pier, S.E.10 (tel. 081/858-3445), in 1954. For £1.60 ($2.65) for adults, 80p ($1.30) for children, the vessel may be boarded from 10am to 6pm Mon. to Sat., from noon to 6pm Sun. It closes at 5pm in winter.

Next to the clipper—and looking like a sardine beside a shark—lies the equally famous *Gipsy Moth IV* (also tel. 081/858-3445). This is the ridiculously tiny sailing craft in which Sir Francis Chichester circumnavigated the globe—solo! You can go on board and marvel at the minuteness of the vessel in which the gray-haired old seadog made his incredible 119-day journey. His chief worry—or so he claimed—was running out of ale before he reached land. The admission to go aboard is 30p (50¢) for adults, 20p (35¢) for children under 16. The *Gipsy* keeps the same hours as the *Cutty Sark* in summer; closed in winter.

The **Royal Naval College** (tel. 081/858-2154) grew up on the site of the Tudor palace in Greenwich in which Henry VIII and Elizabeth I were born. William and Mary commissioned Wren to design the present buildings in 1695 to house naval pensioners, and these became the Royal Naval College in 1873. The buildings are baroque masterpieces, in which the Painted Hall (by Thornhill from 1708 to 1727) and the chapel are outstanding. It is normally open to visitors between 2:30

and 5pm (latest time of entrance, 4:30pm) Mon. to Wed. and Fri. to Sun.; closed Thurs. and certain public holidays. These days are published in daily papers. Admission is free.

The **National Maritime Museum** (tel. 081/858-4422, ext. 230), built around Inigo Jones's 17th-century Palladian Queen's House, portrays Britain's maritime heritage. Actual craft, marine paintings, ship models, and scientific instruments are displayed, including the full-dress uniform coat that Lord Nelson wore at the Battle of Trafalgar. Other curiosities include the chronometer (or sea watch) used by Captain Cook when he made his Pacific explorations in the 1770s. The museum is open from 10am to 6pm Mon. to Sat., from 2 to 6pm Sun. in summer, closing at 5pm in winter; closed January 1, Good Friday, May bank holiday's, and the Christmas holidays. A ticket costs £2 ($3.30) for adults, £1 ($1.65) for children aged 7 to 16.

Old Royal Observatory (tel. 081/858-4422, ext. 221) is worth exploring. Sir Christopher Wren was the architect—after all, he was interested in astronomy even before he became famous. The observatory overlooks Greenwich and the Maritime Museum from a park laid out to the design of Le Nôtre, the French landscaper. Here you can stand at 0° longitude, as the Greenwich Meridian, or prime meridian, marks the first of the globe's vertical divisions. See also the big, red time-ball used in olden days by ships sailing down the river from London to set their timepieces by. There is a fascinating bewilderment of astronomical and navigational instruments, and time and travel become more realistic after a visit here. Hours and prices are the same as for the National Maritime Museum, of which the observatory is a part.

On Sat. and Sun. in Greenwich, there are arts, crafts, and antique markets. Ask at the **Tourist Information Centre,** by the pier and *Cutty Sark* (tel. 081/858-6376), open from 2:30 to 5pm Mon. to Wed. and Fri. to Sun.

Where to Dine

Trafalgar Tavern, Park Row, S.E.10 (tel. 081/858-2437), overlooks the Thames at Greenwich and is surrounded by many attractions. Directly opposite the tavern is the Royal Naval College. Ringed with nautical paintings and engravings, lots of heavy dark wood, and brass artifacts, the restaurant invites you to enjoy traditional English specialities that go well with the 18th-century naval memorabilia. Try the steak and kidney pie, one of the succulent steaks, perhaps chateaubriand. Pheasant and venison are also on the menu. You can also order daily specials, with freshly prepared vegetables. It is open from noon to 3pm and 7:30 to 10:30pm. No dinner is served on Mon., but Mon. lunch is available in summer. Lunch costs from £4.50 ($7.45), with dinners beginning at £12 ($19.80) and going up. The pub is open all day in summer.

RUNNYMEDE

Two miles outside Windsor is the 188-acre meadow on the south side of the Thames, in Surrey, where King John put his seal on the Magna Carta. John may have signed the document up the river on a little island, but that's being technical. Today, Runnymede is also the site of the John F. Kennedy Memorial, 1 acre of English ground given to the United States by the people of Britain. The memorial, a large block of white stone, is hard to see from the road. The pagoda you can see from the road was placed there by the American Bar Association to acknowledge the fact that American law stems from the English system.

The historic site, to which there is free access all year, lies on the Thames, half a mile west of Runnymede Bridge on the south side of A308. If you're taking the M25, exit at junction 13. The nearest rail connection is at Egham, half a mile away. For bus information for the surrounding area, telephone 081/668-7261.

Runnymede Hotel, Windsor Road, Egham, Surrey TW20 0AG (tel. 0784/436171). This four-star hotel stands in 10 acres of landscaped grounds on the banks of the River Thames. The location, near to the site where King John signed the Magna Carta in 1215, is just 17 miles from the heart of London (Waterloo Station can be reached by fast train in approximately half an hour). The hotel was built in 1973, but has undergone extensive, major refurbishment recently, and clients are welcomed with old-fashioned courtesy and a totally new look in decor and ambience. The hotel has 125 bedrooms, some of which are air conditioned. All have private baths and showers, hot beverage facilities, TVs with video, hairdryers, trouser presses, bathrobes, and direct-dial telephones. Charges are £80 ($132) daily in a single and £95 ($156.75) in a double (both prices quoted are in standard accommodation). Breakfast is extra. Luncheon is from £14.75 ($24.35); dinner from £16.95 ($27.95). Meals are served in the River Room, built in two levels, giving each table a view of the garden and river. Two bars are named Anglers and Magna Carta.

SYON PARK

Syon Park lies in Brentford, Middlesex, 9 miles from Piccadilly Circus, on 5 acres of the duke of Northumberland's Thamesside estate. It is one of the most beautiful spots in all of Great Britain. There's always something in bloom. Called "The Showplace of the Nation in a Great English Garden," Syon Park was opened to the public in 1968. A nation of green-thumbed gardeners is dazzled here, and the park is also educational, showing amateurs how to get the most out of their small gardens. The vast flower- and plant-studded acreage betrays the influence of Capability Brown, who laid out the grounds in the 18th century. Particular highlights include a 6-acre rose garden, a butterfly house, and the Great Conservatory, one of the earliest and most famous buildings of its type, built 1822–1829. There is a quarter-mile-long ornamental lake studded with waterlilies and silhouetted by cypresses and willows, even a gardening supermarket, and the Motor Museum, with the Heritage Collection of British cars. With some 90 vehicles, from the earliest 1895 Wolseley to the present day, it has the largest collection of British cars anywhere. Syon is also the site of the first botanical garden in England, created by the father of English botany, Dr. William Turner in 1548. Trees include a 200-year-old Chinese juniper, an Afghan ash, Indian bean trees, and liquidambars.

On the grounds is **Syon House,** built in 1431, the original structure incorporated into the duke of Northumberland's present home. The house was later remade to the specifications of the first duke of Northumberland in 1762–1769. The battlemented facade is that of the original Tudor mansion, but the interior is from the 18th century, the design of Robert Adam. Basil Taylor said of the interior feeling: "You're almost in the middle of a jewel box." In the Middle Ages, Syon was a monastery, later suppressed by Henry VIII. Katherine Howard, the king's fifth wife, was imprisoned in the house before her scheduled beheading in 1542.

The house is open from Easter to the end of September from noon to 5pm Sun. to Thurs. The gardens are open all year except for Christmas and Boxing Day. The gates open at 10am and close at dusk or 6pm. After October, the winter closing hour is 4pm. Admission to the gardens is £1.50 ($2.50) for adults and £1 ($1.65) for children. Admission to Syon House is £2 ($3.30) for adults, £1.50 ($2.50) for children. A combined ticket for house and gardens is £3.25 ($5.35) for adults, £2.25 ($3.70) for children. A separate ticket is required for entrance to the Motor Museum, costing £2 ($3.30) for adults, £1.25 ($2.05) for children. For more information, phone 081/560-0882. Syon Park lies 2 miles west of Kew Bridge (the road is signposted from A315/310 at Busch Corner). By public transport, go to Waterloo Station in London and take British Rail to Kew Bridge Station. From there, catch bus 237 or 267 to the pedestrian entrance to Syon House.

THORPE PARK

One of Europe's leading family entertainment parks, Thorpe Park, Staines Road, Chertsey, Surrey (tel. 0932/562633), lies only 21 miles from central London on the A320 between Staines and Chertsey, with easy access from junctions 11 and 13 on the M25. The entrance fee of £7.99 ($13.20) for adults and £6.99 ($11.55) for children under 14 includes all rides, shows, attractions, and exhibits. Additional charges are made only for roller skate rental and coin-operated amusements. Just a few of the favorite rides and shows are Loggers Leap, Thunder River, Treasure Island, Magic Mill, Phantom Fantasia, the Family Tea Cup Ride, Cinema 180, and the Palladium Theatre. Newer attractions are the Flying Fish, an outdoor roller coaster, Carousel Kingdom, an undercover entertainment area, and A Drive in the Country, a vintage track ride. Free transport is provided around the 500 acres by railway and waterbus. Guests can picnic on the grounds or patronize one of the restaurants or fast foods areas, such as, La Fontana, the French Café, Bavarian Festhalle, or the popular Mississippi Riverboat. The park is open daily from 10am to 6pm from April 7 to October 18. To avoid the busiest times, Mon. to Sat. are recommended for visits from April to July and in September. The nearest mainline station is Staines from Waterloo, and many bus services operate directly to Thorpe Park.

VI

WINDSOR, OXFORD, AND THE HOME COUNTIES

1. WINDSOR

2. ASCOT

3. HENLEY-ON-THAMES

4. INNS ALONG THE THAMES

5. OXFORD

6. WOODSTOCK (BLENHEIM PALACE)

7. HERTFORDSHIRE

8. BUCKINGHAMSHIRE

9. BEDFORDSHIRE (WOBURN ABBEY)

Within easy reach of London, the Thames Valley and the Chiltern Hills are history-rich parts of England, and they lie so close to the capital they can be easily reached by automobile or Green Line coach. You can explore here during the day and return in time to see a show in the West End.

Here are some of the most-visited historic sites in England: the former homes of Disraeli and Elizabeth I, the estate of the duke of Bedford, and of course, Windsor Castle, 22 miles from London, one of the most famous castles in Europe and the most popular day trip for visitors venturing out of London for the first time.

Of course, your principal reason for coming to Oxfordshire is to explore the university city of Oxford, about an hour's drive from London. But Oxford is not the only attraction in the country. The shire is a land of great mansions, old churches, and rolling farmland. In a sense, Oxfordshire is a kind of buffer zone between the easy living in the southern towns and the industrialized cities of the heartland. In the southeast are the chalky Chilterns, and in the west the wool towns of the Cotswolds. In fact, Burford, an unspoiled medieval town west of Oxford, is one of the traditional gateways to the Cotswolds (see Chapter XII). The Upper Thames winds across the southern parts of the county.

The Home Counties are characterized by river valleys and gentle hills. The beech-clad Chiltern Hills are at their most beautiful in spring and fall. This 40-mile chalk ridge extends in an arc from the Thames Valley to the old Roman city of St. Albans in Hertfordshire. The whole region is popular for boating holidays on its 200-mile network of canals.

1. Windsor

A Green Line bus from London will deliver you in about an hour to Windsor, site of England's greatest castle and its most famous boys' school. Green Line buses 700, 701, 702, and 718 leave from Eccleston Bridge behind Victoria Station (see "Buses in Britain," Chapter I). Buses 700 and 702 offer express service. For the return journey, you can either go straight back into London or stop at Hampton Court. Take bus 726 or 718 from Windsor. For further information, telephone 071/668-7261. There are also frequent trains from Paddington Station, London, to Windsor Town Station and Windsor and Eton Riverside Station.

Windsor was called "Windlesore" by the ancient Britons who derived the name from the winding shore along the Thames.

WHAT TO SEE AND DO

Your bus will drop you near the town guildhall, to which Wren applied the finishing touches. It's only a short walk to the castle, up Castle Hill.

Windsor Castle

William the Conqueror ordered a castle built on this spot, beginning a legend and a link with English sovereignty that has known many vicissitudes. King John cooled his heels at Windsor while waiting to put his signature on the Magna Carta at nearby Runnymede; Queen Bess did some renovations; Charles I was imprisoned here before losing his head; Victoria mourned her beloved Albert, who died at the castle in 1861; the royal family spent much of World War II behind its sheltering walls. When Queen Elizabeth II is in residence, the royal standard flies.

The State Apartments contain many works of art, porcelain, armor, furniture, three Verrio ceilings, and several Gibbons carvings from the 17th century. The world of Rubens adorns the King's Drawing Room and in the relatively small dressing room is a Dürer, Rembrandt's portrait of his mother, and Van Dyck's triple look at Charles I. Of the apartments, the grand reception room, with its Gobelin tapestries, is the most spectacular.

The changing of the guard ceremony takes place at 11am daily except Sun., from May to August. In winter, the guard is changed every 48 hours except Sun., so unless you plan to visit in summer, it's wise to phone in advance for information, at the number listed below, extension 252. The Windsor changing of the guard is a much more exciting and moving experience, in my opinion, than the London exercises. In Windsor the guard marches through the town, stopping the traffic as it wheels into the castle to the tune of a full regimental band when the court is in residence. When the queen is not there, a drum and pipe band is mustered.

When the court is at Windsor—six weeks at Easter, June, and three weeks in December—the State Apartments may not be visited. They are open to the public July to late October from 10:30am to 5pm Mon. to Sat., 1:30 to 5pm Sun. Also open January, February, early March, November, and early December, from 10:30am to 3pm Mon. to Sat.; closed Sun. Ticket sales stop 30 minutes before closing, and last admissions are 15 minutes before closing time. Admission is £2.50 ($4.15) for adults, £1 ($1.65) for children. It is always advisable to check what is open before visiting by telephoning 0753/868386.

Queen Mary's Dollhouse

Just about the greatest dollhouse in the world is at Windsor Castle. Presented to the late Queen Mary as a gift, and later used to raise money for charity, the dollhouse is a remarkable achievement and re-creation of what a great royal mansion of the 1920s looked like—complete with a fleet of cars, including a Rolls-Royce. The house is perfect for Tom Thumb and family and a retinue of servants. All is done with the most exacting detail—even the champagne bottles in the wine cellar contain vintage wine of that era. There's a toothbrush suitable for an ant. A minuscule electric iron really works. For late-night reading, you'll find volumes ranging from Hardy to Houseman. In addition, you'll see a collection of dolls presented to the monarchy from nearly every nation of the Commonwealth. Queen Mary's Dollhouse may be viewed for an admission charge of £1.20 ($2) for adults and 50p (85¢) for children, even when the State Apartments are closed.

St. George's Chapel

A gem of the Perpendicular style, this chapel shares the distinction with Westminster Abbey of being a pantheon of English monarchs (Victoria is a notable exception). The present St. George's was founded in the late 15th century by Edward IV on the site of the original Chapel of the Order of the Garter (Edward III, 1348). You enter the nave first with its fan vaulting (a remarkable achievement in English architecture). The nave contains the tomb of George V and Queen Mary, designed by Sir William Reid Dick. Off the nave in the Urswick Chapel, the Princess Charlotte memorial provides an ironic touch. If she had survived childbirth in 1817, she—not her cousin, Victoria—would have ruled the British Empire. In the aisle are the tombs of George VI and Edward IV. The Edward IV "Quire," with its imaginatively carved 15th-century choir stalls (crowned by lacy canopies and Knights of the Garter banners), evokes the pomp and pageantry of medieval days. In the center is a flat tomb, containing the vault of the beheaded Charles I, along with Henry VIII and his third wife, Jane Seymour. Finally, you may want to inspect the Prince Albert Memorial Chapel, reflecting the opulent tastes of the Victorian era. St. George's Chapel is usually open from 10:45am to 3:45 or 4pm Mon. to Sat., and from 2 to 3:45 or 4pm Sun. It is closed during services. Admission is £2 ($3.30) for adults, £1 ($1.65) for children. It is advisable to telephone to check opening hours if you're going to be there at at a time not given as a regular opening time (tel. 0753/865538). It is closed in January and for a few days in mid-June.

Note: Queen Victoria died on January 22, 1901, and was buried beside her beloved Prince Albert in a mausoleum at **Frogmore** (a private estate), near Windsor (open only three days a year, in May). The prince consort died in December 1861.

Exhibition of the Queen's Presents and Royal Carriages

Entered from St. Alban's Street, the redbrick building of the Royal Mews and Burford House were built for Nell Gwynne in the 1670s. They were named for King Charles II's natural son by her, the earl of Burford. When the child was 14 years old, he was created duke of St. Albans, from which the street outside takes its name.

Housed in the mews is the exhibition of the Queen's Presents and Royal Carriages. Displayed are pictures of several members of the royal family, including those of Queen Elizabeth II as colonel-in-chief of the Coldstream Guards riding in the grounds of Buckingham Palace, the duke of Edinburgh driving his horses through a water obstacle at Windsor, and the Queen Mother with Prince Edward, Viscount Linley, and Lady Sarah Armstrong-Jones in the Scottish State Coach. There is also a full-size stable with model horses showing stable kit, harnesses, and riding equipment. In the coach house is a magnificent display of coaches and carriages kept in mint condition and in frequent use. The exhibition of the Queen's Presents includes unique items of interest given to Her Majesty and the Duke of Edinburgh throughout her reign. There is also a collection of pencil drawings of the queen and her family with horses and dogs.

The exhibition is open in November and December and from January to March from 10:30am to 3pm Mon. to Sat; April to October from 10:30am to 5pm Mon. to Sat. and May to October from 10:30am to 3pm Sun. Admission is £1.20 ($2) for adults, 50p (85¢) for children.

Royalty and Empire

At the Windsor and Eton Central Railway Station on Thames Street (tel. 0753/857837), Madame Tussaud's has an exhibition of "Queen Victoria's Diamond Jubilee 1837–1897." A replica of *The Queen,* the engine used to draw the royal coaches, disembarking the life-size wax figures of guests arriving at Windsor for the Jubilee celebration, is at one of the station's platforms. Seated in the Royal Waiting Room are Queen Victoria (in wax, of course), and her family. In one of the carriages, the Day Saloon, are Grand Duke Serge and the Grand Duchess Elizabeth (the queen's granddaughter) of Russia. Waiting in the anteroom is the queen's faithful Indian servant, Hafiz Abdul Karim, the Munshi. Among famous guests portrayed are the prince and princess of Wales (Edward VII and Alexandra), the Empress Frederick of Prussia (Queen Victoria's eldest daughter), and the prime minister, Lord Salisbury. The platform is busy with royal servants, a flower seller, a newsboy, an Italian with a barrel organ, and others who have come to see the arrival of the train. Drawn up on the ceremonial parade ground are the troops of the Coldstream Guards and the horse-drawn carriage that would take the party to the castle. With the sound of military bands in the background and the voices of officers commanding their troops, you really feel you are present for Her Majesty's arrival.

Afterward, at the end of the walkway through the Victorian conservatory, you reach the 260-seat theater where a short audio-visual presentation with life-size animated models gives further glimpses of life during Victoria's reign. The entire visit takes about 45 minutes. The exhibition is open daily from 9:30am to 5:30pm (closed Christmas Day). Admission is £3.95 ($6.50) for adults, £2.95 ($4.85) for children.

Sunday Entertainment

There are often polo matches in **Windsor Great Park**—and at Ham Common —and you may see Prince Charles playing and Prince Philip serving as umpire. The queen often watches. For more information, telephone 0753/860633.

The Town of Windsor

Windsor is largely a Victorian town, with lots of brick buildings and a few remnants of Georgian architecture. In and around the castle are two cobblestone streets, **Church** and **Market,** with their antique shops, silversmiths, and pubs. One shop on Church Street was supposedly occupied by Nell Gwynne, who needed to be within call of Charles II's chambers. After lunch or tea, you may want to stroll along the three-mile, aptly named Long Walk.

Around Windsor Sightseeing Tours

A 35-minute tour of Windsor and the surrounding countryside with commentary is offered in an open-top, double-decker bus. The ten-mile drive starts from Windsor Castle and passes the Royal Mews, the Long Walk, the Royal Farms, Albert Bridge, Eton College, and the Theatre Royal. The departure point is Castle Hill, near the King Henry VIII Gateway to Windsor Castle. Adults pay £3 ($4.95) and children £2 ($3.30). Tickets, along with information about dates of operation and departure times, are available from **Windsorian Coaches,** 103 Arthur Rd. (tel. 0753/860131).

Guided Tours

A 1½ hour guided tour of Windsor Castle and the town leaves from the **Tourist Information Centre** (tel. 0753/852010) in the central station, the one opposite the castle. The walking tour includes a look at the Long Walk, then the Guildhall and Market Cross House, along with the changing of the guard when possible. In the castle precincts you'll visit the Cloisters and the Albert Memorial Chapel, finishing in the State Apartments where no guiding is allowed. Subject to demand, from April to September only, the tours leave at 10:45am and 1:45pm Mon. to Sat., 1:45pm Sun. The cost is £2 ($3.30) for adults and £1.50 ($2.50) for children. All tours are accompanied by a licensed guide.

WHERE TO STAY

For those who decide to stay in Windsor and use it as a base for London sightseeing, London is an easy commute. Trains leave London as late as 10:30 or 11pm, so it's quite easy to take in an early theater and dinner before returning to Windsor for overnight. *Warning:* During the Ascot races and Windsor Horse Show reservations long in advance are necessary.

Expensive Hotels

The **Castle Hotel,** High Street, Windsor, Berkshire SL4 1LJ (tel. 0753/851011), near Windsor Castle, is a solid and long-established hotel with a dignified Georgian facade. It was originally built in the 15th century as a shelter to feed and house the hundreds of workers laboring on the city's foundations and royal buildings. By the 17th century it had changed its name from the Mermaid to the Castle and benefited from the heavy stagecoach traffic that often deposited visitors at its doorstep. In 1986 the entourage of the royal family of Spain was housed in 17 of its best rooms; Princess Anne has dropped in for breakfast; and the duke of Edinburgh has been a guest speaker at functions. Centuries ago the grounds in back of the hotel served as the stable yard for Windsor Castle, but now they support a modern wing containing 46 of the hotel's 85 bedrooms. Each of the accommodations is complete with private bath or shower, color TV, radio, phone, and mini-bar. Singles rent for £74 ($122.10) daily and doubles or twins for £94 ($155.10). The castle also has a car park.

Sir Christopher Wren's House Hotel, Thames Street, Windsor, Berkshire SL4 1PX (tel. 0753/861354), was designed by Christopher Wren in 1676 as his own home. Between Eton and Windsor, the former townhouse occupies a prime position on the Thames, its gardens overlooking swans and boats. The central hall is impressive, with a Queen Anne black marble refectory table. Wren's white-paneled, former study contains his Empire desk, a fireplace, and shield-back Hepplewhite chairs. The bay-windowed main drawing room, decorated with mirrors, sconces, and a formal marble fireplace, opens into a garden and a riverside flagstone terrace for after-dinner coffee and drinks. All of the 38 bedrooms have private baths. Some have fine old furniture, and all are equipped with color TVs, direct-dial phones, and trouser presses. Several units overlook the river. Room 2, which was Sir Christopher Wren's own bedroom, is said to be haunted. Singles with bath range from £80 ($132) daily, and doubles or twins with bath, from £118 ($194.70). Open to nonresidents, the hotel restaurant, the Orangerie, is recommended separately.

Moderately Priced Hotels

Ye Harte & Garter Hotel, 21 High St., Windsor, Berkshire SL4 1LR (tel. 0753/863426), stands on Castle Hill opposite Windsor Castle. An impressive building, the hotel is a combination of two separate inns dating back to the time of Henry VIII. The old Garter Inn, named for the Knights of the Garter, was the setting for scenes in Shakespeare's *Merry Wives of Windsor.* The Garter burned down in the 1800s and was rebuilt as part of one hostelry that included the Hart. The red brick of the present hotel is characteristic of the Victorian era. From the front bedrooms you can watch the guards marching up High Street every morning on their way to change the guard at the castle. Singles cost £46 ($75.90) daily. Doubles go for £67 ($110.55). Breakfast is included. The 50 air-conditioned rooms contain color TVs, direct-dial phones, trouser presses, hot beverage equipment, and other amenities. You can dine in the Apéritif Restaurant or have a drink in the café.

Royal Adelaide Hotel, 46 Kings Rd., Windsor, Berkshire SL4 2AG (tel. 0753/863916), is opposite the famous Long Walk leading to Windsor Castle, five minutes away. An interesting Georgian building, it offers single rooms costing from £55 ($90.75) to £67 ($110.55) daily and doubles and twins from £65 ($107.25) to £80 ($132), and all rates include breakfast. All 42 units, which vary in size, have private baths, radios, TVs, phones, alarms, and hot beverage facilities. There is car parking at the rear for guests, and the hotel is well furnished. A set dinner is available at £12.50 ($20.65) for three courses. The menu is both English and French.

On the Outskirts

On the river road, the A308, from Windsor to Maidenhead, the motorist comes across the **Oakley Court Hotel,** Windsor Road, Water Oakley, Windsor, Berkshire SL4 5UR (tel. 0628/74141), three miles from Windsor and about 20 minutes from Heathrow. This Victorian manor house blossoms as a most attractive riverside hotel. The Gothic house with its turrets and chimneys contains the reception and the living rooms and the restaurant. One modern wing of bedrooms extends from the old house; another, built beside the river, is a 30-foot walk from the main building. Of the 92 rooms, those in the old house have high ceilings, interesting shapes, big baths, and one still contains the original paneling. In the two modern wings, the rooms are of generous size and have baths. All have color TVs, radios with remote control, and phones. There is full room service. Singles rent for £98 ($161.70) to £125 ($206.25) daily, and doubles cost £120 ($198) to £200 (£330), including an English breakfast, VAT, and service.

At Oakley Court's Oak Leaf Restaurant, you can enjoy such specialties as terrine de homard et turbot (terrine of lobster and turbot encased in spinach and served with a mint-and-honey cream) and suprême de volaille blanquette (breast of chicken stuffed with a chicken mousse, prunes, and orange zest, served with a cream and white wine sauce). A set lunch costs £16.67 ($27.50), and a set dinner goes for £25 ($41.25). If you order à la carte, expect to pay from £50 ($82.50). The culinary expertise of Murdo MacSween has made this a popular dining spot, with such notables as Prince Charles and Prince Philip among the customers. Open daily 12:30 to 2:15pm and 7:30 to 10:15pm.

WHERE TO DINE

At Sir Christopher Wren's House Hotel, Thames Street (tel. 0753/861354), already recommended as a hotel, **The Orangerie** is the most elegant and charming restaurant in Windsor with garden terraces. Its anterooms display nymphs whose carved heads gaze out from either side of a neoclassical mantelpiece. The dining room is designed a bit like a greenhouse, with cabriole-legged furniture, lots of chintz, and views through tall French windows of the garden. At dinner a pianist entertains. Full meals, costing from £25 ($41.25), might include a terrine of guinea fowl with macadamia nuts and avocado sauce, mignons of veal filet roasted in a cabbage and cider sauce, or a pair of wood-pigeon breasts fermented in port and served with a plum and blood-orange sauce. Meals are offered from 12:30 to 2pm and 7:30 to 10:30 pm; closed for Sat. lunch. In summer, guests can dine in the garden beside the Thames.

Montmorency Restaurant, Windsor Bridge (tel. 0753/854479), is just on the Eton side of the bridge from Windsor, a building among the boathouses of the college with views over the river and up toward the town and castle. This is an upmarket brasserie owned by Doreen Stanton, who is also owner of the House on the Bridge restaurant opposite. Traditional English dishes, wine, and drinks are served throughout the day. Look for the freshly prepared specials of the day and for a hot roast beef on Sunday. Meals cost from £25 ($41.25). Open daily from 11am to 11pm.

EVENING ENTERTAINMENT

Blazers, William Street (tel. 0753/856222), attracts some of the biggest names on the British cabaret circuit. In plush, comfortable surroundings, you can listen to the cabaret, which begins around 9:45pm, and then later dance until 2am nightly (until midnight on Sun.). A three-course meal costs around £25 ($41.25) per person, plus whatever you order to drink. There's an extensive wine list. Prices will vary, depending on the show, and reservations are essential.

ETON

To visit Eton, home of the most famous public school in the world (Americans would call it a private school), you can take a train from Paddington Station, go by car, or take the Green Line bus to Windsor. If you go by car, you can take the M4 motorway, leaving it at exit 5 to go straight to Eton. However, parking is likely to be a problem, so I advise turning off the M4 at exit 6 to Windsor. You can park there and take an easy stroll past Windsor Castle and across the Thames bridge. Follow Eton High Street to the college. From Windsor Castle's ramparts, you can look down on the river and on the famous playing fields of Eton.

Eton College

Largest of the public (private) schools of England, Eton College was founded by a teenage boy himself, Henry VI, in 1440. Some of England's greatest men, notably the Duke of Wellington, have played on the fields of Eton. Twenty prime ministers were educated here, as well as such literary figures as George Orwell and Aldous Huxley. Even the late Ian Fleming, creator of James Bond, attended. If it's open, take a look at the Perpendicular chapel, with its 15th-century paintings and reconstructed fan vaulting. Visits to the school are possible from Easter to the end of September from 2 to 4:30pm daily; guided tours at 2:15 and 3:15pm; during the summer holidays, from 10:30am to 5pm. Guided tours of the school and museum (see below) cost £2.40 ($4) for adults, £1.80 ($2.95) for children. For information regarding visits, phone 0753/863593.

The Museum of Eton Life

The history of Eton College since its inception in 1440 is depicted in the museum located in vaulted wine cellars under College Hall, which were originally the storehouse for use by the college's masters. The displays, ranging from formal to extremely informal, include a turn-of-the-century boy's room, schoolbooks, sports trophies, canes used by senior boys to apply punishment they felt needful to their juniors, and birch sticks used by masters for the same purpose. Also to be seen are letters written home by students describing day-to-day life at the school, as well as samples of the numerous magazines produced by students over the centuries, known as ephemera because of the changing writers and ideas. Many of the items to be seen were provided by former Etonians. The museum schedule is based on the school year, with hours varying widely. For information, contact the custodian, Eton College (tel. 0753/863593).

Where to Dine

House on the Bridge, 71 High St. (tel. 0753/860914), is in a charming red-brick and terra-cotta Victorian house adjacent to the bridge, beside the river at the edge of Eton. Near the handful of outdoor tables is an almost vertical garden whose plants cascade into the Thames. Well prepared British and international dishes include steak Diane, roast Aylesbury duckling, grilled Dover sole, and crêpes suzette. Many of the most interesting dishes are prepared only for two diners, so it's best to bring a friend. Full meals, costing from £18 ($29.70) to £22 ($36.30) per person, are served daily from noon to 2:30pm and 6 to 11pm.

Eton Wine Bar, 82-83 High St. (tel. 0753/854921), just across the bridge from Windsor, is a charming place with pinewood tables and old church pews and chairs set among antique shops. There is a small garden out back. Soups of the day are often imaginative and sophisticated (for example, watercress vichyssoise). A typical main dish is stuffed eggplant with a Provençal tomato sauce and rice. Each day, two special dishes are featured, and desserts include pineapple and almond flan and damson crunch. Meals cost from £12 ($19.80) up. Wine can be ordered by the glass. Hours are noon to 2:30pm and 6 to 10:30pm Mon. to Thurs., to 11pm Fri. and Sat., and noon to 2pm and 7 to 10pm Sun.

Antico, 42 High St., (tel. 0753/863977), is an old building with beams spreading through several rooms. On your way to the tiny bar you pass a cold table, displaying an array of hors d'oeuvres, fresh fish, and cold meats. There is a wide choice of fish dishes, such as grilled fresh sardines, sole Colbert, or sole with mushrooms, capers, and prawns. Beef filet is a favorite dish. Desserts from the trolley are offered. Meals range from £25 ($41.25) to £30 ($49.50), including VAT and service. Open noon to 2:30pm and 7 to 11pm; closed lunch Sat., all day Sun., and bank holidays.

THINGS TO SEE AND DO NEARBY
Several attractions of interest are in the surrounding area.

One of England's Great Gardens
Savill Garden, Wick Lane, Englefield Green (tel. 0753/860222), is in Windsor Great Park; turn off Wick Road and follow signposts. Started in 1932, the 35-acre garden is considered one of the finest of its type in the northern hemisphere. The display begins in spring with rhododendrons, camellias, and daffodils beneath the trees; then throughout the summer are spectacular displays of flowers and shrubs presented in a natural and wild state. Open all year except at Christmas from 10am to 6 or 7pm, admission is £2 ($3.30) for adults; accompanied children under 16 are admitted free. There is a licensed, self-service restaurant on the premises. The location is 5 miles from Windsor along the A30. Turn off at Wick Road and follow the signs to the gardens.

Adjoining the Savill Garden are the **Valley Gardens,** full of shrubs and trees in a series of wooded natural valleys running down to Virginia water. It's open daily, free, throughout the year.

Windsor Safari Park
Britain's leading Safari Park offers an "African Adventure" for all the family. You can come face to face with some of nature's most dangerous animals and marvel at the range of shows, including the Seaworld Show, which features dolphins, sea lions, and "Winnie"—Britain's only killer whale. Rides include the African Queen Riverboat Ride, where you can journey down the "Congo River" past tribal villages. Other facilities include free safari transport, restaurants, licensed bars, and refreshment kiosks. The park is on the B3022, just 3 miles from Windsor. Take exit 6 on M4, exit 3 on M3, or exit 13 on M25. By rail, go first to Windsor Station where you can catch one of the frequent Beeline or Greenline buses to the park. The all-inclusive admission price for entrance and all shows and attractions is £7.50 ($12.40) adults and £5.95 ($9.80) for children. For more information, call 0753/830886.

The Wellington Ducal Estate
If you'd like to make an interesting day trip to Berkshire, I'd suggest **Stratfield Saye House** (tel. 0256/882882), between Reading and Basingstoke on the A33. It has been the home of the duke of Wellington since 1817, when the 17th-century

house was bought for the Iron Duke to celebrate his victory over Napoleon at the Battle of Waterloo. Many mementoes of the first duke remain in the house, including his billiard table, battle spoils, and pictures. The funeral carriage formerly housed in St. Paul's Cathedral crypt is now in the ducal collection. In the gardens is the grave of Copenhagen, the charger ridden to battle at Waterloo. There are also extensive pleasure grounds together with a licensed restaurant and gift shop.

A short drive away is the **Wellington Country Park** (tel. 0734/326444) with a National Dairy Museum where you can see relics of 150 years of dairying. Other attractions include a riding school, nature trails, and boating and sailing on the lake. In addition, there are a miniature steam railway, the Thames Valley Time Trail, and a deer park.

Stratfield Saye is open May 1 to the last Sun. in September from 11:30am to 5pm; closed Fri. Admission is £3.25 ($5.35) for adults and £1.60 ($2.65) for children. Wellington Country Park is open March to September, daily from 10am to 5pm. Admission is £2.20 ($3.65) for adults, £1 ($1.65) for children. A combined ticket for the house and park costs £4 ($6.60) for adults, £2 ($3.30) for children.

Mapledurham House on the Thames

The Elizabethan mansion home of the Blount family (tel. 0734/723350) lies beside the Thames in the unspoiled village of Mapledurham and can be reached by car from the A4074 Oxford-Reading road. A much more romantic way of reaching the lovely old house is to take the boat that leaves the promenade next to Caversham Bridge at 2pm Sat., Sun., and bank holidays from Easter to the end of September. The journey upstream takes about 40 minutes, and the boat leaves Mapledurham again at 5pm for the journey back to Caversham. This gives you plenty of time to walk through the house and see the Elizabethan ceilings and the great oak staircase, as well as the portraits of the two beautiful sisters with whom the poet Alexander Pope, a frequent visitor here, fell in love. The family chapel, built in 1789, is a fine example of modern Gothic. Cream teas with homemade cakes are available at the house. On the grounds, the last working watermill on the Thames still produces flour.

The house is open from Easter to the end of September from 2:30 to 5pm Sat., Sun., and holidays. The mill is open on the same days from 1:30 to 5pm; Sun. in winter from 2 to 4pm. Entrance to the house costs £2 ($3.30) for adults, £1 ($1.65) for children; to the mill, £1 ($1.65) adults, 50p (85¢) for children.

The boat ride from Caversham costs £2.75 ($4.55) for adults, £1.95 ($3.20) for children for the round trip. Further details about the boat can be obtained from **D&T Scenics Lts.,** Pipers Island, Bridge Street, Caversham Bridge, Reading, Berkshire RG4 8AH (tel. 0734/481088).

---

2. Ascot

While following the royal buckhounds through Windsor Forest, Queen Anne decided to have a racecourse on Ascot Heath. The first race meeting at Ascot was inaugurated in 1711. Since then, the Ascot Racecourse has become a symbol of society, attended by the royal family and members of fashionable circles. Nowadays instead of Queen Anne, you are likely to see Princess Anne, an avid equestrian.

Ascot lies only 28 miles west of London, directly south of Windsor at the southern end of Windsor Great Park (take the A332). There is frequent rail service in London from Waterloo to Ascot Station, about ten minutes from the racecourse.

The **Ascot Racecourse** (tel. 0990/22211) is open throughout the year except for the month of August. There are three enclosures: Tattersalls is the largest, Silver Ring the least expensive, and the third is the Members Enclosure. There are bars and restaurants to suit everybody's taste. Tickets cost £3 ($4.95) to £19 ($31.35) for adults; children under 16 are admitted free if accompanied by an adult. The highlight of the Ascot social season—complete with fancy hats and white gloves—is

Royal Week in late June, but there is excellent racing on the fourth Saturday in July and the last Saturday in September, with more than a million pounds in prize money. There are 13 flat races and 10 National Hunts (point-to-points).

WHERE TO STAY AND DINE

One of the most elegant hotels in the region is the **Royal Berkshire,** London Road, Sunninghill, Ascot, Berkshire SL5 0PP (tel. 0344/23322), 2 miles northeast of Ascot on A322. Its interior decor does justice to its history. Built of russet-colored bricks in the Queen Anne style in 1705, it was lived in for many years by relatives of Sir Winston Churchill. Bedrooms, 82 in all, are often spacious, with amenities including private baths or showers, direct-dial phones, and TVs. A single is priced at £71 ($117.15) to £90 ($148.50) daily, and doubles go for £106 ($174.90) to £140 ($231). Many people visit only for a meal in the Stateroom Restaurant, overlooking the lawns and gardens of the hotel. The food, some of the finest in the area, is made with quality ingredients, often reflecting artistic flair. Lunch costs from £20 ($33) and dinner from £30 ($49.50). There is a good à la carte menu that changes frequently and offers a range of contemporary English dishes. Meals are served daily from 12:30 to 2:30pm and 7:30 to 9:30pm.

Berystede Country House Hotel, Bagshot Road, Sunninghill, Ascot, Berkshire SL5 9JH (tel. 0344/23311), was built by Victorians and includes re-creations of medieval towers, half-timbering, steeply pitched roofs, and a landscaped garden. The entrance hall incorporates the massive lintel and Ionic pilasters of a pseudo-Gothic stone fireplace that, if the weather's cool enough, might be blazing. The hotel has been upgraded, enlarged, and redecorated. Bedrooms, with their high ceilings and chintz, evoke the aura of rooms in a private country house. Each contains a private bath, phone, and color TV, and the more expensive suites boast mahogany reproductions of 18th-century antiques. The rooms, 91 in all, rent for £81 ($133.65) to £125 ($206.25) daily in a single, £96 ($158.40) to £150 ($247.50) in a double or twin. The hotel lies 1¼ miles south of Ascot on A330.

Brockenhurst, Brockenhurst Road, South Ascot, SL5 9HA (tel. 0990/21912), is a small Edwardian hotel (1905) of charm and distinction. It has been improved and expanded, but always with respect to its era. Conveniently located near shops and the rail station, it offers 11 bedrooms, all with private showers or baths. The most expensive are called "executive," and include whirlpool baths, trouser presses, and hairdryers. Each room has a radio, color TV, and direct-dial phone. Singles range from £45 ($74.25) to £69 ($113.85) daily, with doubles renting for £55 ($90.75) to £85 ($140.25), including VAT and a continental, buffet-style breakfast. The hotel has a bar and offers a room service menu.

---

3. Henley-on-Thames

At the eastern edge of Oxfordshire, only 35 miles from London, Henley-on-Thames is a small town and resort on the river. At the foothills of the Chilterns, it is headquarters of the Royal Regatta held annually in July, the premier event among European crews. The regatta dates back to the first years of Victoria's reign.

The Elizabethan buildings, the tearooms, and the inns along the town's High Street live up to one's conception of what an English country town should look like. The life here is serene, and Henley-on-Thames makes for an excellent stopover en route to Oxford. *Warning:* During the Royal Regatta, rooms are virtually impossible to get at the fashionable inns of Henley, unless you've made reservations months in advance.

WHERE TO STAY AND DINE

Dating from the 16th century, the **Red Lion Hotel,** Henley Bridge, Henley-on-Thames, Oxfordshire RG9 2AR (tel. 0491/572161), is a former coaching inn. A bedchamber used to be kept ready for the duke of Marlborough, who would stop over on his way to his palace at Blenheim. The guest list reads like a hall of fame, including such notables as Johnson and Boswell, even George IV, who, it is said, downed more than a dozen lamb chops one night. The redbrick facade, with its climbing wisteria, remains untouched, but most of the interior has been renovated and modernized. A bathless single costs £35 ($57.75) daily, rising to £65 ($107.25) with bath, and bathless doubles go for £68 ($112.20) increasing to £78 ($128.70) with bath. The hotel rents 26 bedrooms, most of them overlooking the Thames. Room facilities include tea or coffee makers, direct-dial phones, and TVs; 21 of the 26 bedrooms have private baths or showers. The hotel also offers ample parking and laundry service. The last dinner is served at 10pm, but room service is provided throughout the day. Guests congregate in the low-beamed lounge and take meals in the Riverside Restaurant, which serves an à la carte lunch or dinner for £20 ($33).

4. Inns Along the Thames

For those who want to anchor into riverside villages with old inns along the Thames, I offer the following suggestions for the motorist. You can watch the peaceful river making its way between the history-laden banks, lined with trees, gardens, and buildings lying somnolent under the English skies.

BRAY-ON-THAMES
Twenty-eight miles from London, you come upon this attractive Thamesside village, with its beautiful old almshouses, timbered cottages, and small period houses. Windsor Castle is just a short jaunt away. The town was once famous for its 18th-century "Vicar of Bray" who cynically changed his religious affiliation to suit every political change that came along.

Where to Dine
In what was a traditional English riverside pub on an attractive stretch of the river, the Roux brothers operate the **Waterside Inn,** Ferry Road (tel. 0628/20691), known for its impeccable cooking (and also for its astronomical prices). The restaurant has been given almost every superlative in the book. The Roux brothers were brought up in the Saône et Loire region of France where their father had a charcuterie (delicatessen), and the boys learned basic cooking skills from him and from their mother. Both first went into private service in England and France, and then opened a London restaurant, Le Gavroche. Michel Roux is in charge of the Waterside operation.

If you select from the à la carte menu, expect to pay around £50 ($82.50) per person, plus wine, if you have been extravagant in your choice of dishes. Actually, you can dine well by ordering the set dinner at £44.50 ($73.45). At lunch, you can enjoy a set meal Mon. to Fri. for £21.50 ($35.50) and Sat. and Sun. for £24.50 ($40.45). Chef Michel has developed some interesting combinations, such as salmon and brill with ginger, a mousse using three different fish, and fileted young rabbit with marrons glacés. Try, if featured, mousseline of chicken with roquefort, or a casolette of crayfish with tagliatelle in a sauce Nantua. The Waterside is open from Tues. dinner to Sun. lunch; hours for lunch are noon to 2pm; dinner 7 to 10pm; closed in January and the Christmas holidays. Reservations are essential.

If the Waterside is too rich for your pocketbook, you should be well pleased with the following, more modestly priced recommendation.

Hinds Head Hotel, High Street (tel. 0628/26151), is on the bend of a very busy, narrow road, but there's ample parking in front of the restaurant. Although calling itself a hotel, the Hinds has no rooms to rent. There is a bar and you can take your pint in with you if you wish, as the wine list is expensive. Portions are large. A three-course lunch has a fish course, followed by roast beef, pork, or lamb, with all the trimmings. The waitresses bring around three sorts of potatoes and then about four different green vegetables. The set lunch on weekdays costs £19 ($31.35); £20

($33) on Sun. A dinner goes for £25 ($41.25). Hours are 12:30 to 2:30pm and 7:30 to 10:30pm; closed for dinner Sun. This is the sort of place to come to on a nice Sunday for a good old English "blow-out" lunch.

STREATLEY-ON-THAMES
This Thameside village has some old buildings and a fine priory church.

Where to Stay and Dine
The Swan Diplomat, High Street, Streatley-on-Thames, Berkshire RG8 9HR (tel. 0491/873737), is a riverside hotel. The Swan has been much enlarged, but still retains much of its old charm. Gardens slope down to the water. The menu offers a high standard of food at a variety of prices. Set lunches cost from £16.50 ($27.25), or you can order à la carte. A specialty, three-course, fixed-price dinner goes for £19.50 ($32.20). Expect to pay from £29.50 ($48.70) if you order your evening meal à la carte. Whether you're touring or just spending a last night before going to Heathrow, this is a good choice. All 46 rooms, each individually designed, have private baths, and a full English breakfast and VAT are included in the rates. The most desirable rooms open onto views of the Thames. Singles cost from £81 ($133.65) daily and doubles from £113 ($186.45). Rooms have direct-dial phones and TVs. There is ample parking on the grounds, plus 24-hour room service. A leisure club with a gym and a sauna, plus rowboats and bicycle rentals, are added features. The hotel lies just off the A329 in Streatley Village. Oxford, Windsor, London, and Heathrow Airport are within an hour's drive.

---

5. Oxford

A walk down the long sweep of The High, one of the most striking streets in England; a mug of cider in one of the old student pubs; a May Day dawn when choristers sing in Latin from Magdalen Tower; the Great Tom bell from Tom Tower, whose 101 peals traditionally signal the closing of the college gates; towers and spires rising majestically; the barges on the upper reaches of the Thames; nude swimming at Parson's Pleasure; the roar of a cannon launching the bumping races; a tiny, dusty bookstall where you can pick up a valuable first edition—all that is Oxford, home of one of the greatest universities in the world. An industrial city, 57 miles from London and the center of a large automobile business as well as a university town, Oxford is best for sightseeing July to September. That's when the students are on vacation and the city is less crowded.

However, at any time of the year you can enjoy a tour of the colleges. The Oxford Information Centre (see below) offers guided walking tours daily throughout the year. Just don't mention the "other place" (Cambridge) and you shouldn't have any trouble.

The city predates the university—in fact, it was a Saxon town in the early part of the 10th century. And by the 12th century Oxford was growing in reputation as a seat of learning—at the expense of Paris. The first colleges were founded in the 13th century. The story of Oxford is filled with conflicts too complex and detailed to elaborate here. Suffice it to say, the relationship between town and gown wasn't as peaceful as it is today. Riots often flared, and both sides were guilty of abuses.

Nowadays, the young people of Oxford take out their aggressiveness by participating in sports. Oxford's most important sporting event, uniting the whole university, is the annual rowing race against the traditional rival, Cambridge.

Ultimately, the test of a great university lies in the caliber of the people it turns out. Oxford can name-drop a mouthful: Roger Bacon, Sir Walter Ralegh, John Donne, Sir Christopher Wren, William Penn, Samuel Johnson, John Wesley, Edward Gibbon, William Pitt, Matthew Arnold, A. E. Housman, Lewis Carroll, T. E. Lawrence, Harold Macmillan, Arnold Toynbee, Graham Greene, and even Dean Rusk

OXFORD

KEY TO NUMBERED SIGHTS:

1. Somerville College
2. Keble College
3. Mansfield College
4. Ruskin College
5. St. John's College
6. Trinity College
7. Wadham College
8. Manchester College
9. St. Catherine's College
10. Worcester College
11. Balliol College
12. New College
13. Nutfield College
14. St. Peter's College
15. Jesus College
16. Exeter College
17. Lincoln College
18. Brasenose College
19. Hertford College
20. All Souls College
21. Queen's College
22. Magdalene College
23. Oriel College
24. University College
25. Corpus Christi College
26. Christ Church College
27. St. Hilda's College

Observatory

River Cherwell

ST. CROSS RD.

LONGWALL ST.

Botanical Gardens

Christ Church Meadows

MANSFIELD RD.

SO. PARKS RD.

PARKS RD.

MERTON ST.

HIGH ST. (A420)

BROAD ST.

ST. ALDATE'S

BANBURY RD.

WOODSTOCK RD.

ST. GILES ST.

BEAUMONT ST.

QUEEN ST.

ST. EBBE'S ST.

GEORGE ST.

NEW RD.

WALTON ST.

NELSON ST.

HYTHE BRIDGE

THAMES ST.

NEW ST.

OXPENS RD.

CANAL ST.

Oxford Canal

Oxford Univ. Press

Oxford Station

River Thames

Many Americans arriving in Oxford ask, "Where's the campus?" If an Oxonian shows amusement when answering, it's understandable. Oxford University is, in fact, made up of 35 colleges. To tour all of these would be a formidable task. Besides, a few are of such interest they overshadow the rest.

PARK AND RIDE

Traffic and parking are a disaster in Oxford, and not just during rush hours. However, there are three large car parks on the north, south, and west of the city's ring road, all well marked. Car parking is free at all times. To and from the car parks buses run every 8 to 10 minutes to the city center—get off at St. Aldate's or Queen Street. There is a charge of 60p ($1) from 9am on, and all day Sat. There is no service on Sunday. The car parks are on the Woodstock road near the Peartree roundabout, on the Botley road toward Faringdon, on the Abingdon road in the southeast, and on the A40 toward London.

TOURS AND TOURIST SERVICES

A tourist reception center for Oxford is operated by **Guide Friday Ltd.** (tel. 0865/790522), at the railway station, Oxford. Their office dispenses maps and brochures and operates tours. Also available is a full range of tourist services, including accommodation references and car rentals. In summer, the office is open daily from 9am to 8pm; in winter, daily from 9am to 4pm. Guided tours of Oxford and the colleges leave from the railway station daily. In summer, aboard open-top, double-decker buses, departures are every 15 minutes. The tour can be a 60-minute panoramic ride, or you can get off at any of the stops in the city. The ticket is valid all day. The tour price is £4 ($6.60).

WHAT TO SEE AND DO

The best way to get a running commentary on the important sightseeing attractions is to go to the **Oxford Information Centre,** St. Aldate's Chambers, St. Aldate's, opposite the town hall, near Carfax (tel. 0865/726871). Walking tours through the city and the major colleges leave daily in the morning and afternoon. They last two hours and cost £2.40 ($3.95). The tour does not include New College or Christ Church. You can also get reservations for entertainment facilities, as well as for Stratford-upon-Avon and London West End theaters (tel. 0865/727855). The center sells a comprehensive range of maps, brochures, souvenir items, as well as the famous Oxford University tee-shirt.

Because there are so many well-known buildings in Oxford (Radcliffe Camera, whose dome competes in a city of spires; Sheldonian Theatre, an early work of Wren's; the Bodleian Library, one of the most important in the world), I have narrowed the sights to a representative list of a few colleges.

For a bird's-eye view of the city and colleges, climb **Carfax Tower.** This is the one with the clock and figures that strikes the hours. Admission is 70p ($1.15) for adults and 30p (50¢) for children. The tower is open from 10am to 6pm Mon. to Sat. and from 2 to 6pm on Sun. from late March to late October. For information, call 0865/250239.

Carfax is the tower left from St. Martin's Church where William Shakespeare once stood as godfather for William Davenant, who also became a playwright. A church had stood on this spot since 1032, until the final one was torn down in 1896. The tower used to be higher, but after 1340 it was lowered, following complaints to Edward III that townspeople threw stones and fired arrows from it during town and gown disputes.

The Oxford Story, Broad Street (tel. 0865/728822), helps the visitor to understand the complexities of Oxford University. It provides an insight into the structure of the colleges, with a look behind the portals at some of the architectural and historical features that might otherwise be missed. It also fills you in on the general background of the colleges and highlights the deeds of some of the famous people who have passed through its portals. The audio-visual presentation is given daily, with an admission charge of £3 ($4.95) for adults and £1.50 ($2.50) for children.

At **Punt Station,** Cherwell Boathouse, Bardwell Road (tel. 0865/515978), you can rent a punt at a cost of £4 ($6.60) per hour, plus a £25 ($41.25) deposit that must be posted. Similar charges are made on rentals at Magdalen Bridge Boathouse and at the Folly Bridge Boathouse. Hours are 10am to 10pm daily.

A Word of Warning

The main business of a university, is, of course, to educate—and unfortunately this function at Oxford has been severely interfered with by the number of visitors who have been disturbing the academic work of the university. So, with deep regret, visiting is now restricted to certain hours and small groups of six or fewer. In addition, there are areas where visitors are not allowed at all, but the tourist office will be happy to advise you when and where you may "take in" the sights of this great institution.

Christ Church

Begun by Cardinal Wolsey as Cardinal College in 1525, Christ Church (tel. 0865/276174), known as The House, was founded by Henry VIII in 1546. Facing St. Aldate's Street, Christ Church has the largest quadrangle of any college in Oxford.

Tom Tower houses Great Tom, the 18,000-pound bell. It rings at 9:05 nightly, signaling the closing of the college gates. The 101 times it peals originally signified the number of students in residence at the time of the founding of the college. The student body number changed, but Oxford traditions live on forever. In the 16th-century Great Hall, with its hammer-beam ceiling, are some interesting portraits, including works by those old reliables, Gainsborough and Reynolds. Prime ministers are pictured, as Christ Church was the training ground for 13 prime ministers: men such as Gladstone and George Canning. There is a separate picture gallery.

The cathedral, dating from the 12th century, was built over a period of centuries. (Incidentally, it's not only the college chapel, but the cathedral of the diocese of Oxford.) The cathedral's most distinguishing features are its Norman pillars and the vaulting of the choir, dating from the 15th century. In the center of the Great Quadrangle is a statue of Mercury mounted in the center of a fish pond. The college and cathedral can be visited from 9:30am to noon and 2 to 6pm in summer, to 4:30pm in winter. Entrance fee is £1 ($1.65) daily.

Magdalen College

Pronounced "maud-len," this college was founded in 1458 by William of Waynflete, bishop of Winchester and later chancellor of England. Its alumni range from Wolsey to Wilde. Opposite the botanic garden, the oldest in England, is the bell tower, where the choristers sing in Latin at dawn on May Day. The reflection of the 15th-century tower is cast in the waters of the Cherwell below. On a not-so-happy day, Charles I—his days numbered—watched the oncoming Roundheads. Visit the 15th-century chapel, in spite of many of its latter-day trappings. Ask when the hall and other places of special interest are open. The grounds of Magdalen are the most extensive of any Oxford college, even containing a deer park. You can visit Magdalen each day from 2 to 6:15pm.

A favorite pastime is to take **Addison's Walk** through the water meadows. The stroll is so named after a former alumnus, Joseph Addison, the 18th-century essayist and playwright noted for his contributions to *The Spectator* and *The Tatler*.

Merton College

Founded in 1264, this college (tel. 0865/276310) is among the trio of the most ancient at the university. It stands near Corpus Christi College on Merton Street, the sole survivor of Oxford's medieval cobbled streets. Merton College is noted for its library, said to be the oldest college library in England, built between 1371 and 1379. There was once a tradition of keeping some of its most valuable books chained. Now only one book is so secured, to show what the custom was like. One of the treasures of the library is an astrolabe (astronomical instrument used for measuring the altitude of the sun and stars), thought to have belonged to Chaucer. You pay only 30p (50¢) to visit the ancient library, as well as the Max Beerbohm Room (the satirical English caricaturist who died in 1956). Both are open from 2 to 4pm Mon. to Sat. (4:30pm March to October), 10am to noon Sat. and Sun., closed between Christmas and the end of the second week in February and for a week at Easter. You can also visit the chapel, dating from the 13th century, at these times.

University College

On The High, University College (tel. 0865/276602) is the oldest one at Oxford, tracing its history back to 1249 when money was donated by an ecclesiastic, William of Durham. More fanciful is the old claim that the real founder was Alfred the Great. Don't jump to any conclusions about the age of the buildings when you see the present Gothic-esque look. The original structures have all disappeared, and what remains today represents essentially the architecture of the 17th century, with subsequent additions in Victoria's day, as well as in more recent times. For example, the Goodhart Quadrangle was added as late as 1962. Its most famous alumnus, Shelley, was "sent down" for his part in collaborating on a pamphlet on atheism. However, all is forgiven today, and the poet is honored by a memorial erected in 1894. The hall and chapel of University College can be visited daily during vacations from 2 to 4pm for a charge of £1 ($1.65).

New College

New College was founded in 1379 by William of Wykeham, bishop of Winchester and later lord chancellor of England. His college at Winchester supplied a constant stream of candidates. The first quadrangle, dating from the late 14th century, was the initial quadrangle to be built in Oxford, forming the architectural design for other colleges. In the antechapel is Sir Jacob Epstein's remarkable modern sculpture, *Lazarus* and a fine El Greco painting of St. James. One of the treasures of the college is a crosier (pastoral staff of a bishop) belonging to the founding father. In the garden you can see the remains of the old city wall and the mound. The college (entered at New College Lane) can be visited daily in summer from 2 to 5pm. Admission is 50p (85¢).

Salter's River Thames Services

From mid-May until mid-September, Salter Brothers run daily passenger boat services on many reaches of the River Thames. Trips are to or from Oxford, Abingdon, Reading, Henley, Marlow, Cookham, Maidenhead, Windsor, Runnymede, and Staines. Combined outings from London can be made in conjunction with train or bus services. Full details can be obtained from **Salter Bros. Ltd.,** Folly Bridge, Oxford (tel. 0865/243421).

WHERE TO STAY

The accommodations in Oxford are limited, although the addition of motels on the outskirts has aided the plight of those who require modern amenities. Recently, some of the more stalwart candidates in the city center have been refurbished as well. In addition, motorists may want to consider some grand country houses on the outskirts of town, which offer the best living in Oxford if you don't mind commuting.

The **Oxford Information Centre,** St. Aldate's Chambers, St. Aldate's (tel. 0865/726871), operates a year-round room-booking service for a fee of £2 ($3.30) and a 7% refundable deposit. If you'd like to seek lodgings on your own, the staff at the center will provide, for a fee, a list of accommodations, maps, and guidebooks.

Expensive Hotels

Randolph Hotel, Beaumont Street, Oxford, Oxfordshire OX1 2LN (tel. 0865/247481), is a refurbished Gothic-Victorian hotel, dating from 1864. For more than a century it has been overlooking St. Giles, the Ashmolean Museum, and the Cornmarket. The lounges, although modernized, are still cavernous enough for dozens of separate conversational groupings, and the furnishings are contemporary. The hotel contains 109 rooms, all with private baths, direct-dial phones, radios, and color TVs. Singles cost £85 ($140.25) per night, and doubles rent for £108 ($178.20). The hotel's Spires Restaurant presents the time-tested and the nouvelle in a high-ceilinged, Victorian dining room. An à la carte dinner costs about £30 ($49.50) per person, while a set dinner goes for £20 ($33), and a set lunch for £15 ($24.75). Hours are daily from 12:30 to 2pm and 7 to 10pm. There is also a coffeeshop with an entrance off the street, serving from 10am to 10pm. The hotel's Chapters bar has a tradition-laden atmosphere. The drink list offers everything from "textbook classics" to "epilogue."

Moderately Priced Hotels

Cotswold Lodge Hotel, 66A Banbury Rd., Oxford, Oxfordshire OX2 6JP (tel. 0865/512121), is a 19th-century building set on a wide avenue lined with stately trees, about a mile from the town center. The outside has Victorian detailing, but the interior has been renovated into functional modern. A newer wing from the 1970s contains additional and comfortable accommodations, each well scrubbed and very pleasant. In all, 52 rooms are rented. In the older section, a scattering of units have flowered wallpaper and some Victoriana. With private baths and direct-dial phones, singles cost from £64 ($105.60) to £70 ($115.50) daily and doubles £80 ($132) to £90 ($148.50). Set-price lunches and dinners are served in the hotel's restaurant.

Welcome Lodge, Peartree Roundabout, Woodstock Road, Oxford, Oxfordshire OX2 8JZ (tel. 0865/54301), is suitable for motorists who want to be within easy reach of the university and shopping districts of Oxford, 2 miles away. Easy to spot, near a large bus stop, the lodge invites with international flags fluttering in the breezes. Its lower-level bedrooms open onto private terraces. The furnishings are in the typical motel style, with compact, built-in necessities. Each of the 95 rooms has a picture-window wall, a private bath with shower, TV, radio, individually controlled heating, and tea-making facilities. Room rates in a single are £50 ($82.50) to £55 ($90.75) daily and from £59 ($97.35) in a double or twin. Special rooms for non-smokers are also offered. A full English breakfast is included in the tariffs. On the grounds are a swimming pool (summer only), the Lodgekeepers Restaurant and bar, the Little Chef Grill, the Granary Self-Service Restaurant, a family shop, and a 24-hour garage.

Oxford Moat House, Godstow Road, Wolvercote Roundabout, Oxford, Oxfordshire OX2 8AL (tel. 0865/59933), one of the Queens Moat Houses Group, incorporates the principles of motel design, with an emphasis on spacious, glassed-in areas and streamlined bedrooms. Its position, at the northern edge of Oxford 2 miles away, is hidden from the traffic at the junction of the A40 and the A34. Although generally patronized by motorists, it can also be reached by bus. In a double or twin, with a full breakfast, you pay £95 ($156.75) daily for two, £80 ($132) in a single. The 155 rooms contain private baths or showers, radios, color TVs, videos, phones, trouser presses, and hot beverage equipment. The Moat House has a swimming pool, squash courts, a whirlpool bath, a sauna, a solarium, and a snooker room.

Eastgate Hotel, Merton Street, The High, Oxford, Oxfordshire OX1 4BE (tel. 0865/248244), stands opposite the ancient Examination Halls and lies within walking distance of Oxford colleges and the city center. Recently refurbished, the Eastgate offers modern facilities while retaining somewhat the atmosphere of an English country house. All 43 rooms have baths, direct-dial phones, color TVs, radios, and tea and coffee makers. Singles cost from £68 ($112.20) to £80 ($132) daily, and twins or doubles go from £78 ($128.70) to £108 ($178.20). Prices include VAT and service. The Ruskin Restaurant offers a selection of roasts and traditional English "fayre," complemented by a choice of wines. A three-course table d'hôte dinner is priced at £15 ($24.75).

Royal Oxford Hotel, Park End Street, Oxford, Oxfordshire OX1 1HR (tel.

0865/248432), is an oldish establishment given a new lease on life by a renovation of its interior. Near Oxford Station, about a 10-minute walk from the center of the city, it is a comfortable and convenient place at which to stay. Of its 25 bedrooms, 12 have private baths, and all have color TVs, phones, and radios. A bathless single goes for £36 ($59.40) daily, a single with bath costing £52 ($85.80). Doubles or twins rent for £46 ($75.90) bathless, £64 ($105.60) with bath. Prices include service and VAT. The bedrooms are well kept, with modern, compact furnishings. Ask about "weekend breaks" when booking.

Budget Hotels

Old Parsonage Hotel, 3 Banbury Rd., Oxford, Oxfordshire OX2 6NN (tel. 0865/310210), is so old it looks like an extension of one of the ancient colleges. Originally a 13th-century hospital named Bethleen, it was restored in the early 17th century. Near St. Giles Church, it is set back from the street behind a low stone wall and sheltered by surrounding trees and shrubbery. However, most of the 35 rooms are in a modern wing that is institutional in character. The owners charge from £28 ($46.26) per person nightly for B&B in a single, from £45 ($74.25) in a twin or double. There is only one room with a private shower; that costs £58 ($95.70) for two persons. The others have hot and cold running water. Each room also has a direct-dial phone. Some of the large front rooms in the older part, with leaded-glass windows, are set aside for travelers. You have breakfast in a pleasant dining room, overlooking the garden. A licensed bar is on the premises.

Dial House, 25 London Rd., Headington, Oxford, Oxfordshire OX3 7RE (tel. 0865/69944), is a 1930s, half-timbered house lying 1½ miles from the heart of Oxford on the main highway to London. A bus stops only a few yards from the door, and, for the motorist, there is off-street parking. The eight bedrooms are immaculately maintained, and all of them have TVs and private baths or showers. Charges range from £35 ($57.75) daily in a single to £42 ($69.30) in a double. The resident owners, Julie and Tony Lamb, are known for maintaining a country house atmosphere. Only breakfast is served in their bright dining room.

Staying in the Environs

A moated stone edifice, **Weston Manor,** Weston-on-the-Green, Oxfordshire OX6 8QL (tel. 0869/50621), is only 8 miles from Oxford, on the A43 Oxford-Northampton road, ideal as a center for touring the district (Blenheim Palace is only 5 miles away). The manor, owned and run by the Osborn family, has existed since the 11th century; portions of the present building date from the 14th and 16th centuries, with later additions in Victoria's day. The estate was an abbey until abbeys were abolished by Henry VIII. Of course, there are ghosts: Mad Maude, the naughty nun who was burned at the stake for her "indecent and immoral" behavior, returns to haunt the Oak Bedrooms. Prince Rupert, during the English Civil War, hid from Cromwell's soldiers in one of the fireplaces, eventually escaping in drag as the "maiden of the milk bucket."

As you enter the driveway, you pass two elm trees, dating back to 1672, and proceed into a formal car-park area. The reception lounge is dominated by a Tudor fireplace and a long refectory table. Most of the bedrooms are spacious, furnished with antiques (often four-posters), old dressing tables, and chests. The hotel rents 37 bedrooms with direct-dial phones, TVs, and private baths or showers. The cost of staying here is from £69 ($113.85) daily in a single, from £89 ($146.85) in a double. Tariffs include an English breakfast and VAT. The Great Hall is one of the most beautiful dining rooms in England, with an open-rafter and beamed ceiling, the lower portion solidly paneled with a rare example of linenfold. There's a minstrels' gallery and a large wrought-iron chandelier. The English food is first rate. A la carte meals average £18 ($29.70), and the big Sunday lunch costs £15 ($24.75). In warm weather, you can enjoy the open-air swimming pool surrounded by gardens.

Studley Priory Hotel, Horton-cum-Studley, Oxfordshire OX9 1AZ (tel. 086735/203), may be remembered by those who saw *A Man for All Seasons*. The former Benedictine priory, a hotel since 1961, was used for background shots for the private residence of Sir Thomas More. It is a stunning example of Elizabethan architecture, although it originally dates from the 12th century. Set in 13 acres of wooded grounds and lived in for around 300 years by the Croke family, the manor, only 7 miles from Oxford, is built of stone in the manorial style, with large halls and long bedroom wings and gable with mullioned windows. The rooms are large and the furnishings tasteful. Guests are received for £65 ($107.25) daily in a single, £75 ($123.75) to £110 ($181.50) in a double. All 19 rooms have private baths or showers, direct-dial phones, and TVs. Room service is provided all day, as is laundry service. There is ample parking. Even if you're not staying over, you may want to visit for lunch or dinner, with a four-course, rather sophisticated meal averaging around £25 ($41.25). Getting here is a bit complicated—so be armed with a good map when you strike out from Oxford. From Oxford, travel to the end of the Banbury Road. At the roundabout take the third exit (toward London). Travel along the "dual-carriageway" for approximately 3½ miles. At the next roundabout take the first exit signposted Horton-cum-Studley—4½ miles. Go through the estate and stay on the same road till you come to "staggered crossroads." Go straight across signposted Horton-cum-Studley—2½ miles. This road will bring you straight into the village, and the hotel is at the top of the hill on the right-hand side.

WHERE TO DINE

A dining and lodging choice supreme, **Le Manoir aux Quat' Saisons,** Great Milton, Oxfordshire OX9 7PD (tel. 0844/278881), 12 miles southeast of Oxford, enjoys a reputation for offering the finest cuisine in the Midlands. The gray-and-honey-colored-stone manor house was originally built by a Norman nobleman in the early 1300s. The connection with France has been masterfully continued to this day by the Gallic owner and chef, Raymond Blanc. His reputation for comfort and cuisine attracts guests from as far away as London—gastronomes who regard the one-hour trek as a delicious excuse for a day in the country. The gabled house that rises today from a mature garden and lawns was built in the 1500s and improved and enlarged in 1908. An outdoor swimming pool, still in use, was added much later. Inside, 21 luxurious bedrooms, each decorated boudoir-style with lots of flowery draperies, ruffled canopies, radio, color TV, phone, springtime colors, and high-quality antique reproductions, cost £150 ($247.50) to £300 ($495) daily, double occupancy.

The main focus of the establishment is a pair of beamed-ceiling dining rooms whose mullioned windows offer views of the garden. You can enjoy such specialties as a soup of Cornish lobster with cumin, a mousse of asparagus with chervil sauce, zucchini flowers stuffed with a sabayon of wild mushrooms, veal cutlet with truffles, breast of wild duck with pear and apples, and scallops poached with herbs. A menu du jour costs £21.50 ($35.50), £28 ($46.20) on Saturday. A menu gourmand is £48 ($79.20). You can also order à la carte. After-dinner coffee is served beside the fire in the lounge. Reservations are a necessity. If you call, an employee will provide directions. Take exit 7 from the artery connecting London with Oxford (the M40). Head along the A329 in the direction of Wallingford, Thame, and Milton Common. Look carefully for signs about a mile later directing you to the manor. Hours are from 12:15 to 2:30pm and 7:15 to 10:30pm daily.

Restaurant Elizabeth, 84 St. Aldate's (tel. 0865/242230), is an intimate and special restaurant that (in spite of its name) owes the inspiration of its cuisine to the continent, notably Spain, France, and Greece. Under the watchful eye of Antonio Lopez, it attracts Oxonians who appreciate good food served in an inviting atmosphere. For appetizers, try either the ttoro (a Basque fish soup served with aïoli), or avgolemono (the Greek national soup—chicken bouillon laced with a beaten egg and lemon juice). Favorite main dishes that I highly recommend include trout stuffed with seafood mousse and coq au vin. Including wine and coffee, plus all the extras, the cost of a dinner is about £28 ($46.20) per person. Wine by the liter, both burgundy and bordeaux, is available. The restaurant is open for dinner from 6:30 to 11pm Tues. to Sat., 7 to 10:30pm Sun. Lunch costs £12 ($19.80), and hours are from 12:30 to 2:30pm. The restaurant is closed Mon.

La Sorbonne, 130A High St. (tel. 0865/241320), in a 1631 building, is tucked away on a narrow lane off The High, one minute's walk from Carfax. True to its name, it provides classic French meals and has done so since 1966. Diners have included Dame Margot Fonteyn, Paul McCartney, and the princess of Wales. A good beginning is the chef's special, moules marinières, offered from October to March only. André Chavagnon, the chef de cuisine and proprietor, offers not only the usual French dishes, but the following specialties as well: jugged hare, wild duck, and tarragon-flavored chicken suprême. A soufflé for two is a specialty. Mr. Chavagnon says: "Soufflés are expensive, but they require a lot of care and attention. When we tried to charge less, everybody wanted one and we couldn't cope." Expect to pay, on an average, about £30 ($49.50) per head à la carte. A set lunch or dinner costs £18 ($29.70). The restaurant is open from noon to 2:30pm and 7 to 11pm Mon. to Sat., noon to 2pm and 7 to 10pm Sun.

Downstairs in the Croute Room, you can eat for about £12 ($19.80), dining on such meals as, for example, onion soup, a dish of the day including vegetables and potatoes, crème caramel, coffee, and a glass of wine. Hours are the same as for the upstairs restaurant.

15 North Parade, at 15 North Parade (tel. 0865/513773), continues to win respect and praise from its patrons; the continental cookery here is first rate. Wicker chairs, subtle lighting, and plenty of photos provide the proper background for the presentation of the ever-changing cuisine. You might begin with a fish soup (similar to what you'd be served in Nice), then follow with roast guinea fowl in a sherry sauce. Care also goes into the vegetables, such as the fresh, crisp-cooked French beans. A set lunch is a bargain at £11.75 ($19.40) weekdays and £14.75 ($24.35) on Sunday. Count on spending £30 ($49.50) and up for dinner. Wines, which are extra, are reasonably priced for the most part. Meals are served from noon to 2pm and 7 to 10:30pm Mon. to Sat., lunch only Sun.

Cherwell Boathouse Restaurant, Bardwell Road (tel. 0865/52746), owned by Tony Verdin, is a virtual Oxford landmark. A French cuisine is offered on two fixed menus at each meal, and the cooks change the menu every two weeks to allow for the availability of fresh vegetables, fish, and meat. Appetizers include soups or fish or meat pâtés, followed by casseroles, pies, and hotpots. There is a very reasonable, even exciting, wine list. For a table d'hôte dinner, the charge is from £15 ($24.75), and Sunday lunch is £9.50 ($15.70). It's recommended that you make a reservation. Children, if they don't order a full meal, are granted half price. The restaurant is open daily from 7:30 to 11:30pm, 12:30 to 2pm Sun. In summer the restaurant also does an all-day cold buffet on the terrace. Before dinner, you can try "punting" on the Cherwell. Punts are rented on the other side of the boathouse.

Bath Place Hotel, 4–5 Bath Place, Holywell Street (tel. 0865/791812), is a bit of a discovery for foreigners, although well-known to Oxonians. It is like a *restaurant avec chambres* in the French sense, both serving tasty continental meals and having eight rooms on the premises, each with bath or shower. B&B charges range from £65 ($107.25) to £85 ($140.25) daily in a single, £75 ($123.75) to £95 ($157.25) in a double or twin. Rooms have TVs and phones.

But most people seek out these 17th-century, converted cottages for the excellent restaurant run by the Fawsitt family. Bath Place was launched in 1989, and has won a successful following. The menu reflects the availability of seasonal produce: English lamb with a caper-studded butter sauce or sea bass from the West Country. A set luncheon costs £16 ($26.40) and an à la carte dinner goes for £30 ($49.50) and up. Meals are served from noon to 2:15pm and 7 to 9:45pm Tues. to Sun.; open until 10:15pm Fri. and Sat. Reservations are always necessary.

Gees, 61 Banbury Rd. (tel. 0865/53540), made its debut in 1988, in what had formerly been Raymond Blanc's Le Petit Blanc. Monsieur Blanc, of course, moved on to the highly rated Le Manoir aux Quat' Saisons. Gees, instead of attempting to imitate such an acclaimed chef, chose instead to chart its own course. The setting is a stylish Victorian conservatory, and the food and service are topnotch. A la carte meals cost from £16 ($26.40) and might include both simple and elaborate dishes. The chef has flair, reflected by his handling of such dishes as chicken grilled with lemon and rosemary or risotto of "fruits of the sea." The steaks are delectable. For an appetizer, if featured, try a salad made with grilled goat cheese or carpaccio. Call for a table from noon to 2:30pm and 6 to 11pm Mon. to Sat., from 11am to 4pm Sun.

THE SPECIAL PUBS OF OXFORD

A short block from The High, overlooking the north side of Christ Church College, **Bear Inn,** Alfred Street (tel. 0865/244680), is an Oxford tradition. Its swinging inn sign depicts the bear and ragged staff, old insignia of the earls of Warwick, who were among the early patrons. Built in the 13th century, the inn has been known to many famous people who have lived and studied at Oxford. Over the years it's been mentioned time and time again in English literature.

The Bear has served a useful purpose in breaking down social barriers, bringing a wide variety of people together in a relaxed way. You might talk with a rajah from India, a university athlete, a titled gentleman—and the latest in a line of owners that goes back more than 700 years. Some former owners developed an astonishing habit: clipping neckties. Around the lounge bar you'll see thousands of the remains of ties, which have been labeled with their owners' names. For those of you who want to leave a bit of yourself, a thin strip of the bottom of your tie will be cut off (with your permission, of course). After this initiation, you may want to join in some of the informal songfests of the undergraduates. Snacks and bar meals are available, costing from £2 ($3.30), and food service is from noon to 2pm and 5:30 to 8:30pm. The pub is open daily from 11am to 2:30pm and 5:30 to 11pm.

Trout Inn, 195 Godstow Rd., near Wolvercote (tel. 0865/54485), lies on the outskirts of Oxford. Hidden away from visitors, the Trout is a private world where you can get ale, beer, and standard English fare. Have your drink in one of the historic rooms, or go outside in sunny weather to sit on a stone wall. On the grounds are peacocks, as well as ducks, swans, and herons that live in and around the river and an adjacent weir pool, who will join with a shoal of chubb fish in turning up for a free feast if you're handing out crumbs. Take an arched stone bridge, stone terraces, architecture with wildly pitched roofs and gables, add the Thames River, and you have the Trout. The Stable Bar, the original 12th-century part, complements the inn's relatively new 16th-century bars. Daily specials are featured, and there is an excellent cold snack bar, with prices ranging from £1.75 ($2.90) to £5.50 ($9.10). Hot meals are served all day in the restaurant. You can dine well for £10 ($16.50). Salads are served in summer and grills in winter. The Trout is open from 11am to 2:30pm and 6 to 11pm Mon. to Sat., from noon to 2pm and 7 to 10:30pm Sun. If you don't have a car, take bus 520 or 521 to Wolvercote, then walk to the pub. On your way there and back, look for the view of Oxford from the bridge.

SHOPPING

An arcade of first-class shops and boutiques, the **Golden Cross** lies between Cornmarket Street and the Covered Market (or between The High and Market Street). Parts of the arcade date from the 12th century. Many buildings remain from the medieval era, along with some 15th and 17th century structures. The market also has a reputation as the Covent Garden of Oxford, where live entertainment takes place on Saturday morning in summer. In the arcade shops you'll find a wide selection of merchandise, including handmade Belgian chocolates, specialty gifts, clothing for both women and men, and luxury leather goods.

THE ENVIRONS OF OXFORD

A Country Inn

Seven miles along the A420 Oxford/Swindon/West Country road, the **White Hart,** Fyfield (tel. 0865/390585), is high on the list of Oxford students who want to celebrate by taking their friends to a romantic inn—once the Fyfield Chantry—

for a superb dinner. It's a public house, dating from the early 15th century, and owned since 1580 by St. John's College (although the present building is leased). In the 1960s the college renovated the inn, successfully restoring its old-world charm. It was once the home of a chantry priest and five almsmen until it was dissolved under Henry VIII. What was the lower chamber for the priest has now been transformed into a raftered dining room; the ancient kitchen is the beamed lounge bar. The menu consists of house specialties, plus the dishes of the day. At lunchtime and in the evening, a wide range of bar snacks is offered. From the à la carte menu, you can order meals ranging in price from £12 ($19.80). The wines, an excellent selection, are extra. Specialties of the White Hart include traditional English food, with emphasis on game. The restaurant is open from 10:30am to 2:30pm and 6 to 11pm; closed Sun. Reservations are advised.

Didcot

A little town 10 miles south of Oxford near the Berkshire border, east of the A34, Didcot is served by trains from Paddington Station in London. Didcot Parkway is a principal intercity station, with good connections to Oxford, Bristol, Reading, and the south coast.

For the railway buff, the place is the home of the **Didcot Railway Centre** (tel. 0235/817200). In the engine sheds are steam locomotives, and on "steaming days" you can roll along in a Great Western Railway train from Didcot Halt, a typical small country station. There is also a re-creation of Brunel's original broad-gauge, Great Western track. In season various other preserved railways in the country send visiting locomotives. Hours are 11am to 5pm; the center is open all year on Sat. and Sun.; from April to the end of September it is open Tues. to Sun. and on bank holidays. Admission charges are £2.30 ($3.80) to £4 ($6.60), depending on the event.

---

6. Woodstock (Blenheim Palace)

The small country town of Woodstock, the birthplace in 1330 of the Black Prince, son of King Edward III, lies on the edge of the Cotswolds. Some of the stone houses here were constructed when Woodstock was the site of a royal palace, which had so suffered the ravages of time that its remains were demolished when Blenheim Palace was built. Woodstock was once the seat of a flourishing glove industry.

BLENHEIM PALACE

This extravagant baroque palace regards itself as England's answer to Versailles. Blenheim is the home of the 11th duke of Marlborough, a descendant of the first duke of Marlborough (John Churchill), an on-again, off-again favorite of Queen Anne. In his day (1650–1722) the first duke became the supreme military figure in Europe. Fighting on the Danube near a village named Blenheim, Churchill defeated the forces of Louis XIV. The lavish palace of Blenheim was built for the duke as a gift from the queen. It was designed by Sir John Vanbrugh, who was also the architect of Castle Howard. Landscaping was carried out by Capability Brown.

The palace is loaded with riches: antiques, porcelain, oil paintings, tapestries, and chinoiserie. But more North Americans know Blenheim as the birthplace of Sir Winston Churchill. His birthroom forms part of the palace tour, as does the Churchill exhibition, four rooms of letters, books, photographs, and other Churchilliana. Today the former prime minister lies buried in Bladon Churchyard, near the palace.

Blenheim Palace is open daily from mid-March through October from 10:30am to 5:30pm; last admittance is at 4:30pm. The admission fee is £4.90 ($8.10) for adults, £2.40 ($3.95) for children.

In the park is the Blenheim Butterfly and Garden Centre. The complex contains a butterfly house containing tropical moths and butterflies in free flight in a virtually natural habitat, a play area, a garden café, a gift shop, and a shop for plants and gardening requirements. The palace is at Woodstock, 8 miles north of Oxford on the A34 road to Stratford-upon-Avon. There is frequent scheduled bus service leaving from Cornmarket Street in Oxford. The bus stops at the park gates. You can go by bus from Victoria Coach Station in London to Oxford, a bus leaving every 20 minutes. The nearest British Rail station is also Oxford.

Where to Stay and Dine

An ancient coaching inn, the **Bear Hotel,** Park Street, Woodstock, Oxfordshire OX7 1SZ (tel. 0993/811511), is reputed to be one of the six oldest such caravanseries in England, dating from the 16th century. The half-stone structure stands in the center of Woodstock, with its courtyard now being used for car parking rather than the rumbling coaches of old. Look for the sign in front with the picture of a huge brown bear. History surrounds you in the 45-bedroom hotel, even such relatively recent history as the hiding away here of Richard Burton and Elizabeth Taylor. They stayed in the Marlborough suite, an attractively decorated sitting room with a mini-bar, plus a bedroom and bath. One of the chambers of the hotel is haunted, legend says. Modern amenities are combined with antiques in the bedrooms, which have bathrooms, hairdryers, trouser presses, radios, color TVs, and phones. The charge is from £72 ($118.80) to £78 ($128.70) daily in a single, from £105 ($173.25) in a double. Blazing hearth fires are found throughout the hotel when the days and nights are cool. You can relax in the big, black-beamed bar or the comfortable lounge for drinks, and enjoy traditional dishes in the dining room. Meals range in price from £13.50 ($22.30) for lunch and £18 ($29.70) for dinner.

There is also the beautifully furnished **Feathers,** Market Street, Woodstock, Oxfordshire OX7 1SX (tel. 0993/812291), a redbrick building where Gordon Campbell-Gray receives guests for his 15 individually decorated bedrooms, all of which have complete baths, color TVs, and direct-dial phones. Singles in this excellent hotel cost from £50 ($82.50) daily, and doubles £75 ($123.75). The two lounges have wood fires. One boasts fine china and valuable old books; the other is oak-paneled with sturdy beams. A multitude of stuffed birds from which the house gets its name adorn the bar; from there you can go into the delightful garden in the courtyard. The food at Feathers is of high quality. Whether you are here for lunch or for a candlelit dinner you're sure to enjoy the well-prepared, simple dishes or such specialties as hot lobster soufflé and English game pie. An exceptionally good set lunch costs £12.50 ($20.65), while complete a la carte dinners go for £18 ($29.70) and up. In summer, you can have a light lunch or afternoon tea in the courtyard garden. Hours are daily from 12:30 to 2:15pm and 7:30 to 9:45pm.

---

7. Hertfordshire

Like a giant jellyfish, the frontier of Greater London spills over into this county, once described by Charles Lamb as "hearty, homely, loving Hertfordshire." This fertile land lies northwest of London and supplies much of that city's food, although industry has crept in. Hertfordshire is sometimes called "the market basket of England."

In spite of its proximity to London, Hertfordshire boasts splendid countryside, from ancient woods to protected meadows, and is home to a host of flora and fauna. *Peter Rabbit* was created here by Beatrix Potter, and George Bernard Shaw found inspiration in the view from his countryside home at Ayot St. Lawrence. As you explore the attractions of the county, you will be trodding in the auspicious footsteps of Good Queen Bess and Henry VIII, who were there before you.

HATFIELD HOUSE

One of the chief attractions of Hertfordshire, and one of the greatest of all English country houses, Hatfield House, Hatfield, Hertfordshire ALG 5NQ (tel. 0707/262823), is just 21 miles north of London on the A1, close to the M1. To build what is now the E-shaped Hatfield House, the old Tudor palace at Hatfield was mostly demolished. The Banqueting Hall, however, remains.

Hatfield was much a part of the lives of both Henry VIII and his daughter, Elizabeth I. In the old palace, built in the 15th century, Elizabeth romped and played as a child. Although Henry was married to her mother, Anne Boleyn, at the time of Elizabeth's birth, the marriage was later nullified (Anne lost her head and Elizabeth her legitimacy). Henry also used to stash away his oldest daughter, Mary Tudor, at Hatfield. But when Mary became queen of England, and set about earning the dubious distinction of "Bloody Mary," she found Elizabeth a problem. For a while she kept her in the Tower of London, but she eventually let her return to Hatfield (Elizabeth's loyalty to Catholicism was seriously doubted). In 1558, while at Hatfield, Elizabeth learned of her ascension to the throne of England.

The Jacobean house that exists today contains much antique furniture, tapestries, and paintings as well as three much-reproduced portraits, including the ermine and rainbow portraits of Elizabeth I. The great hall is suitably medieval, complete with a minstrel's gallery. One of the rarest exhibits is a pair of silk stockings, said to have been worn by Elizabeth herself, the first lady in England to don such apparel. The park and the gardens are also worth exploring. The riding school and palace stables contain an interesting vehicle exhibition and the national (North) collection of model soldiers.

Hatfield is open from March 25 to the second Sun. in October, from noon to 5pm Tues. to Sat., from 1:30 to 5pm Sun. and from 11am to 5pm bank holidays; closed Mon. and Good Friday. Admission is £3.50 ($5.80) for adults, £2.40 ($3.95) for children. The house is across from the station in Hatfield. From London, take Green Line coach 794 or 797, or the fast trains from King's Cross. Luncheons and teas are available from 11am to 5pm in the converted coach house in the old palace yard.

Elizabethan banquets are staged on Tues., Thurs., Fri., and Sat., with much gaiety and music. Guests are invited to drink in an anteroom, then join the long tables for a feast of five courses with continuous entertainment from a group of Elizabethan players, minstrels, and jesters. Wine is included in the cost of the meal, but you're expected to pay for your before-dinner drinks yourself. The best way to get there from London for the feast is to book a coach tour for an inclusive fee starting at £29.50 ($48.70). The Evan Evans agency has tours leaving from Russell Square or even from 41 Tottenham Court Road in London. The coach returns to London after midnight. If you get there under your own steam, the cost is £19.50 ($32.20) on Tues., Thurs., and Fri., and £20.50 ($33.85) on Sat. For reservations, telephone 0707/262055.

HERTFORD

This old Saxon city contains many fine examples of domestic architecture, some of which date from the 16th century. Hertford is reached via the A1 or A10 from London 24 miles away. Samuel Stone, founder of Hartford, Connecticut, was born here.

In the Lee Valley, Hertford goes back to Saxon days. At that time, it stood on the tense border between Saxon England and the Viking strongholds. It grew up because of its strategic position at the junction of four rivers: the Rib, the Lee, the Beane, and the Mimram. It's possible to take riverside walks along the Lee and Beane.

In 911 King Edward fortified the town as a base against the Vikings. Shortly after the Norman Conquest, William built a castle here, whose motte and bailey remain. First a fortress, later a royal palace, the castle today is the center of council offices. The gatehouse was added in the 15th century by Edward IV, and Elizabeth I often stayed at the castle as a child. The gatehouse is open from May to September when brass band concerts can be enjoyed. The grounds are open all year. You can walk beside the massive Norman flint wall with its original 14th-century postern gate. Encircled by roads, the castle stands in the center of town, opening onto Parliament Square.

Where to Stay and Dine

Salisbury Arms Hotel, Fore Street, Hertford, Hertfordshire SG14 1BZ (tel. 0992/583091), has "always been Hertford's principal inn." For 400 years it's been feeding and providing lodgings to wayfarers, or giving a hot grog to the coachman, a stable for his horses. Although the stables have long given way to a car park, a sense of history still prevails. In the cellar is medieval masonry pre-dating the 16th-century structure around it. Cromwell is said to have lodged here, and both Royalists and Roundheads have mounted the Jacobean staircase. The 29 bedrooms now spill over into a modern extension. All have private baths, TVs, phones, and tea and coffee makers. Singles cost £44 ($72.60) daily, with doubles or twins renting for £70 ($115.50). On Fri. and Sat., prices are lowered to £32 ($52.80) per night in a single, £48 ($79.20) in a double or twin. Good, wholesome English "fayre" is provided. There is a well-stocked cellar. Dinners are from £12 ($19.80).

FABDENS PARK

Norman Swallow, artist turned chef/restaurateur, has created **Fabdens Park,** Cold Christmas, near Ware, Hertfordshire SG12 0UE (tel. 0920/463484), 20 miles north of London. This small hotel and restaurant in a lovely 15th-century home has an opulent dining room with only five tables. Emphasis is on top-quality cuisine. Mr. Swallow prepares food with care and flair, traveling to London markets daily to secure the best produce possible. He says he cooks the kind of food he would choose for himself, classical English and French cuisine mainly. You can dine at leisure, and then take coffee in one of the three sitting rooms. A complete meal costs £30 ($49.50) to £35 ($57.75) per person. It is open for dinner only from 7 to 10:30pm Tues. to Sat. Reservations are essential. There are also six suites for rent, all offering the services you would find in a large deluxe hotel. Each unit has a bedroom, bath, and sitting room and is decorated in an individual, romantic style. Each also has a direct-dial phone, color TV, and other amenities, including a full English or a continental breakfast. Butler and maid service is provided all day and most of the night, and Mr. Swallow is on hand to take a personal interest in his guests' well-being. Prices are from £65 ($107.25) daily in a double.

ST. ALBANS

This cathedral city, just 21 miles northeast of London, dates back 2,000 years. It was named after a Roman soldier, the first Christian martyr in England. Don't ask a resident to show you to the **Cathedral of St. Albans.** Here it's still known as "The Abbey," even though Henry VIII dissolved it as such in 1539. Construction on the cathedral was launched in 1077, making it one of the early Norman churches of England. The bricks, especially visible in the tower, came from the old Roman city of Verulamium at the foot of the hill. The nave and west front date from 1235.

The new chapter house, the first modern building beside a great medieval cathedral in the country, which also serves as a pilgrim/visitor center, was opened by the queen in 1982.

The **Verulamium Museum** at St. Michael's (tel. 0727/66100) stands on the site of the Roman city. Here you'll view some of the finest Roman mosaics in Britain. Part of the Roman town wall, a hypocaust, and the outline of houses and shops are still visible. Visit in summer from 10am to 5:30pm Mon. to Sat., 2 to 5:30pm Sun. In winter it is open from 10am to 4pm Mon. to Sat., 2 to 4pm Sun. Admission is £1.20 ($2) for adults, 60p ($1) for children and students. A family ticket costs £2.65 ($4.35).

The **clock tower** at Market Place was built in 1402, standing 77 feet high, a total of five floors. It is open from Easter to mid-September from 10:30am to 5pm Sat. and Sun.

From St. Albans you can visit **Gorhambury,** a classic-style mansion built in 1777 containing 16th-century enameled glass and historic portraits. It's open May to September from 2 to 5pm Thurs. only. Admission for adults is £2 ($3.30); children pay £1 ($1.65). The location is 2½ miles west of St. Albans near the A5.

On the outskirts, the **Mosquito Aircraft Museum,** the oldest aircraft museum in Britain, lies on the grounds of Salisbury Hall, just off the main M25 London–St. Albans road (turn off at junction 22) at London Colney, about 5 miles south of St. Albans. The museum is on the B556. The hall is no longer open to the public, but the museum can be visited from Easter Sun. to the end of October from 10:30am to 5:30pm Sun. and bank holidays, July to the end of September from 2 to 5:30pm Thurs. Displayed is the prototype of the de Havilland "Mosquito" aircraft, which was designed and built at Salisbury Hall in World War II, plus 18 other aircraft of de Havilland origin, as well as memorabilia and relics. Admission is £1 ($1.65) for adults, 40p (65¢) for children. For more information, telephone 0727/22051.

Where to Stay and Dine
St. Michael's Manor Hotel, Fishpool Street, St. Albans, Hertfordshire AL3 4RY (tel. 0727/64444), stands in 5 acres of landscaped gardens, with a private lake, about a 10-minute walk from the heart of St. Albans. At its core is an original manor house dating from the 16th century. To the original structure a William and Mary bow-fronted center section has been added, along with a Georgian-style extension. The grounds of the hotel contain such trees as cedars of Lebanon, hornbeam, and Wellingtonia, and all 26 attractively furnished bedrooms are named after the trees in the garden. The Lilac honeymoon suite, complete with a four-poster bed and lilac decor, is most impressive. All bedrooms have baths or showers, color TVs, and phones. A single costs £60 ($99); doubles or twins, £80 ($132). Prices include a full English breakfast and VAT. Special bed-and-breakfast terms are offered on weekends. A well-prepared English and French menu is presented for both luncheon and dinner to residents and nonresidents. A lunchtime table d'hôte meal with coffee costs £16 ($26.40), and a "chef recommends" dinner goes for £18 ($29.70).

Sopwell House, Cottonmill Lane, St. Albans, Hertfordshire AL1 2HQ (tel. 0727/64477), affiliated with the Best Western reservation system, is a private mansion from the days of George III. Over the years it has known a number of royal personages as guests. Now converted into a hotel of superb taste and comfort, it occupies nearly a dozen Hertfordshire acres. Guests come here to play golf at the neighboring Verulam course, home of the Ryder Cup. Many visitors prefer to anchor in here instead of London, so that they can explore some of the grand mansions previewed in this chapter, notably Hatfield House and Woburn Abbey. There are 70 attractive bedrooms with private baths, TVs, phones, trouser presses, hairdryers, and beverage-making equipment. B&B costs from £63 ($103.95) daily in a single, rising to £80 ($132) to £100 ($165) in a double, with set dinners going for £17.50 ($28.90). The public rooms in the grand 18th-century style are the finest in St. Albans, including the Park Room restaurant with a conservatory opening onto a terrace and the gardens. The location is off A1018, 1½ miles southeast of St. Albans, within easy access to M1, M10, A1, and M25, an easy commute from London.

SHAW'S CORNER
In the village of Ayot St. Lawrence, 3 miles northwest of Welwyn, stands Shaw's Corner (tel. 0438/820307), where George Bernard Shaw lived from 1906 to 1950. The house is practically as he left it at his death. In the hall, for example, his hats are still hanging, as if ready for him to don one. His personal mementos are in his study, drawing room, dining room, and writing hut. The kitchen and scullery are also open to view as well as some first floor rooms on some days. The house is open April to the end of October, 2 to 6pm Wed. to Sat., from noon to 6pm Sun. and bank holidays; closed Good Friday. Admission is £2 ($3.30) for adults, £1 ($1.65) for children.

---

8. Buckinghamshire

This is a leafy county, lying north of the Thames and somewhat to the west of London. Its identifying marks are the wide Vale of Aylesbury, with its sprawling fields and tiny villages, and the long chalk range of the Chilterns. The beech-clad Chilterns run like a spine across the southern part of the shire. In autumn and spring, this part of England is at its most beautiful. The county is bordered by the Thames.

Long associated with the famous, Buckinghamshire was the home of the famous Tory prime minister of Victorian England, Benjamin Disraeli, and, much later, Cliveden was the home of the first woman MP to take her seat in the House of Commons—Lady Nancy Astor. The London branch of the Rothschilds, an international banking family from Frankfurt, has long been associated with the county, from their base at Aston Clinton, a tradition going back to 1851. Eventually six Rothschild mansions were established in the vicinity, including the most impressive, Waddesdon Manor.

Poets and authors have also been associated with Buckinghamshire, including Parliamentarian and blind poet John Milton, who fled London in 1665 to escape the plague. The poet Shelley and his wife Mary (author of *Frankenstein*) lived in the Thames-bordering town of Marlow, as did T. S. Eliot. The American poet, Robert Frost, was attracted to Beaconsfield.

For the tourist, Buckinghamshire has the largest number of National Trust properties of any county in the Thames and Chilterns.

AYLESBURY

The county town of Buckingham, Aylesbury has retained much of its ancient character, especially around the town center with its narrow Tudor alleyways and 17th-century houses. The parish church, St. Mary's, dates from the 13th century and has an unusual spirelet. A short walk from the church takes you to Hickman's Almshouses and the Prebendal Houses, both from the 17th century.

Less than 40 miles from London, Aylesbury is a market town, with Wednesday and Saturday markets held in Friars Square. Gourmets still speak of the succulent Aylesbury ducks and ducklings, a prize-winning dish on any table, although fowls bearing that name are usually raised elsewhere these days.

Six miles northwest of Aylesbury on the Bicester road (A41), **Waddesdon Manor** (tel. 0296/651282) contains an outstanding collection of French royal decorative art of the 17th and 18th centuries, including furniture, Sèvres porcelain, and Savonnerie carpets. Among the paintings are portraits by Reynolds, Gainsborough, and Romney. The manor was built in the late 19th century for Baron Ferdinand de Rothschild and stands in 150 acres of grounds with rare trees and an aviary. Visiting times are from the end of March until the middle of October, from 1 to 5pm Wed. to Sun. It costs £4 ($6.60) to enter the house, grounds, and aviary. Children 10 to 17 are charged £2 ($3.30). Waddesdon Manor lies 6 miles from Aylesbury on the A41 to Bicester. It is 50 miles from London and 25 miles from Oxford, and is accessible from the M25 via A413 to Amersham and Aylesbury. Red River buses run from Aylesbury to Waddesdon Village, and the nearest rail station is also Aylesbury.

Where to Stay and Dine

The Bell, Market Square, Aylesbury, Buckinghamshire HP20 1TX (tel. 0296/89835), adjacent to the county hall of Aylesbury, is a traditional favorite. A Georgian coaching house, it sits in the center of this market town. The 17 bedrooms all have private baths and showers, color TVs, radios, phones, and hot beverage facilities. Singles rent for £68 ($112.20) daily, and doubles go for £90 ($148.50). The cuisine offered here is traditional English cooking. The public bar is cozy with beams and a log fire in cool weather. Cold and hot snacks are available weekdays in the Market Bar. Don't confuse this Bell in the center of town with the Bell Inn at Aston Clinton, just outside Aylesbury, recommended below.

The best restaurant in Aylesbury is **Peebles,** Pebble Lane (tel. 0296/86622), which is run by the capable chef, Jeremy Blake O'Connor. Part of his success is based on his clever use of fresh ingredients, which are subtly flavored and cooked, then attractively presented. The low-ceilinged, wooden beamed restaurant is reached by walking up a cobblestone-paved lane. There is very limited seating in either of the two dining rooms, one with a Victorian stove, so reservations are imperative. A set luncheon goes for £12 ($19.80) weekdays and £14 ($23.10) on Sunday, and dinner costs from £20 ($33) per person. Hours are noon to 2:15pm and 7 to 11pm, 12:30 to 3pm Sun.; closed Mon. and for dinner Sun.

On the Outskirts

Hartwell House, Oxford Road, Aylesbury, Buckinghamshire HP17 8NL (tel. 0296/747444), is a landmark country house. Today's house dates from the 16th to the 18th centuries, part Georgian, part Jacobean. The location is 2 miles southwest of Aylesbury (the nearest rail station) on A418, near the village of Stone, and about 20 miles from Oxford or else an hour's drive from Heathrow Airport outside London.

As you enter the house, you'll be transported into another era, as you wander from the morning room with its rococo ceiling to the oak-paneled bar, pausing in the library where a former tenant, the exiled Louis XVIII (of gargantuan girth), signed the document returning him to the throne of France.

The hotel offers 29 individually decorated bedrooms and 3 sumptuous suites. Another 17 bedrooms are in restored stable buildings. Some of the rooms are huge, and each has a private bath, TV, radio, phone, hairdryer, and trouser press. Prices are from £85 ($140.25) to £95 ($156.75) daily in a single and £115 ($189.75) to £175 ($288.75) in a double. Other facilities include an indoor pool, solarium, sauna, and leisure center. Converted by Historic House Hotels into one of the front-ranking country hotels of England, Hartwell House is also noted for its predominantly British cuisine. Meals, costing from £25 ($41.25), are international in flavor, using whenever possible fresh regional ingredients deftly handled by the chef. A fine wine list is also available.

The Bell Inn, Aston Clinton, Buckinghamshire HP22 5HP (tel. 0296/630252), a *Relais & Châteaux* since 1955, is a former coaching inn believed to have been built at the end of the 18th century. Under the guidance of the Harris family, the inn has won acclaim for its cuisine. Advertised by a large bell instead of an inn sign, it stands unobtrusively by the road 40 miles from London and 4 miles from Aylesbury. It's a mossy brick structure with a Georgian portico. The dining room, with its four seasons murals, is cooly elegant, with polished wood and sparkling glass and silver. You select your meal in a large stone-floored bar while having a drink. Lunch or dinner is a special event. For a beginning, try the "smokies," then go on to the civet de homard or gâteau de gibier. The price of a typical meal is about £35 ($57.75), including half a bottle of the house wine. There are six tastefully decorated bedrooms in the original inn, all with private baths, refrigerators, and mini-bars. Converted from a stable block are 15 more comfortable rooms, arranged around a courtyard across a narrow road from the inn. Such thoughtful touches have been added in the luxuriously appointed baths as bathrobes, bubble-bath, powder, and shampoo; phones, mini-bars, and TVs are also included. Room rates range from £86 ($141.90) to £120 ($198) daily in a single, from £100 ($165) to £175 ($288.75) for a double, including a continental breakfast, VAT, and service. A log fire in the lounge makes for a warm welcome to this old coaching inn.

CLIVEDEN

The former home of Nancy, Lady Astor, Cliveden is now a National Trust property. The house stands on a constructed terrace of mature gardens high above the Thames. The estate's original mansion and the vast sweep of the lawns were created by William Winde in 1666 for the second duke of Buckingham. Later, the father of King George III reared his sons here. After a fire in 1795, the house was redesigned by Sir Charles Barry, the architect of the Houses of Parliment, into its present gracefully symmetrical form. A soaring clock tower was added to one side as a later Victorian folly. When the house was sold by the duke of Southerland to the Astors in 1893, Queen Victoria lamented the passage. The house remained part of the Astor legacy until 1966, repository of a notable collection of paintings and antiques.

The surrounding gardens have a distinguished variety of plantings, ranging from Renaissance-style topiary to meandering forest paths with vistas of statuary and flowering shrubs. Garden features are a rose garden, a magnificent parterre, and an amphitheater where "Rule Britannia" was played for the first time. There are 375 acres of garden and woodland to explore.

The house is open from April 1 to October only, from 3 to 6pm Thurs. and Sun. The grounds are open March to December daily from 11am to 6pm, or sunset if earlier. Admission to the grounds is £2.50 ($4.15); to the house £1 ($1.65). Cliveden is 20 miles west of London, lying 2 miles north of Taplow on the Cliveden Road, off the A40.

A Splurge Stay

Cliveden House, Cliveden, Taplow, Maidenhead, Berkshire SL6 0JB (tel. 06286/68561). In 1984 the National Trust leased the house to Blakeney Hotels, a firm that turned it into one of the most beautiful and luxurious hotels in England. If you wish to experience the sumptuous lifestyle maintained by the Astors you can stay in one of the 31 bedrooms here, all with private baths or showers, direct-dial phones, and TVs. A large staff caters to guests' every need, and amenities include an outdoor swimming pool, sauna, gym, tennis courts, and laundry service. Twins and doubles range from £185 ($305) to £265 ($437) daily. Three single rooms rent for £150 ($248). Breakfast and taxes are included in the rates. An English breakfast is served in a green-and-gold breakfast room fit for Versailles; other meals, costing from £40 ($66), are served dining-room style in the beautiful gilt, mauve, and cream-colored dining room.

MARLOW

This Thamesside town, 35 miles from London, stands on a great loop of the riverbank between Maidenhead and Oxford. Here, along this middle reach of the Thames, is some of the most beautiful rural scenery in England, a land of green fields and deep woods, of stately mansions and parks. It was in these surroundings that Izaak Walton wrote his immortal work on fishing some 350 years ago, *The Compleat Angler*. On the south bank of the river facing Marlow itself stood the inn in which he stayed. That inn still stands and is named after his work.

Where to Stay and Dine

Just 30 miles west of London, **The Compleat Angler Hotel,** Marlow Bridge, Bisham Road, Marlow, Buckinghamshire SL7 1RG (tel. 06284/4444), occupies an emerald-colored swath of lawns stretching down to the banks of the Thames. It has had a distinguished list of clients, including Percy Shelley and his wife, Mary, along with Dame Nellie Melba (for whom the peach dessert was named), J. M. Barrie (author of *Peter Pan*), F. Scott Fitzgerald, and Noël Coward. The reddish brick of its facade incorporates both Georgian and Edwardian elements. Inside, the hotel is a well-organized and impeccably polite world of English chintz, mahogany and oaken antiques, plush carpeting, predictably elegant bars, and very fine dining. Each of the 42 bedrooms is outfitted a lot like those in an elegant, private country home, with real antiques or reproductions, deeply comfortable armchairs and bed, private bath, color TV, radio, and direct-dial phone. Singles cost £100 ($165) daily, and doubles or twins go for £120 ($198) to £135 ($222.75), with service and VAT included.

JORDANS VILLAGE

A peaceful place, **Old Jordans,** Jordans Lane, Jordans Village, Buckinghamshire HP9 2SW (tel. 02407/4586), is a farm dating back to the Middle Ages. But its recorded history starts in the early 17th century when one Thomas Russell, sitting tenant, bought the freehold, signing the deed with his thumbprint. The house was added to over the years, and in the mid-17th century William Penn, founder of Pennsylvania, and other well-known Dissenters stayed here and worshipped. It's full of history, perhaps a little isolated from today's bustle but easily accessible to London and Oxford. Now the property of the Quakers, the house is run as a conference center, but it has 30 simply furnished rooms available for overnight guests. Bathless rooms cost £21.50 ($35.50) daily in a single, £36 ($59.40) in a double. Rooms with bath rent for £32.50 ($53.65) in a single and £50 ($82.50) in a double. All tariffs include a full English breakfast. Lunch, served at 1pm, costs £6 ($9.90) Mon. to Sat., £7 ($11.55) Sun.

On the grounds is the Mayflower Barn, built almost indisputably from timbers from the ship *Mayflower* in which the first Pilgrims sailed to the New World. These days the beams ring to the strains of concert music and recitals performed by top-notch artists.

MILTON'S COTTAGE

The modern residential town of **Gerrards Cross** is often called the Beverly Hills of England, as it attracts many wealthy people. Surrounding this plush section are several tucked-away hamlets, including **Chalfont St. Giles,** where the poet Milton lived during the Great Plague in 1665. He completed *Paradise Lost* here. In this 16th-century cottage are two museum rooms containing 93 rare books, including first editions of *Paradise Lost* and *Paradise Regained* and other Miltoniana, with exhibits of interest to young and old. A cottage garden is a further attraction. The house is open March 1 to October 31 from 10am to 1pm Tues. to Sat., 2 to 6pm Sun., and spring and summer bank holidays; closed Mon. Admission is £1.50 ($2.50) for adults, 60p ($1) for children. For information, write to Milton's Cottage, Dean Way, Chalfont St. Giles, Bucks, P8 4JH (tel. 02407/2313).

West of Gerrards Cross, the town of **Beaconsfield,** with its broad, tree-lined High Street, enjoys many associations with Disraeli.

HUGHENDEN MANOR

Outside High Wycombe, in Buckinghamshire, sits a country manor that gives us not only an insight into the age of Victoria, but acquaints us with a remarkable man. In Benjamin Disraeli we meet one of the most enigmatic figures of 19th-century England. At age 21, Dizzy published anonymously his five-volume novel *Vivian Grey*. But it wasn't his shining hour. He went on to other things, marrying an older widow for her money, although they developed a most loving relationship. He entered politics and continued writing novels, his later ones meeting with more acclaim.

In 1848 Disraeli acquired Hughenden Manor, a country house that befitted his fast-rising political and social position. He served briefly as prime minister in 1868, but his political fame rests on his period as prime minister from 1874 to 1880. He became Queen Victoria's friend, and in 1877 she paid him a rare honor by visiting him at Hughenden. In 1876 Disraeli became the earl of Beaconsfield: He had arrived, but his wife was dead, and he was to die in 1881. Instead of being buried at Westminster Abbey, he preferred the simple little graveyard of Hughenden Church.

Hughenden contains an odd assortment of memorabilia, including a lock of Disraeli's hair, letters from Victoria, autographed books, and especially a portrait of Lord Byron, known to Disraeli's father, are of interest.

If you're driving to Hughenden Manor on the way to Oxford, continue north of High Wycombe on the A4128 for about 1½ miles. If you're relying on public transportation from London, take coach 711 to High Wycombe, then board a Bee Line bus (High Wycombe–Aylesbury 323 or 324). The manor house and garden are open April to October from 2 to 6pm Wed. to Sat. and from noon to 6pm Sun. and bank holidays. It is open in March from 2 to 6pm Sat. and Sun. only; closed Good Friday. Admission is £2.50 ($4.15) for adults, £1.25 ($2.05) for children. For more information, phone 0494/32580.

WEST WYCOMBE

Snuggled in the Chiltern Hills 30 miles west of London, the village of West Wycombe still has an atmosphere of the early 18th century. The thatched roofs have been replaced by tiles, and some of the buildings have been replaced, but the village is still two centuries removed from the present day.

In the mid-18th century Sir Francis Dashwood began an ambitious building program at West Wycombe. His strong interest in architecture and design led Sir Francis to undertake a series of monuments and parks that are still among the finest in the country. He also sponsored the building of a road, using the chalk quarries on the hill to aid in the support of the poverty-stricken villagers. The resulting caves were used by "The Knights of St. Francis of Wycombe," later known as the notorious **Hellfire Club.** A group drawn from the social circle surrounding the prince of Wales, its members "gourmandized," swilling claret and enjoying the company of women "of a cheerful, lively disposition . . . who considered themselves lawful wives of the brethren during their stay."

A visit to West Wycombe wouldn't be complete without a tour of **West Wycombe Park,** seat of the Dashwood family, of both historical and architectural interest. Both George III and Ben Franklin stayed here, but not at the same time. The house is one of the best examples of Palladian-style architecture in England. The interior is lavishly decorated with paintings and antiques from the 18th century. It is owned by the National Trust.

The caves, café, and gift shop are open March until late May from 1 to 6pm Mon. to Sat., late May to early September from 11am to 6pm Mon. to Sat., and early April to late October from 11am to 6pm Sun. and bank holidays. In winter they are open from 1 to 5pm Sat. and Sun. only. The house and grounds are open in June, July, and August, from 2 to 6pm Sun. to Thurs. Admission to the caves is £2 ($3.30) for adults, £1 ($1.65) for children. To visit the house and grounds costs £3.50 ($5.80) for adults and £1.75 ($2.90) for children.

For information on the caves, house, and grounds, call the West Wycombe Park Office, West Wycombe (tel. 0494/24411).

Other sights at West Wycombe include the **Church of St. Lawrence,** perched atop West Wycombe Hill and topped by a huge golden ball. Parts of the church date from the 13th century; its richly decorated interior was copied from a 3rd-century Syrian sun temple. The view from the hill is worth the trek up. Near the church stands the **Dashwood Mausoleum,** built in a style derived from Constantine's Arch in Rome.

---

9. Bedfordshire (Woburn Abbey)

This county contains the fertile, rich Vale of Bedford, crossed by the River Ouse. Most visitors from London head here on a day trip to visit historic Woburn Abbey.

BEDFORD

On the Ouse, Bedford contains many riverside parks and gardens, but is better known for its associations with John Bunyan. In Mill Street stands the 1850 **Bunyan Free Church** (tel. 0234/58075), erected on the site of a barn where Bunyan used to preach. The bronze doors, considered to be artistically outstanding, illustrate ten scenes from *Pilgrim's Progress.* The Bunyan Museum contains the surviving relics of Bunyan and a collection of 169 foreign-language editions of *Pilgrim's Progress.* Open April to October from 2 to 4pm Tues. to Sat.; admission is 50p (85¢) for adults, 30p (50¢) for children.

About a mile south of Bedford, Elstow is close to Bunyan's reputed birthplace. Here you can visit **Elstow Moot Hall,** a medieval timber-frame building originally used as a market hall, now managed as a museum containing a permanent display relating to the life of John Bunyan, including various editions of his work. It is open April to October from 2 to 5pm Tues. to Sat. and bank holidays, and from 2 to 5:30pm Sun. Admission is 40p (65¢) for adults, 20p (35¢) for children. For more information, telephone 0234/228330.

The **Swiss Garden,** Old Warden, near Biggleswade, is an unusual romantic site dating from the early 19th century. It contains the original period buildings and features, together with many interesting plants and trees, some of great rarity. A lakeside picnic area in adjoining woodlands is open at all times. Hours for the garden are April to October, 1:30 to 6pm Wed. to Sun. (last admission at 5:15pm). The garden lies approximately 2½ miles west of Biggleswade adjoining the Biggleswade –Old Warden road about 2 miles west of the A1. For more information, telephone 0234/228330.

Where to Stay and Dine

Woodlands Manor, Green Lane, Clapham, Bedford, Bedfordshire MK41 6EP (tel. 0234/63281), is an owner-run manor house standing in a 3-acre garden 2 miles north of Bedford on A6. Built of honey-colored stone at the turn of the century, this 29-bedroom hotel is the most desirable place to stay in the area. Even though small, it has any number of amenities, such as 24-hour room service and laundry service. Each of the well-furnished bedrooms (some in a modern extension) are well furnished, and often quite large, with color-coordinated decorations. Each has a private bath, phone, TV, and mini-bar. Singles cost from £47 ($77.55) to £71 ($117.15) daily, with doubles going for £62 ($102.30) to £80 ($132). The food, an English and French menu, is excellent. A daily set menu is offered, with lunches for £15 ($24.75) and dinner for £25 ($41.25). An à la carte menu is also changed frequently throughout the year. Quality ingredients are presented with an attention to natural flavors, and service is impeccable.

WOBURN ABBEY

Few tourists visiting Bedfordshire miss the Georgian mansion of **Woburn Abbey,** Woburn, Bedfordshire MK43 0TP, the seat of the dukes of Bedford for more than three centuries. The much publicized 18th-century estate is about 42 miles from London and half a mile from the village of Woburn, which lies 13 miles southwest of Bedford. Its State Apartments are rich in furniture, porcelain, tapestries, silver, and a valuable art collection, including paintings by Van Dyck, Holbein, Rembrandt, Gainsborough, and Reynolds. A series of paintings by Canaletto, showing his continuing views of Venice, grace the walls of the Canaletto Room. Of all the paintings, one of the most notable from a historical point of view is the *Armada Portrait* of Elizabeth I. Her hand rests on the globe, as Philip's invincible armada perishes in the background.

Queen Victoria and Prince Albert visited Woburn Abbey in 1841. Victoria slept in an opulently decorated bedroom. Victoria's Dressing Room contains a fine collection of 17th-century paintings from the Netherlands. Among the oddities and treasures at Woburn Abbey are a Grotto of Shells, a Sèvres dinner service (gift of Louis XV), and a chamber devoted to memorabilia of "The Flying Duchess." Wife of the 11th duke of Bedford, she was a remarkable woman, who disappeared on a solo flight in 1937 (the same year as Amelia Earhart—the duchess was 72 years old at the time).

In the 1950s the present duke of Bedford opened Woburn Abbey to the public to pay off some $15 million in inheritance taxes. In 1974 he turned the estate over to his son and daughter-in-law, the marquess and marchioness of Tavistock, who reluctantly took on the business of running the 75-room mansion that draws hundreds of thousands of visitors a year and employs more than 300 people to staff the shops and grounds.

Today Woburn Abbey is surrounded by a 3,000-acre deer park that includes the famous Père David deer herd, originally from China and saved from extinction at Woburn. The Woburn Wild Animal Kingdom contains lions, tigers, giraffes, camels, monkeys, Prevalski horses, bongos, elephants, and other animals. What would Humphry Repton, the designer of the estate's park in the 19th century, say?

In January, February, and March, the park is open from 10:30am to 3:40pm Sat. and Sun. only and the abbey from 11am to 4:45pm. From April to October, park hours are 10am to 4:45pm daily (to 5:45pm Sun.). The abbey is open from 11am to 5:45pm daily (to 6:15pm Sun.). The last admission to the abbey is 45 minutes before closing time. The charge to enter the park is £2.50 ($4.15) for a car and passengers, 50p (85¢) per person for cyclists and pedestrians. Admission to the abbey is £4.50 ($7.45) for adults, £1.50 ($2.50) for children 7 to 16. Most economical is a family ticket, going for £11 ($18.15) and admitting two adults and two children, with similar reductions for more children.

The deer park admission charge does not apply to visitors purchasing the abbey entrance ticket as they enter the park. When not in use by the duke's family, visitors may see the private apartments at an additional charge of 30p (50¢) for adults, 10p (15¢) for children. For more information, telephone 0525/290666.

Woburn Abbey is hard to reach by public transportation from London, so you may prefer to take an organized tour.

Where to Stay and Dine

After visiting the abbey, a good spot for both food and lodgings is **Bedford Arms,** 1 George St., Woburn, Bedfordshire MK17 9PX (tel. 0525/290441). This is a Georgian coaching inn with a checkered history that blends the old and new at the gates of the estate. Tastefully modernized, it preserves a mellow charm. Its 75-seat Georgian dining room, Hollands, was designed by Henry Holland, architect of Woburn Abbey. Guests are housed in one of the pleasantly furnished bedrooms, all of which contain private baths or showers. Singles cost £65 ($107.25) daily; doubles or twins, £75 ($123.75). Each unit contains coffee-making facilities, radio, phone, automatic alarm system, and color TV. A more recent block provides executive bedrooms with private baths, color TVs, radios, hairdryers, trouser presses, and drinks facilities. This block brings the hotel's complement of bedrooms to 55. The Tavistock adjoining the hotel's main restaurant has been restored, its old beams exposed as well as its inglenook fireplaces. By contrast, a cocktail bar has been designed to create an atmosphere of luxury.

Paris House, Woburn Park (tel. 0525/290692), lies about 2 miles from Woburn on the B528 and is reached by going through the park with grazing deer. A black-and-white timbered structure, said to have been constructed for the Paris Exhibition in the 1870s, on the grounds of the abbey, it is not only scenically located but is without challenge the grandest dining choice in the area. The chef de cuisine and owner, Peter Chandler, is heavily influenced by the cooking of the Roux brothers, the famous master chefs of England. Paris House is a citadel of fine French cuisine, making use of very fresh ingredients deftly handled by a well-trained kitchen staff. The menu is always changing, so it would be useless to recommend specific dishes. The chef has long been known for his tulipe en fantaisie, which is a "sugar fairy" fantasy with fruit and ice cream. Set lunches cost from £15.50 ($25.60) weekdays and £19.50 ($32.15) on Sunday; a table d'hôte dinner, £24 ($39.60). À la carte meals go for £30 ($49.50). The menu is backed up by a good wine list. Open 12:30 to 2pm and 7 to 10pm Tues. to Sat., noon to 2pm Sun.; closed in February. Reservations are necessary.

On the Outskirts

Moore Place Hotel, The Square, Aspley Guise, near Woburn, Bedfordshire, MK17 8DW (tel. 0908/282000), is a gracious Georgian era mansion constructed by Francis Moore in 1786 in this old village 13 miles from Woburn. Exit at junction 13 from the M1. Set in landscaped grounds and restored with sensitivity, Moore Place is a citadel of the good life. Decorations are generally modern but in a style in keeping with the age of the house. A Victorian-style conservatory was added, along with a block of contemporary bedrooms. This makes for a courtyard effect, with a rock garden and water cascade. The 54 beautifully furnished bedrooms, each with private bath, phone, and TV, rent for £75 ($123.75) daily in a single, rising to £95 ($156.75) in a double. In an elegantly modernized setting, the restaurant at the hotel is among the finest in Bedfordshire. Yet its continental and English cookery comes at a relatively modest price: £11.50 ($19) for lunch and £15.50 ($25.60) for dinner. Service is from 12:30 to 2:15pm and 7:30 to 10pm; closed for lunch Sat.

WHIPSNADE WILD ANIMAL PARK

This is the 580-acre breeding park of the Zoological Society of London (which also operates the London Zoo), where the animals roam free in large paddocks and certain species even wander among visitors. On the edge of the Chiltern escarpment in Bedfordshire, Whipsnade lays claim to being the world's first open-air zoo. Many endangered species are here, including the cheetah, Père David deer, oryx, and Indian and white rhinos. There are also 24 species of crane, including the rare and beautiful red-naped or Manchurian crane. There is a lot of walking here to see everything in a single day, but the opportunities for photography are second to none. Exhibits include sea lions, a steam railway, a birds of prey show, a discovery center, and a family center. Animals are in geographical groupings. The park is open daily from 10am to 6pm, to 7pm Sun. and bank holidays; in winter, it closes at sunset. Adults pay £4.50 ($7.45) for admission, and children (aged 4 to 15), £2.70 ($4.45). Cars can be brought into the park for an extra £5 ($8.25). For more information, phone 0582/872171. Take the train from St. Pancras in London to Luton, then the no. 43 bus to Whipsnade Park.

VII

KENT, SURREY, AND SUSSEX

1. KENT'S COUNTRY HOUSES, CASTLES, AND GARDENS

2. CANTERBURY

3. DOVER

4. ROYAL TUNBRIDGE WELLS

5. RICHMOND

6. HASLEMERE

7. GUILDFORD

8. DORKING

9. RYE AND WINCHELSEA

10. HASTINGS AND ST. LEONARDS

11. BATTLE

12. ALFRISTON AND LEWES

13. BRIGHTON AND HOVE

14. ARUNDEL

15. CHICHESTER

Lying to the South and southeast of London are the shires (counties) of Kent, Surrey, and Sussex. They form a most fascinating part of England to explore, and are easy to reach, within commuting distance of the capital.

Of all the centers, **Canterbury** in Kent is of foremost interest, but the old Cinque ports of **Rye** and **Winchelsea** in East Sussex are equally exciting, as is **Brighton** in its own distinctive way. In and around these major meccas are dozens of castles and vast estates, monuments, homes of celebrated men and women, cathedrals, yachting harbors, and little villages of thatched cottages.

The range of accommodations varies from an old-world smugglers' inn at the ancient seaport of Rye to a 16th-century house in Canterbury featured in *David Copperfield*. Throughout the counties of the south coast, you'll discover some superb bargains, as the English themselves come to these coastal shires for the sun and are accustomed to paying reasonable rates.

In the fog-choked cities of northern England, the great dream for retirement is to find a little rose-covered cottage in the south, where the living's easier.

KENT

Fresh from his cherry orchard, the Kentish farmer heads for his snug spot by an inglenook, with its bright-burning fire, for his glass of cherry brandy. The day's work is done. All's right with the world.

We're in what was once the ancient Anglo-Saxon kingdom of Kent, on the fringes of London yet far removed in spirit and scenery. Since the days of the Tudors, cherry blossoms have pinkened the fertile landscape. Not only orchards, but hop fields abound. The conically shaped oasthouses with kilns for drying the hops dot the rolling countryside. Both the hops and orchards have earned for Kent the title of the garden of England. And in England the competition's rough.

Kent suffered severe destruction in World War II, as it was the virtual alley over which the Luftwaffe flew in its blitz of London. After the fall of France, a German invasion was feared imminent. Shortly after becoming prime minister in 1940, Churchill sped to Dover, with his bowler, stogie, walking cane, and pin-striped suit. Once there, he inspected the coastal defense and gave encouragement to the men digging in to fight off the attack. But Hitler's "Sea Lion" (code name for the invasion) turned out to be a paper tiger.

In spite of much devastation, Kent is filled with interesting old towns, mansions, and castles. The country is also rich in Dickensian associations—in fact, Kent is sometimes known as Dickens Country. His family once lived near the naval dockyard at Chatham.

In the cathedral city of Rochester, 30 miles from London, you can visit the **Charles Dickens Centre** and **Dickens Chalet** in Eastgate House, built in 1590. This center, on High Street in Rochester, is open daily from 10am to 5pm. Admission is £1.70 ($2.80) for adults, £1.10 ($1.80) for children. The museum has tableaux depicting various scenes from Dickens's novels, including a Pickwickian Christmas scene, then the fever-ridden graveyard of *Bleak House,* scenes from *The Old Curiosity Shop* and *Great Expectations, Oliver Twist,* and *David Copperfield.* There is clever use of sound and light. Information is also available at the center on various other sights in Rochester associated with Dickens, including Eastgate House and, in the garden, the chalet transported from Gad's Hill Place, where Dickens died, as well as the Guildhall Museum, Rochester Cathedral, and the mysterious "6 Poor Travelers' House." Pick up a brochure that includes a map featuring the various places and the novels with which each is associated. For further information, telephone 0634/843666.

At Broadstairs, the favorite seaside resort of the novelist—"our watering place"—the **Dickens House Museum** stands on the main seafront. This museum (tel. 0843/62853) was once the home of Mary Pearson Strong, on whom Dickens based much of the character of Betsey Trotwood, David Copperfield's aunt. It is open April to October daily from 2:30 to 5:30pm. Admission is 50p (85¢) for adults and 25p (40¢) for children.

At Broadstairs, you can also visit **Bleak House,** Fort Road (tel. 0843/62224), high up on the cliffs. At the peak of his fame, Dickens occupied this mansion which provided the title of one of his greatest works, *Bleak House.* Here he entertained many people famous in art and literature, and he wrote the greater part of *David Copperfield* during his sojourn here. It is open daily Easter to November from 10am to 6pm. From July through September hours are 10am to 9pm. The property also contains a Maritime Museum. Admission is £1.50 ($2.50) for adults, 85p ($1.40) for children under 12. An exhibit, "The Golden Age of Smuggling, 1780–1830," is in the cellar.

At Westerham, at the junction of the Edenbridge and Sevenoaks roads (the A25 and the B2026), an attraction for Canadian readers in particular is the square, red-brick, gabled house where James Wolfe, the English general who defeated the French in the battle for Québec, lived until he was 11 years old. Called **Québec**

KENT, SURREY, AND SUSSEX

House (tel. 0959/62206), a National Trust property, it contains an exhibition about the capture of Québec and memorabilia associated with the military hero, who was born in Westerham on January 2, 1727. The house can be visited from April to October, 2 to 6pm; closed Thurs. and Sat. Admission is £1.50 ($2.50) for adults, 80p ($1.30) for children.

1. Kent's Country Houses, Castles, and Gardens

CHURCHILL'S HOME

For many years, Sir Winston lived at **Chartwell** (tel. 0732/866368), which lies 1½ miles south of Westerham in Kent. Churchill, a descendant of the first duke of Marlborough, was born in grand style at Blenheim Palace on November 30, 1874. Chartwell doesn't pretend to be as grand a place as Blenheim, but it's best preserved as a memorial, administered by the National Trust. The rooms remain as Churchill left them, including maps, documents, photographs, pictures, and other personal mementos. In two rooms are displayed a selection of gifts that the prime minister received from people all over the world. There is also a selection of many of his well-known uniforms. Terraced gardens descend toward the lake with its black swans. In a garden studio are many of Churchill's paintings. Go if you want to see where a giant of a man lived and worked.

The house is open April to October from noon to 5pm on Tues., Wed., and Thurs., from 11am to 5pm on Sat. and Sun. In March and November, hours are 11am to 4pm on Wed., Sat., and Sun. The gardens and studio are not open in March and November, at which time admission to the house only is £2 ($3.30). Otherwise, you pay £3.30 ($5.45) to visit the house and garden, £1.30 ($2.15) to see the garden only, and 40p (65¢) for a visit to the studio. Children are charged half price. The restaurant offers light meals, salads, sandwiches, cakes, and a few hot dishes. It's open from 10:30am on the days the house is receiving visitors.

KNOLE

Begun in the mid-15th century by Thomas Bourchier, archbishop of Canterbury, Knole, at the Tonbridge end of the town of Sevenoaks, just off the A225 (tel. 0732/450608), is one of the largest private houses in England and is considered one of the finest examples of the purely British Tudor-style architecture. It is set in a 1,000-acre deer park.

Henry VIII appropriated the former archbishop's palace from the Catholic Church in 1537. He spent considerable sums of money on Knole, but there is little record of his spending much time here after extracting the palace from the reluctant Archbishop Cranmer. History records one visit only, in 1541. It was a royal palace until Queen Elizabeth I granted it to Thomas Sackville, first Earl of Dorset, whose descendants have lived here ever since. Virginia Woolf, often a guest of the Sackvilles, used Knole as the location for her novel *Orlando*. The building was given to the National Trust in 1946. The Great Hall and the Brown Gallery are Bourchier rooms, early 15th century, both much altered by the Earl of Dorset, who made other additions in about 1603. The earl was also responsible for the Great Painted Staircase. The house covers 7 acres and has 365 rooms, 52 staircases, and 7 courts. The elaborate paneling and plasterwork provide a background for 17th- and 18th-century tapestries and rugs, Elizabethan and Jacobean furniture, and the collection of family portraits.

Knole is open from April to the end of October from 11am to 5pm Wed. to Sat. and bank holidays, from 2 to 5pm Sun.; closed November to March. Last admission is an hour before closing. The gardens are open May to September only on the first Wed. of the month. Admission to the house is £2.50 ($4.15) for adults, £1.30

($2.15) for children. On Fri. (except Good Friday.), extra rooms in Lord Sackville's private apartments are shown, costing adults 50p (85¢); children, 25p (40¢). The park is open daily to pedestrians; cars are allowed to enter when the house is open.

Knole is 5 miles north of Tonbridge and 25 miles from London. Frequent train service is available from London (about every 30 minutes), and then you can take a taxi or walk the remaining 1½ miles to Knole.

IGHTHAM MOTE

A National Trust property, Ightham Mote, Ivy Hatch, Sevenoaks (tel. 0732/810378), is well worth a stop if you're in the area visiting other stately homes and castles. It was extensively remodeled in the early 16th century. The Tudor chapel with its painted ceiling, the timbered outer walls, and the ornate chimneys reflect that period. A stone bridge crosses the moat and leads into the central courtyard overlooked by the magnificent windows of the great hall. The rest of the house is built around the courtyard. From the great hall, a Jacobean staircase leads to the old chapel on the first floor, where you go through the solarium, with an oriel window, to the Tudor chapel.

Unlike many other ancient houses of England lived in by the same family for centuries, Ightham Mote passed from owner to owner, each family leaving its mark on the place. When the last private owner, an American who was responsible for a lot of the restoration, died, he bequeathed the house to the National Trust. It is open April until the end of October from noon to 5:30pm Mon., Thurs., and Fri., 11am to 5:30pm Sun. Admission is £2.80 ($4.60) for adults and £1.40 ($2.30) for children. Ightham Mote is 2½ miles south of Ightham, off the A227, 6 miles east of Sevenoaks.

SQUERRYES COURT

At Westerham, west of Sevenoaks on the A25, is Squerryes Court (tel. 0959/62345), a manor house built in 1681 and owned by the Warde family for 250 years. Besides a fine collection of paintings, tapestries, and furniture, in the Wolfe Room is a collection of pictures and relics of the family of General Wolfe. The general received his military commission in the grounds of the house at a spot marked by a cenotaph. The house and grounds are open from March to September (on Sun. only during March). From April to September you can visit from 2 to 6pm on Wed., Sat., Sun., and bank holidays. Admission is £2.40 ($3.95) for adults, £1.40 ($2.30) for children.

DOWN HOUSE

North of the M25 motorway, Squerryes Court, and Chartwell, Down House, Luxted Road, Downe, Orpington (tel. 0689/59119), was the home of Charles Darwin from 1842 until his death in 1882. The drawing room and old study are restored to how they were when Darwin was working on his famous—and still controversial book—*The Origin of Species*, first published in 1859. The museum also includes collections and memorabilia from Darwin's voyage on H.M.S. *Beagle*. There is a room dedicated to his famous grandfather, Dr. Erasmus Darwin, and a modest exhibit on evolution in the new study, the last room to be added to the house. An important feature of the museum is the garden, retaining original landscaping and a glass house beyond which lies the Sand Walk or "Thinking Path," along which Darwin took his daily solitary walk. Open March 1 to January 31 from 1 to 6pm Tues. to Thurs. and Sat; closed Mon. and Fri. Admission is £1.50 ($2.50) for adults and 50p (85¢) for children. The village of Downe is 5½ miles south of Bromley off A233.

HEVER CASTLE

Built at the end of the 13th century, Hever Castle was then just a fortified farmhouse surrounded by a moat. A dwelling house was added within the fortifications some 200 years later by the Bullen family. In 1506 the property was inherited by Sir Thomas Bullen, father of Anne Boleyn. It was here that Henry VIII courted Anne for six years before she became his second wife and later mother of Elizabeth, who became Queen Elizabeth I of England. In 1538 Hever Castle was acquired by Henry VIII, who granted it to his proxy (fourth) wife, the "great Flanders mare," Anne of Cleves, when he discovered that his mail-order bride did not live up to her Holbein portrait. This luckier Anne did not seem to mind, however. She owned this comfortable castle for 17 years supported by Henry with plenty of money.

In 1903 the castle was purchased by William Waldorf Astor, who spent five years restoring and redecorating it, as well as building a village of Tudor-style cottages connected to the castle, for use by his guests.

Astor was responsible also for the construction of the spectacular Italian gardens with fountains, classical statuary, a maze, and an avenue of yew trees trimmed into fantastic shapes. He also had a 35-acre lake put in, through which the River Eden flows. The castle and its grounds have been used as locations for a number of motion pictures. The forecourt and the gardens were used in filming *Anne of a Thousand Days* in 1969. More recently, Hever Castle was used in *Lady Jane*. Two permanent exhibitions—the Life and Times of Anne Boleyn and the Astors of Hever—are on display.

The castle and grounds are open from March 27 to November 4. The gardens can be entered daily from 11am to 6pm (last entry at 5pm). The castle opens at noon. Admission is £4 ($6.60) for adults, £1.80 ($2.95) for children, to both the castle and the gardens. To visit the gardens only, adults pay £2.70 ($4.45); children £1.60 ($2.65). For further information, call the Hever Castle Estate Office, Hever, near Edenbridge (tel. 0732/865224). The castle is 3 miles southeast of Edenbridge, midway between Sevenoaks and East Grinstead, 20 minutes from the M25 junction 6.

PENSHURST PLACE

A magnificent English Gothic mansion, Penshurst Place, at Penshurst, near Tonbridge (tel. 0892/870307), is one of the outstanding country houses in Britain. In 1338 Sir John de Pulteney, four times lord mayor of London, built the manor house whose great hall forms the heart of Penshurst still, after more than 600 years. The boy king, Edward VI, presented the house to Sir William Sidney, and it has remained in that family ever since. It was the birthplace in 1554 of Sir Philip Sidney, the soldier-poet. In the first half of the 17th century Penshurst was known as a center of literature, attracting such personages as Ben Jonson, who drew inspiration from the estate to write one of his best poems. Today it is the home of William Philip Sidney, Viscount de L'Isle, and Lady de L'Isle. Lord de L'Isle was in Winston Churchill's cabinet in the 1950s and governor-general of Australia in the 1960s.

The Nether Gallery, below the Long Gallery, which contains a suite of ebony and ivory furniture from Goa, houses the Sidney family collection of armor. Visitors can also view the splendid State Dining Room and Queen Elizabeth's Room. In the Stable Wing is an interesting toy museum. Open Tues. to Sun. from April to the first Sunday in October. It is also open on Good Friday. and bank holidays. The gardens, home park, Venture Playground, nature trail, and countryside exhibition are open from 12:30 to 6pm, the house from 1 to 5:30pm. Admission to the house and grounds is £3.50 ($5.80) for adults, £2 ($3.30) for children. Penshurst Place is 33 miles from London and 6 miles west of Tonbridge.

SISSINGHURST CASTLE GARDEN

The writer, V. Sackville-West, and her husband, Harold Nicolson, created the celebrated Sissinghurst Castle Garden, Sissinghurst, 2 miles northeast of Cranbrook (tel. 0580/712850), between the surviving parts of an Elizabethan mansion. The gardens are worth a visit at all seasons. There is a spring garden where bulb flowers flourish, a summer garden, and an autumn garden with flowering shrubs, as well as a large herb garden. The garden is open April to mid-October from 1 to 6:30pm Tues. to Fri., 10am to 6:30pm Sat., Sun., and Good Friday. Admission is £4 ($6.60) for adults and £2 ($3.30) for children on Sunday, dropping to £3.50 ($5.80) for adults and £1.80 ($2.95) for children Tues. to Sat. Meals are available in the Granary Restaurant, open April to mid-October noon to 6pm Tues. to Fri.; 10am to 6pm Sat. and Sun.

LEEDS CASTLE

Once described by Lord Conway as the loveliest castle in the world, Leeds Castle, Maidstone (tel. 0622/765400), dates from A.D. 857. Originally built of wood, it was rebuilt in 1119 in its present stone structure on two small islands in the middle of the lake, and it was an almost impregnable fortress before the invention of gunpowder. Henry VIII converted it to a royal palace.

The castle has strong links with America through the sixth Lord Fairfax who, as well as owning the castle, owned 5 million acres in Virginia and was a close friend and mentor of the young George Washington. The last private owner, the Hon. Lady Baillie, who lovingly restored the castle with a superb collection of fine art, furniture, and tapestries, bequeathed it to the Leeds Castle Foundation. Since then, royal apartments, known as "Les Chambres de la Reine" (the chambers of the queen), in the Gloriette, the oldest part of the castle, have been open to the public. The Gloriette, the last stronghold against attack, dates from Norman and Plantagenet times, with later additions by Henry VIII.

Within the surrounding parkland is a wildwood garden and duckery where rare swans, geese, and ducks can be seen. The redesigned aviaries contain a superb collection of birds, including parakeets and cockatoos. Dogs are not allowed here, but dog lovers will enjoy the Great Danes of the castle and the Dog Collar Museum at the gatehouse, with a unique collection of collars dating from the Middle Ages. A nine-hole golf course is open to the public. The Culpeper Garden is a delightful English country flower garden. Beyond are the castle greenhouses, the maze centered by a beautiful underground grotto, and the vineyard recorded in the *Domesday Book* and now again producing Leeds Castle English white wine.

In the summer, from April to October, Leeds Castle is open daily from 11am to 5pm. From November to March, it is open from 11am to 4pm Sat. and Sun. It is closed for annual open-air concerts June 30 and July 7. Admission to the castle and grounds is £5.20 ($8.60) for adults and £3.70 ($6.10) for children. If you want to visit only the grounds, the charge is £3.70 ($6.10) for adults, £2.20 ($3.65) for children. Car parking is free, with a free ride on a tractor-trailer available for persons who cannot manage the half-mile or so walk from the car park to the castle.

Snacks, salads, cream teas, and hot meals are offered daily at a number of places on the estate, including Fairfax Hall, a restored 17th-century tithe barn with a self-service carvery restaurant and bar.

Kentish Evenings are presented in Fairfax Hall every Sat. throughout the year, starting at 7pm, with a sherry cocktail reception, then a guided tour of the castle. Guests feast on Kentish pâté, followed by broth and roast beef carved at the table, plus seasonal vegetables. The meal is rounded off by dessert, cheese, and coffee. A half bottle of wine is included in the price of £28 ($46.20) per person. During the meal, musicians play a selection of music suitable to the surroundings and the occasion. Advance reservations are required, made by calling the castle. Kentish Evenings finish at 12:30am, and accommodation is available locally.

If you are not driving during your trip, British Rail and several London-based bus tour operators offer inclusive day excursions to Leeds Castle. The castle is 4 miles east of Maidstone at the junction of the A20 and the M20 London-Folkestone roads.

CHILHAM CASTLE GARDENS

In Chilham Village, 6 miles west of Canterbury, Chilham Castle Gardens (tel. 0227/730319), were originally laid out by Tradescant and later landscaped by Lancelot "Capability" Brown. On a former royal property, the gardens are visually magnificent, looking out over the Stour Valley. A Norman castle used as a hunting lodge once stood here. It was frequented by more than one royal personage until King Henry VIII sold it. The Jacobean castle, built between 1603 and 1616 by Sir Dudley Digges (whose descendant was governor-general of Virginia), was reputedly designed by Inigo Jones. It is one of the best examples extant of the architecture of its day and is built around a hexagonal open-ended courtyard. Medieval banquets are held in the Gothic Hall throughout the year.

The castle is not open to the public—only the gardens are. They are open from April 8 to mid-October daily from 11am to 6pm (last entry at 5pm). Admission is £2.30 ($3.80) for adults and £1.15 ($1.90) for children Tues., Wed., Thurs., Sat., and Sun.; £2 ($3.30) for adults and £1 ($1.65) for children Mon. and Fri. There are special events on some weekends in the season for which different admission charges are made. Birds of prey are flown at 3:30pm each afternoon except Mon. and Fri.

The little village of Chilham has a lively small square with a church at one end, the castle at the other, and a mass of half-timbered buildings interspersed with old, redbrick houses. It is on the A252 Canterbury-Maidstone road and the A28 Canterbury-Ashford road.

2. Canterbury

Under the arch of the ancient West Gate journeyed Chaucer's knight, pardoner, prioress, squire, parson, merchant, miller, and cook—spinning tales. They were bound for the shrine of Thomas à Becket, archbishop of Canterbury, who was slain by four knights of Henry II on December 29, 1170. (The king later walked barefoot from Harbledown to the tomb of his former friend, where he allowed himself to be flogged in penance.) The shrine was finally torn down in 1538 by Henry VIII, as part of his campaign to destroy the monasteries. Canterbury, by then, had already been an attraction of long standing.

The medieval Kentish city, on the Stour River, is the mother city of England, its ecclesiastical capital. Mother city is an apt title, as Canterbury was known to have been inhabited centuries before the birth of Jesus Christ. Julius Caesar once went on a rampage near it. Although its most famous incident was the murder of Becket, the medieval city witnessed other major moments in English history—including Bloody Mary's ordering of nearly 40 victims to be burned at the stake. Richard the Lion-Hearted came back this way from crusading, and Charles II passed through on the way to claim his crown.

Canterbury was once completely walled, and many traces of its old fortifications remain. In the 16th century, weavers, mostly Huguenots from northern France and the Low Countries, fled to Canterbury to escape religious persecution. They started a weaving industry that flourished until the expanding silk trade with India ruined it.

The old city is much easier to reach today than it was in Chaucer's time. It lies 56 miles from London, a 1½ hour train ride from Victoria Station or Charing Cross. The city center is closed to cars, but it's only a short walk from several car parks to the cathedral or walking-tour starting point.

From just below the Weavers House, boats leave for half-hour trips on the river with a commentary on the history of the buildings you pass. Umbrellas are provided to protect you against inclement weather. You can get more precise information from the **Tourist Office,** 34 St. Margaret's St. (tel. 0227/766567), a few doors away from St. Margaret's Church.

WHAT TO SEE AND DO

Canterbury Cathedral
The foundation of this splendid cathedral (tel. 0227/762862) in the center of Canterbury dates back to the coming of the first archbishop, Augustine, from Rome

in A.D. 597, but the earliest part of the present building is the great Romanesque crypt built circa 1100. The monastic choir erected on top of this at the same time was destroyed by fire in 1174, only four years after the murder of Thomas à Becket on a dark December evening in the northwest transept, still one of the most famous places of pilgrimage in Europe. The destroyed choir was immediately replaced by a magnificent early Gothic one, and first used for worship in 1185. The cathedral was the first great church in the Gothic style to be erected in England and set a fashion for the whole country. Its architects were the Frenchman, William of Sens, and "English" William who took Sens's place after the Frenchman was crippled in an accident in 1178 that later proved fatal.

This part of the church is noteworthy for its medieval tombs of royal personages such as King Henry IV and Edward the Black Prince, as well as numerous archbishops. To the later Middle Ages belongs the great 14th-century nave and the famous central "Bell Harry Tower." The cathedral stands in spacious precincts amid the remains of the buildings of the monastery—cloisters, chapter house, and Norman water tower, which have survived intact from the Dissolution in the time of King Henry VIII to the present day.

Becket's shrine was destroyed by the Tudor king, but the site of that tomb is in Trinity Chapel, near the high altar. The saint is said to have worked miracles, and the cathedral contains some rare stained glass depicting those feats. Perhaps the most miraculous thing is that the windows escaped Henry VIII's agents of destruction and Hitler's bombs as well (part of the cathedral was hit in World War II), having been removed as a precaution at the beginning of the war. The cathedral library was damaged by a German air raid in 1942, but the main body of the church was unharmed, although a large area of the town of Canterbury was flattened. The replacement windows of the cathedral were blown in, proving the wisdom of having the medieval glass safely stored away. East of the Trinity Chapel is "Becket's Crown," in which there is a chapel dedicated to "Martyrs and Saints of Our Own Time." St. Augustine's Chair, one of the symbols of the authority of the archbishop of Canterbury, stands behind the high altar. The cathedral is open daily from 8:45am to 7pm in summer (closes at 5pm in winter).

Pilgrim's Way

Re-creating the Thomas à Becket pilgrimage of Chaucerian England, **Canterbury Pilgrim's Way,** St. Margaret's Street (tel. 0227/454888), is open daily from 9:30am to 5:30pm, costing adults £2.50 ($4.15) and children £1.50 ($2.50). Visitors are taken on a tour through England of the Middle Ages, and they meet some of Chaucer's pilgrims, including the Wife of Bath. Audio-visual techniques bring these characters to life. Stories of jealousy, pride, avarice, and romance are recounted.

Guided Tours

Guided tours of Canterbury are organized by the **Guild of Guides,** Arnett House, Hawks Lane (tel. 0227/459779), costing £2 ($3.30) with daily tours from April to October.

WHERE TO STAY

Before you can begin any serious exploring, you'll need to find a hotel. You have several possibilities, both in the city and on the outskirts, ranging from craggy Elizabethan houses of historic interest to modern studio-type bedrooms with private baths.

County Hotel, High Street, Canterbury, Kent CT1 2RX (tel. 0227/66266), has been a hotel since the closing years of the reign of Victoria. But its recorded history goes back to the end of the 12th century, when a man named Jacob built a private townhouse on the spot. Over the years it has undergone many changes and alterations, in both its structure and its name. It was first licensed in 1588. Today considered the best in town, it offers 74 bedrooms fully equipped with private bathrooms and showers, color TVs, tea and coffee makers, radios, phones, and bowls of fruit. The rate for a single is £55 ($90.75) daily and a twin or double goes for £68 ($112.20). Period rooms—that is, with a Georgian or Tudor four-poster—are more expensive costing £75 ($123.75) for two. All prices include VAT. For gourmet dining, go to Sullys Restaurant, the hotel's fully air-conditioned dining room (see below). For snacks, vegetarian specialties, salads, and hot dishes, the coffee shop may be your best bet. There is also the Tudor Bar, where you can have aperitifs or after-dinner libations. The hotel has both covered and open car parking.

Chaucer Hotel, Ivy Lane, Canterbury, Kent CT1 1TT (tel. 0227/464427), was originally built around the time of the American Revolution. The location is on a historic street within a few minutes' walk of the cathedral and the Micawber house made famous in *David Copperfield*. Today, a reconstructed Georgian house, the hotel offers 45 comfortably furnished bedrooms, each with private bath or shower, phone, and TV. Your room will lie at the end of a labyrinth of stairs, narrow hallways, and doors; however, the hotel staff will carry luggage and park your car. With service and VAT, singles cost £60 ($99) daily, with doubles going for £75 ($123.75). Don't overlook the possibility of a drink in the Pilgrim's Bar, with its Regency mantel-pieces and French windows open to outdoor terraces in summer. The hotel also has a good restaurant, serving meals until 9:45pm, and it provides 24-hour room service.

Howfield Manor, Chartham Hatch, Canterbury, Kent CT4 7HG (tel. 0227/738294), stands 3¼ miles from Canterbury by the A28. The Dutch-style gables of this brick manor house rise impressively behind a holly and a low enclosing wall of local stone. The oldest section, which dates from 1181, is now used as a restaurant. An ancient well remains from when the manor house was built as a chapel for an Augustinian priory. When Henry VIII dissolved the monasteries of England, the property fell into private hands. It was enlarged in the 17th-century, eventually serving as the farmhouse of a large landowner. Set on five acres of rolling meadows, the house offers 13 tastefully furnished bedrooms that contain such amenities as private baths, alarm clocks, trouser presses, phones, TVs, and hairdryers. For a bed and a full English breakfast, the charge is £60 ($99) daily in a single, £70 ($115.50) in a twin or double. Drinks are served from the Priory Bar and can be taken into the lounge where guests enjoy the plush upholstery and the warmth from a fireplace lined with handmade bricks and dotted with well-polished antique accessories. The hotel's restaurant is one of the best in Canterbury.

Falstaff Hotel, St. Dunstand's St., Canterbury, Kent CT2 8AF (tel. 0227/462138), is a classic Canterbury hostelry, with a history going back to the 1400s. The present building dates from the 18th century, with a modern extension added. Pilgrims of old entered through a flagstone courtyard, as they do today. Public rooms have character resting under beamed ceilings. The hotel rents 25 well-equipped bedrooms, with private baths, phones, and TVs. Even though small, they are well maintained and neatly arranged. Singles range from £58 ($95.70) to £62 ($102.30) daily, with doubles or twins costing from £67 ($110.55) to £72 ($118.80). Two spacious family rooms are also rented. The hotel also operates a good restaurant.

Slatters, St. Margaret's Street, Canterbury, Kent CT1 1AA (tel. 0227/463271), is a record of the city's changing past. Originally, its Jolly Miller Restaurant was built in the 17th century, and many of its old beams and stones are intact. The structure stands on ground once occupied by buildings bombed in World War II. The 26 contemporary bedrooms, with private baths, phones, and TVs, are motel-like. Most of the rooms convert into sitting areas during the day, with armchairs. All rates include breakfast. Singles rent for £36 ($59.40) daily and doubles go for £52 ($85.80) to £75 ($123.75). Parking is available even though you're in the heart of Canterbury, 200 yards from the cathedral. The fully licensed French restaurant serves lunch and dinner. Bar snacks are also available at lunchtime.

Three Tuns, 24 Watling St., Canterbury, Kent CT1 2UD (tel. 0227/67371), is a fine old building that began life as three separate 15th-century houses, built on what was the site of a Roman theater. Additions were made to the structures in the 16th and 17th centuries, and during the 1700s the tavern became known as a coaching inn, popular with people traveling from London to Folkestone and Dover. William and Mary, who later became king and queen of England, stopped over here in 1679, and you can follow their example, even going so far as to stay in the same room, attractively furnished and with a four-poster bed. The hotel rents eight bedrooms, five with private baths. Singles cost £30 ($49.50) daily, and doubles run £42 ($69.30) to £48 ($79.20), with breakfast and VAT included. Each room is equipped with a TV, phone, and hot beverage facilities. The Chapel Restaurant, which serves good fixed-price meals costing £9.50 ($15.70) and £13 ($21.45), is open daily from noon to 2pm and 6:30 to 9pm. The restaurant was the setting for illegal masses during the Civil War, with a secret passage whose entrance can be seen.

Cathedral Gate Hotel, 36 Burgate, Canterbury, Kent CT1 2HA (tel. 0227/464381), is for modern-day pilgrims who want to rest their bones at an inn shouldering up to the cathedral's gateway. Built in 1438, adjoining Christchurch Gate and overlooking the Buttermarket, the hotel has views of the cathedral. In 1620 this former hospice became one of the earliest of the fashionable coffeehouses and teahouses of England. Its facade was added in the 19th century, however. The interior reveals many architectural features of the 17th century. Two curved bay windows overlook the little square in front of the gateway, and rear access leads directly into the cathedral precincts. Mr. and Mrs. C. R. H. Jubber and their children own the hotel and welcome guests to their 25 comfortably furnished rooms, many with private baths. All rooms have direct-dial phones. Those with private bath also have TV. Singles cost £18 ($29.70) to £37 ($61.05) daily; doubles or twins go for £34 ($56.10) to £54 ($89.10). Tariffs include a continental breakfast, and you can also have afternoon tea or supper.

WHERE TO DINE

The most distinguished restaurant in town, **Sully's,** High Street (tel. 0227/766266), is at the most distinguished hotel in Canterbury, the County (already previewed). The seating and comfort level are first rate, and both visitors and locals (the latter usually celebrating some special occasion) frequent this establishment. Considering the quality of the ingredients, the menu offers good value, especially if you stick to the table d'hôte menus: £12 ($19.80) for lunch and £16 ($26.40) for dinner. If you order à la carte, expect to spend from £21 ($34.65) per head. Food service is daily from 12:30 to 2:20pm and 7 to 11pm. You can always count on a selection of plainer, traditional English dishes, but try one of the more imaginatively conceived platters instead. Both English and a continental cuisine are served, and dishes are backed up by a respectable wine list. It's best to call for a table.

George's Brasserie, 71-72 Castle St. (tel. 0227/765658), is an attractive establishment run by a brother and sister, Simon Day and Beverly Holmes, who pride themselves on the cleanliness of their restaurant and the quality of their French food, made only of fresh ingredients. They serve everything from coffee and a croissant to gourmet meals. You can order from the fixed-price menu, costing from £7.95 ($13.10) for lunch, from £10.95 ($18.05) for dinner. On the à la carte listing, numerous appetizers are offered, including a fresh anchovy salad and George's terrines, all served with a basket of French bread. The selection of main dishes changes with the season, but it always includes fish and meat dishes and is served with new potatoes or french fries. Open 10am to 10pm Mon. to Thurs., 10am to 10:30pm Fri. and Sat., with last order time extended for theater-goers.

Tuo e Mio, 16 The Borough (tel. 0227/61471), is a bastion of zesty Italian cookery, the finest in town in its category. Signor R. P. M. Greggio sets the style and plans the menu at his casual bistro. Some dishes are standard, including the pastas, beef, and veal found on most Italian menus. However, a certain flair is shown in the daily specials, based on the shopping for fresh and good quality ingredients on any given day. Try especially the fish dishes including skate, which is regularly featured. Meals cost from £16 ($26.40) to £18 ($29.70). A selection of reasonably priced Italian wines is there to accompany your food selection. Open noon to 2:30pm and

7 to 10:45pm (until 10pm on Sun.); closed Mon., Tues. lunch. Call for a table, especially at lunch. It is closed for two weeks in August and September.

RIDE THE RAILS

In the area is the **Romney, Hythe & Dymchurch Light Railway Co.,** New Romney Station, New Romney (tel. 0679/62353), the world's smallest public railway. The engines are mostly steam driven, the carriages covered so there's no fear of getting wet. The line is 13½ miles long from Hythe (Kent) to New Romney and Dungeness (travel time about an hour), and the trains are one-third-size miniature versions of the kind of trains that ran on English or North American mainline railways in the 1920s. Fares depend on the distance traveled. An ordinary round-trip ticket costs £6 ($9.90) for adults. Otherwise, you can purchase a runabout ticket valid for unlimited travel, costing about £9 ($14.85) per day. Children travel for half the adult fare. Naturally, the ticket includes freedom to travel for a whole day as services permit on the R.H. & D. Railway. It operates daily from Easter to the end of September; March and October on Sat. and Sun. only. Telephone for train times. The railway is reached by road along the A259. The terminal of the railway, Hythe, is near Folkestone, which can be reached by frequent trains from London.

By car, leave Canterbury on the Dover road; 5 miles out turn right and Elham is 5 miles farther. A right turn and another 5 miles will take you to Hythe.

---

3. Dover

Dover, one of the ancient Cinque ports, is famed for its white cliffs. In Victoria's day, it basked in popularity as a seaside resort. Today it is of importance mainly because it is a port for major cross-Channel car and passenger traffic between England and France (usually Calais). Sitting in the open jaws of the white cliffs, Dover was one of England's most vulnerable and easy-to-hit targets in World War II and suffered repeated bombings that destroyed much of its harbor.

This seaport handles more visitors from abroad than any other point of entry to Great Britain. At the **National Tourist Information Centre,** Townwall Street (tel. 0304/205108), I found a small band of dedicated workers tirelessly answering questions and booking accommodations. It is easy to be casual and offhand when dealing with the same old questions time and time again, but these people treat each inquiry as something of vital interest and importance and give endless helpful advice. I am sure they will solve any problem you may have.

WHAT TO SEE AND DO

Hovering nearly 400 feet above the port is **Dover Castle** (tel. 0304/201628), one of the oldest and best known in England. Its keep was built at the command of Becket's fair-weather friend, Henry II, in the 12th century. The castle houses a military museum and a film center. The restaurant is open all year. The ancient castle was called back to active duty as late as World War II. The "Pharos" on the grounds is a lighthouse built by the Romans in the first half of the 1st century. The Romans landed at nearby Deal in 55 B.C. and 54 B.C. The first landing was not successful. The second in 54 B.C. was more so, but after six months they departed, and did not return until nearly 100 years later, in A.D. 43, when they occupied the country and stayed 400 years.

You can visit the keep year round, daily from 10am to 6pm in summer (it closes at 4pm off-season), for an admission of £3 ($4.95) for adults, £1.50 ($2.50) for children.

The **Roman Painted House,** New Street (tel. 0304/203279), is a spectacular, 1,800-year-old Roman mansion (hotel) with exceptionally well-preserved walls and an underfloor heating system. It is famous for its unique Bacchic murals and has won four National Awards for presentation. Open from April until the end of October from 10am to 5pm Tues. to Sun., with an admission of 80p ($1.30) for adults and 40p (65¢) for children.

WHERE TO STAY

The traditional choice is **The White Cliffs,** Waterloo Crescent, Dover, Kent CT17 9BP (tel. 0304/203633), many of whose bedrooms face the Channel. Its facade is impressive, built like a string of attached town houses, with an unbroken seafront balcony and a glass-enclosed front veranda. The 56 bedrooms are comfortable and tranquil, and all have private baths or showers, color TVs, radios, direct-dial phones, and hot beverage facilities. Singles cost from £40 ($66) daily, and doubles begin at £60 ($99) to £66 ($108.90). Rates include breakfast and VAT. Meals and light snacks are available 24 hours a day: dinner costs from £8 ($13.20). A covered garage is available. The hotel is close to the eastern and western docks and the hoverport for travel to and from France and Belgium.

Dover Moat House, Townwall Street, Dover, Kent CT16 1SZ (tel. 0304/203270), stands in the center of town, just a few minutes away from the railway station, the seafront, and the international ferry terminal and hoverport. Its 80 rooms are furnished with queen-size beds, private baths with showers, color TVs, radios, in-house movies, direct-dial phones, hairdryers, mini-bars, and individually controlled air conditioning and heating. Singles begin at £63.50 ($104.80) nightly; the charge is £79.50 ($131.20) for a twin. On the premises are an indoor heated swimming pool and a restaurant with a carvery and salad bar, plus coffeeshop facilities and an English-style bar.

WHERE TO DINE

Finding a good place to eat in Dover is not easy. If you gravitate to typically English, pub-style meals, try **Brittania,** Townwall Street (tel. 0304/203248), across from the Dover Stage Coachotel, near the seafront. It has a bow window, along with gilt and brass nautical accents on its ivory facade. The restaurant is one floor above street level, with a popular pub on the ground floor. Try a prawn cocktail or else a pâté for an appetizer, followed by such main courses as rumpsteak or a mixed grill. Many different salads are offered, including one made with salmon, another with ham. Meals cost from £12 ($19.80). The pub is open from 11am to 11pm Mon. to Sat. The restaurant serves from noon to 2pm and 3 to 9pm Mon. to Sat., from noon to 9pm Sun.

Ristorante al Porto, 43 Townwall St. (tel. 0304/204615), brings Italian flair to Dover. One block from the landing dock of the ferry boats, this Italian-owned restaurant is decorated in a nautical style, with fishnets hanging from the ceiling. It offers one of the largest menus in town, featuring such specialties as steak in a black pepper, cream, and brandy sauce, along with cannelloni or succulent veal in a sauce of mushrooms, garlic, and tomatoes. Try the gelati misti (mixed ice cream) for dessert and a cup of espresso. Expect to pay from £10 ($16.50) for a meal here. However, an à la carte lunch goes for £5.50 ($9.10). Hours re noon to 2:30pm and 7 to 10:30pm; closed Sun.

4. Royal Tunbridge Wells

Dudley, Lord North, courtier to James I, is credited with the discovery in 1606 of the mineral spring that started it all. His accidental find led to the creation of a fashionable resort 36 miles south of London that reached its peak in the mid-18th century under the foppish leadership of "Beau" Nash. Beau or Richard Nash (1674–1761) was a dandy in his day, the final arbiter of what to say and what to wear (for example, he got men to take off their boots and put on stockings). But, of course, most of his time was devoted to Bath. Even so, Tunbridge Wells enjoyed a prime spa reputation from the days of Charles II through Victoria. Because so many monarchs visited it, Edward VII named it Royal Tunbridge Wells in 1919.

The most remarkable feature of Royal Tunbridge Wells is its Pantiles, a colonnaded walkway for shoppers, tea-drinkers, and diners, built near the wells. At the Assembly Hall, entertainment such as opera or vaudeville is presented. The resort is a 50-minute train ride from London.

Canadians touring in the area may want to seek out the grave of the founder of their country's capital. Lt. Col. John By of the Royal Engineers (1779–1836) died at Shernfold Park in Frant East Sussex, near Tunbridge Wells, and is buried in the churchyard there. His principal claim to fame is that he established what was later to be the capital of the Dominion of Canada, the city of Ottawa, and built the Rideau Canal in upper Canada. The canal, some 124 miles long, links the city of Kingston on the St. Lawrence River with the city of Ottawa on the Ottawa River. Between 1826 and 1832 John By successfully constructed this canal through an unexplored wilderness for the British government. At the northern end of the canal he laid out "Bytown." Twenty years later this was renamed Ottawa, and it became the capital of a united Canada. His grave near Royal Tunbridge Wells is marked by a plaque erected by the Historical Society of Ottawa in 1979.

WHERE TO STAY AND DINE

The leading place to stay is the **Spa Hotel,** Mount Ephraim, Royal Tunbridge Wells, Kent TN4 8XJ (tel. 0892/20331). Privately owned, it still retains many of its Georgian charms, although modern amenities have been installed. Standing in 14 acres of its own grounds, the building dates back to 1766; a private home, it was converted to a hotel in 1880. Today it is the property of the Goring family, who rent 76 well-maintained and comfortably appointed bedrooms, charging from £60 ($99) daily in a single, from £76 ($125.40) in a double. Each of these accommodations contains a private bath, TV, and phone. This is the kind of place where guests often check in for long stays. The Chandelier Restaurant serves a combination English and French cuisine, with a set lunch at £15 ($24.75), an à la carte dinner going for £20 ($33). Facilities include a sauna, a solarium, tennis courts, and an indoor swimming pool.

Calverley Hotel, Crescent Road, Royal Tunbridge Wells, Kent TN1 2LY (tel. 0892/26455), is an old stone hotel facing Calverley Park, of special interest in itself. The hotel's large lounge, furnished with comfortable chairs, opens onto the terrace and gardens. The dining room also overlooks the gardens. The 43 bedrooms, on the upper floors, are reached by elevator. Each room has central heating, phone, and radio, and many have private baths or showers. Guests frequently meet in the cocktail bar for drinks before dinner. Overnight rates are £36 ($59.40) in a bathless single, £40 ($66) in a single with bath. VAT and breakfast are included, but you pay an additional £7 ($11.55) for the table d'hôte luncheon and about £8 ($14.85) for dinner, also with VAT included.

Wellington Hotel, Mount Ephraim, Royal Tunbridge Wells, Kent TV4 8BU (Tel. 0892/542911), enjoys a regal position, overlooking the common. The Regency hotel suggests a Charles Addams drawing, with its mansard roof, rows of dormers, and original balconies. Catering mainly to businesspeople and families, it is ideal as a base for visiting the southeast of England. For a luxury, period double room with private bath, the charge is from £60 ($99) per night. Less expensive doubles go for £49 ($80.85) to £55 ($90.75). Singles range from £32 ($52.80) to £41 ($67.65). Rates include VAT, breakfast, and service. The hotel offers 65 bedrooms, 50 with private bath. Rooms also have TVs. A dinner costs from £8.50 ($14.05). The hotel has a health club, sauna, and solarium.

Russell, 80 London Rd., Royal Tunbridge Wells, Kent TN1 1DZ (tel. 0892/544833), is one of the best places for accommodations at the old spa. It is also reasonable in price. Within an easy walk of the Pantiles, it is run by Toni and Kevin Wilkinson. All 21 pleasant and comfortable bedrooms have private baths, TVs, and phones. Singles cost from £54 ($89.10) daily, with doubles or twins going for £66 ($108.90), including a full breakfast and VAT. You should take your meals here, as they are good tasting and offer value for money. A four-course dinner, for example, costs £16 ($26.40).

Thackeray's House, 85 London Rd. (tel. 0892/511921), serves the finest food in Royal Tunbridge Wells, and you get a little history as well, as this is the second-oldest house in the spa, and it was once inhabited by the novelist William Makepeace Thackeray. Bruce Wass, the owner-chef, once worked at one of my favorite restaurants in London, Odin's, before coming here to set up his own place. He has created an elegant atmosphere, backed up by attentive service, for his specialties, which are served from 12:30 to 2:30pm and 7 to 10pm; closed Sun. and Mon. A table d'hôte lunch begins at £15.75 ($26), and a set dinner is offered at £24 ($39.60). Care goes into all his dishes, and many have flair, including an occasional salad with fresh flowers. He reaches perfection with such dishes as tender duck breast served with citrus, or fresh-herb-flavored lamb with baby turnips. For dessert, he is most often cited for his chocolate armagnac loaf, served with a walnut-liqueur sauce.

At a bistro, **Downstairs at Thackeray's,** slightly simpler fare is offered in an informal atmosphere complete with a working inglenook fireplace for winter and courtyard dining for summer. Average prices downstairs are around £8.50 ($14.05) for lunch, from £15 ($24.75) for dinner. Meals are served from 12:30 to 2:30pm and 7 to 11pm; closed Sun. and Mon.

SURREY

This tiny county has for some time been in danger of being gobbled up by the growing boundaries of London and turned into a sprawling suburb. Already some of Surrey's densely populated area is part of Greater London. But Surrey still retains much unspoiled countryside, largely because its many heaths and commons do not make good land for suburbanite houses. Essentially, Surrey is a county of commuters (Alfred, Lord Tennyson was among the first); a worker in the city can travel to the remotest corner of Surrey from London in anywhere from 45 minutes to an hour.

Long before William the Conqueror marched his pillaging Normans across its chalky North Downs, Surrey was important to the Saxons. In fact, early Saxon kings were once crowned at what is now **Kingston-on-Thames** (their Coronation Stone is still preserved near the guildhall).

LIVING IN TUDOR SPLENDOR

The best of England—the best living accommodations, in particular—are to be found in the countryside. There you can sometimes live like a duke or duchess. Transportation facilities are often so good that you can enjoy the best of two worlds, darting into London for all its attractions, while enjoying the better surroundings of rural England.

For those who want to be in the vicinity of Heathrow Airport, yet within easy access of central London, **Great Fosters,** Stroude Road, Egham, Surrey TW20 9UR (tel. 0784/433822), is a perfect choice. It is one of the most impressive old manor houses of England. Built in 1550, at one time it belonged to Elizabeth I and was a hunting lodge in Windsor's Royal Forest. Only 18 miles from London, it still preserves the link to its past. A red brick Tudor building, with stone-mullioned windows, many gables, and towering chimneys, it sits in a private garden, where paths cut through formal grounds of clipped yew hedges, roses, and rhododendrons —and a swimming pool. The architectural features of the interior are in the grand style, as witness the main hall with its carved, black oak, Jacobean fireplace. In the 15th-century tithe barn, with its high vaulted and raftered oak beams, meals are served and an orchestra plays for dancing on Sat. night. The hotel rents 45 bedrooms, each with private bath or shower, phone, and TV. Some of the master bedrooms are in a period style. For example, the gilt-paneled Italian bedroom contains an overscale bed with hand-carved cherubs on the posts. Period-style rooms for two people rent from £120 ($198) daily, and singles from £55 ($90.75). These room rates include a full English breakfast, service, and VAT. Great Fosters is only a half mile from Runnymede and the Kennedy Memorial, and only 7 miles in different directions from Windsor Castle and Hampton Court Palace.

5. Richmond

Want to spend an afternoon in a Thames river town? Richmond is only a 30-minute ride from London, and can easily be reached by tube or Green Line coaches 716 or 716A from Hyde Park Corner. The old town, popular in Victorian times, has good public rail links with London, and it offers the escape many seek from the rush and bustle of the metropolis. If you're feeling light-hearted, take the boat trip down the Thames. Turner himself, art materials in hand, came here for inspiration.

WHAT TO SEE AND DO

Richmond is only 1 mile from Kew and its botanical gardens. You may prefer a combined excursion to Kew Gardens and Richmond on the same day. One of the attractions of the Thames town is the 2,500-acre **Richmond Park,** first staked out by Charles I in 1637. It is filled with photogenic deer and waterfowl. Richmond has long enjoyed associations with royalty, as Henry VII's Richmond Palace stood there (an even earlier manor was razed). Queen Elizabeth I died in the old palace in 1603. Somebody's short-sightedness led to the palace's being carted away, and only a carriageway remains.

If you want to be like the English, you'll climb **Richmond Hill** for a view of the Thames. The setting reminded William Byrd so much of his home on the James River in Virginia, that he named the city founded there in 1737 Richmond.

There are good shops and an excellent theater facing the green on which, in summertime, cricket matches are played. There's also boating on the river. Richmond Park has a public golf course, and you can rent a horse from the local stables. The Richmond Ice Skating Rink has been the nursery of many of England's skating champions. Wimbledon and the Tennis Championships are within easy reach, as is Hampton Court Palace.

At Petersham, the 13th-century **St. Peter's Church** is the burial place of Capt. George Vancouver. The Queen Mother's parents, Lord and Lady Glamis, were married there. It also has some very old wooden box pews. At **St. Anne's Church** at Kew Green, the painters Gainsborough and Zoffany were buried.

From Richmond, you can take bus 65 or 71 to visit historic **Ham House** (disembark at the Fox and Duck Pub across from the grounds of the Ham Polo Club), 8 miles from the heart of London. The house offers an amazing look into the lives of the aristocracy of 17th-century England. Unlike most historic homes in Britain, this one has been maintained almost intact. Much of the house, especially the kitchen (modern for its time), was the work of Elizabeth Murray, Duchess of Lauderdale and Countess of Dysart. Her aim was to create the most sumptuous private residence in Restoration England, complete with elegant French upholstered pieces and ceilings depicting mythological scenes. One of the first private bathrooms in England was installed at Ham House. The house is open daily from 11am to 5pm, charging an admission of £2 ($3.30) for adults, £1 ($1.65) for children. In summer, you can order tea in the 17th-century garden. For more information, phone 081/940-1950.

WHERE TO STAY

A privately owned hotel at the top of Richmond Hill, **The Petersham,** Nightingale Lane, Richmond, Surrey, TW10 6UZ (tel. 081/940-7471), enjoys a view of the Thames that has attracted artists for centuries and has interesting historical features. The Petersham, built as an hotel in 1864, has a spiral stone staircase dominated by ceiling murals. The bedrooms are a blend of old and new, and all have private baths, color TVs, radios, and direct-dial phones. Room service is offered until 10:45pm. The hotel rents 54 bedrooms, in a wide range of styles and sizes. Single rooms at The Petersham cost £80 ($132) daily. Luxury river-view and four-poster rooms for two people are offered at £120 ($198). Rates are reduced on weekends. A "value for money" weekend package is available at £110 ($181.50) with two meals included. Nightingales Restaurant enjoys panoramic views over the river, and both fixed price and à la carte menus are available. The three-course set menu offers a wide choice of international dishes with wines from the hotel's private cellar. Lunch, dinner, or a traditional Sunday lunch cost from £20 ($33). Seasonal specialties are offered based on fresh produce.

WHERE TO DINE

Londoners often go down to Richmond for the day, browse through its art galleries, and then dine out—which must account for the town's number of good restaurants.

Kew Rendezvous, 110 Kew Rd. (tel. 081/940-1334), billing itself with some justification as "the leading Peking-style restaurant in the United Kingdom," is in a building of unique architectural design, just down the road from Kew Gardens. The food is superb, especially if you stick to the chef's specialties and avoid the routine Chinese restaurant fare. Three dishes, designed to delight, include barbecued Peking duck, crispy duck, or a variety of meats on a sizzling iron plate. Also recommended are hot-and-sour Peking soup, sliced beef in oyster sauce, and diced chicken in yellow-bean sauce. If there are six people in your party, you can forgo the above and leave it to the chef, who will prepare you a Peking dinner. Set menus range from £14 ($23.10) to £16 ($26.40) per person. À la carte averages £14 ($23.10). Hours are from noon to 2:15pm and 6 to 11:15pm daily.

---

6. Haslemere

A quiet, sleepy town, Haslemere attracts because early English musical instruments are made by hand there. An annual music festival (see below) is the town's main drawing card. Haslemere is only an hour's train ride from Waterloo Station in London, about 42 miles away.

THE HASLEMERE FESTIVAL

It isn't often that one can hear such exquisite music played so skillfully on the harpsichord, the recorder, the lute, or other early instruments. The Dolmetsch family makes and repairs these instruments, welcoming visitors to their place on the edge of Haslemere. Their instruments and music-making have brought fame to this scenic little Surrey town. They rehearse constantly, preparing for the concerts that are held in July, lasting nine days.

You can get specific information by writing to the **Haslemere Festival Office,** Jesses, Grayswood Road, Haslemere, Surrey GU27 2BS (or telephone 0428/2161 between 9am and 12:30pm daily). During the festival, matinees begin at 3:15pm, evening performances at 7:30pm. For seats in the balcony, prices range from £4 ($6.60) to £6.50 ($10.75), with stall seats going for £2.50 ($4.15) to £5.50 ($9.10).

WHERE TO STAY

On the outskirts of Haslemere, the **Lythe Hill Hotel,** Petworth Road, Haslemere, Surrey GU27 3BQ (tel. 0428/51251), is a 14th-century farmhouse of historic interest set in 14 acres of parkland overlooking National Trust woodlands and just an hour from London, Heathrow, and Gatwick. Across the courtyard is the main hotel, with 32 luxuriously appointed bedrooms and suites, as well as an English restaurant. In the black-and-white timbered farmhouse are five elegant period units, with marble-tile baths. One has a four-poster bed dated 1614. Singles cost from £72 ($118.80) daily, twins and doubles rent for £120 ($198), and 12 suites peak at £150 ($247.50) for two. All tariffs include VAT. Each unit has a phone, TV, and private bath or shower. Downstairs in the farmhouse is the renowned, oak-beamed and paneled Auberge de France Restaurant, offering a classic French cuisine served by candlelight on polished oak tables. Specialties include turbot, fresh Scottish salmon, tournedos de boeuf, and a cellar of fine wines. Dinner costs around £40 ($66) for two persons. Open from 7 to 9:45pm Tues. to Sat.; lunch only Sun.

WHERE TO DINE

Considered the most outstanding French restaurant in Surrey, **Morels,** 25-27 Lower St. (tel. 0428/51462), showcases the talents of a remarkable chef, Jean-Yves Morel. He represents the best of yesterday, yet he is not afraid to experiment with new ideas (mainly those that work). His main street establishment is bright and furnished in modern overtones, but there's nothing about the decor that detracts from the cuisine. Londoners flock here.

Monsieur Morel uses morels in some of his concoctions, perhaps in honor or respect for his own name. His menu, adjusted to the seasons and market conditions, changes every 30 days or so, so it's difficult to recommend specific dishes. A typical one might be chargrilled pigeon breast subtly flavored with a light sauce made with juices of langoustine. Vegetables are done to perfection, and the cheese-board selection rivals those of France. The assiette du chef is a festival for the palate, a perfectly balanced selection of his finest desserts. A set lunch, from 12:30 to 2pm, costs £15 ($24.75), and a table d'hôte dinner, from 7 to 10pm, goes for £18 ($29.70). Count on spending from £30 ($49.50) if dining à la carte. Closed for lunch on Sat. and all day Sun. and Mon.

---

7. Guildford

The old and new meet in the county town on the Wey River, 40 minutes by train from Waterloo Station in London. Charles Dickens believed that its High Street, which slopes to the river, was one of the most beautiful in England. The guildhall has an ornamental projecting clock that dates back to 1683.

Lying 2½ miles southwest of the city, **Loseley House** (tel. 0483/571881), a beautiful Elizabethan mansion visited by Elizabeth I, James I, and Queen Mary, has been featured on TV and in five films. Its works of art include paneling from Henry VIII's Nonsuch Palace, period furniture, a unique carved chalk chimneypiece, magnificent ceilings, and cushions made by Elizabeth I. The mansion is open from the end of May to the end of September from 2 to 5pm Wed., Thurs., Fri. and Sat., charging £3 ($4.95) for adults, £1.50 ($2.50) for children. Lunches and teas are served in the 17th-century tithe barn from 2 to 5pm, and you can tour the farm and visit the farm shop.

WHERE TO STAY AND DINE

About 2 miles southwest of the center of Guildford, the **Post House Hotel,** Egerton Road, Guildford, Surrey GU2 5XZ (tel. 0483/574444), just off the A3 London-Portsmouth road, is surrounded by landscaped grounds. In the 111-bedroom hostelry opened in 1987, a feeling of heritage is conveyed by natural red elm joinery, polished brass fittings, and marble floors. Bedrooms incorporate both living and sleeping areas, and all contain baths and showers, remote-control TVs, radios, direct-dial phones, hot beverage facilities, and mini-bars. The needs of disabled guests have been taken into consideration. Rates range from £85 ($140.25) daily in singles, from £100 ($165) in doubles. The restaurant features traditional English roasts and international dishes. Guests find the hot and cold buffet to be a good value. The coffeeshop, open daily from 6:30 to 11pm, offers family favorites served in an informal atmosphere. There's a health and fitness club with an indoor heated swimming pool and a sun terrace.

Angel Hotel, High Street, Guildford, Surrey GU1 3DR (tel. 0483/64555), is an old coaching inn on the cobbled main street. Its entrance and part of its courtyard are Tudor, and many other original features of this once-busy hostelry have been maintained. Inside, there is lavish paneling, plus a huge, open fireplace as well as exposed beams. Great oak timbers from old ships at Portsmouth were used to support the gallery. Most of the 25 bedrooms, including two family rooms, are simply furnished, although some are quite attractively decorated (these disappear first to those who reserve ahead). Each has a private bath, as well as a phone, radio, TV, and coffee maker. Rates begin at £60 ($99) daily in a single, going up to £76 ($125.40) in a double or twin, including VAT and service. In addition to a well-decorated bar, the hotel has a quick-service coffeeshop as well as a 13th-century restaurant in the crypt, with medieval architecture making for cozy surroundings. The restaurant offers a wide range of dishes, including English roasts, at an average price of £18 ($29.70) per person.

GODALMING

Five miles from Guildford, **Inn on the Lake,** Ockford Road, Godalming, Surrey GU7 1RH (tel. 04868/5575), is a haven of landscaped gardens with ducks drowsing on pools beside the lake. The 20 rooms are decorated with pretty country prints and simple furniture, each with a TV, tea and coffee maker, and radio. Charges are from £45 ($74.25) daily for a single, £70 ($115.50) for a double, including VAT and a large breakfast. Excellent snacks are served in a real old-world bar, where some of the timbers date from Tudor times. In summer, barbecues are held in the garden. For more substantial dinners, fixed-price menus are offered at £13.50 ($22.30) and £17.50 ($28.90) and à la carte with a varied selection of grills, English favorites, and continental dishes. The house was listed in the *Domesday Book* and has Tudor, Georgian, and Victorian associations. Godalming was the starting point for the émigrés who eventually settled Allenton, Georgia, after landing in Savannah.

WISLEY GARDEN

One of the great gardens of England and the world, Wisley Garden (tel. 0483/224234), stands in Wisley near Ripley just off the M25 (Junction 10) on A3 London-Portsmouth road. Every season of the year, this 250-acre garden has a profusion of flowers and shrubbery, ranging from the New Alpine House, with its delicate blossoms in spring, to the Walled Garden with formal flowerbeds in summer, to the Heather Garden's colorful foliage in the fall, and a riot of exotic plants in the glasshouses in winter. This garden is the site of a laboratory where botanists, plant pathologists, and an entomologist experiment and assist amateur gardeners. There is a large gift shop with a wide range of gardening books. Open all year, hours are 10am to 7pm (or sunset if earlier) Mon. to Sat.; closed Sun. Admission is £3 ($4.95) for adults, and £1.20 ($2) for children (6 to 14 years). There is a licensed restaurant and cafeteria in the garden.

8. Dorking

This town, birthplace of Lord Olivier, lies on the Mole River, at the foot of the North Downs. Within easy reach are some of the most scenic spots in the shire, including Silent Pool, Box Hill, and Leith Hill. Three miles to the northwest and 1½ miles south of Great Bookham, off the A246 Leatherhead-Guildford road, stands **Polesden Lacey** (tel. 0372/52048), a former Regency villa containing the Greville collection of antiques, paintings, and tapestries. In the early part of this century it was enlarged to become a comfortable Edwardian country house when it was the home of a celebrated hostess, who frequently entertained royalty there. The 18th-century garden is filled with herbaceous borders, a rose garden, and beech walks, and in all the estate consists of 1,000 acres. The house is open from April to the end of October from 1:30 to 5:30pm Wed. to Sun.; in March and November it's open from 1:30 to 4:30pm Sat. and Sun. only. The charge to visit both the house and garden is £3.50 ($5.80) on Sun. and bank holidays, £3 ($4.95) on other days for adults, with children paying half price. The garden is open daily all year from 11am to sunset. To visit just the gardens, adults are charged £1.50 ($2.50) and children pay 75p ($1.25). A licensed restaurant on the grounds is open from 11am to 4pm on the days the house can be visited.

Where to Stay and Dine

Back in Dorking, **Burford Bridge Hotel,** Box Hill, Dorking, Surrey RH5 6BX (tel. 0306/884561), offers stylish living in a rural town from which a train will zip you into London in less than half an hour. At the foot of the beauty spot of Box Hill, the hotel has a lot of historical associations. Lord Nelson was a frequent patron, and Keats completed *Endymion* here in 1817. Everyone from Wordsworth to Robert Louis Stevenson also frequented the place. You get the best of both old and the new here, including a tithe barn (circa 1600) as well as 48 large bedrooms, renting for £80 ($132) daily in a single, from £120 ($198) in a double. Each room has its own bath or shower, plus a phone and color TV. The restaurant serves good English food, and a bar opens onto a flowered patio with a fountain. In summer, you can enjoy the garden swimming pool and frequent barbecues. The location is 1½ miles north of Dorking on A24.

White Horse Hotel, High Street, Dorking, Surrey, RH4 1BE (tel. 0306/881138). Just 10 miles from Gatwick Airport, you can dine or lodge at a hotel that dates in part from 1500. Once the vicarage of Dorking, the White Horse by tradition was supposed to have been the "Marquis of Granby" in the *Pickwick Papers.* At least Dickens was known to have frequented the bar parlor. An atmospheric place of creaking timbers and low beamed ceilings, the inn offers 68 bedrooms, including 18 family units, each with private bath or shower, phone, radio, TV, and beverage facilities. Some are in a modern annex. A single with bath costs from £65 ($107.25) daily, and a double rents for £80 ($132), including VAT and service. Often called "the most interesting house in Dorking," the inn has a restaurant as well as a Pickwick bar offering à la carte meals for £12 ($19.80) and up. There is also a heated outdoor pool.

After visiting Surrey, you can head south toward the English Channel and the sprawling shires of Sussex.

SUSSEX

If King Harold hadn't loved Sussex so much, the course of English history might have been changed forever. Had the brave Saxon waited longer in the north, he could have marshaled more adequate reinforcements before striking south to meet the Normans. But Duke William's soldiers were ravaging the countryside he knew so well, and Harold rushed down to counter them.

Harold's enthusiasm for Sussex is understandable. The landscape rises and falls like waves. The county is known for its downlands and tree-thickened weald, from which came the timbers to build England's mighty fleet in days gone by. The shires lie south of London and Surrey, bordering Kent in the east, Hampshire in the west, and opening directly onto the sometimes sunny, resort-dotted English Channel.

Like other sections in the vulnerable south of England, Sussex witnessed some of the biggest moments in the country's history. Apart from the Norman landings at Hastings, the most life-changing transfusion of plasma occurred in the 19th century, as middle-class Victorians flocked to the seashore, pumping new spirit into Eastbourne, Worthing, Brighton, even old Hastings. The cult of salt-water worship flourished, and has to this day. Although **Eastbourne** and **Worthing** are much frequented by the English, I'd place them several fathoms below **Brighton** and **Hastings,** which are more suitable for a seaside holiday.

Far more than the resorts, the old towns and villages of Sussex are intriguing, particularly **Rye** and **Winchelsea,** the ancient towns of the Cinque Port Confederation. No Sussex village is lovelier than **Alfriston** (and the innkeepers know it too); **Arundel** is noted for its castle; the cathedral city of **Chichester** is a mecca for theater buffs. Traditionally, and for purposes of government, Sussex is divided into East Sussex and West Sussex. I'll begin in East Sussex, where you'll find many of the inns and hotels within commuting distance of London.

9. Rye and Winchelsea

"Nothing more recent than a Cavalier's Cloak, Hat and Ruffles should be seen in the streets of Rye," said Louis Jennings. He's so right. This ancient town, formerly an island, was chartered back in 1229. Rye, 65 miles below London, near the English Channel, and neighboring Winchelsea were once part of the ancient Cinque Ports Confederation. Rye flourished as a smuggling center, its denizens sneaking in contraband from the marshes to stash away in little nooks (even John Wesley's firm chastisements couldn't stop what was a strongly entrenched tradition).

But the sea receded from **Rye,** leaving it perched like a giant whale out of water, 2 miles from the Channel. Its narrow, cobblestone streets twist and turn like a labyrinth, with buildings jumbled along them whose sagging roofs and crooked chimneys indicate the town's medieval origins. The old town's entrance is **Land Gate,** where a single lane of traffic passes between massive, 40-foot-high stone towers. The parapet of the gate contains holes through which boiling oil used to be poured on unwelcome visitors such as French raiding parties.

Attacked several times by French fleets, Rye was practically razed in 1377. But it rebuilt sufficiently, decking itself out in the Elizabethan style so that Queen Elizabeth I, during her visit in 1573, bestowed upon the town the distinction of Royal Rye. This has long been considered a special place, having attracted any number of famous people, including Charles Lamb (who considered the smugglers "honest thieves") and Henry James, who lived in Lamb House (see details in "What to See and Do," following).

WHAT TO SEE AND DO

Today the city has any number of specific buildings and sites of architectural interest, notably the 15th-century **St. Mary's Parish Church,** with its clock flanked by two gilded cherubs, known as the Quarter Boys from their striking of the bells on the quarter hour. If you're courageous, you can climb a set of wooden stairs and ladders to the bell tower of the church, from which an impressive view is afforded.

Rye Museum, 4 Church Sq. (tel. 0797/223254), is housed in the Ypres Tower, a fortification built around 1250 by order of Henry III as a defense against French raiders. In this ancient building, the museum contains collections of military objects, shipping artifacts, toys, Cinque Ports relics, Victoriana, inn lore, and pottery. From Easter to mid-October, its hours are 10:30am to 1pm and 2:15 to 5:30pm Mon. to Sat. (opens at 11:30am on Sun.). Admission is £1 ($1.65) for adults and 50p (85¢) for children.

Lamb House, the home of Henry James from 1898 to 1916, stands on West Street at the top of Mermaid Street. There are many Jamesian mementos in the house, which is set in walled gardens. It is open April through October from 2 to 5:30pm on Wed. and Sat., charging an admission of £1 ($1.65).

The sister Cinque Federation port to Rye, neighboring **Winchelsea** has also witnessed the water's ebb. It traces its history back to Edward I, and has experienced many dramatic moments, such as sacking by the French. Today it is a dignified residential town. In the words of one 19th-century writer, Winchelsea is "a sunny dream of centuries ago." Its finest sight is a badly damaged 14th-century church, containing a number of remarkable tombs.

On the outskirts, you can visit **Smallhythe Place,** at Tenterden in Kent (tel. 05806/2334), which for 30 years was the country house of Dame Ellen Terry. Ellen Terry, of course, was the English actress acclaimed for her Shakespearean roles who had a long theatrical association with Sir Henry Irving. She died in the house in 1928. This timber-framed house, of a type known as a "continuous-jetty house," was built in the first half of the 16th century. It is filled with Terry memorabilia. The house is on the B2082 near Tenterden, about 6 miles to the north of Rye. The house is open April to October from 2 to 6pm Sat. to Wed. Adults pay £1.70 ($2.80) admission; children 90p ($1.50).

WHERE TO STAY

The leading choice is **Mermaid Inn,** Mermaid Street, Rye, East Sussex TN31 7EU (tel. 0797/223065), one of the most famous of the old smugglers' inns of England, known to that band of cutthroats, the real-life Hawkhurst Gang, as well as to Russell Thorndike's fictional character, Dr. Syn. The hotel rents 28 bedrooms with private baths or showers, phones, and TVs. One of the present rooms, in fact, is called Dr. Syn's Bedchamber, and is connected by a secret staircase—set in the thickness of the wall—to the bar. That room, with a private bath, rents for £88 ($145.20) for two daily, as does the Elizabethan Chamber (with four-poster and private bath). Other rooms—such as the Fleur-de-Lys Chamber and the Tudor Rose Chamber—contain private baths and twin beds, and cost £80 ($132) for two. Terms include breakfast, and a 10% service charge is added. The best rooms are in the main building overlooking the cobblestone street. One, the Smugglers Room, has an oak four-poster.

The Mermaid has sheltered everybody from Elizabeth I to the actor George Arliss. When Elizabeth came to Rye in 1573, the inn had already been operating nearly 150 years. A covered carriageway leads to the car park. In the center of the hotel is a courtyard, where you'll see a pedestal fountain with water flowing down on the heads of water lilies. The Mermaid has also taken over the 16th-century Ship Inn at the foot of Mermaid Street, which, with its 12 bedrooms and restaurant on the first floor, complements the Mermaid.

The George, High Street, Rye, East Sussex TN31 7JP (tel. 0797/222114), is a former coaching inn with a history going back 400 years. It's composed of a trio of 14th-century buildings whose boundaries over the years have grown less distinct. In the 18th century it drew a diverse clientele: some traveling by horse-drawn carriage, others by package boat between London and France. This is one of the most charming small inns in the region. Winding hallways lead to the 22 bedrooms and to a Georgian salon, reserved only for the use of guests, one flight above the antique-laden lobby. Each of the bedrooms contains a private bath, TV, radio, and phone, and has a half-timbered kind of charm. Some of the timbers, capping the ceilings, are said to have come from the wreck of an English ship broken up in Rye Harbour after the defeat of the Spanish Armada. Singles cost from £45 ($74.25), with doubles or twins from £80 ($132), these rates including half board. On the premises, tucked away at the end of narrow hallways and twisted stairwells, is the John Crouch pub, with about eight different kinds of beer and cider on tap. The hotel also has an old-fashioned restaurant and at least two blazing fireplaces in cold weather.

Hope Anchor Hotel, Watchbell Street, Rye, East Sussex TN31 7HA (tel. 0797/222216), at the end of a cobblestone street, is a 17th-century hostelry enjoying panoramic views of the surrounding countryside and overlooking the Strand Quay where yachts can be seen at their moorings. Oak beams and open fires in winter make this a most inviting place to spend a few days. The 17 bedrooms—seven with private baths—are comfortable, all with color TVs and hot beverage facilities. With a full English breakfast included, doubles cost from £49 ($80.85) to £59 ($97.35) daily, and singles £35 ($57.75) to £39 ($64.35). VAT is included. Bar meals are served at lunch, and the restaurant offers an English cuisine, especially fresh fish caught locally. A dinner in the restaurant costs £11 ($18.15).

Durrant House Hotel, East Street, Rye, East Sussex TN31 7LA (tel. 0797/ 223182), is a beautiful Georgian house set on a quiet residential street in the old town behind a cream-colored facade at the end of Market Street. Over the years it has attracted many famous personages, including John Wesley during his evangelistic tours. In more recent times, the renowned artist Paul Nash lived next door until his death in 1946. In fact his celebrated view, as seen in his painting *View of the Rother,* can be enjoyed from the River Room of the hotel. Sir William Durrant, a friend of the duke of Wellington, acquired the house, which is now named after him. In time it was used as a relay station for carrier pigeons; these birds brought news of the victory at Waterloo. The hotel possesses much charm and character. There is a cozy lounge with an arched brick fireplace and, across the hall, a residents' bar. Ten comfortably furnished bedrooms, each with private bath and phone, are rented. Singles cost from £24 ($39.60) to £26 ($42.90) daily, and doubles go for £34 ($56.10) to £50 ($82.50) with an English breakfast included.

WHERE TO DINE

Built in the Georgian era as one of the vicarages for St. Mary's Anglican Church, **The Old Vicarage in East Street,** East Street, Rye, East Sussex TN31 7JY (tel. 0797/225131), is a charming establishment that was converted into a French-style *restaurant avec chambres* in 1979. Although the owners, Sarah and Bill Foster, maintain four beautifully decorated bedrooms upstairs, the establishment is best known for its elegant restaurant. Each of the rooms is suitable for one or two persons and rents, with breakfast included, for £26 ($42.90) to £30 ($49.50) daily per person. Units contain private baths, color TVs, phones, and a carefully assembled kind of panache.

After an aperitif in the cocktail bar, dinner guests proceed into the elegant, blue-and-white dining room, where, within sight of a carved fireplace, guests enjoy a selection of dishes from the classic English cuisine. The menu changes monthly to make the most of the best in local fish and meat. A typical meal listing might include shrimp-and-spinach soup, hot deviled crab, Romney Marsh lamb grilled with rosemary, filet of Rye Bay plaice stuffed with prawns in a fresh cream-and-herb sauce, and escalope of pork in a vermouth sauce, followed by desserts such as vacherin aux fruits and a selection of unusual homemade ice creams. A la carte three-course meals range from £12 ($19.80) to £15 ($24.75). Dinner is served every night from 7 to 9pm. This establishment is not to be confused with a nearby B&B also called the Old Vicarage.

Flushing Inn, Market Street (tel. 0797/223292), is in a 16th-century inn on a cobblestone street. It has preserved the best of the past, including a wall-size fresco in the restaurant dating from 1544 and depicting a menagerie of birds and heraldic beasts. A rear dining room overlooks a carefully tended flower garden. A special feature is the Sea Food Lounge Bar, where sandwiches and plates of seafood are available from £6 ($9.90) to £10 ($16.50). In the main restaurant, luncheons are offered beginning at £9 ($14.85); dinners run from £17 ($28.05). Besides these lunches and dinners, gastronomic evenings are held at regular intervals between October and April. For one of these specially prepared meals, including your apéritif, wine, and after-dinner brandy, you pay £36 ($59.40) per person. Fine wine evenings cost £44 ($72.60) to £56 ($92.40). Open 12:30 to 1:45pm and 7:30 to 9pm; closed Mon. night, all day Tues., for two weeks after Christmas, and for the first two weeks in June. The Flushing Inn has been run by the Mann family since 1960, with the second generation now fully active in the business.

Another choice is offered at the **Landgate Bistro,** 5 Landgate (tel. 0797/222829). Nick Parkin and Toni Ferguson-Lees are known for their fresh local fish, wild duck, rabbit, pigeon, and jugged hare. It's all there in pies, casseroles, and stews, accompanied by fresh seasonal vegetables properly cooked or a salad. A meal will cost £15 ($24.75), plus wine. Food is served from 7 to 9:30pm Tues. to Sat.

---

10. Hastings and St. Leonards

The world has seen bigger battles, but few are as well remembered as the Battle of Hastings in 1066. When William, Duke of Normandy, landed on the Sussex coast and lured King Harold (already fighting Vikings in Yorkshire) southward to defeat, the destiny of the English-speaking people was changed forever. It was D-Day in reverse. The actual battle occurred at what is now Battle Abbey (9 miles away), but the Norman duke used Hastings as his base of operation.

Hastings suffered other invasions—it was razed by the French in the 14th century. But after that blow a Tudor town grew up in the eastern sector, and it makes for a good stroll today. The more recent invasion threat, that of Hitler's armies, never came to pass, although the dragons' dentures put up across the countryside stood waiting to bite into Nazi tanks.

Linked by a 3-mile promenade along the sea, Hastings and St. Leonards were given a considerable boost in the 19th century by that eminent tripper Queen Victoria, who visited several times. Both towns no longer enjoy such royal patronage; rather, they do a thriving business with Midlanders on vacation. Hastings and St. Leonards have the usual shops and English sea-resort amusements. Only 63 miles from London, they are serviced by fast trains from Victoria Station.

WHAT TO SEE AND DO

Hastings Castle

In ruins now, the first of the Norman castles, Castle Hill Road, West Hill (tel. 0424/722022), to be built in England sprouted up on a western hill overlooking Hastings, circa 1067. Precious little is left to remind us of the days when proud knights, imbued with a spirit of pomp and spectacle, wore bonnets and girdles. The fortress was defortified by King John in 1216, and later served as a church. Owned by the Pelham dynasty from the latter 16th century to modern times, the ruins have been turned over to Hastings. It is open daily from 10am to 5pm from Easter to the end of October. Admission is £1.50 ($2.50) for adults, £1 ($1.65) for children. There is now an audio-visual presentation of the castle's history and the famous battle of 1066. From the mount, you'll have a good view of the coast and promenade.

The Hastings Embroidery

A commemorative work, the Hastings Embroidery was first exhibited in 1966. It is a remarkable achievement that traces 900 years of English history through needlework. Depicted are some of the nation's greatest moments (the Battle of Hastings, the coronation of William the Conqueror) and its legends (Robin Hood). In all, 27 panels, 243 feet in length, depicting 81 historic scenes, are exhibited at the town hall, Queen's Road (tel. 0424/722026). The history of Britain comes alive—the murder of Thomas à Becket, King John signing the Magna Carta, the Black Plague, Chaucer's pilgrims going to Canterbury, the Battle of Agincourt with the victorious Henry V, the War of the Roses, the little princes in the Tower, Bloody Mary's reign, Drake's *Golden Hind,* the arrival of Philip's ill-fated Armada, Guy

Fawkes's gunpowder plot, the sailing of the *Mayflower*, the disastrous plague of 1665 and the great London fire of the following year, Nelson at Trafalgar, the Battle of Waterloo, the Battle of Britain, and the D-Day landings at Normandy. Also exhibited is a scale model of the battlefield at Battle, with William's one-inch men doing in Harold's mini-soldiers. These may be viewed October to May, from 11:30am to 3:30pm Mon. to Fri. June to September hours are 10am to 5pm Mon. to Fri.; 10am to 1pm and 2 to 5pm on Sat. Admission is 85p ($1.40) for adults, 45p (75¢) for children.

A Smuggler's Adventure

You can descend into underground haunts of smugglers in days of yore at **St. Clements Caves,** West Hill (tel. 0424/422964). The caves cover 4 acres of passages, caverns, and secret chambers 60 feet below ground. You descend 140 feet down the monk's walk, a candlelit passage into the depths of the caves. There you'll find an exhibition of costumes, weapons, artifacts, and "tools of the trade," which tell the story of smuggling in the 18th century. More than 50 life-size figures are brought to life. It is open from mid-March until the end of October daily from 10am to 6pm, charging adults £2 ($3.30) and children £1.50 ($2.50).

WHERE TO STAY

The most desirable accommodation at either resort is **Royal Victoria,** Marina, St. Leonards, East Sussex TN38 0BD (tel. 0424/445544). The hotel, constructed in 1829, has the most impressive architecture of any establishment in town. It was long a landmark on the seafront, occupying a formidable position, but it needed complete refurbishing. That was done in 1988, and now Royal Victoria is back to its premier position. The hotel offers 28 well-furnished bedrooms, along with 31 impressive, sometimes regal, suites. Standard singles rent for £60 ($99) daily, with doubles costing £85 ($140.25). Suites cost £85 ($140.25) in a single, £110 ($181.50) in a double. The hotel is attractively furnished and decorated, and bedrooms, each with private bath, contain all the modern amenities such as phones and TVs. The hotel offers some of the best food at the resort in its restaurant, which accepts non-residents who reserve. A table d'hôte lunch costs £12.50 ($20.65), with a set dinner going for £16.50 ($27.25). Service is daily from noon to 1:45pm and 7 to 8:45pm.

On the outskirts, one of the best places to stay in the Hastings-Battle district is **Beauport Park Hotel,** Battle Road (A2100), Hastings, East Sussex TN38 8EA (tel. 0424/851222). The hotel is 3½ miles northwest of Hastings at the junction of A2100 and B2159. It looks much older than it is. It was originally erected as the private estate of General Murray, once the governor of Québec (he had previously served under General Wolfe). However, a fire in 1923 swept over it, and it was later reconstructed in the old style. Run as a hotel with 23 rooms, it is surrounded by beautiful gardens (the Italian-style grounds in the rear contain statuary and flowering shrubbery). The living room and lounge are tastefully furnished, and the French windows in the dining room open onto the parklike rear. The B&B rate is £45 ($74.25) daily in a single, £80 ($132) in a double. All units have private baths with showers, direct-dial phones, and TVs. The hotel offers well prepared and handsomely served cuisine. Some of the produce comes from the hotel's own gardens. A set lunch is featured for £11 ($18.15) at which a varied choice is available. The set dinner is £12 ($19.80), and again the choice is wide.

WHERE TO DINE

The leading restaurant, **Röser's,** 64 Eversfield Place (tel. 0424/712218), is a relief to find in what is often considered one of the gastronomic wastelands of southern England. Most diners come here to enjoy the seafood dishes of Gerald Röser, who shows considerable skill in his choice of food offerings, including everything from the classic Dover sole to lamb from Romney Marsh. In season, game dishes are also featured. The cuisine is French inspired, and service is first rate. A set lunch is good value at £15 ($24.75), but you will more likely spend £25 ($41.25) enjoying the evening's à la carte selections. Service is from noon to 2pm and 7 to 10pm; closed Sat. and Mon. lunch, and all day Sun. The wine list is chosen with discretion, and prices tend to be reasonable, as this is not a resort for big spenders.

11. Battle

Seven miles from Hastings, in the heart of the Sussex countryside, is the old market town of Battle, famed in history as the setting for the Battle of Hastings in 1066. King Harold, last of the Anglo-Saxon kings, encircled by his housecarls, fought bravely, not only for his kingdom but for his life. In the battle, Harold was killed by William, Duke of Normandy, and his body was dismembered. To commemorate the victory, William the Conqueror founded **Battle Abbey** at the south end of Battle High Street (tel. 0426/3792), some of the stone for which was shipped from his own lands at Caen in northern France.

During the dissolution of the monasteries in 1537 by Henry VIII, the church of the abbey was largely destroyed. Some buildings and ruins, however, remain in what Tennyson called "O Garden, blossoming out of English blood." The principal building still standing is the Abbot's House, which is leased to a private school for boys and girls and not open to the general public except in the summer holidays. Of architectural interest is the gatehouse, with its octagonal towers, standing at the top of the Market Square. All of the north Precinct Mall is still standing, and one of the most interesting sights of the ruins is the ancient Dorter Range, where the monks once slept.

The town of Battle grew up around the abbey, but even though it has remained a medieval market town, many of the old half-timbered buildings regrettably have lost much of their original character because of stucco plastering carried on by past generations. The abbey is open mid-April to September 30 daily from 10am to 6pm (closes at 4pm the rest of the year). Admission is £1.70 ($2.80) for adults and 85p ($1.40) for children.

WHERE TO STAY

Standing in 30 acres of parkland, **Netherfield Place,** Netherfield Road, Battle, East Sussex TN33 9PP (tel. 04246/4455), built in 1924, is 1¾ miles outside Battle on the A2100, and it's by far the best place to stay. The symmetrical wings of this brick-fronted Georgian mansion extend toward flowering gardens on all sides. Once you pass beneath the cornices of the entrance, you'll discover a world of plush upholstery, comfortable bedrooms, and sun-flooded panoramas. You can enjoy tea or a drink in the glassed-in lounge overlooking the trees outside. The hotel offers 13 cozy bedrooms, each with fully carpeted private bath or shower, attractive wallpaper, tasteful curtains, phone, and TV. The costs begin at £50 ($82.50) daily in a single, £75 ($123.75) in a double. The food is also good and carefully served, prepared with fresh, wholesome produce. Fresh fruit and vegetables come from the hotel's garden. Dinners cost from £17.50 ($28.90).

George Hotel, 23 High St., Battle, East Sussex TN33 0EA (tel. 04246/4466), is an old coaching inn in the center of historic Battle near Battle Abbey. An inn has stood on this site for more than 600 years, and today the George combines modern comfort and a historic, listed building. Yolanda and Dennis Laybourne, the resident owners, have 21 bedrooms, all with private baths, phones, TVs, and hot beverage facilities. Prices, with a continental breakfast included, are £33 ($54.45) daily in singles, £40 ($66) to £43 ($70.95) in doubles. The traditional four-poster bedroom rents for £47 ($77.55) per night. Sat. and Sun. breaks are offered, with £29.50 ($48.90) per person for dinner, bed and breakfast. The hotel has a comfortable bar, with a full snack menu. Open log fires make the place cozy in winter. The spacious restaurant features English and continental dishes. Lunch costs £5.50 ($9.10), and dinner, from £11 ($18.15). There is a private parking area.

WHERE TO DINE

Once a smithy for the village and the 11th-century manor house, the **Blacksmith's Restaurant**, 43 High St. (tel. 04246/3200), is in an oak-beamed building dating back to the 15th century. Owned by Martin and Christine Howe, the restaurant they have created here since 1981 has become a much-talked-of place. Martin was head chef at London's well-known Gay Hussar for 14 years before finding this location in Battle when he felt the need for a place of his own. The result is an informal, low-windowed restaurant with wheel-back chairs and gleaming silver, decorated with antique blacksmith's tools.

There is a small bar where Christine or one of the pleasant local women will take your order from the à la carte menu, costing £14 ($23.10) to £28 ($29.70) for dinner. I sampled roast duck Blacksmith's style, crispy and coated with honey, served with cherry sauce accompanied by vegetables, and finished off with a homemade dessert from the trolley. The meal was not only a delight, but reasonably priced for the generous portions served. Tues. to Fri., a two-course lunch is offered for just £5.50 ($9.10), and a set dinner costs £12.50 ($20.65). Lunch is served noon to 2:30pm Tues. to Fri. and Sun., and dinner is offered 7 to 10:30pm Tues. to Sat. You must reserve a table.

KIPLING'S HOME IN SUSSEX

Rudyard Kipling, the British writer famous for his stories about the days of empire in India, lived his last 34 years—1902 to 1936—at **Bateman's,** a country house half a mile south of Burwash, on the A265, the Lewes-Etchingham road (tel. 0435/882302). The sandstone house, built in 1634, was bequeathed, together with its 300 acres of land and its contents, to the National Trust by Kipling's widow. East and West meet within the house, in Oriental rugs, antique bronzes, and other mementos the writer collected in India and elsewhere. Kipling's library is among the points of interest to be visited. The house is open from April to the end of October from 11am to 6pm Sat. to Wed.; closed Thurs. and Fri. (last admissions at 5:30pm). Admission to the house, a restored watermill, and the attractive garden is £2.80 ($4.60) for adults, £1.40 ($2.30) for children Mon. to Wed., and £3.20 ($5.30) for adults, £1.60 ($2.65) for children on Sat., Sun. and bank holidays.

---

12. Alfriston and Lewes

Nestled on the Cuckmere River, **Alfriston** is one of the most beautiful villages of England. Its High Street, with its old market cross, looks like one's fantasy of what an English village should be. Some of the old houses still have hidden chambers where smugglers stored their loot. Alfriston has several old inns.

During the day Alfriston is likely to be overrun by coach tours (it's that lovely, and that popular). The village lies about 60 miles from London, northeast of Seaford on the English Channel, in the general vicinity of the resort of Eastbourne and the modern port of Newhaven.

You can visit **Drusilla's Zoo Park** (tel. 0323/870234), off the A27. This zoo has won awards. It is not large, but fascinating nonetheless, with a flamingo lake, Japanese garden, and unusual breeds of some domestic animals, among other attractions. Children are especially delighted, as there is a playland covering more than an acre. An English Wine and Food Centre is also part of the complex. The park is open from late March until October daily from 10am to 5pm (until dusk in winter), charging adults £3.75 ($6.20) and children £3.50 ($5.80).

Only about a dozen miles along the A27 toward Brighton lies **Lewes,** an ancient Sussex town worth exploring. Centered in the South Downs, Lewes is 51 miles from London. Since the home of the Glyndebourne Opera is only 5 miles to the east, the accommodations of Lewes are often frequented by cultured guests and are difficult during the Glyndebourne Opera festival, but adequate at other times.

The county town has many historical associations, listing such residents as Thomas Paine who lived at Bull House, High Street, now a restaurant. The half-timbered **Anne of Cleves House** Southover High St. (tel. 0273/474610), so named because it formed part of that queen's divorce settlement from Henry VIII, is now a museum of local history and is cared for by the Sussex Archaeological Society. (Anne of Cleves never lived in the Anne of Cleves House, and there is no proof that she ever visited Lewes.) The museum has a furnished bedroom and kitchen and displays of furniture, local history, the Wealden iron industry, and other local crafts. It is on Southover High Street and is open April to October from 10am to 5pm Mon. to Sat., from 2 to 5pm Sun. Admission is £1.50 ($2.50) for adults, 75p ($1.25) for children.

Lewes, of course, grew up around its Norman castle. From the tower you can obtain a fine view of the countryside. To visit **Lewes Castle and Museum of Sussex Archaeology,** at Westgate (tel. 0273/474379), a joint ticket costs adults £1.50 ($2.50); children 75p ($1.25). The castle and museum are open all year from 10am to 5:30pm Mon. to Sat. (also on Sun., April to October, from 2 to 5:30pm).

WHERE TO STAY AND DINE IN ALFRISTON

The most desirable place to stay is **Deans Place,** Alfriston, Polegate, East Sussex, BN26 5TW (tel. 0323/870248), a historic country home with a modern wing set on its own 5 acres of grounds, with a swimming pool and tennis courts. On the banks of the Cuckmere River, the house lies about 5 miles from the coast. Lounges are spacious and comfortable. Each of the 40 bedrooms is attractively decorated and furnished, with private bath, phone, beverage-making equipment, hairdryer, and TV. Robin and Noori Hilton are the thoughtful hosts, welcoming guests at the rate of £49 ($80.85) to £54 ($89.10) daily in a single, the tariff going up to £79 ($130.35) to £86 ($141.90) in a double. Bar lunches are excellent at midday, and a set dinner is offered for only £13.50 ($22.30), plus an à la carte selection as well.

White Lodge Country House Hotel, Sloe Lane, Alfriston, East Sussex BN26 5UR (tel. 0323/870265). For some 20 years Don and Maureen Denyer lived within its Edwardian-era walls with their children. It was their private home. But in 1984, three weeks after Don retired from a career as a property developer, they transformed their home into one of the most opulently furnished hotels in the region. It stands on 5 acres of gardens, about a five-minute walk from the center. The public rooms are outfitted like French salons, with carved 18th- and 19th-century antiques, many of them gilded. Bronze statues inspired by classical Greek myths are placed about. The daytime dining room is French with Louis XV furniture, centered around a chiseled fireplace of violet-tinged marble. Dinner is served below the reception area in an Edwardian room. A four-course lunch, served daily from 12:15 to 2pm, goes for £9.95 ($16.40); a four-course dinner, from 7:15 to 9:45pm, costs £14.95 ($24.65). Menu specialties, prepared by chefs, include cornets of smoked salmon, grilled lemon sole, and in season, marinated venison. Each of the 20 beautifully furnished bedrooms has a private bath, color TV, hairdryer, phone, lots of flounced and tasseled curtains, and countryside views. Singles rent for £50 ($82.50) daily and doubles or twins from £75 ($123.75).

Star Inn, High Street, Alfriston, East Sussex BN26 5TA (tel. 0323/870495), occupies a building dating from 1450, although it was originally founded in the 1200s, perhaps to house pilgrims en route to Chichester and the shrine of St. Richard. In the center of the village, its carved front still unchanged, it boasts an overhanging second story of black and white timbers and bay windows. The lounges are on several levels, a forest of old timbers. Out back is a motel wing, with studio rooms, all of which have private baths. Each of the 35 rooms has a radio, phone, TV, heating, and built-in wardrobe. A single costs £60 ($99) daily, and a double or twin goes for £82 ($135.30). These rates include VAT and service. A three-course dinner is priced from £12.50 ($20.65).

Moonrakers, High Street (tel. 0323/870472), offers the best food in town. The welcome is warm at this charming little 16th-century restaurant with old beams and a well-prepared cuisine where a homemade taste is emphasized. Elaine Wilkinson is the chef, and she operates the restaurant with her husband, Barry. The menu is changed every few weeks, so I can't recommend specific dishes with any guarantee that they will be served. Fresh fish appears frequently on the menu, and duck dishes are prepared with flair. Count yourself lucky if you're there on the night Elaine decides to prepare beef Wellington. Fresh herbs are used discreetly. A set dinner is served for £17.50 ($28.90). Dinner only is served from 7 to 9pm Tues. to Sat. (slightly later on Sat.). The Moonrakers' wine list is the finest in town. Its annual closing is from mid-January to mid-February, and reservations are essential.

WHERE TO STAY AND DINE IN LEWES

Dating back to 1526. **Shelleys Hotel,** High Street, Lewes, East Sussex BN7 1XS (tel. 0273/472361) is a manor house owned by the earl of Dorset before it was sold to the Shelley family, distant relatives of the poet. Radical changes were made to the architecture in the 18th century. Nowadays, the standards of the management are reflected in the fine antiques, the bowls of flowers, the paintings and prints, the well-kept gardens, and most important, the staff. In the rear is a sun terrace and lawn for tea and drinks. Horse chestnuts and copper beech shade the grounds. The central hall is characterized by Ionic columns, a domed ceiling, and the coat-of-arms of the Shelley family. The bay windows of the front drawing room open onto the rear gardens, and the lounge is paneled. The 21 bedrooms are personal, individually furnished, usually spacious, and most comfortable, with private baths or showers, phones, and TVs. Singles with shower cost from £57.50 ($49.90) daily; doubles with bath/shower, £110 ($181.50). Service and VAT are included in all charges. Room 11 has a 16th-century frieze of Bacchanalian figures and a design of entwining grapes and flowers. You can order meals at Shelleys.

Kenwards, Pipe Passage, 151A High St. (tel. 0273/472343), stands near the Bull House where Thomas Paine lived. It's across the street, a stone-and-brick building reached by a very narrow passage. John and Caroline Kenward welcome you into their little enclave, which is a converted mid-16th-century brewery. In fair weather, you can enjoy a drink in their garden. Under a beamed ceiling, you can later partake of their menu, which uses only fresh seasonal produce. The chef's talent is reflected in such dishes as venison with juniper berries and chicken with orange and coriander. The lemon sole is always reliable. The menu is small, but as Spencer Tracy said of Katharine Hepburn, "it's choice." You can order one of their "surprises" for dessert. The wine list is reasonably priced. A meal is likely to cost from £25 ($41.25) per person. Hours are noon to 2:15pm and 7:30 to 9pm (until 9:30pm on Sat.); closed lunch Sat., dinner Mon., and all day Sun.

---

13. Brighton and Hove

In 1753, when Dr. Russell propounded the seawater cure—even to the point of advocating the drinking of an "oceanic cocktail"—he launched a movement that was to change the life of the average English person, at least his or her vacation plans. Brighton, 53 miles south of London, was one of the first of the great seaside resorts of Europe. The village on the sea from which the present town grew was named Brighthelmstone, and the English eventually shortened it to Brighton.

The original swinger who was to shape so much of its destiny arrived in 1783, after just turning voting age; he was the then prince of Wales, whose presence and patronage gave immediate status to the seaside town.

Fashionable dandies from London, including Beau Brummell, turned up. The construction business boomed, as Brighton blossomed with charming and attractive townhouses, well-planned squares, and crescents. From the prince regent's title came the voguish word "Regency," which was to characterize an era, but it more specifically refers to the period between 1811 and 1820. Under Victoria, and in spite of her cutting off the patronage of her presence, Brighton continued to flourish.

Alas, in this century, as the English began to discover more glamorous spots on the continent, Brighton lost much of its old joie de vivre. It became more aptly tabbed as tatty, featuring the usual run of fun-fair-type English seaside amusements ("let's go down to Brighton, ducky"). Happily, that state of affairs has changed, owing largely to the huge numbers of Londoners moving in (some of whom have taken to commuting, as Brighton lies only one hour with frequent train service from Victoria Station). The invasion is making Brighton increasingly light-hearted and sophisticated. A beach east of the town attracts nude bathers, Britain's first such venture. Introduction of real-life attractions of the flesh has certainly made passé such pictorial representations as were once the big draw on penny machines by the seafront. These, however, still clank and grind away in a museum, where you can take a trip back in time by means of an old penny purchased at the museum's kiosk.

The Lanes, a closely knit section of alleyways off North Street in Brighton (many of the present shops were formerly fishermen's cottages), were frequented in Victoria's day by style-setting curio and antique collectors. Some are still there, although sharing space with boutiques.

At **Hove,** once a separate town but now a part of the Greater Brighton complex, of special interest is the **Engineerium,** in a building that used to house a waterworks. Here you can see a little steam launch, models of engines and steam trucks, old motorbikes, and the Victorian waterworks kept in operative condition.

THE ROYAL PAVILION

Among the royal residences of Europe, the Pavilion at Brighton (tel. 0273/603005), a John Nash version of an Indian mogul's palace, is unique. Ornate and exotic, it has been subjected over the years to the most devastating wit of English satirists and pundits. But today we can examine it more objectively as an outstanding example of the orientalizing tendencies of the romantic movement.

Originally the pavilion was built in 1787 by Henry Holland. By the time Nash had transformed it from a simple classical villa into an Oriental fantasy, the prince regent had become King George IV. He and one of his mistresses, Lady Conyngham, lived in the palace until 1827.

A decade passed before Victoria, then queen, arrived in Brighton. Although she was to bring Albert and the children on a number of occasions, the monarch and Brighton just didn't mix. The very air of the resort seemed too flippant for her—and the latter-day sea-bathing disciples of Dr. Russell trailed Victoria as if she were a stage actress. By 1845 Victoria began packing, and the royal furniture was carted off. Its tenants gone, the pavilion was in serious peril of being torn down. By a narrow vote, Brightonians agreed to purchase it. Gradually, it is being restored to its former splendor, enhanced in no small part by the return of much of its original furniture on loan by the present tenant at Buckingham Palace.

Of exceptional interest is the domed **Banqueting Hall,** with a chandelier of bronze dragons supporting lily-like glass globes. In the Great Kitchen, with its old revolving spits, is a collection of Wellington's pots and pans, his *batterie de cuisine,* from his townhouse at Hyde Park Corner. In the State Apartments, particularly the domed Salon, dragons wink at you, serpents entwine, lacquered doors shine. The Music Room, with its scalloped ceiling, is a salon of water lilies, flying dragons, sunflowers, reptilian paintings, bamboo, silk, and satin.

In the second-floor gallery, look for Nash's views of the pavilion in its elegant heyday. There is also an exhibition of pavilion history, illustrating the damage caused by rainwater, frequent alterations, and the impressive program of repair and reclamation in progress. Currently, the Royal Pavilion is undergoing an extensive program of structural and decorative restoration. This inevitably results in occasional inconvenience to visitors, although the work is, in its own right, absolutely fascinating. The pavilion is open daily October to May from 10am to 5pm, June to September to 6pm; closed Christmas and Boxing Day. Admission is £2.60 ($4.30) for adults, £1.30 ($2.15) for children 5 to 15. A family ticket for one adult and up to four children costs £3.90 ($6.45), for two adults and up to four children £6.50 ($10.75).

SEEING BRIGHTON

A walking tour costs £1.50 ($2.50) for adults, £1 ($1.65) for children. Tours are offered from March to December, but hours are subject to change. For times and places of departure, consult the **Tourist Information Centre,** Marlborough House, 54 Old Steine (tel. 0273/23755), by the Royal Albion Hotel and the bus terminal. Here you can also make reservations for accommodations, reserve tickets for National Express coaches, and pick up a list of current events.

WHERE TO STAY

Dozens of accommodations are to be found in all price ranges. Regrettably, many are establishments, to quote Norman Mailer, "where elderly retired India colonels brood through dinner. . . ." However, that situation is changing now, as the most celebrated relics of yesteryear are experiencing (or have experienced) extensive overhauling. I'll survey the leading hotels, then proceed to a representative sampling of the accommodations awaiting those who must keep expenses trimmed.

Expensive Hotels

The Grand, Kings Road, Brighton, East Sussex BN1 2FW (tel. 0273/21188), is the premier hotel of Brighton. The original Grand was constructed in 1864, and in time entertained some of the most eminent of the Victorians and the Edwardians. This landmark was massively damaged following a terrorist attack on Margaret Thatcher and key figures in the British government. Several colleagues were killed, Mrs. Thatcher narrowly escaped, and entire sections of the hotel looked as if hit by an air raid. That gave its present owners, De Vere Hotels, the challenge to create a new Grand rising from the ashes. Frankly, the new one is better than the old one. It's the most elegant Georgian re-creation in town.

You enter via a glassed-in conservatory and register in public rooms of grandiose proportions, with soaring ceilings and elaborate moldings. The hotel has plushly comfortable furniture in traditional tastes with well-chosen accessories. The 163 rooms, of a very high standard, from a single to the presidential suite, are generally spacious with many amenities, including private baths, color TVs, radios, direct-dial phones, air conditioning, hospitality trays, trouser presses, and hairdryers. A special feature, the sea-view rooms contain mini-bars. There are also units designed for "lady executives," as well as "romantic rooms" with double whirlpool baths. Thoughtfully, some accommodations have been provided with additional facilities for the disabled. Singles rent for £105 ($173.25) daily, and doubles or twins go for £145 ($239.25) to £199 ($328.35), including a full English breakfast and VAT. Hobden's Health Spa is complete with spa pool, steamroom, sauna, solarium, and massage and exercise arena. There is also a hairdressing salon and beautician. Both British and continental cuisine are served in King's Restaurant. The food uses superb ingredients masterfully handled by the kitchen staff. The Victoria Bar is an elegant rendezvous, and Midnight Blues is considered the most sophisticated club at the resort.

Hospitality Inn, King's Road, Brighton, East Sussex BN1 2GS (tel. 0273/206700), is one of the finest accommodations in the south of England. Rising from the seafront, it has been stylishly and often rather luxuriously designed for maximum comfort. Guests wander at leisure through an array of tastefully furnished public rooms, complete with a well-decorated bar lounge. The hotel is perhaps the best equipped in the town, certainly for the athletic, with a gym, an indoor swimming pool, along with a solarium and sauna. Several thoughtful extras with today's modern client in mind were added, including a laundry service and a coffee shop that remains open until 11pm for late arrivals. In all, 204 well-furnished and attractively decorated bedrooms are rented, each with private shower and bath. The air-conditioned bedrooms, which offer mini-bars, TVs, and phones, cost from £99 ($163.35) daily in a single, rising to £119 ($196.35) in a double. Its restaurant, La

Noblesse, is outstanding, and merits a separate recommendation. The Promenade restaurant, overlooking the sea, has an imaginative and well-planned menu. Non-residents can enjoy meals in the restaurants from noon to 2pm and 7 to 11pm; closed Sun.

Brighton Metropole, King's Road, Brighton, East Sussex BN1 2FU (tel. 0273/775432), rises in a neo-Romanesque, redbrick style from a central location on the seafront. The lobby is in a neutral modern style, and the 328 recently refurbished and luxurious bedrooms offer such amenities as private baths and showers, color TVs, radios, direct-dial phones, in-house movies, hairdryers, trouser presses, and tea and coffee makers. Singles cost £99 ($163.35) daily, and doubles and twins go for £130 ($214.50). The hotel also offers 16 suites. On the premises is a leisure club, including an indoor swimming pool, plus an array of dining and drinking facilities, among them the Arundel and Windsor restaurants, the Canon Pub, and the Metro Night Club.

Queens Hotel, 1-5 King's Rd., Brighton, East Sussex BN1 1NS (tel. 0273/21222), one of Brighton's most prestigious hotels, occupies possibly the finest position on the seafront, reputedly on the site of Sake Deen Mahomet's "Indian Vapour Baths," where the first Turkish baths in Britain stood and where the word shampoo originated. This first-class hotel became famous in the 19th century and has had many distinguished guests, even royalty. Each of the 90 bedrooms has a private bath/shower, color TV with in-house movies, radio, direct-dial phone, mini-bar, hairdryer, and personalized safe. Rates are from £75 ($123.75) daily in a single, £95 ($156.75) in a twin or double. Tariffs include a full English breakfast and VAT. Weekend tariff is from £55 ($90.75) per person daily for dinner, bed and breakfast. The sea-facing restaurant offers table d'hôte and à la carte menus. Snacks are also available all day in the Atrium lounge. Hotel facilities include Royales Health Club with pool, Jacuzzi, mini-gym, sunbeds, massage, and Turkish bath. There are numerous places of interest within minutes of the hotel, including the Royal Pavilion.

Moderately Priced Hotels

Granville Hotel, 125 King's Rd., Brighton, East Sussex BN1 2FA (tel. 0273/26302), on Brighton's seafront, offers views over the West Pier and the channel. The 25-room hotel has a black-and-white reception area and lounge reminiscent of Raffles Hotel in Singapore, complete with an elevator and a restaurant. The bedrooms are all comfortably furnished, and some can even be called luxurious. For example, the Granville Room has a handmade, four-poster, antique double bed, sea views, and private bathroom with a double Grecian bath. You may even have a room with a family-size Jacuzzi. Decor by Laura Ashley and Mary Quant appears throughout the hotel. All the units have color TVs, radios, and phones. Singles rent from £50 ($82.50) daily, with doubles ranging from £70 ($115.50) to £95 ($156.75). The hotel's Trogs Restaurant is previewed below.

Old Ship Hotel, King's Road, Brighton, East Sussex BN1 1NR (tel. 0273/29001), in a central position on the seafront, has a paneled interior with comfortable sea-view lounges, an oak-paneled bar, and a spacious sea-facing restaurant that, naturally, specializes in seafood. A well-organized kitchen serves good-tasting meals with selections from an impressive wine list. Each of the 150 accommodations has a color TV, radio, direct-dial phone, and full private bath. Singles cost £70 ($115.50) daily; doubles, £90 ($148.50). All tariffs include an English breakfast and VAT. In 1651 the owner of an earlier manifestation of this hotel saved the life of King Charles II by spiriting him away in his ship. In the Regency heyday, the old ship attracted the Brighton beaumonde.

Budget Hotels

Twenty-One Hotel, 21 Charlotte St., Marine Parade, Brighton, East Sussex BN2 1AG (tel. 0273/686450), is one of the most sophisticated—perhaps the most sophisticated—of the smaller hotels of Brighton. Janet and David Power rent only seven bedrooms in this early-Victorian, white-fronted house a block from the sea. Five of their attractive and well-furnished bedrooms contain private showers and toilets, and all units offer color TVs, direct-dial phones, radios, and hot beverage facilities. Each accommodation has a different color scheme, often in green, pink, or terra-cotta. The basement-level garden suite opens directly onto an ivy-clad courtyard. Singles rent for £35 ($57.75) to £45 ($74.25) daily and doubles go for £45 ($74.25) to £65 ($107.25), including VAT, breakfast, and service. A menu dégustation of four courses, costing £22 ($36.30), is written in French and translated into English. Main courses are likely to include such subtle dishes as sliced breast of duck served pink with a lime sauce or wild poached salmon with fine strips of vegetables. Reservations are essential.

Topps Hotel, 17 Regency Sq., Brighton, East Sussex BN1 2FG (tel. 0273/ 729334), enjoys a diagonal view of the sea from its position beside the sloping lawn of Regency Square. Flower boxes fill the windows of this cream-colored townhouse, whose owners, Paul and Pauline Collins, have devoted years to upgrading it. The establishment contains 12 rooms, all with private baths. Each accommodation is of a different shape and is furnished individually, sometimes with neo-Elizabethan furniture and early 19th-century moldings. Each contains a TV, radio, mini-bar, phone, and trouser press. The hotel charges £39 ($64.35) daily in a single and £65 ($107.25) to £85 ($140.25) in a double, with an English breakfast and VAT included. A small restaurant in the basement serves dinners to clients who reserve by room. Closed during Christmas and the first week in January.

Regency Hotel, 28 Regency Sq., Brighton, East Sussex BN1 2FH (tel. 0275/ 202690), is a typical Regency townhouse built in 1820 with bow windows, a canopied balcony, and a porticoed entrance. The current owners, Mr. and Mrs. Ambrose Simons, have retained the original character of the house while incorporating modern comforts. They rent 14 bedrooms, each with color TV, phone, radio, hairdryer, and tea and coffee maker. Ten have a private shower and toilet, and several of the rooms open onto views across the grassy square and out to sea. The best accommodation, the Regency Suite, has a half-tester bed, complete bath, antique furniture, and a sea-fronting balcony. The public rooms have fireplaces, fine cornices, and paneled doors. Singles rent from £28 ($46.20) to £35 ($57.75) daily, with doubles costing £48 ($79.20) to £58 ($95.70), including tax and a full English breakfast. There is also a licensed bar.

WHERE TO DINE

In a well-preserved, 19th-century building conveniently opening into The Lanes, **English's Oyster Bar and Seafood Restaurant,** 29-31 East St. (tel. 0273/ 27980), is my leading choice for superbly cooked fish. It combines an inviting setting with good food. For years diners have been making such wise selections as half a dozen Colchester native oysters or a hot seafood en croûte with lobster sauce. The chef is known for such specialties as Dover sole and fresh, locally caught plaice. He also offers a seasonal menu, which is available for lunch and dinner every day. You're given a selection of appetizers, plus a choice from at least six main courses. Expect to spend from £18 ($29.70) if you order à la carte. Open noon to 10:15pm Mon. to Sat., 12:30 to 4pm Sun.

Langan's Bistro, 1 Paston Place (tel. 0273/606933), is the latest—and most welcome branch—of this mini-chain of restaurants, which gained fame for its trio of restaurants in London (of which the actor Michael Caine is co-owner). The welcome venture onto the Brighton scene has improved the restaurant lineup here considerably. A meal at Brighton's version of Langan's is not unlike the taste experience you'll sample across the Channel in France. The menu is wisely limited, but it's based on the freshest of ingredients available at the market. You might, for example, begin with a salad made from tiger prawns and scallops, then follow with halibut meunière or a gigot of perfectly done lamb. Desserts are often sumptuous, as reflected by the Grand Marnier-and-orange-flavored crème brûlée. Meals cost £20 ($33), except for the set lunch on Sun. at £12.50 ($20.65). Open 12:30 to 2:30pm and 7:30 to 10:30pm; closed lunch Sat., dinner Sun., all day Mon. Closed for two weeks in August.

La Noblesse, Hospitality Inn, King's Road (tel. 0273/206700), is the flagship restaurant of this previously recommended hotel. The chefs are in fine form, as reflected in their menu of classic dishes, relying on such expensive ingredients as smoked salmon, langoustines, foie gras (can be pan fried with ginger and mango), and oysters. The elegant surroundings in pink, blue, and brass form a proper backdrop for this "night out on the town" choice for Brighton. A continental staff is perfectly trained, serving such dishes as rack of lamb roasted à point (served with morels) and smoked goose breast served on a bed of citrus. The sauces are generally excellent, cooked to bring out natural flavors. Vegetarian meals, such as a vegetable stir-fry medley, are also available. The set lunch is excellent value at £18.50 ($30.55) with a table d'hôte dinner costing £30 ($49.50) including service. Otherwise, you can easily spend £35 ($57.75) ordering à la carte. Meals are served noon to 2:30pm and 7pm to 12:30am; closed lunch Sat., all day Sun. Reservations are always necessary. Wear your "Brighton best" outfit here.

Old Ship Hotel Restaurant, Old Ship Hotel, King's Road (tel. 0273/29001), is a long-enduring favorite with premises opening onto the waterfront, an ideal location. Whenever possible, locally caught fish appears on the menu. Try such dishes as moules marinière (mussels) or fresh salmon from Scotland grilled with saffron. Vegetables, which accompany main dishes, are always fresh and cooked "new style." Sometimes local dishes such as turkey from Sussex appear on the menu but with a French sauce. The best value here is the table d'hôte menu offered at £17.50 ($28.90); otherwise, you'll spend from £25 ($41.25) ordering à la carte. Service is daily, open 12:30 to 2:30pm and 7 to 9:30pm Sun. to Thurs., 12:30 to 2:30pm and 7 to 10pm Fri. and Sat. The wine list is excellent, and reservations are a good idea. Stop in the adjoining pub for a pre- or post-dinner drink.

La Marinade, 77 St. George's Rd., Kemp Town (tel. 0273/600992), is a French restaurant whose cuisine is inspired by the regions of Normandy and Brittany. A two-story restaurant, La Marinade offers a menu showing a certain subtle sophistication in cookery. You get a good range of sensitively cooked dishes, where care has been taken to preserve natural flavors. The white butter sauce, for example, on my recently sampled fish dish was just as good as that served in the Loire Valley. The set lunch menu for £10 ($16.50) is one of the best food values of Brighton. However, should you visit for dinner, count on spending from £20 ($33) à la carte unless you order the table d'hôte dinner for £13.50 ($22.30). Open noon to 2pm and 7:15 to 10pm; closed lunch Sat., dinner Sun., and all day Mon.

China Garden, 88 Preston St. (tel. 0273/25124). The menu is large and satisfying to most diners, and you can eat almost any time—that is, from noon to 11:30pm daily. Dim sum (a popular luncheon choice), however, is offered only until 4pm. Try such dishes as chicken feet in a black-bean sauce, duck's web and mixed meat, perhaps sliced pork Szechuan style. A set dinner is excellent value at £11.50 ($18.15), or you can order à la carte at £20 ($33) per person.

WHERE TO STAY IN HOVE

The leading hotel is **The Dudley,** Lansdowne Place, Hove, Brighton, East Sussex BN3 1HQ (tel. 0273/736266), set near the seafront just a few blocks from the resort's bronze statue of Queen Victoria. Going up marble steps, you register at a carved mahogany desk in the Chippendale style beneath crystal chandeliers and within view of 18th-century antiques and oil portraits of Edwardian-era debutantes. The large and high-ceilinged public rooms emphasize the deeply comfortable chairs, the thick cove moldings, and the chandeliers. The hotel was created when three neighboring houses, each built with bow-fronted facades in the 1820s, were combined into one unit. A bar precedes the entrance to the dining room, where candles and paneling add to the allure of the British and international cuisine. The 80 bedrooms contain private baths, color TVs, radios, phones, and coffee-making equipment, along with high ceilings, tall windows, and conservatively stylish furniture. Depending on the accommodation, singles cost from £65 ($107.25) daily, and doubles or twins go for £85 ($140.25).

Alexandra Hotel, 42 Brunswick Terrace, Hove, Brighton, East Sussex BN3 1HA (tel. 0273/202722), was built in 1830 at the height of the Regency period.

On the Hove seafront, it was at the heart of the Brunswick Estate, which was a small cluster of residences for "people of quality." Before being established as a hotel by a special act of Parliament, the structure at this address was the home of the exiled Austrian diplomat, Prince Metternich. It was one of the first houses in England to have hot and cold running water. The hotel has been fully modernized without detracting from its period atmosphere, with care taken to restore windows and exterior ironwork in the Regency style. Each of the 60 bedrooms has a private bath, color TV, radio and alarm clock, direct-dial phone, tea and coffee maker, hairdryer, and central heating. Many rooms enjoy sea views. A single costs £55 ($90.75) daily, while a double or twin goes for £75 ($123.75), including service and VAT. You can enjoy choice Sussex ale in Alex's Bar and have meals, English or continental cuisine, in the 1830 Restaurant, with its Regency ambience, from noon to 2pm and 7 to 10pm daily. A table d'hôte luncheon costs around £8 ($13.20), with dinner from £11 ($18.15).

Sackville Hotel, 189 Kingsway, Hove, Brighton, East Sussex BN3 4GU (tel. 0273/736292). Its lime and cream-colored, neo-baroque facade was built across the road from the beach in 1902. Today, in a comfortably updated form, it welcomes visitors into a high-ceilinged collection of bedrooms with big windows, sea views, and an assortment of Queen Anne furnishings. Each of the 45 bedrooms contains a private bath, color TV, phone, radio, and reminders of yesteryear. Singles rent for £55 ($90.75) to £65 ($107.25) daily, and doubles go for £70 ($115.50) to £80 ($132). A few units have terraces. A large ground-floor dining room offers a warmly masculine kind of formality with views of the sea and good service and food. An adjacent bar, Winston's, is filled with photographs of Churchill in war and peace.

Courtlands Hotel, 19-27 The Drive, Brighton, East Sussex BN3 3JE (tel. 0273/731055), lies 400 yards from the sea, opening onto the wide thoroughfare known as "The Drive," about a mile from the center of Brighton. It is a comfortable Victorian building, recently modernized, with 53 rooms, all with private baths or showers, phones, and color TVs. This includes units in the Courtlands complex—five particularly agreeable rooms with mini-bars in the cottage and coach-house annex. Bedrooms are spacious and harmonious, with prices set according to plumbing. Rates include a full English breakfast, service, and VAT. Singles cost £52 ($85.80) daily. Doubles rent for £71 ($117.15) to £87 ($143.55). This traditional hotel has more than adequate facilities, including the Golden Dolphin lounge bar and a dining room opening onto gardens. A good cuisine, both international and English, is assured. The hotel has a small children's playground, a solarium, and a heated swimming pool, as well as a games room, and adequate parking.

14. Arundel

This small town in West Sussex, only 58 miles from London, 4 miles from the English Channel, nestles at the foot of one of England's most spectacular castles. The town was once an Arun River port, its denizens enjoying the prosperity of considerable trade and commerce. The harbor traffic is gone, replaced by buses filled with visitors who come to visit the castle.

WHAT TO SEE AND DO

The ancestral home of the dukes of Norfolk, **Arundel Castle** (tel. 0903/883136) is a much-restored mansion of considerable importance. Its legend is associated with some of the great families of England—the Fitzalans and the powerful Howards of Norfolk.

Over the years Arundel Castle suffered destruction, particularly during the Civil War when Cromwell's troops stormed its walls, perhaps in retaliation for the 14th earl of Arundel's (Thomas Howard) sizable contribution to Charles I. In the early 18th century the castle virtually had to be rebuilt. In late Victorian times it was remodeled and extensively restored again. Today it is filled, as you'd expect, with a good collection of antiques, along with an assortment of paintings by old masters such as Van Dyck and Gainsborough.

The castle is open from April 1 to the last Fri. in October, 1 to 5pm Sun. to Fri., opening at noon in June, July, August, and on bank holidays. Last admission is at 4pm; closed Sat. Admission is £3.50 ($5.80) for adults, £2.20 ($3.65) for children 5 to 15 years of age. Surrounding the castle is a 1,100-acre park (scenic highlight: Swanbourne Lake).

In a Georgian cottage in the heart of historic Arundel, the **Arundel Toy and Military Museum** at "Doll's House," 23 High St. (tel. 0903/882908), displays an intriguing family collection spanning many generations of old toys and games, small militaria, dolls, dollhouses, tin toys, musical toys, stuffed bears and frogs, Britain's animals and soldiers, arks, boats, rocking horses, crested military models, an eggcup collection, and other curiosities. Open most days from Easter to October (in winter, Sat. and Sun. only), or it may be seen at any time by arrangement. Admission is £1 ($1.65) for adults, 75p ($1.25) for children. The museum is opposite Treasure House Antiques and Collectors Market.

Arundel Cathedral (the Cathedral of Our Lady and St. Philip Howard), London Road (tel. 0903/882297), stands at the highest point in town. A Roman Catholic cathedral, it was constructed for the 15th duke of Norfolk by A. J. Hansom, who invented the Hansom taxi. However, it was not consecrated as a cathedral until 1965. The interior includes the shrine of St. Philip Howard, featuring Sussex wrought ironwork. Admission is free; it is open daily from 9am to 6pm (closes at dusk in winter). Donations are appreciated.

WHERE TO STAY AND DINE

A former Georgian coaching inn in the center of town, the **Norfolk Arms,** 22 High St., Arundel, West Sussex BN18 9AD (tel. 0903/882101), is just a short walk from the castle. The lounges and dining room are in the typically English country-inn style—that is, unostentatious but unquestionably comfortable. The hotel has been restored with many modern amenities blending with the old architecture. The bedrooms are handsomely maintained and furnished, each with personal touches. All rooms have private bathrooms, color TVs, and phones. It is a moderately priced place, with a B&B rate of £44 ($72.60) daily for singles, £65 ($107.25) for doubles. In the restaurant you can order good English cooking with a luncheon for £9 ($14.85). When available, fresh local produce is offered. You can also dine on a specialty menu for £13 ($21.45), which includes many traditional English dishes.

Pogey's, 25 Tarrant St. (tel. 0903/882222), has brought new life and vitality to what had traditionally been considered a dull restaurant town. In an art deco setting with chrome, you get English food with a flair here. Perhaps lamb with red currant sauce will be featured or magret of duckling in an orange and Cointreau sauce. Try, if offered, suprême of chicken with an asparagus and sweet corn sauce. Full à la carte meals cost from £10 ($16.50) to £20 ($33). A fixed price lunch, when offered, goes for £6 ($9.90) Tues. to Sat., going up to £8 ($13.20) on Sun. Open noon to 3pm and 7 to 11pm Tues. to Sun. The restaurant also operates a wine bar, Thirties, beneath the main dining room, keeping the same hours. Here, typically English food is served, costing from £3 ($4.95) to £5 ($8.25). The wine bar opens onto a floodlit garden, with a life-size chess set as its main feature.

On the Outskirts

Actually, the best place for food and lodging is not in Arundel itself but outside near the village of Amberley, lying north of Arundel, and 1½ miles southwest of Amberley on B2139. Here, a 14th-century castle, portions dating from the 12th, has been turned into **Amberley Castle Hotel,** Amberley, near Arundel, West Sussex BN18 9ND (tel. 0798/831992). Joy and Martin Cummings have operated this deluxe establishment since 1988. From the battlements you'll have views of weald and downland. Elizabeth I herself once held the lease on this castle (from 1588 to 1603), and Cromwell's forces attacked it during the Civil War. Charles II visited the castle on two occasions, in 1651 and 1686.

Each of the 12 sumptuous rooms is named after a castle in Sussex, and the furniture, fabrics, and general decor were selected by Joy herself. Every room has a private Jacuzzi bath, as well as TV, phone, and video library. Two persons pay from £85 ($140.25) to £175 ($288.75) a night, including tax and a full English breakfast. Non-residents who reserve can attend the 12th-century Queen's Room Restaurant, the finest dining room in the area. Service is under a barrel-vaulted ceiling with lancet windows, and the food is a medley of classic French and traditional English. Among the exquisite repertoire, you are likely to be served everything from zucchini flowers filled with crab to a citrus-flavored dish of smoked lambs' tongues. Service is from 7 to 10pm, with meals costing from £20.50 ($33.85) on the table d'hôte or £35 ($57.75) if ordered à la carte. A Sunday lunch is featured from noon to 2pm for £20.50 ($33.85).

---

15. Chichester

According to one newspaper, Chichester might have been just a market town if the Chichester Festival Theatre had not been established in its midst. One of the oldest Roman cities in England, Chichester is in vogue, drawing a crowd from all over the world who come to see its theater's presentations.

Only a 5-minute walk from the Chichester Cathedral and the old Market Cross, the 1,400-seat theater, with its apron stage, stands on the edge of Oaklands Park. It opened in 1962 (first director: Lord Laurence Olivier), and its reputation has grown steadily, pumping new vigor and life into the former walled city.

CHICHESTER FESTIVAL THEATRE AND MINERVA STUDIO THEATRE

The Chichester Festival Theatre offers plays and musicals with all-star casts during the summer season (May to September), and in the winter and spring months, orchestras, jazz, opera, theater, ballet, and a Christmas Show for all the family. The Minerva is a studio theater that offers one of the most adventurous programs during the year in the south and houses a theater restaurant (tel. 0243/782219), society clubroom, and shop. Theater reservations made over the telephone will be held for a maximum of 4 days (call 0243/781312). It is better to mail inquiries and checks to the Box Office, Chichester Festival Theatre, Oaklands Park, Chichester, West Sussex PO19 4AP. MasterCard, Visa, and American Express accepted. In the Chichester Festival Theatre, matinee performances begin at 2:30pm, evening performances at 7:30pm, except first nights which are at 7pm. In the Minerva Studio, matinee performances begin at 2:45pm and evenings at 7:45pm.

How to get there: If you would like to come down from London, 62 miles away, for a matinee, catch the 11:21am train from Victoria Station, which will deliver you to Chichester by 1:01pm, in plenty of time. For an evening performance, board the 4:21pm train from Victoria Station, arriving at 6:06pm. Regrettably, there is no direct late train back to London after the show. Visitors who must return can make a connection via Brighton, arriving at Victoria Station shortly after midnight.

WHERE TO STAY

In Chichester, you have a choice of living either at one of the old inns inside the city or on the outskirts.

Dolphin & Anchor, West Street, Chichester, West Sussex PO19 1QE (tel. 0243/785121), is two old inns joined together. The situation is prime, right at the historic, 15th-century Market Cross and opposite the Chichester Cathedral, a 10-minute walk from the Festival Theatre. The setting blends 19th-century architectural features, including an old coaching entrance, with 20th-century comforts. A more up-to-date wing of bedrooms is also offered. The two-in-one inn has 51 bedrooms, all with baths, TVs, radios, and phones. A single is £60 ($99) daily, a twin going for £74 ($122.10), these tariffs including service and VAT. A few deluxe rooms rent for £85 ($140.25) for two people. There are lounges, bars, the Whig and Tory Restaurant, and the Roussillon Coffee Shop, which serves light meals and grills until 8pm.

Ship Hotel, North Street, Chichester, West Sussex PO19 1NH (tel. 0243/782028), is one of the classic Georgian buildings of the city, only a few minutes' walk from the cathedral, the Chichester Festival Theatre, and many fine antique shops. The Ship was built as a private house in 1790 for Admiral Sir George Murray (one of Nelson's commanders) and still retains an air of elegance and comfort. A grand Adam staircase leads from the main entrance to the 37 bedrooms, (32 with private bathroom), which are all named after historic ships. Rooms have TVs and phones. Single-room prices are £32 ($52.80) to £64 ($105.60) daily, and doubles cost £50 ($82.50) to £85 ($140.25). A full English breakfast is included. Good pub lunches are offered. The Victory Bar is one of Chichester's most popular meeting places. The welcoming restaurant offers excellent value for money with its à la carte and special four-course dinner menus each evening from £12 ($19.80).

Chichester Resort Hotel, Westhampnett, Chichester, West Sussex PO19 4UL (tel. 0243/786351), is a boon to motorists because it's a mile from the city center on the main A27 with large car-parking facilities. A covered passageway connects it to the older White Swan Inn nearby. The attractively styled hotel offers 76 modern bedrooms tastefully furnished, each containing private bathroom, telephone, radio, tea-making facilities, and color TV. The rate is £71.95 ($118.70) daily for a double and £55.95 ($92.30) for a single, including VAT, service, and a full English breakfast. The hotel has a cocktail bar and a restaurant serving a set lunch for £10 ($16.50) and a table d'hôte dinner for £12 ($19.80). There is also an à la carte menu. A health club and swimming pool are on the premises.

WHERE TO DINE

In contrast to its limited number of accommodations, Chichester has several good restaurants, some of which lie in the environs.

Comme Ça, 149 St. Pancras (tel. 0243/788724), is the best French restaurant in town. In fact, it's the best restaurant period. The decor is unpretentious, with a certain French provincial quality. The chef is French, as a look at the menu offerings will reveal. Try feuillete of salmon with chives, sole Comme Ça, perhaps filet of beef with a Dijon mustard sauce. Good quality ingredients are used. Meals cost from £20 ($33), and are served from 12:15 to 2pm and 7:15 to 9:30 or 10pm, depending on business; closed for lunch Sat., dinner Sun., and all day Mon. Reservations are needed.

White Horse, 1 High St., Chilgrove (tel. 0243/535219), lies 6½ miles north of Chichester by the B2141 road to Petersfield. The wine cellar at this informally elegant country restaurant is believed to be one of the most comprehensive in Britain. This is partly because of the careful attention the owners, Barry and Dorothea Phillips, pay to the details of their 18th-century inn, whose patina has been burnished every day since it was first built in 1765. The trio of dining rooms contains old beams, lots of hardwood, and a close attention to the gleaming silver of the table settings. Specialties include wild duck with a black-cherry and port sauce, wild mushroom and chicken vol-au-vent, and veal with a vermouth-and-sorrel sauce. A fixed price lunch costs £14.95 ($24.65), a four-course fixed price dinner going for £19.50 ($32.20). Open noon to 1:45pm and 7 to 9pm; closed Sun., Mon., and all of February.

WEALD AND DOWNLAND OPEN AIR MUSEUM

In the beautiful Sussex countryside at Singleton, 6 miles north of Chichester on the A286 (London road), historic buildings that have been saved from destruction are being reconstructed on a 40-acre downland site. The structures show the development of traditional building from medieval times to the 19th century in the weald and downland area of southeast England. Exhibits include a Tudor market hall; a medieval farmstead and other houses dating from the 14th to 17th centuries; a working watermill producing stone-ground flour; a blacksmith's forge; plumbers' and carpenters' workshops; a toll cottage; a 17th-century treadwheel; agricultural buildings, including thatched barns and an 18th-century granary; a charcoal burner's camp; and a 19th-century village school. The museum is open April to October 31 daily from 11am to 6pm. From November to March, it is open 11am to 5pm Wed. and Sun. only. Admission is £2.80 ($4.60) for adults, £1.25 ($2.05) for children. For further information, phone 0243/63348.

FISHBOURNE

A worthwhile visit only a mile and a half from Chichester is to the remains of the **Roman Palace,** Salthill Road (tel. 0243/785859), the largest Roman residence yet discovered in Britain. Built around A.D. 75, it has many mosaic-floored rooms and even an underfloor heating system. The gardens have been restored to their original 1st-century plan. The story of the site is told both by an audio-visual program and by text in the museum. There is free parking and a cafeteria. The museum is open from March through November. Admission is £2 ($3.30) for adults, £1 ($1.65) for children. Open March, April, and October daily from 10am to 5pm; May to September daily from 10am to 6pm; in November daily from 10am to 4pm; and December to February 10am to 4pm Sun. only. The museum is sited to the north of A259, off Salthill Road, and signposted from Fishbourne Village. Buses stop regularly at the bottom of Salthill Road, and the museum is within a 5-minute walk of British Rail's Fishbourne Station.

WHERE TO STAY ON THE OUTSKIRTS

One of the most interesting ways to attend the theater in Chichester is from a base on the outskirts. That way, you get to enjoy the best of English village life, but can conveniently go into the city whenever you want.

Old Bosham

One of the most charming little villages of West Sussex, Bosham was the site of the first establishment of Christianity on the Sussex coast. The Danish King Canute made it one of the seats of his North Sea empire, and it was the site of a manor (now gone) of the last of England's Saxon kings, Harold, who sailed from here to Normandy on a journey that finally culminated in the invasion of England by William the Conqueror in 1066. Bosham's little church was depicted in the Bayeux Tapestry. Near the harbor, it is reached by a narrow lane. Its graveyard overlooks the boats (a daughter of King Canute is buried inside). The church is filled with ship models and relics, showing the villagers' link to the sea. Bosham is principally a sailing resort, linked by bus service to Chichester. The location is four miles west of Chichester by A259.

Millstream Hotel, Bosham Lane, Bosham, Chichester, West Sussex PO18 8HG (tel. 0243/573234), is set on the road to the village of Bosham and its harbor, off the A27. Completely redecorated, the rooms have different colors, but all are outfitted with floral-patterned wallpaper. The decor is in keeping with the country cottage–type hotel. Beds are comfortable, and each of the 29 rooms has a private bath, phone, and TV. The charge is £85 ($140.25) daily for a double or twin, £55 ($90.75) in a single, with breakfast included in the rates. The cocktail bar at the entrance to the restaurant is tastefully furnished with white bamboo chairs and tables. At the adjoining restaurant, you can order such à la carte dishes as moules (mussels) marinières and roast Sussex lamb with fresh herbs. Dinner costs from £15 ($24.75).

Midhurst

Spread Eagle Hotel, South Street, Midhurst, West Sussex GU29 9NH (tel. 073081/6911), started life as a 15th-century coaching inn, and has been much lived in, altered, and loved ever since. The inn and the market town of Midhurst are so steeped in history that the room you sleep in and the pavement you walk on have a thousand tales to tell. The 41 rooms have beams, small mullioned windows, and unexpected corners, as well as having been modernized with baths, along with radios, color TVs, and phones. The Queen's Suite with four-poster bed goes for £150

($247.50) a night. However, you can rent a double or twin room from £80 ($132) to £120 ($198) or a single from £65 ($107.25), including VAT, service, and a large English breakfast.

Dinner is served in the dining hall, lit by candles that flicker on the gleaming tables. In the winter, log fires blaze. The lounge with its timbered ceiling is where Elizabeth I and her court might have sat to watch festivities in the Market Square outside. The eagle in the lounge is the actual one that decorated the back of Hermann Goering's chair in the Reichstag. It was acquired for its apt illustration of the hotel's name. There are several bars. Midhurst lies only 12 miles from Chichester, only a bit farther from Arundel and Bosham; Brighton is just 36 miles down the road. It's also quite a good place for a first or last night for those boarding a flight at Gatwick Airport outside London.

VIII

HAMPSHIRE AND DORSET

1. PORTSMOUTH AND SOUTHSEA

2. SOUTHAMPTON

3. THE NEW FOREST

4. ISLE OF WIGHT

5. WINCHESTER

6. BOURNEMOUTH

7. SHAFTESBURY

8. WAREHAM

9. DORCHESTER

10. BRIDPORT

11. CHIDEOCK

12. CHARMOUTH

13. LYME REGIS

14. CHEDINGTON

15. SHERBORNE

The images of the countryside seem to be conjured from Burke's *Landed Gentry*. Fireplaces where stacks of logs burn merrily . . . wicker baskets of apples freshly brought in from the orchard . . . milk that doesn't come from bottles . . . ruins of a Roman camp beyond the pear trees, on the crest of a hill . . . a village pub, with two rows of kegs filled with varieties of cider.

You're in Hampshire and Dorset, two shires guarded zealously by the English, who protect their special rural treasures. Everybody knows of Southampton and Bournemouth, but less known is the undulating countryside lying inland. Your car will take you through endless lanes, revealing tiny villages and thatched cottages untouched by the industrial invasion.

The area is rich with legend and with literary and historical associations. Here Jane Austen and Thomas Hardy wrote—and set—their novels. Here King Arthur held court around his Round Table. And from here sailed such memorable ships as the *Mayflower*, Lord Nelson's *Victory*, the D-Day invasion flotilla, and the *QE2* on its maiden voyage.

HAMPSHIRE

This is Jane Austen country—firmly middle class, largely agricultural, its inhabitants doggedly convinced that Hampshire is the greatest spot on earth. Austen wrote six novels of manners, including *Pride and Prejudice* and *Sense and Sensibility*, that earned her a room at the top among 19th-century writers. Her books provided a keen insight into the solid middle-class English who were to build such a powerful empire. Although the details of the life she described have now largely faded ("At five o'clock the two ladies retired to dress, and at half-past six Elizabeth was summoned to dinner"), much of the mood and spirit of Hampshire depicted in her books remains.

Born in 1775, Jane Austen was the daughter of the Oxford-educated rector, the Reverend Mr. George Austen, a typical Hampshire country gentleman, who had much charm but little money. In keeping with a custom of the time, the Austens gave their second son, Edward, to a wealthy, childless family connection, Thomas Knight, whose heir the young man became. It was Edward who gave to his mother and sisters Chawton Cottage (now **Jane Austen's House**) in Chawton, 1 mile southwest of Alton off A31 and B3006 (tel. 0420/83262). The cottage is signposted at Chawton. Visitors can see the surroundings in which the novelist spent the last 7½ years of her life, her period of greatest creativity. In the unpretentious but pleasant cottage, you can see the table on which Jane Austen penned new versions of three of her books and wrote three more, including *Emma* (her "handsome, clever, and rich" heroine, Emma Woodhouse). You can also see the rector's George III mahogany bookcase and a silhouette likeness of the Reverend Austen presenting his son to the Knights. It was in this cottage that Jane Austen became ill in 1816 of what would have been diagnosed by the middle of the 19th century as Addison's disease.

There is an attractive garden in which visitors are invited to have picnics, and an old bakehouse with Ms. Austen's donkeycart. The home is open daily April to October from 11am to 4:30pm for £1 ($1.65) admission; children under 14, 50p (85¢). It is closed Mon. and Tues. in November, December, and March; Mon. to Fri. in January and February; and Christmas Day and Boxing Day.

Hampshire embraces the **New Forest** (don't expect anything in England labeled "new" to be new), the **South Downs**, the **Isle of Wight** (Victoria's favorite retreat), the passenger port and gateway city of **Southampton,** and the naval city of **Portsmouth.**

Going west from Southampton, you'll come to the New Forest, more than 90,000 acres preserved by William the Conqueror as a private hunting ground. William lost two of his sons in the New Forest—one killed by an animal, the other by an arrow. Today it is a vast woodland and heath, ideal for walking and exploring.

Although Hampshire is filled with many places of interest, for our purposes I've concentrated on two major areas that seem to hold the most appeal for visitors: Southampton for convenience of transportation and accommodations and Winchester for history.

1. Portsmouth and Southsea

Virginia, New Hampshire, even Ohio, may have their Portsmouth, but the daddy of them all is the old port and naval base on the Hampshire coast, 70 miles south of London. German bombers in World War II virtually leveled the city, hitting about nine-tenths of its buildings. But the seaport has recovered admirably.

Its maritime associations are known around the world. From Sally Port, the most interesting district in the **Old Town,** "Naval heroes innumerable have embarked to fight their country's battles." That was certainly true on June 6, 1944, when Allied troops set sail to invade occupied France.

Southsea, adjoining Portsmouth, is a popular seaside resort with fine sands, gardens, bright lights, and a host of holiday attractions. Many historic monuments can be seen along the stretches of open space where you can walk on the Clarence Esplanade and look out on the Solent, viewing the busy shipping activities of Portsmouth Harbor.

THE SIGHTS

Some 400 years earlier, an English navy ship didn't fare so well. The *Mary Rose,* flagship of the fleet of men-o'-war of King Henry VIII, sank in the Solent in 1545 in full view of the king. In 1982 a descendant of that monarch, and heir to the throne, Charles, Prince of Wales, watched the *Mary Rose* break the water's surface after almost 4 centuries spent lying on the sea bottom, not exactly shipshape but surprisingly well-preserved nonetheless. Now the remains are on view, but the hull must be kept permanently wet. The hull and the more than 10,000 items brought up by divers constitute one of the most important archeological discoveries of England in many years. Among the artifacts on permanent exhibit are the almost-complete equipment of the ship's barber, with surgeon's cabin saws, knives, ointments, and plaster all ready for use; long bows and arrows, some still in shooting order; carpenters' tools; leather jackets; and some fine lace and silk. Close beside the dock where the hull lies is the *Mary Rose* exhibition in boathouse 5. The artifacts rescued from the ship are stored there. It contains an audio-visual theater and a spectacular two-deck reconstruction of a segment of the ship, including the original guns. A display with sound effects recalls the sinking of the vessel.

To see the *Mary Rose* Ship Hall and Exhibition (tel. 0705/750521), use the entrance to the Portsmouth Naval Base through the Victory Gate (as for H.M.S. *Victory*), and follow the signs. It is open daily from 10:30am to 5:30pm; closed Christmas Day. Admission is £2.80 ($4.60) for adults and £1.80 ($2.95) for children. Family tickets cost £7.40 ($12.20). For information, write to the *Mary Rose* Trust, College Road, H.M. Naval Base, Portsmouth, Hampshire PO1 3LX.

Of major interest is Lord Nelson's flagship, H.M.S. *Victory,* a 104-gun, first-rate ship of the line, now at no. 2 dry dock in Portsmouth Naval Base (tel. 0705/819604). Although she first saw action in 1778, her fame was earned on October 21, 1805, in the Battle of Trafalgar when the English scored a victory over the combined Spanish and French fleets. It was in this battle that Lord Nelson lost his life. The flagship, after being taken to Gibraltar for repairs, returned to Portsmouth with Nelson's body on board (he was later buried at St. Paul's in London). It is open from 10:30am to 5pm Mon. to Sat., from 1 to 5pm on Sun.; closed Christmas Day. Admission is £2.80 ($4.60) for adults, £1 ($1.65) for children, and £4.60 ($7.60) for a family (of four).

The **Royal Naval Museum** (tel. 0705/733060) stands next to Nelson's flagship, H.M.S. *Victory,* and the *Mary Rose* in the heart of Portsmouth's historic naval dockyard. The only museum in Britain devoted exclusively to the general history of the Royal Navy, it contains relics of Nelson and his associates, together with unique collections of ship models, naval ceramics, figureheads, medals, uniforms, weapons, and other naval memorabilia. Special displays include "The Rise of the Royal Navy" and "H.M.S. *Victory* and the Campaign of Trafalgar." Other exhibits feature the Victorian navy, the navy in the early 20th century, the modern navy, and representations of the sailor in popular art and culture. The museum is open daily from 10:30am to 5pm (with some seasonal variations). Admission is £1 ($1.65) for adults, 75p ($1.25) for children. However, entrance is free with a ticket purchased for a tour of H.M.S. *Victory.* The museum complex includes a buffet and souvenir shop.

Portsmouth was the birthplace of Charles Dickens, and the small terrace house of 1804 in which the famous novelist made his appearance on February 7, 1812, and lived for a short time was restored and furnished to illustrate the middle-class taste of the early 19th century. **Charles Dickens's Birthplace Museum** is at 393 Old Commercial Rd., Mile End (tel. 0705/827261). It is open daily from 10:30am to 5:30pm; closed November 1 to the end of February. Admission is 80p ($1.30) for adults, 50p (85¢) for students and children. Family tickets (four persons) are available for £2.10 ($3.45). Last tickets are sold at 5pm.

On the Southsea front, you can see a number of naval monuments, including the big anchor from Nelson's ship, *Victory,* a commemoration of the officers and men of H.M.S. *Shannon* for heroism in the Indian Mutiny, an obelisk with a naval crown in memory of the crew of H.M.S. *Chesapeake,* and a massive column, the **Royal Naval Memorial** honoring those lost at sea in the two world wars, as well as a shaft dedicated to men killed in the Crimean War. There are also commemorations of persons who fell victim to yellow fever in Queen Victoria's service in Sierra Leone and Jamaica. The **Southsea Common,** between the coast and houses of the area, known in the 13th century as Froddington Heath and used for army bivouacs, is a picnic and play area today. Walks can be taken along Ladies' Mile if you want to be away from the common's tennis courts, skateboard and roller-skating rinks, and other activities.

Southsea Castle, built in 1545 as part of the coastal defenses ordered by King Henry VIII, and the D-Day Museum, devoted to the Normandy landings 399 years later, are next door to each other on the Clarence Esplanade of Southsea. The castle, a fortress built of stones from Beaulieu Abbey, houses a museum with displays tracing the development of Portsmouth as a military stronghold, as well as naval history and the archeology of the area. The castle is open daily from 10:30am to 5:30pm; closed January 24–26. Admission is £1 ($1.65) for adults, 60p ($1) for children.

The **D-Day Museum** contains the Overlord Embroidery, showing the complete story of Operation Overlord, as the D-Day action was designated, the men, and the machines that were featured in the invasion operation. The appliquéd embroidery, believed to be the largest of its kind (272 feet long and 3 feet high), was designed by Sandra Lawrence and took 20 women of the Royal School of Needlework 5 years to complete. There is a special audio-visual program with displays, including reconstructions of various stages of the mission with models and maps. You'll see a Sherman tank in working order, Jeeps, field guns, and even a DUKW (popularly called a Duck), that incredibly useful amphibious truck that operated on land and sea. The museum is open daily from 10:30am to 5:30pm; closed December 24–26. Admission is £2.80 ($4.60) for adults, £1.70 ($2.80) for children, and £7.30 ($12.05) for a family ticket of two adults and two children. For information on both Southsea Castle and the D-Day Museum, phone the Visitors' Services Organizer at the city museums office (tel. 0705/827261).

On the northern side of Portsmouth Harbor on a spit of land are the remains of **Portchester Castle** (tel. 0705/378291), built in the late 12th century by King Henry II, plus a Norman church. It is set inside the impressive walls of a 3rd-century Roman fort built as a defense against Saxon pirates when this was the northwest frontier of the declining Roman Empire. By the end of the 14th century Richard II had modernized the castle, making it a secure small palace. Among the ruins are the hall, kitchen, and great chamber of this palace. Portchester was popular with medieval kings, who stayed here when they visited Portsmouth. The last official use of the castle was as a prison for French seamen during the Napoleonic wars. It is open from April 1 to the end of September from 10am to 6pm Tues. to Sun., charging an admission of £1.15 ($1.90) for adults and 60p ($1) for children. From October 1 to March 31, hours are 10am to 4pm Tues. to Sun.

Cross Portsmouth Harbor by one of the ferries that bustle back and forth all day to Gosport. Some departures go directly from the station pontoon to H.M.S. *Alliance* for a visit to the **Royal Navy Submarine Museum** (tel. 0705/529217). The

SOUTHWESTERN COUNTIES

museum traces the story of underwater warfare and life below the seas from the earliest days to the present nuclear age, and contains excellent models, dioramas, medals, and displays from all ages. There is also as much about submariners themselves as about the steel tubes in which they make their homes, and although the museum focuses on British boats, it includes much of international interest. The principal exhibit is H.M.S. *Alliance,* and after a brief audio-visual presentation, visitors are guided through the boat by ex-submariners, experiencing the true feeling of life on board in the artificial world beneath the sea. Midget submarines, both British and others, can be seen outside the museum. Also on display is H.M. *Torpedo Boat No. 1,* better known as *Holland I,* launched in 1901, which sank under tow to the breaker's yard in 1913 and was salvaged in 1982. Admission to the museum is £2.60 ($4.30) for adults and £1.60 ($2.65) for children.

WHERE TO STAY

With fine views of the sea, **The Pendragon,** Clarence Parade, Southsea, Hampshire PO5 2HY (tel. 0705/823201), is a comfortable hotel. All 49 bedrooms have color TVs, radios, phones, hot beverage facilities, and private baths. The rate from £35 ($57.75) per person per day includes dinner, room, and breakfast. The Camelot Restaurant serves traditional English food and wines. The Skylark Bar, whose nautical theme is reflected by a counter resembling a rowboat, attracts both hotel guests and local residents, offering a buffet table at lunch. For a quiet drink, however, you might prefer the Camelot Bar.

Hospitality Inn, South Parade, Southsea, Hampshire PO4 0RN (tel. 0705/731281). Its balconied Victorian facade rises above the boulevard running beside the sea. Restored by its owners, the hotel contains an interior decor that, depending on your room assignment, ranges from contemporary to full-curtained traditional. Each of the 15 bedrooms has been renovated with built-in furniture and tile bath and equipped with such extras as a trouser press and tea-making facilities, TV, and phone. The cost is £58 ($95.70) to £60 ($99) daily, in a single, £67 ($110.55) to £71 ($117.15) in a double. A restaurant serves dinners for £12 ($19.80).

WHERE TO DINE

In old Southsea, **Bistro Montparnasse,** 103 Palmerston Rd. (tel. 0705/816754), comes as a bit of a surprise. It is generally conceded to serve the best food in the area. This is a French bistro enclave, with candles glowing on the tables and music played in the background to get you in the mood for a well-rounded selection of dishes. Fresh produce is competently and delicately prepared. The cooking is familiar fare, the menu a sort of list of the way we used to eat. Some of the dishes, such as veal flavored with Calvados and cream, betray a Norman influence. Meals cost from £14 ($23.10) to £16 ($26.40), and service is only at dinner and never on Sun. Hours are from 7 to 10:30pm. Some good house wine is available by the carafe.

WHERE TO STAY AND DINE IN THE ENVIRONS

Dating from 1715, **The Old House Hotel,** the Square, Wickham, Fareham, Hampshire PO17 5JG (tel. 0329/833049), 9 miles from Portsmouth, is a handsome early Georgian house. The location is at the junction of the A333 and the A32. Wickham is only 2 miles north of the M27 motorway, linking Brighton through Portsmouth to Bournemouth. It is thought to have been the first house of its architectural type built in the village, surrounded by low, medieval timber structures around the square. The paneled Georgian rooms on the ground and first floors of the hotel contrast with the beamed bedrooms on the upper floors, once the servants' quarters. All the nine bedrooms contain period furniture, many pieces original antiques. An additional three bedrooms are in an annex 50 yards from the main property in a building dating from the 16th century. Annex rooms contain all the facilities of the main hotel. The individually decorated units have private baths, radios, phones, and TVs. Singles are priced at £70 ($115.50) daily and doubles at £90 ($148.50) for B&B, service, and VAT. Hotel bedrooms are available only Mon. to Fri. The restaurant occupies what was once a timber-frame outbuilding with stables, adjacent to a garden overlooking the Meon River. It serves a French provincial cuisine, a complete meal costing from £21 ($34.65). The menu changes weekly, and care goes into the selection of the freshest vegetables and seasonal produce. Lunch is served from 12:30 to 2pm and dinner from 7:30 to 9:30pm; closed lunch Sat. and Mon., all day Sun. The hotel's bar, with a French provincial ambience, is open exclusively for hotel and restaurant guests. Owners Richard and Annie Skipwith, who converted a private residence into this fine hotel in 1970, recommend making reservations in advance.

BROADLANDS

The home of Lord Mountbatten of Burma until his assassination in 1979, Broadlands, Romsey (tel. 0794/516878), lies on the A31, 72 miles southwest of London. Lord Mountbatten lent the house to the then Princess Elizabeth and Prince Philip, Mountbatten's nephew, as a honeymoon haven in 1947, and in 1981 Prince Charles and Princess Diana spent the first part of their honeymoon here. Broadlands is owned by Lord Romsey, Lord Mountbatten's eldest grandson, who has created a fine exhibition and audio-visual show depicting the highlights of his grandfather's brilliant career as a sailor and statesman. The house, originally linked to Romsey Abbey, was purchased by Lord Palmerston in 1736. It was later transformed into an elegant Palladian mansion by Capability Brown and Henry Holland. Brown landscaped the parkland and grounds, making the river (the Test) the main object of pleasure. The house is open April 12 to September 30 daily from 10am to 4pm; closed Fri., except Good Friday, until August 1. Admission is £4 ($6.60) for adults, £2.50 ($4.15) for children.

2. Southampton

To many North Americans, England's No. 1 passenger port, home base for the *Queen Elizabeth 2,* is the gateway to Britain. Southampton is a city of wide boulevards, parks, and shopping centers. It was rebuilt after German bomb damage, which destroyed hundreds of its old buildings.

In World War II, some 3½ million men embarked from here (in the World War I, more than twice that number passed through Southampton). Its supremacy as a port has long been recognized and dates from Saxon times when the Danish conqueror, Canute, was proclaimed king here in 1017.

Southampton was especially important to the Normans and kept them in touch with their homeland. It shares the dubious distinction of having imported the bubonic plague in the mid-14th century, which wiped out a quarter of the English population. On the Western Esplanade is a memorial tower to the Pilgrims, who set out on their voyage to the New World from Southampton on August 15, 1620. Both the *Mayflower* and the *Speedwell* sailed from here but were forced by storm damages to put in at Plymouth, where the *Speedwell* was abandoned. The memorial is a tall column with an iron basket on top—the type used as a beacon before lighthouses.

If you're waiting in Southampton between boats, you may want to use the time to explore some of the major sights of Hampshire that lie on the periphery of the port—the New Forest, Winchester, the Isle of Wight, and Bournemouth in neighboring Dorset.

WHERE TO STAY

Considered the finest hotel in Southampton, **Polygon Hotel,** Cumberland Place, Southampton, Hampshire SO9 4GP (tel. 0703/330055), is a favorite with tourists and business travelers. It bears the name of a district known as the Polygon that was popular with visiting nobility in the 18th century. The present hotel was built in the early part of this century to replace a 19th-century hostelry. The Polygon has been modernized and refurbished to a good standard. The 119 bedrooms all have private baths, mini-bars, color TVs, radios, phones, and hot beverage facilities. They rent for £72 ($118.80) daily for a single, £94 ($155.10) for a twin-bedded room. The Polygon overlooks the town's Watts Park and civic center, and is within easy reach of the main shopping area.

Post House, Herbert Walker Avenue, Southampton, Hampshire SO1 0HJ (tel. 0703/330777), rises 10 floors tall. It was built near the new docks to overlook the harbor, but is only 5 minutes away from the city center. You can unload your luggage under a sheltered drive and walk into the reception area. The rooms, 130 in all, are handsome and spacious, with fine built-in pieces, picture-window walls, private baths, phones, radios, and TVs. Twin or double rooms cost £88 ($145.20) daily, and singles go for £78 ($128.70). Rates include service and VAT. Among the facilities of the hotel are a heated, open-air swimming pool and a residents' lounge with color TV. The Harbour Bar adjacent to the restaurant offers an intimate atmosphere.

Dolphin Hotel, 35 High St., Southampton, Hampshire SO9 2DS (tel. 0703/339955), which dates back to the 13th century, was Jane Austen's choice, and even Thackeray's when he was writing *Pendennis*. In time, Queen Victoria arrived in a horse-drawn carriage at this Georgian inn and coaching house. A classic brick building, with a pair of bow windows, it is in the center of the city, and is approached through an arched entrance, over which rests a coat-of-arms of William IV and Queen Adelaide. The 74 bedrooms vary widely in size, but are generally spacious and well furnished. All have private baths, TVs, and phones. Singles cost £58 ($95.70) daily; doubles and twins £73 ($120.45). The lounge is nicely paneled. The open staircase holds a rare collection of naval uniform prints. Meals at the Dolphin are quite good, with a table d'hôte dinner beginning at £12 ($19.80). Drinks are served in the Nelson Bar.

Southampton Moat House, 119 Highfield Lane, Portswood, Southampton, Hampshire SO9 1YO (tel. 0703/559555), stands in a residential area on the outskirts of the city. This modern hotel, a member of Queens Moat Houses group, offers 70 comfortable accommodations and efficient service. Its restaurant, Hamilton's, serves both table d'hôte and à la carte menus, which are complemented by a comprehensive wine list. Lunch and dinner will cost from £15 ($24.75) for a three-course meal. Rooms are from £60 ($99) daily in a single and £85 ($140.25) in a double, including an English breakfast and VAT. Accommodations contain private baths, phones, and TVs.

WHERE TO DINE

Southampton isn't distinguished for its gastronomy. However, there have been some improvements, as exemplified by the selections below.

Geddes, Town Quay (tel. 0703/221159), is the best restaurant in town. Contained within the redbrick walls of a historic warehouse, it was originally designed by Scottish architect John Geddes as a ship's chandler and warehouse. Back then, the sea came up to its foundations. In spite of the rustic exterior, the interior is decorated in a French Regency style. There is a wine cellar with 600-year-old walls, once part of the medieval Southampton Wall. A fixed price three-course lunch goes for £13.50 ($22.30), with à la carte dinners ranging from £20 ($33) per person without wine. Continental-style main dishes are likely to include such fare as a timbale of seafood mousse wrapped in smoked salmon, venison in red currant sauce, and breast of chicken with a blue cheese mousse stuffing. Lunch is from noon to 2:30pm Mon. to Fri., dinner from 7 to 10:30pm Mon. to Sat.

Kuti's, 70 London Rd. (tel. 0703/221585), is the best Indian restaurant in all of Hampshire. Decorated in a flamboyant style, with murals from India, it invites you to partake of its wares. It pays homage to the many different cuisines of India, giving you a wide choice. Sample a vegetarian thali or tandoori chicken, along with a host of other dishes. Some items may be familiar to you; others come as delightful, zesty surprises. A set lunch costs from £7.50 ($12.40), with dinners averaging around £12 ($19.80). Open daily from noon to 2:30pm (at which time a buffet lunch is served) and from 6 to 11:30pm.

3. The New Forest

The New Forest came into the limelight in the times of Henry VIII, who loved to hunt here, as deer abounded. Also, with his enthusiasm for building up the British naval fleet, he saw his opportunity to supply oak and other hard timbers to the boatyards at Buckler's Hard on the Beaulieu River for the building of stout-hearted men-o'-war. Today you can visit the old shipyards, the museum with its fine models of men-o'-war, pictures of the old yard, and dioramas showing the building of these ships, their construction, and their launching. It took 2,000 trees to build one man-o'-war.

Stretching for about 92,000 acres, the New Forest is a large tract, 14 miles wide and 20 miles long. William the Conqueror laid out the limits of this then-private hunting preserve. Those who hunted without a license faced the executioner if they were caught, and those who hunted but missed had their hands severed.

Nowadays, the New Forest is traversed by a motorway to the southwest. However, I'd suggest you stop a moment and relax.

This used to be a forest, but now the groves of oak trees are separated by wide tracts of common land that is grazed by ponies and cows, hummocked with heather and gorse, and frequented by rabbits. Away from the main arterial roads, where signs warn of wild ponies and deer, there is a private world of peace and quiet.

BEAULIEU ABBEY—PALACE HOUSE

This stately home is in the New Forest (tel. 590/612345). The abbey and house, as well as the National Motor Museum, are on the property of Lord Montagu of Beaulieu, at Beaulieu, 5 miles southeast of Lyndhurst and 14 miles south of Southampton. The ruins of a Cistercian abbey, founded on this spot in 1204, can be explored today. Palace House was the great gatehouse of the abbey before it was converted into a private residence in 1538. The house is surrounded by gardens.

On the grounds, the **National Motor Museum,** is one of the most comprehensive motor museums in the world, with more than 250 vehicles. It traces the story of motoring from 1895 to the present. Famous autos include four land-speed record-holders, among them Donald Campbell's *Bluebird*. The collection's foundation was Lord Montagu's family collection of vintage cars. A special feature is called "Wheels": In a darkened environment, visitors can travel in specially designed "pods," each of which carries up to two adults and one child along a silent electric track. The pods move at a predetermined but variable speed, and are capable of rotating almost 360°. By this means, the visitor is introduced to a variety of displays spanning 100 years of motor development. Sound and visual effects are integrated into individual displays. In one sequence, visitors experience the smell, noise, and visual thrill of a Grand Prix race.

All facilities are open Easter to September daily 10am to 6pm, October to Easter daily 10am to 5pm; closed Christmas Day. Admission to the motor museum, palace and gardens, abbey ruins, and exhibition of monastic life costs £5.25 ($8.65) for adults, £3.50 ($5.80) for children. For further information, contact the Visitor Reception Manager, John Montagu Building, at the number above.

BUCKLER'S HARD

This historic 18th-century village on the banks of the River Beaulieu is where ships for Nelson's fleet were built, including the admiral's favorite, *Agamemnon,* as well as *Eurylus* and *Swiftsure*. The **Maritime Museum** (tel. 0590/616203) reflects the shipbuilding history of the village. Its displays feature shipbuilding at Buckler's Hard; Henry Adams, master shipbuilder; Nelson's favorite ship; Buckler's Hard and Trafalgar; and models of Sir Francis Chichester's yachts and pieces of his equipment. The cottage exhibits are a re-creation of 18th-century life in Buckler's Hard. Here you can stroll through the New Inn of 1793 and a shipwright's cottage of the same period, or look in on the family of a poor laborer at home. All these displays include village residents and visitors of the late 18th century.

The museum is open Easter to May daily from 10am to 6pm; June to September to 9pm; and September to Easter to 4:30pm. Admission is £1.95 ($3.20) for adults, £1.20 ($2) for children. The walk back to Beaulieu, 2½ miles along the riverbank, is well marked through the woodlands. During the summer you can take a half-hour cruise on the River Beaulieu in the present *Swiftsure,* an all-weather, catamaran cruiser.

WHERE TO STAY AND DINE

My list of recommendations for food and lodgings begins with the finest establishment in the entire area.

New Milton

Chewton Glen Hotel, Christchurch Road, New Milton, Hampshire BH25 6QS (tel. 0425/275341), is a gracious country house on the fringe of the New Forest. It's within easy reach of Southampton and Bournemouth. After leaving the village of Walkford, follow the signpost off the A35 New Milton–Christchurch road, through parkland to a private car park. There are 58 rooms in the old house and a new wing, each equipped with private bath, phone, and TV. In the old house, the magnificent staircase leads to well-furnished chambers opening onto lovely views over the spacious grounds. In the new wing, you find yourself on the ground level with French doors opening onto your own private patio. Here the decor is in muted colors, the rooms named for the heroes of novels written by Captain Marryat (he was the author of *The Children of the New Forest*). There is no single occupancy rate. Doubles range from £125 ($206.25) to £180 ($297) daily, excluding VAT. Suites for two cost from £200 ($330) to £330 ($544.50). Everywhere log fires burn and fresh flowers add fragrance. Guests can swim in an open-air, heated swimming pool. The garden sweeps down to a stream and then to rhododendron woods. In addition there are a tennis court, a nine-hole golf course, an indoor swimming pool, a sauna, and a Jacuzzi.

In the dining room, the standard of cooking and the presentation is high. Particular emphasis is placed on fresh ingredients. The chef favors a modern cuisine, complemented by excellent sauces and velvety-smooth desserts. The set meal of three courses is changed daily. A set lunch is £18 ($29.70), going up to £20 ($33) on Sun. A set dinner costs £37.50 ($61.90).

Lyndhurst

Lyndhurst Park Hotel, High Street, Lyndhurst, Hampshire SO43 7NL (tel. 042128/3923), is a large old country house set in five acres of beautiful gardens, with an outdoor heated swimming pool and all-weather tennis court. The 59 bedrooms all have private baths, color TVs with in-house video, direct-dial phones, radio-alarms, tea and coffee makers, hairdryers, and trouser presses. They rent for £52 ($85.80) to £58 ($95.70) daily in a single, £62 ($102.30) to £82 ($135.30) in a double, including VAT and an English breakfast. There are two bars, one with beams, high-backed settles, and harnesses decorating the brick walls. The hotel has an oak-paneled restaurant, where a wide selection of dishes is offered at both lunch and dinner. A four-course dinner with coffee will cost about £14 ($23.10).

Crown Hotel, 9 High St., Lyndhurst, Hampshire SO43 7NF (tel. 042128/2922), stands on a spot where there has been a hostelry for centuries, on the main street of the village opposite the church with its tall spire. The present building is a mere 100 years old, and the 42 bedrooms are snug with baths, color TVs, radios, phones, and mini-bars. Singles cost from £50 ($82.50) daily, and doubles or twins from £78 ($128.70), including VAT and a full English breakfast. Much local produce is used in the dining room, including venison. The specialty is a rich concoction of meat, mushrooms, and onions cooked in red wine and cream with red currants and brandy. A set lunch or dinner costs from £14.50 ($23.95). There are also à la carte selections. Sunday lunch is well patronized by the local people. It also does substantial bar meals.

Brockenhurst

New Park Manor, Lyndhurst Road, Brockenhurst, Hampshire SO42 7QH (tel. 0590/23467), is a former royal hunting lodge dating from the days of William the Conqueror. It is the only hotel in the New Forest itself. In 1666 King Charles II made New Park his favorite hunting lodge on his return from exile in France, and came here accompanied by Nell Gwynne. Now a modern country hotel, the manor has 25 bedrooms. The original rooms have been preserved, including such features as beams and open log fires. The owners have installed central heating throughout, and the bedrooms contain baths, color TVs, phones, and tea and coffee makers. The price for B&B is £39.50 ($65.20) to £46 ($75.90) per person daily. Included in the tariff is the use of a swimming pool in a sheltered corner of the garden (heated in summer) and a hard tennis court. Riding from the hotel's stables is available. The candlelit restaurant, with its log fire, specializes in flambé cookery. The chef often uses fresh garden produce, which is backed up by a good wine list. The hotel lies half a mile off the A337 Lyndhurst-Brockenhurst road past the 500-year-old thatched lodge to the manor.

Carey's Manor, Lyndhurst Road, Brockenhurst, Hampshire SO42 7RH (tel. 0590/23551), is a manor house built of red brick. Its origins are in the days of Charles II, who used to come here when Carey's was a hunting lodge. Greatly extended in 1888, the building became a country hotel in the 1930s. Much improved in recent years, it is better than ever. The old house is still filled with character, as exemplified by its mellow, time-worn paneling and carved oak staircase. The bedrooms, 80 in all, are well furnished, although they differ in style and location. Some are in the restored main building, while others are in the garden wing. Each accommodation contains private bath or shower, phone, radio, TV, hairdryer, and trouser press. Singles cost from £80 ($132) daily, with doubles renting for £120 ($198). The hotel also serves good food, a modern British and French cuisine. Carey's is ideal as a resort, with an indoor swimming pool, gym, solarium, and sauna. The hotel, about a 90-minute drive from London, stands on 5 acres of landscaped grounds.

Balmer Lawn Hotel, Lyndhurst Road, Brockenhurst, Hampshire SO42 7ZB (tel. 0590/23116), is a former hunting lodge, set back from the main highway, its grounds blending with those of the New Forest. The site is on the A337, the Lyndhurst-Lymington road, about a mile outside of Brockenhurst. It has both an indoor and outdoor swimming pool, along with a sauna and a gym. Its 58 bedrooms, with private baths or showers, phones, and TVs, come in a variety of styles and shapes, but all are comfortable and well kept. Singles range from £70 ($115.50) to £80 ($132) daily, with doubles renting for £90 ($148.50) to £100 ($165). The hotel is also a good choice for dining. It offers bar meals at lunch and full course meals at night.

One of the best restaurants in the area is **Le Poussin,** 57 Brookley Rd., Brockenhurst (tel. 0590/23063), which lies in back of a double-fronted shop in the center of the village. Continental waiters have a certain flair as they present the day's French specialties. To guarantee the freshness of their ingredients, Caroline and Alexander Aitken (he's the chef) also opened their own deli. The chef offers at least four different versions of venison. One specialty—Fruits of the New Forest—contains hare, wild rabbit, and venison with a game sauce. Desserts are often sumptuous. A set lunch is excellent value at £7.50 ($12.40), and à la carte dinners cost from £30 ($49.50). Open noon to 2pm and 7 to 10pm; closed lunch Sun. and all day Mon. Reservations are necessary.

Beaulieu

Montagu Arms, Palace Lane, Beaulieu, Hampshire, SO42 7ZL (tel. 0590/612324), was built with locally made bricks and tiles as well as timbers from the

New Forest. Its origins are from the 13th century. This time-tested favorite combines the comfort of a country manor house with the cozy hospitality of a mellow wayside inn. The hotel staff keeps up an old English garden, which is well sheltered and filled with some rare plants. The main lounge overlooks this garden, and the dining room, serving good food and wine, is oak beamed and paneled. In one of the three bars, the counter was fashioned with an old wine press. The 24 bedrooms are immaculately kept and modernized, all with private baths, phones, and TVs. Singles cost £47 ($77.55) to £60 ($99) daily, and twins and doubles go for £70 ($115.50) to £115 ($189.75), including VAT, service, and a full English breakfast. You can have a set lunch in the dining room for £15 ($24.75); a set dinner, from £22 ($36.30).

Buckler's Hard

Master Builders House Hotel, Buckler's Hard, Beaulieu, Hampshire SO4 7XB (tel. 0590/616253), 2½ miles south of Beaulieu, is a lovely 18th-century main house that was once the home of master shipbuilder Henry Adams, who was responsible for many of the wooden walls that dominated the seaways of the world. Today there is a wing that accommodates guests in 23 rooms with baths, color TVs, phones, and hot beverage facilities. Singles rent for £50 ($82.50), doubles and twins for £68 ($112.20) to £77 ($127.05), including VAT and a full English breakfast. The space in the main building is devoted to the Yachtsman Buffet Bar, which provides good, ample snack meals, and to the restaurant with its wide windows overlooking the busy river.

---

4. Isle of Wight

Four miles across the Solent from the south coast towns of Gosport, Lymington, and Portsmouth, the Isle of Wight is known for its sandy beaches and its ports, favored by the yachting set. The island, which long attracted such literary figures as Alfred, Lord Tennyson and Charles Dickens, is compact in size, measuring 23 miles from east to west, 13 miles from north to south. You can take regular ferryboats over. Hydrofoils, which are faster, cross the Solent in just 20 minutes from Southampton, and hovercraft take just 8 minutes from Southsea.

The price of a round-trip ticket on the ferry from Southampton to Cowes is from £4.70 ($7.75) to £8.70 ($14.35) per passenger. Taking a car for the day costs from £11 ($18.15) to £30.25 ($49.90), depending on the size of the vehicle. The ferry from Lymington to Yarmouth for a day round trip costs £4 ($6.60) for adults, £2 ($3.30) for children. Transport of an average car, round trip, is £31.40 ($51.80).

The more unusual way of reaching the island is by ferry from Portsmouth Harbor or by hovercraft from Southsea, both of which take you to Ryde, the railhead for the island's communications system. A train that services the island meets the ferry at the end of an 800-yard pier. Arriving in Yarmouth, via Lymington, however, is something else—a busy little harbor providing a mooring for yachts and also for one of the lifeboats in the Solent area.

Visitors who'd like to explore the Isle of Wight just for the day can take an **Around the Island Rover** bus trip, for which tickets may be purchased on the bus. This enables anyone to board and leave the buses at any stop on the island. The price is £4.95 ($8.15) for adults per day and £2.50 ($4.15) for children. It also gives passage on the island's only railway, running from the dock at Ryde to the center of Shanklin, a distance of 12 miles. For further information, phone 0983/523821.

Ryde, on the northeast of the island, was established as a seaside resort in Victorian times. The Church of All Saints, designed by Sir Gilbert Scott, dominates the town with its 200-foot spire. **Cowes** is the premier port for yachting in Britain. Henry VIII ordered the castle built there, but it is now the headquarters of the Royal Yacht Squadron. The seafront, the Prince's Green, and the high cliff road are worth exploring. Hovercraft are built in the town, and it's also the home and birthplace of the well-known maritime photographer, Beken of Cowes. It's almost *de rigueur* to wear oilskins and wellies, leaving a wet trail behind you.

Along the southeast coast are the twin resorts of **Sandown,** with its new pier complex and theater, and **Shanklin,** at the southern end of Sandown Bay, which has held the British annual sunshine record more times than any other resort. Keats once lived in Shanklin's Old Village. Farther along the coast, **Ventnor** is called the "Madeira of England," because it rises from the sea in a series of steep hills.

On the west coast, the sand cliffs of **Alum Bay** are a blend of many different colors, a total of 21 claimed. The Needles, three giant chalk rocks, and the Needles Lighthouse, are further features of interest at this end of the island. If you want to stay at the western end of Wight, consider **Freshwater Bay. Newport** is the island's capital, a bustling market town lying in the heart of the island.

WHAT TO SEE AND DO

Long a favorite of British royalty, the island has as its major attraction **Osborne House** (tel. 0983/20022), Queen Victoria's most cherished residence, lying a mile southeast of East Cowes. Prince Albert, with his characteristic thoroughness, contributed to many aspects of the design of the Italian-inspired mansion, which stands in lush gardens, right outside the village of Whippingham. The rooms have remained as Victoria knew them, right down to the French piano she used to play and with all the cozy clutter of her sitting room. Grief-stricken at the death of Albert in 1861, she asked that Osborne House remain as it was, and so it has. Even the turquoise scent bottles he gave her, decorated with cupids and cherubs, are still in place. It was in her bedroom at Osborne House that the queen died on January 22, 1901. The house is open from Easter to the end of October daily from 10am to 5pm. Admission is £4 ($6.60) for adults, £2 ($3.30) for children.

A completely different attraction, **Carisbrooke Castle** (tel. 0983/522107) is where Charles I was imprisoned by the Roundheads in 1647. This fine medieval castle is in the center of the island, 1½ miles southwest of Newport. Everybody heads for the Well House, concealed inside a 16th-century stone building. Donkeys take turns treading a large wooden wheel connected to a rope that hauls up buckets of water. The castle is open from mid-March to October 1 daily from 10am to 6pm Mon. to Sat. In winter it closes at 4pm. Admission is £2.30 ($3.80) for adults, £1.15 ($1.90) for children.

You have a choice of several bases on the Isle of Wight unless you're what the English call a "day-tripper."

WHERE TO STAY AND DINE

Ryde

A good anchor on the Isle of Wight is **Hotel Ryde Castle,** Esplanade, Ryde, Isle of Wight PO33 1JA (tel. 0983/63755), an accommodation on the seafront, looking out on the Solent. The original castle (circa 1540) was ordered built by Henry VIII as part of the defenses against the Spanish. With its crenellated, ivy-clad exterior and its well-kept public rooms and bedrooms, the hotel attracts families as well as single visitors. The 18 units have private baths, color TVs, phones, radios, hairdryers, and tea and coffee makers. Double bedrooms have four-poster beds. The charge for B&B is £45 ($74.25) per person daily, with half board costing £55 ($90.75). Both table d'hôte and à la carte meals are offered in the dining room, where full use is made of fresh fish caught locally and island farm produce. The bar lounge offers a wide range of snacks for lunch.

Some of the best dining on the island is at **Biskra House,** 17 St. Thomas's St., Isle of Wight PO33 2XX (tel. 0983/67913), which also offers rooms, nine in all. Each has a TV, phone, and either a shower or bathtub. Singles rent for £30 ($49.50) daily, with doubles costing from £48 ($79.20) to £58 ($95.70) with VAT and breakfast included. There are two restaurants within Biskra House. A cellar restaurant is Italian, serving full meals daily from noon to 2pm and 7 to 10:30pm, costing from

£10 ($16.50) to £15 ($24.75) per person. On the street level is a French restaurant, which has a fixed price menu at £13.50 ($22.30), serving from noon to 2pm and 7 to 9:30pm; closed Sun. and Mon. evenings. Fresh lobster is often featured, and steak Diane is prepared at your table.

Shanklin

A good bargain is provided by **Bourne Hall Country Hotel,** Luccombe Road, Shanklin, Isle of Wight, PO37 6RR (tel. 0983/862820). Because of the old village, with its thatched cottages, and the Chine, two of the leading attractions on the island, many visitors prefer to make their base at Shanklin. At Bourne Hall they receive a warm welcome from Mr. and Mrs. Shears, who have one of the best equipped houses in the area, complete with two swimming pools, a sauna, a solarium, and a Jacuzzi. Rooms, 28 in all, are comfortably furnished with private baths, phones, and TVs. From February to December, B&B guests are received and charged from £28 ($46.20) daily in a single, rising to £65 ($107.25) in a double.

Luccombe Chine House, Luccombe Chine, Shanklin, Isle of Wight PO37 6RH (tel. 0983/862037), stands on about 10 acres of grounds opening onto Luccombe Bay. It's small and choice, with only eight bedrooms, half a dozen of which contain four-poster beds. Each room is immaculately kept and well furnished, containing a private bath or shower, hot beverage facilities, TV, and hairdryer. B&B charges range from £21 ($34.65) to £27 ($44.55) per person nightly. It's a good base from which to explore the Isle of Wight. The food is also good, with meals costing from £11 ($18.15).

Sandown

Standing in its own garden, **St. Catherine's Hotel,** 1 Winchester Park Rd., Sandown, Isle of Wight PO36 8HJ (tel. 0983/402392), is just a few minutes' walk from Sandown's sandy beach, leisure center, and pier complex, with its sun lounges and theater. St. Catherine's was built in 1860 of creamy Purbeck stone and white trim, for the dean of Winchester College; a modern extension was added for streamlined and sunny bedrooms. The brightly redecorated lounge has matching draperies at the wide bay windows. There are card tables and a small library of books. Adjacent is a cozy, fully stocked bar and a spacious comfortable dining room. The 21 bedrooms have duvets, white furniture, and built-in headboards. All the rooms contain private baths or showers, color TVs, and phones. Stuart and Marlene Barker welcome you, charging £26.50 ($43.75) per person per night for half board or £18.50 ($30.55) per person for B&B. VAT is included in the rates.

Freshwater Bay

Once the home of Alfred, Lord Tennyson, **Farringford Hotel,** Bedbury Lane, Freshwater Bay, Isle of Wight, PO40 9PE (tel. 0983/752500), has an old-fashioned country ambience. A holiday, recreational estate, it has at its core a fine stone manor house and is surrounded by cottages on 33 acres of landscaped grounds. It's adapted to the taste of the English, but everyone is accommodated from March until after Christmas. Half board goes from £34 ($56.10) to £44 ($72.60) per person daily including VAT and service. The hotel rents 68 bedrooms, each with private bath or shower, TV, and phone. Dinner is four courses of well-cooked, simple dishes, and lunch can be a snack in the bar lounge. There is a nine-hole golf course free to hotel guests, as well as tennis courts, a swimming pool, a croquet lawn, and a sports pavilion.

Chale

A 17th-century coaching inn, **The Clarendon Hotel and Wight Mouse Inn,** Chale, Isle of Wight PO38 2HA (tel. 0983/730431), lies on the most southerly part of the island, where the vegetation is almost tropical. From here, you have views over the Channel to the mainland coast. The Clarendon is a cheerful place at which to spend the night. The 14 rooms are beautifully furnished with antiques, and all have color TVs as well as tea and coffee makers. John and Jean Bradshaw offer a half-board rate of £30 ($49.50) per person daily. The meals are ample, with many fresh ingredients. In their pub, the Wight Mouse Inn, open all day, every day for hot meals and drinks throughout the year, they serve a large selection of beers, including real ales, and 365 (one for every day of the year) whiskies, in addition to the more usual drinks. Live entertainment is provided nightly year round. Children are most welcome here.

Totland Bay

With the colored sands of Alum Bay and the Needles nearby (two of the attractions of the Isle of Wight), **Country Garden,** Church Hill, Totland Bay, Isle of Wight PO39 0ET (tel. 0983/754521), is ideally situated. It's the most charming place to stay at Totland Bay (and about this there is little dispute). It also has a restaurant open to the public, with meals costing from £12 ($19.80) and up. The food is good, and local produce is used whenever possible. From its well-landscaped, 2-acre garden, you'll have views of the Dorset coastline (coming up in the next section). Country Garden was successfully converted from a once-private Victorian home. A total of 18 bedrooms, each attractively and comfortably furnished, are rented to guests at a rate of £35 ($57.75) daily in a single, going up to £75 ($123.75) for the best doubles. Each accommodation has a private bath as well as many up-to-date amenities, such as phone and TV. Other facilities include an indoor swimming pool, a sauna, and a solarium.

5. Winchester

The most historical city in all of Hampshire, Winchester is big on legends—it's even associated with King Arthur and the Knights of the Round Table. In the Great Hall, all that remains of Winchester Castle, a round oak table, with space for King Arthur and his 24 knights, hangs on the wall. But all that spells undocumented romance. What is known, however, is that when the Saxons ruled the ancient kingdom of Wessex, Winchester was the capital.

The city is also linked with King Alfred, who is honored today by a statue, and is believed to have been crowned here. The Danish conqueror, Canute, came this way too, as did the king he ousted, Ethelred the Unready (Canute got his wife, Emma, in the bargain). The city is the seat of the well-known Winchester College, whose founding father was the bishop of Winchester, William of Wykeham. Established in 1382, it lays claim to being the oldest public (private) school in England.

Traditions are strong in Winchester. It is said (although I've never confirmed the assertion) that if you go to St. Cross Hospital, now an almshouse, dating from the 12th century, you'll get ye olde pilgrim's dole of ale and bread (and if there's no bread, you can eat cake!). Winchester, 65 miles from London, is essentially a market town, on the downs on the Itchen River.

WINCHESTER CATHEDRAL

For centuries Winchester Cathedral (tel. 0962/853137) has been one of the great mother churches of England. The present building, the longest medieval cathedral in Britain, dates from 1079, and its Norman heritage is still in evidence. When a Saxon church stood on this spot, St. Swithun, bishop of Winchester and tutor to young King Alfred, suggested modestly that he be buried outside. When he was later buried inside, it rained for 40 days. The legend lives on: just ask a resident of Winchester what will happen if it rains on St. Swithun's Day, July 15.

Of the present building, the nave with its two aisles is most impressive, as are the chantries, the reredos (late 15th century), and the elaborately carved choir stalls. Of the chantries, that of William of Wykeham, founder of Winchester College, is perhaps the most visited (it's found in the south aisle of the nave). The cathedral also contains a number of other tombs, notably those of Jane Austen and Izaak Walton (exponent of the merits of the pastoral life—*The Compleat Angler*). The latter's tomb is to be found in the Prior Silkestede's Chapel in the South Transept. Jane Austen's grave is marked with a commemorative plaque. Winchester Cathedral contains in chests the bones of many of the Saxon kings and the remains of the Viking conqueror, Canute, and his wife Emma in the presbytery. The son of William the Conqueror, William Rufus (who reigned as William II), is also believed to have been buried at the cathedral. There are free guided tours at 11am and 3pm Mon. to Sat. from April to the end of October.

The crypt is flooded for a large part of the year, and at such times it is closed to the public. When it's not flooded, there are regular tours at 10:30am and 2:30pm daily except Sun. The cathedral library and the newly opened Triforium Gallery are open during the summer 10:30am to 1pm and 2 to 4:30pm Tues. to Sat., 2 to 4:30pm Mon. The library comprises Bishop Morley's 17th-century book collection and an exhibition room containing the 12th-century Winchester Bible. The Triforium shows sculpture, woodwork, and metalwork from 11 centuries and affords magnificent views over the rest of the Cathedral. Admission to library and Triforium Gallery is £1 ($1.65) for adults and 50p (85¢) for children. No admission fee for entry to the cathedral is charged but a donation of £1.50 ($2.50) is suggested.

WHERE TO STAY

Accommodations are limited, but adequate. I'll survey the most expensive recommendations first.

Expensive Hotels

Lainston House, Sparsholt, Winchester, Hampshire SO21 2LT (tel. 0962/863588), is a fine, restored 17th-century William and Mary manor house, lying 3½ miles northwest of Winchester, along the A272. Visitors are struck with the beauty of the redbrick structure as they approach via a long, curving, tree-lined drive. It sits in 63 acres of rolling land, linked with the name Lainston in the *Domesday Book* of 1086. Inside the stately house, elegance is the keynote, with Delft-tile fireplaces, oak and cedar paneling, molding, and cornices of the original owners preserved, set off with period pieces. From the reception areas, done in soft pastels and antiques, you go up the mahogany and oak staircase to some of the 32 bedrooms, which are equally attractive. These and the units in the annex are carpeted and have well-equipped bathrooms, plus radios, phones, color TVs, and mini-bars. Charges are £85 ($140.25) daily in a single room, £100 ($165) for a standard or double, and £140 ($231) for a deluxe room. In either of the two dining rooms, you can order such specialties as roast partridge or roast loin of lamb rolled with a herb stuffing. Meals cost £30 ($49.50) to £35 ($57.75).

Wessex Hotel, Paternoster Row, Winchester, Hampshire SO23 9LQ (tel. 0962/861611), is a modern structure adjacent to the grounds of Winchester Cathedral. Two stories high, built of natural brick, it turns most of its walls of windows toward a view of the Norman Tower. The lounges and reception areas are built on several open levels. The coffeeshop is contemporary in design, and the cocktail lounge and restaurant are traditional with leather furniture, mahogany and brass. The hotel has 93 bedrooms and one suite, with 27 accommodations facing the cathedral. The rooms are warmed by soft materials and have such amenities as direct-dial phones, color TVs, radios, hairdryers, and 24-hour room service. A single begins at £74 ($122.10) daily and a double at £90 ($148.50). The coffeeshop is open from 10am until 10pm daily, and the main restaurant has large picture windows overlooking the cathedral and its grounds. Both traditional English and French cuisines are served.

Moderately Priced Hotels

Royal Hotel, St. Peter Street, Winchester, Hampshire SO23 8BS (tel. 0962/840840) is a fine old hotel, built at the end of the 17th century as a private house. It has a modern extension overlooking gardens. For 50 years it was used by nuns from Brussels as a convent before being turned into a hotel. As a hotel, however, it soon became the center of the city's social life. It's only a few minutes' walk to the cathedral, yet still enjoys a secluded position. Best of all is the garden hidden behind high walls. Its 59 bedrooms contain phones, TVs, and private baths or showers. Singles go from £68 ($112.20) to £75 ($123.75) daily and the best doubles for £80 ($132) to £92 ($151.80). These prices include a traditional English breakfast, VAT, and service. Meals are served in a small, formal dining room, with a view of the private garden. A set dinner costs £15 ($24.75).

Budget Hotels
Stratton House, Stratton Road, St. Giles Hill, Winchester, Hampshire SO23 8JQ (tel. 0962/863919), is a lovely old Victorian house (circa 1890) set in an acre of ground in an elevated position on St. Giles Hill, overlooking the city. It is about a 5- to 10-minute walk from the center. Six single, double, twin-bedded, and family units are available throughout the year. The charge for B&B is from £16 ($26.40) daily in a single, £30 ($49.50) to £34 ($56.10) in a double. All bedrooms have TVs and hot beverage facilities. An evening meal can be arranged for another £8 ($13.20). There is ample parking in a private courtyard, and free pick-up is possible if you arrive at the train or bus station.

WHERE TO DINE
The best restaurant in town, **Brann's,** 9 Great Minster St. (tel. 0962/864004), overlooks Winchester Cathedral. It is both a restaurant (upstairs) and a wine bar downstairs. At the wine bar customers may enjoy lighter meals at less expensive prices. David C. Brann, who has had a long and distinguished history in the restaurant business, is aided by his wife and business partner, Barbara, a former actress. Their aim is to produce high quality, affordable meals using fresh, seasonal ingredients. In that, they succeed admirably. There are always daily specials to look forward to that prevent the menu from becoming dull, even to diners who eat at Brann's every day. The welcome is always courteous, but never stuffy or pretentious. The decor is elegant but comfortable. Casual dress is not frowned upon, but they do like guests in the restaurant upstairs to wear a jacket and tie in the evening. The wine bar menu features excellent dishes such as Brann's fish chowder followed by tandoori chicken with dark almond sauce. Meals here cost from £8 ($13.20). In the restaurant, typical dishes are likely to include chicken breast stuffed with tarragon and lemon and glazed with Pernod, roast best end of English lamb with rosemary sauce and spinach mousse, or grilled breast of English duckling, marinated with soy, ginger, and honey. Lunch goes for £15 ($24.75), with dinner costing £25 ($41.25). Service is daily from noon to 3pm and 6 to 10:30pm. They are closed on bank holidays. Reservations are recommended.

In an atmosphere of another century, **Elizabethan Restaurant,** 18 Jewry St. (tel. 0962/853566), offers you an opportunity to dine under hand-hewn beams by candlelight. The street-level bar is for drinks and snacks, while the more formal dining room is one floor above. The restaurant sits in the upper reaches of the village, in a building originally dating from 1509. Well run, the kitchen offers an excellent English cuisine with many French-inspired dishes. Try, for example, roast beef or lobster thermidor. A tourist menu costs only £8.50 ($14.05) for three courses, but you must order it by 8pm. After that, à la carte dinners cost from £18 ($29.70). Meals are served daily from noon to 2:30pm and 6 to 10:30pm.

DORSET

This is Thomas Hardy country. You may have read *Far from the Madding Crowd* or *Tess of the D'Urbervilles* (or seen the movies based on them), and know Dorset is the Wessex of Hardy novels. Some of the towns and villages, although altered considerably, are still recognizable from his descriptions. However, he changed the names to protect the innocent. Bournemouth, for example, became Poole, Weymouth converted to Budmouth. "The last of the great Victorians," as he was called, died in 1928 at the age of 88. While his tomb rests in a position of honor in Westminster Abbey, his heart was buried in his beloved Dorsetshire.

One of England's smallest shires, Dorset lies between the old seaport of **Poole** in the east to **Lyme Regis** in the west (known to Jane Austen). Dorset is a southwestern county, bordering the English Channel. It's big on cows, and Dorset butter is served at afternoon tea. Mainly it is a land of farms and pastures, with plenty of sandy heaths and chalky downs.

The most prominent tourist center of Dorset is the Victorian seaside resort of **Bournemouth.** If you don't anchor there, you might also try a number of Dorset's other seaports, villages, and country towns. For the most part, we'll hug closely to the impressive coastline.

Incidentally, Dorset, as the vacation-wise English might tell you if they wanted to divulge a secret, is a budget traveler's friend.

6. Bournemouth

The south coast resort at the doorstep of the New Forest didn't just happen: It was carefully planned and manicured, a true city in a garden. Flower-filled, park-dotted Bournemouth contains great globs of architecture inherited from those arbiters of taste, Victoria and her son, Edward. Its most distinguished feature is its chines (narrow, shrub-filled, steep-sided ravines) along the zigzag coastline. The real walking English strike out at, say, Hengistbury Head, making their way past sandy beaches, both the Boscombe and Bournemouth Piers, to Alum Chine, a distance of 6 miles, and a traffic-free walk to remember.

It is estimated that of the nearly 12,000 acres that Bournemouth claims for its own, about one-sixth is turned over to green parks and flowerbeds, such as the Pavilion Rock Garden, through which amblers pass both day and night. The total effect, especially in spring, is striking, and helps explain Bournemouth's long-established popularity with the garden-loving English. Bournemouth was discovered back in Victoria's day, when sea-bathing became a firmly entrenched institution, often practiced with great ritual. Many of the comparatively elegant villas that exist today (now largely bed-and-breakfast houses and hotels) were once private homes.

Bournemouth, along with Poole and Christchurch, forms the largest urban area in the south of England. It also has some 20,000 students attending the various schools and colleges, who explore, in their off-hours, places written about or painted by such poets and artists as Shelley, Beardsley, and Turner.

The resort's amusements are wide and varied. At the Pavilion Theatre, for example, you can see West End–type productions from London. The Bournemouth Symphony Orchestra is justly famous in Europe. And there's the usual run of golf courses, band concerts, variety shows, and dancing.

Bournemouth is about 104 miles from London, easily reached in about one hour and 40 minutes on an express train from Waterloo Station. It makes a good base for exploring a historically rich part of England. On its outskirts are the New Forest, Salisbury, and Winchester, and the Isle of Wight (15 miles away, the former seaside retreat of Victoria).

WHERE TO STAY

Expensive Hotels

The Carlton Hotel, Meyrick Road, East Overcliff, Bournemouth, Dorset BH1 3DN (tel. 0202/22011). Its staff defines it as Edwardian, although in parts it evokes art deco with its rounded balconies and horizontal detailing. More easily defined as a vacation resort than just an ordinary hotel, it sits atop a seaside cliff lined with private homes and other hotels. The Carlton boasts a luxury restaurant and cocktail bar, elegant lounges, a boutique, a swimming pool, and a health and beauty spa. There, a sudsy whirlpool, a gymnasium, and a trained staff contribute to healthy vacations. The hotel contains 66 comfortably modernized bedrooms, each with private bath, radio, and color TV. Double occupancy costs £128 ($211.20) daily, singles, £88 ($145.20). Lunch goes for £14.50 ($23.95), and dinner costs £23 ($37.95).

Royal Bath Hotel, Bath Road, Bournemouth, Dorset BH1 2EW (tel. 0202/ 25555), was built in the Victorian era to simulate a French château, with towers and bay windows looking out over the bay and Purbeck Hills. It's opening date in fact was June 28, 1838, the day of Victoria's coronation. After the teenage prince of Wales (later—a long time later—Edward VII) stayed here, the hotel added "royal" to its name. Over the years it has attracted everybody from Oscar Wilde to Rudolf Nureyev, and most definitely the great prime minister, Disraeli. In its own 3 acres of cliff-top gardens is a heated swimming pool. The rate is £70 ($115.50) to £77 ($127.05) daily in a single, £112 ($184.80) to £150 ($247.50) in a twin, inclusive of breakfast, service, and taxes. The table d'hôte lunch is £15 ($24.75), and dinner is £22 ($36.30). The resident band plays for a dinner-dance Sat. evenings. For health enthusiasts, there is a sauna bath, as well as Swedish massages and special diets. Every bedroom, 135 in all, has a private bath, phone, and TV (the large accommodations contain sitting areas as well).

Moderately Priced Hotels

The **Bournemouth Highcliff Hotel,** 105 St. Michael's Rd., West Cliff, Bournemouth, Dorset BH2 5DU (tel. 0202/557702). Built by the Victorians along a clifftop at the edge of the sea, this hotel boasts a rhythmically massive facade dotted with jutting bay windows and a glassed-in conservatory. Its high-ceilinged interior has been tastefully renovated into a subtly updated format, retaining most of the elegant ceiling moldings but replacing the antiques with conservatively modern counterparts. The hotel premises offer heated swimming pool, tennis court, sauna, solarium, putting green, and games room. A tastefully elegant restaurant serves well-prepared food in a grand manner, with formal service. The 107 refurbished bedrooms contain private baths, phones, and TVs, with singles costing £75 ($123.75) daily; doubles £110 ($181.50).

The **Norfolk Royale Hotel,** Richmond Hill, Bournemouth, Dorset BH2 6EN (tel. 0202/551521), one of the oldest prestige hotels of the resort, built a few blocks from the seafront and the shopping area in the center of town, has undergone a major £5-million renovation program, restoring it to its former Edwardian elegance. Disregarding what lies on its periphery, it is like a country estate, with a formal entrance and a rear garden and fountain shaded by trees. The public rooms are geared to holiday guests, with two bars. The 95 bedrooms and suites have been luxuriously appointed with the traditional styles of the Edwardian period blending with modern comforts such as private baths, phones, and TVs. Rates start at £72.50 ($119.65) per person daily for bed and an English breakfast, with special weekend rates from £48 ($79.20) per person. Among the special features of the hotel are the swimming pool covered with a glass dome and the Orangery restaurant set in the terraced gardens.

Langtry Manor Hotel, 26 Derby Rd., East Cliff, Bournemouth, Dorset BH1 3QB (tel. 0202/23887), originally called the Red House, was built in 1877 for Lillie Langtry, the famous Jersey Lily, as a gift from Edward VII to his favorite mistress. The house contains all sorts of reminders of its illustrious inhabitants, including initials scratched on a windowpane and carvings on a beam of the entrance hall. On the half-landing is the peephole through which the prince could scrutinize the assembled company before coming down to dine, and one of the fireplaces bears his initials. The owner has furnished the hotel in the Edwardian style, and on Sat. a six-course Edwardian dinner is served. There is no menu; the dishes are just produced for inspection. Other evenings, dinner is a more usual three-course affair at £18 ($29.70). The 30 bedrooms range from ordinary twins to the Lillie Langtry suite, Lillie's own room, with a four-poster bed draped in Nottingham lace and a double heart-shaped bathtub, or you can rent the Edward VII suite, furnished as it was when His Royal Highness lived in this spacious room. The huge, carved oak fireplace has handpainted tiles showing scenes from Shakespeare. The four-poster bed can be made up as either twins or a large double bed. Rooms have private baths or showers, TVs, mini-bars, and phones. Singles range from £42 ($69.30) to £52 ($85.80) daily, with doubles costing £75 ($123.75) to £92 ($151.80).

WHERE TO DINE

You may want to go more than once to **Sophisticats,** 43 Charminster Rd. (tel. 0202/291019), which is among the leading restaurants at this south coast resort. In a shopping section, about 1½ miles from the heart of Bournemouth, Sophisticats tempts its diners with its excellent fresh fish, and you can order any number of veal and beef dishes (sometimes the latter will be prepared in the Indonesian style). Appetizers are filled with flavor and texture, and a highly desirable finish to a meal is to order a dessert soufflé (but let the waiter know in time). Service is from 7 to 10pm Tues. to Sat., with meals costing from £15 ($24.75). Make sure you reserve a table.

Crust, Hampshire House, Bourne Avenue, the Square (tel. 0202/21430), is one of the best centrally located restaurants in Bournemouth, waking up sleepy local tastebuds with some really good food at fair prices. Look for the daily specials on a blackboard menu. You might begin with moules marinière or Stilton mushrooms with garlic mayonnaise, then follow with king prawns wrapped in bacon and cooked in garlic butter or poached halibut with crab and lobster sauce. Wilf Wilshaw and his staff keep this pleasant little place open daily from noon to 3pm and 6:30 to 11pm, offering a set lunch for £6.50 ($10.75) and dinner priced from £12 ($19.80) to £20 ($33).

WHERE TO STAY AND DINE AT POOLE

An iron fence separates the flower-filled urns of the flagstone forecourt of the **Mansion House,** 11 Thames St., Poole BH15 1JN (tel. 0202/685666), from the street. The neoclassical detailing and fan-shaped windows that pierce the red brick of the establishment's facade are the pride and well-maintained joy of the owners. You'll probably be offered a glass of sherry as you register near the sweeping staircase of the entrance vestibule. A pair of bars offers both formal and rustic decors. An upstairs lounge and graciously furnished bedrooms provide plenty of quiet, well-decorated corners for relaxation. The 19 bedrooms, with baths, air conditioning, TVs, and phones come with many thoughtful extras and cost £70 ($115.50) daily in a single, £85 ($140.25) to £95 ($156.75) in a double. Excellent modern English cuisine is served at around £22 ($36.30) for dinner. The house was built more than 200 years ago by an English entrepreneur engaged in cod-fishing off the coast of Newfoundland.

KINGSTON LACY

An imposing 17th-century mansion, Kingston Lacy (tel. 0202/883402), at Wimborne Minster, on the B3082 Wimborne-Blandford road, 1½ miles west of Wimborne, was the home for more than 300 years of the Bankes family, who had as guests such distinguished persons as King Edward VII, Kaiser Wilhelm II, Thomas Hardy, George V, and Wellington. The house contains a magnificent collection of artworks, tapestries, and furnishings brought from abroad by Sir Charles Barry (designer of the House of Commons) at the request of William Bankes, a friend of Lord Byron. The present house was built to replace Corfe Castle, the Bankes family's home that was destroyed in the Civil War. During her husband's absence in pursuit of duties as chief justice to King Charles I, Lady Bankes led in the defense of the castle, withstanding two sieges before being forced to surrender to Cromwell's forces in 1646 through actions of a treacherous follower. The keys of Corfe Castle hang in the library at Kingston Lacy. The house, set in 250 acres of wooded park, is open from April to the end of October noon to 5:30pm Sat. to Wed. The park is open from 11:30am to 6pm. Admission to the house and garden is £4 ($6.60) for adults, £2 ($3.30) for children. The park and garden can be visited for £1.20 ($2) for adults, 60p ($1) for children.

7. Shaftesbury

The origins of this typical Dorsetshire market town date back to the 9th century when King Alfred founded the abbey and made his daughter the first abbess. King Edward the Martyr was buried there, and King Canute died in the abbey but was buried in Winchester. Little now remains of the abbey, but the ruins are beautifully laid out. The museum adjoining St. Peter's Church at the top of Gold Hill gives a good idea of what the ancient Saxon hilltop town was like.

Today, ancient cottages and hostelries cling to the steep cobbled streets, thatched roofs frown above tiny paned windows, and modern stores vie with the street market in the High Street and the cattle market off Christy's Lane.

The town, right on the A30 from London, is an excellent center from which to visit Hardy Country (it appears as Shaston in *Jude the Obscure*), Stourhead Gardens, and Longleat House.

WHERE TO STAY AND DINE

A Georgian house with Victorian additions, **The Royal Chase Hotel,** Shaftesbury, Dorset SP7 8DB (tel. 0747/3355), has had varied occupants. Once a button-making factory and then a monastery, it is now a delightfully informal Best Western hotel run by George and Rosemary Hunt and manager Liz Thomas (with the hotel for many years). All 35 rooms have private baths, TVs, and phones, and go for £35 ($57.75) per person per night, including a full breakfast, early-morning tea, newspaper, service, and VAT. The hotel offers an indoor swimming pool, an exercise center, and a Turkish steam room.

A meal in the elegant Byzant Restaurant will cost from £15 ($24.75) and includes several local dishes such as local trout, seasonal game, and venison marinated in sherry. Dinner is served nightly from 7 to 10:30pm. A more informal restaurant, Country Kitchen, serves light meals, snacks, and children's favorites throughout the day. They serve Thomas Hardy's Ale, featured in the *Guinness Book of Records* as the strongest beer brewed in a bottle. Even for less fanatical drinkers, the bar, dominated by an open-kitchen range and decorated with Dorsetshire bygones, is an attraction. There are traditional bar games, shove ha'penny, and table skittles at which to pitch your skill.

In the Environs

Plumber Manor, Sturminster Newton, Dorset DT10 2AF (tel. 0258/72507), a Jacobean manor house in 600 acres of farmland, stands less than 2 miles southwest of Sturminster Newton by A357 on Hazelbury Bryan Road. It has been lived in by the Prideaux-Brune family since the early 17th century. The present inhabitants, Richard Prideaux-Brune and his wife, Alison, open the lovely old place to guests. Downstairs, a large hall from which the staircase rises is decorated with family portraits. A comfortable lounge is furnished with antiques. There's a bar to serve the restaurant, made up of three connecting dining rooms where guests can sample the excellent cooking of Brian Prideaux-Brune, Richard's brother. Upstairs, a gallery leads to 6 of the 16 bedrooms, all with private baths, TVs, and phones, opening onto views over the gardens and the countryside. Ten more large units in a long, low stone barn across the stable block (large umbrellas are provided to make the crossing if necessary) are well designed, with wide window seats and views over the gardens, modern baths, and well-chosen furnishings. Guests are accepted here on half-board terms. Per person rates for half board range from £65 ($107.25) to £80 ($132), the latter for single occupancy of a double room.

Dinner is a three-course meal costing from £25 ($41.25), including VAT. Try the English lamb or roast pheasant in port sauce. All main courses are served with fresh vegetables. The restaurant is closed to non-residents on Mon. in winter. On those days, a set meal is served for residents. Plumber Manor has a family atmosphere, with the Prideaux-Brunes treating their clientele as house guests.

8. Wareham

This historic little town on the Frome River is about a mile west of Poole Harbor. Many find it a good center for touring the South Dorset coast and the Purbeck Hills. It contains remains of early Anglo-Saxon and Roman town walls, plus the Saxon church of St. Martin with its effigy of T. E. Lawrence (Lawrence of Arabia).

The district was known to Lawrence, who died in a motorcycle crash in 1935. His former home, **Clouds Hill,** lies 7 miles to the west of Wareham (a mile north of Bovington Camp). It is extremely small. From April to October, it is open from 2 to 5pm Wed., Thurs., Fri., and Sun., charging an admission of £1.70 ($2.80). From November to March, it is open from 1 to 4pm Sun. only.

WHERE TO STAY AND DINE

In what was a 16th-century priory, the **Priory Hotel,** Church Green, Wareham, Dorset BH20 4ND (tel. 09295/551666), has as a backdrop the rectangular bulk of the nearby village church. Beside the River Frome, the hotel has a well-tended garden adorned by graceful trees. Inside, a warmly paneled bar and a sumptuous lounge filled with antiques open onto views of the lawn. The 17 bedrooms are tastefully furnished with antiques and complementary textiles. Each has its own bath, mini-bar, TV, direct-dial phone, and many extras. Singles go for £45 ($74.25) to £115 ($189.75), with breakfast included. French-inspired meals are served in the wood-ringed dining room, while less formal fare is featured in the basement restaurant.

9. Dorchester

Thomas Hardy, in his 1886 novel *The Mayor of Casterbridge,* gave Dorchester literary fame. But it was known to the Romans; in fact, its Maumbury Rings, south of the town, is considered the best Roman amphitheater in Britain, having once resounded with the shouts of 12,000 spectators screaming for gladiator blood. Dorchester, a country town, was the setting of another bloodletting, the "Bloody Assize" of 1685, when Judge Jeffreys condemned to death the supporters of the Duke of Monmouth's rebellion against James II.

But it is mostly through Hardy that the world knows Dorchester. Many of his major scenes of love and intrigue took place on the periphery of Dorchester. The land was best known to Hardy, since he was born in 1840 at **Higher Bockhampton,** 3 miles northeast of Dorchester. His home, now a National Trust property, may be visited by the public March to October daily from 11am to 6pm or dusk, whichever is earlier. But to go inside, you must make an appointment with the tenant. You may write in advance to **Hardy's Cottage,** Higher Bockhampton, Dorchester, Dorset, England, or telephone 0305/62366. You approach the cottage on foot, a 10-minute walk after parking your vehicle in the space provided in the wood. The admission is £1.70 ($2.80).

You may also want to browse around the **Dorset County Museum,** High West Street (next to St. Peter's Church), with its gallery devoted to memorabilia of Thomas Hardy. In addition, you'll find an archeological gallery with displays and finds from Maiden Castle, Britain's largest Iron Age hill fort, plus galleries on the geology, local history, and natural history of Dorset. The museum is open 10am to 5pm Mon. to Sat. Admission is £1.20 ($2) for adults, 60p ($1) for children 5 to 16 years of age (children under 5 free).

WHERE TO STAY AND DINE

In business more than 3 centuries, **Kings Arms Hotel,** 30 High East St., Dorchester, Dorset DT1 1HF (tel. 0305/65353), has great bow windows above the porch and a swinging sign hanging over the road, a legacy left over from its days as a coaching inn. An archway leads to the courtyard and parking area at the back of the hotel. All the 31 rooms have been refurbished and have private baths, radios, TVs, phones, and hot beverage facilities. An overnight stay will cost £49 ($80.85) daily in a single, up to £125 ($206.25) in a twin. A full English breakfast and VAT are included in the tariffs. In addition to the main bar, there is a bistro overlooking the conservatory. Lunch snacks are served in both the bar and the bistro. Lunch and dinner are available in the restaurant, where the price for dinner is £12 ($19.80) to £24 ($39.60), including VAT.

In the Environs

Summer Lodge, Evershot, Dorset DT2 0JR (tel. 0935/83424), is a country-house hotel 12 miles north of Dorchester, where its resident owners, Nigel and Margaret Corbett, provide care, courtesy, and comfort. Once home to the heirs of the earls of Ilchester, the country house, in the village of Evershot, stands on 4 acres of secluded gardens. Evershot appears as Evershed in *Tess of the D'Urbervilles,* and author Thomas Hardy designed a wing of the house. In this relaxed, informal atmosphere, guests rent 17 rooms with views either of the garden or over the village rooftops to the fields beyond. Although centrally heated, the hotel offers log fires in winter. Guests sit around the fire getting to know each other in a convivial atmosphere. All rooms have private baths and phone (six have TVs). Rates range from £80 ($132) daily in a single to £125 ($206.25) to £152 ($250.80) in a double, including a full English breakfast, afternoon tea, a five-course dinner with coffee, and VAT. Mrs. Corbett, who does the cooking, specializes in traditional English dishes the way they should be done, placing the emphasis on homegrown and local produce. In addition to the dining room with its French windows opening onto a terrace, the Corbetts have a bar and a TV room, plus a heated outdoor pool and an all-weather tennis court.

Yalbury Cottage Country House Hotel and Restaurant, Lower Bockhampton, near Dorchester (tel. 0305/62382), is a thatch-roofed cottage with inglenooks and beamed ceilings in a small country village in the heart of Hardy country and, in fact, within walking distance of Thomas Hardy's cottage and of Stinsford Church, where his heart is buried. The hotel has eight luxuriously furnished and equipped bedrooms overlooking the gardens or fields beyond, reflecting a mood of tranquility. Each has private bath, color TV, phone, hot beverage facilities, ironing center, hairdryer, bathrobes, and other small touches for the guests' added comfort. The renowned restaurant is open, evenings only, for both residents and non-residents. Mouth-watering sauces and lightly cooked fresh vegetables enhance traditional English and continental dishes. Breakfast, a five-course dinner, and after-dinner coffee cost from £59 ($97.35) to £66 ($108.90) per person per day. Dinner is only £22.50 ($37.15) per person.

10. Bridport

In Thomas Hardy's fictional Wessex terrain, Bridport was Port Bredy. The town lies inland, although there is a harbor a mile away at the holiday resort of West Bay, near the end of Chesil Beach. Bridport is 150 miles from London, 38 miles from Exeter. Ropes and fishing nets are Bridport specialties. Many a man dangled from the end of a Bridport dagger—that is, a rope—especially when some home-grown rebels were carted off to Dorchester to face Hanging Judge Jeffreys.

An interesting excursion from Bridport is to visit **Parnham** at Beaminster (tel. 0308/862204). One of the loveliest houses in Dorset, it stands in a wooded valley beside the River Brit. Since Tudor times it has been surrounded by sweeping lawns and magnificent trees, along with terraces and falling water. In 1976 John Makepeace, internationally known designer and furniture maker, bought Parnham, made it his home, and set up his workshop in the former stables. Here his team of craftspeople make the unique pieces of exquisite, commissioned furniture, Makepeace designs, and on which his reputation is based. The well-restored rooms of the great house display recently completed pieces from the workshop, and there are monthly exhibitions by Britain's leading contemporary artists, designers, and craftspeople. The ornate plastered ceilings, paneled walls, and stone fireplace are a splendid setting for the best of 20th-century design and construction.

Light lunches and teas with homemade cakes and local clotted cream are served in the 17th-century licensed buttery. The house, gardens, exhibitions, and work-shop are open from April to October 10am to 5pm on Wed., Sun., and bank holidays. Admission is £2.75 ($4.55) for adults, £1.50 ($2.50) for children. Parnham is on the A3066, 5 miles north of Bridport.

WHERE TO STAY AND DINE

One of the most desirable places to stay in Bridport just happens to be a bargain as well. From February to October, **Roundham House**, Roundham Gardens, West Bay Road, Bridport, Dorset DT6 4BD (tel. 0308/22753), receives guests. It lies a mile south of Bridport by B3157. Near the sea, Roundham may be your sunny dream of a Dorset holiday. A beautifully kept country home, it rents a total of only eight bedrooms. Each is well furnished with either a private bath or shower, as well as a number of other amenities, including hairdryer, phone, and TV. Your hosts, Mr. and Mrs. R. David Moody, provide many thoughtful extras for their guests. From July to September, a single room rents for £29.50 ($48.70) daily, a double or twin going for £42 ($69.30). Off-season reductions are granted. Some rooms are suitable for families. It's best to take the half-board rate ranging from £32 ($52.80) to £41 ($67.65) per person daily. A table d'hôte menu at £12.50 ($20.65) provides good value and is made with fresh ingredients.

Haddon House, West Bay, Bridport, Dorset DT6 4EL (tel. 0308/23626), in the environs of Bridport, was built in the Regency style. It lies within a short walk of the harbor and the beaches of West Bay, which is about 1½ miles south of Bridport on B3157. Paul and Helen Loud are superb hosts, seeing to the needs of their guests and welcoming them into a homelike setting. They have 13 well furnished bed-rooms to rent, each with private bath or shower and many amenities such as phone, TV, and beverage-making equipment, along with trouser press and hairdryer. At this fully licensed hotel, they receive guests all year, charging from £33.50 ($55.30) daily in a single, rising to £47 ($77.55) in a double. The hotel adjoins an 18-hole golf course. Haddon House also offers good food with meals ranging from £10.50 ($17.35) to £15 ($24.75).

11. Chideock

Chideock is a charming village a mile west of Bridport. It's a hamlet of thatched houses, with a dairy farm in the center. About a mile away from the coast, it's a gem of a place for overnight stopovers, or especially longer stays. The countryside, with its rolling hills, makes excursions a temptation.

WHERE TO STAY AND DINE

In this village of winners, the 15th-century **Chideock House Hotel**, Chideock, Dorset DT6 6JN (tel. 0297/89242), is perhaps the prettiest thatched house. Set near the road, with a protective stone wall, the house opens onto a rear garden of flowers, shrubs, and fruit trees. A driveway through the gardens leads to a large car park. You go directly into the beamed lounge with its two fireplaces, one an Adam fireplace with a wood-burning blaze on cool days. Most of the nine bedrooms have private baths, and all have TVs and tea and coffee makers. You can stay here on a B&B basis at a cost beginning at £20 ($33.00) per person daily. The cuisine is a local favorite with the best dessert table in town and offers a good table d'hôte or à la carte menu, served from 7 to 9pm daily. The house quartered the Roundheads in 1645, and the ghosts of the village martyrs still haunt, as their trial was held at the hotel. Resident owners are Derek and Jenny Hammond.

12. Charmouth

On Lyme Bay, Charmouth, like Chideock, is another winner. A village of Georgian houses and thatched cottages, Charmouth contains some of the most dramatic coastal scenery in West Dorset. The village lies to the west of Golden Cap, which is, according to the adventurers who measure such things, the highest cliff along the coast of southern England. The location is 22 miles from Dorchester.

WHERE TO STAY AND DINE

The most desirable place to stay is **White House,** 2 Hillside, Charmouth, Dorset DT6 6PJ (tel. 0297/60411). It lies in this small coastal town once visited by Jane Austen gathering material for *Persuasion.* The White House is a Georgian home, with much of its period architecture, including bow doors, well preserved. It is tastefully furnished in a traditional style in keeping with the character of the house. Mr. and Mrs. Balfour took this place, constructed in 1827, and turned it into a most comfortable place at which to stay. Each of their seven handsomely furnished bedrooms has a private bath or shower, along with direct-dial phone, color TV, and hot beverage facilities. For B&B, a person pays from £38.50 ($63.55) nightly. Bar lunches are available during the day, and at night home-cooked dishes, with a selection of carefully chosen wines, are offered.

13. Lyme Regis

On Lyme Bay near the Devonshire border, the resort of Lyme Regis is one of the most attractive centers along the south coast. For those who shun such big, commercial holiday centers as Torquay or Bournemouth, Lyme Regis is ideal—the true English coastal town, with a highly praised mild climate. Seagulls fly overhead; the streets are steep and winding, walks along Cobb Beach brisk and stimulating, the views, particularly of the craft in the harbor, photogenic. Following Lyme Regis's career as a major seaport (the Duke of Monmouth landed here to begin his unsuccessful attempt to become king), one finds it was a small spa for a while, catering to such visitors as Jane Austen.

The seaside town was the location of the film *The French Lieutenant's Woman,* and the actors stayed in the town's two main hotels.

The town also boasts the 1979–1981 world champion and best-dressed town crier four different years, the latest being 1987. Richard Fox is just maintaining a tradition that has been handed down for 1,000 years in Lyme Regis when he announces the local news. He'll also take visitors on a 2-hour tour of the resort on Tues. at 3pm to see the Cobb, the harbor from which ships sailed to fight the Spanish Armada. The walk heads up old Broad Street. Mr. Fox can be reached at Flat 2, 22A Broad Street (tel. 02974/3568).

The surrounding area is a fascinating place for fossils. In 1810 at the age of 11 Mary Anning discovered one of the first articulated ichthyosaur skeletons. She went on to become one of the first professional fossilists in the country. Books telling of walks in the area and the regions where fossils can be seen are available at the local **information bureau** in the guildhall on Bridge Street (tel. 02974/2138).

WHERE TO STAY AND DINE

The most desirable place to stay is **Alexandra Hotel,** Pound Street, Lyme Regis, Dorset DT7 3HZ (tel. 02974/2010). Built in 1735, it was originally the home of the Dowager Countess Poulett and was later owned by duc du Stacpoole. But by the turn of the century it had reverted from an aristocratic address to a hotel. Today it has been discreetly modernized but with an awareness of its original character. Its gardens occupy 1½ acres. The hotel's attractively furnished bedrooms, 26 in all, have private baths, direct-dial phones, color TVs, radios, and tea and coffee makers. Rooms rent for £40 ($66) daily in a single, rising to £80 ($132) to £86 ($141.90) in a double. Both table d'hôte and à la carte meals are offered in the hotel's excellent dining room. Dinner costs from £15 ($24.75).

Mariners Hotel, Silver Street, Lyme Regis, Dorset DT7 3HS (tel. 02974/2753), a coaching inn dating from 1641, has been preserved and refurbished to become a fine hotel. The resident proprietors are proud, and rightly so, of the view from their lounge and some of the bedrooms of the Dorset coastline all the way to the lighthouse at Portland Bill, 25 miles away. All 15 bedrooms have private baths within or outside the units and contain phones and TVs. Although modernized, the accommodations retain their 17th-century charm of crooked beams and irregularly shaped rooms. Singles rent for £45 ($74.25) daily, with doubles costing £88 ($145.20). In the restaurant, you can either order table d'hôte or à la carte menus. The floodlit garden features a 340-year-old tulip tree, the third oldest in the country. The building occupied by the hotel was immortalized by Beatrix Potter in her painting of "Susan the Cat and Stumpy the Dog" and featured in *Tales of Little Pig Robinson* published in 1902.

Kersbrook Hotel, Pound Road, Lyme Regis, Dorset DT7 3HX (tel. 02974/2596), was built of stone in 1790 and is crowned by a thatch roof. It sits on a ledge above the village, which provides a panoramic view of the coast, on its 1½ acres of gardens redone according to the original 18th-century plans. The public rooms have been refurnished with antique furniture, re-creating old-world charm yet with all modern facilities. Mr. and Mrs. Eric Hall Stephenson are the resident proprietors, offering half-board rates ranging from £36 ($59.40) to £38 ($62.70) per person daily in a double or £47 ($77.55) in a single. All 12 bedrooms are comfortably furnished and contain private baths or showers. The hotel is justifiably proud of its pink, candlelit restaurant, serving table d'hôte and à la carte meals daily from 7:30 to 9:30pm, with an extensive wine list. The chef is known as an artist in the kitchen.

Royal Lion, Broad Street, Lyme Regis, Dorset DT7 3QF (tel. 02974/5622), is an old coaching inn, once known as the White Lion. On the side of a hill, it climbs up from the sea, with country furnishings in the oak-beamed bar and lounge. The 30 bedrooms are also country style, including one with a canopied bed used regularly by Edward VII when he was prince of Wales (his mistress, Lillie Langtry, was born in Lyme Regis). Accommodations contain private baths, TVs, and phones. A room and a large breakfast costs from £30 ($49.50) per person daily, including VAT and an early-morning cup of tea brought up with the daily papers. Ordered separately, a dinner will cost around £12 ($19.80), and you're given a choice of fresh local fish along with grilled meat dishes. There is a separate buffet bar.

---

14. Chedington

Chedington, 17 miles from Dorchester, is known to mapmakers and geographers as the meeting place of two of England's famous streams, the Axe and the Parrett. Motorists can more easily locate it near Winyard's Gap, a few yards from the A3565, which stretches between Crewkerne and Dorchester. The legendary King

Alfred is said to have found solace in this countryside from the pressures of ruling his kingdom. For a visit here, the following hotel is recommended.

WHERE TO STAY AND DINE

Chedington Court, Chedington, near Beaminster, Dorset DT8 3HY (tel. 093589/265), is a Jacobean manor house set in 10 acres of terraces, gardens, and lawns. It contains mullioned windows, boldly angled gables, and steep slate roofs. This manor was converted into a 10-room hotel in 1981 by the establishment's owners, Philip and Hilary Chapman. Much of the style and some of the grandeur of the Victorians have been preserved. There's a glassed-in conservatory laden with mimosa and plumbago. The bedrooms are individually furnished, sometimes with antiques, canopied beds, and fireplaces, along with some elegant accessories and such conveniences as phone and TV. One contains satinwood furniture that long ago was contained in an oceangoing suite aboard the *Queen Mary*. Doubles cost £55 ($90.75) to £70 ($115.50) per person daily for half board, including service and VAT. The fresh and flavorful meals served in the dining room from 7 to 9pm are a high point of the day. Each is personally and carefully prepared by Hilary and her assistant and served in a room with a panoramic view over the Dorset Hills.

15. Sherborne

A little gem of a town, with well-preserved medieval, Tudor, Stuart, and Georgian buildings, Sherborne is in the heart of Dorset in a setting of wooded hills, valleys, and chalk downs. It was here that Sir Walter Ralegh lived before the vicissitudes of power dislodged him forever.

Sherborne Old Castle (tel. 0935/812730), half a mile east of the town, was built in the early 12th century by the powerful Bishop Roger de Caen, but it was soon seized by the Crown about the time of the death of King Henry I in 1135 and the troubled accession to the throne of Stephen. The castle was given to Sir Walter Ralegh by Queen Elizabeth I. The gallant knight built Sherborne Lodge in the deer park close by (now privately owned). The buildings were mostly destroyed in the Civil War, but you can still see a gatehouse, some graceful arcades, and decorative windows. The castle ruins can be visited daily from March 17 to October 14, 10am to 6pm. From October 15 to March 16, hours are 10am to 4pm. Closed three days at Christmas and New Year's Day.

Sherborne Castle (tel. 0935/813182) was built by Sir Walter Ralegh in 1594, when he decided that it would not be feasible to restore the old castle to suit him. His new home was an Elizabethan residence, a square mansion, which later owners gussied up with four Jacobean wings to make it more palatial. After King James I had Ralegh imprisoned in the Tower of London, the monarch gave the castle to a favorite Scot, Robert Carr, so that the Raleghs were banished from their home. It became the property of Sir John Digby, first earl of Bristol, in 1617 and has been the Digby family home ever since. The mansion was enlarged by Sir John in 1625, and in the 18th century the formal Elizabethan gardens and fountains of the Raleghs were altered by Capability Brown, who created a serpentine lake between the two castles. The 20 acres of lawns and pleasure grounds around the 50-acre lake are open to the public. In the house are fine furniture, china, and paintings by Gainsborough, Lely, Reynolds, Kneller, and Van Dyck, among other artists. From Easter Sat. to the end of September the house is open from 2 to 5:30pm on Thur., Sat., Sun., and bank holidays. Admission to the castle is £2.70 ($4.45) for adults, £1.35 ($2.25) for children; to the grounds only, £1 ($1.65) for adults, 50p (85¢) for children.

Sherborne Abbey is worth visiting to see the splendid fan vaulting of the roof, as well as the many monuments, including Purbeck marble effigies of medieval abbots and the Elizabethan four-posters and canopied Renaissance tombs. A baroque statue of the earl of Bristol, standing between his two wives, was carved in 1698. The church is open daily from 8am to 6pm in summer, 4pm in winter. Many of the abbey's medieval monastic buildings are still in existence, used today to house a school. This British public school was the setting of a novel by Alec Waugh, *The Loom of Youth,* and for M.G.M.'s film *Goodbye, Mr. Chips.*

At **Cerne Abbas,** a village south of Sherborne, stands the Pitchmarket, where Thomas and Maria Washington, uncle and aunt of America's George Washington, once lived.

WHERE TO STAY AND DINE

Convenient to motorists because of its location at the side of the A30, the **Post House Hotel,** Horsecastles Lane, Sherborne, Dorset DT9 6BB (tel. 0935/813191), is a 60-bedroom modern hotel offering standardized comfort and renewed bathrooms. Accommodations are carpeted and attractively upholstered, containing mini-bars, phones, tea makers, and color TVs. Singles rent for £56 ($92.40) to £66 ($108.90) daily and doubles for £66 ($108.90) to £74 ($122.10) with breakfast included. A bar and restaurant are on the premises.

Eastbury Hotel, Long Street, Sherborne, Dorset DT9 3BY (tel. 0935/813131), is a 12-room Georgian townhouse hotel, lying in its own walled garden close to the 8th century abbey and Sherborne's two castles. Built in 1740 in the reign of George II, it has a traditional ambience, with its own library of antiquarian books. Beautifully restored, it still maintains its 18th-century character. Each bedroom with its own bath, color TV, direct-dial phone, along with several other amenities, maintains an individual character. The charge is from £55 ($90.75) daily in a single, rising to £78 ($128.70) in a double. The best, fresh English produce is served in the dining room, which has an extensive wine list. Meals begin at £12 ($19.80).

IX

DEVON

1. EXETER

2. DARTMOOR

3. CHAGFORD

4. TORQUAY

5. TOTNES

6. DARTMOUTH

7. PLYMOUTH

8. MILTON DAMEREL

9. CLOVELLY

10. LYNTON-LYNMOUTH

11. THE TAW VALLEY

The great patchwork quilt area of the southwest of England, part of the "West Countree," abounds with cliffside farms, rolling hills, foreboding moors, semitropical plants, and fishing villages. The British approach sunny Devon with the same kind of excitement one would normally reserve for hopping over to the continent. Especially along the coastline, the British Riviera, many of the names of the seaports, villages, and resorts have become synonymous with holidays in the sun: Torquay (Torbay), Clovelly, Lynton-Lynmouth.

Many small towns and fishing villages do not allow cars to enter. Car parks are provided on the outskirts, but sometimes there is a long walk to the center of the harbor. In high season, from mid-July to mid-September, the more popular villages get quite crowded, and one needs reservations in the limited number of hotels available.

It's easy to involve yourself in the West Country life, as lived by the British vacationers. Perhaps you'll go pony trekking across moor and woodland, past streams and sheep-dotted fields, stopping at local pubs to soak up atmosphere and ale. Chances are your oddly shaped bedroom will be in a barton (farm) mentioned in the *Domesday Book* or in a thatch cottage neither straight, level, nor true.

When a Devonian invites you to walk down the primrose path, he or she means just that. The primrose is practically the shire flower of this most beautiful of counties. Devon is a land of jagged coasts—the red cliffs in the south facing the English Channel, the gray cliffs in the north opening onto the Bristol Channel.

It's the lazy life in south Devon, as you sit in the orchard, enjoying the view of the coast from which Ralegh and Drake set sail. Almost every little hamlet is geared to accommodate tourists, who flock here in great numbers from early spring to late fall. There is much to see and explore. The tranquil life prevails.

North Devon is Lorna Doone country. Much of the district is already known to those who have read Victorian novelist R. D. Blackmore's romance of the West Country, *Lorna Doone*.

The bay-studded coastline is mysterious. Pirates and smugglers used to find havens in crooked creeks and rocky coves. The ocean crashes against the rocks, and the meadows approach so close to the cliff's edge that you wonder why they don't go spilling into the sea, sheep and all. The heather-clad uplands of Exmoor, with its red deer, extend into north Devon from Somerset, a perfect setting for an English mystery. Favorite bases are Clovelly and the twin resorts of Lynton and Lynmouth.

Aside from the shores, a great many of the scenic highlights appear in the two national parks: **Dartmoor** in the south, **Exmoor** in the north.

A SPECIAL BUS TICKET

The two main bus companies in Devon and Cornwall combine to offer a **Key West ticket,** granting unlimited travel anywhere on the two networks for any 7 consecutive days at a cost of £16 ($26.40) for adults and £11 ($18.15) for children under 14. A family ticket—two adults and two children—costs £32 ($52.80). You can plan your journeys from the maps and timetables available at any Western National/Devon General office when you purchase your ticket. Further information may be obtained from Devon General Ltd., Belgrave Road, Exeter, Devon EX1 2LB (tel. 0392/439333).

---

1. Exeter

The county town of Devonshire, on the banks of the River Exe, Exeter, 201 miles from London, was a Roman city founded in the 1st century A.D. Two centuries later it was encircled by a mighty stone wall, traces of which remain today. Conquerors and would-be conquerors, especially the Vikings, stormed the fortress —none was more notable than William the Conqueror. Irked at Exeter's refusal to capitulate (perhaps also because it sheltered Gytha, mother of the slain Harold), the Norman duke brought Exeter to its knees on short notice.

Under the Tudors, the city grew and prospered. Sir Walter Ralegh and Sir Francis Drake cut striking figures strolling through Exeter's streets. In May 1942 the Germans bombed Exeter, destroying many of the city's architectural treasures. Exeter was rebuilt, but the new, impersonal-looking shops and offices couldn't replace the Georgian crescents and the black-and-white timbered buildings with their plastered walls. Fortunately, much was spared, including the major architectural treasure, the cathedral.

EXETER CATHEDRAL

Owing its present look to the Decorated style of the 13th and 14th centuries, the Exeter Cathedral Church of St. Peter actually goes back to Saxon times. Even Canute, the Viking conqueror, got in on the act of rebuilding around 1017. The cathedral of Bishop Warelwast came into being in the early 12th century, and the north and south towers serve as reminders of the Norman period. The remarkable feature of the present Gothic building is the tierceron vaulting of the nave and quire, 300 feet long and unbroken by any central tower or spire. The cathedral did suffer damage in the 1942 German bombings, losing its St. James's Chapel, which subsequently has been restored. But most of the treasures remained intact, including the rows of sculpture along the west front; the 14th-century Minstrels' Gallery, its angelic figures with early English musical instruments in hand; and the carved oak 14th-century bishop's throne. The Dean and Chapter, who own the cathedral, re-

CORNWALL AND DEVON

Isles of Scilly

St. Martin's
Tresco
Bryher
Samson
Hugh Town   St. Mary's
St. Agnes

Atlantic Ocean

0   kms.   16
0   miles   10

N

SOMERSET

Bristol Channel

Ilfracombe
Barnstaple
Bideford
Clovelly
Barnstaple Bay
Great Torrington
So. Molton
Chulmleigh
Tiverton

DEVON

Okehampton
Moretonhampstead
Lydford
Tavistock
Bovey Tracey

Exeter
Seaton
Exmouth
Teignmouth
Torquay
Newton Abbot
Brixham
Ivybridge
Dartmouth

CORNWALL

Newquay
St. Austell
St. Ives
Penzance
Land's End
Helston
Falmouth
Mount's Bay

Polperro
Millbrook
Plymouth

English Channel

M5
30
361
38
30
30
30
30
38

quest that visitors make a donation of at least £1 ($1.65) per adult. The cathedral is open from 7:15am to 5:30pm Mon. to Fri., from 7:15am to 3pm Sat., and from 8:30am to 6:30pm Sun.

EXETER MARITIME MUSEUM

At the Haven (tel. 0392/58075), the maritime museum has a collection of more than 200 small craft, many of which are on display, and shelters the world's largest collection of English and foreign craft, coming from places that range from the Congo to Corfu. The larger boats afloat in the canal basin can be boarded. There are canoes, proas, and boats that have been rowed across the Atlantic, and you can go aboard the oldest working steamboat or even picnic on a Hong Kong junk or an Arab dhow. This is an active museum, and the ISCA members who maintain the boats sail some of them during the summer months. Five colorful Portuguese chatas that carry a maximum of six passengers are available for rent at the museum from May to September. The boats are rowed along the 3 miles of navigable water on the historic canal at a charge of £2.50 ($4.15) per hour. The museum is open every day of the year except Christmas and Boxing Day from October to June 10am to 5pm, July to September to 6pm. Adults pay an admission of £3 ($4.95); children, £1.75 ($2.90). Note: Occasionally, individual boats used for special events or sailing may not be on display.

OTHER ATTRACTIONS

Much of the old remains. The **Exeter Guildhall,** a colonnade building on High Street (tel. 0392/265500), is regarded as the oldest municipal building in the kingdom. The earliest reference to the guildhall is contained in a deed of 1160. The Tudor front that straddles the pavement was added in 1593. Inside is a fine display of silver in the gallery. It contains a number of paintings as well, including one of Henrietta Anne, daughter of Charles I (she was born in Exeter in 1644). The ancient hall is paneled in oak. Subject to mayoral commitments, the guildhall is open throughout the year from 10:30am to 5pm Mon. to Sat., and admission is free.

Just off "the High" is a green historic oasis. At the top of Castle Street stands an impressive Norman gatehouse from William the Conqueror's castle. Although only the house and walls survive, the view from here and the surrounding gardens is spectacular. Just by the gatehouse is a charming Regency villa, adapted from an earlier house and now known as **Rougemont House Museum,** home of Exeter's costume and lace, in Castle Street (tel. 0392/265858), which is open daily from 10am to 5:30pm. The museum features costumes displayed in period rooms (these change twice a year), along with one of the largest lace collections in Europe. It charges £1.70 ($2.80) for adults and 70p ($1.15) for children.

St. Nicholas Priory, the Mint, off Fore Street (tel. 0392/265858), is open from 10am to 5:30pm Tues. to Sat., charging adults 65p ($1.05) and children 30p (50¢). This is the guest wing of a Benedictine priory founded in 1070. You will see fine plaster ceilings and period furniture.

The **Underground Passages** just of Exeter's High Street were built to carry the medieval water supply into the city. Now by entering the new underground interpretation center, visitors are able to see a video presentation and introductory exhibition before taking a guided tour, making this one of the most unusual museums in the country. Admission free, the center (tel. 0392/265213) is open daily year round from 10am to 4pm.

On the Outskirts

Powderham Castle, Powderham (tel. 0626/890243), lies 8 miles south of Exeter off the A379 Dawlish road. A castle was built here in the late 14th century by Sir Philip Courtenay, sixth son of the second earl of Devon, and his wife, Margaret, granddaughter of Edward I. Their magnificent tomb is in the south transept of

Exeter Cathedral. The castle suffered damage during the Civil War and was restored and altered in the 18th and 19th centuries. The castle contains many family portraits and fine furniture, including a remarkable clock that plays full tunes at 4pm, 8pm and 12 o'clock, some 17th-century tapestries, and a chair used by William III for his first council of state at Newton Abbot. The staircase hall contains some remarkable plasterwork set in bold relief against a turquoise background, more than 2 centuries old, as well as a detailed pedigree of the Courtenay family, a document more than 12 feet high. The chapel dates from the 15th century, with hand-hewn roof timbers and carved pew ends. Powderham Castle is a private house lived in by Lord and Lady Courtenay and family. From May to early September the castle is open from 2 to 5:30pm Sun. to Thurs. Admission is £2.75 ($4.55) for adults, £1.75 ($2.80) for children 8 to 16. There is a tea room for light refreshments.

WHERE TO STAY

Buckerell Lodge, Topsham Road, Exeter, Devon EX2 4SQ (tel. 0392/52451), is about the finest place to stay in the area, lying a mile southeast of the center on the B3182. The origins of the house go back to the 12th century, but it has been altered and changed beyond recognition over the years. Often a choice of commercial travelers, it's also a tourist favorite, especially in summer. The look today is Regency, and the bedrooms are well decorated and nicely equipped with private baths, phones, and TVs, coming in a range of styles and sizes. In all, 54 bedrooms are rented, costing £64 ($105.60) daily in a single, £76 ($125.40) in a double. During the day you can dine on lighter fare such as soups and salads, and in the evening you can order such traditional English fare as roast beef and Yorkshire pudding, served from 7 to 9:45pm, costing £20 ($33) for a complete meal.

Rougemont Hotel, Queen Street, Exeter, Devon EX4 3SP (tel. 0392/54982), is imbued with a stylish flair that none of its competitors provides. Fairly recently, this great, old-fashioned Victorian hotel, opposite the central railway station, underwent a metamorphosis, emerging as a solid place at which to stay. Its neoclassical architecture is a background for the contemporary furnishings. Much of the comfort and tasteful decor are found in the 66 bedrooms. Singles rent from £60 ($99) daily and doubles from £69.50 ($114.70), including VAT and an English breakfast. Amenities include telephones, radios, TVs, private baths, and air conditioning. A fixed price dinner costs £12.50 ($20.65). Guests gather in the Adam-style Drake's Bar for drinks. A good stock of wine comes from the cellar, which, incidentally, was once a debtors' prison.

Royal Clarence Hotel, Cathedral Yard, Exeter, Devon EX1 1HD (tel. 0392/58464), a Georgian building, escaped destruction during the war. It is a hotel full of history, recently refurbished. All of the 56 bedrooms have private baths, phones, and TVs, and many overlook the 14th-century cathedral. A single rents for £60 ($99) to £78 ($128.70) daily, a double going for £105 ($173.25), with VAT included. Comfortable lounges display a mixture of antiques, gilt mirrors, and modern pieces. In the restaurant, a table d'hôte lunch costs £12.50 ($20.65) and a set dinner costs £16 ($26.40). You can also order à la carte.

Devon Motel, Exeter Bypass, Matford, Exeter, Devon EX32 8XU (tel. 0392/59268), lies on the outskirts of the city at the western sector of the bypass on the A38. It is convenient to the airport and as a stopping-off point for those headed for the West Country. You drive your car into your own open garage, and your bedroom and private bath are directly overhead. Singles pay £44 ($72.60) to £49 ($80.85) daily and doubles £57 ($94.05) to £62 ($102.30), including a full English breakfast and VAT. Some cheaper singles are in the old part of the hotel and are without bath, but all doubles and units in the new wing have private baths, phones, and TVs. Inside, all is compact and built-in, with a picture window overlooking the meadows beyond. On the premises are a restaurant and bars. An à la carte dinner costs from £12 ($19.80).

White Hart Hotel, 65-66 South St., Exeter, Devon EX1 1EE (tel. 0391/79897), a coaching inn in the 17th and 18th centuries, is one of the oldest inns in the city. It is said that Cromwell stabled his horses here. The hotel is a mass of polished wood, slate floors, oak beams, and gleaming brass and copper. The 61 bed-rooms combine old and new, containing color TVs, baths or showers, and phones. Guests are housed in either the old wing or a more modern one. Some units are considered deluxe, and the most expensive are private suites. The single rate begins at £44 ($72.60) daily with bath or shower, going up to £48 ($79.20). Doubles or twins with bath cost from £64 ($105.60). All tariffs include a full English breakfast. Suites are more expensive. The dining room offers good English and continental dishes in a well-appointed atmosphere. The hotel has a wine cellar, which supplies the Ale & Port House (a bar with waiter service where you can feast on traditional English fare), plus the well-known Bottlescreu Bills wine bar, which offers beefsteak-and-oyster pie or, in summer, barbecued steak in the wine garden. The hotel is owned by one of London's most famous wine merchants, their only—to date—hotel venture. You may want to patronize the bar even if you're not a guest. It is open from 11am to 11pm Mon. to Sat., 11am to 3pm and 6 to 10:30pm Sun.

St. Olaves Court Hotel, Mary Arches Street, Exeter, Devon EX4 3AZ (tel. 0392/217736), is such a favorite that it's almost considered a special address. A Georgian mansion, it lies in the center of Exeter, having been constructed as a home by a rich merchant, circa 1830. The location is ideal, within a short walk of the cathedral. You can hear the church bells. The house has been discreetly furnished, in part with antiques. Each of the 17 bedrooms has been individually decorated, containing such amenities as hot beverage facilities, TV, radio, and private bath or shower. Singles pay from £34 ($56.10) to £52 ($85.80) daily, with doubles charged £41 ($67.65) to £67 ($110.55). A trouser press, hairdryer, and what the English call a "hospitality tray" are found in every room, some of which are equipped with Jacuzzis. The hotel also features a good English cuisine, serving meals until 9:30pm. Reserve early, as the fame of this place is growing.

WHERE TO DINE

Tudor House, Tudor Street (tel. 0392/73764), is the choice place for dining. Exeter suffered for years without a really fine restaurant until the chef de cuisine and owner, Jean Cooke, opened this imaginative dining room. Housed in a Tudor build-ing, the restaurant has a gracious beamed interior with well-chosen furnishings and trappings. The food is a happy marriage of traditional and modern. The restaurant is sophisticated enough to have vegetarian meals, but it will also cater to the gent want-ing a good steak with sauce. Homemade soups often have flair in their selection of ingredients, and main dishes are fresh and perfectly cooked. The menu is likely to change in the lifetime of this edition, but you'll be assured of getting the best of modern British cuisine. A set lunch is modestly priced at £10 ($16.50), with à la carte dinners costing from £20 ($33). Service is from noon to 2pm and 7 to 9:45pm Tues. to Sun. (closed lunch Sat.). Reservations are needed.

A short walk from the cathedral, the **Ship Inn,** Martin's Lane (tel. 0392/72040), was often visited by Sir Francis Drake, Sir Walter Ralegh, and Sir John Haw-kins. Of it Drake wrote: "Next to mine own shippe, I do most love that old 'Shippe' in Exon, a tavern in Fyssh Street, as the people call it, or as the clergie will have it, St. Martin's Lane." The pub still provides tankards of real ales, lager, and stout and is still loved by both young and old. A large selection of snacks is offered in the bar every day, while the restaurant upstairs provides more substantial English fare. At either lunch or dinner, you can order from a wide selection including French onion soup, whole grilled lemon sole, and five different steaks. The price of the main courses includes vegetables, roll, and butter. Portions are large, as in Elizabethan times. Expect to spend from £6 ($9.90) to £10 ($16.50) for a three-course meal. The restaurant is open from noon to 2pm Mon. to Sat. and from 6:30 to 10pm Mon. to Sat. Sun. hours are noon to 2pm and 7 to 9pm. The bar is open from 11am to 2:30pm and 5 to 11pm Mon. to Sat., from noon to 2pm and 7 to 10:30pm Sun.

Coolings Wine Bar, 11 Gandy St. (tel. 0392/434183). In one of the older and more interesting little streets of the city, this is a beckoning place with beams above the checked cloths of the tables. Some of the dining space is in the cellars of the old building. All the food is prepared on the premises, and that includes a good selection of cold meats, pies, and quiches, as well as chicken Waldorf and sugar-baked ham, each served with a variety of salads, then two or three daily hot dishes, chalked up on the blackboard. Meals cost around £6 ($9.90). The place is open from 11am to 2:30pm and 5:30 to 11pm Mon. to Sat.

WHERE TO STAY AND DINE OUTSIDE EXETER
Perhaps the finest way to enjoy the cathedral city of Exeter, especially if you have a car, is to live on the outskirts, from 10 to 19 miles from the heart of the city.

At Bickleigh
In the Exe Valley, 4 miles south of Tiverton and 10 miles north of Exeter, lies Bickleigh, a hamlet with a river, an arched stone bridge, a mill pond, and thatch-roofed cottages—epitome of English charm, one of the finest spots in all of Devon.
Bickleigh Cottage Country Hotel, Bickleigh Bridge, Bickleigh, Devon EX16 8RJ (tel. 08845/230), is a thatched, 17th-century, nine-room hotel with a riverside garden leading down to the much photographed Bickleigh Bridge. Add to this image swans and ducks gliding by to get your leftover crumbs from tea on the lawn. Mr. and Mrs. Stuart Cochrane, the owners, charge from £15 ($24.75) per person nightly for B&B. In a room with a private bath, the rate is from £17.50 ($28.90) per person nightly. Meals are good and nourishing. The raspberries and gooseberries come fresh from the garden, topped with generous portions of Devonshire cream. Dinner is priced from £8.50 ($14.05). Inside, the rooms are cozy, with oak beams and old fireplaces. Bus 354 runs between Exeter and Tiverton, if you don't have a car.

At Ottery St. Mary
This sleepy little market town, where Coleridge *(The Rime of the Ancient Mariner, Kubla Khan)* was born, lies in the Otter River Valley, only 10 miles east of Exeter. See the almost perfectly preserved church from the 14th century. The old cloth town makes a good base for exploring the south Devon coastline, particularly if you center at the following medium-priced recommendation:
Salston Hotel, Ottery St. Mary, near Exeter, Devon EX11 1RQ (tel. 04081/5581), an old manor house, lies 1½ miles off the main A30 London road, and a mile from Ottery St. Mary. The hotel is officially listed as a building of historical and architectural interest. It was once the home of the Coleridge family. Even though it has lost most of its acreage and original furnishings, the exterior is intact—a rambling three-story brick hotel with chimneys and gables. The lounge is large, with two bay windows opening onto the gardens. A ballroom, built for the visit of Princess Alexandra of Teck (that name may send you rushing to your history books), has a Tudor fireplace. The 27-room Salston has added an extension with luxury rooms. Each of its rooms has a shower, hairdryer, mini-bar, phone, and TV. B&B charges in a single cost from £50 ($82.50) daily, with doubles going for £62 ($102.30). Spa fans will find a health studio run in conjunction with the Salston, plus two squash courts. There is a 20- by 48-foot swimming pool, plus an adjoining Norwegian pine cabin with sauna, solarium, and massage and relaxing room.

At South Zeal
South Zeal lies 17 miles west of Exeter. The village is signposted from the A30, near Sticklepath.
The Oxenham Arms, South Zeal, Okehampton, Devon EX20 2JT (tel. 0837/840244). Its conversion to an inn in 1487 earmarks this place as one of the oldest continuously licensed inns in England. Its history predates that era by hundreds of years, however, as a massive Celtic standing-stone testifies. The establishment is owned by Louisiana-born James Henry and his English wife, Patricia. The carefully

preserved inn was originally built in the 12th century as a monastery. The mullioned windows and chiseled granite of the facade, coupled with the beamed and paneled interior, hint that this is no ordinary pub hotel. Inside, clusters of antiques and open fireplaces add a note of charm. Nature lovers appreciate the garden, whose shrubs are accessible via the old monastery's steps. All but two of the eight rooms contain private baths. For stays of one or two nights, the rate for B&B ranges from £18 ($29.70) to £25 ($41.25) per person daily, depending on the plumbing. The half-board tariff is also attractively priced at £30 ($49.50) to £35 ($57.75) per person daily. The dining room is open to non-residents, the charge being £8.50 ($14.05) to £12.50 ($20.65) for a fixed-price lunch or dinners. Menu specialties include tasty bar food as well as more formal dishes such as pot pie of mixed shellfish, Devonshire squab pie, and fresh fish. There's a dart board, plus several kinds of English ale in the atmospheric bar.

2. Dartmoor

Antiquity-rich Dartmoor's foreboding landscape is for the experienced walker only. The land of this granite mass sometimes rises to a height of 2,000 feet above sea level. The national park is a patchwork quilt of mood changes: gorse and purple heather, Dartmoor ponies, gorges with rushing water.

Accommodation information is operated by the **Dartmoor Tourist Association,** 8 Fitzford Cottages, Tavistock (tel. 0252/3501). Local information centers will also provide a list of accommodations.

Some 13 miles west from Exeter, the peaceful little town of **Moretonhampstead,** perched on the edge of Dartmoor, makes a good center. Moretonhampstead contains much that is old, including a market cross and several 17th-century colonnaded almshouses.

The much visited Dartmoor village of **Widecombe-in-the-Moor** is only 7 miles from Moretonhampstead. The fame of the village stems from an old folk song about Tom Pearce and his gray mare, listing the men who were supposed to be on their way to Widecombe Fair when they met with disaster: Bill Brewer, Jan Stewer, Peter Gurney, Peter Davy, Daniel Whiddon, Harry Hawke, and Old Uncle Tom Cobley. Widecombe also has a parish church worth visiting. Called the **Cathedral of the Moor,** whose roster of vicars begins in 1253, the house of worship in a green valley is surrounded by legends. When the building was restored, a wall-plate was found bearing the badge of Richard II (1377–1399), the figure of a white hart.

Transmoor Link, a public transport bus service, usually operates throughout the summer and is an ideal way to get onto the moor to explore the 500 miles of footpaths, bridleways, and more than 90,000 acres of common land with public access. The country is rough and on the high moor you should always make sure you have good maps, a compass, and suitable clothing and shoes. Don't be put off, however. Unless you are an experienced hiker, it is unlikely that you will go far from the well-trodden paths.

Information on Transmoor Link and on bus links between various towns and villages on Dartmoor is available from the Transport Co-ordination Centre (tel. 0392/272123).

The **Dartmoor National Park Authority** (DNPA) runs guided walks of varying difficulty, ranging from 1½ hours up to 6 hours for a trek of some 9 to 12 miles. All you have to do is turn up suitably clad at your selected starting point, and there you are. Details are available from DNP information centers or from the Dartmoor National Park Authority Headquarters, Parke, Haytor Road, Bovey Tracey, Devon TQ13 9JQ (tel. 0626/832093). The charge for walks is £1 ($1.65) to £2 ($3.30).

Throughout the area are stables where you can arrange for a day's trek across the moors. For horseback riding on Dartmoor there are too many establishments to list. All are licensed, and you are accompanied by an experienced guide. The moor can be dangerous, with sudden fogs descending without warning on treacherous marshlands. Prices are around £3 ($4.95) per hour, £8 ($13.20) for a half day, and £14 ($23.10) for a full day. Most riding stables are listed in a useful free publication, *The Dartmoor Visitor*, which also contains details of guided walks, places to go, accommodations, local events, and articles about the national park. *The Dartmoor Visitor* is obtainable from DNP information centers and tourist information centers or by post. Send an International Reply Coupon to the DNPA headquarters (address above).

Museum of Dartmoor Life, Dartmoor Centre, West Street, Okehampton (tel. 0837/52295). The market town of Okehampton owes its existence to the Norman castle built by Baldwin de Bryonis, the sheriff of Devon, under orders from his uncle, William the Conqueror, in 1068, just 2 years after the Conquest. The Courtenay family lived there for many generations until Henry VIII beheaded one of them and dismantled the castle in 1538. The museum is housed in an old mill with a waterwheel and is part of the Dartmoor Centre, a group of attractions around an old courtyard. Also here are working craft studios, a Victorian cottage tea room, and a Dartmoor National Park tourist information center. Museum displays cover all aspects of Dartmoor's history from prehistoric times, including geology, industries, living conditions, crafts, farm tools and machinery, and some old vehicles—a Devon box wagon of 1875, a 1922 Bullnose Morris motorcar, a 1937 motorcycle. There is a reconstructed cider press, a blacksmithy, and a tourist information center. The museum is open March to December from 10am to 5pm Mon. to Sat. (and on Sun. in July and August). Admission is 80p ($1.30) for adults, 40p (65¢) for children.

WHERE TO STAY AND DINE

A Jacobean-style mansion, the **Manor House Hotel,** Moretonhampstead, Devon TQ13 8RE (tel. 0647/40355), is set in 270 acres of private parkland on the edge of Dartmoor National Park. In the grounds are an excellent 18-hole championship golf course, a par-3 course, a putting green, and tennis and squash courts. Built by the second viscount Hambledon as a hunting lodge in 1907, the hotel is renowned for its open log fires, oak paneling, and superb cuisine. All of the 69 bedrooms have private baths, color TVs, radios, direct-dial phones, trouser presses, and hot beverage facilities. Prices quoted for half board are £80 ($132) to £87 ($143.55) daily for singles in high season, £55 ($90.75) to £70 ($115.50) in low season. Doubles and twins, also for half board, pay £140 ($231) to £160 ($264) in high season, £95 ($156.75) to £120 ($198) off-season. Prices include VAT, service charge, and golf privileges. Bar snacks can be enjoyed at lunch, and Devonshire cream teas are available every afternoon. From the terrace, you can watch the River Bovey meandering through grounds or set out on a walk along its bank to the lakes and gardens.

The Castle Inn, Lydford, near Okehampton, Devon EX20 4BH (tel. 082282/242), is a 16th-century inn next to Lydford Castle. The low inn, with its pink facade and row of rose trellises, is the hub of the village, along with the all-purpose grocery store and post office. The inn's owners, David and Susan Grey, have maintained the character of the commodious rustic lounge with its valuable collection of old furniture and accessories, including wing chairs, grandfather clocks, and antique prints. One room is called the "Snug," containing a group of high-backed oak settles arranged in a circle. The inn is the home of the famous Lydford pennies, hammered out in a Saxon mint in the reign of Ethelred the Unready (around A.D. 1000). Seven of the pennies are displayed in the Foresters' Bar, where meals are served buffet style, from noon to 2pm daily, a great spread set out on a long table. The cost depends on your selection of a main course. Buffet salads at lunch cost about £5 ($8.25) with a main course. Snacks are available as well. A three-course dinner will run about £15 ($24.75). For a bed and a large country-style breakfast, the charge is £27 ($44.55) to £32 ($52.80) daily in a single, £42 ($69.30) in a double or twin, depending on the plumbing. The 10 bedrooms are not large but are well planned and attractively furnished, often with mahogany and marble Victorian pieces, each room with its own color scheme, TV, and phone. Two are suites.

Holne Chase Hotel, Ashburton, near Newton Abbot, Devon TQ13 7NS (tel. 03643/471), is a white-gabled country house, within sight of trout- and salmon-fishing waters. You can catch your lunch and take it back to the kitchen to be cooked. Although the mood of the moor predominates, Holne Chase is surrounded by trees, lawns, and pastures, a perfect setting for walks along the Dart. It's off the main Ashburton-Princetown road, between Holne Bridge and New Bridge. Every bedroom in the house is named after a tributary of the River Dart. B&B ranges from £50 ($82.50) to £60 ($99) daily in a single and from £60 ($99) to £100 ($165) in a double. Accommodations contain private baths, phones, and TVs. The 14-room house is furnished in period style, a refurbished bar also being done in the style of the rest of the hotel. The cooking combines the best of English fare with specialty dishes that are made all the better whenever produce from the gardens is used or fresh fish from the Dart River and Torquay. Devon beef and lamb are also featured. The old cellars hold a good selection of wines.

Cherrybrook Hotel, Two Bridges, Yelverton, Devon PL20 6SP (tel. 0822/88260), is a small family-run hotel in the center of the Dartmoor National Park, on the high moor but within easy driving distance of Exeter and Plymouth. It was built in the early 19th century by a friend of the Prince Regent, given permission to enclose a large area of the forest of Dartmoor for farming. Part of the farm was later leased to a gunpowder-manufacturing company, whose remains can still be seen. The lounge and bar with their beamed ceiling and slate floors are a reminder of these times. John and Susan Reynolds rent seven double, single, and family rooms, all of which have private showers and toilets, charging £20.50 ($33.85) per person daily for B&B. You can dine here also, paying around £10 ($16.50) for a four-course dinner and coffee.

A VISIT TO AN ABBEY

Constructed in 1278, **Sir Francis Drake's House,** Buckland Abbey, Yelverton (tel. 0822/853607), was originally a Cistercian monastery. It was dissolved in 1539 and became the country seat of Sir Richard Grenville and later Sir Francis Drake (two great sailors). It remained in the Drake family until 1946 when the abbey and grounds were given to the National Trust. The abbey is now a museum, housing exhibits including Drake's drum, banners, and other artifacts. (You probably won't get a chance to beat Drake's drum, but if you do, remember the words of Henry Newbold's poem: "Drake will quit the port of heaven and come to England's aid once more.") The abbey lies 3 miles west of Yelverton off the A386. It is open from April to the end of October 10:30am to 5:30pm (to 5pm in October); closed Thurs. The rest of the year it is open on Wed., Sat., and Sun. from 2 to 5pm. Admission is £3.20 ($5.30) for adults, £1.60 ($2.65) for children. Light snacks are available daily.

---

3. Chagford

Six hundred feet above sea level, Chagford is an ancient Stannary Town. With the moors all around, it is a good base for exploration of the region of North Dartmoor. It is 20 miles from Exeter, Torquay, and Plymouth. Chagford overlooks the Teign River in its deep valley and is itself overlooked by the high granite tors. There's good fishing in the Teign (ask at your hotel). From Chagford, the most popular excursion is to **Postbridge,** 6 miles to the southwest, a village with a prehistoric clapper bridge.

Near Chagford stands **Castle Drogo,** in the hamlet of Drewsteignton (tel. 06473/3306). This massive granite castle was designed and built by Sir Edwin Lutyens and the castle's owner, Julius Drewe, in the early 20th century. It stands high above the River Teign, with views over the moors. The family can trace its origins back to the Norman Conquest. Drewe, who wanted to create a home worthy of his noble ancestors, found the bleak site high above the moors, and he and Lutyens created a splendid modern castle. The tour includes the elegant library, the drawing room, the dining room with fine paintings and mirrors, and a chapel, along with a vaulted-roof gunroom and a garden. There is a restaurant open daily from 11am to 5:30pm. The castle is open from April to October 11am to 5:30pm, to 4:30pm in October, Sat. to Thurs., charging an admission of £3.40 ($5.60) for adults, half price for children. If you wish to visit only the grounds, the fee is £1.50 ($2.50) for adults, half that for children.

WHERE TO STAY AND DINE

A mile from the edge of Dartmoor in beautiful countryside, the **Gidleigh Park Hotel,** Chagford, Devon TQ13 8HH (tel. 06473/2367), is 2 miles from Chagford, northwest by Gidleigh Road. A visit to this hotel, a *Relais & Chateaux,* is highly recommended. Its American owners, Kay and Paul Henderson, have renovated and refurnished the house with flair and imagination. In a park of 40 acres, the mansion is Tudor style. Large beech and oak trees abound. Inside, the oak-paneled public rooms and the open log fires invite a return to yesterday. The windows open onto views of the garden and the Teign Valley, with Dartmoor lying beyond. Most of the bedrooms, 14 in all, are on the second floor and are approached by a grand staircase. All rooms contain private baths, color TVs, and phones. Room rates depend on the size of the room and its view, and are from £175 ($288.75) to £275 ($453.75) daily for double occupancy, and £140 ($231) to £240 ($396) for single occupancy. This includes dinner, morning tea and newspaper, continental breakfast, service, and tax. The hotel has a three-room thatched cottage with two bathrooms across the river, 350 yards from the hotel. It is available for two, three, or four people. Excellent meals costing from £40 ($66) are served in an oak-paneled dining room. The menu is changed daily, and only the best and freshest products are used. Dining here has been called a memorable experience. In fact, the restaurant here has been called "one of the best in the West Country," and its wine list has received numerous awards.

How to get there: From Chagford Square turn right into Mill Street at Lloyds Bank. After 200 yards, fork right and down the hill to the crossroads. Cross straight over onto Holy Street, following the lane passing Holy Street Manor on your right and shifting into low gear to negotiate two sharp bends on a steep hill. Over Leigh Bridge, turn a sharp right into Gidleigh Park. A half-mile drive will bring you to the hotel.

Great Tree Hotel, Sandy Park, Chagford, Devon TQ13 8JS (tel. 0647/432491), lies 1½ miles northeast of Chagford. Formerly an old hunting lodge, it is a comfortable 12-bedroom country house set in 18 acres of private grounds. Bedrooms are country style, with private baths or showers, TVs, radios, phones, and tea and coffee makers. The charge is from £36 ($59.40) per person daily, with a full English breakfast included. Beverley and Nigel Eaton-Gray, the proprietors, offer a four-course dinner made with homegrown produce, so far as possible, costing £18.50 ($30.55). Meals are served in their Whitewater restaurant. There are bar snacks at lunch and Devonshire cream teas on the terrace or by the log fire in winter.

Easton Court Hotel, Easton Cross, Chagford, Devon TQ13 8JL (tel. 06473/3469), is known to many a discerning visitor, and ever since it was established as a hotel in the 1920s by an American, Carolyn Cobb, this Tudor house has known its share of literary and theatrical celebrities. Alec Waugh wrote *Thirteen Such Years* here, and Patrick Leigh Fermor penned *The Traveller's Tree.* But it is best known as the place where Evelyn Waugh wrote *Brideshead Revisited.* An 11-hour video cassette of the entire TV series is available to guests. The guestbook reads like a Who's Who of yesteryear: Robert Donat, Margaret Mead, Ralph Richardson, C. P. Snow, Richard Widmark, John Steinbeck. Here is the atmosphere that usually fits in with a preconceived impression of a country place in England: an ancient stone house with a thatched roof, heavy oak beams, an inglenook where log fires burn in cold weather, and a high-walled flower garden. The seven bedrooms are snug and comfortable, sheltering 15 guests at a time with private baths or showers, plus phones and TVs (on request). Your hosts charge £52 ($85.80) per person daily for half board, depending on the season. British and international dishes are served, including coq au vin, steak and mushroom pie, and curried prawns. Meals, open to non-residents who reserve, cost from £15 ($24.75).

---

4. Torquay

In 1968, the towns of Torquay, Paignton, and Brixham joined to form "The English Riviera" as part of a plan to turn the area into one of the super three-in-one resorts of Europe. The area today—the birthplace of mystery writer Agatha Christie—opens onto 22 miles of coastline and 18 beaches.

To follow up on the Riviera label, Torquay (Torbay) would definitely be the Cannes section, whereas Paignton invites family fun (long, safe beaches), and Brixham is a busy fishing port.

Torquay is set against a backdrop of the red cliffs of Devon, with many sheltered pebbly coves. With its parks and gardens, including numerous subtropical plants and palm trees, it is often compared to the Mediterranean, a setting you hardly expect in England. At night, concerts, productions from the West End (the D'Oyly Carte Opera appears occasionally at the Princess Theatre), vaudeville shows, and ballroom dancing keep the holiday-makers—and many honeymooners—entertained.

If you suddenly long for an old Devonshire village, you can always ride the short distance to **Cockington,** still in the same borough, which contains thatched cottages, an old mill, a forge, and a 12th-century church.

Furthermore, if you want to visit one of the great homes of England, you can call on **Oldway,** in the heart of Paignton (tel. 0803/296244). Started by the founder of the Singer sewing-machine dynasty, Isaac Merritt Singer, and completed the year after he died (1875), the neo-classic mansion is surrounded by about 20 acres of grounds and Italian-style gardens. Inside, if you get the feeling you're at Versailles, you're almost right, as some of the rooms were copied. Open all year, Oldway may be visited Mon. to Sat. from 9am to 1pm and 2 to 5:15pm (on Sat. and Sun. from 2:30 to 5pm, May to September only). Admission is free. The gardens are always open.

WHERE TO STAY

The leading five-star hotel in the West Country, **The Imperial,** Park Hill Road, Torquay, Devon TQ1 2DG (tel. 0803/294301), dates from the 1860s. Ever since then, it's always been known as the finest hotel along the south coast of England. It sits within 5½ acres of subtropical gardens opening onto rocky cliffs, with views of the Channel. Inside, a world unfolds of soaring ceilings, marble columns, and ornate plasterwork, enough to make a former visitor, Edward VII, feel at home. Its exterior, however, makes it look far younger than its years, as it was sheathed in the mid-1950s in a weatherproof shell of aluminum and concrete. Each of the 163 bedrooms enjoys lots of well-ordered space, traditional furniture, private bath, phone, TV, radio, and mini-bar. Each accommodation has a private balcony suspended high above a view taking in offshore islands with black rocks and sheer sides. Singles rent for £91 ($150.15) daily and doubles or twins for £170 ($280.50). Included in the rates are the full use of the sporting facilities, dancing in the ballroom every night except Sunday, and entrance to La Pigalle nightclub.

The Ballroom Restaurant is a world of crystal chandeliers and tasteful decor, serving a menu, either table d'hôte or à la carte, of both British and international dishes, backed up by a fine wine list. Hours are daily from 12:30 to 2:30pm for lunch. If you go for dinner, served from 7 to 9pm, it's important to reserve a table. The hotel also contains one of the most modern sports facilities in town, complete with Jacuzzi, a pair of all-weather tennis courts, a "pitch and putt" machine, two squash courts, and an exercise room.

Palace, Babbacombe Road, Torquay, Devon TQ1 3TG (tel. 0803/200200), ranks along with the Imperial as the most desirable accommodation at this seaside resort. This Victorian hotel was built when life was on a grand scale, as reflected by its spacious public rooms with their molded ceilings and columns. With all its many improvements in recent years, it should ride into the next century in a premier position. A four-star hotel, it is luxurious in appointments and facilities. Its public facilities, in fact, are the most impressive in Torquay, with both in- and outdoor swimming pools along with in- and outdoor tennis courts, even a nine-hole golf course. All its bedrooms, some 134 in all, not counting suites, are well furnished, with private baths, phones, and TVs. Singles rent for £53 ($87.45) and up on a daily rate, with doubles costing from £90 ($148.50). The hotel occupies 25 choice acres of real estate in Torquay, sweeping down to Anstey's Cove.

Palm Court Hotel, Sea Front, Torquay, Devon TQ2 5HW (tel. 0803/ 284881), a Victorian crescent built facing south onto the esplanade overlooking Torquay, offers style and good living. Two lounges are wood-paneled with leaded-glass windows. In the dining room is a minstrels' gallery. There are two up-to-date bars and a coffeeshop, open all day. All rooms have been modernized and have color TVs, hot beverage facilities, central heating, phones, and radios. Of the 72 bedrooms, 53 have private baths. The highest tariffs are charged from July to September. Depending on the plumbing, B&B costs £23 ($37.95) to £26 ($42.90) per person per night. The half-board rate is £31 ($51.15) to £34 ($56.10) per person. The hotel has an elevator. With garden chairs and tables on the sun terrace outside the coffeeshop, the Palm Court becomes a social center. At night the colored flood-lighting around the bay evokes a Riviera atmosphere.

Homers, Warren Road, Torquay, Devon TQ2 5TN (tel. 0803/213456). The Victorians who built this house set it near the top of steeply inclined gardens overlooking Tor Bay. The 14 bedrooms are furnished with phones, color TVs, private baths, and such touches as antique mirrors and patterned wallpaper. The accommodating owners charge £36 ($59.40) daily in a single, £72 ($118.80) in a double, with a full breakfast. English and French specialties are served in the hotel's restaurant, the dishes prepared with fresh ingredients. A fixed-price lunch costs £12 ($19.80); dinner, £25 ($41.25).

On the outskirts, **Orestone Manor,** Rockhouse Lane, Maidencombe, Torquay, Devon TQ1 4SX (tel. 0803/328098), lies in this small village about 3½ miles north of Torquay by A379. Sometimes the best way to enjoy a bustling seaside resort is from afar, nestling in a country home. Orestone Manor provides such an opportunity from March to December. In one of the loveliest valleys in south Devon, this gabled manor house, constructed in the early 17th century as a private home, enjoys a tranquil rural setting, standing on 2 acres of well-landscaped gardens. The 20 bedrooms are handsomely and comfortably furnished, with private baths and several amenities such as phones, TVs, and beverage-making facilities. The single rate is from £29 ($47.85) nightly, rising to £80 ($132) in a double. Good and tasty bar lunches are provided Mon. to Sat., and a set dinner, correctly prepared and using fresh ingredients, is £18 ($29.70).

WHERE TO DINE

Considered by some as the finest independent dining spot in town, **Remy's,** 3 Croft Rd. (tel. 0803/292359), serves food at reasonable prices. The name of the place, in a Victorian building, comes from its owner and chef de cuisine, Remy Bopp of France. Here is a chef who sets great store by his raw ingredients, whether they be fresh fish from a local fisherman or vegetables from the market. Everything is home-made, including bread, ice cream, sorbet, and pastries. Food-wise guests also enjoy his carefully selected collection of French wines. Meals are served from 7 to 9:30pm Mon. to Sat., costing from £16 ($26.40) and up; closed Sun., Mon., and for the first two weeks in August.

Mulberry Room, 1 Scarborough Rd., Torquay, Devon TQ2 5UJ (tel. 0803/ 213639). Lesley Cooper is one of those inspired cooks, and she'll feed you well in her little dining room, seating some two dozen diners at midday. The restaurant is situated in the dining area of one of Torquay's Victorian villas and faces onto a patio of plants and flowers, with outside tables for summer lunches and afternoon teas.

You can even stay here in one of the three bedrooms, each simply but comfortably furnished and well kept. B&B charges range from £11.50 ($19) to £15.50 ($25.60) daily, making it one of the bargains of the resort. The vegetarian will find comfort here, while regular diners feast on her baked lamb or honey-roasted chicken among other dishes. Traditional roasts draw the Sunday crowds. The choice is wisely limited so that everything served will be fresh. A set lunch ranges in price from £6.50 ($10.75) to £9.50 ($15.70), with Sat. dinner going for £15 ($24.75). She is open for lunch 12:15 to 2:30pm Wed. to Sun. only; dinner 7:30 to 9pm Sat. only.

5. Totnes

One of the oldest towns in the West Country, the ancient borough of Totnes rests quietly in the past, seemingly content to let the Torquay area remain in the vanguard of the building boom. On the River Dart, 12 miles upstream from Dartmouth, Totnes is so totally removed in character from Torquay that the two towns could be in different countries. Totnes has several old historic buildings, notably the ruins of a Norman castle, an ancient guildhall, and the 15th-century church of St. Mary, made of red sandstone. In the Middle Ages, the old cloth town was encircled by walls, and the North Gate serves as a reminder of that period.

WHERE TO STAY

A historic former coaching inn, **Royal Seven Stars,** the Plains, Totnes, Devon TQ9 5DD (tel. 0803/862125) dates for the most part back to 1660, although its origins go back 500 years before that. The hotel has an interesting porch over its entrance and overlooks a square in the town center, near the banks of the River Dart. The interior courtyard, once used for horses and carriages, is now enclosed in glass, with an old pine staircase. With antiques and paintings, the hotel's own heraldic shield, hand-carved chests, and a grandfather clock, the courtyard forms an inviting entrance to the inn. The 18 bedrooms have been modernized, and 12 have private baths, built-in furniture, and comfortable beds. A four-poster room is also rented for £68 ($112.20) for two per night. All have color TVs, phones, hot beverage facilities, and central heating. Charges, which include a big English breakfast, are £32 ($52.80) to £42 ($69.30) daily in a single, £44 ($72.60) to £52 ($85.80) for a double, with VAT included. A buffet bar is open for lunch all year as well as for supper May to September. A three-course lunch or four-course dinner can be enjoyed in the Brutus Room, open all year. Lunch costs £8 ($13.20), and dinner, around £15 ($24.75) for non-residents. A dinner-dance and cabaret show is presented in the Star-lite Room most Sat. evenings.

WHERE TO DINE

An intimate rendezvous for diners, **The Elbow Room,** 6 North St. (tel. 0803/863480), is in a converted one-time cider press and adjoining cottage. The original 300-year-old stone walls have been retained and decor matched to them to give a unique atmosphere. Mr. and Mrs. R. J. Savin provide a standard of food and service that attracts gourmets. Mrs. Savin combines technical skill with inspiration and a flair for the unusual in the selection, preparation, and presentation of her appetizers, main courses, and homemade desserts. Main courses are accompanied by, and inclusive of, fresh vegetables. The menu is restricted to a maximum of ten international dishes, ranging from chicken with almonds (a suprême of fresh chicken served in a fresh cream and Grand Marnier sauce, garnished with flaked almonds and apple) to whisky steak Dijonnaise (prime filet of English beef served in a whisky, herb mist, and mushroom sauce). A lunch menu with a selection of roasts costs from £8 ($13.20) for three courses. In the evening, à la carte meals range from £15 ($24.75) to £20 ($33) for three courses. The restaurant is open from noon to 2pm and 6:30 to 9:30pm Tues. to Sat. Mr. Savin presides over the restaurant with charm and expertise.

WHERE TO STAY AND DINE IN THE ENVIRONS
In and around this area is some of south Devon's finest scenery. The hamlets are especially pleasing.

At North Huish
Just 2½ miles south of the A38, near Avonwick, Charles and Carol Trevor-Roper welcome guests to **Brookdale House,** North Huish, South Brent, Devon TQ10 9NR (tel. 054882/402), a comfortable hotel decorated in traditional country-house style to match the elegance of the large marble open fireplaces and decorative plaster cornice work in the spacious public rooms. The six bedrooms in the main house and two in adjacent Brookdale cottage all contain bathrooms and are tastefully furnished, with easy chairs, color TVs, direct-dial phones, hairdryers, trouser presses, and hot beverage facilities. The charge for B&B is £65 ($107.25) daily for single occupancy, £75 ($123.75) to £100 ($165) in a double or twin. The house has a large, comfortable lounge, a reading room, and a cozy paneled bar where you can order a snack lunch and drinks. The restaurant offers dishes making use of local produce, including Devon lamb and beef, game, salmon from the River Dart, and fresh fish from Brixham and Plymouth, together with fresh vegetables, clotted cream, local cheeses, and stone-ground flour. A set dinner costs £25 ($41.25). Brookdale House is closed in January.

At Stoke Gabriel
About 4 miles southeast of Totnes sits the little village of Stoke Gabriel, one of the loveliest in Devon. Famous as a fishing hamlet, it lies on a creek of the River Dart. Dartmouth is only 6 miles south of the village (equidistant to Torquay).
Gabriel Court Hotel, Stoke Gabriel, near Totnes, Devon TQ9 6SF (tel. 080/428206), is a manor house owned by the same family from 1487 until 1928, when it was converted into a hotel. Michael and Eryl Beacom run a hotel of quality, offering good value. The house, on the banks of the Dart River, standing in a terraced Elizabethan garden, has a heated swimming pool and a lawn tennis court. The 3-acre site is a setting for the white-painted house, which offers 23 well-furnished rooms, 19 with private bath. Eight of these accommodations are in a modern extension. Rooms have TVs and phones. Including an English breakfast, rates are £60 ($99) daily in a double, or from £35 ($57.75) to £45 ($74.25) in a single (the higher price for use of a double room). Gabriel Court enjoys a reputation for its well-cooked English food, enhanced all the more by fruit and vegetables from the garden, as well as trout and salmon from the Dart and poultry from nearby farms. The hotel also has a bar. In winter, there are log fires in the lounges, and the house is also centrally heated. The hotel is closed in February.

---

6. Dartmouth

At the mouth of the River Dart, this ancient seaport, 36 miles from Exeter, is the home of the Royal Naval College. Traditionally linked to England's maritime greatness, Dartmouth sent out the young midshipmen who ensured that Britannia ruled the waves. You can take a river steamer up the Dart to Totnes (book at the kiosk at the harbor). The view along the way is of Devon's most beautiful river.

Dartmouth's 15th-century castle was built during the reign of Edward IV. The town's most noted architectural feature is the Butterwalk, lying below Tudor houses. The Flemish influence in some of the houses is pronounced.

WHERE TO STAY

A coaching inn since 1639, the **Royal Castle Hotel**, 11 the Quay, Dartmouth, Devon TQ6 9PS (tel. 08043/4004), has slept a host of visitors, including Sir Francis Drake, Queen Victoria, Charles II, and Edward VII (bedrooms named after them commemorate their visits). Horse-drawn carriages (as late as 1910) would dispatch their passengers in a carriageway, now enclosed to make the reception hall. Everywhere you look, you see reminders of the inn's rich past. The glassed-in courtyard, with its winding wooden staircase, has the original coaching horn and a set of 20 antique spring bells connected to the bedrooms. Many of the rooms opening off the covered courtyard and the rambling corridors have antiques. All 20 units have been recently restored and have private baths, color TVs, direct-dial phones, and central heating. Prices range from £35 ($57.75) daily in a single, from £80 ($132) in a double, including the Royal Castle breakfast and VAT. The meals, taken in the restaurant under a beautiful Adam ceiling, are excellent, in the best English tradition. Dinner costs from £15 ($24.75). A favorite place to settle in is the Galleon Bar, once two old kitchens, with double fireplaces and large hand-hewn beams said to have been salvaged from Armada ships. There is another pub-style bar, with settles, popular with the locals. Guests lounge on the second floor in a room with a bay window overlooking the harbor.

Dart Marina Hotel, Sandquay, Dartmouth, Devon TQ6 9PS (tel. 08043/2580), is an ochre-walled establishment at the edge of its own marina, within a 3-minute walk of the center of town. It was originally built as a clubhouse for the marina, but was expanded into a full-fledged hotel. Warmly masculine, its public rooms are sheathed with paneling crafted from glowing pine interspersed with yard upon yard of upholstery. From the bar, the yachting set can view their craft through large windows. Of the 33 comfortable bedrooms, all have private baths, several contain balconies, and each has a color TV, radio, phone, and coffee-making equipment. Singles cost from £66 ($108.90) to £86 ($141.90) daily, and doubles or twins go for £82 ($135.30) to £110 ($181.50).

WHERE TO DINE

Considered the best restaurant in town, **The Carved Angel**, 2 South Embankment (tel. 08043/2465), serves specialties that are usually more akin to the creative cuisine of the continent than to the traditional cookery of England. Co-owner and chef Joyce Molyneux welcomes visitors to her stylishly simple riverside restaurant, the kitchen of which is partially screened from the dining room by plants. It was a former Victorian storefront. The restaurant is behind a half-timbered, heavily carved facade rising opposite the harbor. Inside, a central statue of a carved angel is ringed with a decor of neutral colors. Typical dishes include beef marinated in orange and ginger and served with bay leaves on a skewer, and Dart salmon with rhubarb. The fish soup Provence style is superb. Full meals cost £28.50 ($47.05) to £35 ($57.75), with a fixed-price lunch going for £18.50 ($30.55) to £22 ($36.30). Meals are served from 12:30 to 1:45pm and 7:30 to 9:30pm; closed Sun. night and all day Mon.

Mansion House, Mansion House Street (tel. 08043/5474), occupies an 18th-century townhouse and has a skilled chef and owner, Richard Cranfield, whose cuisine we've enjoyed many times at other locations. The townhouse-like dining room on the second floor (first to the British) is elegantly appointed and furnished, a proper, pristine background for a chef de cuisine who presents an imaginative and well-balanced menu. That menu is deliberately and wisely kept short, so that food can be fresh and in season. The helpful staff might suggest such dishes as turbot stuffed with mushrooms and foie gras, accompanied by deep-fried vegetables, or perhaps garlic-flavored sirloin from Scotland. But, as befits its location in Dartmouth, the menu emphasizes fresh seafood. Dishes for the vegetarian are also possible. Where the 18th-century mayor of Dartmouth entertained his friends at ballroom dances, guests dine today from 12:30 to 1:30pm and 7:30 to 9:30pm. The house is closed for lunch Sat. and all day Sun. and Mon. A set luncheon costs £19.50 ($32.20), with a table d'hôte dinner going for £20.50 ($33.85). A la carte dinners cost from £25 ($41.25), and reservations are necessary. A bistro-style wine bar is on the ground floor.

Horn of Plenty, Gulworthy, Devon PL19 8JD (tel. 0822/832528), is 3 miles west of Tavistock on the A390. As you drive along that road from Tavistock to Callington, you will see a small sign pointing north along a leafy drive to the solid Regency house where Sonia Stevenson operates what the French call a *restaurant avec chambres.* You can stay in one of the spacious, warm, and elegant bedrooms, six in all, that have been installed over the old stables of the house, paying £68 ($112.20) daily in a single, £75 ($123.75) in a double. All accommodations have color TVs, hot beverage facilities, phone, and a well-stocked mini-bar. You can return after a day of touring around the country to enjoy one of Sonia's well-prepared dinners which might include young grouse with red-currant jelly or an Alsatian choucroute with boiled bacon and frankfurters, served with Alsatian wines. You can expect to pay from £25 ($41.25) for dinner. Lunch at £18 ($29.70) is served from noon to 2pm except on Thurs., Fri., and Christmas Day. Dinner is from 7 to 9:30pm every day except Christmas.

7. Plymouth

The historic seaport of Plymouth is more romantic in legend than in reality. But this was not always so. In World War II, the blitzed area of greater Plymouth lost at least 75,000 buildings. The heart of present-day Plymouth, including the municipal civic center on the Royal Parade, has been entirely rebuilt—the way that it was done the subject of much controversy.

For the old you must go to the Elizabethan section, known as the **Barbican,** and walk along the quay in the footsteps of Sir Francis Drake (once the mayor of Plymouth) and other Elizabethan seafarers, such as Sir John Hawkins, English naval commander and slave trader. It was from here in 1577 that Drake set sail on his round-the-world voyage. An even more famous sailing took place in 1620 when the Pilgrims left their final port in England for the New World. That fact is commemorated by a plaque at the harbor.

Legend has it that while playing bowls on Plymouth Hoe (Celtic for "high place"), Drake was told that the Spanish Armada had entered the sound and, in a masterful display of confidence, finished the game before going into battle. A local historian questions the location of the bowls game, if indeed it happened, starring Sir Francis. I am told that the Hoe in the 16th century was only gorse-covered scrubland outside tiny Plymouth and that it is more likely that the officers of the Royal Navy would have been bowling (then played on a shorter green than today) while awaiting the Armada arrival at the Minerva Inn, Looe Street, 20 yards from the house where Sir Francis lived, about 2 minutes' walk from the Barbican. My informant says that other captains, knowing that it would take about 20 minutes to ready their ships to sail against the Spanish, may have sent their executive officers to prepare while they finished their drinks and game. Doubt is cast on Drake's display of such insouciance, however, the feeling being that "5 feet 2 inches of red-haired impetuosity as he was, he'd have been off like a flash!"

Of special interest to visitors from the United States is the final departure point of the Pilgrims in 1620, the already-mentioned Barbican. The two ships, *Mayflower* and *Speedwell,* that sailed from Southampton in August of that year, put into Plymouth after they suffered storm damage. Here the *Speedwell* was abandoned as unseaworthy, and the *Mayflower* made the trip to the New World alone. The Memorial Gateway to the Waterside on the Barbican marks the place, tradition says, whence the Pilgrims' ship sailed.

The Barbican is a mass of narrow streets, old houses, and quayside shops selling antiques, brasswork, old prints, and books. Fishing boats still unload their catches at the wharves, and passenger-carrying ferryboats run short harbor cruises. A trip includes a visit to Drake's Island in the Sound, the dockyards, and naval vessels, plus a view of the Hoe from the water.

A cruise of Plymouth Harbour costs £2.50 ($4.15) for adults and £1.25 ($2.05) for children. Departures are from February to November, with cruises leaving every half hour from 10am to 4pm daily. These **Plymouth Boat Cruises** are booked at the Phoenix Wharf, the Barbican (tel. 0752/662338).

The **Barbican Craft Centre,** White Lane (tel. 0752/662338), in the Barbican, has workshops and showrooms where you can watch and talk to the people engaged in crafts. You'll see such sights as a potter throwing a special design or a glass-blower fashioning a particular glass. Woodcarvers, leather workers, and weavers are also busy, and you can buy their products at reasonable prices, even commissioning your own design if you're lucky.

WHERE TO STAY

Still a major base for the British navy, Plymouth is an interesting stopover.

Duke of Cornwall Hotel, Millbay Road, Plymouth, Devon PL1 3LG (tel. 0752/266256), is a Victorian Gothic building that survived World War II bombings. Constructed in 1863, it was regarded by Sir John Betjeman as the finest example of Victorian architecture in Plymouth. The 70 bedrooms, all with private baths, color TVs, radios, phones, and coffee-making facilities, have been refurbished. Nine are master bedrooms, one with an antique four-poster bed. A single costs from £47.50 ($78.40) daily, and a double goes for £55 ($90.75). Tariffs include a full English breakfast and VAT. The hotel dining room is of an elegant contemporary style with a circular ceiling supporting a fine chandelier. Lunch costs £7.50 ($12.40), and dinner from £10.50 ($17.35).

Plymouth Moat House Hotel, Armada Way, Plymouth, Devon PL1 2HJ (tel. 0752/662866), might have upset the departure of our forebears—if they'd known how luxurious the hotel would be, they might never have sailed. It's one of the most distinguished hotels in West Country, overlooking the harbor and the Hoe. Rising like a midget skyscraper, it contains 215 good-size bedrooms with long double beds. Singles cost £70 ($115.50) daily, and doubles go for £80 ($132). The rooms are well-furnished with air conditioning, wide picture windows, TVs, radios, phones, and private baths. Babysitting is available. A covered swimming pool is on the grounds, and there's a sauna and sun terrace as well, with garden tables set up for poolside refreshments. On the top floor is the Penthouse, a carvery with views across Plymouth Sound, and on the ground floor there's a specialty fish and meat restaurant, Mongers.

Astor Hotel, 14 Elliott St., the Hoe, Plymouth, Devon PL1 2PS (tel. 0752/225511), was originally built by Victorians as the private home of a prosperous sea captain. In 1987 it received a major restoration, and today it contains 56 comfortable bedrooms, each with private bath, radio, color TV, phone, and coffee-making facilities. With breakfast included, singles cost £45 ($74.25) daily; doubles or twins, £68 ($112.20). Reduced rates can be arranged for stays of two nights or more, providing that half board is accepted. The hotel lies near the Hoe on a street lined with 19th-century buildings. On the premises is a series of well-decorated public lounges, plus a cozy and accommodating pub separated from the reception desk by a fan-shaped trio of glass doors.

Mayflower Post House, Cliff Road, the Hoe, Plymouth, Devon PL1 3DL (tel. 0752/662828), is situated on a hilltop above the bay. This nine-story hotel was constructed in 1970, its clientele divided equally between tourists and business-related travelers. The hotel contains 106 bedrooms, all but a dozen of which face the sea. Each unit has a TV, radio, private bath, mini-bar, and phone. Singles cost £62 ($102.30) daily, and doubles or twins rent for £72 ($118.80), with VAT and service included. On the premises is a pub, the Boston Bar, with a separate entrance, along with a free-form, heated outdoor pool (open daily from April to October) and a restaurant with wide-angle views of the sea.

Novotel Plymouth, Marsh Mills Roundabout, 270 Plymouth Rd., Plymouth, Devon PL6 8NH (tel. 0752/221422), is suitable for motorists, especially those with children, lying at the entrance to the city on the A38. Set in landscaped gardens with ample parking, it offers 100 bedrooms, each soundproof with private bath or shower, color TV, and direct-dial phone. Two children under 16 sharing a room with their parents receive not only the room but breakfast free. There's also a swimming pool, plus a children's play area. B&B rates are £58 ($95.70) daily in a single, rising to £72 ($118.80) in a double. A grill restaurant is open daily from 6am to midnight.

WHERE TO DINE

The most distinguished restaurant in Plymouth is **Chez Nous,** 13 Frankfort Gate (tel. 0752/266793). The owner and chef, Jacques Marchal, is a master in the kitchen, borrowing heavily from the past if he wants to, but also daring to express his creative talent by showing diners what he is capable of. The type of cooking is called *la cuisine spontanée*—that is, based on the use of fresh produce changing with the seasons. Chez Nous is quite pretty and cozy, lying in a shopping complex. Look for the specials of the day on the blackboard menu. Aided by a classic and rather elegant wine list, the food is likely to include such dishes as scallops steamed with ginger, seaman's pie, and pork with prunes. Fish, generally, is the preferred main dish to order here. Desserts and appetizers are also prepared with care. Fresh, quality ingredients are a hallmark of the cuisine. Lunch costs from £21.50 ($35.50) on the table d'hôte, with most à la carte dinners going for £30 ($49.50). It is open from 12:30 to 2pm and 7 to 10:30pm Tues. to Sun.; closed the first three weeks in September and again in February.

Barbican Wine Lodge, the Quay, Barbican (tel. 0752/660875), lies right on the quayside, across the water from the customs house. The lodge is an old building with wooden floors softened by sawdust. Vintage wines are stacked in racks behind the bar under an oak-beamed ceiling. There is a good ambience, plus a set lunch menu, or you can order à la carte. The lodge specializes in fish bought locally each day, including brill, turbot, red mullet, John Dory, oysters, and mussels when in season. Live music is presented each evening and jazz on Sun. at lunch. The Wine Lodge is open from 10am to 11pm daily. Meals cost from £11 ($18.15). Parking is available on the quay.

For a change of pace, try **China Garden,** 17-19 Derry's Cross (tel. 0752/664472), which is the finest Chinese restaurant in the area, charging remarkably low prices considering the quality of its cookery. The cooking is inspired by the cuisine of Peking (now Beijing), and you get the legendary Peking duck, along with tasty spareribs and other delicacies—even that which is not so delicate (beef and red-hot peppers). In addition to à la carte items, the menu is divided into a series of "feasts." Lunch begins at £4.60 ($7.60), with a table d'hôte dinner costing from £11 ($18.15) per head, including VAT. A la carte meals range from £12 ($19.80). Service is efficient and accurate, and lunch is from noon to 2:30pm, dinner 6 to 11:30pm. On Fri. and Sat., only dinner is served, 6 to midnight, and Sun. hours are only from 6 to 11pm. It's highly recommended, and located just outside the center of town.

8. Milton Damerel

If you're taking the A39 north from Cornwall, consider a stopover deep in the heart of north Devon in the hamlet of Milton Damerel. As you reach the junction with A3072, head eastward to Holsworthy. There you will connect with the A388 going north. The turnoff for Milton Damerel is signposted.

WHERE TO STAY AND DINE

A mile north on the A388, the **Woodford Bridge Hotel,** Milton Damerel, Holsworthy, Devon EX22 7LL (tel. 040926/481) is a pretty, 15th-century, whitewashed inn with thatched roof, lots of wood paneling, and 14 bedrooms. The bar, where a good selection of snacks is offered, is popular with the locals. There is also an elegant dining room, where you can enjoy well-prepared dishes, including fresh local produce, game, sea bass, and other courses. A table d'hôte dinner with three choices for each course goes for £12.50 ($20.65), while a meal chosen à la carte can cost £12.50 ($20.65) to £25 ($41.25). The hotel's owner has decorated the accommodations with chintz and dainty lamps. Rooms contain private bath or shower, phone, and TV. Rents are from £41 ($67.65) daily in a single, depending on the plumbing. Doubles or twins on the same basis cost from £68 ($112.20). Breakfast and VAT are included in the tariffs.

---

9. Clovelly

This is the most charming of all Devon villages and is one of the main attractions of the West Country. Starting at a great height, the village cascades down the mountainside, with its narrow, cobblestone High that makes travel by car impossible. (You park your car at the top and make the trip by foot.) Supplies are carried down by donkeys. Every yard of the way provides views of tiny cottages, with their terraces of flowers lining the main street. The village fleet is sheltered at the stone quay at the bottom.

To avoid the climb back up the slippery incline, go to the rear of the Red Lion inn and "queue up" for a Land Rover. In summer, the line is often long, but considering the alternative, it's worth the wait. Two Land Rovers make continuous round-trips, costing 40p (65¢) per person each way.

Tip: To avoid the flock of tourists, stay out of Clovelly from around 11 in the morning till teatime. After tea, settle in your room, and have dinner, perhaps spend the night in peace and contentment. The next morning after breakfast, you walk around the village or go for a swim in the harbor, then visit the nearby villages during the middle of the day when the congestion sets in. Bideford, incidentally, is 11 miles away.

WHERE TO STAY

A warning: It's hard to get a room in Clovelly. Advance reservations, with a deposit, are imperative during the peak summer months, although you can always telephone in advance and just possibly get a bed.

New Inn, Main Street, Clovelly, Devon EX39 5TQ (tel. 02373/303), about halfway down the High Street, is the village pub, a good meeting place at sundown. It offers the best lodgings in the village, in two buildings on opposite sides of the steep street (but only a 12-foot leap between their balconies). B&B ranges from £16.50 ($27.25) to £20.50 ($33.85) per person daily, inclusive. The inn rents 20 bedrooms, five with private bath or shower. If you're only stopping over, then this little country inn is recommended for meals. A wide choice of moderately priced meals is offered in the oak-beamed dining room. The local fare, including Devonshire cream, is featured whenever possible. Locally caught lobsters are also prepared by the chef. Motorists can park in the car park. It is advisable to pack an overnight case, as the luggage has to be carried down (but is returned to the top by donkey).

Red Lion, the Quay, Clovelly (near Bideford), Devon EX39 5TF (tel. 02373/237), an 18th-century inn, may well have the best location in the village—at the bottom of the steep cobbled street, right on the stone seawall of the little harbor. Rising three stories, it is an unspoiled country inn, the life centering on an antique pub where the villagers gather to satisfy their thirsts over pints of ale. Most of the bedrooms look directly onto the sea. All have hot and cold running water and adequate furnishings. The cost is from £16.50 ($27.25) per person nightly, including breakfast. One double room is rented for £40 ($66), containing a private bath. Rooms are equipped with hot beverage facilities. Other meals are available in the sea-view dining room, where lunch is served from noon to 2pm, and dinner from 7 to

8pm costs from £8.50 ($14.05). The manager can arrange for boating in the bay, and suggests that the Red Lion is not suitable for children under 7 years of age.

10. Lynton-Lynmouth

The north coast of Devon is set off most dramatically in Lynton, a village some 500 feet high. It lies 206 miles from London and 59 miles from Exeter. It is a good center for exploring the moody Doone Valley and that part of Exmoor that spills into the shire from neighboring Somerset. The Valley of Rocks, west of Lynton, offers the most spectacular scenery.

The town is joined by a cliff railway to its sister, Lynmouth, about 500 feet lower. The rivers of East and West Lyn meet in Lynmouth, a resort popular with the English. For a panoramic view of the rugged coastline, you can walk on a path halfway between the two towns that runs along the cliff. From Lynton, or rather from Hollerday Hill, you can look out onto Lynmouth Bay, Countisbury Foreland, and Woody Bays in the west.

WHERE TO STAY AND DINE

Set high on a cliff, **Tors Hotel,** Lynmouth, Lynton EX35 6NA (tel. 0598/53236), opens onto a view of the coastline and the bay of Lynmouth. It was built in the fashion of a Swiss château, with more than 40 gables, Tyrolean balconies jutting out to capture the sun (or the moon), black-and-white timbered wings, and some 30 chimneys. Surrounding the hotel are a terrace and a heated swimming pool. The interior has been modernized, and much attention has been paid to the 35 comfortable bedrooms, each with private bath or shower, TV, and phone. Singles rent for £35 ($57.75) to £53 ($87.45) daily, and doubles cost £55 ($90.75) to £69 ($113.85). All tariffs include VAT and a full English breakfast. A set lunch costs £7 ($11.55), a set dinner going for £14 ($23.10). The hotel is open from March to mid-November.

Hewitt's Hotel and Restaurant, North Walk, Lynton, Devon EX35 6HJ (tel. 0598/52293), is named for the gentleman, Sir Thomas Hewitt, who helped construct the funicular rail that links the twin resorts. In the latter 19th century, he also built a home for himself, and that place today is one of the most successful little inns in Lynton, operated by Susan and Robert Mahon. Lying in some two dozen acres of grounds, it opens onto beautiful vistas of Lynmouth Bay (best enjoyed while seated on a sunny terrace). The old house is filled with architectural character, as exemplified by its grand staircase, time-mellowed paneling, antiques, and stained-glass windows. The most desirable of the 10 bedrooms have private balconies, although all of them are well furnished and comfortably appointed. Most of them also contain private baths. The hotel is "for all seasons," and the country-house atmosphere can be enjoyed for £30 ($49.50) daily in a single, rising to £70 ($115.50) in the best doubles. Bar lunches are far above average, and dinner is among the best served at the resort. In fact, it is reason enough to stay here, and you won't be overcharged either, as meals cost from £16 ($26.40). A medley of British and continental dishes are served.

The **Rising Sun Hotel,** the Harbour, Lynmouth, Lynton, Devon EX35 6EQ (tel. 0598/53223), is perhaps one of the most colorful thatched inns in England, especially as it's right at the end of the quay at the mouth of the Lyn River. Not only is the harbor life spread before you, but you can bask in the wonder and warmth of an inn in business for more than 600 years. In bedroom after bedroom, with crazy levels and sloping ceilings, you'll have views of the water, the changing tides, and bobbing boats. It is a lovely old place, where the staircase is so narrow and twisting that it requires care to negotiate. Ceilings are low and floorboards creak. Behind the inn, halfway up the cliff, is a tiny garden bright with flowers in summer, where you can sit and gaze out over the thatch roofs to the sea. Hugo Jeune, the owner, has refurbished the place and added more rooms by joining two adjacent properties, and he has rooms available nearby in Shelley's Cottage, where the poet honeymooned with Harriet in 1812. R. D. Blackmore wrote part of *Lorna Doone* while staying at the hotel. The inn rents 16 bedrooms, 2 with four-poster beds, but all with private bath or shower, and each with phone and TV. Guests are charged from £32 ($52.80) to £37 ($61.05) per person daily for B&B, service, and VAT. Two persons can rent Shelley's Cottage for £90 ($148.50) daily. Half board is available for £47 ($77.55) to £52 ($85.80) per person daily. It's a delight dining at the Rising Sun, as everything is 101% British in the dining room, with its deeply set window and fireplace. See the original 14th-century fireplace in the bar.

Bath Hotel, Lynmouth, Devon EX35 6EL (tel. 0598/52238), is a solid building between the busy street and the towering cliffs. B&B begins at £21.50 ($35.50) to £28.50 ($47.05) per person daily in a room with bath. Many of the 24 bedrooms have views over the river and out to the sea. A good set dinner is served in the restaurant for £11.50 ($19), with lobster and salmon specialties. Sunday lunch offers cuts from a roast, traditional vegetables, and an old-fashioned dessert.

---

11. The Taw Valley

The River Taw rises high on Dartmoor, as do many other West Country rivers, and makes its way northwest through beautiful moorland scenery and mid-Devon farmlands, finally emptying into the sea at Barnstaple. The river and area are the settings for Henry Williamson's world-renowned books, *Salar the Salmon* and *Tarka the Otter,* as well as being highly productive of sea trout, salmon, and brown trout. This is an unspoiled rural valley between Exmoor and Dartmoor. It retains a peaceful atmosphere away from the pressures of modern life, and it's populated with hospitable people.

Many visitors have never heard of such little towns as Crawleigh, Chulmleigh, Winkleigh, Crediton, and Eggesford, so I recommend a trip through the valley. Fishing opportunities abound.

WHERE TO STAY AND DINE

An old coaching inn built in the early 1800s is now the **Eggesford House Hotel** (Fox and Hounds), Eggesford, Chulmleigh, Devon EX18 7JZ (tel. 0769/80345), lying halfway between Exeter and Barnstaple. The coaching inn formed part of the large Eggesford Country Estate, home of the earls of Portsmouth. The Forestry Commission presently owns the majority of the estate's 7,000 acres, with beautiful walks and scenery provided. The hotel, set in its own grounds of some 30 acres, is approached by a sweeping drive through woodlands. Owned by David and Sheila Ingyon and their family, it has recently undergone considerable renovation but retains its attractive inherent characteristics. All 20 bedrooms are beautifully appointed and have baths, color TVs, and phones. B&B costs from £27.50 ($45.40) per person daily, rising to £37.50 ($61.90) for half board. If your heart is set on experiencing the peace and tranquility of the mid-Devon countryside, sampling some of the best salmon and trout fishing in the whole area, and spending the autumn and winter evenings beside a crackling fire, eating and drinking with locals, or experiencing the pleasure of sleeping in a four-poster bed, this is the place for you. Fishermen and early risers can select their accommodations from a range of fully modernized country cottages adjacent to the main hotel buildings. The hotel is open all year.

CORNWALL

1. LOOE

2. POLPERRO

3. FOWEY

4. TRURO

5. PORTLOE

6. ST. MAWES

7. FALMOUTH

8. PENZANCE

9. THE ISLES OF SCILLY

10. NEWLYN, MOUSEHOLE, AND LAND'S END

11. ST. JUST-IN-PENWITH

12. ST. IVES

13. PORT ISAAC

14. TINTAGEL

15. BOLVENTOR

The ancient duchy of Cornwall is the extreme southwestern part of England, often called "the toe." But Cornwall is one toe that's always wanted to dance away from the foot. Although a peninsula, it is a virtual island—if not geographically, then spiritually. Encircled by coastline, it abounds with rugged cliffs, hidden bays, fishing villages, sandy beaches, and sheltered coves where smuggling was once practiced. Many of the little seaports with their hillside-clinging cottages resemble towns along the Mediterranean, yet Cornwall retains its own distinctive flavor.

The true Cornish people are generally darker and shorter than the English. Their Celt-Iberian origin still lives on in superstition, folklore, and fairy tales. King Arthur, of course, is the most vital legend of all. When Cornish people speak of King Arthur they're not just handing out a line to tourists. To them, Arthur and his knights really existed, romping around Tintagel Castle, now in ruins—Norman ruins, that is—lying 300 feet above the sea, 19 miles from Bude.

The ancient land had its own language up until about 250 years ago, and some of the old words ("pol" for pool, "tre" for house) still survive. The Cornish dialect is more easily understood by the Welsh than by those who speak the Queen's English.

The Cornish, like the Welsh, are great miners (tin and copper) and they're fond of the tall tale. Sometimes it's difficult to tell when they're serious. One resident told me that he and his wife had been walking in the woods at twilight, but had lost their way. He claimed that the former owner of the estate (in Victoria's day) appeared suddenly in a dog-carriage and guided them back to where they'd taken the wrong turn. If this really had happened, I wouldn't be surprised—at least not in Cornwall.

I suggest berthing at one of the smaller fishing villages, such as East and West Looe, Polperro, Mousehole, or Portloe—where you'll experience the true charm of the duchy. Many of the villages, such as St. Ives, are artists' colonies. Except for St. Ives and Port Isaac, most of my recommendations lie on the southern coast, often called the Cornish Riviera, which strikes many foreign visitors as being the most intriguing. However, the north coast has its own peculiar charm.

1. Looe

After your visit to Plymouth, about 15 miles away in Devon, you can either take the Tamar Suspension Bridge to Cornwall, or else cross by ferry from Plymouth. You'll soon arrive in the ancient twin towns of East and West Looe, connected by a seven-arched stone bridge that spans the river. In the jaws of shrub-dotted cliffs, the fishing villages present a stark contrast to Plymouth. Houses scale the hills, stacked one on top of the other in terrace fashion.

In both fishing villages you can find good accommodations. Fishing and sailing are two of the major sports and the sandy coves, as well as East Looe Beach, are spots for seabathing. Beyond the towns are cliff paths and downs worth a ramble.

Looe is noted for its shark-angling, but you may prefer simply walking the narrow, crooked medieval streets of East Looe, with its old harbor and 17th-century guildhall. If you wish, you can strike out from Looe on the cliff walk, a distance of 4½ miles, to Polperro. The less adventurous will drive.

WHERE TO STAY

Space and prices are at a premium in July and August. Some hotels are so heavily booked that they can demand Saturday-to-Saturday clients only.

Hannafore Point Hotel, Marine Drive, Hannafore, West Looe, Cornwall PL13 2DG (tel. 05036/3273), is a rambling, many-gabled structure commanding an advantageous view of the harbor, overlooking miles of Cornish coastline and one of the most beautiful bays in England. In addition to the older bay-windowed chambers, newer sections have walls of glass for viewing the harbor and St. George's Island. The entrance opens onto several levels of comfortable lounges and bars, with cantilevered stairs and balconies. The 38 modern bedrooms all include either private baths or showers, and most of the front rooms have their own balcony. Each room has a direct-dial phone, color TV, radio, hairdryer, and hot beverage facilities. B&B rates vary depending on the view, location of the room, and the time of the year. From May to the end of October, a single costs from £51 ($84.15) to £53.50 ($88.30) daily, and a double or twin goes for £79 ($130.35) to £94 ($155.10). That panoramic view adds to the pleasure of dining in the Headland Restaurant, where fresh ingredients are used in the fine Cornish and French cuisine. The hotel has an elevator, and there is a comprehensive activity center with an indoor pool on the premises. Hannafore Point is in the main center for shark and deep-sea fishing, and is ideal for exploring either Cornwall or parts of Devon.

Fieldhead Hotel, Portuan Road, Hannafore, West Looe, Cornwall PL13 2DR (tel. 05036/2689), was originally built in 1896 as a private home. Now operated as a hotel, one of the most recommendable in the area, it sits in 2 acres of gardens opening onto a view of the sea with a heated, outdoor swimming pool. Closed in January, it otherwise receives guests in its 14 well-furnished bedrooms. All of these accommodations offer private baths or showers, color TVs, and phones. Depending on the season, B&B overnight rates range from £20 ($33) to £27 ($44.55) per person for occupancy of a double or twin room. Single residents pay a daily supplement of £8 ($13.20).

Talland Bay Hotel, Talland-by-Looe, Cornwall PL13 2JB (tel. 0503/72667), lies 4 miles southwest of Looe by the A387. A country house dating from the 16th century, set on 2½ acres, it is under the domain of Polly and Ian Mayman, who will indicate local beaches and the croquet lawn. Its thick, white walls shelter two sides of a rectangular swimming pool whose borders are ringed with flagstones and a semi-tropical garden. Views from the 23 tastefully furnished bedrooms include the sea and rocky coastline. All units contain private baths, color TVs, radios, and phones. Some of the bedrooms are in an annex. The charge for half board is from £38 ($62.70) to £66 ($108.90) per person daily. The food is the best in the area, featuring excellently prepared seafood. Even if you aren't staying here, you may want to reserve a table. A la carte meals cost around £20 ($33) per person. A much frequented buffet lunch is served by the pool in summer. The restaurant is open from 12:30 to 2pm Mon. to Sat., from 12:45 to 1:30pm Sun., and from 7:15 to 9pm seven days a week. The hotel is closed from January to mid-February.

Commonwealth Manor Hotel, St. Martin's Road, East Looe, Cornwall PL13 1LP (tel. 05036/2929), is a family-operated, country-house hotel, about a 12-minute walk from the harbor and the center of the resort. Well maintained, it operates like a little inn, containing 11 bedrooms with private baths and TVs. From March to October, guests receive a warm welcome here and are shown to one of the well-furnished and comfortably appointed bedrooms. With a full English breakfast included, charges are from £29 ($47.85) to £37 ($61.05) daily in a single, going up to £50 ($82.50) to £58 ($95.70) in a double. Opening onto the Looe River Valley, Commonwealth Manor stands on a wooded hillside in some 3 acres of private grounds with a heated swimming pool. Meals are good, using fresh ingredients, with dinners going for about £12 ($19.80).

WHERE TO STAY AND DINE OUTSIDE LOOE

Peacefully secluded 5 miles from Looe, the **Old Rectory Country House Hotel,** St. Keyne, near Liskeard, Cornwall PL14 4RL (tel. 0579/42617), is in the countryside of southeast Cornwall, which is known for its natural beauty. The owners have brought the hotel to a high standard to complement the original architecture, with use of paneled doors, marble fireplaces, Persian rugs, velvet sofas, and crystal. Meals are served on Wedgwood china in the elegant dining room where home-prepared meals and a selection of table wines are served. All eight bedrooms have baths or showers, color TVs, electric blankets, and hot beverage facilities. Two rooms also contain four-posters. B&B costs from £24 ($39.60) per person nightly, with singles paying a £6 ($9.90) supplement. The approach to the hotel is by a winding drive off the little-used B3254 to the rear of the house. The hotel overlooks 3 acres of gardens with views across the valley.

Well House, St. Keyne, Liskeard, Cornwall PL14 4RN (tel. 0579/42001), is another one of those *restaurant avec chambres* found occasionally in the West Country. This one, in fact, surfaces near the top. Lying about 3 miles from Liskeard, Well House stands in 5 acres of gardens opening onto vistas of the Looe Valley. It offers an all-weather tennis court and a swimming pool, as well as seven beautifully furnished bedrooms, each with private bath and shower. Overnight B&B charges are from £48 ($79.20) daily in a single, rising to £95 ($156.75) in a double. Nicholas Wainford, the owner, provides many thoughtful extras, such as fresh flowers in the bedrooms. But it is mainly for the cuisine that guests flock to the place, which they can do from 12:30 to 2pm and 7 to 9pm Tues. to Sun. A set luncheon goes for £18 ($29.70), with a five-course table d'hôte dinner offered for £24 ($39.60). You're ushered into a grand contemporary dining room, with an almost formal staff, where you can peruse the brief but delectable menu. Carefully prepared and elegantly presented, the food is made with tip-top ingredients and combines the best of both British and continental dishes. The menu is imaginative but not dangerously so. You feel that each dish was carefully thought out and perfected before appearing on the menu.

---

2. Polperro

This ancient fishing village, 28 miles from Plymouth, is reached by a steep descent from the top of a hill. Motorists in summer are forbidden to take their cars down unless they are booked in a hotel. Why? Because otherwise they'd create too much of a traffic bottleneck in July and August. At one time it was estimated that nearly every man, woman, and child in the village spent time salting down pilchards for the winter or smuggling. Today, tourists have replaced the contraband.

You'd have to search every cove and bay in Cornwall to turn up a village as handsome as Polperro, which looks, in some parts, almost as if it had been removed intact from the 17th century. The village is tucked in between some cliffs. Its houses—really no more than fishermen's cottages—are bathed in pastel-wash. A small river, actually a stream called the Pol, cuts its way through Polperro. The heart of the village is its much photographed, much painted fishing harbor, where the pilchard boats, loaded to the gunnels, used to dock.

There's a large car park, the price based according to the length of your stay. For those unable to walk, a horse-drawn bus carries visitors to the town center.

WHERE TO STAY

Receiving guests from March to October, **Lanhael House,** Langreek Road, Polperro, Cornwall PL13 2PW (tel. 0503/72428), is one of the best of the moderately priced accommodations at the resort. Roy and Sandra Pauls's modernized house dates from the 17th century, but today it has many amenities, including a swimming pool and a terrace to capture the sun of the Cornish coast. The six bedrooms are comfortable and attractively furnished, and two contain private baths. The charge, depending on the plumbing, ranges from £18 ($29.70) daily in a single and from £32 ($52.80) in a double. There is limited car parking as well.

Claremont, Fore Street, Polperro, Cornwall PL13 2RG (tel. 0503/72241), is a 17th-century cottage with postwar additions. It lies behind a white facade on the main street leading to the center of the village. Service and access to the owners of this pleasant hotel are probably the most compelling reasons to check in. It sits above the village, offering a view over its rooftops for guests to enjoy between Easter and October. The 10 bedrooms are all comfortably furnished and have private baths, costing from £35 ($57.75) daily for doubles, £16.50 ($27.25) for singles. The French owners, Nellie Peyrin and Gilles Couturier, serve genuine French cooking from 7:30 to 9pm, a dinner costing from £9.95 ($16.40). Bar meals range from £3.95 ($6.50).

WHERE TO DINE

Good English cookery is offered at **The Kitchen,** Fish na Bridge (tel. 0503/72780), a pink cottage about half way down to the harbor from the car park. Once a wagon builder's shop, it is now a restaurant run by Vanessa and Ian Bateson. Ian is the chef, except Vanessa makes all the homemade desserts, as well as bakes the bread. Reservations are essential. Everything is homemade from the best fresh ingredients available. The menu changes seasonally and is biased toward local fresh fish. Typical dishes include crab in filo pastry, seafood provençale, and lobster. Dinner is offered nightly in summer from 7 to 9:30pm, costing from £15.50 ($25.60), with a vegetarian menu at £13 ($21.45) and lobster menu at £21 ($34.65). In winter, dinner is only on Fri. and Sat. Closed all of January.

The Captain's Cabin, Lansallos Street (tel. 0503/72292), one of the mellow old structures of town, a 16th-century fisherman's cottage, invites you to dine among antiques and brass in the beamed low-ceilinged dining room. The owner, Lesley Jacobs, and her staff offer a comprehensive cuisine. The chef has a fine reputation for his local fish dishes, from among which you might choose crab mornay, lobster thermidor, or grilled lemon sole. The wide variety of fresh local fish is brought in daily by the fishermen of Polperro. At lunchtime, 11:30am to 2:30pm, you can order à la carte meals for around £6.50 ($10.75), or special snacks and sandwiches such as fresh crab and salad. At dinner there are à la carte listings and chef's specials, as well as two set meals: three courses for £9.95 ($16.40), and four courses for £12.95 ($21.35). Dinner is served from 7 to 11pm. The Cabin is open daily all year, including holidays.

WHERE TO STAY AND DINE IN THE ENVIRONS

If you find the busy activity of the two little harbors of Looe and Polperro too much for you, then you can live in far greater style at two of England's outstanding inns, just outside. **Pelynt,** about 3 miles north of Polperro, is a small, sleepy village; and **Lanreath,** lying off the road to West Looe, is another peaceful community.

Jubilee Inn, Jubilee Hill, Pelynt, Cornwall PL13 2JZ (tel. 0503/20312), was built in the 16th century, but it took its name from the time it was restored in connection with the tribute paid to Queen Victoria's Jubilee celebration. Only the best handmade Victorian furnishings were used in the restoration, even in the bedrooms. Nine well-furnished rooms are rented with baths, TVs, and phones, costing £55 ($90.75) to £63 ($103.95) per person daily for half board. The food is good, and the vegetables come fresh from the inn's own garden. Sun. lunch is served for £8.50 ($14.05). Otherwise, you have lunch in the bar, where hot and cold dishes are offered. Dinner is à la carte and will cost £15 ($24.75) to £20 ($33), depending on what you choose and how much. The inn is a comment on, rather than a monument to, the past. The lounge has a hooded fireplace, with a raised hearth, Windsor armchairs, antique porcelain, and copper bowls filled with flowers cut from the garden behind the building. The dining room is elegantly Victorian, with mahogany chairs and tables. A circular, glass-enclosed staircase takes you to the bedrooms. Fitting onto the outside, the winding stairway has been built to serve as a combined tower and hothouse.

Punch Bowl Inn, Lanreath, near Looe, Cornwall PL13 2NX (tel. 0503/20218), has had a checkered career since it was first licensed in 1620, serving in turn as a courthouse, coaching inn, and rendezvous for smugglers. Today, its old fireplaces and high-backed settles, as well as its 14 bedrooms (some with four-posters), provide hospitality to travelers from abroad and to the English. The B&B rate is from £18 ($29.70) to £24 ($39.60) per person daily with bath, from £13 ($21.45) to £17.50 ($28.90) per person without bath. There is a modern lounge, TV room, air-conditioned cocktail bar, and an additional bedroom wing. Even if you're not stopping over, owners Harvey and Sylvia Frith invite you to sample the fare or drinks in one of the kitchens (really bars, among the few "kitchens" licensed in Britain as "bars"). In the Stable Restaurant, with its Tudor beams and fireplace, you eat à la carte, choosing to have just a bowl of soup, or perhaps you'd like a steak. Meals cost £7 ($11.55) to £16 ($26.40). Food is served from noon to 2pm and 7 to 9:30pm daily.

3. Fowey

Called the Dartmouth of Cornwall, Fowey, 34 miles from Plymouth, is a town of historical interest (one of the most ancient seaports in the West Country). Once the Fowey Gallants sailed the seas and were considered invincible when raiding French coastal towns. However, occasional retaliation was inevitable. At the time of the Armada, Fowey sent more ships than London, 277 miles away. With its narrow streets and white-washed houses, it has remained unspoiled over the years, enjoying a sheltered position on a deep-water channel. Its creeks and estuary attract sailors and fishermen. If you climb up to St. Catherine's Point, you'll be rewarded with a view of the harbor. Sandy beaches and coves are there to explore as well (there's also an 18-hole golf course within easy reach of Carlyon Bay).

WHERE TO STAY AND DINE

A Georgian house, **Marina Hotel,** the Esplanade, Fowey, Cornwall PL23 1HY (tel. 072683/3315), has shutters and sweeping verandas stretching across its symmetrical facade. It is under the direction of David and Sheila Johns. Originally built for a bishop of Truro, the house sits on top of a well-constructed retaining wall that rises steeply above the boats moored in the estuary of the Fowey (pronounced "foy") River. The modernized interior still retains some of the best of the original architectural features, as well as a walled garden running to the water's edge. A well-managed restaurant is on the premises, and if by chance you arrive by boat, the hotel will provide you with a mooring. Some of the comfortable and big-windowed bedrooms have a private balcony. Half-board rates range from £34 ($56.10) to £44 ($72.60) per person daily, but for stays of 2 days or longer, prices are reduced by around 12%. From March to October, guests are received in 11 bedrooms, with private baths or showers, TVs, and phones.

Food for Thought, on the town quay (tel. 072683/2221). The sprawling stone walls that contain this establishment were originally built as the village customs house. Since its renovation by Martin Billingsley, this warmly decorated restaurant has been known for some of the best seafood in town. Directly on the water, the snug-ceilinged dining room serves succulent lobster and Scottish crayfish. The dishes are usually inspired by recipes prepared in France across the Channel and include crab-stuffed chicken breast served with a saffron sauce, a mixed-fish tart, and grilled fresh Fowey sea bass. Full à la carte meals cost from £25 ($41.25), and a three-course fixed-price dinner, with service, drinks, and VAT included, comes to £15.50 ($25.60). Meals are served only from 7 to 9:30pm Mon. to Sat. Reservations are necessary. The restaurant is closed January and February.

4. Truro

This ancient town on the Truro River, 52 miles from Plymouth and 295 miles from London, is the only cathedral city in Cornwall, the ecclesiastical center of Cornwall. The cathedral church of St. Mary was begun in 1880 in the Early English style (the spires are in the Norman Gothic design). The town is within 8 to 20 miles of the Cornish beaches. It can be used as a base to explore the countryside, which ranges from bleak Bodmin Moor to fertile farmland and the Winter Roseland of the Falmouth Estuary.

Trelissick Garden (tel. 0872/862090) lies on both sides of the B3289 south of Truro, overlooking King Harry Passage. The entrance is just off the King Harry Ferry up the hill and beyond the circular tower. In this beautiful wooded park with peaceful walks through the well-tended trees and shrubs, the rhododendrons are a splash of color in late spring. Upon arrival, you pick up a map and set out on a woodland walk that will take you through the plantations to the banks of Lamouth Creek and all along the edge of the River Fal and Channals Creek before you return to the center of the garden, about a 1-hour stroll. Then you can visit the gardens, where the vegetation is more controlled.

The restaurant here (tel. 0872/863486) is open daily at 11am for coffee and from 12:15 to 2:15pm for lunch, with afternoon teas served until 6pm. The emphasis is on wholesome, fresh food, such as homemade soup and Cornish ice creams and clotted cream. A lunch costs £6 ($9.90) Mon. to Sat., £8.50 ($14.05) for a three-course meal on Sun., which includes a roast and coffee. You can also have sherry Cornish cider or one of the various lagers.

The garden is open April to October from 11am to 6pm Mon. to Sat., 1 to 6pm (or to sunset if earlier) on Sun. Entry to the park and woodland walk is free. To visit the gardens costs adults £2.20 ($3.65), and children pay half price.

WHERE TO STAY AND DINE

A very special and charming place is **Alverton Manor,** Tregolls Road, Truro, Cornwall TR1 1XQ (tel. 0872/76633), which was originally built around 1820 and later became an Anglican convent. Built of honey-colored stone and capped with a slate roof, it was in derelict condition until its restoration began in 1987. After its transformation, it has been turned into the finest hotel and restaurant in Cornwall. The manor sits on sloping land in a garden of 6 acres, less than a mile north of the center of Truro along A39. Open all year, it contains 25 individually decorated bedrooms, most with high ceilings and either arched or rectangular, mullioned leaded windows. All accommodations have private baths, TVs, and phones and come with a continental breakfast included. Singles ranges from £65 ($107.25) to £95 ($156.75) daily, with doubles costing from £90 ($148.50) to £125 ($206.25). Meals are a delight, a sophisticated continental cuisine using top quality ingredients deftly handled by an accomplished chef. A set lunch costs from £8.50 ($14.05), with dinners going from £23 ($37.95). The dining room is pastel colored and often sunny, and filled with French-inspired furniture in cherrywood. Reservations are needed.

A gracefully detailed late Victorian house, the **Carlton Hotel,** 49 Falmouth Rd., Truro, Cornwall TR1 2HL (tel. 0872/72450), has twin gables overlooking a pleasant garden and a spacious modern bedroom wing. Twenty-eight of the establishment's 32 rooms contain private baths, color TVs, and phones. Conveniently close to the center of town, the hotel charges £30 ($49.50) daily in a single, £45 ($74.25) in a double, with breakfast included. Snacks as well as more formal lunches and dinners are available.

Aside from the cuisine served at Alverton Manor, the best food is found not in Truro, but at **Long's,** Redruth Road, Blackwater (tel. 0872/561111), lying 7 miles west of Truro by A390. Ann (she's the chef) and Ian Long have long enjoyed acclaim for serving some of the finest food in the West Country, and, considering the quality of the cooking and the ingredients, at a very reasonable price as well. To their Georgian building in the heart of the village they have brought a warming touch in a decor of pastel hues. Try her rabbit pâté, followed by a spicy, perfectly seasoned lamb in a pastry case. Her chocolate praline mousse is delectable. Actually, you never know what you're getting until you arrive, as Mrs. Long is very much an inspired chef. Hers is an individualized version of modern British cuisine. Open for dinner only from 7:30 to 10pm Wed. to Sat., costing from £16 ($26.40), and for lunch only 12:30 to 2pm Sun., with a set menu offered for £10.50 ($17.35). Reservations are necessary.

5. Portloe

If you really want to get away from it all and go to that hidden-away Cornish fishing village, then Portloe is for you. It lies 15 miles from Truro. On the slope of a hill, opening onto Veryan Bay, it is reached by a road suitable for cars—but chances are you may get sidetracked and spend the rest of the afternoon on byways, opening and closing gates to keep the cattle from straying.

Portloe is an ideal stopover on the south Cornish coast if you're traveling in July and August, when the popular tourist centers, such as Looe and St. Ives, are overrun.

WHERE TO STAY

A prestigious inn, the **Lugger Hotel,** Portloe, Cornwall TR2 5RD (tel. 0872/ 501322), is a 17th-century establishment at the top of the harbor slip, with a bay and boats as part of the scene. It is believed to have been a smugglers' hideaway in its early days, but today, the Powell family runs it as a modernized, sparkling clean hotel on the water's edge. The 19 bedrooms all have private baths or showers and toilets, color or TVs, radios, central heating, tea and coffee makers, and direct-dial phones. The charges are from £44 ($72.60) to £49 ($80.85) per person daily for a bed, an English breakfast, dinner, and VAT. Accommodations in the main building and the 19th-century bedroom wing are traditionally furnished in Tudor or Victorian style. The restaurant, which is open to nonresidents for dinner, has a panoramic view of the cove. A cocktail bar occupies the original inn parlor, and the hotel also has lounges, a sauna, and a solarium. Guests are allowed reduced greens fees at nearby Truro Golf Club. The hotel is open from mid-March to early November, with room rates reduced for stays of more than two days.

6. St. Mawes

Overlooking the mouth of the Fal River, St. Mawes is often compared to a port on the French Riviera. Because it's sheltered from northern winds, subtropical plants grow here. From the town quay, you can take a boat to Frenchman's Creek, Helford River, and other places. St. Mawes is noted for its sailing, boating, fishing, and yachting. Half a dozen sandy coves lie within 15 minutes by car from the port. The town, built on the Roseland Peninsula, makes for interesting walks, with its color-washed cottages and sheltered harbor. On Castle Point, Henry VIII ordered the construction of St. Mawes Castle. Falmouth, across the water, is only 2 miles away, Truro 18 miles, and London 300 miles.

WHERE TO STAY AND DINE

The highest-rated hotel is the **Tresanton,** 27 Lower Castle Rd., St. Mawes, Cornwall TR2 5DR (tel. 0326/270544). It is really three buildings, the oldest one dating from the 18th century. One is on the roadside, another halfway up, and the third—the main part of the hotel—on top of the hill and away from the traffic noise. The upper level has spacious veranda terraces—so there are a lot of places to sit outside among the flowers, looking across the bay. To quote a reader, it's "quite simply the most charming and delightful hotel I have ever stayed in." The owners are Graham and Maureen Brockton. The 21 bedrooms are fresh and bright, furnished for the most part in the French country-house manner. All have private baths, phones, and TVs, and are stocked with sewing kits, tissues, books to read, whatever. All accommodations face the sea. A single with dinner and B&B rents from £61 ($100.65) daily, while a similar double goes for £118 ($194.70) to £180 ($297). The lounge has an open fireplace and comfortable chairs. The dining room, also overlooking the sea, has attractive murals and a decor designed to carry the eye from the house to the sun terraces, the subtropical gardens, and the sea beyond. The menu wisely emphasizes fish dishes.

The **Idle Rocks,** Tredenham Road, St. Mawes, Cornwall TR2 5AN (tel. 0326/ 270771), is a solid old building right on the sea wall, with gaily colored umbrellas and tables lining the terrace. Water laps at the wall, and the site opens onto views over the river and the constant traffic of sailing boats and dinghies. The bar serves tasty lunch snacks, including fresh seafood caught locally. The bedrooms mostly have sea or river views, and they're equipped with central heating, hot beverage facilities, color TVs, radios, and intercoms. The main hotel building contains 15 of the rooms, with 9 more being in an annex. All have private baths or showers. Singles rent for £42 ($69.30) to £52 ($85.80) daily, depending on the location of the room. Doubles cost from £85 ($140.25) to £100 ($165). The higher priced units are in the main building. Tariffs include a full English breakfast and VAT. Half board is offered for £50 ($82.50) to £60 ($99) per person. The hotel is open from mid-March to the first of January. Golf is available at Truro Golf Club at reduced greens fees.

A colorful inn on the seafront, **The Rising Sun,** the Square, St. Mawes, Cornwall TR2 5DJ (tel. 0326/270233), is made of a row of fishermen's cottages with a flagstone terrace out front. It oozes with tasteful charm. Known as one of Cornwall's best inns, it was recently redecorated. B&B charges in a single are £32 ($52.80) per day, rising to £72 ($118.80) in a double, the latter with private bath or shower. The inn rents 12 bedrooms, 9 with private baths or showers, and each with phone and TV. The inn also has a reputation for good food, and you may want to patronize its facilities even if you don't spend the night. The dining room is tastefully decorated, and a table d'hôte dinner costs from £18 ($29.70). During the day you can enjoy tasty bar meals, and, on Sunday, of course, a traditional roast. There are both a cocktail bar and a public bar, the latter enjoyed by the locals.

---

7. Falmouth

A lot of cutthroat ship wreckers used to live in the area. In fact, when John Killigrew, a leading citizen, started to build a lighthouse on Lizard Head, they protested that the beacon in the night would deprive them of their livelihood and "take away God's Grace from us." Falmouth, 26 miles from Penzance, is built on a promontory overlooking the estuary of the Fal. Today it is a favorite base for the yachting set, who consider it one of the most beautiful harbors in Europe. On a small peninsula, Falmouth's old section overlooks the land-locked inner harbor. The newer part, center for most of the hotels, faces the bay and commands a panorama from St. Anthony's Lighthouse to Pendennis Castle. Warmed in winter by the Gulf Stream, Falmouth has become a year-round resort. Many find it a good center for touring the rugged Cornish coastline. It's possible, for example, to take a ferry from Falmouth to St. Mawes, a 20-minute ride.

Pendennis Castle, once part of Henry VIII's coastal defense system, dates from 1544, when the central circular keep was completed on the site of a prehistoric fortress. Since Tudor days it has protected the entrance to Falmouth Harbour. Youth Hostels Association runs a hostel in the old barrack block, but the castle can be visited daily from Good Friday to the end of September from 10am to 6pm, from 10am to 4pm the remainder of the year. Admission is £1.30 ($2.15) for adults, 65p ($1.05) for children. For information, phone 0326/316594.

During most of the year, sightseeing craft ply up and down the River Fal from the Prince of Wales Pier in Falmouth to the town quay in Truro.

WHERE TO STAY

From its 5 acres of gardens, the **Falmouth Hotel,** Castle Beach, Seafront, Falmouth, Cornwall TR11 4NZ (tel. 0326/312671), rises in an impressively eclectic mélange of 19th-century styles. Considered the biggest and most important hotel in town, it contains 73 comfortably modernized rooms, each with its own bath, phone, radio, and color TV. Singles or doubles rent for £35 ($57.75) per person daily, with breakfast included. There's a choice of bars and restaurants, plus a heated swimming pool and a garden bordering the water. The hotel often hosts business conferences for local companies.

Greenbank Hotel, Harbourside, Falmouth, Cornwall TR11 2SR (tel. 0326/312440), hangs tenaciously to the old days of the Post Office Packet Services (1688–1850). Beside the shore road, this hotel overlooks the water with its own landing pier. Over the years it has been expanded, but it remains traditional, having attracted many famous guests, including Florence Nightingale. The spacious lounges have views of the harbor, and the 43 rooms are comfortably furnished, each with private bath or shower, TV, and phone. In a single, the rate ranges from £35 ($57.75) to £65 ($107.25) daily, increasing to £70 ($115.50) to £105 ($173.25) in a double or twin. The hotel has a hairdressing and beauty salon, as well as a water-view dining room favored by local yachting people and serving old-fashioned English food. Lunches cost from £9 ($14.85); dinners, from £15 ($24.75).

Penmore Manor Hotel, Mongleath Road, Falmouth, Cornwall TR11 4PN (tel. 0326/211411), is an 18th-century Georgian mansion a mile from the center of Falmouth. After the owners acquired the property, they embarked on an enthusiastic campaign to upgrade it, and today they work hard to make their guests happy, serving flavorful meals in the dining room and arranging a variety of outside activities. There are 42 rooms in the main building and extensions. Each accommodation has a private bath, radio, phone, and color TV. Singles cost £44 ($72.60) to £53 ($87.45) daily, and doubles go for £65 ($107.25) to £88 ($145.20), with a full breakfast included. The Fountain Leisure Club provides guests with indoor and outdoor heated swimming pools, spa bath, sauna, mini-gym, croquet lawn, and even giant chess. The view from the trio of lounges includes 5 acres of woodland and Falmouth Bay.

WHERE TO STAY IN THE ENVIRONS

Budock Vean Hotel, Golf and Country Club, Mawnan Smith, Falmouth, Cornwall TR11 5LG (tel. 0326/250288), 5 miles southwest by Trescobeas Road (off the B3291), stands among the pines and subtropical vegetation sloping sharply to the Helford River. You come to an old stone house with a stout front door and bright welcoming hall. Some bedrooms are in the old house, others in the new wing, and all have baths, phones, and toilets. A few units have views over the gardens and down to the distant river, and others overlook the private golf course. B&B costs from £60 ($99) per person daily in summer. Tariffs drop to £37 ($61.05) per person in winter. VAT is included in the tariffs. Meals are a selection of international and English dishes. The hotel has an indoor, heated swimming pool. In winter, a log fire burns on the open grate. The main attraction for many guests is the 18-hole golf course free to residents. Closed in January and February.

Riverside, Helford, near Helston, Cornwall, TR12 6JU (tel. 032623/443), owned by Susan Darrell, is a small, French provincial–style restaurant in two 18th-century cottages beside the Helford River. There are 12 tables with a capacity of 36 diners. Furnishings are in keeping with the cottage style of the house. Try the bourride, a Provençal fish stew with aïoli and rouille. Main courses include chicken Georgian style, with grapes and oranges, or guinea fowl with rosemary. Desserts offers such fare as a toothsome walnut treacle tart and iced lemon soufflé. The set price of £24 ($39.60) includes VAT and service. A table is yours for the evening, so there's no rushing to clear up for the next serving. Reservations are essential. Meals are served daily from 7:30 to 9:30pm; closed from November to early March. Riverside also has overnight accommodations. The seven double rooms have private baths, and there are some with TV and some with fine views. The charge is £65 ($107.25) to £82 ($135.30) per night for two persons, with a continental breakfast, VAT, and service all included.

POLDARK MINE

Three miles north of Helston on the B3297 is the **Poldark Mine and Heritage Complex,** Wendron (tel. 0326/573173). As you have driven around Cornwall, the old workings of the tin mines will have been evident everywhere. Here you have the chance of visiting a mine and walking through the old workings, which extend for several miles beneath the surface. Recent extension of the area open to the public into newly discovered caverns has made the tour of the mine last 3 hours. There are extensive heritage museums depicting the living conditions of the 18th-century mining community, the history of tin, and the famous Holman collection. One museum houses the largest collection of flatirons in Europe and perhaps the world.

Amid prize-winning gardens are restaurants, Cornish craft shops, picnic areas, and children's play areas. The mine and heritage complex is open daily from April to October 10am to 6pm. Last admissions are 4:30pm, but allow 3 hours for your visit. Admission to the mine is £3.75 ($6.20) for adults, £2.25 ($3.70) for children.

The mine and surrounding area are of particular interest to readers and television viewers of the "Poldark" series, filmed from novels by Winston Graham.

8. Penzance

This little Gilbert and Sullivan harbor town is the end of the line for the Cornish Riviera Express. A full 280 miles southwest from London and 77 miles from Plymouth, it is noted for its equable climate (it's one of the first towns in England to blossom with spring flowers) and the summer throngs that descend for fishing, sailing, and swimming. Overlooking Mount's Bay, Penzance is graced in places with subtropical plants, as well as palm trees.

The harbor is used to activity of one sort or another. Those pirates in *The Pirates of Penzance* were not entirely fictional. The town was raided by Barbary pirates, destroyed in part by Cromwell's troops, sacked and burnt by the Spaniards, and bombed by the Germans. In spite of its turbulent past, it offers tranquil resort living today.

The most westerly town in England, Penzance makes a good base for exploring Land's End, the Lizard peninsula, St. Michael's Mount, the old fishing ports and artists' colonies of St. Ives, Newlyn, and Mousehole—even the Isles of Scilly.

WHAT TO SEE AND DO

Three miles east of Penzance, **St. Michael's Mount** is reached at low tide by a causeway. Rising about 250 feet from the sea, St. Michael's Mount is topped by a partially medieval, partially 17th-century castle. At high tide the mount becomes an island, reached only by motor launch from Marazion. A Benedictine monastery, the gift of Edward the Confessor, stood on this spot in the 11th century. The castle, with its collections of armor and antique furniture, is open, weather and tide permitting, from the end of March to the end of October, 10:30am to 4:45pm Mon. to Fri. It charges £2.60 ($4.30) for adults and £1.30 ($2.15) for children. In winter, you can only go over when the causeway is dry. There is a tea garden on the island, as well as a National Trust restaurant, both of which are open in summer. *Warning:* The steps up to the castle are steep and rough, so wear stout shoes.

From Penzance, take bus 20, 21, or 22, then get off at Marazion, the town opposite St. Michael's Mount. To avoid disappointment, it is a good idea to telephone the office of St. Michael's Mount (tel. 0736/710507) to learn the state of the tides, especially during the cooler months.

The **Minack Theatre** in Porthcurno, 9 miles from Penzance, is unique. It's carved out of the Cornish cliff-face with the Atlantic as its impressive backdrop. In tiered seating, similar to that of the theaters of ancient Greece, 550 people can watch the show and the rocky coast beyond the stage. The theater's season of plays and musical shows begins at the end of May and continues until mid-September. There is an exhibition hall that houses a permanent record of the life and work of Rowena Cade. This exhibition center is open from Easter to October 30 and includes a chance to visit the theater outside of performance times. Seats cost £3.50 ($5.80) purchased at the box office. When no performance is on, admission to the center and to see the theater is £1.20 ($2). For details, phone 0736/810694 during the season. To reach Minack, leave Penzance on the A30 heading toward Land's End. After 3 miles, bear left onto the B3283 and follow signposts to Porthcurno.

WHERE TO STAY

The Queen's Hotel, the Promenade, Penzance, Cornwall TR18 4HG (tel. 0736/62371), opens onto good views across Mounts Bay. Lying on the only promenade in Cornwall, this Victorian hotel is decorated and furnished with many antiques. Paintings from Newlyn Art School adorn many of the walls. The hotel offers 71 comfortably furnished bedrooms with private baths and such amenities as color TVs, free in-house video systems, direct-dial phones, and beverage-making equipment. A single begins at £38 ($62.70) nightly, with doubles going for £68 ($112.20). Fresh local seafood is a specialty of the Promenade Restaurant where dinners cost from £14.50 ($23.95). A bar buffet is offered Mon. to Sat. for £4 ($6.60). Or else you can dine in the hotel's bar, brasserie, and restaurant, the Strollers. The hotel also has such health facilities as a gymnasium, a sauna, and a Jacuzzi, as well as a hairdressing salon.

Built in 1660, the **Abbey Hotel,** Abbey Street, Penzance, Cornwall TR18 4AR (tel. 0736/66906), is a well-preserved place that is frequented by discerning guests. The bonus is its situation—on a narrow side street on several terraces directly overlooking Penzance Harbour. The seven bedrooms and baths are stylishly furnished. You can take only your room and breakfast at the Abbey, or have dinner in the restaurant downstairs. Singles cost from £50 ($82.50) daily, a double or twin going from £60 ($99) to £85 ($140.25), including a full English breakfast and VAT. Behind the hotel, which is built close to the street, is a tiny formal garden on two tiers, each with a view of the water. Here the herbs are grown that are used to spice the delicately flavored meats in the restaurant downstairs. The owners, Michael and Jean Cox, have brought their vitality, style, and charm into the hotel business. Mrs. Cox is the former international model, Jean Shrimpton. Sample dishes from their dinner menu include homemade soups, mackerel pâté, fresh local fish dishes, and generally a roast joint. Everything is fresh and delicately cooked, a dinner costing from £16.50 ($27.25).

The **Georgian House,** Chapel Street, Penzance, Cornwall TR18 4AE (tel. 0736/65664), once the home of the mayors of Penzance, and reputedly haunted by the ghost of Mrs. Baines, who owned it hundreds of years ago, has been completely renovated into a cozy, intimate hotel. Denise and Michael Hardman welcome guests to their 12 bright, clean bedrooms, all with hot and cold water basins, color TVs, and tea and coffee makers. Six of the rooms contain private baths or showers and toilets. Rates are £13.50 ($22.30) to £17 ($28.05) per person daily for B&B in a bathless room, rising to £18.50 ($30.55) with private bath. The house is centrally heated, with a comfortable reading lounge, a licensed bar with a nautical motif, and an intimate dining room where good Cornish meals are served from April to October, although the house takes guests all year. Parking is available in the courtyard at the rear of the premises.

WHERE TO DINE

Down a narrow cobblestone street opposite Lloyds Bank, **Harris's Restaurant,** 46 New St. (tel. 0736/64408), is owned and run by a husband-and-wife team, Roger and Anne Harris. It's a warm, candlelit place with a relaxed atmosphere. Light lunches, costing from £8 ($13.20), served upstairs, include crab Florentine, lobster salad, and salad niçoise. Dinner is more elaborate, offering such dishes as breast of duckling in a port wine sauce, filet steak with a red wine and wild-mushroom sauce, and medallions of venison. Expect to pay up to £20 ($33) for a complete dinner. Lunch is served from noon to 1:45pm Tues. to Sat., and dinner from 7 to 10pm Mon. to Sat. (Tues. to Sat. in winter).

Berkeley, Abbey Street (tel. 0736/62541), lies on a side street near the Abbey Hotel. It was designed and built by the Morris family at the rear of Admiral Benbow's Restaurant and Bar. A sophisticated rendezvous, it has exposed stone, plush banquettes, and touches of glitter. Some of the taped jazz music and much of the atmosphere will evoke a setting of some 50 years ago. You get good honest cookery here, not flights of fancy. For example, try the whole Dover sole cooked in butter with lemon juice or breast of chicken fried in butter and seasoned with fresh sage, perhaps scallops Breton style. The restaurant only serves dinner, and is open 7:30 to

10:30pm Mon. to Sat. (closed on off-season Mon.). A full à la carte dinner costs from £22 ($36.30).

---

9. The Isles of Scilly

Perhaps the most interesting and scenic excursion from Penzance is a day trip to the Isles of Scilly, which lie off the Cornish coast about 27 miles west-southwest of Land's End. There are five inhabited and more than 100 uninhabited islands in the group. Some consist merely of a few square miles of land while the largest, St. Mary's, encompasses some 30 square miles. Two of these islands attract tourists, St. Mary's and Tresco.

These islands were known to the early Greeks and the Romans, and in Celtic legend they were inhabited entirely by holy men. There are more ancient burial mounds on these islands than anywhere else in southern England, and artifacts found establish clearly that people lived here more than 4,000 years ago. Today there is little left of this long history to show the visitor. Now these are islands of peace and beauty where early flowers are the main export and tourism the main industry.

St. Mary's is the capital, with about seven-eighths of the total population of all the islands, and it is here that the ship from the mainland docks at Hugh Town. However, for the day visitor, I recommend the helicopter flight from Penzance to **Tresco,** the neighboring island, where you can enjoy a day's walk through the 735 acres, mostly occupied by the **Abbey Gardens.**

HOW TO GET THERE

You can travel via the **Isles of Scilly Steamship Company Ltd.,** Quay Street, Penzance (tel. 0736/62009), with daily departures from April to October. The trip from Penzance to Hugh Town, St. Mary's, takes about 3 hours. Steamships leave Penzance daily at 9:15am and return from Scilly at 4:45pm. In winter, there is a restricted service. A same-day, round-trip ticket costs £24 ($39.60) for adults, £12 ($19.80) for children. You can buy an onward ticket for Tresco, including the ferry and landing charges, at £3.50 ($5.80).

British International Helicopters, at the Penzance Heliport (tel. 0736/63871), operates a year-round helicopter service to St. Mary's and Tresco. Flight time is 20 minutes. The standard fare from Penzance to the islands is £33 ($54.45) each way. Flights start at 7:50am July to September, and at 8:45am the remainder of the year. They continue regularly throughout the day, with the last flight back to Penzance at 6:15pm in summer, 3:40pm otherwise. For people arriving in Penzance by train, there is a bus service between the railway station and the heliport. The cost is £1 ($1.65), and travel time is about 5 minutes.

British Rail runs express trains from Paddington Station, London, to Penzance. BritRail Passes can be used. Travel time is about 5 hours. There are special offers on the Night Riviera Express.

For those who wish to travel to Penzance by road, there is good **express bus service.** The Rapide costs from £26 ($42.90) round-trip for the journey from London, about 8 hours each way. The buses are fitted with toilets and have reclining seats and a hostess who dispenses coffee, tea, and sandwiches. The buses are run by National Express from Victoria Coach Station, 172 Buckingham Palace Rd., London, S.W.1 (tel. 071/7300-0202).

WHAT TO SEE AND DO ON TRESCO

No cars or motorbikes are allowed on the island, but walking or bicycling is pleasant. Bikes can be rented by the day. The hotels use a special wagon towed by a farm tractor to transport guests and luggage from the harbor.

The **Abbey Gardens,** mentioned above, are the most outstanding feature of

Tresco. Here you can enjoy a day's walk through the 735 acres. These gardens were started by Augustus Smith in the mid-1830s. When he began work, the area was a barren hillside, a fact visitors find hard to believe.

The gardens are a collector's dream, with more than 5,000 species of plants from some 100 different countries. The old abbey, or priory, is a ruin said to have been founded by Benedictine monks in the 11th century, although some historians date it from A.D. 964. Of special interest in the gardens is **Valhalla,** a collection of nearly 60 figureheads from ships wrecked around the islands. There is a rather eerie atmosphere surrounding these gaily painted figures from the past, each one a ghost with a different story to tell. Hours are 10am to 4pm daily. Admission is £2.50 ($4.15).

After a visit to the gardens, walk through the fields, along paths, and across dunes thick with heather. Flowers, birds, shells, and fish are so abundant that Tresco is a naturalist's dream and a walker's paradise. Birds are so unafraid that they land within a foot or so of you and feed happily.

The phone number for **information** to do with Tresco is 0720/22849. Call it to find out about boat schedules, possible changes in hours and prices at the abbey, and other matters.

WHERE TO STAY ON TRESCO

The top hostelry here is the **Island Hotel,** Tresco, Isles of Scilly, Cornwall TR24 0PU (tel. 0720/22883), a modern establishment on the northeast side of the island with views that have been compared to those seen in the Greek islands. The building blends with the sea and the rocks, and long, low extensions have been added to an original cottage. Some rooms overlook the sea, some face inland. All the 41 units are comfortably furnished with easy chairs and storage spaces, private baths, toilets, drying racks, color TVs, phones, and razor points. Managers John and Wendy Pyatt charge rates that vary considerably, according to location and time of year. Depending on your room assignment and the time of year, charges for half-board range from £58 ($95.70) to £102 ($168.30) per person daily. Understandably, 1-night stays are not encouraged, a 3-night minimum being preferred. The hotel is closed from October to March.

The only other hotel on Tresco is the **New Inn,** Tresco, Isles of Scilly, Cornwall TR24 0PU (tel. 0720/22844). This pub, built of stone and standing on the island's road, has an outdoor area for those who wish to picnic and drink a glass of ale. Inside, the bar is the meeting place for locals and tourists alike. Lunch snacks are available, a bar meal costing £6 ($9.90) for two courses. Dinners are £13 ($21.45) to £15 ($24.75). The pictures in the bar are worth a look. They show many of the ships that sank or foundered around the islands in the past, as well as some of the gigs used in pilotage, rescue, smuggling, and pillage. The inn has 12 rooms, all twins and doubles with private bathrooms. Here, too, there is a wide range of prices. Accommodation prices vary from £16.50 ($27.25) per person daily for B&B until mid-April, after which a dinner, bed, and breakfast tariff applies until mid-October. The prices range from £32 ($52.80) to £45 ($74.25) during that time. The inn has a heated outdoor swimming pool.

WHAT TO SEE AND DO ON ST. MARY'S

Expert diver Mark Groves, who runs **Underwater Island Safaris,** "Nowhere," Old Town (tel. 0720/22732), has worked as a diver in both the Caribbean and the Red Sea. He can entertain both the experienced and the inexperienced diver. A diving safari costs from £22 ($36.30) for three hours of instruction and diving, including gear rental. Diving for qualified persons takes place on many of the historic and beautiful drop-offs. Waterskiing is also offered.

Cars are available but hardly necessary. The **Island Bus Service** has a basic charge of 50p (85¢) from one island point to another. However, sightseers can circumnavigate the island, paying £1 ($1.65) for the privilege. Children are charged half fare.

Bicycles are one of the most practical means of transport. **Buccabu Bicycle Ren-**

tals, the Strand, St. Mary's (tel. 0720/22289), is the major rental agency. The cost, depending on the type of bicycle you want, ranges from £4 ($6.60) to £20 ($33) per day, the latter the price for a tandem bike.

The **Isles of Scilly Museum** on St. Mary's (tel. 0270/22337) is open daily in summer from 10am to noon, 1:30 to 4:30pm, and 7 to 9pm. Winter hours are from 2 to 4pm only on Wed. Admission is 50p (85¢). The museum shows the history of the islands from 1500 B.C. with artifacts from wrecked ships, drawings, and relics discovered in the Scillies.

The **Tourist Information Office** on St. Mary's offers service (tel. 0720/22536).

WHERE TO STAY ON ST. MARY'S

A substantial stone structure, the **Hotel Godolphin,** Church Street, St. Mary's, Isles of Scilly, Cornwall TR21 0JR (tel. 0720/22316), gives the impression, as you approach, of being the private house it once was—it has been turned into a hotel with skillful additions, creating a fine hostelry in town. There are 31 bedrooms, 27 of which have private baths. All have color TVs, radios, intercoms, phones, hot beverage facilities, and central heating. The best rooms overlook the garden. Open March to October, the hotel charges £40 ($66) to £52 ($85.80) daily in a double. The hotel's name comes from the name of the estate on which the building stands, originating when Queen Elizabeth I gave the island to Francis Godolphin in 1571.

Star Castle Hotel, the Garrison, St. Mary's, Isles of Scilly TR21 0JA (tel. 0720/22317), is in a structure built as a castle in 1593 in the shape of an eight-pointed star. It was erected for the defense of the Isles of Scilly against attacks by Spain in retaliation for the 1588 defeat of the Armada. Because of the purpose of the original building, the hotel has views out to sea as well as over the town and the harbor. The great kitchen has a huge fireplace where a whole ox could be roasted. An early Prince of Wales (later King Charles II) took shelter here in 1643 when he was being hunted by Cromwell and his parliamentary forces. In 1933 another Prince of Wales was here to officiate at the opening of the castle as a hotel. This was the man who succeeded to the throne as King Edward VIII but was never crowned.

The hotel has 24 bedrooms, 16 of which are in the garden annex comprising two wings facing each other across the lawns. These are extra-large units, each with bath and opening directly onto the gardens. Of the 8 double or twin rooms in the castle, 5 have private baths and the remainder have hot and cold running water and include the rampart guard house. These are much favored for their isolation, in the points of the star overlooking the sea and the town, although the bathroom is a few yards away—across the ramparts. Charges range from £39 ($64.35) to £57 ($94.05) per person daily. All tariffs include a full English breakfast and dinner. There is a glass-covered, heated swimming pool, and the garden has many sheltered places for you to relax. Lunch and dinner orders are taken in the Cellar Bar. Typical English food is served daily from noon to 1:30pm and 6:45 to 8pm, and many of the vegetables come from the hotel's large gardens.

Carnwethers Country Guest House, Pelistry Bay, St. Mary's, Isles of Scilly, Cornwall TR21 0NX (tel. 0720/22415), is a modernized, two-story farmhouse with a one-story extension, standing on top of a hill looking down to fields, beach, and the sea. Pelistry Bay is a secluded part of St. Mary's island, the sandy beach well sheltered. You can walk at low tide across to the nearby uninhabited island of Tolls. The hostelry is owned and operated by Roy and Joyce Graham, with Joyce personally supervising the kitchen. For dinner, although the choice is limited, traditional English fare is offered. Dinner, served at 6:30pm, includes only fresh local produce and home-grown vegetables. Breakfast is a substantial meal, the marmalade being a particular pride of the house. Half board costs £24 ($39.60) to £30 ($49.50) per person daily in spring and fall, £27 ($44.55) to £36 ($59.40) in high season. All the rooms have private baths or showers, plus TVs. VAT is included in the rates. All the rooms are spotless, warm, and comfortable. The main lounge is in two parts, one for conversation and reading, the other containing a library full of books about the island. There is a separated bar lounge in its own grounds with a croquet lawn. A heated outdoor swimming pool is in operation from May to September. Sauna and a games room are also available.

---

10. Newlyn, Mousehole, and Land's End

From Penzance we head south to two of Cornwall's most charming villages.

NEWLYN

From Penzance, a promenade leads to Newlyn, a mile away, another fishing village on Mount's Bay. The late Stanhope Forbes founded an art school in Newlyn. The village has an artists' colony, attracting both the serious painter and the amateur sketcher. From Penzance, Newlyn is reached by taking bus 1 or 1B. For a dining or overnighting recommendation, try the following.

Where to Stay and Dine

Higher Faugan Hotel, Newlyn, Penzance, Cornwall TR18 5NS (tel. 0736/62076), lies three-quarters of a mile south of Penzance on the B3315. The structure was built in 1904 by painter Alexander Stanhope Forbes, whose work is now in demand, as is that of his wife, Elizabeth Adela Forbes, and many other artists from the "Newlyn" school. The spacious country-house hotel is the property of Michael and Christine Churchman. The building's granite walls, big windows, and steep roofs are surrounded by 10 acres of lawn, garden, and woodland, all of which can be covered on foot by adventurous visitors. Amenities include a heated outdoor swimming pool, a putting green, a hard tennis court, a billiards room, and a cultivated dining room serving beautifully prepared specialties. A dozen well-furnished bedrooms are offered, each with private bath, phone, TV, and coffee-making facilities. B&B is priced at £30 ($49.50) to £39 ($64.35) per person daily, and half board goes for £38 ($62.70) to £49 ($80.85) per person.

MOUSEHOLE

In a sheltered cove off Mount's Bay, Mousehole (pronounced mou-zel) is 3 miles south of Penzance, 321 miles from London. The hordes of tourists who flock here haven't changed it drastically: The gulls still squawk, the cottages still huddle close to the harbor wall (although they look as if they were built more to be photographed than lived in), the fishermen still bring in the day's catch, the old salts sit around with their pipes talking about the good old days, and the lanes are as narrow as ever. About the most exciting thing that's occurred around here was the arrival in the late 16th century of Spanish galleons, whose sailors sacked and burned the village. An artists' colony is home to both painters and potters.

The village's odd name, according to linguistic historians, is derived from a now-extinct Mediterranean language probably used by the Phoenicians when they landed here more than 2,000 years ago. Roughly translated, it means "watering place."

Where to Stay and Dine

Carn Du Hotel, Raginnis Hill, Mousehole, Cornwall TR19 6SS (tel. 0736/731233), has twin bay windows gazing over the top of the village onto the harbor with its bobbing fishing vessels. Andrew and Sigrid Field are the rulers of this panoramic aerie, whose seven double and twin bedrooms offer private baths, radios, and much comfort. Half board in low season is £30.50 ($50.35) daily per person, rising to £34.50 ($56.95) in high season. The meals, going for £11.50 ($19), are straightforward and fresh, usually accompanied by a bottle of wine from the cellars. You might precede your meal with a drink in one of the lounges. The Fields will arrange sporting options for active vacationers but won't mind if you prefer to sit and relax. The establishment is open from March to mid-January.

Tavis Vor Hotel, the Parade, Mousehole, Cornwall TR19 6PR (tel. 0736/ 731306), opens onto a marvelous view overlooking the harbor and St. Michael's Mount. Almost directly opposite is a small island on which there are the remains of a monastery. The first building on the sea side when you enter Mousehole, Tavis Vor is a seven-bedroom hotel set on its own grounds. Ample parking is provided (a rarity in Mousehole), and there is direct access to the beach from the grounds of the hotel. Most of the bedrooms contain a private bath. Overnight tariffs for B&B range from £18.50 ($30.55) per person. The hotel, which remains open all year, specializes in traditional English cooking. Meals cost from £10 ($16.50).

Where to Stay and Dine in the Environs

Lamorna Cove Hotel, Lamorna Cove, Cornwall TR19 6XH (tel. 0736/ 731411), lies 5 miles from Penzance. This is one of the most perfect Cornish coves, seemingly inaccessible down a winding, narrow road, dropping always toward the sea until you suddenly emerge onto the sea wall of the tiny cove. The owners have added to the old stone building, once a tiny chapel for Cornish miners, with a bell tower. They once even blasted several tons of rock from the cliff face to provide more room. The bar is in the chapel. A large dining room runs the length of the building, and there are several lounges full of comfortable chairs, with a log fire in winter. Accommodations, 18 in all, are in the main hotel, with baths or showers, TVs, phones, and some with balconies. There are also two cottages, one suitable for four, the other for five persons. A rocky garden clings to the cliffside and then surrounds a small swimming pool with a sun terrace overlooking the sea. In high season, a single costs from £55 ($90.75) daily, and a double or twin begins at £120 ($198), these tariffs including a full breakfast, dinner, VAT, and service. If you don't have the time to stay at the hotel, the bar lunches can be well recommended. On Sun., a traditional luncheon is served. Dinners at £15 ($24.75) are quite a feast.

LAND'S END

Craggy Land's End, where England comes to a stop, is where you'll find the last of everything. It lies 9 miles west of Penzance and is reached by bus. America's coast is 3,291 miles away to the west of the rugged rocks that tumble into the sea beneath Land's End.

Publicity says that "Everyone should stand here, at least once." Given the romantic concept that this is the piece of England closest to America, the most distant point you can go on mainland England, this is so. It must still retain some of its mystique, even if "big business" has now opened the Land's End Heritage Museum, the Man and the Sea Exhibition, and the Worzel Gummidge Exhibition, not to mention a video theater with continuous performances and the First and Last Craft Workshop from which to buy your first and "last" souvenirs. True, the area needs an injection of money. As anyone standing on those jagged cliffs can see, the pounding they take causes much damage to the coastline. Better to ignore the commercial aspect and enjoy the cliff walks and spectacular views. If you want to research the ancient traditions of Cornish folklore, there are other places far more dedicated to research than this tourist trap.

Where to Stay and Dine

State House Hotel, Land's End, Sennen, Cornwall TR19 7AA (tel. 0736/ 871844), is set behind a white façade within a complex of buildings rising from the scrubby landscape at the very tip of England. The hotel has a panoramic clifftop position, exposed to the wind and sea spray. Each of its 34 bedrooms is handsomely furnished with a private bath, beverage-making equipment, phone, and TV. The prices of the rooms are £100 ($165) daily in a double and £55 ($90.75) in a single. In winter, these tariffs include dinner and B&B. However, in summer it includes only B&B. Singles occupying a double room pay a surcharge costing from £10 ($16.50) to £15 ($24.75) daily. A fixed-price lunch is served daily from noon to 2pm, costing £8 ($13.20), with a table d'hôte dinner from 7 to 9:30pm going for £15 ($24.75).

11. St. Just-in-Penwith

Between Sennen and St. Ives lie some of the finest dining recommendations in the area. Actually, there are two places in Cornwall called St. Just. This one is St. Just-in-Penwith. (The other, outside St. Mawes, is St. Just-in-Roseland.) St. Just-in-Penwith was a tin-mining town in the last century. Its main attraction is its church, just off a triangle-shaped square, with a pinnacled tower from the 15th century. The town is named for St. Just-in-Penwith, a saint of the mid-5th century.

DINING AT BOTALLACK

The **Count House Restaurant,** Botallack (tel. 0736/788588), 2¼ miles northwest of St. Just-in-Penwith by the B3306, is the most southwesterly place to eat on the English mainland to be recommended in this guide. Overlooking the Atlantic, the building occupied by the restaurant was constructed around 1820 as a carpenter's workshop for the nearby tin mine, with the adjoining Georgian house, formerly the counting house for the mine, being the private home of owners Graham and Helen Ashton. The restaurant is constructed from local stone with a high-beamed roof. Paintings by local artists and antique prints displayed in the restaurant can be purchased. You dine at well-spaced tables, choosing from a menu that changes weekly and features fresh fish and produce from local farms and markets. Full dinners cost from £15 ($24.75) to £20 ($33) per person. From April to October, hours are 7:30 to 9:30pm Tues. to Sat; from November to March, 7:30 to 9:30pm Wed. to Sat. All year, Sun. lunch is served from 12:30 to 2:30pm.

12. St. Ives

This north coast fishing village, with its sandy beaches, is England's most famous art colony. Only 20 miles from Land's End, 10 from Penzance, but 319 miles from London, it is a village of narrow streets and well-kept cottages. The artists settled in many years ago and have integrated with the fishermen and their families.

The art colony was established long enough ago to have developed several schools or "splits," and they almost never overlap—except in a pub where the artists hang out, or where classes are held. The old battle continues between the followers of the representational and the devotees of the abstract in art, with each group recruiting young artists all the time. In addition, there are the potters, weavers, and other craftspeople—all working, exhibiting, and selling in this area. There are several galleries to visit, with such names as the Sail Loft.

A word of warning: St. Ives becomes virtually impossible in August, when you're likely to be trampled underfoot by busloads of tourists, mostly the English themselves. However, in spring and early fall, the pace is much more relaxed, and a visitor can have the true experience of the art colony.

PARK AND RIDE

During the summer months, many of the streets in the center of town are closed to vehicles. You may want to leave your car in the **Lelant Saltings Car Park,** 3 miles from St. Ives on the A3074, and take the regular train service into town, an 11-minute journey. Departures are every half hour. It's free to all car passengers and drivers, and the car-park charge is £2.25 ($3.70) per day. Or you can use the large **Trenwith Car Park,** close to the town center, for 50p (85¢) and then walk down to the shops and harbor or take a bus costing 35p (60¢) for adults and 20p (35¢) for children.

BARBARA HEPWORTH MUSEUM

At Trewyn Studio and Garden, on Barnoon Hill (tel. 0736/796226), the former home of Dame Barbara Hepworth contains a museum of sculpture by the artist from 1929 until her death in 1975, together with photographs, letters, and other papers documenting her life and background. The garden, too, contains sculpture and is well worth a visit. The museum is open in summer from 10am to 5:30pm Mon. to Sat., in winter to 4:30pm. Admission is 50p (85¢) for adults, 25p (40¢) for children. There is limited parking some 200 yards away.

WHERE TO STAY

Standing on its own 70 acres, **Tregenna Castle Hotel,** St. Ives, Cornwall TR26 2DE (tel. 0736/795254), was really once a castle. It was optimistically earmarked by Von Ribbentrop to be Hitler's British Berchtesgaden. Approached by a long driveway, it crowns a hill high above the fishing village of St. Ives. While the interior is spacious and a good background for gracious living, the grounds contain gardens and lawns, an open-air, heated swimming pool with a flagstone edging for sunbathers, three lawn tennis courts, three hard courts, and an 18-hole golf course. The 73 bedrooms usually are of good size, handsomely maintained with contemporary furniture, and each has a private bath, phone, and TV. They rent from £44 ($72.60) daily in a single, from £87 ($143.55) in a double.

Porthminster Hotel, the Terrace, St. Ives, Cornwall TR26 2BN (tel. 0736/795221), is a leading Cornish Riviera resort. On the main road into town, it is set in a beautiful garden, within an easy walk of Porthminster Beach. Large and imposing, Porthminster, like Tregenna Castle, has long been the traditional choice for visitors to St. Ives. With its staunchly Victorian architecture, it is warm and inviting. The hotel, a Best Western affiliate, offers 50 well-furnished bedrooms, each with private bath or shower, TV, and phone. Singles rent for £35 ($57.75) to £40 ($66) daily, with doubles costing £68 ($112.20) to £78 ($128.70). Extra facilities at the hotel include a sun lounge, a solarium, and a sauna, as well as a swimming pool that sees action from June to September. Bar lunches go for £5.50 ($9.10), with dinners costing from £12 ($19.80).

Pedn-Olva Hotel, the Warren, St. Ives, Cornwall TR26 2EA (tel. 0736/796222). From the car park above, all you can see of the hotel is the roof and chimneys, and then you pass through the practical lobby to the lounges and restaurant before coming on the magnificent view over the bay that is the outstanding feature of this establishment. There are sun terraces with lounges and umbrellas and a swimming pool for those who do not wish to walk down the rocky path to Porthminster Beach. If you crave solitude, however, scramble down the rocks to sunbathe just above the gentle rise and fall of the sea. The hotel rents 24 comfortably furnished bedrooms containing private baths or showers, TVs, and phones. Singles cost from £40 ($66) daily, with doubles renting for £82 ($135.30). A set dinner costs £11.50 ($19).

Garrack Hotel, Higher Ayr, Burthallan Lane, St. Ives, Cornwall TR26 3AA (tel. 0736/796199), from its 2-acre knoll, commands a panoramic view of St. Ives and Portmeor Beach. The vine-covered little hotel, once a private home, is reached by heading up a narrow lane. It's one of the friendliest and most efficiently run small, medium-priced hotels on the entire coast, with every room furnished in a warm, homelike manner. The atmosphere in the living room is inviting, with a log-burning fireplace, antiques, and comfortable chairs. The Garrack belongs to Mr. and Mrs. Kilby, who are proud of their meals (see my dining recommendations). The Kilbys have added a wooden leisure building to the hotel with a swimming pool that has a Jacuzzi whirlpool and swim jet, a solarium, and a sauna, all with changing rooms and a small bar overlooking the lovely bay. On a patio, you can sunbathe. There is a honeymoon suite, plus a launderette. Depending on the season and the room, rates for B&B range from £28 ($46.20) to £35 ($57.75) per person daily. Fifteen of the 21 rooms have private baths or showers, and all accommodations are equipped with phones and color TVs.

WHERE TO DINE

The dining room at the **Garrack Hotel,** Higher Ayr, Burthallan Lane (tel. 0736/796199), the domain of Mr. and Mrs. Kilby, produces an excellent cuisine and, when possible, uses fresh ingredients from their own garden. The hotel dining room, open to non-residents, offers regular à la carte listings, plus a cold buffet or snacks at the bar, and an £12 ($19.80) dinner from 7 to 8:30pm. The menu features some of the finest of English dishes, such as roast shoulder of lamb with mint sauce, fried fillet of plaice, and a wide sampling of continental fare, such as filet of bass meunière and escalopes de veau Cordon Bleu. Live lobsters swim in the Kilbys' sea-water tank until being removed for preparation and cooking to order. Of course, if you order cold lobster salad, a little prior notice is required. Two trolleys are at your service, one with continental cheeses and two antique cheeseballs covering half a Stilton wheel or a farmhouse Cheddar cheese, and the other with a wide choice of desserts. (You can have Cornish cream with any dessert, if you wish.) The Kilbys' son Michael joined his parents in the operation of the hotel and restaurant after completing a training period with Claridges in London. Coffee-shop style food is available throughout the day from 11am until 10pm in the small leisure center.

---

13. Port Isaac

The most unspoiled fishing village on the north Cornish coastline is Port Isaac, 9 miles from Wadebridge. This Atlantic coastal resort retains its original character, in spite of the intrusions of large numbers of summer visitors. By all means wander through its winding, narrow lanes, gazing at the whitewashed fishermen's cottages with their rainbow trims. The location is 14 miles from Tintagel and 266 miles from London.

WHERE TO STAY AND DINE

The leading choice is **Port Gaverne Hotel,** Port Gaverne, Port Isaac, Cornwall PL29 3SQ (tel. 0208/880244), which was built in the 17th century as a coastal inn sheltering fishermen looking for refuge from their seagoing labors. Today, under the administration of Frederick and Marjorie Ross, it caters to vacationing families and couples. It boasts a sheltered cove for boating and swimming, and can arrange shark fishing, pony trekking, and country hikes. Its painted facade is draped with vines, and inside you'll find a trio of comfortably atmospheric bars for relaxing beside a fireplace (one of them is a modified baking oven). Clusters of antiques, stained glass, and early photographs of Cornwall add sometimes bittersweet grace notes. Dinners are served by candlelight and include locally caught lobster, fish, or crab in season, as well as locally raised lamb and beef. Bar snacks are also available, with dinners costing from £15 ($24.75). The 18 comfortably furnished bedrooms rent for £32 ($52.80) to £36 ($59.40) per person daily. Tariffs include a full English breakfast. Each unit has its own bath, TV, and phone. The hotel is closed from mid-January to mid-February.

Slipway Hotel, Harbourfront, Port Isaac, Cornwall PL29 3RH (tel. 0208/880747), was originally built in 1527, with major additions added in the early 1700s. This waterside building has seen more uses than any other structure in town, everything from fishermen's cottages to the headquarters of the first bank here. Once the building was a lifeboat station for rescuing sailors stranded on stormy seas. This establishment is one of the few at Port Isaac that offers private parking. The establishment rents 10 bedrooms, 5 with private baths. Double rooms cost from £22 ($36.30) to £24.50 ($40.45) per person daily for B&B, depending on the facilities. The hotel is better known for its restaurant. Its main dining room is high ceilinged, containing a mistrel's gallery occupying the cellar and part of the ground floor. At lunch, only bar snacks are available, but dinner is served nightly in the restaurant from 7:30 to 9:30pm, a three-course meal costing from £16 ($26.40).

---

14. Tintagel

On a wild stretch of the Atlantic coast, Tintagel is forever linked with legends of King Arthur and Merlin. The 13th-century ruins of **Tintagel Castle** (tel. 0840/770328), popularly known as King Arthur's Castle, stand 300 feet above the sea on a rocky promontory. It is open from 10am to 6pm Tues. to Sun. from Good Friday to September 30. Hours during other months are from 10am to 4pm. Admission is £1.30 ($2.15) for adults, 65p ($1.05) for children. The colorful writing of Lord Tennyson in *Idylls of the King* greatly increased the interest in Tintagel, as had the works of Geoffrey of Monmouth. The ruins, which date from Geoffrey's time, are the remains of a castle built on the foundations of a Celtic monastery from the 6th century, a long, steep, tortuous walk from the car park. In summer, many visitors make the ascent to Arthur's lair via 100 rock-cut steps. You can also visit Merlin's Cave.

The **Old Post Office** (tel. 0208/4281) at Tintagel is a National Trust property. It was once a 14th-century manor, but since the 19th century it has had connections with the post office. In the village center, it has a genuine Victorian post room. It is open daily April 1 to September 30 from 11am to 5:30pm and in October from 11am to 4:45pm. Admission is £1.40 ($2.30) for adults and 70p ($1.15) for children.

If you become excited by legends of Knights of the Round Table, you can go to **Camelford,** 5 miles inland from Tintagel. The market hall there dates from 1790, but more interestingly, the town claims to be Camelot.

WHERE TO STAY

As you approach Tintagel from Boscastle, **Bossiney House Hotel,** Bossiney, Tintagel, Cornwall PL34 0AX (tel. 0840/770240), stands in an inviting spot half a mile northeast of Tintagel on B3263. Two brothers, Colin and Bob Savage, and their families operate the hotel, and everybody combines to make guests feel welcome. The hotel is comfortable with a TV lounge and a well-stocked bar/lounge, which has a fine view of surrounding meadows marching right up to the tops of the cliff as well as the wide expanse of lawn with a putting green. The 19 rooms are comfortably furnished and 16 contain baths or showers. The large dining room, where a big English breakfast is served and you can enjoy other well-prepared meals brought to you by smiling Cornish women, is so situated as to give a view of the front, side, and back lawns. Guests pay from £28.75 ($47.45) to £38 ($62.70) per person daily for a room and half board, depending on the season. On the grounds is a Scandinavian log chalet with a heated swimming pool, a sauna, and a solarium.

Trebrea Lodge, Trenale, near Tintagel, Cornwall PL34 0HR (tel. 0840/770410), may appear a dignified stately home, but in truth it looks and feels inside like an old Cornish farmhouse. It dates back to 1315 and was lived in by the same family for more than 600 years. The house, owned by Jill and Richard Radford, looks straight out across fields to the sea, and each bedroom has a good view. The nine rooms are available in many sizes, and each has a private bath or shower, color TV, radio, intercom, and even a baby-listening service. Evenings are cozy in the drawing room around an open fire. The original first-floor drawing room has been restored, and there is a traditional Victorian smoking room in addition to the bar. You can have drinks in another lounge with a fireplace. Dining is most informal, and all food is homemade by Mrs. Radford, who has mastered true English recipes. The cost is from £32 ($52.80) per person daily for half board. The lodge is open from February to mid-November.

15. Bolventor

This village in central Cornwall near Launceston is visited by the fans of Daphne du Maurier, as it was the setting for her novel *Jamaica Inn* (see below). The inn is named for the Caribbean island where the one-time owner of the inn had become prosperous from sugar on his plantation there. Opposite the inn, a small road leads to Dozmary Pool, where the "waves wap and the winds wan," into which Sir Bedivere threw Excalibur at King Arthur's behest.

Jamaica Inn, Bolventor, Launceston, Cornwall, PL15 7TS (tel. 056686/ 250), is a long, low building beside the main A30 road across Bodim Moor. Built in 1547 as a coaching inn, it today has a room dedicated to the memory of Daphne du Maurier and her novel, *Jamaica Inn,* mentioned above. The hotel has welcoming bars, a grill restaurant with waitress service (open only in the evening), and a bar open daily in summer from 11am to 11pm and in winter from 11am to 2:30pm and 6 to 10:30pm. If you're passing through, snacks are available from 9:30am to 10pm. There are seven bedrooms (doubles and twins), including a four-poster room. Each room has a private bath. Rates range from £35 ($57.75) daily for double occupancy, with the four-poster room costing £50 ($82.50).

XI

WILTSHIRE, SOMERSET, AND AVON

1. SALISBURY

2. CASTLE COMBE

3. LACOCK

4. EXMOOR NATIONAL PARK

5. DUNSTER

6. TAUNTON

7. GLASTONBURY

8. WELLS

9. THE CAVES OF MENDIP

10. BATH

11. BRISTOL

12. THORNBURY

For our final look at the "West Countree," we move now into Wiltshire, Somerset, and Avon, the most antiquity-rich shires of England. When we reach this area of woodland and pastoral scenes, London seems far removed—even divorced from the bucolic life here.

Most people seem to agree that the West Country, a loose geographical term, begins at Salisbury, with its ancient origins and notable Early English cathedral. Nearby is Stonehenge, England's oldest and most mysterious prehistoric monument, and Avebury, an important prehistoric site. Both Stonehenge and Salisbury are in Wiltshire.

Somerset is even more varied—rich not only in historical cities, but also in wild scenic grandeur, especially in Exmoor, home of the red deer, with its varied terrain and picturesque villages. The legendary burial place of King Arthur at Glastonbury and the cathedral city of Wells also await you on your visit to Somerset. The old Roman city of Bath and the seaport of Bristol are the main targets in the county of Avon.

WILTSHIRE

When you cross into Wiltshire, you'll be entering a county of chalky, grassy uplands and rolling plains. Much of the shire is agricultural, and a large part is devoted to pastureland. Wiltshire produces an abundance of England's dairy products, and is noted for its sheep raising. In this western shire, you'll traverse the Salisbury Plain, the Vale of Pewsey, and the Marlborough Downs (the last gobbling up the greater part of the land mass).

1. Salisbury

Long before you've come to the end of the 83-mile trek from London, the spire of Salisbury Cathedral comes into view—just as John Constable painted it so many times. The 404-foot pinnacle of the Early English and Gothic cathedral is the tallest in England. But Salisbury is also a fine base for touring such sights as Stonehenge.

Salisbury, or New Sarum, lies in the valley of the Avon River. Filled with Tudor inns and tearooms, it is known to readers of Thomas Hardy as Melchester and to the Victorian fans of Anthony Trollope as Barchester.

SALISBURY CATHEDRAL

You can search all of England, but you'll find no purer example of the Early English, or pointed, style than Salisbury Cathedral. Its graceful spire has already been mentioned, but the ecclesiastical building doesn't depend totally on the tower for its appeal. Construction began as early as 1220, then took 38 years to complete, which was jet-age speed in those days (it was customary to drag out cathedral-building for 3 centuries at least). The spire began soaring at the end of the 13th century. Despite an ill-conceived attempt at revamping in the 18th century, the architectural harmony of the cathedral was retained.

The cathedral's octagonal chapter house (note the fine sculpture) is especially attractive, dating from the 13th century. It also contains one of the four surviving original texts of Magna Carta, together with treasures from the diocese of Salisbury and manuscripts and artifacts belonging to the cathedral. There is a charge of 25p (40¢) per person to visit the chapter house. The cloisters enhance the beauty of the cathedral. The close, with at least 75 buildings in its compound (some from the early 18th century and others predating that), is exceptionally large, setting off the cathedral most fittingly. A donation of £1 ($1.65) is asked of each visitor. For more information call 0722/28726.

The cathedral has a good **brass rubbing center** where you can choose from a selection of exact replicas molded perfectly from the original brasses. The small charge made for each rubbing includes the cost of materials and a donation to the church from which it comes. The center is open at the cathedral from early June to early September from 10am to 5pm Mon. to Sat., from 2 to 5pm Sun.

One of the most distinguished nearby houses is **Mompesson House,** the close (tel. 0722/335659), built by Charles Mompesson in 1701, while he was member of parliament for Old Sarum. An outstandingly beautiful example of the Queen Anne style, it is well known for its fine plasterwork ceilings and paneling. There is also a magnificent collection of 18th-century drinking glasses. It is open April to October from noon to 5:30pm dusk Sat. to Wed., charging an admission of £2 ($3.30) for adults, £1 ($1.65) for children.

Also in the close is the **Regimental Museum of the Duke of Edinburgh's Royal Regiment** (Berkshire and Wiltshire), the Wardrobe, 58 the Close (tel. 0722/336222, ext. 2683), an elegant house, the origins of which date from 1254. One of the finest military museums in the country, it has exhibits telling the story of nearly

250 years of this famous regiment, including uniforms, pictures, weapons, and other militaria. Admission is £1.30 ($2.15) for adults, 70p ($1.15) for children. It is open from February to the end of November 10am to 4:30pm Mon. to Fri. It is also open on Sun. from April to October and on Sat. in July and August.

TOURS
Leisurely guided walks through the city and car tours of the surrounding countryside, including Stonehenge and Avebury and even farther afield, are run by **Wessexplore.** Telephone Don Cross at 0722/26304 for information. Regular guided walks of about 1½ hours' duration take you through the city, visiting St. Thomas's Church and the cathedral close. The starting point is the **Tourist Information Bureau** in Fish Row. Departures from May to September are daily at 8:30am. The cost is £1 ($1.65) for adults, 50p (85¢) for children. An entire family can go for a guided walk for £2 ($3.30).

WHERE TO STAY
An inn-collector's gem, the **Rose and Crown,** Harnham Road, Salisbury, Wiltshire SP2 8JQ (tel. 0722/27908), 1½ miles from the heart of town by the A3094, is a half-timbered, 13th-century hostelry. The river Avon winds its way within a few feet of the Rose and Crown, and beyond the water you can see the tall spire of the cathedral. The lawns and gardens between the inn and the river are shaded by old trees, and chairs are set out so you can enjoy the view and count the swans. The inn, part of the Queens Moat House Hotels chain, contains both a new and an old wing. The new wing is modern, but to me, the old wing is more appealing, with its sloping ceilings, and antique fireplaces and furniture. Each of the 28 bedrooms has a private bath or shower, phone, color TV, radio, and hot beverage facilities. A single rents for £66.50 ($109.75) daily, a double or twin with bath goes for £92.50 ($152.65) including an English breakfast, service, and VAT. You can have lunch overlooking the river. The fare is English. A set luncheon goes for £9.50 ($15.70) and a dinner from £12 ($19.80). Across the courtyard (where there's free parking) are two taverns. You can easily walk over the arched stone bridge to the center of Salisbury from here in 10 minutes or so.
Grasmere, 70 Harnham Rd., Salisbury, Wiltshire SP2 8JN (tel. 0722/338388), is a late Victorian house beautifully restored and operated by the previously recommended Rose and Crown. It stands near the confluence of the Nadder and Avon rivers in 1½ acres of grounds. Constructed in 1896 for Salisbury merchants, the house still suggests a family home. Architectural features were retained as much as possible, including a "calling box" for servants in the dining room. Grasmere rents only five bedrooms, but each is rather luxuriously furnished and contains a private bath, color TV, and phone. A trio of them overlook the cathedral, a view witnessed by John Constable. Singles rent for £36 ($59.40) daily, with doubles costing £48 ($79.20).
White Hart, 1 St. John's St., Salisbury, Wiltshire SP1 2SD (tel. 0722/27476), combines the best of the old and the new worlds. The White Hart has been a Salisbury landmark since Georgian times. Its classic facade is intact, with tall columns crowning a life-size effigy of a hart. The older accommodations are traditional, but a new part has been added, making a total of 68 bedrooms, each with a private bath or shower, TV, and phone. It's in the rear, opening onto a large car park—like a motel. New-wing units are tastefully conceived and decorated. The highest prices are charged from April to the end of October. Singles cost from £70 ($115.50) daily and doubles from £95 ($156.75). Service and VAT are included in the tariffs. You can have your before-dinner drink in Wavell's Bar, followed by a meal for around £14 ($23.10).
King's Arms Hotel, 9 St. John's St., Salisbury, Wiltshire SP1 2SB (tel. 0722/27629), is a former coaching inn, in black-and-white Tudor style, with leaded-glass windows, an old pub sign out front, and a covered entrance, formerly a coach setting-down point. It is unsophisticated without being self-consciously so. The

King's Arms charges from £36 ($59.40) daily for a single room, from £52 ($85.80) in a double. Rooms contain private baths or showers, phones, and TVs. A special feature of the hotel is the William and Mary four-poster suite. No one seems to know the age of the inn, although it is generally recognized that it was built before the cathedral. Conspirators helping Charles II flee to France were thought to have met here in the mid-17th century. The hotel contains a good restaurant, fine old oak beams, the original ironwork, a priest's hiding hole, and the Elizabethan fireplace. Have a pint of ale in the oak-beamed pub, sitting in a high-backed settle, warming yourself in front of the open fire.

Cathedral Hotel, 7 Milford St., Salisbury, Wiltshire SP1 2AJ (tel. 0722/20144), is in the heart of Salisbury, across the street from the old Red Lion. An 18th-century building, it lies near the cathedral and shops, and is family owned and managed. Its bedrooms have been renovated, and all 30 of them have color TVs, radios, direct-dial phones, and intercoms, and 19 have private baths. Singles are priced at £28 ($46.20) daily, and doubles rent for £62 ($102.30). The rooms are large and well furnished and maintained. Add to that an elevator to take your luggage upstairs, plus helpful personnel, and you have a good place to stay, with a full English breakfast, VAT, and service charge included in the rates. The Cathedral Bar, with traditional pub atmosphere, serves a hot and cold buffet at lunchtime, and the restaurant offers good food. You can have drinks in either the Cathedral Bar or the Milford Lounge Bar.

Red Lion Hotel, Milford Street, Salisbury, Wiltshire SP1 2AN (tel. 0722/233340), is too stately to roar. But since the 1300s, it has been putting up wayfarers who rumbled in stagecoaches from London across the Salisbury Plain to the West Country. Cross under its arch into a courtyard with a hanging, much-photographed creeper, a red lion, and a half-timbered facade, and you'll be transplanted back to the old days. However, the Red Lion has stayed abreast of the times and has been modernized, including the addition of an elevator. Run by two families who have owned it since 1913, the inn offers 59 comfortable bedrooms, each with private bath or shower and an individual decor. Each accommodation also has a remote-control color TV, radio, hot beverage facilities, direct-dial phone, hairdryer, and mini-bar. Singles rent for £50 ($82.50) daily with doubles or twins costing from £75 ($123.75). Many patronize the hotel just for its continental and English cuisine. An à la carte luncheon costs from £7.50 ($12.40), with a three-course dinner going for £12.50 ($20.65). The restaurant has a wattle and daub wall dating from 1230, and the antique-filled hotel is also noted for its clocks, including a skeleton organ clock in the reception hall. Meals are served daily from 12:30 to 1:45pm and 7 to 9pm.

The New Inn, 43 New St., Salisbury, Wiltshire SP1 2PH (tel. 0722/27679), is an upmarket B&B, one of the finest in Salisbury. But, contrary to its name, it isn't new at all. It's a 15th-century building whose walled garden backs up to the cathedral close wall. The center of the inn is the serving bar, which is a common counter for three outer rooms—one, a tiny sitting area; another, a tavern with high-backed settles and a fireplace; and the third, a lounge. In addition to serving food and drink, it rents eight double bedrooms, each attractively and comfortably furnished, with a private bath. Only nonsmokers are accepted, however. B&B costs from £40 ($66) to £50 ($82.50) daily for two.

WHERE TO DINE

The best restaurant in town is **Crustaceans,** 2 Ivy St. (tel. 0722/333948), which, as the name suggests, specializes in fish. From the north of Scotland all the way to the Isles of Scilly (off the coast of Cornwall), an array of fresh fish tempts diners from 7 to 10:30pm Mon. to Sat. Meals cost from £20 ($33) and up, and reservations are needed. Barry Allen makes good use of the fish he buys, and tries to preserve its flavor while awakening the tastebuds with various sauces and means of preparation. Lemon and Dover sole are specialties. But you'll find the complete array of fish here, everything from langoustines and tiger prawns to Devonshire turbot. A comprehensive wine list includes Californian wines. Lunch is also served from noon to 2pm Tues. to Sat.

To Wilton House

To Railway Station

To Stonehenge

FISHERTON ST.

CASTLE ST.

ENDLESS ST.

SALT LANE

WINCHESTER ST.

CHURCHILL WAY

CRANE ST.

NEW CANAL

NEW ST.

CATHERINE ST.

BROWN ST.

GIGANT ST.

CULVER ST.

MILFORD ST.

NORTH WALK

WEST WALK

ST. ANN ST.

EXETER ST.

To Southampton

Avon

Fish Pond

CHURCHILL WAY

N

SALISBURY

0   meters   250
0   feet   750

KEY TO NUMBERED SIGHTS:

1. Shoemakers' Hall
2. Theatre
3. Bus Station
4. St. Thomas' Church
5. North Gate
6. St. Ann's Gate
7. Museum
8. Joiners' Hall
9. King's House
10. Harnham Gate
11. Salisbury Cathedral
12. Post Office
13. Tourist Information Centre
14. Market Place
15. Guildhall

Haunch of Venison, Minster Street (tel. 0722/22024), deserves its popularity. Right in the heart of Salisbury, this creaky-timbered, 1320 chophouse serves some excellent dishes, especially English roasts and grills. Stick to its specialties and you'll rarely go wrong. Diners with more adventurous palates will sample a bowl of game soup. The pièce de résistance of the inn is its local New Forest haunch of venison, with chestnut puree and red-currant jelly. Meals cost from £15 ($24.75) up. For a bargain lunch, enjoy the bar snacks, including game pie made with venison. The centuries have given a gleam to the oak furnishings, and years of polishing have worn down the brass. Twisting steps lead to tiny, cozy rooms (there is one small room with space for about four to sit where you can saturate yourself in the best of England's yesterdays and todays). Two windows of the barroom overlook St. Thomas's cloisters. Dancing fires are kept burning in the old fireplace; heavy beams are overhead; antique chairs encircle the tables. The restaurant is open daily for lunch from noon to 2pm; dinner is served from 7 to 10:30pm, except Sun. night, when only the bar is open and no food is served.

Harper's Restaurant, 7-9 Ox Row, Market Square (tel. 0722/333118), is run by its chef-patron, Adrian Harper, who prides himself on specializing in "real food," homemade and wholesome. The pleasantly decorated restaurant offers such à la carte selections as Harper's pâté with whole-meal toast, smoked, peppered filet of mackerel, and Sicilian fish soup. Main dishes include breast of chicken cooked in fresh tarragon, brandy and cream, and grilled lamb steak Tikka with tandoori style mint sauce and vegetables. Luscious desserts complete the menu. Expect to pay from £10 ($16.50) for an à la carte meal. Fixed-price menus are also offered, costing £6.30 ($10.40) at lunch and £11 ($18.15). Special menus for children, costing £2.50 ($4.15), include fish fingers, beefburgers, or sausages, all with french fries, beans, and ice cream. Harper's is open from noon to 2pm and 6:30 to 10pm Mon. to Sat. It's best to reserve a table.

On the Outskirts

Silver Plough, Pitton, near Salisbury (tel. 072272/266), lies just off the A30 road from London to Salisbury. Originally a farmhouse, it's a pretty country pub with a restaurant added. The pub has a reputation for country wines and English cheeses. You can sup at least 12 varieties and eat home-baked cottage loaves with a wide selection of cheese for your lunch, in the beamed lounge bar, hung with tankards, coachhorns, and other country memorabilia. In addition to the cheese served for lunch in the pub, the restaurant is also open. The bar, incidentally, serves a full snack menu of homemade dishes, featuring steak and kidney pie, grilled steak, and various pastas. There is also a dining room, where the chef does succulent grills and roasts for the set meals or else provides you with an à la carte dinner. He prepares smoked salmon, pheasant, and fish dishes. The owners pride themselves on providing everything from a simple ploughman's lunch to a full meal, a set dinner costing from £17.50 ($28.90). Hours are noon to 2:30pm and 7 to 10pm daily. The Silver Plough has known many famous visitors, but apart from displaying a signed letter from Queen Victoria, the management prefers to stick to its quiet, country atmosphere and to concentrate on making its guests feel at home.

SIDE TRIPS FROM SALISBURY

In this area rich in reminders of England's heritage, traces have been found of human occupation long beyond the dawn of history—Neolithic people, Iron Age habitation, Romans, Saxons, Danes, Normans, and English people of today, all have left their mark on the land.

Old Sarum

About 2 miles north of Salisbury off the A345 is Old Sarum (tel. 0722/335398), the remains of what is believed to have been an Iron Age fortification. The earthworks were known to the Romans, who called it Sorbiodunum, and later to the Saxons. The Normans, in fact, built a cathedral and a castle in what was then a walled town of the Middle Ages. Parts of the old cathedral were disassembled to erect the cathedral at New Sarum. It is open from Good Friday to the end of September from 10am to 6pm Tues. to Sun.; off-season from 10am to 4pm. Admission is 80p ($1.30) for adults, 40p (65¢) for children.

Wilton House

In the town of Wilton, 2½ miles to the west of Salisbury, is one of England's great country estates, Wilton House (tel. 0722/743115), the home of the earl of Pembroke. The stately house dates from the 16th century, but has seen modifications over the years, as late as Victoria's day. It is noted for its 17th-century state rooms by Inigo Jones. Many famous personages have either lived at or visited Wilton. It is believed that Shakespeare's troupe entertained here. Plans for the D-Day landings at Normandy were laid out here by Eisenhower and his advisers, in the utmost secrecy, with only the silent Van Dycks in the Double Cube room as witnesses. The house is filled with beautifully maintained furnishings and displays some of the finest paintings in England, including works by Rembrandt, Rubens, and Reynolds. There are exhibitions of 7,000 model soldiers; the Pembroke Palace dollhouse; a historic tableau of dolls and toys through the ages, together with a unique collection of tiny dolls' clothes; and a 400-sq.-ft. model railway with models of Salisbury Cathedral and Wilton House. There is also a huge adventure playground for children.

The estate lies in the midst of 20 acres of grounds, with giant cedars of Lebanon, the oldest of which were planted in 1630. The Palladian Bridge was built in 1737 by the ninth earl of Pembroke and Roger Morris. Wilton House can be visited from Easter to mid-October from 11am to 6pm Tues. to Sat. and on bank holidays, from 1 to 6pm Sun. Last admission is 5:15pm. You can walk through with guides in attendance; however, guided tours are by appointment only. An inclusive ticket to the house, grounds, and exhibitions costs adults £3.80 ($6.25) and children under 16 £2.80 ($4.60). To visit just the grounds is £1.40 ($2.30) for adults and £1 ($1.65) for children. From Salisbury, take bus 60 or 61.

Stonehenge

Two miles west of Amesbury, at the junction of the A303 and the A344/A360, and about 9 miles north of Salisbury is the renowned Stonehenge, believed to be anywhere from 3,500 to 5,000 years old. This huge circle of lintels and megalithic pillars is the most important prehistoric monument in Britain.

Some Americans have expressed their disappointment after seeing the concentric circles of stones. Admittedly, they are not the pyramids, and some imagination has to be brought to bear on them. Pyramids or not, they represent an amazing engineering feat. Many of the boulders, the bluestones in particular, were moved many miles (perhaps from southern Wales) to this site by the ancients. If you're more fanciful, you can always credit Merlin with delivering them on clouds from Ireland.

The widely held view of the 18th- and 19th-century romantics that Stonehenge was the work of the Druids is without foundation. The boulders, many weighing several tons, are believed to have predated the arrival in Britain of that Celtic cult. Recent excavations continue to bring new evidence to bear on the origin and purpose of Stonehenge. Controversy surrounds the prehistoric site especially since the publication of *Stonehenge Decoded,* by Gerald S. Hawkins and John B. White, which maintains that Stonehenge was an astronomical observatory—that is, a Neolithic "computing machine" capable of predicting eclipses.

Others who discount this theory adopt Henry James's approach to Stonehenge, which regards it as "lonely in history," its origins and purposes (burial ground? sunworshipping site? human sacrificial temple?) the secret of the silent, mysterious Salisbury Plain.

Admission is £1.70 ($2.80) for adults, 85p ($1.40) for children. From April 1 to September 30, hours are daily from 10am to 6pm. From October to March 31, hours are daily from 10am to 4pm. Your ticket permits you to go inside the fence surrounding the site to protect the stones from vandals and souvenir hunters. You can go all the way up to a short rope barrier about 50 feet from the stones. If you don't have a car, you can take a bus from the Salisbury train station. There are also organized bus tours out of Salisbury.

Longleat House

Between Bath and Salisbury, Longleat House (tel. 09853/551), owned by the sixth marquess of Bath, lies 4 miles southwest of Warminster, 4½ miles southeast of Frome on the A362. The first view of this magnificent Elizabethan house, built in the early Renaissance style, is romantic enough, but the wealth of paintings and furnishings within its lofty rooms is enough to dazzle.

A tour of the house, from the Elizabethan great hall, through the library, the state rooms, and the grand staircase, is filled with variety. The state dining room is full of silver and plate, and fine tapestries and paintings adorn the walls in rich profusion. The library represents the finest private collection in the country. The Victorian kitchens are open during the summer months, offering a glimpse of life below the stairs in a well-ordered country home. Various exhibitions are mounted in the stable yard. Events are staged frequently in the grounds, and the safari park contains a vast array of animals in open parklands, including Britain's only white tiger.

A maze, believed to be the largest in the world, was added to the attractions by Lord Weymouth, son of the marquess. It has more than 1½ miles of paths among yew trees. The first part is comparatively easy, but the second part is very complicated, with bridges adding to the confusion. It knocks the Hampton Court maze into a cocked hat, as the British say.

Longleat House is open from Easter to the end of September daily from 10am to 6pm, to 4pm the rest of the year. The safari park is open mid-March to early November from 10am to 6pm (last cars admitted at 5:30pm or sunset if earlier). Admission to Longleat House is £3 ($4.95) for adults and £1.50 ($2.50) for children. The Safari Park costs £4 ($6.60) for adults and £3 ($4.95) for children. Special exhibitions and rides require separate admission tickets. Discount tickets for all attractions cost £8 ($13.20) for adults and £6 ($9.90) for children.

Stourhead

After Longleat, you can drive 6 miles down B3092 to Stourton, a village just off the B3092, 3 miles northwest of Mere (A303). Stourhead (tel. 0747/840348), a Palladian house, was created in the 18th century by the banking family of Hoare. The magnificent gardens became known as *le jardin anglais* in that they blended art and nature. Set around an artificial lake, the grounds are decorated with temples, bridges, islands, and grottoes, as well as statuary. The house is open from April 1 to November 4 noon to 5:30pm Sat. to Wed. Admission is £3 ($4.95) for adults and £1.50 ($2.50) for children. The gardens are open from 8am to 7pm and can be visited separately for an admission of £3 ($4.95) for adults and £1.50 ($2.50) for children. The gardens are also open in winter (November to February), charging £2 ($3.30) for adults and £1 ($1.65) for children.

Avebury

One of the largest prehistoric sites in Europe, Avebury lies on the Kennet River. It gained in popularity with visitors once the government had to rope off the sarsen circle at Stonehenge. Explorers are able to walk the 28-acre site at Avebury, winding in and out of the circle of more than 100 stones, some weighing up to 50 tons. They are made of sarsen, a sandstone found in Wiltshire. Inside this large circle are two smaller ones, each with about 30 stones standing upright. Native Neolithic tribes are believed to have built these circles. The village of Avebury, some of which is in the ownership of the National Trust, has been called the Ancient Capital of England.

Dating from before the Conquest, **Avebury Manor** (tel. 06723/203) was built on the site of a Benedictine cell. An early Elizabethan manor house, it stands beside the great stone circle of Avebury. Original oak-paneled rooms and plaster-work ceilings, fine oak furniture, and early paintings fill the house. The manor is steeped in history. The attic and anterooms have been chosen to take you back in time. There you will see wax figures of the notorious William Sharington, the staunch royalist Sir John Stawell, and Sir Richard Holford, all once owners of the house. Additional attractions include musket and Tudor archery displays. Replica jewelry and dress of the Elizabethan period, atrifacts of torture, and exhibitions of Civil War arms are displayed. Within the grounds, visitors can see an Elizabethan market square full of craft workshops, music-making minstrels, jugglers, strolling players, lords and ladies, and jesters. There is also an adventure playground, plus falconry demonstrations. Surrounding gardens and parkland are equally intriguing. The manor is open from Easter to October, 10am to 6pm every day. The manor lies 1½ miles from the A4, London-Bath road, and 9 miles from junction 15, Swindon exit on the M4, and 6 miles from Marlborough.

Avebury Museum (tel. 06723/250), founded by Alexander Keiller, houses one of Britain's most important archeological collections. It began with Keiller's material from excavations at Windmill Hill and Avebury, and now includes artifacts from other prehistoric digs at West Kennet, Long Barrow, Silbury Hill, West Kennet Avenue, and the Sanctuary. It is open from Good Friday to the end of September daily 10am to 6pm, from 10am to 4pm off-season. Admission is 85p ($1.40) for adults, and 45p (75¢) for children.

The Great Barn Museum of Wiltshire Rural Life (tel. 06723/555), housed in a 17th-century thatched barn, is a center for the display and interpretation of Wiltshire life during the last 3 centuries. There are displays on cheese making, blacksmithing, thatching, sheep and shepherds, the wheelwright and other rural crafts, as well as local geology and domestic life. From mid-March to the end of October, it is open daily from 10am to 5:30pm. The remainder of the year, it is open from 1 to 4:30pm Sat. and 11am to 4:30pm Sun. Admission is 95p ($1.55) for adults, 50p (85¢) for children, and £2.25 ($3.70) for a family ticket.

After sightseeing—and still in the same vicinity—you may be ready for a bite to eat. The **Stones Restaurant,** High Street (tel. 06723/514), has made an impact on the palates in the area since its opening in 1984 by Dr. Hilary Howard and Michael Pitts. They specialize in freshly made, original, high-quality food (no additives) served in attractive surroundings at reasonable prices. You can have a meal for around £6 ($9.90), including drinks. A wide range of cakes, desserts, and cold savories is available throughout the day, supplemented at lunch by a full, hot-food menu, which can be accompanied by the local, prize-winning ale, Bunce's Best. Other drinks are available, including coffee, tea by the pot, fruit juices, and bottled beer. There is an exceptional range of handmade, unpasteurized English and Welsh cheeses. In summer, queues get long at lunch, so it's best to arrive early (lunch starts at noon), and to avoid Sunday lunch entirely. Cream teas at Stones are famous, with their own scones and jam plus clotted cream brought from Cornwall. Stones is open daily April until the end of October from 10am to 6pm.

---

2. Castle Combe

Once voted Britain's prettiest village, Castle Combe was used for location shots for *Dr. Dolittle,* with Rex Harrison. About 9½ miles from Bath, this little Cotswold village is filled with shops selling souvenirs and antiques. The village cottages are often set beside a trout stream, and are made of stone with roofs laden with moss. The church is unremarkable except for its 15th-century tower. An old market cross and a triple-arched bridge are much photographed.

WHERE TO STAY AND DINE

Set in 26 acres of gardens and parklands, the **Manor House,** Castle Combe, Wiltshire SN14 7HR (tel. 0249/782206), is on a country estate whose original manor was the 14th-century baronial seat in Castle Combe. To the south, the lawns sweep down to the trout-stocked River Bybrook where fishing is permitted. Antiques and period pieces adorn the oak-paneled public rooms, with the main lounge having an 18th-century frieze depicting Shakespeare's Falstaff. The 35 bedrooms, all with baths or showers, TVs, and phones, are individually furnished. Some are in the Cotswold Mews Cottages at the entrance to the grounds. A double room costs from £90 ($148.50) to £200 ($330) and a single £90 ($148.50). The hotel offers an extensive menu, with dinner costing from £23.50 ($38.80). Although casual informality prevails during the day, the general manager requests that men wear jackets and ties for dinner. The hotel has an outdoor, heated swimming pool and an all-weather tennis court.

---

3. Lacock

This is a National Trust village, with a 13th-century abbey and adjoining 16th-century houses and gardens. Within an easy drive of Bath, it contains a delightful 14th-century inn, **Sign of the Angel,** 6 Church St., Lacock, Wiltshire SN15 2LA (tel. 024973/230), ideal for a meal. This small inn offers good meals in an atmosphere that makes you feel you have stepped back into Shakespeare's time. Before an open fire on nippy days, food is served under a heavily beamed ceiling. Roasts are often featured on the menu. A set dinner runs from £20 ($33) per person, and a reservation is essential. Lunch is served from 1 to 1:30pm and dinner from 7:30 to 8pm (one sitting only). The Sign of the Angel is closed for luncheon on Sat. and for dinner on Sun. (it also shuts down for the Christmas holidays). The inn offers six bedrooms in the main building and four in a garden cottage, each with private bath, TV, and phone. A single rents for £55 ($90.75) daily, with doubles going for £80 ($132). No guests under 12 are permitted. Exit at junction 17 and follow the signs for Chippenham and Warminster. The village of Lacock is signposted 3 miles south of Chippenham on the A350. Follow the local traffic signs into the village. The inn is in the bottom corner of the village.

SOMERSET

When writing about Somerset, it's difficult to avoid sounding like the editor of *The Countryside Companion,* waxing poetic over hills and valleys, dale and field. Mendip's limestone hills undulate across the countryside. The irresistible Quantocks are the pride of the west, especially lovely in spring and fall. Here, too, is the heather-clad **Exmoor National Park,** a wooded area abounding in red deer and wild ponies, much of its moorland 1,200 feet above sea level. Somerset opens onto the Bristol Channel, with Minehead the chief resort, catering primarily to the English.

Somerset is rich in legend and history, and is particularly fanciful about its associations with King Arthur and Queen Guinevere, along with Camelot and Alfred the Great. Its villages are noted for the tall towers of their parish churches.

A quiet, unspoiled life characterizes Somerset. You're likely to end up in an ivy-covered old inn, talking with the regulars by the fireside, or you may stop at a large estate that stands in a woodland setting, surrounded by bridle paths and sheep walks (Somerset was once a great wool center). Maybe you'll settle down in a 16th-century thatched, stone farmhouse, set in the midst of orchards in a vale. Somerset is reputed (and I heartily concur) to have the best cider anywhere. When you lounge under a shady Somerset apple tree, downing a tankard of refreshingly chilled golden cider, all those you've drunk in the past taste like apple juice.

My notes on Somerset, accumulated over many a year, would easily fill a book. But because space is limited I've confined myself in the main to just some highlights.

4. Exmoor National Park

The far west of Somerset forms most of the Exmoor National Park. In addition to the moor, the park includes the wooded valleys of the rivers Exe and Barle, the Brendon Hills, and the sweeping stretch of coast from Minehead to the boundary of Devon. This is more of the land of Blackmore's *Lorna Doone*. You can walk up Badgworthy Water from Malmsmead to Doone Valley, divided by the Somerset-Devon line, or visit tiny Oare Church and see the window through which Carver Doone shot Lorna at her wedding. The moors, which rise to 1,707 feet at Dunkery Beacon, invite walkers and pony trekkers. Ponies and wild deer roam freely.

Visit England's smallest complete church at Culbone and the centuries-old clapper bridge over the River Barle at Tarr Steps. Some of England's prettiest villages are within the national park, and some lie along its borders. Selworthy, an idyllic little town, is in Exmoor, as is Allerford, with its pack-horse bridge and its walnut tree, both of them owned and preserved by the National Trust.

Minehead, a fine resort, is just outside the park's northeastern boundary, but in some ways, the little villages which have that town as a focal point have more charm.

BILBROOK

Near Washford, **Dragon House,** Bilbrook, Somerset TA24 6HQ (tel. 0984/40215), is reached by driving from the A39 a short distance southeast of Minehead, then through a wide gateway into the inn's driveway and walking into the charming house, with a comfortable lounge and cozy bar. This 17th-century inn was once a smugglers' drinking den and, in contrast, later a Methodist preaching house. Everything is spotlessly clean, with old furniture lovingly polished and gleaming in the firelight. The 10 beamed bedrooms are individually furnished in country-cottage style, with good beds and some antiques. One has a half-tester bed. All the units have radios, TVs, bath, or showers, and views over the moors or the garden. From the elegant hall, an ancient staircase leads to a gallery around the first floor off which many of the bedrooms are open. Staircases lead to other units with dormer windows in the roof. Guests are accepted at half-board rates ranging from £48 ($79.20) to £58 ($95.70) per person daily. At lunch, excellent bar meals are served. For dinner in the antique-furnished dining room, you face a well-chosen menu of English and continental dishes. Try the local, farm-raised trout, which can be cooked "in so many ways." Perhaps the honey-roast duck or roast quail will appeal to you, even a vegetarian menu.

MIDDLECOMBE

About 1½ miles west of Minehead on the A39, **Periton Park,** Middlecombe, Minehead, Somerset TA24 8SW (tel. 0643/706885), is reached by a long, winding drive through rhododendron clumps and tall trees. The Victorian house is set high above its 30 acres of pasture and woodland. The house dates from 1875 when it was constructed by the owner of a local bakery. Ever since, it's been affectionately called Bun Castle by its neighbors. Owners Ian and Christine Dodd rent seven well-furnished rooms, each with private bath, TV, and phone. B&B costs £52.50 ($86.65) daily in a single and £75 ($123.75) in a double. Mr. Dodd is known for his martinis, and you might want to order one before going into the dining room for an excellent English meal at £16.50 ($27.25).

WINSFORD

Actually in Exmoor National Park but near Minehead is the **Royal Oak Inn,** Winsford, Somerset TA24 7JE (tel. 064385/455). This thatched 15th-century inn facing the village green is to many the epitome of West Country inns, catering to a farming-hunting-shooting population from near and far. If you're there on a Tues., you get a sense of the nature of local farmers and residents by observing those who attend meetings of the National Westminster Bank officials in the lounge. In season, the bar and restaurant teem with elegantly dressed hunters and shooters who descend on the moors annually, interspersed with locals in sensible tweeds, backpackers with heavy boots, and tourists trying to blend into the landscape. The hotel rents 14 rooms, each with bath, phone, and TV. Double rooms with bath cost from £115 ($189.75) per night, with breakfast included. Perhaps you might prefer the Royal Oak Suite if it's available; minor royalty often stays here, and the charge is £140 ($231) for two. Some rooms are across the courtyard. The restaurant offers such selections as fisherman's pot and a choice of fresh or saltwater fish. Roast rack of Exmoor lamb is a specialty. Meals cost from £17 ($28.05).

---

5. Dunster

The village of Dunster lies in Somerset near the eastern edge of Exmoor National Park, 3 miles southeast of Minehead, just off the A39. It grew up around the original Dunster Castle, constructed as a fortress for the de Mohun family whose progenitor came to England with William the Conqueror. The village, about 4 miles from the Cistercian monastery at Cleeve, has an ancient priory church and dovecote, a 17th-century gabled yarn market, and little cobbled streets along which whitewashed cottages gleam proudly.

WHERE TO STAY AND DINE

On the site of what has been a hostelry for weary travelers for more than 600 years, **Luttrell Arms,** 36 High St., Dunster, Somerset TA24 6SG (tel. 0643/821555), is the outgrowth of a guesthouse the Cistercian abbots at Cleeve had built in the village of Dunster. It was named for the Luttrell lords of the manor, who bought Dunster Castle and the property attached to it in the 14th century. The hotel has, of course, been provided with the amenities expected by modern travelers, but from its stone porch to the 15th-century Gothic hall with hammer-beam roof (now divided), it still retains a feeling of antiquity. The 25 bedrooms, all with private baths or showers, phones, and TVs, are comfortably appointed and attractively decorated in keeping with the hotel's long history. Four of the accommodations have four-poster beds. Singles rent for £68 ($112.20) daily, and doubles, £87 ($143.55). A lounge is upstairs, while downstairs you can enjoy a drink in the timbered Tudor bar, with its large inglenook fireplace. This was once the kitchen of the hostelry. A meal in the dining room, costing from £12 ($19.80), can be ordered from a varied menu. Depending on the season, you might choose guinea fowl or baked sugared ham with Somerset cider sauce. A buffet lunch is offered Mon. to Sat. You can also order bar food.

DUNSTER CASTLE

On a tor (high hill) from which you can see the Bristol Channel, Dunster Castle (tel. 0643/821314) stands on the site of a Norman castle granted to William de Mohun of Normandy by William the Conqueror shortly after the conquest of England. The 13th-century gateway built by the de Mohuns is all that remains of the original fortress. In 1376 the castle and its lands were bought by Lady Elizabeth Luttrell and belonged to her family until given to the National Trust in 1976, together with 30 acres of surrounding parkland. The first castle was largely demolished during the Civil War, and the present Dunster Castle is a Jacobean house built in the lower ward of the original fortifications in 1620, then rebuilt by Salvin in 1870 to look like a castle. Terraced walks and gardens command good views of Exmoor and the Quantock Hills.

Outstanding among the contents within are the 17th-century panels of embossed painted and gilded leather depicting the story of Antony and Cleopatra, and a remarkable, allegorical 16th-century portrait of Sir John Luttrell shown wading naked through the sea with a female figure of peace and a wrecked ship in the background. The 17th-century plasterwork ceilings of the dining room and staircase and the finely carved staircase balustrade of cavorting huntsmen, hounds, and stags are also particularly noteworthy. The castle and grounds can be visited from April to the end of September 11am to 5pm Sun. to Thurs. (last admission at 4:30pm); in October hours are 2 to 4pm (last admission at 3:30pm). Admission to both the castle and grounds is £3.50 ($5.80) for adults, £1.50 ($2.50) for children. To the grounds only, admission is £1.70 ($2.80) for adults, 70p ($1.15) for children.

COMBE SYDENHAM HALL

Between Dunster and Taunton, on the B3188 just south of Monksilver, you can visit Combe Sydenham Hall (tel. 0984/56284), which was the home of Elizabeth Sydenham, wife of Sir Francis Drake. It stands on the ruins of monastic buildings that were associated with nearby Cleeve Abbey. At the hall, you can see a cannon ball that legend says halted the wedding of Lady Elizabeth to a rival suitor in 1585. The gardens include Lady Elizabeth's Walk, which circles around ponds originally laid out when the knight was courting his bride-to-be. The valley ponds are fed by springwater and are full of rainbow trout (ask about the fly-fishing and tuition). Woodland walks are possible to Long Meadow with its host of wildflowers. Also to be seen are a deserted hamlet whose population reputedly was wiped out by the Black Death and a historic corn mill, presently being restored. In the hall's tearoom, smoked trout and pâté are produced on oak chips, as in days of yore, and there are a shop and car park. The hall is open in July, August, and September are from 11am to 4pm and in April, May, June, and October from 11am to 3pm Mon. to Fri. The country park hours in July, August, and September are from 11am to 6pm., and in April, May, June, and October from 11am to 5pm Sun. to Fri. Admission is £2.50 ($4.15) for adults, £1.80 ($2.95) for children.

Combe Sydenham is 5 miles south of Watchet on the B3188 road between Monksilver and Elsworthy. Incidentally, it was from Watchet, a few miles east of Minehead along the coast, that Coleridge's Ancient Mariner sailed.

COLERIDGE COTTAGE

Across the Quantock Hills to the east of the area just previewed, the hamlet of Nether Stowey lies on the A39, at the northern edge of Quantock Forest. Here you can visit Coleridge Cottage (tel. 0278/732662), home of Samuel Taylor Coleridge when he wrote *The Rime of the Ancient Mariner*. During his 1797–1800 sojourn here, he and his friends, William Wordsworth and sister Dorothy, enjoyed exploring the Quantock woods. The cottage, at the west end of Nether Stowey on the south side of the A39 and 8 miles west of Bridgwater, has its parlor and reading room open to visitors from April to the end of September from 2 to 5pm Tues. to Thurs. and on Sun. Admission to the National Trust property is £1 ($1.65).

---

6. Taunton

The historic county town of Somerset in the Vale of Taunton Deane, Taunton is one of the best centers for exploring West Somerset. Taunton Castle was the scene of Judge Jeffreys' Bloody Assize after the end of the Monmouth rebellion at the Battle of Sedgemoor. The castle dates from the 11th and 12th centuries, and the east gatehouse is now a hotel (see below). The castle also houses a museum (look for the picture of Judge Jeffreys in the great hall). Even more interesting than the castle is the Church of St. Mary Magdalene, with its soaring tower, completed in 1514.

Taunton is 168 miles from London and 50 miles from Bristol.

WHERE TO STAY AND DINE

Beauty and history are combined at the **Castle Hotel,** Castle Green, Taunton, Somerset TA1 1NF (tel. 0823/272671), in the center of Taunton. Nature lovers usually opt for one of this establishment's four garden suites, whose windows look out over a landscape originally designed in the 12th century. The plantings and nearby archeological ruins are not the only attraction here. Some of the hotel's thick walls were built as part of a Norman fortress. Later architects designed the newer sections in a crenellated pattern whose windows barely peek out from behind cascades of climbing wisteria. The 35 bedrooms benefit from a recent upgrading, which filled them with softly upholstered, tasteful furniture and many amenities of modern life, such as private baths, phones, and TVs. Charges are from £78 ($128.70) to £130 ($214.50) daily in a single, £100 ($165) to £180 ($297) in a double. After an apéritif in the Rose Room, you can head for the elegant restaurant. There the chef applies French-inspired nouvelle cuisine techniques to traditional English ingredients for such imaginative specialties as rabbit pithivier, red mullet, and succulent lamb, beef, and venison dishes. The restaurant charges £26 ($42.90) for a set dinner, or else you might pay up to £38 ($62.70) for an elaborate à la carte meal. Hours are from 7:45am to 10pm Mon. to Sat. 8:15am to 10pm Sun.

---

7. Glastonbury

The goal of the medieval pilgrim, **Glastonbury Abbey** (tel. 0458/32267), once one of the wealthiest and most prestigious monasteries in England, is no more than a ruined sanctuary today. But it provides Glastonbury's claim to historical greatness, an assertion augmented by legendary links to such figures as Joseph of Arimathea, King Arthur, Queen Guinevere, and St. Patrick.

It is said that Joseph of Arimathea journeyed to what was then the Isle of Avalon, with the Holy Grail in his possession. According to tradition, he buried the chalice at the foot of the conically shaped Glastonbury Tor, and a stream of blood burst forth. (You can scale this more than 500-foot-high hill today, on which rests a 15th-century tower.)

At one point, the saint is said to have leaned against his staff, which immediately was transformed into a fully blossoming tree. A cutting alleged to have survived from the Holy Thorn can be seen on the abbey grounds today. It blooms at Christmastime. Some historians have traced this particular story back to Tudor times. Joseph, so it goes, erected a church of wattle in Glastonbury. The town, in fact, may have had the oldest church in England, as excavations have shown.

The most famous link—popularized for Arthurian fans in the Victorian era by Tennyson—concerns the burial of King Arthur and Queen Guinevere on the abbey grounds. In 1191 the monks dug up the skeletons of two bodies on the south side of the Lady Chapel, said to be those of the king and queen. In 1278, in the presence of Edward I, the bodies were removed and transferred to a black marble tomb in the choir. Both the burial spot and the shrine are marked today.

A large Benedictine Abbey of St. Mary grew out of the early wattle church. St. Dunstan, who was born nearby, was the abbot in the 10th century, later becoming archbishop of Canterbury. Edmund, Edgar, and Edmund "Ironside," three early English kings, were buried at the abbey.

In 1184 a fire destroyed most of the abbey and its vast treasures. It was eventually rebuilt after much difficulty, only to be dissolved by Henry VIII. Its last abbot, Richard Whiting, was hanged by the neck at Glastonbury Tor. Like the Roman forum, the abbey for years was used as a stone quarry.

The modern-day pilgrim to Glastonbury can visit the ruins of the lady chapel, linked by an Early English "Galilee" to the nave of the abbey. The best-preserved building on the grounds is a 14th-century, octagonal abbot's kitchen, where oxen were once roasted whole to feed the wealthier of the pilgrims (that is, the biggest donors). You can visit the ruins and museum from 9:30am till dusk or 6pm for £1 ($1.65) for adults, 50p (85¢) for children under 16.

Glastonbury may be one of the oldest inhabited sites in Britain. Excavations have revealed Iron Age lakeside villages on its periphery. Some of the discoveries may be viewed in a little museum in the High Street.

After the destruction of its once great abbey, the town lost prestige. It is a market town today. The ancient gatehouse entry to the abbey is a museum, its principal exhibit a scale model of the abbey and its community buildings as they stood in 1539, at the time of the dissolution.

SOMERSET RURAL LIFE MUSEUM

The history of the Somerset countryside since the early 19th century is illustrated in this museum based in the abbey farm, Chilkwell Street, Glastonbury (tel. 0458/32903). The centerpiece of the museum is the abbey barn, home barn of Glastonbury Abbey, built around 1370. The magnificent timbered room, stone tiles, and sculptural details (including the head of Edward III), make it special. There is also a Victorian farmhouse comprising exhibits illustrating farming in Somerset during the "horse age" and domestic and social life in Victorian times. In summer there are demonstrations of buttermaking, weaving, basketwork, and many other traditional craft and farming activities, which are rapidly disappearing. The museum is open from 10am to 5pm weekdays (2pm to 6pm on Sat. and Sun.; 2:30pm to 5pm in winter). Admission is £1 ($1.65) for adults, 25p (40¢) for children. There is a museum shop and tearoom.

WHERE TO STAY AND DINE

If you're one of the lucky few who can stay over in this town rich in history, you can lodge where the wealthy pilgrim of yore did.

The George & Pilgrims Inn, 1 High St., Glastonbury, Somerset BA6 9DP (tel. 0458/31146), is one of the few pre-Reformation hostelries still left in England. Once it offered hospitality to Glastonbury pilgrims; now it accepts modern travelers. In the center of town, the inn has a facade that looks like a medieval castle, with stone-mullioned windows with leaded glass. Some of the 12 bedrooms were formerly monks' cells, others have four-posters, veritable carved monuments of oak. You may be given the Henry VIII Room, where the king watched the burning of the abbey in 1539. The owners charge £42 ($69.30) daily for a single, from £55 ($90.75) to £75 ($123.75) in a double, all rooms with private baths, direct-dial phones, and TVs. VAT and an English breakfast are included. You could be drawn to the old kitchen, which is now the Pilgrim's Bar, with its old oak beams. Even if you don't stay over, you may want to stop in for dinner in the Georgian Restaurant to enjoy the à la carte or table d'hôte menus, both of which feature traditional local dishes, or homemade fare in the snack bar. Dinners cost from £15 ($24.75).

Number 3 Restaurant and Hotel, 3 Magdalene St., Glastonbury, Somerset BA6 9EW (tel. 0458/32129). Only dinner is served in this pleasant, family-run restaurant and hotel. That makes an evening meal here something of an event for the loyal clientele of this Georgian-style dining room, run by John and Ann Tynan. Specialties include several lobster dishes (they have their own tanks), scallops in Smitain sauce topped with langoustine, loin of Somerset lamb served with orange-and-ginger sauce, venison with blackberry and port wine sauce, and wild Scottish salmon with lime sauce. There are also special vegetarian dishes. Fixed-price meals begin at £24 ($39.60) for dinner. A super wine list contains descriptions of each of the carefully selected vintages. There are two outdoor tables for warm-weather dining. The restaurant also has six double bedrooms, tastefully and individually decorated and with private baths, TVs, and phones, costing £40 ($66) to £55 ($90.75) daily, breakfast included.

8. Wells

To the south of the Mendip Hills, the cathedral town of Wells is a medieval gem. It lies only 21 miles from Bath, 123 from London. Wells was a vital link in the Saxon kingdom of Wessex—that is, important in England long before the arrival of William the Conqueror. Once the seat of a bishopric, it was eventually toppled from its ecclesiastical hegemony by the rival city of Bath. But the subsequent loss of prestige has paid off handsomely today. After experiencing the pinnacle of prestige, it fell into a slumber—hence, much of its old look remains. Wells was named after the wells in the town, which were often visited by pilgrims to Glastonbury in the hope that their gout could be eased by its supposedly curative waters.

WELLS CATHEDRAL

Begun in the 12th century, Wells Cathedral is a well-preserved example of the Early English style of architecture. The medieval sculpture (six tiers of hundreds of statues recently restored) of its west front is without peer in England. The western facade was completed in the mid-13th century. The landmark central tower was erected in the 14th century, with its attractive fan vaulting attached later. The inverted arches were added to strengthen the top-heavy structure.

Much of the stained glass dates from the 14th century. The fan-vaulted Lady Chapel, also from the 14th century, is in the Decorated style. To the north is the vaulted chapter house, built in the 13th century. Look also for a medieval astronomical clock in the north transept. There is no charge to enter the cathedral. However, visitors are asked to make voluntary donations of £1.50 ($2.50) for adults, 75p ($1.25) for students and children. For information, telephone the cathedral offices (tel. 0749/74483).

After a visit to the cathedral, walk along its cloisters to the moated Bishop's Palace. The great hall, built in the 13th century, is in ruins. Finally, the street known as Vicars' Close is one of the most beautifully preserved streets in Europe.

The Cloister Restaurant and Cathedral Shop are adjacent to the cathedral.

WHERE TO STAY

Your best choice is the **Swan Hotel,** Sadler Street, Wells, Somerset BA5 2RX (tel. 0749/78877). Set behind a stucco facade on one of the town's main arteries, this place was originally built in the 15th century as a coaching inn. It faces the west front of Wells Cathedral. The inn offers 32 comfortable and attractive bedrooms, each with private bath, color TV, phone, and a refreshing color scheme. Several of the accommodations contain four-poster beds. Depending on the accommodation, singles cost from £48.75 ($80.45) daily, and doubles or twins run £68.50 ($113.05) to £75 ($123.75), with a full English breakfast included. The spacious and elegantly accessorized public rooms stretch out to the left and right of the entrance as you enter. Both ends contain a blazing and baronial fireplace, beamed ceilings, and paneling. The restaurant, the Bishop's Kitchen, is recommended separately.

Star Hotel, 14 High St., Wells, Somerset BA5 2SQ (tel. 0749/73055), had its origins somewhere in the 16th century, but it is best associated with the great coaching era. The cobbled carriageway is still a feature and leads to the dining room—once the stables. The hotel front was restored in the Georgian period. The hotel has been modernized, yet retains its old charm and unhurried pace. Copper and brass are extensively used for decoration, and several original stone walls and timbers have been exposed. The inn rents 16 bedrooms, with private baths or showers and TVs. A single costs from £32 ($52.80) daily with bath or shower, and a double with the same plumbing goes for £44 ($72.60). Tariffs include VAT and an English breakfast. The inn has a reputation for good food, a set dinner costing £11.50 ($19).

Crown Hotel, Market Place, Wells, Somerset BA5 2RP (tel. 0749/73457), was built in the 15th century as a coaching inn. In Elizabethan times it witnessed a number of additions. William Penn, the founder of Pennsylvania, preached from a bedroom window here in 1685. A plaque commemorating this is on the hotel wall. You'll find open beams in at least one of the bedrooms. All 15 accommodations contain private baths, TVs, and phones, and cost £45 ($74.25) to £50 ($82.50) daily in a single, £65 ($107.25) to £75 ($123.75) in a double. These terms include a full English breakfast and VAT. A table d'hôte lunch costs £6.50 ($10.75), with a set dinner going for £10.95 ($18.05). They also have a coffeeshop serving light snacks. The Crown is just 2 minutes from Wells Cathedral.

Red Lion Hotel, Market Place, Wells, Somerset BA5 2RP (tel. 0749/72616), is an early 15th-century inn close to the cathedral and the Bishop's Palace. A bathless single costs £29 ($47.85) per day, a single with bath going for £36 ($59.40). Doubles are priced at £49.50 ($81.70) with baths. There are 29 bedrooms within the hotel with private baths or showers. The dining room serves good English cooking, charging £12.50 ($20.65) for dinner.

WHERE TO DINE

One of the leading choices is **The Bishop's Kitchen** (Ridènes Restaurant), the Swan Hotel, Sadler Street (tel. 0749/77312). Owned and operated by this previously recommended hotel, the restaurant is reached via a separate entrance that funnels in from an alleyway in back. Of the several cozy rooms, some are heated with stone-sided fireplaces. Many visitors claim that the most charming pub in town can be found here, and you might be tempted to linger for a drink before heading in for dinner. In a warmly decorated room redolent of antique paneling and beamed ceilings, you can enjoy full meals priced from £18.50 ($30.55) at dinner, but only £9 ($14.85) for lunch. These are served daily from 11:30 to 3pm and 7pm to midnight. Typical menu items include filet steak Diane, veal marsala, and darne of salmon.

---

9. The Caves of Mendip

The great Caves of Mendip are two natural sightseeing attractions in Somerset, both easily reached by heading west out of Wells.

WOOKEY HOLE

Just 2 miles from Wells, you'll first come to **Wookey Hole Caves & Mill** (tel. 0749/72243), the source of the Axe River. In the first chamber of the caves, you can see, as legend has it, the Witch of Wookey turned to stone. These caves are believed to have been inhabited by prehistoric people at least 60,000 years ago. A tunnel, opened in 1975, leads to the chambers unknown to early man and previously accessible only to divers.

Leaving the caves, you follow a canal path to the mill, where paper has been made by hand since the 17th century. Here you can watch high-quality paper being made by skilled workers according to the traditions of their ancient craft. Also in the mill is housed a Fairground by Night exhibition, a colorful assembly of relics from the world's fairgrounds, and an Edwardian Penny Pier Arcade where old pennies can be exchanged for new to play the original machines. There is also a museum covering the history of the caves from prehistoric times to modern cave-diving expeditions, as well as a giant working waterwheel.

Adults pay £4.10 ($6.75), children under 17 being charged £2.85 ($4.70), for a guided tour lasting two hours. Free parking is provided, and visitors can use the self-service restaurant and picnic area. Wookey Hole Caves is open all year round except the week before Christmas; from 9:30am to 5:30pm in summer and 10:30am to 4:30pm in winter.

CHEDDAR CAVES

A short distance from Bath, Bristol, and Wells is the village of Cheddar, home of Cheddar cheese. It lies at the foot of Cheddar Gorge, within which are the **Cheddar Caves,** underground caverns with impressive formations. There is a museum displaying prehistoric artifacts dating from when the caves were the home of Cheddar Man, whose 9,000-year-old skeleton is also on display. A climb up the 274 steps of Jacob's Ladder offers views over Somerset, and, on a clear day, you may even see Wales. The caves are open all year daily, from Easter until the end of September 10am to 5:30pm; 10:30am to 4:30pm the rest of the year; closed December 24 and 25. Admission is £3.50 ($5.80) for adults and £2 ($3.30) for children. Adults and children over 12 can also go adventure caving, taking tours of a subterranean world beyond the showcaves at a cost of £4.50 ($7.45). Overalls, helmets, and lamps are provided.

AVON

Avon is the name that has been given to the area around the old port of Bristol and the spa at Bath, an area that used to be in Somerset.

10. Bath

In 1702 Queen Anne made the 115-mile trek from London to the mineral springs of Bath, thereby launching a fad that was to make the city the most celebrated spa in England. Of course, Victoria-come-lately eventually hiked up too, to sample a medicinal cocktail (which you can still do today), but Bath by then had passed its zenith.

The most famous personage connected with Bath when it was the pinnacle of fashion was the 18th-century dandy, Beau Nash. He was the final arbiter of taste and manners (one example: he made dueling déclassé). The master of ceremonies of Bath, he cut a striking figure as he made his way across the city with all the plumage of a bird of paradise. While dispensing (at a price) trinkets to the courtiers and aspirant gentlemen of his day, Beau was carted around in a liveried carriage. The gambler was given the proper setting for his considerable social talents by the 18th-century architects John Wood the Elder and his son. These architects designed a city of stone from the nearby hills, a feat so substantial and lasting that Bath today is the most harmoniously laid-out city in England.

Their work done, the Georgian city on a bend of the Avon River was to attract a following among leading political and literary figures—Dickens, Thackeray, Nelson, Pitt. Canadians may already know that General Wolfe lived on Trim Street, and Australians may want to visit the house at 19 Bennett Street where their founding father, Admiral Philip, lived. Even Henry Fielding came this way, observing in *Tom Jones* that the ladies of Bath "endeavour to appear as ugly as possible in the morning, in order to set off that beauty which they intend to show you in the evening." And Jane Austen used Bath as the setting of her "gothic" novel, *Northanger Abbey*.

Bath has had two lives. Long before its Queen Anne, Georgian, and Victorian popularity, it was known to the Romans as Aquae Sulis. The foreign legions founded their baths here (which may be visited today), so they might ease rheumatism in the curative mineral springs.

Remarkable restoration and careful planning have ensured that Bath retains its handsome look today. The city suffered devastating destruction from the Baedeker air raids of 1942.

For information go to the **Bath Tourist Information,** Colonnades Shopping Centre, Bath Street (tel. 0225/462831), opposite the Roman baths. Hours in summer are from 9:30am to 7pm Mon. to Sat. and from 10am to 6pm Sun. In winter, hours are from 9:30am to 5pm Mon. to Sat. only.

WHAT TO SEE AND DO

The major sights today are the abbey, the Pump Room, and the Roman baths. But if you're intrigued by architecture and city planning, you may want to visit some of the buildings, crescents, and squares. The North Parade, where Goldsmith lived, and the South Parade, where Fanny Burney (English novelist and diarist) once resided, represent harmony, the work of John Wood the Elder. The younger Wood, on the other hand, designed the Royal Crescent, an elegant half-moon row of town houses copied by Astor architects for their colonnade in New York City in the 1830s. Queen Square is one of the most beautiful squares (both Jane Austen and Wordsworth lived here), showing off quite well the work of Wood the Elder. And don't miss his circus, built in 1754, as well as the shop-flanked Pulteney Bridge, designed by Robert Adam and compared aptly to the Ponte Vecchio of Florence.

Bath Abbey
Built on the site of a much larger Norman cathedral, the present-day abbey is a fine example of the late Perpendicular style. When Queen Elizabeth I came to Bath in 1574, she ordered that a national fund be set up to restore the abbey. The west front is the sculptural embodiment of a Jacob's Ladder dream of a 15th-century bishop. When you go inside and see its many windows, you'll understand why the abbey is called the "Lantern of the West." Note the superb fan vaulting, achieving at times a scalloped effect. Beau Nash was buried in the nave and is honored by a simple monument totally out of keeping with his flamboyant character. Hours are 9am to 5:30pm Mon. to Sat. (visiting times on Sun. depend on services). Visitors are requested to make a donation, at least 50p (85¢), more if you can afford it.

Pump Room and Roman Baths
Founded in A.D. 75 by the Romans, the baths were dedicated to the goddess Sul Minerva. In their day they were an engineering feat, and even today are considered among the finest Roman remains in the country. They are still fed by the only hot spring water in Britain. After centuries of decay, the baths were rediscovered in Victoria's reign, and the site of the Temple of Sulis Minerva has been recently excavated and is now open to view. The museum connected to the baths contains many interesting objects from Victorian and recent digs (look for the head of Minerva). Coffee, lunch, and tea, usually with music from the Pump Room Trio, can be enjoyed in the 18th-century pump room, overlooking the hot springs. There's a drinking fountain serving hot mineral water. The Pump Room, Roman Baths, excavations, and museum are open daily in July and August from 9am to 7pm. At other times from March to October inclusive, they are open daily from 9am until 6pm. From November to February, they are open from 9am to 5pm, except on Sun., when opening is at 10am. Admission is £3.25 ($5.35) for adults, £1.50 ($2.50) for children. For more information, phone 0225/461111, ext. 2785.

Bath International Festival
Bath's graceful Georgian architecture provides the setting for one of Europe's most prestigious international festivals of music and the arts. For 17 days in late May and early June each year the city is filled with more than 1,000 performers. The festival is built around a base of classical music, jazz, and the contemporary visual arts, with orchestras, soloists, and artists from all over the world. In addition to the main music and art program, there is all the best in talks and tours. Ticket prices are £4 ($6.60) for lunch recitals and range from £5 ($8.25) to £25 ($41.25) for evening concerts and operas. Full details can be obtained from Bath Festival, 1 Pierrepont Place, Bath BA1 1JY (tel. 0225/462231). In the United States, full details and tickets are available from Keith Prowse, 234 W. 44th St., New York, NY 10036 (tel. 212/398-1430).

The Theatre Royal
The Theatre Royal, Sawclose, has been restored and refurbished with plush red-velvet seats, red carpets, and a painted proscenium arch and ceiling, and is now regarded as one of the most beautiful theaters in Britain. It is a 1,000-seat theater with

a small pit from which grand circles of seats rise to upper levels. Beneath the theater, reached from the back of the stalls or by a side door, are the theater vaults. There you will find a pleasant bar in one of the curved vaults with stone walls. In the next vault is the brasserie, and a Japanese restaurant is beside the stage door.

The theater advertises lists of forthcoming events, with a repertoire that includes, among other offerings, West End shows. The box office (tel. 0225/448844) is open from 9:30am to 8pm Mon. to Sat.

A Georgian House

No. 1 Royal Crescent (tel. 0225/428126) gives you the chance to see inside a Bath townhouse that has been redecorated and furnished by the Bath Preservation Trust so that it appears as it might have toward the end of the 18th century. The house is positioned at one end of Bath's most magnificent crescent. It is open to the public from March to the end of October from 11am to 5pm Tues. to Sat. and from 2 to 5pm on Sun., from November to Christmas from 11am to 3pm Tues. to Sat. Last admissions are 30 minutes before closing. Closed Mon. except bank holidays and during the Bath Festival. Admission is £1.50 ($2.50) for adults, £1 ($1.65) for children.

The American Museum

Some 2½ miles outside Bath you get a glimpse of life as lived by a diversified segment of American settlers until Lincoln's day. It was the first American museum established outside the United States. In a Greek Revival house, designed by a Georgian architect, Claverton Manor, the museum (tel. 0225/460503) sits proudly in its own extensive grounds high above the Avon valley. Among the authentic exhibits —shipped over from the States—are a New Mexico room, a Conestoga wagon, an early American beehive oven, the dining room of a New York townhouse of the early 19th century, and (on the grounds) a copy of Washington's flower garden at Mount Vernon. There is a permanent exhibition in the New Gallery of The Dallas Pratt Collection of Historical Maps. You can visit the museum from the end of March to the end of October from 2 to 5pm Tues. to Sun. There is an American arboretum on the grounds. Admission to the house and gardens is £4 ($6.60) for adults, £3 ($4.95) for children.

Walking Tours

A good look at Bath is provided by the **Mayor's Corps of Honorary Guides** in the free walking tours of the city. The guides are all unpaid volunteers acting in an honorary capacity to point out the beauties of their city. They don't accept tips. Tours, lasting about 2 hours, leave from the abbey churchyard, outside the Pump Room. Visitors see the historical and architectural features of the city, but are not shown into any buildings. From May to October, tours are offered at 10:30am Sun. to Fri. and at 2:30pm on Sun. and Wed.; from May to September, at 7pm on Tues., Fri. and Sat.; and from November to April, at 10:30am Sun. to Fri. and at 2:30pm Sun. The tours are arranged by the Guides Corps in conjunction with the Bath City Council (tel. 0225/461111, ext. 2786).

WHERE TO STAY

In accommodations, Bath offers a wide choice—some in architectural landmarks.

Expensive Hotels

The Royal Crescent Hotel, 16 Royal Crescent, Bath, Avon BA1 2LS (tel. 0225/319090), is a special place, standing proudly in the center of the famed Royal Crescent, a Georgian colonnade of townhouses designed by John Wood the Younger in 1767. Long regarded as the premier hotel of Bath, the 45-room hotel has attracted the rich and famous (everybody from Jane Austen in days of yore to King Hussein of Jordan more recently). Crystal chandeliers, period furniture, and paintings add to the rich adornment. The bedrooms, including the Jane Austen Suite, are often lavishly decorated with trappings such as four-poster beds and half testers. Room facilities include a private bath or shower, direct-dial phone, TV, and air conditioning. Singles rent for £95 ($156.75) daily, with doubles costing £170 ($280.50). Nine of the accommodations are suites, for which two persons are charged from £235 ($387.75) to £340 ($561) nightly. The food is excellent, and served in the lavishly decorated Dower House. Reservations are vital for rooms or meals.

Bath Spa Hotel, Sydney Road, Bath, Avon BA2 6JF (tel. 0225/444424), is a restored 19th-century mansion, lying a 10-minute walk from the center of Bath with the added advantage of 180 parking spaces. Behind a facade of Bath stone, it lies at the end of a tree-lined drive on 7 acres of landscaped grounds, with a Victorian grotto and a Grecian temple. Winston Churchill in World War II visited when it was the headquarters of the Admiralty. In its long history, it had served many purposes (once a hostel for nurses) before being returned to its original grandeur. Today, it has 103 well-furnished rooms and 7 suites, each with phone, TV, private bath or shower, and mini-bar. One person (in a double room) pays £100 ($165) per night, with twins renting for £125 ($206.25). Suites begin at £175 ($288.75) for two persons. Tariffs include service and VAT. Guests have use of activity facilities, including a swimming pool, gym, and tennis court. The drawing room of what once was an English general's house (he served in India) is today restored. It is representative of the new style of the hotel, which uses log fireplaces, elaborate moldings, oak paneling, and staircases to create country-house charm. The general called his home Vellore House, and the name is today remembered in the restaurant where an international cuisine is served.

The Priory Hotel, Weston Road, Bath, Avon BA1 2XT (tel. 0225/331922), was converted from one of Bath's Georgian houses in 1969. It stands in 2 acres of formal gardens with manicured lawns and flowerbeds, a swimming pool, and a croquet lawn. The 21 bedrooms are individually decorated and furnished with antiques, and each has color TV, direct-dial phone, and easy chairs. My personal favorite is Clivia (all rooms are named after flowers or shrubs), a nicely appointed duplex within a circular turret. Prices start at £82 ($135.30) daily for singles, with standard twins and doubles renting from £110 ($181.50). Deluxe rooms for two cost from £160 ($264). All tariffs include a full English breakfast and VAT. The restaurant consists of three separate dining rooms, one in a small salon in the original building. The others have views over the garden. The menu is varied and reflects seasonal availability. Grouse, partridge, hare, and venison are served in season in several recipes, as is the succulent best end of lamb roasted with herb-flavored breadcrumbs. The average dinner price is £28 ($46.20). A three-course luncheon is offered for £18 ($29.70), and on Sun. traditional roasted meats are featured. The Priory is known for its wine list.

Queensberry Hotel, Russel Street, Bath, Avon BA1 2QT (tel. 0225/447928). Much of the beauty of this place derives from the many original fireplaces, ornate ceilings, and antiques, which the creators of the property, Stephen and Penny Ross, have preserved. Each of three interconnected townhouses that form this hotel was constructed in the early Georgian era. Today, 24 bedrooms are rented, each with a private bath, phone, TV, antique furniture, and carefully chosen upholstery in keeping with the character of the house. Open since 1988, Queensberry has already become one of Bath's most important hotels. Depending on their location, doubles cost from £80 ($132) to £120 ($198) daily, with singles going for £75 ($123.75). The least expensive doubles, although spacious, are in the basement. VAT and a continental breakfast are included in the price. The hotel doesn't have a restaurant but has a stylish bar where light meals are offered both at lunch and in the evening. However, the staff aids in securing restaurant reservations, and you can always dine at Queensberry's sister hotel, the award-winning Homewood Park, 5 miles outside Bath.

Fountain House, 9-11 Fountain Buildings, Lansdown Road, Bath, Avon BA1 5DV (tel. 0225/338622). The three buildings that compose this hotel are a trio of Regency, neoclassic, white-fronted structures, each of which dates from 1735. British entrepreneur Robin Bryan created an all-size hotel that has been favorably compared to the most prestigious properties in England. Each suite contains reproduction antiques, lots of color-coordinated chintz, at least one bedroom, a sitting room, a private bath, and a minibar, as well as all the electronic equipment you'd expect in such an elegant hotel, including TV and phone. One-bedroom suites cost from £98 ($161.70) to £138 ($227.70) daily for two persons, whereas a two-bedroom suite, suitable for four persons, rents for £165 ($272.25). The hotel stands within 100 yards of Milsom Street, the city's main shopping and historical thoroughfare. It doesn't serve a formal breakfast. Instead, all ingredients are delivered in a basket to the door, and clients prepare their own breakfasts at their own pace.

Moderately Priced Hotels
Lansdown Grove Hotel, Lansdown Road, Bath, Avon BA1 5EH (tel. 0225/315891), is a well-run hotel outside the center of the city, set on the northern slopes with views, 600 feet above sea level. Its drawing room is informal, with flowering chintz draperies, a large gilt-and-marble console, and comfortable armchairs. The 45 bedrooms all have private baths or showers, color TVs, mini-bars, phones, hairdryers, and trouser presses. Singles cost from £62 ($102.30) daily, and doubles from £95 ($156.75). All rates include VAT and a full English breakfast. It's a pleasure to eat in the sunny dining room, with its bay window that opens onto the garden. Before-dinner drinks are available in the cocktail bar. The hotel, a Best Western affiliate, offers a car park as well as a covered garage.

Francis Hotel, Queen Square, Bath, Avon BA1 2HH (tel. 0225/424257), as part of Queen Square, stands as the first major work of John Wood, the architect and creator of Bath's most prestigious buildings. Originally six private residences dating from 1729, the Francis was opened as a private hotel by Emily Francis in 1884 and has offered guests first-class service for more than 100 years. Many bedrooms overlook Queen Square—named in honor of George II's consort, Caroline. The Francis is an example of 18th-century taste. The public rooms contain shell-shaped niches, moldings, some 18th-century antiques, a cocktail bar, and the Edgar Restaurant, which offers a wide array of both British and international food. Each of the well-furnished bedrooms, 93 in all, has a private bath, color TV, phone, and radio. Singles cost from £70 ($115.50) daily, and doubles or twins rent from £100 ($165).

Dukes Hotel, Great Pulteney Street, Bath, Avon BA2 4DN (tel. 0225/463512). A short walk from the heart of Bath, this building dates from 1780 but has been completely restored and rather elegantly furnished and modernized. Many of the original Georgian features, including cornices and moldings, have been retained. Twenty-two attractively furnished bedrooms are rented, and all but two have complete private baths. Amenities include electric trouser presses, direct-dial phones, color TVs, and hairdryers. The owner, Peter F. Yarker, charges from £35 ($57.75) to £55 ($90.75) daily in a single and £55 ($90.75) to £90 ($148.50) in a double, depending on the room assignment. Guests can relax in a refined drawing room or else patronize the cozy bar. A varied menu is also offered.

Pratt's Hotel, South Parade, Bath, Avon BA2 4AB (tel. 0225/460441), once the home of Sir Walter Scott, is convenient for sightseeing. It is on a wide street with a large car park close by. Several elegant terraced Georgian townhouses were joined into a comfortable place with warm, cheerful lounges, a bar, and a high-ceilinged dining room. The 46 bedrooms all have private baths, color TVs with in-house movies, radios, telephones, trouser presses, and tea and coffee makers. A single goes for £58 ($95.70) daily and a twin or double for £75 ($123.75). All rates include a full English breakfast and VAT. Children under 15 sharing a room with two adults stay free. English and French cuisine is served in the dining room, where dinner costs from £18 ($29.70).

Apsley House Hotel, 141 Newbridge Hill, Bath, Avon BA1 3PT (tel. 0225/336966), is a charming private hotel in a building dating back to the reign of William IV, just a mile from the center of Bath. It's set in its own gardens, stately, with a square tower, arched windows, and a walled garden with south views. All seven rooms are luxuriously appointed with private baths or showers, phones, and TVs.

The Alpine and Romantic rooms cost from £105 ($173.25) daily for two people, while the Champagne, Gold, Melissa, Ondine, and Ballerina rooms go for £90 ($148.50). Tariffs include a full English breakfast, service, and VAT. If you would like to have dinner in the handsome dining room, expect to spend £20 ($33) for the three-course menu. Drinks are served in an intimate cocktail bar, and there is a comfortable lounge. To reach the hotel, take the A4 to Upper Bristol 1 Road and fork right at traffic signals into Newbridge Hill.

Budget Hotels

Laura Place Hotel, 3 Laura Place, Great Pulteney St., Bath, Avon BA2 4BH (tel. 0225/463815), was built the same year as the French Revolution (1789). The hotel won a civic award for the restoration of its stone facade. Set on a corner on a residential street overlooking a public fountain, it lies within a 4-minute walk of the Roman Baths and Bath Abbey. The place is skillfully decorated with antique furniture and fabrics evocative of the 18th century. The house is owned by Patricia Bull, who rents 10 comfortable bedrooms. Seven of these offer private baths. With VAT and breakfast included, singles range from £20 ($33) to £32 ($52.80) daily, with doubles going for £42 ($69.30) to £68 ($112.20).

Sydney Gardens Hotel, Sydney Road, Bath, Avon BA2 6NT (tel. 0225/464818), is reminiscent of the letters of Jane Austen, who wrote to friends about the long walks she enjoyed in Sydney Gardens, a public park just outside the city center. In 1852, an Italianate Victorian villa was constructed here of gray stone on a lot immediately adjacent to the gardens. Today Stanley and Diane Smithson maintain six rooms to rent, each of which has a private bath and comes with a good breakfast included in the price. Single rooms cost £50 ($82.50) to £55 ($90.75) daily, doubles £60 ($99). No meals other than breakfast are served, since the center of town with its many dining spots lies within a 10-minute walk. There's also a footpath running beside a canal for an additional pedestrian adventure.

Number Ninety Three, 93 Wells Rd., Bath, Avon BA2 3AN (tel. 0225/317977), is a small and well-run guesthouse operated by Christopher Pollard. He provides an alternative to the high-priced hotels of Bath by operating a traditional B&B, British style. The place is small but immaculately kept and well maintained. Five bedrooms, each with private bath or phone, are rented, costing from £21 ($34.65) to £28 ($46.20) daily in a single and from £36 ($59.40) to £40 ($66) in a double. The elegant Victorian house serves a traditional English breakfast, and the location is within walking distance of the city center. An evening meal can be arranged at 6:30pm.

Luxury Living in the Environs

Ston Easton Park, Ston Easton, near Farrington Gurney BA3 4DF (tel. 076121/631), lies 1¼ miles south of Farrington Gurney on the A37. From the moment you pass a collection of stone out-buildings and the century-old beeches of its 30-acre park, you know you've come to a very special place. The mansion was created in the mid-1700s from the shell of an existing Elizabethan house, and in 1793 Sir Humphry Repton designed the landscape. In 1977, after long years of neglect, Peter and Christine Smedley acquired the property and poured money, love, and labor into its restoration. Now, it is one of the great country hotels of England. A pair of carved mahogany staircases ringed with ornate plaster detailing might be considered works of sculpture. A sunflower-colored, formal dining room contains museum-quality oil portraits, grandeur, and exquisite attention to detail. The chef prepares superb food, offering imaginative menus. A lunch costs £19.50 ($32.20), and a dinner goes for £29.50 ($48.70). Guests who return early from sightseeing enjoy tea in the hotel garden beside one of the four cascades. The sheer volume of antiques filling the place is staggering. There's a manorial library, as well as a drawing room suitable for a diplomatic reception, and 20 tasteful bedrooms filled with flowers, plus upholstery, and antiques. Each room has a private bath or shower, phone, and TV. Singles cost from £70 ($115.50) daily, doubles and twins rent for £115 ($189.75) to £195 ($321.75), and junior suites for two persons are priced at £230

($379.50) to £270 ($445.50). Children under 12 aren't accepted. The hotel is 11 miles southwest of Bath, 13 miles southeast of Bristol, and 5 miles north of Wells.

Hunstrete House, Hunstrete, Chelwood, near Bristol, Avon BS18 4NS (tel. 07618/490490), is a *Relais & Châteaux,* lying 8½ miles west of Bath. This 18th-century house is set in 90 acres of private parkland. The village of Hunstrete was first recorded in A.D. 936 when King Athelstan passed through on his way to the abbey in Glastonbury. The fine Georgian house has 24 bedrooms with private baths. Six units are in the Courtyard House, attached to the main structure and overlooking a paved courtyard with its Italian fountain and flower-filled tubs. Swallow Cottage, which also adjoins the main house, has its own private sitting room, double bedroom, and bath. Units in the main house are individually decorated and furnished in attractive colors. They vary in size as reflected by the rates. All rooms have private baths, phones, and TVs. Doubles cost £100 ($165) to £155 ($255.75), up to £175 ($288.75) in a suite. A single person will pay from £85 ($140.25). Tariffs include a continental breakfast, VAT, and service. Part of the pleasure of staying at Hunstrete is the contemporary and classical cuisine. A three-course dinner at £32 ($52.80) gives diners a wide and delectable choice. A heated swimming pool lies in a sheltered corner of the walled garden.

Homewood Park, Hinton Charterhouse, Bath, Avon BA3 6BB (tel. 0225/723731), is set in 10 acres of garden, just 5 miles south of Bath on the A36 Bath-Warminster road. Stephen and Penny Ross, who ran the successful Popjoy's restaurant in Bath, have converted the property and now offer 15 bedrooms with private baths, phones, and TVs. This small, family-run hotel was built in the 18th century, then subsequently enlarged in the 19th century. Overlooking the Limpley Stoke Valley, it is a large Victorian house, its grounds adjoining the 13th-century ruin of Hinton Priory. The B&B rate is from £65 ($107.25) daily in a single to £145 ($239.25) in a double. Of course, most visitors come here for the cuisine, served in a dining room facing south, overlooking the gardens. The French and English cooking is prepared with skill and flair, and you should expect to spend from £17.50 ($28.90) to £30 ($49.50) for a three-course dinner. You can play tennis and croquet in the garden. Riding and golfing are nearby, and beautiful walks in the Limpley-Stoke Valley lure guests.

WHERE TO DINE

Bath enjoys a reputation as a gourmet citadel of Britain.

Popjoy's, Beau Nash House, Sawclose (tel. 0225/460494), is housed in a 1720 Georgian building that was once the home of the notorious Beau Nash, the "King of Bath." The restaurant is named after Julianna Popjoy, Nash's last mistress. Her ghost is said to haunt the drawing room. When Nash died in 1761, Julianna vowed never again to sleep in a bed, and spent the rest of her life gathering herbs and living in a hollow tree in Wiltshire. In 1982 Popjoy's was restored exactly as it had been in 1720, even down to scraping the centuries of paint from the walls to discover the original colors. Everything is freshly prepared in the basement kitchen. A set dinner is priced at £22.50 ($37.15), while à la carte meals cost from £25 ($41.25). A la carte lunches cost from £6 ($9.90). Meat comes from Devon, fish daily from Cornwall, and fresh vegetables from local farmers. Menus lean toward the new way of cooking using less fat, less cream, and no flour in sauces. The wine list (they buy their wine from 16 different wine merchants) is more than 100 strong. The menu is changed every 8 weeks, and ever since the place reopened in 1983, there has hardly been an empty seat. The house wine is specially bottled in France and imported for the restaurant. It is open from noon to 2pm and 6 to 10:30pm Tues. to Sat. (except Sat. lunch).

Hole in the Wall, 16 George St. (tel. 0225/425242). You enter what looks like the living room of a Georgian townhouse, where a hostess greets you, takes your name and order for a drink and presents you with the impressive menu, and even helps plan your meal if you prefer. All the selections are especially prepared for you. When your table is ready, you descend into an old-world dining room, with an attractive decor that includes a great fireplace. The benches, tables, and chairs are antiques. The menu is changed frequently. The cooking is classical Italian, and the superb use of fresh ingredients and fresh fish is a strong feature. The menu is à la carte with a meal costing between £15 ($24.75) and £25 ($41.25), depending on choice. Daily specials are also available. Lunch is served from noon to 2:30pm and dinner from 6:30 to 11:15pm. Closed Sun.

Tarts Restaurant, 8 Pierrepont Pl., (tel. 0225/330280), is a bistro located on two different levels of a rustic cellar. It offers a French-inspired cuisine, and perhaps the finest wine list in Bath. The bistro contains room for 45 diners. Menus are constantly changing based on seasonal availability of ingredients. You might try, for example, roast guinea fowl with a Thai sauce (coconut, lime, mild chiles, cream, and ginger) or filet steak poivrade in a red wine cream with crushed peppercorns and a game stock. For an appetizer, sample, if featured, a rillette (coarse pâté) of fresh and smoked salmon with condiments. All desserts, including ice cream, are made on the premises. Watch for the day's specials. Meals cost from £26 ($42.90) at dinner but you can lunch here at two-thirds the price. Service is from noon to 2:30pm and 6:45 to 10:45pm Mon. to Sat. Reservations are vital.

Woods, 9-13 Alfred St. (tel. 0225/314812). The elegant Georgian building that contains this restaurant is also the home of one of Bath's antique emporiums. Diners climb a flight of steps to reach this restaurant, and once inside find carefully prepared daily specials described on a blackboard. American jazz from the 1930s might accompany a meal here. The chef offers a vegetarian dish of the day in addition to regular meat and fish specialties. These might include calves' liver with kidneys and coriander, filet of English lamb cooked pink, and a homemade fish pie. Full meals, costing from £15 ($24.75), are served at lunch and dinner from noon to 2:15pm and 6:30 to 10:15pm Mon. to Sat.

Chikako's, Theatre Royal, Sawclose (tel. 0225/464125). Its intimacy, coupled with its flavorfully light-textured Japanese specialties, attracts a clientele beyond the patrons of the theater in which it is housed. The low-slung, Japanese-style lacquered tables have depressions beneath to allow all the leg-dangling comfort of the West. Some of the meals are cooked on a hotplate plugged directly into your table. A bevy of waiters bring fresh slices of prawn, halibut, mackerel, seasonal vegetables, chicken, pork, salmon, and beef. Sake, tea, and Japanese beer are the preferred drinks, but wine is also available. The menu includes a full range of Japanese cuisine (teriyaki is a favorite). Food is served amid a simple decor of bamboo, rice paper, and lacquerwork. Meals cost £12 ($19.80) to £20 ($33). It is open daily from 6 to 11pm.

The Moon and Sixpence, 6A Broad St., (tel. 0225/460962), is one of the leading restaurants and wine bars of Bath. The restaurant occupies a stone-built structure with an extended conservatory and sheltered patio. Just off Broad Street, it has a cobbled passageway leading you past a fountain into its courtyard. At lunch a large cold buffet with a selection of hot dishes is featured in the wine bar section. In the upstairs restaurant overlooking the bar, full service is offered. A three-course lunch costs from £10.75 ($17.75). Main courses are likely to include such dishes as filet of lamb with caramelized garlic or medallions of beef filet with a fresh herb and shallot hollandaise. Look for the daily specials on the continental menu. Dinners cost from £20 ($33). Hours are daily from noon to 2:30pm for lunch and from 5:30 to 10:30pm (until 11pm on Fri. and Sat.) for dinner. Call for a reservation.

11. Bristol

Bristol, the largest city in the West Country, is a good center for touring western Britain. Its location is 10 miles west of Bath, just across the Bristol Channel from Wales, 20 miles from the Cotswolds, and 30 miles from Stonehenge. This historic inland port is linked to the sea by 7 miles of the navigable Avon River. Bristol has long been rich in seafaring traditions and has many links with the early colonization of America. In fact, some claim that the new continent was named after a Bristol town clerk, Richard Ameryke. In 1497 John Cabot sailed from Bristol, which led to the discovery of the northern half of the New World.

WHAT TO SEE AND DO

In Bristol, the world's first iron steamship and luxury liner has been restored to her 1840 glory. She's the 3,443-ton S.S. *Great Britain,* and was created by Isambard Brunel, a Victorian engineer. Visitors can go abroad this "floating palace" daily from 10am to 6pm in summer, to 5pm in winter, for an admission of £2.10 ($3.45) for adults, £1 ($1.65) for children. For information, phone 0272/260680.

At the age of 25 in 1831, Brunel began a Bristol landmark, a suspension bridge over the 250-foot-deep Avon Gorge at Clifton.

Bristol Cathedral, College Green (tel. 0272/264879), was begun in the 12th century and was once an Augustinian abbey. The central tower was added in 1466. The chapter house and gatehouse are good examples of late Norman architecture, and the choir is magnificent. The cathedral's interior was singled out for praise by Sir John Betjeman, the late poet laureate.

Another church, **St. Mary Redcliffe,** 10 Redcliffe Parade West (tel. 0272/291962), was called "the fairest, the goodliest, and most famous parish church in England" by such an authority as Elizabeth I. Built in the 14th century, it has been carefully restored. One of the chapels is called "The American Chapel," where the kneelers show the emblems of all the states of the U.S. The tomb and armor of Admiral Sir William Penn, father of the founder of Pennsylvania, are in the church.

Cobbled King Street is known for its **Theatre Royal,** built in 1776 and now the oldest working playhouse in the United Kingdom. It is the home of the Bristol Old Vic. Backstage tours leave the foyer at noon every Fri. and Sat. Phone 0272/250250, box office, or 0272/277466, administration.

Guided walking tours are conducted in summer, and these last about 1½ hours, leaving from Neptune's statue. The tour departs at 2:30pm Sat. and at 7pm Thur. Guided tours are also conducted through Clifton, a suburb of Bristol, which has more Georgian houses than the just-previewed Bath.

Additional information on special walks is provided by **Bristol Tourist Information,** 14 Narrow Quay (tel. 0272/260767).

WHERE TO STAY

A modern city-center hotel, the **Holiday Inn,** Lower Castle Street, Bristol, Avon BS1 3AD (tel. 0272/294281), is ideal for the business traveler, but also suitable to the visitor who makes it to this part of the West Country. The heated swimming pool is impressive, and the foyer is spacious. Public areas are comfortable and stylish, in the tradition of this popular chain. The Restaurant Panache serves an à la carte menu as well as snacks from 7am to 10pm. The 284 bedrooms are uniformly furnished, bright, and cheerful, with double beds (doubles have two) and good tile bathrooms, TVs, phones, and air conditioning. Singles cost £80 ($132) to £85 ($140.25) daily and the double tariff is £95 ($156.75) to £100 ($165).

Grand Hotel, Broad Street, Bristol, Avon BS1 2EL (tel. 0272/291645). Built by the Victorians in the grand manner, this 178-room hotel sits on a street in the commercial heart of town. The architectural detailing that causes it to be considered one of the most noteworthy hotels in town includes rows of fan-shaped windows, intricate exterior corniches, lavishly ornate crystal chandeliers, two bars (one in a nautical theme), and a pair of comfortable restaurants, including the Brass Nails, serving good food. Dinner costs from £13.60 ($22.45). Each of the refurbished bedrooms has a TV, radio, phone, and private bath, as well as coordinated fabrics. Singles cost from £62.50 ($103) to £82.50 ($136.15), with breakfast included.

Bristol Hilton, Redcliffe Way, Bristol, Avon BS1 6NJ (tel. 0272/260041). Set conveniently amid the commercial bustle of the center of town, this modern hotel offers an imaginative decor. Its split-level restaurant is set inside the brick-lined walls of a former 16th-century glass kiln refurbished in the style of a French brasserie, offering both lunch and dinner and featuring English and French specialties. Lunch or dinner costs from £14.50 ($23.95). Many of the 200 bedrooms are outfitted in pastels, and all contain private baths, radios, phones, in-house video, TVs, and tea and coffee makers. Singles cost £78 ($128.70) daily, and doubles go for £93 ($153.45).

WHERE TO DINE

In cellars once used by monks, **Harvey's Restaurant,** 12A Denmark St. (tel. 0272/277665), is in a house that has belonged to Harvey's since the company was founded in 1796. The cellars date from far earlier, as they were originally part of a monastery dissolved and sacked by order of Henry VIII. Today the subterranean chambers house what is arguably the best restaurant in Bristol, with one of the finest and longest wine lists in Europe. The French chef offers a lunch selection for £13.75 ($22.70), and à la carte dinner can cost from £20 ($33). Specialties include beef Wellington, roast ribs of lamb with garlic and herbs, and veal medallions prairie. Food is served from noon to 2:30pm and 7 to 11:15pm Tues. to Fri., from 6:30 to 11:15pm Sat.; closed Sun.

The rest of the historic building is Harvey's Wine Museum. The main gallery is lined with huge sherry butts; there are displays of silver decanter labels and old wine bottles. The glass gallery contains many engraved and decorated glasses and goblets. There are family documents, passports, and watches belonging to Victorian and Edwardian Harveys. In the Unicorn, a reconstructed medieval inn, visitors are sustained with a glass of sherry. The museum is open on Fri. from 10am to noon or by appointment. If you lunch here, you may be able to arrange a visit to this place.

Lettonie, 9 Druid Hill, Stoke Bishop (tel. 0272/686456), is run by Martin Blunos and Siân Blunos, who insist on high quality ingredients. Both imbue their subtle restaurant with a simple elegance, and they are known for producing some of the most memorable meals in the area. Try, as for example, guinea fowl in a prune and brandy sauce, followed by one of their luscious desserts, perhaps a terrine of mixed chocolates. Service is top rate, as is the welcome. Lunch is served from noon to 2pm, costing £12.50 ($20.65), with a set dinner offered at £19 ($31.35) from 7 to 10:30pm. It is closed for dinner on Sun. and all day Mon. It's possible to dine à la carte for about £25 ($41.25) per person. Reservations are essential. The wine list is carefully selected and moderate in price.

Some of the most creative cookery in town is found at **Michael's,** 129 Hotwell Rd., Bristol, Avon BS8 4RU (tel. 0272/276190), run by Michael McGowan. His charming and well-patronized restaurant is near Clifton on a highway leading toward the Avon Gorge. In his pleasant bar, decorated like an Edwardian parlor, an open fire burns. The dining room is also bright and inviting. Michael's menu is imaginative, and he likes to change it, depending on the availability of seasonal produce. Service is informal and enthusiastic. Sunday lunch is offered in winter only, for £8.95 ($14.75) and up from noon to 2:30pm. Dinner is served from 7 to 11:30pm Mon. to Sat. Expect to pay about £22 ($36.30) to £25 ($41.25) per person. Always call for a table. There's no smoking in the dining room. If you want a cigarette, stick to the bar. Michael offers simple, bathless accommodations in a five-story Regency house overlooking the Avon Gorge and the suspension bridge. Rooms have hot and cold running water, and guests can use a kitchen and communal lounge. Two with showers are available. The price is from £17 ($28.05) per person per night.

12. Thornbury

Twelve miles from Bristol, Thornbury is known for its castle (now a hotel, see below). Many of the crenellations and towers were built in 1511 as the last defensible castle ever constructed in England. Its owner was beheaded by Henry VIII for "certain words" spoken in haste. Henry confiscated the lands and, to celebrate, stayed here for 10 days with Anne Boleyn in 1535. Later, Mary Tudor spent 3 years of her adolescence here.

Thornbury Castle, Thornbury, near Bristol, Avon BS12 1HH (tel. 0454/ 418511), is a genuine Tudor castle (built 1511) and once owned by Henry VIII. It is surrounded by trees and thick stone walls. Maurice C. R. Taylor, who was a music publisher, TV producer, and real estate developer, has brought many improvements to the property. He rents 18 bedchambers, 8 of which contain four-posters. Rooms, which have private baths, phones, and TVs, are superbly accessorized with fine furniture and many amenities. Singles rent for £75 ($123.75) daily, with doubles costing £80 ($132) to £180 ($297). Dining is some of the finest in Avon in one of the hotel's two dining rooms. Lunch costs from £16.50 ($27.25) per person and is served from noon to 2pm daily. Dinner, from £26.50 ($43.75) per person, is served from 7 to 9:30pm. Specialties include Scottish smoked salmon with a salad dressed in walnut oil, breast of chicken with an apricot and basil filling, and hot butterscotch pudding.

XII

THE COTSWOLDS

1. TETBURY

2. MALMESBURY

3. CIRENCESTER

4. PAINSWICK

5. CHELTENHAM

6. ROYAL SUDELEY CASTLE

7. BIBURY

8. CLANFIELD

9. BURFORD AND MINSTER LOVELL

10. SHIPTON-UNDER-WYCHWOOD

11. CHIPPING NORTON

12. BOURTON-ON-THE-WATER

13. STOW-ON-THE-WOLD

14. LOWER SWELL

15. THE SLAUGHTERS

16. MORETON-IN-MARSH

17. BROADWAY

18. CHIPPING CAMPDEN

The Cotswolds, a stretch of limestone hills, is a pastoral land dotted by ancient villages and deep wooded ravines. This bucolic scene in the middle of southwest England, about a 2-hour drive from London, is found mainly in Gloucestershire, with portions in Oxfordshire, Wiltshire, and Worcestershire. The wolds or plateaus led to this area's being given the name Cotswold, old English for "God's high open land."

Cotswold lambs used to produce so much wool they made their owners very rich—wealth they invested in some of the finest domestic architecture in Europe, built with honey-brown Cotswold stone. The wool-rich gentry didn't neglect their churches either. Often the simplest of villages will have a church that in style and architectural detail seems to rank far beyond the means of the hamlet.

If possible, try to explore the area by car. That is the best way to survey the winding goat paths, rolling hills, and sleepy hamlets, with names such as Stow-on-the-Wold, Wotton-under-Edge, Old Sodbury, Chipping Campden, Shipton-under-

Wychwood, and Upper and Lower Slaughter (often called "The Slaughters"). These most beautiful of English villages keep popping up on book jackets and calendars.

1. Tetbury

In the rolling Cotswolds, Tetbury was never in the mainstream of tourism. However, ever since an attractive man and his lovely bride moved there and took up residence in the Macmillan place, a Georgian building on nearly 350 acres, it is now drawing crowds from all over the world. Charles and Diana may one day be king and queen of England. Their nine-bedroom mansion, Highgrove, lies just outside the town on the way to Westonbirt Arboretum. The house cannot be seen from the road, but you might see Princess Di shopping in the village.

The town has a 17th-century market hall and a lot of antique shops, along with boutiques (one called Diana's). Its inns, even before the royal couple moved in, were not cheap, and the prices have certainly not dropped since that time.

WHERE TO STAY AND DINE

Dating from 1596, **The Close,** 8 Long St., Tetbury, Gloucestershire GL8 8AQ (tel. 0666/502272), takes its name from a Cistercian monastery that was on this site. It was once the home of a wealthy Cotswold wool merchant. It is built of the honey-brown Cotswold stone, with gables and stone-mullioned windows. The ecclesiastical-type windows in the rear overlook a garden with a reflection pool, a haven for doves. Inside, you'll find a Georgian room with a domed ceiling (once it was an open courtyard), where before-dinner drinks are served and you can peruse the menu. Dining is in one of two rooms. Candlelight on winter evenings, floral arrangements, sparkling silver and glass are just the background for the fine food. The cooking is superb, and an à la carte menu offers specialty dishes. A set dinner costs from £25.50 ($42.10) per person. Fixed-price menus are offered for lunch for £14.95 ($24.65). Most of the 15 bedrooms, all with private baths, phones, and TVs, are spacious and handsomely furnished with antiques. A single room is priced at £75 ($123.75) daily and a double at £160 ($264). A continental breakfast, service, and VAT are included.

The Snooty Fox, Market Place, Tetbury, Gloucestershire GL8 8DD (tel. 0666/52436), is a desirable hotel in the commercial heart of Tetbury. It was originally built in the 16th century as a coaching inn. The Victorians added a high front porch under which flowers grow in what used to be watering troughs for horses. A stone-walled lounge with comfortable chairs and a Gothic fireplace opens off the reception area. There's a popular pub inside, with an amusing caricature of a snooty fox in full riding regalia, and one of the most elegant restaurants in town. In warm weather, tables are set at the edge of the market square beneath the 19th-century iron overhang. Three of the hotel's 12 bedrooms contain antique beds with canopies, and the rest are comfortably and tastefully furnished in a more modern style. Each has a private bathroom, color TV, radio, phone, hairdryer, trouser press, and hot beverage facilities. Singles cost from £66 ($108.90) to £84 ($138.60) daily and doubles from £86 ($141.90) to £108 ($178.20). VAT and a continental breakfast are included.

Calcot Manor, Calcot, Tetbury, Gloucestershire GL8 8YJ (tel. 066689/391), stands 3½ miles west of Tetbury on the A4135. It was originally a farmhouse, and on the grounds is a 14th-century tithe barn, among the oldest in Britain. The thick stone walls of the main house shelter a flowering terrace where tea and drinks are served in good weather. Tastefully decorated public rooms mix touches of modernism with clusters of flowers and English antiques. Meals are relaxing, with continental touches gathered from the Ball family's combined catering experience in Switzerland and France. The food is the finest served in the area. Dinner, daily from 7:30 to 9:30pm, goes for £32 ($52.80). Wife and mother Barbara, husband Brian, and son Richard add gracious touches to the establishment. The 13 bedrooms with bath are furnished with antiques, rich fabrics, and modern conveniences such as phones and TVs. Four contain whirlpool baths, and one has a four-poster bed. Views from many of the rooms encompass a sweep of lawn and the Cotswold countryside. With early morning tea and a full English breakfast, singles cost from £70 ($115.50) daily, and doubles rent for £85 ($140.25) to £120 ($190). Children over age 12 only are accepted.

---

2. Malmesbury

At the southern tip of the Cotswolds, the old hill town of Malmesbury is encir-·cled by the Avon River. In the center of England's "Middle West," it makes a good base for touring the Cotswolds. Cirencester is just 12 miles away; Bibury, 19 miles; and Cheltenham, 28 miles. Malmesbury is a market town, with a fine market cross. Its historical fame is reflected by the Norman abbey built there on the site of King Athelstan's grave.

Malmesbury is considered the oldest "borough" in England, as it was granted its charter by Alfred the Great in 880. In 1980 it celebrated its 1,300th anniversary. Some 400 years ago the Washington family lived there, leaving their star-and-stripe coat-of-arms on the church wall. In addition, Nancy Hanks, Abraham Lincoln's mother, came from Malmesbury. The town still has members of the family, noted for their lean features and tallness. The Penns of Pennsylvania also originally came from Malmesbury.

WHERE TO STAY AND DINE

In the heart of town adjoining the 13th-century Norman abbey, **The Old Bell,** Abbey Row, Malmesbury, Wiltshire SN16 0BW (tel. 0666/822344), is arguably the oldest hotel in England, having been a hostelry for more than 700 years. Historical connections link it with Nancy Hanks and with the family of George Washington. Its facade is wisteria-covered stone, with six gables and three towering chimneys; an iron picket fence guards the flowers and shrubbery. The inn opens onto a formal garden, with graveled monks' walks leading to the rear back wall, with its little stone gazebo bordering the Avon below. Architecturally, much remains of the original building, including a 13th-century window. The 35 bedrooms are all individually styled and have private baths, color TVs, phones, hairdryers, trouser presses, and hot beverage facilities. With breakfast, singles cost £58 ($95.70) daily, and doubles run £80 ($132), including VAT. The inn is often used by sportsmen, especially during Sat. hunts. The dining room serves lunch for £10.50 ($17.35), and dinner for £17.50 ($28.90).

An even better accommodation is found on the outskirts at **Whatley Manor,** Easton Grey, Malmesbury, Wiltshire SN16 0RB (tel. 0666/822888), which lies about half a mile east of Easton Grey on B4040. Easton Grey itself is 2 miles west of Malmesbury on B4040. This 18th-century manor house is one of the most desirable country house hotels in Wiltshire. By the River Avon, it was once a farmhouse but has been successfully converted into an upmarket Cotswold stone manor hotel. It rents 29 well-furnished, often most spacious, bedrooms, each with private bath or shower, phone, and TV. Some of the accommodations are found in the old court house on the grounds. The tariff in a single is from £62 ($102.30) nightly, with doubles costing from £86 ($141.90). The hotel has formal gardens, beautifully kept, on 10 acres of land. Facilities include an outdoor, heated swimming pool, a sauna, a solarium, and a Jacuzzi, plus an all-weather tennis court, table tennis, and snooker rooms. Even if you aren't staying here, consider candlelight dining nightly from 7:30 to 9pm with a set dinner going for £23 ($37.95). You can also visit for lunch, with a set menu costing from £12.50 ($20.65). Service is from 12:30 to 1:45pm. The cooking is both British and international.

3. Cirencester

Don't worry about how to pronounce the name of the town. Even the English are in disagreement. Just say "siren-sess-ter" and you won't go too far wrong. Cirencester is often considered the unofficial capital of the Cotswolds, probably a throwback to its reputation in the Middle Ages when it flourished as the center of the great wool industry.

Even in Roman Britain, five roads converged on Cirencester, which was called Corinium in those days. In size, it ranked second only to London. Today it is chiefly a market town, a good base for touring, as it lies 34 miles from Bath, 16 from the former Regency spa at Cheltenham, 17 from Gloucester, 36 from Oxford, and 38 from Stratford-upon-Avon. The trip from London is 89 miles.

Corinium Museum, Park Street (tel. 0285/655611), houses one of the finest collections of archeological remains from the Roman occupation, all found locally in and around Cirencester. Mosaic pavements found here on Dyer Street in 1849 and other mosaics are the most important exhibits. Provincial Roman sculpture, such as figures of Minerva and Mercury, pottery, and artifacts salvaged from long-decayed buildings provide a link with the remote civilization that once flourished here. The museum has been completely modernized to include full-scale reconstructions and special exhibitions on local history and conservation. It is open from 10am to 5:30pm Mon. to Sat., from 2 to 5:30pm Sun. Admission is 80p ($1.30) for adults, 40p (65¢) for children.

The restored 19th-century, two-cell jail, or **Cirencester Lock-up** as it was called in its heyday, on Trinity Road (tel. 0285/655611), is open daily by arrangement, so visitors can see interpretive displays including architectural conservation in the Cotswolds. Details of the exhibits here may be acquired at the Corinium Museum (see above).

Cirencester Parish Church, dating back to Norman times and Henry I, is the Church of John the Baptist, overlooking Market Place. (Actually, a church may have stood on this spot in Saxon times.) In size, the Cirencester church appears to be a cathedral—not a mere parish church. The present building represents a variety of styles, largely Perpendicular, as in the early-15th-century tower. Among the treasures inside are a 15th-century pulpit and a silver-gilt cup given to Queen Anne Boleyn 2 years before her execution.

WHERE TO STAY AND DINE

A delightful country-house atmosphere prevails at **Stratton House Hotel,** Gloucester Road, Stratton, Cirencester, Gloucestershire GL7 2LE (tel. 0285/651761), at Stratton, 1¼ miles northwest on the A417, a building that is part Jacobean and part Georgian. This mellow old house, which stands in its own beautiful grounds with a walled garden and herbaceous borders, is inviting and comfortable. The 26 bedrooms are large and have private baths or showers, phones, TVs, hairdryers, and trouser presses. In the dining and drawing rooms, some fine antique furniture and oil paintings may be seen. B&B rates range from £45 ($74.25) daily in a single to £58 ($95.70) in a double. These tariffs include an English breakfast and a well-served dinner with a wide choice of British dishes. There is a timbered-beam bar, and in winter log fires blaze in this barn and in the main hall.

The **Fleece Hotel,** Market Place, Cirencester, Gloucestershire GL7 2NZ (tel. 0285/658507). Its half-timbered facade hints at its origins as an Elizabethan coaching inn. Later it was enlarged by the Georgians. On warm days its flowering courtyard offers one of the most pleasant dining spots in town. Inside, a handful of open fireplaces warm the beamed interior whenever it's chilly. The staff offers clients French-inspired dinners priced from £18.50 ($30.55), enjoyed in an attractive restaurant or in the establishment's congenial wine bar, where local residents shuffle through a dusting of sawdust. The 23 comfortably modernized bedrooms contain old-fashioned hints of yesteryear such as quilted bedcoverings. Each has a private bath, phone, color TV, radio, and coffee-making facilities, with B&B costing £55 ($90.75) daily in a single, £85 ($140.25) in a double.

In the Environs

For food and lodging, one of the best choices lies in the environs. **The Pear Tree at Purton,** Church End, Purton, Swindon, Wiltshire SN5 9ED (tel. 0793/772100), is an English country restaurant with 18 well-furnished bedrooms, costing from £75 ($123.75) in a single or £85 ($140.25) to £125 ($206.25) nightly in a double. The individually decorated rooms have private baths, direct-dial phones, color TVs, hairdryers, trouser presses, and free sherry and mineral water, and open onto views of the garden and countryside. Each accommodation—three with four-poster beds—is named after a famous Purtonian, such as Anne Hyde, mother of Queen Mary and Queen Anne. The house was formerly the vicarage for the twin-towered parish Church of St. Mary's. A Cotswold stone house, it lies 3 miles from junction 16 of the M4 and 5 miles from Swindon. Set in 7½ acres, it looks out over a traditional Victorian garden and beyond the rolling hills to the source of the Thames.

Francis and Anne Young run the best restaurant in the area. The cuisine is inspired by France, although the recipes and cooking are distinctly English. The best of seasonal produce is featured, including local beef, lamb, and pork. Seafood is brought fresh from Devon, and many of the herbs used to flavor the dishes come from the establishment's own garden. Dining is in an attractive conservatory, and service is daily from noon to 2:30pm and 7 to 9:30pm (until 10pm on Fri. and Sat.). A set lunch goes for £12.50 ($20.65) weekdays or £13.50 ($22.30) on Sun. A table d'hôte dinner costs £18.50 ($30.55), and reservations are necessary. To dine à la carte costs from £22 ($36.30).

4. Painswick

The sleepy little town of Painswick, 4 miles northeast of Stroud, is considered a model village. All of its houses, while erected at different periods, blend harmoniously, as the villagers used only Cotswold stone as their building material. The one distinctive feature on the Painswick skyline is the spire of its 15th-century parish church. The church is linked with the legend of 99 yew trees, as well as its annual Clipping Feast (not the yew trees—rather, the congregation joins hands and circles around the church as if it were a Maypole, singing hymns as they do). Ancient tombstones dot the churchyard.

WHERE TO STAY

At the rear of the Painswick church stands the **Painswick Hotel,** Kemps Lane, Painswick, Gloucestershire GL6 6YB (tel. 0452/812160). Completely refurbished, this beautiful Georgian house, with a 19th-century facade, was once a royal vicarage and is encircled by terraces of formal gardens. The hotel reception area was once the private chapel. I think this hotel offers exceptional value. Many readers have reported it to be the highlight of their Cotswold tour. In rooms, cuisine, and service, it merits consideration enough to rate a major detour from wherever else you were going. All rooms have private baths, TVs, and phones. Rates for bed and an English breakfast are £45 ($74.25) daily in a single, £70 ($115.50) in a double, with VAT included. There are 16 rooms in all, in the main building and in a newer wing. The hotel has high standards of cuisine and service in its half-paneled dining room.

Before Columbus sailed on his quest for a new route to China, there was a market hall in Painswick, supported by stone pillars. In Shakespeare's time,

Gloucestershire stone masons turned the hall into one of the most beautiful houses in the town. Today, right in the middle of Painswick, that market hall is **Thorne,** Friday Street, Painswick, Gloucestershire, GL6 6QJ (tel. 0452/812476), the home of Barbara Blatchley. Barbara welcomes guests to this handsome, beautifully appointed house on a fairly selective basis, as she has only two twin guestrooms, complete with bathrooms and central heating. The charge is from £40 ($66) per person per day for bed, breakfast, and dinner, with wine and cocktails. Meals are served in the beam-ceilinged dining room, where two of the market pillars dating from 1400 are part of the wall. Top-quality farm produce and fresh vegetables are used in preparation of meals. If you arrive at the railway station in Stroud, Barbara will arrange to have you picked up at no extra charge. A qualified "Blue Badge Guide," she will also take guests to such places as Bath, Stratford-upon-Avon, Oxford, and Stonehenge at arrangements to be agreed upon.

WHERE TO DINE

An excellent restaurant, **The Country Elephant,** New Street (tel. 0452/813564), serves fine, English country-style cuisine. Owned and operated by Kenneth and Marril Gibson, the restaurant has a distinct personal touch. Marril does the cooking, buying the freshest ingredients locally. There is a cozy bar with an open log fire, and in the pleasantly decorated dining room you may enjoy filet of beef with oysters, fresh trout or sole, or pork filet with apricot and Stilton mousse, all cooked to order and served with a selection of fresh seasonal vegetables. Appetizers, both hot and cold, are imaginative. The dessert trolley is tempting. Meals cost from £21 ($34.65). Kenneth has composed an interesting and reasonably priced wine list to suit most palates. The restaurant is open for dinner from 7 to 10pm Tue. to Sat.

5. Cheltenham

In a sheltered area between the Cotswolds and the Severn Vale, some 100 miles from London, a mineral spring was discovered by chance. Legend has it that the Cheltenham villagers noticed pigeons drinking from a spring and observed how healthy they were (the pigeon has been incorporated into the town's crest). Always seeking a new spa, George III arrived in 1788 and launched the town. The Duke of Wellington also came, to ease his liver disorder. Even Lord Byron came this way, proposing marriage to Miss Millbanke.

Cheltenham is one of England's most fashionable spas. Its architecture is mainly Regency, with lots of ironwork, balconies, and verandas. Attractive parks and open spaces of greenery make the town especially inviting. The main street, the Promenade, has been called "the most beautiful thoroughfare in Britain." Rather similar are such thoroughfares as Lansdowne Place and Montpelier Parade. The design for the dome of the Rotunda was based on the Pantheon in Rome. Montpelier Walk, with its shops separated by caryatids, is one of the most interesting shopping centers in England.

The waters are still taken from the beautiful **Pittville Pump Room,** West Approach Drive, Pittville (tel. 0242/512470), one of the spa's finest Regency buildings. Cheltenham Waters are the only natural, consumable alkaline waters in Great Britain. On Sunday from the end of May until the end of September, the Pittville Pump Room is open for a host of activities, including brunch, afternoon cream teas, live classical music, Landau carriage rides around the city, and brass bands playing in Pittville Park—it's real, traditional England. The Gallery of Fashion is also situated in the pump room, depicting the social history of Cheltenham Spa. Memorabilia includes photographs and prints of when the U.S. Army was stationed at Pittville in the 1940s. There is free entrance to the pump room, which is open all year. Admission to the gallery is 50p (85¢). Hours from April to October are from 10:30am to 5pm Tue. to Sun.

The **Cheltenham Art Gallery and Museum,** Clarence Street (tel. 0242/

237431), houses one of the foremost collections of the arts and crafts movement, notably the fine furniture of William Morris and his followers. One section is devoted to Edward Wilson, Cheltenham's native son who died with Captain Scott on the Antarctic Expedition of 1910. Admission free, it is open from 10am to 5:20pm Mon. to Sat.

Cheltenham is the cultural center of the Cotswolds. Its restored **Everyman Theatre,** Regent Street (tel. 0242/572573), is the only professional repertory theater in Gloucestershire, offering a mixed program of musicals, dramas, comedies, and classics. The box office is open from 10am to 8pm Mon. to Sat.

The International Festival of Music and the Festival of Literature take place each year in July and October, respectively, attracting internationally acknowledged performers and orchestras.

Cheltenham is also the winner of "Beautiful Britain in Bloom," and many visitors come here just to see its gardens from spring to autumn.

Escorted coach tours of the Cotswolds take place every Tue., Thur., and Sun. from June until the end of December. Full details are available at the **Tourist Information Centre,** 77 Promenade (tel. 0242/522878). The center also has a free room-booking service and has an information board, showing room availability.

WHERE TO STAY

The best hostelry at the spa is **Queens Hotel,** Promenade, Cheltenham, Gloucestershire GL50 1NN (tel. 0242/514724). At the head of the Regency Promenade, this hotel looks down on the Imperial Gardens. Architecturally, it is imposing, built in 1838 in the style of the Roman temple of Jupiter. This distinguished hotel has a Regency decor and an unusually fine staircase. There are 77 bedrooms, all with private baths, phones, radios, and color TVs. Accommodations at the back are quieter. Everything is well furnished, although decidedly old-fashioned. A single rents for £70 ($115.50) daily, and a double for £92 ($151.80), including service and VAT. The restaurant serves a luncheon from £12 ($19.80). A complete set dinner is £18 ($29.70).

Hotel De la Bere and Country Club, Southam, Cheltenham, Gloucestershire GL52 3NH (tel. 0242/237771), is 3 miles northeast on the A46. The building on this property has origins in 1500. Constructed of Cotswold stone, it stands near the racecourse. For 3 centuries, the property was owned by the De la Bere family. It was converted into a hotel in 1972, and every effort has been made to ensure that the original charm of the building still remains. The restaurant, the Elizabethan Room, and the Royalist Room are all paneled in oak, and there is also a great hall, complete with its minstrel's gallery. The menu is impressive, and there are some interesting first courses. Dinner à la carte costs £18 ($29.70), with a fixed-price menu available for lunch at £11 ($18.15) and for dinner at £15 ($24.75). The 57 bedrooms, five of which boast double four-poster beds, all have private baths, color TVs, phones, and hot beverage facilities. They have all been tastefully decorated and furnished to preserve their individual charm and character. Single bedrooms cost from £60 ($99) daily, and doubles or twins go for £105 ($173.25).

Greenway, Shurdington, near Cheltenham, Gloucestershire GL51 5UG (tel. 0242/862352), is an elegant and beautifully furnished Cotswold country house in a garden setting lying in the village of Shurdington, less than 4 miles southwest of Cheltenham on A46. Ivy clad, this is a Cotswold showpiece. Restored with sensitivity and decorated and furnished to a high standard, Greenway rents rooms in both its main house and in a converted coach house. Original paintings and antiques abound throughout the hotel. On a chilly day, open fires beckon. Guests are almost assured of comfort here. Some 18 well-furnished bedrooms are rented, each with private bath or shower, TV, and phone. Singles cost £85 ($140.25) daily, with doubles going from £105 ($173.25) to £185 ($305.25). The dining room is elegantly appointed with an extension added in the Victorian conservatory style. The cooking is superb, using quality produce and good, fresh ingredients that are handled deftly. Lunch is from 12:30 to 2pm Sun. to Fri., and dinner is from 7:30 to 9:30pm Mon. to Sat. (at 7:30pm only Sun.). Lunches cost from £9 ($14.85) to £15 ($24.75) with a table d'hôte dinner going for £25 ($41.25). Service is formal, on target, and polite, all at the same time.

WHERE TO DINE

A good place to eat along the A40 is **Twelve Suffolk Parade,** 12 Suffolk Parade (tel. 0242/584544). The continental meals served here are worthy of those served in a charming French restaurant. Under the giant basket of ferns hanging in the center of the dining room, you can enjoy such typical dishes as chicken breast with curried mango sauce and rice flavored with cardamom and coriander, individual casseroles of sole with shrimp, and fresh, hot homemade garlic bread, while you sip one of the excellent French wines. Set lunches cost £10 ($16.50). Dinners go for around £18 ($29.70). Hours are noon to 2pm and 7:30 to 10:30pm Tue. to Sat. Hours are 7:30 to 10:30pm only on Sun.; closed Sun. lunch and Mon. Reservations are needed.

Le Champignon Sauvage, 24 Suffolk Rd. (tel. 0242/573449), is one of the leading restaurants of this old spa. David Matthias is a chef of considerable talent. He wisely limits his selection of dishes every night for better quality control. The style is French with English overtones. On some nights Mr. Matthias allows his imagination to roam a bit, so dining here is always a surprise, a pleasant one usually. He might stuff a wild rabbit with herbs or stuff a lamb with offal and eggplant. This "wild mushroom" serves lunch from 12:30 to 1:30pm and dinner from 7:30 to 9:15pm. It is closed for lunch on Sat. and all day Sun. A set luncheon costs £9.50 ($15.70) with a table d'hôte dinner going for £15.50 ($25.60). To dine à la carte costs from £25 ($41.25) per person. Reservations are essential.

For some spa devotees, the best dining is found in the environs at **Redmond's at Malvern View,** Cleeve Hill (tel. 0242/2017), lying 4 miles northeast at Cleeve Hill on A46. Redmond Hayward achieved local renown when he operated the premier dining room at Cheltenham. Now in his new location his country inn remains a choice dining place. Mr. Hayward keeps his selections of food items limited. That way, he can give his discriminating diners the best of local produce and well-chosen ingredients to go with his fine wine list. His constantly changing menu reflects the wide range of his repertoire and has an international flavor. Whatever your selection of a main course—perhaps chicken breast with an orange-flavored vanilla sauce—save room for one of his soufflés, which tend to be light-as-a-feather delights. Everything, certainly the soufflés, is prepared fresh and to order. Lunch is 12:30 to 2pm and dinner from 7:15 to 10pm daily. A set lunch costs £13.50 ($22.30), rising to £14.50 ($23.95) on Sun. A set dinner costs £22.50 ($37.15) or else you'll spend about £25 ($41.25) if ordering à la carte. The restaurant is closed Sat. lunch, dinner Sun., and all of Mon. Reservations are needed.

---

6. Royal Sudeley Castle

Sudeley is a 15th-century castle in the Cotswolds village of Winchcombe, 6 miles northeast of Cheltenham. The history of the castle dates back to Saxon times, when the village was the capital of the Mercian kings.

One of England's finer stately homes, Sudeley Castle attracts visitors from all over the world. There are works of art by Constable, Turner, Rubens, Van Dyck, and many others. The gardens are formal and surrounded by rolling farms and parkland. The Queen's Garden (replanted with old-fashioned roses) dates from the time when Katherine Parr, sixth wife of Henry VIII, lived and died at Sudeley. Her tomb is in a chapel on the property. There are several permanent exhibitions, some magnificent furniture and glass, and many relics from the castle's past. Waterfowl are to be found on the Moat Pond and peacocks strut around the grounds.

In an area to the right of the keep as you enter the castle are workshops for talented local artisans who use traditional skills to produce stained glass, textiles, wood and leather articles, and marbled paper, among other items. There is also a design exhibition illustrating the use of such work in country houses.

The castle is open from Easter to the end of October daily from noon to 5pm. The grounds are open from 11am. Admission to the castle, exhibitions, and grounds is £3.75 ($6.20) for adults, £1.95 ($3.20) for children. A family ticket for two adults and two children costs £10 ($16.50). For more information, phone 0242/602308.

The present owner of Sudeley Castle, Lady Ashcombe, an American by birth, has lived here for more than 25 years.

If you'd like to stay near the castle, **Isbourne House,** Castle Street, Winchcombe, Cheltenham, Gloucestershire GL54 5JA (tel. 0242/602281), is an excellent choice. Edward Saunders and his colleague, Dick Whittamore, receive guests in a part Georgian, part Elizabethan Cotswold-stone house surrounded by a well-kept garden, stone walls, and wrought-iron gates. They operate an extremely high standard B&B, providing a full-platter English breakfast in the morning. Only two rooms are available, one with complete bath and toilet, the other with a shower and hand basin. Charges are from £34 ($56.10) to £42 ($69.30) daily in a double. On 24 hours notice, elegant dinners can be provided. Sometimes guests can be introduced to country pastimes such as horse shows or fox hunting English-style.

7. Bibury

On the road from Burford to Cirencester, Bibury is one of the loveliest spots in the Cotswolds. In fact, the utopian romancer of Victoria's day, poet William Morris, called it England's most beautiful village. On the banks of the tiny Coln River, Bibury is noted for **Arlington Row,** a gabled group of 15th-century cottages, its biggest and most-photographed drawing card. The row is protected by the National Trust.

Arlington Mill Museum on the Cirencester-Burford Road (A433) (tel. 028574/368) dates from the 17th century and was in use as a mill until 1914. Mill machinery, agricultural implements, cobbler's and blacksmith's equipment, printing and weaving devices, and Victorian costumes and wedding finery are on display. There are William Morris and John Keble rooms, and you can see arts and crafts exhibits, including furniture. There is also pottery for sale. The museum is open from mid-March to October daily 10:30am to 7pm (or dusk, if earlier), from November to February on Sat. and Sun. Admission is £1.80 ($2.95) for adults, £1 ($1.65) for children.

WHERE TO STAY

Bibury is a good base for touring the old wool towns of the North Cotswolds.

Bibury Court Hotel, Bibury, Gloucestershire GL7 5NT (tel. 028574/337), is a Jacobean manor house built by Sir Thomas Sackville in 1633 (parts of it date from Tudor times). Its 8 acres of grounds are approached through a large gateway, the lawn extending to the encircling Coln River. The house was privately owned until it was turned into a hotel in 1968. The structure is built of Cotswold stone, with many gables, huge chimneys, leaded-glass stone-mullioned windows, and a formal graveled entryway. Inside there are many country manor furnishings, and antiques, as well as an open, stone, log-burning fireplace. In 17 rooms with baths, TVs, and phones, the rent is from £38 ($62.70) daily in a single, £52 ($85.80) to £60 ($99) in a double. Many of the rooms have four-poster beds, original oak paneling, and antiques. Meals are an event in the Coach House Restaurant, where dinners are priced from £18 ($29.70). Lunch bar meals cost from £5 ($8.25). After tea and biscuits in the drawing room, walk across the lawn along the river where you'll find a doorway leading to a little church.

Swan Hotel, Bibury, Gloucestershire GL7 5NW (tel. 028574/204), is a scene-stealer. Before you cross over the arched stone bridge spanning the Coln, pause and look at the vine-covered facade. Yes, it's the same view that has appeared on many a calendar. The former coaching inn will bed you down for the night in one of its 24 handsomely appointed chambers, all with baths and showers, phones, and TVs, charging £38.50 ($63.55) daily in a single, £68.50 ($113.05) in a double. A traditional English breakfast and VAT are included. All rooms have been modernized, and there are many comforts. The special feature of the Swan is the small stretch of trout stream reserved for guests. If you're just passing through for the day, you may want to stop over and order the £13.50 ($22.30) lunch or the £16.50 ($27.25) dinner. When you see the gardens at the Swan, your exploring days may be over.

8. Clanfield

Clanfield lies at the foot of the Cotswolds, near the upper reaches of the Thames. In the heart of "hunting country," it is convenient to Cheltenham and the Newbury race courses. Golf and fishing are available nearby. Clanfield lies 20 miles from Oxford, 8 miles from our last stopover in Burford, and 16 miles from Swindon, and also makes a center for visits to Blenheim Palace, Stratford-upon-Avon, Henley-on-Thames, and the Cotswold Wild Life Park, only a 10-minute drive from the following recommendation.

WHERE TO STAY AND DINE

A fine example of a 16th-century manor house, **The Plough,** Bourton Road, Clanfield, Oxfordshire OX8 2RB (tel. 036781/222), is widely considered to be the most attractive building in this area. The first-class restaurant is decorated in soft pastel shades, complemented by fine crystal and silver settings. A set three-course lunch is offered, costing £15 ($24.75), and dinners can be ordered à la carte for around £30 ($49.50), VAT included. The restaurant is open daily from 12:30 to 2:30pm and 7:30 to 9:30pm. You can enjoy drinks in the lounge bar in front of a huge fireplace, amid a wealth of beams and lots of old-world charm. The Plough has six beautiful, individually decorated bedrooms, two with showers in the bathrooms and the remaining with whirlpool baths. One room, Honeysuckle, has a four-poster bed, and another, Primrose, is made elegant by a canopied bed. All rooms have color TVs, trouser presses, hairdryers, and direct-dial phones. Bed and a full English breakfast costs £68 ($112.20) daily in a single, £115 ($189.75) in a double, with VAT included.

9. Burford and Minster Lovell

In Oxfordshire, as you go east or west along the A40, you can make interesting stops at Burford, right on the highway, or Minster Lovell, a short distance to the north of the main road.

BURFORD

The gateway to the Cotswolds, this unspoiled medieval town, built of Cotswold stone, is 19 miles to the west of Oxford, and 75 miles from London. Its fame rests largely on its early Norman church (c. 1116) and its High Street, lined with coaching inns. Oliver Cromwell passed this way, as did Charles II and Nell Gwynne. Burford was one of the last of the great wool centers, the industry surviving into

Victoria's reign. You may want to photograph the bridge across the Windrush River, where Queen Elizabeth I once stood. Burford is definitely equipped for tourists, as the antique shops along The High will testify.

Where to Stay and Dine

Whether you're staying over or simply stopping off for lunch, there's a choice of some romantic old inns.

Bay Tree Hotel, Sheep Street, Burford, Oxfordshire OX8 4LW (tel. 099382/ 3137), would astonish the former owner of this 400-year-old, stone-gabled home. Surely Sir Lawrence Tanfield would never have predicted that this stately old house would become a peaceful setting for retreat-seekers. In his time, he was the unpopular Lord Chief Baron of the Exchequer to Elizabeth I—and was not noted for his hospitality. But time has erased the bad memory, and the splendor of this Cotswold manor house remains. The house has oak-paneled rooms with stone fireplaces, where logs burn in chilly weather. There is a high-beamed hall with a minstrel's gallery. Room after room is furnished tastefully. The 20th-century comforts, such as TVs, phones, and baths in all 22 bedrooms, have been discreetly installed. And the beds are a far cry from the old rope-bottom contraptions of the days of Queen Elizabeth I. Try to get one of the rooms overlooking the terraced gardens at the rear of the house. The charge is £60 ($99) daily in singles, £95 ($156.75) in doubles.

Lamb Inn, Sheep Street, Burford, Oxfordshire OX8 4LR (tel. 099382/3155), is a thoroughbred Cotswold house, built solidly in 1430 of thick stones, with mullioned and leaded windows, many chimneys and gables, and a slate roof mossy with age. It opens onto a stone-paved rear garden, with a rose-lined walk and a shaded lawn. B&B costs from £45 ($74.25) per person daily. The 13 bedrooms are a mixture of today's comforts, such as good beds and plentiful hot water, and antiques. The public living rooms contain heavy oak beams, stone floors, window seats, Oriental rugs, and fine antiques (Chippendale, Tudor, Adam, Georgian, Jacobean). In the drinking lounge, a special beer, made in an adjoining brewery, is served. Light lunches and snacks are served in the bars and lounges, or in the garden in summer. Dinner as well as a traditional Sun. lunch are offered in the beamed dining room with a garden view. If you're dining here in the right season, you can feast on treats of the rivers or forest, such as salmon, trout, and venison.

Golden Pheasant Hotel, 91 High Street, Burford, Oxfordshire OX8 4RV (tel. 099382/3223), has both the oldest set of property deeds surviving in Burford, as well as a location on main street. In the 1400s it was the private home of a prosperous wool merchant, but began serving food and drink in the 1730s when it used to both brew and serve beer. Like many of its neighbors, it is capped with a slate roof and fronted with light-gray hand-chiseled stones. Inside, within view of dozens of old beams and a blazing fireplace, a candlelit restaurant serves both French and English specialties. The hotel offers 12 bedrooms, a pair with four-poster beds, but each with private bath, radio, TV, phone, and coffee-making equipment. Depending on the season, and with an English breakfast included, singles range from £45 ($74.25) to £55 ($90.75) daily and doubles or twins from £58 ($95.70) to £78 ($128.70).

MINSTER LOVELL

From Oxford along the A40, you pass through Witney. Soon after, you turn right at the Minster Lovell signpost, about half a mile off the highway between Witney and Burford. Long since passed by the main road, the village is visited because of **Minster Lovell Hall and Dovecote** (tel. 0993/775315). In ruins, the hall dates from the 1400s. The medieval dovecote with nesting boxes survives. An early Lovell is said to have hidden in the moated manor house and subsequently starved to death after a battle in the area. The hall and dovecote can be visited from Good Fri. to the end of September daily from 10am to 6pm, from 10am to 4pm off-season; closed Mon. Admission is 85p ($1.40) for adults, 40p (65¢) for children. The legend of the mistletoe bough originated in the village by the River Windrush. Minster Lovell is mainly built of Cotswold stone, with thatched or stone-slate roofs.

It's rather a pity that there is a forest of TV antennas, but the place is still attractive to photographers.

Where to Stay and Dine
The Old Swan Hotel, Main Street, Old Minster, Minster Lovell, Oxfordshire OX8 5RN (tel. 0993/774441), has been an inn for some 6 centuries. It offers a blend of Cotswold stone and half timbering. The Swan and the manor house (now in ruins) were once the two most important buildings in the village. Richard III was entertained by the Lovell family in the manor house, while his servants slept at the Swan. Polished flagstone floors and traditional log fires are remainders of those times. Today, the Old Swan offers modern comfort in historic surroundings. All 10 bedrooms have private baths, phones, mini-bars, and color TVs, renting for £48.50 ($80.05) daily in a single for B&B, or else £80 ($132) in a double. A four-poster suite for two rents for £92 ($151.80). Prices include a full English breakfast and VAT. In the beamed candlelit restaurant you can enjoy fine food, some of which is grown in the gardens of the hotel. A lunch costs from £12.50 ($20.65), with a fixed-price dinner going for £17.50 ($28.90). The inn is owned by a nearby conference center, Minster Lovell Mill, which contains 50 bedrooms. The conference center, made of honey-colored Cotswold stone, was once a very old mill. During the week it is filled with conventioneers, but on weekends it rents rooms to the general public at the same rates as the Old Swan.

10. Shipton-under-Wychwood

Taking the A361 road, en route from Burford to Chipping Norton, you arrive after a turn-off at the little village of Shipton-under-Wychwood in Oxfordshire. It's about 4 miles north of Burford; but don't blink or you'll pass it right by.

WHERE TO STAY AND DINE
The site of a hospice for dispensing aid to the poor operated by monks as part of the Bruern Abbey in the 13th century, **The Shaven Crown,** High Street, Shipton-under-Wychwood, Oxfordshire OX7 6BA (tel. 0993/830330), was built of rugged Cotswold stone during the reign of Queen Elizabeth I. It is on the main village road, and opens onto a triangular village green in the shadow of a church. Most of the nine rooms overlook a cobblestone courtyard and garden and have some antiques. Private baths have been installed in all bedrooms, as have phones and TVs. The charge for B&B is £26 ($42.90) daily in a single and £59 ($97.35) in a double. Half board is offered for £39.50 ($65.20) per person per day if you stay 2 or more days.

11. Chipping Norton

Just inside the Oxfordshire border is Chipping Norton, another gateway town to the Cotswolds. Since the days of Henry IV it has been an important market town, and its main street is a curiosity: built on a slope with one side higher than the other.

Chipping Norton was long known for its tweed mills. Also seek out its guildhall, its church, and its handsome almshouses, and search for the nearby prehistoric Rollright Stones, more than 75 stones forming a circle 100 feet in diameter—the "Stonehenge of the Cotswolds." Chipping Norton lies 11 miles from Burford, 20 miles from Oxford, and 21 miles from Stratford-upon-Avon.

WHERE TO STAY AND DINE
The town's best-known inn is the **White Hart,** High Street, Chipping Norton, Oxfordshire OX7 5AD (tel. 0608/642572), which stands in the center of this Cotswold town. Its facade overlooking the market place, the White Hart traces its origins

to Richard II in the 13th century. However, its stone exterior is from the 18th century. Once it was a favorite stopover for wayfarers between London and Worcester. The hotel still retains many of its historical mementos in its public rooms. In winter, fires greet guests as they did when this was a stopover for the coaching trade. The hotel has been modernized with many amenities, yet some of its Regency style is still intact. Guests gather for drinks in a stone-clad bar, with a log fire, before heading for the restaurant, serving British cookery. The bedrooms, 21 in all, are well furnished and comfortably appointed. Each unit contains a private bath or shower, color TV, and phone. There are only two singles, which rent for £37.50 ($61.90) a night. Standard doubles go for £55 ($90.75), rising to £75 ($123.75) in a four-poster bedroom.

The leading restaurant in town is **Vittles,** 7 Horsehair (tel. 0608/644490), which is a Cotswold stone cottage graced with a bay window, lying only a short walk from the market place. Ian and Eve Chapman (he's the chef and she directs service in the dining room) are the owners. Here diners enjoy traditional eating in elegant and stylish surroundings, with courteous service. The food is in the modern British style. Service is from noon to 1:45pm Mon. to Fri., and from 6:30 to 11pm Mon. to Sat.; closed Sun. A light lunch costs from £8 ($13.20) to £10 ($16.50), with a three-course dinner ranging from £15 ($24.75) to £25 ($41.25). A reasonably priced wine list of around 80 selections is also available, and reservations are needed.

An Old Mill in the Environs

Mill House Hotel & Restaurant, Kingham, Oxfordshire, OX7 6UH (tel. 060871/8188). In A.D. 1086 reference was made in the *Domesday Book* to a mill worth 44 pence in lease value situated at "Corsingham of the King." This same mill is a fine regional hotel today, where the nostalgia of days gone by merges with today. The Mill House Hotel envelops all that and it has been possible to infuse modern amenities without detracting from the original purpose of the buildings. There are comfortable lounges with log fires and old stone floors and oak beams. In the bar, the original ovens of the old bakehouse line the wall. The 21 bedrooms, all with private baths and showers, color TVs, radios, and phones, have been refurbished to a high standard as has the enlarged restaurant, now one of the finest in the Cotswolds. The B&B rate is £60 ($99) to £80 ($132) daily in a double, £45 ($74.25) in a single. The hotel has a winning chef, who offers excellent à la carte and fixed-price menus, and the wine list is based on some 175 bins. Even if you're a resident, you may want to call for a reservation. Lunch is daily from 12:30 to 2pm, with dinner served from 7 to 9:45pm. Dinners begin at £18 ($29.70). This establishment stands in some 10 acres of ground bounded by a trout stream.

---

12. Bourton-on-the-Water

In this scenic Cotswold village, you can be like Gulliver, voyaging first to Brobdingnag, then to Lilliput. If you imagine Bourton-on-the-Water as Brobdingnag, you can then visit Lilliput, at the **Old New Inn,** High Street (tel. 0451/20467). In the garden is a near-perfect and most realistic model village. It's open daily from 9:30am till dusk, and costs £1 ($1.65) for adults, 90p ($1.50) for children.

Bourton-on-the-Water is 85 miles from London, lying on the banks of the tiny Windrush River. If you're coming to the Cotswolds by train from London, the nearest rail station is in Moreton-on-Marsh, 8 miles away. Buses make connections with the trains, however.

Among the attractions in the area, **Birdland,** Rissington Road (tel. 0451/20689), is a handsomely designed garden set on about 8½ acres, containing some 1,200 birds of 361 different species. Included is the largest and most varied collection of penguins in any zoo, with underwater viewing. In the tropical house are hummingbirds. Many of the birds are on view in captivity for the first time. From March to November the hours for seeing these exotic birds and flowers are 10am to

6pm; other months, 10am to 4pm. Admission is £2.50 ($4.15) for adults and £1.80 ($2.95) for children up to 14.

WHERE TO STAY

Bourton-on-the-Water offers a handful of quite good accommodations.

Old New Inn, High Street, Bourton-on-the-Water, Cheltenham, Gloucestershire GL54 2AF (tel. 0451/20467), can lay claim to being the leading hostelry in the village. Right in the center, overlooking the river, it's a good example of Queen Anne design (the miniature model village in its garden was referred to earlier). Hungry or tired travelers are drawn to the old-fashioned comforts and cuisine of this most English inn. The B&B rate is from £25 ($41.25) per person nightly, including service charge and VAT. The 24 rooms are comfortable, with homelike furnishings, soft beds. Nine rooms have private baths. Non-residents are also welcome here for meals, with lunches at £5 ($8.25) and dinner from £15 ($24.75). You may want to spend an evening in the pub lounge, playing darts or chatting with the villagers.

Old Manse Hotel, Victoria Street, Bourton-on-the-Water, Cheltenham, Gloucestershire GL54 2BX (tel. 0451/20082), is reminiscent of the setting of Nathaniel Hawthorne's *Mosses from an Old Manse*. A gem architecturally, the ivy-covered hotel is by the slow-moving river that wanders through the village green. Built of Cotswold stone, with chimneys, dormers, and small-paned windows, it has been modernized inside, and all 12 rooms have private baths, color TVs, radios, and phones. The charge is £60 ($99) daily for two persons in a twin with private bath, £40 ($66) in a single. A continental breakfast is included in the rates. The inn's best feature is the stone fireplace in the dining room, and the wood-paneled bar is nice too. Dining is a treat here. The manse is closed during the first week in January.

Chester House Hotel and Motel, Victoria Street, Bourton-on-the-Water, Cheltenham, Gloucestershire GL54 2BS (tel. 0451/20286), is a weathered, 300-year-old, Cotswold-stone house built on the banks of the Windrush River. Owned and managed by the Davies family, the hotel is a convenient place at which to stay. It blends an old building with a row of stables converted into a comfortable motel. All the 23 bedrooms have private baths or showers, color TVs, and direct-dial phones. B&B rates are from £28 ($46.20) per person daily. The hotel also has an intimate bar and a stone-walled restaurant with a full restaurant license for serving drinks. Diners are served a reliable English cuisine, including Cotswold lamb. Guests are received from mid-February to mid-November.

A MUSEUM AT NORTHLEACH

Opened in 1981, the **Cotswold Countryside Collection,** Fosseway (Cotswold District Council) (tel. 0451/60715), is a museum of rural life displays. You can see the Lloyd-Baker collection of agricultural history, including wagons, horse-drawn implements, and tools, as well as a "seasons of the year" display. A Cotswold gallery records the social history of the area. "Below Stairs" is an exhibition of laundry, dairy, and kitchen. The museum's home was a house of correction, and its history is displayed in the reconstructed cellblock and courtroom. The museum is open daily from 10am to 5:30pm (from 2 to 5:30pm on Sun.). Admission is 80p ($1.30) for adults, 40p (65¢) for children. Northleach lies off the A40 between Burford and Cheltenham.

---

13. Stow-on-the-Wold

This Cotswold market town is unspoiled, in spite of the busloads of tourists who stop off en route to Broadway and Chipping Campden, about 10 miles away. The town is the highest in the Cotswolds, built on a wold about 800 feet above sea level. In its open market square, you can still see the stocks where offenders in days gone by were jeered at and punished by the townspeople with a rotten egg in the face. The final battle between the Roundheads and the Royalists took place in Stow-on-the-Wold. The town, which is really like a village, is used by many for exploring not only the Cotswold wool towns but also Stratford-upon-Avon, 21 miles away. The nearest rail station is at Moreton-in-Marsh, 4 miles away.

WHERE TO STAY AND DINE

Wyck Hill House, Burford Road, Stow-on-the-Wold, Cheltenham, Gloucestershire GL54 1HY (tel. 0451/31936), dates from 1720 when its stone walls were begun as the manor house for the parish church of Wyck-Rissington. After a long and varied history, it was discovered in 1984 by two Texas-born Anglophiles who restored it to elegance before selling it to a small exclusive hotel group. One wing of the manor house, it was discovered, rested on the foundations of a Roman villa. Today, Wyck Hill is one of the most sophisticated country hotels in the region, lying on 100 acres of grounds and gardens 2 miles south of Stow-on-the-Wold. The opulent interior pays attention to 18th-century authenticity. Room after room leads onto paneled libraries and Adam sitting rooms. Well-furnished bedrooms, 32 in all, are in the main hotel, in the coach house annex, or in the orangery. Accommodations range in price from £80 ($132) to £150 ($247.50) for two persons daily. Excellent food is also served, a three-course luncheon costing £14.50 ($23.95), an à la carte dinner going for around £28 ($46.20).

Stow Lodge Hotel, the Square, Stow-on-the-Wold, Cheltenham, Gloucestershire GL54 1AB (tel. 0451/30485), dominates the market place, but is set back far enough to maintain its aloofness. Its gardens, honeysuckle growing over the stone walls, diamond-shaped windows, gables, and many chimneys, capture the best of country living, while letting you anchor right into the heart of town. Mr. and Mrs. Jux, the owners, who are partners with their daughter and son-in-law, Mr. and Mrs. Hartley, offer 22 ample, well-furnished bedrooms, all with private baths, radios, phones, TVs, central heating, and hot beverage facilities. Depending on the season, the daily rate in a double or twin ranges from £50 ($82.50) to £67 ($110.55) with a full English breakfast included. Arrange to have your afternoon tea out back by the flower garden. The owners discovered an old (approximately 1770) open stone fireplace in their lounge and since have offered log fires as an added attraction.

The Grapevine Hotel, Sheep Street, Stow-on-the-Wold, Cheltenham, Gloucestershire GL54 1AU (tel. 0451/30344), mingles urban sophistication with reasonable prices, rural charm, and intimacy. Known both for its hotel and restaurant, it is one of the most innovative and charming places to stay in this much-visited village. It was named after the ancient vine whose tendrils shade and shelter the beautiful conservatory restaurant. The reading room, comfortable lounge, and cozy bar with Victorian accessories create a warm ambience for tea, bar snacks, or dinner. Full meals feature English, French, and Italian cuisine and are served from 7 to 9:30pm daily. Bar snacks are served at midday. Dinners are more elaborate, costing from £22 ($36.30) and including, perhaps, turkey scallops with white wine sauce, beef filet topped with Stilton, or, for the vegetarian, garlic mushroom mille-feuilles.

The transformation of a pair of Cotswold-stone-sided houses into this hotel was the personal statement of Sandra Elliott. She supervised the decor of the 17 bedrooms, each with a private bath or shower, tasteful furnishings, color TV, phone, radio, hairdryer, and tea and coffee makers. The dinner, bed, and breakfast rate is £44 ($72.60) per person daily, with B&B going for £33 ($54.45) per person. A "bargain break" rate is also available.

The Fosse Manor Hotel, Fosse Way, Stow-on-the-Wold, Cheltenham, Gloucestershire GL54 1AX (tel. 0451/30354). Its stone walls and neo-Gothic gables are almost concealed by strands of ivy, which threaten to engulf even the windows. It lies about a mile south of Stow-on-the-Wold along the A429 near the site of an ancient Roman road that used to bisect England. From your high stone-sided window, you might enjoy a view of a landscaped garden with a sunken lily pond, flagstone walks, and an old-fashioned sundial. Inside, the interior is conservatively modernized with such touches as a padded and upholstered bar and a dining room. The 20 bedrooms are homelike, with matching fabrics and wallpaper. Accommodations have private baths or showers, TVs, and phones, and two of the rooms are favorites of honeymooners. Overnight rates are £35 ($57.75) to £45 ($74.25) in a single, £58 ($95.70) to £85 ($140.25) in a double, including breakfast, VAT, and service.

14. Lower Swell

Near Stow-on-the-Wold, Lower Swell and Upper Swell are twins, both small Cotswolds villages. The hamlets are not to be confused with Upper and Lower Slaughter.

WHERE TO STAY AND DINE
You may want to anchor in for the night or stop for a meal at the **Old Farmhouse Hotel,** Lower Swell, Stow-on-the-Wold, Cheltenham, Gloucestershire GL54 1LF (tel. 0451/30232). A small, intimate hotel in the heart of the Cotswolds, it is 1¼ miles west of Stow-on-the-Wold on B4068. It was converted from a 16th-century farmhouse. The hotel has been completely refurbished and the original fireplaces restored, once again blazing with log fires. The relaxed atmosphere, together with excellent food and wine, has made this a popular stop for visitors, so reserving a room before arrival is strongly recommended. The owner has 13 bedrooms to rent, all with color TVs and 11 with private baths. Two accommodations under the eaves share a bath. All the units are different because of the building's farmhouse origin. All prices include a cooked English breakfast and service. The B&B rate in a double or twin-bedded room ranges from £42 ($69.30) daily with a shared bath up to £68 ($112.20) with a private bath. Dinner is served daily from 7pm, with last orders taken at 9pm. The table d'hôte menu is changed daily, costing £12.50 ($20.65). The hotel has a secluded walled garden and ample private parking.

15. The Slaughters

Midway between Bourton-on-the-Water and Stow-on-the-Wold are the twin villages of Upper and Lower Slaughter. Don't be put off by the name because these are two of the prettiest villages in the Cotswolds. Actually the name "Slaughter" was a corruption of "de Sclotre," the original Norman landowner. The houses are constructed of honey-colored Cotswold stone, and a stream meanders right through the street, providing a home for the ducks that wander freely about, begging scraps from kindly visitors. In Upper Slaughter you can visit a fine example of a 17th-century Cotswold manor house.

WHERE TO STAY AND DINE
In its own private grounds, surrounded by flower beds and shady trees, the **Lower Slaughter Manor,** Lower Slaughter, Cheltenham, Gloucestershire GL54 2HP (tel. 0451/20456), is steeped in a thousand years of history, yet it offers the facilities of a modern, first-class hotel. Even before the Norman Conquest a manor house stood on this spot, becoming at some period a convent housing the nuns of the Bridgetine Order of Syon for a few centuries. A reminder of those days is a decorated ceiling on which pious words are used as a motif. After the break-up of religious houses and expulsion of the nuns, the house was given to the high sheriff of Gloucestershire in 1608, and he rebuilt it much as it is today. The west wing was added, as was the stable block with its central clock tower and great stone fireplace.

The 19 bedrooms are handsome and spacious, all with baths, color TVs, radios, and direct-dial phones. Some have four-poster beds. Double rooms are rented for single occupancy for £75 ($123.75) nightly for bed, early morning tea, a continental breakfast, and VAT. As a double, the charge is £90 ($148.50) to £155 ($255.75). The four-poster rooms cost £165 ($272.25). In the manor's restaurant you can enjoy traditional English country cooking, with each meal cooked fresh using locally grown produce, herbs from the house's gardens, honey from Cotswold bees, local free-range eggs, and homemade preserves. Guests can use the heated, indoor swimming pool with a sauna and a solarium, or in good weather, the croquet lawn and tennis court.

Lords of the Manor Hotel, Upper Slaughter, Cheltenham, Gloucestershire GL54 2JD (tel. 0451/20243), is a 17th-century house standing on several acres of rolling fields and gardens that include a stream flowing through the grounds in which guests fish for brown trout. Modernized in its amenities, the hotel has still been successful in maintaining the quiet country-house atmosphere of 300 years ago. The 30 guestrooms are equipped with private baths, phones, and TVs, and many rooms have views of the Cotswold hills. Half of the rooms are in a sympathetically converted old barn and granary. Rates, which include a full English breakfast, VAT, and service, range from £90 ($148.50) to £135 ($222.75) daily for a double, depending on the plumbing. Singles cost from £65 ($107.25). The walls in the lounge bar are hung with family portraits of the original lords of the manor. Another bar overlooks the garden, and chintz and antiques are everywhere. The country atmosphere is carried into the dining room as well, with its antiques and mullioned windows. All the well-prepared dishes are fresh and homecooked. You'll pay an average of about £25 ($41.25) for an à la carte dinner with dessert and coffee. The cooking is modern English with some French influence.

16. Moreton-in-Marsh

As it's connected by rail to Paddington Station in London (83 miles away), Moreton-in-Marsh is an important center for train passengers headed for the Cotswolds. It is very near many of the villages of interest—Bourton-on-the-Water, 8 miles; Stow-on-the-Wold, 4 miles; Broadway, 8 miles; Chipping Campden, 7 miles; Stratford-upon-Avon, 17 miles away.

Each of the Cotswold towns has its distinctive characteristics. In Moreton-in-Marsh, look for the 17th-century market hall and its old curfew tower, and then walk down its High Street, where Roman legions trudged centuries ago (the town once lay on the ancient Fosse Way). Incidentally, if you base here, don't take the name Moreton-in-Marsh too literally. Marsh derives from an old word meaning border.

WHERE TO STAY

In a 300-year-old structure, the **Manor House Hotel,** High Street, Moreton-in-Marsh, Gloucestershire GL56 0LJ (tel. 0608/50501), is complete with its own ghost, a priest's hiding hole, a secret passage, and a moot room used centuries ago by local merchants to settle arguments over wool exchanges. On the main street, it is formal, yet gracious, and its rear portions reveal varying architectural periods of design. Here, the vine-covered walls protect the garden. Inside are many living rooms, one especially intimate with leather chairs and a fireplace-within-a-fireplace, ideal for drinks and the exchange of "bump-in-the-night" stories. The hotel has a heated indoor pool, a spa bath, and a sauna. You can't miss on most of the 38 bedrooms, as they are tastefully furnished, often with antiques or fine reproductions. Many have fine old desks set in front of window ledges, with a view of the garden and ornamental pond. Rooms contain private baths or showers, color TVs, and phones. Singles cost from £30 ($49.50) to £51 ($84.15) daily, with doubles paying from £72 ($118.80) to £82 ($135.30). A favorite nook is the bar, with its garden view through leaded Gothic windows. Evening meals in the two-level dining room are candlelit. A table d'hôte lunch goes for £12 ($19.80), and dinner is £18 ($29.70).

Redesdale Arms, High Street, Moreton-in-Marsh, Gloucestershire GL56 0AW (tel. 0608/50308), owned by Michael C. Elvis and Patricia M. Seedhouse, a long-enduring favorite, is one of the best-kept coaching inns in the Cotswolds. It has been a landmark along the old Fosse Way for some 2 centuries. Some of the look of 1774 is still evident, but the inn has been considerably upgraded. Guests gravitate to the bar, where drinks are served in front of a 6-foot-high stone fireplace in winter. In warmer months, the courtyard is a favorite spot for having a leisurely snack or drink. Each of the 17 bedrooms is tastefully and individually furnished. All of the units contain private baths, phones, and TVs. Singles rent for £44.50 ($73.45) daily, with doubles costing £65 ($107.25). The inn is also well known for its meals: a three-course dinner costs £12.95 ($21.35); a full à la carte meal is also offered. Bar snacks are available at lunch and in the evening and on Sun., you can enjoy the classic English roast lunch in full for £9.50 ($15.70). The dining room is open seven days a week.

The White Hart Royal Hotel, High Street, Moreton-in-Marsh, Gloucestershire GL56 0BA (tel. 0608/50731), is a mellow old Cotswold inn. It's also another one of the hostelries graced by Charles I (in 1644), who did a lot of sleeping around. The inn provides the amenities of today without compromising the personality of yesteryear. There are 18 well-furnished bedrooms, with hot and cold running water (9 with private bath), innerspring mattresses, and a few antiques intermixed with basic 20th-century pieces. Rooms are equipped with phones and TVs. Singles cost £52 ($85.80) daily, and twins or doubles with bath go for £75 ($123.75). All rates include service and VAT. The bar is built of irregular Cotswold stone. You can have drinks in front of the 10-foot open fireplace.

17. Broadway

This is the best-known Cotswold village. Its wide and beautiful High Street is flanked with honey-colored stone buildings with mullioned windows remarkable for the harmony of their style and design. Overlooking the Vale of Evesham, Broadway is virtually mobbed with tourists in summer, a major stopover for bus tours. That it retains its charm in spite of the invasion is a credit to its character.

Broadway lies near Evesham at the southern tip of Hereford and Worcester. Many of the prime attractions of the Cotswolds as well as Shakespeare Country lie within easy reach of Broadway. Stratford-upon-Avon is only 15 miles away. The nearest rail stations are at Evesham and Moreton-in-Marsh.

WHERE TO STAY

For lodgings, Broadway has the dubious distinction of sheltering the most expensive inn in the Cotswolds. Even the guesthouses can command a good price—and get it.

Lygon Arms, High Street, Broadway, Hereford and Worcester WR12 7DU (tel. 0386/852255), a many-gabled structure whose mullioned windows look right out on the road in the center of town, basks in its reputation as one of the greatest old English inns. In the rear it opens onto a private garden, with 3 acres of lawns, trees, and borders of flowers, stone walls with roses, and nooks for tea or sherry. The oldest portions, built of fieldstone with a mossy slate roof, date from at least 1532, but builders many times since have made their additions. King Charles I reputedly drank with his friends in one of the oak-lined chambers, and later, his principal enemy, Oliver Cromwell, slept here on the night before the Battle of Worcester. Today, an earlier century is evoked by the almost overwhelmingly charming cluster of antique-laden public rooms. These include cavernous fireplaces, smoke-stained paneling, 18th-century pieces, and polished brass. You dine in the oak-paneled great hall, with a Tudor fireplace, a vaulted ceiling, and a minstrels' gallery. Many but not all the 62 rooms are in the antique style. A new wing offers more 20th-century styling. If you choose to stay here, singles cost from £90 ($148.50) to £115 ($189.75) daily, and doubles, £132 ($217.80) to £195 ($321.75), with a continental breakfast and VAT included. Each room contains a private bath or shower, radio, TV, phone, hairdryer, and trouser press. New for your visit will be a country club adjoining the old inn.

The club building was created from an 18th-century abattoir, formerly owned by pie makers and the site of the only butchery in England run by a clergyman. Many health and leisure facilities are available here, including a large swimming pool, a sauna, beauty therapy facilities, and a gym. Guests of the Lygon Arms receive a complimentary membership.

Dormy House, Willersey Hill, Broadway, Hereford and Worcester WR12 7LF (tel. 0386/852711), 2 miles southeast of Broadway on the A44, is a manor house standing high on a hill above the village, with views in all directions. Its spectacular position has made it a favorite place for those who desire either a meal, afternoon tea, or lodgings. Halfway between Broadway and Chipping Campden, it was created from a sheep farm. The owners transformed it, furnishing the 17th-century farmhouse with a few antiques, good soft beds, and full central heating, extending these amenities to an old adjoining timbered barn, which they converted into studio rooms, with open-beamed ceilings. All of the 48 accommodations have color TVs, clock radios, and private baths. Units in the main house include suites, even a penthouse, renting for £125 ($206.25). Singles cost £49 ($80.85) to £65 ($107.25) daily, depending on the standard of the room. Doubles, ranging from small to twin to four-poster units, are priced from £90 ($148.50) to £115 ($189.75). Rates include a full English breakfast and VAT. The establishment serves excellent cuisine, a table d'hôte luncheon costing £16 ($26.40), and a fixed-price dinner going for £23 ($37.95) both with coffee included. The cellar contains a superb selection of wines. Bar meals range from around £5 ($8.25). Bowls of fresh flowers adorn tables and alcoves throughout the hotel.

Buckland Manor, Buckland, Broadway, Gloucestershire WR12 7LY (tel. 0386/852626), about 2 miles south of Broadway via the B4632, across the county line in Gloucestershire, is an imposing slate-roofed manor house ringed with fences of Cotswold stone, green lawns, lambs, and daffodils. Its jutting chimneys rise a few steps from the Buckland church, with its darkened stone tower. The core of the manor house was erected in the 13th century, with wings added in succeeding centuries, especially the 19th. Adrienne and Barry Berman poured labor, love, and money into making this an exquisitely furnished property, with 11 bedrooms to rent. The Oak Room, with a four-poster bed and burnished paneling, occupies what used to be a private library. In each of the rooms, leaded windows overlook gardens and grazing land with Highland cattle and Jacob sheep. Even the oversize bathrooms each contain at least one antique, as well as carpeting and modern plumbing, and all the rooms have color TVs and phones. Doubles cost from £135 ($222.75) to £210 ($346.50) per night. There are no singles; however, single occupancy of a double room ranges from £125 ($206.25) to £150 ($247.50). Prices include early morning tea, a full English breakfast, and VAT. French-inspired meals, served in the elegant dining room with a baronial fireplace, cost from £20 ($33). Children under 12 are not accommodated. The hotel is closed for 3 weeks between January and February.

Broadway Hotel, the Green, Broadway, Hereford and Worcester WR12 7AB (tel. 0386/852401), is right on the village green, perhaps one of the most colorful houses in Broadway. It is a converted 15th-century house, formerly used by the abbots of Pershore, combining the half-timbered look of the Vale of Evesham with the stone of the Cotswolds. While keeping its old-world charm, the hotel has been modernized and converted to provide comforts. All 24 rooms have private baths or showers, color TVs, hot beverage facilities, central heating, and bedside phone. A single costs £33 ($54.45) daily, and doubles go for £62 ($102.30) to £76 ($125.40). All tariffs include an English breakfast, service, and VAT. One of the rooms with full private bath has a four-poster bed. The cooking is fine, the service personal, the dining room attractive, the bedrooms pleasantly furnished. The comfortable cocktail bar is well stocked.

Collin House Hotel and Restaurant, Collin Lane, Broadway, Hereford and Worcester WR12 7PB (tel. 0386/858354), was a 16th-century farmhouse built of Cotswold stone. Transformed into a hotel, it sits on a country lane in 8 acres of gardens and orchards. The seven cozy bedrooms are named for flowers that grow here in profusion. Large structural timbers, tasteful wallpaper, private baths, and mullioned windows make the rooms attractive. Wild Rose, with its sloped ceiling, is probably the most romantic. Singles cost £38 ($62.70) daily, with doubles going for £75 ($123.75), with a full English breakfast (minimum two nights). A bar offers seating beside an inglenook fireplace. Traditional English food, flavorfully and freshly prepared, is served in the evening by candlelight in a room with stone-rimmed windows and ceiling beams. A three-course evening meal costs £16.50 ($27.25). At noon informal bar lunches are served beside the fire. The hotel lies a mile west of Broadway along the A44. From Broadway, follow the signs to Evesham before turning right onto Collin Lane.

WHERE TO DINE

Set back from the main street, **Hunter's Lodge Restaurant,** High Street (tel. 0386/853247), is surrounded by its own lawns, flowerbeds, and shady trees. The stone gables are partially covered with ivy, and the windows are deep-set with mullions and leaded panes. There is a formal entrance, with a circular drive and a small foyer furnished with antiques. The Swiss chef/proprietor is Kurt Friedli. His wife, Dottie, greets you, discusses the menu, and makes sure you have everything you want in the way of food and service. That might include rabbit casserole, wild duck with orange and fresh cream, or two quails on a skewer grilled with bacon and apples and finished with apple brandy. In summer you can eat in the garden. Dottie says she doesn't try to make "every chair pay the maximum." If somebody wants only one course, that's all right with her. Three courses at dinner will cost from £20 ($33) per person. Lunch is lighter and simpler—perhaps chicken liver pâté followed by sea bream with herb butter and vegetables, topped off by a homemade dessert, a meal costing about £12 ($19.80). Lunch is served from 12:30 to 2pm and dinner from 7:30 to 10pm; closed on Sun. night and all day Mon.

---

18. Chipping Campden

The English themselves, regardless of how often they visit the Cotswolds, are attracted in great numbers to this town. Off the main road, it's easily accessible to major points of interest, and double-decker buses frequently run through here on their way to Oxford (36 miles away) or Stratford-upon-Avon (12 miles away).

On the northern edge of the Cotswolds above the Vale of Evesham, Campden, a Saxon settlement, was recorded in the *Domesday Book.* In medieval times, rich merchants built homes of Cotswold stone along its model High Street, described by the historian G. M. Trevelyan as "the most beautiful village street now left in the island." The houses have been so well preserved that Chipping Campden to this day remains a gem of the Middle Ages. Its church dates from the 15th century, and its old market hall is the loveliest in the Cotswolds. Look also for its almshouses. They and the market hall were built by a great wool merchant, Sir Baptist Hicks, whose tomb is in the church.

WHERE TO STAY AND DINE

Here are several good choices, all in the medium-priced range.

Noel Arms Hotel, High Street, Chipping Campden, Gloucestershire GL55 6AT (tel. 0386/840317), may make you a snob. You just may assume a title for the night, dreaming that this is your personal manor house, with its staff of servants. Dating back to the 14th century, the Noel Arms is a famous establishment. All 26 rooms have private baths, direct-dial phones, TVs, and tea and coffee makers. Singles rent for £41.50 ($68.50) daily, doubles going for £55 ($90.75), and doubles with four-poster beds costing £65 ($107.25). Included in the prices are a full English breakfast and VAT. Rooms are divided between the main building and an annex. You can drive your car under the covered archway and into the old posting yard, where parking is private. The food here always draws praise. Lunch averages £8

($13.20) and dinner runs £13.50 ($22.30) to £16.50 ($27.25), if you order from the à la carte menu. The food is traditional English: poached salmon, roast sirloin of beef with Yorkshire pudding, roast leg of lamb with onion sauce, steak hollandaise, apple and loganberry pie. There's a private sitting room for residents, but you may prefer the lounge, with its 12-foot-wide fireplace. The adjoining room is the public tavern—public in the sense that it's frequented by the locals. It's almost too quaint: old worn curved settles where you can drink beer from mugs of pewter, and soak up an atmosphere enhanced by racks of copper, brass pans, medallions, and oak tables and chairs worn from centuries of use.

Cotswold House Hotel, the Square, Chipping Campden, Gloucestershire GL55 6AN (tel. 0386/840330), is a stately, formal Regency house dating from 1800. Right in the heart of the village, opposite the old wool market, it is run by Mr. and Mrs. Robert Greenstock. They have brought a high taste level to this handsome old house, set in 1½ acres of tended, walled garden with shaded seating. They are rightfully proud of the winding Regency staircase in the reception hall. All 15 bedrooms, each with private bath, TV, and phone, have been renovated. They are individually furnished with themes ranging from Gothic to French to military, with many others included along the way. There is even an Indian Room complete with tiger's head. Singles rent for £65 ($107.25) to £75 ($123.75) daily, and doubles or twins run £59 ($97.35) to £72 ($118.80). A deluxe four-poster room goes for £81.50 ($134.50). All tariffs include full breakfast and VAT. You can dine either in the restaurant, which serves first-class food, a combination of the best of English and French, in a formal, elegant room, or else in Greenstocks All-Day Eaterie, open daily from 9:30am to the last orders at 9:30pm. Here light dishes and meals are served.

Kings Arms Hotel, the Square, Chipping Campden, Gloucestershire GL55 6AW (tel. 0386/840256), stands right in the center. It is partly Georgian, partly much older, a pretty house with a large garden from which come the fresh vegetables for your good dinner. All the 14 accommodations are well furnished and spotlessly clean but only two have a private bath. TV and phones are in the communal rooms. Singles cost £25 ($41.25) a night, with doubles going for £40 ($66) to £50 ($82.50). This hotel has a high reputation for its cooking, and over the years has won many awards. The traditional, English-style Sun. lunch is offered at £9.95 ($16.40). However, a regular set dinner is featured at £14.50 ($23.95). Bar snacks, incidentally, are an inexpensive way to sample some gourmet dishes here.

In the Environs

Even more desirable than the accommodations of Chipping Campden are those of **Charingworth Manor Hotel,** Charingworth, near Chipping Campden, Gloucestershire GL55 6NS (tel. 038678/555), which traces its origins back to Tudor days. Actually, a manor of some sort stood on this spot at the time of the *Domesday Book*. In the 1930s the house was host to such illustrious guests as T.S. Eliot, author of *The Wasteland*. The hamlet of Charingworth lies 3¼ miles east of Chipping Campden. Charingworth rents 19 bedrooms, of which 7 luxuriously furnished rooms and one sumptuous suite are situated in the main house. Equally well-appointed rooms lie in the converted east wing. Jacobean additions were made onto the manor, and today's country home has been completely restored with sensitivity to preserve its old character. All its bedrooms have private baths and many amenities such as phones and TVs. Singles rent for £80 ($132) nightly, with doubles costing £95 ($156.75) to £195 ($321.75). Guests can enjoy cocktails as well as first-class wines and formal service. With its honey-colored stone and slate roofs, this manor house stands on its own 55 acres of grounds.

XIII

STRATFORD AND THE HEART OF ENGLAND

1. STRATFORD-UPON-AVON

2. WARWICK

3. KENILWORTH CASTLE

4. COVENTRY

5. HEREFORD AND WORCESTER

6. SHROPSHIRE

7. STAFFORDSHIRE

So close to London, so rich in fascination, the Shakespeare Country in the heart of England is the district, other than London, most visited by North Americans. Many who don't recognize the county name, Warwickshire, know its foremost tourist town, Stratford-upon-Avon, birthplace of England's greatest writer.

The county and its neighboring shires form a land of industrial cities, green fields, and sleepy market towns—dotted with buildings, some of which have changed little since Shakespeare's time. Here are many of the places that have magic for overseas visitors, not only Stratford-upon-Avon, but also Warwick and Kenilworth castles, as well as Coventry Cathedral.

Those who have time to penetrate deeper into the chapter will find elegant spa towns, such as Great Malvern, historic cathedral cities such as Hereford and Worcester, and industrial archeology at Stoke-on-Trent (the famous potteries). Scenery in Shropshire ranges from untamed borderlands to gentle plains that give way in the north to wooded areas and meres.

1. Stratford-upon-Avon

This town has a phenomenal tourist trade. Actor David Garrick really launched it in 1769 when he organized the first of the Bard's birthday celebrations. It is no secret by now, of course, that William Shakespeare was born in Stratford-upon-Avon on April 23, 1564. Surprisingly little is known about his early life, as the frankest of his biographers concede. Perhaps because documentation is so lacking about the writer, much useless conjecture has arisen (did Elizabeth I really write the plays?).

But the view that Francis Bacon or anyone else wrote Shakespeare's works would certainly stir up *The Tempest,* if suggested to the innkeepers of Stratford-upon-Avon. Admittedly, however, some of the stories and legends connected with Shakespeare's days in Stratford are largely fanciful, invented belatedly to amuse and entertain the vast number of literary fans making the pilgrimage.

Today's magnet, in addition to Shakespeare's birthplace, is the Royal Shakespeare Theatre, where Britain's foremost actors perform in a long season that lasts from Easter until January. Stratford-upon-Avon is also a good center for trips to Warwick Castle, Kenilworth Castle, Sulgrave Manor (ancestral home of George Washington), and Coventry Cathedral. The market town lies 91 miles from London, 40 from Oxford, and 8 from Warwick.

GETTING THERE

A service allowing you to spend the entire day (or several days) in Stratford and Shakespeare's Country is the **Shakespeare Connection "Road and Rail Link,"** leaving from London's Euston Station Mon. to Fri. at 8:40, 10:10, and 10:40am and 12:40, 4:40, and 5:10pm; on Sat. at 8:40 and 10:40am and 12:40, 4:40, and 5:10pm; and on Sun. at 9:40am and 6:10pm. This is a safe, sure way to attend the Royal Shakespeare Theatre and return to London on the same day. If you only want to attend the evening performance at the theater, again the Shakespeare Connection is your best bet, trains leaving London at 4:40 or 5:10pm Mon. to Sat. Returns to London are timed to fit theater performances, with departure at 11:15pm from either the Guide Friday Ltd. office at the Civic Hall, 14 Rother St., or just opposite the theater. The service is the fastest way of reaching Stratford from London, journey time averaging 2 hours. It is operated by **British Rail** and **Guide Friday** (tel. 0789/294466). Prices are £20 ($33) for a one-way fare, £22.50 ($37.15) for a round-trip ticket valid for 3 months. Ask for a Shakespeare Connection ticket at London's Euston Station or at any British Rail London Travel Centre. BritRail pass holders using the service simply pay the bus fare to Stratford-upon-Avon from Coventry, £4.50 ($7.45) one way, £6 ($9.90) for a round-trip ticket.

TOURS AND TOURIST SERVICES

A tourist reception center for Stratford-upon-Avon and Shakespeare's Country is operated by **Guide Friday Ltd.,** the Civic Hall, 14 Rother St. (tel. 0789/294466). The center dispenses free maps and brochures on the town and area and operates tours. Also available is a full range of tourist services, including accommodation booking, car rental, and theater tickets. In summer, the center is open daily from 9am to 7pm. In winter, hours are from 9am to 5:30pm Mon. to Fri., from 9am to 4pm Sat., and from 9:30am to 4pm Sun.

Guided tours of Stratford-upon-Avon leave the Guide Friday Tourism Centre daily. In summer, aboard open-top double-decker buses, departures are every 15 minutes from 9:30am to 5:30pm. The tour can be a 1-hour panoramic ride, or you can get off at any or all of the Shakespeare's Birthplace Trust properties. Anne Hathaway's Cottage and Mary Arden's House are the two logical stops to make outside the town. Tour tickets are valid all day for you to hop on and off the buses. The price for these tours is £4 ($6.60) per person. Tours are also offered to Warwick Castle, Kenilworth Castle, and Charlecote Park, costing £7 ($11.55) per person; Cotswold Country Villages, £10 ($16.50) per person; Cotswold Country Pubs, £10 ($16.50) per person; and Blenheim Palace and Bladon (the Churchill story tour), £10 ($16.50) per person. Tour prices do not include entrance fees at the stops made.

Caught Without a Room?

During the long theater season, the hotels in Stratford-upon-Avon are jam-packed, and you may run into difficulty if you arrive without a reservation. However, you can go to the **Tourist Information Centre** (tel. 0789/293127) from April to the end of October 9am to 5:30pm; November to the end of March from 10:30am to 4:30pm Mon. to Sat. A staff person who is experienced in finding accommodation for travelers in all budget categories will telephone and endeavor to book a room for you in the price range you are seeking. The fee for room reservations made is 10% of the first night's stay (B&B rate only) deductible from the visitor's final bill.

It is also possible to reserve accommodation if you write well enough in advance. By writing to the Information Centre, you'll be spared having to get in touch with several hotels on your own and running the risk of getting turned down. If you do write, specify the price range and the number of beds required. The center often gets vague letters, and the staff doesn't know whether to book you into a private suite at the Shakespeare Hotel or else lend you a cot to put in front of the Royal Shakespeare Theatre: do be specific. For this postal "book-a-bed-ahead" service, the charge is £2.65 ($4.35), payable in pounds sterling only. The complete address is The Information Centre, Judith Shakespeare's House, 1 High St., Stratford-upon-Avon, Warwickshire, CV37 6AU.

WHAT TO SEE AND DO

Besides the attractions on the periphery of Stratford, there are many Elizabethan and Jacobean buildings in this colorful town—many of them administered by the **Shakespeare Birthplace Trust**. One ticket—costing £5 ($8.25) for adults, £2 ($3.30) for children—will permit you to visit the five most important sights. You should pick up the ticket if you're planning to do much sightseeing (obtainable at your first stopover at any one of the Trust properties). The properties are open all year except Good Fri. morning, December 24 to December 26, and the morning of January 1. From March 25 to October 27, hours are from 9am to 6pm Mon. to Sat., from 10am to 6pm Sun. From October 28 to March 30, hours are from 9am to 4:30pm Mon. to Sat. On Sun. in winter, only Shakespeare's Birthplace and Anne Hathaway's Cottage are open, hours being from 1:30 to 4:30pm. The other three properties (Mary Arden's House, Hall's Croft, and New Place/Nash's House) are closed on Sun. in winter. Last admissions all year are 30 minutes before closing time.

For further information concerning the Trust's activities, send a stamped (English postage, please), self-addressed envelope to the Director, the Shakespeare Centre, Henley Street, Stratford-upon-Avon, Warwickshire CV37 6QW (tel. 0789/204016).

Shakespeare's Birthplace

On Henley Street, the son of a glover and whittawer, the Bard was born on St. George's day (April 23) in 1564, and died 52 years later on the same day. Filled with Shakespeare memorabilia, including a portrait, and furnishings of the writer's time, the Trust property is a half-timbered structure, dating from the early years of the 16th century. The house was bought by public donors in 1847 and preserved as a national shrine. You can visit the oak-beamed living room, the bedroom where Shakespeare was born, a fully equipped kitchen of the period (look for the "babyminder"), and a Shakespeare Museum, illustrating his life and times. Later, you can walk through the garden out back. It is estimated that some 660,000 visitors pass through the house annually. If visited separately, admission is £2 ($3.30) for adults, 80p ($1.30) for children. Next door to the birthplace is the modern Shakespeare Centre, built to commemorate the 400th anniversary of the Bard's birth. It serves both as the administrative headquarters of the Birthplace Trust and as a library and study center. An extension to the original center, opened in 1981, includes a visitors' center providing reception facilities for all those coming to the Birthplace.

Anne Hathaway's Cottage

One mile from Stratford-upon-Avon, in the hamlet of Shottery, is the thatched, wattle-and-daub cottage where Anne Hathaway lived before her marriage to the poet. In sheer charm, it is the most interesting and most photographed, it would seem, of the Trust properties. The Hathaways were yeoman farmers, and—aside from its historical interest—the cottage provides a rare insight into the life of a fami-

GLOUCESTER, WORCESTER, AND WARWICK

ly of Shakespeare's day. If the poet came a-courtin', he must have been treated as a mere teenager, as he married Miss Hathaway when he was only 18 years old and she much older. Many of the original furnishings, including the courting settle and utensils, are preserved inside the house, which was occupied by descendants of Shakespeare's wife until 1892. After a visit through the house, you'll surely want to linger in the garden and orchard. You can either walk across the meadow to Shottery from Evesham Place in Stratford (pathway marked), or else take a bus from Bridge Street. The admission is £1.70 ($2.80) for adults, 70p ($1.15) for children.

New Place/Nash's House

This site is on Chapel Street, where Shakespeare retired in 1610, a prosperous man to judge from the standards of his day. He died there 6 years later, at the age of 52. Regrettably, only the site of his former home remains today, as the house was torn down. You enter the gardens through Nash's House (Thomas Nash married Elizabeth Hall, a granddaughter of the poet). Nash's House has 16th-century period rooms and an exhibition illustrating the archeology and history of Stratford. The heavily visited knott garden adjoins the site, and represents the style of a fashionable Elizabethan garden. New Place itself has its own great garden, which once belonged to Shakespeare. Here, the Bard planted a mulberry tree, so popular with latter-day visitors to Stratford that the cantankerous owner of the garden chopped it down. The mulberry tree that grows there today is said to have been planted from a cutting of the original tree. The admission is £1.20 ($2) for adults, 50p (85¢) for children.

Mary Arden's House and the Shakespeare Countryside Museum

This Tudor farmstead, with its old stone dovecote and various outbuildings, was the girlhood home of Shakespeare's mother. It is situated at Wilmcote, 3 miles from Stratford. The house contains rare pieces of country furniture and domestic utensils. The barns, stable, cowshed, and farmyard are used to display an extensive collection of farming implements and other bygones illustrating life and work in the local countryside from Shakespeare's time to the present century.

Visitors also see the neighboring Glebe Farm whose interior evokes farm life in late Victorian and Edwardian times. A working smithy and displays of country crafts are added attractions. Light refreshments are available, and there is a picnic area. Admission is £2 ($3.30) for adults, 80p ($1.30) for children.

Hall's Croft

This house is on Old Town Street, not far from the parish church, Holy Trinity. It was here that Shakespeare's daughter Susanna lived with her husband, Dr. John Hall. Apart from that association, Hall's Croft is a Tudor house of outstanding character with a particularly beautiful walled garden. Dr. Hall was widely respected and built up a large medical practice in the area. Exhibits illustrating the theory and practice of medicine in Dr. Hall's time are on view in the house, which is furnished in the style of a middle-class Tudor home. The admission is £1.20 ($2) for adults, 50p (85¢) for children. Visitors to the house are welcome to use the adjoining Hall's Croft Club, which serves morning coffee, lunch, and afternoon tea.

There are other interesting sights not administered by the Trust foundation. They include the following attractions.

Holy Trinity Church

In an attractive setting near the Avon, the parish church of Stratford-upon-Avon is distinguished mainly because Shakespeare was buried in the chancel ("and curst be he who moves my bones"). The Parish Register records his baptism and burial (copies of the original, of course). No charge is made for entry into the church, described as "one of the most beautiful parish churches in the world," but visitors wishing to view Shakespeare's tomb are asked to donate a small sum, 40p (65¢) for adults and 25p (40¢) for students toward the restoration fund. Hours from November to March 31 are 8:30am to 6pm Mon. to Sat. and from 2 to 5pm Sun.

Harvard House

Not just of interest to Harvard students and alumni, Harvard House on High Street (tel. 0789/204507) is a fine example of an Elizabethan townhouse. Rebuilt in 1596, it was once the home of Katherine Rogers, mother of John Harvard, founder of Harvard University. In 1909 the house was purchased by a Chicago millionaire, Edward Morris, who presented it as a gift to the American university. With a profusion of carving, it is the most ornate house in Stratford. Its rooms are filled with period furniture, and the floors, made of the local flagstone, are authentic. Look for the Bible Chair, used for hiding the Bible during the days of Tudor persecution. Harvard House, charging admission of £1 ($1.65) for adults, 50p (85¢) for students and children, is open April through September Mon. to Sat.

A Brass-Rubbing Center

At the **Royal Shakespeare Theatre Summer House,** Avonbank Gardens (tel. 0789/297671), open from March until the end of October daily 11am to 4pm, you can explore brass rubbing. Admission is free. Medieval and Tudor brasses illustrate the knights and ladies, scholars, merchants, and priests of a bygone era. The Stratford collection contains a large assortment of exact replicas of brasses. The charge made for the rubbings includes the special paper and wax required, and any instruction you might need.

A Motor Museum

Stratford-upon-Avon Motor Museum, 1 Shakespeare St. (tel. 0789/69413), just around the corner from Shakespeare's birthplace, is a small but interesting museum started in 1974 by Bill Meredith-Owens, internationally known motor rally driver. The Roaring Twenties era is portrayed and consists of many Rolls-Royces (some specially built for the maharajas of India), Bugattis, early Jaguars, and many others. They also have a specialty bookshop where maintenance books on the old models and vintage cars are for sale. Admission is £2 ($3.30) for adults, £1 ($1.65) for children. The museum is open April to October daily from 9am to 6pm, and November to March from 10am to 4pm; closed Christmas Day.

ATTENDING THE THEATER

The **Royal Shakespeare Company** has three theaters in Stratford-upon-Avon, including its most important, the Shakespeare Theatre (tel. 0789/295623), built on the banks of the Avon. Seating 1,500, it is the number one theater for Shakespearean productions. The season runs from early April to late January. In an average season, five Shakespearean plays are staged.

Usually, you'll need advance reservations. There are two successive booking periods, each one opening about 2 months in advance. If you wait until your arrival in Stratford, it may be too late to get a good seat. Tickets can be booked through New York agents Edwards and Edwards or Keith Prowse, or direct with the theater box office by telephone with payment by major credit card. The price of seats generally ranges from £5 ($8.25) to £26 ($42.90). A small number of tickets are always kept back for sale on the day of a performance. You can phone from anywhere and make a credit card reservation, picking up your ticket on the day it is to be used, but there is no cancellation once your reservation is made.

The **Swan Theatre,** opened in 1986, seating 430, performs many Restoration comedies and later writers' work. The interior of the Swan Theatre reflects the style of an Elizabethan playhouse and replaces the Victorian interior of the Memorial Theatre built in 1879, which had been destroyed by fire in 1926. The original art gallery, library, and the collections escaped the fire and now display an exhibition of stagecraft from medieval mummers to the present day, with costumes, props, and photographs from Royal Shakespeare Company productions. The Swan Theatre, which uses the same box office as the Shakespeare Theatre, presents a repertoire of five plays each season, with tickets ranging from £8 ($13.20) to £19 ($31.35).

A third theatre in Stratford-upon-Avon, **The Other Place,** is temporarily closed for restoration work, but will reopen in 1991.

The **RSC Collection** is open all year except Christmas and Boxing days, from 9:15am to 8pm Mon. to Sat. and from noon to 5pm on Sun. (Sun. November to March, 11am to 4pm). Admission: adults, £1.50 ($2.50), children, £1 ($1.65). Theater tours of the Royal Shakespeare and Swan Theatres are at 1:30pm and 5:30pm (excluding matinee days) and four times on Sun., production schedules permitting. Prices of tours are: adults, £2.80 ($4.60), children, £2 ($3.30).

For information on the RSC Collection and Theatre Tours, telephone 0789/296655, extension 421.

WHERE TO STAY

Expensive Hotels

Welcombe Hotel, Warwick Road, Stratford-upon-Avon, Warwickshire CV37 0NR (tel. 0789/295252), is one of England's great Jacobean country houses, placed about a 10-minute ride from the heart of Stratford-upon-Avon. The home once belonged to Sir Archibald Flower, the philanthropic brewer who helped create the Shakespeare Memorial Theatre. Converted into a hotel, it is surrounded by 157 acres of grounds. It is reached by a formal entrance on Warwick Road, a winding driveway leading to the main hall. There's even an 18-hole, 6,202-yard golf course on the estate. Guests gather on fair days for afternoon tea or drinks on the rear terrace, with its Italian-style garden and steps leading down to flowerbeds. The public rooms are heroic in size, with high mullioned windows providing views of the park. The 76 bedrooms—some big enough for tennis matches—have pleasant furnishings, private baths, TVs, and phones. A single room with bath rents for £80 ($132) to £95 ($156.75), all prices including a full breakfast and VAT. You can order either table d'hôte meals or from the à la carte menu.

Ettington Park Hotel, Alderminster, Stratford-upon-Avon, Warwickshire CV37 8BS (tel. 0789/740740), a Victorian Gothic mansion, is one of the most sumptuous retreats in the Shakespeare Country—maybe *the* most sumptuous. This mansion opened as a hotel in 1985, but it has a history stretching over 9 centuries. The land is a legacy of the Shirley family, whose 12th-century burial chapel stands near the hotel. With its baronial fireplaces and conservatory and its charming staff, the place is like a grand private home. Restorers have brought back the beauty of the Adam ceilings, the stone carvings, and the ornate staircases. A new wing, assembled with the same stone and neo-Gothic carving as that of the original house, stretches toward a Renaissance-era garden arbor entwined with vines. The giant sequoias, ancient yews, and cedars have been incorporated into lawns and terraced gardens, whose flowers and ferns cascade into the waters of a rock-lined stream.

The 49 bedrooms contain dozens of memories of another era, yet the most modern comforts are concealed behind antique facades, including a private bath with every room, TV, and phone. With a full breakfast, doubles cost from £125 ($206.25) daily. In the dining room, the Shirley family crest is inlaid in hundreds of marquetry depictions in the carved and burnished paneling. The cuisine is a medley of English and French specialties, a fixed-price dinner costing from £27.50 ($45.40). The waters of a Jacuzzi foam into an indoor swimming pool under a Gothic skylight. Downstairs, there's a sauna. To get here, don't go to the village of Ettington, as the name of the hotel suggests. Head instead along the A34 between Stratford-upon-Avon and Oxford to the village of Alderminster.

The Shakespeare, Chapel Street, Stratford-upon-Avon, Warwickshire CV37 6ER (tel. 0789/294771), is filled with historical associations. Its original core dates from the 1400s, but it has seen many additions in its long life. It's been called both the Four Gables Hotel and the Five Gables Hotel. In the 1700s a demure facade of Regency brick was added to conceal the intricate timber framing, but in the 1880s, with a rash of Shakespearean revivals, the hotel was restored to its original Tudor look. Residents relax in the post-and-timber-studded public rooms, within sight of fireplaces and playbills from 19th-century productions of Shakespeare's plays. The hotel restaurant serves well-prepared lunches and dinners, and one of the most charming pubs in town, the Froth and Elbow, lies on the hotel's street level. Many of the bedrooms, 70 in all, were named by the noted actor, David Garrick. The oldest are capped with hewn timbers, with bathrooms built between the 400-year-old timbers. Modern comforts have been added, including mini-bars, TVs, and phones. Even the newer accommodations are at least 40 to 50 years old and have rose and thistle patterns carved into many of their exposed timbers. Single rooms cost from £75 ($123.75) to £82 ($135.30) daily, and doubles and twins go for £105 ($173.25) to £120 ($198).

Alveston Manor Hotel, Clopton Bridge, Stratford-upon-Avon, Warwickshire CV37 7HP (tel. 0789/204581), is a black-and-white timbered manor, conveniently placed for attending the theater, just a 2-minute walk from the Avon. It has a wealth of chimneys and gables, a hodgepodge of styles, everything from an Elizabethan gazebo to Queen Anne windows. Tracing the building's ancestry involves one in early English history, as its origins predate the arrival of William the Conqueror. A Ping-Pong game of ownership has been played with Alveston, which was mentioned in the *Domesday Book*. Rooms in the manor house are for those who gravitate to old slanted floors, overhead beams, and antique furnishings. However, in the modern block, attached by a covered walk through the rear garden, rooms have built-in pieces, and a color-coordinate decor. Each of the 108 accommodations has a private bath or shower, TV, and phone. In a single room, the rate is £70 ($115.50) to £85 ($140.25) daily, increasing to £90 ($148.50) to £110 ($181.50) in a double or twin. Service and VAT are included. In the newer block, a number of large rooms are rented to three or four persons. The lounges are in the manor; and guests gather in the Cedar Room with a view of the centuries-old tree at the top of the garden— said to have been the background for the first presentation of *A Midsummer Night's Dream*. In the main living room, with its linenfold paneling, logs burn in the Tudor fireplace. Food is served in the softly lit Tudor Restaurant, with its oak beams and leaded-glass windows. A set dinner costs £16.50 ($27.25).

Moat House International, Bridgefoot, Stratford-upon-Avon, Warwickshire CV37 6YR (tel. 0789/414411), is a four-star hotel standing in 5 acres of landscaped lawns on the banks of the River Avon. It is one of the flagships of Queens Moat Houses, a hotel chain in Britain. The hotel has recently undergone a total refurbishment program, and now every bedroom has a high standard of comfort. Nearly 250 bedrooms are offered, each with private bath or shower, air conditioning, direct-dial phone, color TV, video, and hairdryer. Rates for a single begin at £75 ($123.75) nightly, going up to £99 ($163.35) in a double, with VAT and a full English breakfast included. The hotel offers an array of drinking and dining facilities, including the Warwick Grill, which features a British and continental menu. You can also dine in the Tavern, which has a carvery of hot and cold roasts. You can drink in the Tavern Pub and in the Actors, which doubles as a night club. In addition, a riverside restaurant seats 200 persons. The location overlooks the Royal Shakespeare Theatre, which can be reached by barge. The hotel has its own leisure complex with a swimming pool, a sauna, a solarium, a mini-gym, and a Jacuzzi.

Moderately Priced Hotels

White Swan, Rother Street, Stratford-upon-Avon, Warwickshire CV37 6NH (tel. 0798/297022), is a cozy, intimate hotel, one of the most atmospheric in Stratford. It was in business for more than 100 years before Shakespeare appeared on the scene. The gabled medieval front would present the Bard with no surprises, but the modern comforts inside would surely astonish him, even though many of the rooms have been preserved. Paintings dating from 1550 hang on the lounge walls. All the 42 bedrooms are well appointed and have private baths or showers, color TVs, radios, and phones. Singles rent for £70 ($115.50) daily, and doubles go for £86 ($141.90). The hostelry has a spacious restaurant, where good food is served. The oak-beamed bar is a popular meeting place (see "Special Pubs," below).

The Falcon, Chapel Street, Stratford-upon-Avon, Warwickshire CV37 6HA (tel. 0789/205777), is a blending of the very old and the very new. At the rear of a black-and-white timbered inn, licensed a quarter of a century after Shakespeare's death, is a contemporary bedroom extension, joined by a glass-covered passageway. In the heart of Stratford, the Falcon faces the Guild Chapel and the New Place Gardens. The bedrooms in the mellowed part have oak beams, diamond leaded-glass windows, some antique furnishings, and good reproductions. One arrives at the rear portion to unload luggage, just as horse-drawn coaches once dispatched their passengers. All 73 bedrooms have private baths, radios, TVs, phones, electric trouser presses, and hot beverage facilities. Rates include full English breakfast, space for your car, VAT, and service charge. A single with bath is £60 ($99) daily, and a double or twin with bath costs £82 ($135.30). The social lounges are tasteful and comfortable—some of the finest in the Midlands. In the intimate Merlin Lounge is an open copper-hooded fireplace where coal and log fires are kept burning under beams salvaged from old ships (the walls are a good example of wattle and daub, typical of Shakespeare's day). The Oak Lounge Bar is a forest of weathered beams, and on either side of the stone fireplace is the paneling removed from the poet's last home, New Place. A set luncheon or dinner costs £14 ($23.10).

The Swans Nest, Bridgefoot, Stratford-upon-Avon, Warwickshire CV37 7LT (tel. 0789/66761), presents a Georgian facade with tall, narrow windows looking out over the Avon with its swans. Most of the bedrooms, however, are in a modern, red-brick extension whose walls encircle courtyards. The complex sits in its own gardens on a low, flat area beside a canal, not far from the Royal Shakespeare Theatre. The River Bar offers a view of the planting outside. The Bewick Restaurant serves food in a room lined with early-19th-century paintings. Fixed-price lunches and dinner cost £8.95 ($14.75) and £14 ($23.10) respectively. The 60 bedrooms are comfortably modern and filled with tasteful furnishings. Each unit has its private bath, color TV, radio, phone, and hot beverage facilities. Singles cost £62 ($102.30) nightly and doubles from £75 ($123.75).

Arden Hotel, 44 Waterside, Stratford-upon-Avon, Warwickshire CV37 6BA (tel. 0789/294949), has a nearly symmetrical, red-brick main section dating from the Regency period. Over the years, a handful of adjacent buildings and a modern extension have been added to enlarge the capacity. Today the modernized interior contains a well-upholstered cocktail lounge and pub, a dining room with big front windows, a covered garden terrace, and 45 comfortable bedrooms. Each unit has a private bath, phone, color TV and hot beverage facilities. With an English breakfast included, singles cost £65 ($107.25) daily and doubles go for £100 ($165). A fixed-price dinner in the restaurant goes for £18 ($29.70). The hotel is convenient for theater-goers because of its position across the street from the side entrance of the Royal Shakespeare.

Dukes, Payton Street, Stratford-upon-Avon, Warwickshire CV37 6UA (tel. 0789/69300), was formed when two Georgian townhouses were united and restored to create this little charmer. In the center of Stratford, it has a large garden, yet is close to Shakespeare's birthplace. A family operated inn, Dukes offers attractively decorated public areas and bedrooms that have been restored to an impressive degree of comfort and coziness. The hotel offers 22 bedrooms, each with private bath or shower as well as a direct-dial phone and TV. Charges for an overnight stay range from £70 ($115.50) daily in a single to £85 ($140.25) in a double. The building reflects taste in its well-chosen pieces of furniture, often antique. Dukes also serves a good English and continental cuisine.

Budget Hotels

Grosvenor House Hotel, 12-14 Warwick Rd., Stratford-upon-Avon, Warwickshire CV37 6YT (tel. 0789/69213), is a pair of Georgian residences joined to form a hotel of 51 bedrooms, all with either a private bath or shower. It is a member of the Best Western hotel group. Lawns and gardens to the rear of the hotel lend attraction. All bedrooms have color TVs, radios, tea and coffee makers, and phones. Singles rent for £45 ($74.25) daily, and doubles go for £66 ($108.90), including service, VAT, and a full English breakfast. There is a large free car park for guests. The informal bar (open until midnight) and terrace offer relaxation before or after you lunch or dine in the large restaurant, whose floor-to-ceiling windows look onto the gardens. The Grosvenor is a short stroll from the intersection of Bridge Street and Waterside so that you're right at riverside Bancroft Gardens and the Royal Shakespeare Theatre.

The Stratford House, Sheep Street, Stratford-upon-Avon, Warwickshire CV37 6EF (tel. 0789/68288), a Georgian house, stands 100 yards from the River Avon and the Royal Shakespeare Theatre. It is a small hotel of only 10 bedrooms, all with private bath or shower. The hotel is owned by Sylvia Adcock, who extends a warm welcome to North American clients. The house is furnished tastefully and with style, somewhat like a private home, with books and pictures along with a scattering of antiques. Everything is spotlessly maintained. On the side is a walled courtyard, with flowering plants. The B&B rate is from £45 ($74.25) to £55 ($90.75) daily in a single, £70 ($115.50) to £80 ($132) in a double. The price includes a full English breakfast and VAT. All bedrooms have color TVs, phones, and tea and coffee makers. Both hotel guests and outsiders can dine in the garden restaurant, Shepherd's, recommended separately.

Stratheden Hotel, Chapel Street, Stratford-upon-Avon, Warwickshire CV37 6EP (tel. 0789/297119), is a small, tuck-away hotel in the very heart of Stratford-upon-Avon. It was built in 1673 with a tiny rear garden and top-floor rooms with slanted, beamed ceilings. It has been in the Wells family for the past quarter century. The house has improved in both decor and comfort, with fresh paint, curtains, and good beds. Seven of the 10 rooms have private showers and toilets, with B&B costing £15 ($24.75) to £23 ($37.95) per person nightly. The entry hallway has a glass cupboard, holding family heirlooms and collector items. The dining room, with a bay window, has an overscale sideboard that once belonged to the "insanely vain" Marie Corelli, the eccentric novelist, poet, and mystic who wrote a series of seven books, beginning with *A Romance of Two Worlds* and ending with *Spirit and Power and Universal Love.* Queen Victoria was one of her avid readers. The Victorian novelist (1855–1924) was noted for her passion for pastoral paintings and objets d'art. You can see an example of her taste in bedchamber furniture: a massive mahogany tester bed in one of the rooms.

Victoria Spa Lodge, Bishopton Lane, Stratford-upon-Avon, Warwickshire, CV37 9QY (tel. 0789/67985), is a large house dating from 1837 and lying 1½ miles from the center of town, situated by a canal. Originally opened as a spa, it once had Queen Victoria's eldest daughter, Princess Vicky, as a guest. The famous cartoonist, Bruce Bairnsfather, also resided here. Paul and Dreen Tozer are accommodating hosts. Their seven bedrooms are tastefully decorated with Laura Ashley wallpaper and matching quilts. Color TVs and hot beverage facilities are in all rooms. Four rooms also have private baths or showers. B&B ranges from £17.50 ($28.90) to £22 ($36.30) per person nightly. A full English breakfast is served in a cheerful and antique-filled dining room. Meals and light refreshments are available on request.

WHERE TO DINE

In the best position in town, the **Box Tree Restaurant,** in the Royal Shakespeare Theatre, Waterside (tel. 0789/414999), has walls of glass providing an unobstructed view of the Avon and its swans. The meals and service are worthy of its unique position. The restaurant is open on matinee days from noon to 2pm, when a three-course table d'hôte luncheon costs £12.50 ($20.65). Evening hours are 5:45pm to midnight when a three-course, pre-theater dinner is featured. During intermission, there is a snack feast of smoked salmon and champagne. After each evening's performance you can dine by flickering candlelight. Classical French, Italian and English cuisine is served. Dinner and supper are à la carte and cost from £18.25 ($30.10) to £25 ($41.25) per person. Be sure to book your table in advance, especially on the days of performances (there's a special phone for reservations in the theater lobby).

Also overlooking the Avon, the **River Terrace Restaurant** in the theater is open to the general public as well as to play-goers. A coffeeshop and licensed restaurant serves typical English and pasta dishes, morning coffee, and afternoon teas, which are offered on a self-service basis. Meals cost £4 ($6.60) to £8.50 ($14.05). It's open from 10:30am to 9:30pm Mon. to Sat., to 5:30pm Sun. The restaurant has the same phone as the Box Tree (above).

Shepherd's Garden Restaurant, Stratford House Hotel, Sheep Street (tel. 0789/68288), is appropriately stylish for its role as host to many of the directors and actors from the Royal Shakespeare Theatre. Light and airy, it has a skylit conservatory look, with draping vines and plants. Windows open onto a view of a walled garden. You are served British cookery here among the finest in Stratford-upon-Avon. For an appetizer, you might begin with smoked chicken and mango with a curried mayonnaise, going on to either fresh salmon with a chive and butter sauce or roast rack of lamb with a mild garlic sauce. These are only examples of what type of food is served, as the menu, based on the use of fresh ingredients, changes frequently. Lunch, served from noon to 2pm, costs from £12.50 ($20.65), with dinner, from 6 to 9:30pm, going for £18 ($29.70) and up. Closed Sun. dinner and Mon.

Hussain's, 6A Chapel St. (tel. 0789/67506), stands across from the Shakespeare Hotel and historic New Place. Dining here has been compared to a visit to a private Indian home, and the restaurant has many admirers—some of whom consider it the finest dining spot in Stratford-upon-Avon. At least it pleased Ben Kingsley, star of *Gandhi.* The owner, Noor Hussain, has selected a well-trained, alert staff, who welcome guests into their domain, often advising about special dishes. Against a setting of pink crushed-velvet paneling, you can select from an array of dishes from northern India. Herbs and spices are blended imaginatively in the kitchen to give dishes a distinctive flavor. Regular meals cost from £12.50 ($20.65), and set dinners are offered at £22 ($36.30) for two persons. Many tandoori dishes are offered, along with various curries with lamb or prawn. It is open daily from noon to 2pm for lunches and from 5:15pm to 11:45pm for dinner.

Sir Toby's, 8 Church St. (tel. 0789/68822), constructed of red brick, lies away from the busy center. It's cozy and intimate, with limited seating. In summer, a few tables are placed outside for al fresco dining. Mr. and Mrs. Watkins welcome diners to their establishment only in the evening from 5:30 to 9:30pm and never on Sun. They take pride in their good home cooking and also cater to the vegetarian palate, blending the best of the past with the cooking techniques of today. You might also visit for a pre-theater meal because of its early opening. Meals cost from £15 ($24.75) and up.

Da Giovanni, 8 Ely St. (tel. 0789/297999), is an intimate spot, favored by actors. The yellow-brick cottage is graced with an Italianate facade that shelters the entrance to a cocktail lounge with antiques. Da Giovanni is in the trattoria style, its menu beginning fittingly enough with minestrone. The classic Italian menu includes such pasta dishes as lasagne and cannelloni, and such main dishes as escalope pietmontese and scampi provençale. A good Italian dessert is the zabaglione, although at least two persons must order it. A selection of excellent continental ices is also featured, everything from Italian cassata to mela stregata. Expect to pay from £15 ($24.75) for a complete dinner. A 10% service charge is added. It's closed on Sun., but open other days from 12:30 to 2pm and 6 to 11:30pm.

SPECIAL PUBS

Affectionately known as the Dirty Duck, it's really the **Black Swan,** Waterside (tel. 0789/297312). By whatever bird it's called, it's been popular since the 18th century as a hangout for Stratford players. The autographed photographs of its patrons, such as Lord Laurence Olivier, line the wall. The front lounge and bar crackles with intense conversation. In the spring and fall an open fire blazes. In the Dirty Duck Grill Room, typical English grills, among other dishes, are featured. You're faced with a dozen appetizers, most of which would make a meal in themselves. Main dishes include braised kidneys or oxtails or honey-roasted duck. Meals cost from £12 ($19.80). Hours are from 11am to 4pm and 5:30 to 11pm Mon. to Sat., from noon to 2pm only on Sun. In fair weather, you can drink while sitting in the front garden and watch the swans on the Avon glide by.

After visiting the Black Swan, you may be ready to call on the **White Swan,** Rother Street (tel. 0789/297022), one of the most atmospheric pubs in Stratford-upon-Avon, found in a hotel previously recommended. Once you step inside, you're drawn into a world of cushioned leather armchairs, old oak settles, oak paneling, and fireplaces. It is believed that Shakespeare may have come here to drink back when it was called Kings Head. Today you can go here for food and drink from 10:30am to 2:30pm and 6 to 11pm Mon. to Sat., from noon to 3pm and 7 to 10:30pm Sun. At lunch you can partake of the food offerings, including hot dishes of the day along with fresh salads and sandwiches, light meals costing from £5 ($8.25).

WHERE TO STAY AND DINE IN THE ENVIRONS

Ettington

Some 6½ miles southeast of Stratford-upon-Avon on the A422, **Chase Country House Hotel,** Banbury Road, Ettington, Stratford-upon-Avon, Warwickshire CV37 7NZ (tel. 0789/740000), has a somewhat notorious history as the former home of an Irish gunrunner. It's contained within a high-gabled mansion of elaborate brickwork upon which a Victorian architect unleashed Gothic fantasies in 1867. The establishment today contains 12 comfortably traditional bedrooms, priced at £60 ($99) to £65 ($107.25) daily for a single and £72 ($118.80) to £75 ($123.75) for a double, with a full breakfast included. Each unit has a phone, radio alarm, color TV, and private bath. The highlight of the hotel, however, is that it provides some of the best food in the area. Typical English dishes include Wiltshire fritters with a spicy sauce, an appetizing mélange of Cotswold fish (smoked on the premises using smoldering English oak in smoke pots), and braised oxtail. A heavenly dessert is called Athol Brose, concocted from cream, whisky, and honey layered with oat flakes. Meals are priced from £20 ($33), reasonable for such a commendable restaurant. Reservations are important. Hours are 12:30 to 2:30pm (to 1:30pm on Sun.) and 7:30 to 9pm. Closed to non-residents for lunch on Sat. and for dinner on Sun.

Wilmcote

In the tiny village where Shakespeare's mother, Mary Arden, lived stands the **Swan House Hotel,** the Green, Wilmcote, Stratford-upon-Avon, Warwickshire CV37 9XJ (tel. 0789/67030). Really an upgraded village pub-hotel, the white-painted Swan is tranquil, offering not only fresh bedrooms at low prices, but good meals as well. It's owned by Ian and Diana Sykes, who have made the inn homelike. It has 12 bedrooms, all with private baths or showers, color TVs, and hot beverage facilities. A single rents for £32 ($52.80) daily, and a double goes for £52 ($85.80). All tariffs are inclusive of an English breakfast, service, and VAT. A four-poster room is available. In the popular beamed bar with an open fire and the original well, they serve a range of homemade hot and cold bar snacks. The bar offers four real ales at lunch or in the evening. The restaurant is a good setting for à la carte meals. English cuisine is prepared with French overtones, using fresh local produce.

Alcester

A magnificent, 115-room Palladian country house, **Ragley Hall** (tel. 0789/762090), built in 1680, is the home of the marquess and marchioness of Hertford and their family, lying 9 miles from Stratford-upon-Avon. The house has been lovingly restored and appears as it probably looked during the early 1700s. Great pains were taken to duplicate color patterns and in some cases even the original wallpaper patterns. Ragley Hall's vast and spacious rooms boast priceless pictures, furniture, and works of art that have been collected by 10 generations of the Seymour family. While possessing a museumlike quality in the sense that its artifacts are properly displayed and lighted, and have great historical importance, Ragley Hall is indeed a private home.

Perhaps the most spectacular attraction is the lavishly painted south staircase hall. The present marquess commissioned muralist Graham Rust to paint the modern trompe l'oeil work on the subject, *The Temptation,* but this religious theme stops with the lavishly evil Devil offering a gold circlet to Christ in the central ceiling medallion.

The house is open from Easter Sat. until the end of September, noon to 5pm Tue. to Thur. and Sat. and Sun., and on bank holidays. The park, gardens, Adventure Wood, and Farm and Woodland Walk are open from 10am to 6pm. In July and August the garden and park only are also open on Mon. and Fri. The Adventure Wood is closed Mon. to Fri. in September. Admission to the house, garden, and park is £3.50 ($5.80) for adults, £2.20 ($3.65) for children. For the park and gardens only adults pay £2.50 ($4.15) and children £1.50 ($2.50).

Ten centuries of history are lodged at **Billesley Manor Hotel,** Billesley, near Alcester, Warwickshire B49 6NF (tel. 0789/400888), 3 miles west of Stratford-upon-Avon by the A422. Set in 11 acres of English gardens, the manor offers a traditional welcome combined with modern comfort. The old blends with the new, from the oak panels and carved fireplaces to an indoor, heated swimming pool. Accommodations, 41 in all, range from four-poster to modern bedrooms, all with spacious baths, color TVs, trouser presses, and direct-dial phones. Rates are from £85 ($140.25) daily in a single and from £125 ($206.25) in a double or twin. Tariffs include a full English breakfast, VAT, and service. You can relax in front of a roaring log fire in manorial splendor, and the wood-paneled restaurants serve excellent fare, backed up by a fine wine list. There are tennis courts, a croquet lawn, and a golf "pitch and putt" course. Hot-air ballooning, riding, shooting, and fishing can be arranged.

---

2. Warwick

Most travelers approach Warwick via the A46 from Stratford-upon-Avon, 8 miles away. The town, 92 miles from London, stands on the Avon.

Visitors seem to rush through Warwick to see Warwick Castle; then they're off on their next adventure, traditionally to the ruins of Kenilworth Castle. But the historic center of medieval Warwick deserves to be treated with greater respect. It has far more to offer than a castle.

In 1694 a fire swept through Warwick, destroying large segments of the town, but it still retains a number of Elizabethan and medieval buildings—along with some fine Georgian structures. (Very few traces remain, however, of the town walls, except the East and West Gates.) Warwick looks to Ethelfleda, daughter of Alfred the Great, as its founder. But most of its history is associated with the earls of Warwick, a title created by the son of William the Conqueror in 1088. The story of those earls —the Beaumonts, the Beauchamps (such figures as "Kingmaker" Richard Neville) —makes for an exciting episode in English history too detailed to document here.

WARWICK CASTLE

Perched on a rocky cliff above the Avon, this magnificent 14th-century fortress encloses a stately mansion in the grandest late-17th-century style. The importance of the site has been recognized from earliest times. The first defense works of significance at Warwick were built by Ethelfleda, daughter of Alfred the Great, in A.D. 915. Her fortifications were further developed by the construction of a motte and bailey castle on the orders of William the Conqueror in 1068, two years after the Norman Conquest. There are now no remains of the Norman castle except the castle mound, as this was sacked by Simon de Montfort in the Barons' War of 1264.

The Beauchamp family, the most illustrious medieval earls of Warwick, are responsible for most of the castle as it is seen today, and much of the external structure remains unchanged from the mid-14th century. When the castle was granted to Sir Fulke Greville by James I in 1604, he spent £20,000 (an enormous sum in those days) converting the existing castle buildings into a luxurious mansion. The

Grevilles have held the earl of Warwick title since 1759, when it passed from the Rich family.
The state rooms and great hall house fine collections of paintings, furniture, arms, and armor. The armory, dungeon, torture chamber, ghost tower, clock tower, and Guy's tower give vivid insights into the castle's turbulent past and its important part in the history of England. The private apartments of Lord Brooke and his family, who in recent years sold the castle to Madame Tussaud's company, of waxworks fame, are open to visitors to display a carefully constructed Royal Weekend House Party of 1898. The major rooms contain wax models of the time: young Winston Churchill, the Duchess of Devonshire, Winston's widowed mother, Jennie, and Clara Butt, the celebrated singer, along with the Earl and Countess of Warwick and their family. In the Kenilworth bedroom, the Prince of Wales, later to become King Edward VII, reads a letter, and in the red bedroom, the Duchess of Marlborough prepares for her bath. Among the most lifelike of the figures is a little uniformed maid, bending over a bathtub to test the temperature of the water. Surrounded by gardens, lawns, and woodland, where peacocks roam freely, and skirted by the Avon, Warwick Castle was described by Sir Walter Scott in 1828 as "that fairest monument of ancient and chivalrous splendor which yet remains uninjured by time."

Don't miss the re-created Victorian Rose Garden, originally designed by Robert Marnock in 1868. It fell into disrepair, and a tennis court was built on the site among the trees. In 1980 it was decided to restore the garden, and as luck would have it, Marnock's original plans were discovered in the County Records Office. Close by the rose garden is a Victorian alpine rockery and water garden. The romantic castle is, throughout the year, host to various special events, colorful pageants such as those created by the members of the Sealed Knot and the French Foot Grenadiers. There are regular appearances of the magnificent Red Knight on his splendid warhorse, and traditional Morris Dancers perform on the lawns. Some form of live entertainment is presented almost every day on the grounds in summer.

Warwick Castle, Castle Hill (tel. 0926/495421), is open from 10am to 5:30pm daily from March 1 to October 31 and from 10am to 4:30pm from November 1 to February 28 except Christmas Day. Admission is £4.99 ($8.25) for adults, £3.25 ($5.35) for children.

OTHER SIGHTS

St. Mary's Church

Destroyed in part by the fire of 1694, this church on Old Square with its rebuilt battlemented tower and nave is considered among the finest examples of the work of the late 17th and early 18th centuries. The Beauchamp Chapel, spared from the flames, encases the Purbeck marble tomb of Richard Beauchamp, a well-known earl of Warwick who died in 1439 and is commemorated by a gilded bronze effigy. The most powerful man in the kingdom, not excepting Henry V, Beauchamp has a tomb considered one of the finest remaining examples of Perpendicular Gothic as practiced in England in the mid-15th century. The tomb of Robert Dudley, Earl of Leicester, a favorite of Elizabeth I, is against the north wall. The Perpendicular Gothic choir dates from the 14th century, as do the Norman crypt and the chapter house. For more information, get in touch with the Warwick Parish Office, Old Square Warwick (tel. 0926/400771).

Lord Leycester Hospital

At the West Gate, this group of half-timbered almshouses was also spared from the Great Fire. The buildings were erected in about 1400, and the hospital was founded in 1571 by Robert Dudley, Earl of Leicester, as a home for old soldiers. It is still in use by ex-servicemen and their wives today. On top of the West Gate is the attractive little chapel of St. James, dating from the 12th century, although much restored. The hospital, on High Street (tel. 0926/491422), can be visited from

10am to 5:30pm Mon. to Sat. for £1.50 ($2.50) for adults, 50p (85¢) for children. Off-season, it closes at 4pm. Last admission is 15 minutes before closing.

Warwick Doll Museum

In one of the most charming Elizabethan buildings in Warwick, this doll museum, Oken's House, Castle Street (tel. 0926/495546), is near St. Mary's Church. Its seven rooms contain an extensive collection of dolls in wood, wax, and porcelain. The house once belonged to Thomas Oken, a great benefactor of Warwick. The museum is open from Easter to the end of September 10am to 5pm Mon. to Sat. and 2 to 5pm Sun. Admission is 75p ($1.25) for adults, 50p (85¢) for children.

Warwickshire Museum

At the market place, this museum (tel. 0926/410410 ext. 2500) was established in 1836 to house a collection of geological remains, fossils, and a fine grouping of British amphibians from the Triassic period. There are also displays illustrating the history, archeology, and natural history of the county, including the famous Sheldon tapestry map. It is open from 10am to 5:30pm Mon. to Sat. and 2:30 to 5pm on Sun. in summer.

St. John's House

At Coten End, not far from the castle gates, there is a display of domestic life and costumes, and the house in which these exhibitions are displayed is a fund of beauty itself, dating from the early 17th century. A Victorian schoolroom is furnished with original 19th-century school furniture and equipment. During term time, Warwickshire children, dressed in replica costumes, can be seen enjoying Victorian-style lessons. Groups of children also use the Victorian parlor and the kitchen. As it is impossible to display more than a small amount at a time, a study room is available where you can see objects from the reserve collections. The costume collection is a particularly fine one, and visitors can study the drawings and photos that make up the costume catalog. These facilities are available by prior appointment only (see below). Upstairs is a Military Museum, tracing the history of the Royal Warwickshire Regiment from 1674 to the present day. The house is open from 10am to 12:30pm and 1:30 to 5:30pm Tue. to Sat., and also from 2:30 to 5pm Sun. May to September. Admission is free. For more information and for appointments in the study room, telephone the Keeper of Social History (tel. 0926/410410, ext. 2021).

WHERE TO STAY

Many prefer to seek lodgings in Warwick, then commute to Stratford-upon-Avon.

Hilton National Hotel, Warwick Bypass, the A46 Stratford Road, Warwick, Warwickshire CV34 6RE (tel. 0926/499555), is at the elbow junction of a network of highways, making it popular with commercial travelers. It has a hutch-style, low-slung modern design of earth-colored brick, an octagonal dining room, and a functional series of interconnected bars, lounges, and public areas, as well as a heated indoor swimming pool. The establishment hosts many conferences and sales meetings for local companies. Foreign visitors find that its standardized comfort and easy-to-find location make it a good base for touring Warwick and the surrounding regions. The hotel rents 150 well-furnished rooms, each with private bath, phone, and TV, as well as 24-hour room service. Charges are from £75 ($123.75) in a single and £96 ($158.40) in a double.

Lord Leycester Hotel (Calotels), Jury Street, Warwick, Warwickshire CV34 4EJ (tel. 0926/491481), was a manor house belonging in 1726 to Lord Archer of Umberslade. Years later, it was converted into an inn under the sign of the three tuns, and later still it became once more a private residence. In 1926, it was turned into a hotel, an identity it retains today. The 52 bedrooms provide comfortable accommodation, all with private baths or showers. Singles rent for £42 ($69.30) daily, and doubles or twins go for £58 ($95.70). Tariffs include a full English breakfast and VAT. All rooms have color TVs, radios, phones, and tea and coffee makers. A small à la carte menu is offered in the dining room, or you can have snacks in the Tavern Bar. A large car park is found at the rear of the hotel, whose position is central, within walking distance of the castle and other historic buildings of Warwick.

The Westgate Arms, 3 Old Bowling Green St., Warwick, Warwickshire CV34 4DD (tel. 0926/492362). The original structure on this site was built in 1315, but the black-and-white building you see today dates from 1964. Its position near the castle ensures a busy summer trade in its rambling bars, dining room, and 10 comfortably refurbished bedrooms, costing £59.50 ($98.20) daily for a single and £80.50 ($132.85) for a double. If you come to dine, after passing through a loosely defined cocktail lounge/pub/social center, you enter a conservatively decorated room. In the center, a service area contains facilities for chefs to prepare the popular flambéed specialties of the house. A five-course, fixed-price dinner costing £16.25 ($26.80) is a traditional favorite, and a table d'hôte luncheon goes for £10.25 ($16.90). There are also some interesting à la carte dishes.

WHERE TO DINE

One of the best restaurants in town is **Randolph's,** 19-21 Coten End (tel. 0926/491292). It's in a black-and-white half-timbered building that encompasses a former cluster of narrow cottages. Within a cozily beamed dining room, Rodolf and Gillian Prymaka prepare elegantly sophisticated dishes that rely heavily on fresh ingredients and years of culinary training. You might enjoy the house-style goose in marsala wine sauce, calves' kidneys on homemade pasta with madeira sauce, perfectly prepared vegetables, and fresh-baked bread. A favorite choice among the establishment's loyal clientele is thick-sliced beef aged three weeks. Desserts run a tempting gamut from calorie-conscious but flavorful afterthoughts to diet-breaking fantasies. Full meals, priced from £25 ($41.25), are served only in the evening from 7:45 to 9:30pm Mon. to Sat.

---

3. Kenilworth Castle

In magnificent ruins, this castle—the setting of Sir Walter Scott's romance *Kenilworth*—once had walls that enclosed an area of 7 acres. It lies 5 miles north of Warwick, 13 from Stratford-upon-Avon. In 1957 Lord Kenilworth presented the decaying castle to England, and limited restoration has since been carried out.

The castle dates back to the days of Henry I, having been built by one of his lieutenants, Geoffrey de Clinton. Of the original castle, only Caesar's Tower, with its 16-foot thick walls, remains. Edward II was forced to abdicate at Kenilworth in 1327, before being carried off to Berkeley Castle in Gloucestershire, where he was undoubtedly murdered. In 1563 Elizabeth I gave the castle to her favorite, Robert Dudley, Earl of Leicester. The earl built the gatehouse, which was visited on several occasions by the queen. After the Civil War, the Roundheads were responsible for breaching the outer walls and towers, and blowing up the north wall of the keep. This was the only damage caused following the Earl of Monmouth's plea that it be "slighted with as little spoil to the dwellinghouse as might be."

From Good Fri. to the end of September, the castle is open daily from 10am to 6pm. In other months, hours are from 10am to 4pm Tue. to Sun. The castle is closed December 24–26 and January 1. Admission is £1.15 ($1.90) for adults, 60p ($1) for children under 16. For information, phone 0926/52078.

WHERE TO STAY AND DINE

In the old part of Kenilworth, **Clarendon House Hotel,** 6-8 Old High St., Kenilworth, Warwickshire CV8 1LZ (tel. 0926/57668), is a family-run hotel and restaurant. The oak tree around which the original ale house was built in 1430 is still supporting the roof of the building today. The present owners welcome guests to spend the night in any of the 30 bedrooms, all of which are tastefully decorated.

Twenty rooms have private baths or showers, and each has a phone and a TV. Depending on the plumbing, singles range from £43 ($70.95) to £46 ($75.90) daily, with doubles paying £62 ($102.30) to £67 ($110.55). Tariffs include VAT, service, and a full English breakfast.

Before the evening meal, guests gather in the timbered and oak-paneled Royalist Retreat Bar and lounges. The hotel's Castle Tavern restaurant is housed in what was once the inn stable. The oddly timbered room is decorated with antique maps and armor, constant reminders that a Cromwellian garrison once stayed at the inn during a seige of Kenilworth Castle. Game is a specialty at the Clarendon House, and in season you may dine on such specialties as jugged hare, pheasant georgienne (marinated in madeira wine with oranges, grapes, and walnuts), grouse, or mallard (wild duck cooked in red wine, mushrooms, and *fines herbes*). A complete dinner, inclusive of VAT, is available for around £15 ($24.75) à la carte, but there is also an interesting table d'hôte menu of four courses for £10.50 ($17.35). You can dine from 7 to 9:30pm Sun. to Thur., from 7 to 10pm on Fri. and Sat. Sun. luncheon of three courses is available at £8 ($13.20), served from noon to 1:30pm.

Restaurant Bosquet, 97A Warwick Rd. (tel. 0926/52463), is a tiny terraced townhouse restaurant owned and operated by Bernard Lignier, a Frenchman, who does the cooking, and his English wife, Jane. The à la carte menu is changed with the seasons but consists mainly of French dishes, such as sweetbreads, loin of lamb with tarragon, fish according to the market, and game according to the season. There is a good selection of reasonably priced regional French wines. An à la carte meal of three courses goes for £25 ($41.25) per person. The set lunch or dinner menu, at £15 ($24.75), is changed regularly and also includes seasonal produce. The restaurant is open noon to 2pm and 7 to 10pm; closed lunch Sat., all day Sun., and for 3 weeks in July and August. It is essential to make reservations, as the place is quite small. Bosquet is something of a culinary oasis in Kenilworth.

4. Coventry

Coventry has long been noted in legend as the ancient market town through which Lady Godiva made her famous ride, giving birth to a new name in English: Peeping Tom. The Lady Godiva story is clouded in such obscurity that the truth has probably been lost forever. It has been suggested that the good lady never appeared in the nude, but was the victim of scandalmongers, who, in their attempt to tarnish her image, unknowingly immortalized her.

Coventry is 19 miles from Stratford-upon-Avon, and only 11 from Warwick and 6 from Kenilworth, but 100 miles from London.

WHAT TO SEE AND DO

This Midlands city, home of motorcar and cycle manufacturing, is principally industrial, but you'll want to pay it a visit to see Sir Basil Spence's controversial **Coventry Cathedral,** consecrated in 1962. The city was partially destroyed during the blitz in the early 1940s, but the rebuilding was miraculous. No city more than Coventry seems to symbolize England's power to bounce back from adversity.

The cathedral grew up on the same site as the 14th-century Perpendicular building. Many Coventry residents have maintained that the foreign visitor is more likely to admire the structure than the Britisher, who perhaps is more attached to traditional cathedral design.

Outside is Sir Jacob Epstein's bronze masterpiece, *St. Michael Slaying the Devil.* Inside, the outstanding feature is the 70-foot-high altar tapestry by Graham Sutherland, said to be the largest in the world. The floor-to-ceiling abstract stained-glass windows are the work of the Royal College of Art. The West Window is most interesting, with its engraved glass, rows of stylized saints and prophets with angels flying around between them.

In the undercroft of the cathedral is a visitor center, The Spirit of Coventry. There you can see the Walkway of Holograms, three-dimensional images created with laser light, depicting the Stations of the Cross. It is an exciting walk through sound, light, and special effects including a bombed house. The treasures of the cathedral are on show. An audio-visual on the city and church includes the fact that 450 aircraft dropped 40,000 firebombs on the city in one day.

The cathedral is open daily in summer from 9:30 to 7pm, closing at 5:30pm in winter. The 14th-century tower of the old cathedral costs £1 ($1.65) for adults to visit, 50p (85¢) for children. Admission to the visitor center is £1.25 ($2.05) for adults, 75p ($1.25) for children 6 to 16.

After visiting the cathedral, you may want to have tea in Fraters Restaurant nearby.

St. Mary's Guildhall, Bayley Lane (tel. 0203/225555). Up a flight of steps leading from a small yard off Bayley Lane is one of the most attractive medieval guildhalls in England, dating from 1342. It was originally built as a meeting place for the guilds of St. Mary, St. John the Baptist, and St. Catherine. It is now used for the solemn election of the lord mayors of the city and for banquets and civic ceremonies. Above the north window is an arras (tapestry), added in the 15th century, and a beautiful oak ceiling with its original 14th-century carved angels, which was rebuilt in the 1950s. There is a minstrel's gallery and a treasury, and off the armoury, Caesar's Tower, where Mary Queen of Scots was imprisoned in 1569. By appointment only, you can also see a magnificent collection of 42 original watercolors by H. E. Cox, depicting Coventry before the bombings of 1940. City pensioners conduct guided tours.

Ford's Hospital, Greyfriars Lane (tel. 0203/223838), is a house built in the very early 16th century to house the poor of the city. Today it is a wealth of old beams and mullioned windows restored during 1953. It is now the home once more of elderly Coventry residents. There is a beautiful inner courtyard surrounded by timbered walls hung with geraniums, ferns, and ivy in summer. It is open from 10am to 5pm throughout the year, and is well worth a visit. Admission is free.

Museum of British Road Transport, St. Agnes Lane, Hales Street (tel. 0203/832425), is some 5 minutes' walk from Coventry Cathedral in the city center. It houses the largest municipally owned collection in the United Kingdom, possibly in the world. The oldest car is an original Daimler, dating from 1897 (the first English Daimler was built in Coventry only a year before). The museum also displays some of the most antique vehicles still running—six of them are regular participants in the annual London-Brighton run (only vehicles manufactured before 1905 are eligible). Curiosities include a 1910 Humber taxi whose mileage is listed at more than one million. Exhibits are diversified, as the museum has the ambitious task of covering the total history of transport in the Midlands, internationally recognized as the home of the British transport industry. Indeed, Coventry has been the home of some 124 individual motor vehicle manufacturers, many of which are represented in the collections. Among the military vehicles is the staff car in which Montgomery rode into Berlin after the defeat of the Nazis. Special exhibitions include a period street scene for the formative years of motoring (1895–1899); the Royalty in the Road display featuring both Queen Mary's 1935 limousine and King George VI's 1947 state landaulette; a history of the cycle exhibit for 1818–1987; and the most recent innovation, a hi-tech audio-visual display featuring Thrust 2, the current holder of the world land-speed record, relating the entire history of this important story from 1898 to today. The museum is open daily throughout the summer from 10am to 5pm (April to October), and on Fri., Sat., and Sun. from 10am to 4pm (November to March). Admission is £2 ($3.30) for adults, £1 ($1.65) for children.

WHERE TO STAY AND DINE

A modern structure, the **De Vere Hotel,** Cathedral Square, Coventry, West Midlands CV1 5RP (tel. 0203/633733), is considered the best in town, standing next to the cathedral. Just off the Coventry inner ring road, it is in the center of the city. For such a provincial hotel, it has a first-class standard of comfort and service. Attracting a large business clientele, the hotel sounds an elegant tone in its public rooms, including the traditional Bentleys Restaurant, with its own conservatory area built out on to Cathedral Square. In addition, Daimlers, the hotel's biggest bar, is decorated in art deco style and offers a comprehensive snack and light-meal service. The 180 bedrooms are spacious and equipped with rosewood furnishings, and each unit was designed as a twin-bedded studio with private bath and double-glazed windows to keep out traffic noises. Each accommodation has a phone and TV. Twins range in price from £89 ($146.85) to £141.50 ($233.50) daily, the latter for a VIP suite, and singles pay £72 ($118.80) to £122.50 ($202.15). These rates include breakfast and VAT.

Hotel Leofric, Broadgate, Coventry, West Midlands CV1 1LZ (tel. 0203/21371), named for Lady Godiva's husband, attracts far more business people than tourists. However, if you're overnighting in Coventry, it's a good choice, lying only 2 or 3 minutes from the cathedral, overlooking the famous statue of Lady Godiva. Each of the 91 bedrooms has a private bath, TV, phone, and radio. The regular rate in a single is from £54 ($89.10) daily, increasing to £72 ($118.80) in a double or twin. Tariffs include VAT. The Leofric's Carving Room is perhaps the best value in Coventry and serves traditional English food. A three-course meal is offered at £12.50 ($20.65). The coffeeshop, Peep-in-Tom's, is named after the legendary figure who took a look at Lady Godiva. For a before-dinner drink, I'd recommend one of the specials in Ray's Bar.

On the outskirts, **Ansty Hall,** Ansty, Coventry, West Midlands CV7 9HZ (tel. 0203/612222), offers even better living, at least for the traditionalist. The location is in a 1600s house set on about 9 acres of grounds at the village of Ansty, which lies about half a mile from junction 2 of the busy M6. Behind a pristine red-brick facade, the architectural character of the house is set as you enter a spacious reception hall paneled in oak. The hotel is small, with only 13 bedrooms, but each accommodation has been brought up to date with modern amenities such as a private bath or shower, direct-dial phone, and TV. Some units are more spacious than others, almost like a small suite. B&B ranges from £62 ($108.50) daily in a single, going up to £105 ($173.25) in a double. The hotel also serves good British food with dinners costing from £20 ($33), but you must arrive for dinner by 9:30pm.

5. Hereford and Worcester

The Wye Valley contains some of the most beautiful river scenery in Europe. The river cuts through agricultural country, and there is no population explosion in the sleepy villages. Wool used to be its staple business. Today, fruit growing and dairy farming are important.

The old county of Herefordshire has now combined with Worcestershire to form "Hereford and Worcester"-shire. Worcestershire's name, of course, has become famous around the world because of its sauce familiar to gourmets and Bloody Mary drinkers. It is one of the most charming of Midland counties, covering a portion of the rich valleys of the Severn and Avon.

Herefordshire's Black Mountains border the Welsh Brecon Beacons National Park, and between the two cathedral cities of Hereford and Worcester the ridge of the Malverns rises from the Severn Plain.

If you wish to use your BritRail Pass to travel to the heart of England, you can take the train from Paddington Station in London. The train takes you through many of the previously mentioned towns and villages, and you can stop and visit Windsor, Henley-on-Thames, and Oxford, not to mention the numerous Cotswold villages such as Chipping Campden. It must be one of the best train rides in the country, and you can also take a side trip by bus from Evesham to Stratford-upon-Avon. Or take the bus back from Stratford to Oxford via Woodstock, then the train back into London.

HEREFORD

One of the most colorful old towns in England, the ancient Saxon city of Hereford, on the Wye River, was the birthplace of both David Garrick and Nell Gwynne. Dating from 1079, the red-sandstone Hereford Cathedral, lying between West Street and King Street (tel. 0432/59880) contains all styles of architecture, from Norman to Perpendicular. One of its most interesting features is a library of chained books—more than 1,600—as well as one of the oldest maps in existence, the Mappa Mundi of 1290. There is also a treasury of the crypt.

Hereford is surrounded by both orchards and rich pasturelands. Hence it has some of the finest cider in the world, best sampled in one of the city's mellow pubs. Hereford cattle sold here are some of the finest in the world too.

The Old House, High Town (tel. 0432/268121, ext. 207), is preserved as a Jacobean period museum, with the appropriate furnishings. The completely restored half-timbered structure was built in 1621. Furnished in 17th-century style on three floors, the house includes a kitchen, hall, and bedrooms with four-poster beds. It was originally part of Butcher's Row. The house is open all year from Mon. to Sat. Summer hours are from 10am to 1pm and 2 to 5:30pm. In winter, it is open only from 10am to 1pm. Admission is 60p ($1) for adults, 30p (50¢) for children. A joint ticket costing £1 ($1.65) admits you to both The Old House and Churchill Gardens Museum.

The **Churchill Gardens Museum and Hatton Gallery,** Venns Lane, Aylestone Hill (tel. 0432/267409), which can be visited on a joint ticket combined with the Old House (see above), stand on the outskirts. Set in a large park, the center displays fine furniture, costumes, and paintings of the 18th and 19th centuries. The Hatton Gallery is devoted to the work of a local artist, Brian Hatton, killed in World War I. It is open from 2 to 5pm Tue. to Sun. all year. The museum lies at the top of Aylestone Hill, off the main Worcester Road (A465), a 10-minute walk from the city center.

The Cider Museum and King Offa Cider Brandy Distillery, Pomona Place, Whitecross Road (the A438 to Brecon) (tel. 0432/354207), tells the story of traditional cider making right through to modern factory methods. Displays include orcharding, a 17th-century French beam press, a cooper's shop, an old farm cider house, traveling cider makers' "tack" that used to be trundled from farm to farm, and the original champagne cider cellars with their tiers of bottles. Also on view are a 1920s press house and factory bottling line and the great oak vats of the Napoleonic period. The King Offa Distillery has been granted the first new license to distill cider brandy in the United Kingdom in more than 250 years, and visitors can see it being produced from the beautiful copper stills brought from Normandy. The museum shop sells cider, cider brandy, cider brandy liqueur, and Royal Cider, the real wine of old England, as well as a good selection of gifts and souvenirs. The museum is open from 10am to 5:30pm seven days a week from April to the end of October, from 1 to 5pm Mon. to Sat. from November to March. Admission is £1.50 ($2.50) for adults, £1 ($1.65) for children. The museum is 5 minutes' walk from the city center and a quarter of a mile from the city Ring Road on the A438 to Brecon.

Where to Stay

Green Dragon Hotel, Broad Street, Hereford, Hereford and Worcester HR4 9BG (tel. 0432/272506), hides behind an 18th-century Georgian facade, although this former coaching inn is considerably older. Near the cathedral, it retains many traditional old features, including some early 17th-century paneling made of Herefordshire oak. The 88 bedrooms are adequate enough, with private baths or showers, color TVs, and in-house movies. Singles cost from £65 ($107.25) to £70 ($115.50) nightly, with doubles going for £81 ($133.65) to £92 ($151.80). The paneled restaurant offers both English and continental dishes.

Hereford Moat House, Belmont Road, Hereford & Worcester HR2 7BF (tel. 0432/354301), lies off the A65, southwest of the city. The hotel has been expanded and much improved in recent years until now it offers 60 well-furnished and comfortable bedrooms, each with private bath or shower, direct-dial phone, and TV. A favorite with business clients, the hotel rents singles for £55 ($90.75) to £60 ($99) daily, with doubles costing £68 ($112.20) to £72 ($118.80). Room service is 24 hours a day, and there is ample parking. The restaurant is stylishly decorated, serving a British and French cuisine, with meals costing from £13 ($21.45).

Where to Dine

Fat Tulip, The Old Wye Bridge, 2 St. Martin's St. (tel. 0432/275808), is the best dining option that has happened to Hereford in many a year. Kevin and Susan Powles have set for themselves a formidable task: waking up the tastebuds of sleepy Hereford. Alongside the Wye River, they operate with good teamwork this casual and much frequented "English bistro." Everything tastes homemade and somehow captures the essence of the country in Mr. Powles' choice of fresh ingredients— quail, smoked marlin, crabmeat pancakes, or roast pigeon, the latter a delectable dish served with an onion confit. Meals cost from £22 ($36.30). Lunch is daily from noon to 2pm and dinner from 7 to 9:30pm Mon. to Sat. Reservations are needed.

Effy's, 96 East St. (tel. 0432/59754), is reached by heading up a narrow street (off Broad Street). It is housed behind a storefront-style facade. Inside, the atmosphere warms considerably, with a fantasy of pink-and-green latticework along with fresh flowers and a garden out back. There's even a second floor for additional seating, as there are only a few tables downstairs (which means that reservations are important). Some dishes are really excellent, and the cookery has imaginative flair. Try such offerings as pigeon breasts in garlic butter, trout meunière, or a chicken-and-zucchini casserole, finished off by, say, apple and plum pie, perhaps one of the homemade ice creams (made with fresh fruit). Dishes offered, of course, will depend on the season and what is particularly fresh on any given day. Dinner, costing from £15 ($24.75), is served from 7 to 11pm Tue. to Sat.

WORCESTER

This historic cathedral city, known for its gloves and porcelain, stands 27 miles from Birmingham, 26 miles from Stratford-upon-Avon, and 124 miles from London.

Worcester Cathedral, set high on the bank of the River Severn, celebrated its 900th anniversary in 1984. The original crypt is still in daily use, and the quire, rebuilt in 1224, has contained the tomb of King John since 1216. The chapter house, with its single central supporting column, is one of the oldest and finest in England. The cathedral, which has a long tradition of the finest choral music, is open daily from 7:45am to 6pm.

A visit to the **Royal Worcester Porcelain Factory,** Severn Street (tel. 0905/23221), is worthwhile. A tour costs £2.25 ($3.70) for adults, £1.25 ($2.05) for children over 8, allowing you to see the craftspeople at work. Unfortunately it's necessary to book ahead if you wish to take a tour (for "same day" tour, phone before 10am), but everyone can enjoy browsing in the shop at the factory. There you can buy examples of their craft. Many pieces are "seconds," all marked as such and sold at moderate prices. Most of the time you won't be able to tell why. There is also a magnificent museum.

The city is rich in other sights, including the **Commandery,** Sidbury (tel. 0905/355071), founded in the 11th century as the Hospital of St. Wulstan, becoming over the years a fine 15th-century, timber-frame structure that was the country home of the Wylde family. Charles II used the house as headquarters for the 1651 Battle of Worcester. The great hall has a hammerbeam roof and a minstrels' gallery. England's premier **Civil War Centre** is now situated here, with audio-visual displays and regular "living history" encampments with 17th-century costumes and crafts. The house is open from 10:30am to 5pm Mon. to Sat. and 2 to 5pm on Sun. Admission is £1.70 ($2.80) for adults, 85p ($1.40) for children, or £4.30 ($7.10) for a family ticket. The Commandery has canalside tea rooms, a picnic area, and a Garden of Fragrance.

You can also see **Queen Anne's Guildhall,** High Street, built in 1724, with statues honoring Charles I and Charles II, erected by the Royalists. Walking tours of the city are offered in summer. Pump Room teas are available on certain dates. Ask at the Tourist Information Centre at the guildhall for details (tel. 0905/723471).

Where to Stay and Dine

Fownes, City Walls Road, Worcester, Hereford and Worcester WR1 2AP (tel. 0905/613151), is the best place to stay in town, a glove factory in the days of Queen Victoria. It has been successfully converted until now it offers 61 well-furnished bedrooms, each with private bath or shower, direct-dial phone, and TV. Within easy walking distance of Worcester Cathedral, the hotel opens onto a canal. Most bedrooms are spacious, decorated with pastel colors and containing thoughtful extras. Singles range from £65.50 ($108.10) per night, climbing to £83.50 ($137.80) in a double. Extra facilities include a sauna and laundry service. King's Restaurant, the hotel's dining room, is credited with offering the finest cuisine in town.

Brown's Old Cornmill, 24 Quay St. (tel. 0905/26263), is a richly atmospheric dining room in a building constructed as a grain mill in the late 1700s. Today, subtly modernized reminders of an agrarian society surround you as you enjoy flavorful meals. You might begin with a warm salad of bacon and scallops, following with roast quail garnished with cognac and grapes or a plump chicken breast loaded with herb-and-cheese stuffing. Fish is popular here, with several preparations of Dover sole, as well as imaginative dishes of salmon and turbot. Fixed-price lunches begin at £16.95 ($27.95), and dinner at £24 ($39.60). A special Sun. lunch menu is offered for £14 ($23.10). Service is from 12:30 to 1:45pm and 7:30 to 9:30pm Mon. to Sat., from 12:30 to 2pm Sun.; closed Sat. at lunch, Sun. evening, and bank holidays.

Where to Stay and Dine at Abberley

The Elms Hotel, Abberley, near Worcester, Hereford and Worcester WR6 6AT (tel. 0299/896666), is on the A443 12 miles northwest of Worcester on the border of the old county of Herefordshire. Queen Anne was on the throne when this magnificent country house was built in 1710. Twelve acres of rolling parkland surround formal gardens, and there are tennis courts, a putting green, and a croquet lawn for the use of the guests. This is a warm country house where open log fires burn in the comfortably furnished lounges to welcome visitors. The 25 bedrooms are mostly large, some with four-poster beds. All have private baths or showers, radios, phones, and color TVs. Much antique and good English furniture is used. Bathrooms are supplied with such accessories as hairdryers. Rates for single rooms with bath start at £80 ($132), £95 ($156.75) in the adjoining coach house, £105 ($173.25) in the newly refurbished main house, or £115 ($189.75) for a four-poster bedroom. All tariffs include a full English breakfast, VAT, and service. Brooke Room Restaurant is open daily for lunch from 12:30 to 2pm and for dinner from 7:30 to 9:30pm. It's an elegant and restful place. Using only the finest and freshest ingredients and the lightly flavored sauces of nouvelle cuisine, the chef admits that larger portions are served here than are usual in such restaurants, in order to satisfy the hearty country appetites of the local clientele. You can enjoy the view of the raised gardens, floodlit at night, through the arched windows while you wait for your freshly prepared meal to be served. Luncheon is £13.95 ($23); dinner, £22 ($36.30). There is a good wine list.

Museums in the Environs

Sir Edward Elgar's Birthplace, Crown East Lane, Lower Broadheath (tel. 090566/224), about 3 miles west of Worcester, is a brick cottage surrounded by stables and a coach house built by his father and uncle in the early 19th century. Nowadays the house contains a museum of photographs and drawings, original musical scores, and mementos of his youth. Musicians and conductors come from afar to check his music and their interpretations of it. To reach the house, drive out of Worcester on the A44 toward Leominster. After 2 miles, turn off to the right at the sign. The house is in the village, half a mile along a side road. Admission is £2 ($3.30) for adults, 50p (85¢) for children. It's open from 10:30am to 6pm in summer, from 1:30 to 4:30pm in winter; closed Wed. and from mid-January to mid-February.

Avoncroft Museum of Buildings, Stoke Heath, Bromsgrove (tel. 0527/ 31886), is 11 miles from Worcester and 21 miles from Stratford-upon-Avon. It is open daily from 11am to 5:30pm in June, July, and August. Hours are the same in April, May, September, and October, but it's closed Mon. In March and November, it's open from 11am to 4:30pm Tue. to Thur. and Sat. and Sun.; closed altogether in December, January, and February. Admission is £2.30 ($3.80) for adults, £1.15 ($1.90) for children. A family ticket admitting two adults and two children goes for £6 ($9.90). The museum is an open-air site where a variety of historic buildings have been saved from destruction and reconstructed. There are a windmill in working order; a merchant's timber-framed house from the 15th century; an Elizabethan house; a cockfight theater, a stable, a wagon shed, and an ice house, all from the 18th century; chain- and nailmaking workshops; a blacksmith's forge; an 18th-century dovecote with doves; a three-seater earth closet (outdoor toilet); and an early 19th-century tollhouse. The displays give a fascinating insight into the construction of buildings erected by English forebear. The 14th-century Guesten Hall roof from Worcester is being reconstructed on a new building that, as well as displaying the roof, will serve as an exhibition hall for the museum. Free car parking is available, and there is also a picnic area.

Nearby, **Hanbury Hall** (tel. 052784/214) is a Wren-style, red-brick building erected in the early 18th century. It is remarkable for its painted ceilings and magnificent staircase by Thornhill. It is open from 2 to 5pm Sat. and Sun. from April to October (including all of Easter weekend). From May to the end of September, hours are from 2 to 6pm Wed. to Sun. and bank holidays. Admission is £2.20 ($3.65) to £1.10 ($1.80) for children. Tea is served in the building.

THE MALVERNS

The beautiful, historic Malverns, once part of the ancient kingdom of Mercia, lie to the west of Worcester. Great Malvern became important in the 19th century as a spa town, and much of the Victorian splendor remains. The Malvern Hills stretch for 9 miles, with six townships lying along their line, making this a splendid walking center for your visit to the shire of Hereford and Worcester. The largest Priory Church in the area dates from the 15th century and has some fine stained glass. The monks' stalls have superb misericords and medieval titles. You can wander through Great Malvern, Malvern Link, West Malvern, Malvern Wells, Little Malvern, and several other hamlets on a walking tour.

Two miles out of Great Malvern to the left as you leave on the Ledbury road is **St. Wulstan's Church** where Sir Edward Elgar, who lived throughout his life in the Malvern area, is buried with his wife and daughter. There is a bronze bust to the composer in Priory Park, and he lived at Craeglea on the Malvern Wells road and at Forli in Alexandra Road. It was here that he composed the *Enigma Variations, Sea Pictures,* and the *Dream of Gerontius.*

Water is still bottled at **Holy Well,** above Malvern Wells, and you can visit the place where monks are reputed to have wrapped the infirm in cloths steeped in the waters to cure their ills. St. Anne's Well is also open to view above the town, but you have to be hardy to climb the 200-odd steps to taste the waters.

Where to Stay and Dine at Malvern Wells

Great Malvern has many fine accommodations, but discriminating travelers over the years have retreated instead to Malvern Wells, 2 miles south on the A449. There they find peace and tranquility with views over the Severn and Evesham Vales. Not only does Malvern Wells possess one of the most charming hotels in the area, it also has the finest and most acclaimed cuisine.

The **Cottage in the Wood Hotel,** Holywell Road, Malvern Wells, Great Malvern, Hereford and Worcester WR14 4LG (tel. 0684/573487), is considered the best place to stay at Malvern Wells. Owned and run by John and Sue Pattin, the hotel is a Georgian building originally constructed as part of a much larger estate. The property lies in 7 acres of lawn, gardens, and woodlands stretching down the hillside commanding 30-mile views across the Severn Valley to the Cotswolds. The public rooms are decorated with antiques and reproductions, and upholstered sofas and chairs allow for relaxing near open fires. The 20 bedrooms are scattered through the older main house and a pair of more recently converted outer buildings. Each has a private bath, direct-dial phone, and TV. Accommodations cost £50 ($82.50) daily in a single, £66 ($108.90) to £100 ($165) in a double. The flavorful meals served in the dining room cost from £15 ($24.75).

Restaurant Croque-en-Bouche, 221 Wells Rd. (tel. 0684/565612), opposite the filling station, is run by Robin and Marion Jones in what was the bakery and grocer's shop in a five-story Victorian building. There is still an old oven in the basement where wine is now stored. In the nice old house is a small bar where Robin offers a list of aperitifs, including the house drink of raspberry liqueur with sparkling white burgundy. Dinner at £26 ($42.90) starts with a huge tureen of homemade soup, followed by a choice for the fish course, such as cannelloni with crab and coriander. The main course might be venison or wild rabbit niçoise. The cheeseboard is well supplied with British products, and you can finish with a crème brûlée or sorbet made with fresh fruits. As there are only Robin and Marion to look after you, you must reserve a table. Coffee is served, and since smoking is not permitted in the dining room, smokers adjourn to the bar at this stage. The restaurant is open from 7:30 to 9:30pm Wed. to Sat.

LEDBURY

Hope End Country House Hotel, Hope End, Ledbury, Hereford and Worcester HR8 1JQ (tel. 0531/3613) lies at Wellington Heath, 2 miles north of Ledbury. Elizabeth Barrett Browning lived here during her first 23 years. It is owned and operated by John and Patricia Hegarty, who come from local families. John's ancestor helped build the canal and bring the railway to Ledbury, and Patricia's family has lived here for more than 500 years. The house, refurbished in English country style, is furnished with antiques, and paintings and other art adorn the walls of the drawing room. The nine bedrooms have phones, and all have adjoining baths. The charge for B&B, VAT, and service ranges from £80 ($132) to £120 ($198) for two persons, the latter price for one of the larger rooms or in the suite across the courtyard under the minaret. Patricia enjoys a reputation for her cuisine and has written a widely acclaimed book on English cookery. She specializes in providing wholesome and fresh foods and bakes her own brown bread. Fresh fruit and vegetables come from the large walled garden. Fresh eggs, local beef and lamb, fish and game, and a wide selection of English cheeses make meals a pleasure. Five-course dinners include such appetizers as haddock hotpots with cider, followed by wild duck, or lamb. Dinner costs from £25 ($41.25). Closed Mon. and Tue., the inn operates from March to November.

EVESHAM

A delightful market town on the Avon River, Evesham is known for its riverside parks. It contains several interesting buildings, including a 16th-century bell tower. It is a center of a famous fruit- and vegetable-growing region, and in springtime the Vale of Evesham is a mass of blossoms. Six miles southeast of Broadway and 14 miles northeast of Stratford-upon-Avon, it makes a good center for touring both the Cotswolds and the Shakespeare Country.

Evesham Hotel, Coopers Lane, off Waterside, Evesham, Hereford and Worcester WR11 6DA (tel. 0386/765566), lies down a small lane beside the River Avon to Evesham. It is owned and run by the Jenkinson family. John is general manager, and there is always a Jenkinson on duty. A dwelling has stood on the site since the 16th century, and the mulberry trees and cedars of Lebanon date back almost that far. The lounges and the restaurant look out over the gardens to the trees. There is a modern bar where the usual drinks are served, plus an amazing selection of malt whiskies and brandies. In the Cedar Restaurant, dinner, from 7 to 9:30pm daily, is a well-prepared à la carte event. You choose your meal from such dishes as pheasant

Normandie or vegetarian hotpot. All are served with a selection of fresh vegetables and followed by homemade desserts. The meal price for three courses is £15 ($24.75). At lunch, from 12:30 to 2pm, a buffet offers homemade soup, selections from a serve-yourself buffet, and coffee, all costing around £8 ($13.20). The 40 bedrooms are warm and comfortable, with color TVs radios, phones, hot beverage facilities, and private bathrooms. An added wing has well-equipped units with views over the garden. It's attached to the main house by a fully enclosed and heated corridor. The cost for B&B is £50 ($82.50) daily in a single, £70 ($115.50) in a double, and £82 ($135.30) in a family suite. All tariffs include VAT and a full English breakfast, or a continental breakfast served in your room if you prefer. Other facilities include an indoor, heated pool.

6. Shropshire

Immortalized by A. E. Housman's *A Shropshire Lad,* this hilly county borders Wales, which accounts for its turbulent history. The bloody battles are over today, and the towns of Shropshire, with their black-and-white timbered houses, are peaceful and quiet. The county makes a good base for touring in the Welsh mountains.

When Parliament redistricted and even renamed some of the shires of England in 1973, the name of Shropshire was changed back to a much older name—Salop. However, in this case, the name just didn't catch on, and you'll find the county still called Shropshire on recent maps and by most of its inhabitants.

SHREWSBURY

Lying within a horseshoe bend of the Severn River, Shrewsbury is the capital of Shropshire. The river almost encloses the town. Known for its cakes and ale, Shrewsbury contains one of the best-known schools in England. It was also the birthplace of Charles Darwin.

Considered the finest Tudor town in England, Shrewsbury is noted for its black-and-white buildings of timber and plaster, including Abbot's House from 1450 and the tall gabled Ireland's Mansion from 1575 standing on High Street. It also has a number of Georgian and Regency mansions, some old bridges, and handsome churches, including the Abbey Church of Saint Peter and St. Mary's Church. The city lies 164 miles from London and 39 miles from Stoke-on-Trent.

Shrewsbury Castle, built by a Norman earl, Roger de Montgomery, in 1083, stands in a dominating position where the River Severn almost surrounds the town. It houses the Shropshire Regimental Museum, including the collections of the King's Shropshire Light Infantry, the Shropshire Yeomanry Cavalry, and the Shropshire Royal Horse Artillery. The collections represent more than 300 years of regimental service and include a lock of Napoleon's hair and an American flag captured in 1814 when the White House was seized and burned in the War of 1812. The castle is open daily from 10am to 5pm. Admission is 60p ($1). For more information, phone 0743/58516.

Rowley's House Museum, on Barker Street (tel. 0743/61196), is housed in a fine 16th-century timber-frame house and an adjoining brick mansion. This museum includes displays on art, local history, Roman and prehistoric archeology, geology, costumes, and natural history. The great treasures include the fine Hadrianic forum inscription and silver mirror, both from the nearby Roman city of Viroconium (Wroxeter). The museum is open from 10am to 5pm Mon. to Sat. year round and also from noon to 5pm Sun. from Easter to mid-September. Admission is 60p ($1) for adults, 30p (50¢) for children.

Clive House Museum on College Hill (tel. 0743/54811), townhouse of Clive of India when he served as major of Shrewsbury in 1762, contains period rooms and local pottery and porcelain, early watercolors, and textiles, and has a garden. Hours are 2 to 5pm on Mon., 10am to 1pm and 2 to 5pm Tue. to Sat. Admission is 30p (50¢) for adults, 15p (25¢) for children.

Where to Stay and Dine

Prince Rupert Hotel, Butcher Row, Shrewsbury, Shropshire SY1 1UQ (tel. 0743/236000), is a hotel of character—part of it dating from the 15th century—right on a quiet side street in the center of town. Its front has four peaked gables and, in summer, a wealth of flowerboxes. The facade is characterized by peaked gables on the Old Church Street entrance. Even though the interior has been modernized, it still has exposed beams and uneven floors. A favorite gathering spot is the lounge, which is tapestried. There are two restaurants, including the Cavalier, which has a reputation for fine cuisine. The 63 air-conditioned rooms are bright and fresh, with compact, well-maintained baths, phones, and TVs. Singles range in price from £58 ($95.70) daily, and doubles or twins begin at £73 ($120.45). Guests have included Margaret Thatcher and her husband, Denis, and George C. Scott, who stayed here for 7 weeks when he made a film based on Dickens's *A Christmas Carol*.

Lion Hotel, Wyle Cop, Shrewsbury, Shropshire SY1 1UY (tel. 0743/53107), is a red-brick structure, once a famous posting inn, standing in the center of town near English Bridge. In part the hotel dates from the 15th century, and oak beams and paneling from that period remain. Many famous people have stayed here, including Dickens, Jenny Lind, and De Quincey, who described the hotel's Adam ballroom in his *Confessions of an Opium Eater*. Dickens stayed in what is now the beamed Dickens Suite, where you can read his comments on his sojourn here, which he described as "the strangest little rooms, the ceilings of which I can touch with my hands." The cost is £100 ($165) nightly for two persons. The 59 bedrooms are well furnished, with baths or showers, TVs, and phones. Singles cost £55 ($90.75) daily, and doubles go for £75 ($123.75) to £85 ($140.25), all tariffs including VAT and service. The restaurant with its 1920s decor serves both table d'hôte and à la carte meals. Dinner is from £12.95 ($21.35). The hotel has two bars, the Oak bar featuring a buffet at lunch.

LUDLOW

Looking down on the Teme River, this mellow old town was once a Norman guardian of the Welsh border, with lots of history whispering through its quiet lanes and courts and the Georgian and Jacobean timbered buildings. The two little princes who died in the Tower of London lived here, and it was once the refuge and home of the first wife of Henry VIII, Catherine of Aragon. You can visit the Church of St. Laurence where the unhappy queen prayed.

The most colorful street is known as "Broad," rising from the old Ludford Bridge to Broadgate, the one remaining gateway from walls erected in the Middle Ages. See, in particular, the Butter Cross and Reader's House. A. E. Housman's grave is in the cemetery here. The location is 162 miles from London and 29 miles from Shrewsbury.

Where to Stay and Dine

The Feathers, Bull Ring, Ludlow, Shropshire SY8 1AA (tel. 0584/875261), is one of England's most famous Elizabethan inns. Built in 1603 as a private residence, it is characterized by its half-timbered front and richly decorated interior. The 36 bedrooms are bright and cheerful, and all of them contain private baths, as well as phones, radios, TVs, trouser presses, and tea and coffee makers. Colors are in harmony, with Welsh tapestry bedspreads. Singles go for £65 ($107.25) nightly, and doubles or twins cost £95 ($156.75) to £105 ($173.25), including an English breakfast. If possible, ask for one of the units with a four-poster bed. The Richard III restaurant, with its original fireplace, is in the old-world style, serving good food and drink. Dinners go for £18 ($29.70) and up. There are also two fully licensed bars, and polished brass and copper set the right decorative tone. In the James I lounge, you can enjoy a carved mantelpiece and an elaborately ornamented plaster ceiling.

IRONBRIDGE

Ironbridge Gorge is the location of an intriguing complex of museums, the birthplace of the Industrial Revolution.

The Iron Bridge was the first in the world made of that metal, which was cast at Coalbrookdale in 1779 and gave its name to the area. Abraham Darby I, ironmaster, first smelted iron using coke as a fuel at the Old Furnace in Coalbrookdale, thus paving the way for the first iron rails, iron bridge, iron boat, iron aqueduct, and iron-framed building. The Ironbridge Gorge Museum spreads over some 6 square miles of the Severn Gorge, encompassing a unique series of industrial monuments and displays.

The **Ironbridge Gorge Museum,** Ironbridge, Telford (tel. 095245/3522), in-cludes the Blists Hill Open Air Museum with a re-creation of a 19th-century town with costumed demonstrators, the Coalbrookdale Museum and Darby Furnace of Iron with a sound-and-light display, the Coalport China Museum, the Jackfield Tile Museum, the Severn Warehouse (now the Museum of the River), and many other smaller museums, including the Bedlam Furnaces, the 1779 Iron Bridge (first in the world) with its original tollhouse, Rosehill House (the restored 19th-century home of the Darby family), the Long Warehouse Library and Archives, and the Elton Gal-lery with charming exhibitions. A ticket to all the attractions is £6.50 ($10.75) for adults, £3.80 ($6.25) for children. A family ticket for two adults and up to five chil-dren costs £18.50 ($30.55). All the sites are open from 10am to 6pm daily from mid-February to the end of October. The Ironbridge Gorge was declared a World Heritage Site by UNESCO in 1987.

7. Staffordshire

Stoke-on-Trent is the name of the five towns known as the Potteries, the "Five Towns" of Arnold Bennett's novels. The Potteries are known throughout the world for the excellence of their fine porcelain and china.

The so-called Black Country of steelworks and coal mines has almost disap-peared, although you can visit a coal mine and descend in the "cage" to the worked-out seams.

Within easy reach of the industrial town of Dovedale is a valley with some of England's most beautiful scenery, forming part of the wild country of Peak District National Park.

Unless you have endless time and can match local bus routes to your schedule, you'll find it difficult exploring the "Five Towns" without a car.

STOKE-ON-TRENT

Because of the worldwide interest in the making of pottery, this town has found itself something of a tourist attraction. It's the home of the pottery made famous by Josiah Wedgwood, along with other well-known names such as Coalport, Minton, and Spode. It lies 162 miles from London and 58 miles from Liverpool.

The **Wedgwood Visitor Centre,** at Barlaston (tel. 0782/204141), charges adults £1.75 ($2.90) and children £1 ($1.65) for admission, and is open from 9am to 5pm Mon. to Fri., 10am to 4pm on Sat. The center is also open on public holidays with the exception of the Christmas period. In the demonstration hall, you can watch the clay pots being formed on the potter's wheel, see how the raised motifs so well known on Wedgwood Jasper are made and added to the pieces, as well as wit-ness how plates are turned and fired, then painted. Craft operatives are happy to answer your questions about their special occupation. There's a continuous film show in the large cinema, and the beginning of the movie is announced on the pub-lic address system. In the shop you can see samples of all the sorts of items made at the factory and purchase souvenirs. Prices are the same as elsewhere, but they do sometimes have items of discontinued lines and some "seconds" available at re-duced prices.

The museum was redesigned and enlarged in 1985 and features "living" dis-plays including Josiah Wedgwood's Etruria factory and his Victorian showroom. Other room settings can also be seen. When you need a rest, there is a lounge with a snack cafeteria where a selection of light refreshments can be had at reasonable prices. Here you can write your postcards home and have them franked with a special stamp to say they were mailed at the Wedgwood Centre.

Royal Doulton, Nile Street, Burslem, near Stoke-on-Trent (tel. 0782/ 575454). You will walk for nearly a mile and negotiate some 250 steps during the tour of this pottery factory, but you will see exactly how plates, cups, and figures are made from basic raw materials. The gift shop has slightly imperfect articles on sale alongside quality goods, and you can browse through the Sir Henry Doulton Gallery, tracing the company's history since 1815 and containing a collection of Doulton's historical figures. Tours of the factory are at 10:30am and 2pm, costing £2 ($3.30). The gallery is open Mon. to Fri. from 9am to 4:15pm. Advance reservations are advisable. Call Sandra Baddeley, the tour organizer.

John Beswick, Gold Street, Longton, near Stoke-on-Trent (tel. 0782/ 313041). Since 1896, the John Beswick Studios of Royal Doulton have built a reputation for fine ceramic sculpture. Most renowned for its authentic studies of horses, birds, and animals, the studio also creates the famed Character and Toby Jugs of Royal Doulton. You may be lucky enough to see Peter Rabbit in the making during a visit. The 1½-hour tour ends in the factory shop so you can indulge your purchasing whims. Tours depart at 10:15am and 2pm Mon. to Fri., costing £2 ($3.30). Advance reservations are essential (call Joan Barker).

Spode, Church Street, Stoke-on-Trent (tel. 0782/744011), is yet another factory that offers guided tours, available at 10am and 2pm Mon. to Thur., and at 10am Fri. Again, advance reservations are essential. The cost is £1.25 ($2.05) for a standard tour and £6 ($9.90) for a connoisseur tour. The shop is open from 9am to 5pm Mon. to Thur., from 9am to 4pm Fri., and from 9am to 1pm Sat.

Moorcroft Pottery, W. Moorcroft, Sandbach Road, Burslem, Stoke-on-Trent (tel. 0782/214323), is an interesting alternative to the world-famous names. Founded in 1898 by William Moorcroft, who produced his own special brand of pottery and was his own exclusive designer until his death in 1945, the pottery is special in that decoration is part of the first firing, giving it a higher quality of color and brilliance than, say, Spode. Today, design is in the hands of William's son, John, who carries on the personal traditions of the family firm, creating clear floral designs in bright, clear colors for what has been described as the art nouveau of the pottery world. There is much to admire and buy in the factory seconds shop. The factory and the restored bottle oven are open from 10am to 5pm Mon. to Fri. and from 9:30am to 4:30pm Sat. There is always someone around to explain the various processes and to show you around the museum, with its collections of early Moorcroft. Factory tours take place on Wed. and cost £1 ($1.65).

Afterward, a visit to the past is in order. The **Gladstone Pottery Museum,** Uttoxeter Road at Longton (tel. 0782/319232), is a 19th-century pottery factory restored as a museum, with craftspeople demonstrating daily in original workshops. Galleries depict the rise of the Staffordshire pottery industry; tile history; sanitary ware with washstand bowls and jugs plus toilets of all shapes, sizes, colors, and decoration. There are replicas of a potter's house and a factory manager's office. Admission to the museum is £2.50 ($4.15) for adults, £1.75 ($2.90) for children. It is open March to October from 10am to 5pm Mon. to Sat. and from 2 to 5pm Sun. From October to February, visits are possible from 10am to 4pm.

Stoke-on-Trent City Museum and Art Gallery, Bethesda Street, Hanley (tel. 0782/202173), has departments of fine arts, decorative arts, natural history, archeology, and social history. In addition, it houses one of the largest and finest collections of ceramics in the world. It's open from 10am to 5pm Mon. to Sat., 2 to 5pm Sun. Admission is free.

Minton Museum, London Road (tel. 0782/744766), is the starting point for a 1½-hour conducted tour through the major departments of the renowned pottery firm. A telephone call or a letter in advance is advised if you would like to join the £2 ($3.30) conducted tour, which includes a visit to the department where Minton's celebrated raised gold designs are produced. Visitors will also have the opportunity of seeing free-hand painting of the highest order. Details are available of a service offered by Minton enabling customers to commission a special handpainted, personalized plate featuring an illustration of their own choice. The cost is around £200 ($330), and delivery takes 3 to 4 months. Ask the museum curator or factory guides.

The **Chatterley Whitfield Mining Museum** at Tunstall, Stoke-on-Trent (tel. 0782/813337), is a unique museum of mining with an underground gallery showing the history of mining from early times to the modern day. Tours underground are led when possible by ex-miners who vividly relate their experiences working in a coal mine. Visitors are "kitted out" with lamp and helmet, and stout shoes are recommended. Chatterley Whitfield was the first colliery to produce one million tons of coal in a year. Coal was mined here for 140 years before its transformation into a museum in 1979. Other displays and attractions include a steam-winding engine, pit ponies, locomotives, a shire horse, colliery canteen, museum shop, and a large car park. In addition to these, Chatterley Whitfield now houses the National Mining Collection brought from Lound Hall in Nottinghamshire. Hours are from 10am to 4pm daily, or evening tours by special arrangement. Tours cost £3.50 ($5.80) for adults, £2.50 ($4.30) for children.

Where to Stay and Dine

For those who wish to visit the Staffordshire Potteries and stay overnight in this industrial part of the country, I offer the following suggestions.

Crown Hotel, 38 High St., Stone, Staffordshire ST15 8AS (tel. 0782/813535), is a solid 18th-century coaching inn, rebuilt by Henry Holland on the site of a far more ancient staging post dating to 1579 and known as one of the most important in the country in the reign of Charles II. Today the coach yard is roofed in to provide for the lofty paneled dining room. The sleek "carriages" of today's travelers are housed in a large yard behind the hotel. Some of the 29 accommodations are in the main hotel, reached by a fine galleried oak staircase; others are in an annex at the back. All units have baths (showers only in the newer part), color TVs, and hot beverage facilities. Prices run from £62 ($102.30) daily in a double with bath, £38 ($62.70) in a single. Prices include VAT, service, and an enormous breakfast. Dinner in the paneled dining hall includes main-course specials such as salmon and steaks. Dinners are from £12 ($19.80). At lunch, a buffet provides substantial meals.

Haydon House Hotel, Haydon Street, Basford, Stoke-on-Trent, Staffordshire ST4 6JD (tel. 0782/711311), is a turn-of-the-century privately owned townhouse in the heart of the pottery district. It offers singles with bath for £55 ($90.75) daily, and doubles with bath or shower go for £65 ($107.25). All 30 units have color TVs, radios, and phones. Six private apartments, called Glebe Mews, have lots of antiques and cost from £98 ($161.70) per day for two persons. If you make a reservation in advance, you may be able to get the antique four-poster bedroom. The Townhouse bar and dining room are Victorian in style and comfort, with antique clocks (83 in all), lending a club atmosphere to the hotel. Haydon House is noted for good food prepared by an award-winning chef. A three-course luncheon chosen from the ample list of dishes will cost from £14.50 ($23.95) up. The table d'hôte dinner, at £14.50 ($23.95), allows you to choose from five appetizers and five main dishes, plus dessert or cheese, then coffee. The à la carte menu is more extensive, including specially prepared steak dishes. English teas are served from 3 to 5pm in the Conservatory.

STAFFORD

The county town of Staffordshire was the birthplace of Izaak Walton, the British writer and celebrated fisherman. Long famous as a boot-making center, it contains many historic buildings, notably St. Chad's, the town's oldest church; St. Mary's, with its unusual octagonal tower; and the Ancient High House, the largest timber-frame townhouse in England. The location is 142 miles from London and 17 miles from Stoke-on-Trent.

In the Staffordshire countryside at Shallowford, between Stafford and Eccleshall, lies **Izaak Walton Cottage** (tel. 0785/760278). Walton is best remembered as the author of *The Compleat Angler*. The period garden of his cottage has been planted with 17th-century herbs and flowers, as well as plants. Admission is

50p (85¢) for adults, 25p (40¢) for children. It is open from 12:30 to 5:30pm Tue. to Sun. from mid-March to October. In winter, it's open only on Sat. and Sun. from 12:30 to 4:30pm.

Where to Stay and Dine

Tillington Hall Hotel, Eccleshall Road, Stafford, Staffordshire ST16 1JJ (tel. 0785/53531), a country house hotel that has been extensively remodeled and renovated, stands in its own grounds just a mile from the center of the county town, yet less than half a mile from the M6 motorway (exit 14). There are 90 bedrooms, each with private baths, color TVs, radios, direct-dial phones, trouser presses, hairdryers, and hot beverage facilities. The charge is from £70 ($115.50) daily in a single, £84 ($138.60) for a twin-bedded room. All tariffs include a full English breakfast, service, and VAT. Luncheon and dinner in the Potters Table Restaurant costs from £12 ($19.80).

LICHFIELD

Fans of Samuel Johnson pay a pilgrimage here to this historic city where he was born in 1709, son of an unsuccessful bookseller and parchment maker. The city is noted for its cathedral, whose three spires are known as "Ladies of the Vale." The tallest spire rises more than 250 feet, and the west front of the cathedral was built from about 1280. You can walk around the beautiful close and see a bit of the Vicars Close, with its half-timbered houses, along with the 17th-century Bishops Palace. The location is 128 miles from London and 30 miles from Stoke-on-Trent.

Dr. Johnson's Birthplace on Breadmarket Street (tel. 0543/264972) contains mementos and pictures of the author and his contemporaries. It is open daily from 10am to 5pm. Admission is 75p ($1.24) for adults, 40p (65¢) for children.

Across the street from Dr. Johnson's Birthplace stands the **Heritage Centre & Treasury,** Breadmarket Street (tel. 0543/256611), in Lichfield's Market Square. The former parish church has been transformed into a treasury and exhibition room with a coffeeshop and a gift shop. The exhibition tells the story of Lichfield through its people and events, including an audio-visual presentation of the Civil War. The treasury displays examples of the silversmithing art showing civic, regimental, and church plate. Ancient charters are displayed in the Muniment Room. The center is open daily from 10am to 5pm. Admission is 85p ($1.40) for adults, 40p (65¢) for children.

You can also visit the **guildhall** behind the Heritage Exhibition. Over the city dungeons dating from the Middle Ages, the guildhall was rebuilt in 1846. Prisoners were jailed here before they were burned at the stake in market square.

Incidentally, market days are Fri. and Sat. in Lichfield.

Where to Stay and Dine

George Hotel, Bird Street, Lichfield, Staffordshire WS13 6PR (tel. 0543/414822), is the most desirable place to stay in town. In the center of Lichfield, this hotel has a regal look to it. In the vicinity of the cathedral, the Georgian inn offers 38 handsomely furnished and equipped bedrooms, each with its own private bath or shower as well as direct-dial phone and TV. The hotel has many amenities, including plenty of towels and toilet articles. Singles rent for £68 ($112.20) to £76 ($125.40) daily, and doubles cost £86 ($141.90) to £95 ($156.75). Have a drink in the lovely old bar before going in to dinner (but do so before 9:30pm). The George is also known for serving some of the best food in town, both a British and an international menu, with dinners costing from £12 ($19.80).

TUTBURY

Once a stronghold of the Anglo-Saxon kings of Mercia, and mentioned in the *Domesday Book,* Tutbury is a small town on the Dove River, lying 4 miles north of Burton-upon-Trent. It has a fine Norman church and the ruins of Tutbury Castle.

Ye Olde Dog and Partridge, High Street, Tutbury, Staffordshire DE13 9LS (tel. 0283/813030), has been a village inn for so long there is no clear record of its beginnings. Charming in appearance, it has an ornate black-and-white timbered facade, bay windows, and leaded glass, surviving elements from the 15th century. A coaching house in the 18th and 19th centuries, it offers a more modernized hospitality today. Inside, the inn still has a wealth of old timbering and fireplaces, maintaining a traditional character. All the bedrooms have private baths, color TVs, mini-bars, and direct-dial phones. A single costs from £54 ($89.10) daily and a double or twin, from £66 ($108.90). All tariffs include a full breakfast and VAT. The inn has an intimate wine bar and carvery open seven days a week. The carvery is known for the quality of its roast beef.

XIV

CAMBRIDGE AND EAST ANGLIA

1. CAMBRIDGE

2. ELY

3. THAXTED

4. SAFFRON WALDEN

5. DEDHAM

6. NEWMARKET

7. CLARE

8. LONG MELFORD

9. LAVENHAM

10. WOODBRIDGE

11. ALDEBURGH

12. EAST BERGHOLT

13. NORWICH

14. SHIPDHAM

15. NORTH NORFOLK

The four counties of East Anglia—Essex, Suffolk, Norfolk, and Cambridge-shire—are essentially low-lying areas, in parts of which the bucolic life still reigns supreme.

East Anglia was an ancient Anglo-Saxon kingdom, under heavy domination of the Danes for many a year. Beginning in the 12th century, it became the center of a great cloth industry that brought it prosperity, as the spires of some of its churches testify to this day. Essentially, it is a land of heathland, fens, marshes, and broads in Norfolk.

Cambridge is the most visited city in East Anglia, and you will not want to miss it. Ely is one of England's most important cathedrals.

Don't neglect to also pass through Suffolk and Essex—Constable country, containing some of the finest landscapes in England. Norwich, one of the major cit-ies of East Anglia, is less visited, but the fortunate few who go that far toward the North Sea will be rewarded.

CAMBRIDGESHIRE

Cambridgeshire is the westernmost county of East Anglia. This area still has fen country. In the time of Hereward the Wake, the fens covered most of East Anglia, but they were gradually drained by landowners to create farmland. Wicken Fen (on the A1123) and Woodwalton Fen (off the B1040 at Ramsey) are two of the few such areas that have been preserved.

Cambridge is the most visited city in East Anglia. The other top attraction is Ely Cathedral, just north of Cambridge. Cambridge is easily reached from London by frequent trains from St. Pancras station.

1. Cambridge

Cambridge is a collage of visual images: A young couple lying in an open green space between colleges; rowing under the Bridge of Sighs; spires and turrets; drooping willows, and punting on the Cam; dusty secondhand bookshops; daffodils swaying in the meadows; carol singing on Christmas Eve in King's College Chapel; dancing till sunrise at the May balls; narrow lanes where Darwin, Newton, and Cromwell once trod; The Backs, where the lawns of the colleges sweep down to the Cam River; the tattered black robe of an upperclassman, hanging by a thread to his shoulder as it flies in the wind.

We're in the university city of Cambridge, which, along with Oxford, is one of the ancient seats of learning in Britain. The city on the banks of the Cam River is also the county town of Cambridgeshire, 55 miles northeast of London, 80 miles from Oxford. In many ways, the stories of Oxford and Cambridge are similar—particularly the age-old conflict between town and gown. But Oxford is an industrial city, sheltering a thriving life beyond the campus; what Cambridge industry has is high tech.

There is much to see and explore in Cambridge—so give yourself time to wander, even aimlessly. For those pressed, I'll offer more specific direction.

ORIENTATION

The center of Cambridge is a pedestrian mall, so park your car at one of the many car parks (they get more expensive as you get nearer the city center), and take the opportunity to visit some of the colleges spread throughout the city. King's College might be number one on your list, especially the chapel that houses *The Adoration of the Magi* by Rubens. Follow the courtyards through to the "Backs" (the college lawns) and walk through to Trinity (where Prince Charles studied) and St. John's, including the Bridge of Sighs.

There are many other historic buildings in the city center, all within walking distance, including Great St. Mary's Church (from which the original Westminster chimes come), St. Bene't's Church, the Round Church, the Fitzwilliam Museum (one of the largest and finest provincial museums), the Folk Museum, and the modern Kettles Yard Art Gallery.

For a more detailed insight into the life and times of Cambridge, both town and gown, join one of the guided tours from the **Cambridge Tourist Information Centre,** Wheeler Street (tel. 0223/322640), which is behind the guildhall. The center has a wide range of information, including data on public transportation in the area and on different sightseeing attractions.

TOURS AND TOURIST SERVICES

A tourist reception center for Cambridge and Cambridgeshire is operated by **Guide Friday Ltd.** at Cambridge Railway Station (tel. 0223/62444). The center, on the concourse of the railway station, dispenses free maps and brochures of the city and area and operates tours. Also available is a full range of tourist services, including accommodation booking. In summer the tourist center is open daily from 9am to 6:30pm, closing at 4pm in winter. Guided tours of Cambridge leave the center daily. In summer, aboard open-top, double-decker buses, departures are every 15 minutes from 9am to 6pm. In winter, departures are hourly. The tour can be a 1-hour panoramic ride or you can get off at any of the many stops, such as King's College Chapel or the American Cemetery, then rejoin the tour when you wish. Tickets are valid all day for you to hop on and off the buses. The price of this tour is £3.50 ($5.80) per person.

CAMBRIDGE UNIVERSITY

Oxford University predates Cambridge. But in the early 13th century scholars began coming up to Cambridge. The choice of the market town as a seat of learning just happened—coming about because a core of masters and students, dissatisfied with Oxford, gathered here. Eventually, Cambridge won partial recognition from Henry III, rising and slumping with the approval or disdain of subsequent English monarchs. Cambridge consists of 31 colleges for both men and women. Most of the college buildings date from the 19th century, but there are also some older sites. Colleges are closed to the public for exams from mid-April until the end of June.

King's College Chapel

The teenaged **Henry VI** founded the college on King's Parade in 1441. The Perpendicular Chapel, however, is not only the crowning glory but one of the architectural gems in England inherited from the Middle Ages. The chapel, owing to the chaotic vicissitudes of English kings, wasn't completed until the early years of the 16th century. Its most characteristic features are its magnificent fan vaulting—all of stone—and its great windows, most of which were fashioned by Flemish artisans between 1517 and 1531 (the west window, however, dates from the late Victorian period). The stained glass, in hues of blues, reds, and ambers, reflects biblical stories. The long range of the windows, reading from the first on the north side at the west end right around the chapel back to the first on the south side, tells the story of the Birth of the Virgin, the Annunciation, the Birth of Christ, the Life, Ministry, and Death of Christ, the Resurrection, the Ascension, the Acts of the Apostles, and the Assumption. The upper range contains Old Testament parallels to these New Testament stories. The rood screen is from the early 16th century. Henry James called King's College Chapel "the most beautiful in England." It is open during vacation time from 9:30am to 5:45pm Mon. to Sat., and from 10:30am to 5:45pm Sun. During term time the public is welcome to choral services, which are at 5:30pm Mon. to Sat. (service said on Mon.), and at 10:30am and 3:30pm Sun. In "term" the chapel is open to visitors from 9:30am to 3:45pm daily, from 2 to 3pm and from 4:30 to 5:45pm on Sun.; closed December 26 to January 1. It may be closed at other times for recording sessions.

There is an exhibition in the seven northern side chapels showing why and how the chapel was built. Admission to the exhibition is £1 ($1.65) for adults, 50p (85¢) for children.

Peterhouse

This college on Trumpington Street is visited largely because it is the oldest Cambridge college, having been founded as early as 1284. The founding father was Hugh de Balsham, the bishop of Ely. Of the original buildings, only the hall remains, but this was restored in the 19th century and now contains stained-glass windows by William Morris. Old Court was constructed in the 15th century, but refaced in 1754, and the chapel dates from 1632. Ask permission to enter at the porter's desk.

Trinity College

On Trinity Street, Trinity College—the largest at Cambridge (not to be confused with Trinity Hall)—was founded in 1546 by Henry VIII from a number of smaller colleges that had existed on the site. The courtyard is the most spacious one in Cambridge, built when Thomas Nevile was master. Sir Christopher Wren designed the library. For admission to the college, apply at the porter's lodge, or telephone 0223/338400 for information.

Emmanuel College

On St. Andrew's Street, Emmanuel (tel. 0223/334200) was founded in 1584 by Sir Walter Mildmay, a chancellor of the exchequer to Elizabeth I. It is of interest at least to Harvard students, as John Harvard, founder of that university, studied here. With its attractive gardens, it makes for a good stroll. You might even visit the chapel designed by Sir Christopher Wren and consecrated in 1677. Both the chapel and college are open daily from 9:30am to 12:15pm and 2 to 6pm.

Queens' College

On Queens' Lane, Queens' College (tel. 0223/335511) is considered by some old Cantabrigians as the loveliest in the architectural galaxy. Dating back to 1448, it was founded, then refounded, by two English queens, one the wife of Henry VI, the other the wife of Edward IV. Its second cloister is the most interesting, flanked with the half-timbered president's lodge, dating from the first half of the 16th century. The college may be visited during the day from mid-March to mid-October. An admission fee of 45p (75¢) is charged and a short printed guide issued. Normally, individual visitors are admitted from 1:45 to 4:30pm daily, but during July, August, and September, the college is also open to visitors from 10:15am to 12:45pm daily. Entry and exit is by the old porters' lodge in Queens' Lane only. The old hall and chapel are usually open to the public when not in use.

St. John's College

On St. John's Street, the college was founded in 1511 by Lady Margaret Beaufort, mother of Henry VII. A few years earlier she had founded Christ's College. Before her intervention, an old monk-run hospital had stood on the site of St. John's. The impressive gateway bears the Tudor coat-of-arms, and Second Court is a fine example of late Tudor brickwork. But its best-known feature is the Bridge of Sighs crossing the Cam, built as late as the 19th century, patterned after the bridge in Venice. It connects the older part of the college with New Court, a Gothic revival on the opposite bank from which there is an outstanding view of the famous "backs." The Bridge of Sighs is closed to visitors but can be viewed from the neighboring Kitchen Bridge. Wordsworth was an alumnus of St. John's College. The chapel is open from 9am to 4pm Mon. to Fri., from 9am to noon on Sat. On Sun., the chapel is open to visitors attending the choral service.

Other College Sights

The above are only a representative selection of some of the more interesting colleges. **Magdalen College** on Magdalene Street was founded in 1542; **Pembroke College** on Trumpington Street was founded in 1347; **Christ's College** on St. Andrew's Street was founded in 1505; and **Corpus Christi College** on Trumpington Street dates from 1352. Only someone planning to stop in Cambridge for a long time will get around to them.

A Word of Warning: Unfortunately, because of the disturbances caused by the influx of tourists to the university, Cambridge has regretfully had to limit visitors, and even exclude them from various parts of the university altogether, and, in some cases, even charge a small fee for entrance. Small groups of up to six people are gener-

CAMBRIDGE

KEY TO NUMBERED SIGHTS

1. Jesus College
2. Magdalen College
3. St. John's College
4. Trinity College
5. Sidney Sussex College
6. Christ's College
7. Clare College
8. King's College
9. Corpus Christi College
10. Emmanuel College
11. Selwyn College
12. Peterhouse College
13. Pembroke College
14. Downing College
15. Newnham College

ally admitted with no problem, and you can inquire from the local tourist office about visiting hours here.

OTHER SIGHTS

However, colleges aren't the only thing to see in Cambridge, as you'll assuredly agree if you explore the following attractions.

The Fitzwilliam Museum

On Trumpington Street, near Peterhouse, this museum (tel. 0223/332900) was the gift of the viscount Fitzwilliam, who in 1816 gave Cambridge University his paintings and rare books—along with £100,000 to build the house in which to display them. He thereby knowingly or unknowingly immortalized himself. Other gifts have since been bequeathed to the museum, and now it is one of the finest in England. It is noted for its porcelain, old prints, archeological relics, and oils (17th-century Italian, including Titian, Veronese, and Tintoretto; Rubens; Van Dyck; French impressionists; and a superb collection of 18th- and 19th-century British paintings). The museum is open from 10am to 5pm Tue. to Sat., from 2:15 till 5pm Sun.; closed Mon., Good Fri., December 14 to 31, and New Year's Day. Admission is free.

Great St. Mary's

Great St. Mary's, opposite King's College Chapel on King's Parade, is the university church (tel. 0223/350914). It is built on the site of an 11th-century church, but the present building dates largely from 1478. It was closely associated with events of the Reformation. The cloth that covered the hearse of King Henry VII is on display in the church. A fine view of Cambridge may be obtained from the top of the tower. Admission is 50p (85¢) for adults, 20p (35¢) for children.

BOAT RENTALS

Punting on the Cam (nothing to do with football) is a traditional pursuit of students and visitors in Cambridge, but there are other types of boating available if you don't trust yourself to stand up and pole a punt under and around the weeping willow trees. Upriver, you can go all the way to Grantchester, a distance of about two miles, made so famous by Rupert Brooke. Downstream, you pass along the Backs behind the colleges of the university.

Scudamore's Boatyards, Granta Place (tel. 0223/359750), by the Anchor Pub, has been in business since 1910. All craft rent for £4.80 ($7.90) per hour, including punts, canoes, and rowboats. A £30 ($49.50) deposit, payable with cash or credit card, is required. There is a maximum of six persons per punt. Also offered is a chauffeured punt where a moonlighting student, dressed in a traditional punter's costume, rows you past the back view of several historic buildings, lecturing as he rows. The cost of this 45-minute guided tour is £3.50 ($5.80) per person.

PERSONALIZED TOURS

The person to know if you're in the Cambridge area is Mrs. Isobel Bryant, who operates **Heritage Tours** from her 200-year-old cottage, Manor Cottage, Swaffham Prior (tel. 0638/741440). A highly qualified expert on the region, she will arrange tours starting from your hotel or Cambridge railway station to, for instance, Lavenham with its thatched and timbered houses, to the fine medieval churches of the Suffolk villages, to Ely Cathedral, and to one of the grand mansions nearby with their many treasures. The charge of £75 ($123.75) for the day covers up to three passengers and all travel expenses, including the services of the driver/guide. Lunch in a village pub and admission fees add £5 ($8.25) per person.

Mrs. Bryant can also arrange accommodation with local families in their country houses. The charges range from £30 ($49.50) to £60 ($99) for two persons per night in double rooms with private baths, these tariffs including a full English breakfast. Often dinner can be arranged at around £10 ($16.50) per person, including wine. Rooms without private baths rent from £12 ($19.80).

There are also walking tours around the colleges of Cambridge costing £20 (\$33) for a family-size party, lasting about 2 hours. There is also a tour of Newmarket, headquarter of the horseracing industry. That tour includes getting to watch training gallops, a visit to the Racing Museum or a stud stable, seeing the bloodstock-sales center, and being shown the Jockey Club. For a group of 12 or more persons, a whole-day tour costs £15 (\$24.75) per person, a half-day tour going for £8 (\$12.30) per person. A shorter tour can be arranged for individuals or a family group. If you want lunch at a private manor house with Cordon Bleu cooking, the cost will be £8.50 (\$14.05) per person, with wine included, for groups of 12 or more. All prices include VAT.

BICYCLE RENTALS

The most popular way of getting around in Cambridge, next to walking, is bicycling. **Geoff's Bike Hire,** 65 Devonshire Rd. (tel. 0223/65629), has bicycles for rent for £4 (\$6.60) per day or £10 (\$16.50) per week. A deposit of £15 (\$24.75) is required. Hours are from 9am to 5:30pm Mon. to Sat. It is also open on Sun. in summer.

WHERE TO STAY

Accommodations are limited in scope and facilities, although generally adequate for the purpose. Much of the overload in summer is siphoned off by little guesthouses, filled at term time with scholars, but otherwise freed when most visitors arrive in July and August.

Moderately Priced Hotels

The Garden House, Granta Place, Mill Lane, Cambridge, Cambridgeshire CB2 1RT (tel. 0223/63421), is a modern hotel set between the riverbank and a cobblestone street in the oldest part of town, a short stroll from the principal colleges. The hostelry, next door to the boatyard where you can rent punts, has a series of outdoor terraces on which drinks and afternoon tea are served in good weather. The earth-tone brick and stained-wood exterior harmonizes with the wall coverings in the bar lounge of the hotel, where comfortable sofas and chairs tempt visitors. Well-furnished bedrooms have private baths, radios, color TVs, mini-bars, phones, soundproof windows, hot beverage facilities, and hairdryers. Most of the 118 rooms have balconies and river views. Standard singles cost £72 (\$118.80) daily, with doubles going for £82 (\$135.30) to £96 (\$158.40), with VAT and a continental breakfast included. The hotel's Le Jardin Restaurant overlooks the river and gardens and offers fixed-price and à la carte menus, including vegetarian meals, at lunch and dinner. Also a selection of hot and cold light meals is available in the Riverside Lounge, accompanied in the evening by piano music. When weather permits, the Cocktail Bar serves drinks outside on the terrace and lawn. The hotel has ample free parking.

University Arms Hotel, Regent Street, Cambridge, Cambridgeshire CB2 1AD (tel. 0223/351241), is a traditional hotel near the city center and the university. The present building contains 115 tastefully decorated bedrooms, most of which overlook Parker's Piece on which one of England's greatest cricketers, Sir Jack Hobbs, learned to play. Each bedroom has its own phone, central heating, private bath, electric razor outlets, radio, and color TV. The single rate is £65 (\$107.25) daily, and a twin-bedded room is £80 (\$132). These prices include service, VAT, and an English breakfast. The spacious oak-paneled restaurant features both table d'hôte and à la carte menus. Lunch costs from £8 (\$13.20) and dinner from £13 (\$21.45). The Octagon Lounge, with its stained-glass domed ceiling and open log fire, is a popular place to meet for tea. *Tip:* The hotel porter can arrange a guided tour for you.

Cambridgeshire Moat House, Bar Hill, Cambridge, Cambridgeshire CB3 8EU (tel. 0954/780555), is 5 miles from the center of Cambridge on the A604 road, a modern three-star hotel with heated, indoor swimming pool, sauna, three squash courts, two outside tennis courts, an 18-hole championship golf course, putting green, and helipad. There are 100 bedrooms, all with private baths, color TVs, radios, direct-dial phones, hairdryers, and hot beverage facilities. Singles cost £70 ($115.50) daily, and twins £87 ($143.55). Prices include a full English breakfast, VAT, and the use of all sports facilities. Residents are charged for golf, £8 ($13.20) per person per day on weekdays, and £10 ($16.50) per person per day on weekends. There are both table d'hôte and à la carte menus available in the restaurant. Bar meals are also served daily.

Post House Hotel, Lakeview Bridge Road, Impington, Cambridge, Cambridgeshire CB4 4PH (tel. 0223/237000), near a highway intersection at Impington, lies 2 miles north of Cambridge on the B1049 where it intersects with the A45. Its wings partially embrace a grassy courtyard, lying a short walk from a small artificial lake. Its large public rooms soar above the dozens of sofas and chairs, ending in a peaked summit. On the premises are a heated, indoor swimming pool, a Jacuzzi, a sauna, and a lobby bar. The hotel restaurant, the Churchill, has mahogany paneling, reproductions of paintings created by Sir Winston himself, portrait busts, and photos of the famous statesman at various periods of his life. Each of the 120 bedrooms offers a big-windowed view of the outdoors and is equipped with private bath or shower, a TV, phone, and mini-bar. Singles cost £77 ($127.05) to £85 ($140.25) daily, and doubles or twins go for £90 ($148.50) to £105 ($173.25).

Budget Hotels

Arundel House, 53 Chesterton Rd., Cambridge, Cambridgeshire CB4 3AN (tel. 0223/67701), occupies one of the finest sites in Cambridge, overlooking the River Cam and open parkland. It's only a few minutes' walk from the city center and the university colleges. This 19th-century terraced hotel has 88 bedrooms, most with private baths. All have color TVs, radios, direct-dial phones, hairdryers, and hot beverage facilities, as well as a videotaped guide to Cambridge on an in-house video channel. Video films can also be played in your room. Singles cost £25 ($41.25) to £42 ($69.30) daily, and doubles run £37 ($61.05) to £58 ($95.70). All room rates include a continental breakfast and VAT. The hotel has a cocktail bar and a small garden with outdoor tables and an attractive Victorian-style restaurant offering table d'hôte or à la carte menus. Bar meals are also available. A fixed-price, three-course lunch is £7.50 ($12.40); a table d'hôte dinner, £10.50 ($17.40). There's a coin-operated launderette on the premises.

Gonville Hotel, Gonville Place, Cambridge, Cambridgeshire CB1 1LY (tel. 0223/66611), stands on its own grounds, opposite Parkers Piece, only a 5-minute walk from the center of the city. It's not unlike a country house—ivy covered, with shade trees and a formal car entry. In 1973 it was gutted and rebuilt as a commercial hotel, intending to attract business people as well as tourists in summer. Singles go for £55 ($90.75) daily and doubles for £72 ($118.80). Prices include VAT, service charge, and an English breakfast. Each of the 62 bedrooms has a private bath, phone, and TV. Central heating is provided throughout, plus air conditioning in the restaurant, where you can get a set lunch for £9 ($14.85) or dinner for about £12 ($19.80). You can also order à la carte. The quality of comforts is good.

Regent Hotel, 41 Regent St., Cambridge, Cambridgeshire CB2 1AB (tel. 0223/351470), reopened in 1985 to receive paying guests in its 19 attractive and comfortable furnished bedrooms, 15 of which contain private baths. All units have a phone, color TV, and radio. Only breakfast is served, but there's a cocktail bar on the street level. It's one of the nicest of the moderately priced small hotels of Cambridge. Depending on the plumbing, singles cost £29 ($47.85) to £41 ($67.65) daily, doubles or twins £42.50 ($70.15) to £53 ($87.45). Right in the city center, overlooking Parker's Piece, the house was built in the 1840s as the original site of Newham College. When the college outgrew its physical plant, the building became a hotel.

WHERE TO DINE

Midsummer House, Midsummer Common (tel. 0223/69299), is one of the dining discoveries of Cambridge, lying near the River Cam. The preferred dining is in an elegant conservatory, but you can also find a smartly laid table upstairs. The menu is wisely limited, and quality control seems much in evidence here. The chef, Hans Schweitzer, knows the French school well; except every dish seems to bear his own special imprint, and that is quite good. Attired in funeral black, the waiters will come to your assistance, as you peruse the menu for the freshest or most exciting selection on any given day. Chef Schweitzer displays his considerable talents in the set luncheon going for £13.50 ($22.30) or the table d'hôte dinners costing from £21.50 ($35.50) to £27.50 ($45.40). Sun. lunch is £15 ($24.75). The restaurant serves from noon to 2pm and 6:30 to 9:30pm Tues. to Sun. There is no dinner on Sun. and no lunch offered on Sat.

Upstairs, 71 Castle St. (tel. 0223/312569), is an authentic Middle Eastern and Moroccan eatery, one of the best in this part of England. The location, above Waffles, lies on a hillside road above the most historic part of Cambridge, about a 5-minute walk from the center. The cookery is genuine, reflecting the varied background of the kitchen staff. You might begin with the famous harira, a Moroccan beef soup with lentils. The stuffed eggplant (called aubergine on the menu) is filled with nuts and various aromatic spices and is usually a delight, as is filet of trout in a lime sauce with pistachios. The prize offering, however, is the lamb couscous, which is flavored with ginger, among other spices, and topped with a rich sauce. It's presented for your pleasure in an earthenware tajine. A la carte meals in this former Victorian townhouse cost £15 ($24.75) and are served from 6:30 to 10:30pm Tue. to Sun. (closes at 9:30pm on Sun.). A set dinner is priced from £8 ($13.20). They finish your repast with a cardamom- and orange-water-flavored coffee. Reservations are advised.

Charlie Chan, 14 Regent St. (tel. 0223/61763), is generally conceded to be the finest Chinese restaurant in Cambridge, although this is a debated point, other devotees of Oriental cookery having their own favorites. Nevertheless, in frequent visits on my part this place has proved to be reliable and capable in spite of its large selection of dishes. It is a long, corridor-like restaurant, with pristine decor, consisting of, among other elements, tile floors. It lies on a busy commercial street near one of its major rivals, Shao Tao. The specialties I've most enjoyed include an aromatic and crispy duck, lemon chicken, and prawn with garlic and ginger. It's best to go with a party—that way you can sample many different dishes. A la carte meals range in price from £20 ($33) per person, although a set meal costs only £9 ($14.85). Hours are noon to 2:15pm and 6 to 11pm daily.

Twenty Two, 22 Chesterton Rd. (tel. 0223/351880). Who would expect to find one of the best restaurants in Cambridge in this quiet residential and hotel district? In the vicinity of Jesus Green, it has up to now been an address jealously guarded by the locals who "don't want tourists to spoil it." Decorated in pink and gray tones, it is an exponent of the best of contemporary English and continental cookery, relying on the freshest ingredients in any season. The menu is ever-changing, based on the shopping for any given week. Michael Sharpe, the chef and owner, uses time-tested recipes along with his own inspiration of the moment. A set dinner is offered from 7:30 to 9:30pm Tue. to Sat. for £16.50 ($27.25).

Restaurant Angeline, 8 Market Passage (tel. 0223/60305), is set along a commercial passageway in the heart of town behind a narrow facade, found between Sidney and Market streets, just two blocks east of Trinity College. The multiple nationalities of its owners, coupled with its French chef, make this one of the most varied restaurants in town. Upstairs, there's a bar for drinking, lots of upholstery, and attractive fixed-price lunches costing from £5 ($8.25). The more elaborate dinners, at £16 ($26.40), might include Wiltshire roast duck, trout meunière, and grilled Dover sole, fresh salmon, and several preparations of lamb. Full meals are served from noon to 2:30pm and 6 to 11pm, except Sun. evening.

EVENING ENTERTAINMENT AND PUBS

An outstanding attraction in Cambridge is the **Arts Theatre,** 6 St. Edward's Passage, adjacent to the city center and the Tourist Information Office and fitted into a maze of lodging houses and shops. It provides Cambridge and the surrounding area with its most important theatrical events. Almost all of the leading stars of the British stage have performed here at one time or another. Call 0223/352000 to find out what's playing. Seats for most productions are £8 ($13.20) to £10 ($16.50).

Cambridge Arms, 4 King St. (tel. 0223/359650), is a popular student haunt in the center of town. The place has plenty of atmosphere and doesn't neglect its food in favor of dispensing beer and ale. In fact, it has good lunch meals, including the chef's daily specials for £3.50 ($5.80) and also grilled steaks and cold buffet dishes. Hot and cold snacks are available from £1 ($1.65), and hours are from 11am to 11pm Mon. to Sat., and from noon to 3pm and 7 to 10:30pm Sun.

Perhaps the most popular pub outing you can take from Cambridge is to the hamlet of **Grantchester,** lying 2 miles from the university city and reached by going along the A603. One of the most beautiful villages in the shire, Grantchester has an old church and gardens leading down to water meadows. It was made famous by Rupert Brooke, the famed pre–World War I English poet, who is best known today for his sonnet, *The Solider.* He was a charming and romantic character, and his life, which ended prematurely in 1915, has inspired many books.

Even if you've never heard of Brooke, you may enjoy spending a late afternoon here, wandering through the old church and then heading, as everybody does, including Cambridge students and their professors, to **The Green Man,** 59 High St., Grantchester (tel. 0223/841178), a coaching inn with a history of some 4½ centuries. On a winter's night, the mellow old pub welcomes you with an open fire. But in summer you may want to retreat to the beer garden in back, and from there you can stroll down to the river. If you're in Grantchester at lunch or dinner, you can enjoy a good spread, including fresh salads, pâtés, English cheese, and desserts, with filling meals costing from £4 ($6.60). Hours are from 11am to 2:30pm and 6 to 11pm Mon. to Sat. and from noon to 3pm and 7 to 10:30pm Sun.

---

2. Ely

The top attraction in the fen country, outside of Cambridge, is Ely Cathedral. The small city of Ely lies 70 miles from London, only 16 miles north of Cambridge. Ely used to be known as the Isle of Ely, until the surrounding marshes and meres were drained. The last stronghold of Saxon England, Ely was defended by Hereward the Wake, until his capitulation to the Normans in 1071.

ELY CATHEDRAL

The near-legendary founder of the cathedral was Etheldreda, the wife of a Northumbrian king who established a monastery on the spot in 673. The present structure dates from 1081. Seen for miles around, the landmark octagonal lantern town is the crowning glory of the cathedral. It was erected in 1322, following the collapse of the old tower, and represents a remarkable engineering achievement. Four hundred tons of lead and wood hang in space, held there by timbers reaching to the eight pillars.

You enter the cathedral through the Galilee West Door, a good example of the Early English style of architecture. The already-mentioned lantern tower and the octagon are the most notable features inside, but visit the lady chapel. Although it has lost much of its decoration over the centuries, it's still a handsome example of the Perpendicular style, having been completed in the mid-14th century. The cathedral is open from 7am to 7pm daily in summer, from 7:30am to 6pm daily in winter. Visitors are asked to pay an entry fee of £2.20 ($3.65) to help save the cathedral from ruin. The refectory and shop are open daily. For information, telephone 0353/667735.

ELY MUSEUM

The story of a fenland city and its people are told at the Ely Museum, 28C High St. (tel. 0353/66655), which is open from 10:30am to 1pm and 2:15 to 5pm Tue.

to Sat. (from 2:15 to 5pm only Sun.). Admission is 80p ($1.30) for adults and 40p (65¢) for children. Artifacts gathered throughout the area are displayed there, including a rare collection of 17th-century Ely trade tokens. A gallery presents old films of Ely and the surrounding fenland.

WHERE TO STAY AND DINE

Right in the center of the town, **Lamb Hotel,** 2 Lynn Rd., Ely, Cambridgeshire CB7 4EJ (tel. 0353/663574), is a former coaching inn with ample car parking available. In the shadow of the cathedral, this Queens Moat House hotel offers 32 renovated bedrooms with private baths or showers, TVs, phones, and hot beverage facilities. The B&B rate in a double or twin is £68 ($112.20) daily, and a single costs £52 ($85.80). Tariffs are inclusive of an English breakfast and VAT. A table d'hôte lunch or dinner costs from £10 ($16.50). Sun. lunch is an event when a roast topside of beef in the Merrie Olde England style is wheeled out. In the 1400s this place was known as the "Holy Lambe," a stopping-off spot for wayfarers, often pilgrims, through East Anglia.

Old Fire Engine House, St. Mary's Street (tel. 0353/662582), opposite St. Mary's Church, is one of the finer restaurants in East Anglia, worth a detour. It enjoys an interesting setting in a walled garden, in a complex of buildings with an art gallery. The restaurant was converted from a fire station. All the good English cooking is the result of the staff, a harmonious combination of unusual people who really care about food preparation. Materials are all fresh. Soups are served in huge bowls, and accompanying them is a coarse-grained crusty bread. Main dishes include duck with orange sauce, jugged hare, steak and kidney pie, baked stuffed pike, casserole of rabbit, and pigeon with bacon and black olives. Desserts include fruit pie and cream, although I'd recommend the syllabub. A meal costs from £13 ($21.45). In summer you can dine outside in the garden, even order a cream tea. Ann Ford owns the place, and not only does some of the cooking and serves, but still has time to talk to customers. It's open daily from 10:30am to 5:30pm and 7:30 to 9pm (last entry), from 12:30 to 5pm Sun. Do try for a table if you're just passing. This place is quite popular with locals and people coming out from Cambridge, especially on weekends, so it's better to make a reservation.

A TOUR TO GRIME'S GRAVES

On the B1108, off the main A1065 from Swaffham to Mildenhall road east of Ely, you can visit Grime's Graves (tel. 0842/810656), 3 miles northeast of Brandon (Norfolkshire). This is well worth the short detour, as it is the largest group of Neolithic flint mines in the country. This is fir-wooded country with little population, and it's easy to imagine yourself transported back to ancient times. The mines are well signposted, and you soon find yourself at a small parking lot presided over by a custodian who will open up one or several of the shafts. Climb down the ladder of the pit and imagine what must have been going on even before the time of the Anglo-Saxons. Restoration has been carried out during the intervening years, and it is now possible to see where work took place and, if you're lucky, you may find a worked flint of your own to present to the custodian. It's best to have a flashlight handy. The climb down is perpendicular, so it's only for the stout-hearted.

The mines are close to the air force bases known to countless American air crews during World War II. Hours are from 10am to 6pm Tue. to Sun. from Good Fri. to September 30, from 10am to 4pm in winter. Admission is 85p ($1.40) for adults, 40p (65¢) for children.

AN AIRCRAFT MUSEUM

Part of the Imperial War Museum (tel. 0223/833963) is housed at Duxford Airfield at junction 10 of the M11 motorway. It was a former Battle of Britain station and the U.S. Eighth Air Force base in World War II. In hangars that date from World War I, you'll find a huge collection of historic civil and military aircraft from both world wars, including the only B-29 Superfortress in Europe. Other exhibits include midget submarines, tanks, and a variety of field artillery pieces, as well as a special historical display on the U.S. Eighth Air Force.

The museum is open daily from 10am; closed Christmas and New Year's Day. Admission is £4.50 ($7.45) for adults and £2.25 ($3.70) for children in summer. Special charges are made for special events and parking is free.

ESSEX

Even though it borders London, and is industrialized in places, Essex still contains unspoiled rural areas and villages. Most motorists pass through it on the way to Cambridge. A land of rolling fields, there are many seaside towns and villages in the east, because Essex opens onto the North Sea.

The major city is **Colchester,** in the east, known for its oysters and roses. Fifty miles from London, it was the first Roman city in Britain, the oldest recorded town in the kingdom. Parts of its Roman fortifications remain. A Norman castle has been turned into a museum, containing a fine collection of Roman Britain. Among the former residents of Colchester were King Cole, immortalized in the nursery rhyme, and Cunobelinus, the warrior king, known to Shakespearean scholars as Cymbeline.

However, Colchester is not the pathway of most visitors—so I have concentrated instead on tiny villages in the western part of Essex, including Saffron Walden and Thaxted, which are representative of the best of the shire. You can explore all of them quite easily on your way to Cambridge or on your return trip to London. Roughly, they lie from 25 to 30 miles south of Cambridge.

A BASE OUTSIDE LONDON

Just 22 miles from London's West End, **Brentwood Moat House,** London Road, Brentwood, Essex CM14 4NR (tel. 0277/225252), is 2 minutes from Intersection 28 on the M25 motorway. This four-star hotel is on the London side of Brentwood, three-quarters of a mile from the center of town. The hotel, a Tudor building of historical interest, dates back to the 16th century and was associated with Catherine of Aragon and used by Henry VIII as a hunting lodge. The 39 bedrooms offer excellent facilities, with private baths, color TVs, radios, electric trouser presses, phones, hairdryers, and 24-hour room service. In the main building, original Tudor bedrooms include four-poster beds. Singles are priced at £82 ($135.30) to £88 ($145.20) daily, and doubles go for £102 ($168.30) to £106 ($174.90). The special Tudor rooms are more expensive. The character of the Moat House is preserved with original oak beams, period windows, and inglenook fireplaces. A warm atmosphere prevails.

3. Thaxted

Some 43 miles north of London, the Saxon town of Thaxted sits on the crest of a hill. It contains the most beautiful small church in England, whose graceful spire can be seen for miles around. Its bells ring out special chimes to parishioners who attend their church. Dating back to 1340, the church is a nearly perfect example of religious architecture.

Thaxted also has a number of well-preserved Elizabethan houses and a wooden-pillared Jacobean guildhall.

WHERE TO STAY AND DINE

About 4 miles southwest of Thaxted, **Whitehall,** Church End, Broxted, Thaxted, Essex CM6 2BZ (tel. 0279/850603), lies on the B1051 road. In the 18th century, almost 28,000 acres of prime farmland were attached to this property. By the 1900s the countess of Warwick, then its mistress, entertained King Edward VII within its baronial walls. Today, in an elegantly simplified format, guests are still entertained more or less royally. Ten elegant bedrooms are rented, each differently furnished in 18th-century style. All have private baths, phones, TVs, many thoughtful extras, and views over the 300-year-old yew trees of an ancient walled garden. Singles cost from £70 ($115.50) daily and doubles from £105 ($173.25), with a full breakfast included.

A medieval brewhouse with a soaring ceiling is the setting for specialties prepared with fresh ingredients. A tempting fixed-price dinner is offered for £28.50 ($47.05).

4. Saffron Walden

In the northern corner of Essex, a short drive from Thaxted, is the ancient market town of Walden, renamed Saffron Walden because of the fields of autumn crocus that used to grow around it. Although it lies only 44 miles from London, it still hasn't succumbed to heavy tourist traffic. Residents of Cambridge, 15 miles to the north, escape to this old borough for their weekends.

Many of the houses in Saffron Walden are distinctive in England, in that the 16th- and 17th-century builders faced their houses with parget—a kind of plasterwork (sometimes made with cow dung) used for ornamental facades. The 14th-century Sun Inn and many 15th- and 16th-century, timber-framed houses with pargetting can be viewed, as can the Perpendicular-style Church of Saffron Walden, the largest in Essex. Saffron Walden is one of the few market towns in England to retain its medieval street pattern.

One mile west of Saffron Walden (on the B1383) is **Audley End House** (tel. 0799/22399), considered one of the finest mansions in all of East Anglia. This Jacobean house was begun by Sir Thomas Howard, treasurer to the king, in 1605, built on the foundation of a monastery. James I is reported to have said, "Audley End is too large for a king, though it might do for a Lord Treasurer." The house has many outstanding features, including an impressive great hall at whose north end is a screen dating from the early 17th century, considered one of the most ornamental in England. Rooms decorated by Robert Adam contain fine furniture and works of art. A "Gothick" chapel and a charming Victorian ladies' sitting room are among the attractions. The park surrounding the house was landscaped by Capability Brown. It has a lovely rose garden, a river and cascade, and a picnic area. In the stables, built at the same time as the mansion, is a collection of agricultural machinery, a Victorian coach, old wagons, and the estate fire wagon. It's all open from April 1 to the end of September daily from 1 to 6pm. The grounds are open from noon to 5pm. Admission to the house is £3.50 ($5.80) for adults, £1.75 ($2.90) for children.

WHERE TO STAY AND DINE

In the center of this Cromwellian market town stands the **Saffron Hotel,** 10-18 High St., Saffron Walden, Essex CB10 1AY (tel. 0799/22676). Dating from the 16th century, the Saffron combines modern comforts with old-world charm, as reflected by its individually designed and decorated rooms. All 21 rooms have color TVs, phones, tea and coffee makers, and central heating, and 16 contain private baths. Most units overlook High Street or the inner courtyard with its patio garden. Stories abound locally about the Saffron Hotel ghost. B&B rates are £28 ($46.20) daily in a bathless single, £44 ($72.60) in a single with complete bath or shower. Doubles with private bath rent for £58 ($95.70). Prices are reduced for children sharing rooms of adults. Tariffs include a continental breakfast and VAT. The hotel's restaurant is known locally and is decorated in the Regency style. Dining is by candlelight overlooking a floodlit patio garden. A three-course menu with several choices on each course costs £15 ($24.75). There is also an à la carte menu. The cuisine at the Saffron is among the best in the area, combining traditional English dishes with more ambitious specialties. Meals are served from noon to 2pm and 7:30 to 9:30pm; closed Sat. lunch and all day Sun. You can also order from an excellent bar menu.

---

5. Dedham

Remember Constable's *Vale of Dedham*? In this little Essex village on the Stour River, you're in the heart of Constable country. Flatford Mill is only a mile farther down the river. The village, with its Tudor, Georgian, and Regency houses, is set in the midst of the water meadows of the Stour. Constable immortalized its church and tower. Dedham is right on the Essex-Suffolk border, and makes a good center for exploring both North Essex and the Suffolk border country. The location is 63 miles from London and 8 miles from Colchester (Essex).

About three-quarters of a mile south of the village center is **Castle House** (tel. 0206/322127), home of Sir Alfred Munnings, the president of the Royal Academy (1944–1949) and painter extraordinaire of racehorses and animals. The house and studio contain sketches and other works, and are open early May to early October from 2 to 5pm Sun., Wed., and bank holidays, as well as on Thur. and Sat. in August. Admission is £1.50 ($2.50) for adults, 25p (40¢) for children.

WHERE TO STAY AND DINE

Small and exclusive, **Maison Talbooth,** Stratford Road, Dedham, Colchester, Essex CO7 6HN (tel. 0206/322367), has 10 bedrooms, each really a spacious suite. This Victorian country house was handsomely restored, and each accommodation has been distinctively furnished by one of England's best-known decorators. High-fashion colors abound: antiques are mixed discreetly with reproductions—and the original architectural beauty has been preserved. The super-luxury suite, with a sunken bath, goes for £120 ($198) nightly for two persons and has a draped bed. Other suites, each with its own theme, start as low as £80 ($132) for two. One person pays from £75 ($123.75) to £100 ($165). When you arrive, you're welcomed by your hostess who takes you to your suite, where fresh flowers, fruit, and a private bar are standard, as are private baths, phones, and TVs. A continental or cooked breakfast is brought in the morning. In an informal, yet stylish, drawing room, guests mingle with the hostess, making you feel as if you're a guest in her country home.

Maison Talbooth's nearby restaurant, **Le Talbooth,** Gun Hill (tel. 0206/323150), is in a hand-hewn, hand-plastered, half-timbered weaver's house set in beautiful gardens on the banks of the River Stour in Constable country. Le Talbooth was featured in Constable's *Vale of Dedham*. You descend a sloping driveway leading past flowering terraces. A well-mannered staff will usher you to a low-ceilinged bar for an aperitif. Taller guests are cautioned to beware of low ceiling beams, which add a rich atmospheric note of another era. Owner Gerald Milsom has brought a high standard of international cooking to this rustically elegant place, where a well-chosen wine list complements the good food. An à la carte menu changes six times a year, and special dishes change daily, as they reflect the best produce available at the market. Food is cooked to order to preserve natural flavors. Main dishes are likely to range from garlic-studded Scottish beef filet to roast breast of partridge. Lunch is priced from £16 ($26.40) and dinner from £40 ($66). Hours are daily from noon to 2pm and 7 to 9pm. Reservations are vital.

Dedham Vale Hotel, Stratford Road, Dedham, Colchester, Essex CO7 6HW (tel. 0206/322273), is less glamorous than owner Gerald Milsom's other hotel—the nearby Maison Talbooth, previewed above—but this vine-covered Edwardian house offers six attractive bedrooms to overnight guests in a peaceful bucolic setting.

Each unit has a private bath, phone, TV, radio, and a comfortable collection of traditional furniture. With a continental breakfast included, singles cost £75 ($123.75) daily, and doubles go for £95 ($156.75). VAT and service are included. On chilly mornings, a fire blazes in the Regency-style fireplace in the restaurant. The bar offers views of a flowering terrace and floor-to-ceiling murals of Constable's East Anglia. Many nonresidents who drop in head for the Terrace Restaurant. There, the protective glass canopy of an Edwardian conservatory shelters the napery and cut flowers of an increasingly popular dining spot. One of Constable's great-nieces occupied one of the upstairs bedrooms here, when this was a convalescent home. The hotel is within easy reach of the ports of Harwich and Felixstowe for journeys to the continent.

SUFFOLK

The easternmost county of England—a link in the four-county chain of East Anglia—Suffolk is a refuge for artists, just as it was in the day of its famous native sons, Constable and Gainsborough. Through them, many of the Suffolk landscapes have ended up on canvas in museums.

A fast train can make it from London to East Suffolk in approximately an hour and a half. Still, its fishing villages, dozens of flint churches, historic homes, and national monuments remain far removed from mainstream tourism in England.

The major towns of Suffolk are **Bury St. Edwards,** the capital of West Suffolk, and **Ipswich** in the east, a port city on the Orwell River. But to capture the true charm of Suffolk, you must explore its little market towns and villages. Beginning at the Essex border, we'll head toward the North Sea, highlighting the most scenic villages as we move easterly across the shire.

6. Newmarket

This old Suffolk town, 62 miles from London, has been famous as a racing center since the time of King James I. Visitors can see Nell Gwynne's House, but mainly they come to visit Britain's first and only **National Horseracing Museum,** 99 High St. (tel. 0638/667333). The museum is housed in the old subscription rooms, early-19th-century rooms used for placing and settling bets. Visitors will be able to see the history of horseracing over a 300-year period. There are fine paintings of famous horses, pictures on loan from Queen Elizabeth II, and copies of old Parliamentary Acts governing races. There is also a replica of a weighing-in room, plus explanations of the signs used by the ticktack men who keep the on-course bookies informed of changes in the price of bets. A continuous, 53-minute, audiovisual presentation shows races and racehorses.

To make history come alive for the museum visitor, they offer popular tours of this historic town. You are taken by a guide to watch morning gallops on the heath, through the town where you'll see bronzes of stallions from the past, and other points of interest. An optional tour of a famous training establishment is offered, plus a visit to the Jockey Club Rooms, known for a fine collection of paintings. Reservations are necessary, but the tour, which lasts a whole morning, is conducted April to October. The museum is open from 10am to 5pm Tue. to Sat., from 2 to 5pm Sun. Closed Mon. except bank holidays in August. Equine tours are available. Admission is £2 ($3.30) for adults, 50p (85¢) for children. The museum is closed from December to March, but those with a special interest in seeing it during those months can telephone.

The National Stud (tel. 0638/663464), lying beside Newmarket's July Race

Course, 2 miles southwest of the town, is *the* place for those who wish to see some of the world's finest horseflesh, as well as watch a working thoroughbred breeding stud in operation. A tour lasting about 1¼ hours lets you see many mares and foals, plus horses in training for racing. Tours are possible at 11:15am and 2:30pm Mon. to Fri. as well as at 11:15am Sat. when there is racing in Newmarket during the racing season, April to September. Reservations for tours must be made at the National Stud office from 9am to 1pm or 2 to 5pm Mon. to Fri. or by phoning the number given above. Admission is £2.75 ($4.55) for adults, £1.50 ($2.50) for children.

WHERE TO STAY AND DINE
The town's best inn is the **Newmarket Moat House,** Moulton Road, Newmarket, Suffolk CB8 8DY (tel. 0638/667171), a member of Queens Moat Houses, lying near Newmarket Heath, close to the center of town. For some time now a favorite of the English horseracing world, it houses devotees of the "sport of kings" in one of its 44 well-appointed bedrooms. Contemporary in styling, it offers a private bath or shower in each of its units, plus phone and TV. Singles begin at £60 ($99) daily, with standard doubles priced at £72 ($118.80) to £76 ($125.40). The cooking is a combination of English and French, and full dinners cost from £16 ($26.40). You should arrive for dining no later than 9:30pm, however.

If you'd like to find a place in the environs, there is none better than **Swynford Paddocks,** Six Mile Bottom, Cambridgeshire CB8 0UE (tel. 063870/234), lying 6 miles from Newmarket on the A1304. Many guests use it as a base for exploring Cambridge. This well-appointed country house, one of the finest in the area, lies on a 60-acre stud farm surrounded by beautiful grounds. Once it was a favorite retreat of Lord Byron. But now it has been intelligently converted into a first-class hotel and restaurant (open to non-residents, but you should call first). The hotel rents only 15 handsomely equipped and attractive bedrooms each with private bath or shower, TV, and phone. Singles cost £60 ($99) daily and doubles or twins go for £90 ($148.50). That's expensive, but you get a lot of quality here. A first-rate English and French cuisine is served, with dinners costing from £18.50 ($30.55).

---

7. Clare

Lying 58 miles from London, but only 26 miles east from Cambridge, the small town of Clare holds to the old ways of East Anglia. Many of its houses are bathed in Suffolk pink, the facades of a few demonstrating the 16th- and 17th-century plasterwork technique of pargeting. The Stour River, which has its source a few miles away, flows by, marking the boundary of Suffolk and Essex. The little rail station has fallen to the economy axe. The nearest station is now at Sudbury, where Gainsborough was born. The journey by road from London takes about 2 hours, unless you succumb to the scenery and the countryside along the way.

Ancient House Museum (tel. 0787/277865), directly across from the churchyard, is a splendid example of pargeting and has many notable architectural features and fascinating exhibits, leading to a deeper understanding and appreciation of the rural life of Suffolk. The museum is open from Easter to October from 2:30 to 4:30pm Wed. to Sun., as well as from 11am to 12:30pm on Sun. Admission is 60p ($1) for adults, 30p (50¢) for children.

WHERE TO STAY AND DINE
One of the oldest inns in England, **The Bell Hotel,** Market Hill, Clare, Sudbury, Suffolk CO10 8NN (tel. 0787/277741), was known as the Green Dragon when it served the soldiers of Richard de Clare, one of William the Conqueror's barons. Later it became a posting house, but in time the old stable became bedrooms. Today, this 16th-century coaching inn, with its characteristic black and white timbered facade, rents 10 bedrooms, 7 with private baths, in the main building, and 11 bedrooms (each with private bath) in an annex. B&B rates range from £38

($62.70) to £57 ($94.05) daily in a single and £58 ($95.70) to £98 ($161.70) in a double. The rooms have traditional styling, and the beds are comfortable. Some of the accommodations also contain four-poster beds. The beamed dining room, with its high-backed chairs and large brick fireplace, is ideal for winter meals. Lunch costs from £10.50 ($17.35), with dinners going for £12 ($19.80).

---

8. Long Melford

Long Melford has been famous since the days of the early clothmakers. Like its sister, Lavenham (coming up), it grew in prestige and importance in the Middle Ages. Of the old buildings remaining, the village church is often called "one of the glories of the shire." Along its 3-mile-long High Street—said to boast the highest concentration of antique shops in Europe—are many private homes erected by wealthy wool merchants of yore. While London seems far removed here, it is only 61 miles to the south. Cambridge is 34 miles away.

Of special interest are Long Melford's two stately homes, one of which being **Melford Hall.** Standing in Long Melford on the east side of A134, this National Trust property was favored by Beatrix Potter. Her Jemima Puddleduck still occupies a chair in one of the bedrooms upstairs, and others of her figures are on display. The house, built between 1554 and 1578, contains paintings, fine furniture, and Chinese porcelain. The principal rooms and gardens can be visited from May to the end of September from 2 to 6pm Wed., Thur., Sat., Sun., and bank holidays. From April to October, hours are from 2 to 6pm only on Sat. and Sun. Admission is £2.20 ($3.65) for adults, £1.10 ($1.80) for children.

Kentwell Hall, whose entrance is north of the green in Long Melford on the west side of the A134, about half a mile north of Melford Hall, has been restored by its owners, the barrister Patrick Phillips and his wife. At the end of an avenue of linden trees, the hall is a red-brick Tudor mansion surrounded by a broad moat. A 15th-century moat house, interconnecting gardens, a brick-paved maze, and a costume display are of interest, and there are also rare-breed farm animals to be seen. The hall hosts regular re-creations of Tudor domestic life, including the renowned annual events for the weeks June 24 to July 15 and small events over holiday weekends. The public can visit this family home and its grounds over Easter weekend, on Sun. from mid-April to mid-June, and Wed. to Sat. from mid-July to the end of September. Hours are 2 to 6pm. During bank holidays, when special rates apply, hours are from 11am to 6pm. Admission when no special event is on is £2.75 ($4.55) for adults, £1.60 ($2.65) for children.

WHERE TO STAY

An opportunity to experience life in one of the great old inns of East Anglia is provided at the **Bull Hotel,** Hall Street, Long Melford, Sudbury, Suffolk CO10 9JG (tel. 0787/78494). Built by a wool merchant, it is probably Long Melford's finest and best-preserved building, dating back to 1540. Improvements and interior modernization have been undertaken. Incorporated into the general hotel is a medieval weavers' gallery and the open hearth with its Elizabethan brickwork. The 25 bedrooms are a goodly mixture of the old and new—each with phone, TV, and private bath or shower. A single room with bath rents for £65 ($107.25) daily, and a double with bath for £95 ($156.75). The Cordell Room is the outstanding part of the Bull, with its high beamed ceilings, trestle tables, settles, and handmade chairs, as well as a 10-foot fireplace. Food is served from noon to 2:30pm and 7 to 9:30pm daily.

Black Lion Hotel, the Green, Long Melford, Suffolk CO10 9DN (tel. 0787/312356), is a fully restored 17th-century coaching inn overlooking one of Suffolk's loveliest village greens. The nine individually decorated rooms all have baths, direct-dial phones, tea and coffee facilities, and color TVs. Single rooms cost from £40 ($66) daily and doubles from £55 ($90.75) to £75 ($123.75) all including either continental or full English breakfasts. An added bonus is the hotel's well-patronized

Countrymen restaurant which offers excellent food and a well-chosen wine list. Lunch costs from £10 ($16.50) and dinner from £17.50 ($28.90).

WHERE TO DINE

The most highly rated restaurant in town is **Chimneys,** Hall Street (tel. 0787/79806). The guiding light behind this place is Sam Chalmers, who was chef at the highly acclaimed Le Talbooth in Dedham. Right in the heart of town, he opened this place with its oak beams and brick walls. The house is from the 16th century, and in the back is a "secret garden." This establishment represents modern British cookery at its best. With the help of a carefully chosen and reasonably priced wine list—from both California and European vineyards—guests can select from a constantly changing repertoire. On any given night you are likely to enjoy such English exotica as pressed lambs' tongues with a Cumberland sauce or wild pigeon in port wine. Try also, if featured, a smoked fish ravioli or mussels with oyster sauce. Desserts can be unusual, such as the poppy-seed parfait. It is closed Mon. and for dinner on Sun. Otherwise, hours are noon to 2pm and 7 to 9:30pm. A set lunch is good value at £12.50 ($20.65) or £13.75 ($22.70) on Sunday, but you can count on paying from £30 ($49.50) for an à la carte dinner.

9. Lavenham

Once a great wool center, Lavenham is considered a model village of East Anglia. It is filled with a number of half-timbered Tudor houses, washed in the characteristic Suffolk pink. The prosperity of the town in the days when wool was queen is reflected in the **guildhall,** on the triangular main "square," built from wool-trading profits. Inside are exhibits on the textile industry of Lavenham, showing how yarn was spun, then "dyed in the wool" with woad (the plant used by the ancient Picts to dye themselves blue) and following on to the weaving process. There is also a display showing how half-timbered houses were constructed.

Church of St. Peter and St. Paul, at the edge of Lavenham, contains interesting carvings on the misericords and the chancel screen, as well as ornate tombs. This is one of the "wool churches" of the area, built by pious merchants in the Perpendicular style with a landmark tower.

Lavenham lies only 7 miles from Sudbury, 11 miles from Bury St. Edmunds, and 66 miles from London.

WHERE TO STAY AND DINE

Linked to the Middle Ages, **The Swan,** High Street, Lavenham, Sudbury, Suffolk CO10 9QA (tel. 0787/247477), is a lavishly timbered inn, probably one of the oldest and best-preserved buildings in this relatively unmarred village. Its success has necessitated incorporating an adjoining ancient wool hall, which provides a high-ceilinged and timbered guesthouse and additional raftered, second-story bedrooms, opening onto a tiny cloistered garden. The Garden Bar opens onto yet another garden, with old stone walls and flowerbeds. Londoners often visit on September-to-March weekends for dinner and chamber music concerts. All 47 accommodations contain private baths, phones, and TVs. A single rents for £80 ($132) to £85 ($140.25) daily and doubles, £100 ($165) to £115 ($189.75). The bedrooms vary in size, according to the eccentricities of the architecture. Most have beamed ceilings and a mixture of traditional pieces that blend well with the old. The more expensive rooms contain four-poster beds. There are nearly enough lounges for guests to try a different one every night of the week. Meals in the raftered, two-story-high dining room have their own drama, as you sit on leather-and-oak chairs with brass studding. Even if you're not spending the night, you can sample the three-course luncheon priced at £13.50 ($22.30). Evening table d'hôte dinners go for £16.95 ($27.95). From the à la carte menu, you can order such specialties as roasted goose breast in a rich sauce with crispy bacon and mushrooms or rosettes of

English lamb with avocado served with a fresh basil wine sauce with chopped toma-toes. Expect to spend from £25 ($41.25). In World War II, Allied pilots (who made The Swan their second home) carved their signatures into the bar, a longish room with a timbered ceiling and a fine weapon collection.

The Great House, Market Place, Lavenham, Sudbury, Suffolk CO10 9QZ (tel. 0787/247431), is the finest spot for dining. Behind a Georgian facade and opening onto the market place, it is also attractively decorated, with Laura Ashley prints, an inglenook fireplace, and old oak beams. A Texan owner, John O. Spice, has wisely hired a Frenchman, Régis Crépy as his chef-de-cuisine. He is assisted by his wife, Martine. He is an inventive chef, as reflected by such dishes as marinated smoked salmon with cucumber puree and sour cream, sauté of sweetbreads with a wild mushroom sauce, and medallions of lamb filet in lime sauce. Meals are served daily from noon to 2:30pm and 7 to 10:30pm. The least expensive way to dine here is to order the set lunch at £7.50 ($12.40) or the table d'hôte dinner at £13.50 ($22.30). A la carte menus are also available, an evening meal costing around £22 ($36.30). The house also rents four elegantly decorated bedrooms (suites, actually) for £45 ($74.25) to £60 ($99) daily in a single, £62 ($102.30) to £68 ($112.20) in a double for B&B. Rooms contain private baths or showers, TVs, and phones.

10. Woodbridge

A yachting center, 12 miles from the North Sea, Woodbridge is a market town on a branch of the Deben River. Its best-known resident was Edward FitzGerald, the Victorian poet and translator of the *Rubáiyát* of Omar Khayyám (some critics con-sider the Englishman's version better than the original). The poet died in 1883 and was buried 4 miles away at Boulge.

Woodbridge is a good base for exploring the East Suffolk coastline and excur-sions to Constable's Flatford Mill, coming up. But first, a look at my moderately priced accommodation and dining recommendation, which is some 1½ miles from the Woodbridge rail station.

WHERE TO STAY AND DINE

On the A12 road near Woodbridge, **Seckford Hall,** Woodbridge, Suffolk IP13 6NU (tel. 0394/385678), captures the spirit of the days of Henry VIII and his strong-willed daughter, Elizabeth (the latter may have held court here). The estate is built of brick, now ivy covered, and adorned with crowstepped gables, mullioned windows, and ornate chimneys—pure Tudor. The hall was built in 1530 by Sir Thomas Seckford, a member of one of Suffolk's first families. You enter through a heavy, studded Tudor door into a flagstone hallway with antiques. The butler will show you to your bedroom. Owners Mr. and Mrs. Michael Bunn have seen to it that your stay is like a house party. All 34 bedrooms have private baths, phones, and TVs. A single room rents from £59 ($97.35) daily, a double or twin from £70 ($115.50), and a four-poster unit from £75 ($123.75) and up. Charges include a full English breakfast, service, and tax. One room is high-ceilinged with a monumental 1587 four-poster bed. In summer, reservations are helpful for those desiring bed, break-fast, and evening dinner. (Non-residents can stop by for dinner, which is à la carte. Best to phone first.)

If you arrive before sundown, you may want to stroll through a portion of the 34-acre gardens with a rose garden, herbaceous borders, and greenhouses. At the bottom of the garden is an ornamental lake, complete with weeping willows and paddling ducks. At 4pm, you can have a complete tea in the great hall. Sip your brew slowly, savoring the atmosphere of heavy beams and a stone fireplace. Your chair may be Queen Anne, your table Elizabethan. Dinner will be announced by the butler.

Good English meals are served in a setting of linenfold paneling and Chippendale and Hepplewhite chairs. After-dinner coffee and brandy are featured in the Tudor Bar. Other facilities include a heated, indoor swimming pool.

---

11. Aldeburgh

Pressed against the North Sea, Aldeburgh is a favorite resort of the in-the-know traveler, even attracting Dutch people who make the sea crossing via Harwich and Felixstowe, now major entry ports for traffic from the continent. Benjamin Britten, the renowned composer (1913–1976) and author of such works as *Death in Venice* and *Billy Budd,* lived here, and various of his works, notably operas, had their first performances at the Aldeburgh Festival. He founded the festival in 1946, and it still takes place in June, featuring internationally known performers. Other concerts and events also take place throughout the year. The Snape Maltings Concert Hall nearby is generally regarded as one of the more successful of the smaller British concert halls, and it also contains the Britten-Pears School of Advanced Musical Studies, established in 1973.

Less than 100 miles from London, the town dates from Roman times, and has long been known as a small port for North Sea fisheries. There are two golf courses, one at Aldeburgh and another at Thorpeness, 2 miles away. A yacht club opens onto the River Alde 9 miles from the river's mouth. Two bird sanctuaries are also nearby, Minsmere and Havergate Island. Both are famous for their waterfowl, and they are managed by the Royal Society for the Protection of Birds.

Constructed on a shelf of land at the level of the sea, the High or main street of town, runs parallel to the often-turbulent waterfront. This main street sits below a cliff face that rises some 55 feet. A major attraction is the 16th-century **Moot Hall Museum** (tel. 072885/2158). The hall dates from the time of Henry VIII, but its tall, twin chimneys are later additions. The timber-frame structure contains old maps and prints. It's open from Easter to June 2:30 to 5pm on Sat. and Sun. only, but from July to September it's open daily. Admission is 30p (50¢) for adults, free to children.

Aldeburgh also contains the nation's northernmost Martello tower, erected to protect the coast from a feared invasion by Napoleon.

WHERE TO STAY AND DINE

In August, during music festivals, and at the time of the regatta, accommodations tend to be fully booked. Do reserve far in advance during these times.

Wentworth Hotel, Wentworth Road, Aldeburgh, Suffolk IP15 5BD (tel. 0728/452312), is a traditional country-house hotel, with tall chimneys and gables, overlooking the sea. Many rooms open onto good views. Since 1920 the Pritt family have welcomed the world to their hotel, including Sir Benjamin Britten and his beloved friend, Peter Pears. The novelist E. M. Forster, whose books, *Room with a View* and *Maurice,* have been filmed, also came this way. In summer tables are placed outside so guests can enjoy the sun, but in winter the open fires in the lounges, even the cozy bar, are a welcome sight. Many come here anytime except in January to enjoy the good food and wine. Others, seeking accommodations are housed in any of 31 bedrooms, each well appointed, with TV and bath, and most with private bath. Rates range from £38 ($62.70) daily in a single, £90 ($148.50) in a double.

Brudenell Hotel, the Parade, Aldeburgh, Suffolk IP15 5BU (tel. 0728/452071), is right on the waterfront. Built at the beginning of the 20th century, it was remodeled and redecorated. The interior is pleasant, and from the 47 bedrooms there are many with a view of the sea. All of the rooms have private bathrooms. Every room has a TV, radio, tea and coffee makers, and central heating, as well as good beds. The dining room, with an all-glass wall overlooking the coast, is an ideal spot for a three-course luncheon costing £7.25 ($11.95). Dinner goes for £13 ($21.45). Rates are from £42 ($69.30) per person per night inclusive of dinner, accommodation, breakfast, service, and tax.

12. East Bergholt

The English landscape painter John Constable (1776–1837) was born at East Bergholt. Near the village is **Flatford Mill** (tel. 0206/298283), subject of one of his most renowned canvases. The mill, in a scenic setting, was given to the National Trust in 1943, and since has been leased to the Field Studies Council for use as a residential college. Weekly courses are arranged on all aspects of the countryside and the environment. None of the buildings contains relics of Constable, nor are they open to the general public, but students of all ages and capabilities are welcome to courses. The fee for 1 week is inclusive of accommodation, meals, and tuition. Details may be obtained from The Warden, Field Studies Council, Flatford Mill Field Centre, East Bergholt, Colchester, Essex CO7 6UL.

THE LOCAL PUB

Cited by numerous writers as one of the unmarred inns of East Anglia, the **Red Lion Inn,** the Street (tel. 0206/298332), traces its ancestry back to around 1500. The family-run pub has an enclosed children's garden. There is a wide range of bar meals, costing £1.75 ($2.90) to £5 ($8.25), including the best ploughman's lunch in the area. Steaks are offered in the evening. Hours are from noon to 3pm and 7 to 11pm Mon. to Sat., from noon to 3pm and 7 to 10:30pm Sun. A short stroll from Flatford Mill and the heart of Constable land, the inn is opposite a historic church with a bell cage on the ground, where the bells are hand-rung. The Red Lion is reached by turning off the A12 Colchester-Ipswich road. Ask about B&B accommodations, costing £20 ($33) per person daily.

NORFOLK

Bounded by the North Sea, Norfolk is the biggest of the East Anglian counties. It's a low-lying area, with fens, heaths, and salt marshes. An occasional dike or windmill makes you think you've been delivered to the Netherlands. One of the features of Norfolk is its network of broads, miles and miles of lagoons—shallow in parts—connected by streams.

Summer sports people flock to Norfolk to hire boats for sailing or fishing. From Norwich itself, **Wroxham,** capital of the broads, is easily reached, only 8 miles to the northeast. Motorboats regularly leave from this resort, taking parties on short trips. Some of the best scenery of the broads is to be found on the periphery of Wroxham.

13. Norwich

Norwich, 109 miles from London and 20 miles from the North Sea, still holds to its claim as the capital city of East Anglia. The county town of Norfolk, Norwich is a charming and historic city, despite encroachments by industry. It is the most important shopping center in East Anglia and is well provided with hotels and entertainment. In addition to its cathedral, it has more than 30 medieval parish churches built of flint.

There are many interesting hotels in the narrow streets and alleyways, and a big open-air market, busy every weekday, where fruit, flowers, vegetables, and other goods are sold from stalls with colored canvas roofs.

WHAT TO SEE AND DO

Assembly House, Theatre Street, is a Georgian building restored to provide a splendid arts and social center. The **Maddermarket Theatre** (tel. 0603/620917), the home of the Norwich Players, is an 18th-century chapel converted by Nugent Monck in 1921 to an Elizabethan-style theater. It stands behind Stranger's Hall on St. John's Alley. On the outskirts of the city, the buildings of the University of East Anglia are modern in design and include the Sainsbury Center.

There is a **tourist information center** at the guildhall, Gaol Hill (tel. 0603/666071).

Norwich Castle

In the center of Norwich, on a partly artificial mound, sits the castle, formerly the county gaol (jail). Its huge 12th-century Norman keep and the later prison buildings are used as a civic museum and headquarters of the county-wide Norfolk Museums Service (tel. 0603/222222, ext. 71224).

The museum's art displays include an impressive collection of pictures by artists of the Norwich School, of whom the most distinguished were John Crome, born 1768, and John Sell Cotman, born 1782. The Castle Museum also contains the greatest specialist collection of British ceramic teapots in the world and unrivaled collections of Lowestoft porcelain and Norwich silver. Rare prehistoric gold jewelry and other archeological finds help to illustrate Norfolk's wealth and importance and the life of its people. A set of dioramas shows Norfolk wildlife in its natural setting. You can also visit a geology gallery and a permanent exhibition "Norfolk in Europe."

The Castle Museum is open daily from 10am to 5pm (on Sun. 2 to 5pm). Charges are: £1 ($1.65) for adults, 20p (35¢) for children. There's a cafeteria open from 10am to 4:30pm Mon. to Sat., as well as a bar serving from 10:30am to 2:30pm.

Norwich Cathedral

Principally of Norman design, the cathedral dates from 1096. It is noted primarily for its long nave, with its lofty columns. Its spire, built in the late Perpendicular style, rises 315 feet, and shares distinction with the keep of the castle as the significant landmarks on the Norwich skyline. On the vaulted ceiling are more than 300 bosses (knoblike ornamental projections) depicting biblical scenes. The impressive choir stalls with the handsome misereres date from the 15th century. Edith Cavell—"Patriotism is not enough"—the English nurse executed by the Germans in World War I, was buried on the cathedral's Life's Green. The quadrangular cloisters go back to the 13th century, and are among the most spacious in England. A donation of 50p (85¢) is requested.

The cathedral visitors' center includes a refreshment area and an exhibition and film room with tape/slide shows about the cathedral. Admission is free. The cathedral can be visited from October to May 7:30am to 6pm daily and from June to September 7:30am to 7pm daily.

A short walk from the cathedral will take you to **Tombland,** one of the most interesting old squares in Norwich.

Sainsbury Centre for Visual Arts

The Sainsbury Centre for Visual Arts (tel. 0603/592470) was the gift in 1973 of Sir Robert and Lady Sainsbury, who contributed their private collection to the University of East Anglia, 3 miles west of Norwich on Earlham Road. Along with their son, David, they gave an endowment to provide a building to house the collection. The center, designed by Foster Associates, was opened in 1978, and since then the building has won many national and international awards. Features of the structure are its flexibility, allowing solid and glass areas to be interchanged, and the superb quality of light, which allows optimum viewing of works of art. The Sainsbury Collection is one of the foremost in the country, including modern, ancient, classical, and ethnographic art. It is especially strong in works by Francis Bacon, Alberto Giacometti, and Henry Moore. Other displays at the center include the Anderson collection of art nouveau and the university aggregation of 20th-century abstract art and design. There is also a regular program of special exhibitions. The center (tel. 0603/592470) is open from noon to 5pm; closed Mon. Admission is 50p (85¢) for adults, 25p (40¢) for children. The restaurant on the premises offers a self-service buffet from 10:30am to 2pm and a carvery service from 12:30 to 2pm Mon. to Fri. A conservatory coffee bar serves light lunches and refreshments from noon to 4:30pm Tue. to Sun.

The Mustard Shop

The Victorian-style Mustard Shop, 3 Bridewell Alley (tel. 0603/627889), is a wealth of mahogany and shining brass. There is an old cash register to record your purchase, and the standard of service and pace of life also reflect the personality and courtesy of a bygone age. In the Mustard Museum is a series of displays illustrating the history of the Colman Company and the making of mustard, its properties and origins. There are old advertisements, as well as packages and "tins." You can browse in the shop, selecting whichever of the mustards you prefer. Really hot, English-type mustards are sold, as well as the continental blends. Besides mustards, the shop sells aprons, tea towels, chopping boards, pottery mustard pots, and mugs. The shop and museum are open from 9am to 5:30pm Mon. to Sat.

U.S. Air Force Memorial

A memorial room honoring the **Second Air Division of the Eighth United States Army Air Force** is part of the Central Library, Bethel Street (tel. 0603/222222, ext. 52). A memorial fountain also honoring the United States airmen who were based in Norfolk and Suffolk in World War II, many losing their lives in the line of duty, is in the library courtyard. The fountain incorporates the insignia of the Second Air Division and a stone from each state of the United States. Books, audiovisual materials, and records of the various bomber groups are in the library. There is no admission charge, but contributions are used for the upkeep of the memorial. Hours are daily from 9am to 5pm.

WHERE TO STAY

Norwich is better equipped than most East Anglian cities to handle guests who arrive without reservations. The **Norwich City Tourist Information Centre** maintains an office at the guildhall, Gaol Hill, opposite the market (tel. 0603/666071). Each year a new listing of accommodations is drawn up, including both licensed and unlicensed hotels, B&B houses, and even living arrangements on the outskirts.

In business since 1272, the **Maids Head Hotel,** Tombland, Norwich, Norfolk NR3 1LB (tel. 0603/761111), claims to be the oldest continuously operated hotel in the United Kingdom. In the most ancient part of the city and next to Norwich Cathedral, it has two parts, Elizabethan and Georgian, to its architectural personality. The Georgian section has a prim white entry and small-paned windows. The 82 bedrooms offer phones, TVs, private baths or showers, with fresh fruit, newspapers, and the traditional services such as shoe cleaning, breakfast served in bed, and afternoon cream teas. The four-poster Queen Elizabeth I room (where the Tudor monarch allegedly once slept) is much sought after. Singles with shower cost £60 ($99), and singles with bath £85 ($140.25). A double with bath and shower costs £75 ($123.75) to £98 ($161.70). An English breakfast is included in all the tariffs. Meals are served in the Courtyard Carvery at lunch with an extensive buttery service all day. The Georgian paneled Minstrel Room offers dinner each night. Lunches cost from £8 ($13.20) and dinners from £13 ($21.45).

Post House Hotel, Ipswich Road, Norwich, Norfolk NR4 6EP (tel. 0603/56431), is 2 miles from the center of the city on the A140 Ipswich road and 1 mile from the All London road. Free parking space is provided for 200 cars. The hotel charges £78 ($128.70), also including VAT and service. Each of the 120 bedrooms has a private bath, phone, TV, radio, tea and coffee maker, and a mini-bar. The rooms have combined sitting areas, with sofas and armchairs. The coffeeshop, which stays open till 10:30pm, reflects Norfolk's ties with agriculture (sturdy farming tools decorate the walls); the main restaurant specializes in traditional English fare, such as game in season, smoked fish, and potted meats. The Punch Bar is decorated with early *Punch* cartoons and drawings. Guests enjoy an activity center with indoor pool, gym, solarium, and sauna.

   Hotel Nelson, Prince of Wales Road, Norwich, Norfolk NR1 1DX (tel. 0603/ 760260), is modern with a waterside setting, close to Thorpe Station, behind a four-store facade pierced with horizontal rows of glass. Each of its 121 bedrooms has its own private bath, TV, phone, and a view of either the river or a pleasant courtyard. Accommodations cost £65 ($107.25) daily in a single, £84 ($138.60) in a double. A nautical theme is predictably carried out in most of the public rooms. There are a sauna and an exercise room on the premises, plus a cocktail lounge and two restaurants. One of these, the Quarterdeck, brings back memories of Norwich's most famous son, Horatio, Admiral Lord Nelson, after whom the hotel is named. The nautical name also stems, of course, from the heroic naval exploits of Nelson, even up to his death at the Battle of Trafalgar. At the Quarterdeck (or should I say "on" it?), you get fast, cheerful service and a choice of dishes such as Cromer fish pie or beef-and-beer casserole with mushrooms and noodles. The restaurant is open daily from 10:30am for coffee and drinks, from noon to 2pm for lunch, and from 5:30 to 10:30pm for informal dinners, costing from £12.50 ($20.65). The hotel is near the railway station and Foundry Bridge, and there's free parking.

   Embassy Lansdowne Hotel, 116 Thorpe Rd., Norwich, Norfolk NR1 1RU (tel. 0603/620302), has been refurbished and refurnished extensively, but without taking away from the previous high standards of service and atmosphere. Two semi-detached cottages on the hotel grounds have been made into 44 bedrooms, with modern conveniences just like in the main building, but with original features, including bay windows and wooden beams as well as a private garden. Rooms contain private baths, TVs, and phones. Single rooms rent for £48 ($79.20) daily, while doubles peak at £70 ($115.50). The reception area's chandeliers light the way up the elegant staircase to the restaurant.

WHERE TO DINE

   Adlard's, 79 Upper St. Giles St. (tel. 0603/633522), is run by its chef and owner, David Adlard, who is clearly the culinary star of Norwich. In stylish surroundings, David, aided by his wife, Mary, offers a clean, crisp decor of green and white, with candlelit tables and a collection of paintings. Service is correct in every way, but also relaxed enough to make diners comfortable. He specializes in modern British cookery, bringing his own interpretation to every dish. These are likely to include poached salmon suprême with a chive-flavored butter sauce, rosette of lamb with an artichoke mousse, or pheasant with a game mousse accompanied by madeira sauce. Dinner is served Tue. to Sat., a table d'hôte going for £22.50 ($37.15). A la carte dinners cost from £30 ($49.50) per person, and reservations are essential.

   Green's Seafood Restaurant, 82 Upper St. Giles St. (tel. 0603/623733), serves the finest fresh fish dishes in Norwich. By the glow of candlelight, you can also enjoy some well-seasoned meat dishes, but it is the fish that attracts. You might begin with a well-flavored fish soup, then follow with poached scallops in red wine sauce or turbot with a creamy prawn sauce. Grilled Dover sole is a perennial favorite. Hours are 12:15 to 2:15pm and 7 to 11pm; closed lunch Sat., Sun., and Mon. Dinner costs from £22 ($36.30) per person, and reservations are needed.

   Marco's, 17 Pottergate (tel. 0603/624044), serves the best Italian food in the region, accompanied by salad greens and herbs that owner Marco Vessalio grows in a nearby kitchen garden. The pasta is homemade and concocted into tempting specialties, including gnocchi and a range of tagliatelle. One of Signor Vessalio's chicken, veal, or beef dishes might follow a steaming bowl of minestrone or pasta.

Lunch and dinner are served Tue. to Sat.; closed August, as well as some holidays. Hours are from 12:30 to 2pm and 7:30 to 10pm. A set lunch costs £12.50 ($20.65), and à la carte dinners go for £22 ($36.30).

Brasted's, 8-10 St. Andrews Hill (tel. 0603/625949), offers a lovely home in the oldest part of Norwich, within an easy stroll of both the cathedral and castle. After exploring the two major sights of Norwich, you can come here to sample the savory cooking of John Brasted, for whom the restaurant is named. The owner and chef de cuisine, Mr. Brasted, knows how to combine the best of yesterday with modern cooking techniques and innovations. As you enjoy the rather flamboyant interior, you can peruse the menu. You'll probably settle for one of the fresh fish dishes of East Anglia. Other dishes, including vegetables and desserts, seem equally well prepared. Brasted's is open from noon to 2pm and 7 to 10:30pm; closed lunch Sat. and all day Sun. Count on spending from £25 ($41.25) for a meal here.

14. Shipdham

As you negotiate a sharp bend around the churchyard in Shipdham village, near Thetford, you come to an open gateway leading to the wide graveled front yard of **Shipdham Place**, Church Close, Shipdham, Norfolk IP25 7LX (tel. 0362/820303). Ring the bell, and you will be welcomed into an old country house that was once the rectory. It dates back to the 17th century, with an elegant Regency block that was added in 1800. There are two lounges with comfortable chairs and a drinks trolley. You are trusted to help yourself and enter your drinks in the book for payment at departure. Behind the house, a garden is at the disposal of guests. You can take coffee on the terrace on a warm summer evening. Upstairs, the eight bedrooms with private baths and phones come in varying shapes and sizes. Some have sloping ceilings. All are decorated in pretty country prints, and fresh fruit and flowers are placed in your room on arrival. Rates vary from £30 ($49.50) per night for a single room to £77 ($127.05) for the big double rooms at the front of the house, which have large baths and walk-in closets. All tariffs include VAT and breakfast. It is mainly for the cuisine that Mr. and Mrs. Alan Poulton, the hosts, are known. Dishes are likely to include roast Norfolk partridge with bread sauce, potted Norfolk crab, and saddle of new-season English lamb. Dinner is served from 7:30 to 9:30pm. The location is 5 miles north of Thetford along the A1075.

15. North Norfolk

This part is already well known by members of the American Eighth Air Force, for many Liberators and Flying Fortresses took off and landed from this corner of the country. Their captains and crews sampled most of the local hostelries at one time or another. Now it is just feathered birds that fly overhead, and the countryside is peaceful.

WHAT TO SEE AND DO
This area is of considerable scenic interest. Norfolk, especially, provides an alternative to the vastly overcrowded West Country in summer, and it's extremely convenient for a weekend out of London, as it lies only a 3-hour drive away. Some good values are offered in the way of accommodations and food.

Sandringham
Some 110 miles northeast of London, Sandringham (tel. 0553/772675) has been the country home of four generations of British monarchs, ever since the prince of Wales (later King Edward VII) purchased it in 1861. The son of Queen

Victoria, along with his Danish wife, Princess Alexandra, rebuilt the house, standing on 7,000 acres of grounds, and in time it became a fashionable rendezvous of British society. The red-brick Victorian Tudor mansion consists of more than 200 rooms, and in recent times some of the rooms have been opened to the public, including two drawing rooms and a dining room. Sandringham joins Windsor Castle and the Palace of Holyroodhouse in Edinburgh as the only British royal residences that can be examined by the public. Guests can also visit a lofty saloon with a minstrels' gallery.

A group of former coach houses houses a museum of big-game trophies and a collection of cars, including the first vehicle purchased by a member of the royal family, a 1900 Daimler Tonneau that belonged to Edward VII. The house and grounds are open, except when Her Majesty or members of the royal family are there, from April 29 to September 30, Sun. to Thur. inclusive. The house and grounds are always closed on Fri. and Sat. Hours are 11am (noon on Sun.) to 4:45pm for the house; 10:30am (11:30am on Sun.) to 5pm for the grounds. Admission to the house and grounds is £2.20 ($3.65) for adults, £1.40 ($2.30) for children. To visit the grounds only, adults pay £1.70 ($2.80); children £1 ($1.65). The house is closed from the third week in July to the end of the first week in August, and the grounds and house are both closed for all by the first and last three or four days of that period. The 70-acre gardens are richly planted with azaleas, rhododendrons, hydrangeas, and camellias.

Sandringham lies 50 miles from Cambridge and 8 miles from King's Lynn. There is a bus service between King's Lynn and Sandringham.

Blickling Hall

A long drive, bordered by massive yew hedges towering above and framing your first view of this old house, leads you to Blickling Hall, near Aylsham (tel. 0263/733084). A great Jacobean house built in the early 17th century, it is perhaps one of the finest examples of such architecture in the country. The long gallery has an elaborate 17th-century ceiling, and the Peter the Great Room, decorated later, has a fine tapestry on the wall. The house is set in ornamental parkland with a formal garden and an orangery. Meals and snacks are available. It is open from April until the end of October from 1 to 5pm, with the gardens, shop, and restaurant opening at noon; closed Mon. and Thur. Admission to the house and gardens is £4 ($6.60) for adults, £2 ($3.30) for children; £2 ($3.30) for adults and £1 ($1.65) for children to the gardens only.

Norfolk Lavender Ltd.

At **Caley Mill** at Heacham (tel. 0485/70384) you can see how lavender is grown, the flowers harvested, and the essence distilled before appearing prettily packaged as perfume, aftershave, and old-fashioned lavender bags to slip between your hankies. Much of the lavender is grown on the nearby Sandringham royal estate, so you may end up with a regal product. The house and grounds are open all year. Hours are from 10am to 5pm Mon. to Fri. from January to Easter, from 10am to 5:30pm daily from Easter to October, and from 10am to 5pm Mon. to Sat. from November to Christmas. The tours cost £1 ($1.65) for adults, free for children. The Miller's Cottage Tea Room serves cream teas, homemade cakes, and light lunches from Easter to the end of May in the afternoon only. From May to Christmas, the tea room is open at the same time as the shop. The best time to see the lavender in bloom is late June to mid-August.

The Thursford Collection

Just off the A148, which runs from King's Lynn to Cromer, at Thursford Green, Thursford, near Fakenham (tel. 0328/878477), George Cushing has been collecting and restoring steam engines and organs for more years than you'd care to remember. His collection is now a trust, and the old painted giants are on display, a paradise of traction engines with impeccable pedigrees such as Burrells, Garretts, and Ruston Proctors. There are some static engines, the sort that run merry-go-rounds at funfairs, but the most flamboyant exhibits are the old show business musical organs, the Wurlitzers and concert organs with their brilliant decoration, moving figures, and mass of windpipes. The organs play throughout the afternoon. There is a children's play area, and a Savages Venetian Gondola switchback ride with Gavoili organ, which operates daily. It was built at nearby Kings Lynn, and Disneyland has been after it for years. On many days during the summer, the 2-foot-gauge steam railway, the Cackler, will take you around the wooded grounds of the museum. There is a refreshment café and a souvenir shop to buy photographs, books, and records of the steam-organ music. The collection is open daily from Easter until the end of October. Times of opening vary, so you'll need to call first. Adults pay £4 ($6.60) admission, and children £2 ($3.30).

The North Norfolk Railway
This steam railway plies from Sheringham to Weybourne. The station at Sheringham (0263/822045) opens daily at 10am from Easter to October. Admission to the station and museum is free from October to March. From Easter to the end of September, admission is 50p (85¢) for adults, 30p (50¢) for children. There are two museum displays of railway paraphernalia, steam locomotives, and historic rolling stock. The round trip to Weybourne by steam train takes about 45 minutes through attractive countryside. Days and times of departure vary, so you should phone between 10am and 5pm before you go there. A ride on a steam train between Weybourne and Sheringham is £2.50 ($4.15) for adults for a round trip, £1.50 ($2.50) for children.

WHERE TO STAY AND DINE
Almost on the edge of the sea but protected from its worst ravages, **The Maltings,** the Street, Weybourne, near Holt, Norfolk NR25 6SY (tel. 026370/731), is a delightful country pub in the best tradition. The 21 bedrooms are simple and comfortable with private baths, color TVs, and phones, and cost £35 ($57.75) daily in a single, from £55 ($90.75) in a double. Rates include a large English breakfast, VAT, and service. The original building dates back to the 16th century, and the flint walls and stout plain exterior bear witness to those times. The elegant restaurant has à la carte choices, including most of those haute cuisine dishes that you crave, along with a Taste of England menu when a succulent set lunch will cost £8.50 ($14.05); a set dinner, £15 ($24.75).

Blakeney Hotel, the Quay, Blakeney, near Holt, Norfolk NR25 7NE (tel. 0263/740797). As its address indicates, the hotel is right on the quay overlooking the harbor and across the flats from Blakeney Point where migrating birds rest on their way south. The village and neighboring Cley built many of the Elizabethan sailing ships, and the hotel bar is named for one of them, *Revenge.* The 51 rooms of this hotel, built in 1923, are cozy, with private baths, color TVs, phones, and radios. Singles cost £38 ($62.70) to £52 ($85.80) daily, and doubles run £76 ($125.40) to £104 ($171.60). Breakfast is included. There is an indoor swimming pool, and the lounge has panoramic windows with views over the flats to the sea.

Congham Hall, Lynn Road, Grimston, King's Lynn, Norfolk PE32 1AH (tel. 0485/600250), is just the place if you'd like to center around the King's Lynn area. Far better than anything you'd find in town, Congham Hall lies at Grimston, more than 6 miles northeast by A148. One of the most scenic and beautiful of the country house hotels of East Anglia, Congham Hall is set on 40 acres of its own parklike grounds complete with paddocks and orchards. Trevor and Christine Forecast brought taste and refinement to converting this Georgian manor into a small hotel of charm and character. Their facilities include a hard tennis court and a heated swimming pool along with a sauna and solarium. The house is tastefully decorated, and the well-furnished bedrooms offer much comfort. They also contain private baths or showers, phones, TVs, and hairdryers among other amenities. The Forecasts rent 10 bedrooms and one suite, with standard singles priced from £65 ($107.25) daily, with doubles going for £85 ($140.25). Their menu is varied, and the wine list well chosen. Meals begin at £12.50 ($20.65), going up to £32 ($52.80) for an elaborate repast.

Old Rectory, Great Snoring, Fakenham, Norfolk NR21 0HP (tel. 0328/ 820597). The history of this old house is shrouded in mystery, but in 1500 it was believed to be hexagonal with stone-mullioned windows and heraldic shields of the then owners, the Shelton family, carved on the oaken front door. The Victorians did their bit to restore the house, but it still remains a solid part of the medieval village life. Rosamond Scoles and her family have six comfortable and elegantly furnished rooms for guests. Overnight is £48 ($79.20) daily in a single, £72 ($118.80) in a double, all with bath, including a leisurely and substantial breakfast. There is a large lounge for guests, where a woodstove burns, and the light flickers on antique wood-work. Dinner is three courses, cheese, and coffee for £15.50 ($25.60) per person. Picnic hampers are provided for luncheon al fresco if you wish. Old Rectory is li-censed, so you can enjoy a sherry before dinner or a nightcap by the fire before retiring to your bed.

Elderton Lodge, Cromer Road, Thorpe Market, North Walsham, Norfolk NR11 8TZ (tel. 026379/547). At a point 21 miles from Norwich, turn off the A149 road to the former dower house of the big estate with wide views over the farmlands. The entrance hall of the hotel is full of family memorabilia, and there's a large lounge bar, off which you'll find a conservatory in which light meals are served. Many of the eight bedrooms have private baths, while guests in bathless units share large, elegant corridor facilities. A single costs from £20 ($33) daily, and a double begins at £46 ($75.90). All rates include a full breakfast and VAT. The set dinner menu at £11.50 ($19) includes grilled trout with almonds, lamb cutlets with pâté and red-currant sauce, or breast of chicken with madeira sauce.

Links Country Park Hotel and Golf Club, Sandy Lane, West Runton, near Cro-mer, Norfolk NR27 9QH (tel. 026375/691), is 24 miles from Norwich and 42 miles from King's Lynn. You don't need to be a golfer to enjoy this country hotel, with its large, comfortable public rooms and bars. Despite the fact that it's sur-rounded by the golf course, there are views out over the sea and plenty of places to walk. The 32 bedrooms are spacious and comfortable with TVs, phones, and private baths, and hot beverage facilities. Half-board charges are £130 ($214.50) daily in a double, £45 ($74.25) in a single. There is an elegant restaurant with good set menus. Next to the clubhouse is the Fairways Grill Room, a lofty place decorated with plaques and the names of past winners of golf tournaments, with plenty of ta-bles and chairs, plus a good but simple menu.

XV

EAST MIDLANDS

1. NORTHAMPTONSHIRE
2. LEICESTERSHIRE
3. DERBYSHIRE
4. NOTTINGHAMSHIRE
5. LINCOLNSHIRE

The East Midlands is a mixture of dreary industrial sections and some of Britain's noblest scenery, such as the Peak District National Park, centered in Derbyshire. Byron said that scenes there rivaled those of Switzerland and Greece. Many pleasant surprises are in store for you, from the tulip land of Lincoln to the 18th-century spa of Buxton in Derbyshire, from George Washington's ancestral home at Sulgrave Manor in Northamptonshire to what remains of Sherwood Forest.

1. Northamptonshire

The shire, in the heart of the Midlands, has been inhabited since Paleolithic times. Traces have been found of Beaker and other Bronze Age people, and remains of a number of Iron Age hill-forts can still be seen. Two Roman roads—Watling Street and Ermine Street—ran through the county, and relics of Roman settlements have been discovered at Towcester, Whilton, Irchester, and Castor. In the 7th century, invasion by West Saxons and Anglians contributed a racial mix. In 655, the first abbey was established at Medehamstede, now Peterborough.

It was under the aegis of the Danes in the 9th century that the city of Northampton became the seat of administration for a borough which had almost the same boundaries as the shire does today and as recorded in the *Domesday Book*. In the Middle Ages, castles and manor houses dotted a country rich in cattle, sheep farming, and the production of leatherwork.

SULGRAVE MANOR

On your way from Oxford to Stratford-upon-Avon, if you take the A34 north, you can visit Sulgrave Manor, the ancestral home of George Washington. First, you'll come to Banbury. Follow the A422 east from Banbury into Northamptonshire toward Brackley, but turn off to the left after a short distance onto the B4525, which will take you to the tiny village of Sulgrave. Signs will lead you to Sulgrave Manor, a small Tudor manorial house built in the mid-16th century.

As part of Henry VIII's plan to dissolve monasteries, he sold the priory-owned manor in 1539 to Lawrence Washington, who had been mayor of Northampton. George Washington was a direct descendant of Lawrence (seven generations removed). The Washington family occupied Sulgrave for more than a century. In 1656 Col. John Washington left for the New World.

In 1914 the manor was purchased by a group of English people in honor of the friendship between Britain and America. Over the years, major restoration has taken place (a whole new wing had to be added), with an eye toward returning it as much as possible to its original state. The Colonial Dames have been largely responsible for raising the money. From both sides of the Atlantic the appropriate furnishings were donated, including a number of portraits—even a Gilbert Stuart original of the first president. On the main doorway is the Washington family coat-of-arms—two bars and a trio of mullets—which is believed to have been the inspiration for the "Stars and Stripes."

The manor is open from March to December 10:30am to 1pm and 2 to 5:30pm; closed Wed. Otherwise the hours are 10:30am to 1pm and 2 to 4pm; closed in January. Admission is £2 ($3.30) for adults, £1 ($1.65) for children. For more information, telephone 029576/205.

Where to Stay and Dine

Across from Sulgrave Manor is the **Thatched House Hotel,** Manor Road, Sulgrave, near Banbury, Northamptonshire OX17 2SE (tel. 029576/232), a long, low group of thatched 17th-century cottages, with a front garden full of flowers. Even if you're just passing through, it's a good place to stop for tea following your visit to Sulgrave Manor. Cream teas, served from 3:30 to 5:30pm and costing £1.80 ($2.95), consist of scones with thick cream and jam, and strawberries in season. Tea is served at a table in either the beamed living room or dining room, furnished with antiques. If you're lucky enough to stay over, Ron Walpole, the owner and manager, has modernized the seven bedrooms, installing private baths in all the doubles. Two singles on the second floor share a bath. Each unit has a TV and a tea and coffee maker. Depending on the plumbing, singles range from £25 ($41.25) to £35 ($57.75) daily, and doubles cost £60 ($99). Rates include a full English breakfast and VAT. Lunches cost £6.50 ($10.75) to £7.25 ($11.95). Dinner goes for £10.50 ($17.35), when you can feast on such dishes as medallion of English lamb flavored with herbs or roast guinea fowl in a sherry sauce. Food is served daily from noon to 2pm and 7:30 to 9:30pm.

NORTHAMPTON

The administrative and political center of Northamptonshire was a favorite meeting place of Norman and Plantagenet kings, fortified after 1066 by Simon de Senlis (St. Liz). Here King John was besieged by the barons trying to force policy changes that finally resulted in the Magna Carta. During the Wars of the Roses, Henry VI (before he achieved that note) was defeated and taken prisoner, and during the Civil War, Northampton stuck with Parliament and Cromwell. The town, on the River Nene, has long been an important center for the production of boots and shoes, as well as other leatherwork, pursuits that are traced through the centuries in two of the city's museums. Northampton lies 69 miles from London and 41 miles from Oxford.

Central Museum and Art Gallery, Guildhall Road (tel. 0604/34881), displays the history of Northampton from earliest times right up to the present day with objects, sound, and film. The museum also displays English Oriental ceramics, Old Masters, sculpture, and British 19th- and 20th-century art. It is open from 10am to 5pm Mon. to Sat. (to 8pm Thur.). Admission is free.

Museum of Leathercraft, Old Blue Coat School, Bridge Street (tel. 0604/34881), traces the history of leather use from ancient Egyptian times to the present. Missal cases, 16th-century caskets, and modern saddles are displayed, with exhibits of costumes, luggage, and harnesses. It is open from 10am to 5pm Mon. to Sat. with no admission charge.

Where to Stay and Dine

Northampton Moat House Inn, Silver Street, Northampton, Northampton-shire NN1 2TA (tel. 0604/22441), is a concrete-and-glass structure, attracting mainly the business client, drawn to its good location just off the Inner Ring Road (West). A first-class motor hotel, it checks you in and out smoothly and efficiently. The atmosphere isn't stiff at all—in fact it's rather informal, and the public lounges are attractively decorated. You can dine in a coaching-house atmosphere in the Sad-dle Room, with its large stone fireplace and heavy beams. The menu is international, and guests dine by candlelight, enjoying soft music from a piano player. A resident band entertains on Sat. night from September to June. The 138 rooms are well fur-nished and comfortable, each with private bath or shower and toilet, along with color TV, radio, phone, and wall-to-wall carpeting. Singles cost £68 ($112.20) dai-ly; doubles, £82 ($135.30).

Westone Moat House, Ashley Way, Weston Favell, Northampton, Northamp-tonshire NN3 3EA (tel. 0604/406262), is a big 19th-century mansion that has seen much modernization. A favored spot here is the cocktail lounge, which has ele-gance, its windows opening onto the terrace and grounds. All 65 bedrooms have private baths, color TVs, radios, phones, and hot beverage facilities. B&B costs £59 ($97.35) daily in a single, £69 ($113.85) in a double or twin. Traditional English dishes are among the offerings in the restaurant, which has good food, fine service, and a bright decor. The location is 3 miles east off A45.

ALTHORP HOUSE

The mansion that was the girlhood home of the princess of Wales, Althorp, Northampton (no phone calls allowed), is the residence of Lord Spencer, the father of the former Lady Diana Spencer who married Prince Charles. The entrance lodge is 5 miles northwest of Northampton, beyond the village of Harlestone. Althorp is about a 1½-hour drive from London on the A428 from Northampton to Rugby. Built in 1508 by Sir John Spencer, the house has undergone many alterations over the years.

It contains a collection of pictures by Van Dyck, Reynolds, Gainsborough, and Rubens, as well as fine and rare French and English furniture, along with Sèvres, Bow, and Chelsea porcelain. The collection is quite as magnificent as that in better-known stately homes. The house is open daily from 1 to 5pm, except in July and August when hours are 11am to 6pm. Wed. is Connoisseur's Day, when extra rooms are shown and the tour is longer. Admission to the house and grounds on regular days is £2.75 ($4.55) for adults, £1.75 ($2.90) for children, rising to £3.75 ($6.20) for adults and £2 ($3.30) for children on Connoisseurs' Day. The grounds and lake can be visited separately for 50p (85¢) for adults, 25p (40¢) for children. A gift shop, wine shop, and tea room are maintained at Althorp. The present countess helps in the gift shop, and Lord Spencer's own favorite sideline is the excellent cellar and wine shop.

STOKE BRUERNE

On the Grand Union Canal, the **Canal Museum,** at Stoke Bruerne near Towcester in Northamptonshire (tel. 0604/862229), is just south of the Blisworth Tunnel (take the A508 from the M1 junction 15 or the A5). The three-story cornmill has been restored and adapted to give an insight into the working lives of canal boatmen and their families. On display is a full-size replica of a "butty" boat cabin complete with cooking range, brassware, lace curtains, traditional ware, tools, and teapots. There is also an early semidiesel Bolinder boat engine, a boat-weighing machine once used to determine canal toll charges. You can buy posters, books, illustrations of canal life, hand-painted traditional canalware, models, and badges in a shop at the museum. It is open from 10am to 6pm; closed on Mon. from October to Easter and open till 4pm Tue. to Sun. Admission is £1.50 ($2.50) for adults, £1 ($1.65) for children. A family ticket will cost you £4 ($6.60).

The Boat Inn, Grand Union Canal (tel. 0604/862428), started as a row of humble cottages in the 17th century and has gradually progressed without losing its original character. It's still a limestone building with a thatched roof overlooking Grand Union Canal and the Stoke Bruerne Waterways Museum. The public house is the oldest part. It has stone floors and open fires. Bar food is served here. The restaurant offers a full range of dishes, including venison and grouse in season. A three-course meal, finished off with a choice from the dessert trolley or the cheeseboard, then coffee and mints, will cost around £15 ($24.75), including VAT. The "Great British Sunday Lunch," roast beef with Yorkshire pudding, of course, costs £8.95 ($14.75) for adults, £5.95 ($9.80) for children. Hours are 11am to 3pm and 6 to 11pm. The Woodward family has owned and run The Boat Inn since 1877.

Cruises are available on the Woodwards' canal narrow boat, *Indian Chief.* A 25-minute trip to Blisworth Tunnell Mouth and back costs 85p ($1.40) for adults, 55p (90¢) for children. The boat has music, video, fully stocked bar, soft drinks, tea, coffee, and snacks. You can also hire a chauffeur-driven Rolls-Royce for sightseeing or for airport pick-up, costing £25 ($41.25) per hour.

AT WEEDON

True to its name, the **Crossroads Hotel,** High Street, Weedon, Northamptonshire NN7 4PX (tel. 0327/40354), lies near the M1, the A5, and the A45. The owners have created a little nook where imagination and good taste reign. The clock tower of the hotel, standing in the garden, is a sign of hospitality. Inside there is a collection of old clocks throughout the dining room and lounges. The antique collection in the dining room is enhanced with stuffed fish, horse prints, birds in cages, a Victorian carved sideboard, old bicycles hanging from the ceiling, and etched mirrors. There's a large brick oven, and best of all, excellent meals are offered. The house specialty is "Wendy's famous steak, kidney, and mushroom pie," served with vegetables. A fixed-price menu costs from £12 ($19.80). In the Garden House, 50 first-rate rooms are offered, all with private baths, color TVs, phones, trouser presses, hairdryers, and hot beverage facilities. The cost of singles at the hotel is £60 ($99) to £65 ($107.25) daily. Doubles range from £70 ($115.50) to £80 ($132). All tariffs include VAT and a full English breakfast. The·Parlour serves breakfast, morning coffee, and afternoon tea. The Crossroads is an affiliate of Best Western.

2. Leicestershire

Virtually ignored by most North American tourists, this eastern Midland county was, according to legend, the home of King Lear. Whatever the truth of that, Leicestershire is rich in historical associations. It was at Bosworth Battlefield that the last of the Yorkist kings, Richard III, was killed in 1485, irrevocably changing the course of English history.

LEICESTER

Although the county town is a busy industrial center, it was once a Roman settlement and has Roman remains and an archeological museum that remind one of those days.

It also has a Norman castle-hall, a period museum, a 15th-century guildhall

(Shakespeare is said to have played here), and many interesting gardens. On the abbey park and grounds are the remains of Leicester Abbey, Cardinal Wolsey's grave, a boating lake, paddling pool, riverside walks, ornamental gardens, and an aviary.

For details of guided tours and local excursions, ask at one of the **tourism and information centers:** 2-6 St. Martin's Walk (tel. 0533/511300) or St. Margaret's Bus Station (tel. 0533/532353). The location is 107 miles from London and 26 miles from Nottingham.

Where to Stay and Dine

Grand Hotel, Granby Street, Leicester, Leicestershire LE1 6ES (tel. 0533/ 555599), is aptly named indeed. Built in 1898 when no expense was spared, the interior decoration is magnificent, oak and mahogany paneling abound, and the welcome matches the setting, with the emphasis placed on making your stay as comfortable as possible and offering you good value for money. In the Grand Carving Room, decorated in a '20s style, you can choose from succulent joints of meat generously carved by the chef to satisfy the heartiest appetite. The 91 refurbished bedrooms have a bright, cheery decor, and all have private baths, color TVs, and phones. Singles cost from £65 ($107.25) to £75 ($123.75) daily, and twins from £72 ($118.80) to £100 ($165).

In the Environs

Rothley Court Hotel, Westfield Lane, Rothley, Leicester, Leicestershire LE7 7LG (tel. 0533/374141), is 5 miles north of Leicester on the B5328 road, just off the A6 between Leicester and Loughborough. The hotel is on the edge of Charnwood Forest, a royal hunting ground for centuries and in the heart of the Quorn hunting area. In 1231, Henry III granted the manor and "soke" (right to hold court under feudal law) to the Knights Templar. The chapel erected next to the existing abbey around 1240 is believed to be second only to the Temple in London as the best-preserved Templar chapel in Britain. In the 16th century the Babington family bought the place, and this may be the only estate of that family to remain intact after discovery of the so-called Babington plot to overthrow Elizabeth I and put Mary Queen of Scots on the English throne. Images of Nubian slaves in the coffee lounge and on the half-landing above reflect the family's association with Kitchener of Khartoum. The hotel offers 36 bedrooms with color TVs, radios, and direct-dial phones, as well as modern baths. Singles rent for £75 ($123.75) to £80 ($132) daily, and doubles or twins for £90 ($148.50) to £130 ($214.50), all tariffs including a full English breakfast and VAT. There are comfortable lounges and a bar overlooking the gardens on down to the brook. A set luncheon costs £12 ($19.80), while dinner goes for around £18.50 ($30.55), VAT included.

TOURING THE COUNTRY

As long as people continue to read Sir Walter Scott's *Ivanhoe,* they will remember **Ashby-de-la-Zouch,** a town that retains a pleasant country atmosphere. Mary Queen of Scots was imprisoned in an ancient castle here.

Belvoir Castle

On the northern border of Leicestershire overlooking the Vale of Belvoir (pronounced "beaver"), Belvoir Castle has been the seat of the dukes of Rutland since the time of Henry VIII. Rebuilt by Wyatt in 1816, the castle contains paintings by Holbein, Reynolds, and Gainsborough, as well as tapestries in its magnificent state rooms. Seven miles west-southwest of Grantham, between the A607 to Melton Mowbray and the A52 to Nottingham, the castle was the location of the movies *Little Lord Fauntleroy* and Steven Spielberg's *Young Sherlock Holmes,* and in summer it is the site of medieval jousting tournaments. From late March to early October, it is open from 11am to 6pm Tue. to Sat.; from 11am to 7pm Sun. During October, it is open only on Sat. and Sun., from noon to 6pm. Admission is £2.80 ($4.60) for adults, £1.60 ($2.65) for children. Further details are available from Estate Office, Belvoir Castle, Grantham, Lincolnshire (tel. 0476/870262).

Bosworth Battlefield

Bosworth Battlefield Visitor Centre and Country Park, Sutton Cheney, Market Bosworth, Leicester (tel. 0455/290429), lies between the M1 and the M6, close to Nuneaton. The 1485 battle it commemorates is considered one of England's three most important battles (the other two being the one at Hastings in 1066 and the Battle of Britain in 1940). The Battle of Bosworth ended the War of the Roses between the houses of York and Lancaster, ending with the death of King Richard III, last of the Yorkists, and the proclamation of the victor, Henry Tudor, a Welsh nobleman who had been banished to France to thwart his ambition. Henry landed at Milford Haven and marched across country to Leicestershire where King Richard was encamped, defeated the monarch, and became King Henry VII, initiating the Tudor dynasty. Today, the appropriate standards fly where the opponents had their positions, and in a three-quarters of a mile walk along the marked battle trails, you can see the whole scene of the fighting. In the center are exhibitions, models, book and gift shops, a cafeteria, and a film theater where an audio-visual introduction with an excerpt from the Lord Laurence Olivier film of Shakespeare's *Richard III* is presented.

The center is open from Easter to the end of October from 2 to 5:30pm Mon. to Sat., and from 1 to 6pm Sun. and bank holidays. Admission to the exhibition is £1.20 ($2) for adults, 80p ($1.30) for children. The battle trails can be visited all year without charge during daylight hours. Special medieval attractions are held in July, August, and September. Special charges apply on main event days.

Melton Mowbray

Other interesting towns to visit in Leicestershire include Melton Mowbray, a market town that claims to be the original home of Stilton cheese and is renowned for its pork pies. The location is 15 miles from Leicester and 113 miles from London.

Melton Carnegie Museum, Thorpe End (tel. 0664/69946), depicts the past and present life of the area, with special exhibits on Stilton cheese and Melton pork pies. It's open Easter to September from 10am to 5pm Mon. to Sat., from 2 to 5pm on Sun. October to Easter, hours are 10am to 4:30pm Mon. to Fri. and 10:30am to 4pm on Sat.; closed Christmas Day, Boxing Day, January 1, and Good Friday.

WHERE TO STAY AND DINE Outside Melton Mowbray, you come upon one of the great country house hotels of England, **Stableford Park Country House Hotel,** Stapleford, Melton Mowbray, Leicestershire LE14 2EF (tel. 057284/522). Bob Payton, who is famous in London for his Chicago Pizza Pie Factories, and his wife, Wendy, restored a 16th-century mansion and turned it into what many discerning guests consider the premier hotel of the Midlands. It was restored and decorated in a style far grander, perhaps, than the Victorian aristocrats enjoyed in their heyday. It's the kind of place you head for if you'd like to go on a fox hunt, red coat and all. In chilly weather, open fires greet you in many of the sumptuous public rooms. Set in its own sprawling park and gardens, Stapleford Park was a former seat of the earls of Harborough. While riding one day, Mr. Payton spotted what was called a "distinguished old pile," bought it, and set about transforming it into his country showcase. Each of the 30 elegant bedrooms has a beautiful private bath and many luxurious amenities, such as air conditioning, phone, TV, and mini-bar. Singles begin at £95 ($156.75) nightly, with doubles costing a peak £185 ($305.25), except for suites, which are more expensive. Naturally, this celebrated restaurateur would settle only for a deluxe restaurant on his premises, with dinner served until 11pm. Room service is available 24 hours a day. The location is 5 miles east of Melton Mowbray by B676 on the Stapleford Road.

Hambleton Hall, Hambleton, Leicestershire LE15 8TH (tel. 0572/756991), 3 miles east of Oakham by the A606 road, stands on a promontory of Rutland Water, a huge artificial lake. Humbleton Hall is a century-old house built as a hunting box, now restored to a high standard of luxury and comfort. This *Relais & Châteaux* hotel is run more like a country home. It's a tranquil place, comfortably decorated and furnished, and kept supplied with fresh flowers. Terraced gardens run down to the water. The 15 bedrooms, all with phones, radios, and color TVs, as well as private baths, cost from £100 ($165) to £190 ($313.50) daily for two, from £95 ($156.75) for singles. A continental breakfast is included in the rates. Guests can relax in the comfortable lounge or small bar and enjoy meals in the large dining room with fresh napery, crystal, and bright silver. A set dinner costs £30 ($49.50).

3. Derbyshire

The most magnificent scenery in the Midlands is found within the borders of this county, lying between Nottinghamshire and Staffordshire. Derbyshire has been less defaced by industry than its neighbors. The north of the county, containing the **Peak District National Park,** is by far the most exciting for touring, as it contains waterfalls, hills, moors, green valleys, and dales. In the south the land is more level, and the look becomes, in places, one of pastoral meadows.

Some tourists avoid this part of the country, because it is ringed by the industrial sprawl of Manchester, Leeds, Sheffield, and Derby. To do so, however, would be a pity, and this part of England contains the rugged peaks and leafy dales that merit a substantial detour, especially Dovedale, Chee Dale, and Millers Dale.

HISTORIC HOMES

Near Bakewell, 10 miles north of Matlock, stands one of the great country houses of England, **Chatsworth,** the home of the 11th duke of Devonshire and his duchess, the former Deborah Mitford (sister of Nancy and Jessica). With its lavishly decorated interiors and a wealth of art treasures, it takes in 175 rooms, the most spectacular of which are open to the public. Visiting hours are 11am to 4:30pm daily from March to October (tel. 024688/2204) for information. Admission to the house and garden is £4 ($6.60) for adults and £2 ($3.30) for children.

On this spot the eccentric Bess of Hardwick built a house, which eventually held Mary Queen of Scots prisoner upon orders of Queen Elizabeth I. Most of that structure was torn down, and the present building, with many, many additions, dates from 1686. Capability Brown (who seems to have been everywhere) worked on the landscaping at one time. But it was Joseph Paxton, the gardener to the sixth duke, who turned the garden into one of the most celebrated in Europe. Queen Victoria and Prince Albert were lavishly entertained here in 1843. The house contains a great library and such paintings as the *Adoration of the Magi* by Veronese and *King Uzziah* by Rembrandt. On the grounds you can see spectacular fountains, and there is a playground for children in the farmyard.

Hardwick Hall, Doe Lea, Chesterfield (tel. 0246/850430) lies 9½ miles southeast of Chesterfield. The approach from M1 is at Junction 29. The house was built in 1597 for Bess of Hardwick, a woman who acquired four husbands and an estate from each of them. It is particularly noted for its architecture ("more glass than wall"). The high great chamber and long gallery crown an unparalleled series of late 16th-century interiors, including an important collection of tapestries, needlework, and furniture. The house is surrounded by a 300-acre country park, which is open daily all year. Walled gardens, orchards, and an herb garden are just part of its attractions. The house is open from the first of April until mid-September from 1 to 5:30pm on Wed., Thur., Sat., and Sun. Admission to the hall and garden is £4 ($6.60) for adults and £2.10 ($3.45) for children.

Melbourne Hall, at Melbourne (tel. 0332/862502), 8 miles south of Derby, originally built by the bishops of Carlisle (1133), stands in one of the most famous formal gardens in Britain. The ecclesiastical structure was restored in the 1600s by one of the cabinet ministers of Charles I and enlarged by Queen Anne's vice chamberlain. It was the home of Lord Melbourne, who was prime minister when Victoria ascended to the throne. He was born William Lamb, and Melbourne Hall was also the home of Lord Byron's friend, Lady Caroline Lamb. Lady Palmerston later inherited the house, which contains an important collection of pictures, antique furniture, and works of art. A special feature is the beautifully restored wrought-iron pergola by Robert Bakewell, noted 18th-century ironsmith. The house is open from 2 to 5pm in August (except on August 6, 13, and 20). Admission is £2 ($3.30) for adults, 75p ($1.25) for children. The garden can be visited from April to September 2 to 6pm on Wed., Sat., Sun., and bank holidays. Admission to the garden is £2 ($3.30).

OTHER PLACES TO SEE

Royal Crown Derby, 194 Osmaston Rd., in Derby (tel. 0332/47051). In case this is your special favorite in the pottery world, I suggest a trip into the center of Derby to take the 2-hour tour of the only factory allowed to use both the words "royal" and "crown" in its name, a double honor granted by George III and Queen Victoria. At the end of the tour, you can treat yourself to a bargain in the gift shop and visit the Royal Crown Derby Museum, which is open from 9:30am to 12:30pm and 1:30 to 4pm Mon. to Fri. Tours, lasting 1½ hours, take place at 10:30am and 1:45pm Mon. to Fri. costing £2 ($3.30). If you want to take a tour, you must call and arrange a time.

National Tramway Museum, Crich, near Matlock (tel. 0773/852565). One young 70-year-old whom I know spends as much of his free time as his wife will allow in this paradise of vintage trams—electric, steam, and horse-drawn, from England and overseas, including New York. Your admission ticket is £3 ($4.95) for adults and £1.70 ($2.80) for children. This ticket allows you unlimited rides on trams, which make the 2-mile round trip to Glory Mine with scenic views over the Derwent Valley via Wakebridge, where a stop is made to visit the Peak District Mines Historical Society display of lead mining. It also includes admission to various tramway exhibitions and displays and to the tramway period street, an ongoing project. Hours are 10am to about 6pm. It's open Sat. and Sun. and bank holidays from early April to November, Mon. to Thur. from early May to early November, and Fri. from mid-July to early September.

Peak District Mining Museum, the Pavilion, Matlock Bath (tel. 0629/583834), is open daily throughout the year except Christmas Day from 11am to 4pm (until 5pm in summer). Admission is 80p ($1.40) for adults, 50p (85¢) for children. The exhibition traces 2,000 years of Derbyshire lead mining and has as its centerpiece a giant water-pressure engine that was used to pump water from a lead mine in the early 19th century. It was recovered from a chamber 360 feet underground by members of the society. A popular feature for young visitors is a simulated mine level and climbing shaft through which they can crawl.

BUXTON

One of the loveliest towns in Britain, Buxton was developed in the 18th century to rival the spa at Bath. However, long before that its waters were known to the Romans, whose settlement here was called Aquae Arnemetiae. The thermal waters were pretty much forgotten after that until the reign of Queen Elizabeth I, when the baths were reactivated, and even Mary Queen of Scots was brought here by her caretaker, the earl of Shrewsbury, to "take the waters." Buxton today is mostly the result of the 18th-century development carried out under direction of the duke of Devonshire. The location is 172 miles from London and 38 miles from Derby.

What to See and Do

The Crescent, modeled on the one in Bath but with more elegant classical lines, was originally a hotel complex, but it is now occupied by a hotel and the county library. The pump room of the spa has become the **Buxton Micrarium,** the Crescent (tel. 0298/78662), a world of microscopic animals and plants. Open daily from April to November from 10am to 5pm, the Micrarium charges adults £2 ($3.30) and children £1 ($1.65) for admission. Perhaps the most outstanding feature of recent restoration in Buxton is the Edwardian opera house, for years the local movie palace, now restored in all its marble, velvet, and ornamental plaster opulence. The annual opera festival held here bids fair to become a rival of Glyndebourne.

Water from the nine thermal wells is no longer available for spa treatment except in the hydrotherapy pool at the Devonshire Royal Hospital. It is also used in the swimming pool at the 23-acre **Pavilion Gardens,** but if you want a drink of spa water, you can purchase it at the tourist information center or help yourself at the public fountain across the street.

Poole's Cavern, Buxton Country Park, Green Lane, in Buxton (tel. 0298/26978), is a cave that was inhabited by Stone Age people, who may have been the first to marvel at the natural vaulted roof bedecked with stalactites. Explorers walk through the spacious galleries, viewing the incredible horizontal cave, electrically lighted. It is open daily from Easter until the first week in November from 10am to 5pm, charging £2.20 ($3.65) for adults, £1.20 ($2) for children.

Some 20 minutes away in Grin Low Woods is **Solomon's Temple,** a folly built in 1895 on a tumulus that dates from the Neolithic Age. Climb a small spiral staircase inside the temple for impressive views over Buxton and the surrounding country.

The **tourist information center,** the Crescent, arranges guided walks lasting 1½ hours. You can take the Spa Heritage Trail around the conservation area of the town, including the Crescent and the Pavilion Gardens, and the Vera Britten Walk. Guides can also be booked for bus tours. Phone 0298/25106 for details.

Where to Stay and Dine

Hartington Hotel, 18 Broad Walk, Buxton, Derbyshire SK17 6JR (tel. 0298/22638), is a substantial Georgian building overlooking Pavilion Gardens and a lake. Your view is of the River Wye, the gardens, and the surrounding hills, a pastoral setting, yet close to the town center. The hotel has been fully adapted to provide service and comfort, and as a thoughtful extra, some ground-floor bedrooms with private bath or shower have been added and made suitable for disabled guests. The well-proportioned living room is furnished in a homelike style, with some antiques. The dining room is dignified and has a garden view. All 17 bedrooms have radios, tea and coffee makers, and hot and cold running water, and 7 have private baths and TVs. Rent for a single starts at £25 ($41.25) daily, with doubles costing from £38 ($62.70) to £45 ($74.25). Evening meals are available starting at £9 ($14.85). All rates include VAT. The same family has run the hotel for more than 30 years.

ASHBOURNE

This old market town has a 13th-century church, a 16th-century grammar school, and ancient almshouses. It lies 146 miles from London and 14 miles from Derby.

For a superb cuisine and a limited number of accommodations, I recommend **Callow Hall,** Mappelton Road, Ashbourne, Derbyshire DE6 2AA (tel. 0335/43404), lying less than a mile west of the center going along Union Street. Set in an area of great beauty, with views over the Dove Valley, Callow Hall is a Victorian country home enjoying its own garden setting. The thoughtful owners, the Spencer family, operate these premises, and they have renovated and restored 14 bedrooms, each with bath or shower. Singles rent from £45 ($74.25) to £70 ($115.50) daily, with doubles costing from £75 ($123.75) to £100 ($165), including a full English breakfast. The bedchambers have pieces of antique furniture but modern amenities too, including trouser presses, phones, TVs, and hairdryers. In other words, you'll be looking good as you make your appearance in the dining room, one of the most outstanding in the area. The family has long been known in Ashbourne as bakers, and naturally their expertise is reflected in their dessert menu. However, appetizers and main meat courses get equal billing here. Lamb appears in imaginative ways, and, in season, you can also order jugged hare. It is open for dinner from 7:30 to 9:30pm Mon. to Sat. and for lunch from 12:30 to 2:30pm Sun. A set lunch ranges in price from £10 ($16.50) to £12.50 ($20.65), with dinners costing from £18.50 ($30.55). The food is mainly continental, and always made with good, fresh British ingredients.

DOVEDALE/THORPE

Overhung by limestone crags, this beautiful wooded valley forms part of the Peak District National Park, with its views of Thorpe Cloud, a conical hill 900 feet high. It's best explored on foot. Fishermen know of its River Dove trout stream, because of its associations with such anglers as Izaak Walton and Charles Cotton. Thorpe lies 151 miles from London and 16 miles from Derby.

Izaak Walton Hotel, Dovedale, Thorpe, Derbyshire DE6 2AY (tel. 033529/555), is a comfortable hotel in what was originally a 17th-century farmhouse, lying a mile west of Thorpe. Most of the rooms have views over the dales and peaks of Derbyshire. This is ideal rambling country, with Dovedale spreading before you. All 34 bedrooms have baths and have been recently refurbished, containing phones and TVs. A singles costs £43 ($70.95) daily; a double, £72 ($118.80). These tariffs include service, an English breakfast, and VAT. A table d'hôte luncheon costs £9.50 ($15.70) and a set dinner £13.50 ($22.30). This country is for the fisherman, but if that's not your sport, it is a good center for touring, with Haddon Hall, Chatsworth House, and Hardwick Hall, to name but a few, lying within easy reach.

WHERE TO STAY AND DINE ELSEWHERE IN DERBYSHIRE

An Elizabethan mansion, **Riber Hall,** Riber, Matlock, Derbyshire DE4 5JU (tel. 0629/582795), 3 miles southeast of Matlock by the A615, is owned and operated by the Biggin family. The symmetrically gabled, stone-walled structure is ringed with acres of lawns and forests, with a walled garden closer in where guests can contemplate the foothills of the Pennines. The house was built in the 1400s, and by the 1970s it was so derelict it required massive restoration. Each of the 11 bedrooms is attractively furnished with antiques, chintz, mullioned windows, and appropriate accessories. Wedgwood bone china and cut glass are used throughout. Most units have exposed beams and carved Jacobean four-poster beds. Each has a private bath, phone, TV, fresh flowers, and baskets of fruit, and five have whirlpool baths. Singles cost from £58 ($95.70) daily, and doubles, from £78 ($128.70), with a continental breakfast included. A rather formal elegant restaurant with an intricately carved oak mantelpiece serves outstanding meals accompanied with a selection of fine wines. Typical dishes include French-inspired versions of crêpes stuffed with foie gras, breast of partridge in puff pastry, fresh trout and salmon, and scallops with ginger. A la carte meals cost from £22 ($36.30). Guests play on an all-weather tennis court.

The Rutland Arms Hotel, the Square, Bakewell, Derbyshire DE4 1BT (tel. 0629/812812) is a beautiful, early-Georgian building situated in the center of the small market town of Bakewell. Set in the heart of the Peak District National Park, with the famous Chatsworth House and Haddon Hall nearby, the hotel is steeped in history. Past patrons include Jane Austen, who stayed at the hotel and wrote part of her famous novel *Pride and Prejudice*. Of course, the famous Bakewell pudding was a result of a culinary mishap in the kitchens. The most glamorous accommodation in the hotel is the Jane Austen Suite, which costs £75 ($123.75) per night. All rooms have private baths, phones, and TVs, and the tariff includes a full English breakfast and VAT. Special rates are available on request for weekend breaks. A number of the rooms are located in the hotel courtyard. The hotel has a comfortable lounge and cocktail bar, and its Four Seasons Restaurant has a reputation for an excellent cuisine. The restaurant offers full à la carte and table d'hôte menus with a selection of vegetarian dishes available on request. The dishes are made with fresh local produce, and local game is included when in season. A total of 36 bedrooms are rented, costing £40 ($66) for a single and £50 ($82.50) for a double. Some family rooms for three or four rent for £65 ($107.25) per night.

**YORKSHIRE / DERBYSHIRE
LINCOLNSHIRE / LANCASTER**

*North York Moors
National Park*

Helsmley

Castle
Howard

YORKSHIRE

A 54

York

A 19

North Sea

N
W — *E*
S

HUMBERSIDE

HIRE

A 1

A 19

Lincoln

LINCOLNSHIRE

NOTTINGHAMSHIRE

Boston

*The
Wash*

Stamford

Cavendish Hotel, Baslow, Bakewell, Derbyshire DE4 1SP (tel. 024688/2311), lying alongside A619, built as the celebrated Peacock Inn in the 1780s, was restored in 1975 and extended in 1984. It has 24 well-equipped bedrooms, a commendable dining room, and drawing rooms with roaring log fires. The Cavendish is set on the duke of Devonshire's Chatsworth estate. You look out upon the cavern-filled Derbyshire Peak District from your room, which has such amenities as TV, clock-radio, mini-bar, bathroom, and shower. All rooms have twin or double beds and rent from £70 ($115.50) to £85 ($140.25) daily. Lunch or dinner costs £18 ($24.70) to £25 ($41.25). In the newer wing of the hotel, for which the builders found secondhand stone to match exactly that in the original old fishing inn, the Mitford Rooms were named to honor the duchess of Devonshire, each unit named after members of her Mitford family: Deborah, Diana, Jessica, Lucy, Nancy, Pamela, Sydney, Unity, Valkyrie, and Vivian. The duchess did the original Cavendish in 1975 and its sister hotel, the Devonshire Arms, at Bolton Abbey in 1981, borrowing furnishings from Chatsworth and also having much of the furniture made by hand in the Chatsworth workshop.

4. Nottinghamshire

"Notts," as it is called, lies in the heart of the East Midlands, offering towns rich in folklore or bustling market towns. Many famous people came from Nottingham, notably the outlaw from Sherwood Forest, Robin Hood, and his merry band. But it was also home to the romantic poet Lord Byron, whose ancestral home at Newstead Abbey can be visited. More than a century ago, D. H. Lawrence, author of *Sons and Lovers* and *Lady Chatterley's Lover,* was born in a tiny miner's cottage in Eastwood, which he later immortalized in his writings.

Sherwood Forest is probably the most famous woodland in the world. It isn't the green haven it used to be, but it did provide in its time excellent cover for its world-famous bandit and his band, Robin Hood and his Merry Men, including Friar Tuck and Little John. Actually very little of it was forest, even in its heyday. The area consists of woodland glades, fields, and agricultural land, along with villages and hamlets.

The **Sherwood Forest Visitor Centre,** Sherwood Forest Country Park at Edwinstowe (tel. 0623/823202), near Mansfield, stands in the area just by the Major Oak, popularly known as Robin Hood's tree. It's in the center of many marked walks and footpaths through the woodland. There's an exhibition of life-size models of Robin and the other well-known outlaws, as well as a shop with books, gifts, and souvenirs. The center, some 18 miles north of Nottingham city off the A614, will provide as much information as remains about Friar Tuck and Little John, along with Maid Marian and Alan-a-Dale, as well as the other Merry Men. Little John's grave can be seen at Hathersage, Will Scarlet's at Blidworth. Robin Hood is believed to have married Maid Marian at Edwinstowe Church, close to the visitor center. The Major Oak nearby (mentioned above) is 30 feet in circumference, so that outlaws could easily have hidden in the hollow trunk.

At the center, Robin Hood's Larder offers light snacks and meals, with an emphasis on traditional English country recipes, appropriately named. It is open at various hours, depending on the center's opening days and times, but food and drinks are available from machines when the restaurant is closed.

There is a full program of events taking place on the center site and in the area. The center also contains a tourist information center, one of the national network in England. The center is open from April to September 10:30am to 5pm Mon. to Sat.; from October to March, 10:30 to 4:30pm.

NOTTINGHAM

The county town is a busy industrial city, 121 miles north of London and 72 miles from Manchester. On the north bank of the Trent, Nottingham is one of the most pleasant cities in the Midlands, and some of its many attractions are detailed below.

What to See and Do

Overlooking the city, **Nottingham Castle** was built by the duke of Newcastle on the site of a Norman fortress in 1679. After restoration in 1878, it was opened as a provincial museum (tel. 0602/483504), surrounded by a charmingly laid-out garden. See, in particular, the History of Nottingham Gallery, the ceramics, and the collection of medieval Nottingham alabaster carvings. The works of Nottingham-born artists are displayed in the first-floor gallery, and you can purchase regional crafts in the museum shop. The castle is open from April to September daily from 10am to 5:45pm, from October to March 10am to 4:45pm; closed Christmas Day. Admission is free except on Sun. and bank holidays, when adults pay 40p (65¢) and children 20p (35¢).

For £1 ($1.65) for adults and 30p (50¢) for children, you'll be taken on a conducted tour at the castle of Mortimer's Hole and underground passages. King Edward III is said to have led a band of noblemen through these secret passages, surprising Roger Mortimer and the queen, killing Mortimer, and putting his lady in prison. A statue of Robin Hood stands at the base of the castle.

Brewhouse Yard Museum consists of five 17th-century cottages at the foot of Castle Rock, presenting a panorama of Nottingham life in a series of furnished rooms and shops. Some of them, open from cellar to attic, have much local history material on open display, and visitors are encouraged to handle these exhibits. The most interesting features are in a series of cellars cut into the rock of the castle instead of below the houses, plus an exhibition of a Nottingham shopping street, 1919–1939, with 11 shops for services that are local to the city. This is not a typical folk museum, but attempts to be as lively as possible, involving both visitors and the Nottingham community in expanding displays and altering exhibitions on a bimonthly basis. Open all year, the admission-free museum (tel. 0602/483504, ext. 3600) may be visited from 10am to 5pm; closed Christmas Day.

An elegant row of Georgian terraced houses, the **Museum of Costume and Textiles,** 51 Castle Gate (tel. 0602/483504), presents costumes from the 18th century to about 1960 in period settings, textiles, embroideries, and lace (one of the city's industries). You'll see everything from the 1632 Eyre map tapestries of Nottinghamshire to "fallals and frippery." The admission-free museum is open daily from 10am to 5pm.

On the outskirts of Nottingham, at Ravenshead, **Newstead Abbey** (tel. 0623/793557) was once Lord Byron's home. It lies 11 miles north of Nottingham on the A60 (the Mansfield road). Some of the original Augustinian priory, bought by Sir John Byron in 1540, still survives. In the 19th century the mansion was given a neo-Gothic restoration. Mementos, including first editions and manuscripts, are displayed inside, and later you can explore a parkland of some 300 acres, with waterfalls, rose gardens, a Monk's Stew Pond, and a Japanese water garden. Admission to the grounds and gardens is 90p ($1.50) for adults, 45p (75¢) for children. To visit the abbey, the charge is £1.20 ($2) for adults, 20p (35¢) for children. The abbey is open from Good Friday to September 30 daily from 11:30am to 6pm (last entrance at 5pm). The gardens are open daily all year from 10am to dusk.

Also on the outskirts of Nottingham, **Wollaton Hall,** Wollaton Park (tel. 0602/281333), is a well-preserved Elizabethan mansion, the most ornate in England (finished in 1588), housing a natural history museum, with lots of insects, invertebrates, British mammals, birds, reptiles, amphibians, and fish. The mansion is open April to September daily from 10am to 7pm (on Sun. from 2 to 5pm); from October to March, 10am to dusk (1:30 to 4:30pm Sun.); closed Christmas Day. Admission is free except on Sun. and bank holidays when adults pay 30p (50¢) and children 10p (15¢). The hall is surrounded by a deer park and garden. See the camellia house with the world's earliest (1823) cast-iron front. The bird dioramas here are among the best in Britain. The hall is just a few minutes' drive from the center of Nottingham, or else you can go by city bus.

Where to Stay

Albany Hotel, St. James's Street, Nottingham, Nottinghamshire NG1 6BN (tel. 0602/470131), is a large tower block of 139 bedrooms in the heart of the city. Flanked by multistory car parks, it offers good rooms, each with private bath, double-glazed windows, air conditioning, and central heating, as well as color TV, radio, direct-dial phone, and coffee maker. Singles rent for £72 ($118.80) nightly and doubles go for £88 ($145.20). In the hotel's carvery, guests can carve as much as they wish from hot and cold joints, or else patronize the more expensive Four Seasons, which, in honor of its namesakes, changes its menu and floral decorations quarterly. Along with seasonal specialties, continental dishes are featured. The Forum, the lounge and cocktail bar, is another rendezvous.

Nottingham Moat House, 296 Mansfield Rd., Nottingham, Nottinghamshire NG5 2BT (tel. 0602/602621), stands on the A60 Nottingham-Mansfield road, a little less than a mile from the city center. A bustling, modern hotel, it is well maintained and run, and there's plenty of room to park your car. Attracting business people (and likely to be heavily booked on weekdays), it offers 173 well-furnished, streamlined rooms for £55 ($90.75) daily in a single, £69 ($113.85) in a double, including private baths with showers, color TVs, radios, direct-dial phones, hot beverage facilities, trouser presses, and hairdryers. Have a before-dinner drink in the Savoy Bar, featuring glass domes and floral displays, before dining in the Steak Bar or the Colonial Restaurant. A meal in either costs about £6 ($9.90) to £10.50 ($17.35).

Strathdon Thistle Hotel, 44 Derby Rd., Nottingham, Nottinghamshire NG1 5FT (tel. 0602/418501), a favorite of traveling business people, lies about 5 miles from the M1, in the center of the city. Of the 69 bedrooms (the majority of which are singles), 23 come with private tile baths, the rest with showers, although all have color TVs, phones, radios, and coffee makers. Singles costs £54 ($89.10) to £62 ($102.30), and doubles or twins go for £69 ($113.85) to £77 ($127.05). The rate depends on the day of the week, Sat. and Sun. being cheaper. Some rooms have shower only. Drinks are ordered in the Boston Bean Co. bar, a combination American saloon and diner. In the hotel's restaurant, good table d'hôte evening meals cost from £12 ($19.80), a set luncheon £10.50 ($17.35), or you can order à la carte. The cuisine consists of some international dishes, along with traditional English fare.

Where to Dine

Shogun, 95 Talbot St. (tel. 0602/475611). Someone, anybody, just had to come up with a name like this for a Japanese restaurant. Shogun is considered the leading restaurant in the Nottingham district. Yet, unlike the prices in Japan, the tariffs here are very reasonable. For example, a table d'hôte lunch goes for only £6.50 ($10.75), a set dinner costing from £12.50 ($20.65). Of course, you can spend a lot more by ordering à la carte, at least £15 ($24.75) per person. Service is from noon to 1:45pm and 7 to 11pm Mon. to Sat. While admiring the samurai armor, you can order the classic dishes of the Japanese kitchen. The menu offers a choice of interesting, well-prepared dishes such as sashimi and sushi. You can also order beef, chicken, or fish teriyaki. Service is the most professional in the city. The location couldn't be more convenient. It's on a road leading out of the city in the direction of the motorway (the M1) in a red-brick, turn-of-the-century, warehouse setting with a sophisticated decor.

SOUTHWELL

This ancient market town, about a half-hour drive from Lord Byron's Newstead Abbey, is a good center for exploring the Robin Hood country. Byron once belonged to a local amateur dramatic society here. An unexpected gem is the old twin-spired cathedral, **Southwell Minster,** which many consider the most beautiful church in England. James I found that it held up with "any other kirk in

Christendom." Look for the well-proportioned Georgian houses across from the cathedral.

Saracen's Head, Market Place, Southwell, Nottinghamshire NG25 0HE (tel. 0636/812701), is a historic coaching inn, where both Charles I and James I dined. In fact, Charles I was made a prisoner here before the Scots handed him over to the Parliamentarians. After he was beheaded, the name of the inn was changed from King's Arms to Saracen's Head. Commanding the junction of the main ancient thoroughfares of the town, the old hostelry also frequently entertained Byron. Today the inn still has an old atmosphere, such as cozy bars with exposed beams and paneling. From the cellar emerges a selection of wines to complement meals, offered in the restaurant from both an à la carte and a table d'hôte menu. The 27 redecorated and refurbished bedrooms contain private baths with shower, TVs, radios, and phones. Doubles cost from £75 ($123.75) daily, and singles rent for £60 ($99), including service and VAT.

NEWARK-ON-TRENT

Here is an ancient riverside market town, on the Roman Fosse Way, lying about 15 miles across flatlands from Nottingham. King John died at **Newark Castle** in 1216. Constructed between the 12th and 15th centuries, the castle—now in ruins—survived three sieges by Cromwell's troops before falling in 1646. From its parapet, you can look down on the Trent River and across to Nottingham. The delicately detailed parish church here is said to be the finest in the country. The town contains many ancient inns, reflecting its long history.

On the banks of the River Trent, a short walk from Newark Castle, is **Millgate Folk Museum,** 48 Millgate, Newark, Nottinghamshire NG24 4TS (tel. 0636/79403), in a building that housed a 19th-century oil-seed mill and then a warehouse. Today it contains portrayals of social and industrial life in the area from around 1800 to World War II. Agricultural, malting, and printing implements are displayed, and a series of furnished rooms depicts domestic life in those times. The museum, for which there is no admission fee, is open from 10am to 5pm Mon. to Fri. all year, and from 1 to 5pm on Sat., Sun., and bank holidays from Easter to October.

THE DUKERIES

In the Dukeries, portions of Sherwood Forest, legendarily associated with Robin Hood, are still preserved. These are vast country estates on the edge of industrial towns. Most of the estates have disappeared, but the park at **Clumber**—covering some 4,000 acres—is administered by the National Trust, which has preserved its 18th-century beauty, as exemplified by Lime Tree Avenue. Rolling heaths and a peaceful lake add to the charm. You can see **Clumber Chapel,** built in 1886–1889 as a chapel for the seventh duke of Newcastle. It is open from 10am to 5pm daily; closed Christmas Day. There is no admission charge, but entry costs £2 ($3.30) for cars, £5 ($8.25) for minibuses and house trailers. There are stables with a stable tower clock dated 1763, a classical bridge over the lake, lodges, and pleasure grounds, as well as fishing, bicycle rental, a shop, and a restaurant. The park is open all year. Clumber Park is 5 miles southeast of Clumber Park Stableyard, Worksop, close to the A1 (tel. 0909/476592).

EASTWOOD

Because of the increased interest in D. H. Lawrence these days, many literary fans like to make a pilgrimage to Eastwood, his hometown. The English novelist was born there on September 11, 1885. Mrs. Brown, a member of the D. H. Lawrence Society, conducts parties of visitors around the "Lawrence country," hoping at the end they'll make a donation to the society. If you're interested in taking a tour, write her in advance—Mrs. M. Brown, D. H. Lawrence Society, c/o 8A Victoria St., Eastwood, Nottingham, NG16 3AW (tel. 0773/718139).

The Victoria Street address is the Lawrence birthplace, which has been turned into the **D. H. Lawrence Information Centre and Museum** (tel. 0773/763312), now authentically depicting a miner's home as it was in 1885, with an audio-visual presentation. The Eastwood Library houses a unique collection of Lawrence's works and the headstone from his grave on the French Riviera. The museum is open daily April to October from 10am to 5pm, November to March from 10am to 4pm; closed Christmas Eve to New Year's Day. Admission is 50p (85¢) for adults, 25p (40¢) for children.

SCROOBY

This is a tiny village of some 260 inhabitants where in 1566 William Brewster, a leader of the Pilgrims, was born. His father was bailiff of the manor and master of the postes, so it may have been in the manor house that the infant Brewster first saw the light of day. The original house dated from the 12th century, and the present manor farm, built on the site in the 18th century, has little except historical association to attract.

Brewster Cottage, with its pinfold where stray animals were impounded, lies beside the village church of St. Wilfred. But it's uncertain whether Brewster ever lived there.

The village also contains Monks Mill on the River Ryton, now almost a backwater but once a navigable stream down which Brewster and his companions may have escaped to travel to Leyden in Holland and on to their eventual freedom.

In the 18th century the turnpike ran through the village, and there are many stories of highwaymen, robberies, and murders. The body of one John Spencer dangled for more than 60 years as a reminder of the penalties of wrongdoing. He'd attempted to dispose of the bodies of the keeper of the Scrooby tollbar and his mother in the river.

Search for Pilgrim Roots

Many North Americans who trace their ancestry to the Pilgrims come to this part of England to see where it all started. The Separatist Movement had its origin in an area north of Nottingham and south of York, and the towns from which its members came are all in a small area. They include **Blyth** (the one in Nottinghamshire, not the one in Northumberland), **Scrooby, Austerfield, Bawtry,** and **Babworth.** Besides William Brewster, who is identified with Scrooby, William Bradford was born in a manor house still standing in Austerfield. The churches at Scrooby and Babworth welcome North Americans.

Blyth is the most beautiful of the villages, with a green surrounded by well-kept old houses, looking a lot like a New England village, which is no surprise. The parish church was developed from the 11th-century nave of a Benedictine priory church. On the green is a 12th-century stone building which was once the Hospital of St. John.

5. Lincolnshire

This large East Midlands county is bordered on one side by the North Sea. Its most interesting section is Holland, in the southeast, a land known for its fields of tulips, its marshes and fens, and windmills reminiscent of the Netherlands. Although much of the shire is interesting to explore, time is too important for most visitors to linger long. Foreign tourists, particularly North Americans, generally cross the tulip fields, scheduling stopovers in the busy port of Boston before making the swing north to the cathedral city of Lincoln, lying inland.

BOSTON

This old seaport in the riding of Holland has a namesake that has gone on to greater glory, and perhaps for this reason it is visited by New Englanders. At Scotia Creek, on a riverbank near Boston, is a memorial to the early Pilgrims who made an unsuccessful attempt in 1607 to reach the promised land. They were imprisoned in the guildhall in cells that can be visited today. A company left again in 1620—and fared better, as anybody who has ever been to Massachusetts will testify. Part of the ritual here is climbing the **Boston Stump,** a church lantern tower with a view for miles around of the all-encircling fens. In the 1930s the people of Boston, U.S.A., paid for the restoration of the tower, known officially as St. Botolph's Tower. Actually, it's not recommended that you climb the tower, as the stairs aren't in good shape. The tower, as it stands, was finished in 1460. The city officials were going to add a spire, making it the tallest in England. But because of the wind and the weight, they feared the tower would collapse. Therefore, the tower became known as "the Boston Stump." An elderly gentleman at the tower assured me it was the tallest in England —that is, 272½ feet tall. Boston is 116 miles north from London, and 34 miles southeast of Lincoln.

The center of Boston is closed to cars, and you will have to walk to visit the church and the guildhall.

Where to Stay and Dine

The town's leading hotel is **White Hart,** Bridge Foot, Boston, Lincolnshire PE21 8SH (tel. 0205/64877), a Regency building constructed along the river and lying a short distance from the historic center. This old coaching inn has been newly refurbished and redecorated. Its 23 bedrooms are pleasantly and attractively furnished, renting for £37.50 ($61.90) nightly in a single, the cost rising to £53 ($87.45) in a double, including an English breakfast. Eighteen of the comfortable bedrooms have private baths or showers, and each contains phone and TV. There is a free car park through the coaching courtyard at the rear of the hotel. White Hart offers some of the best food and drink in town in its two bars and one restaurant, the latter specializing in steak. Bar snacks are served from noon to 2pm Mon. to Sat., and meals in the restaurant, costing from £15 ($24.75), are offered from noon to 2:30pm and 6 to 10pm.

New England Hotel, 49 Wide Bargate, Boston, Lincolnshire PE21 6SH (tel. 0205/65255), stands in the town center and is especially busy on market days. The location is near the market place and the Boston Stump, opening onto a large car park. Ales and wines are dispensed in the Pilgrim Bar, and at lunch, the place is often a beehive of activity. This three-story Victorian building houses one of the most frequented restaurants in town, Chaucers, offering a menu that includes roasts, grills, and seafood. The average price for lunch is £9.50 ($15.70) per person, with dinner costing around £13 ($21.45). The hotel also rents 25 bedrooms, each with a private bath, color TV, phone, and tea and coffee maker. Singles range from £48 ($79.20) daily, and doubles cost £58 ($95.70). Families are catered to, especially those with small children.

LINCOLN

One of the most ancient cities of England, and only 135 miles north of London, Lincoln was known to the Romans as Lindum. Some of the architectural glory of the Roman Empire still stands to charm the present-day visitor. The renowned **Newport Arch** (the North Gate) is the last remaining arch left in Britain that still spans a principal highway. For a look at the Roman relics excavated in and around Lincoln, head for the **Greyfriars City and County Museum,** Broadgate (tel. 0522/ 30401), open from 10am to 5:30pm Mon. to Sat., 2:30 to 5pm on Sun. Admission is 50p (85¢) for adults, 25p (40¢) for children.

Two years after the Battle of Hastings, William the Conqueror built a castle on the site of a Roman fortress. Used for administrative purposes, parts of the castle still remain, including the walls, the 12th-century keep, and fragments of the gateway tower. In addition, you can visit the High Bridge over the Witham River, with its half-timbered houses (you can have a meal in one of them). This is one of the few medieval bridges left in England that has buildings nestling on it.

Visit also the **Museum of Lincolnshire Life,** Burton Road (tel. 0522/ 528448), the largest folk museum in the area, with displays ranging from a Victorian schoolroom to locally built steam engines. It's open from 10am to 5:30pm Mon.

to Sat., 2 to 5:30pm Sun. Admission is 80p ($1.30) for adults, 40p (65¢) for children.

Lincoln Cathedral

No other English cathedral dominates its surroundings as does Lincoln. Visible from up to 30 miles away, the minster's three towers are an arresting sight. The central tower is 271 feet high, making it the second tallest in England, giving just one foot to its near neighbor, Boston Stump, mentioned earlier. Lincoln's central tower once carried a huge spire, which, prior to heavy gale damage in 1549, made it the tallest in the world at 525 feet. Mon. to Sat. in summer, there are accompanied tower trips.

Construction on the original Norman cathedral was begun in 1072 and it was consecrated 20 years later. It sustained a major fire and then, in 1185, an earthquake. Only the central portion of the West Front and lower halves of the western towers survive from this period. The present cathedral represents the Gothic style, particularly the Early English and Decorated periods. The nave is 13th century, but the black font of tourni marble originates from the 12th century. In the Great North Transept is a rose medallion window known as the Dean's Eye. Opposite it, in the Great South Transept, is its cousin, the Bishop's Eye. East of the high altar is the Angel Choir consecrated in 1280 and so called after the sculpted angels high on the walls. The exquisite wood carving in St. Hugh's Choir dates from the 14th century. Lincoln's roof bosses, dating from the 13th and 14th centuries, are handsome. A mirror trolley assists visitors in their appreciation of these features that are some 70 feet above the floor. In the cloister are oak bosses. These are easier to see, although there is also a mirror.

In the Seamen's Chapel (Great North Transept) is a window commemorating Lincolnshire-born Captain John Smith, one of the pioneers of early settlement in America and the first governor of Virginia. The library and north walk of the cloister were built in 1674 to designs by Sir Christopher Wren. Viewing of the fine restoration work, newly completed in the Wren Library, is available by appointment. An exhibition of manuscripts is shown in the Medieval Library.

In the treasury, open from Easter to the end of September 2:30 to 4:30pm Mon. to Sat., there is fine gold and silver plate from the churches of the diocese.

The cathedral is open from 7:30am daily, closing at 6pm in winter (Sunday 5pm) and 8pm in summer. The suggested donation to the cathedral is £1.50 ($2.50). Guided tours are conducted Mon. to Sat., but not in January or February except by prior appointment.

An extensive range of gifts, including facsimiles of the Lincoln Magna Carta, are available in the two minster gift shops and refreshments served in the cloister coffee shop.

Where to Stay

White Hart Hotel, Bailgate, Lincoln, Lincolnshire LN1 3AR (tel. 0522/526222), was named after the emblem of Richard II because he visited the region shortly before the hotel's construction and probably stayed at an inn erected on the site. A letter from 1460 reported on a visit to the inn by a London woman who paid sixpence for her room and complained that her bed was lumpy. The facade covering the inn dates from the 1700s when it was a luxurious private home. Its life as a modern hotel began in 1913 when the live-in owners started accepting paying guests, but only if they came with ironclad references from mutual friends. It is surrounded by ancient cobblestone streets usually reserved for pedestrians. The cathedral and the oldest part of Lincoln lie a short walk from the doorstep. Once through a revolving mahogany door, you enter a large and finely proportioned lounge filled with fine antiques, rare and unusual clocks, and display cabinets of rare silver, glass, and porcelain. The hotel also bears the honor of having hosted several meetings between Churchill and Eisenhower in the darkest days of World War II. The Georgian main dining room offers elegant furnishings and well-prepared lunches and dinners. If you elect to overnight here, you'll be following in the footsteps of Lloyd George, Edward VIII, and Margaret Thatcher. Each of the 52 accommodations includes a well-accessorized private bath, phone, TV, some kind of antique furniture, and windows overlooking the old city. To reach your room, you negotiate a labyrinth of narrow halls and stairways. With breakfast included, singles cost £70 ($115.50) daily, and doubles go for £100 ($165).

Eastgate Post House, Eastgate, Lincoln, Lincolnshire LN2 1PN (tel. 0522/520341), is a hotel attached to a Victorian mansion (now the Eastgate Bar). Eastgate occupies a historic site: in fact, when workmen were digging its foundations in the mid-1960s, they discovered the remnants of the north tower of the East Gate of Roman Lincoln. The hotel is well sited, overlooking Lincoln Cathedral. A preserved part of the Roman city wall is included in the rear garden. All 71 bedrooms have private baths, showers, color TVs, radios, mini-bars, and hot beverage facilities. Rates are £72 ($118.80) daily in a single, £88 ($145.20) in a double or twin, including service and VAT. Breakfast, lunch, and dinner are served in the Palatinate Restaurant, which also overlooks the cathedral. The cost of a table d'hôte lunch is £9.50 ($15.70) and dinner goes for £14 ($23.10). You can choose from an à la carte menu also. The coffeeshop serves grills and snacks. Free parking for up to 120 vehicles is found at the front and rear of the hotel.

Grand Hotel, St. Mary's Street, Lincoln, Lincolnshire LN5 7EP (tel. 0522/24211), is an extensively remodeled hotel with suitable amenities and a cooperative staff. You'll pay £50 ($82.50) daily for a double with private bath, £38 ($62.70) for a single with bath. The West bar and the lounges are streamlined, but the Tudor bar pays homage to the past. The 48 bedrooms are compact, with many built-in features and coordinated colors along with private baths or showers, TVs, and phones. The Grand is easy to spot just opposite the bus depot. It's a long walk to the cathedral, but you can hop a bus. The food is a topnotch bargain, both in price and taste. From 7 to 8:30pm, a table d'hôte dinner is offered for £9.75 ($16.10). The food is not only good and typically English, but the portions are ample. You can also lunch at the Grand daily from noon to 2pm. A buttery is open from 11am to 10pm.

D'Isney Place Hotel, Eastgate, Lincoln, Lincolnshire LN2 4AA (tel. 0522/538881), is a small, family-owned hostelry close to the cathedral, the minster yard, the castle, and the Bailgate shops. It was built in 1735 and later extended. The cathedral close's wall and towers, constructed in 1285, form the southern boundary of the house gardens. Each of the 18 rooms is uniquely decorated, with a large bath, radio, phone, color TV, and hot beverage facilities. Some units have four-poster beds and Jacuzzi baths. The proprietors charge £40 ($66) daily for a single, from £60 ($99) for a double. There is car-parking space.

Where to Dine

Harveys Cathedral Restaurant, 1 Exchequergate, Castle Square (tel. 0522/510333), lies in the heart of the old town, a short walk from the cathedral and the castle. My favored dining spot in the city, it is run by Adrianne and Bob Harvey. This stately Georgian building until recently was reputed to be haunted, but the cozy Victorian decor has routed any dismal spirits. The motto of the Harveys is "simple lunches—superb dinners," and they live up to this with a lunch menu offering traditional English dishes such as farmhouse chicken pie and beef in Guinness, followed by Victorian sherry trifle. Lunch will cost around £7 ($11.55) to £10 ($16.50). In the evening the restaurant is candlelit and reservations are essential. The Harveys offer a table d'hôte menu at £18 ($29.70). This includes a special soup or fruit dish; an appetizer course; a selection from seven main dishes, including French and "Taste of England" specialties; cheeses; and desserts or ice cream. Almost everything the Harveys serve is homemade, and all ingredients are fresh. If you're in Lincoln over a weekend, take in a traditional Sun. lunch here. You won't taste better roast beef anywhere, but remember to reserve your table. The restaurant is open from noon to 1:45pm and 7:30 to 9:30pm daily.

Whites of Lincoln, the Jews House, 15 the Strait (tel. 0522/524851), is a stone-fronted building, said to be the oldest lived-in house in Europe. Dating from the 12th century, it has a low-beamed ceiling, a cast-iron fireplace, and an array of medieval features. Two of the massive ceiling beams are known to be the original, dating from 1180. The menu is a stylish, French-inspired collection of dishes that change with the season. Typical dishes might be fresh breast of wood pigeon on a bed of artichokes or a gratin of langoustine on a bed of spinach with a champagne and port wine sauce. Desserts are much in demand here, including the special one, charlotte royale (it's filled with a double-cream lemon mousse). Lunch will cost from £6.50 ($10.75), while dinners go for £15 ($24.75) to £20 ($33). The restaurant is open daily from noon to 2pm for lunch, from 2 to 5pm for tea, and for dinner from 7:30 to 8:45 Mon. to Sat. Reservations are much appreciated.

STAMFORD

This charming stone-built market town, lying 92 miles from London, 50 miles from Lincoln, is visited chiefly for **Burghley House,** Stamford (tel. 0780/52451), the home of the Cecil family for more than 400 years. The house, a mile east of Stamford just off A1, was built in 1564 on the remains of a monastery founded in 1158. Ten years later, and again in 1589, additions were made. At this magnificent Elizabethan house you will see a collection of more than 400 works of art, mainly Italian of the baroque period. There are also splendid examples of furniture, tapestries, and decoration from the 16th and 17th centuries. It is said that nobody has slept in the Queen Elizabeth I bedroom since the monarch was last here. From the window you can see a lime tree she planted in the 16th century. The present growth sprang from the roots of the original tree. The kitchen found in the oldest part of the house is huge. A whole ox could be roasted on the spit. The house is open Easter to October 7 daily from 11am to 5pm. Admission is £3.30 ($5.45) for adults, £2 ($3.30) for children.

Where to Stay and Dine

Lady Anne's Hotel, 37-38 High St., St. Martin's without Stamford, Lincolnshire PE9 2LJ (tel. 0780/53175), is named after Lady Anne Cecil, a young and favorite sister of the ninth earl of Exeter. She lived in the original building for many years, but it has seen many changes before emerging as a country hotel. The 28 bedrooms come in a wide range: some have very small showers while others are light and airy with baths and toilets. All have TVs and phones. Depending on the plumbing, singles range from £30 ($49.50) to £39.50 ($65.20) daily, and doubles run as high as £60 ($99), with more expensive suites offered. These rates are inclusive of tea or coffee, a morning paper, and a large English breakfast. Outside is a car park, and inside there's a welcoming log fire in the bar. The cottagey dining room has a menu of grills and fish dishes, including trout cooked in white wine and butter. In season, venison pie and pheasant are specialties. Expect to spend from £10 ($16.50) for a meal.

WANSFORD-IN-ENGLAND

Instead of staying in Stamford, an ideal alternative lies just off the A1 road to the north in a village of stone houses with a wide, typical English main street. At the **Haycock Hotel,** Great North Road, Wansford, 8½ miles west of Peterborough by A47 in Cambridgeshire PE8 6JA (tel. 0780/782223), a stone in the garden dates the present building from 1632, although an inn has existed on this site for many years. The inn is built around a courtyard with stone archways and mullioned windows. It is said that Mary Queen of Scots, on her way to imprisonment in 1586 at Fotheringhay, visited the inn. In later years Queen Victoria stopped by when she was still a princess. Many of the 51 bedrooms have four-posters, and all have private baths, phones, and color TVs. Your overnight charge includes early-morning tea and a newspaper, then a full English breakfast. Singles range from £74 ($122.10) daily, and twins and doubles go for £110 ($181.50). Menus are à la carte in the dining room, a meal averaging about £20 ($33).

GRANTHAM

This market town stands in the middle of rich farming country, 29 miles from Lincoln and 113 miles from London. A corner site on North Parade was the childhood home of Britain's first woman prime minister, Margaret Thatcher. Her father, Alfred Roberts, ran a busy greengrocer's shop on the ground floor, and the family lived in rooms above the business. Margaret was born there on October 13, 1925. The family moved to a nearby house in 1944, but Mr. Roberts continued with the store until he sold it in 1959.

In the Middle Ages, Grantham was a prosperous wool-trade town. Isaac Newton attended King's School here in the 17th century, and his initials can still be seen on the wooden sill of the old schoolroom built of Ancaster stone. The 283-foot spire of St. Wulfram's parish church rises as a local landmark and can be seen for miles around. The town has many old inns and a medieval market cross.

Belton House, Grantham, a National Trust property, 3 miles northeast of Grantham on A607 Grantham-Lincoln road (tel. 0476/66116), is one of the finest Restoration country houses in Britain, built in 1684. The original architect was probably William Wynde, whose work resembles that of Wren. The house today appears very much as it did originally. The saloon and red drawing room are particularly finely carpeted, and the Tyrconnel Room has a rare painted floor apparently from the early 19th century. The library contains a fine barrel-vaulted ceiling by James Wyatt. Oriental porcelain and chinoiserie are part of the attractions. Throughout the house hang portraits of the initial owners, the Brownlow family. The house is open April to October from 1 to 5:30pm Wed. to Sun. Admission is £3.20 ($5.30) for adults, £1.60 ($2.65) for children.

Where to Stay and Dine

Angel and Royal, High Street, Grantham, Lincolnshire NG31 6PN (tel. 0476/65816), is reportedly one of the oldest inns in Britain, tracing its origins back to the 1100s. Today its stone facade is much more modern, at least from the 1400s. Head through an arch and you enter a stone-paved courtyard lying between two wings of the structure, with tables and chairs placed outside in fair weather. Its 13th-century stone-walled restaurant and bar is one of the most popular in town, offering lunch daily from 12:30 to 2pm, costing from £8 ($13.20), and dinner from 7 to 10pm, costing from £15 ($24.75) and including such classic English fare as beef sirloin with Yorkshire pudding. Tasty bar snacks are also available. The hotel rents 24 well-appointed bedrooms, each with private bath or shower, phone, and TV. Rates begin at £58 ($95.70) daily in a single, £75 ($123.75) in a double, but ask about weekend bargain breaks that are much cheaper.

The most desirable place to dine in the area is **Barkston House,** Barkston, Grantham, Lincolnshire NG32 2NH (tel. 0400/50555), lying less than 4 miles north of Grantham on A607. This is a *restaurant avec chambres.* Actually it offers only two bedrooms, so it's best to reserve well in advance. Singles pay £35 ($57.75) nightly, with doubles going for £52 ($85.80). Originally a Georgian farmhouse, Barkston excels in English cookery. Vegetables are perfectly crisp, and main courses are composed of fresh and well-chosen ingredients. Natural flavors are enhanced by the kitchen staff. The wine list is limited, but well chosen, and, most important, reasonable in price. Dinner is served from 7:30 to 9:15pm Mon. to Sat., costing from £20 ($33) per person. Lunch is from noon to 2pm Tues. to Fri. only, when a set menu is offered for only £8.50 ($14.05). Reservations are important.

XVI

CHESHIRE, LIVERPOOL, AND THE LAKES

1. CHESTER
2. NANTWICH
3. LIVERPOOL
4. CARTMEL
5. KENDAL
6. WINDERMERE
7. AMBLESIDE
8. RYDAL
9. GRASMERE
10. HAWKSHEAD AND CONISTON
11. KESWICK
12. BORROWDALE
13. BASSENTHWAITE
14. ULLSWATER
15. BRAMPTON

The northwest of England is one of the special parts of the country. Its remoteness is part of its charm. Have you ever seen one of those English-made films depicting life in the Lake District? A soft mist hovers over the hills and dells, sheep graze silently on the slope of the pasture, and a foggy enchantment fills the air.

One of England's most popular summer retreats in Victoria's day was the northwest part of the Lake District. It enjoyed vogue during the flowering of the Lake Poets, including Wordsworth, who was ecstatically moved by the rugged beauty of this area. In its time the district has lured such writers as Coleridge, Charles Lamb, Shelley, Keats, Tennyson, Matthew Arnold, and Charlotte Brontë.

The county of Cheshire lies south of Lancashire. I suggest a pilgrimage to the ancient city of Chester near the Welsh border, with its medieval walls.

CHESHIRE

This county is low lying and largely agricultural. The name it gave to a cheese—and a cat—(Cheshire) has spread across the world. This northwestern county borders Wales, which accounts for its turbulent history. The towns and villages of Cheshire form a good base for touring North Wales, the most beautiful part of that little country.

1. Chester

Chester is ancient, having been founded by a Roman legion on the Dee River in the 1st century A.D. It reached its pinnacle as a bustling port in the 13th and 14th centuries, declining thereafter following the gradual silting up of the river. The upstart Liverpudlians captured the sea-trafficking business. The other walled medieval cities of England were either torn down or badly fragmented, but Chester still retains 2 miles of fortified city walls.

The main entrance into Chester is Eastgate, itself dating back to only the 18th century. Within the walls are half-timbered houses and shops, some from the days of the Tudors. Chester is freakish architecturally in that some of its builders kept to the black-and-white timbered facades—even when erecting buildings during the Georgian and Victorian periods.

WHAT TO SEE AND DO
The Rows are double-decker layers of shops—one tier on the street level, the other stacked on top and connected by a footway. The upper tier is like a continuous galleried balcony. Shopping upstairs is more adventurous, and rain is never a problem. Thriving establishments operate in this traffic-free paradise: tobacco shops, restaurants, department stores, china shops, jewelers, even antique dealers. For the most representative look, take an arcaded walk on Watergate Street.

At noon and 3pm Tues. to Sat., April to September, at the City Cross, the town crier issues his news (local stuff on sales, exhibitions, and attractions in the city) at the top of his not-inconsiderable voice, to the accompaniment of a hand bell—at the junction of Watergate, Northgate, and Bridge Streets. Eastgate Street is now a pedestrian way, and musicians often play beside St. Peter's Church and the Town Cross.

Chester Cathedral
The present building founded in 1092 as a Benedictine abbey was created as a cathedral church in 1541. Considerable architectural restorations were carried out in the 19th century, but older parts have been preserved. Notable features include the fine range of monastic buildings, particularly the cloisters and refectory, the chapter house, and the superb medieval woodcarving in the quire (especially the misericords). Also worth attention are the long south transept with its various chapels, the consistory court, and the medieval roof bosses in the lady chapel. A freestanding bell tower, the first to be built in England since the Reformation, was completed in 1975 and may be seen southeast of the main building. The cathedral is open daily from 7am to 6:30pm. Facilities include a refectory, a bookshop, and an audio-visual presentation. For more information, phone 0244/324756.

Discover Chester
Head first for the **tourist information center,** Town Hall, Northgate Street (tel. 0244/324324), which provides a wide range of services, including a booking

desk for local or nationwide accommodations. Maps or free leaflets can be picked up, and arrangements made for coach tours or walking tours of Chester (including a ghost hunter tour).

In a big Victorian building opposite the Roman amphitheater, the largest uncovered in Britain, the **Chester Visitor Centre,** Vicars Lane (tel. 0244/351609), only minutes from the city center, offers a number of services to visitors from 9am to 9pm daily (until 7pm in winter). A visit to a life-size Victorian street complete with sounds and smells helps your appreciation and orientation to Chester. The center has a gift shop, a licensed restaurant serving meals and snacks all day, and a currency exchange. Entrance to the center is free.

A Walk on the Wall

In the center of town, you'll see the Eastgate clock, the most photographed timepiece in the world after Big Ben. Climb the stairs near it, which lead up to the top of the city wall, and you can follow it on a walk looking down on Chester today from a path of the past. The wall passes through centuries of English history. You pass a cricket field, see the River Dee, which was formerly a major trade artery, and get a look at many old buildings of the 18th century, some undergoing renovation. Flower-filled back gardens are lovely from this height. The wall also goes past some Roman ruins, and it is possible to leave the walkway to explore them. The walk is charming and free.

Chester Zoo

Just off the A41 on the outskirts of Chester, the Chester Zoo (tel. 0244/380280), 2 miles from the center of the city, is world-famous for its wide collection of mammals, birds, reptiles, and fish, as well as for its 110 acres of gardens. Many rare and endangered species breed freely in spacious enclosures, and the zoo is particularly renowned for the most successful breeding group of chimpanzees and orangutans in Europe. The gardens are worth seeing in any season, with 160,000 plants in the spring and summer bedding displays alone. A waterbus, a popular summer feature, allows you to observe the hundreds of waterbirds who make their home here. The zoo has several facilities if you get hungry or thirsty during your visit: the licensed Oakfield Restaurant, the Jubilee self-service cafeteria, the Oasis snackbar, and the Rainbow kiosk for either meals or snacks and drinks. The zoo is open daily from 10am to dusk; closed Christmas Day. Admission is £3.80 ($6.25) for adults, £1.90 ($3.15) for children 3 to 15.

WHERE TO STAY

One of the most luxurious hotels in the north of England, the **Chester Grosvenor Hotel,** Eastgate Street, Chester, Chesire CH1 1DE (tel. 0244/324024), lies in a fine, half-timbered building in the heart of Chester and has a well-deserved reputation. It is owned and named after the family of the dukes of Westminster. The history and origin of the hotel can be traced back to the reign of Queen Elizabeth I. Started as a Tudor inn, it became a political headquarters in Hanoverian days and later went on to be a glittering mecca for the Regency and Victorian set, continuing to be a social center in the Edwardian era. Prince Albert visited here, and guests more recently have ranged from Princess Diana to Prince Rainier.

The high, marble-floored foyer of the hotel, with its 200-year-old chandelier, carved wooden staircase, and antiques, sets the tone. The 83 air-conditioned bedrooms are large and well furnished, all with radios, color TVs, direct-dial phones, mini-bars, and private baths equipped with such amenities as hairdryers. Rates begin at £95 ($156.75) daily for singles, £145 ($239.25) for doubles or twins. VAT is included. The grand hotel has the finest drinking and dining facilities in the entire county. Its formal restaurant, Arkle, and its more informal La Brasserie will be previewed later. Other amenities include a sauna, a gym, a solarium, and a business center.

Crabwall Manor, Parkgate Road, Mollington, Chester, Cheshire CH1 6NE (tel. 0244/851666). Chester's only country-house hotel, Crabwall Manor traces its origins back to the 16th century. Most of the present building, however, dates from the early 1800s. The location is 2¼ miles northwest of Chester on the A540. Standing in 11 acres of private grounds and gardens, the well-managed hotel rents 48 sensitively furnished bedrooms, each with private bath or shower, direct-dial phone, and color TV. Most of the rooms are quite large and show a certain flair in their decoration, and the bathrooms are first class, with bidets and separate showers for the most part. Rates range from £70 ($115.50) daily in a single, going up to £85 ($140.25) in a double, with suites costing more. The finest of contemporary English and French dishes are offered in a split-level restaurant. Non-residents can also visit to enjoy the harmonious flavors, the subtle sauces, and the well-chosen meat, fowl, and fish that are served daily from 12:30 to 2pm and 7 to 9:30pm. Set lunches cost £12 ($19.80) to £13.50 ($22.30) with a table d'hôte dinner offered for £25 ($41.25). You can also dine à la carte.

Mollington Banastre, Parkgate Road, Chester, Cheshire CH1 6NN (tel. 0244/851471), lies 2 miles northwest on A540. This successfully converted Victorian mansion, now turned into a country-house hotel, one of the leading ones in Cheshire, is affiliated with the Best Western reservation system. A gabled house, it offers a health and leisure complex, along with a trio of restaurants and 67 well-furnished bedrooms, each with private bath, direct-dial phone, and TV. Equipped with all the modern amenities, these rent for £72 ($118.80) daily in a single, going up to £90 ($148.50) in a double. In addition, the hotel also has a pub on its grounds.

Rowton Hall Hotel, Whitchurch Road, Rowton, Chester, Cheshire CH3 6AD (tel. 0244/335262), is a stately home, 2 miles from the city center, which offers overnight accommodation for motorists. The gracious house, built in 1779 with a later wing added, stands in an 8-acre garden, with a formal driveway entrance. The Hall has comfortable traditional and contemporary furnishings. All 42 bedrooms have private baths, phones, and TVs, a single renting for £62 ($102.30) daily and a double for £78 ($128.70). All prices include a full English breakfast and VAT. The good English meals are served in the oak-paneled dining room with a Tudor fireplace. The hotel stands on the site of the battle of Rowton Moor, which was fought in 1643 between the Roundheads and the Cavaliers.

Blossoms Hotel, St. John Street, Chester, Cheshire CH1 1HL (tel. 0244/323186), has been in business since the mid-17th century, although the present structure was rebuilt late in Victoria's day. Each of the traditionally furnished 69 bedrooms is equipped with central heating, and all have private baths, phones, radios, color TVs, and coffee makers. The price for B&B in a single begins at £68 ($112.20) daily and in a double at £95 ($156.75). The old open staircase in the reception room sets the tone of the hotel. Dinner is served in the Egerton Room from 7 to 9:30pm daily, offering both a carving table selection at £10.50 ($17.35) and an à la carte menu. These menus are available for lunch as well as dinner. The Snooty Fox, a traditional English pub with a hunting decor, is open for lunch from 11am to 2:30pm Mon. to Sat., noon to 2pm Sun.

WHERE TO DINE

The premier restaurant in this part of England is **Arkle Restaurant,** Chester Grosvenor Hotel, Eastgate Street (tel. 0244/324024), the formal restaurant of this already previewed grand hotel. This 45-seat gourmet restaurant has a superb chef de cuisine and a talented, 40-strong team preparing the finest food with the freshest ingredients. Here you get modern British and continental cooking prepared with subtle touches and a certain lightness as reflected by the sauces and the cooking of meats and vegetables. For the ultimate food experience, the kitchen will prepare a special, six-course dinner menu (the restaurant manager will describe the succulent feast) at a cost of £35 ($57.75) per person. Otherwise, a set lunch costs £13.50 ($22.30) for two courses, £17.50 ($28.90) for three courses. To dine à la carte is about £40 ($66) per person. You are likely to be served such dishes as roast filet of halibut with crab sausages, and cutlet of Norfolk duckling with morels and shallot fondue. Desserts are equally luscious and tempting. Arkle has an award-winning cheese selection and unique breads (a choice of at least six daily) and cheese biscuits are homemade. You can partake of this grand cuisine from noon to 2:30pm Tue. to Sat., and 7:30 to 10pm Mon. to Sat.

La Brasserie, Chester Grosvenor Hotel, Eastgate Street (tel. 0244/324024), is perhaps the best all-around dining choice in Chester, not only for convenience but for price and quality. In the same building as this prestigious hotel, which has already been previewed, along with its formal restaurant, Arkle, La Brasserie is open daily from 6:30am to 11:30pm. Regardless of your schedule, you couldn't ask for more convenient dining hours than that. In a delightfully art nouveau setting, the Brasserie daily offers a three-course set lunch at £9.75 ($16.10) served from 11:30am to 2:30pm and a three-course table d'hôte dinner for £14.50 ($23.95) from 6:30 to 11pm. Main dishes are likely to include poached filet of salmon with a dill sauce, roasted guinea fowl with green cabbage, and veal steak with Marsala sauce.

Abbey Green, 2 Abbey Green, Northgate Street (tel. 0244/313251), is the premier vegetarian restaurant of Northwest England. In soft pastel tones, evocative of the "Mauve Era" of the 1890s, the restaurant is open from noon to 2:30pm and 6:30 to 10pm Mon. to Sat. (closed Mon. dinner). Meals cost from £12 ($19.80). There are many thoughtful extras to this restaurant, including wheelchair access, a non-smoking section, and helpings scaled down to kid-size. For its inspiration, the menu roams the world, including such Middle Eastern treats as hummus and pita bread, or tostados from Mexico. Flavors appear in unusual combinations, perhaps inspired by the imagined cuisine on some South Seas islands. The place is popular so you should call and reserve a table. It's in the center, in a brick building from the 1700s.

---

2. Nantwich

The old market town on the Weaver River lies only 15 miles southeast of the county town of Chester, and can easily be tied in with a visit to that city. The town is particularly outstanding because of its black-and-white timbered houses. The most spectacular one, Churche's Mansion, is a dining recommendation.

WHERE TO STAY

With its striking appearance, **Rookery Hall,** Worleston, Nantwich, Cheshire CW5 6DQ (tel. 0270/626866), is a structure whose Italianate facade and massive proportions would appear at home in the Loire Valley in France. More a château than a manor house, it was built in the 1700s but radically altered in 1867 into the high-Victorian design that stands today. Guests are welcomed to the 11 handsomely furnished bedrooms, each with a private bath, direct-dial phone, TV, and comfortable amenities. With a full English breakfast and a four-course dinner, single rooms cost £97.50 ($106.90) daily, and doubles rent for £165 ($272.25). While you enjoy panoramic views of the surrounding countryside, you can sample well-prepared food, which includes a combination of English dishes and modern French cuisine. The lavishly paneled dining room is a suitable setting for meals based on traditional English cookery with a modern twist. Try Cheshire sausages on a bed of leeks, rack of Welsh lamb with homegrown mustard-seed sauce, and bread-and-butter pudding with honey ice cream. The location is 2½ miles north of Nantwich by the A51 and on the B5074.

WHERE TO DINE

The most enchanting old restaurant in Cheshire, **Churche's Mansion Restaurant,** Hospital Street (tel. 0270/625933), lies in Nantwich at the junction of Newcastle Road and the Chester bypass. Many years ago Dr. and Mrs. E. C. Myott learned that this historic home of a wealthy Elizabethan gentleman had been advertised for sale in America, and asked the town council to step in and save it. Alas, no English housewife wanted such a gloomy and dark home, so the Myotts attended the sale and outbid the American syndicate that wanted to transport it to the United

States. Dr. Myott said that "our friends thought we were mad." They sought out the mysteries of the house: a window in the side wall, inlaid initials, a Tudor well in the garden, a long-ago love knot with a central heart (a token of Richard Churche's affection for his young wife). Today the house is widely known and recommended for its quality meals. Lunch costs from £8.50 ($14.05) and dinners from £16.50 ($27.25). Tariffs include VAT and coffee. Hours are from noon to 2pm and 7 to 9:30pm daily. It is advisable but not absolutely necessary to make reservations.

---

3. Liverpool

Liverpool, with its famous waterfront on the River Mersey, is a great shipping port and industrial center that gave the world everybody from the fictional Fannie Hill to the Beatles. King John launched it on its road to glory when he granted it a charter in 1207. Before that it had been a tiny 12th-century fishing village, but it quickly became a port for shipping men and materials to Ireland. In the 18th century it grew to prominence as a port as a result of the sugar, spice, and tobacco trade with the Americas. By the time Victoria came to the throne, Liverpool had become Britain's biggest commercial seaport. Recent refurbishing of the Albert Docks, establishment of a Maritime Museum, and the conversion of warehouses into little stores, similar to those in Ghirardelli Square in San Francisco, have made this an up-and-coming area once again, with many attractions for visitors.

Liverpudlians, as they are called, are rightly proud of their city, with its new hotels, two cathedrals, shopping and entertainment complexes (as exemplified by St. John's Centre, a modern pedestrian precinct), and the parks and open spaces (2,400 acres in and around the city, including Sefton Park with its Palm House). Liverpool's main shopping street, Church, is traffic-free.

Liverpool is easily reached by car, following the M1, the M6, and the A5080 from London right to the coast city in the west where the River Mersey joins the Irish Sea. Trains go from Euston or Kensington Olympia Stations from London or the Rapide bus from Victoria Coach Station goes direct to Liverpool. The city lies 219 miles from London and 35 miles from Manchester.

WHAT TO SEE AND DO

Liverpool today has a wealth of things for the visitor to see and enjoy—major cathedrals, waterfront glories restored, cultural centers, even the places where the Beatles began their meteoric rise to fame and fortune.

The Cathedrals

Attracting many Liverpool visitors is the great new (as cathedrals go) Anglican edifice, the **Cathedral Church of Christ,** Saint James Mount (tel. 051/709-6271), largely completed 74 years after it was begun in 1903. On a rocky eminence overlooking the River Mersey, the cathedral might possibly be the last Gothic-style one to be built on earth. Dedicated in the presence of Queen Elizabeth II in 1978, it is the largest church in the country (the fifth largest in the world). England's poet laureate at the time, Sir John Betjeman, hailed it as "one of the great buildings of the world." Its vaulting under the tower is 175 feet high, the highest in the world, and its length of 619 feet makes it one of the world's longest. The architect, who won a competition in 1903 for the building's design, was Giles Scott. He went on to rebuild the House of Commons, gutted by bombs, after World War II. He personally laid the last stone on the highest tower pinnacle. The organ of the world's largest Anglican cathedral contains nearly 10,000 pipes, the biggest found in any church. The tower houses the highest (219 feet) and the heaviest (31 tons) ringing peals of bells in the world, and the Gothic arches are the highest ever built.

In 1984, a visitor center and refectory was opened, the dominant feature being an aerial sculpture of 12 huge sails, with a ship's bell, clock, and light that changes color on an hourly basis. Full meals may be taken in the charming refectory. The cathedral can be visited from 9am to 6pm daily. Tours of the tower are offered from noon to 4:30pm Mon. to Sat., from 4 to 5pm Sun. The tours cost adults £1.50 ($2.50), children (accompanied by an adult), 50p (85¢).

Half a mile away from the Anglican cathedral stands the Roman Catholic **Metropolitan Cathedral of Christ the King,** Mount Pleasant (tel. 051/709-9222), but any notion that they glower at each other from that distance is dismissed by the name of the road that joins them—Hope Street. The sectarian strife of earlier generations has been ended, and a change in attitude, called by some the "Mersey Miracle," was illustrated clearly in 1982 when Pope John Paul II drove along Hope Street to pray in both cathedrals. The Metropolitan Cathedral is so called because Liverpool is, in Catholic terms, the mother city, the "metropolis" of the north of England. Construction of the cathedral to the design of Sir Edwin Lutyens was started in 1930, but when World War II halted progress in 1939, not even the granite and brick vaulting of the crypt was complete. At the end of the war it was estimated that the cost of completing the structure as Lutyens had designed it would be some £27 million. Architects throughout the world were invited to compete to design a more realistic project to cost about £1 million and to be completed in 5 years. Sir Frederick Gibberd won the competition and was commissioned to oversee the construction of the circular cathedral in concrete and glass, pitched like a tent at one end of the piazza that covered all the original site, crypt included. Between 1962 and 1967 the construction was completed, providing seating for a congregation of more than 2,000, all within 50 feet of the central altar. Above the altar rises a multi-colored glass lantern weighing 2,000 tons and rising to a height of 290 feet. This has been called a "space age" cathedral.

The Metropolitan Cathedral is open daily from 8am to 6pm (to 5pm Sun. in winter). It has a bookshop, a tea room, and tour guides.

On the Waterfront

Albert Dock, Albert Dock Co. Ltd. (tel. 051/708-7334), is a showpiece development on Liverpool's waterfront. Built of brick, stone, and cast iron, it opened in 1846, saw a long period of decline, and has been renovated and refurbished so that it is now England's largest grade 1 listed building, a designation for landmark buildings. The dockland warehouses now contain quality shops, restaurants, cafés, an English pub, and a cellar wine bar. One pavilion houses the main building of the Merseyside Maritime Museum (see below) and another is the home of the Tate Gallery Liverpool, the national collection of modern art in the north of England (see below). Albert Dock shopping is open daily from 10am to 6pm, bars and restaurants are open until 11pm. There's no charge for going there and strolling around, and car parking is available.

Merseyside Maritime Museum, Albert Dock (tel. 051/207-0001), set in the historic heart of Liverpool's magnificent waterfront, is a large museum providing a unique blend of floating exhibits, craft demonstrations, working displays, and special events. In addition to restored waterfront buildings, exhibitions show the story of mass emigration through Liverpool in the last century, shipbuilding on Merseyside, and many other aspects of Liverpool's maritime heritage. You can see a restored piermaster's house and a working cooperage, and you can take a steamboat trip around the historic Albert Dock complex. The museum is open daily from 10:30am to 5:30pm (last admission at 4:30pm). Admission is £1.50 ($2.50) for adults, 75p ($1.25) for children. A smörgåsbord restaurant, a coffeeshop, a waterfront café, gift shops, and ample parking space are among the facilities. There is wheelchair access to all floors of the main museum building and most areas of the Maritime Park. Disabled visitors are made most welcome.

Tate Gallery at Albert Dock (tel. 051/709-3223), opened in 1988, housing the national collection of 20th-century art in the north of England. It is the first gallery in England devoted entirely to modern art. The gallery was a decision of the board of directors at the Tate Gallery in London to move more than 85 percent of its modern collections from vaults to the gallery in Liverpool where all the world could see these "hidden treasures." Lack of space in London made it impossible to show the collection. So, this new "Tate Gallery of the North" came into being. Some of the world's greatest modern artists, such as Picasso and Dali, but also Magritte and Rothko, are likely to be on display at any time, along with a changing array of temporary exhibitions and events. The gallery is open from 11am to 7pm Tues. to Sun., charging no admission. It closes at 6pm in winter. However, the price of special exhibitions is £2 ($3.30).

The Beatles Story, Britannia Pavilion, Albert Dock (tel. 051/709-1963), opened in 1990, telling the saga of the Beatles—how they met, why they split up, and who and what were the people and places that inspired their music. It is open daily from 10am to 6pm, charging adults £2.50 ($4.15) and children £1.50 ($2.50).

You can take the famous **Mersey Ferry** from the pier head to both Woodside and Seacombe. Services operate daily from early morning to early evening throughout the year. Further information is obtained from the Mersey Ferries, Victoria Place, Seacombe, Wallasey (tel. 051/630-1030).

Other Sights

Museum of Labour History, former county sessions house, William Brown Street (tel. 051/207-0001, ext. 279), traces what it was like to live and work in Merseyside over the last 150 years, with people struggling for legal and political rights, establishing trade unions, and improving their working conditions. It is open from 10am to 5pm Mon. to Sat. and 2 to 5pm Sun.; closed New Year's Day, Good Friday, and the three Christmas holidays. Admission is free.

Walker Art Gallery, William Brown Street (tel. 051/207-0001), has one of the finest collections of paintings outside London. It is known for its European pictures and sculptures from 1300 to the present. Open from 10am to 5pm Mon. to Sat., and 2 to 5pm Sun., it is closed New Year's Day, Good Friday, and for the Christmas holidays. Admission is free.

Where the Beatles Began

Whether or not they're Beatles fans, most visitors who come to Liverpool want to take a look at where Beatlemania began in the Swinging Sixties. Mathew Street is the heart of Beatleland, and **Cavern Walks** (tel. 051/236-9082) is a shopping development and tour service built on the site of the former Cavern Club where the Beatles performed almost 300 times. John Doubleday's controversial statue of the group is in the central piazza of the cavern complex, surrounded by shops and restaurants. The outside of Cavern Walks was decorated by Cynthia Lennon, John's first wife. Another controversial statue of John, Paul, George, and Ringo, this one by Liverpool sculptor Arthur Dooley, is opposite the building facade. Farther along Mathew Street is the John Lennon Memorial Club and the **Beatles Shop,** 31 Mathew St. (tel. 051/236-8066), open from 9:30am to 5:30pm, 10:30am to 4pm Sun. from April to the end of December. Around the corner on Stanley Street is a statue of Eleanor Rigby, seated on a bench.

Tours

A daily £2 ($3.30) sightseeing tour gives a brief introduction to Liverpool, while for £4 ($6.60), Beatles fans can take a 2-hour guided tour of famous locations such as Penny Lane and Strawberry Fields. For those who prefer to "do it themselves," a Beatles map can be purchased for £1 ($1.65). Details are available from the **Merseyside Tourism Board.** Its information centers are at Clayton Square Shopping Centre, opposite the main railway station (tel. 051/709-3631), and the Albert Dock (tel. 051/708-8854). Both centers are open every day.

WHERE TO STAY

The "grand hotel" of Liverpool, the **Brittania Adelphi Hotel,** Ranelagh Place, Liverpool, Merseyside L3 5UL (tel. 051/709-7200), built in 1914, is known for its fine rooms and good cuisine. Past the elegant entrance, you enter a world of marble corridors, molded ceilings, and dark polished wood. However, these traditional features are complemented by a range of modern amenities. The hotel has been completely refurbished, offering 376 bedrooms, each with private bath or shower, color TV, and phone. The well-furnished and attractively appointed bedrooms cost £48 ($79.20) to £75 ($123.75) daily in a single and £85 ($140.25) in a twin or double. Facilities include three restaurants, four bars, a disco, hair and beauty salons, and a health club with swimming pool, gym, solarium, and Jacuzzi. There is garage space for 100 cars.

Liverpool Moat House, Paradise Street, Liverpool, Merseyside L1 8JD (tel. 051/7090181), is, in the opinion of some, the leading hotel of Liverpool. In the center of the city, it is one of the most comfortable hotels in Merseyside, with an efficient modernity. Bedrooms are spread across seven floors, 258 in all, each with private bath or shower, air conditioning, TV, and direct-dial phone. Most often favored by commercial travelers, it also lures sightseers drawn to the attractions of "new Liverpool." Singles rent for £72 ($118.80) nightly, with doubles costing from £92 ($151.80), with even more expensive suites available. The hotel has a number of facilities, including solarium, gym, indoor swimming pool, and garden. Its coffeeshop stays open until 10:30pm for late arrivals. It also offers a good restaurant serving British and French dishes, with meals costing from £15 ($24.75).

Atlantic Tower, 30 Chapel St., Liverpool, Merseyside L3 9RE (tel. 051/627070), enjoys one of the most advanced architectural designs of any hotel in Liverpool. Showcased in a high rise that evokes the bows of a great luxury liner, Atlantic Tower is considered one of the two or three top hotels in the city. You check into a spacious lobby and are shown to one of the 222 well-furnished bedrooms, each with private bath or shower, air conditioning, direct-dial phone, and TV. Often opening onto views of the River Mersey, bedrooms rent for £67.50 ($111.40) to £75 ($123.75) in a single and £75 ($123.75) to £85 ($140.25) in a double. You can dine in the Stateroom Restaurant, enjoying drinks in a bar that resembles a Pullman coach.

Trials, 56-62 Castle St., Liverpool, Merseyside L2 7LQ (tel. 051/2271021), is another leading hotel of Liverpool, but it's much smaller, with only 20 suites. Rather luxurious, this hotel of charm and character was created from a centrally located Victorian structure that had once been a bank. Now beautifully converted to its new role, Trials is often the choice of the most discriminating visitor to Liverpool. The accommodations are split level, actually plush suites, with Jacuzzis, private baths or showers, phones, trouser presses, hairdryers, and TVs. From Sun. to Thur., the accommodations rent for £80 ($132) daily in a single to £100 ($165) in a double. On Fri. and Sat., each suite goes for £50 ($82.50) daily in a single and £60 ($99) in a double. With a unique character, Trials Restaurant offers a grand cuisine served in first-class surroundings. The hotel has 24-hour room service.

WHERE TO DINE

Consistently good food is served at **Jenny's Seafood Restaurant,** the Old Ropery, Fenwick Street (tel. 051/236-0332). In the vicinity of the harbor, it has a basement room that is both pleasantly decorated and softly illuminated. All this forms a backdrop for the good-tasting fresh seafood that is brought in daily. Everything I've sampled has been of fine quality and well prepared. The service, on my latest rounds, was excellent. Expect to pay £12.50 ($20.65) to £21 ($34.65) for a full meal. The restaurant is closed Mon. evening, for lunch Sat., and all day Sunday, but it is open from noon to 2:15pm and 7 to 10pm; closed Sun., dinner Mon., lunch Sat., and the two weeks in August.

Far East, 27-35 Berry St. (tel. 051/7093141), is considered the finest Chinese restaurant in Liverpool. Liverpool is particularly famous for its Chinese restaurants, not surprising as the city has one of the largest Chinese populations in Europe and its own "Chinatown." Here you might enjoy a dim sum lunch, later returning in the evening for more haute Chinese fare. You face a bewildering array of Cantonese specialties, including chile-flavored large prawns. The chefs also do marvelous things with duck. You can sample its fares daily from noon to 11:30pm, with a set lunch offered for only £5 ($8.25) and a set dinner for £6 ($9.90). However, you are likely to get carried away with the à la carte specialties and spend at least £12 ($19.80).

Armadillo, 20-22 Matthew St. (tel. 051/2364123), is one of the leading independent restaurants of Liverpool. In a converted warehouse, it stands across the street from the site of the famous Cavern, where the Beatles got their start. The selection of fresh, good-tasting British food leans toward the vegetarian at times, but top-quality meat, poultry, and fish dishes are served as well. This place, owned by Martin Cooper, seems to be near the top of everybody's list of favorite restaurants in Liverpool. A set lunch costs only £8.50 ($14.05), with à la carte dinners priced from £16 ($26.40). Hours are from 11:45 to 3pm and 7:30 to 10:30pm; closed Sun., dinner Mon.

THE LAKE DISTRICT

Driving in the wilds of this northwestern shire is fine for a start, but the best activity is walking, which is an art—practiced here by both young and old with a crooked stick. Don't go out without a warning, however. There is a great deal of rain and heavy mist. Sunny days are few. When the mist starts to fall, try to be near an old inn or pub, where you can drop in for a visit and warm yourself beside an open fireplace. You'll be carried back to the good old days, as many places in Cumbria have valiantly resisted change. If you strike up a conversation with a local, just make sure you know something about hounds.

The far northwestern part of the shire, bordering Scotland, used to be called Cumberland. Now part of Cumbria, it is generally divided geographically into a trio of segments: the Pennines, dominating the eastern sector (loftiest point at Cross Fell, nearly 3,000 feet high); the Valley of Eden; and the lakes and secluded valleys of the west—by far the most interesting. The Lake District, so beautifully described by the Romantic Lake poets, enjoys many literary associations. Wordsworth was a native son, having been born at Cockermouth.

The largest town is Carlisle in the north—not a very interesting tourist center, but possible as a base for explorations to **Hadrian's Wall.** The wall stretches from Wallsend in the east to Bowness on the Solway, a distance of about 75 miles. It was built in the 2nd century A.D. by the Romans.

4. Cartmel

The village of Cartmel, lying some 6 miles south of the southern end of Lake Windermere, is 2 miles northwest of Grange-over-Sands, a resort that gained popularity in Victorian times. Cartmel's 12th-century priory and the racecourse made it an attraction then as now.

WHERE TO STAY AND DINE

Opened in 1985 by John Tovey, who created the Miller Howe Hotel in Windermere, recommended below, the **Uplands Country House Hotel,** Haggs Lane, Cartmel, near Grange-over-Sands, Cumbria LA11 6HD (tel. 05395/36248), stands in 2 acres of garden with views to the Morecambe Bay estuary. The hotel is run by Tom and Diana Peter in partnership with Mr. Tovey, from whom they learned their innkeeping skills in 12 years of employment at the hotel in Windermere. Uplands has five comfortable double bedrooms, all with TVs, phones, clocks, hairdryers, and private baths. Half board costs £62 ($102.30) in a single to £115 ($189.75) in a double. Tom is an excellent chef, producing country-style, three-course luncheons costing £12 ($19.80). Even if you don't stay here, it's worth a stop just to dine, a four-course meal costing £20 ($33). You might choose as an appetizer mushroom-and-marsala quiche or stuffed cheese peach with bacon roll, followed by filet of sea bass, roast sirloin of Lakeland beef, or roast local wood pigeon. For dessert, the strawberry and kiwi fruit meringue slice is just right if it's available. The hotel is closed in January and February.

5. Kendal

A market town, Kendal contains the ruins of a castle where Catherine Parr, the last wife of Henry VIII, was born. With its 13th-century parish church, Kendal makes a good stopover en route to the lakeside resort of Windermere, about 9 miles away. Kendal is 270 miles from London.

The town was also associated with George Romney, the 18th-century portrait painter (Lady Hamilton was his favorite subject) who used to travel all over the Lake District trying to get someone to sit for him. He held his first exhibition in Kendal, married and had children there. He deserted them in 1762, not returning until the end of his life. He died in Kendal in 1802.

Abbot Hall, Kirkland, a handsome stone Georgian mansion, houses the **Abbot Hall Art Gallery** and the **Museum of Lakeland Life and Industry** (tel. 0539/722464), operated by the Lake District Art Gallery and Museum Trust. The gallery, laid out in 18th-century rooms, contains portraits by Romney and Gardner and Lake District watercolors. The museum exhibits period rooms, costumes, printing, weaving, and local industries, as well as Queensgate, a reconstructed Victorian street scene, and a farming display. Recently added are the Arthur Ransome room and Arts and Crafts Movement rooms. The gallery and museum are open from 10:30am to 5pm Mon. to Fri., from 2 to 5pm Sat. and Sun. Admission is £1.50 ($2.50) for adults, 75p ($1.25) for children.

Kendal Museum of Archaeology and Natural History, Station Road (tel. 0539/721374), one of the oldest museums in Britain, now administered by the Abbot Hall Art Gallery, traces the story of people of the area since the Stone Age, as well as Kendal's development as a wool town. Realistic constructions take the visitor on a tour of the major wildlife habitats in the district. The museum also contains a world wildlife gallery with specimens of birds, animals, and insects, pointing out the ecological problems of the modern world. The museum is open 10:30am to 5pm Mon. to Fri., 2 to 5pm Sat. and Sun. From the spring bank holiday weekend to October 31, it is open from 10:30 to 5pm Sat. It's closed during the Christmas holidays, New Year's Day. Admission is £1.50 ($2.50) for adults, 75p ($1.25) for children. Family tickets at £4 ($6.60) are available.

WHERE TO STAY

With a name harking back to Kendal's heyday as a wool town, the **Woolpack Hotel,** Stricklandgate, Kendal, Cumbria LA9 4ND (tel. 0539/23852), offers modern conveniences in this motel-like establishment. All 53 rooms are equipped with private baths, TVs, and phones, and some are suites, which are ideal for families of three or more. Children under 12 are accommodated at no charge when sharing their parents' rooms. All the rooms are decorated in pastel colors to add to the cheerful atmosphere. Convenient parking is provided. Singles range upward from £58 ($95.70) daily, while doubles begin at £72 ($118.80). VAT, service, and a full English breakfast are included in the tab. Meals cost from £15 ($24.75).

WHERE TO DINE

In a converted former grocery store, **Moon,** 129 Highgate (tel. 0539/29254), is known for serving the best food in Kendal. Admittedly, the competition here isn't too keen, but this place excels, nevertheless. Run by Val Macconnell, the restaurant

THE LAKE DISTRICT

serves succulent meat, fish, vegetarian, and wholefood dishes, and does so exceedingly well. Good old-fashioned flavors and modern cooking techniques combine to offer a tempting array of British food selections daily from 6 to 10pm, to 10:30pm Fri. and Sat. Meals cost from £12 ($19.80) and are likely to include everything from smoked mackerel pâté with a gooseberry sauce to a vegetable ragout. The restaurant is attractively decorated in a bistrolike format.

---

6. Windermere

The grandest of the lakes is Windermere, the largest one in England, whose shores wash up against the adjoining towns of Bowness and Windermere. Both of these lakeside resorts lie on the eastern shore of Windermere, which is 274 miles from London and 10 miles from Kendal. A ferry service connects Hawkshead and Bowness. Windermere, the resort, is the end of the railway line. From either town, you can climb Orrest Head in less than an hour for a panoramic view of England's lakeland. From that vantage point, you can even see Scafell Pike, rising to a height of 3,210 feet—the peak pinnacle in all of England.

Windermere Steamboat Museum, Rayrigg Road, Windermere (tel. 09662/5565), is a working museum. It was founded and developed by George Pattinson, who discovered the fascination of steam many years ago and now has probably the best and most comprehensive collection of steamboats in the country. The wet boatsheds house some dozen boats, including the veteran *Dolly,* probably the oldest mechanically powered boat in the world, dating from around 1850. It was raised from the lake bed in the early 1960s and run for several years with the original boiler and steambox.

Also displayed is the *Esperance,* an iron steam yacht registered with Lloyds in 1869, as well as many elegant Victorian and Edwardian steam launches. Attached to the boathouses is the speedboat *Jane,* dating from 1938, the first glider-plane to take off from the water in 1943, and the hydroplane racer *Cookie*—all jostling Beatrix Potter's rowing boat and other Lakeland craft for position. Boats that have been added to the collection include the steam launch *Kittiwake,* the motorboat *Lady Hamilton,* and the fast speedboat *Miss Windermere IV.*

The museum is open from Easter to October, charging an admission of £2 ($3.30) for adults and £1.20 ($2) for children. The *Osprey* is regularly in steam, and visitors can make a 45-minute trip on the lake at £2.75 ($4.55) for adults, £1.75 ($2.90) for children.

It's also possible to make trips on Ullswater and on Coniston, and there is regular steamer service around Windermere, which serves the outlying villages as well as operating for visitors in summer.

WHERE TO STAY AND DINE

A clientele from all over the world comes to **Miller Howe Hotel,** Bayrigg Road, Windermere, Cumbria LA23 1EY (tel. 09662/2536), an inn bearing the unique imprint of its creator, former actor John Tovey. At the beginning of the 1970s he selected a country estate overlooking Lake Windermere, with views of the Langdale Peaks, and converted it to provide stylish accommodations and an exquisite cuisine. His large, graciously furnished rooms have names—no numbers—and he treats guests as if they were invited to a house party. Each accommodation is provided with binoculars to help absorb the view better, and even copies of *Punch* from the 1890s. Each of the 13 air-conditioned bedrooms has a private bath or shower, plus a portable TV and phone provided upon request. Antiques are used lavishly throughout the house. Rates per person, including a full English breakfast, dinner, and VAT, range from £64 ($105.60) to £110 ($181.50) daily. The hotel is closed from mid-December to mid-March. Dinner at Miller Howe is worth the drive up from London. While Tovey is famed as a pastry chef, he is equally known for his original appetizers and main dishes. Even if you can't stay the night, at least consider a meal here, for which you must reserve. The set meal of five courses will cost £27.50 ($45.40) per person, including coffee and VAT. Regional dishes using local produce are a special feature. You might try Lake District lamb, fresh salmon, game pies (in season), Lancashire cheese, and Cumbria sausage. Men must wear coats and ties in the dining room. Dinners are served daily at 8:30pm only, at 7:30 and 9:30pm Sat.

Langdale Chase Hotel, Windermere, Cumbria LA23 1LW (tel. 05394/32201), on the A591 between Windermere and Ambleside, is a great old lakeside house—built for grandeur—comparable to a villa on Lake Como, Italy. The story goes back to 1930 when the dynamic Ms. Dalzell and her mother took over the country estate, with its handsomely landscaped gardens, and decided to accept paying guests while retaining an uncommercial house-party atmosphere. Waterskiing, rowing, lake bathing, tennis, croquet on the grounds, and fishing attract the sportsminded. The rate for B&B ranges from £35 ($57.75) daily in a single. In a double or twin, the rent is £85 ($140.25). The 28 bedrooms have excellent furniture, private baths, phones, and TVs. The interior of the Victorian stone château, with its many gables, balconies, large mullioned windows, and terraces, is a treasure house of antiques. The main lounge hall looks like a setting for one of those English drawing-room comedies. The house was built in part with bits and pieces salvaged from the destruction of a nearby abbey and castle—hence, the ecclesiastical paneling. On the walls are distinctive paintings, mostly Italian primitives, although one is alleged to be a Van Dyck. The dining room ranks among the finest in the Lake District—with guests selecting tables that are good vantage points for lake viewing. The cuisine is highly personal, mostly a liberated English fare, supported by a fine wine list. Open to nonresidents, the dining room charges from £9 ($14.85) for a set lunch, from £20 ($33) for a set dinner.

Cedar Manor, Ambleside Road, Windermere, Cumbria LA23 1AX (tel. 09662/3192), is one of the most desirable country-house hotels in the area. In Victoria's day, it was an impressive lakeside home with gables and chimneys. But since those times it was converted into a small hotel of exceptional merit. Each of the 12 bedrooms, containing private bath or shower and TV, is well furnished and maintained, renting for £40 ($66) daily in a single or £80 ($132) in a double. A cedar tree, perhaps from India, has grown in the garden for some 2 centuries, and from that tree the hotel takes its name. Meals are good and wholesome, offering excellent value at a cost of £16 ($16.40) per person for five courses.

Roger's, 4 High St. (tel. 09662/4954), is one of the most acclaimed restaurants in the Lake District. Some diners prefer it to the highly touted viands served at Miller Howe. The stellar French dining room of Cumbria, Roger's carries the name of its skilled chef de cuisine, Roger Pergl-Wilson. For almost a decade he has been going strong at this location (a part of England where restaurants seem to have a high mortality rate). That means he's doing something right. You can judge for yourself from 7 to 9:30pm Mon. to Sat. A table d'hôte dinner—superb value—costs £18.50 ($30.55), but you are most likely to spend from £23 ($37.95) ordering à la carte. Homegrown ingredients go into the cookery whenever possible. Regardless, everything tastes fresh here, as care goes not only into the preparation but the presentation, which is polite and efficient without being overly formal. Deer from the field, salmon from the rivers, char from Lake Windermere, and quail from the air—everything seems deftly handled here. Always call for a reservation.

7. Ambleside

A good and idyllic retreat, Ambleside is one of the major centers attracting pony-trekkers, fell-hikers, and rock-scalers. The charms are essentially there year round, even in late autumn when it's fashionable to sport a mackintosh. Ambleside is superbly perched, at the top of Lake Windermere. Traditions are entrenched, especially at the Rushbearing Festival, an annual event. The resort lies 278 miles from London and 14 miles from Kendal.

WHERE TO STAY AND DINE

Half a mile south of Ambleside, **Rothay Manor,** Rothay Bridge, Ambleside, Cumbria LA22 0EH (tel. 05394/33605), on the A593, is like a French country inn, where the star is the cuisine, combined with a dedicated chef in the kitchen, well-selected French wines, and 15 comfortable, centrally heated bedrooms and three suites. Each unit has a bath or shower, phone, and TV. The price for B&B is £60 ($99) daily in a single, £94 ($155.10) in a double. The rooms are individually decorated, with a free use of vibrant colors. Most of them have shuttered French doors opening onto a sun balcony, with a mountain view. Throughout the estate you'll find an eclectic combination of antiques (some Georgian blended harmoniously with Victorian), flowers, and "get-lost" armchairs. The manor is also a restaurant open to non-residents. The spacious dining room is decked with antique tables and chairs. Appointments are flawless, and incorporate fine crystal, silver, and china. At night candles burn in silver holders. Buffet lunches are served from noon to 2pm every day except Sun. Dinners, from 8 till 9pm, are more ambitious, costing £22 ($36.30).

Kirkstone Foot, Kirkstone Pass Road, Ambleside, Cumbria LA22 9EH (tel. 05394/32232), is a 17th-century manor house whose lodging facilities have been increased with the construction of several slate-roofed and self-catering apartments in the surrounding parklike grounds. The original building is encircled by a well-tended lawn, while the interior is cozily furnished with overstuffed chairs and English paneling. The restaurant offers home-cooked English meals under the direction of the co-owner, Jane Bateman, who personally runs this fine establishment along with her husband, Simon. Fresh produce is used whenever possible. The comfortable accommodations, 16 in the main house and 16 in the outlying units, are tastefully decorated in a family style of coziness, with color TVs, radios, private baths or showers, and phones. For a full English breakfast and a five-course dinner, expect to pay from £32 ($52.90) to £42 ($69.30) per person daily. If you're staying in one of their flats, you can visit for dinner for another £16 ($26.40) per person.

The Riverside Hotel, near Rothay Bridge, Under Loughrigg, Ambleside, Cumbria LA22 9LJ (tel. 05394/32395), is a small country hotel, beautifully situated in a riverside setting. Secluded, on a quiet lane away from traffic noise, it is still only a few minutes' walk from the center of Ambleside. The hotel is owned and run by Jim and Jean Hainey, who accommodate guests and provide good meals. All 10 bedrooms have private baths, phones, color TVs, radios, hairdryers, and central heating. The charge for bed and half board is £36 ($59.40) per person daily.

Nanny Brow Hotel, Clappersgate, Ambleside, Cumbria LA22 9NF (tel. 0966/32036), is set on a hill about a mile west of Ambleside of the A593. This 21-bedroom hotel with eight suites was once a private home but has now been turned into one of the most successful little hotels in the Ambleside area. The Tudor-style gabled house is reached via a steep tree-flanked drive. Once you arrive, you find a country-house setting with a lovely sitting room with intricate cove moldings and, if the weather merits it, a log fire. Rooms are in both the main house and a garden wing, the latter offering first-rate accommodations (some of the suites have half-tester beds). The rooms contain private baths or showers, and other amenities include coffee makers, phones, and color TVs along with lots of comfortable charm. B&B costs £38 ($62.70) daily in a single, £74 ($122.10) in a double. You can also take full board here, costing £55 ($90.75) per person, including a six-course dinner. The food is well prepared, using fresh ingredients. Other facilities include a solarium and a whirlpool bath.

Wateredge Hotel, Waterhead, Ambleside, Cumbria LA22 0EP (tel. 05394/32332). Derek and Pamela Cowap took two 17th-century fishermen's cottages and formed this hotel, which has all the modern amenities but yet somehow manages to maintain much of its original character. Set on beautiful gardens overlooking Lake Windermere, the hotel also serves some of the best food in the area. Public rooms contain many little nooks for reading and conversation, and there is also a cozy bar. However, on sunny days guests prefer to anchor in one of the chairs on the lawn. The 23 rooms vary in size and appointments; some are spacious, others much smaller. Each has a private bath or shower, phone, and TV. Half-board terms are from £45 ($74.25) per person daily. A set dinner costs about £18 ($29.70), and it is offered nightly from 7 to 8:30pm. If hotel guests don't take all the tables, non-residents can call and see if they too can join the dining party. Fresh produce is used, and the quality of cooking is high. In winter a log fire will greet you.

Riverside Lodge Country House, near Rothay Bridge, Ambleside, Cumbria LA22 0EH (tel. 05394/34208), is an old and charming property run by Alan and Gillian Rhone who offer personal service. Theirs is an early Georgian house on the river bank, a short walk from the center, standing near the foot of Loughrigg Fell on 3 acres of grounds. It's featured in the book, *Famous Lakeland Homes,* by Kathleen Eyres. Bonnie Prince Charlie rested here in 1745. The lodge has some beamed ceilings and offers five well-furnished bedrooms, some with river views. Each has a private bath, phone, and color TV. Half board costs from £39 ($64.35) to £42 ($69.30) per person nightly. Have a drink in the intimate lounge with its open fire before going in to the dining room overlooking the river. Mrs. Rhone prepares an appetizing English cuisine.

8. Rydal

Between Ambleside (at the top of Lake Windermere) and Wordsworth's former retreat at Grasmere is Rydal, a small village on one of the smallest lakes, Rydal Water. The village of Rydal is noted for its sheep-dog trails at the end of summer. The location is 1½ miles north of Ambleside on A591.

Rydal Mount, off A591, 1½ miles north of Ambleside (tel. 05394/33002), was the home of William Wordsworth from 1813 until his death in 1850. Part of the house was built as a farmer's lake cottage around 1575. A descendant of Wordsworth's still owns the property, now a museum containing many portraits, furniture, and family possessions as well as mementos and books of the poet. The 3½-acre garden was landscaped by Wordsworth and contains rare trees, shrubs, and other features of interest. The house is open daily from 9:30am to 5pm from March to October, from 10am to 4pm from November to February; closed Tue. in winter. Admission is £1.80 ($2.95) for adults, 80p ($1.30) for children 5 to 16.

The village of Rydal is noted for its sheep-dog trials at the end of summer.

WHERE TO STAY AND DINE

Built in the 17th century as a wayfarer's inn, the **Glen Rothay Hotel,** Rydal, Ambleside, Cumbria LA22 9LR (tel. 05394/32524), lies between Rydal and Ambleside along the A591 and adjoining Dora's Field, immortalized by Wordsworth. Set back from the highway, it has a stucco-and-flagstone facade added by Victorians. Inside, the place has been modernized, but original detailing remains, including beamed ceilings and paneling. Much of the business derives from a popular street-level pub. There is also a more formal cocktail lounge, with a fireplace and comfortable armchairs, as well as a dining room serving solid English food. The 11 comfortable bedrooms upstairs have private baths or showers, central heating, and coffee makers, and a few offer four-poster beds. Half board ranges from £32 ($52.80) to £40 ($66) per person daily.

9. Grasmere

On a lake that bears its name, Grasmere was the home of Wordsworth from 1799 to 1808. He called this area "the loveliest spot that man hath ever known."

The poet lived with his sister, Dorothy (the writer and diarist), at **Dove Cottage,** which is now a museum administered by the Wordsworth Trust. Wordsworth, who followed Southey as poet laureate, died in the spring of 1850, and was buried in the graveyard of the village church at Grasmere. Another tenant of Dove Cottage was Thomas De Quincey (*Confessions of an English Opium Eater*). For a combined ticket costing £3 ($4.95) for adults, £1.35 ($2.25) for children, you can visit both Dove Cottage and the Wordsworth Museum. This houses the Wordsworth treasures, manuscripts, paintings, and memorabilia. There are also various special exhibitions throughout the year, exploring the art and literature of English Romanticism. The property is open daily from 9:30am to 5:30pm; closed from mid-January to mid-February. For further information, phone 09665/544; 09665/268 for Dove Cottage Restaurant information.

WHERE TO STAY AND DINE

In this hiking and rock-scaling center, you'll find the following recommendations, beginning first with the most expensive, then descending in price level.

Michael's Nook, Grasmere, Cumbria LA22 9RP (tel. 09665/496; turn off the A591 at the Swan Hotel), is a country-house hotel, once a private residence, standing in its own secluded garden of 3 acres. A lakeland home of stone, honoring a hill shepherd, Michael, subject of a Wordsworth poem, it contains much fine mahogany woodwork and paneling, exemplified by its elegant staircase. Throughout the house, owned by Grasmere antiques dealer Reg Gifford and his wife, Elizabeth, are many fine antiques, enhanced by the glow of log fires or vases of flowers. The handsomely decorated bedrooms, nine doubles and two suites, are individually furnished with such amenities as bath herbs, hairdryers, sandalwood sachets in drawers, and lavender-scented closets. One room, decorated with flowered chintz, has a four-poster bed. All units have private baths and showers, phones, and TVs. The minimum booking is usually three nights, but shorter visits will be accommodated where possible. The tariffs range from £170 ($280.30) in a standard double with bath, £224 ($369.60) in a superior double with bath, the rates including dinner, breakfast, service, and VAT.

Only about 20 persons are served in the intimate dining room, which accepts reservations from non-residents for both lunch and dinner. Care and attention to detail go into preparation of the meals, with menus changing daily. You might choose from poached prawns, Loch Linnhe in cream sauce flavored with Drambuie, perhaps sautéed calves' liver in shallot-and-vinegar sauce. An attractive staff serves the tables. Lunch is priced at £21 ($34.65) and is served at 12:30pm daily; dinner, at 7:30pm daily, costs £31.50 ($52), VAT included. In summer, dinner sittings are at 7 and 9pm on Sat.

Wordsworth Hotel, Stock Lane, Grasmere, Cumbria LA22 9RP (tel. 09665/592), stands in the heart of the village and is owned by Reg Gifford of Michael's Nook Country House Hotel. An old stone lakeland house (once the 19th-century Rothay Hotel), the Wordsworth has been gutted and rebuilt to provide 35 large bedrooms with views of the fells and river, as well as modern baths, TVs, phones, air conditioning, and comfortable chairs. Singles rent for £50 ($82.50) daily; doubles, £115 ($189.75). There is a four-poster bedroom with beams and dormer windows. The original master bedroom has a Victorian bathroom, with a brass towel rail and polished pipes and taps. There are several lounges, with sink-in armchairs grouped around log fires. A buffet lunch is served in the cocktail lounge, including the chef's hot dish of the day. A set six-course dinner in the Prelude Restaurant at £19 ($31.35) is likely to include a light fruit or vegetable appetizer, then soup, a choice of two meat dishes, followed by dessert or cheese, along with coffee and mints. The à la carte menu is more ambitious, and a three-course meal of, say, smoked-haddock and cheese soufflé, clear beef broth with quail eggs, breast of chicken stuffed with walnuts, and rich chocolate-fudge cake costs around £20 ($33). Each dish is carefully explained on the menu so you know what you're getting. Meals are served daily from 12:30 to 2pm and 7 to 9pm, to 9:30pm Fri. and Sat. The hotel has a large, heated swimming pool, a whirlpool, a sauna, a solarium, a games room, and a mini-gym.

White Moss House, Rydal Water, Grasmere, Cumbria LA22 9SE (tel. 09665/295), is an old lakeland cottage off the main A591 between Grasmere and Rydal Water. It overlooks the lake and the fells, where you're welcomed by Peter and Susan Dixon as a house guest to be pampered with morning tea in bed, your bedcovers turned down at night, and your culinary preferences remembered and adhered to. The rooms are comfortably furnished and well heated in nippy weather. In all there are only five accommodations, so advance booking is essential. These units have private baths, color TVs, direct-dial phones, radios, trouser presses, hairdryers, and such bathroom amenities as soap, shampoo, and herbal bath salts. The rent is £53 ($87.45) to £71 ($117.15) per person nightly including an elegant, if large, breakfast and a dinner to satisfy a gourmet. There's also Brockstone, their cottage annex, a 5-minute drive along the road, where two, three, or four guests can be accommodated in utter peace. Dinner is a leisurely affair beginning at 8pm. You're served five courses likely to include a roast of lamb with an orange and red-currant sauce or quail with a chicken and brown-rice stuffing. For dessert, I hope Mrs. Beeton's chocolate pudding is featured. If you're not a resident, dinner will cost from £21.95 ($36.20), but you must reserve a table early.

The Red Lion Hotel, Red Lion Square, Grasmere, Cumbria LA22 9SS (tel. 09665/456), is a 200-year-old coaching inn in the heart of the village. It's only a short stroll to Dove Cottage, once the home of William Wordsworth, and it's as-sumed that the poet often stopped for a meal, drink, or to warm himself by the fire. Recently refurbished, the hotel offers 36 bedrooms, all with private baths, phones, and TVs. B&B costs from £32 ($52.80) daily in a single, £62 ($102.30) in a double, including VAT. There's an elevator to all floors. Enjoy a drink or lunch in the light and airy surroundings of the Easdale Bar, or try the Lamb Inn and Buttery for a more traditional pub atmosphere. In the dining room, you'll be served some of the finest fare in the district, a set meal costing from £14 ($23.10) or you can order à la carte.

Swan Hotel, on A591, Grasmere, Cumbria LA22 9RF (tel. 09665/551), has been renovated so that only the shell of the old building remains. However, there have been inns on this site for 300 years. Sir Walter Scott used to slip in for a secret drink early in the morning, and Wordsworth mentioned the place in *The Waggoner*. In fact, in one of the lounges is the poet's tapestry chair. The 36 rooms contain built-in furniture and good beds along with private bath, phone, and TV. Singles cost from £64 ($105.80) daily, and twins begin at £80 ($132), with service and VAT included. The restaurant serves daily from noon to 2pm and 7 to 9pm, providing both table d'hôte and à la carte meals.

---

10. Hawkshead and Coniston

Discover for yourself the village of Hawkshead, with its 15th-century grammar school where Wordsworth went to school for 8 years (he carved his name on a desk that still remains). The location is 283 miles from London and 19 miles from Kendal. Near Hawkshead, in the vicinity of Esthwaite Water, is the 17th-century **Hill Top Farm,** former home of Beatrix Potter, the author of the Peter Rabbit books, who died in 1943.

At **Coniston,** 4 miles away from Hawkshead, you can visit the village associated with John Ruskin. Coniston is a good base for rock climbing. The Coniston Old Man towers in the background at 2,633 feet, giving mountain climbers one of the finest views of the Lake District.

John Ruskin, poet, artist, and critic, was one of the great figures of the Victorian age and a prophet of social reform, inspiring such diverse men as Proust, Frank Lloyd Wright, and Gandhi. He moved to his home, **Brantwood** (tel. 05394/41396), on the east side of Coniston Water, in 1872 and lived there until his death in 1900. The house today is open for visitors to view much Ruskiniana, including some 200 pictures by him. Also displayed are his coach and boat, the *Jumping Jenny*. A video program tells the story of Ruskin's life and work.

An exhibition illustrating the work of W.J. Linton is laid out in his old printing room. Linton was born in England in 1812 and died at New Haven, Connecticut, in 1897. Well known as a wood engraver and for his private press, he lived at Brantwood, where he set up his printing business in 1853. He published *The English Republic,* a newspaper and review, before immigrating to America in 1866, where he set up his printing press in 1870. The house is owned and managed by the Education Trust, a self-supporting registered charity. It is open daily from mid-March to mid-November from 11am to 5:30pm, Wed. to Sun. only in winter. Admission is £2.25 ($3.70) for adults and £1.25 ($2.05) for children, with a family ticket costing £6 ($9.90). Part of the 250-acre estate is open as a nature trail, costing 50p (85¢) for adults, 35p (60¢) for children, if the walk is taken separately. The Brantwood stables, designed by Ruskin, have been converted into a tea room and restaurant, the Jumping Jenny. Also in the stable building is the Lakeland Guild Craft Gallery, which follows the Ruskin tradition in encouraging contemporary craftwork of the finest quality.

Literary fans may want to pay a pilgrimage to the graveyard of the village church, where Ruskin was buried; his family turned down a chance to have him interred at Westminster Abbey.

WHERE TO STAY AND DINE AT HAWKSHEAD

The most desirable accommodation is found at **Tarn Hows,** Hawkshead, Cumbria, LA22 0PR (tel. 09666/696), which lies about 1½ miles by B5285, the Coniston road. Secluded enough to be called a retreat, Tarn Hows Hotel is named after a scenic attraction of the Lake District. The hotel itself lies in one of the most beautiful sections of Cumbria. Owned by the Moore family, the hotel offers 23 bedrooms, each well kept and furnished in a homelike, comfortable fashion. B&B rates begin at £30 ($49.50) per person per night. Accommodations are equipped with private baths or showers, phones, radios, and hot beverage facilities. The staff at the hotel, based on reader reports, show a personal interest in their guests. They also serve good food from 7pm with last orders taken at 8:45pm. These are correctly prepared dishes that appeal to a variety of tastes.

The best place for food in the area is **Grizedale Lodge,** Grizedale, Hawkshead, Cumbria LA22 0Q1 (tel. 09666/532), which is a Lakeside country *restaurant avec chambres.* Many people come here just to dine, as the cuisine is topnotch. Margaret Lamb is considered one of the finest chefs in the Lake District, and her considerable talents are reflected by her five-course evening meals based on the best of English and continental dishes. During the day guests order bar lunches but at night they can enjoy a memorable meal in a tranquil setting for only £15 ($24.75) per person. Service is personable. Bar lunches are served daily from 12:30 to 1:45pm and dinner from 7 to 10:30pm. Mrs. Lamb and her husband, Jack, also offer six handsomely furnished bedrooms for guests, each with private bath, phone, and TV. Half-board terms cost from £38 ($62.70) per person daily. Guests are received every month but January.

WHERE TO STAY AND DINE AT CONISTON

The most popular, traditional, and attractive pub in the village is the **Coniston Sun Hotel,** Coniston, Cumbria LA21 8HQ (tel. 05394/41248). In reality, it is a country-house hotel of much character, dating from 1902, although the inn attached to it is from the 16th century. Standing on its own grounds above the village, it lies at the foot of Coniston Old Man. Donald Campbell made this place his headquarters during his attempt on the world water-speed record. Each of the 11 bedrooms is decorated with style, and two of them contain four-posters. Each unit also has a private bath, phone, color TV, and hot beverage facilities. B&B costs from £25 ($41.25) to £30 ($49.50) per person daily. A four-course dinner is offered for £15.50 ($25.60), including coffee and VAT. Fresh local produce is used whenever possible in the candlelit restaurant. Log fires take the chill off a winter evening, and guests relax informally in the lounge.

11. Keswick

Lying 22 miles north of Windermere and 294 miles from London, Keswick opens onto Derwentwater, one of the loveliest lakes in the district. Robert Southey, poet laureate, lived for four decades at Greta Hall, and was buried at Crosthwaite Church. Coleridge lived here too, depending on Southey for financial aid. Sir Hugh Walpole, the novelist, in a different era also resided near Keswick.

Keswick is the natural geographical starting point for car tours and walks of exploration in the northern Lake District, including the John Peel country to the north of Skiddaw (quiet and little known), Borrowdale, Buttermere, and Crummock Water, as well as Bassenthwaite, Thirlmere, and Ullswater.

WHERE TO STAY

Brundholme Country House, Brundholme Road, Keswick, Cumbria CA12 4NL (tel. 07687/74495), is your best choice. Coleridge wrote that this Regency villa (restored and opened as a hotel in 1988) was "in a delicious situation." He was referring to the views over Keswick to the enveloping hills. The owner, Ian Charlton, is also the chef de cuisine, aided by his wife, Lynn, and a well-chosen staff, perhaps one of the most helpful in the area. Wordsworth was also known to visit this house above the River Greta. The small hotel offers 11 well-furnished bedrooms, each with private bath or shower, phone, and TV. Rates range from £35 ($57.75) to £55 ($90.75) per person nightly for B&B. Many of the bedrooms are quite large, but all are comfortable.

This country-house hotel is mainly known for its French and English cuisine, using, when available, local produce such as char (a succulent fish found in Lake Windermere) or trout from Borrowdale. The local game from Cumberland is reputedly the best in England. Try such specialties as homemade soups, jugged hare, and Cumberland ham. Meals are served daily from 12:15 to 1:30pm and 7:30 to 8:30pm. A set lunch (very good value) is offered at £9.50 ($15.70) to £13.45 ($22.20), with a table d'hôte dinner priced from £15 ($24.75) to £19 ($31.35). Reservations are important. The hotel also has a garden.

A tranquil retreat is **Grange Country House,** Manor Brow, Ambleside Road, Keswick, Cumbria CA12 4BA (tel. 07687/72500). Set in its own gardens, it stands on a hilltop where it receives guests in every month but December and January. The hotel has 11 attractively furnished and well-kept bedrooms, each with private bath or shower, phone, and TV. Charges are from £26 ($42.90) per person nightly for B&B. This charming hotel dates from the 1800s, and guests are welcomed in chilly weather by log fires. Many of its rooms open onto beautiful views of the lakeland hills. The hotel, directed by Jane and Duncan Miller, also offers a first-rate cuisine. Guests can dine here for £13.50 ($22.30) in the evening. The house is furnished in part with antiques.

The Keswick, Station Road, Keswick, Cumbria CA12 4NQ (tel. 07687/72020), set in its own 4½ acres of landscaped gardens, stands near public parks in a residential district of town, about a 5-minute walk from the center. Its rhythmical bay windows and its somber stone walls evoke the very essence of a Victorian hotel. Inside, tall ceilings, a collection of blue willow porcelain, and antique reminders of a grander age lie in secluded crannies and on the landings of stairwells. The 64-room hotel contains a well-upholstered collection of high-ceilinged bedrooms with private baths or showers, color TVs, radios, phones, and welcoming trays. Singles cost from £65 ($107.25) daily, and doubles or twins go for £87 ($143.55). Many of the bedrooms are flooded with sunlight from bay windows that encompass views of the manicured grounds. Families are especially welcomed. The restaurant, also opening onto views, serves both English and international dishes.

Skiddaw Hotel, Main Street, Keswick, Cumbria CA12 5BN (tel. 07687/72071), has an impressive face and entrance marquee built right onto the sidewalk in the heart of Keswick. The owners have refurbished the interior, retaining the best features in combination with modern facilities. The 40 bedrooms are compact and eye-catching, with baths, phones, color TVs, and hot beverage facilities. They rent for £22 ($36.30) daily in a single, £38 ($62.70) in a double. Guests gather in the lounge or the popular cocktail bar with an art nouveau ambience. Meals feature well-prepared English cuisine, available à la carte all day. In addition, a chef's special, such as Lancashire hot pot, is offered for lunch. Dinner costs from £8 ($13.20) to £14 ($23.10). There is a wide selection of wines.

12. Borrowdale

If you head south from Keswick for 3½ miles along the B5289, you come to one of the most charming spots in the Lake District. This beautiful lakeland valley begins near Great Gable at a height of 2,949 feet, opening out to enfold Derwentwater. Traditionally, it has been a center of rambling and rock climbing. It also contains one of the best-known hotels in the Lake District (see below).

WHERE TO STAY AND DINE

Since 1987, the Stakis hotel chain has run the **Stakis Lodore Swiss Hotel,** Borrowdale, Keswick, Cumbria CA12 5UX (tel. 059684/285), overlooking Derwentwater. With its spike-capped mansard tower, symmetrical gables, and balcony-embellished stone facade, it looks a lot like a hotel you might find in the foothills of Lake Geneva. When it was constructed in the 19th century, its owners were Swiss. The old tradition of good rooms, good food, and service continues today. The hotel sits amid fields where cows graze. The interior has been modernized, and each of the 70 well-furnished bedrooms contains direct-dial phone, hairdryer, private bath, mini-bar, radio, color TV with in-house video, and coffee makers. Half-board rates range from £45 ($74.25) to £70 ($115.50) daily in a single and £85 ($140.25) to £135 ($222.75) in a double. The food is exceptional for the area, with a set dinner costing from £20 ($33). Dishes include roast topside of English beef with Yorkshire pudding, Morecambe Bay shrimp, and plaice sautéed in butter. Call for a reservation, especially at dinner. Food is served from 12:30 to 2pm and 7:30 to 9:30pm daily. Facilities include an indoor and outdoor swimming pool, a solarium, a beauty salon, and a garden. The hotel closes in January and February.

Borrowdale Hotel, Borrowdale, Keswick, Cumbria CA12 5UY (tel. 059684/224), standing on B5289, is a lakeland stone building, circa 1866, with log fires welcoming you when the weather is not kind. It was originally a coaching inn. Its 34 rooms are comfortable, many opening onto views. All have private baths or showers, toilets, color TVs, radios, intercoms, phones, baby-listening units, and hairdryers. Some traditional four-poster beds are available. The tariff for half board, inclusive of VAT, is £38 ($62.70) to £50 ($82.50) daily in a single, £75 ($123.75) to £100 ($165) in a double. The main attraction of the hotel is its restaurant. A traditional English lunch on Sun. costs from £9 ($14.85). During the rest of the week, bar lunches with a choice of 25 main courses cost in the £6 ($9.90) range. The seven-course dinner, consisting of appetizer, main, and dessert courses, each having a choice of at least six different dishes, starts at £16 ($26.40). Cuisine from all parts of the globe is offered, and the menu is changed daily. If you wish to have the daily roast, the chef will carve it at your table from a silver trolley.

13. Bassenthwaite

With its fine stretch of water in the shadow of the 3,053-foot Skiddaw, Bassenthwaite makes a good center for exploring the western Lake District. The location is 300 miles from London, 7 miles from Keswick.

WHERE TO STAY AND DINE

Rich in history, the **Armathwaite Hall Hotel,** Bassenthwaite, Cumbria CA12 4RE (tel. 059681/551), 1½ miles west on the B5291, was originally built in the 1300s as a house for Benedictine nuns. During the Middle Ages it was plundered frequently, leaving the sisters wretchedly poor. By the 17th century a series of wealthy landowners had completed the severe Gothic design of its stately facade, and in 1844 an architecturally compatible series of wings were added. In the 1930s it was converted into a hotel, and Sir Hugh Walpole, who once stayed here, found it "a house of perfect and irresistible charm." Ringed with almost 140 acres of woodland, some of it bordering the lake, the place offers a magnificent entrance hall filled with hunting trophies and sheathed with expensive paneling. There's also a whimsically modern cocktail lounge whose veneer-clad, Gay '90s bar contrasts with one of the most neo-baroque fireplaces in the district. A Victorian billiard room is lined with old engravings, and a first-class restaurant offers a view of the lake. An indoor swimming pool is ringed with stone walls and sheltered from the rain with a roof of wooden trusses. Each of the handsomely furnished bedrooms, 42 in all, contains private bath, color TV, radio, and phone. Singles range from £50 ($82.50) to £90 ($148.50) daily, and doubles or twins go from £96 ($158.40) to £170 ($280.50), with breakfast included.

14. Ullswater

A 7-mile sheet of water, stretching from Pooley Bridge to Patterdale, Ullswater is the second-largest lake in the district. Incidentally, it was on the shores of Ullswater that Wordsworth saw his "host of golden daffodils." The market town of Penrith lies 7 miles to the east and London is 296 miles away. While housed in the area, it is easy to explore several places of archeological interest, such as Hadrian's Wall, east of Carlisle, or Long Meg stone circle near Penrith.

WHERE TO STAY AND DINE

A *Relais & Chateaux* for the past quarter of a century, **Sharrow Bay Country House Hotel,** Howtown, Lake Ullswater, near Penrith, Cumbria CA10 2LZ (tel. 08536/301), is the second oldest member of that prestigious group in Britain. It is an unusual Victorian house that was a private home until it was purchased by Francis Coulson in 1949. Realizing its potential, he began restoration work on the structure, with its low angled roof and wide eaves, sleeping on the floor while the work was in progress. Three years later he was joined by Brian Sack, and together they turned Sharrow into one of England's finest eating places. This was also the first Country House Hotel to be created in Great Britain. The hotel offers 30 antique-filled bedrooms, 18 in the gatehouse and cottages. Of these, eight units in the main house and all in the cottages have private baths. Some accommodations, as well as the drawing room, open onto views of the lakes, trees, or Martindale Fells. Each of the individually decorated bedrooms has a name rather than a number and comes with a phone and TV. The daily terms range from £84 ($138.60) to £110 ($181.50) per person daily for room, dinner, a full English breakfast, service, and VAT.

The six-course £32.50 ($53.65) set menu contains a formidable list of choices. I recently counted 28 appetizers, including the chef's specialty, mousseline of fresh salmon with hollandaise sauce. The carefully chosen main courses seemed designed to make the best of home-grown food items, including roast Lancashire guinea fowl, a roast stuffed shoulder of young English lamb, or even a Cumberland ham from a cold-table selection. The dessert selections are among the best you'll find in northwest England, including a fresh-strawberry, hazelnut, and brandy cream roulade. A feature as well is the Sharrow homemade cream ices, including prune and armagnac. Brian Sack is the dining room host, with an efficient staff. If you're motoring through the area, I suggest you call ahead and make a reservation for the £20.50 ($33.85) set luncheon. Meals are served from 1 to 1:45pm and 8 to 8:45pm daily. Either for a meal or a room, you should write or telephone in advance. Closed December, January, and February.

---

15. Brampton

One of the best centers for the Lake District is at Brampton, which is only 4 miles from the Roman Wall and 11 miles from the M6 Motorway and Carlisle. London lies 317 miles away.

WHERE TO STAY AND DINE

On the A689 road, the **Farlam Hall Hotel,** Brampton, Cumbria CA8 2NG (tel. 06956/234), 2¾ miles south of Brampton, is a good base for visiting the Roman Wall, the Lake District, and the Yorkshire Dales. A *Relais & Chateaux,* Farlam Hall is listed as a building of architectural and historic interest. It was just a farmhouse when it was erected in the 17th century, but in 1826 it changed hands and became a noted Border manor house. It stands in 4 acres of grounds, with some fine old trees, a stream, and a small lake. John Wesley is said to have preached in the house, and George Stephenson, inventor of the steam railroad engine, stayed here. The hotel is run by the Quinion and Stevenson families, who have set high standards of service and cuisine. Barry, an advanced Cordon Bleu chef, is in charge of the kitchens, offering such dishes as roast Lancashire duckling with honey, almond, and raisin sauce. All ingredients are freshly brought in from the nearby coast or the local farms. Dinner is graced by the Quinion women, who serve the tables in full evening dress. Dinner in the formal dining room, with white linen cloths and napkins and silver table service, is at 8pm, costing £22 ($36.30). Men are expected to wear jackets and ties. Accommodations consist of 13 bedrooms, all doubles and twins, with private baths or showers, TVs, direct-dial phones, and hairdryers. Furnishings are antique, and everything is comfortable. There are views of the gardens and the lake. An overnight stay, including an English breakfast, dinner, and VAT, costs from £70 ($115.50) to £80 ($132) daily in a single, £120 ($198) to £160 ($264) in a double.

XVII

YORKSHIRE AND NORTHUMBRIA

1. YORK

2. NORTH YORKSHIRE

3. WEST YORKSHIRE

4. DURHAM

5. TYNE AND WEAR

6. NORTHUMBERLAND

For the connoisseur, the northeast of England is rich in attractions. **Yorkshire,** known to readers of *Wuthering Heights* and the works of James Herriot (*All Creatures Great and Small*), embraces both the moors of North Yorkshire and the Dales. With the radical changing of the old county boundaries, the shires are now divided into North Yorkshire (the most interesting from the tourist point of view), West Yorkshire, South Yorkshire, and Humberside.

Away from the cities and towns the beauty of Yorkshire is wild and remote. It's characterized by limestone crags, caverns along the Pennines, mountainous uplands, rolling hills, the chalkland wolds, moorlands, broad vales, lazy rivers, and tumbling streams. Yorkshire has some 100 miles of shoreline, with rocky headlands, cliffs, sandy bays, sheltered coves, fishing villages, bird sanctuaries, and yachting havens.

Across this vast region came the Romans, the Anglo-Saxons, the Vikings, medieval religious orders, and England's kings, lords of the manor, craftspeople, hill farmers, and wool makers—all leaving their mark. You can still see Roman roads and pavements, great abbeys and battle-scarred castles, stately homes, open-air museums, and craft centers, along with parish churches, old villages, and cathedrals.

Northumbria is made up of the counties of Northumberland, Cleveland, and Durham. Tyne and Wear is one of the more recently created counties, with Newcastle upon Tyne as its center.

The Saxons who came to northern England centuries ago carved out this kingdom, which at the time stretched from the Firth of Forth in Scotland to the banks of the Humber in Yorkshire. Again, this slice of England has more than its share of industrial towns, but vast tracts of that ancient kingdom remain natural and unspoiled.

The whole area evokes ancient battles and bloody border raids. Roman relics, border castles, Saxon churches, and monastic ruins abound in Northumbria, none more notable than Hadrian's Wall, one of the wonders of the Western world. The finest stretch of the wall lies within the Northumberland National Park between the stony North Tyne River and the county boundary at Gilsland.

1. York

Few cities in England are as rich in history as York. It is still encircled by its 13th-and 14th-century city walls—about 2½ miles long—with four gates. One of these, Micklegate, once grimly greeted visitors coming up from the south with the heads of traitors. To this day, you can walk on the footpath of the walls of the Middle Ages.

The crowning achievement of York is its minster, or cathedral, which makes the city an ecclesiastical center topped only by Canterbury. In spite of this, York is one of the most overlooked cities on the cathedral circuit. Perhaps foreign visitors are intimidated by the feeling that the great city of northeastern England is too far north. Actually, it lies about 195 miles north of London on the Ouse River, and can easily be tied in with a motor trip to Edinburgh. Or after visiting Cambridge, a motorist can make a swing through a too-often-neglected cathedral circuit: Ely, Lincoln, then York.

There was a Roman York (Hadrian came this way), then a Saxon York, a Danish York, a Norman York (William the Conqueror slept here), a medieval York, a Georgian York, a Victorian York (the center of a flourishing rail business), and certainly now a 20th-century York. A generous amount of 18th-century York remains, including Richard Boyle's restored Assembly Rooms.

WHAT TO SEE AND DO

The best way to see York is to go to the **tourist information center,** DeGrey Rooms, Exhibition Square (tel. 0904/621756) at 10:15am and 2:15pm daily from April to the end of October, where you'll be met by a volunteer guide who will take you on a 1½-hour walking tour of the city, revealing its history and lore through numerous intriguing stories. There is no charge. Additional tours are made at 7pm daily during June, July, and August. From November to March, there is a daily walking tour at 10:15am.

At some point in your exploration, you may want to visit **the Shambles,** once the meat-butchering center of York, dating back before the Norman Conquest. But this messy business has given way, and the ancient street survives. It is filled with jewelry stores, cafés, and buildings that huddle so closely together you can practically stand in the middle of the pavement, arms outstretched, and touch the houses on both sides of the street.

Recently, special interest has been focused on discoveries of the Viking era, from 867 to 1066, when the city was known as Jorvik, the Viking capital and a major Scandinavian trade center (see below). Incidentally, the suffix "gate" used for streets and sites in York is from the Scandinavian word for "street," a holdover from that Vikings era.

York Minster

One of the great cathedrals of the world, York Minster traces its origins back to the early 17th century. The present building, however, dates from the 13th century. Like the minster at Lincoln, York Cathedral is characterized by three towers, all built in the 15th century. The central tower is lantern shaped, in the Perpendicular style. Its towers stand at the converging point of several streets: the High, Duncombe Place, Minster Yard, and Petergate.

Perhaps the distinguishing characteristic of the cathedral is its medley of stained glass from the Middle Ages—in glorious blues, ruby reds, forest greens, and honey ambers. See in particular the large east window, the work of a 15th-century Coventry glass painter. In the north transept is an architectural gem of the mid-13th century, the "Five Sisters," with its lancets. The choir screen, from the late 15th century, has an impressive line-up—everybody from William the Conqueror to the overthrown Henry VI.

The chapter house is open from 10am to 5pm Mon. to Sat., 1 to 5pm Sun., costing adults 50p (85¢) and children 20p (35¢). The shop is open from 9am to

5pm Mon. to Sat., 1 to 4pm Sun. The refurbished foundations is open from 10am to dusk Mon. to Sat., 1pm to dusk Sun., costing £1.40 ($2.30) for adults, 60p ($1) for children. The crypt is open from 10am to 5pm Mon. to Sat., 1 to 5pm Sun. Adults pay 50p (85¢) for admission and children 20p (35¢). At a reception desk near the entrance to the minster, parties can be put in touch with a guide, if one is available, for a conducted tour. Gifts toward the maintenance of the minster are requested. For information, telephone 0904/624426.

From the top of the central tower on a clear day, there are unrivaled views of York and the Vale of York. It is a steep climb up a stone spiral staircase and not recommended for the very elderly, very young, or anyone with a heart condition or breathing difficulties. In winter, the tower is open only on Saturday and Sunday, providing the weather is suitable. A climb costs adults £1 ($1.65), and children pay 50p (85¢).

The Treasurer's House

In the minster yard, the Treasurer's House (tel. 0904/624247) stands on a site where there's been a building since Roman times. The main part of the house was rebuilt in 1620 as the official residence of the treasurer of York Minster, and was lived in as a private home until 1930. It has a magnificent series of rooms with fine furniture, glass, and china of the 17th and 18th centuries. An audio-visual program describes the work of the medieval treasurers and some of the personalities with which this York house is associated. The house has an attractive small garden. It is open from April until the end of October daily from 10:30am to 5pm (last entry at 4:30pm). Admission is £2 ($3.30) for adults, £1 ($1.65) for children. On some evenings in summer, the house is open from 7:30 to 9:30pm when you can enjoy coffee by candlelight in the great hall. An attractive shop and licensed restaurant serving Yorkshire specialties are open the same hours as the house.

York Castle Museum

On the site of York's castle, the York Castle Museum, Eye of York, off Tower Street (tel. 0904/653611), is one of the finest folk museums in the country. Its unique feature is a re-creation of a Victorian cobbled street, "Kirkgate," named for the museum's founder, Dr. John Kirk. He acquired his large collection while visiting his patients in rural Yorkshire at the beginning of this century. The period rooms range from a neoclassical Georgian dining room through an overstuffed and heavily adorned Victorian parlor, to the 1953 sitting room with a brand-new television set purchased to watch the coronation of Elizabeth II. In the Debtors' Prison, former prison cells display craft workshops. There is also a superb collection of arms and armor, and the Costume Gallery, where displays are changed regularly to reflect the variety of the collection. Half Moon Court is an Edwardian street, with a gypsy caravan and a pub (sorry, the bar's closed!). During the summer, you can visit a watermill on the bank of the River Foss.

The museum is open April to October from 9:30am to 6:30pm Mon. to Sat. (from 10am on Sun.). From November to March, hours are 9:30am to 5pm Mon. to Sat. (from 10am on Sun.). Last admission is an hour before closing, and it is recommended that you allow at least 2 hours for a visit to this museum. Admission is £3 ($4.95) for adults, £1.50 ($2.50) for children.

National Railway Museum

The first national museum to be built away from London, the National Railway Museum, Leeman Road (tel. 0904/621261), has attracted millions of visitors since it opened in 1975. Adapted from an original steam locomotive depot, the museum gives visitors a chance to look under and inside steam locomotives or see how Queen Victoria traveled in luxury. In addition, there's a full-size collection of railway memorabilia, including an early 19th-century clock and penny machines for purchasing tickets on the railway platform. On display are more than 20 full-size locomotives. One, the *Agenoria*, dates from 1829 and is a contemporary of Stephenson's well-known *Rocket*. It's almost identical to the first American locomotive, the *Stourbridge*

Lion, sent to the United States from England in 1828. Items on exhibition change from time to time, but there is always a fine selection of the beautifully colored, British steam locomotives on display. *Mallard,* the fastest steam locomotive in the world, is in the museum when it's not at work on the railroad. Of several royal coaches, the most interesting is the century-old Royal Saloon, in which Queen Victoria rode. It's like a small hotel, with polished wood, silk, brocade, and silver accessories.

The museum can be visited from 10am to 6pm Mon. to Sat., 11am to 6pm Sun.; closed some public holidays. Admission is £3 ($4.95) for adults, £1.50 ($2.50) for children.

Jorvik Viking Centre

At Coppergate (tel. 0904/643211) is the Viking city discovered many feet below the present ground level. It was reconstructed exactly as it stood in A.D. 948. In a "time car," you can travel back through the ages to 1067 when Normans sacked the city, and then ride slowly through the street market peopled by faithfully modeled Vikings. You can go through a house where a family lived and down to the river to see the ship chandlers at work and a Norwegian cargo ship unloading. At the end of the ride, you pass the Finds Hut where thousands of artifacts are displayed. Departures on the time train are at regular intervals from 9am to 7pm daily in summer (until 5:30pm in winter). Admission is £3 ($4.95) for adults, £1.50 ($2.50) for children.

Theatre Royal

Finally, Theatre Royal, St. Leonard's Place (tel. 0904/623568), is an old traditional theater building with modern additions to house the box office, bars, and restaurant. It is worth inquiring about the current production as the Royal Shakespeare Company includes York in its tours, the Arts Council presents dance, drama, and opera, and visiting celebrities appear in classics. There is also an excellent resident repertory company.

Seats go from £4 ($6.60) in the gallery to £10 ($16.50) in the dress circle.

WHERE TO STAY

Expensive Hotels

Middlethorpe Hall Hotel, Bishopthorpe Road, York, North Yorkshire YO2 1QB (tel. 0904/641241), on the outskirts of York near the race course, is set in 26 acres of park reached along the A19 road. Built in 1699, the stately, red-brick, William and Mary country house had fallen into disrepair during a period of use as a nightclub before it was purchased by Historic House Hotels and beautifully restored, both inside and out. Fresh flowers are used profusely, with lots of antiques providing the ambience of a manor house of other days nicely blended with modern amenities. As befits such a house, there is an elegant drawing room, plus a library. The hotel has 30 bedrooms, including three suites, each of which is done in its own decor and style. All the rooms have up-to-date bathrooms, phones, and TVs. Rooms are divided between the main house and restored outbuildings. Singles rent from £80 ($132) daily and standard twins and doubles for £108 ($178.20) to £120 ($198). Guests find in their room such niceties as homemade cookies and bottles of Malvern water, as well as bathrobes. Meals are served in two restaurants, one oak-paneled and one a grill room. A choice of either international or English traditional meals is offered, a table d'hôte dinner costing £25.90 ($42.75).

Bilbrough Manor, Bilbrough, York, North Yorkshire YO2 3PH (tel. 0937/834002), is one of the loveliest places to stay—or to dine—in the environs of York. The location is 4 miles southwest of York. The imposing neo-Gothic walls and multiple chimneys that rise today were built in 1901 as a replacement for a dilapidated manor house. However, its foundations go back to the 13th century. The hotel sits near the village church.

The public rooms are sumptuous with paneling and baronial fireplaces, along with deep chintz-covered sofas. Each of the 12 individually furnished bedrooms is elegant and unique, with many thoughtful accessories. These include private bath or shower, color TV, radio, hairdryer, and trouser press. Singles rent for £85 ($140.25) daily, and twins or doubles run £135 ($222.75), including an English breakfast and VAT. Even if you don't reside here, you might want to dine, sampling superb viands the chef cooks in the modern French and British tradition, and food is served in a historic paneled dining room. Service is on Wedgwood, and the menu changes frequently, but always fresh quality ingredients are used. A certain artistry is reflected both in the food preparation and in the presentation of dishes. Meals are served from noon to 1:45pm and 7 to 9:30pm, costing from £35 ($57.75) per person. Table d'hôte luncheons go for £13 ($21.45). Always call for a reservation.

Viking Hotel, North Street, York, North Yorkshire YO1 1JF (tel. 0904/659822), is a 187-bedroom, modern hotel within the ancient city walls, overlooking the River Ouse, with the attractions of York only a few minutes' walk away. The bedrooms, many with views toward the minster, have private baths, color TVs, direct-dial phones, trouser presses, hairdryers, and hot beverage facilities. A single room costs from £65 ($107.25) daily, while £86 ($141.90) will buy a double or twin unit, inclusive of an English breakfast, VAT, and service. The hotel's two restaurants offer a variety of dining. The Regatta is for à la carte meals, the Carving Room for traditional roasts and à la carte choices. Each eating place has a bar and offers a welcoming atmosphere.

The Judges Lodging, 9 Lendal, York, North Yorkshire YO1 2AQ (tel. 0904/638733). The earliest historical fact about this charming house is that it was the home of a certain Dr. Wintringham in 1710. At the beginning of the 19th century it is listed as having been a judges' lodging, used when they traveled north from the London Inns of Justice. Drive around the sweeping drive, then up the broad stone steps to the stout front door. You will be greeted by the butler who will register your name and then lead you up a circular wooden staircase, the only one of its type in the United Kingdom, to one of the 13 bedrooms. All bedrooms have private baths or showers, phones, and TVs. Some have four-poster beds. If you want to spoil yourself, you can book the large Prince Albert suite, a twin-bedded room with three large windows overlooking the minster. Prince Albert actually slept in the room once. Hand-embroidered sheets and French embroidered linen in the bathrooms are an additional elegant touch. Each room has a different decor and is named accordingly. One is known as the Queen Mother Room, and in fact it is with her blessing that the coffee cups you will use at dinner come from Clarence House. Singles cost from £45 ($74.25) daily, while doubles and twins are priced at £85 ($140.25). Rates include VAT and a full English breakfast.

There are two dining rooms, where candles flicker and the carefully trained French staff will attend to your every need. Dinner will cost from £18 ($29.70). All meat, fish, and vegetables are brought in fresh. Down in the old cellars where they found bits of Roman pottery, antique pieces of glass, and other relics of the house's varied past, there is a cocktail bar, open to the public.

Moderately Priced Hotels

Mount Royale Hotel, 119 The Mount, York, North Yorkshire YO2 2DA (tel. 0904/628856), is excellent for the money, and the food is good too. The Mount Royale is only minutes from the city center. Built in 1833, it is carefully furnished with some antiques blended with modern pieces. The owners took over the house next door, increasing their bedroom capacity to 20 units, each with bath, phone, and TV, costing from £69 ($113.85) daily in a single, £88 ($145.20) in a double or twin, including VAT and a large breakfast. The hotel has a swimming pool. The menu consists of roast joints with interesting accompaniments. The extensive set menu, costing £25 ($41.25), carries supplements for such items as fresh out-of-season asparagus or strawberries. The dining room opens onto an attractive garden. Justifiably popular with locals, the restaurant requires advance reservations.

Dean Court Hotel, Duncombe Place, York, North Yorkshire YO1 2EF (tel.

0904/625082), is an ancient building lying right beneath the towers of the minster. All 41 rooms have bathrooms or showers, phones, radios, and color TVs. The owner has done a lot to bring the facilities up to standards expected today. Singles rent for £50 ($82.50) to £55 ($90.75) daily for B&B, and doubles are charged £85 ($140.25) to £110 ($181.50). Snacks are served in a coffee lounge from 10am to 8pm (to 10pm in summer).

Budget Hotels

Beechwood Close Hotel, 19 Shipton Rd., York, North Yorkshire YO3 6RE (tel. 0904/658378). On the A19, north of the city, Beechwood is a large house surrounded by trees, a garden with a putting green, and free parking space. Mr. and Mrs. Spink and Mr. and Mrs. Blythe run a small hotel with 14 bedrooms, all with private baths, central heating, TVs, phones, and hot beverage facilities. The charge for a bed and a good Yorkshire breakfast is from £27 ($44.55) per person daily, including VAT. Good dinners or bar meals are served in the dining room overlooking the garden. The hotel is a 15-minute walk to the minster, either by road or along the river. However, a bus stop is close by.

Heworth Court, 76-78 Heworth Green, York, North Yorkshire YO3 7TQ (tel. 0904/425156), is a three-story, red-brick house that provides one of the best of the reasonably priced accommodations of York. Only 16 rooms are rented by its owner, but they are agreeably furnished, each with private bath or shower, phone, and TV. Charges are from £35 ($57.57) daily in a single, rising to £55 ($90.75) in a double. The location is on the east side of the city on the A1036. Some of the bedrooms open onto a courtyard. The hotel also offers a commendable cuisine, and you can order dinner until 9:30pm.

Abbots Mews Hotel, 6 Marygate Lane, Bootham, York, North Yorkshire YO3 7DE (tel. 0904/634866), was converted from a series of 1800s coach driver's cottages. The setting, as the name suggests, is in a mews. What at one time had been a Victorian coach house with stables is now a highly recommendable hotel and restaurant, one of the best of the reasonably priced ones in York. The hotel is also well located, lying close to the historic district. Mr. and Mrs. Dearnley offer 47 bedrooms, each with private bath or shower and such thoughtful extras as phone and TV. All year, guests are received and charged £35 ($57.75) daily in a single, rising to £54 ($89.10) to £66 ($108.90) in a double with an English breakfast. The food served here is also recommendable, and you can order dinner until 9:30pm.

Hudson's Hotel, 60 Bootham, York, North Yorkshire YO3 7BZ (tel. 0904/621267), just minutes' walking distance from the minster, is a 28-bedroom hotel offering personal service. The owner converted two Victorian houses into the main hotel building in 1981 and later added an extension in the Victorian style. All accommodations have private baths, color TVs, direct-dial phones, and tea and coffee makers. B&B costs from £35 ($57.75) to £40 ($66). Hudson's has its own large car park.

Cottage Hotel, 3 Clifton Green, York, North Yorkshire YO3 6LH (tel. 0904/643711), comprises two Victorian houses that have been refurbished and extended to provide accommodations overlooking the village green of Clifton, about 10 minutes' walk from York Minster. The hotel has 20 handsome bedrooms, each with a private bath, color TV, direct-dial phone, and hot beverage facilities. Singles rent for £35 ($57.75) daily, with doubles or twins costing £55 ($90.75) and family rooms from £60 ($99). In the restaurant and bar are the 400-year-old timber beams rescued from Micklegate. Hand-pulled real ale is among the beverages served in the bar, to the accompaniment of firelight in cool weather. The hotel provides parking for its guests.

WHERE TO DINE

19 Grape Lane, 19 Grape Lane (tel. 0904/636366), in the heart of York, is spread across two floors. With such a name, you expect a very British restaurant, but actually the cooking is French inspired, including such dishes as roast duck in a black cherry sauce, pheasant Normande, or bouillabaisse. The menus are wisely limited, so that every dish will be fresh. The wine list is ever growing, and service is thoughtful and considerate. It is open from 12:30 to 1:45pm and 7:30 to 10:30pm Tue. to Sat., serving a set lunch for £9.50 ($15.70) and a table d'hôte dinner for £17.50 ($28.90). A la carte meals average £18 ($29.70) and beyond. The location is on a cobbled lane off Petergate.

McCoy's at York, 17 Skeldergate (tel. 0904/612191), continues the restaurant renaissance that is occurring in a city long known for "having only bad places to eat." This bistro arrives as a welcome change. It is casual and informal, but very professional nonetheless. Run by the McCoy brothers, this restaurant occupies converted premises in a river-bordering, former warehouse. Cooking is of a very high standard, and there's a wide medley of dishes from which to choose, including the famous McCoy's sausage with onion sauce and Yorkshire pudding. The fish is especially good, including an unusually generous portion of lemon sole. You might also try tarragon-flavored halibut in a red pepper sauce. Desserts usually are praised, including a sticky toffee pudding or "jam roly-poly." The wine list is not long but well chosen, and a house wine is featured. Service is daily from noon to 2:15pm and 7 to 10:30pm, with meals costing from £15 ($24.75). You're served in air-conditioned comfort, and vegetarians and families with children (special helpings for them) are welcomed.

Kites, 13 Grape Lane (tel. 0904/641750), lies only about a five-minute walk from the minster, in the heart of York, on a small street near Stonegate. To reach it, walk up a narrow staircase to the second floor. This is a simple York bistro where the food is good and the atmosphere and service unpretentious. It has many devotees, attracted to its eclectic brand of cookery that is international in scope. For example, one recipe might have been a dish served in the Middle Ages in England (perhaps with adaptations) and another one from Thailand. The baked trout in tahini might have come from Beirut in the old days, or else the filet of beef flavored with tarragon from France. Fondues, fresh salads, and herbs from the owner's garden are part of the features here. A children's menu is provided, as are vegetarian meals. It is open daily from noon to 2pm and 6:30 to 10:30pm, to 11pm Sat.; closed Sun. Call for a table.

Tony's Greek Restaurant, 39 Tanner Row (tel. 0904/659622), is a family-run restaurant. Tony Sideras, assisted by his wife, June, attends to the restaurant and the comfort and satisfaction of guests. His daughter, Maria, cooks the authentic and tasty Greek dishes. An à la carte menu is offered, a three-course meal with wine costing around £13.50 ($22.30) to £15.50 ($25.60), with VAT included. Among the appetizers are halloumi (goat's-milk cheese gently fried), and fresh mushrooms cooked in red wine, with coriander. Main dishes include herb-flavored rack of lamb, moussaka (layers of eggplant, zucchini, and potato, with a minced beef sauce, topped with a béchamel sauce), and a vegetarian dish. All selections are served with fresh vegetables cooked in herbs. The meal is rounded off by Greek pastries, Greek yogurt with honey, or a selection of sorbets. Also offered is a traditional meze, a complete meal consisting of 16 authentic Greek specialties served in four courses. The cost of this is £10.50 ($17.35) per person. The restaurant is open for dinner from 6:30 to 10:30pm Mon. to Thur., to 11pm on Fri. and Sat.; closed Sun. Reservations are advisable.

A YORK PUB CRAWL

Known for the best location of any pub in York, **Kings Arms,** King's Straithe (tel. 0904/659435), is a popular riverside pub. Right near the Ouse Bridge, the location is on the left bank of the river. This historic public house, one of charm, character, and intimacy, is filled with beamed ceilings, brick walls, and a mellow atmosphere. A board records flood levels at the Ouse. In summer, tables are placed outside along the river. Your hosts serve a full range of Samuel Smith's draft and bottled beers, traditionally brewed in Tadcaster, only 10 miles from York. Bar meals cost from £4 ($6.60). You can order burgers, homemade curries, or steak and kidney pie. The pub is open from 11am to 11pm Mon. to Sat., noon to 3pm and 7 to 10:30pm Sun.

The Black Swan, Peaseholme Green (tel. 0904/626236), is a fine timbered frame house, the home of the lord mayor of York in 1417. The mother of General James Wolfe of Québec also lived here. One of the oldest inns in the city, it offers pub meals, which can be enjoyed in front of a log fire in a brick inglenook. Food consists of sandwiches, homemade soups, and Yorkshire puddings filled with beef stew. Meals cost from £4 ($6.60). The pub is open daily from 11am to 11pm, noon to 3pm and 7 to 10:30pm Sun. You can also stay here, as the pub rents three bedrooms, each with private bath or shower, for £17.50 ($28.90) per person daily.

Ye Olde Starre Inne, Stonegate (tel. 0904/623063), lies on a pedestrian street in the heart of Old York. It is York's oldest licensed pub, dating back to 1644. Some inn (of one kind or another) might have stood on this spot since 900 A.D. In a pub said to be haunted by an old lady, a little girl, and a cat, you enter into an atmosphere of cast-iron tables, an open fireplace, oak Victorian settles, and time-blackened beams. Of course, you can come here to drink, but many visitors also eat here, as the pub offers a wide array of homemade food. These might include beef in beer, lamb in cider, or a Lancashire hotpot, even roast beef and Yorkshire pudding. You can also enjoy a salad bar, with both cheese, fish, and meat salads. Meals cost from £6 ($9.90). Everything might be washed down with hand-pulled ale. In fair weather, guests fill the tables in a courtyard. Hours are from 11am to 11pm Mon. to Sat., from 7 to 10:30pm Sun.

A SIDE TRIP TO CASTLE HOWARD

In its dramatic setting of lakes, fountains, and extensive gardens, Castle Howard at Malton in North Yorkshire (tel. 065384/333), the 18th-century palace designed by Sir John Vanbrugh, is undoubtedly the finest private residence in Yorkshire. Principal location for the TV series "Brideshead Revisited," this was the first major achievement of the architect who later created the lavish Blenheim Palace near Oxford. The Yorkshire palace was begun in 1699 for the third earl of Carlisle, Charles Howard, whose descendants still call the place home. The striking facade is topped by a painted and gilded dome, reaching more than 80 feet into the air. The interior boasts a 192-foot "long gallery," as well as a chapel with magnificent stained-glass windows by the 19th-century artist Sir Edward Burne-Jones. Besides the collections of antique furniture, porcelains, and sculpture, the castle contains a number of important paintings, including a portrait of Henry VIII by Holbein, and works by Rubens, Reynolds, and Gainsborough.

The seemingly endless grounds around the palace also offer the visitor some memorable sights, including the domed Temple of the Four Winds, by Vanbrugh, and the richly designed family mausoleum by Hawksmoor. There are two rose gardens, one with old-fashioned roses, the other featuring modern creations. The stable court houses the Costume Galleries, the largest private collection of 18th- to 20th-century costumes in Britain. The authentically dressed mannequins are exhibited in period settings.

Castle Howard is open to the public daily from March 20 to October 31. The grounds are open from 10am; the cafeteria, house, and Costume Galleries from 11am. It all closes at 5pm, with last admission to the house and galleries at 4:30pm. Admission is £4.50 ($7.45) for adults, £2 ($3.30) for children. You can enjoy sandwiches, hot dishes, and good wines in the self-service cafeteria. The location is 15 miles northeast of York (3 miles off the A64; it's signposted). It lies 5 miles southwest of Malton off the A64, York-Scarborough road.

2. North Yorkshire

Yorkshire, known to readers of *Wuthering Heights* around the world, is now divided into three counties—West Yorkshire, South Yorkshire, and North Yorkshire. For those seeking legendary untamed scenery, I'd recommend a tour of North Yorkshire, which also takes in the just-previewed historic cathedral city of York.

North Yorkshire contains England's most varied landscape. Its history has been turbulent, often bloody, and many relics of its rich past are still standing, including ruined abbeys. Yorkshire is little known to the average North American visitor, but many an English traveler is familiar with its haunting moors, serene valleys, and windswept dales.

The hospitality of the people of Yorkshire is world renowned, and if a pudding that originated there doesn't accompany a slab of roast beef, the plate looks naked to the British. The people of Yorkshire, who speak an original twang often imitated in English cinema, are, in general, hard-working and industrious, perhaps a little contemptuous of the easy living of the south. But they are decidedly open to strangers, providing you speak to them first.

HARROGATE

If you head west from York for 20 miles, you reach Harrogate, North Yorkshire's second-largest town after York itself. In the 19th century Harrogate was a fashionable spa. Most of its town center is surrounded by a 200-acre lawn called "the Stray." Boutiques and antique shops—which Queen Mary used to frequent— make Harrogate a shopping center of excellence, particularly along Montpellier Parade. Harrogate is called England's floral resort, deserving such a reputation because of its gardens, including Harlow Car Gardens and Valley Gardens. The former spa has an abundance of guesthouses and hotels, including the expensive Swan where Agatha Christie hid out during her mysterious and still-unexplained disappearance in the 1920s. Harrogate is 211 miles from London.

Where to Stay

The Old Swan Hotel, Swan Road, Harrogate, North Yorkshire HG1 2SR (tel. 0423/500055), is the spot where the late mystery writer Agatha Christie suddenly surfaced after a mysterious 11-day disappearance that was the subject of the film *Agatha,* featuring Dustin Hoffman. One of the most famous hotels in northern England, The Old Swan offers comfort, good food, fine wines, and impeccable service. It has been modernized, yet retains the atmosphere of a country home. There are 137 bedrooms, including 10 suites, all with private baths and showers, color TVs, phones, and tea and coffee makers. The tariff for a twin-bedded room is £72 ($118.80) to £100 ($165) daily, £38 ($62.70) to £85 ($140.25) in a single, both rates including VAT. You may dine in the Wedgwood Room or in the à la carte restaurant, The Library, serving good dishes, including traditional British food, cooked and presented in a modern idiom.

Majestic Hotel, Ripon Road, Harrogate, North Yorkshire HG1 2HU (tel. 0423/568972). Encircled by gardens, this enormous, red-brick and stone, Victorian architectural monument dates from 1900. It stands on a hillside above the commercial center, yet is convenient to the pump rooms and royal baths. Behind its ornate facade it has been thoroughly modernized with upholstered comfort but with enough Victorian embellishments, such as lobby pillars, to make it interesting. The hotel offers 156 well-furnished bedrooms, each with private bath, color TV, radio, phone, and tea and coffee maker. With high ceilings and conservative furnishings, singles rent for £80 ($132) daily, and doubles or twins are priced at £100 ($165). The hotel also has a health center, a pool, squash courts, and an outdoor tennis court. The Regency Bar takes its theme from the Georgian era. Later, guests patronize the dining room, decorated in an art nouveau style.

Crown Hotel, Crown Place, Harrogate, North Yorkshire HG1 2RZ (tel. 0423/567755). When Lord Byron stayed here in 1806, the poem he composed, "Ode to a Beautiful Quaker," became feted all over England. During World War II, several of its floors served as the Air Ministry. But the history of the Crown goes far back before that, having been a coaching inn in the 18th century. Next to the historic pump rooms, the hotel today is an elaborate Georgian building crafted of gray stone and Corinthian columns set at the edge of a traffic circle. Popular for its conference facilities, the hotel also offers a stately collection of public rooms, including a high-ceilinged reception area. After guests have a drink in the Brontë Bar, they head for the Ripley Restaurant, which is a paneled dining room ringed with cove moldings. Each of the 116 conservatively modernized bedrooms contains private bath or shower, color TV, radio, phone, and coffee maker. Singles rent for £75 ($123.75) daily, and doubles or twins go for £92 ($151.80).

Grant's Hotel, 3-7 Swan Rd., Harrogate, North Yorkshire HG1 2SS (tel. 0423/560666), was created when five, stone-fronted, Victorian townhouses were joined together into one well-appointed unit. Until Pam and Peter Grant took it over, it had been considered an eyesore, a run-down tenement hotel. Today she dispenses hospitality and charm in equal doses. This is a professionally minded establishment, with a street-level bar and a whimsical basement restaurant named Chimney Pots, serving well-flavored new British–style cuisine amid Victorian-inspired wallpaper and pink napery. Each of the 37 bedrooms is cozy and tastefully decorated, with private bath, color TV, radio, direct-dial phone, and tea and coffee maker. There is a selection of four-poster beds and a half-tester. With VAT and a full English breakfast, singles cost £55 ($90.75) daily and doubles or twins from £75 ($123.75). Children sharing a room with their parents are charged for meals only.

Fern Hotel, Swan Road, Harrogate, North Yorkshire HG1 2SS (tel. 0423/523866), set behind a large copper beech tree and a small formal garden, has a gray stone facade, parts of the original detailing, and lots of well-upholstered comfort. Built by Victorians, it contains 32 bedrooms, each of which is well furnished with several amenities including color TV, phone, private bath or shower, and coffee maker. Singles cost £30 ($49.50) to £52 ($85.80) daily, and doubles or twins go for £50 ($82.50) to £85 ($140.25). VAT and an English breakfast are included. On the premises is a high-ceilinged restaurant, the Portico, serving wholesome food.

Where to Dine

Hodgson's Restaurant, Russell Hotel, 29-35 Valley Drive (tel. 0423/509866), is often cited as the best restaurant at the spa. In an oak-paneled dining room, you can sample savory wares. An interesting blend of modern and classical British dishes is presented, but only for dinner, served from 7 to 10:30pm Tue. to Fri. A set dinner costs from £22 ($36.30) with à la carte meals averaging £25 ($41.25). Inside this warmly decorated Victorian hotel, you can sample such dishes as Aylesbury duck in an orange sauce, or stuffed loin of pork or a perfectly done pair of roast quail. The wine list is reasonably priced and well selected.

Millers, 1 Montpelier Mews (tel. 0423/530708). In your search for that Harrogate antique in the spa's antique shop district, you'll stumble upon this excellent choice of a restaurant. Simon Gueller, one of the co-owners, is a chef of considerable skill, and he operates this deservedly popular and comfortable restaurant. Fish is his specialty, and he does many dishes exceedingly well. It's hard to classify his cuisine, other than to say it's new British cookery. For example, scallops might appear with a flavoring of chile and green ginger. In fact, the cuisine is characterized by its use of herbs and spices, which somehow blend into harmonious dishes without any flavor overwhelming the palate. Time was those palates at Harrogate weren't too hard to please, but a new generation has demanded more excitement and imagination in cooking, and Millers delivers. Desserts are refreshing and "creative endings" to meals. Service is Mon. to Sat.; closed Mon. dinner, from noon to 2pm and 7 to 10pm with meals costing around £25 ($41.25). Reservations are needed.

Drum and Monkey, 5 Montpelier Gardens (tel. 0423/502650). Come here for some of the best fish dishes in the spa, prepared with skill. In the heart of Harrogate, the restaurant is a bustling place. It's usually filled downstairs, where many patrons prefer to eat at the bar. Tables are freely shared with those savoring Dover sole, salmon, grilled mackerel, whatever swims. If you're here for lunch, try the "dressed" crab salad. For a main course, try grilled Dover sole or else grilled lobster, perhaps the "fruits of the sea" platter in garlic butter. Poached salmon trout is invariably a winner. Meals range in price from £15 ($24.75), but could go much higher, depending on your fish selection. It is open from noon to 2:30pm and 7 to 10pm Mon. to Sat.

MOORS AND DALES

The rural landscape is pierced with ruins of once-great abbeys and castles. North Yorkshire is a land of green hills, valleys, and purple moors. Both the Yorkshire Dales and the Moors are wide-open spaces, two of Britain's finest national parks, with a combined area of some 1,200 square miles. However, the term "national" can be misleading, as the land is managed by foresters, farmers, and private landowners. In fact, more than 90% of the land is in private ownership. The Dales rise toward Cumbria and Lancashire to the east, and the Moors stretch to the eastern coastline.

From Harrogate, our last stopover, you can enjoy the region's wildest scenery by heading out on day trips, or staying at one of the inns coming up. You can discover white limestone crags, drystone walls, fast-rushing rivers, and isolated sheep farms or clusters of sandstone cottages.

Malhamdale receives more visitors annually than any dale in Yorkshire. Of the priories and castles to visit, two of the most interesting are the 12th-century ruins of **Bolton Priory,** and the 14th-century pile, **Castle Bolton,** to the north in Wensleydale. **Richmond,** the most frequently used town name in the world, stands at the head of the Dales. The Norman towers of Richmond Castle, the country's best-known fortress, dominate the cobbled market town. The Georgian Theatre here, which was constructed in 1788, has a resident amateur company of the highest quality.

In contrast, the Moors, on the other side of the Vale of York, have a wild beauty all their own, quite different from that of the Dales. They are bounded by the Cleveland and Hambleton Hills. The white horse of Kilburn can be seen, hewn out of the landscape. Both **Pickering** and **Northallerton,** two market towns, serve as gateways to the Moors. Across the Moors are seen primordial burial grounds and stone crosses. The best-known trek in moorland is the 40-mile hike over bog, heather, and stream from Mount Grace Priory inland to Ravenscar on the seacoast. It's known as **Lyke Wake Walk.**

The beauty and seclusion along the southern border of today's park made this area attractive to the founders of four great abbeys. The Cistercians established **Rievaulx** ecclesiastical community near Helmsley and **Fountains Abbey** near Ripon as well as **Byland Abbey** near the village of Wass. The Bendictines were also here, establishing **Ampleforth Abbey** near **Coxwold,** one of the most attractive villages in the Moors. Rievaulx, Fountains, and Byland Abbeys are in ruins, but Ampleforth still works as a monastery and well-known Roman Catholic boys' school. Although most of Ampleforth's buildings are of 19th- and 20th-century construction, these contain artifacts from earlier monastic times.

Along North Yorkshire's 45 miles of coastline are such traditional seaside resorts as **Filey, Whitby,** and **Scarborough,** the latter claiming to be the oldest seaside spa in Britain, standing on the site of a Roman signaling station. It was founded in 1622, following the discovery of mineral springs with medicinal properties. In the 19th century, its Grand Hotel, a Victorian structure, was acclaimed as "the best in Europe." The Norman castle on big cliffs overlooks the twin bays.

In and Around Helmsley

This attractive town, where a market is held every Friday, is a good center for exploring the surrounding area. Called the key to Ryedale, it is the mother town of the district, standing at the junction of the roads from York, Pickering, Malton, Stokesley, and Thirsk. On the southern edge of the North York Moors National Park, Helmsley is well known as a center for walking and "pot-holing." It is in a section that contains many places of interest: remains of Bronze and Iron Age existence on the moors, prehistoric highways, Roman roads, and, of course, the ruins of medieval castles and abbeys. Beyond the main square of the town are the ruins of its castle, built between 1186 and 1227, and its impressive keep.

A good reason for selecting Helmsley as a stopover is that it is near York and well located, but with hotel rates far below those of the larger city. York lies 24 miles from Helmsley, and London is a drive of 234 miles.

Three miles northwest of Helmsley are the ruins of **Rievaulx** (pronounced "reevo") **Abbey** (tel. 04396/228), named for Rye Vallis, valley of the River Rye. The first Cistercian house in northern England, the abbey was founded in 1131 by monks who came over from Clairveaux in France. At its peak it had 140 monks and 500 lay brothers. Its size, architecture, and setting make even the abbey ruins among the most impressive in the country. The land was given by Walter l'Espec, a Norman knight who later entered the community as a novice, and died and was buried here. It is open from 10am to 6pm Good Friday to September 30, from 10am to 4pm in winter; closed Mon. Admission is £1.40 ($2.30) for adults, 70p ($1.15) for children.

Rievaulx Terrace, a property of the National Trust, is a landscaped, grassy terrace about half a mile long, which was laid out in the mid-18th century by Thomas Duncombe of Duncombe Park. It lies 2 ½ miles northwest of Helmsley on the Stokesley Road (B1257). After a woodland walk, you emerge onto a wide lawn near a circular "temple" known as the Tuscan Temple. The walk along the terrace gives frequent views of the abbey ruins in the valley below. At the opposite end from the Tuscan Temple is the Ionic Temple, whose interior is beautifully decorated and furnished, with a classically painted ceiling and furniture of gilded wood with rosevelvet upholstery. In the basement are two rooms originally used by servants to prepare food for guests above. The Ionic Temple was planned by Thomas Duncombe III as a banqueting house and a place of rest and refreshment after the long carriage ride from Duncombe Park. It is open from 10:30am to 6pm daily from Good Friday to the end of October. Admission is £1.50 ($2.50) for adults, 70p ($1.15) for children. For information, phone 0439/340.

Black Swan, Market Place, Helmsley, North Yorkshire YO6 5BJ (tel. 0439/70466), has stood since the 16th century overlooking the market place. Incorporating Tudor, Georgian, and Elizabethan houses, this hotel offers 38 well-furnished bedrooms, each with private bath, radio, TV, phone, and tea and coffee makers. These rent from £70 ($115.50) daily in a single, from £105 ($173.25) in a twin, including service and VAT. A wing of bedrooms overlooks the walled garden. Public rooms are full of character, with open fires, paneling, and time-aged beams. In the traditionally furnished restaurant, you can enjoy such Yorkshire dishes as jugged hare and sirloin Helmsley. A dinner costs from £16.50 ($27.25) to £25 ($41.25). The hotel also has two bars.

In and Around Ripon

Ripon has an ancient tradition of a watchman blowing a curfew horn in the center of town every night at 9, a custom dating back to 886. This cathedral city, 27 miles north of Leeds by road, was once a Saxon village where a Celtic monastery was founded in 651. London is 222 miles away.

WHAT TO SEE AND DO Beneath the central tower of **Ripon Cathedral,** a Norman archbishop's church dating from 1154, is the original crypt built by St. Wilfrid more than 1,300 years ago, one of the oldest buildings in England. The original plaster is still on the walls. It was built the same size and shape as was traditionally believed to be the layout of the tomb from which Jesus rose from the dead.

Archbishop Roger built the nave of the Norman cathedral, the north transept, and part of the choir stalls. The twin towers of the west front are Early English, from about 1216, and the library (once the lady loft) is from sometime in the 14th century. The canons stalls were hand-carved, completed in 1495. Two sides of the tower date from the original construction in 1220, but in 1450 an earthquake caused the other two sides to collapse. They were reconstructed, and the central tower and south transept were added at the beginning of the 16th century. The completion of all the work was never carried out, as King Henry VIII took away all the cathedral endowments. Until 1664 the towers had tall spires, but they were removed to prevent fires caused by lightning.

Today the cathedral is a lively Christian center, with a study center and a choir school. It is the mother church of the Diocese of Ripon, which spreads over most of the Yorkshire Dales to the fifth-largest city in England, Leeds. For further information, telephone 0765/4108.

Ripon Prison and Police Museum, St. Marygate (tel. 0765/3706), is a fascinating exhibition of the history of police work from the time of the wakeman of Ripon (the watchman of the town in the Middle Ages) up to the wonders of modern technology as they pertain to fighting crime. The building in which the museum is housed started life as a prison, built in 1815. In 1887 it became a police station and continued so until its retirement in 1956. Now it has displays of life in both phases of its existence, including some of the punishment devices so popular in days past. The museum is open from 1:30 to 5pm daily from May to the end of September. In July and August hours are 11am to 5pm Tues. to Sat. and bank holidays. Admission is 75p ($1.25) for adults, 50p (85¢) for children.

Fountains Abbey and **Studley Royal,** Fountains, 4 miles southwest of Ripon off the B6265 (tel. 076586/333), stands on the banks of the River Skell. The abbey was founded by Cistercian monks in 1132, and is the largest monastic ruin in Britain. In 1987, it was awarded world heritage status. The ruins provide the focal point of the 18th-century landscape garden at Studley Royal, one of the few surviving examples of a Georgian green garden. It is known for its water gardens, ornamental temples, follies, and vistas. The garden is bounded at its northern edge by a lake and 400 acres of deer park. The abbey and gardens are open daily except December 24 and 25 and Fri. in November, December, and January. From January through March and in November and December it is open daily from 10am to 5pm (or dusk). From April to June and in September, it is open daily from 10am to 7pm, and in July and August daily from 10am to 8pm. October sees daily openings from 10am to 6pm (or dusk). Admission to the abbey and gardens is £2.40 ($3.95) for adults and £1 ($1.65) for children. A family ticket—two adults, two children—costs £5.80 ($9.55).

Newby Hall, northeast of the River Ure between Ripon (4 miles) and Boroughbridge (3½ miles), is one of Yorkshire's renowned Adam houses, a very fine example of 18th-century interior decoration—recently restored to its original beauty.

Surrounding this beautiful family home of Mr. and Mrs. Robin Compton are 25 acres of award-winning gardens containing many rare and unusual plants and shrubs. Originally built for Sir Edward Blackett, circa 1695, in the style of Sir Christopher Wren, the house was remodeled and extended by Robert Adam to exhibit antique sculpture, tapestries, and furniture collected by its then owner William Weddell. The Gobelins tapestries completed for the drawing room in 1776 were one of only five sets made for English patrons, and the Newby set is the only one of the five to have a dove-gray and not a rose-pink background. The tapestry for the sofas and chairs was designed to echo the floral theme of the wall tapestries; this set of Chippendale furniture is unique in that it retains its original upholstery. Other attractions include the Woodland Discovery Walk, Adventure Gardens for children, 10¼-inch miniature railway for rides alongside the river, the Newby Shop and licensed restaurant, picnic area, and plant stall. Open April 1 to September 30 11am to 5:30pm Tue. to Sun. and bank holidays (hall and railway noon to 5pm), with last admission at 5pm. Admission to hall and gardens is £3.60 ($5.95) for adults, and £2 ($3.30) for children. For further information, telephone 0423/322583.

WHERE TO STAY AND DINE AT RIPON The **Ripon Spa Hotel,** Park Street, Ripon, North Yorkshire HG4 2BU (tel. 0765/2172), opened its doors in 1909 with high hopes. Its owner hoped that Ripon would, like Harrogate, attracts hundreds of guests coming here to "take the spa waters." That didn't happen, nevertheless the hotel endured, attracting those who use it as a base for exploring the surrounding Yorkshire countryside, including Fountains Abbey. The same family has run the hotel for half a century, welcoming guests in their 40 old-fashioned rooms, which still have plenty of modern comforts such as private baths or showers, color TVs, phones, radios, and tea and coffee makers. British to the core, the hotel charges £44 ($72.60) to £60 ($99) daily in a single, £60 ($99) to £80 ($132) in a double or twin. Ask about "Two-Day Breaks" including dinner, bed, and breakfast available throughout the year. The hotel stands right outside the center of Ripon on 7 acres of private gardens. The public rooms overlook these gardens. Good British cookery is served in an elegant and spacious dining room, and guests also enjoy the Turf Tavern, named for its association with Ripon Racecourse.

Unicorn Hotel, Market Place, Ripon, North Yorkshire HG4 1BP (tel. 0765/2202), is a coaching inn and posting house. It has welcomed travelers for some 400 years with Yorkshire warmth and hospitality, and the same is true today. It's directly opposite the obelisk where the 1,000-year-old tradition of setting the watch by blowing the horn takes place each evening. The facade of the inn is in Victorian style, with square bay windows and an elaborate front entrance. All 33 bedrooms have private facilities, TV, central heating, tea and coffee maker, and phone. Singles rent from £39 ($64.35) daily, and doubles or twins from £52 ($85.80), these tariffs including VAT and a full English breakfast. The English and French cuisine in the Royal Charter Restaurant is Cordon Bleu, and in addition, bar lunches are served in a typically English pub with locally brewed real ale.

Thirsk

This pleasant old market town, lying in the Vale of Mowbray north of York, has a fine parish church. But what makes it such a popular stopover for visitors is the fame brought to the village by James Herriot, author of *All Creatures Great and Small* and other books about his experiences as a veterinarian serving this area of Yorkshire. Mr. Herriot still practices in Thirsk, and visitors can photograph his office, perhaps getting a picture of his partner standing in the door. The location is 227 miles from London and 24 miles from York.

If you'd like to stay over, **Golden Fleece,** Market Place, Thirsk, North Yorkshire YO7 1LL (tel. 0845/23108), is a traditional hotel in the center of town, opening onto the cobbled marketplace. This has been a famous hostelry in England for more than 300 years, once attracting coachdrivers on the high road from York to Darlington. The interior is beautifully kept, with antique furniture, old brasses, and big open hearths. There are 22 bedrooms, 6 with private baths and one with a four-poster bed. All units have color TVs, radios, phones, razor sockets, central heating, and hot beverage facilities. Singles cost from £46 ($75.90) daily and doubles begin at £55 ($90.75). In the Mail Coach Restaurant, you can enjoy an old English cuisine, and the Paddock Bar is a comfortable place to have drinks, perhaps a pint of full-bodied Yorkshire ale.

Hawes

The natural center of the Yorkshire Dales National Park is Hawes, England's highest market town and the capital of Wensleydale. It is also the home of the cheese of that name. It's on the Pennine Way, which is popular with hikers. You can watch traditional ropemaking at W. R. Outhwaite and Son (tel. 09697/487). Hawes lies on a good road, the A684, about midway between the A1 to the east and the M6 to the west. The situation is 65 miles from York and 253 miles from London.

Upper Dales Folk Museum, Station Yard (the old train station) (tel. 09697/494), traces folk life in the area of the Upper Dales. Peat-cutting and cheese-making, among other occupations, are depicted. The museum is open from 11am to 5pm Mon. to Sat., 2 to 5pm Sun. from March 20 to the end of July and during September. In August, hours are from 10am to 6pm Mon. to Sat., 2 to 5pm Sun. In October, it is open only from noon to 5pm; closed in winter. Admission is 75p ($1.25).

You don't need to travel far from Rookhurst for beautiful Dales scenery. Gayle, originally a Celtic settlement, is divided by Duerley Beck, with two lovely waterfalls, a ford and an old stone bridge, beloved of artists and photographers.

WHERE TO STAY AND DINE Simonstone Hall, Hawes, North Yorkshire DL8 3LY (tel. 09697/667255), former home of the earls of Wharncliffe, is 1½ miles north of Hawes—rural but not isolated. The place once attracted such guests as Lillie Langtry and Disraeli. Constructed in 1733, the building has been converted and restored, so that today it is a comfortable family-run, country-house hotel. There are 10 spacious bedrooms with private baths, phones, and TVs. Two persons can stay here on half-board terms, costing from £97.50 ($160.90) to £124.25 ($205), depending on the time of year. The owners, Mr. and Mrs. J. R. Jeffryes, are happy to have guests relax in the large, south-facing, paneled drawing rooms, which have comfortable, mostly antique furnishings. You can have drinks in the Tawny Owl Bar and enjoy good food in the hotel's dining room. Expect to pay about £16.50 ($27.25) for a four-course dinner. This can be complemented with good wines from the extensive cellar.

3. West Yorkshire

This county, carved out of a piece of the old county of Yorkshire, is dominated by the industrial city of Leeds, which, even though a respectable town with lots of Victorian architecture, is hardly on most foreign visitors' agenda for a tour of England. West Yorkshire might easily be one of the "forgotten counties" of England were it not for its two major attractions, Haworth, home of the Brontës, and Harewood House, one of the country's most stately homes.

HAWORTH
In West Yorkshire, this ancient stone village lying on the high moors of the Pennines—45 miles west of York via Leeds and 21 miles west of Leeds itself—is world-famous as the home of the Brontë family. The three sisters—Charlotte, Emily, and Anne—distinguished themselves as English novelists. They lived a life of imagination at a lonely parsonage at Haworth.

Anne wrote two novels, *The Tenant of Wildfell Hall* and *Agnes Grey*. Charlotte's masterpieces, *Jane Eyre* and *Vilette,* depicted her experiences as a governess; *Jane Eyre* enjoyed popular success in its day and is now considered a classic of British fiction.

But it is Emily's fierce and tragic *Wuthering Heights* that is best loved, a novel of passion, intensity, and primitive power. With scenes of unforgettable, haunting melancholy, the book has come to be appreciated by later generations. Haworth is the most visited literary shrine in England, after Stratford-upon-Avon.

From Haworth, you can walk to Withens, the "Wuthering Heights" of the immortal novel. In Haworth, Charlotte and Emily are buried in the faily vault under the church of St. Michael's.

The parsonage where they lived has been preserved as the **Brontë Parsonage Museum** (tel. 0535/42323), housing their furniture, personal treasures, pictures, books, and manuscripts. It may be visited April to September daily from 11am to 5:30pm, 4:30pm October to March. It is closed from January 22 to February 9 and at Christmas. Admission is £1.50 ($2.50) for adults, and 30p (50¢) for children.

On the Haworth Moor stands a Brontë landmark, **Ponden Hall,** Stanbury, near Keighley (tel. 0535/44154), a distance of some 3 miles from Haworth. It lies half a mile from the main road on the wide rough track that is the Pennine Way. An Elizabethan farmhouse built in 1560 and extended in 1801, this reputedly is the model for Thrushcross Grange, Catherine's home after her marriage to Edgar Linton.

Today the hall provides a farmhouse accommodation, a hand-loom weaving studio, a residential weaving course, a bunkhouse accommodation, as well as camping.

The village of Haworth has frequent bus and train service to Keighley, Bradford, and Leeds in West Yorkshire.

Where to Stay and Dine

The **tourist information center,** at 2-4 West Lane in Haworth (tel. 0535/42329), offers an accommodation-booking service, and the office is open daily from 9:30am to 5:30pm April until the end of October, from 9:30 to 5pm November to March.

A reminder: You must not expect such amenities as private baths, air conditioning, and the like in the lower-priced places. Just as in the United States, you get what you pay for.

Old White Lion Hotel, 6 West Lane, Haworth, Keighley, West Yorkshire BD22 8DU (tel. 0535/42313), stands at the top of a cobblestone street. It was built around 1700 with a solid stone roof almost next door to the church where the Reverend Brontë preached and to the parsonage where the family lived. Joyce and Keith Bradford welcome tourists from all over the world to their warm, cheerful, and comfortable hotel. Although full of old-world charm, all 15 rooms are fully up to date, including, for example, private baths and TVs. The double rate is £42 ($69.30) daily, with singles costing £28 ($46.20). VAT is included. Dinners, except Sunday, are à la carte, and good local meats and fresh vegetables are used. Meals cost £10 ($16.50) in the evening. Bar snacks include the usual favorites—ploughman's lunch, hot pies, fish, and sandwiches.

Weaver's Restaurant, 15 West Lane (tel. 0535/43822), was once cottages for weavers but it has now been turned into the best restaurant in the Brontë hometown. In the words of one satisfied diner, "It's the only game in town as far as food is concerned." British to the core, it not only has an inviting atmosphere but serves excellent food made with fresh ingredients. Jane and Colin Rushworth have a great talent in the kitchen, and you can sample very English wares at dinner from 7 to 9:30pm Tue. to Sat. It serves lunch in winter from 12:30 to 1:30pm, costing £9.50 ($15.70). Dinners cost from £12 ($19.80) and up, and include such classic dishes as Yorkshire pudding with gravy. Try, if featured, one of the Gressingham ducks, which are widely praised in the U.K. for the quality of their meat. For your final course, you might select a Yorkshire cheese or one of the superb, made-in-house desserts. The style of the place is informal. The restaurant is likely to be closed for a certain time each summer for vacation, so call in advance to check. You should always reserve a table at any rate. The place tends to be popular, and with good reason.

LINTON (NEAR WETHERBY)

One of the most desirable accommodations in West Yorkshire—worth a detour—is **Wood Hall Hotel,** Linton, near Wetherby, West Yorkshire LS22 4JA (tel. 0937/67271). It could be your center for exploring the Yorkshire Dales. A Georgian mansion with a Jacobean addition, it overlooks the River Warfe. It is set in more than 100 acres of parkland and woodland overlooking the Wharfe Valley. The handsome house offers 22 luxurious bedrooms, each individually designed with private bath or shower, phone, and TV. All rooms are doubles costing from £95 ($156.75) to £105 ($173.25). Single occupancy of a double ranges from £75 ($123.75) to £95 ($156.75). The hotel restaurant is the finest in the area, serving from 12:30 to 2pm and 7 to 9:30pm, to 10pm Fri. and Sat., and to 9pm on Sun.; closed Sat. lunch. The dining room is elegantly decorated, serving a sophisticated British cuisine. A set dinner costs from £25 ($41.25), and reservations are needed.

HEBDEN BRIDGE

Deep in the heart of the South Pennines lies this little town, which was a busy fustian (a stout, mainly cotton, fabric) weaving center during and after the Industrial Revolution. It became an important site for the industry because of its position at the junction of the Calder and Hebden valleys and was a shipping station on the Rochdale Canal, which connected Halifax on the east and Rochdale on the west.

Hebden Bridge is 7 miles south of Haworth and about 25 miles east of Leeds. The canal is being restored, and already trips from Hebden Bridge are possible.

Hebden Lodge Hotel, New Road, Hebden Bridge, West Yorkshire HX7 8AD (tel. 0422/845272), overlooking the historic canal moorings, is a Victorian building with modern amenities. You are welcomed by the owners, Robert and Christine Nicholas, to 13 bedrooms with showers, color TVs, radio alarms, and hot beverage facilities. Prices range from £25 ($41.25) daily in a single to £55 ($90.75) in a double or twin, with a full English breakfast included. Mr. Nicholas is also the chef, preparing and cooking fresh produce with both lunch and dinner menus changed daily. He offers a large choice of well-prepared dishes.

HAREWOOD HOUSE AND BIRD GARDEN

In West Yorkshire, at junction of A61 and A659, midway between Leeds and Harrogate and 5 miles from the A1 at Wetherby, stands the home of the earl and countess of Harewood. One of the treasure houses of England, this 18th-century house was designed by John Carr and has always been owned by the Lascelles family. The fine Adam interior has superb ceilings and plasterwork, and furniture made especially for Harewood by Chippendale. There are also important collections of English and Italian paintings and Sèvres and Chinese porcelain.

The Capability Brown landscape includes a 4½-acre bird garden that borders the lake. It contains exotic species from all over the world, including penguins, macaws, flamingos, and snowy owls; there is a tropical rainforest exhibition as well. The spacious grounds offer terraces, lakeside and woodland walks, exhibitions, shops, and a restaurant and cafeteria. Car parking is free, and there is a picnic area, plus an adventure playground for the children.

Harewood is open daily from 10am to 5pm from Easter to the end of October. The house, bird garden, and adventure playground are also open on Sun. in November, February, and March. Admission is £2 ($3.30) for adults and £1 ($1.65) for children. For further facts, phone visitor information (tel. 0532/886225).

4. Durham

This densely populated county of northeast England is too often pictured as a dismal, forbidding place, with coalfields, ironworks, mining towns, and shipyards. Yet it contains valleys of quiet charm and a region of wild moors in the west. Therefore if you have the time, it would be interesting to explore the Durham Dales, especially Teesdale with its waterfalls and rare wildflowers, and Weardale with its brown-sandstone villages.

DURHAM

The county town is built on a sandstone peninsula. Its treasure is the **Cathedral of Durham** (tel. 091/386-4266), which ranks among the most beautiful buildings in the world. Its solid towers dominate the neighboring countryside from its sandstone pinnacle surrounded by the River Wear. Inside, the massive and bold incised piers in the nave and the ribbed vaults (this was the first great church in northern Europe to develop this feature) give it a feeling of solidarity and security. The church was named for St. Cuthbert, the greatest north country saint, who was first buried at Lindisfarne in A.D. 687. After being hauled around for many years, his body was interred where it now lies behind the high altar. From May to September, the cathedral is open from 7:15am to 8pm, to 6pm other months. Visitors can explore the treasury, with its relics of St. Cuthbert, along with precious books and silver plate, from 10am to 4:30pm Mon. to Sat., 2 to 4:30pm Sun. Admission is 60p ($1) for adults and 10p (15¢) for children. The Monks' Dormitory is open from 11am to 3pm Mon. to Sat., from 2 to 4pm Sun., charging adults 25p (40¢) and children 10p (15¢). An audio-visual display is open from 11am to 3pm Mon. to Sat., charging adults 40p (65¢) and children 20p (35¢). Finally, visitors can climb the tower, which is normally open from 9:30am to 4pm Mon. to Sat. Admission is 50p (85¢) for adults and 25p (40¢) for children (payable to the steward in the south transept). Once at the top, you'll have a sweeping view over Durham and its castle.

From Framweigate Bridge, below the massive church, is a peaceful riverside walk, known locally as the Banks. It leads you through trees beneath the castle and then up a steep path to the cathedral. It's quite a challenge for the faint-hearted, but well worth the effort for the fit.

In the shadow of the cathedral is the **Church of St. Mary le Bow,** now containing the **Durham Heritage Centre,** which is open from May to September from 2 to 4:30pm; closed Fri. It presents changing exhibitions and audio-visual presentations of the city's history, plus rubbings of replicas of monumental brasses. Admission is 50p (85¢) for adults, 20p (35¢) for children.

Adjoining the cathedral is **Durham Castle** (tel. 091/374-3800), which was founded by the Normans and was the home of the prince-bishops until it was given to Durham University in 1832. Except on the occasion of university or other functions, the castle is open to visitors all year. From July to September, hours are 10am to noon and 2 to 4:30pm Sat. and Sun. only. During the rest of the year, it is open from 2 to 4pm on Mon., Wed., and Sat. Admission is £1.25 ($2.05) for adults and 55p (90¢) for children.

Where to Stay and Dine

Royal County Hotel, Old Elvet, Durham, County Durham DH1 3JN (tel. 0385/386-6821), is a Georgian hostelry tracing its origins to Cromwellian times. With a well-conceived refurbishment program, this four-star hotel offers attentive service to the guest. There are 149 bedrooms, all with private baths, TVs, video channels, radios, direct-dial phones, and hot beverage facilities. You're given your choice of accommodations in either the older building with its traditional furnishings or in the new block of rooms, many with views over the river and the city of Durham. Rates range from £75 ($123.75) daily in a single, from £90 ($148.50) in a double, and tariffs include an English breakfast. An à la carte menu is served in the air-conditioned County Restaurant, and the Brasserie offers table d'hôte meals and light snacks.

BARNARD CASTLE

Near the River Tees in the town of Barnard Castle stands the **Bowes Museum** (tel. 0833/690606), at the eastern end. It was built in 1869 by John Bowes and his wife, the countess of Montalbo, to house and display their art collection. Here you'll find masterpieces by Goya and El Greco, plus other paintings, fine tapestries, and ceramics. There are also collections of French and English furniture, superb costumes, musical instruments, a children's gallery, and many other exhibits of interest. The noted silver swan performs its mechanical marvels once or twice daily. A tea room and ample parking are found on the premises. It is open all year, daily from 10am to 5pm, 2 to 5pm Sun., charging £1.55 ($2.55) for adults, 70p ($1.15) for children. It closes at 4pm from November to February and entirely for a week around Christmas. The café is open daily from April to September. Barnard Castle lies 258 miles from London and 68 miles from Leeds.

Where to Stay and Dine

Blagraves House Restaurant, 30 the Bank (tel. 0833/37668), occupies a 15th-century house with a dining room that has been richly decorated. They invite you to come by and "taste our food," which I've found to be excellently prepared and wholesome. Fresh local produce and good service characterize the establishment. Meals are offered for £15 ($24.75) to £20 ($33). Main dishes are likely to include beef with Stilton cheese and a walnut sauce on chicken with mangoes. Lunch is served only on Sun. from noon to 1:30pm, and dinner is from 7 to 9:30pm Tue. to Sun.

DURHAM AND NORTHUMBERLAND

NORTH SEA

Holy Island

Bamburgh Castle

Northumberland

Alnwick

Alnmouth

National Park

Longhorseley

NORTHUMBERLAND

A 696

A 68

A 1

Hadrian's   Wall

A 69

Haltwhistle

Haydon Bridge   Hexham

TYNE AND WEAR

Newcastle upon Tyne

Blanchland

Durham

A 19

DURHAM

N
W — E
S

A 66

Yorkshire Dales
National Park

Rose and Crown Hotel, Romaldkirk, Teesdale, County Durham DL12 9EB (tel. 0833/50213), lies in a dale that often escapes the notice of the traveler in the north, at Romaldkirk, an attractive village set around a fine green with a water pump and punitive stocks (not in use today!). Higher up the dale, the River Tees goes over a sheer drop of 69 feet, and downstream is Barnard Castle and the Bowes Museum. In the main building are well-furnished bedrooms, one with a four-poster bed. All have private baths or showers, color TVs, radios, and phones, and across the court-yard in a modern extension, units have the same amenities, plus hot beverage facilities. The hotel rents nine bedrooms and two suites. An overnight stay costs £45 ($74.25) daily in a single, £70 ($115.50) in a double, which includes a full English breakfast and a morning paper. There is a comfortable lounge, and the two bars have roaring log fires. Bar lunches are served Mon. to Sat., with complete dinners in the restaurant costing £16.50 ($27.25).

BLANCHLAND

Near Consett, the village of Blanchland dates from the mid-12th century. It's a cobbled square with houses and little village shops. The post office still shows the arms of Queen Victoria over the mailbox. The village is 298 miles from London and 24 miles from Newcastle-on-Tyne.

The Lord Crewe Arms Hotel, Blanchland, near Consett, County Durham DH8 9SP (tel. 043475/251), was the priory of the now-destroyed Abbey of Blanchland, and the bars are to be found in the crypt of the old building. You can walk through one of the enormous chimneys with a priest's hole above your head. All 18 rooms have baths, TVs, and phones, costing from £62 ($102.30) daily in a single and from £80 ($132) in a double, including a traditional breakfast and VAT. Some bedrooms are in the annex opposite the old building. Rooms are decorated with fresh flowers, and a glass of sherry will be waiting to greet you. A four-course dinner at £20 ($33) is likely to include seafood vol-au-vent, roast duckling, or grouse in season, followed by a homemade dessert. There are also bar snacks for those who want to stop for a short while en route to Hadrian's Wall or Scotland.

BEAMISH

West of Chester-le-Street, 8 miles southwest of Newcastle-on-Tyne and 12 miles northwest of Durham City, lying just off the A693, is Beamish, the North of England Open Air Museum. Here the way of life of the people of the region has been re-created. You can step into the "living" past to visit a dentist's home and surgery, a solicitor's office, a working public house, and fully stocked cooperative shops. A tram ride away is the Colliery Village where guided tours are given underground at a real "drift" mine, bread is baked in a coal-fired oven, and a winding engine is often in steam. Meet the pigs, cattle, and poultry in the farmyard at home farm and step into the farmhouse kitchen where the farmer's wife goes about her daily chores. There's the Railway Station, too, complete with signal box, rolling stock, and steam locomotives. An average visit takes 4½ hours. Beamish is open April through October daily 10am to 6pm; November through March 10am to 5pm Tue. to Sun. Last admission is always 4pm. In summer charges are £4.50 ($7.45) for adults and £3.50 ($5.80) for children, and in winter £2.50 ($4.15) for adults and £1.50 ($2.50) for children. For more information, phone 0207/231811.

---

5. Tyne and Wear

In the county of Tyne and Wear, industrial Newcastle upon Tyne is the dominant focus, yet outside the city there is much natural beauty. Cattle graze on many a grassed-over mining shaft. There is the scenic beauty of the moors and the rugged coastline. Americans are interested in the ancestral home of George Washington (see below), and Newcastle itself merits a stopover, particularly for motorists heading to Scotland.

The National Trust administers two sites in the region surrounding Newcastle. **Gibside Chapel,** at Burnopfield (tel. 0207/542255), built in the classical style of James Paine in 1760, is an outstanding example of Georgian church architecture. A stately, oak-lined avenue leads to the door of the chapel, which is the mausoleum of the Bowes family. The interior is decorated in delicate plasterwork and is furnished with paneled pews of cherrywood and a rare mahogany three-tiered pulpit. Hours are 2 to 6pm Tue. to Sun. from April 1 to September 30. The entrance fee is £1.50 ($2.50) for adults, 75p ($1.25) for children. A shop, refreshment stand, and picnic area are here. The location is 6 miles southwest of Gateshead and 20 miles northwest of Durham between Rowlands Gill and Burnopfield.

Washington Old Hall (tel. 091/416-6879) is the ancestral home of the first president of the United States, and the place from which the family took its name. President Carter visited the manor house in 1977. The interior of the house, which dates back to 1183, is furnished with period antiques and a collection of Delftware. Relics of the Washingtons are also on display. It is open April to September from 1 to 5:30pm, charging adults £1.50 ($2.50) for admission and children 75p ($1.25). It is open in October from 1 to 5:30pm on Wed., Sat., and Sun. only. The location is in Washington on the east side of the A182, 5 miles west of Sunderland (2 miles from the A1). South of Tyne Tunnel, follow signs for Washington New Town District 4 and then Washington Village.

NEWCASTLE UPON TYNE

An industrial city, Newcastle is graced with some fine streets and parks, as well as many old buildings. After crossing its best-known landmark, the Tyne Bridge, you enter a steep city that sweeps down to the Tyne, usually on narrow lanes called "chares." Once wealthy merchants built their townhouses right on the quayside, and some of them remain.

For years Newcastle has been known as a shipbuilding and coal-exporting center, and gave rise to the expression of suggesting the absurdity of shipping coals to Newcastle. The location is 276 miles from London and 95 miles from Leeds.

Dominating the skyline, **St. Nicholas Church of England Cathedral** rises to a soaring crown spire. It is England's most northerly cathedral and is situated close to the central station and the castle. The provost says that "the cathedral is one of the gems among the glorious churches of Northumberland." The present building is substantially from the 14th century, the spire being a 15th-century construction. The cathedral has a refectory open at lunch and also a gift shop.

The keep of the so-called New Castle, built by Henry II in 1170, contains the **Keep Museum,** on St. Nicholas Street, with a collection of medieval relics. It's open April to September from 9:30am to 5:30pm Tue. to Sun., October to March to 4:30pm Tue. to Sun.

Where to Stay

The premier hotel of the city is **Gosforth Park Thistle,** High Gosforth Park, Newcastle upon Tyne, Tyne and Wear NE3 5HN (tel. 091/2364111), although it lies on the outskirts on B1318 (some 5 miles north of Newcastle on A6125). Once you get there, the effort proves worth it. With sleek contemporary styling, it welcomes guests into 178 well-furnished bedrooms, each with private bath or shower, direct-dial phone, TV, in-house feature films, hairdryer, and trouser press. Catering largely to a business clientele, the executive rooms are the most desirable and expensive. Singles rent for £82 ($135.30) daily, with doubles costing £100 ($165). The hotel has a number of drinking and dining facilities as well as an activity center with a pool and gym.

County Thistle Hotel, Neville Street, Newcastle upon Tyne, Tyne and Wear NC99 1AH (tel. 091/232-2471), is a refurbished hotel in the center of town. A dominant figure of the Newcastle scene, it was built directly opposite the railway station and heralded the coming of the industrial age. Under the Thistle group, the hotel has 115 bedrooms each well maintained and all with private baths or showers, direct-dial phones, and color TVs. The charge for singles begins at £65 ($107.25) daily, and doubles and twins cost from £95 ($156.75). The hotel's reception lobby has as its focal point a sweeping staircase, complemented by limed oak furnishings and potted plants. Excellent meals are served in the candlelit Café Mozart, the windows of which look out on the arches of Newcastle's old buildings. Inventive cooking, combining modern and traditional dishes, is served, with meals from £12 ($19.80).

Where to Dine

21 Queen Street, Quayside (tel. 091/222-0755), is stylish and elegant, the city's leading restaurant, run with determination by its proud owner, Terence Laybourne. His cuisine bears no resemblance to the fare that was served in Newcastle for decades. He has brought imagination and plenty of finesse to the kitchen of this restaurant, which has earned him acclaim. Part of the once-decaying but now redeveloped quayside at Princes Wharf, the restaurant is decorated in soft, soothing colors of land and sea. His wife, Susan, guides the dining room with a skilled hand. You might enjoy, as most diners do, one of the fresh fish dishes that appear daily on the menu. The style of cuisine is modern British-French. You can also sample such dishes as honey-roasted duck and herb-flavored lamb that evoke memories of Provence. For dessert, try if featured the melting chocolate cake flavored with Grand Marnier. A set lunch for £12.50 ($20.65) is perhaps the city's outstanding dining value, although you can pay as much as £30 ($49.50) per head in the evening. Service is from noon to 2pm and 7 to 11pm; closed lunch Sat., and all day Sun. and Mon. Reservations are always essential.

In a city long known for its Chinese eateries, **Dragon House,** 30-32 Stowell St. (tel. 091/232-0868), has surfaced near the top. It offers the largest menu in the city, at least 200 separate dishes, ranging from stir-fried chicken with oyster sauce to roast duck Hong Kong style. Barry Yu, the owner, oversees a restaurant staff that is equally adept at preparing classic Chinese cookery as they are in inventing new dishes. They always seem to manage to come up with interesting flavor combinations. Bowing to modern tastes, they also offer a health and vegetarian menu. Fortified by Korean-grown ginseng, you can peruse the menu from noon to 2pm and 6pm to midnight Mon. to Sat., from noon to midnight Sun. A set lunch is a steal at £4 ($6.60), and you can return for a table d'hôte dinner costing from £11.50 ($19) to £16 ($26.40). A la carte orders average £16 ($26.40). Reservations are needed, and you can dine in air-conditioned comfort.

Fisherman's Lodge, Jesmond Dene (tel. 091/2813281), is considered by some as one of the finest restaurants in Tyne and Wear, lying as it does in a wooded parkland next to Ouse Burn. Fresh fish dishes—an array of scampi, halibut, crab, and lobster—are there to tempt. The kitchen staff is equally adept at classic or more modern fish preparations. You can enjoy a lager or a glass of wine in a relaxing bar lounge before tackling the menu. If someone in your party doesn't like fish, there are many well-prepared meat dishes as well. Meals are served from noon to 2pm and 7 to 11pm; closed Sat. lunch and all day Sun. A set lunch is a good value at £13.50 ($22.30), although you are likely to spend from £25 ($41.25) for an à la carte dinner. Reservations are necessary.

6. Northumberland

Unfortunately, most motorists zip through this far northeastern county of England on their way to Scotland, missing the beauty and historic interest of the Border section. Because it is so close to Scotland, Northumberland was the scene of many a bloody skirmish. The county now displays a number of fortified castles that saw action in those battles. Inland are the valleys of the Cheviot Hills, lying mostly within the Northumberland National Park and the remainder of the Border Forest Park, Europe's largest planned forest.

Northumberland's coast is one of Britain's best-kept secrets. Here are islands, castles, tiny fishing villages, miles of sands, as well as golf and fishing among the dunes, and birdwatching in the Farne Islands—in all, an area of outstanding natural beauty.

Wallington Hall, at Cambo, 12 miles west of Morpeth on the B6342 and 6 miles northwest of Belsey off the A696, dates from 1688, but the present building reflects the great changes brought about in the 1740s when Daniel Garrett completely refashioned the exterior of the house. The interior is decorated with rococo plasterwork and furnished with fine porcelains, furniture, and paintings. Travelers may also visit the museum and enjoy an extensive display of dollhouses. The coach house contains an exhibit of ornate carriages. The main building is surrounded by 100 acres of woodlands and lakes, including a beautifully terraced, walled garden and a conservatory restaurant, shop, and information center. The grounds are open all year; the house, April 1 to October 28 from 1 to 5:30pm; closed Tue. Last admission is half an hour before closing time. Admission to the house and grounds is £3 ($4.95); to the grounds only, £1.50 ($2.50). Children pay half price. For more information, telephone 067074/283.

Seaton Delaval Hall at Whitley Bay (tel. 091/237-1493), the enormous country home of Lord Hastings near Whitley Bay, represents the architecture of Sir John Vanbrugh, builder of Blenheim Palace and Castle Howard. Many consider this English baroque hall the masterpiece of the playwright/architect. It looks like the stage settings for 14 Roman tragedies piled one on top of another. Walk over and look through a window, and you can almost imagine knights and wenches feasting at long tables and drinking mead. The house is open to view from May to September from 2 to 6pm Wed. and Sun., charging adults an admission of £1 ($1.65); children, 50p (85¢). The hall is half a mile from the coast of Seaton Sluice between Blyth and Whitley Bay, 10 miles from Newcastle, reached via Northumbrian buses 363 and 364, which run half-hourly.

Farne Islands are a group of small islands off the Northumbria coast, which provide a summer home for at least 20 species of seabirds as well as for one of the largest British colonies of gray seals. St. Cuthbert died here in 687, and a chapel built in the 14th century is thought to be on the site of his original cell. Only Inner Farne and Staple Island are open to the public. Visiting season extends from April through September, but access is more controlled during the breeding season. From mid-May to mid-July, you can visit Staple Island from 10:30am to 1:30pm daily, and Inner Farne from 2 to 5pm daily. From April 1 to mid-May and from mid-July until the end of September hours for both Staple Island and Inner Farne are from 10am to 6pm. Tickets are obtained on the island. During the peak season, adults pay £2.50 ($4.15) and children are charged £1.50 ($2.50). During the rest of the season, the admission is £2 ($3.30).

The best way to get to this most famous bird and animal sanctuary in the British Isles is to telephone or write Billy Shiel, the Farne Islands boatman, at 4 Southfield Ave., Seahouses, Northumberland (tel. 0665/720308). He has been taking people in his licensed boat for the past 40 years, so he knows the tides and the best places to film seals, puffins, and guillemots. He runs 2½-hour trips in his 60-passenger craft at a cost of £3.50 ($5.80) per person.

Incidentally, these are the islands where Grace Darling and her father made their famous rescue of men from a foundered ship (see below).

HOLY ISLAND

The site of the Lindisfarne religious community during the Dark Ages, Holy Island is only accessible for 10 hours of the day, high tides covering the causeway at other times. For crossing times, check with local information centers.

Lindisfarne Castle, on Holy Island, was built about 1550 as a fort to protect the harbor. In 1903 it was converted by Sir Edwin Lutyens into a comfortable home for Edward Hudson, the founder of *Country Life.* It is open from April to the end of September from 1 to 5:30pm; closed Fri., except Good Friday. In October it's open only on Wed., Sat., and Sun. Admission is £2.80 ($4.60) for adults and £1.40 ($2.30) for children.

At Lindisfarne, you can stay at the **Lindisfarne Private Hotel,** Holy Island, Northumberland TD15 2SQ (tel. 0289/89273). This is a fine, substantial frame building with a trio of tall chimneys. It's run by members of the Massey family, who conduct it more like a private home than a hotel. Centrally heated bedrooms contain hot and cold running water (a few with private baths) and are decorated with personality, providing a homelike atmosphere. The charge ranges from £22.50 ($37.15) to £25 ($41.25) per person daily for bed, breakfast, and evening dinner. Boating excursions can be arranged to the Farnes.

BAMBURGH CASTLE

Guarding the British shore along the North Sea, the castle at Bamburgh (tel. 06684/208) stands on a site that has been occupied since the 1st century B.C. The Craggy Citadel where it stands was a royal center by A.D. 547. The Norman keep has stood for 8 centuries, the remainder of the castle having been restored toward the end of the 19th century. This was the first castle to succumb to artillery fire, the guns of Edward IV. You can visit the grounds and public rooms daily from April to early October: 1 to 5pm in April, May, June, and September; 1 to 6pm in July and August; and 1 to 4:30pm in October. Admission is £2.10 ($3.45) for adults, 90p ($1.50) for children. There is a tea room. The castle is the home of Lord and Lady Armstrong and their family. It lies 16 miles north of Alnwick and 6 miles from Belford.

Nearby is the **Grace Darling Museum** at Bamburgh (tel. 0665/720037), which has various mementos, pictures, and documents relating to the heroic Grace Darling, including the boat in which she and her father, who was keeper of the Longstone lighthouse in the Farne Islands, rescued nine people from the S.S. *Forfarshire,* which foundered in 1838. It's open daily from Easter to mid-October from 11am to 6pm. Admission is free, but donations to the Royal National Lifeboat Institution are gratefully accepted.

HADRIAN'S WALL

This wall, which extends across the north of England for 73 miles, from the North Sea to the Irish Sea, is particularly interesting for a stretch of 10 miles west of Housesteads. Only the lower courses of the wall are preserved intact; the rest were reconstructed in the 19th century with the original stones. From several vantage points along the wall, you have incomparable views north to the Cheviot Hills along the Scottish border, and south to the Durham moors.

The wall was built following a visit of the Emperor Hadrian in A.D. 122. He wanted to see the far frontier of the Roman Empire, and he also sought to build a dramatic line between the so-called civilized world and the barbarians. Legionnaires were ordered to build a wall across the width of the island of Britain.

The wall is a premier Roman attraction in Europe, ranking among many people with Rome's Colosseum. The western end can be reached from Carlisle, with a good museum of Roman artifacts, and the eastern end from Newcastle upon Tyne (some remains are seen on the city outskirts and a good museum at the university). South Shields, Sights at Housesteads, Chester, Corbridge, and Vindolanda are all good forts to visit in the area.

At Housesteads (English Heritage) you can visit a **Roman fort** (tel. 0434/344363), built about A.D. 130 to house an infantry of 1,000 men. Called Vercovicium in Latin, the fort held a full-scale military encampment, the remains of which can be seen today. The fort is open April 1 to September 30 from 10am to 6pm; during other months from 10am to 4pm. Admission is £1.40 ($2.30) for adults and 70p ($1.15) for children.

Just west of Housesteads is **Vindolanda** (tel. 0434/344277), another fort south of the wall at Chesterholm. The building is very well preserved, and there is also an excavated civilian settlement outside the fort with an interesting museum of artifacts of everyday Roman life. Hours are daily from 10am to 5pm or dusk. Admission is £2 ($3.30) for adults, £1 ($1.65) for children.

Not far from Vindolanda is the **Roman Army Museum,** Carvoran, on

Hadrian's Wall near Greenhead, which traces the growth and influence of Rome from her early beginnings to the development and expansion of the empire, with special emphasis on the role of the Roman army and the garrisons of Hadrian's Wall. A barracks room shows basic army living conditions. Realistic life-size figures make this a striking visual museum experience. Admission is £1.50 ($2.50) for adults, £1.10 ($1.80) for children. For information, phone 06972/485.

Within easy walking distance of the Roman Army Museum lies one of the most imposing and high-standing sections of Hadrian's Wall, Walltown Crags, where the height of the wall and magnificent views to north and south are impressive.

HAYDON BRIDGE

Between Haltwhistle (9 miles) and Hexham (6 miles), the **Anchor Hotel**, John Martin Street, Haydon Bridge, Northumberland NE47 6AB (tel. 043484/227), is ideally situated for visitors to the wall and its surroundings. This riverside village pub was once a coaching inn on the route from Newcastle to Carlisle. The cozy bar is much used by locals. In the country dining room, wholesome evening meals are served. Dinner costs from £12 ($19.80). You can also spend the night in one of the 12 bedrooms, 10 with private baths, phones, and TVs. Charges range from £25 ($41.25) to £31 ($51.15) daily in a single and £36 ($59.40) to £42 ($69.30) in a double.

HEXHAM

Above the Tyne River, this historic old market town is characterized by its narrow streets, old market square, a fine abbey church, and its Moot Hall. It makes a good base for exploring Hadrian's Wall and the Roman supply base of Corstopitum at Corbridge-on-Tyne, the ancient capital of Northumberland. The **tourist office**, at Hallgate (tel. 0434/605225), has masses of information on the wall for walkers, drivers, campers, and picnickers.

Abbey Church of St. Wilfrid is full of ancient relics. The Saxon font, the misericord carvings on the choir stalls, Acca's Cross, and St. Wilfrid's chair are well worth seeing. The location is 304 miles from London and 21 miles from Newcastle upon Tyne.

Where to Stay and Dine in the Environs

The best accommodations are found not in Hexham itself, but in satellite villages and small towns, as exemplified by the following.

For a stay in a stately home, I recommend **Langley Castle**, Langley, Hexham, Northumberland NE47 5LU (tel. 043484/8888), not far southwest of Haydon Bridge and about 7 miles west of Hexham, in 10 acres of woodland on the edge of Northumberland National Park. The castle, built in 1350, was mainly uninhabited after being damaged in 1400 in the English-Scottish war, until its purchase in the late 19th century by Cadwallader Bates, a historian, who spent the rest of his life restoring the property with great care to its original beauty. Such medieval features are here as the 1350 spiral staircase, stained-glass windows, huge open fireplaces, 7-foot-thick walls, and many turrets. Today the only medieval fortified castle home in England receives paying guests in eight luxuriously appointed bedrooms of varying sizes and amenities. All the units have baths, direct-dial phones, color TVs, and radios, and some have whirlpools or saunas. Rents range from £65 ($107.25) to £85 ($140.25) daily, depending on the season and the features of the room, the prices based on double occupancy. Prices include breakfast and VAT. The hotel has an elegant drawing room, with an adjoining oak-paneled bar. Local specialties are served in the intimate restaurant.

Hadrian Hotel, Wall, near Hexham, Northumberland NE46 4EE (tel. 043481/232), is the ideal place to stay when visiting Hadrian's Wall. It's an ivy-covered building erected of stones taken from the wall. The owners have completely refurbished the place, and it now has two Jacobean-style bars serving good bar meals specializing in seafood. The restaurant has an à la carte menu offering such specialties as stuffed guinea fowl Emperor Hadrian and roast chicken Northumbrian.

Meals cost from £15 ($24.75) and up. The nine attractive bedrooms have baths or showers, toilets, TVs, phones, radio alarms, and hot beverage facilities. Three units have four-poster beds. Singles cost from £20 ($33) to £26 ($42.90) daily and doubles or twins £32 ($52.80) to £40 ($66). The hotel has a private residents' garden and beer gardens.

George Hotel, Chollerford, Humshaugh, near Hexham, Northumberland NE46 4EW (tel. 043481/611), stands on the banks of the Tyne, a creeper-covered country hotel with gardens leading to the riverbank. It's a convenient base for visiting Hadrian's Wall. The hotel dates from the 18th century, when the original structure was built of Roman stone. The 54 bedrooms are pleasantly appointed and have private baths, color TVs, phones, and mini-bars. Rates are from £60 ($99) daily for a single, from £85 ($140.25) for twins or doubles. All tariffs include an English breakfast and VAT. The hotel has an activity club with heated, indoor swimming pool, sauna, spa bath, and solarium. The Fisherman's Bar is where locals gather for a traditional pub welcome and bar snacks served at lunch. A set buffet luncheon in the restaurant costs from £10 ($16.50); dinner, from £15.95 ($26.30). An à la carte menu is also available, complemented by a large wine list.

LONGHORSLEY

Linden Hall Hotel, Longhorsley, Morpeth, Northumberland NE65 8XF (tel. 0670/516611), a converted 19th-century mansion, is set in 300 acres of woods and parkland near Longhorsley, 6 miles northwest of Morpeth by the A1 onto the A697. A sweeping staircase leads to rooms with modern beds, except in the honeymoon suites, which are furnished with four-posters. All 45 units have baths, color TVs, radios, phones, and baby-listening service, with some antique furniture used to advantage. Ten ground-floor rooms grouped around a sunny cobblestone courtyard are suitable for physically handicapped guests. All rates include a full English breakfast, VAT, and service. A single costs £75 ($123.75) daily, a double or twin going for £86 ($141.90) to £96 ($158.40). The chef offers a wide menu with some original appetizers. An array of fish dishes is offered nightly. Vegetables fresh from the field accompany main dishes in summer. There is also a good selection of wines. A meal costs around £18 ($29.70) to £25 ($41.25), including dessert.

On the estate in the restored granary is the Linden Pub, a casual place with a log fire and a collection of those large enameled signs that used to advertise tobacco, Camp coffee, and cocoa. As well as serving North Country ales, the pub provides good bar food. They often have barbecues in the courtyard in summer, when guests can indulge in such pursuits as quoits, boule, and garden draughts.

ALNMOUTH

A seaside resort on the Aln estuary, Alnmouth attracts sporting people who fish for salmon and trout in the Coquet River or play on its good golf course. The location is 314 miles from London and 37 miles from Newcastle upon Tyne.

Schooner Hotel, Northumberland Street, Alnmouth, Northumberland NE66 2RS (tel. 0665/830216), is a well-preserved Georgian inn, only a few minutes' walk to the water. The hotel is adjacent to the nine-hole Village Golf Course, the second oldest in the country, and also lies near an 18-hole championship course. The hotel has a squash court and a solarium. All 24 bedrooms have baths, color TVs, and direct-dial phones. Singles cost £24 ($39.60) to £35 ($57.75) daily, and doubles go for £40 ($66) to £62 ($102.30). Guests can count on the good meals: set luncheons are priced at £6.50 ($10.75) and set dinners at £10.50 ($17.35). The hotel has a grill room, dining room, the Seahunter Bar, the Chase Bar, and the Long Bar, as well as a residents' lounge.

ALNWICK

Set in the peaceful countryside of Northumberland, this ancient market town has had a long history. It lies 320 miles from London and 34 miles from Newcastle upon Tyne. A good center for touring an area of scenic beauty, Alnwick is visited chiefly today by travelers wanting to see the local historic architecture.

What to See and Do

In the town of Alnwick, 30 miles north of Newcastle, **Alnwick Castle** (tel. 0665/510777), the largest castle in England after Windsor, is the seat of the duke of Northumberland. This border fortress dates from the 11th century, when the earliest parts of the present castle were constructed by Yvo de Vescy, the first Norman baron of Alnwick. A major restoration was undertaken by the fourth duke in the mid-19th century, and Alnwick remains relatively unchanged to this day. The rugged medieval outer walls do not prepare the first-time visitor for the richness of the interior, decorated mainly in the style of the Italian Renaissance.

Most of the castle is open to the public during visiting hours. You can tour the principal apartments, including the armory, guard chamber, and library, where you can view portraits and landscapes painted by such masters as Titian, Canaletto, and Van Dyck. You may also visit the dungeons and the interesting Museum of Early British and Roman Relics. From the terraces within the castle's outer walls, you can look across the broad landscape stretching over the River Aln.

The castle is open May to September from 1 to 5pm; closed Sat. from April 29 to June 23 and September 2 to October 5. Admission is £2.20 ($3.65) for adults and £1 ($1.65) for children.

Cragside, designed in the late 19th century by architect Richard Norman Shaw for the first Lord Armstrong, is a grand estate stretching across 900 acres on the southern edge of the Alnwick Moor. Here groves of magnificent trees and fields of rhododendrons frequently give way to peaceful ponds and lakes. The Victorian house is open only for part of the season, but the grounds alone are worth the visit. At Rothbury, the house is just 13 miles southwest of Alnwick. The park is open from April 1 to the end of October daily 10:30am to 7pm, to 4pm Sat. and Sun. from November to the end of March. Admission to the park only is £2 ($3.30) for adults and £1 ($1.65) for children. The house is open from April to the end of October 1 to 5:30pm Tue. to Sun. (last entry half an hour before closing). Admission to both house and park is £3.50 ($5.80) for adults, £1.75 ($2.90) for children. For more information, phone 0669/20333.

Dunstanburgh Castle (English Heritage), on the coast 9 miles northeast of Alnwick, about 1½ miles east of Embleton (which is the castle's address), was begun in 1316 by Thomas, Earl of Lancaster, and enlarged later in the 14th century by John of Gaunt. The ruins of the gatehouse, towers, and curtain wall stand on a promontory high above the sea. You can reach the castle on foot only, either by walking from Craster in the south or across the Dunstanburgh Golf Course from Embleton and Dunstan Steads in the north. The castle is open from Good Friday to the end of September; 10am to 6pm Tue. to Sun., to 4pm October to the end of March; closed Christmas and New Year's. Admission is 85p ($1.40) for adults, 40p (65¢) for children.

Where to Stay and Dine

The White Swan, Bondgate Within, Alnwick, Northumberland NE66 1TD (tel. 0665/602109), has a history going back to medieval days when it entertained highwaymen and passengers on the Edinburgh-London stagecoaches. A neoclassic coaching inn, just inside an ancient town gate, the Hotspur, it has also become the permanent home of the music room of the S.S. *Olympic,* sister ship of the *Titanic.* This beautiful paneled room was removed from the ship and completely reconstructed at the hotel. The hotel has 41 bedrooms, with baths and showers, phones, and TVs, and some of these are in a modern block and others in the older, more traditional part of the inn. Singles begin at £54 ($89.10) daily, and doubles peak at £75 ($123.75) including a full breakfast, service, and VAT.

CORNHILL-ON-TWEED

This border village, on the River Tweed, faces Coldstream on the Scottish shore. The location is 345 miles from London and 59 miles from Newcastle upon Tyne.

Tillmouth Park Hotel, Cornhill-on-Tweed, Northumberland TD12 4UU (tel. 0890/2255), built in 1882, is an imposing Victorian mansion, occupying a secluded position in its own parkland gardens overlooking the River Till at the heart of a 1,000-acre estate. It stands about 9 miles from Berwick, 3 miles from Cornhill-on-Tweed, and 4 miles from Coldstream. Monumental and impressive, it rises four stories high, with many wings, gables, and chimneys, including a porch emblazoned with heraldic devices. In spite of its size, there are only 13 bedrooms, each one comfortable, all containing private baths, TVs, and phones. Ask for the Sir Walter Scott room with its twin four-posters. Edwardian furnishings grace some of the chambers, which rent for £50 ($82.50) daily for one person, £75 ($123.75) for a double. Honeymooners ask for the garden suite. Modernity, as reflected by a cocktail bar, has been blended with tradition, as represented by a galleried lounge with a stone fireplace.

PART TWO

SCOTLAND

XVIII

INTRODUCING SCOTLAND

1. THE COUNTRY

2. FLYING TO SCOTLAND

3. GETTING AROUND SCOTLAND

4. FAST FACTS FOR SCOTLAND

In Scotland, a land of bagpipes and clans, you'll find some of the grandest scenery in Europe. You'll first encounter the Lowlands, but in the distance the fabled Highlands loom. You'll discover lochs and glens, heather-covered moors, pastel houses and graystone cottages, mountains, and rivers and streams filled with trout and salmon. Eagles soar and deer run free. Lush meadowlands are filled with sheep; rocky coves and secret harbors wait to be discovered. You'll hear the sound of Gaelic, see a Shetland pony, and perhaps attend a Highland gathering. You'll find quiet contemplation or else enjoy an activity-filled calendar.

Many visitors think of Scotland as Edinburgh and search no further, but if you travel northward, you'll find the real Scotland, along with overwhelming hospitality and a sense of exploration.

A small nation, Scotland is only 275 miles long and some 150 miles wide at its broadest point. No one lives more than 40 miles from salt water. In spite of the smallness of size, however, Scotland has extended its influence far and wide. Inventors came from Scotland, including Alexander Graham Bell, and explorers, including Mungo Park and David Livingstone. Scotland gave the world such entrepreneurs as Andrew Carnegie, poets such as Robert Burns and novelists such as Sir Walter Scott. But, curiously, for a long time its most famous resident has been neither man nor woman—it's the Loch Ness monster!

Scotland has its own legal system and issues its own currency. However, English and Scottish banknotes have equal value and are accepted in both countries. The Church of Scotland is separate from that of England. The language of the Scot is said to be nearer original English than what is spoken in England today.

If you go by road or rail, you will hardly be aware of crossing out of England into Scotland. The border is just a line on a map. But, even though the two countries have been joined constitutionally since 1707, Scotland is very different from England. It is very much its own country. But remember that scotch is a whisky (spelled without an *e*) and *not* the name of the proud people who inhabit the country. They are called Scots or Scottish. Even if you forget and call them Scotch, they'll forgive you—what they won't forgive is you calling them English.

1. The Country

This northernmost country of the three that make up the island of Great Britain (Scotland, England, and Wales) has for centuries been the home of a spirited, independent people, who were tough enough and brave enough to live in this mostly rugged land and to maintain their freedom from outside control up to the time a Scotsman, King James VI, went to sit on the British throne as James I in 1603.

Scotland is the oldest geological formation of Great Britain, divided physically into three regions: the granite Highlands, including lochs, glens, and mountains, plus the hundreds and hundreds of islands to the west and north; the Central Lowlands, where three valleys and estuaries (firths) of the Clyde, Forth, and Tay rivers make up a fertile belt from the Atlantic Ocean to the North Sea; and the Southern Uplands, the smooth, rolling moorland, broken with low crags and threaded with rivers and valleys, between the central plain and the English border.

From the last Ice Age, humankind has lived in what is today Scotland, as attested by cairns, standing stones, brochs, cromlechs, and burial chambers. Eventually Celts moved in. They may have come here via Ireland, but they were probably not Irish Celts, being more closely related to those of Cornwall, Wales, and Brittany—Celt-Iberians. They were dubbed Picts (from the Latin *pictor* or painter) by the Roman invaders, who came to what they called Caledonia in the early part of the 1st century A.D. The Picts were so named because they painted their bodies blue, it is claimed. At any rate, the Romans didn't have much luck against the wild, fierce inhabitants of Caledonia and before long pulled back south and built Hadrian's Wall, leaving the northern reaches to the short, dark Picts.

A different breed of Celt, the Dalriad Irish, called Scots, moved in before A.D. 500, bringing with them Christianity. These people were red- and sandy-haired with fair skin. They settled first in the Argyll peninsula, which they named Scotia. The Scotians and Celt-Iberians (Picts) became mixed over the centuries, but in the Highlands, some of the small, dark strain still exists in almost pure form.

Religion has a strong place in the lore and history of this country, from Druids to Roman Catholicism to staunch and puritanical Presbyterianism. The early centuries of Scotland were marked by strong leadership by monks and abbots, but by the time of the Reformation, John Knox and his militant Calvinism took over in many areas. Presbyterianism is still the major religion in the country, despite the link with England.

The country had its own kings and their battling cohorts by the time of William the Conqueror. Sometimes the Scots banded together to battle the English, at other times joining the neighbors to the south to fight each other. The first Irish invaders started new families, which, when they split from the original homesteads and resettled, formed *clans,* the Gaelic word meaning "family" or "children of." The clan designation allowed them to trace their origins even when they moved to distant places. There was a strong hierarchy within each clan, with a chief at its head, followed by lesser chieftains, gentlemen, and then plain clansmen. The various families warred among themselves for territory, rights and honor. The fighting among the clans abated in 1609 when, on the island of Iona, the statutes of Iona were signed by most of the clan chiefs. Sporadic fighting continued for years, but the last real clan battle—Macdonalds versus Macintoshes—took place in 1688.

The power of the great lords of Scotland was broken in 1603, when the son of Mary Queen of Scots assumed the throne of England upon the death of Elizabeth, but all was not peace and goodwill between Scots and English. Religion again stirred strife when King James II was ousted from the throne and his Roman Catholic descendants tried to restore their title and their religion to England and Scotland. Because many Highlanders had rallied to the cause of Bonnie Prince Charlie's claims to the throne (1745), the wearing of the tartan, the distinguishing plaid material denoting the wearer's clan affiliation, was banned until 1782.

As a result of the strife and defeat of anti-English forces, many Scots fled to other parts of the world during the troubled 1700s, becoming an integral part of the development of the United States and other countries.

THE PEOPLE

Scotland is a country of hospitable people, who are descended from an interesting mixture of bloodlines: Celt-Iberian (Pict), Roman, Norse, Saxon, Irish Celtic, Jute, Angle, Norman, and French, with perhaps a few more sources thrown in, what with the seafarers of many nations who have come here through the centuries.

At one time, in parts where the Celtic heritage was strongest, the language of the country was Gaelic and even today is still used in some remote parts. That language is still remembered in a few words and phrases, as it is seen in place names. The later Gaelic was always much like Erse or Irish Gaelic, although there are similarities to the languages that were once the native tongues of Cornwall and Brittany and the one that is still widely spoken in Wales.

Scotland has a population today of some 5,200,000 people, about 75% of whom live in the Central Lowland area, the fertile strip that stretches from the Firth of Forth to the Firth of Clyde, where most of the industry of the country is found. Outside the big cities of Edinburgh and Glasgow, people live in small towns and on farms, some even in the tiny crofts clinging to steep hillsides in the western Highland county.

Scotland's deepest traditions appear to the outsider to be based on the clan system of old, with tartans, bagpipes, and all such things playing a large part in the thinking of people when they talk about the country. This is a romantic memory, however, and the fact is that many of the Scots—Lowlanders—have little or no connection with the clansmen of earlier times.

Many of the Scots were laden with a lasting guilt feeling by the preachings of John Knox and the forced adherence for a long time to teachings of the kirk and harsh Scottish Presbyterianism. Although the customs have changed in resort areas, brought about by the coming of many tourists to the country, there is still a strain of puritanism that can be seen in Sunday closings, with many of the people of the country observing the Sabbath as a day of rest.

The strength and independent spirit of the Scots has been carried by their people who have spread all over the world, making good in many fields. Many, however, have stayed home and made their mark from the place where Bronze Age aborigines began the long journey into modern Scotland.

TARTANS AND KILTS

Today the clans, the ancient families, and those who enjoy common ancestry are identified mainly by their tartans, the word first recorded in 1471 to describe the previously named "chequered garment" or "mantle." The kilt has a much older history as a style of dress. It was recorded in Bronze Age frescoes in Crete and worn by soldiers such as the Romans.

After the 1745 rebellion led by Bonnie Prince Charlie, the checkered, multicolored cloth was banned. However, when Sir Walter Scott invited King George IV to visit Scotland, the king arrived in a kilt, wearing pink tights underneath. Thus the tartan came back into fashion, helped in no small part by Prince Albert, consort to Queen Victoria.

There are some 300 clan designs today. Many kilt shops throughout Scotland will help you determine if your family has its own tartan.

Garb o' the Gods

Few people realize that from 7 to 10 yards of tartan wool cloth goes into the average kilt. Even fewer non-Scots know what is actually worn beneath the voluminous folds strapped over the muscular thighs of a parading Scotsman. For a Highlander, the answer to that question is "nothing," an answer that is true for any

defender of the ancient tradition that only a Stewart can wear a Stewart tartan, that only a MacPherson can wear a MacPherson tartan, and that only a Scotsman looks good in a kilt. Of course, any true Scot would wager his claymore (sword) that only a foreigner would stoop to wearing "unmentionables" (that's underpants to us) beneath his kilt.

Alas, commercialism has reared its ugly head with the introduction of undergarments to match the material making up the swirling folds of the kilts of bagpipe players. Nevertheless, salesmen in shops specializing in Highland garb tell the story of a colonel, the 11th earl of Airlie, who had heard that the soldiers of his elite Highland Light Infantry were mollycoddling themselves with undershorts. The next day, his eyebrows bristling, he ordered the entire regiment to undress under his watchful eye. To his horror, he saw that half a dozen of his soldiers had disgraced the regiment by putting on "what only an Englishman would wear." He publicly ordered the offending garments removed. When he gave the order next day to "drop your kilts," not a soldier in the regiment had on "trews" (close-cut tartan shorts).

It was no doubt a long time before a similar level of indiscretion may have manifested itself among the Highland Light Infantry, if indeed it ever has. Even with the general decline of standards today, the mark of a man in the Highlands is still whether he can abide drafts up against his thighs and the feel of rough cloth against tender flesh.

If you're not fortunate enough to be of Highland extraction, or if you are distantly Scottish but can't discover possible clan connections, there is still hope. Long ago, Queen Victoria authorized two "Lowland" designs as suitable garb for Sassenachs (Saxons—Englishmen and, more remotely, Americans). If, during your jaunts in the Highlands, you decide to wear a kilt and a true Scot sees you in a Sassenach tartan, he or she will probably assume that you are also wearing "unmentionables."

ANCESTRAL ROOTS

If you have a name beginning with "Mac" (which simply means son), or if your name is Donaldson, or Shaw, or one of the dozens and dozens of other Scottish names, you may have been descended from a clan. This was a group of kinsmen ruled over by a chief and claiming a common ancestry. MacDonald is, in fact, one of the oldest clans, dating back to the 13th century. Clans and clan societies have their own museums throughout Scotland, and local tourist offices will have details about where to locate them. Some of the more prominent ones are previewed in this guide.

In bookstores throughout Scotland, you can also purchase clan histories and maps. In Edinburgh and Glasgow, genealogical firms specialize in tracing Highland family histories.

If you'd like to do it yourself (a lot cheaper), you may want to go to the **General Register Office for Scotland,** New Register House, Edinburgh, Lothian EH1 3YT. You can write them for a full list of their search fees and a full extent of their records before going there yourself. Scottish ancestor hunters come here bitten by the genealogy bug, and seats get crowded in summer. The house has on record details of every birth, marriage, and death in Scotland since 1855. It also has census returns for every decade from 1841 to 1891. They also have such data as the recordings of foreign marriages of Scots, adopted children's registers, and war registers.

2. Flying to Scotland

Until recently, most North Americans reached Scotland by flying first to the bustling airports of London, then going on to Scotland via train, rented car, or plane. Since most visitors combine trips to Scotland with visits to England, this is probably the most often-used travel pattern for North American visitors, especially since the choice of airlines flying into London from North America is greater than that flying from any other country. The keen transatlantic competition often leads to less expensive airfares (and consequent savings for you).

Among the many airlines flying to London from North America is the premier airline of the United Kingdom, **British Airways,** with 21 different routes between the United States and the United Kingdom. British Airways is joined in the transatlantic sweepstakes with such competing carriers as **American, Delta, Pan Am,** and **Virgin Atlantic.** (The many ways of getting to London are presented in Chapter I.)

Many visitors, however, are increasingly attracted to the idea of flying directly to Scotland. To answer this need, in 1990, many airlines caught on to the idea of promoting Scotland as a viable (and profitable) destination in itself.

Foremost among them was British Airways, which added three nonstop flights to Glasgow from New York every week throughout the year. Flights depart from JFK airport every Fri., Sat., and Sun. at 8:30pm, flying nonstop to Glasgow for an early (7:45am) arrival the next morning. Westbound flights return to New York the same day at noon. Many visitors appreciate the avoidance of the crowds at London airports, and often begin and end their trips to Great Britain from Scotland.

As for prices and promotions, British Airways charges very nearly the same amount to Glasgow as it does for flights to its English destinations of London and Manchester. This makes it especially tempting for APEX passengers to land at London and depart from Glasgow (or vice versa) after winding their way through the British countryside by car or by train.

Passengers departing from the Midwest for the vales of Scotland might opt for **American Airlines'** daily nonstop flights to Glasgow from Chicago. Serving the entire Midwest and much of the West Coast, American's widebodied 767s depart from O'Hare airport every evening at 8:40pm, arriving the next morning in Glasgow at 10:15am. Chicago's vast airport facilities make it a useful connecting point for flights throughout the central and western States, and most of Canada as well.

Another contender is **Northwest Airlines'** flight 34, which for many years flew from Boston to the isolated Scottish airport of Prestwick. In 1990, it altered its flight plans to fly instead to the more centrally located airport at Glasgow. Boston is Northwest's main hub to its five destinations in Europe, and many visitors appreciate the ability to avoid both New York and London on their way to the rural beauties of Scotland.

A QUESTION OF FARES

Because many of their passengers prefer to land at London's Heathrow and depart from Glasgow's Abbotsinch, British Airways applies the same promotions and rock-bottom APEX fares to a triangular, "open-jawed" ticket that it applies to simpler round-trip tickets between New York and London.

Most of the fares already discussed in Chapter I, "Flying to England," apply with only slight modifications to BA's flights from New York to Glasgow. At presstime, a nonrefundable, APEX round-trip ticket between New York and Glasgow cost between $490 and $712, depending on the day of the week and the season. This ticket required a 30-day advance purchase, and a delay of between 7 and 21 days before returning to New York. Passengers who preferred to land in London and depart from Glasgow paid a few dollars less than those printed above, because of the greater flexibility (and slightly lower prices) of flights into London.

Many passengers wait until moments before flight time, then call an airline to get the discounted prices of remaining unbooked tickets. For this type of passenger, BA offers discounted tickets available 3 days or less prior to flight time. Depending on the season, round-trip tickets from New York to Glasgow cost around $540 in high season, and a bit less in winter.

All classes of service on BA's other flights are also available on BA's flights from New York to Glasgow. A talk with a BA reservations agent will present any special promotional deals available at the time of your intended departure.

From Chicago, American Airlines offers its least expensive APEX tickets to passengers who pre-reserve their tickets 30 days in advance, and who stay abroad for between 7 and 21 days. Flying in both directions between Mon. and Thur. in low season (which is usually the cold-weather months) will cost a passenger around $538. Flying both directions on a midsummer weekend will cost around $718 round trip.

Additional promotions, special fares, and special savings come and go with the seasons. The best way is to telephone a reservations agent for the airlines directly. For toll-free reservations and information, call British Airways at 800/247-9297, American Airlines at 800/433-7300, and Northwest Airlines at 800/225-2525.

---

3. Getting Around Scotland

From Newcastle upon Tyne, the A68 heading northwest takes you to where England meets Scotland, an area long known as "Carter Bar." At this point, all of Scotland lies before you, and an unforgettable land it is.

I recommend to visitors that they approach the Border Country after a stopover in the York area of England. That way, they can start exploring Scotland in the east with Edinburgh as their goal, then go up through Royal Deeside and on to Inverness, crossing over and down the west side of Glasgow, emerging at Gretna Green, near Carlisle in England's Lake District. The Border Country is a fitting introduction to Scotland, as it contains many reminders of the country's historic and literary past. A highlight of the tour is a visit to Abbotsford, the house Sir Walter Scott built on the banks of the salmon-filled River Tweed. However, if you enter Scotland from the west of England, you'll travel through Dumfries and Galloway—the Land of Burns, former home of Scotland's national poet, Robert Burns.

Burns knew well the southwestern corner of Scotland, which is bounded by an indented coastline of charm, which attracts many artists to the secluded life that prevails there. Distances aren't long, but many motorists traveling in Scotland find so much to see that they take 2 or 3 days to cover about 100 miles. At Ayr, Troon, and Prestwick (with its international airport), you'll find sandy beaches and golf courses, good fishing, and pony trekking. Farther north, you'll come to the land of the lochs and glens. Maybe you'll even spot the Loch Ness monster, Nessie, along the way.

By Train

For information on traveling by train in Scotland, see Chapter I, Section **3**, "Traveling Within Britain."

By Bus

The cheapest means of transport in Scotland is bus (or coach). **Scottish Citylink Coaches,** which link Glasgow and Edinburgh with the popular tourist centers of Aviemore and Inverness, is a good bet. It takes only 3 hours to reach Aviemore from Edinburgh, 3½ hours to Inverness from the capital. Other popular runs are offered, including links between Glasgow and Fort William, Inverness and Ullapool, and Glasgow and Oban. For information, get in touch with **Highland Scottish,** Seafield Road, Inverness (tel. 0463/237575), or **Scottish Citylink Coaches,** Buchanan Bus Station, Glasgow (tel. 041/3329191), and **St. Andrew Square Bus Station,** Edinburgh (tel. 031/557-5717).

By Ferry

You can use a variety of special excursion fares to reach Scotland's islands, available from Caledonian MacBrayne for the Clyde and the islands of the west or from P&O Scottish Ferries, serving Orkney and Shetland. Caledonian MacBrayne sails to 23 Hebridean or Clyde islands. The fares, times of departure, and other requirements are so complicated that a special book is published by the Highlands and Islands Development Board. It details all the data you need for road, rail, sea, and air travel throughout Scotland. Updated annually, it is available throughout the country. The title is *Getting Around the Highlands and Islands.*

Helpful contacts are **Caledonian MacBrayne,** the Ferry Terminal, Gourock

PA19 1QP, Renfrewshire (tel. 0475/33755); and **P&O Scottish Ferries,** Orkney and Shetland Services, Jamieson's Quay, Aberdeen, Aberdeenshire AB9 8DL (tel. 0224/572615).

By Car
See Chapter I, Section 3, for information on car rentals in Britain.

WHERE TO GO
The French, the second partner in the "Auld Alliance," used to call it *Le Grand Tour d'Écosse,* or the grand tour of Scotland. Johnson and Boswell made the tour, and visitors, most often North American, continue to follow in their footsteps to this day. But, since many are faced with miles of grand scenery, including mist-shrouded glens and mountains, heathered moorlands, and timeless islands, they must make tough decisions about what to see and what to save for another day.

Some prefer to plan their tours around the grand castles of Scotland, whose lo-cations range from the Borders to the Highlands. Each of these unique and magnificent properties will be documented in the chapters ahead. They include Blair Castle, the home of the 10th duke of Atholl, who still has a private army; Floors Castle, home of the duke and duchess of Roxburghe; Glamis Castle, setting for Shakespeare's *Macbeth;* Dunrobin Castle, home of the earls and dukes of Sutherland for eight centuries; Scone Palace, home of the earls of Mansfield for more than four centuries; and Hopetoun House, Scotland's greatest Adam mansion.

For those with a very limited time schedule, I'll outline some popular itinerar-ies through Scotland. The first is for those motorists entering Scotland through the southeast, known as "the Borders." At Newcastle-on-Tyne (in England), I suggest you take the A696 in the direction of Otterburn. It becomes the A68 and will lead you right into Jedburgh and Melrose, the heart of the Border Country with its an-cient abbeys. From Melrose, take the A6091 west in the direction of Galashiels. The road runs into the A7 north. At Galashiels, turn west onto the A72 in the direction of Peebles. This will take you through the Tweed Valley, with all its associations with Sir Walter Scott, the novelist. From Peebles, it is but a short drive along a secondary road, the A703, leading into the capital of Scotland, Edinburgh, which many critics consider one of the most beautiful cities of Europe.

While based in Edinburgh, you can take many interesting excursions in every direction. Among these, you can cross the Forth Bridge, taking the southern coastal road along the Forth. You can head east, to the ancient Kingdom of Fife. You can visit the fishing villages of East Neuk, eventually reaching the capital of golf, St. An-drews, if you've continued to follow the coastal road. You will be at a point 49 miles from Edinburgh. There are several ways to return to Edinburgh. If you're rushed for time, you can take the A91 west. In the vicinity of Loch Leven and its historic castle, this becomes an express highway, heading back to Edinburgh across the Forth Bridge.

The second excursion requires stopovers of at least 3 nights. You can leave Edin-burgh on the express highway, the M9, that goes to Stirling, 37 miles away, where you'll be within sight of the famous castle in about an hour. You can spend an hour or two walking around its old town with its castle, before heading for the Trossachs, one of the most beautiful scenic areas of Scotland. The A84 heads west in the right direction, but eventually you must cut onto the A821, going via Callander. The Trossachs have been called "Scotland in miniature." The Trossachs take in such de-lights as Loch Katrine and, the most famous of all, Loch Lomond. Sometimes this is called Rob Roy country and Lady of the Lake country, because Sir Walter Scott used the area as a setting for his novels. You can either overnight in the Trossachs or con-tinue west to Loch Lomond.

The next day you can leave Loch Lomond and, along its western shore, connect with A83, which will take you to Inveraray, a small holiday resort, seat of the duke of Argyll at Inveraray Castle. From Inveraray, you can head north along the A819 to Dalmally, which lies along the A85. Continue west from Dalmally until you reach the junction with the A82. There you can head north, going through Glen Coe, site of the infamous 1692 massacre. If you stay on the A82, you'll reach Fort William, which has the greatest concentration of hotels in the area.

After a night in Fort William, continue north along the A82 until you reach the junction of Invergarry. There you can turn west along the A87, the road to the isles, which will take you to the Kyle of Lochalsh, where frequent ferries ply back and forth to Skye, the most visited of Scottish islands. Skye deserves at least a day and night, more if you can spare it.

If you have the time and can add another 2 days to your schedule, head back to Invergarry. Instead of turning south to Fort William, continue on the road north to Inverness. The distance from Invergarry to Inverness is 41 miles. The A82 will take you along the western bank of Loch Ness where, as you drive along, you can try to spot the monster rearing its head from the water.

If you take this motor jaunt, you will not by any means have seen Scotland. There's the granite city of Aberdeen and the great northeast, including Royal Deeside, site of Balmoral Castle where the queen herself takes some of her holidays. There's Glasgow, the biggest city of Scotland and its cultural center, a place filled with art treasures and far better as a sightseeing attraction than its former grim industrial reputation suggests. There's the Robert Burns country, centering around Ayr, then the southern Lowlands of Dumfries and Galloway, bordering England.

All of these attractions have been documented in this guide. The itinerary suggestions are only for those in a hurry. Perhaps if your time is too pressed, you'll return again at some future date and see the other parts as well, for each is rich in attraction, lore, and adventure.

---

4. Fast Facts for Scotland

The aim of this "grab bag" section is to make your adjustment to the Scottish way of life easier. It is maddening to have your trip marred by an incident that could have been avoided had you been tipped off earlier. To prevent that from happening, I'll try to anticipate the addresses, data, and information that might come in handy on all manner of occasions.

For more specific listings, refer to "Fast Facts" in the sections on Glasgow, Edinburgh, and Inverness. For general information, see "Fast Facts for Britain" in Chapter I.

BABYSITTERS: They're most often called "childminders" in Britain. The fame of the Scottish "nanny" has traveled around the world, and if you're traveling with small children, your best bet is to ask your hotel to recommend someone as a babysitter. Expect to pay the cost of travel to and from your hotel.

BANKS: Hours can vary widely from town to town. Most banks are open Mon. to Wed. from 9:30am to 12:30pm and 1:30 to 3:30pm. On Thur. some banks, especially in cities, are also open from 4:30 to 6pm. On Fri., hours are often 9:30am to 1:30pm. One of the most reliable banks is the Bank of Scotland, with branches throughout the country.

BAR AND PUB HOURS: Basically, you can get a drink from 11am to 11pm, but this can vary widely, depending on the discretion of the local tavern owner. Not all pubs are open on Sun. Those that keep Sun. hours generally stay open from 12:30 to 2:30pm and 6:30 to 11pm. Hotel residents can usually purchase alcoholic drinks outside regular hours.

BUSINESS HOURS: Business hours are 9am to 5pm Mon. to Fri. The lunch break lasts an hour, but most places stay open all day.

CIGARETTES: Most U.S. brands are available in major cities and towns. *Warn-*

ing: Smoking is banned at an increasing number of places, including many B&B houses, which accept only non-smokers as guests. Make sure you enter a "smoker" on the train. Also, in most buses you can smoke only in specially designated sections. Some restaurants restrict smoking, as do certain theaters and other public places. Check carefully before lighting up to avoid embarrassment.

CLIMATE: Temperatures can range from 30° to 110° in Britain; so no Britisher will ever really advise you about the weather—far too uncertain. The Lowlands of Scotland usually have a moderate year-round temperature. In spring, the average temperature is 53° F rising to about 65° F average in summer. By the time the crisp autumn has arrived, the temperatures have dropped to spring levels. In winter the average temperature is 43° F. Temperatures in north Scotland are colder, especially in winter, and you should dress accordingly. It rains a lot in Scotland, but perhaps not as much as age-old myths would have it: The rainfall in Edinburgh is exactly the same as that in London. But you should always take your raincoat with you. See "Weather."

CLOTHING SIZES: Regardless of what the charts say, these can vary widely. If you're making serious purchases, it is always better, if possible, to try on a garment. Women will find hosiery sizes the same as in America. Likewise, men will find suits and shirts the same size.

CURRENCY: The currency in Scotland is the pound sterling (£) made up of 100 pence (p), which is used throughout the United Kingdom. Scotland issues its own pound notes, but English and Scottish money are interchangeable.
   At this writing $1 = approximately 57p (or £1 = $1.65), and this was the rate of exchange used to calculate the dollar values given in this guide (generally rounded to the nearest quarter). This rate fluctuates from time to time and may not be the same when you travel to Scotland.

CUSTOMS: Chances are, you will be entering Scotland from England. If that is so, you will not go through customs again when crossing into Scotland, as there are no border formalities, since it is part of the same country of Great Britain. However, if you're flying from a foreign country directly into Scotland, you will have to clear customs, which will be your entry into Great Britain. For details about what you may import or take out of the country, see "Fast Facts for Britain."

DENTISTS: You can find one listed in the yellow pages of the telephone book or you can ask at your hotel. Appointments are usually necessary, but if you are in pain a dentist will generally fit you in.

DOCTORS: Hotels have their own list of local practitioners, for whom you'll have to pay. If not, dial "0" (zero) and ask the operator for the local police, who will give you the name, address, and phone number of a doctor in your area. Emergency treatment is free, but if you're admitted to a hospital, referred to an outpatient clinic, or treated for an already-existing condition, you will be required to pay. You will also pay if you visit doctors at their offices or if a doctor makes a "house call" to your hotel. Be safe. Take out adequate medical/accident insurance or extend your existing insurance to cover you while you're abroad.

DOCUMENTS FOR ENTRY: While every U.S. citizen needs a valid passport to enter Britain, no entry visa is required. Canadian citizens also need a passport.

DRUGSTORES: In Scotland they're called "chemist" shops. Every police station in the country has a list of emergency chemists. Dial "0" (zero) and ask the operator for the local police. Emergency drugs are normally available at most hospitals, but you'll be examined to see that the drugs you request are really necessary.

ELECTRICAL APPLIANCES: The electrical current of Scotland is 240 volts, AC (50 Hz). Some international hotels are specially wired to allow North Americans to plug in their 120-volt appliances, but you'll usually need a transformer plus an adapter plug for your electric razor, hairdryer, or soft contact lens sterilizer. Ask at the electrical department of a large hardware store for the size converter you'll need.

EMBASSIES AND HIGH COMMISSIONS: Since Scotland is not a separate nation, it does not have embassies located within its borders. Nations of the world maintain their embassies in London. If you must contact the embassy of your country, refer to "Fast Facts" in Chapter I.

EMERGENCY: For police, fire, or ambulance, dial 999. Give your name, address, and phone number, and state the nature of the emergency. Misuse of the 999 service will result in a heavy fine (cardiac arrest, yes; dented fender, no).

ETIQUETTE: In short, be normal and polite. The Scots do not like hearing other conversations. In pubs, you are not expected to buy a round unless someone has bought you a drink; don't talk religion or politics.

FILM: All types are available, especially in Glasgow, Inverness, and Edinburgh. Processing takes about 24 hours, and many places will do it almost while you wait. There are few restrictions on the use of your camera, except when notices are posted as in churches, theaters, and certain museums. If in doubt, ask.

HAIRDRESSERS: Ask at your hotel. You should tip the "hairwasher" 50p (85¢) and stylist £1 ($1.65), more if you have a tint or permanent. Hairdressing services for women are available in most department stores, and for men, at the main railway stations in Edinburgh and Glasgow.

HOLIDAYS: Christmas Day, Boxing Day (December 26), New Year's Day, January 2, Good Friday and Easter Monday, May Day, spring bank holiday, and the first Mon. in August. A major event on the Scottish calendar is Burns' Night, honoring the poet. Throughout the land at various suppers, the national bard's poems are recited and, of course, haggis is brought in, piping hot.

LIBRARIES: Every town has a public library, and as a visitor you can use the reference sections. Lending, however, is restricted to local citizens.

LOST PROPERTY: Don't give up hope if you leave your prize possessions on a bus or in a taxi—or elsewhere. Report the loss to the police first, and they will advise you where to apply for its return. Taxi drivers are required to hand lost property to the nearest police station.

For lost passports, credit cards, or money, report the loss and circumstances immediately to the nearest police station. For lost passports, you should then contact your embassy (see "Embassy and High Commission"). For lost credit cards, report to the appropriate organization; the same holds true for lost travelers checks.

LUGGAGE STORAGE: You may want to make excursions throughout Britain, taking only your essentials along. Very few B&B hotels have space to store lots of luggage, and you might want to return to a different hotel. It's possible to store suitcases at most railway stations. At stations, you must be prepared to allow luggage to be searched for security reasons. Be warned: if you object to a search, you could be viewed with suspicion.

MAIL DELIVERY: Have your mail addressed "Poste Restante" at any of the big towns, or give your hotel address. A letter generally takes about 7 to 10 days to arrive in the United States. When claiming personal mail, always carry identification.

MEASURES: For the measurement of distance, Scotland uses miles and inches. For other measures, it's the metric system; refer to the chart on metric measures in Chapter I.

MEDICAL SERVICES: Medical treatment is free only for unforeseen emergency conditions that arise during your stay in Scotland. You'll need to consult a physician privately for any other medical treatment you require. The larger hotels will put you in touch with a house doctor should you need one. The same holds true for dental emergencies. However, you'll normally pay a charge for any treatment.

PETS: See "Customs." It is illegal to bring in pets, except with veterinary documents, and even then they are subject to a quarantine of 6 months. Hotels have their own rules, but generally do not allow dogs in restaurants or public rooms and often not in the bedrooms either.

POLICE: The best source of help and advice in emergencies is the police (dial "0" zero, and ask for the police for non-life-threatening situations, or dial 999 for emergencies). If the local police can't assist, they will have the address of a person who can. Losses, theft, and other crimes should be reported immediately to the police.

POLITICS: There are two main parties, Conservative and Labour. The conservatives believe in free enterprise and freedom of the individual to make his or her own decisions, with some government support. Labour believes in state ownership and control, with the state providing maximum support for the individual. The Liberals and SDP have joined in an uneasy alliance to form the Social Democratic and Liberal Party, but have not yet made any noticeable impact. The Labour Party is very strong in Scotland, particularly around the central district, taking in Glasgow, where most of the people live.

POST OFFICE: Post offices and sub post offices are centrally situated and are open from 9am to 5pm Mon. to Fri., from 9am to noon Sat.

RELIGION: Times of services are posted outside the various places of worship. Scotland is in the main a Protestant nation, but in the larger cities all major faiths are represented. Nearly all the churches in Scotland are hospitable to visitors.

REST ROOMS: These are usually found at signs saying "Public Toilets." They are clean, often have an attendant, and may be used with confidence. Hotels can be used, but they discourage non-residents. Garages (filling stations) do not always have facilities for the use of customers. There's no need to tip, except in hotels where there is an attendant.

SAFETY: This is not a serious problem for the average visitor going to Scotland. Most of the country is extremely safe, and its people are among the most honest in

Europe. However, caution should always be used. Never leave your car unlocked and always protect your valuables. Many areas in and around Glasgow are dangerous, with dozens of muggings reported weekly. Whenever you're traveling in an unfamiliar city or country, stay alert and be aware of your immediate surroundings. Also see the safety warning in "Fast Facts for Britain."

SENIOR DISCOUNTS: These are available only to holders of a British pension book.

SHOE REPAIRS: Many of the large department stores of Scotland have "shoe bars" where repairs are done while you wait.

SHOPPING: Your best buys are in tartans, knitwear, tweeds, and whisky. There is a wide array of cashmere and lambswool knitwear, along with an excellent selection of Harris tweeds for both women and men. Collectors still go to Scotland for antiques, and it is also known for its silver and sports equipment. Edinburgh crystal is legendary.

STORE HOURS: In general, stores are open from 9am to 5:30 or 6pm Mon. to Sat. Most stores close early one day each week, often on a Tue. or Wed. afternoon. The night for late shopping is Thur., when stores remain open until 7pm in Glasgow or until 8pm in Edinburgh.

TAXES: There is no local sales tax. However, Great Britain imposes a standard Value Added Tax (called VAT for short) of 15%. Most Common Market countries already have a tax similar to VAT. In Scotland, hotel rates and meals in restaurants are taxed 15%. The extra VAT charge will show up on your bill unless otherwise stated. It is in addition to the service charge. Should the service charge be 15%, you will, in effect, be paying 30% higher than the prices quoted. The service charges, if included as part of the bill, are also taxable.

   If you make a major purchase at a shop that participates in the retail Export Scheme, you can get your VAT refunded. Ask the shopkeeper for a form and a stamped, addressed envelope. When you leave the country, customs will sign and stamp your form, and you must mail it back to the shopkeeper. Keep the goods in question in your handbag so you can produce them if asked. But be warned: lines at the customs window are long, and you should allow yourself extra time. When shopkeepers receive your form, they will mail you your refund.

   As part of an energy-saving scheme, the British government has also added a special 25% tax on gasoline ("petrol").

TELEPHONES: Phone numbers in Scotland don't have much consistency of pattern. (It's what the Scots call a "real hotch-potch.") Next-door neighbors may have a six-digit number and an eight-digit number. You'll need all the figures, which can go all the way to 10. Consult directory enquiries to aid you. Dial 192, give the operator the town where you want the number, the subscriber's name, and then the address.

   If you're calling from a pay phone, the machine will accept all British coins except 1p. Put your money in first, wait for it to register, then dial your number. Phone booths contain detailed instructions about how to make a call in Scotland. Of course, if you're still confused, you can dial the operator for assistance. You'll see special phone booths used only by phone-card holders. These useful phone cards, which are sold at post offices and even at the tourist board, function somewhat like a credit card. They are sold in denominations of £1, £2, £4, £10, and £20. You put your card into the phone box and make your call. The card is valid until all of its units have been used.

TELEX AND FAX: Telexes and Fax are common in Scotland but still mostly restricted to business premises and hotels. If your hotel has a telex, or Fax, they will send messages for you. You may need to arrange the receipt of an expected message in advance.

TIME: Britain is based on Greenwich Mean Time, with BST, British Summer Time (GMT + 1 hour) used roughly from April to October. When Edinburgh or Glasgow is noon, New York is 7am, Chicago is 6am, Denver is 5am, and Los Angeles an early 4am.

TIPPING: Many establishments add a service charge. If the service has been good, it is usual to add an additional 5% to that. If no service is added to the bill, give 10% for less-than-good service; otherwise, 15% or more. If service is bad, tell them and don't tip! Scotland is one of the few countries of Europe where I've had helpful personnel refuse tips.

TOURIST INFORMATION: There are more than 160 tourist information centers in Scotland. All are well signposted in their cities or towns, and some are closed in winter. For more specific listings refer to Edinburgh or Glasgow.

If you wish to write for information about Scotland, the address is the Scottish Tourist Board, 23 Ravelston Terrace, Edinburgh, Midlothian EH4 3EU.

WEATHER: This is of vital concern in Scotland. It can seriously affect your travel plans. For reports covering the whole of Scotland, call 031/246-8021 in Edinburgh or 041/246-8021 in Glasgow. For weather forecasts in the Edinburgh area, call 031/246-8091, and in Glasgow and the environs, 041/246-8091.

XIX

SOUTHERN SCOTLAND

1. THE BORDER COUNTRY
2. BURNS COUNTRY
3. DUMFRIES AND GALLOWAY

The gentlest part of Scotland is the Southern Uplands, that section connected on the east with Sir Walter Scott and on the west with the celebrated poet of the people, Robert Burns. This is a land of smooth, rolling moors, between the English border and the central plain of Scotland, where the country's population is massed. In southern Scotland, low hills break the terrain, which is threaded with deep valleys and rushing rivers.

The Border Country is a fit introduction to Scotland, containing as it does many reminders of the historic and artistic past of Scotland. Salmon and tweed are the major products of the eastern borderland.

The Burns Country, in the southwestern corner of the country, is where the poet lived, wrote, and died. The gentle climate and secluded life known to Burns still prevail.

There's good fishing in the rivers and the sea in southern Scotland, and pony-trekking is an activity in the low hills and valleys. Sandy beaches and golf courses combine with traces of prehistoric and historic people to form a fascinating and easily traversed region.

1. The Border Country

Castles in romantic ruins and Gothic skeletons of abbeys stand as reminders—in this ballad-rich land of plunder and destruction—of interminable battles that raged between England and the proud Scots. For a long time the Border Country was a no-man's-land.

This is also the land of Sir Walter Scott, that master of romantic adventure in a panoramic setting, who died in 1832. Today he is remembered for such works as *Rob Roy, Ivanhoe,* and *The Bride of Lammermoor.*

Southeast Scotland contains the remains of four great abbeys, built by King David I in the mid-12th century: Dryburgh (where Scott is buried), Melrose, Jedburgh, and Kelso.

The Borders is also the home of the celebrated "Common Ridings" gatherings commemorating major events of the past.

JEDBURGH

Jedburgh lies on the River Jed, 325 miles from London, 48 from Edinburgh. This royal burgh and border town is famous for its ruined **Jedburgh Abbey,** founded by King David in about 1138 and considered one of the finest abbeys in Scotland. Inside is a small museum, containing fragments of medieval works. The abbey is open April to September from 9:30am to 7pm or dusk Mon. to Sat., 2 to 7pm or dusk Sun. From October to March it keeps the same hours, except it is closed on Thur. afternoon and all day Fri. Admission is £1 ($1.65) for adults and 50p (85¢) for children.

On Queen Street, you can visit the **Mary Queen of Scots House** (tel. 0835/ 63331), where she stayed in 1566 for 6 weeks. After a long ride to Hermitage Castle where the earl of Bothwell lay wounded, the queen suffered a stomach hemorrhage that nearly killed her. The house, recently refurbished to commemorate Mary's 400th anniversary, is now a Mary Queen of Scots Visitor Centre, telling a thought-provoking story of her life. It is open from Easter to November 10am to 5pm Mon. to Sat., 1 to 5pm Sun. Admission is £1 ($1.65) for adults, 50p (85¢) for children.

Castle Jail Museum, Castlegate (tel. 0835/63254), stands on the site of Jedburgh Castle. When it was opened in 1823, it was considered a "modern reform jail." Charging 60p ($1) for adults, 30p (50¢) for children, it is open from 10am to 5pm Mon. to Sat., from 1 to 5pm Sun.

Where to Stay and Dine

Jedforest Hotel, Camptown, Jedburgh, Roxburghshire, TD8 6PJ (tel. 08354/274). The hotel is ideally situated on the main A68 just 4 miles south of Jedburgh and with easy motoring distance of all the attractions of the Border towns. A sweeping, tree-lined driveway leads you to this old manor house set in 30 acres of wooded pastureland alongside the River Jed, with a mile of its own private fishing for residents. The hotel has four bedrooms with showers housed in an annex and a purpose-built bungalow separated from the main hotel that offers eight rooms, each with hot and cold running water. All rooms throughout have color TVs, electric blankets, trouser presses, hairdryers, and hot beverage facilities. Breakfast is included. Prices start from £25 ($41.25) for single and £19 ($31.35) per person for double or twin rooms. The hotel hosts a half-timbered pub with two bars. The Lounge Bar, with an open coal fireplace, is an ideal cozy setting to relax, have a drink, and sample an extensive bar menu; or try the public bar where you can turn your hand to such sports as pool and darts.

The Carters' Restaurant, Abbey Place (tel. 0835/63414), is a pub with a downstairs dining room built of old abbey stones lying in the center of the village. The building has had a long history—a local grammar school from 1779, before finding its present role. This is the favorite gathering place of the people of Jedburgh, who know that its owner, Michael Wares, serves good food and drink. Soups, bar snacks, and coffee are served daily in the lounge bar. The restaurant offers either British or continental dishes daily from £7.50 ($12.40). Lunches are served daily from noon to 2pm. Dinners are more elaborate, presented from 6 to 9pm Mon. to Thur. to 10 on Fri. and Sat. Fish is fresh from Eyemouth, accompanied, if you wish, by a tomato-and-coleslaw salad. The pub is open from 11am to 11pm Mon. to Thur., to midnight Fri. and Sat. On Sun. it closes from 3 to 6pm. The establishment also has an outdoor patio with a medieval well, now converted to a wishing well.

KELSO

Another typical historic border town, Kelso lies northeast of Jedburgh on the A698, at the point where the Teviot meets the Tweed. **Kelso Abbey,** now in ruins, was the earliest and the largest of the border abbeys. In the town's marketplace, the "Old Pretender," James Stewart, was proclaimed king, designated James VIII.

Kelso is also the home of the duke of Roxburghe, who lives at **Floors Castle,** built in 1721 by William Adam and lying north of Kelso. Part of the castle, which is open to the public, contains superb French and English furniture, porcelain, tapestries, and paintings by such artists as Gainsborough, Reynolds, and Canaletto. There are a licensed restaurant, coffeeshop, and gift shop as well as a walled garden and garden center. The castle was a major location for the film *Greystoke,* concerning the Tarzan legend. The house is open in May, June, and September from Sun. to Thur. In July and August, it is open Sun. to Fri. Otherwise, it is closed to individuals. The house opens at 11:30am, the last guests being shown through at 4:45pm. The grounds and gardens may be visited from 10:30am to 5:30pm. Admission is £2.50 ($4.15) for adults, £1.50 ($2.50) for children. For further information, phone 0573/23333. Kelso lies 44 miles from Edinburgh and 68 miles north of Newcastle-on-Tyne.

A Historic Home on the Outskirts

Seat of the earl of Haddington, **Mellerstain** (tel. 057381/225) lies in the Borders, although it is most often visited on a day trip from Edinburgh, 37 miles away. One of Scotland's famous Adam mansions, it is near Gordon, 9 miles northeast of Melrose and 7 miles northwest of Kelso. It's open from May to September from 12:30 to 4:30pm Mon. to Sat. Admission is £2.50 ($4.15) for adults, £1 ($1.65) for children.

Mellerstain enjoys associations with Lady Grisell Baillie, the Scottish heroine, and Lord Haddington is her descendant. William Adam built two wings of the house in 1725, and the main building was designed by his more famous son, Robert, some 40 years later. You're shown through the interior, with its decorations and ceilings by Robert Adam, and are allowed to view the impressive library as well as paintings by old masters and antique furniture. Later, from the garden terrace, you can look south to the lake, with the Cheviot Hills in the distance, a panoramic view. Afternoon tea is served, and souvenir gifts are on sale.

Where to Stay

Ednam House Hotel, Bridge Street, Kelso, Roxburghshire TD5 7HT (tel. 0573/24168), is a conversion of a Georgian house into a 32-room hotel often referred to as "that lovely place beside the river." The hotel, lying on the fringe of Kelso, has a good atmosphere, and the bedrooms are well kept, some with river views. Built in 1761, the hotel was purchased from the duke of Roxburghe in 1928, and it is one of the finest examples of Georgian architecture in the Borders. A few of the bedrooms are spacious and airy, although late arrivals might be given the more cramped quarters. Accommodations come equipped with private baths, phones, and TVs, and B&B costs £29 ($47.85) daily in a single, £68 ($112.20) in a double. Rates include a full Scottish breakfast. For those wanting to chance it with the highly unreliable Scottish sun, there is a terrace.

Sunlaws House Hotel, Heiton, Kelso, Roxburghshire TD5 8JZ (tel. 05735/331), lies 3 miles southwest from Kelso by the A698. The manorial walls of this late-19th-century castle rise on 200 acres of woodland, lawns, and gardens. The building was erected as the family home of the Roxburghe family, who valued its location on the trout-filled Teviot River. In 1982 it was converted, with the blessing of the duke and duchess, into a country hotel. Sunlaws maintains 6 bedrooms within the old stable block and another 16 units within the main house. Each has a private bath or shower, phone, and TV. Amid a subdued but elegant decor, the hotel has four low-burning fireplaces even in summer. Many of the guests come for shooting and fishing; others to watch the wildlife, especially deer. A glassed-in conservatory offers clusters of wicker chairs for enjoying drinks or tea when the weather is fine. A tennis court and croquet lawn are on the grounds. With breakfast included, singles rent for £50 ($82.50) to £80 ($132) daily, and doubles run £77 ($127.05) to £130 ($214.50), depending on the accommodation.

Where to Dine

Marlefield Country House Hotel, Eckford, near Kelso Roxburghshire TD5 8ED (tel. 05734/561), is a country-house hotel and restaurant, some 4 centuries old, set in a 4-acre garden in the Cheviot Hills. From Edinburgh, take the A68 through Dalkeith, Pathhead, Earlston, and Newtown St. Boswells, then take a left turn at A698 (signposted Kelso, 2 miles before Jedburgh). Turn right at the Eckford sign and follow the hotel signs.

Serving the best food for miles around, the hotel's dining room offers such continental dishes as lobster bisque with cognac, scampi in a langoustine cream sauce, and veal Zuricher style. A set lunch is good value at £8.50 ($14.05), with a traditional Sun. lunch tallying up at £10.50 ($17.35). A set dinner is offered at £15.50 ($25.60). A la carte orders cost from £22 ($36.30) per person, and service is from noon to 2pm and 7 to 9:30pm. Call for a reservation.

You can also lodge here in comfort, as the hotel offers seven double- or twin-bedded accommodations, all with private baths, TVs, and phones. Two persons pay from £65 ($107.25) a night. Single occupancy of a double is £45 ($74.25). There is also a suite, costing two persons £110 ($186.50) a night. Bedrooms are graciously styled in the finest Scottish manor house tradition.

DRYBURGH

Sir Walter Scott is buried at **Dryburgh Abbey.** These Gothic ruins are surrounded by gnarled yew trees and cedars of Lebanon, said to have been placed there by knights returning from the Holy Land during the years of the Crusades. Near Dryburgh is "Scott's View," over the Tweed to his beloved Eildon Hills, considered one of the most beautiful views in the region. Admission is £1 ($1.65) for adults, 50p (85¢) for children. The abbey ruins are open mid-March to mid-October from 9:30am to 6:30pm Mon. to Sat., from 2 to 6:30pm Sun. Winter closing is at 4pm. The location is 5 miles southeast of Melrose, near St. Boswells.

ST. BOSWELLS

This old village, 40 miles from Edinburgh, stands on the Selkirk-Kelso road, near Dryburgh Abbey. It lies 4 miles from Melrose and 14 miles from Kelso. Because of the following hotel, many motorists prefer to make St. Boswells their headquarters for touring the Borders.

Dryburgh Abbey Hotel, Newton Street, St. Boswells, Roxburghshire TD6 0RQ (tel. 0835/22261), stands beside the ruins from which it takes its name. On the outskirts of St. Boswells, the red-sandstone hotel is surrounded by well-kept grounds near the River Tweed. Built in the Scottish-baronial manor style, the abbey hotel has all the amenities associated with the traditional country-house hotel. Modern conveniences have been slipped in, however. The hotel offers 28 well-furnished bedrooms, 20 with private baths or showers, and each with TV. Singles cost from £28.50 ($47.05) to £39.50 ($65.20) daily, with doubles going for £75 ($123.75) to £95 ($156.75).

MELROSE

Lying 4 miles from Dryburgh Abbey and 37 miles from Edinburgh, Melrose enjoys many associations with Sir Walter Scott. This border town, as mentioned, is also famous for its ruined Melrose Abbey, in Melrose in the Valley of the Tweed. You can visit the ruins of the beautiful Cistercian abbey, founded in 1136, in which the heart of Robert I (the Bruce) is said to have been buried. Look for the beautiful carvings and tombs of other well-known Scotsmen buried in the chancel. In Scott's *The Lay of the Last Minstrel,* the abbey's east window received rhapsodic treatment, and in *The Abbot* and *The Monastery,* Melrose appears as "Kennaquhair." It is open April to September from 9:30am to 7pm Mon. to Sat., from 2 to 7pm Sun. October to March, hours are 9:30am to 4pm, Mon. to Sat., 2 to 4pm Sun. Admission is

£1.25 ($2.05) for adults, 60p ($1) for children. For more information, phone 089682/2562.

Burt's Hotel, Market Square, Melrose, Roxburghshire TD6 9PN (tel. 089682/2285), is an 18th-century inn in the center of town, within walking distance of the abbey. It was built in 1722 between the main square and a garden and offers a taste of small-town Scottish flavor. The hotel offers 21 comfortable rooms, 18 of which contain baths. All the units have color TVs, phones, and hot beverage facilities. Accommodations in singles cost £32 ($52.80) daily; doubles, £54 ($89.10). All tariffs include breakfast. There's an elegant restaurant overlooking the garden and an attractive bar. Inexpensive bar lunches are tasty, and you can also take lunch in the restaurant. Bar suppers are also good, or if you prefer, an à la carte dinner in the restaurant, costing from £14 ($23.10), might include any item from duckling with cherries to medallions of Hungarian-style pork.

At sunset you can stroll along the banks of the River Tweed, or perhaps walk along a public footpath on a hill overlooking the town.

ABBOTSFORD

This was the home of Sir Walter Scott that he built and lived in from 1812 until he died. It contains many relics collected by the author. Especially interesting is his study, with his writing desk and chair. In 1935 two secret drawers were found in the desk. One of them contained 57 letters, part of the correspondence between Sir Walter and his wife-to-be. The Scott home is open from mid-March to October 31 10am to 5pm Mon. to Sat., 2 to 5pm Sun., charging £1.80 ($2.95) for adults, 90p ($1.50) for children. For more information, telephone 0896/2043. The house lies near Melrose, just off the A7, south of the junction with the A72, some 2½ miles southeast of Galashiels.

TRAQUAIR HOUSE

At Innerleithen, in Peeblesshire, Traquair is considered the oldest inhabited and most romantic house in Scotland. Dating back to the 10th century, it is rich in associations with Mary Queen of Scots and the Jacobite risings. Its treasures include glass, embroideries, silver, manuscripts, and paintings. Of particular interest is a working brewhouse equipped as it was 2 centuries ago. The great house is still lived in by the Stuarts of Traquair. The house is open 1:30 to 5:30pm, the grounds and restaurant 10:30am to 5:30pm, from Easter to late May on Sun. and Mon. only, and daily from May 27 to the end of September. In July and August, hours are extended from 10:30am to 5:30pm (last entrance at 5:15pm). Admission is £2.75 ($4.55) for adults, £1.25 ($2.05) for children. There are crafts workshops on the grounds as well as a restaurant/tea garden, woodland and River Tweed walks, and a maze. To make inquiries, telephone 0896/830323.

Innerleithen, 30 miles from Edinburgh, is a modest little mill town, but the unmarred beauty of the River Tweed valley as seen from the town's surrounding hillsides remains constant. The famous Ballantyne cashmeres are manufactured here, and annual games and a Cleikum ceremony take place here in July. Scott's novel, *St. Ronan's Well,* is identified with the town.

PEEBLES

This royal burgh and county town, 23 miles from Edinburgh, is a market center in the Valley of the Tweed. Scottish kings used to come here when they went to hunt in Ettrick Forest. The town is noted for its large woolen mills.

Peebles is also known as a "writer's town." John Buchan, Baron Tweedsmuir, the Scottish author and statesman who died in 1940 and is remembered chiefly for writing the Stevensonian adventure story *Prester John* in 1910, lived here. He was also the author of *The Thirty-Nine Steps* (1915), the first of a highly successful series of secret-service thrillers. In 1935 he was appointed governor-general of Canada. Robert Louis Stevenson once lived at Peebles, and drew upon the surrounding countryside in *Kidnapped,* first published in 1886.

On the north bank of the Tweed stands **Neidpath Castle** (tel. 0721/20333), a mile west of Peebles on the A72 road. This is an early 14th-century, L-shaped tower house, with a magnificent situation above the river. A rock-cut well and a pit prison are within the 11-foot-thick walls. The castle was besieged by Cromwellian forces in 1650, and soon after the Civil War it was upgraded for 17th-century living. However, by late in the 18th century it had become more or less a ruin. It is open from the Thur. before Easter until September 30 from 11 to 5pm Mon. to Sat., 1 to 5pm Sun. Admission is £1 ($1.65) for adults, 50p (85¢) for children.

Where to Stay and Dine

Cringletie House Hotel, Eddleston, Peebles, Peeblesshire EH45 8PL (tel. 0721/233), 3 miles north on the A703, is an imposing country hotel, with towers and turrets, standing on 28 acres of private grounds. It's like a small French château, built of red sandstone. Your hosts, Mr. and Mrs. Stanley Maguire, receive you in their baronial mansion. The hotel rents 13 spacious and comfortable bedrooms, each with private bath or shower, TV, and phone. The B&B rate is from £35 ($57.75) per person daily. The public rooms are rich in character and style, as befits a Victorian mansion. There is an elevator as well. Mrs. Maguire is in charge of the hotel's restaurant. In elegant surroundings, you are given a limited but well-selected choice of dishes. The food is made even more enjoyable by the attentive service. In season the vegetables come fresh from Mrs. Maguire's garden. She has her own style of cooking, and her special dishes include a delectable smoked haddock mousse. A Sun. luncheon costs £11.50 ($19), and a four-course dinner, served from 7:30 to 8:30pm, goes for £18.50 ($30.55). Lunch is à la carte Mon. to Sat. You can be punctual, because of the short hours of serving (the food is freshly cooked), and you'll need a reservation of course, particularly if you aren't a guest of the hotel. The restaurant and hotel are closed from the beginning of January to mid-March.

The Tontine, High Street, Peebles, Peeblesshire EH45 8AJ (tel. 0721/20892), was originally constructed in 1807 by a group of hunters, who sold shares in its ownership to their friends. Several decades ago it was transformed into a private hotel. Flowerboxes adorn its stone lintels and a stone lion guards the fountain in its forecourt. Inside, a cozy and rustic bar, the Tweeddale Shoot Bar, evokes a much older shooting club from the 16th century. The Adam-style dining room is considered one of the architectural gems of Peebles, containing tall fan-topped windows, Scottish antiques, and a minstrel's gallery. Each of the 37 bedrooms is contained within an angular modern wing built in back of its 19th-century core, jutting toward views of the banks of the nearby River Tweed. Units are equipped with TVs, radios, private baths or showers, and coffee makers. Singles rent for £44 ($72.60) daily and twins for £62 ($102.30). Reductions are made for stays of 2 nights or more, providing half board is taken.

2. Burns Country

As Sir Walter Scott dominates the Borders, so does Robert Burns the country around Ayr and Prestwick. There are, in addition, a string of famous seaside resorts stretching from Girvan to Largs. Some of the greatest golf courses in Britain, including Turnberry, are found here, and Prestwick, of course, is one of the major airports of Europe.

AYR

Ayr is the most popular resort on Scotland's west coast, lying 81 miles from Edinburgh and 35 miles from Glasgow. A busy market town, it offers 2½ miles of sands and makes for a good center for touring the Burns Country. This royal burgh is also noted for its manufacture of fabrics and carpets, so you may want to allow time to browse through its shops. With its steamer cruises, fishing, golf, and racing, it faces the Isle of Arran and the Firth of Clyde.

Ayr is full of Burns associations. The 13th-century **Auld Brig o'Ayr,** the poet's "poor narrow footpath of a street. Where two wheelbarrows tremble when they meet," was renovated in 1910. A Burns museum is housed in the thatched **Tam o'Shanter Inn** in Ayr High Street, an alehouse in Rabbie's day.

The **Auld Kirk** of Ayr dates from 1654 when it replaced the 12th-century Church of St. John. Burns was baptized in the kirk.

Ayr is also the birthplace of the famous road builder **John L. MacAdam,** whose name was immortalized in road surfacing.

For centuries Ayr has been associated with horse racing, and it now has the top racecourse in Scotland. One of the main streets of the town is named Racecourse Road for a stretch near the town center.

In the Tarbolton village, 7½ miles northeast of Ayr off the A758, is the **Bachelors' Club** (tel. 0292/541940), a 17th-century house where in 1780 Burns and his friends founded a literary and debating society, now a property of the National Trust for Scotland. In 1779 Burns attended dancing lessons there, against the wishes of his father. There also, in 1781, he was initiated as a Freemason in the Lodge St. David. Eleven months later he became a member of Lodge St. James, which continues today in the village. Yule Lithgow says the Bachelors' Club is open for visitors from noon to 5pm from April until the end of October, and he will arrange to show it at other times if you telephone him at 0290/50503. Admission is £1 ($1.65) for adults, 50p (85¢) for children. Tarbolton is 6 miles from Prestwick Airport.

Where to Stay

Station Hotel, Burns Statue Square, Ayr, Ayrshire KA7 3AT (tel. 0292/263268). Its Edwardian red-sandstone exterior is considered one of the landmarks of town. Inside, relatively few modernizations have managed to retain the antique gilded wall sconces and the darkened paneling of another time. This isn't the most modern hotel in town, but many visitors consider its high ceilings, elaborate detailing, and old world charm more than enough reason to check in. Just a few paces from the railway station, the hotel contains 70 comfortable bedrooms, many quite spacious. Each has a phone, private bath, and TV. The overnight charge for B&B ranges from £50 ($82.50) daily in a single, going up to £65 ($107.25) in a double, with breakfast and VAT included.

The Pickwick Hotel, 19 Racecourse Rd., Ayr, Ayrshire KA7 2TD (tel. 0292/260111). It may seem ironic to have a hotel commemorating a character in a Charles Dickens novel in a town noted for its memories of Rabbie Burns. But this early Victorian hotel, set on its own grounds, does just that. The Pickwick is really a large-size house, renting 15 well-furnished private bedrooms that contain either a private shower or else a complete bath. The B&B rates are £42 ($69.30) daily in a single and £62 ($102.30) in a double, including a full Scottish breakfast, VAT, and service. Each unit bears a Dickensian title. All rooms have color TVs, radios, drink dispensers, trouser presses, and hot beverage facilities. In the paneled Pickwick Club, you can soak up much Dickensian atmosphere. The food is simple but well prepared, a lunch costing around £9.50 ($15.70) and a dinner from £13.50 ($22.30).

Caledonian Hotel, Dalblair Road, Ayr, Ayrshire KA7 1UG (tel. 0292/269331), is centrally situated, just a few hundred yards from Ayr's seashore. It offers 114 refurbished bedrooms with private baths, color TVs, phones, radios, hairdryers, and tea and coffee makers. Singles rent for £55 ($90.75) daily and doubles for £72 ($118.80). Many of the rooms open onto views of the sea. The rooms are decorated in pastels with lightwood furniture. The hotel boasts a good restaurant, serving a Scottish and French cuisine, a continental-style café, and a fully equipped leisure complex. The hotel's location is near several championship golf courses.

Belleisle House Hotel, Doonfoot Road, Ayr, Ayrshire KA7 4DU (tel. 0292/42331), is a country-house hotel lying on A719, approximately 2 miles south of Ayr. Standing in a public park with two golf courses, it is a stone-built structure that was once owned by the Magistrates of Ayr. Note some of the interior paneling and ornate carvings, often depicting scenes in *Tam O'Shanter,* by Robert Burns. Fireplaces add to the traditional Scottish country-house ambience. The hotel rents 17 bedrooms, 14 with private bath. Rates range from £43 ($70.95) daily in a single, rising to £62 ($102.30) in a double. The hotel has two dining rooms, one inspired by the music room of Marie Antoinette at Versailles, the other by her bedroom. The good Scottish cooking is excellent, with both restaurant and bar meals served. Open all year, it extends a special welcome to children.

ALLOWAY

Some 3 miles from the center of Ayr is where Robert Burns, Scotland's national poet, was born on January 25, 1759, in the gardener's cottage—the "auld clay biggin"—his father, William Burns, built in 1757. More than 100,000 people visit the **Burns Cottage and Museum** (tel. 0292/41215) annually, and it still retains some of its original furniture, including the bed in which the poet was born. Chairs displayed here were said to have been used by Tam o'Shanter and Souter Johnnie. Beside the cottage is a museum, open April to October from 9am to 5pm Mon. to Sat., from 2 to 5pm Sun. From November to March, the hours are 10am to dusk daily; closed Sunday. Admission to the cottage and the museum is £1.50 ($2.50) for adults, 75p ($1.25) for children. A family ticket sells for £3.50 ($5.80).

The Auld Brig over the Ayr, mentioned in *Tam o'Shanter,* still spans the river, and Alloway Auld Kirk, also mentioned in the poem, stands roofless and "haunted" not far away. The poet's father is buried in the graveyard of the kirk.

Alloway is dominated by the **Burns Monument and Gardens** (tel. 0292/41321). The monument is a Grecian-style building erected in 1823, containing relics, books, and manuscripts associated with Robert Burns, dating back to the 1820s. It's open April to October daily from 9am to 7pm and November to March from 10am to 5pm. Admission is included in the entrance fee to Burns's Cottage and Museum. The monument is 2 miles south of Ayr on the B7024.

Land o'Burns Centre, Murdochs Lane (tel. 0292/43700), presents a multiscreen of highlights of Burns's life, his friends, and his poetry. Information is available from the personnel, and a well-stocked gift shop is there, plus a tea room. The Russians are particularly fond of Burns and his poetry, and many come annually to visit the cottage and pore over his original manuscripts. Admission to the theater is 50p (85¢) for adults, 30p (50¢) for children. Hours in July and August are daily from 10am to 6pm, June and September to 5:30pm, October and May to 5pm.

Where to Stay

Burns Monument Hotel, Monument Road, Alloway, Ayrshire KA7 4PQ (tel. 0292/42466), is a 190-year-old inn that overlooks the River Doon and the bridge, "Brig o' Doon," of *Tam o'Shanter.* The historical inn, with riverside gardens and a white-washed bar, offers nine rooms attractively decorated, bright and cheerful, some opening onto river views. All bedrooms have private baths and TVs. B&B averages £38 ($62.70) daily in a single and from £60 ($99) in a double.

Balgarth Hotel, 8 Dunure Rd., Doonfoot, Ayr, Ayrshire KA7 4HR (tel. 0292/42441), 2 miles south of Ayr on the A719 coastal road to the fishing village of Dunure, is within easy reach for touring the Burns Country and southwest Scotland. The hotel stands within its own grounds, complete with beer garden overlooking the Clyde and Carrick Hills, and offers special rates to golf enthusiasts with access to Royal Troon, Turnberry, and other scenic courses on the Ayrshire coast. The 15 rooms are bright and well furnished, with TVs, phones, and private baths. The tariff for B&B is from £26 ($42.90) daily in a single, from £42 ($69.30) in a double, including VAT.

CULZEAN CASTLE AND COUNTRY PARK

One of Robert Adam's most notable creations, built around an ancient tower of the Kennedys, Culzean (tel. 06556/274; pronounced Cullane), 12 miles south-southwest of Ayr, dates mainly from 1777 and is considered one of the finest Adam houses in Scotland. The castle, with a view of Ailsa Craig to the south and overlooking the Firth of Clyde, is well worth a visit and is of special interest to Americans because of General Eisenhower's connection with it and its National Guest Flat. In

1946 the guest flat was given to the general for his lifetime in gratitude for his services as Supreme Commander of Allied Forces in World War II. Culzean stands near the golf courses of Turnberry and Troon, a fact that particularly pleased the golf-loving Eisenhower. An exhibition of Eisenhower memorabilia includes sound and audio-visual spectacles, and is seen by more than 100,000 people a year. To illustrate his career, there is a capsule history of World War II demonstrated with wall maps. Mementos of Eisenhower include his North African campaign desk and a replica of the Steuben glass bowl given him by his cabinet when he retired from the presidency.

From April to October the castle is open daily from 10am to 5:30pm. Last admission is half an hour before closing. The charge is £2.40 ($3.95) for adults, £1.20 ($2) for children.

In the castle grounds is **Culzean Country Park,** which in 1969 became the first such park in Scotland. It has an exhibition center in farm buildings by Adam. The 563-acre grounds include a walled garden, an aviary, a swan pond, a camellia house, and an orangery as well as a deer park, miles of woodland paths, and beaches. It has gained an international reputation for its visitor center (Adam's home farm) and related visitor and educational services. The park and all facilities are open April to the end of October 10:30am to 5:30pm and the park is open November to the end of March 9:30am to dusk. Cars are charged £4 ($6.60) to enter the park between April and October. It is open to walk-in customers all year round. For information, phone 06556/269.

After leaving Culzean Castle, you might want to take a short drive to see **Souter Johnnie's Cottage** in Kirkoswald (tel. 06556/603), 4 miles west of Maybole on the A77. This thatched cottage was the home of the village cobbler, John Davidson (Souter Johnnie), at the end of the 18th century. Davidson and his friend Douglas Graham of Shanter Farm were subjects in the Burns poem *Tam o'Shanter.* The cottage contains Burnsiana and contemporary cobblers' workshop and tools. In the churchyard are the graves of Tam o'Shanter and Souter Johnnie, two of his best-known characters. In the garden, the converted alehouse provides shelter for the Thom figures of Tam o'Shanter, Souter Johnnie, the innkeeper, and his wife. The cottage is open from the end of March to the end of September daily from noon to 5pm (other times by appointment). Admission is £1 ($1.65) for adults, 50p (85¢) for children.

TURNBERRY

On the Firth of Clyde, Turnberry was originally part of the Culzean Estate owned by the marquess of Ailsa. It began to flourish after the marquess consented early in this century to allow the Glasgow and South Western Railway to develop golfing facilities, resulting in railway service, a recognized golfing center, and a first-class hotel. From the original two 13-hole golf courses, the complex has developed into the two 18-hole courses, Ailsa and Arran, known worldwide. The Ailsa, one of the most exacting courses yet devised, has been the scene of numerous championship tournaments and PGA events, including the 1986 British Open Championship.

The two courses are named for the Isle of Arran and Ailsa Craig, which can be seen across the waters of the firth. **Ailsa Craig** is a 1,110-foot-high rounded rock 10 miles offshore, a nesting ground and sanctuary for seabirds. Granite for the stones used in the Scottish game of curling used to be taken from this rock.

There was once a Turnberry Castle about 6 miles south of the golfing locale. Only scant remains exist to mark the place that many historians say was the birthplace of Robert the Bruce in 1274. Turnberry lies 97 miles from Edinburgh and 15 miles from Ayr.

Where to Stay and Dine

Turnberry Hotel and Golf Courses, Maidens Road, Turnberry, Ayrshire KA26 9LT (tel. 0655/31000), is a remarkable Edwardian property that has undergone one of the most complete glamorizations of any hotel in Scotland. The owners spent millions of dollars on the infrastructure and decor without diminishing the aura of a more opulent era, as reflected by the oak paneling and molded high ceilings. From afar, one can see the hotel's white facade, its red-tile roof, and its dozens of gables. In World War II the corridors of the structure were transformed into a military hospital, but today the property is once again considered one of the grand hotels of Britain. The public rooms contain scores of Waterford crystal chandeliers, Ionic columns, a medley of pastel colors, and lots of well-polished oak. Each of the 21 suites and 94 bedrooms is furnished in an elegant 19th-century style, the most luxurious in the region. The marble-sheathed bath with each accommodation is loaded with extras; the rooms include color TVs, radios, phones, 24-hour room service, and views of the surrounding lawns and forests. High-season rates, with a full Scottish breakfast included, range from £130 ($214.50) daily in a single and £160 ($264) in a double or twin. Service and taxes are included. Fixed-price dinners cost from £24 ($39.60). Facilities include an indoor swimming pool, a sauna, a health club, a gym, and a solarium.

PRESTWICK

Prestwick is the oldest recorded baronial burgh in Scotland. But most visitors today aren't concerned with that ancient fact—rather, they fly in, landing at Prestwick's International Airport, which is in itself a popular sightseeing attraction, as spectators gather to watch planes take off and land from all over the world.

Behind St. Ninian's Episcopal Church is **Bruce's Well,** the water from which is reputed to have cured Robert the Bruce of leprosy. The **Mercat Cross** still stands outside what used to be the Registry Office and marks the center of the oldest part of Prestwick, dating back to at least 983. Prestwick is a popular holiday town, and is considered one of Scotland's most attractive resorts, with its splendid sands and golf courses. Prestwick opens onto views of Ayr Bay and the Isle of Arran and lies 78 miles from Edinburgh and 32 miles from Glasgow.

Where to Stay

Towans Hotel and Motel, Powmill Road, Prestwick, Ayrshire KA9 2NY (tel. 0292/77831). The original building faces a side lawn and then looks out over the Firth of Clyde to the Isle of Arran. Much of the accommodation is in a modern hotel/motel block that blends with the old. The owners, conscious of the needs of international travelers passing through Prestwick Airport, are geared to catering for early and late arrivals. The 53 rooms have private baths, and tea and coffee makers. Breakfast is served from 4am, and the dining room has a local reputation for well-cooked meals. B&B costs from £40 ($66) to £45 ($74.25) per person daily. All meals are extra, but you can make as much tea and coffee as you want in your room.

Parkstone Hotel, Central Esplanade, Prestwick, Ayrshire KA9 1QN (tel. 0292/77286), is a white-walled Victorian building with cookie-cutter gingerbread set under its steep eaves. Its modernized interior has a pub in back, whose view of the sea attracts a lunch crowd. The hotel is the property of Stewart and Sandra Clarkson, who maintain their 15-room establishment in good order. All the rooms in this century-old hostelry have private baths and color TVs. Singles rent for £36 ($59.40) daily, rising to £53 ($87.45) in a double or twin, all tariffs including a full breakfast, VAT, and service. A set dinner costs from £10.50 ($17.35) per person. In cold weather, a coal fire burns in an oak-paneled room near the reception desk.

TROON

This holiday resort looks out across the Firth of Clyde to the Isle of Arran. It offers several golf links, including the Old Troon course. Bathers in summer find plenty of room on its 2 miles of sandy beaches, stretching from both sides of its harbor. The broad sands and shallow waters make it a safe haven also. From here you can take steamer trips to Arran and the Kyles of Bute.

Troon is mostly a 20th-century town, its earlier history having gone unrecorded. It takes its name from the curiously shaped promontory that juts out into the Clyde estuary on which the old town and the harbor stand. The promontory was called "Trwyn," the Cymric word for nose, and later this became the Trone and then Troon.

Fullarton Estate, on the edge of Troon beyond the municipal golf course, is the ancestral seat of the dukes of Portland.

A massive statue of Britannia stands on the seafront as a memorial to the dead of the two world wars. On her breastplate is the lion of Scotland emerging from the sea. Troon lies 77 miles from Edinburgh and 31 miles from Glasgow.

Where to Stay and Dine

Marine Highland Hotel, Troon, Ayrshire KA10 6HE (tel. 0292/314444). Because of its widespread reputation as the best hotel within an easy drive of Prestwick Airport, 5 minutes away, many guests check in here to recover from jet lag. The hotel's red-sandstone exterior rises from flat grasslands, a short stroll from the sea, whose waters can be seen from the windows of many of the public rooms. With dozens of turrets, chimneys, and gables, it resembles a Victorian village, especially since the surrounding golf course prevents any significant building nearby. Inside, the comfortably modernized interior still offers glimpses of Victoriana. There are two restaurants, fairways, and Crosbie's Brasserie, offering some of the best food in Troon. Meals cost from £8 ($13.20) to £17 ($28.05). Each of the 72 comfortably furnished bedrooms contains private bath, color TV, and phone. They cost £76 ($125.40) daily in a single, £115 ($189.75) in a double. The hotel was upgraded and refurbished in 1987, when a leisure and sports center, available to guests, was added.

3. Dumfries and Galloway

Southwestern Scotland is often overlooked by motorists rushing north. But this country of Burns is filled with many rewarding targets—a land of unspoiled countryside, fishing harbors, artists' colonies of color-washed houses, and ruined abbeys and castles dating from the days of the border wars.

It's a fine touring country, and the hotels are generally small, of the Scottish provincial variety, but that usually means a reception from a smiling staff and good traditional Scottish cookery, using the local produce.

I've documented the most important centers below, but have included some off-beat places for those seeking a more esoteric trip.

LOCKERBIE

A border market town 13 miles from Dumfries, 74 miles from Edinburgh, Lockerbie lies in the valley of Annandale, offering fishing and golf. It's a good center for exploring some sightseeing attractions in its environs.

Lockerbie was the scene in 1593 of a battle that ended one of the last great Border family feuds. The Johnstones routed the Maxwells, killing Lord Maxwell and 700 of his men. Many of the victims had their ears cut off with a cleaver, a method of mutilation that became known throughout the Border Country as the "Lockerbie Nick."

Of interest are the remains of **Lockmaben Castle,** 3½ miles west of Lockerbie, said to have been the boyhood home (some historians say the birthplace) of Robert the Bruce. This castle, on the south shore of Castle Loch, was captured and recaptured 12 times and also withstood six attacks and sieges. James IV was a frequent visitor, and Mary Queen of Scots was here in 1565. The ruin of the early-14th-century castle is on the site of a castle of the de Brus family, ancestors of Robert the Bruce. However, the charming hamlet of Lochmaben, with its five lochs, is reason enough to visit, regardless of who was or was not born there. Admission is free. Telephone 0387/53862 to inquire about visiting.

If you're heading north to Lockerbie on the A74, I'd suggest a stopover in the village of Ecclefechan. There you can visit **Carlyle's Birthplace,** 5 miles southeast of

Lockerbie on the Lockerbie-Carlisle road. Even though the historian, critic, and essayist Thomas Carlyle isn't much read these days, the "arched house" in which he was born in 1795 is interesting in itself, containing mementos and manuscripts of the author. It's open from Easter until the end of October, daily from noon to 5pm, charging an admission of £1 ($1.65) for adults, 50p (85¢) for children. For more information, telephone 05763/666.

Where to Stay and Dine

Lockerbie House Country Hotel, Boreland Road, Lockerbie, Dumfriesshire DG11 2RG (tel. 05762/2610), is a former family mansion from the Georgian era that has been turned into a family-operated hotel. The comfort and character of its past life has been maintained in the conversion. The hotel is situated in a 78-acre park and woodland, with such wildlife as roe deer. It lies a half a mile from the main A74 London-Glasgow road, and a mile north of Lockerbie on the B723, 25 miles north of Carlisle across the border in England. Public rooms are large and comfortable, as befits a Scottish country house, and the 30 bedrooms are well furnished, each with private bath or shower, TV, and phone. B&B costs £42 ($69.30) daily in a single, rising to £78 ($128.70) in a double. The hotel dining room serves a British and French cuisine, with lunches costing from £8.50 ($14.05) and dinner ranging from £15 ($24.75) to £20 ($33).

Dryfesdale House Hotel, Lockerbie, Dumfriesshire DG11 2SF (tel. 05762/2427), was built in 1831 and was originally a Church of Scotland manse. This hotel offers traditional comfort with logfires and tranquil surroundings. There is a choice of 16 bedrooms, 15 of which have private baths or showers, TVs, and phones. Several of the units are quite spacious and six are adapted to accommodate disabled persons. Singles range from £36 ($59.40) daily, doubles £55 ($90.75). The hotel, known for its good food and wines, is fully licensed with two old-world bars. The sun lounge and dining room open onto good views, and the hotel stands on 5 acres of grounds. The owners, the Smith family, are always available to help. The hotel lies a mile northwest by A74.

MOFFAT

An Annandale town, Moffat thrives as a center of a sheep-farming area, symbolized by a statue of a ram in the wide High Street, and has been a holiday resort since the mid-17th century, because of the curative properties of its water. It was here that Robert Burns composed the drinking song "O Willie Brew'd a Peck o' Maut." Today people visit this border town on the banks of the Annan River for its good fishing and golf. The town lies 61 miles from Edinburgh and 60 miles from Glasgow.

North of Moffat is spectacular hill scenery. Five miles northwest is a huge, sheer-sided, 500-foot-deep hollow in the hills called the **Devil's Beef Tub,** where Border cattle thieves, called reivers, hid cattle lifted in their raids.

Northeast along Moffat Water, past White Coomb, which stands 2,696 feet high, is the **Grey Mare's Tail,** a 200-foot hanging waterfall formed by the Tail Burn dropping from Loch Skene. It is under the National Trust for Scotland.

Where to Stay and Dine

Annandale Hotel, High Street, Moffat, Dumfriesshire DG10 9HF (tel. 0683/20013), has been a coaching inn since the 18th century, housing travelers who crossed through the Border Country en route to Edinburgh. However, the inn has been modernized and the amenities provided around here have improved considerably since the old days. Eleven of the 24 bedrooms contain private baths, and three of these have showers. Singles, if bathless, begin at £32 ($52.80) per night, rising to £38 ($62.70) with bath or shower. Doubles, with bath or shower, cost from £55 ($90.75). The rooms, including the public ones, are immaculately kept. The proprietors have built up a good reputation for their cuisine, which includes Scottish specialties. The last dinner is served at 9pm, and the cost is from £10 ($16.50). It's in the center of town, but provides ample car parking on its own grounds.

Beechwood Hotel, Harthope Place, Moffat, Dumfriesshire DG10 9RS (tel. 0683/20210), was originally built as the 19th-century headquarters of "Miss Thompson's Private Adventure Boarding Establishment and School for Young Ladies." Today it is a charming country hotel and restaurant. It lies behind a dark facade of chiseled stone at the end of a narrow rural lane. A "tea lawn," smooth as a putting green, is the site for outdoor refreshments on sunny days. Each of the seven bedrooms contains a private bath and a certain amount of homespun charm along with such modern amenities as phone and TV. Singles rent for £45 ($74.25) daily and doubles for £62 ($102.30). If you just want to stop in for a meal (and you'll be welcome if you phone in advance), lunch is from noon to 1:30pm, dinner, 7:30 to 9pm. A fixed-price dinner costs £16.50 ($27.25).

Moffat House Hotel, High Street, Moffat, Dumfriesshire DG10 9HL (tel. 0683/20039), is considered one of the town's most architecturally noteworthy buildings, because of its construction in 1751 by John Adam. It sits within a garden in the center of town behind a chiseled facade of red and black stone, with a pair of symmetrical wings stretching out on either side. Ancient trees shelter its rear from the winds blowing in from the farmlands beyond. Each of the 20 modernized bedrooms contains comfortable and functional furniture, and all offer private baths or showers, TVs, and phones. With breakfast included, per-person rates are £32 ($52.80) daily in a single, £26 ($42.90) in a double. The hotel offers some of the best food in town, especially at night when the chef prepares an international menu. Bar suppers are served from 6 to 9pm Mon. to Thur., from 5 to 9:30pm Fri. and Sat. However, dinner in the regular restaurant, costing from £14 ($23.10), is served from 7 to 8:45pm only, and is likely to feature a bill of fare including a haunch of venison, mallard duck in cherry sauce, and pheasant in an orange-pepper sauce.

A Castle Hotel at Beattock

Two miles north of Moffat along the A74, near the village of Beattock, the most luxurious accommodations in the area are found at the **Auchen Castle Hotel,** Beattock, Dumfriesshire DG10 9SH (tel. 06833/407), a Victorian mock-castle, really a charming country house, built on the site of Auchen Castle. It's one of the most tranquil oases in the Scottish Lowlands, with terraced gardens, a trout-filled loch, and vistas from its windows. The 24 bedrooms are often spacious and invariably comfortable, and each has a private bath or shower, phone, and TV. Rates are £39 ($64.35) daily in a single, from £58 ($95.70) in a double, including a cooked breakfast, service, and VAT. Rooms are spacious and well appointed in the annex. The lofty dining room is exceptional for the area, its windows overlooking flowering ornamental grounds in late spring. Simple dishes are appetizingly good because of the materials used. Roast Scottish beef is preferred by many. The well-appointed tables and efficient staff complement the atmosphere. Lunch is from noon to 2pm and dinner from 7 to 9pm. Bar lunches only are offered, and a dinner goes for £16 ($26.40).

DUMFRIES

A county town and royal burgh 59 miles from Ayr, this Scottish Lowland center enjoys associations with Robert Burns and James Barrie. In a sense it rivals Ayr as a mecca for admirers of Burns. He lived in Dumfries from 1791 until his death in 1796, and it was here that he wrote some of his most famous songs, including "Auld Lang Syne" and "Ye Banks and Braes of Bonnie Doon." The location is 80 miles from Edinburgh.

What to See and Do

In **St. Michael's Churchyard,** a burial place for at least 900 years, stands the **Burns Mausoleum.** The poet was buried there along with his wife, Jean Armour, as well as five of their children. Burns died in 1796, but his remains weren't removed to the tomb until 1815. In the 18th-century church of St. Michael's you can still see the pew used by the Burns family.

The poet died at what is now called the **Robert Burns House,** a simple, unpretentious stone structure, which can be visited by the public; it contains personal relics and mementos relating to Burns. His death may have been hastened by icy dips in well water that the doctor prescribed. The house is on Burns Street (formerly Mill Vennel). The **town museum,** the **Globe Inn,** and **the Hole in the Wa' Tavern** all contain Burns relics, and a statue of him stands in the High Street. You can stroll along **Burns' Walk** on the banks of the River Nith.

St. Michael's is the original parish church of Dumfries and its founding is of great antiquity. The site was probably sacred before the advent of Christianity. It appears that a Christian church has stood there for more than 1,300 years. The earliest written records date from the reign of William the Lion (1165–1214). The church and the churchyard are interesting to visit because of all their connections with Scottish history, continuing through World War II.

From St. Michael's, it's a short walk to the Whitesands, where four bridges span the Nith. The earliest of these was built by Devorgilla Balliol, widow of John Balliol, father of a Scottish king. The bridge originally had nine arches but now has six and is still in constant use as a footbridge.

The summer only **tourist information office,** Whitesands (tel. 0387/53862), is near the bridge. The wide esplanade was once the scene of horse and hiring fairs and now is a fine place to park your car and explore the town. Tour buses park here.

The **Mid Steeple** was built in 1707 as municipal buildings, courthouse, and prison. The old Scots "ell" measure of 37 inches is carved on the front of the building. A table of distances on the building includes the mileage to Huntingdon, England, which in the 18th century was the destination for Scottish cattle drovers driving their beasts south for the markets of London.

At the **Academy,** J.M. Barrie was a pupil, and he later wrote that he got the idea for *Peter Pan* from his games in the nearby garden.

Where to Stay

Cairndale Hotel, English Street, Dumfries, Dumfriesshire DG1 2DF (tel. 0387/54111), is most reliable, a fine and substantial choice. Its bedrooms have been attractively decorated, with special care paid to modern amenities. All of the color-coordinated chambers contain private baths, color TVs, clock-radio alarms, direct-dial phones, hairdryers, and hot beverage facilities. Executive rooms and suites also contain queen-size beds, mini-bars, trouser presses, and whirlpool baths. Singles rent for £54 ($89.10) daily, and doubles go for £64 ($105.60), including breakfast, VAT, and service. You have a choice of two bars, and guests quickly decide which one they'll make their local. The public lounges are handsomely decorated, and you can select your own favorite nook, perhaps a comfortable chair upholstered in velvet. Dinner, served until 9pm, is generally quite good, including such dishes as roast sirloin of Galloway beef, Arbroath smokies, mealed herring with Arran sauce, and Ecclefechan flan with Drambuie cream. A three-course table d'hôte lunch goes for £7.50 ($12.40) and a four-course dinner for £13.95 ($23). The hotel is owned and managed by the Wallace family, who also run their own butcher business.

Station Hotel, 49 Lovers Walk, Dumfries, Dumfriesshire DG1 1LT (tel. 0387/54316), is among the most traditional hotels of Dumfries, lying a few steps from the gingerbread-fringed train station. The hotel was built of hewn sandstone at the turn of the century when trains were the most comfortable way to travel. Its design of heavy timbers, polished paneling, soaring ceilings, and open fireplaces reminds visitors of alpine hotels in Switzerland. However, the welcome and dinner menu at The Dining Room are purely Scottish (see below). Before dinner, drinks can be enjoyed in the lounge bar, followed by dinner in a high-ceilinged room framed on one side with bay windows overlooking century-old trees and the station. The 32 modernized bedrooms are accessible via long corridors of old-fashioned design. Each contains a private bath, phone, tea-maker, color TV, comfortable bed, and electric trouser press. Singles cost from £52 ($85.80) daily, and doubles peak at £62 ($102.30).

Waverley Hotel, 19 St. Mary's Street, top of English Street, Dumfries,

Dumfriesshire DG1 2DF (tel. 0387/54848), is a good bargain, close to the station, about a 5-minute walk to the center of town. The owners, J. and J. V. Meikle, offer 35 bedrooms with hot and cold running water, central heating, color TVs, and shaving points. Four have private baths. Some family rooms are available, and there is a reduction for children sharing their parents' room. Singles cost from £16 ($26.40) to £22 ($36.30) daily, and doubles or twins run £30 ($49.50) to £32 ($52.80), the higher prices charged for rooms with baths, including VAT and a full breakfast. Drinks can be enjoyed in one of the two bars. In the evening, a "high tea" menu is offered, giving you a choice of steaks, salads, fish, and bacon and eggs, a meal starting at £5 ($8.25). Everything tastes homemade in the dining room.

Where to Dine

Bruno's, 5 Balmoral Rd. (tel. 0387/55757). It may seem quixotic to recommend an Italian restaurant in the seat of Rabbie Burns, but Bruno's serves some of the best food in town. It is most unassuming, and that is part of its charm. Its minestrone is first rate, and its pastas such as lasagne are homemade. The chef doesn't serve the most imaginative Italian dishes ever sampled—in fact the repertoire is most familiar, such as saltimbocca alla romana and pollo alla diavola, but it's done with a certain flair. The veal is particularly tender, and the tomato sauce well spiced and blended. Steak au poivre is also excellent. It will cost from £14 ($23.10) per person, but it's worth it. A set three-course meal for £10.95 ($18.05) is popular. There is also a special pasta supper for £4.75 ($7.85). Bruno's serves only dinner, from 6:30 to 10pm; closed Tue.

The Dining Room, Station Hotel, 49 Lovers Walk (tel. 0387/54316), was part of *the* grand hotel of town when it was built, and it still lives up to its high standards. Today the restaurant evokes the Edwardian age. It's a big-windowed dining room where the Victorian gingerbread of the train station is on view. The decor of the restaurant is high-ceilinged. The table d'hôte menu at £15 ($24.75) per person includes a satisfying array of specialties such as local salmon, haggis, cock-a-leekie soup, chicken "whisky sour," and local trout in a sauce of smoked salmon and mushrooms. A polite member of the uniformed staff might help turn the dinner, served daily from 7 to 9pm, into a grand occasion. Reservations are suggested.

Burns's Favorite "Howff"

Globe Inn, 56 High St. (tel. 0387/52335), was a favorite haunt of Burns, who used an old Scottish word, *howff,* to describe his local. He not only imbibed here, but he had a child with the barmaid, Anna Park. The pub, in business since 1610, is reached down a narrow, flagstone passageway off High Street. It has a separate restaurant. You can go here for meals, drink, or to play a nightly game of dominoes. A little museum is devoted to Burns, and on windowpanes upstairs you can see verses he scratched with a diamond. In this convivial atmosphere, you can order cooked bar lunches Mon. to Sat., beginning at £4 ($6.60). That means such items as homemade soups and steak and kidney pie. The pub is open from 11am to 11pm Mon. to Sat., from 12:30 to 2:30pm and 6:30 to 11pm Sun.

Excursions from Dumfries

Based in Dumfries, you can set out on treks in all directions to some of the most intriguing sightseeing goals in the Scottish Lowlands.

South on the A710 leads to the village of New Abbey, dominated by the red-sandstone ruins of **Sweetheart Abbey,** the Cistercian abbey founded in 1273 by Devorgilla, mother of John Balliol, the "vassal king." When her husband, John Balliol the Elder, died, she became one of the richest women in Europe. Most of Galloway, with estates and castles in England and land in Normandy, belonged to her. Devorgilla founded Balliol College, Oxford, in her husband's memory. She kept his embalmed heart in a silver-and-ivory casket by her side for 21 years until her death in 1289 at the age of 80, when she and the casket were buried beside Balliol in the front of the abbey altar. So the abbey gained the name of "Dulce Cor," Latin for "sweetheart," which has since become a part of the English language.

Built into a wall of a cottage in the village is a rough piece of sculpture showing three women rowing a boat—an allusion to the bringing of sandstone across the Nith to build the abbey.

Also at New Abbey, the **Shambellie House Museum of Costume,** on the A710 (tel. 038785/375), is in a Victorian country home that was designed by David Bryce. Now housing a branch of the National Museum of Scotland, it has a collection of fashionable clothing given by Charles Stewart. Open from mid-May to mid-September and charging no admission, it may be visited from 10am to 5:30pm Thur. to Sat. and on Mon., from noon to 5:30pm Sun.

Directly south from New Abbey on the A710 to Southerness are the **Arbigland Gardens and Cottage** at Kirkbean (tel. 038788/213), 15 miles to the southwest of Dumfries. This is where John Paul Jones, one of the founders of the American navy, was born. You can visit the woodland with its water gardens arranged around a secluded bay, walking in the pathways where the great admiral once worked as a boy. The gardens are open May to September 2 to 6pm Tue., Thur., and Sun., charging adults £1 ($1.65), children 50p (85¢).

Or, alternatively, you can head south from Dumfries on the B725 to **Caerlaverock Castle,** Glencaple Road, near the mouth of the River Nith, 2 miles south from Glencaple. Once the seat of the Maxwell family, this impressive ruined fortress dates back to the 1270s. In 1300 Edward I laid siege to it. In 1640 it yielded to Covenanters after a 13-week siege. The castle is triangular with round towers. The interior was reconstructed in the 17th century as a Renaissance mansion, with fine carving. The castle is open April to September daily from 9:30am to 7pm, 2 to 7pm Sun.; October to March daily from 9:30am to 4pm, 2 to 4pm Sun. Admission is 60p ($1) for adults, 30p (50¢) for children.

Near the castle is the Caerlaverock National Nature Reserve, between the River Nith and Lochar Water. It is a noted winter haunt of wildfowl, including barnacle geese.

After leaving the castle, continue east along the B725 to the village of **Ruthwell,** about 10 miles southeast of Dumfries. There at the early-19th-century Ruthwell Church you'll see one of the most outstanding crosses of the Dark Ages. Standing 18 feet high, the cross is believed to date from the 8th century. Engraved with carvings, it bears the earliest-known specimen of written English (a Christian poem in Runic characters).

North from Dumfries on the A76 takes you to **Lincluden College,** 2 miles away. This is the richly decorated remains of a 15th-century collegiate church.

Four miles away, still following the A76, is **Ellisland Farm** (tel. 038774/426), where Robert Burns made his last attempt at farming, renting the spread from 1788 to 1791. The present occupants·of the house will show you through the Burns Room. It was at this farm that Burns wrote *Tam o'Shanter.* Call for an appointment.

Continuing north, still on the A76, you reach **Thornhill,** a country resort—familiar to Burns—overlooking the River Nith. From here, it's possible to branch out for excursions in many directions.

The main target is **Drumlanrig Castle** (tel. 0848/30248), the seat of the duke of Buccleuch and Queensberry, built between 1679 and 1691. It lies 3 miles north of Thornhill, off the A76. This pink castle contains some outstanding paintings, including a Rembrandt, a da Vinci, and a Holbein. In addition, it is further enriched by Louis XIV antiques, silver, porcelain, and relics related to Bonnie Prince Charlie. The castle stands in a parkland ringed by wild hills, and there's even an adventure woodland playground. The gardens are being gradually restored to their 1720 magnificence. There's a working crafts center in the old stable yard, with independent craft workers in a variety of skills. Meals are served in the old kitchen hung with gleaming copper. The castle is open from 11am to 5pm Mon. to Wed. and on Sat., from 2 to 6pm Sun., from the end of May to mid-August. The grounds can be visited daily from the end of April to the end of September. Last entry is 45 minutes before closing. Admission is £3 ($4.95) for adults, £1 ($1.65) for children.

Of almost equal interest, **Maxwelton House** (tel. 08482/385) lies 3 miles south of Moniaive and 13 miles north of Dumfries on the B729. It was the stronghold of the earls of Glencairn in the 14th and 15th centuries. But it is more remembered today as the birthplace (1682) of Annie Laurie of the Scottish ballad. From Maxwelton you can see that the braes are just as bonnie as ever. The braes, of course, refer to the neighboring hillsides. The house and an agricultural museum are open from 2 to 5pm Mon. to Thur. in July and August. The garden and chapel are open from April to September at those same hours. The house can be visited at other times by appointment. Admission for house, garden, and museum is £1.75 ($2.90) for adults, £1.25 ($2.05) for children; to the garden only, 75p ($1.25).

Back on the A76, you can branch northwest on the B797, heading in the direction of Mennock Pass. There, at **Wanlockhead,** you'll be in the highest village in Scotland. Once this village was a gold-mining center and known as "God's Treasure House." Gold was mined here for the Scottish crown jewels.

CASTLE DOUGLAS

An old cattle and sheep market town, Castle Douglas makes a good touring center for Galloway. It lies about 8 miles southwest of Dumfries, and 98 miles from Edinburgh, at the northern tip of Caringwark Loch. On one of the islets in the loch is an ancient lake dwelling known as a "crannog."

The favorite excursion is to **Threave Castle,** 1½ miles west on an islet in the River Dee west of town, the ruined 17th-century stronghold of the Black Douglases. The four-story tower was built between 1639 and 1690 by Archibald the Grim, Lord of Galloway. In 1455 Threave Castle was the last Douglas stronghold to surrender to James II, who employed "Mons Meg" (the famous cannon now in Edinburgh Castle) in its subjection. Over the doorway projects the "gallows knob" from which the Douglases hanged their enemies. The castle was captured by the Covenanters in 1640 and dismantled. Owned by the National Trust, the site must be reached by a half-mile walk through farmland and then by small boat across the Dee. Last sailing to the castle is at 6pm. Threave Castle is open from 10am to 7pm Mon. to Sat., from 2 to 7pm Sun. from April to the end of September. The cost is 75p ($1.25) for adults and 50p (85¢) for children.

Threave Garden (tel. 0556/2575) is built around Threave House, a 19th-century baronial mansion a mile west of Castle Douglas, off the A75. They are both under the protection of the National Trust of Scotland, which uses them as a school for gardening. The year-round garden is at its best in April when the daffodils bloom and in June, with rhododendrons and the rock garden in flower. There is a visitor center and a restaurant. The garden is open daily from 9am to sunset and the visitor center from 9am to 6pm. Admission is £2.20 ($3.65) for adults, £1.10 ($1.80) for children.

Where to Stay and Dine

Douglas Arms, King Street, Castle Douglas, Kirkcudbrightshire DG7 1DB (tel. 0556/2231), is a 200-year-old coaching inn, but it has been turned into a modernized hotel, right in the center of town. Behind a rather stark, two-story facade, the public rooms are bright and cheerful, giving you a toasty feeling on a cold night. Bedrooms have color-coordinated schemes, and such gadgets as razor sockets. Seventeen of the 26 rooms contain private baths. The B&B rate ranges from £20 ($33) to £25 ($41.25) per person daily, the higher charge for accommodations with private bath. Dinner is served until 9pm, and of course, trout and salmon are featured along with good beef and lamb. A set dinner costs from £12 ($19.80).

King's Arms, St. Andrew's Street, Castle Douglas, Kircudbrightshire DG7 1EL (tel. 0556/2626), is a good place to stop over, enjoying either a room, a meal, or a drink in the trio of tartan-clad bars, featuring a malt whisky collection. The restaurant serves homecooked meals using fresh fish and tender beef. Main courses are often shellfish, lobster, pheasant, and venison. A set meal costs from £14 ($23.10). It is attractively decorated and the staff is helpful. The 14 bedrooms are comfortable but modest, and some chambers contain TVs, private baths and toilets, or else showers and toilets. Singles cost £20 ($33) daily, and doubles rent for £50 ($82.50), including breakfast, VAT, and service. There is a sheltered and secluded sun garden at the rear of the hotel, which is a rendezvous for coffee, tea, or a sundowner. Everything is maintained well, and parking is provided.

ROCKCLIFFE

An attractive seaside village, Rockcliffe has a bird sanctuary on its offshore Rough Island. From its sand-and-rock beach, you can look out to the Lake District mountains on the distant horizon. The distance is 20 miles from Dumfries and 100 miles from Edinburgh.

Baron's Craig Hotel, Rockcliffe, Dalbeattie, Kircudbrightshire DG5 4QF (tel. 055663/225), is a stately country home, built of granite, and set back from the shoreline of Solway Firth. Because of its position sheltered from the cold north wind, its gardens bloom profusely in season. Lawns and grounds—nearly 12 acres —are well maintained. The public rooms are spacious and airy, brightly decorated and welcoming. In the modern bar you can select your favorite whisky. The owners have paid special attention to the 27 bedrooms, decorating them in warm, pleasing colors to suggest in summer a holiday atmosphere. From April to October, it rents singles (bathless) for £38 ($62.70) daily, going up to £52 ($85.80) with bath. A bathless double costs £68 ($112.20), rising to £90 ($148.50) with bath, including breakfast. Twenty-two of the rooms contain private baths, and each accommodation has phone and TV.

Even if you're not staying here, you might want to drive down to enjoy the hotel's fine cookery. The dining room overlooks the water, and table appointments have style. At lunch the menu is considerably shortened, but still quite good, a bar lunch costing from £5 ($8.25). In the evening, however, a table d'hôte is offered at £18 ($29.70) from 7 to 9pm. The menu is based on good local ingredients, and dishes are acceptably prepared.

KIRKCUDBRIGHT

Stewartry's most ancient burgh, Kirkcudbright (pronounced Kir-coo-bree) lies at the head of Kirkcudbright Bay on the Dee Estuary, 108 miles from Edinburgh and 28 miles from Dumfries. This intriguing old town contains color-washed houses inhabited in part by artists. In fact, Kirkcudbright has been called the "St. Ives (Cornwall) of Scotland."

In the old town graveyard are memorials to Covenanters and to Billy Marshall, the tinker king who died in 1792 at the age of 120, reportedly having fathered four children after the age of 100.

Maclellan's Castle, built in 1582 for the town's provost, Sir Thomas Maclellan, easily dominates the center of town. Kirkcudbright is an attractive town which is the center of a lively group of weavers, potters, and painters who work in the 18th-century streets and lanes.

The **Tolbooth,** a large building, dates back to the 16th and 17th centuries, and in front of it is a **Mercat Cross** of 1610. The Tolbooth is a memorial to John Paul Jones (1747–1792), the gardener's son from Kirkbean who became a slave trader, a privateer, and in due course one of the founders of the American navy. For a time, before his emigration, he was imprisoned for murder in the Tolbooth.

Art exhibitions are regularly sponsored at **Broughton House,** High Street (tel. 0557/30437), a 17th-century mansion that once belonged to artist E. A. Hornel. The house contains a large reference library with a Burns collection, along with pictures by Hornel and other artists, plus antiques and other works of art. You can stroll through its beautiful garden. Broughton is open Easter to mid-October from 11am to 1pm and 2 to 5pm Mon. and Wed. to Sat., from 2 to 5pm Sun. In winter it is open by prior arrangement only. Admission is 80p ($1.30) for adults, 40p (65¢) for children.

In addition, the **Stewartry Museum,** St. Mary Street (tel. 0557/30797), contains a fascinating collection of antiquities, depicting the history and culture of Galloway. It's open Easter to October from 11am to 4pm Mon. to Sat., 11am to 5pm in July and August. Admission is 50p (85¢) for adults, 25p (40¢) for children.

North of town is the ruined **Tongland Abbey,** one of whose abbots, John

Damian, once tried to fly from the battlements of Stirling Castle wearing wings of bird feathers, in the presence of James IV. He landed in a manure pile.

Dundrennan Abbey, 7 miles southeast of Kirkcudbright, the ruins of a rich Cistercian house founded in 1142, includes much late Norman and Transitional work. Dundrennan is a daughter abbey of Rievaulx Abbey in Yorkshire and the mother abbey of Glenluce and Sweetheart Abbeys. The small village is partly built of stones "quarried" from the abbey. Mary Queen of Scots, after escaping from Loch Leven and being defeated at the Battle of Langside, spent her last night in Scotland at the abbey in May 1568. She went to England to seek help from Elizabeth, who imprisoned her instead. The transept and choir, a unique example of the Early Pointed style, remain.

In accommodations, I suggested the **Selkirk Arms,** Old High Street, Kircudbright, Kircudbrightshire DG6 4JG (tel. 0557/30402), where Robert Burns stayed when he composed the celebrated Selkirk Grace. (The grace was actually given on St. Mary's Isle, the seat of the Douglases, earls of Selkirk, and, in part, it went as follows: "But we ha'e meat, and we can eat, and sae the Lord be thankit.") The hotel, a two-story, 18th-century building, has 16 bedrooms, and the furnishings are in keeping with the character of the house. It has an inviting atmosphere and a helpful staff. You will be the guests of John and Sue Morris. The bedrooms have been recently refurbished and all have private baths or showers, color TVs, phones, and tea and coffee makers. The daily rate for B&B is £36 ($59.40) in a single, £56 ($92.40) in a double. The restaurant offers a wide range of fresh local produce, such as Galloway beef, lamb, venison, salmon, and scallops. Bar lunches and suppers are also available. The hotel has ample parking and a spacious garden in the rear. Private salmon fishing is offered on the River Dee. The neighborhood evokes memories of John Paul Jones, and there are little art galleries displaying the works of local painters.

GATEHOUSE-OF-FLEET

This sleepy former cotton town, on the Water of Fleet, was the Kippletringan in Sir Walter Scott's *Guy Mannering,* and Burns composed "Scots Wha Hae wi' Wallace Bled" on the moors nearby and wrote it down in the Murray Arms Hotel there.

The town's name probably dates from 1642 when the English government opened the first military road through Galloway to assist the passage of troops to Ireland. In 1661 Richard Murray of Cally was authorized by Parliament to widen the bridge and to erect beside it an inn that was to serve as a tollhouse, with the innkeeper responsible for the maintenance of a 12-mile stretch of road. This is believed to have been the original house on the "gait," or road, which later became known as the "gait house of Fleet," and by 1790 it was being written in its present form and spelling. The ancient "gait house" is now part of the Murray Arms Hotel, used as a coffeeroom, and is probably the oldest building still in existence in the town.

West of Gatehouse, on the road to Creetown, is the well-preserved, 15th-century tower of the McCullochs, with its sinister "murder hole" over the entrance passage. Through this trapdoor, boiling pitch was poured onto attackers.

The location of Gatehouse is 113 miles from Edinburgh and 33 miles from Dumfries.

Cardoness Castle was originally the seat of the McCulloch family, one of whom, Sir Godfrey McCulloch, was the last person in Scotland to be executed, at Edinburgh in 1697, by the "Maiden," the Scots version of the guillotine. The castle is on the A75, a mile southwest of Gatehouse-of-Fleet. It is open from 9:30am to 7pm Mon. to Sat., from 2 to 7pm Sun., April to the end of September. The remainder of the year, closing time is 4pm. Admission is 60p ($1) for adults, 30p (50¢) for children.

Where to Stay and Dine

Cally Palace Hotel, Gatehouse-of-Fleet, Kircudbrightshire DG7 2DL (tel. 05574/341), is a large 18th-century mansion standing in 100 acres of gardens and wooded parkland, 1½ miles south by A75. Especially popular with more mature travelers, it is an oasis of peace and quiet—most comfortable, more suited for someone who wishes to spend a few days in Galloway than the fleeting overnight motorist. The public lounges are overscale with some fine period pieces, and a sun patio looks out onto a swimming pool. Amenities include a bar, table tennis, and pool, in addition to tennis, putting, croquet, sauna, game fishing, loch boating, and dancing at certain times of the year. All of its 55 rooms contain private baths or showers. Some of the bedrooms have balconies opening onto the grounds. Rooms come in widely varying styles and sizes, but all have color TVs and hot beverage facilities. Depending on the room assignment, half-board tariffs range from £48 ($79.20) to £54 ($89.10) per person nightly. A dinner-dance is held on Sat. night.

Murray Arms, High Street, Gatehouse-of-Fleet, Kircudbrightshire DG7 2HY (tel. 05574/207), is a long, low, white-painted building that was once a posting inn in the 18th century, its coffeehouse dating back even earlier, to 1642. Burns wrote his stirring song "Scots Wha' Ha'e" while staying at the inn, the occasion still commemorated by the Burns Room with its Leitch pictures. The inn has been considerably updated and modernized by the laird of the Cally Estate, and that is as it should be, since it was James Murray of Cally who made the Murray Arms into a coaching inn so long ago. Now it's back in the same family after a long departure. Standing by an old clock tower, the inn has long been known for its food and hospitality. In addition to three bars, the house has a sun lounge opening onto a roof terrace. The 12 rooms are modestly furnished, and singles range from £34 ($56.10) daily, doubles from £68 ($112.20). All the rooms contain private baths, TVs, and phones. You can stop in for a complete dinner in its attractively decorated restaurant opening onto the garden. From 7:30 to 9pm daily, you can order a table d'hôte meal for £14.50 ($23.95). Specialties include Galloway beef and fresh Solway Firth salmon. The Lunky Hole lounge and food bar is open from noon to 9:45pm daily and serves a wide variety of hot and cold food.

NEWTON STEWART

Sometimes called "the gateway to Galloway" and the "heart of Galloway," this small town on the River Cree was made a burgh or barony in 1677 after a son of the second earl of Galloway built some houses beside the ford across the river and gave the hamlet its present name. When the estate was later purchased by William Douglas, he changed the name to Newton Douglas, but it didn't stick. The town has a livestock market and woolen mills. Cree Bridge, built of granite in 1813 to replace one swept away by a flood, links the town with **Minnigaff** where there is an old church with carved stones and some memorials.

Newton Stewart is associated with Scott, Stevenson, and Burns. Today it is chiefly a center for touring, especially north for 9 miles to the beauty spot of **Loch Troolin** in the Glen Trool Forest Park, 200 square miles of magnificently preserved splendor. On the way to Loch Trool you go through the village of Glentrool, where you'll find the first car park for those wanting to take the Stroan Bridge walk, a distance of 3½ miles. The hearty Scots, of course, walk the entire loch, all 4½ miles of it.

Newton Stewart lies 131 miles from Edinburgh and 87 miles from Glasgow.

Where to Stay and Dine

Newton Stewart has a wide range of accommodations, making it one of the best bases for touring Galloway. **Kirroughtree,** Newton Stewart, Wigtownshire DG8 6AN (tel. 0671/2141), lies 1½ miles northeast on A712. This is an early Georgian manor house, once the seat of the Herons of Galloway, built in 1719 and full of traditional character, with certain Spanish features. The hotel has been completely refurbished and is now a luxurious country-house hotel. All 22 bedrooms are attractively furnished and have baths, color TVs, and phones. Rates range from £45 ($74.25) per person daily for B&B, the price including VAT and free golf at several courses. There are two elegant dining rooms with period furnishings. The hotel is fully licensed and has a cozy cocktail bar. This place is ideal for those who want complete peace as it is surrounded by some 8 acres of gardens with some 10,000 ornamental shrubs and trees and views of the Galloway countryside and Solway Firth. It also offers pony trekking and many pleasant walks, plus shooting, deer stalking, and salmon and trout fishing. Closed January 4 to February 4.

The Bruce, 88 Queen St., Newton Stewart, Wigtownshire DG8 6JL (tel. 0671/2294), is an exemplary, up-to-date hotel. Although not lavish in appointments, it is modern and efficiently run, maintaining a good standard of comfort, but keeping its prices reasonable—from £34 ($56.10) daily in a single, from £54 ($89.10) in a double. The decor is bright, and the bedrooms well designed. All of the 17 bedrooms contain private baths, TVs, and phones. Guests enjoy a bar and congenial company, composed mainly of locals who frequent the Bruce. The restaurant, also in the modern style, offers a cold table at lunch daily from 12:30 to 2pm. Dinners, when the menu is more varied, are quite interesting, and everything tastes homecooked from fresh produce. A table d'hôte, served from 7:30 to 9pm, goes for £15 ($24.75).

WHITHORN

Ten miles south of Wigtown, you come upon Whithorn, a town with ancient crosses and tombstones including the 5th-century **Latinus Stone,** the earliest Christian memorial in Scotland. St. Ninian, the son of a local chieftain, founded a monastery here in A.D. 397 and built his "Candida Casa" or "White House," probably the first Christian church in Scotland. In the 12th century, Fergus, Lord of Galloway, built a priory. The church and monastery were destroyed in the 16th century. Excavations in the ruins have revealed fragments of wall covered in pale plaster believed to be from Ninian's Candida Casa. The ruins are entered through the Pend, a 17th-century arch on which are carved the Royal Arms of Scotland.

A moorland walk to the west coast 2½ miles away leads to **St. Ninian's Cave** in Port Castle Bay, used by the missionary as a retreat.

The **Isle of Whithorn,** 3 miles southeast of the town, is where St. Ninian landed about A.D. 395 on his return from studying in Rome to bring Christianity to Scotland. The ruins of a plain 13th-century chapel are here but no signs of an earlier church. On the point of the promonotory are the remains of an Iron Age fort and a late-17th-century tower.

Chapel Finian, near the shore road on the way from Whithorn to Glenluce, is a small chapel or oratory probably dating from the 10th or 11th century, in an enclosure about 50 feet wide.

Whithorn lies 52 miles from Edinburgh and 72 miles from Dumfries.

Just outside Whithorn is the **Castlewigg Hotel,** Whithorn, Wigtownshire DG8 8DL (tel. 09885/213), a small licensed country hotel under the personal supervision of its owners. Castlewigg is 2 miles north of Whithorn on the A746, with views to the north toward Newton Stewart and to the east to Fleet Bay. More than 200 years old, the hotel building was the dower house of Castle Wigg, which lies in ruins, not open to the public, a mile or so off the road. The hotel rents seven bedrooms, five with private baths. Bedrooms cost from £17 ($28.05) to £21 ($34.65) per person nightly for B&B. Guests enjoy the residents' lounge with color TV, the spacious, colorful dining room, and the lounge bar. Dinner costs around £12 ($19.80). You can order such dishes as venison in red wine and port, as well as rainbow trout. The hotel specializes in hunting and fishing holidays. The Castlewigg sits in 7 acres of grounds, about 150 yards from the main road, so there's ample parking.

PORTPATRICK

Until 1849 steamers sailed the 21 miles from Donaghdee in Northern Ireland to Portpatrick, which became a "Gretna Green" for the Irish. Couples would land on Saturday, have the banns called on Sunday, and marry on Monday. When the harbor became silted up, Portpatrick was replaced by Stranraer as a port.

Commanding a clifftop to the south are the ruins of **Dunskey Castle,** a grim keep built in 1510 by John Adair.

Ten miles south of Portpatrick is the little village of **Port Logan.** In the vicinity is **Logan House,** the seat of the McDouall family, which could trace their ancestry so far back that it was claimed they were as "old as the sun itself." This family laid out the world-famous gardens at Logan.

Logan Botanic Garden (tel. 077686/231), an annex of the Royal Botanic Garden, Edinburgh, contains a wide range of plants from the temperate regions of the world. Cordylines, palms, tree ferns, and rhododendrons grow well in the mild climate of southwest Scotland. The garden is open April 1 to October 31 daily from 10am to 6pm. Admission charges are 60p ($1) for adults and 30p (50¢) for children. The site is 14 miles south of Stranraer off the B7065 road. A licensed restaurant and toilet facilities are available.

The ancient church site of **Kirkmadrine** lies in the parish of Stoneykirk, south of Portpatrick. The site now has a modern church, but there is an ancient graveyard and early inscribed stones and crosses, including three of the earliest Christian monuments in Britain, showing the chi-rho symbol and inscriptions dating from the 5th or early 6th century. There was an early Christian monastery and, in the Middle Ages, a parish church.

Portpatrick lies 141 miles from Edinburgh and 80 miles from Dumfries.

Where to Stay and Dine

Instead of going to the larger town, Stranraer, you might prefer to stay at the **Knockinaam Lodge Hotel,** Portpatrick, Portpatrickshire DG9 9AD (tel. 077681/ 471), 3¼ miles southeast off the A77, built as a Victorian holiday house in 1869 and enlarged in 1901. It stands on a little terraced bay right at the foot of a deep and thickly wooded glen, surrounded on three sides by cliffs, looking out to sea and the distant Irish coast. In the heat of World War II, Sir Winston Churchill chose the lodge for a secret meeting with General Eisenhower. The prime minister enjoyed a long hot bath (in a tub that's still here) while smoking a cigar. Knockinaam is run in the best country-house tradition by the resident owners. Containing only 10 bedrooms, all with phones, TVs, and private baths or showers, the hotel's rate is from £65 ($107.25) per person daily for dinner, bed, and breakfast, VAT included. There is a garden with lawns running down to a private sandy beach. The lodge serves the best food in the area. All ingredients used in the kitchen are fresh. You can dine in the restaurant overlooking the sea as it breaks over the rocks at the end of the garden, enjoying tender Galloway beef, lobsters, scallops, and other local dishes, accompanied by homegrown vegetables. Both à la carte and table d'hôte meals are cooked to order. Service is polite and efficient. Lunch, daily from noon to 1:30pm, is offered for £15 ($24.75); set dinner, from 7:30 to 9pm, costs £28 ($46.20), including VAT. The lodge is open from mid-March to January.

STRANRAER

The largest town in Wigtownshire, Stranraer is the terminal of the 35-mile ferry crossing from Larne, Northern Ireland.

Stranraer lies 132 miles from Edinburgh and 75 miles from Dumfries.

An early chapel, built by a member of the Adair family near the 16th-century **Castle of St. John,** in the heart of town, gave the settlement its original name of Chapel, later changed to Chapel of Stranrawer and then shortened to Stranraer. The name is supposed to have referred to the row or "raw" of original houses on the "strand" or burn, now largely buried beneath the town's streets. The Castle of St. John became the town jail and in the late 17th century held Covenanters during Graham of Claverhouse's campaigns of religious persecution.

Three miles from Stranraer on A75 are **Castle Kennedy Gardens** and **Lochinch Castle** (tel. 0775/2024), a late-19th-century Scots baronial mansion. In the grounds of Lochinch Castle are the White and Black lochs and the ruins of Castle Kennedy, which was built during the reign of James IV but burned down in 1716. The gardens, restored in the middle of the 19th century, contain the finest pinetum in Scotland. Go in the right season and you can wander among rhododendrons, azaleas, and magnolias. The castle is not open to the public, but the gardens are, daily from 10am to 5pm April to September. Admission is £1.50 ($2.50) for adults, 50p (85¢) for children. Light refreshments are available.

Where to Stay and Dine

North West Castle, Royal Crescent, Stranraer, Wigtownshire DG9 8EH (tel. 0776/4413), overlooks Loch Ryan and the departure quay for Northern Ireland. The oldest part of the house was built in 1820 by Capt. Sir John Ross, R.N., the Arctic explorer. Of course, to honor the brave man your bedroom window should face northwest, an allusion to his search for the "North West Passage." The hotel owners will give you a brochure that relates the exploits and disappointments of the explorer. The original building has been altered and extended to meet the hotel's popularity. At last count, a total of 77 rooms are offered, all with private baths, phones, and TVs. Singles cost from £40 ($66) daily, and doubles run £55 ($90.75) to £100 ($165). Many of the best rooms are in the two modern wings. The lounges are cozy and pleasantly furnished, and the dining room is impressive, serving mainly continental fare with Scottish overtones. Fresh local ingredients are used. The bars downstairs are well stocked—I prefer the Explorers' Lounge with its views of the harbor. Further facilities include a garden, sauna, and solarium, plus curling rink, games room, indoor swimming pool, and dancing to a live band most Sat. nights.

George Hotel, George Street, Stranraer, Wigtownshire DG9 7RJ (tel. 0776/2487), stands right in the heart of town. Many of its guests are embarking for Northern Ireland in the morning. Of the 31 bedrooms, 15 contain private baths. Singles cost £23 ($37.95) to £30 ($49.50) nightly, and doubles go for £40 ($66) to £46 ($75.90), including VAT, service, and a full breakfast. Most of the rooms contain such amenities as razor sockets and radios. Color-coordinated schemes are used in the bedrooms, and the baths are spotlessly clean. A cooperative staff will give touring advice. The hotel's restaurant is also good, making use of local produce, the cooking and service quite acceptable. The lighting is subdued and the ingredients fresh, the emphasis placed on "Taste of Scotland" dishes, costing £13 ($21.45) for four courses and coffee.

XX

EDINBURGH, GLASGOW, AND CENTRAL SCOTLAND

1. EDINBURGH

2. DAY TRIPS FROM EDINBURGH

3. THE KINGDOM OF FIFE

4. GLASGOW AND THE CLYDE

5. THE TROSSACHS AND LOCH LOMOND

Scotland has often been compared to a sandwich in that the central belt is considered the meatier part. Within a relatively small compass of land, you can visit not only the capital at Edinburgh but also enjoy such beauty as the Trossachs (the Scottish lake district), the silver waters of Loch Lomond, or take in the cragginess of Stirling Castle. Central Scotland should be treated as far more than just a gateway to the Highlands.

Edinburgh, often called the fairest city in Europe, is our first stopover. While based there you can take many day trips, such as to the seaside and golfing resort of North Berwick. The Scots suggest you take a "look aboot ye."

From Edinburgh, on the opposite shore of the Firth of Forth, reached by bridge, the Kingdom of Fife is rich in treasures, such as Falkland Palace, the hunting retreat of the Stuart kings, and the unspoiled fishing villages along the coast, collectively known as "East Neuk."

To the west of Edinburgh, a distance of some 40 miles, the industrial city of Glasgow is more and more a goal for visitors. It is rich in its own attractions, and from there you can set out on a tour in many directions, including the glens and hills associated with the outlaw Rob Roy. Also on Glasgow's doorstep is the scenic estuary of the Firth of Clyde. You can cruise down the Clyde on a paddle-steamer.

1. Edinburgh

Scotland's capital city is Edinburgh, off the beaten path for those doing the mad whirlwind tour of Europe, as it lies 373 miles north of London. The city is associated with John Knox, Mary Queen of Scots, Robert Louis Stevenson, Sir Arthur Conan Doyle (creator of Sherlock Holmes), David Hume, Alexander Graham Bell, Sir Walter Scott, and Bonnie Prince Charlie—to name drop a bit.

From the elegant Georgian crescents of the New Town, to the dark medieval "wynds" of the Old Town, down the wide, magnificent Princes Street (Stevenson's "liveliest and brightest thoroughfare"), Edinburgh is a powerful attraction. Of course it's not as sophisticated as Paris, nor as fast-paced as London. And it's banal to call it the Athens of the North, although the Greek Revival movement of the 19th century made many of the buildings look like pagan temples.

Most travelers know that since World War II Edinburgh has been the scene of an ever-growing international festival, with its action-packed list of cultural events. But that shouldn't be your only reason for visiting the ancient seat of Scottish royalty. Its treasures are available all year. In fact, the pace the rest of the time—when the festival-hoppers have gone home—is more relaxed. The prices are lowered, and the people themselves, under less pressure as hosts, return to their traditional hospitable nature.

GETTING THERE

Edinburgh is about an hour's flying time from London (see "Flying to Scotland" in Chapter XVIII). It also is about 2 hours by bus or rail from the major international airport of Scotland, Prestwick, and it lies in the center of most of the rail and bus lines leading from Scotland to England. Edinburgh's improved airport, connected by frequent 30-minute bus rides to midtown, receives flights only from within the British Isles and the rest of Europe.

Edinburgh is well connected by rail and bus to other points in Britain. The second-class, round-trip fare from London to Edinburgh is £115 ($189.75). This ticket has no restrictions of any kind. An Inter-City Saver Ticket, which has many restrictions as to departure time, costs from £59 ($97.35) to £63 ($103.95) round trip.

The least expensive way to go is by bus from London, the trip from Edinburgh taking about 8 hours and costing around £16.50 ($27.25) for a one-trip ticket.

GETTING AROUND

Edinburgh doesn't benefit from a modern underground (subway, to Americans) system, so you'll find **buses** will probably be your chief method of transport in the Scottish capital. The fare you pay is determined by the distance you ride. The minimum fare is 20p (35¢) for one stage or less, and the maximum fare is £1.10 ($1.80) for 30 or more stops. (A stage is not a stop. It's a distance of about half a mile in which a number of stops usually exist.) Children up to 14 years of age pay 20p (35¢) to 60p ($1), according to the number of stages, and children under 5 travel free.

The Edinburgh city officials have devised several types of term bus passes for extended tourist visits to their city. The **Edinburgh Freedom Ticket** allows 1 day of unlimited travel on city buses at £1.40 ($2.30) for adults and £1 ($1.65) for children. Another form of extended ticket is a **TouristCard,** allowing unlimited travel on all city buses for a time period of between 2 and 13 days, plus special discounts at certain restaurants and for tours of selected historical sites. A two-day TouristCard costs £3.50 ($5.80) for adults and £2.40 ($3.95) for children. A 13-day TouristCard goes for £11.75 ($19.40) for adults and £8.65 ($14.30) for children.

For daily commuters or for diehard enthusiasts, a **RidaCard** season ticket allows unlimited travel for adults on all buses at £5.50 ($9.10) for adults for one week and £19.50 ($32.20) for four weeks. Travel must begin on a Sun. Prices for children are £3.50 ($5.80) for one week, £12.30 ($20.30) for four weeks.

These tickets and further information may be obtained at the **Waverley Bridge Transport Office,** Waverley Bridge in Edinburgh (tel. 031/554-4494), or the **Lothian Region Transport Office,** 14 Queen St., Edinburgh EH2 1JL (tel. 031/554-4494).

As a last resort, try hailing a cab or waiting at a taxi stand. Meters begin at 80p ($1.30).

EDINBURGH FAST FACTS

Besides the information given in "Fast Facts" for Britain and "Fast Facts" for Scotland, I will also list some data applicable specifically to Edinburgh.

AMERICAN EXPRESS: The office in Edinburgh is at 139 Princes St. (tel. 031/225-7881).

CONSULATES: The place to go for emergency problems such as lost passports is the **American Consulate, 3** Regent Terrace (tel. 031/556-8315). The **Australia Consulate** is at 80 Hanover St. (tel. 031/226-6271). Canada doesn't operate a consulate in Edinburgh, but has one in Glasgow.

DENTAL CARE: For a dental problem, go to the **Dental Surgery School, 31** Chambers St. (tel. 031/225-9511). Hours are 9 to 10:15am and 2 to 3:15pm Mon. to Sat.

EMERGENCIES: Call 999 in an emergency to summon police, an ambulance, or firefighters.

HOSPITAL: Go to the **Royal Infirmary of Edinburgh, 1** Lauriston Place (tel. 031/229-2477).

INFORMATION: Help for tourists is at 5 Waverley Bridge (tel. 031/226-6591).

LAUNDERETTE: Try **Bendex Laundrette** 13 South Clerk St. (tel. 031/667-5844), which is open from 8am to 6:30pm Mon. to Fri., 8am to 2pm Sat., 9am to 1:30pm Sun.

LOST PROPERTY: If you have lost property (or had it stolen), go to **Police Headquarters** on Fettes Avenue (tel. 031/331-3131).

MEDICAL CARE: In a medical emergency, you can seek help from the **Edinburgh Royal Infirmary,** Lauriston Place (tel. 031/229-2477).

PHARMACY: The most popular place is **Boots,** 48 Shandwick Place (tel. 031/225-6757), which is open from 8:45am to 9pm Mon. to Sat., 11am to 4:30pm Sun.

POST OFFICE: **Edinburgh Branch Post Office,** 2-4 Waterloo Place (tel. 031/550-8314), is open from 9am to 5:30pm Mon. to Thur., 9:30am to 5:30pm Fri., 9am to 12:30pm Sat.

WHERE TO STAY

Searching for suitable lodgings isn't too difficult in Edinburgh, as the city offers a wide range of accommodations at different price levels throughout the year. However, during the 3-week period of the festival, the establishments fill up with international visitors, so it's prudent to reserve in advance. To take care of on-the-spot bookings, the **Edinburgh Tourist Centre,** Waverley Market Complex, 3 Princes St. (tel. 031/557-1700), compiles an investigated and lengthy list of small hotels and guest houses. The emphasis is on well-managed, clean, comfortable, and hospitable guesthouses, usually catering to anywhere from 2 to 12 visitors, some for as little as £12 ($19.80) per person. The bureau's hours during the peak season, May 1 to September 30, are 8:30am to 8pm Mon. to Sat., 11am to 8pm Sun. (to 9pm July and August). A £1 ($1.65) booking fee and a 10% deposit are charged. There's also an information and accommodation desk at Edinburgh Airport.

You can write in advance, enclosing your requirements and the fee, but you should allow about 4 weeks' notice, especially during the summer and particularly during the festival weeks.

Assuming you arrive in Edinburgh when the accommodations aren't fully booked or that you will reserve a room in advance, I've prepared a representative sampling of the leading candidates, from expensive to budget.

Expensive Hotels

Edinburgh Sheraton, 1 Festival Square, Edinburgh, Lothian EH3 9SR (tel. 031/229-9131). Town leaders still praise the development of what had been a railway siding into one of the most glamorous hotel and office complexes in Scotland. Its figurehead, sheathed in the same kind of beige limestone that covers many of the city's historic buildings, is a glistening modern hotel, one of the best in Edinburgh. The hotel is elegantly appointed, with long corridors and soaring public rooms. Designers drew upon local loyalties by choosing appropriate tones of thistle and mauve for much of the carpeting. This, coupled with acres of wood trim, a central location, big-windowed views of Edinburgh Castle, and a well-chosen staff, makes this the most appealing modern hotel in the Scottish capital. The 263 spacious, well-upholstered rooms offer 24-hour room service, double glazing on the windows, color TV and easy contact with a team of concierges. The prices of accommodations are reasonable, considering the quality of the hotel. Singles range from £75 ($123.75) to £115 ($189.75) daily, with twins or doubles costing £100 ($165) to £155 ($255.75). More glamorous and more expensive suites are also available. A plushly modern cocktail bar is a favorite rendezvous for dozens of local residents, while the restaurant, with its views over the fountain on Festival Square, presents well-prepared main courses and a lavish Sun. buffet. A leisure center offers a swimming pool, whirlpool, sauna, and fully equipped gym. The hotel is only a short walk from Princes Street.

Caledonian Hotel, Princes Street and Lothian Road, Edinburgh, Lothian EH1 2AB (tel. 031/225-2433), part of the Norfolk Capital Hotels group, is the city's premier traditional hostelry, with commanding views over Princes Street Gardens and up to the castle from its prime site at the west end of the main thoroughfare and shopping street of the city. The Caledonian is an Edinburgh landmark. Built of salmon-pink sandstone, one of only three such buildings in the city, the hotel has been the subject of considerable investment recently. There are 238 well-appointed rooms, all with mini-bars, color TVs, in-house video, direct-dial phones, and baths. The charges vary from £90 ($148.50) daily in a standard single to £145 ($239.25) for a deluxe double, with VAT included. The public areas have been totally renovated, decorated in pastel shades reminiscent of an age of Edwardian splendor. There are two bars: a traditional Edinburgh pub, Platform 1, where live entertainment is presented on weekends, and the Pullman Bar, where you can enjoy a drink. For elegant dining, try the Pompadour Restaurant (see below under "Where to Dine"). There are less formal meals to be had in the Gazebo Restaurant, and a traditional British afternoon tea is served in the hotel's lounge. Food and drink are good value, with a substantial buffet from the Gazebo's hot and cold table costing around £13.50 ($22.30).

Royal Terrace Hotel, 18 Royal Terrace, Edinburgh, Lothian EH7 5AQ (tel. 031/557-3222), has been called "the country-house hotel in the city." Offering 100 luxurious double bedrooms, it was formed from three four-story Georgian townhouses, rising on an elegant crescent, about a 10-minute stroll from Waverley Station. Rooms are furnished in fine British styling, and they have a host of amenities, including hairdryers, color TVs, phones, in-house movies, three direct-dial phones, and 24-hour room service. Each has a marble bathroom, and some contain whirlpool baths, even four-poster beds. Two persons pay from £100 ($165) a night, or else triples are rented at £115 ($189.75). The restoration, while providing the most up-to-date comfort, retained much of the period styling, with oil paintings, antiques, open Adam fireplaces, carpets, and Viennese crystal chandeliers. The hotel has a glass-enclosed patio restaurant as well.

Roxburghe Hotel, 38 Charlotte Square, Edinburgh, Lothian EH2 4HG (tel. 031/225-3921), is an Adam building of dove-gray stone, a stately townhouse opening directly onto a tree-filled square. While only four floors high (including a row of dormered mansard windows), it is nevertheless the first choice for a number of discriminating people. The hotel is central, a short walk from Princes Street. The atmosphere is traditional, as reflected in the drawing room, with its ornate ceiling and woodwork, and tall arched windows opening toward the park. The furnishings are often antique, with groups of Chippendale chairs. All of the 76 bedrooms, reached by elevator, have private baths or showers, color TVs, clock radios, phones, trouser presses, and tea and coffee makers, plus amenities such as sewing kits, shower caps, and foam baths, as well as baskets of fruit. The units are handsomely traditional, a favorite scheme being Wedgwood blue-and-white, Adam-style paneling. In high season, singles cost £52 ($85.80) to £70 ($115.50) daily, and twins go for £75 ($123.75) to £115 ($189.75), all with a continental breakfast, service, and VAT included. A place to congregate for drinks is the Consort Bar, with its festive decor. A dining room serves not only good meals, but gives diners a view of the square.

George Hotel, 19 George St., Edinburgh, Lothian EH2 2PB (tel. 031/225-1251), is concentrated quality. A member of the Inter-Continental Hotels Group, the George is only short blocks from Princes Street, in the midst of a number of boutiques and bus, rail, and air terminals. Between April 1 and October 1 the highest rates are in effect: £85 ($140.25) to £105 ($173.25) daily in a single with bath, £120 ($198) to £132 ($217.80) in a twin or double-bedded room, also with bath. All prices include VAT. All of the bedrooms have been refurnished and redecorated, containing private baths or showers, color TVs, radios, direct-dial phones, and hot beverage facilities. The hotel has 24-hour room service. The public rooms have retained the style, elegance, and old-fashioned comfort of a country house. The Carvers Table offers a selection of prime Scottish beef, roast lamb, or roast pork. Le Chambertin, the hotel's exclusive French restaurant, is open Mon. to Sat. (refer to my dining recommendations).

King James Thistle Hotel, 107 St. James Centre, 1 Leith St., Edinburgh, Lothian EH1 3SW (tel. 031/556-0111), in the heart of Edinburgh just off the end of Princes Street, is a restyled and refurbished hostelry with comfortable bedrooms and many amenities. Each of the 147 bedrooms has private bath, direct-dial phone, color TV with in-house video, radio, trouser press, hairdryer, and hot beverage facilities. In addition, 24-hour room service and parking adjacent to the hotel are provided. Rooms cost from £85 ($140.25) to £95 ($156.75) daily in a single, from £120 ($198) to £130 ($214.50) in a double, VAT and service included. You can dine in the Brasserie St. Jacques on good French cuisine. The Boston Bean Company is a blend of an American saloon and a cocktail bar, reminiscent of early Americana. The style in both the brasserie and the bar is relaxed.

Carlton Highland Hotel, 1–29 North Bridge, Edinburgh, Lothian EH1 1SD (tel. 031/556-7277), was originally built as one of Edinburgh's leading department stores. But in 1984 a team of entrepreneurs converted it into a plushly comfortable hotel. Its Victorian turrets, Flemish-style gables, and severe gray stonework rise imposingly from a street corner of the Royal Mile, a few paces from Waverley Station. The hotel's interior was altered into a bright and airy milieu of hardwood paneling, pastel colors, and modern conveniences. On the premises is a bar, as well as a pair of engaging restaurants. One of them, Quills, is designed like a private library from the 19th century. In the basement is an exercise room along with swimming pool, whirlpool, sauna, two squash courts, and aerobics studio. Each of the 207 bedrooms contains a kind of Scandinavian simplicity and comfort, as well as many amenities such as a private bath, phone, mini-bar, color TV, coffee maker, and hairdryer. With VAT and breakfast included, singles cost £80 ($132) to £90 ($148.50) daily and doubles or twins £160 ($264) to £170 ($280.50).

Hilton National, Bells Mills, 69 Belford Road, Edinburgh, Lothian EH4 3DG (tel. 031/332-2545), once known as Ladbroke Dragonara, is a contemporary accommodation set beside the Water of Leith outside the historic district of Edinburgh. A section of it was a grain mill in Victoria's day, and that old commitment is still honored by the naming of the Granary Bar, which has a certain elegantly rustic quality. Public rooms are generous in space, and the hotel offers 143 well-furnished bedrooms, each with private shower or toilet, direct-dial phone, TV, and clock radio. Some of the rooms—called Gold Star—are the most elegant of all. Singles range in price from £105 ($173.25) to £132 ($217.80) daily, with doubles going for £135 ($222.75) to £165 ($272.25). Late arrivals will find dinner served until 10pm as well as 24-hour room service.

Moderately Priced Hotels

Old Waverley Hotel, 43 Princes St., Edinburgh, Lothian EH2 2BY (tel. 031/556-4648), has turn-of-the-century origins, but it can be an ideal stopover for those desiring a central, comfortable establishment, which has been refurbished to provide modern amenities, with personnel giving efficient service. All of the 66 bedrooms have private baths, phones, and TVs. The B&B rate in a single costs £60 ($99) to £65 ($107.25) daily. In a double, the B&B charge is from £85 ($140.25) to £90 ($148.50), including VAT and service. The lounges on the second floor have been given that contemporary look. Some of the rooms look onto Princes Street and, at night, the floodlit castle. The hotel has a good restaurant serving à la carte and table d'hôte meals.

Donmaree Hotel, 21 Mayfield Gardens, Edinburgh, Lothian EH9 2BX (tel. 031/667-3641), is a formally elegant Victorian villa ringed with hedges and rose borders along with a small but impeccably manicured lawn. The location is on a busy street with other Victorian homes with rooms to rent, but they are not as good as the Donmaree. Dating from 1869, the hotel has been extensively refurbished to its Victorian best. It offers 17 beautifully furnished bedrooms, all with private baths or showers, color TVs, phones, and hot beverage facilities. With a full Scottish breakfast included, singles cost from £43 ($70.95) daily, with doubles or twins priced from £50 ($82.50) to £70 ($115.50). The location is only 15 minutes from Princes Street. It is an individual hotel with much to recommend it, not the least of which is its highly rated restaurant.

Mount Royal Hotel, 53 Princes St., Edinburgh, Lothian EH2 2DG (tel. 031/225-7161), is right in the middle of the famed thoroughfare, complete with its major shops. A modern world emerges as you climb the spiral staircase or take an elevator to the second floor, with its reception rooms and lounges, and floor-to-ceiling windows opening onto views of the Old Town. In reality, Mount Royal is a remake of an old hotel, providing 158 streamlined bedrooms with a view. The emphasis is utilitarian—not on frills, although the comfort is genuine. In summer, singles with bath go for £78 ($128.70) to £95 ($156.75) daily, twins with bath cost £100 ($165) to £118 ($194.70). Prices include a continental breakfast, service, and VAT. The main dining room serves reasonably priced lunches and dinners, offering both a carving table and à la carte menus. The lounge on the second floor, with floor-to-ceiling windows offering views over the Scott Memorial and Princes Street, provides a wide range of savory and sweet snacks and beverages throughout the day.

Crest Hotel, Queensferry Road, Edinburgh, Lothian EH4 3HL (tel. 031/332-2442), stands on the road leading to the airport and the Forth Road Bridge. A modern, recently refurbished building, it is easily accessible in a city where parking is difficult. It offers views over the Firth of Forth and the floodlit cathedral. The 118 well-furnished bedrooms come with private baths, color TVs, radios, phones, and trouser presses. The standard rate for a single is £75 ($173.25) to £80 ($132) daily, and for a double, £85 ($140.25) to £105 ($173.25), including VAT and service. The Corinthian Restaurant offers a three-course lunch, costing £12 ($19.80), and a full menu in the evening for £16 ($26.40).

Howard Hotel, 32-36 Great King St., Edinburgh, Lothian EH3 6QH (tel. 031/557-3500). Three Georgian terrace houses have been combined to create a comfortable resting place at one of the finest hotels in Edinburgh. Singles, renting for £80 ($132) daily, include a full breakfast, VAT, and service. Doubles cost £120 ($198). The decor is a combination of both traditional and modern. The 25 rooms have private baths, hot beverage facilities, color TVs, radios, and direct-dial phones. After relaxing in the lounge, you might want to patronize an elegant restaurant in the basement, known as No. 36. A three-course luncheon goes for £9.50 ($15.70). Specialties include such dishes as smoked Scottish salmon and pan-fried Scottish sirloin. At dinner, two courses from a wide selection will cost from £18 ($29.70). Across the passage in the basement is the Claret Jug, with paneled walls and touches of red, along with dark wood wheelback chairs. At lunch a popular cold buffet is served in the bar, with ample portions of cold poultry and meat. At the back is a car park.

The Bruntsfield Hotel, 69-74 Bruntsfield Place, Edinburgh, Lothian EH10 4HH (tel. 031/229-1393). Its neo-Gothic facade overlooks an expanse of city park. Like the other 19th-century buildings lining this residential street, it is built of evenly spaced rows of honey-colored stones, reflecting the prosperity of their original owners. Inside, the hotel is neat and stylish, with a formal milieu of French-inspired armchairs and pastel shades of peach and blue. Just across the street lie the trees and putting greens of what are reputed to be the world's oldest golf course, the Bruntsfield Links. There's an attractive restaurant on the premises, The Potting Shed, along with a bar. The hotel also has a more formal restaurant, The Park. The 52 bedrooms are comfortably renovated, each with private bath, color TV, radio, direct-dial phone, trouser press, hairdryer, tea and coffee maker, and in-house movies. With a full Scottish breakfast and VAT, singles range from £50 ($82.50) to £62 ($102.30) daily, doubles or twins from £70 ($115.50) to £78 ($128.70).

Barnton Thistle Hotel, 562 Queensferry Rd., Edinburgh, Lothian EH4 6AS (tel. 031/339-1144), stands at a crossroads lying between Edinburgh and the airport. An architectural curiosity, it is Victorian with a balconied tower rising in the center. However, the bedrooms are up to date. This long-established hotel has its devotees. It attracts largely a commercial clientele, but is suitable for visitors as well, especially in summer. There are generous public areas, including two bars serving spirits. Fifty bedrooms are rented, and each is well furnished and maintained, with complete bath or shower, direct-dial phone, TV, and trouser press, as well as hot beverage facilities. Singles rent from £62 ($102.30) daily, with doubles costing £95 ($156.75). The hotel has a lot of facilities and extras ranging from a sauna to a secretarial service. Its restaurant serves international food, and there is live music with dancing on Sat. A coffee shop stays open until 10pm for late arrivals.

Commodore Hotel, West Marine Drive, Cramond Foreshore, Edinburgh, Lothian EH4 5EP (tel. 031/336-1700), was originally built in the 1960s and has nearly doubled in size since then. It sits on the banks of the Forth River, a short distance from the Forth River Bridge, across which the traffic of the main autoroute, M8, is funneled. The hotel occupies grounds between the river and a parkland. Each of its 50 well-furnished bedrooms overlooks either the park or river. Each of the accommodations has big windows, color TV, private bath, and phone. With VAT and a continental breakfast included, singles rent for £54 ($89.10) to £65 ($107.25) daily, with doubles costing £82 ($135.30). The hotel lies within a 15-minute drive north of Princes Street. Golfers appreciate the nearby access to a local course known as Silver Knowes. This hotel is a member of a chain, Friendly Hotels, which is firmly entrenched in Scotland as a leader of moderately priced hotels.

Ellersly House, 4 Ellersly Rd., Edinburgh, Lothian EH12 6HZ (tel. 031/337-6888), an Edwardian country house, lies 2½ miles west of the city center along A8. Standing in secluded gardens, it is about a 5-minute ride from the center. Staying here has been compared to the "privacy of a home." This country house stands in a dignified residential section close to the vicinity of the Murrayfield rugby grounds. It is one of the best of the moderately priced hotels of Edinburgh. It rents 55 well-equipped bedrooms, each with private bath or shower, direct-dial phone, and TV. Accommodations are either in the main house or an annex. After a refurbishment program, the hotel is better than ever. Singles rent for £65 ($107.25) daily, with doubles costing £85 ($140.25). The hotel possesses a well-stocked wine cellar and offers good-tasting meals, with dinner going for £15 ($24.75). Service is first class.

Braid Hills Hotel, 134 Braid Rd., Edinburgh, Lothian EH10 6JD (tel. 031/447-8888), is a stone house with turrets and gables in the Edwardian style, however, it dates from the 1880s in Victoria's reign. It is one of the best of the country-house-type hotels lying right outside Edinburgh, opening onto views of the city. The location of this long-established hotel is about 15 minutes from Princes Street. It offers

68 rooms, each well furnished and containing such amenities as private bath or shower, direct-dial phone, TV, and trouser press. Singles rent for £65 ($107.25) daily, with twins or doubles costing £78 ($128.70), including breakfast. Its restaurant features Scottish and continental cuisine, with both table d'hôte and à la carte menus.

Budget Hotels

Clarendon, 18 Grosvenor St., Edinburgh, Lothian EH12 5EG (tel. 031/337-7033), is a hotel for all seasons. It is found in a row of similar buildings, converted terrace houses, and it has been refurbished and equipped to a high standard. It is a tranquil welcoming choice, offering 51 bedrooms, each with private bath or shower. The single rate ranges from £50 ($82.50) to £55 ($90.75) daily, with doubles going for £75 ($123.75) to £80 ($132). Each accommodation has a color TV, direct-dial phone, and hot beverage facilities. Owned by Scottish Highlands Hotels, this West End selection is an easy stroll to the shops and attractions of Princes Street. A Scottish cuisine is served in its restaurant, with dinners provided until 9:30pm. Meals cost from £10 ($16.50) to £18 ($29.70).

Thrums Private Hotel, 14 Minto St., Edinburgh, Lothian EH9 1RQ (tel. 031/667-5545), takes the fictional name of J. M. Barrie's designation of his hometown of Kirriemuir. The proprietors, Mr. and Mrs. J. Maloney, run a choice establishment that is well decorated and furnished. The staff is helpful. The hotel consists of two buildings with 14 bedrooms, most with private baths or showers and all with color TVs, radios, tea and coffee makers, electric blankets, phones, and hairdryers. Singles rent for £20 ($33) to £30 ($49.50) daily, and doubles with bath cost £39 ($64.35) to £44 ($72.60). Family rooms are also offered. Tariffs include a full Scottish breakfast, VAT, and service. A small bar is available to residents. The hotel operates an à la carte restaurant for lunches and dinners, a three-course meal costing from £5 ($8.25) to £15 ($24.75). Good fresh produce is used in the preparation of all meals. A peaceful garden and car park can be used by hotel guests.

Teviotdale House, 53 Grange Loan, Edinburgh, Lothian EH9 2ER (tel. 031/667-4376). Some visitors rate this Victorian townhouse, on a main bus route leading to the heart of the city, as the finest B&B accommodation in Edinburgh. Jane Coville has acquired the property, and her attention to detail has earned her an enviable reputation. All seven bedrooms have private showers, hot and cold running water, toilets, TVs, hairdryers, and restful beds. Breakfast may be the highlight of your dining for the day. Each meal is homecooked with fresh ingredients, including smoked salmon, kippers, and home-baked bread and scones. The charge for B&B is from £21.50 ($35.50) to £37 ($61.05) daily, according to the season and size of the room. The house lies about 10 minutes from Princes Street, Waverley Station, and Edinburgh Castle.

The Nova Hotel, 5 Bruntsfield Crescent, Edinburgh, Lothian EH10 4EZ (tel. 031/447-6437), is in a quiet cul-de-sac near the city center, with a view over Bruntsfield Links in front and the Pentland Hills to the back. Visitors are welcomed to its 10 large, well-appointed bedrooms, all with baths and showers, toilets, direct-dial phones, color TVs, hairdryers, trouser presses, hot beverage facilities, and full central heating. Rents are £29.50 ($48.70) to £35 ($57.75) daily in a single, £52 ($85.80) to £62 ($102.30) in a double or twin, and £70 ($115.50) in a family room with up to three occupants. On the ground floor, guests enjoy the cocktail bar, and the public bar also provides an inviting atmosphere.

Castle and Country House Hotels

To fulfill your fantasy, you might want to spend your first night in Scotland in a real castle or a baronial country house surrounded by gardens and spacious grounds.

Dalhousie Castle, Bonnyrigg, Edinburgh, Lothian EH19 3JB (tel. 0875/20153), dates back to the 13th century, and over its long history it has entertained such illustrious guests as Edward I, Henry IV, Oliver Cromwell, Sir Walter Scott, and Queen Victoria. Today it is the family seat of the Ramsays of Dalhousie, who have converted it into a luxurious hotel, yet retained some of its finest architectural features. It lies off the A7 Carlisle-Edinburgh road, just outside the village of Bonnyrigg, only 8 miles from Edinburgh. A turreted and fortified house, with ramparted terraces and battlements, it offers such delights as a dungeon restaurant, which offers many local Scottish dishes. The 25 rooms all have private baths, color TVs, phones, radios, and plenty of space in which to sit and relax. Two of the suites have four-poster beds. In high season, a single rents for £72 ($118.80) daily, whereas a double or twin ranges from £92 ($151.80) to £110 ($181.50).

For true palatial living, you might want to take one of the two-room suites with double or twin beds, costing £150 ($247.50) to £180 ($297). A full breakfast is included in the tariffs. The castle overlooks the banks of South Esk, from which came the red sandstone to build it. The hotel can arrange salmon and trout fishing, horseback riding, and shooting.

Borthwick Castle, North Middleton, Gorebridge, Midlothian EH23 4QY (tel. 0875/20514), is in a pastoral valley only 12 miles south of Edinburgh, just off the A7. This noble twin-tower keep, built in 1430, is the finest example of its kind in Britain today. It was here that the ill-fated Mary Queen of Scots sought refuge with her third husband, the earl of Bothwell, in 1567. In 1650 the castle was besieged by the forces of Oliver Cromwell, and the damage inflicted by cannon fire can still be seen. All 10 bedchambers have private baths and are centrally heated. The apartments once occupied by the Scottish queen and her beloved Bothwell, both with four-poster beds, are available to guests. Room rates are £95 ($156.75) to £155 ($255.75) daily for a twin or double, including VAT. The higher price is for the Mary Queen of Scots four-poster or the Earl of Bothwell four-poster. Dine by candlelight and log fire in the stone-vaulted great hall, with its minstrel's gallery and hooded fireplace. A five-course, two-choice dinner menu is available for £35 ($57.75). Borthwick Castle is known for the excellence of its cuisine and personal service, its authentic medieval ambience, and the re-creation of a gracious lifestyle of other days.

Dolphinton House Hotel, Dolphinton, near West Linton, Peeblesshire EH46 7AB (tel. 0968/82286), dates from 1801 when it was built on the site of an older manor. For more than 4 centuries the Mackenzie clan held control here in this redsandstone mansion now converted to a comfortable hotel, only 26 miles southwest of Edinburgh. It lies 7 miles east of Biggar and 3 miles west of West Linton on the A702 (the main Edinburgh-Carlisle Road). The ambience is one of an old-fashioned country house. The atmosphere of a Victorian house is created by the use of Ayrshire lace, antique prints, and Laura Ashley wallpapers, among other touches. With a full Scottish breakfast, singles rent for £45 ($74.25) daily, with a twin or double going for £75 ($123.75). The 12 well-furnished bedrooms have private baths, phones, and TVs.

For £20.50 ($33.85), you'll be served a five-course Scottish gourmet dinner and coffee. Arthur and Susan Bell see that the menu of their chef is changed daily, its offerings based on the season. Local produce is used whenever possible, including game from the moors, fish from lochs and rivers, and beef, lamb, and kid from Border pasturelands. Herbs come from a walled garden. The hotel stands on 186 acres, which embrace the remains of an Iron Age fort.

WHERE TO DINE

The Scots are hearty eaters—and you may like the sizes of their portions as well as the quality of their fare, with choices from river, sea, and loch. You can dine on a cock-a-leekie soup, fresh Tay salmon, haggis, neeps, tatties, and whisky, Aberdeen Angus filet steak, potted hough, poacher's soup, and good old stovies and rumbledethumps. If none of the above tempts you, you'll find that French cuisine has made an inroad at many of the first-class hotels.

Expensive Restaurants

Pompadour Restaurant, Caledonian Hotel, Princes Street and Lothian Road (tel. 031/225-2433), is one of the finest in Edinburgh, on the mezzanine floor of the famous hotel, serving fine Scottish and French cuisine. The restaurant has been refurbished, with gray wall panels interspersed with panels of floral-patterned silk. The chef blends cuisine moderne with traditional menus in this intimate, luxurious place. A special daily menu reflects the best produce available from the markets that day, and Scottish salmon, venison, and other game are often included in a meal. Both the lunch and evening menus feature the fresh produce from the local Scottish and French markets—items such as goose liver with wild mushrooms, filet of lamb with spinach and rosemary, and charlotte of marinated salmon filled with seafood. A set lunch costs £16.50 ($27.25); a set dinner with extras goes for £35 ($57.75). An à la carte meal costs from £35 ($57.75). There is a non-smoking area. Lunch is served from 12:30 to 2pm, dinner from 7:30 to 10:30pm. No lunch is served on Sat. or Sun. On Sat. night there is dancing to a small combo, with piano music presented on other nights. Jackets and ties are requested for men, and reservations are required.

L'Auberge, 56 St. Mary's St. (tel. 031/556-5888), in the vicinity of Royal Mile, is ranked as among the top three or four restaurants in Edinburgh. As its name suggests, the cuisine is French, backed up by a carefully chosen wine list. Service is perhaps the most polished in the Scottish capital. Game and fish are specialties, and each dish—whether from the moors, loch, or sea—is individually prepared. Some of the main dishes taste as if you've been transported to the Périgord region of France. The restaurant, lying between Cowgate and Canongate, always requires a reservation. Meals cost from £12 ($19.80) to £18 ($29.70) at lunch, with dinners priced from £20 ($33) to £30 ($49.50). Service is daily from noon to 2pm and 7 to 9:30pm.

Le Chambertin, George Hotel, 21 George St. (tel. 031/225-1251), provides a top-level French cuisine in intimate surroundings, between 12:30 and 2:30pm Mon. to Fri. A meal, inclusive of wines, is available for £18.95 ($31.25) and £24.95 ($41.15) à la carte. Dinners cost from £15 ($24.75). In the evening, guests can select from a wide choice of wines, including some special bottles from the Chambertin district of France. The à la carte menu is well balanced and features many traditional dishes and also, subject to availability, lobster, mussels, oysters, and many other specialties.

Moderately Priced and Budget Restaurants

Martins, 70 Rose St., North Lane (tel. 031/225-3106), cooks, as one diner put it, "the pick of the market." Martin and Gay Irons, the owners, have a knack for picking chefs who show more than just promise: They deliver. You can get a set lunch for only £7.50 ($12.40), which has to be one of the food bargains of Edinburgh, considering the skill of the cookery and the quality of the ingredients used. However, in the evening, expect to spend from £25 ($41.25). The fish dishes (most often from the U.K.) served here are one of the reasons for visiting this establishment. But if you want something really Scottish, see if roast venison (offered with a sauce made with bramble vinegar) is on the menu: a most delectable dish. Meals in imaginative concoctions and light in texture are served Tues. to Sat. (except lunch on Saturday) at their establishment from noon to 2pm and 7 to 10pm (stays open half an hour later on Fri. and Sat. Reservations are necessary.

Donmaree Hotel Restaurant, 21 Mayfield Gardens (tel. 031/667-3641), previously recommended for its rooms, is also an outstanding restaurant in Edinburgh, with superb food and service. The location is a residential neighborhood behind a gray stone facade. Inside, it's beautifully decorated in the spirit of its Victorian origins. Under the direction of Mr. and Mrs. Galt, it has received a darkly authentic gloss from the 19th century with antiques and several oil portraits. A table d'hôte luncheon is offered for only £9.50 ($15.70). Dinners cost from £18 ($29.70). The chef might offer a pot-roasted pheasant, roast rack of lamb marinated in honey and red wine, or roast duckling with an orange and Curaçao sauce. Hours are daily from 12:30 to 2pm and 6:30 to 10pm. Reservations are desired. The location is 15 minutes from Princes Street.

Alp Horn Restaurant, 167 Rose St. (tel. 031/225-4787), in an antique, stone building on a street famous for its variety of pubs, provides a meal that is like a vacation in Switzerland. The wooden door opens to reveal an interior accented with checked gingham curtains, potted plants, and simple wooden tables and chairs. As you'd expect, the menu offers air-dried meats (Grisons style), several fondues, venison in season, and a version of Rösti, the famous potato dish of Switzerland. All of this might be capped off with a slice of Apfel Strudel. Lunch is served from noon to 2pm, dinner from 6:30 to 10pm, Mon. to Sat. Full meals cost from £18 ($29.70).

Cosmo Ristorante, 58A North Castle St. (tel. 031/226-6743), is one of the most heavily patronized Italian restaurants in the Scottish capital. Courtesy, efficiency, and good cookery are featured here. In season you can ask for mussels as an appetizer. Soups and pastas are always reliable. However, remember that the cost of your pasta is doubled if you order it as a main course. On the other hand, the portions are also doubled. I've found the veal dishes the best cooked and a good value, although you may be attracted to the seafood. The cassata siciliana is well made and not unbearably sweet. Expect to pay £18 ($29.70) to £25 ($41.25) for a complete meal. The restaurant serves from noon to 2:15pm for lunch and from 7 to 10:15pm for dinner Tue. to Sat.

The Oyster Bar at the Café Royal, 17 W. Register St. (tel. 031/556-4124), is by far the best-maintained section of this historic establishment, a famous building that also contains the Café Royal pub. The Oyster Bar corner evokes images of baronial castles in the windswept Highlands. These are enjoyed to the sights and aromas of well-prepared lunches and dinners. An entire wall of this elegantly Victorian room is devoted to full-size depictions of 19th-century Scotsmen in full dress, each set into a stained-glass window. It's best to reserve a table. Full meals cost from £15 ($24.75). The restaurant specializes in seafood, as its name implies. You might like the salmon with mussels, shrimp, Camembert, and white wine, or else the steak in black-butter sauce. You can also select trout Celopatra (in this case with capers, prawns, and lemons), grilled sardines, and sole cardinal. Open daily from 12:30 to 2:30pm and 7 to 10:30pm.

Whigham's Wine Cellars, 13 Hope St. (tel. 031/225-8674), lie in a basement. Before the premises became a fashionable wine-cellar restaurant, wine was actually bottled here. Whigham's has been in business since the mid-18th century, and it used to ship wines to the American colonies. Walk across its mellowed, old stone floors until you find an intimate alcove. A range of continental wines is offered. Each day, you can make your selection from an assortment of appetizers and plats du jour. Their smoked fish (not just salmon) is exceptional, and meals come to £12 ($19.80). Hours are from 11am to midnight Mon. to Sat.

Cousteau's Bar and Seafood Restaurant, 47 Hill St., Northlane (tel. 031/226-3355), is an inviting, little-known restaurant. Obviously the emphasis is placed on the freshness and quality of the fish, all of which comes from Scottish waters. Oysters are often available, and a savory opener would be the mussels marinières au gratin or perhaps crab en chemise. You might order turbot, grilled or poached salmon, or trout. Most seasonal fish are available, and the prices vary with weather conditions. Expect to pay from £18 ($29.70) per person for a meal. There are simple desserts and a good wine list, which is perhaps a little expensive. Open from noon to 2pm and 6 to 11pm Mon. to Sat.

Chinese and Indian Restaurants

The Dragon's Castle, 21 Castle St. (tel. 031/225-7327), is the oldest established Chinese restaurant in Edinburgh. Its success has been attributed to the fact that it opened in an auspicious year—the Year of the Dragon in the Chinese zodiac calendar. Cantonese and Pekinese cuisine is served, as well as seafood and a selection of European dishes, in case you're not feeling Chinese. Menus list a choice of 10 set meals, for two to six people, costing either £11 ($18.15) or £13.50 ($22.30) per person. Prices for main dishes ordered individually are reasonable. The restaurant is open from noon to 11:30pm Mon. to Thur., noon to 11:45pm Fri. and Sat., and 12:30 to 11pm Sun. Three-course business lunches are offered during the week from noon to 2pm, costing only £5 ($8.25).

Verandah Tandoori, 17 Dalry Rd. (tel. 031/337-5828), in the vicinity of the Haymarket depot, offers better than average food from North India and Bangladesh.

A much-awarded restaurant, it deserves its good reputation. Vegetarians, of course, flock here, and you can select from a wide range of classic and tandoori food items made with excellent, fresh ingredients. It is open for lunch daily from noon to 2:30pm and dinner from 5 to 11:45pm, the latter ideal for both early bird dinners and late evening suppers. The prices are reasonable, with a set luncheon or dinner costing only £9.50 ($15.70).

Szechuan House, 95 Gilmore Place (tel. 031/229-4655). Unlike London, Edinburgh doesn't abound in Szechuan restaurants, but there is one. You don't come here for elegant trappings, but what you get is some of the best Chinese food in Edinburgh. Vegetarians can also dine happily here, although most items seem to be concocted into zesty, savory platters from poultry and fish, especially chicken, duck, and prawns. My favorite menu selection is whimsically titled "bang-bang" chicken. You'll find the usual array of Chinese dishes along with some surprises such as a soup made with fish heads. But that might be left for only the adventurous palate. Meals cost from £9 ($14.85). Service is from 5:30pm to 2am Tue. to Sun.

Indian Cavalry Club, 3 Atholl Place (tel. 031/228-3282). There are those who consider this the best Indian restaurant in Scotland. The name alone may attract you to this well-run place. The decor might suggest one of the old Hollywood movies, starring Gary Cooper or Errol Flynn. You face a vast menu in your armchair culinary tour of the subcontinent. Actually, some of the dishes are inspired by Burma and Nepal. Of course, all the familiar fare, including vindaloo dishes and tandooris, is there, but there are many imaginative and unusual presentations as well. Vegetarians will find much to please their palates as well. Service is daily from noon to 2:30pm and 5:30 to 11:30pm. A set luncheon is good value at £5.95 ($9.80), with a table d'hôte dinner going for £12.95 ($21.35). You can also order à la carte.

Where to Dine and Drink at Leith

In the northern regions of Edinburgh, Leith is the old port town, opening onto the Firth of Forth. Once it was a city in its own right until it was slowly absorbed into Edinburgh. After decades of decay, parts of it are gradually being restored into modernized "flats," along with a collection of restaurants, wine bars, and pubs.

Vintners Room, the Vaults, 87 St. Giles St., Leith (tel. 031/554-6767), is the leading restaurant of Leith, installed in vaults where wine merchants of old stored their vintages. Tim and Sue Cumming are not necessarily trying to make any earth-shaking statement in cuisine here; instead they seem to concentrate on good wholesome food well prepared and served. Against a tasteful decor, with plasterwork, guests peruse the menu which on any given night might include these old favorites: salmon in puff pastry, coq au vin, or grilled oysters with bacon. You dine in air-conditioned comfort, paying £8.50 ($14.05) for the set luncheon (the single best food value in Leith), or else you can order a £11.50 ($19) set menu. Otherwise, à la carte dinners cost from £18 ($29.70). Open from noon to 2:30pm and 6:30 to 10pm; closed Sat. lunch and Sun. dinner. Reservations are needed.

Skipper's Bistro, 1A Dock Place (tel. 031/554-1018), is one of the foremost restaurants in the port area, a former pub that has been skillfully gentrified by Allan and Jen Corbett. Today the walls are covered with an alluring shade of red designed to show off the well-polished brass, the antique chairs, and the marble-top-bars. Fish is a specialty. Meals cost £12.50 ($20.65) for two courses, £14 ($23.10) for three courses. Coffee rounds off the flavor of the meals, which might include a marinade of kipper, trout au gratin, scallops thermidor, and a mousseline of seafood. Lunch is served daily from 12:30 to 2pm, and dinner from 7:30 to 10pm. This place lies off Commercial Street near a canal.

Waterfront Wine Bar, 1C Dock Place (tel. 031/554-7427), is a pleasant place whose brick and stone walls are adorned with old prints, maps, photographs, and other nautical memorabilia. A large vine acts like a pergola, letting dappled sunlight play across the tables. During the summer you can be seated at a table on a floating raft. Wine lovers enjoy vintage wine by the glass and a large selection by the bottle. Food is available, with an array of daily specials listed on the blackboard, perhaps including a prawn salad or lamb kebabs. The establishment charges from £13

($21.45) for a full meal. Food is served from noon to 2:30pm Mon. to Fri., noon to 3pm Sat. Dinner is from 6 to 9:30pm Mon. to Thur., 6 to 10pm Fri. and Sat.; closed Sun. It lies off Commercial Street toward the water.

Dining at Cramond

At least once you should get out into the countryside surrounding Edinburgh. One way to do this is to take bus 41 for about 5 miles from the West End to the little Scottish village of Cramond. Few visible traces remain today of its Roman occupation.

Quietly nestling on a sloping street is the **Cramond Inn,** on Cramond Glebe Road (tel. 031/336-2035), which has been serving food and drinks to wayfarers for 300 years (it was known to Robert Louis Stevenson). Picture upholstered booths, some upholstered beer-barrel chairs, a collection of local watercolors, a low ceiling, large, foot-square old beams, dark oak and creamy-colored walls, recessed windows, a small stone fireplace—and you'll begin to get the feel of the inn. The restaurant can serve 60 diners, but you'd better call in advance as it's most popular. The steak and kidney pie is excellent, but I'm drawn to the haggis (with "neeps and tatties" and a dram of whisky), the famed dish of Scotland, made with an assortment of chopped meats, oatmeal, and spices. For an appetizer, the smoked haddock and prawn chowder is a favorite. A specialty of the house is medallion of venison with rowan jelly. Bar lunches are served in the lounge bar from noon to 2pm Mon. to Sat., 12:30 to 2:30pm Sun. The dining room serves lunch from noon to 2:30pm and dinner from 7 to 10pm Mon. to Sat. Meals cost from £10 ($16.50) to £15 ($24.75).

WHAT TO SEE AND DO

Before leaving the Scottish capital, you'll want to take a look at both the Old Town and the New Town. Each has different attractions—the Old Town is largely medieval; the New Town, Georgian.

Those on the most rushed of schedules may have time to see only the most important attractions. These include (1) Edinburgh Castle, (2) the Palace of Holyroodhouse, (3) a walk along the Royal Mile, (4) the National Gallery of Scotland, and (5) a look at the Gothic Scott Monument in the East Princes Street Gardens.

A good place to begin exploration is on the Royal Mile of the Old Town, a collective term for Canongate, Lawnmarket, and the High.

Edinburgh Castle

It is believed that the ancient city grew up on the seat of the dead volcano, Castle Rock. History is vague on possible settlements, although it is known that in the 11th century Malcolm III (Canmore), and his Saxon queen, Margaret, occupied a castle on this spot. The good Margaret was later venerated as a saint. St. Margaret's Chapel was built in the Norman style, the present oblong structure dating principally from the 12th century. The 5-ton **Mons Meg,** a 15th-century cannon that formerly sat outside the tiny chapel, is now to be found in the French Prisons.

Inside the castle (tel. 031/225-9846) you can visit the **state apartments**—particularly Queen Mary's Bedroom—where Mary Queen of Scots gave birth to James VI of Scotland (later James I of Britain). The great hall with its hammer-beam ceiling was built by James IV. It displays armaments and armor. Scottish Parliaments used to convene in this hall.

The highlight, however, is the Crown Chamber, which houses the Honours of Scotland, used at the coronation of James VI, along with the sceptre and the sword of state of Scotland. The French Prisons can also be viewed. Turned into a prison in the 18th century, these great storerooms housed hundreds of Napoleonic soldiers during the early 19th century. Many of them made wall carvings that you can see today.

The castle may be visited from April to the end of September 9:30am to 5:05pm (last ticket sold) Mon. to Sat. and 11am to 5:05pm Sun., from October to the end of March 9:30am to 4:20pm Mon. to Sat. and 12:30 to 3:35pm Sun. Admission is £2.20 ($3.65) for adults £1.10 ($1.80) for children.

Your entrance ticket to the castle includes entry to the galleries of the **Scottish United Services Museum** (tel. 031/225-7534). These are situated on the west side of Crown Square and in the North Hospital block. This national museum deals with the history of the navy, army, and air force at all periods. It is considered unique and comprehensive, the longest established collections of British armed forces historical material in the United Kingdom. The exhibitions alone are the largest single part of the areas in the castle open to the public. The Scottish regiments of the British Army figure strongly, and displays in the North Hospital block deal with the story of the Scottish soldier in an exciting fashion. In other sections, uniforms, equipment, badges, and medals present more traditional displays.

The Camera Obscura, Castlehill (tel. 031/226-3709), is right beside the castle at the head of the Royal Mile. It's at the top of the Outlook Tower and offers a magnificent view of the surrounding city. Trained guides point out the landmarks and talk about Edinburgh's history. In addition, there are several exhibitions, all with an optical theme, and a shop selling books, crafts, and records. Hours from November to March are 9:30am to 5pm daily, from April to October 9:30am to 6pm daily. Admission is £2.20 ($3.65) for adults, £1.10 ($1.80) for children.

Along the Royal Mile

Ideally, if you have the time you should walk the full length of the Royal Mile —all the way to the Palace of Holyroodhouse at the opposite end. Along the way you'll see some of the most interesting old structures in Edinburgh, with their turrets, gables, and towering chimneys. Of all the buildings that may intrigue you, the most visited are John Knox's House and **St. Giles' Cathedral.**

Although it still bears the name "cathedral," which it once was, St. Giles' is now properly titled the High Kirk of Edinburgh (tel. 031/225-4363). Founded in 1120, the interior dates mainly from the 15th century. It contains the Thistle Chapel, designed by Sir Robert Lorimer and housing beautiful stalls and notable heraldic stained-glass windows. The chapel is open from 10am to 5pm daily. John Knox, the leader of the Reformation in Scotland, was minister of St. Giles' from 1560 to 1572.

Lady Stair's House, Lady Stair's Close, Lawnmarket, was built in 1622 by a prominent merchant burgess. It takes its name from a former owner, Elizabeth, the Dowager-Countess of Stair. Today it is a treasure house of portraits, relics, and manuscripts relating to three of Scotland's greatest men of letters: Robert Burns, Sir Walter Scott, and Robert Louis Stevenson. The house is open 10am to 5pm Mon. to Sat., to 6pm from June to September. During the festival it's open from 2 to 5pm Sun. For information, telephone 031/225-2424, ext. 6593. Admission is free.

As an Old Town complement to the New Town Georgian House (see below), the National Trust for Scotland has a 1620 tenement in the Royal Mile. **Gladstone's Land,** 477B Lawnmarket (tel. 031/226-5856), is a four-story building with two floors furnished as they might have been in the 17th century. On the ground floor, reconstructed shop booths display replicas of goods of the period. It is open from 10am to 5pm Mon. to Sat. (last entry at 4:30pm); 2 to 5pm Sun., April to the end of October. Admission is £1.80 ($2.90) for adults, and 90p ($1.50) for children.

Museum of Childhood, 42 High St. (tel. 031/225-2424), stands just opposite John Knox's House on the Royal Mile. It was the first museum in the world to be devoted solely to the history of childhood. Five galleries contain nearly every facet of the world of children, ranging from antique toys and games to exhibits on health, education, costumes, and many other items representing the childhood experience of members of different nationalities and periods. Because of the youthful clientele it naturally attracts, visitors are warned that it has been described as "the noisiest museum in the world." It is open from 10am to 6pm June to September, to 5pm the rest of the year, and from 2 to 5pm on Sun. during the Edinburgh Festival. Admission is free.

Across the street at 45 High St. is **John Knox House** (tel. 031/556-9579), dating back to the late 15th century. Even if you're not interested in the reformer who founded the Scottish Presbyterian Church, you may want to visit his house, as it is characteristic of the "lands" that used to flank the Royal Mile. All of them are gone now, except Knox's house, with its timbered gallery. Inside you'll see the tempera ceiling in the Oak Room, along with exhibitions of Knox memorabilia. The house may be visited from 10am to 4:30pm Mon. to Sat. Admission is £1 ($1.65) for adults, 50p (85¢) for children. The price includes a 12-minute video on the life and times of Knox and Mary Queen of Scots.

After leaving John Knox's House, continue along the Canongate in the direction of the Palace of Holyroodhouse. At 163 Canongate stands one of the handsomest buildings along the Royal Mile. The **Canongate Tolbooth** (tel. 031/225-2424) was constructed in 1591 and was once the courthouse, prison, and center of municipal affairs for the burgh of Canongate. It houses the People's Story, a museum of the life and work of Edinburgh's inhabitants. Starting with Trade Incorporations and Friendly Societies, it looks at how people organized themselves at work and in political and social campaigns, as well as at housing, health, and welfare, and at how people spent their leisure time—sports, movies, dancing, the pub, and the tea room. It is open from 10am to 6pm Mon. to Sat., 2 to 5pm Sun. from June to September. During other months, this admission-free museum is open from 10am to 5pm Mon. to Sat.

Across the street at 142 Canongate is **Huntly House** (tel. 031/225-2424, ext. 6689), an example of a restored 16th-century mansion. It is now Edinburgh's principal museum of local history. You can stroll through period rooms and reconstructions from 10am to 5pm Mon. to Sat., until 6pm from June to September. During the festival it is also open from 2 to 5pm Sun. Admission is free.

The Palace of Holyroodhouse

At the eastern end of the Royal Mile, the palace (tel. 031/556-1096) was built adjacent to an Augustinian abbey, established by David I in the 12th century. The nave, now in ruins, remains today. James IV founded the palace nearby in the early part of the 16th century, but of his palace only the north tower is left. Much of what you see today was ordered built by Charles II.

In the old wing occurred the most epic moments in the history of Holyroodhouse, when Mary Queen of Scots was in residence. Mary, who had been queen of France and widowed while still a teenager, decided to return to her native Scotland. She eventually entered into an unsuccessful marriage with Lord Darnley, but spent more time and settled affairs of state with her secretary, David Rizzio. Darnley plotted to kill the Italian, and he and his accomplices marched into Mary's supper room, grabbed Rizzio over her protests, then carried him to the Audience Chamber, where he was murdered with 56 stab wounds. A plaque marks the spot of his death on March 9, 1566.

Darnley himself was to live less than a year after, dying mysteriously in a gunpowder explosion. Mary, of course, was eventually executed on the order of her cousin, Elizabeth I. One of the most curious exhibits in Holyroodhouse is a piece of needlework by Mary, depicting a cat-and-mouse scene (Elizabeth's the cat).

The state apartments also contain some fine 17th-century Flemish tapestries, especially a whole series devoted to Diana, as well as some Gobelins. In the great gallery are 89 portraits, depicting Scottish kings, including Macbeth, painted by a Dutchman, De Wet. (They either all looked surprisingly similar in the face, or else De Wet used the same model for the lot of them.) Three of the state rooms, which were built as the private suite of Charles II, have been furnished with 17th-century furniture, much of which is original to the palace, including a magnificent state bed and more tapestries.

The palace suffered long periods of neglect, although it basked in glory at the ball in the mid-18th century thrown by Bonnie Prince Charlie. The present queen and Prince Philip live at Holyroodhouse whenever they visit Edinburgh. When they're not in residence, you can visit the palace, usually all year except for 2 weeks at the end of May and 3 weeks from the middle of June. Hours are 9:30am to 5:15pm Mon. to Sat., 10:30am to 4:30pm Sun. In winter, the palace is closed at 3:45pm and on Sun. Adults pay £2 ($3.30) to enter, but when the state apartments are closed, the cost is £1.50 ($2.50) for the Historical Rooms tour.

The New Town

At some point, the Old Town became too small. The burghers decided to build a whole new town across the valley, where the marsh was drained and eventually turned into public gardens. Princes Street is the most striking boulevard. Architecturally, the most interesting district of the New Town is the north side of Charlotte Square, designed by Robert Adam. The young architect James Craig shaped much of the Georgian style of the New Town, with its crescents and squares.

At no. 7 Charlotte Square, a part of the northern facade, is the restored building known simply as the **Georgian House** (tel. 031/225-2160). It is a prime example of Scottish architecture and interior design in the zenith of the New Town. Originally the home of John Lamont, 18th chief of the Clan Lamont, the house is under the auspices of the National Trust for Scotland. The furniture in this Robert Adam house is mainly Hepplewhite, Chippendale, and Sheraton, all dating from the 18th century. In a ground-floor bedroom is a sturdy old four-poster with an original 18th-century canopy. The dining room table is set for a dinner on fine Wedgwood china, and the kitchen is stocked with gleaming copper pots and pans. The house is open from 10am to 4pm Mon. to Sat., 2 to 4pm Sun., from April to October. Admission is £1.90 ($3.15) for adults, 95p ($1.55) for children.

The Gothic-inspired **Scott Monument** lies in the **East Princes Street Gardens.** It is the most famous landmark of Edinburgh, completed in the mid-19th century. Sir Walter Scott's heroes are honored by small figures in the monument. You can climb the tower from May to October 9am to 6pm Mon. to Sat. for 60p ($1). In winter you must scale the monument before 3pm. Closed Sun. At West Princes Street Gardens is the first-ever **Floral Clock,** which was constructed in 1904.

Art Treasures

For the art lover, Edinburgh has a number of masterpieces, and many visitors come here just to look at the galleries. Of course, the principal museum is the **National Gallery of Scotland,** on the Mound (tel. 031/556-8921), in the center of Princes Street Gardens. Although the gallery is small as national galleries go, the collection came about with great care and was expanded considerably by bequests and loans. A few paintings are of exceptional merit. I'll highlight a representative sampling.

Italian paintings include Verrocchio's *Madonna and Child,* Andrea del Sarto's *Portrait of a Man,* and Domenichino's *Adoration of the Shepherds.* However, perhaps the most acclaimed among them is Tiepolo's *Finding of Moses.* A spectacular sculpture acquisition is Bernini's posthumous bust of *Monsignor Carlo Antonio Pozzo,* archbishop of Pisa.

The Spanish masters are less well represented but shine forth in El Greco's *Saviour,* Velázquez's *Old Woman Cooking Eggs,* an early work by that great master, and *Immaculate Conception* by Zurbarán, his friend and contemporary.

The Flemish School emerges notably in Rubens's *Feast of Herod* and the Dutch in Rembrandt's *Woman in Bed,* superb landscapes by Cuyp, Ruisdael, and Hobbema, and in one of the gallery's more recent acquisitions, *Interior of St. Bavo's Church, Haarlem,* by Pieter Saenredam, his largest and arguably finest painting, bought in 1982. Hans Holbein the Younger's *Allegory of the Old and New Testaments* has added a new dimension to the representation of early northern painting in the gallery.

Among the paintings on loan to the gallery since World War II, from the duke of Sutherland, are two Raphaels: *The Holy Family with a Palm Tree* and *The Bridgewater Madonna.* Titian gives us his favorite subject, Venus, this time rising from the sea, but he's even more masterly in his Diana canvases. A rare feature of the gallery is the *Seven Sacraments* paintings by Poussin, the 17th-century French painter, also on loan.

The most valuable gift to the gallery since its founding, the Maitland Collection, includes Cézanne's *Mont St. Victoire,* as well as works by Degas, Van Gogh,

Renoir, Gauguin, and Seurat, among others. Gauguin's *Vision of the Sermon,* a key work in the development of modern painting, is one of the gallery's masterpieces. A recent acquisition is an early Monet, *Shipping Scene—Night Effects.* Cézanne's *Big Trees* is one of the most notable acquisitions in recent years.

The great English painters are represented by excellent examples— Gainsborough's *The Hon. Mrs. Graham,* Constable's *Dedham Vale,* along with works by Turner, Reynolds, and Hogarth. The building houses the national collection of the Scottish school, including many Ramsays, Raeburns, and Wilkies, none finer than Henry Raeburn, at his best in the whimsical *The Rev. Robert Walker Skating on Duddingston Loch.*

The Department of Prints and Drawings contains examples of many of Europe's greatest masters and draws its changing exhibition programs from the permanent collections.

The gallery is open from 10am to 5pm Mon. to Sat., 2 to 5pm Sun. During the festival, hours are 10am to 6pm Mon. to Sat., 11am to 6pm Sun. Admission is free. This gallery is one of the three national galleries of Scotland.

Scotland's national collection of 20th-century art is at the **Scottish National Gallery of Modern Art,** Belford Road (tel. 031/556-8921). In 1984 it moved from its temporary home in the Royal Botanic Garden into a former school building completed in 1828, which has been converted into an art gallery. It is set in 12 acres of grounds just 15 minutes' walk from the west end of Princes Street. The collection is truly international in scope and quality despite its modest size. Major sculptures sited outside the building include pieces by Henry Moore, Hepworth, and Bourdelle. Inside, the collection ranges from a fauve Derain and cubist Braque and Picasso to recent works by Richard Long, Baselitz, and Lucian Freud. There is naturally a strong representation of English and Scottish art. Highlights of the collection include works by Vuillard, Matisse, Miró, Magritte, Léger, Jawlensky, Kirchner, Kokoschka, Dix, Ernst, Ben Nicholson, Dubuffet, Pollock, Beuys, Balthus, Hanson, De Andrea, Lichtenstein, Kitaj, and Hockney. Prints and drawings can be studied in the Print Room by appointment only.

The licensed café also sells coffee and nonalcoholic drinks as well as light refreshments and salads. Gallery hours are 10am to 5pm Mon. to Sat., 2 to 5pm Sun. These hours are extended during the Edinburgh Festival. The only bus that actually passes the gallery is the infrequent no. 13. However, buses 18, 20, and 41 pass along Queensferry Road, leaving only a 5-minute walk up Queensferry Terrace and Belford Road to the gallery. Admission is free.

Housed in a red stone Victorian Gothic building by Rowand Anderson, the **Scottish National Portrait Gallery,** 1 Queen St. (tel. 031/556-8921), at the east end of Queen Street, gives you a chance to see what the famous people of Scottish history looked like. The portraits, several by Gainsborough and Reynolds, include everybody from Mary Queen of Scots to James VI and I, from Sir Walter Scott to Rabbie Burns, from Flora Macdonald to Ramsay MacDonald. Charging no admission, the gallery is open from 10am to 5pm daily and from 2 to 5pm Sun.

National Museums of Scotland

Two long-established museums were combined in 1985 to form a union with one administration (tel. 031/225-7534), international collections in the arts and sciences, and a treasure trove of Scottish material. Displays range through the decorative arts, ethnography, natural history, technology, geology, archeology, and other sciences. They were formerly the Royal Scottish Museum and the National Museum of Antiquities. Now they form part of the National Museums of Scotland. The Chambers Street building at the city center near the Royal Mile, begun in 1861 and one of the finest examples of Victorian architecture in Edinburgh, houses the international collections in the arts and sciences. The Findlay Building, on Queen Street, at the east end of the city center, opened in 1890, contains collections of Scottish memorabilia from prehistoric times to the present. The collections were initiated more than 200 years ago by the Society of Antiquaries.

Hours for the two buildings of the Royal Museum are 10am to 5pm Mon. to

Sat., 2 to 5pm Sun. Admission to both is free, except for some special temporary exhibitions. To reach the Chambers Street branch, centrally situated about a 10-minute walk southward from Waverly Station, one of some 23 Lothian Region buses can be used. The Queen Street branch is also about a 10-minute walk from Waverly Station, this time to the north and about 5 minutes from the bus station. You can take one of 11 Lothian Region buses to reach it.

Scotch Whisky Heritage Centre

At 358 Castlehill, Royal Mile (tel. 031/220-0441), this center is privately funded by a conglomeration of Scotland's biggest whisky distillers. It highlights the economic effect of whisky on both Scotland and the world and illuminates the centuries-old traditions associated with whisky making, showcasing the exact science and art form of distilling. A 7-minute movie is shown and visitors ride in a whisky barrel through theatrical presentations of the history and traditions of Scotch whisky making to the present day. The center's shop stocks a wide range of Scotch whiskies and other gifts.

June to September it is open daily from 9am to 6:30pm. The rest of the year it is open daily from 10am to 5pm. Admission is £2.50 ($4.15) for adults and £1.25 ($2.05) for children.

Lauriston Castle

This fine country mansion standing in extensive grounds overlooking the Firth of Forth lies on the outskirts of Edinburgh about 3¼ miles northwest of Princes Street. If going by car, take the Queensferry Road (A90), as if heading for the Forth Road Bridge, but turn off to the right at the Quality Street junction (look for directional signs pointing to Lauriston Castle). Then proceed down Cramond Road South until you come to the entrance on the right to the castle. If using public transport, take the Lothian Region bus 41 from the Mound, Hanover Street, or George Street.

The house is associated with John Law (1671–1729), the founder of the first bank in France, and its collections are strong in English Georgian and French Louis styles of furniture. The house gives one a good picture of the leisured lifestyle of the wealthy middle class prior to World War I. Look for the Derbyshire Blue John ornaments and the Crossley wool "mosaics." The house is open from 11am to 1pm and 2 to 5pm Sat. to Thur. from April to October. From October to March, it is open from 2 to 4pm Sat. and Sun. only. Visits are by guided tour only, each tour lasting approximately 50 minutes and the last one beginning 40 minutes before closing time. Admission is £1.10 ($1.80) for adults, 50p (85¢) for children. For more information, telephone 031/336-2060.

THE FESTIVAL

The highlight of Edinburgh's year—some would say the only time when the real Edinburgh emerges—comes in the last 3 weeks of August during the **Edinburgh International Festival.** Since 1947 the festival has brought to Edinburgh artists and companies of the highest international standard in all fields of the arts, including music, opera, dance, theater, exhibition, poetry, and prose, and "Auld Reekie" takes on a cosmopolitan air.

During the period of the festival, one of the most exciting spectacles is the **Military Tattoo** on the floodlit esplanade in front of Edinburgh Castle, high on its rock above the city. Vast audiences thrill to the delicate maneuvers of the famous Scottish regiments, the precision marching of military units from all parts of the world, and of course the stirring skirl of the bagpipes and the swirl of the kilt.

Less predictable in quality but infinitely greater in quantity is the **Edinburgh Festival Fringe,** an opportunity for anybody—whether an individual, a group of friends, or a whole company of performers—to put on their own show wherever they can find an empty stage or street corner. Late-night reviews, outrageous and irreverent contemporary drama, university theater presentations, maybe even a full-length opera—Edinburgh gives them all free rein. As if that were not enough,

Edinburgh has a **Film Festival**, a **Jazz Festival**, a **Television Festival**, and a **Book Festival** (every second year) at the same time.

Ticket prices vary from £1 ($1.65) up to about £21 ($34.65) a seat, but if you move fast enough, there are not many events that you cannot see for £2.50 ($4.15).

Information can be obtained at the following places: **Edinburgh Festival Society,** 21 Market St., Edinburgh EH1 1BW (tel. 031/226-4001); **Edinburgh Festival Fringe,** 180 High St., Edinburgh EH1 1BW (tel. 031/226-5257); **Edinburgh Military Tattoo,** The Tattoo Office, 22 Market St., Edinburgh EH1 1QB (tel. 031/225-1188); **Edinburgh Film Festival,** Department M, Edinburgh International Film Festival, The Filmhouse, 88 Lothian Rd., Edinburgh EH3 9BX (tel. 031/228-6382); **Edinburgh Jazz Festival,** 116 Canongate, Edinburgh EH8 8DD (tel. 031/557-1642); **Edinburgh Television Festival,** 17 Great Poulteney St., London W1R 3DG (tel. 01/437-5100); **Edinburgh Book Festival,** 25A South West Thistle Street Lane, Edinburgh EH2 1EW (tel. 031/225-1915); and **Edinburgh Accommodation Bureau,** Tourist Accommodation Service, Waverley Market, Waverley Bridge, Edinburgh EH1 1BP (tel. 031/557-2727).

TOURS

If you want a quick introduction to the principal attractions in and around Edinburgh, then consider one or more of the tours offered by **Lothian Region Transport,** 14 Queen St. (tel. 031/220-4111). You won't find a cheaper way to hit the highlights. The coaches leave from Waverley Bridge, near the Scott Monument, and operate throughout the year, with rather more curtailed service in the winter months.

The main tour of Edinburgh is the Edinburgh Classic Tour, which runs every day, every 15 minutes, on a journey which lasts just under an hour around the historical parts of old Edinburgh. Passengers may leave the coach at any point on the route to visit a place of interest, such as the Castle or Holyrood Palace, and board a subsequent coach as it comes along to continue the tour. Normally open-top, double-deck coaches are used on this tour, and live commentaries are given on all LRT tours.

Other tours of Edinburgh in the program are Historic Edinburgh, which lasts 2½ hours and includes a conducted visit to either Edinburgh Castle or Holyrood Palace, and the Sea, City and Hills which takes almost 2 hours and is a drive around the perimeter of the city giving panoramic views over Edinburgh and its environs.

There is also a wide selection of journeys that operate away from Edinburgh. These are on a special program called the Waverley Series, composed of full-day and half-day excursions to destinations throughout Scotland.

Full details of all tours are available from LRT at Waverley Bridge, or 14 Queen St., Edinburgh (tel. 031/220-4111).

SHOPPING

There are big and beautiful stores along Princes Street, facing the gardens and the castle, but there is just as much opportunity for seeking out souvenirs along the Royal Mile.

Along Princes Street

Next to Waverley Station is **Waverley Market Shopping Centre,** offering something for everyone, all under one roof in the center of Edinburgh, on three levels. A food court has tempting snacks, and unique handmade items can be bought in the craft center. The market is open seven days a week, from 9am to 6pm Mon. to Sat. (to 7pm Thur.) and 11am to 5pm Sun.

Jenners, Princes Street at the corner of South St. David's Street (tel. 031/225-2442). Everyone in Edinburgh has probably been to Jenners at least once. One of the oldest independent stores in the world, Jenners, with its elegant Victorian facade, celebrated its 150th anniversary in 1988. The store is known for its fine selection of quality merchandise made in Scotland, international fashion, and wide range of Scottish foods.

Debenham's, 112 Princes St. (tel. 031/225-1320). This, along with Jenners, competes for the honor of the best department store in Edinburgh. Its modernized Victorian shell stocks a wide array of Scottish and international merchandise behind a marble-covered front.

Tartan Gift Shops, 96 Princes St. (tel. 031/225-5551). If you've ever suspected that you might be Scottish, this establishment will show you a chart indicating the place of origin within this country of your family name. You'll then be faced with a bewildering array of hunt and dress tartans for your personal use. The high-quality wool is sold by the yard as well as in the form of kilts for both men and women. There's also a line of lamb's-wool and cashmere sweaters, and all the accessories to round out your perfect image as a Scot. The staff here is helpful. The shop is on two levels of a Princes Street building, in a format that the staff calls "seven steps up, seven steps down."

Laura Ashley, 126 Princes St. (tel. 031/225-1218). Would it be possible to say more about Laura Ashley? In her lifetime, she was credited more than anyone else with bringing English chintz back into style, as well as ruffled English blouses and dresses. This particular branch of her worldwide empire specializes in garments ranging from those for babies from birth through children's wear, bridal, and adult fashions in sizes 10 to 16 (United Kingdom sizing).

The Millshop, 134C Princes St. (tel. 031/225-2319), one of 25 such shops throughout the United Kingdom, sells knitwear, skirts, giftware, and travel rugs. In addition to regular shop hours Mon. to Sat., the shop also is open from 11am to 5pm Sun.

Romanes & Paterson, 62 Princes St. (tel. 031/225-4966), "Specialists in Scottish Woolen Goods," is the flagship store of The Edinburgh Woollen Mill. It sells the complete range of company products, pure, new, wool knitwear and garments, and has a large selection of tartans and associated products. There is a range of children's kilts plus a variety of sweaters and accessories for men. The Romanes & Paterson Coffee Shop on the second floor overlooks Princes Street with views of the Scott Monument and Edinburgh Castle. It offers a selection of specialty coffees, teas, and homebaking. The store is open 9am to 5:30pm Mon. to Sat., 12:30 to 5pm Sun.

Along the Royal Mile

Scottish Craft Centre, Acheson House, 140 Canongate (tel. 031/556-8136), was founded as a charity some 40 years ago to encourage the highest standards of Scottish craft work. It has a constantly changing exhibition of contemporary Scottish crafts—and everything is for sale. It is open from 10am to 5:30pm Mon. to Sat. At your leisure, you can browse among all sorts of typically Scottish products, including knitwear, pottery, glass, and jewelry. Everything is reasonably priced.

John Morrison, 461 Lawnmarket (tel. 031/225-8149), is a marvelous place at which to shop for a tartan. Orders can be mailed throughout the world if you can't take immediate delivery of your Highland dress. Women can order an authentic, hand-tailored kilt or else a semikilt or a kilt skirt. The store also provides evening sashes and stoles to match a skirt. The store specializes in kilts for men, a heavy hand-woven worsted in one's favorite tartan. To go with it, there are doubles and jackets. That's followed up with accessories—a jabot and cuffs along with kilt hose, a tie, and plain green undertrews to answer the eternal question.

The Scottish Shop, 336-340 Lawnmarket (tel. 031/226-4272). Convenient to Edinburgh Castle, this Highland-inspired gift shop lies near the top of the Royal Mile. It sells a wide variety of woolen goods, walking sticks, thistle-shaped wine glasses, jewelry, and many other souvenir items.

The Shetland Connection, 491 Lawnmarket (tel. 031/225-3525). The owner of this shop, Moira-Anne Leask, is viewed as a boon to some of the knitting industries in the Scottish islands. A battalion of crofters knit the traditional Fair Isle and soft mohair sweaters especially for her shop, which sits on the Royal Mile not far from Edinburgh Castle. Many of the designs follow her own directives. These include sweaters, hats, gloves, and scarves, each made of 100% wool. The store is open daily from 10am to 6pm.

Forsyth's of Edinburgh, 183 Canongate (tel. 031/556-6399), has an extensive selection of high-quality woolens at good prices for the value. The staff is helpful and polite, and the shop has clothes and knitwear "of Scottish character for ladies and gentlemen."

Along Victoria Street

Victoria Street is called a terrace in the Old Town. In the shadow of the castle, you can enter it from the Royal Mile, walking down a steep hill until you reach Grassmarket. However, you can catch your breath along the way by dropping in at the following shop.

John Nelson, 22 Victoria St. (tel. 031/225-4413). This art lover's dream carries a well-indexed list of antique prints and maps, including many historical maps of Scotland and the Americas. In addition, if you're looking for depictions of anything from ivy-covered ruins to antique portrayals of birds and flowers, this is the place. Most of the prints range from 1760 to 1880, while the maps cover the cartographer's skill between 1560 and 1880. Hours are 10am to noon and 1:30 to 5pm Mon. to Fri., from 10am to 1pm and 2 to 4pm on Sat.; closed Tue.

Other Shopping Suggestions

Jewelry: One of the best jewelry shops in the city is **Robert Anthony,** 108B Rose St. (tel. 031/226-4550). It has a large selection of gold chains and antique and second-hand jewelry. If you're not interested in an expensive purchase, you might buy one of the souvenir nine-karat gold items of Edinburgh, including Highland dancers or Scottish bagpipes.

Brass: For choice items in brass, go to **Top Brass,** 77 Dundas St. (tel. 031/557-4293). Each of the one-of-a-kind items from this well-stocked shop comes from within a 100-mile radius of Edinburgh. Co-owners Nick Carter and Tom O'Donnell scour the Highlands and northern England for the best brassware of the 19th and early 20th centuries, polishing it to a soft luster. The owners offer an array of brass bed frames, fire fenders, light fixtures, chandeliers, and antique hardware. Larger items can be packaged and shipped.

Dolls: For the collector and enthusiast, **Geraldines of Edinburgh M.O.C.,** 35A Dundas St. (tel. 031/556-4295), merits a stop. It presents both original, limited edition, and reproduction porcelain dolls in many shapes and sizes. Also porcelain teddies with soft bodies are for sale.

Brass Rubbing: For beautiful wall hangings and other gifts, you can make your own brass rubbings or buy them ready-made at the **Scottish Stone & Brass Rubbing Centre,** Trinity Apse, Chalmers Close (near the Royal Mile), which is open from 10am to 5pm Mon. to Sat. (to 6pm from June to September). You can visit the center's collection of replicas molded from ancient Pictish stones, rare Scottish brasses, and medieval church brasses. No experience is needed to make a rubbing—the center will show you how and supply materials. For information, phone 031/556-4364.

Scotland's Clan Tartan Centre

Whether you have a clan to your name or would like to borrow one, the **James Pringle Woollen Mill,** 70-74 Bangor Rd., Leith (tel. 031/553-5161), is the place to find it. The mill produces a large variety of top-quality wool items, including a range of Scottish knitwear such as cashmere sweaters, tartan and tweed ties, travel rugs, tweed hats, tam-o'-shanters—what have you. In addition, the mill has the only Clan Tartan Centre in Scotland, where more than 2,500 sets and trade designs are accessible through their research facilities offered for your use. A free audio-visual presentation shows the history and development of the tartan. The James Pringle Woollen Mill and its Clan Tartan Centre are open from 9am to 5:30pm Mon. to

Sat.; April to the end of December also Sun. from 10am to 5:30pm. You can visit free, as well as taking advantage of free taxi service to the mill from anywhere in Edinburgh (ask at your hotel).

Visit to a Crystal Factory

Lead crystal from Scotland is shipped around the world. The maker is **Edinburgh Crystal,** based at Eastfield, Penicuik (tel. 0968/75128), about 10 miles south of Edinburgh, just off the A701 to Peebles, devoted entirely to handmade crystal glassware. Tours of the factory, during which you can watch the glassmakers at work, are available from 9am to 3:30pm Mon. to Fri. Crystal gifts and tableware may be purchased at the large factory shop, open from 9am to 5pm Mon. to Sat., 11am to 5pm Sun. A spacious restaurant, Pentland View, serves traditional "Scottish fayre." The crystal factory dates back to the 1860s. The Peter Anderson Woollen Mill Shop is also on the premises.

PUBS AND EVENING ENTERTAINMENT

Unless you arrive in Edinburgh at festival time, the old city doesn't have a very exciting nightlife. Many Scots go to bed early. However, after touring during the day, you can still find some amusement.

Folk Music

Forrest Hill Bar, 25 Forrest Rd. (tel. 031/225-1156), is also known as Sandy Bell's. Informal music and singing sessions happen there, and for anyone visiting Edinburgh, it's a good place to start off and get the feel of the folk scene. It's best to go between 9pm and 1am nightly. Music is presented on most nights but definitely on Thur., Fri., Sat., and Sun. morning. Lager costs from £1.30 ($2.15).

Folk music is presented in many clubs and pubs in Edinburgh, but these strolling players tend to be somewhat erratic or irregular in appearances. It's best to read notices in pubs such as the Forrest Hill Bar and talk to the tourist office to see where the *ceilidh* will take place the night of your visit.

The Best of the Pubs

Deacon Brodie's Tavern, 435 Lawnmarket (tel. 031/225-4402), established in 1806, is the neighborhood pub along the Royal Mile. It perpetuates the memory of Deacon Brodie, good citizen by day, robber by night. Mr. Brodie, it is believed, was the inspiration for Robert Louis Stevenson's *The Strange Case of Dr. Jekyll and Mr. Hyde.* Brodie ended up on the gallows on October 1, 1788. The tavern and wine cellars contain a cocktail and lounge bar. This traditional pub setting has lots of atmosphere, making it popular with visitors and locals alike. The tavern is open from 11am to 11pm Mon. to Sat. Inexpensive snacks are served from 11am to 2:30pm, costing from £3 ($4.95), including cottage pie, Scotch eggs, cheese, and the ploughman's special.

Ma Scott's, 202 Rose St. (tel. 031/225-7401), is a corner pub with tufted settles placed back to back. It still has its Victorian water fountains on the bar. After a revamp, the pub, formerly known as Scott's, was named after its hearty empress who once commanded authority over the rugby players drawn to its precincts. In a totally unpretentious atmosphere, right off Princes Street, you can enjoy good drinks, bar snacks, and dinners. Meals cost from £6 ($9.90). In summer, it's open at noon Mon. to Sat. On Mon., Tue., and Wed. it shuts down at 11:30pm, on Thur. at midnight, and on Fri. and Sat. at 1am. In winter, hours are reduced across the board by about half an hour.

Guildford Arms, W. Register Street (tel. 031/556-1053), dates back to the "mauve era" of the late 1890s. This Victorian-Italianesque corner pub, still harboring its oldtime memories, has one of the most intriguing decors of any pub in Edinburgh—or Scotland, for that matter. Next door to the world-famed Café Royal, it lies near the King James Hotel. It still has seven arched windows with etched glass, plus an ornate ceiling, as well as a central bar and around-the-wall seating. It's large, bustling, and at times can be a bit rough, but it's got plenty of character. Hours are 11am to 11pm Mon. to Sat., 12:30 to 2:30pm and 6:30 to 11pm Sun. Bar lunches, offered only from noon to 2pm, cost from £4 ($6.60).

Black Bull, 12 Grassmarket (tel. 031/225-6636). Because of this establishment's location on a shop-lined street below the Royal Mile, it is often overlooked by visitors. You can take a shortcut on foot from Edinburgh Castle by descending a steep flight of stone steps, but most pub crawlers enjoy window shopping along the city streets. The pub is decorated like a scarlet version of a Victorian railway car, with tasseled lampshades, a country Victorian mantelpiece, and an ascending series of platforms leading up to the carved bar. Of course, the head of a black bull is one of the pub's focal points. The place jumps at night to the recorded music of whatever group is hot at the time. During the day, lunches, and good ones at that, cost from £3.50 ($5.80). These might be accompanied by a glass of vintage port or a tart cider pulled from a tap. The pub is open from 11am to 11pm daily.

Abbotsford Pub and Restaurant, 3 Rose St. (tel. 031/225-5276). Since both the downstairs pub and the upper-level restaurant are among the most popular establishments of their kind in Edinburgh, no one will mind if you drop in just for a drink. Of course, you might be so entranced by the Victorian ambience that you'll decide to stay for dinner as well. The businesses are in a red-sandstone building on one of the most popular nightlife streets of Edinburgh. The paneling of the lower section is full grained and well polished, in keeping with the ornately detailed plaster ceiling and the rectangular bar area in the center of the room. A fire burns in chilly weather. Upstairs, some of the most generous portions in the city are served of the hearty, reasonably priced meals. Waitresses are helpful as they place the dishes on the napery-covered tables. Lunches begin at £6 ($9.90) and might include helpings from a cold table, roast lamb, roast beef, or a mixed grill. Dinners are more elaborate, costing from £12 ($19.80), and including such dishes as roast duck in orange sauce, fried haddock, or haggis with mashed turnips, finished off with a Scotch whisky trifle. You'll find this establishment near the rear entrance to Jenners Department Store. The pub and restaurant are open from 11am to 2:30pm and 5 to 11pm; closed Sun.

Kenilworth, 152-154 Rose St. (no phone), is an intriguing bar named after the novel by Sir Walter Scott. Originally built as a private home, the structure was sold to a brewery in 1904, lavishly decorated, and turned into a popular pub in the Edwardian style. In 1981 its owners initiated a piece-by-piece renovation of each detail of the elaborately crafted interior. Even the exquisite blue-and-white wall tiles were carefully and accurately reproduced by a ceramics factory in Glasgow. The tiles, coupled with the rows of stained-glass windows, a massive wooden bar, a coal-burning fireplace, and a jukebox, make for an attractive bar. The clientele is likely to include a cross section of representatives of most of the performing arts in Edinburgh. Ales cost from £1.50 ($2.50), and hours are 11am to 11pm daily.

Theaters

Royal Lyceum Theatre, Grindlay Street (tel. 031/229-9697), has a resident company that enjoys an enviable reputation for its presentations, which may range from Shakespeare to an exciting new Scottish playwright. The theater is in a beautiful Victorian building dating from 1883 that contains a restaurant, three bars, and facilities for the disabled.

King's Theatre, 2 Leven St. (tel. 031/229-1201), is the premier theater of Edinburgh, offering a wide repertoire of classical entertainment, including ballet and opera. West End productions from London are also presented here.

Traverse Theatre, 112 West Bow, Grassmarket (tel. 031/226-2633), is one of the few theaters in Britain funded solely to present new plays by British writers and first translations into English of international works. This is a small theater with a big reputation. A bar and restaurant are open Tue. to Sun. Theater tickets are £5 ($8.25).

Playhouse Theatre, 18-22 Greenside Place (tel. 031/557-2590 for the box office), is the biggest entertainment center in the city. Pop concerts featuring top stars of both England and America have been held here. Musical productions are presented, along with visiting ballet and opera companies. Perhaps you'll be fortunate enough to see the Scottish Ballet performing *Swan Lake.*

Music

Usher Hall, Lothian Road (tel. 031/228-1155), is Edinburgh's premier classical, choral, and popular music concert hall. It is the setting for such musical events as Gilbert and Sullivan highlights and soloists from the former D'Oyly Carte Opera Company.

The Queen's Hall, Clerk Street (tel. 031/668-2019), is home to the Scottish Chamber Orchestra and a major venue for the Edinburgh International Festival. It also plays host to a full range of concerts, from classical to rock music, including a Friday night jazz club. A restaurant is open 10am to 5pm and before concerts Mon. to Sat., serving vegetarian and meat dishes, homebaked goods, and salads. There is full bar service at lunch and on concert nights.

Films

Chances are, language won't be a problem.

The leading cinema houses include **Filmhouse,** located on Lothian Road (tel. 031/228-2688). You can also see films at **Cannon,** also on Lothian Road (tel. 031/229-3030).

Another leading cinema is **Dominion,** Newbattle Terrace (tel. 031/447-2660). If you don't like what's playing at any of the above, try the **Odeon Cinema,** Clerk Street (tel. 031/667-7331).

---

2. Day Trips from Edinburgh

Within easy reach of Edinburgh lie some of the most interesting castles and mansions in Scotland.

STIRLING

Almost equidistant from Edinburgh and Glasgow, Stirling is dominated by its impressive castle, perched on a 250-foot basalt rock on the main east-west route across Scotland formed by the River Forth and the River Clyde and the relatively small section of land between them. The ancient town of Stirling, which grew up around the castle, lies in the heart of an area so turbulent in Scottish history that it was called "the cockpit of Scotland," the scene of several battles. One of the most memorable of these was the Battle of Bannockburn in 1314, when Robert the Bruce defeated the army of Edward II of England.

Stirling can easily be reached by car or train from either Glasgow or Edinburgh. From Edinburgh, a bus takes about an hour and a half to travel the distance of 37 miles.

Stirling is the central crossroads of Scotland, giving easy access by rail and road to all its major towns and cities. If you use it as a base, it is also only a short drive to many attractions, including Loch Lomond, the Trossachs, and the Highlands. The town center boasts several shopping facilities, including the Thistle Centre indoor shopping precinct.

What to See and Do

On the right bank of the Forth, **Stirling Castle,** Upper Castle Hill (tel. 0786/62517), dates from the Middle Ages, when its location on a dividing line between the Lowlands and the Highlands caused it to become known as "the key to the

Highlands." There are traces of earlier (7th century) royal habitation of the Stirling area, but it became a firm part of written history when Scots bled wi' Wallace and were led by Bruce during the Wars of Independence (from England) in the 13th and 14th centuries. The castle became an important seat of Kings James IV and James V, both of whom added to the structures, the latter following classic Renaissance style, then relatively unknown in Britain. Here Mary Queen of Scots lived as an infant monarch for the first 4 years of her life.

After the final defeat of Bonnie Prince Charlie's army, stopped here in 1746, the castle became an army barracks and headquarters of the Argyle and Sutherland Highlanders, one of Britain's most celebrated regiments.

The castle and visitors' audio-visual center are open from 9:30am to 6pm Mon. to Sat., 10:30am to 5:30pm Sun. from April to the end of September, from 9:30am to 5:30pm Mon. to Sat. and 12:30 to 4:20pm Sun. from October to the end of March. Last tickets are sold 45 minutes before closing times. Admission is £1.50 ($2.50) for adults, 75p ($1.25) for children. A family ticket is available for £4 ($6.60).

Also at the castle, you can visit the **Museum of the Argyll and Sutherland Highlanders** (tel. 0786/75165). It presents an excellent exhibition of colors, pipe banners, and regimental silver, along with medals (some of which go back to the Peninsular War). Admission-free, it is open April to September from 10am to 5:30pm Mon. to Sat., from 11am to 5pm Sun. October hours are 10am to 4pm. Closed November to April.

The **Church of the Holy Rude** on St. John Street is said to be the only church in Scotland still in use that has witnessed a coronation. The date was 1567 when the 13-month-old James VI was crowned. John Knox preached the sermon. The church dates from the early 15th century, and in its day it attracted none other than Mary Queen of Scots. It is open daily from 10am to 5pm from May to September.

Also of interest are the **Auld Brig** over the Forth, dating from the 14th century, and the palace built by James V in the 16th century.

One of the most interesting excursions is to **Bannockburn,** a name that looms large in Scottish history. It was here that Robert the Bruce, his army of 6,000 outnumbered three to one, defeated the forces of Edward II in 1314. Before nightfall Robert the Bruce had won back the throne of Scotland. The battlefield lies off the M80, 2 miles south of Stirling.

At the **Bannockburn Heritage Centre,** Borestone, near Stirling (tel. 0786/812664), and audio-visual presentation tells the story of these events. The queen herself came here in 1964 to unveil an equestrian statue of the Scottish hero. An exhibition, "The Kingdom of the Scots," traces the history of Scotland from the earliest times to the Union of Crowns. The site is open all year, but the Heritage Centre and shop are open only from April 1 to October 28 daily from 10am to 6pm. The last audio-visual showing is at 5:30pm. Admission is £1.10 ($1.80) for adults and 55p (90¢) for children. At Borestone, where Robert the Bruce commanded his forces, you can see Stirling Castle and the Forth Valley.

Where to Stay and Dine

Park Lodge Hotel, 32 Park Terrace, Stirling, Stirlingshire FK8 2JS (tel. 0786/74862). Set across the street from a city park, within a residential neighborhood uphill from the center of town, this hotel is contained in a 19th-century Italianate mansion. Built of stone blocks and slates, it has a Doric portico, a Georgian-era core dating from 1825, and century-old climbing roses and wisteria, along with Tudor-style chimney pots. Frankly, the hotel qualifies as the most stylish in town. Anne and Georges Marquetty house guests in one of their nine upstairs bedrooms, and later suggest they dine at one of the elegant tables of their restaurant (see below). Each bedroom contains a private bath or shower, color TV, phone, and an array of antique furnishings (Room 6 has a four-poster bed). Singles cost from £55 ($90.75) daily, and doubles or twins begin at £70 ($115.50), with breakfast included. You might enjoy tea in a walled garden behind the hotel, with its garden room, drawing room, widely spaced iron benches, and terra-cotta statues. Just on the other side of tall casement windows, a pair of French-inspired salons reek of such expensive luxuries as marble fireplaces, elaborate draperies, and cabriole-legged armchairs.

The Heritage, 16 Allan Park, Stirling, Stirlingshire FK8 2QG (tel. 0786/ 73660). Its culinary sophistication and its beautiful decor rank it as one of the most sought-after restaurants in the entire district (it also rents rooms). Near the center of town, the location is on a quiet residential street. You enter a gentleman's parlor, richly outfitted with somber walls and enviable antiques, for a drink before descending to the low-ceilinged basement restaurant. Amid a French-inspired decor, you'll taste some of the best cuisine in town, prepared with finesse by Georges Marquetty. In his youth he worked as an executive chef in Paris, and later he spent 12 years in Cincinnati with his British wife, Anne (there he was voted one of the leading chefs of America).

At his Scottish place, full meals cost from £12 ($19.80) and are served from noon to 2pm (except Sun.) and 6 to 9:30pm. Specialties include Parisian crayfish, foie gras with truffles, veal scallop with Parma ham and cheese, and rack of lamb. Reservations are important. Upstairs, four handsomely furnished double or twin bedrooms rent for £55 ($90.75) daily, with breakfast included.

DUNBLANE

A small cathedral city on the banks of the Allan Water, Dunblane lies about 7 miles north of Stirling, on the road to Perth. It is 42 miles from Edinburgh and 33 miles from Glasgow. Dunblane takes its name from the Celtic Church of St. Blane, which once stood on the site now occupied by the cathedral.

Sports enthusiasts are attracted to the area because of its golfing, fishing, and hunting possibilities.

What to See and Do

An excellent example of 13th-century Gothic ecclesiastical architecture, **Dunblane Cathedral** was spared the ravages of attackers who destroyed other Scottish worship centers. Altered in the 15th century and restored several times in the 19th and 20th centuries, the cathedral may have suffered the most from neglect subsequent to the Reformation. A Jesse Tree window is in the west end of the building, and of interest are stalls, misericords, a pulpit with carved figures of early ecclesiastical figures, and other striking features, including the wooden, barrel-vaulted roof with colorful armorials. A Celtic stone from about A.D. 900 can be seen in the north aisle.

Bishop Robert Leighton, an outstanding leader of the 17th century who did much to resolve religious bickerings, is represented by his personal library in a 1687 structure on the grounds of the old manse. It is of interest because of the bishop's material on the 17th century and the effects of the troubled times on Scotland. The **Cathedral Museum,** the Square, is in the dean's house and contains articles and papers pertaining to both the cathedral and the town. Admission-free, it is open Easter weekend and June to September from 10:30am to 12:30pm and 2:30 to 4:30pm Mon. to Sat. The story of Dunblane and its ancient cathedral is displayed here in this 1624 house, and you can also visit an enclosed garden with a restored old well.

Where to Stay and Dine

Cromlix House, Kinbuck, Dunblane, Perthshire FK15 9JT (tel. 0786/ 822125), is a fine country-house hotel 3¼ miles north of Dunblane by A9 just beyond the village of Kinbuck. The manor, built in 1880, is set in a 5,000-acre estate that has belonged to the Eden family for more than 400 years. The hotel, which opened in 1982, is on the B8033 road, just off the A9, about 20 minutes from Gleneagles, which has made it popular with golfers seeking a secluded hideaway. Guests can walk through the forests and farmland surrounding the hotel, and tennis is available, as well as fishing on three private lakes and hunting. The manor has an elegant drawing room with big bow windows and a lounge where family photos are displayed. Antiques are among the furnishings of the public rooms and the bedrooms. Bouquets of fresh flowers and open fires in cool weather add to the comfort of the place. The 14 bedrooms (8 with sitting rooms) are carpeted and have complete and spacious bathrooms, phones, color TVs, and radios. Singles cost from £85 ($140.25) to £120 ($198) daily, and doubles from £120 ($198) to £190 ($313.50). All rates include a full Scottish breakfast, VAT, and service. In addition to a second-floor library, guests are invited to visit the chapel and the gun room.

Eating by candlelight in the dining room, which has an open fireplace, is a culinary experience. No formal menus are presented, and guests are served as they would be in a family home. The freshest local ingredients are used. Your meal might include Scottish beef or lamb, game from the estate, or locally caught salmon. Traditional country-house recipes are used skillfully by the chef, who adds special touches to please the most discerning palates. The food will taste even better accompanied by some of the good wines from the cellar, especially the vintage bordeaux. Expect to pay from £32 ($52.80) for dinner. If you're not a guest at the house, reservations for dinner are necessary. Lunch, costing £7 ($11.55) to £20 ($33), is served by prior arrangement only, and dinner hours are 7 to 9:30pm.

DOUNE

Lying 41 miles from Edinburgh and 35 miles from Glasgow, this small market town with its 15th-century castle is a good center for exploring the Trossachs. The Rivers Teith and Ardoch flow through Doune.

What to See and Do

Doune Castle (tel. 0786/50000), on the banks of the River Teith, stands 4 miles west of Dunblane. Once it was a royal palace. Now owned by the earl of Moray, it was restored in 1883, making it one of the best preserved of the medieval castles of Scotland. The castle is open from 9:30am to 7pm Mon. to Fri., 2 to 7pm Sat. and Sun. April to September. In other months opening times are the same, with closing at 4pm. Admission is £1 ($1.65) for adults, 50p (85¢) for children.

After visiting the castle, guests can drive 1½ miles to the **Doune Motor Museum,** which charges £2 ($3.30) for adults, £1 ($1.65) for children. The motor museum contains about 40 vintage and post-vintage motor cars, including the second-oldest Rolls-Royce in the world. It is open daily from April 1 to October 31. In April and May hours are 10am to 4:30pm, June to August the hours are 10am to 5pm, and in September and October the last admissions are again at 4:30pm. For more information, telephone 0786/841203.

South of Doune lies **Blair Drummond Safari and Leisure Park** (tel. 0786/841456). You meet the typical cast of safari animal characters here, and the park also offers a jungle cruise, a giant Astroglide, and an amusement arcade, as well as a pets' farm and performing sea lions show. Open from mid-March to October, the park can be visited from 10am daily, with last admission at 4:30pm. Adults pay £3.50 ($5.80), children 3 to 14 are charged £2.50 ($4.15), and children under 3 get in free. A safari bus is available for visitors with three-wheeler or soft-top cars, costing £3.80 ($6.25) for adults, £2.80 ($4.60) for children. You can have refreshments at the Watering Hole Bar or in the Ranch Kitchen (tel. 0786/841430), or use one of the picnic areas. To reach the park, take exit 10 off the M9 onto the A84 near Stirling.

Where to Stay and Dine

The Woodside, Stirling Road, Doune, Perthshire FK16 6AB (tel. 0786/841237), is a stone structure standing on the A84 main Stirling-Oban road. In the heart of Perthshire, it was originally a coaching inn and dates back to the 18th century. It contains 12 well-furnished bedrooms with private baths, direct-dial phones, and color TVs. Singles cost from £32 ($52.80) daily, and doubles, from £46 ($75.90), including a full breakfast. The lounge is brightened by red plush seating and is brimful with antiques. The lounge bar has an open fire and offers a selection of more than 100 malt whiskies. You can enjoy a selection of traditional salad dishes on the bar luncheon menu with soused herring and homemade pâté salads. Grilled Aberdeen Angus steaks are also served. The dining room overlooks the garden, and you sit in high-backed carved Edwardian chairs, enjoying such specialties as venison, salmon, and fresh lobster in season. Dinner is likely to run about £10 ($16.50) to £15 ($24.75).

LINLITHGOW

In this royal burgh, a country town in West Lothian, 18 miles west of Edinburgh, Mary Queen of Scots was born. The roofless **Palace of Linlithgow,** site of her birth in 1542, can still be viewed here today, although it is but a shell of its former self. Once a favorite residence of Scottish kings, the palace was built square-shaped. In the center are the remains of a royal fountain erected by James V. The suite occupied by the queen was in the north quarter, but this was rebuilt for the homecoming of James VI (James I of Great Britain) in 1620. The palace was burned in 1746, destroying one of the gems in the Scottish architectural crown. The great hall is on the first floor, and a small display shows some of the more interesting relics of architecture. The castle is open from 9:30am to 7pm Mon. to Sat. and 2 to 7pm Sun. April to September, closing at 4pm in winter. Admission is £1 ($1.65) for adults, 50p (85¢) for children. For information, phone 031/2262570.

South of the palace stands the medieval **Church of St. Michael,** considered one of the best examples of a medieval parish church remaining in the country. The golden crown is of late vintage, having taken the place of one from the Middle Ages that fell in 1820. It is open from June to September daily from 10am to noon and 2 to 4pm, charging no admission. Winter hours are the same, but it is open only Mon. to Fri. For information, phone 0506/842195.

From Linlithgow, it is but a 3½-mile drive east on the Queensferry Road (A904) to the **House of the Binns** (tel. 050683/4255), the historic home of the Dalyells. The mansion, with its fine Jacobean plaster ceilings, portraits, and panoramic vistas, receives visitors on Easter weekend and then from May to the end of September from 2 to 5:30pm Sat. to Thur. The parkland is open from 10am to 7pm. Admission is £2.20 ($3.65) for adults, £1.10 ($1.80).

Where to Dine

Champany, on the A904, 2 miles northeast of Linlithgow (tel. 050683/4532), was once a farmhouse, but the stone building has been converted into one of the finest places for dining in Scotland. The dining room is circular, with a steep hexagonal ceiling. Victorian mahogany furniture adds a sedate touch. They specialize in grills, and you'll find the best steaks in Britain here. The owner, Clive Davidson, a South African (his wife, Anne, was born in Dundee), once had a butcher shop, and he is an expert on beef, usually the Scots blue-gray, his favorite being the "pope's eye." He insists that his steaks are 1¼ inches thick, and his meat is hung for at least 4 weeks, which adds greatly to its flavor. He also prepares spit-roasted Norfolk duck, along with an assortment of oysters, salmon, and lobsters that are kept in a pool on the premises. Even the french fries are freshly prepared. Next door to the main dining room is a chophouse, which has less expensive cuts, attracting the family trade. You can choose your own cut and watch it being grilled. A set lunch goes for £10 ($16.50). Dinner is à la carte, costing around £22 ($36.30) per person for a complete meal. There is also a raw bar. Open from 12:30 to 2:15pm and 7 to 10pm daily, except that the dining room is closed Sun. (the chophouse is open).

HOPETOUN HOUSE

This is considered by some as "Scotland's finest stately home," and it is an outstanding example of Scottish, 18th-century architecture. It is the seat of the marquess of Linlithgow, whose ancestors were once governors-general of Australia and viceroys of India. Set in the midst of beautifully landscaped grounds, laid out along the lines of Versailles, the mansion (tel. 031/331-2451) lies near the Forth Road Bridge at South Queensferry, off the A904, 12 miles from Edinburgh. You can wander through splendid state apartments filled with 18th-century tapestries, unique Cullen furniture, paintings, statuary, and other works of art. From a rooftop viewing platform, you look out over a panoramic view of the Firth of Forth. The house stands on extensive grounds and woodland areas with fine walks, nature trails, deer parks, and seasonal wild flowers. Hopetoun is open from April 13 to September 30 daily from 10am to 5:30pm. Admission to the house and grounds is £2.80 ($4.60) for adults, £1.40 ($2.30) for children.

NORTH BERWICK

This royal burgh, created in the 14th century, was once an important Scottish port. In East Lothian, 24 miles east from Edinburgh, it is today a holiday resort popular with the Scots and an increasing number of foreigners. Visitors are drawn to its golf courses, beach sands, and harbor life on the Firth of Forth. You can climb the rocky shoreline or enjoy the heated outdoor swimming pool in July and August.

At the **information center,** Quality Street (tel. 0620/2197), you can pick up data on how to take boat trips to the offshore islands, including **Bass Rock,** a breeding ground inhabited by about 10,000 gannets and one or two crusty lighthouse keepers. The volcanic island is a mile in circumference. It's possible to see the rock from the harbor. The viewing is even better at **Berwick Law,** a volcanic lookout point surmounted by the jawbones of a whale.

Some 2 miles east of the resort on the A198 stand the ruins of the 14th-century, diked and rose-colored **Tantallon Castle,** rising on cliffs. This was the ancient stronghold of the Douglases from the time of its construction in the 14th century until its defeat by Cromwell's forces in 1651. Overlooking the Firth of Forth, the castle ruins are still formidable, with a square, five-story central tower and a dovecote, plus the shell of its east tower, a D-shaped structure with a wall from the central tower. Tantallon Castle can be visited from 9:30am to 7pm Mon. to Sat. and on Sun. from 2 to 7pm from late March to the end of September, closing at 4pm from October to the end of March; closed Wed. and Thurs. mornings. Admission is £1 ($1.65) for adults, 50p (85¢) for children.

Where to Stay and Dine

The premier hotel is **The Marine,** Cromwell Road, North Berwick, East Lothian EH39 4LZ (tel. 0620/2406). Steep roofed and rambling, it is composed of gray stone blocks and ringed with a wall and rows of trees. Golfers appreciate the view over the West Links Course, some of whose putting greens come close to the hotel's massive foundations. Inside, there's the aura of an Edwardian country house, with well-ordered rows of chintz-covered sofas and large bay windows turned toward panoramas of sand and sea. On the premises is a bar lined with antique golfing photos. Good Scottish cooking along with international dishes are a feature of the restaurant. Other facilities include two tennis courts, a solarium, and a sauna. Each of the 83 well-furnished bedrooms contains a private bath, color TV, radio, and phone. Singles rent for £60 ($99) to £70 ($115.50) daily and doubles or twins for £75 ($123.75) to £85 ($140.25).

GULLANE

Lying 19 miles from Edinburgh in East Lothian, Gullane, with a population of around 2,000 people, is really a pocket of posh. Not only does it have one of the great country hotels of Scotland (see below), but it also is home to a small restaurant (also see below) that some food critics have suggested is "the best in Scotland."

Where to Stay and Dine

About 5 miles from North Berwick, an excellent place to stay is **Greywalls Hotel,** Muirfield, Duncur Road, Gullane, East Lothian EH31 2EG (tel. 0620/842144). An Edwardian country house, designed as a private home by the renowned architect of his day, Sir Edwin Lutyens, it was visited from time to time by King Edward VII, who admired the views across the Firth of Forth and south to the Lammermuir Hills. The gardens of the house were laid out by Gertrude Jekyll, who often worked with architect Lutyens in supplying a complete Edwardian home package. Today Greywalls is the property of Giles and Ros Weaver. They have combined the atmosphere of a home with the amenities of a delightful country-house hotel. In the paneled library, guests relax on comfortable sofas before a blazing log fire (in cool weather). The garden room, another of the hotel's four lounge areas, is done in bamboo furnishings. There is also a small bar. The 24 bedrooms, all with private baths, vary in size: some smaller ones are simply decorated and others, more spacious, are furnished with period pieces. Singles cost from £70 ($115.50) daily, and doubles, from £100 ($165) to £120 ($198), including a full Scottish breakfast. The hotel has a hard tennis court and a croquet lawn, with 10 golf courses within 5 miles.

The food served in the elegant dining room reflects culinary expertise. Light French-style dishes are made almost as appealing to the eye as to the palate. Specialties include fresh seafood. Other tasty main courses might be venison, breast of pheasant, smoked duck, or local beef. Meals cost £14 ($23.10) to £25 ($41.25). Men are required to wear jackets and ties in the dining room, which is open daily from 12:30 to 2pm and 7:30 to 9pm. Greywalls is open from April to the end of October.

La Potinière, Main Street, Gullane (tel. 0620/843214), is a small and pretty restaurant beautifully run by David and Hilary Brown. The excellent food produced by Hilary, using so far as possible local ingredients, is complemented by a fine choice of wines from the cellar supervised by David. A fixed-price luncheon of four set courses is served at 1pm except Wed. and Sat., costing £13.50 ($22.30) Mon. to Sat., £14.50 ($23.95) Sun. The first course is usually a light and subtly flavored soup, followed by a fish dish, perhaps a mousseline, or by one of Hilary's creations. The main course can range from steak to turkey to lamb, but all done with flair and providing a taste treat. Cheese and dessert wind up the meal. On Sat. only a special dinner is served, starting at 8pm and costing £21 ($34.65). Reservations for this five-course gourmet's delight are made well in advance. No smoking is permitted in the dining room. The restaurant is closed for a week sometime in June and all of October.

DIRLETON

Another popular excursion from Edinburgh, 2 miles northeast of Gullane along A198, is to this little town that vies for the title of "prettiest village in Scotland." The town plan, drafted in the early 16th century, is essentially unchanged today. Dirleton has two greens shaped like triangles, with a pub opposite Dirleton Castle, placed at right angles to a group of cottages. Dirleton is a preservation village and is subject to careful control on any development. It's on the Edinburgh-North Berwick road (the A198), 21 miles from Edinburgh.

A rose-tinted structure with surrounding gardens, **Dirleton Castle** is in the village of Dirleton. It was started in the 13th century by the wealthy Anglo-Norman de Vaux family, and looks like a fairytale fortification with its towers, arched entries, and oak ramp similar to the drawbridge that once protected it. The castle was built with prison, bakehouse, and storehouses carved from the bedrock. Ruins of the great hall and kitchen can be seen, as well as what's left of the lord's chamber where the de Vaux family lived. You can see the windows and window seats, a wall with a toilet and drains, and other household features. The 16th-century main gate has a hole through which boiling tar or water could be poured to discourage unwanted visitors.

The castle's **country garden** and bowling green are still in use, with masses of flowering plants rioting in the gardens and bowlers sometimes seen on the green. A 17th-century dovecote with 1,100 nests stands at the east end of the garden. A small gate at the west end leads onto one of the village greens.

The castle can be visited from April to September, from 9:30am to 7pm Mon. to Sat., and from 2 to 7pm Sun.; October to March, from 9:30am to 4pm Mon. to Sat., and from 2 to 4pm Sun. Admission to the castle and gardens is £1 ($1.65) for adults and 50p (85¢) for children.

Where to Stay and Dine

The Open Arms, Dirleton, East Lothian EH39 5BG (tel. 062085/241), will receive you in keeping with the promise of its name. This old stone hostelry has been transformed into a handsome restaurant, serving the finest food in the area. It lies off the A198. Overlooking the castle ruins, the hotel is owned by Arthur Neil, who has built up an enormous local reputation for serving Scottish dishes. Try, for example, cranachan (served with shortbread, this is a concoction of oatmeal, heavy cream, and brambles). Cold Scottish salmon is served encased in pastry, and is one of the inn's specialties. Another specialty of 40 years' standing is a stew made of fresh mussels and onions. On one recent occasion, the luncheon menu featured a first for me— smoked mackerel with gooseberry-cream sauce. Before having, say, a venison casserole in red wine sauce, you might begin with a real "Taste of Scotland" specialty, lentil broth with oatmeal, about which, the Scots say, you can "stand up your spoon in it." The people who serve are informed and skillful. The light-luncheon menu costs £7 ($11.55). A table d'hôte luncheon on Sun. costs £10 ($16.50). Hours are 12:30 to 2:15pm. In the evening, between 7 and 10pm an à la carte dinner is offered for £20 ($33) and up.

The Open Arms will also receive you as an overnight guest. However, it's small, only seven double or twin bedrooms, each with private bath, color TV, phone, and, joy of joys, room service available at no extra cost. A room rented for single occupancy costs £60 ($99) to £70 ($115.50) daily, £90 ($148.50) to £100 ($165) for two persons, including a full breakfast, service, and VAT. Log fires crackle and blaze, and it must surely be a golfer's paradise, as it's surrounded by eight courses.

DALKEITH

This small burgh in Midlothian, 7 miles southeast of Edinburgh, is the site of **Dalkeith Palace**, rebuilt and redesigned by Sir John Vanbrugh, circa 1700. Such monarchs as George IV, Victoria, and Edward VII have stayed here during visits to Edinburgh.

Visitors flock here for **Dalkeith Park,** Dalkeith (tel. 031/663-5684), to explore the woodland and riverside walks in and around the extensive grounds of the palace. Luring guests are nature trails and an adventure woodland play area, a tunnel walk, and an Adam bridge. The park is open daily from 11am to 6pm, April 2 to October 31. During November the park is open only on Sat. and Sun. from 11am to dusk. To reach the park, go 7 miles south of Edinburgh on the A68. The price of admission is 75p ($1.25). A ranger service offers regular guided walks.

---

3. The Kingdom of Fife

North of Forth from Edinburgh, the county of Fife still likes to call itself a "kingdom." Its name, even today, suggests the romantic episodes and pageantry during the reign of the early Stuart kings. Within this shire lay 14 of Scotland's 66 royal burghs. Many of the former royal palaces and castles, either restored or in ruins, can be visited today, and I've previewed the most important ones, coming up.

As Edinburgh is so near, the temptation is to set up headquarters in one of the city's many elegant hotels or B&B houses and explore Fife from that base. However, serious golfers may want to stay at one of my recommended hotels in St. Andrews.

DUNFERMLINE

This ancient town was once the capital of Scotland. It is easily reached by the Forth Road Bridge, opened by Queen Elizabeth II in 1964. Dunfermline lies 5 miles northwest of the Forth Bridge, a distance of 14 miles northwest of Edinburgh.

Dunfermline Abbey (tel. 0383/724586) stands on a site occupied by a Christian house of worship for some time. The Celtic Culdee Church dated back to the 5th and 6th centuries and was rebuilt in 1072. Traces of both buildings are visible beneath gratings in the floor of the old nave. In 1150 the existing church was replaced by a large abbey, the nave of which remains, an example of Norman architecture. Later, St. Margaret's shrine, the northwest baptismal porch, the spire on the northwest tower, and the flying buttresses were added. When Dunfermline was the capital of Scotland, 22 royal persons were interred within the abbey. Except for the sepulchers of Queen Margaret and King Robert the Bruce, no visible memorial or burial places are known. The tomb of Robert the Bruce lies beneath the pulpit. The abbey church is open April to September from 9:30am to 5pm Mon. to Sat., 2 to 5pm Sun. From October to March it closes at 4pm.

The **Royal Palace** witnessed the birth of King Charles I and James I. Only the southwest wall remains of this once-gargantuan edifice. The last king to reside here was Charles II, in 1651.

Andrew Carnegie, the American industrialist and philanthropist, was born here in 1835. The **Andrew Carnegie Birthplace Museum,** Moodie Street (tel. 0383/724302), lies at the corner of Moodie Street and Priory Lane and comprises the 18th-century weaver's cottage in which he was born and a memorial hall provided by his wife. It was completely refurbished in 1984. Displays tell the story of the weaver's son from Dunfermline who emigrated to America to become one of the richest men in the world and one of the most generous private benefactors of his era. Admission is free, and the museum is open April to October from 11am to 5pm Mon. to Sat., from 2 to 5pm Sun. From November to March, it is open daily from 2 to 4pm.

From the fortune he made in steel, Mr. Carnegie gave away more than $400 million before his death in 1919. Dunfermline, as his birthplace, received the first of the 2,811 free libraries he provided throughout Britain and the United States. It also received public baths and **Pittencrieff Park and Glen,** so rich in history and natural charm. A statue in the park honors the hometown boy who once worked as a bobbin boy in a cotton factory.

Where to Stay and Dine

The best choice, for either a meal or a bed, is the **King Malcolm Thistle Hotel,** Queensferry Road, Dunfermline, Fife KY11 5DS (tel. 0383/722611). Modern, pastel colored, and fairly stylish, this hotel sits on a roundabout a mile south of Dunfermline on the A823. Named after the medieval king of Fife (and later of Scotland) Malcolm Canmore, it was built in 1972 but thoroughly revamped in 1989. Each of its well-furnished bedrooms, 48 in all, contains a private bath, color TV with video, trouser press, hairdryer, and phone. With VAT included, singles range from £49 ($80.85) to £58 ($95.70) daily; doubles or twins from £58 ($95.70) to £68 ($112.20) daily; special low season and weekend rates are also available. On the premises is an elegant, glass-sided bar and restaurant in an appealing design. Accessible via a separate entrance lies the Canmore Vaults Bar.

CULROSS

This old royal burgh has been renovated by the National Trust for Scotland, and is one of the most beautiful in the country. As you walk its cobbled streets, admiring its whitewashed houses, you'll feel you're taking a stroll back into the 17th century. Many of the cottages have crow-stepped gables and red pantiled roofs.

Set in tranquil walled gardens, **Culross Palace** was built in the village between 1597 and 1611, containing a series of paintings on its wooden walls and ceilings. It has been restored and may be visited, April to September, from 9:30am to 7pm Mon. to Sat., from 2 to 7pm Sun. From October to March it's open from 9:30am to 4pm Mon. to Sat., from 2 to 4pm Sun. Admission is £1 ($1.65) for adults, 50p (85¢) for children. The palace, which stands in the village on the Firth of Forth, lies between Kincardine and Dunfermline (A985).

The other important attraction nearby is **Culross Abbey,** a Cistercian monastery whose founding father was Malcolm, Earl of Fife, in 1217. Parts of the nave are still intact, and the choir serves as the Culross parish church. There is also a central tower. The abbey is open from the Saturday before Easter to the last Saturday in August only. Hours are Sat. and Sun., 10am to 4pm.

FALKLAND

Owned by the National Trust of Scotland, **Falkland Palace and Garden** (tel. 3337/57397) was once the hunting palace of the Stuart kings. This royal burgh of cobblestone streets and crooked houses lies at the northern base of the hill of East Lomond, 21 miles north of Edinburgh and 11 miles north of Kirkcaldy on the A912.

Since the 14th century Falkland has been connected with Scottish kings. Originally a castle stood on the site of today's palace, but it was replaced in the 15th century. Falkland then became a favorite seat of the Scottish court. A grief-stricken James V died here. Mary Queen of Scots used to come to Falkland for "hunting and hawking." It was also here that Francis Stuart, fifth Earl of Bothwell, came with his men and tried to seize his cousin, James VI, son of Mary Queen of Scots. Bullet marks may be seen on the front of the towers of the gatehouse (1593). Cromwell's forces occupied Falkland in 1654.

The royal chapel and apartments are open April 1 until the end of October from 10am to 6pm Mon. to Sat., from 2 to 6pm Sun. Admission is £2.40 ($3.95) for adults and £1.20 ($2) for children. To visit only the gardens costs £1.50 ($2.50) for adults and 75p ($1.25) for children. The gardens have been laid out to the original royal plans. At Falkland is the oldest royal tennis court in the United Kingdom.

Where to Stay and Dine

Covenanter Hotel, the Square, Falkland, Fife KY2 7BU (tel. 0337/57224), has been a popular inn since the early 18th century. With modest modernization, it offers a good standard of accommodation. It's built ruggedly of local stone, with high chimneys, wooden shutters, and a Georgian entry. The location is on a small square, opposite the church and palace. You enter a white hall with a circular staircase leading to the lounges and bedrooms. The dining room is strictly "old style," and for before-dinner drinks there is an intimate pub, the Covenanter Cocktail Bar. Pub luncheons go for £6 ($9.90), and a set evening meal costs £12.50 ($20.65). B&B in the four rooms with private baths and TVs cost from £34 ($56.10) daily in a single, £50 ($82.50) in a double.

THE EAST NEUK

Within a half hour's drive of St. Andrews are some of the most beautiful and unspoiled fishing villages of eastern Scotland.

Anstruther

This is an important port and a summer resort, with the **Scottish Fisheries Museum** (tel. 0333/310628) down by the harbor. Here you can follow the fisherfolk through every aspect of the fishing industry from the days of sail to modern times. Experience the life of the "herring drifters" on board the old *Reaper,* berthed in the harbor, and don't miss the aquarium. The museum is open April to October from 10am to 5:30pm Mon. to Sat., from 10am to 4:30pm the rest of the year. Sun. hours are from 11am to 5pm in summer, 2 to 4:30pm in winter. Admission is £1.60 ($2.65) for adults, 80p ($1.30) for children.

Across the harbor, you can visit a floating exhibit in the old *North Carr* Lightship. Entrance is free.

Isle of May, a nature reserve, lies in the Firth of Forth, and is accessible by boat from Anstruther. It is a bird observatory and a field station, and contains the ruins of a chapel from the 12th century as well as an early-19th-century lighthouse.

From the museum, you can walk to the tiny hamlet of Cellardyke, which is really old Anstruther, with many charming stone houses.

Anstruther lies 46 miles from Edinburgh and 34 miles from Dunfermline.

WHERE TO STAY AND DINE Originally a Scottish manse, **Craw's Nest Hotel,** Bankwell Road, Anstruther, Fife KY10 3DS (tel. 0333/310691), was converted into a popular hotel, with beautiful views over the Firth of Forth and May Island. To the original building, many extensions were added under the direction of the owner, Mrs. Edward Clarke, and her son-in-law, Ian Birrel. The black-and-white building is step-gabled, standing behind a high stone wall. The 50 bedrooms are handsomely equipped and appointed, costing from £32 ($52.80) per person nightly for B&B. Each of the units contains private bath, phone, and TV. Public areas are simply decorated and cozy, including a lounge bar as well as a bustling public bar. The food is good, and the wine is priced reasonably in the hotel's dining room. The hotel is just 10 minutes from St. Andrews.

Smuggler's Inn, High Street East, Anstruther, Fife KY10 3DQ (tel. 0333/310506), stands in the heart of town, a warmly inviting inn that evokes memories of smuggling days around here. The original inn that stood on this spot dates back to 1300. In Queen Anne's day it was a well-known tavern. The ceilings are low, the floors uneven, and of course, the stairways are winding. Overlooking the harbor, eight rooms are rented daily for £24 ($39.60) in a single, £46 ($75.90) in a double, with private baths or showers and TVs. The owners offer à la carte dinners for £14 ($23.10) and bar suppers, both served daily from 7 to 10:30pm. Bar lunches or suppers cost from £6.50 ($10.75). If available, ask for the local Pittenweem prawns.

Elie

With its step-gabled houses and little harbor, this is my favorite village along the coast. Elie and its close neighbor, **Earlsferry,** overlook a crescent of golden sand beach, with more swimming possibilities to be found among sheltered coves. The name Elie is believed to be derived from the "ailie," or island, of Ardross, which now forms part of the harbor and is joined to the mainland by a road. A large stone building, a former granary, at the harbor is a reminder of the days when Elie was a busy trading port.

Earlsferry, to the west, got its name from an ancient ferry crossing, which Macduff, Thane of Fife, is supposed to have used on his escape from Macbeth.

East of the harbor at Elie stands a stone structure known as the **Lady's Tower,** used by Lady Janet Anstruther, a noted 18th-century beauty, as a bathing cabaña.

Another member of the Anstruther family, Sir John, added the interesting **Bell Tower** to the parish church that stands in the center of the village.

Beyond the lighthouse, on a point of land to the east of the harbor, lies **Ruby Bay,** so named because garnets can be found there. Still farther along the coast is **Fossil Bay,** where a variety of fossils can be found.

Nearby is a good golf course, and there are rock-ribbed sands for bathing.

A SPECIAL PUB If you're passing this way, I suggest that you drop in at the **Ship Inn** (tel. 0333/330246) on the Toft, there to enjoy a pint of lager, real ale, or glass of whisky from a large selection. In summer you can sit out in fair weather, overlooking the water. In colder months, a fireplace burns brightly. The pub has a nautical atmosphere, and doesn't do much in the way of food, but the owners prepare homemade soups in winter and "filled rolls" are available all day, costing from 60p ($1), with lager going for £1.40 ($2.30). Hours are 11am to midnight Mon. to Sat., 12:30 to 2:30pm and 6:30 to 11pm Sun. The building occupied by the pub dates from 1778, and a bar has been in business here since 1830.

Crail

Considered the pearl of the East Neuk of Fife, Crail is an artists' colony, and many painters have found cottages around this little harbor. Natural bathing facilities lie at Roome Bay, and there are many beaches nearby. The Balcomie Golf Course, in good condition, is one of the oldest in the world.

The Croma Hotel, 33-35 Nethergate, Crail, Fife KY10 3TU (tel. 0333/50239), is a guesthouse near the harbor with 11 bedrooms. It's the home base of all-American ball player Jack Healy and his attractive wife, Rosemarie, originally from Ireland. The Chart Room is fully licensed, and it's Jack's domain. Rosemarie has decorated the dining room in rose, pink, and white and used Windsor chairs set in front of the bay window. Many of the artists who live in this little fishing village come here for drinks and evening meals. The Healys charge from £15 ($24.75) per person daily for B&B in one of their bedrooms. They serve an evening meal for £10 ($16.50). You can also have a bar meal in the Chart Room. The hotel is closed from November to mid-March.

ST. ANDREWS

On a bay of the North Sea 51 miles from Edinburgh and 14 miles from Dundee, St. Andrews is sometimes known as the "Oxford of Scotland." Founded in 1411, the **University of St. Andrews** is the oldest in Scotland and the third oldest in Britain. At term time you can see the students in their characteristic red gowns.

The Sights

The university's most interesting buildings include the tower and church of St. Salvator's College and the courtyard of St. Mary's College, dating from 1538. An ancient thorn tree, said to have been planted by Mary Queen of Scots, stands near the college's chapel. The church of St. Leonard's College is also from medieval days. The Scottish Parliament in 1645 met in the old university library, now the Psychology Department. A library building opened in 1976 contains nearly half a million books, with many rare and ancient volumes. Guided tours of the university are run twice daily in summer, usually in July and August. For information about them, go to the tourist office at South Street (tel. 0334/72021).

The historic sea town in northeast Fife is also known as the home of golf in Britain. The world's leading golf club, the **Royal & Ancient** (tel. 0334/72112), was founded here in 1754. All of St. Andrews's four golf courses—the Old, the New, the Jubilee, and the Eden—are open to the public. Of course, the hallowed turf of the Old Course is the sentimental favorite. The clubhouse is not open to nonmembers, but in common with the rest of Scotland there's no problem in playing a round on the courses. It is advisable to reserve with the starter, however, or you may not get on. To play the Old Course, a current handicap certificate and/or letter of introduction from a bona fide golf club must be presented. By the 18th hole on the Old Course, there are links rooms with lockers, showers, and changing facilities, as well as meals and refreshments.

The old gray royal burgh of St. Andrews is filled with many monastic ruins and ancient houses; regrettably, they represent but a few more skeletons of medieval St. Andrews.

In the area of a Celtic settlement of St. Mary of the Rock, other ecclesiastical centers culminated in **St. Andrews Cathedral and Priory** (tel. 0334/72563). To explore it, follow South Street to the end. The early cathedral Church of St. Rule Regulus may have been built in the late 11th century and modified in the mid-12th century. In the 1160s the larger cathedral was founded. Built in both the Romanesque and Gothic styles, it was the largest church in Scotland, establishing St. Andrews as the ecclesiastical capital of the country. Today the ruins can only suggest the former beauty and importance of the cathedral. The east and west gables and a part of the south wall of the nave remain, and standing also is "the Pends," part of the old entrance gateway to the cathedral precinct. There is a collection of early Christian and medieval monuments, as well as artifacts discovered on the cathedral site. It is open April to September from 9:30am to 7pm Mon. to Sat., from 2 to 7pm Sun. From October to March hours are from 9:30am to 4pm Mon. to Sat., from 2 to 4pm Sun. Admission is free.

Holy Trinity Church ("the town kirk"), a beautifully restored medieval church, stood originally in the grounds of the now-ruined cathedral, near the 12th-century St. Regulus Tower with its 108-foot accessible stairway to the top and a fine view of the city. It was removed to the present site in 1410 and considerably altered after the Reformation of 1560. It was restored to its present condition in the early 20th century, with much fine stained glass and carvings.

Also of great interest nearby is the ruined, 13th-century **Castle of St. Andrews,** northwest of the cathedral on a rocky headland, with its bottle dungeon and secret passages. Founded in the early part of the 13th century, it was reconstructed at several periods in its history. Cardinal Beaton's murder in 1546 set off the first round of the Reformation struggle. It is open from 9:30am to 6:30pm Mon. to Sat., 2 to 6:30pm Sun., mid-March to mid-October. Winter closing is at 4pm. It charges 60p ($1) for admission.

Where to Stay and Dine

Today, you can fare much better than Samuel Johnson and James Boswell, who, heading for the Hebrides, stopped off here for a meal of "rissered haddocks and mut chops."

In hotels, many dedicated golfers prefer the **St. Andrews Old Course Hotel,** Old Station Road, St. Andrews, Fife KY16 9SP (tel. 0334/74371), as it overlooks the 17th fairway, the "Road Hole" of the Old Course. Fortified by finnan haddie and porridge, a real old-fashioned Scottish breakfast, you can face that diabolical stretch of greenery where nearly all of the world's golfing greats have played and the Scots have been whacking away since early in the 15th century. The hotel is not ancient—far from it: It's very contemporary, its balconies affording top preview seats at all tournaments. Some £15 million was spent to transform the hotel into one of world-class standard. The facade is being altered to keep it in line with the more traditional buildings of St. Andrews. The 108 bedrooms and 17 suites were remodeled and refurbished, and each has such facilities as a private bath, phone, and TV. B&B in a single ranges from £135 ($222.75) daily, rising to £205 ($338.25) in a double or twin.

The hotel offers an array of facilities, including health spa, whirlpool, massage salons, Turkish bath, beauty therapy salons, pool, changing and locker rooms, and pro shop. The hotel offers two restaurants, one à la carte and pricey, the other less expensive. Both maintain a high standard of Scottish and French cuisine. A four-course table d'hôte menu costs £22 ($36.36). Try to pay a pre-dinner visit to the Jigger Inn adjoining the hotel. In a former stationmaster's house, the pub evokes days of yore.

The Rusack's, 16 Pilmour Links, St. Andrews, Fife KY16 9JQ (tel. 0334/74321), sits at the edge of the famous 18th hole. Rusack's was originally built in 1887 by Josef Rusack, a German from Silesia who recognized the potential of St. Andrews as a golf capital. He placed advertisements on the front pages of British newspapers, which at the time was considered revolutionary. The hotel stands behind stone walls capped with neoclassical gables and slate roofs. Inside, chintz picks up the tones from the bouquets of flowers sent in fresh twice a week. Between panels and Ionic columns of the public rooms, racks of lendable books re-create the library of a private country house. Fireplaces and armchairs add to the allure. Upstairs, the bedrooms, 50 in all, contain some carved antiques, modern conveniences, spacious charm, color TVs, private baths or showers, and phones. Singles cost £80 ($132) to £85 ($140.25) daily, and doubles or twins rent for £125 ($206.25) to £150 ($247.50).

The nightlife contained within the hotel partially explains why the crew and actors of *Chariots of Fire* stayed here during its filming. The Champions Bar in the basement, overlooking the links, golf-related photos, trompe l'oeil racks of books, vested waiters, and evening folksinging. The Chesterfield sofas are full of animated clients from 11am to 11pm, and light meals and snacks are served as well. The hotel's formal restaurant serves daily specials along with local game, meat, and fish, accompanied by a wine list from a well-stocked cellar.

Some golfers prefer the cozy retreat of **Rufflets Country House Hotel,** Strathkinness Low Road, St. Andrews, Fife KY16 9TX (tel. 0334/72594), on the B939, a mile and a half from St. Andrews. Of the 21 bedrooms, each is equipped with private bath or shower, phone, radio, color TV, hot beverage facilities, and alarm clock, and all are well furnished in a warm, homelike way. Set in a garden of about 10 acres, this country house is substantial. The furnishings throughout are tasteful, as is the decor. The most modern bedrooms are in the newer wing, although traditionalists request space in the handsome main building, and those in the know reserve well in advance, as Rufflets is very popular with the British. Singles rent from £50 ($82.50) daily, and doubles cost from £80 ($132) to £100 ($165). The hotel is closed from January to mid-February. Even if you aren't staying here, you may want to call and reserve a table at the Rufflets Hotel Restaurant, overlooking a well-designed garden. Excellent, fresh ingredients are used in the continental and Scottish dishes, and everything I've sampled here has been accurately cooked. The service, too, is polite and efficient. A dinner costs from £18 ($29.70). Lunch is served daily from 12:30 to 2pm, dinner from 7 to 9pm.

St. Andrews Golf Hotel, 40 the Scores, St. Andrews, Fife KY16 9AS (tel. 0334/72611). A combination of greenery, sea mists, and tradition makes this 19th-century property a winner even with nongolfers. Brian and Maureen Hughes, the owners, recently embarked on a redecorating program that made a pleasant hotel even better. There are a pair of cocktail bars, a sauna, a solarium, and 23 handsome bedrooms. Each contains a private bath, color TV, phone, radio, and thoughtful extras. Singles rent for £50 ($82.50) daily, and doubles go for £80 ($132). Bar lunches are served Mon. to Sat., and dinner costs from £17.50 ($28.90). Nearby are tennis courts to add the possibility of another sport to the ubiquitous golf facilities of the region.

If you're seeking less formality, a favorite eating spot for years has been the **Grange Inn,** at Grange, about a mile and a half from St. Andrews on the A959 (tel. 0334/72670). In this country cottage, with its charming garden, an old-fashioned hospitality prevails. Tempting dishes are served, some of them continental in flavor, but all of them well cooked and pleasantly served. B&B in one of the two twin-bedded rooms costs £28.50 ($47.05) per person daily. Try such dishes as ravioli stuffed with crabmeat, an array of roasts, lamb cutlets, and steamy soups. Many of the dishes are based on regional recipes. In the restaurant, an inexpensive fixed-price lunch is offered for £8.50 ($14.05), served from 12:30 to 2pm daily. A la carte dinners, from 7 to 9:30pm, cost from £20 ($33). Bar lunches and suppers are served in the pub part of the premises. You can enjoy country cooking and meet the locals at the same time. Dishes are individually priced, a meal costing from £6 ($9.90).

In the Environs

The Peat Inn, Cupar, Fife KY15 5LH (tel. 033484/206), 6 miles southwest of St. Andrews on the B940, is in an old inn/post office built in 1760, where David Wilson prepares exceptional cuisine. The restaurant is run by David and his wife, Patricia, who have built up a reputation for serving high-quality meals in comfortable surroundings. The ingredients David uses in preparation of the dishes are almost all locally grown, even the pigeons, a specialty, coming from a St. Andrews farm. Pigeon is offered in a pastry case with wild mushrooms, or you can order the plump breasts in an Armagnac and juniper sauce. Other dishes are wild duck, crab, and lobster salad, grouse in season, sometimes even woodcock. The inn has a worthy wine selection too. Dinner costs from £25 ($41.25); lunch goes for £14.50 ($23.95). The restaurant is open from 1 to 2:30pm and 7 to 9:30pm Tue. to Sat. Reservations are required. The inn offers accommodation in eight beautifully furnished suites, costing around £98 ($161.70) daily for double occupancy. The establishment is closed for 2 weeks in January and 2 weeks in November.

---

4. Glasgow and the Clyde

The city that was once called "the ugly duckling of Europe" has turned into a swan. Today, a restored Glasgow is known as Europe's grandest surviving Victorian city, and is also one of Britain's leading cultural centers, home of the Scottish

National Orchestra, Scottish Ballet, Scottish Opera, and the BBC Scottish Symphony Orchestra.

The commercial capital of Scotland, and Britain's third-largest city, Glasgow is very ancient, making Edinburgh, for all its wealth of history, seem comparatively young. Glasgow was founded by St. Kentigern, also called St. Mungo, who selected the site 1,400 years ago for his church. The village that became the city grew up beside a ford 20 miles from the mouth of the River Clyde. It was a medieval ecclesiastical center and seat of learning. The ancient city is buried beneath 19th-century Glasgow, which has undergone vast urban renewal.

In 1136 a cathedral was erected. In 1451 the university was started—the second established in Scotland. Commercial prosperity began in the 17th century when its merchants set out to dominate the trade of the western seas. The Clyde was widened and deepened, and the city's expansion engulfed the smaller towns of Ardrie, Renfrew, Rutherglen, and Paisley, whose roots are deep in the Middle Ages.

Glasgow contains major sightseeing attractions—enough to make the city a worthy goal for many visitors, and it's also a good center for touring central Scotland. For example you can sail on Loch Lomond and Loch Katrine on the same day, and the resorts along the Ayrshire coast are only an hour away by frequent train service. From Glasgow you can also explore the Burns Country, the Stirling area, Culzean Castle, and the Trossachs.

The location is 46 miles from Edinburgh and 221 miles from Manchester.

ORIENTATION

Monumental Glasgow—that is, Victorian City and Merchant City, along with the Central Station—Scotland's largest city, lies on the north bank of the River Clyde, which runs through the metropolis. The ancient center of Glasgow has as its core the great Glasgow Cathedral, a perfect example of pre-Reformation Gothic architecture which, in part, dates back to the 12th century. Behind it lies the Necropolis, burial ground of many Victorian merchants. Across the square is Provand's Lordship, the oldest house in the city (built in 1471). Down High Street can be found the Tolbooth Steeple (1626) at Glasgow Cross, while nearer the River Clyde is Glasgow Green, Britain's first public park (1662).

From Ingram Street, South Frederick Street will take you to George Square, with its many statues, including one dedicated to Sir Walter Scott. This is the center of modern Glasgow.

Over the centuries the city headed west, first to Merchant City, a compact area of imposing buildings. This is the location of the National Trust for Scotland's show and visitor center at Hutcheson's Hall. The broad pedestrian thoroughfare of Buchanan Street, Argyle Street, and Sauchiehall Street are the heart of the shopping district.

Glasgow's West End is just a short taxi journey from the city center. It is easily accessible from any part of the city and close to the M8 motorway (inner ring road) and the Clydeside Expressway. An extensive network of local bus routes serves the West End. The Glasgow underground operates a circular service; by boarding at any station on the system passengers can reach the four stations serving the district—Kelvinbridge, Hillhead (the most central), Kelvin Hall, and Patrick.

The West End is the finest example in Britain of a great Victorian city. The terraces of the Park Conversation Area rise to afford excellent views of the West End. Across Kelvingrove Park is the Art Gallery and Museum. Nearby, the tower of the University of Glasgow dominates Gilmorehill. Beyond is the Hunterian Art Gallery, home to a famous collection of Whistlers. Just a few strides away is Byres Road, a street of bars and shops, along with restaurants. To the north is the botanic gardens.

A little more than 3 miles southwest of the city center lies the Pollok Country Park and the Pollok Estate. An extensive network of bus services passes close by the park area, which is also served by two suburban rail stations. An electric bus service is in operation from the Country Park Gates on Pollokshaws Road to Pollok House and the Burrell Collection Gallery. The Burrell Collection is housed in the heavily wooded Pollok Country Park, Scotland's top tourist attraction and the focal point of any visit to the South Side. Nearby is the 18th-century Pollok House.

Extensive parklands and greenery characterize the southern environs of the city. In addition to the Pollok Country Park and Estate, there is Haggs Castle Golf Club, home of the Glasgow Open, and Bellahouston Park, scene of the historic papal visit in 1983. En route to the Burrell Collection, you cross by the 148-acre Queens Park, honoring Mary Queen of Scots, where panoramic views of the city are possible from the hilltop. Close to Maxwell Park is the Haggs Castle Museum, located in a 400-year-old building.

TRANSPORTATION

West of the city, the **Glasgow Airport** is at Abbotsinch (tel. 041/887-1111). You can use the regular city-link bus service to the city center. From **Prestwick Airport,** there is infrequent bus service. For information, phone 041/332-7133. There is, however, regular service to Glasgow from the Prestwick Bus Station, and frequent train service from Prestwick to the Glasgow Central Station.

Taxis can be called to your address (call 041/332-6666 or 041/429-2900). A surcharge of one-third the meter fare is added if the taxi is hired to travel outside the city limits of Glasgow.

Glasgow has a good **bus** network. The Travel Centre for city transport is at St. Enoch Square (tel. 041/226-4816). If you're planning to tour the environs by bus, you might need to contact the Buchanan Bus Station, Buchanan Street (tel. 041/332-7133). There is a limited **underground** (subway) system. Fares begin at 40p (65¢). For more information, get in touch with the Travel Centre, St. Enoch Street (tel. 041/226-4826).

For **British Rail,** the headquarters in Glasgow is at the Central Station and the Queens Street Station (for questions, phone 041/204-2844).

GLASGOW FAST FACTS

AMERICAN EXPRESS: The office is at 115 Hope St. (tel. 041/226-3077). Open from 9am to 5pm Mon. to Fri., from 9am to noon Sat.

AUTOMOBILE SERVICE: For 24-hour service, call 041/812-0101.

BANKS: Most banks are open from 9:30am to 3:30pm Mon. to Fri. All branches have extended hours on certain days (it varies from bank to bank).

EMERGENCY: Dial 999 to report a fire, or summon the police or an ambulance.

FAX/TELEX: Many offices along High Street and newsagents will send a Fax for you: Try Lexus, 181 Pitt St. (tel. 041/221-5266). Telemessages may be sent from post offices or private phones.

GAY SWITCHBOARD: Call 041/221-8372 daily from 7 to 10pm. Details about the gay scene in Glasgow are available. The Lesbian line is reached at 041/348-4596, from 7 to 10pm Mon. only.

MEDICAL: The major hospital is the Royal Infirmary, 84 Castle St. (tel. 041/552-3535).

PHARMACY: A late-night pharmacy is at 1795 Paisley Road West (tel. 041/882-8535).

POST OFFICE: The main branch is at 1-5 George Square (tel. 041/242-4193), and hours are 8:30am to 5:30pm Mon. to Fri., 9am to 12:30pm Sat.

TELEPHONES: The old public boxes still take coins, whereas newer ones take British Telecom cards. These can be purchased at most newsagents and shops in units of 10, 20, 40, and 100p.

TOURIST INFORMATION: Greater Glasgow Tourist Board, 35-39 St. Vincent Place (tel. 041/227-4880), is the most helpful office in the country. Hours are from 9am to 9pm Mon. to Sat., from 10am to 6pm Sun., June to September. During other months, hours are from 9am to 6pm Mon. to Sat. only.

WHERE TO STAY

Expensive Hotels

The leading hotel in the city is **Holiday Inn,** 500 Argyle St., Anderston, Glasgow, Lanarkshire G3 8RR (tel. 041/226-5577). Its illuminated sign and soaring profile add a vivid accent to the Glasgow city skyline from its perch at the Anderston exit to the M8. Its 298 well-equipped bedrooms are among the finest in the city, each containing a private bath, phone, color TV with free in-house movies, and air conditioning. After work, dozens of local residents unwind in one of the popular bars scattered throughout the cavernous lobby, where open fireplaces compete with fountains and lots of plants for visual supremacy. The hotel contains four squash courts, a mini-gym, a whirlpool, and a sauna, plus a large indoor pool. A trio of restaurants complete the designation of this place as a village within a city. Singles range from £95 ($156.75) daily and doubles from £105 ($173.25).

One Devonshire Gardens, 1-3 Devonshire Gardens, Glasgow, Lanarkshire G12 0UX (tel. 041/339-2001). In 1880, house no. 1 was built as an upper-crust private home, but by the early 1980s it had degenerated into a seedy rooming house. In 1986 a professional designer bought it and embarked on a major restoration, which made it more elegant than it was in its heyday. Behind its sandstone facade he added such Georgian touches as cove moldings patterned into laurel and urn motifs, along with masses of floral-patterned chintz, comfortable seating arrangements, and a scattering of antiques, all against a backdrop of deep-blue walls. At the sound of the doorbell, a pair of chambermaids clad in Edwardian costumes of frilly aprons and dust bonnets will appear at attention to welcome you. Each of the eight upstairs bedrooms, which have been individually designed, is impeccably furnished in the best of period taste and offers double bed, private bath, and lots of luxurious accessories as well as such amenities as private bath, phone, and TV. Singles rent for £104 ($171.60) daily, doubles £130 ($214.50). Breakfast, VAT, and service are included. The success of the first venture led to the acquisition of nos. 2 and 3, bringing the room count to 27. The newer rooms have the same facilities and are priced the same. For a separate recommendation of the restaurant, see the section coming up. The location is in the Hyndland district of Glasgow, just west of the center, amid a neighborhood of stone-sided Victorian houses.

The Albany, Bothwell Street, Glasgow, Lanarkshire G2 7EN (tel. 041/248-2656), is a modern, well-equipped, four-star hotel in the heart of the city. It has 254 well-appointed bedrooms and suites, all with private baths, direct-dial phones, color TVs, air conditioning, hot beverage facilities, hairdryers, trouser presses, mini-bars, and electronic door-locking systems. Singles rent for £95 ($156.75) daily, with a double or twin going for £110 ($181.50). Sometimes weekend bookings mean "Leisure Break" tariff reductions. The Albany has two restaurants and a trio of bars catering to many tastes. During the week, it is filled mainly with commercial travelers, but on weekends it is likely to be patronized by vacationers intent on exploring the sights of Glasgow.

The Copthorne Hotel, George Square, Glasgow, Lanarkshire GD 1DS (tel. 041/332-6711), is a landmark hotel in the center near the Queen Street Station where trains depart for the north of Scotland. Its high-ceilinged design was originally constructed as the North British Hotel, until foreign investors renovated it into a format more luxurious than it was originally. The hotel's role in history was played when Winston Churchill met here in Room 21 with Harry Hopkins, FDR's envoy, in 1941. The pivotal meeting that took place is credited with securing Hopkins's support for the Lend-Lease Bill. When the public rooms of the hotel were renovated, designers searched for antiques and glistening marble panels. Each of the 142 rooms offers in-house movies, plush carpeting, and an upgraded decor. Singles are priced from £76 ($125.40) daily and doubles £88 ($145.20) with VAT included. The more formal dining room is called Windows on the Square, while La Mirage Café and Bar is one of the most alluring spots in Glasgow for a drink or a light meal. Everywhere, rows of potted palms and ornate accessories are shown in their best light against the tastefully modernized background.

Stakis Grosvenor Hotel, Grosvenor Terrace, Great Western Road, Glasgow, Lanarkshire G12 0TA (tel. 041/339-8811). When a team of engineers used a revolutionary technique of impregnating the decaying sandstone of this hotel's neoclassical facade with a combination of fiberglass and concrete, the city offered them an architectural award. It was at this time that the Greek-owned Stakis company almost completely gutted the interior, reconstructing it in a casino-style sweep of crystal chandeliers and brassy accents. Today the hotel is considered one of the most comfortable in town, offering elegant dining in a pink- and mauve-colored restaurant whose picture windows look across the street toward an iron fence surrounding the botanical gardens, 10 minutes from the city center. Lacy curtains cover the dozens of fan-shaped windows illuminating the russet-colored leather on the deep armchairs of the upper lobby and the downstairs bar. The 95 well-furnished bedrooms, each with private bath or shower, phone, and TV, rent for £100 ($165) daily in a double and from £85 ($140.25) in a single, with breakfast and taxes included. Reduced weekend rates are often offered.

The White House Hotel, 11-13 Cleveden Crescent, Kelvinside, Glasgow, Lanarkshire G12 0PA (tel. 041/339-9375), lies in Glasgow's west end in a classical Georgian crescent just off Great Western Road. The hotel consists of three houses in a private crescent designed by the famous architect, John Burnet, Sr. The owner, Ian Ferguson, has been the creator of the transformation to a Georgian-style apartment hotel. There are 32 suites ranging from executive single and double to mezzanine split-level suites and mews cottages. All the units are furnished to a high standard and have remote control color TVs, in-house movies, direct-dial phones, bath/showers with toilets, and fully fitted kitchens. The accommodations rent for £70 ($115.50) daily in singles, £86 ($141.90) in doubles, and £90 ($148.50) to £100 ($165) for two in mews cottages. Rates are fully inclusive. Discounts are available on weekends.

The **Kelvin Park Lorne Hotel,** 923 Sauchiehall St., Glasgow, Lanarkshire (tel. 041/334-4891), in the West End, is contemporary in styling and appointments. It also offers one of the best restaurants in Glasgow. Many guests go for a drink in the stylish cocktail bar, which is a tribute to the famed designer, Charles Rennie Mackintosh. His name came into American media exposure at the auction of the estate of the late pop artist Andy Warhol. At that time, a Mackintosh table owned by Warhol sold for a record $275,000. Later they patronize Newbery's restaurant, honoring Fra Newbery, the mentor of Mackintosh. Newbery's offers a set menu at £14 ($23.10) as well as excellent à la carte selections for £20 ($33). Typical dishes include duckling in orange sauce, salmon braised in Madeira, or else herb-flavored lamb. There is also a vegetarian menu. Each of the 80 bedrooms, all with private baths, TVs, and phones, are beautifully furnished. Some accommodations offer four-posters. Midweek charges range from £56 ($92.40) to £82 ($135.30) daily in single, with doubles or twins costing £66 ($108.90) to £92 ($151.80). Substantial weekend reductions are likely to be granted (always inquire when reserving a room if discounts are offered).

Moderately Priced and Budget Hotels
Officially opened in 1883, the **Central Hotel,** 99 Gordon St., Glasgow, Lanarkshire G13 SF (tel. 041/221-9680), was the grandest hotel Glasgow had seen. Near

the rail station whose commerce and transport changed the face of Scotland, it was the queen of the city's most famous street. Now revamped and restored to its former glory, it is owned by Friendly Hotels, who specialize in offering excellent rooms at affordable prices. Today the Central is the unquestioned leader in its price bracket. The massive baronial wooden staircase leading from the lobby to the upper floors was painstakingly stripped and refinished as part of the continuing restoration of this historic hotel.

The Central contains 229 bedrooms, each with private bath or shower, and prices are determined by the fixtures and age of the accessories. Each bedchamber, however, is comfortable and high ceilinged. Singles range from £52 ($85.80) to £64 ($105.60) daily, doubles from £70 ($115.50) to £80 ($132), with VAT and a continental breakfast included. Sandblasting of the facade revealed scores of heretofore concealed details, such as elaborate Victorian cornices and pilasters. The hotel's finest hour might have been the transmission shortly after World War II of the first TV broadcast on a private line extending from London to a bedroom on the fourth floor of this hotel. Its bar with its old panels has a good selection of Highland malts, and the Entresol Restaurant serves freshly prepared Scottish food.

At the edge of town, the **Stakis Pond Hotel,** 2-4 Shelley Rd., Glasgow, Lanarkshire G12 0XP (tel. 041/334-8161), a 137-bedroom modern hotel, is a good bet for a comfortable, bargain-conscious stay. It's set in a green area beside a duck-filled pond. Part of the benefits include the use of the glass-walled indoor pool, exercise machines, and saunas. Each of the functional and sunny bedrooms has a private bath and a video-equipped TV. Singles cost from £82 ($135.30) daily and doubles or twins from £92 ($151.80). The hotel's pine-paneled steakhouse offers generous portions of well-prepared meals served in a salad bar/carvery format. One of the hotel's bars is on a glassed-in balcony above the swimming pool.

Hospitality Inn, 36 Cambridge St., Glasgow, Lanarkshire G2 3HN (tel. 041/ 332-3311), a downtown high-rise hotel, is among the best in the moderately priced category. Its reception area has the kind of tropical-inspired waterfall you'd expect to find in the Caribbean. However, the flavor of its bar and restaurant is satisfyingly Scottish. Each of the 306 conservatively styled bedrooms has a TV, phone, radio, wake-up alarm, and full bath. Accommodations, which are suitable for one or two persons, cost £85 ($140.25) daily in a studio and £95 ($156.75) in a deluxe room. Some of the more expensive units hold up to four persons. The prices at this hotel can go down on weekends. Ask before booking. The Prince of Wales dining room is a study in soft greens and airy spaciousness. The gardenlike coffeeshop offers one of the best food bargains in Glasgow, a carvery lunch costing £8.50 ($14.05). The bar remains open for residents every night until 1am, and room service is available on a 24-hour basis. There's even a basement car park, plus lots of in-house services, such as a resident hairdresser.

Beacons Hotel, 7-8 Park Terrace, Glasgow, Lanarkshire G3 6BY (tel. 041/ 332-9438), is an architectural period piece that has been converted into one of the best middle-bracket hotels in Glasgow. Constructed in 1856, the hotel was originally two private townhouses for well-to-do Glaswegians. After a successful renovation, it now has 36 pleasantly furnished bedrooms, each with private bath, color TV, radio, direct-dial phone, hairdryer, and tea-making facilities. Singles rent for £50 ($82.50) to £60 ($99) daily, while doubles or twins cost from £75 ($123.75) to £95 ($156.75). Unusual for such a small hotel, the Beacons has 24-hour room service. It also has a basement restaurant, the Diva.

Babbity Bowster, 16-18 Blackfriars St., Glasgow, Lanarkshire G1 1PJ (tel. 041/552-5055), in the heart of Glasgow in an area known locally as Merchant City, is a small but delightful hotel that doubles as an art gallery. Named for an ancient Scottish fertility dance, the hotel, the work of brothers Tom and Fraser Laurie, is in a Robert Adam building once used as a fruit and flower shop. The work of Glaswegian artists is displayed in the upstairs restaurant, with the frequently changed exhibits containing pictures for sale. Among items not for sale is the ceramic logo that contains the hotel's name and a picture of dancing Scots. Babbity Bowster has only six bedrooms for rent, charging from £42 ($69.30) daily in a single, £54 ($89.10) in a double. The restaurant has a reputation for good food, attracting students and teachers from Strathclyde University up the road. The menu changes daily. Traditional Scottish ales, Murphy's stout from Cork, and whisky are served, and musical events are also presented in the first-floor restaurant on some Sun. evenings.

Staying in the Environs

The former residence of Sir James Lithgow, the **Gleddoch House Hotel,** Langbank, Renfrewshire PA14 6YE (tel. 047554/711), was converted in 1974 to a deluxe hotel set on large grounds, including farmlands, riding stables, golf course, and gardens. The 33 rooms are named for birds—Golden Eagle, Mallard, Osprey —and have good baths, plus radios, phones, color TVs, hairdryers, trouser presses, and hot beverage facilities. A single room costs £85 ($140.25) to £95 ($156.75) daily and a double runs £120 ($198), with a Scottish breakfast included in the rates. Weekend charges are lower. The paneled hallway is bright with a roaring fire, and there's a cozy bar. The residents' sitting room is upstairs. Breakfast is a leisurely, help-yourself affair. At lunch, you can order smoked trout and salmon mousse, clear Highland game broth, and perhaps a traditional warm pudding. A set lunch costs from £15 ($24.75). In the evening, you can dine from an à la carte menu, although I recommend the fixed-price dinner for £28 ($46.20). The five set courses change daily, and might include home-cured salmon, Scottish lamb, duck, or beef, and one of the tempting hot or cold desserts. Many guests prefer to have lunch in the Golf Club House. There are a sauna and a plunge pool, as well as horseback riding.

To get there, drive west along the A8/M8 from Glasgow and the Erskine Bridge toward Greenock and Gourock. Turn left at the sign for Langbank on the B789, going left again under the railway bridge and then steeply up the hill to the hotel entrance on the right.

WHERE TO DINE

The high-ceilinged restaurant of **One Devonshire Gardens,** 1 Devonshire Gardens (tel. 041/339-2001), recommended as a hotel above, has become one of Glasgow's most charming and unusual dining rooms since its inception in 1986. You dine amid flowery Victorian-inspired wallpaper, served by chambermaids dressed in frilly aprons and muslin mob caps. You go first to the drawing room, elegantly decorated, where drinks are served as you peruse the menu of fresh British cuisine. Reservations are needed, and it's open from noon to 2pm and 7 to 11pm. A fixed-price menu at both sessions offers an ample choice, and quality ingredients are handled with care and finesse in the kitchen. The lunch cost is £18.50 ($30.55), and dinner goes for £28.50 ($47.05). Perhaps you'll begin with a curried-parsnip soup, then follow with terrine of brill and trout, going on to rack of Borders lamb.

Fountain, 2 Woodside Crescent, Charing Cross (tel. 041/332-6396), attracts a clientele of expense-account lunchers and Glasgow's most fashionable people. It is a formal restaurant. You can select from many popular British and French dishes, including grills, salmon, duck, and good fresh vegetables. Typical dishes are likely to include trois filets verge (slices of salmon, turbot, and sole, poached with watercress and garnished with stars of puff pastry), rosettes of beef Eugénie (three slices of beef filet with fresh tomato "en concasse") and a basil-flavored hollandaise. Dessert might be a mousse of fresh kiwi and strawberries covered with a Chantilly-cream sauce. A set lunch costs £10.50 ($17.35), and a set dinner starts at £16 ($26.40), the price depending on your main-dish choice. You can also dine à la carte, for around £21 ($34.65) to £35 ($57.75) per person. The wine list is excellent, and the proprietor makes an effort to find wines from different regions, as well as the traditional bordeaux and burgundies. Meals are served from noon to 2:30pm and 7 to 11pm Mon. to Fri., dinner only Sat.

Rogano, 11 Exchange Place (tel. 041/248-4055), is considered one of the most perfectly preserved art deco interiors in Scotland. Its decor dates from 1934, when Messrs. Rogers and Anderson combined their talents and their names to create an ambience that has hosted virtually every star of the British film industry since the invention of the talkies. The doorman and bartender have been employed for decades. In an ambience filled with birchwood veneers, lapis lazuli clocks, etched mirrors, spinning ceiling fans, cozy semicircular banquettes, and dozens of potted palms, you can enjoy dinners ranging from £20 ($33) per person. However, a set lunch costs only £10.50 ($17.35). The array of menu items in the restaurant, changing every 2 or 3 months, is likely to include both Scottish and international specialties, with an emphasis on seafood. There are at least six varieties of temptingly rich desserts. A less expensive menu is offered downstairs in the Café Rogano, where meals cost from £11 ($18.15). The main restaurant, for which reservations are needed, is open from noon to 2:30pm and 7 to 10:30pm Mon. to Sat. The café is open from noon to 11pm Mon. to Thur., to midnight Fri. and Sat.

The Colonial Restaurant, 25 High St. (tel. 041/552-1923), lies a few paces from the Talbooth Steeple tower behind a deceptively simple facade underneath a trussed ceiling. Here Scottish-born Peter Jackson has distinguished himself as one of the best chefs of Scotland. The decor is not exceptional, but the cookery is first rate. For example, you might begin with a mousse of white asparagus and go on to select such elegant fare as salmon tartar with cucumber, steamed filet of brill in a wine sauce, or pigeon with peaches. A set luncheon at £6.50 ($10.75) is one of the dining bargains of Glasgow. A table d'hôte dinner goes for £22.50 ($37.15); however, you are likely to spend from £25 ($41.25) if ordering à la carte in the evening. Hours are noon to 2:30pm and 6 to 10:30pm; closed Mon. at dinner, Sat. at lunch, and all day Sun.

Ubiquitous Chip, 12 Ashton Lane, at Hillhead (tel. 041/334-5007), is run by Ron Clydesdale, a devotee of pure Scottish cooking. The flippantly named restaurant enjoys an enviable national reputation for both its food and its fine wines. The ingenuity of the chef is reflected in a wide range of dishes offered. If you wish, you can eat in the dining room, but the covered courtyard is my favorite place year round. Such Scottish recipes are on the menu as haggis and neeps, smoked Loch Tay eel, and macerated Scottish beef with tapenade just for appetizers. Fresh fish, lamb, grouse, guinea fowl, and several excellent beef dishes are among the main courses. In addition, there is always at least one vegetarian dish on the menu. The serving staff is young and enthusiastic and will tell you how the various foods are prepared. Count on spending from £16 ($26.40) for a satisfying meal. The Chip, as it's called, is open from noon to 2:30pm and 5:30 to 11pm Mon. to Sat.

The Carvery, The Albany Hotel, Bothwell Street (tel. 041/248-2656), lies on the lobby level of this prestigious hotel, but the price of its meal is low considering what you get. Within a brick-lined ambience of napery-covered tables and pinpoint lighting, you can select from one of Glasgow's most amply stocked buffets for £10.95 ($18.05) per head. The buffet is spread on an altarlike centerpiece, laden with dishes both hot and cold. It's augmented with carved roasts and joints produced by uniformed chefs. No advance reservations are accepted, and service is daily from noon to 2pm and 5:30 to 10pm. Evening meals Sun. are from 6:30 to 10pm.

The Buttery, 652 Argyle St. (tel. 041/221-8188), is the perfect hunt-country restaurant, with oak panels, racks of wine bottles, and an air of baronial splendor. The bar in the anteroom used to be the pulpit of a church. The waitresses wear high-necked costumes of which John Knox would have approved. Everywhere you look, you see 19th-century accessories. The Oyster Bar in the outer section serves lunches Mon. to Fri. for around £11.50 ($19) apiece. Menus include smoked salmon, rare roast beef, a terrine of Scottish seafood, and, of course, oysters. The more formal inner room serves an elegant menu, with full meals costing from £20 ($33). In the formal restaurant, hours are noon to 2:30pm (no lunch Sat.) and 7 to 10pm. The bar, however, stays open until 11pm. Reservations in the main dining room are suggested. The restaurant is closed Sun.

The Belfry, 652 Argyle St. (tel. 041/221-0630). Each element of decor in this place, on the basement level of the Buttery, just previewed, came from a church in northern England, including the pews and pulpits. Lots of illuminated stained glass creates a cozy ambience. It's probably the only pub in Glasgow that affords a contemplation of Christ in majesty by patrons while they enjoy a pint of ale. The cramped and partially exposed kitchen produces daily specials such as poached salmon in a lemon mayonnaise, smoked mackerel pâté, and a chicken-and-broccoli pie. The establishment keeps the Sabbath holy, but it is open Mon. to Fri. for lunch and dinner (Sat., it's open for dinner only) from noon to 2:30pm and 6 to 10pm (to 11pm Fri. and Sat.). Full meals cost from £12 ($19.80) and can be accompanied by a choice from the wine list.

In the Environs
October, 128 Drymen Rd., Bearsden (tel. 041/942-7272), is much favored by young Glaswegian professionals who seek style, flair, palate-exciting ingredients, and a reasonable price—all wrapped up in one restaurant. The chef de cuisine, Ferrier Richardson, satisfies those tastes admirably. He is a much-awarded chef, having been voted "Scottish Master Chef" and having served on the British National team for the Asian Food Olympics in 1990. Lunch is a relatively modest affair, offered daily noon to 2pm, but at dinner from 7 to 10pm the kitchen goes to work. Service is only Tue. to Sat. and dinners cost from £25 ($41.25), including wine, with a set lunch offered for £10.50 ($17.35). It is hard to characterize the cookery as it seems to roam around the world at leisure, taking from something here, borrowing from something there. Nevertheless, the final result is worthy. Vegetarians will also find dishes to suit their needs here, too. Call for a reservation. The restaurant lies in a suburb of Glasgow, a 15-minute ride out by car or taxi.

WHAT TO SEE AND DO
In Glasgow, the center of the city is **George Square,** dominated by the city chambers, which Queen Victoria opened in 1888. Of the statues in the square, the most imposing is that of Sir Walter Scott on an 80-foot column. Naturally, you'll find Victoria along with her beloved Albert, plus Robert Burns.

Cathedral of Glasgow, near the center of the city on Castle Street, first built in 1136, burned down in 1192, but was rebuilt soon after. The Laigh Kirk, the vaulted crypt said to be the finest in Europe, remains to this day. Visit the tomb of St. Mungo in the crypt where a light always burns. The edifice is one of mainland Scotland's few complete medieval cathedrals, dating from the 12th and 13th centuries. Formerly a place of pilgrimage, 16th-century zeal purged it of all "monuments of idolatry." For the best view of the cathedral, cross the Bridge of Sighs into the necropolis, the graveyard containing almost every type of architecture in the world. The graveyard is built on a rocky hill and dominated by a statue of John Knox. It was first opened in 1832, and the first person to be buried there was a Jew—typical of the mixing of all ethnic groups in this cosmopolitan city where tolerance reigns until the local rival football teams meet. The necropolis is full of monuments to Glasgow merchants, among them William Miller (1810–1872), who wrote "Wee Willie Winkie."

To visit the cathedral, walk to the eastern end of Cathedral Street, running in back of Queen Street Station. From April to September, the admission-free cathedral is open from 9:30am to 7pm Mon. to Sat., from 2 to 5pm Sun. In winter, hours are 9:30am to 4pm Mon. to Sat., 2 to 4pm Sun.

Glasgow Art Gallery and Museum, Kelvingrove (tel. 041/357-3929), headquarters of Glasgow Museums and Art Galleries, is the finest municipal gallery in Britain. The art gallery contains a superb collection of Dutch and Italian old masters and French 19th-century paintings. Displayed are works by Giorgione (*The Adulteress Brought Before Christ*), Rembrandt (*The Man in Armour*), Millet (*Going to Work*), and Derain (*Blackfriars*). Dali's *Christ of St. John of the Cross* is on display. Scottish painting is of course well represented in the four galleries of British painting from the 17th century to the present day. The museum has an outstanding collection of European arms and armor, displays from the ethnography collections featuring the Eskimo and Native North American, Africa, and Oceania, as well as a large section devoted to natural history. There are major new exhibits on the natural history of

Scotland, featuring plant life, animal life, and geology. There are also small, regularly changing displays from the decorative art collections of silver (especially Scottish), ceramics, glass, and jewelry, plus furniture and other decorative art items by Charles Rennie Mackintosh and his contemporaries. The museum is open from 10am to 5pm Mon. to Sat., from 2 to 5pm Sun. Teas and light lunches are available in the museum. Admission is free.

Burrell Collection, Pollok Country Park, 2060 Pollokshaws Rd. (tel. 041/649-7151), opened in 1983, is Glasgow's greatest sightseeing attraction. Some critics consider it the most eminent private art collection in Europe. It is housed in a building opened in 1983 to display the rich treasures left to Glasgow by Sir William Burrell, a wealthy shipowner, who had a life-long passion for art collecting. A vast aggregation of furniture, textiles, ceramics, stained glass, silver, art objects, and pictures—especially 19th-century French art—can be seen. Reconstructed from Sir William's home, Hutton Castle at Berwick-upon-Tweed, are the dining room, hall, and drawing room arranged around the courtyard. Included are artifacts from the ancient world, Asian art, and European decorative arts and paintings. The collection may be visited from 10am to 5pm Mon. to Sat., 2 to 5pm Sun. It's closed on Christmas and New Year's Day. Admission is free. There's a restaurant, and you can roam through the surrounding lawns of the park. The collection lies 3 miles southwest of the center. From the center of Glasgow, take bus 21, 23, or 45.

Haggs Castle, 100 St. Andrews Dr. (tel. 041/427-2725), is a branch of the Glasgow Museums and Galleries designed especially for children. It explores the changing lifestyles of the 400 years of the castle's existence. In the castle is a reconstructed kitchen from 1585, a room that shows how an inhabitant lived in the 17th century, and a Victorian nursery. An 18th-century cottage in the grounds is used as an activities workshop, and children who visit can take part in sessions, which include weaving, archery, butter-making, and sewing samplers. The castle is open from 10am to 5pm Mon. to Sat., from 2 to 5pm Sun. Admission is free.

Pollok House, Pollok Country Park, 2060 Pollokshaws Rd. (tel. 041/632-0274), the ancestral home of the Maxwells, was built circa 1750 and has additions from 1890 to 1908 designed by Robert Rowand Anderson. The house and its 360 acres of parkland were given to the city of Glasgow in 1966. Today it contains one of the finest collections of Spanish paintings in Britain, with works by El Greco, Goya, and Murillo, among others. Also on display are paintings by William Blake, together with British and European furniture, ceramics, and silver. The house is open from 10am to 5pm Mon. to Sat., from 2 to 5pm Sun. Admission is free.

Provand's Lordship, 3 Castle St. (tel. 041/552-8818), opposite the cathedral, is the oldest house in Glasgow. It was built in 1471 by Bishop Andrew Muirhead as the manse for priests serving the adjacent St. Micnolas' Hospital (demolished in the 18th century) but has been in secular hands since the Reformation of 1560. It has associations with Mary Queen of Scots. It is now a museum in the care of Glasgow Museums and Art Galleries, with period room displays. The house is open from 10am to 5pm Mon. to Sat., from 2 to 5pm Sun. Admission is free.

People's Palace, Glasgow Green (tel. 041/554-0223), provides a visual record of the rise of Glasgow. The palace was built originally as a cultural center for the people of the East End of Glasgow, and it was constructed between 1895 and 1897. Exhibitions trace the foundation of the city in 1175–1178. Such turbulent interludes as the reign of Mary Queen of Scots are represented by the personal relics of the queen herself. The bulk of the collections are from the 19th century, representing Victorian Glasgow, including posters, programs, and props from the music hall era. Also displayed are items relating to trades and industries, the Glasgow potteries and stained-glass studios, trade unions, newspapers, and similar matters. Paintings of Glasgow by John Knox and others may be seen, plus portraits of Glaswegians from St. Mungo to Billy Connelly. The city museum may be visited from 10am to 5pm Mon. to Sat., from 2 to 5pm Sun. Admission is free. There is a tea room in the Winter Gardens.

The park in which the palace is situated, **Glasgow Green,** is the oldest public park in the city. Once a common pasture for the early town, it has witnessed much history. Seek out, in particular, Nelson's monument, the first of its kind in Britain; the Saracen Fountain, opposite the palace; and Templeton's Carpet Factory, modeled on the Doge's Palace in Venice.

Miss Toward's Tenement House, 145 Buccleuch St. (tel. 041/338-0183), has been called a "Glasgow flat that time passed by." Until her death, Agnes Toward was an inveterate hoarder of domestic trivia. She lived in an 1892 building on Garnethill, not far from the main shopping street, Sauchiehall. For 54 years she lived in this flat that is stuffed with the artifacts of her era, everything from a porcelain "jawbox" sink to such household aids as Monkey Brand soap. After her death, the property eventually came into the care of the National Trust for Scotland, which realized that it was a virtual museum of a vanished era. Approached through a "wally close," the museum is open from the first of April until the end of October from 2 to 5pm, from November to March from 1 to 4pm Sat. and Sun. only. Admission is £1.10 ($1.80) for adults, 55p (90¢) for children.

Royal Highland Fusiliers Museum, 518 Sauchiehall St. (tel. 041/332-5639), displays 300 years of the infantry of Glasgow and Ayrshire. Relics, such as weapons, mementos, medals, pictures, and uniforms trace the saga of the regiment's history from 1678. The regiment served under 15 monarchs on five continents. The museum is open from 9am to 4:30pm Mon. to Thurs. and 9am to 4pm on Fri., charging no admission.

Hunterian Museum, University of Glasgow, University Avenue (tel. 041/330-4221), is in the main university buildings on Gilmorehill, 2 miles west of the heart of the city. This museum is Glasgow's oldest, having opened its door in 1807. The museum is named after William Hunter, its early benefactor who donated his private collections to get the exhibition going. It has one of the world's finest collections of coins and medals, going back more than 2,000 years. Cleopatra and Alexander the Great are two of the personalities depicted on exhibits. The museum's other main displays include archeological and geological finds, among them distance slabs from the Antonine Wall built between the River Clyde and the Firth of Forth in A.D. 142 as the northern boundary of the Roman Empire. Alongside its ornamental carvings is a statement of a detachment of the "VI Victorious, Loyal and Faithful Legion," announcing that it had completed 3,666½ paces of the wall. The museum has a bookstall, a coffeehouse in the 18th-century style, and temporary exhibitions. It is open from 9:30am to 5pm Mon. to Fri., to 1pm Sat. Admission is free.

Hunterian Art Gallery (tel. 041/330-5431) is in a separate building from the museum, opposite the university. It has paintings by Chardin, Rembrandt, Reynolds, Pissaro, Sisley, and Stubbs, as well as some outstanding works (paintings, prints, furniture, and ceramics) by James McNeill Whistler and Charles Rennie Mackintosh, including the Mackintosh House, a reconstruction of the architect's home on three levels, with his own furniture and decorated in the original style. The main gallery exhibits 18th-century British portraits and 19th- and 20th-century Scottish paintings, with works by McTaggart, the Glasgow Boys, Scottish Colourists, Gillies, Philipson, and others. Temporary exhibitions, selected from the largest collection of artists' prints in Scotland, are presented in the print gallery, which also houses a permanent display of printmaking techniques. Contemporary sculpture is displayed in an outdoor courtyard. Hours are 9:30am to 5pm Mon. to Fri., to 1pm Sat. The Mackintosh House closes from 12:30 to 1:30pm Mon. to Sat. Closed on Sun. and public holidays. Admission is free except for the Mackintosh House, which costs 50p (85¢) Mon. to Fri. afternoons and Sat.

Museum of Transport, Kelvin Hall, 1 Bunhouse Rd. (tel. 041/357-3929), contains a fascinating collection of all forms of transportation and related technology. Displays include a simulated Glasgow street of 1938 with period shop fronts and appropriate vehicles and a reconstruction of one of the Glasgow Underground stations. An authentic motor car showroom has a display of mass-produced automobiles. Superb and varied ship models in the Clyde Room reflect the significance of Glasgow and the River Clyde as one of the world's foremost areas of ship-building and engineering. The museum is open from 10am to 5pm Mon. to Sat., from 2 to 5pm Sun. Admission is free, and there is a self-service cafeteria.

Although it has much industry and a lot of stark commercial areas, Glasgow contains many gardens and open spaces.

Chief among these is **Bellahouston Park,** Paisley Road West, 171 acres of beauty with a sunken wall and rock gardens as well as wildlife. It's open all year daily from 8am to dusk. Here you'll find the **Bellahouston Sports Centre** (tel. 041/427-5454), which is a base for a variety of indicated trails that make up runners' training courses.

Glasgow Botanic Gardens, Great Western Road (tel. 041/334-2422), cover 40 acres—an extensive collection of glasshouse plants, in particular orchids, begonias (the national collection), and ferns, as well as herb gardens. It, too, is open all year, from 7am to dusk daily. The Glasshouses can be visited from 1 to 4:45pm. The Kibble (Crystal) Palace, containing a splendid grove of tree ferns, opens at 10am. Admission is free.

Linn Park, on Clarkston Road, is 212 acres of pine and woodland, with many lovely walks along the river. Here you'll find a nature trail, pony rides for children, an old snuff mill, and a children's zoo. The park is open all year daily from 8am to dusk.

Greenock is an important industrial and shipbuilding town on the Clyde Estuary, lying west of the center of Glasgow. It was the birthplace in 1736 of James Watt, inventor of the steam engine. The huge Cross of Lorraine on Lyle Hill above the town commemorates Free French sailors who died in the Battle of the Atlantic during World War II.

SHOPPING

Shops in Glasgow are open from 9am to 5:30pm Mon. to Sat. Many stores also opt to stay open late on Thurs., usually until 8pm.

The principal shopping district is **Sauchiehall Street,** Glasgow's fashion center, containing many shops and department stores where you'll often find quite good bargains, particularly in woolen goods. The major shopping area, about three blocks long, has been made into a pedestrian mall.

The most luxurious shopping is at **Princes Square,** which is also the name of a deluxe shopping center that has been glassed in around a sandstone courtyard from long ago. Prince Charles came to Glasgow in 1989 to open the center officially. Designer shops with a wide range of chic, international merchandise are found on the main levels.

The Barras, the weekend market of Glasgow, takes place about a quarter of a mile east of Glasgow Cross. With free admission, it is held all year from 9am to 5pm Sat. and Sun. Rich in stalls and shops, this century-old market has some 800 traders selling their wares. You can not only browse for that special treasure but also become a part of Glasgow life and be amused by the buskers.

The Highland House of Lawrie, 110 Buchanan St. (tel. 041/221-0217). There's possibly no more prestigious store in Scotland than this elegant haberdashery. Despite its aristocratic clientele, prices are more reasonable than you might expect, and the welcome offered by the experienced sales staff is genuinely warm-hearted. Don't be fooled by the array of crystal and gift items offered for sale on the street level, because the real heart and soul of the establishment lies on the lower level. There, carefully constructed tweed jackets, tartan accessories, waistcoats, and sweaters are sold to both men and women. Each is impeccably crafted by kilt-making experts. Most of the merchandise is, of course, crafted from top-quality wool and suitable even in the dampest of Highland weather. Men's kilts contain as much as 8 yards of material pleated to carry out the plaid pattern. Women's hand-stitched kilts are also sold, as are those for children. Don't overlook the tweed blazers for men, which are reasonable in price. The business was founded in 1881, and today it is the oldest established kiltmaker in Scotland.

Fraser's Department Store, 45 Buchanan St. (tel. 041/221-3880), is

Glasgow's version of Harrods Department Store. The Glasgow store contains a soaring Victorian-era glass arcade rising four stories. Inside, you'll find everything from clothing to Persian rugs, from crystal to handmade local artifacts of all kinds. Even a quick visit to see the Victorian embellishment is worthwhile—and you'll surely see something you want to buy.

William Porteous & Co. Ltd., 9 Royal Exchange Place (tel. 041/221-8623), is a long-established bookstore specializing in travel guides and maps for Scotland and the remainder of the United Kingdom and Europe. They also have Scottish souvenir books and prints and carry all the main British and foreign newspapers and magazines.

Henry Burton & Co., 111 Buchanan St. (tel. 041/221-7380), one of the city's most prestigious men's outfitters, is in a slightly cramped, two-story building filled with well-crafted clothes. Established in 1847, the store has a helpful staff, which offers competent advice as needed. Most of the garments are for men, but a limited selection of knitwear for women is sold also.

The following recommendations are not specific shops but rather areas where you can find stores by the dozens:

The **Argyll Arcade** stands at 30 Buchanan St. Even if the year of its construction (1827) was not set in mosaic tiles above the entrance, you'd still know that this is an old collection of shops. Most of the businesses set beneath the glass canopy sell watches and jewelry, both antique and modern. In fact the arcade contains what is said to be the largest single concentration of retail jewelers in Europe, surpassing even those of Amsterdam. The fame of the arcade has traveled far beyond Glasgow. It seems to be a Scottish tradition that a wedding ring becomes lucky when purchased within the arcade's narrow confines. Whether or not this is true, the rents charged here are higher than for comparable stores in Glasgow, even exceeding the exorbitant amounts charged along London's fashionable Bond Street.

Since the arcade is officially classified as a historic structure, a portion of its rents goes toward maintaining it in mint condition. Over the years the locale has given rise to many legends, including that of a pair of ghosts said to inhabit Sloan's pub. Today, beneath the curved glass ceiling, an impressive security system is maintained, designed to protect the area's two dozen shops and their multi-million-pound inventories against wrongdoers in the milling pedestrian traffic.

Victorian Village, 57 West Regent St. (tel. 041/332-0703). Antique lovers will want to browse through this warren of tiny shops in this somewhat claustrophobic cluster. Much of the merchandise isn't particularly noteworthy, but there are many exceptional pieces. Several of the owners stock reasonably priced articles of 19th-century provenance. Other shops sell old jewelry and clothing, a helter-skelter of artifacts.

A Covent Garden–type shopping complex, the **Briggait,** is in the Victorian building that once housed Glasgow's fish market. It offers a wide and exclusive range of merchandise from designer fashion to traditional Scottish products, a choice of restaurants, a continuous program of exhibitions, and regular entertainment on Sat. and Sun. The Briggait is closed Tues.

PUBS AND EVENING ENTERTAINMENT

Glasgow, not Edinburgh, is the cultural center of Scotland. Still, for many Glaswegians the best evening is to be spent drinking at their favorite pub (my selections coming up). Cultural Glasgow is well represented, however, in the list of places to go for an evening's entertainment.

Theaters

The Theatre Royal, at Hope Street and Cowcaddens Road (tel. 041/331-1234), is the home of the Scottish Opera, which long ago attracted attention on the world scene. The building, designed by C. J. Phipps, opened in 1895 and was completely refurbished as a home for the Scottish Opera, reopening in 1975. It offers 1,547 comfortable seats and has spacious bars and buffets on all four levels. It has been called "the most beautiful opera theatre in the kingdom" by the *Daily Tele-*

graph, which noted its splendid Victorian Italian-Renaissance plasterwork and glittering chandeliers. But it is not the decor that attracts opera-goers. Rather, it is the ambitious repertoire. The box office is open from 10am to 6pm Mon. to Sat. The Theatre Royal is also home to the Scottish Ballet, and hosts visiting theater and dance companies from around the world.

Citizens Theatre, at Gorbals and Ballater Streets (tel. 041/429-0022), was founded after World War II by James Bridie, a famous Glaswegian whose plays are still produced. The theater is home to one of the United Kingdom's most prestigious repertory companies. All seats cost £5 ($8.25).

Pavilion Theatre, 121 Renfield St. (tel. 041/332-1846), is still alive and well, specializing in rock/pop concerts, plays, all types of variety shows, and a pantomime season.

Mitchell Theatre, Granville Street (tel. 041/221-3198), has earned a reputation for small-scale entertainment, ranging from dark drama to dance, as well as conferences and seminars. A modern little theater, it adjoins the well-known Mitchell Library.

Glasgow Arts Centre, 12 Washington St. (tel. 041/221-4526), is part of Strathclyde Regional Council's Community Education Service. The center always seems to be doing or presenting something interesting, including productions aimed at children. Its activities range from theatrical productions to folk concerts.

Tron Theatre, 63 Trongate (tel. 041/552-4267), occupies one of the three oldest buildings in Glasgow, the former Tron Church. Tron Theatre has transformed the old structure, with its famous Adam dome, into a small theater presenting the best of contemporary drama, dance, and music events. The Tron also has a restored Victorian bar/café, serving traditional homecooked meals, including vegetarian, and a fine selection of wines and malt whiskies. The bar/café is open from noon to midnight Tue. to Sat., 6:30pm to 11pm Sun. Performances in the theater run Tue. to Sun. at 7:30pm with occasional late-night shows at 10pm.

Favorite Pubs

Corn Exchange, 88 Gordon St. (tel. 041/248-5380), opposite Central Station, was the corn exchange in the mid-19th century, but since 1988 it's been one of the most popular pubs of Glasgow. Amid dark paneling and high ceilings, guests can enjoy a pint of lager for £1.30 ($2.15). The pub is open from 11am to midnight Mon. to Sat., closing from 2:30 to 6:30pm Sun. Food is served from 11:30am to 2:30pm Mon. to Sat., with meals costing from £5 ($8.25).

Archie's Bar, 27 Waterloo St. (tel. 041/221-3210), is an excellent modern bar, with a self-service area, offering cold meats and salads, along with four or five hot dishes, including steak pie, ham, and fruit pies. Expect to spend from £4 ($6.60). Archie's is open from noon to 10pm Mon. to Sat.

Pot Still, 154 Hope St. (tel. 041/333-0980), is the best place to go in Glasgow to sample malt whisky. A selection of more than 100 single-malt (unblended) whiskies, many at a variety of different strengths, can be tasted (perhaps not on the same night). You can also order malt whiskies at a variety of maturities—that is, years spent in casks. Many prefer the malt whisky that has been aged in a sherry cask. On one shelf is displayed a Dalmore and a Springbank whisky, each bottled more than half a century ago. They are to be looked at—never sampled. The Still runs from 11am to midnight Mon. to Sat. You can also enjoy good bar food at lunch, including cold meat salads or sandwiches. Light meals cost from £3.50 ($5.80).

Bon Accord, 153 North St. (tel. 041/248-4427), is a real ale drinker's local. The brand names of what emerges on hand-pump may be unfamiliar to North Americans, but the tastes will probably delight. Of course, the pub is likely to satisfy your taste in malt whisky as well, perhaps introduce you to a new bottle. The place is clean and tidy, pleasantly decorated, a safe haven. Bar snacks cost from £3.50 ($5.80). It is open from 11am to midnight Mon. through Sat., from 11am to 2:30pm and 6:30 to 11pm Sun.

5. The Trossachs and Loch Lomond

"The Trossachs" is the collective name given that wild Highland area lying east and northeast of Loch Lomond. Both the Trossachs and Loch Lomond are said to contain Scotland's finest scenery in moor, mountain, and loch. The area has been famed in history and romance ever since Sir Walter Scott included vivid descriptive passages in *The Lady of the Lake* and *Rob Roy*.

In Gaelic, the Trossachs means "the bristled country," an allusion to its luxuriant vegetation. The thickly wooded valley contains three lochs—Vennachar, Achray, and Katrine. The best centers for exploring are the villages of the Trossachs and the gateways of Callander and Aberfoyle.

Legendary Loch Lomond, the largest and most beautiful of Scottish lakes, is known for its "bonnie banks." Lying within easy reach of Glasgow, the loch is about 24 miles long. At its widest point, it stretches for 5 miles. At Balloch in the south the lake is a Lowland loch of gentle hills and islands. But as it moves north, the loch changes to a narrow lake of Highland character, with rugged steep hillsides.

CALLANDER

For many, this small burgh, 16 miles northwest of Stirling by road and 52 miles from Edinburgh, makes the best base for exploring the Trossachs and Loch Katrine, Loch Achray, and Loch Vennachar. For years motorists—and before them passengers traveling by bumpy coach—stopped here to rest up on the once-difficult journey between Edinburgh and Oban.

Callander stands at the entrance to the **Pass of Leny** in the shadow of the Callander Crags. The Teith and Leny rivers meet to the west of the town.

Four miles beyond the Pass of Leny, with its beautiful falls, lies **Loch Lubnaig** ("the crooked lake"), divided into two reaches by a rock and considered fine fishing waters. Nearby is **Little Leny,** the ancestral burial ground of the Buchanans.

More falls are found at **Bracklinn,** 1½ miles northeast of Callander. In a gorge above the town, Bracklinn is considered one of the most scenic of the local beauty spots. Other places of interest include the **Roman Camp,** the **Caledonian Fort,** and the **Foundations of St. Bride's Chapel.** The tourist office on Leny Road (tel. 0877/30342), will give you a map pinpointing the above-recommended sights. While there, you can also get directions for one of the most interesting excursions from Callander, to **Balquhidder Church,** 13 miles to the northwest, the burial place of Rob Roy.

Where to Stay and Dine

The leading hotel is **Roman Camp,** Main Street, Callander, Perthside FK17 8BG (tel. 0877/30003), once a 17th-century hunting lodge with pink walls and small gray-roofed towers, built on the site of what was believed to have been a Roman camp. The dukes of Perth once came to this turreted establishment, lodging here for "hunting and hawking." Entering through a gate, the modern-day traveler drives up a splendid driveway, with shaggy Highland cattle and sheep grazing on either side and well-manicured yew hedges. A river runs through the 20-acre estate. In summer, flowerbeds are in bloom. Inside you are welcomed to a country house furnished in a gracious manner. There are 14 bedrooms and 3 suites, with 7 of the units on the ground floor and 1 adapted for use of disabled guests. Two of the bedrooms contain showers, while 12 have private bath/showers. All have hairdriers, radios, direct-dial phones, TVs, and hot beverage facilities. The charge is from £60 ($99) daily for single occupancy, from £75 ($123.75) for a double. Prices include VAT and service. The dining room was converted in the '30s from the old kitchen. The ceiling design is based on the old Scottish painted ceilings of the 16th and 17th centuries, which were a feature of houses around the time the Roman Camp hunting lodge was built. The meals—Scottish country-house fare—are served until 8:30 in the evening. There is a small cocktail bar, but the library, with its plasterwork and paneling, remains undisturbed. The hotel is open all year round.

Pinewood Hotel, Leny Road, Callander, Perthshire FK17 8AP (tel. 0877/30111), a former Victorian "gentleman's house," stands in its own attractive gardens with pine trees. A double driveway leads from the main West Highland route. The hotel offers 16 comfortably furnished bedrooms, 8 with private baths or showers, color TVs, and phones. Singles rent for £18.50 ($30.55) per person daily, with doubles costing from £35 ($57.75). There are also some family rooms available. Tariffs include a full Highland breakfast. There is a choice of bar meals, or you can have a more formal dinner in the restaurant, which offers a four-course, multichoice menu using seasonal, fresh, local and traditional produce, complemented by a carefully chosen wine list.

ABERFOYLE

Looking like an alpine village, in the heart of the Rob Roy country, this small holiday resort, 55 miles from Edinburgh, 26 miles from Glasgow, and 19 miles from Stirling, is the gateway to the Trossachs, near Loch Ard. A large crafts center contains a wealth of gift items related to the Highlands.

Where to Stay and Dine

Bailie Nicol Jarvie Hotel, Aberfoyle, Perthshire FK8 3SZ (tel. 08772/202), is an old-fashioned hotel on the road between Loch Ard and Aberfoyle. If you're passing through the Trossachs, it makes a suitable overnight stopover. The hotel takes its name from Nicol Jarvie, the Glasgow magistrate who used to visit the outlaw Rob Roy at a former inn on this site. The hotel is one of character, and it was recently refurbished. All its 38 bedrooms contain private baths. Many of the rooms have high ceilings and are furnished in comfortable pieces. The B&B rate is £26 ($42.90) per person nightly, increasing to £41 ($67.65) per person for half board. Lovers of antiquity are drawn to Bailie Bar, a cocktail lounge hung with weaponry. The hotel serves good country meals, using farm produce when available. It's open all year.

For dining, **Braeval Old Mill** (tel. 08772/711) is the obvious choice, lying a mile east of Aberfoyle on A81 (the Callander Road). Overlooking a golf course, this topnotch restaurant is housed in a former stone mill. Owners Fiona and Nick Nairn (he's the chef) kept an antique waterwheel to remind diners of the building's former function. They serve dinner from 7 to 9:30pm Tue. to Sun., Sun. lunch from noon to 2pm, with meals costing from £16 ($26.40). The set lunch goes for £10.50 ($17.35), and reservations are always advised. Mr. Nairn's repertoire embraces both traditional and modern British dishes in a changing menu based on the availability of only fresh produce, which he uses deftly.

THE TROSSACHS

The Duke's Pass (A821) north from Aberfoyle climbs through the Achray Forest, past the **David Marshall Lodge** information center, operated by the Forestry Commission, where you can stop for snacks and a view of the Forth Valley. The road runs to the Trossachs—the "bristly country"—between lochs Achray and Katrine.

Loch Katrine, at the head of which Rob Roy MacGregor was born, owes its fame to Sir Walter Scott, who set his poem *The Lady of the Lake* there. The loch is the principal reservoir of the city of Glasgow. A small steamer, *Sir Walter Scott*, plies the waters of the loch, which has submerged the Silver Strand of the romantic poet. Sailings are from early May to the end of September between Trossachs Pier and Stronachlachar. Round-trip fare is £2.60 ($4.30) for adults, £1.50 ($2.50) for children. Complete information as to the sailing schedules is available from the Strathclyde Water Department, Lower Clyde Division, 419 Balmore Rd., Glasgow G22 6NU (tel. 041/355-5333).

Trossachs Hotel, Trossachs, Perthshire FK17 8HY (tel. 08776/232), became famous in Victoria's heyday. Built on the site of one of the old posting inns of Scotland that dated from the 18th century, it was erected by Lady Willoughby as a castle in 1826, converting to a hotel in 1852. After a long career the hotel, now mellowed with time, is still going strong. Rooms come in a variety of styles. At least 100 rooms, all doubles or twins, are rented (more will be added to this roster when renovations are completed). The hotel charges £28 ($46.20) per person daily for B&B, the cost rising to £38 ($62.70) per person for half board. The dining room, hung with shields, is draped with the plaids of ancient clans and has a timbered ceiling. The hotel is right in the heart of the Trossachs, 2 miles from Loch Katrine where you can sail on the loch steamship, *Sir Walter Scott*.

LOCH LOMOND

This largest of Scotland's lochs was the center of the ancient district of Lennox, in the possession of the branch of the Stuart family from which sprang Lord Darnley, second husband of Mary Queen of Scots and father of James VI of Scotland, who was also James I of England. The ruins of Lennox Castle are on Inchmurrin, one of the 30 islands of the loch—one having ecclesiastical ruins, one noted for its yew trees planted by King Robert the Bruce to ensure a suitable supply of wood for the bows of his archers. The loch is fed by at least 10 rivers from west, east, and north. On the eastern side is Ben Lomond, rising to a height of 3,192 feet.

The song "Loch Lomond" is supposed to have been composed by one of Bonnie Prince Charlie's captured followers on the eve of his execution in Carlisle Jail. The "low road" of the song is the path through the underworld that his spirit will follow to his native land after death more quickly than his friends can travel to Scotland by the ordinary high road.

The road from Dumbarton to Crianlarich runs along the western shore of the loch. However, the easiest way to see the loch is not by car but by the **Countess Fiona,** which sails daily from Easter until the end of September. Built in 1936 for the Caledonian Steam Packet Company, she is now owned by Alloa Brewery Company and sails from Balloch Pier. A full cruise, round-trip ticket costs £12 ($19.80) for adults, £6 ($9.90) for children. For further information, phone 041/226-4271 for a recorded message or sailing times.

Balloch

At the southern end of Loch Lomond, Balloch is the most touristy of the towns and villages around the lake. It lies only a half-hour drive from the heart of Glasgow, and there is regular train service from Glasgow to Balloch Station. The town grew up on the River Leven, as it leaves Loch Lomond, flowing south to the Clyde. Today it is visited chiefly by those wanting to take boat trips on the *Countess Fiona*, which leaves in season from Balloch Pier. The most popular time to visit is during the Highland Games held here every year.

Balloch Castle Country Park is set on 200 acres along the "bonnie banks." The present Balloch Castle, replacing one that dates from 1238, was constructed in 1808 for John Buchanan of Ardoch. Built in the "castle-Gothic" style, it has a visitor center, which explains the history of the property. The site has a walled garden, and the trees and shrubs, especially the rhododendrons and azaleas, reach the zenith of their beauty in late May and early June. You can also visit a "Fairy Glen." The location is about three-quarters of a mile from the center of Balloch, and it is open all year daily from 8am to dusk, charging no admission.

WHERE TO STAY AND DINE Your best bet is the **Balloch Hotel,** Balloch Road, Balloch, Dunbartonshire G83 8LQ (tel. 0389/52579). When it was built, this white-walled establishment sat isolated at a point where the river flowed into Loch Lomond. In 1860, the Empress Eugénie, wife of Napoléon III, slept in the Inchmoan Room during her tour of Scotland. Today the warmly decorated pub and adjoining restaurant are filled with engravings of scenes from Scottish history. Well-prepared and plentiful food make this one of the most alluring stopovers in the area. Meals in the restaurant begin at £8 ($13.20), and pub lunches are cheaper. If you'd like to make the Balloch your base for exploring Loch Lomond, 13 comfortable bedrooms with private baths or showers rent for £52 ($85.80) daily in a double, £33 ($54.45) in a single. All units contain color TVs, phones, and tea and coffee makers.

Luss

This village on the western side of Loch Lomond is the traditional home of the Colquhouns. Among its stone cottages, on the water's edge, is a branch of the **Highland Arts Studios of Seil.** Cruises on the loch or boat rentals may be arranged at a nearby jetty.

Colquhoun Arms Hotel, Luss, Alexandria, Dunbartonshire G83 8NY (tel. 043686/282), is a yellow-and-white former coaching inn, sitting close to the road under the canopy of large trees. The modernized interior is filled with light-grained paneling, plaid carpeting, a pool table, an attractively lit dining room, a lounge bar, and a pub. The owner is Norwegian-born H. L. Weibye, a local businessman. The 24 rooms are bathless, except for 6 units. Bathless singles cost £22 ($36.36) daily and similar doubles go for £35 ($57.75). Doubles with bath rent for £44 ($72.60). Bar meals cost from £6.50 ($10.75), while full dinners in the dining room start at £12 ($19.80).

Inverbeg

This hamlet on the western shore of Loch Lomond stands in a beauty spot of Scotland, reached in about 40 minutes from Glasgow. The location is about 3 miles north of Luss. The hamlet is known for its oldtime ferry inn (see below), the second-oldest youth hostel in Scotland, and several well-known art galleries. A small fleet of Loch Lomond cruisers can usually be seen in the harbor of Inverbeg Bay, and a ferry to Rowardennan and Ben Lomond plies the route three times a day in summer.

The Inverbeg Inn, Luss, Loch Lomond, Dunbartonshire G83 8PD (tel. 043686/678). The site on which this inn stands has always been important as the ferryboat landing that services the western end of Loch Lomond. The roadside building that a visitor can see today was constructed in 1814. Earlier inns probably stood on the same site. Today, directed by the Bisset family, the establishment serves savory pub lunches as well as more formal restaurant meals throughout the year. The first thing a cold-weather visitor might see is a blazing fire heating the reception room near the entrance. About half of the comfortably furnished bedrooms look out over a garden in the rear. Depending on the plumbing and the season, singles cost from £32 ($52.80) to £36 ($59.40) daily with doubles going for £38 ($62.70) to £58 ($95.70). Seven of the rooms contain private baths. Fixed-price evening meals cost from £12 ($19.80), with pub lunches going for half that or less. You might want to stop in only for a meal.

Tarbet

On the western shores of Loch Lomond, Tarbet is not to be confused with the larger center of Tarbert, headquarters of the Loch Fyne herring industry. Loch Lomond's Tarbet is merely a village and a summer holiday base with limited accommodations. In the distance you can see the majesty of Ben Lomond. King Haakon of Norway came this way in the 13th century, devastating the countryside. To the north, now the site of the Inveruglas power station, the Clan MacFarlane had their rallying point.

Boats can be launched from the pier, and Tarbet is one of the stops on the route of the steamship *Countess Fiona.*

Tarbet Hotel, Tarbet, Arrochar, Dunbartonshire G83 7DE (tel. 03012/228). Local historians say that some form of hotel has stood on this spot for the past 400 years. A coaching inn was built on the site in 1760, and in the Victorian era a baronial facade and military-style crenelations were added. The exterior suggests that the interior might be as antique as the stone facade. However, the present owners have modernized the inside. A cozy cocktail lounge looks past a row of yew trees onto the lake. Good food is served in the spacious dining rooms, and there are 91 simple but comfortable rooms to rent. Of these, 72 contain private baths or showers. A bathless single goes for £18 ($29.70) daily, increasing to £35 ($57.75) in a similar double. Rooms with bath cost £28 ($46.20) in a single, rising to £52 ($85.80) in a double. The hotel is closed in January.

XXI

NORTHEAST SCOTLAND

1. EXPLORING TAYSIDE
2. THE GRAMPIAN REGION

Covering the regions of Tayside and Grampian, northeast Scotland beckons the visitor with much scenic grandeur, although some come just to hit the Whisky Trail. Three of Scotland's most important cities, Dundee, Aberdeen, and Perth, are tucked away in this corner, and the section also contains three of the country's best-known salmon rivers, the Dee, the Spey, and the Tay.

The land is riddled with historic old castles, and will give you a view of Highland majesty—imposing, grand, tumultuous, including Queen Victoria's favorite view. The best known of the traditional Highland gatherings takes place at Braemar.

---

1. Exploring Tayside

The trouble with exploring Tayside is that you may find it so fascinating in scenery you'll never make it on to the Highlands. Carved out of the old counties of Perth and Angus, Tayside is named for its major river, the 119-mile-long Tay. Its tributaries and dozens of lochans and Highland streams are some of the best salmon and trout waters in Europe. One of the loveliest regions of Scotland, Tayside is filled with heather-clad Highland hills, long blue lochs under tree-clad banks, and miles and miles of walking trails.

It is a region dear to the Scots, a symbol of their desire for independence, as exemplified by the Declaration of Arbroath and the ancient coronation ritual of the "Stone of Destiny" at Scone. In cities, Perth and Dundee are among the leading six centers of Scotland.

Tayside also provided the backdrop for many novels by Sir Walter Scott, including *The Fair Maid of Perth, Waverley,* and *The Abbot.*

Its golf courses are world-famous, ranging from the trio of 18-hole courses at Gleneagles to the open championship links at Carnoustie.

We'll begin our trip in an offshoot southern pocket of the county at Loch Leven, then take in Perth and its environs, heading east to Dundee, and later along the fishing villages of the North Sea, cutting west again to visit Glamis Castle, finally ending our journey of exploration even farther west in the lochs and glens of the Perthshire Highlands.

LOCH LEVEN

"Those never got luck who came to Loch Leven." This proverbial saying sums up the history of the ruined Douglas Fortress, **Loch Leven Castle,** on Castle Island, dating from the late 14th century. Among its more ill-fated prisoners, none was more notable than Mary Queen of Scots. Within its forbidding walls she signed her abdication on July 24, 1567. However, she effected her escape from Loch Leven on May 2, 1568. Thomas Percy, seventh Earl of Northumberland, supported her cause. For his efforts he, too, was imprisoned and lodged in the castle for 3 years until he was handed over to the English, who beheaded him at York. The castle is open from 9:30am to 7pm Mon. to Sat., 2 to 7pm Sun., April to September, closed in winter. Admission to the castle is free, but the charge for the ferry is 60p ($1) for adults, 30p (50¢) for children.

Lying to the north of Dunfermline (head toward Kinross), the loch has seven islands. Loch Leven Castle, of course, is in ruins. So is the **Priory of Loch Leven,** built on the site of one of the oldest Culdee establishments in Scotland, and lying on St. Serf's, the largest of the islands in the loch.

In Kinross, 25 miles north of Edinburgh, you can make arrangements to visit Loch Leven Castle by boat, the only means of access.

Where to Stay and Dine

Nivingston House, Cleish, Kinross-shire KY13 7LS (tel. 05775/216), lies on the B9097, 2 miles south of Kinross at Cleish. It serves some of the finest food in Tayside. The place is run by Pat and Allen Deeson, who offer 17 modernized rooms with private baths or showers, phones, and TVs for £60 ($99) daily in a single, £75 ($123.75) in a double, both with breakfast included.

However, most visitors arrive to sample the wares of the kitchen. I've never had the same meal here twice, as one must depend on the inspiration of the chef. But that's hardly a problem. Meals, costing £14 ($23.10) for lunch and £22.75 ($37.55) for dinner, are concocted principally from local produce, such as fish, Scottish lamb and beef, and veal, as well as charcoal-grilled sardines. Try, if featured, his fish terrine and the king prawns, or the delectable house pâté. Desserts are luscious, your selection made from a trolley wheeled to your table. Hours are daily from noon to 2pm and 7 to 9pm. Always reserve a table. The hotel stands on 10 acres of grounds.

PERTH

From its majestic position on the Tay, the ancient city of Perth was the capital of Scotland until the middle of the 15th century. Here the Highland meets the Lowland. Sir Walter Scott chose the royal burgh as a setting for *The Fair Maid of Perth*. It lies 44 miles from Edinburgh and 64 miles from Glasgow. The tourist information center is at the Round House, Marshall Place (tel. 0738/38353).

What to See and Do

The main sightseeing attraction of "the fair city" is the **Kirk of St. John the Baptist,** on St. John's Place, of which the original foundation, it is believed, dates from Pictish times. However, the present choir dates from 1440 and the nave from 1490. In 1559 John Knox preached his famous sermon here attacking idolatry, and it caused a wave of iconoclasm to sweep across the land. The church was restored as a World War I memorial in the mid-1920s. In the church is the tombstone of James I, who was murdered by Sir Robert Graham.

Black Watch Regimental Museum, Balhousie Castle, Hay Street (tel. 0738/2128, ext. 8530), contains the memorabilia of the 42nd and 73rd Highland Regiments. You get to see 2½ centuries of British military history, including paintings, silver, and uniforms. Admission is free, but it's appreciated if you make a donation to the museum fund. From April to the end of September it is open 10am to 4:30pm

Mon. to Fri., from 2 to 4:30pm Sun. and bank holidays. Winter hours are 10am to 3:30pm Mon. to Fri.

John Dewar & Sons, the internationally renowned distillers of Dewar's White Label Scotch whisky, have a massive bottling complex at Inveralmond, on the outskirts of Perth. Inveralmond is one of the largest establishments of its kind in Scotland, and as many as 350,000 bottles are filled there in one day. Organized tours are given for visitors wishing to see the bottling and dispatch processes. You are advised to phone 0738/21231 for information.

The Fair Maid's House, North Port (tel. 0738/25976), was the old Glover's House that Sir Walter Scott chose as the home of his heroine in the already-mentioned novel, *The Fair Maid of Perth.* Now a craft shop, it sells high-quality Scottish crafts, including woolen goods, silver, glass, and pottery. It is open from 10am to 5pm Mon. to Sat. Upstairs houses a studio where Highland character dolls are made by Sheena MacLeod. Visitors are welcome, but hours are irregular, so call first to see if it's open.

Branklyn Garden, Dundee Road (A85), has been called the finest 2 acres of private garden in Scotland. Established in 1922 by Mr. and Mrs. John Renton, it was bequeathed to the National Trust for Scotland. It has a superb collection of rhododendrons, alpines, and herbaceous and peat-garden plants from all over the world. Open daily from March to the end of October, it can be visited from 10am to sunset for an admission of £1.20 ($2) for adults and 60p ($1) for children. For information, phone 0738/25535.

You can watch glassmakers at work at the **Caithness Glass factory,** at Inveralmond (tel. 0738/37373), where there is also a visitor center. Of special interest is the intricate art of paperweight making. Glassmaking can be observed from 9am to 4:30pm Mon. to Fri. The factory shop and restaurant are open from 9am to 5pm Mon. to Sat. and 1 to 5pm Sun.

Where to Stay

Station Hotel, Leonard Street, Perth, Perthside PH2 8HE (tel. 0738/24141). Its fortunes were assured when most of the traffic from the Highlands began funneling over the nearby George Street Bridge, completed just 3 years before the American Revolution. The nearby street corner became known as the "hub of the universe," and later stagecoaches made it a major stopover. Built as the grandest hotel in Perth in 1890, it has been restored by the Friendly Hotel chain. The hotel has entertained everybody from Queen Elizabeth II to Margaret Thatcher. It is set behind a severely dignified, gray-sandstone facade, containing 70 comfortable bedrooms. Each accommodation has a private bath or shower, TV, mini-bar and hot beverage facilities. Singles range from £42 ($69.30) to £52 ($85.80) daily, with doubles costing £52 ($85.80) to £58 ($95.70), with VAT and a continental breakfast included. Each room is different from its neighbor, charmingly so, and each has high ceilings evoking the age of Victoria. You register in a lobby darkly paneled in mahogany and upholstered in pastel colors. One of the hotel's highlights is a baronial staircase handcarved from Canadian hardwood.

Royal George, Tay Street, Perth, Perthside PH1 5LD (tel. 0738/24455), gets the "royal" in its name from a long ago visit by Victoria. The stone facade and landscaped garden you see today, however, dates from around 1910. Each bedroom is solidly furnished, evoking the 19th century with high ceilings, big windows, and wood detailing. Each bedroom has a private bath or shower, TV, and phone. With breakfast included, singles rent for £50 ($82.50) daily, with doubles costing from £68 ($112.20). On the premises is Helen MacGregor's, a bar named after the legendary mistress of Rob Roy. In the Ox and Claret, traditional cookery, including Scottish beef, is a specialty.

Where to Dine

Timothy's, 24 St. John St. (tel. 0738/26641), has a convivial informality, and also serves some of the best food in this ancient city, far superior to that I've encountered in the dining rooms of the staid Victorian hotels. Try the Scottish smörgåsbord offered by the owners, Caroline and Athole Laing. Roast beef (served rare and tender), smoked trout, tasty sausages, crabmeat wrapped in smoked salmon, and homemade soups (such as nettle or dandelion) are well prepared. Perhaps you might like to try salmon caught in the River Tay, only about 55 yards away, brought here fresh each morning and served at lunch and dinner during the season. The fresh oysters from Loch Fyne are luscious. Top-quality local produce is used, including garden fruit and vegetables. In summer, the Laings even decorate the smörgåsbord with fresh nasturtiums, borage, and marigold flowers. Athole wears his kilt every evening to give visitors to Perth a warm Scottish welcome. Caroline, who does all the cooking, makes a special "pudding" every day, such as fresh raspberry-cream soufflé in summer and a steamy hot, fruit-spiced sponge in winter. She's known for her Scottish trifle, made the old-fashioned way—no jelly, but lots of fruit, sherry, and cream. For a complete meal, including a glass of wine, expect to pay from £5 ($8.25) at lunch and from £8 ($13.20) at dinner. Meals are from noon to 2:30pm and 7 to 10pm Tue. to Sat., and it's necessary to call for a reservation.

SCONE

On the River Tay, Old Scone, 2 miles from Perth, was the ancient capital of the Picts. On a lump of granite called the "Stone of Destiny" the monarchs of the Dark Ages were enthroned. The British sovereign to this day is still crowned on the stone, but in Westminster Abbey. Edward I moved the stone there in 1296. Charles II was the last king crowned at Scone; the year: 1651.

Scone Palace (tel. 0783/52300), the seat of the earl of Mansfield and birthplace of David Douglas of fir tree fame, was largely rebuilt in 1802, incorporating the old palace of 1580. Inside is an impressive collection of French furniture, china, ivories, and 16th-century needlework, including bed hangings executed by Mary Queen of Scots. A fine collection of rare conifers is found on the grounds in the Pinetum. Rhododendrons and azaleas grow profusely in the gardens and woodlands around the palace. To reach the palace, head northeast of Perth on the A93. It lies 2 miles from the center of Perth. The site is open from Good Friday to mid-October from 9:30am to 5pm Mon. to Sat., 1:30 to 5pm Sun. Admission is £3 ($4.95) for adults, £2 ($3.30) for children, including entrance to both the house and grounds.

Where to Stay and Dine

The Murrayshall, New Scone, Perthshire PH2 7PH (tel. 0738/51171), an elegant country-house hotel and restaurant, lies 1½ miles east of New Scone by A94. Set in 300 acres of parkland, it was completely refurbished in 1987, and reopened as one of the showpieces of Perthshire. A Victorian mansion, it offers its own 18-hole, par 73 golf course, interspersed with trees, water hazards, and white-sanded bunkers. The hotel is traditionally styled, both in its public rooms and in its 19 bedrooms, each with private bath, phone, color TV, and quality furniture. The size of the rooms varies, as does the decorating. Twins or doubles cost from £95 ($156.75) to £115 ($189.75) daily, with singles going for £65 ($107.25) to £75 ($123.75). Dinner is another £25 ($41.25), and it's a worthy choice—in fact, the finest dining in the area. Chef Bruce Sangster is the excitement behind the Old Master's restaurant, named for the walls hung with Dutch masters. The menu provides Scottish flavor and French inspiration in cooking, with vegetables and herbs from the hotel's own garden used. Local ingredients are used whenever possible in the preparation of the food, which is served in the candlelit restaurant daily from noon to 2pm and 7 to 9:30pm. Non-residents are welcome, but must reserve.

Balcraig House, New Scone, Perth, Perthshire PH2 7PG (tel. 0738/51123), is 1½ miles northeast of Perth along the A94. A country house, built in the 19th century when Queen Victoria sometimes stayed at Scone Palace nearby, Balcraig is run today as an elegant country-house hotel. The owners have created a relaxed, luxurious atmosphere amid delightful scenery. Fresh flowers, polished woodwork, crystal chandeliers, and a collection of tapestries provide the ambience, adding to the elegance of the drawing room. The 10 bedrooms, all with well-equipped bathrooms,

color TVs, hairdryers, phones, and radios, are individually decorated. One I especially like is the Rose Room, which has a fine four-poster bed. All the units are well-
maintained. A single costs £65 ($107.25) daily, while doubles are priced from £90
($148.50) to £115 ($189.75). The house has a private garden, a tennis court, and
greens for croquet and boules. Baby-sitting can be arranged, and you can go pony-
trekking through the estate. The cuisine here is highly recommended, with the emphasis on traditional Scottish fare artistically presented. Most of the produce is
homegrown or obtained locally from first-class purveyors. Your poached salmon, as
a change of pace, might come with a hazelnut hollandaise sauce. Meals cost from
£18 ($29.70). The wine cellar is impressive.

GLENEAGLES

This famous golfing center and sports complex is on a moor between Strath
Earn and Strath Allan. The center gets its name from the Gaelic Gleann-an-Eaglias,
meaning glen of the church. **St. Mungo's Chapel,** higher up the glen than the internationally known golf courses and hotel, has monuments of the Haldane family,
whose ancestral castle ruins made way—and provided the stones—for the building
of the later family seat constructed in 1624.

Gleneagles has four 18-hole golf courses connected with the hotel: King's
Course, the longest one; Queen's Course, next in length; Prince's Course, shortest
of all; and Glendevon, the newest of the quartet, built in 1980. They are considered
the best in Scotland. The sports complex is one of the most splendid in Europe.

Gleneagles provides a good—but far from inexpensive—base from which to
explore the major attractions of central Scotland. It is in the ancient Royal Burgh of
Auchterarder of many centuries ago, strategically placed on the road that led from
the royal residence at Scone to Stirling Castle. Today it is on the A9, about halfway
between Perth and Stirling, a short distance from the village of Auchterarder. It lies
55 miles from Edinburgh and 45 miles from Glasgow. The tourist information center is at 90 High St. (tel. 0764/63450).

Where to Stay and Dine

The Gleneagles Hotel, Auchterarder, Perthshire PH3 1NF (tel. 0764/
62231), stands in its own 830-acre estate, 1½ miles southwest of Auchterarder by
A9. Built in 1924, it is the only five-star hotel in Scotland. The service and decor are
incomparable in the country. Each of the 236 luxurious bedrooms has a spacious
bath, color TV, in-house video, mini-bar, direct-dial phone, and 24-hour room service. The rooms have fine furnishings, and the hills and glens of the surrounding
countryside make splendid views. The price of singles, including VAT, ranges from
£85 ($140.25) to £95 ($156.75) daily; doubles £140 ($231) to £170 ($280.50).
Guests can dine in the Strathearn Restaurant, paying from £20 ($33) for a table
d'hôte lunch, and from £27.50 ($45.40) for a table d'hôte dinner. The emphasis is
on regional dishes, and piano music is played in the evening. The gourmet restaurant
is the Conservatory Restaurant, which has magnificent views. Hours are 7:30 to
10:30pm daily.

The hotel's country club, enclosed in a glass dome to provide a year-round
tropical climate, offers to members and hotel guests use of swimming pool, whirlpool, Turkish bath, saunas, plunge pool, and children's pool. If you're really hardy,
you can use the Canadian hot tubs outdoors. Champneys, the health spa, includes
various treatment rooms for health, beauty, and massages. There are also squash
courts, gym, snooker tables, tennis courts, croquet lawns, and bowling green, not to
mention fishing on the River Tay. In the country club, you can have steak and salads
at the Brasserie, and there's also a cocktail bar. In addition there is The Gleneagles
Jackie Stewart Shooting School and The Gleneagles Mark Phillips Equestrian Centre, both equipped to the highest standards. For the coddling of golfers, The Dormy
House (old name for a clubhouse) sits beside the 18th greens of the King's and
Queen's courses. Here is another restaurant and bar in addition to showers and
changing rooms.

Auchterarder House, Auchterarder, Perthshire PH3 1DZ (tel. 0764/63646), a mile from Gleneagles, sits in its own grounds off the B8062 between Auchterarder and Crieff. A fine example of 1830s architecture and construction in the Scots Jacobean style, the mansion house has been completely restored and the interior refurbished to a high standard of luxury by its present owners, Ian and Audrey Brown. The house has elegant public rooms and 11 comfortable bedrooms, all with private baths and other amenities calculated to please a discerning clientele, such as TVs and phones. Singles pay from £75 ($123.75) to £95 ($156.75) daily, and doubles £100 ($165) to £140 ($231). Afternoon tea is served in the glass conservatory with its miniature fountain and goldfish pond. You can enjoy drinks in the handsome bar, which was the chapel of the house in other days. Lunch and dinner are served in the Victorian dining room or in the library. You can choose from a French and British menu. Dinner will cost £32 ($52.80) to £40 ($66), the price including canapes, coffee, and petit fours.

Free courtesy car service is offered from Gleneagles Station, and the staff will help arrange tours of the area as well as sports activities, including golf. You may be content, however, just to browse around the 20 acres of grounds, where a fine collection of rare shrubs, trees, and rhododendrons is nurtured.

CRIEFF

At the edge of the Perthsire Highlands, Crieff makes a pleasant stopover with possibilities for fishing and golf. This small burgh, 18 miles from Perth and 60 miles from Edinburgh, was the seat of the court of earls of Strathearn until 1747. In its market place, gallows were once used to execute Highland cattle rustlers.

You can take a "day trail" into Strathearn, the valley of the River Earn, the very center of Scotland. Highland mountains meet gentle Lowland slopes, and moorland mingles with rich green pastures. North of Crieff, the road to Aberfeldy passes through the narrow pass of the Sma'Glen, with hills rising on either side to 2,000 feet. The glen is a well-known beauty spot.

In addition, you can explore a distillery, glassworks, and a pottery center. The tourist information center is on High Street (tel. 0764/2578), but open in summer only.

What to See and Do

Glenturret Distillery Ltd., Glenturret, the Hosh (tel. 0764/2424), is Scotland's oldest distillery, established in 1775. On the banks of the River Turret, it is reached from Crieff by taking the A85 toward Comrie. At a point three-quarters of a mile from Crieff, turn right at the crossroads. The distillery is a quarter of a mile up the road. It is all signposted. Visitors can see the milling of malt, mashing, fermentation, distillation, and cask filling, followed by a free "wee dram" dispensed at the end of the tour. Visitors are welcome March to December from 9:30am to 5:30pm Mon. to Sat. (last full tour at 4:30pm). Tours through the distillery are at frequent intervals. In January and February, only the shop is open, from 2 to 4pm. The Glenturret Heritage Centre incorporates a 100-seat audio-visual theater and an Exhibition Display Museum. The distillery shop has the full range of the Glenturret Pure Single Highland Malt Scotch whisky and the Glenturret malt liqueur, together with an extensive range of souvenirs. At the Smugglers Restaurant and Whisky Tasting Bar you can taste older Glenturret whiskies, such as 10-year-old, high-proof, 12- and 15-year-old, and the Glenturret malt liqueur. The guided tours, taking about 25 minutes, cost £1.25 ($2.05) for adults, 70p ($1.15) for youngsters 12 to 17 years old. Under 12s are admitted free. Admission to the Heritage Centre is 50p (85¢), the presentation lasting about 20 minutes.

Stuart Strathearn, Muthill Road (tel. 0764/4004), is a factory welcoming visitors wanting to see how handmade crystal is produced. From June to September it is open daily from 9am to 7pm. From October to May, it closes at 5pm. You can see the traditional craftsperson's skill in the Stuart Crystal film demonstrated by factory glassworkers. The shop on the premises has a large selection of Stuart Crystal and its own engraved crystal giftware. On the grounds of the factory is a picnic area, plus a children's playground.

Crieff Visitors Centre, 14 Comrie St. (tel. 0764/5151), which opened in 1985, was built by Buchan's Thistle Potteries and Perthshire Paperweights, two medium-size craft factories, to enable visitors to see their skills in manufacturing pottery and glass. Buchans established the Thistle Potteries more than a century ago and is the last survivor of the famous Portobello potteries. Visitors can go on escorted tours through the factory Mon. to Fri., seeing all the elements of the process. Perthshire Paperweights has recently been designed to allow visitors to watch the processes. It is also open during working hours, but Fri. afternoon is the least interesting time, because the staff is only preparing the next week's glass. The center has a large showroom displaying the products of both factories, including both firsts and seconds in pottery, although all paperweight seconds are destroyed. There is a modern licensed restaurant. Hours are 9am to 6pm daily, although factory tours are only possible during normal production hours.

Three miles south of Crieff, you can visit the gardens of **Drummond Castle** (tel. 076481/257), a mile north of Muthill, seat of the late earl of Ancaster. The gardens were originally laid out about 1630 by John Drummond, second Earl of Perth. Around 1830, the parterre was Italianized and embellished with figures and statues from Italy. Probably one of the most interesting pieces of statuary is the sundial, designed and built by John Mylne, Master Mason to King Charles I. The grounds are open daily from 2 to 6pm (last entry at 5pm) from May to the end of August. In September, they are open only on Wed. and Sun. from 2 to 6pm. Admission is £1.20 ($2) for adults, 60p ($1) for children.

Where to Stay and Dine

Murraypark Hotel, Connaught Terrace, Crieff, Perthshire PH7 3DJ (tel. 0764/3731), is small, offering 14 rooms with private baths and phones, but its standards are first rate. The bedrooms have a pleasing decor and are comfortably furnished. Singles rent from £24 ($39.60) for B&B, and doubles go for £58 ($95.70). Before dinner, you can meet in the bar after having strolled around the hotel, enjoying views across Strathearn. Meals are based on country-house fare, costing from £13.50 ($22.30).

COMRIE

An attractive little village in Strathearn, 25 miles from Perth, Comrie stands at the confluence of the Earn, Ruchill, and Lednock rivers. The A85 runs through the village to Lochearnhead, Crianlarich, and on to Oban and the western seaboard. It's a convenient place to stop overnight for travelers crossing Scotland. Waterskiing, boating, and sailing are available on Loch Earn in summer.

On the A85, the **Scottish Tartans Museum,** Drummond Street (tel. 0764/70779), is the only museum devoted entirely to tartans and Highland dress. There are more than 400 tartans on display together with models, prints, and pictures depicting Highland attire. There is a reconstructed weaver's cottage with occasional demonstrations of hand-spinning and hand-weaving, as well as a garden featuring plants, shrubs, and trees used in past times to dye tartan. The museum is open from 10am to 5pm Mon. to Sat., 2 to 4pm Sun., from April to October. In winter, visits are possible during office hours (ring the bell) Mon. to Fri. as well as from 10am to 12:30pm Sat. The Scottish Tartans Society undertakes research inquiries on a fee basis using its archives, *The Register of All Publicly Known Tartans.* There is a shop selling authentic tartan goods, plus a mail order service. Admission to the museum is £1.25 ($2.05) for adults, 75p ($1.25) for children.

Where to Stay and Dine

The Royal Hotel, Melville Square, Comrie, Perthshire PH6 2DN (tel. 0764/70200), was awarded the "royal" after the visit of Her Majesty, Queen Victoria. It's not, as you might imagine, a Victorian hotel, but rather an L-shaped stone inn dating back to 1765, with white trim and six bedroom dormers. Its cocktail bar with copper-top tables, furnished and decorated in the proprietor's own Gordon tartan, is noted for its selection of malt whiskies, and on the walls are framed prints and photographs with signatures of numerous famous guests who have stayed here over the years, including that of "Monty," Lloyd George, actress Sarah Bernhardt, and Queen Victoria's faithful servant, John Brown. The dining room is equally attractive, with an open log fire. The bedrooms are comfortable, consisting of one with a four-poster bed, plus 10 more units, all of which have private baths, direct-dial phones, color TVs, radios, hot beverage facilities, and electric blankets with controls. The charge per person for B&B is £24 ($39.60) daily, £37 ($61.05) per person for a bed and half board. The spacious residents' lounge is well appointed, and the cocktail bar has been refurbished. You can dine à la carte in the dining room, with silver service. A table d'hôte dinner costs £14 ($23.10). Lunch is served daily from noon to 2pm, and dinner hours are from 7 to 9pm Sun. to Thur., from 7 to 10pm Fri. and Sat.

DUNDEE

This royal burgh and old seaport is an industrial city, one of the largest in Scotland, lying on the north shore of the Firth of Tay. When steamers took over the whaling industry from sailing vessels, Dundee took the lead as homeport for the ships from the 1860s until World War I. Long known for its jute and flax operations, the fame of Dundee today is linked with the production of the rich Dundee fruit-cakes and Dundee marmalades and jams.

Spanning the Firth of Tay is the **Tay Railway Bridge,** opened in 1888. Constructed over the tidal estuary, the bridge is some 2 miles long, one of the longest in Europe. There is also a road bridge a mile and a quarter long, with four lanes and a walkway in the center.

Although many travelers pass through the city en route to Glamis Castle, 12 miles north, there are some interesting sights in Dundee.

What to See and Do

At Victoria Dock, the frigate *Unicorn* (tel. 0382/200900), a 46-gun ship of war launched in 1824 by the Royal Navy and now the oldest British-built ship afloat, has been in large part restored and visitors can explore all four decks: the quarterdeck with 32-pound carronades; the gundeck with its battery of 18-pound cannons and the captain's quarters; the berth-deck with officers' cabins and crew's hammocks; and the orlop deck and hold. Various displays portraying life in the sailing navy and the history of the *Unicorn* make this a rewarding visit. The ship is open daily from 10am to 5pm (to 4pm Sat.) from April to mid-October. There is limited opening Mon. to Sat. in winter. Admission is £1.25 ($2.05) for adults, 75p ($1.25) for children.

The McManus Galleries, Albert Square (tel. 0382/23141), designed by Sir George Gilbert Scott and built in 1867, house an art collection of national importance, including fine examples of 19th- and 20th-century Scottish paintings, prints, drawing, sculptures, furniture, clocks, glass, ceramics, and silver. There are also three galleries telling the story of life in Tayside from prehistoric times to the Industrial Revolution and on into the 20th century. The archeology gallery also has a significant display of material from ancient Egypt and breaks new ground by including contemporary artwork in the display design. The building is one of Scotland's finest examples of Victorian Gothic architecture. The galleries are open from 10am to 5pm Mon. to Sat. Admission is free.

For a spectacular view of Dundee, the Tay bridges across to Fife, and the mountains to the north, go to **Dundee Law,** a 572-foot hill a mile north of the city. The hill is an ancient volcanic plug.

About 5 miles east of the city center on the seafront, at **Broughty Ferry,** a little fishing hamlet, later the terminus for the ferry that crossed the Firth of Tay until the bridges were built, is **Broughty Castle** (tel. 0382/76121), a 15th-century estuary fort. Besieged by the English in the 16th century and attacked by Cromwell's army under General Monk in the 17th century, it was eventually restored as part of Britain's coastal defenses in 1861. Its gun battery was dismantled in 1956, and it is now a museum with displays on local history, arms and armor, seashore life, and Dundee's whaling story. The observation area at the top of the castle provides fine views of the Tay estuary and northeast Fife. The castle is open from 10am to 1pm and 2 to 5pm Mon. to Thur. It is open on Sun. July to September only, from 2 to 5pm. Closed Fri. Admission is free.

Where to Stay and Dine

Angus Thistle Hotel, 101 Marketgait, Dundee, Angus OD1 1QU (tel. 0382/26874), is a glass-and-concrete structure. Don't stay here seeking historical romance, but if you want a comfortable accommodation, you'll find all the amenities. The furnishings throughout are well maintained, 53 rooms and 5 suites have private baths, phones, and TVs. In a single, the rate is from £55 ($90.75) daily. A double rents for £85 ($140.25). VAT and service are included. The hotel also has three bars and a main dining room serving a standard cuisine, with meals costing from £10 ($16.50).

ARBROATH

Samuel Johnson wasn't that much impressed with Scotland on his jaunt there, but he did say that the view of Arbroath repaid him for some of the hardships suffered in his journey. Arbroath is a popular coastal resort with a fishing harbor and rugged, red-sandstone cliffs weathered into grotesque shapes. Smugglers once used the sandstone caves along the coast. Arbroath "smokies" (smoked haddock) are one of the fish delicacies along the east coast of Scotland.

The "Fairport" of Sir Walter Scott's *The Antiquary,* the royal burgh of Arbroath lies 17 miles northeast of Dundee and 72 miles from Edinburgh.

Associated with the Declaration of Arbroath of 1320, when the Scottish Parliament met here and drew up a famous letter to send to the pope asserting Scotland's independence from England, **Arbroath Abbey,** High Street, was founded as a priory in 1178 by William the Lion to honor his late friend, Thomas à Becket, murdered in Canterbury 8 years earlier. The red-sandstone abbey, a rich and influential ecclesiastical center, became dilapidated after the beginning of the 17th century, but it was once again in the news in 1951 when the Stone of Scone, stolen from Westminster Abbey, turned up on the altar here. For more information, phone 031/244-3101. Hours are the same as for the museum described below.

The Abbot's House, within the precincts of Arbroath Abbey (tel. 0241/78756), has been restored as a museum, with a collection of relics and stone sculpture. April to the end of September hours are 9:30am to 7pm Mon. to Sat., 2pm to 7pm Sun. The remainder of the year the hours are the same, except for a 4pm closing. Admission charges are 60p ($1) for adults, 30p (50¢) for children.

Where to Stay and Dine

Letham Grange, Colliston, Arbroath, Angus DD11 4RL (tel. 0241/024189), is by far the best place to stay in the area, but you have to journey nearly 5 miles northeast of Arbroath along A933. A Victorian country house, now turned into a hotel of charm and character, it has been sensitively restored and now welcomes guests. The grange is set on a 350-acre private estate near an 18-hole golf course. All year guests are received, and they are housed and fed well. The 20 bedrooms are not only comfortable, but immaculately maintained and well furnished, each with private bath or shower, TV, and phone. Guests are charged from £56 ($42.40) daily in a single, the cost rising to £85 ($140.25) in a double. The food is good, using quality ingredients, and the service and attention are first class. Meals can be ordered from an à la carte menu, a combination of Scottish and continental dishes. You may want to photograph the hotel, as it's one of those Scottish Victorian piles with a crescent-shaped, pillared, Georgian portico from which rises a square tower. It dates from the age when newly prosperous Victorians had unlimited funds to spend on their castles in the north. The hotel is sports oriented, with fishing and riding as well as the previously mentioned golf available.

KIRRIEMUIR

This town of narrow streets is the birthplace of Sir James M. Barrie, the "Thrums" of his novels. The Scottish dramatist and novelist was born in 1860, son of a linen manufacturer. **Barrie's Birthplace,** 9 Brechin Rd. (tel. 0575/72646), a property of National Trust for Scotland, contains manuscripts and mementos of the writer. A little wash house outside the four-room cottage was used by the young Barrie as his first theater. Besides his creation of *Peter Pan,* Barrie also wrote such stage successes as *The Admirable Crichton* and *Dear Brutus.* The house is open from 11am to 5:30pm Mon. to Sat., 2 to 5:30pm Sun. Easter week, and then May to the end of September. Admission is £1 ($1.65) for adults, 50p (85¢) for children.

Where to Stay and Dine

Thrums Hotel, 25 Bank St., Kirriemuir, Angus DD8 4BE (tel. 0575/72758), built in the 19th century, is almost next to the Barrie birthplace. The hostelry is like an inn, standing in the heart of town, with 11 pleasantly kept rooms. Everything about the hotel is well maintained. You might like it so much you'll choose it as a center for exploring Tayside. The charge for bathless accommodations is £18 ($29.70) per person daily, rising to £23 ($37.95) per person for a room with private bath, including breakfast. Should you just be passing through Kirriemuir, Thrums is ideal for lunch. It suitably honors Barrie by offering some old-fashioned and traditional Scottish cookery, including Tayside salmon, Angus steaks, and cloutie dumpling. Lunch, daily from noon to 2pm, costs £7.50 ($12.40), and dinner, from 6:30 to 9:30pm, runs around £13 ($21.45).

GLAMIS CASTLE

After Balmoral Castle, most visitors to Scotland want to see Glamis Castle at Glamis (pronounced Glaams), for its architecture, its Shakespearian link (Macbeth was thane of Glamis at the beginning of the play), and its link with the Crown. For 10 centuries it has been connected to British royalty. Queen Elizabeth, the Queen Mother, was brought up here; her daughter, now Queen Elizabeth II, spent a good deal of her childhood here; and Princess Margaret, the Queen's sister, was born here, becoming the first royal princess born in Scotland in 3 centuries. The existing castle dates in part from the middle of the 14th century, but there are records of a castle's having been in existence in the 11th century, at which time it was one of the hunting lodges of the kings of Scotland. King Malcolm II was carried there mortally wounded in 1034 after having been attacked by his enemies while hunting in a nearby forest.

Glamis Castle has been in the possession of the Lyon family since 1372, when it formed part of the dowry of Princess Joanna, daughter of King Robert II, when she married John Lyon, secretary to the king. The castle was altered in the 16th century and restored and enlarged in the 17th, 18th, and 19th centuries. It contains some fine plaster ceilings, furniture, and paintings.

The present owner, the Queen's cousin, is the 18th earl of Strathmore and Kinghorne. He lives at the castle with his family. He is the direct descendant of the first earl.

The castle is open to the public, who have access to the royal apartments and many other rooms, and also to the gardens and grounds, open daily from noon to 5:30pm (last tour at 4:45pm) from the end of April to mid-October. Admission to the castle and gardens is £3 ($4.95) for adults, £1.50 ($2.50) for children. If you wish to visit the grounds only, the charge is £1.20 ($2) for adults, 60p ($1) for children. For further details, get in touch with the Administrator, Estates Office (tel. 030784/242).

Also in Glamis, you may want to visit the **Angus Folk Museum,** Kirkwynd Cottages (tel. 030784/288), run by the National Trust for Scotland. From the former county of Angus, rich in folklore, were collected domestic utensils, agricultural implements, furniture, and clothing. The museum is open daily from 11am to 5pm (last entry 30 minutes earlier), Easter weekend and then May 1 to September 30. Admission is £1.30 ($2.15) for adults, 60p ($1) for children.

DUNKELD

A cathedral town, Dunkeld lies in a thickly wooded valley of the Tay River, at the edge of the Perthshire Highlands, 58 miles from Edinburgh and 14 miles from Perth. Once a major ecclesiastical center, it is one of the seats of ancient Scottish history. It was an important center of the Celtic church, for example.

Founded in A.D. 815, the **Cathedral of Dunkeld** was converted from a church to a cathedral in 1127 by David I. The 14th and 15th centuries witnessed subsequent additions. The cathedral was first restored in 1815, and at that time traces of the 12th-century structure clearly remained, as they do to this day. The cathedral can be visited daily from 9:30am to 7pm in summer, from 9:30am to 4pm in winter. Admission is free.

The National Trust for Scotland has been effective in restoring many of the old houses and shops around the market place and cathedral that had fallen into decay. The trust owns 20 houses on High Street and Cathedral Street. Many of these were constructed in the closing years of the 17th century during the rebuilding of the town following the Battle of Dunkeld. The trust has opened an **Ell Shop,** which is open from 10am to 1pm and 2 to 4:30pm Mon. to Sat. from Easter weekend to May 31 and September 1 to December 22. Hours are from 10am to 6pm Mon. to Sat. and 2 to 5pm Sun. from June 1 to the end of August.

The **Scottish Horse Museum,** the Cross, has exhibits tracing the history of the Scottish Horse Yeomanry in the museum in one of the "little houses of Dunkeld," all Jacobean cottages well preserved and maintained. From the time of the raising of the cavalry force in Scotland and South Africa in 1900 to its amalgamation with the Fife and Forfar Yeomanry in 1956, the Scottish Horse mounted yeomanry regiment was the only such fighting body besides the Lovat Scouts. The museum is open from 10am to 4pm daily, but takes a 1-hour break for lunch on Sun., from Easter to the end of September. Admission is 50p (85¢) for adults, free for children.

Shakespeare fans may want to seek out the oak and sycamore in front of the destroyed **Birnam House,** a mile to the south. This was believed to be a remnant of the Birnam wood to which the Bard gave everlasting literary fame in *Macbeth*. In Shakespeare's drama, you may recall, the "woods of Birnam came to Dunsinane."

The tourist information center is at the Cross (tel. 03502/688), but open in summer only.

Where to Stay

Stakis Dunkeld House Hotel, Dunkeld, Perthshire PH8 0HX (tel. 03502/ 771), offers the quiet dignity of life in a Scottish country house. Built by the seventh duke of Atholl for his duchess in the 19th century, the house was erected on the banks of the Tay, and the surrounding grounds—280 acres in all—were planted with trees and flowering bushes, making for a parklike setting. You reach the house by going down a long drive. Guests can fish for trout and salmon on the grounds. The house is well preserved and beautifully kept, and, as befits such a place, accommodations come in a wide range of styles, space, and furnishings. Singles cost £75 ($123.75) to £85 ($140.25) daily, doubles or twins go for £110 ($181.50) to £120 ($198), and all rates include VAT. The hotel, extensively restored and expanded, now offers 92 first-class bedrooms, each with private bath, phone, and TV. It is ranked as one of the leading leisure and sporting hotels in the country. Its restaurant is the finest in the area, paying homage to its Taste of Scotland dishes, but also serving an international cuisine as well. Facilities include all-weather tennis courts and an indoor swimming pool. Archery and fishing are also popular.

Cardney House, Dunkeld, Perthshire PH8 0EX (tel. 03504/222), is an elegant 18th-century manor on a private estate outside Dunkeld, 3 miles from the town on the A923 Blair Gowrie road. The house is surrounded by hills, forests, and lochs, and on the grounds rare and beautiful shrubs are grown, as well as orchids, stephanotis, and lemon and orange trees. Here you are received like the guest at a private party at a country home by the charming and hospitable hosts, Commander and Mistress MacGregor of Cardney, who because of "crippling taxes" now receive paying guests. The gracious home is well furnished, often with antiques, and the atmosphere is one of refinement and tranquility, a style set so admirably by the proprietors. They have available now only two singles and six doubles, charging £28 ($46.20) per person daily for half board, including VAT. Dinner, a Cordon Bleu cuisine, is served until 10 in the evening, and you definitely feel you are dining family style. The food is well prepared and beautifully served, and meals are complemented by a first-class wine cellar. Guests relax freely in the lounges, which are furnished with family treasures, often antiques. There's an elevator. During the day, shooting and fishing expeditions can be arranged. Mistress Mariquita MacGregor is an active concert singer, and musical evenings are given regularly at Cardney.

Where to Dine

Kinnaird House, Kinnaird Estate, on B898 northwest of Dunkeld (tel. 079682/440), brings a style of restaurant and a high-caliber cuisine never experienced in Dunkeld before. John Webber, the chef, has prepared meals for some of the golden palates of Europe, notably at Clieveden, former seat of Lady Astor. Now he's turned his considerable talent to this luxurious dining room. He cooks in the modern, post-nouvelle British and continental style, depending on fresh ingredients with changing menus based on the season. Lobster, Scottish salmon, the best of local beef, pork, and poultry go into his kitchen and turn up like delicate artwork on the plate. The establishment offers a set lunch for £13 ($21.45) and a table d'hôte dinner beginning at £25 ($41.25). Service is from 12:30 to 2pm and 7:30 to 9pm, when reservations are essential.

PITLOCHRY

After leaving Edinburgh, many motorists stop here, 71 miles away, for the night before continuing on the Highland road to Inverness. However, once they discover the charms of Pitlochry, they want to linger. This popular holiday resort center is a touring headquarters for the Valley of the Tummel.

It is particularly renowned for its **Pitlochry Festival Theatre,** Scotland's "theatre in the hills." (Telephone 0796/2680 for information.) Founded in 1951, the festival theater draws people from all over the world to its repertoire of plays, usually presented from May until late October. Performances in the evening begin at 8, and on Wed. and Sat. there is a matinee at 2pm. A theater next to Pitlochry's dam and salmon ladder opened in 1981.

Pitlochry Dam was created because a new power station was needed, but in effect the engineers created a new loch. The famous **salmon ladder** was built to help the struggling salmon upstream. An underwater portion of the ladder—a salmon-observation chamber—has been enclosed in glass to give sightseers a look. An exhibition (tel. 0796/3152) is open here from Easter to late October daily from 9:45am to 5:30pm, charging adults 50p (85¢), and children, 25p (40¢).

Pitlochry doesn't just entertain visitors, although it would appear that way in summer. It also produces scotch whisky and tweeds.

The tourist information center is at 22 Atholl Rd. (tel. 0796/2215).

Where to Stay and Dine

The Green Park Hotel, Clunie Bridge Road, Pitlochry, Perthside PH16 5JY (tel. 0796/3248), lies about half a mile from the center, at the northwest end of Pitlochry, and it's one of the best hotels in the area. Against a backdrop of woodland, the white-painted mansion with its carved eaves enjoys a scenic position, its lawn reaching to the shores of Loch Faskally, the only hotel so situated. Visitors who reserve well in advance get one of the half dozen or so rooms in the garden wing, all enjoying a view of the loch. All 37 rooms contain private baths or showers, TVs, and phones. It's customary to stay here on half-board terms, costing £39 ($64.35) to £46 ($75.90) per person daily. Guests enjoy drinks in a half-moon-shaped lounge overlooking the water. Many diners come here during festival season to enjoy the good food and wine. The hotel is supervised by Anne and Graham Brown. Dinner is served until 8:30pm, and many traditional Scottish dishes are featured. The Green Park is open from mid-March until November 1.

Pitlochry Hydro Hotel, Knockard Road, Pitlochry, Perthshire PH16 5JH (tel. 0796/2666), was originally known by the English gentry who came here in summer to enjoy the fresh air of the Perthshire Highlands. Built in the Scottish-baronial-mansion style, the hotel has kept up with modern improvements. It stands on large, well-manicured grounds, and offers, at latest count, 70 rooms with private baths, phones, and TVs. Ask for one of the turreted corner rooms when making a reservation. Singles cost £52 ($85.80) daily, and doubles go for £82 ($135.30), including a full Scottish breakfast, VAT, and service. A set dinner costs £12 ($19.80). The hotel has an indoor swimming pool and other leisure facilities.

Pine Trees Hotel, Strathview Terrace, Pitlochry, Perthshire PH16 5QR (tel. 0796/2121), is a charming, country-house hotel built in 1892 on 14 acres of private grounds, only about a 15-minute walk to the town center and the golf course, home of the Highland Open Championships. A well-appointed family-run hotel, Pine Trees has spacious, comfortable public rooms, an atmosphere of warmth and relaxation, and an enviable reputation for good food and wine. The 18 bedrooms have private baths or showers, TVs, and phones, and prices in the high season are £34 ($56.10) to £40 ($66) daily in a single, £60 ($99) to £70 ($115.50) in a double. Bar lunches and full luncheon and dinner menus are offered, with fresh and smoked salmon always on the menu. Trout and salmon fishing can usually be arranged.

Excursions from Pitlochry

From the town you can make excursions in almost any direction. Heading northwest for 3 miles on the A9, you come to the **Pass of Killiecrankie,** where "Bonnie Dundee" and his Jacobites won their victory over the armies of General Mackay fighting for King William in 1689. This is one of the scenic highlights of the area.

A **visitors center** (tel. 0796/3233) stands near the site of the famous battle. It presents an interesting exhibition and is also a center for rangers and naturalists. Dedicated Scots will answer questions on walks, whatever, which are possible in the area. The exhibition, visitors center, shop, and snackbar are open from 10am to 5pm daily from Easter weekend to May 25 and September 1 to the end of October, from 9:30am to 6pm daily from May 26 to the end of August.

If time remains, try to see another attraction, **Queen's View,** where Victoria herself picnicked in 1844. At the eastern end, Victoria looked down the length of the loch toward Schiehallion. The view is reached by taking the B8019 for 2½ miles northwest of Pitlochry. An obelisk commemorates the visit of the queen. The beauty spot, the Linn of Tummel, along with 40 acres, came to the National Trust for Scotland during World War II. It is filled with magnificent woodland walks, in which you can enjoy the Douglas fir, spruce, larch, oak, and sycamore.

BLAIR ATHOLL

Eight miles to the northwest of Pitlochry stands the gleaming white **Blair Castle** (tel. 079681/207), the home of the duke of Atholl, just off the A9. Built in Scottish baronial style and dating from 1269, it has the distinction of being the last castle in the British Isles to be besieged. Today, in more than 32 rooms open to the public, you can see impressive collections of furniture, paintings, china, lace, Masonic regalia, arms and armor, and Jacobite relics. It is open Easter week through the third Sun. in October. Hours are 10am to 6pm Mon. to Sat., from 2 to 6pm Sun. Last entry is at 5pm. Admission is £3 ($4.95) for adults, £2 ($3.30) for children. The duke of Atholl has the only official private army in Great Britain, known as the Atholl Highlanders.

For both food and lodging, you might prefer a stopover in Blair Atholl to Pitlochry. If so, I'd recommend the **Atholl Arms,** Blair Atholl, Perthside PH18 5SG (tel. 079681/205). Once lords and ladies who couldn't find room at Blair Castle stayed here, and some of the grand balls of old Perthshire were held here. Now the Atholl Arms is a roadside inn, built of stone and gabled with large bays, attracting motorists en route to Inverness. A cocktail lounge has been redecorated, and there's a public bar as well, attracting the locals. The ballroom has been turned into an arched-roof restaurant, complete with a minstrels' gallery. There's also a more intimate dining room with antiques and mahogany chairs. Both rooms offer a substantial menu. The 30 bedrooms are individually styled and well fitted, and each one I inspected had a completely different character. The rate is £29 ($47.85) daily in a single, £58 ($95.70) in a twin or double, each including a private bath or shower, phone, and TV. Rates include VAT, service, and a full breakfast. Bar snacks are served at lunch, and a four-course table d'hôte dinner, costing £12.50 ($20.63), is offered in the evening.

KILLIN

Just over the border from Tayside in the central region, Killin is a village on the Dochart at the lower end of Loch Tay. Lying 45 miles west of Perth by road, and 72 miles from Edinburgh, Killin is both a summer holiday resort and a winter sports center. The **Falls of Dochart** are world-famous, but the town is also noted for beauty spots, and there are sights of historical interest as well.

Killin Church contains a font more than 1,000 years old. Less than a quarter of a mile from the church stands an upright stone, said to mark the grave of Fingal. An island in the Dochart was the ancient burial place of the MacNab Clan.

The ruins of **Finlarig Castle** contain a beheading pit near the castle gate that was written about in Scott's *The Fair Maid of Perth.* Perched 1,000 feet above the loch, the castle was the seat of "Black Duncan of the Cowl," a notoriously ruthless chieftain of the Campbell Clan.

The summer-only tourist information center is on Main Street (tel. 05672/254).

Where to Stay and Dine

Bridge of Lochay, Killin, Perthshire FK21 8TS (tel. 05672/272), retains some of its 16th-century character, although it has seen many alterations and additions since that time. Half a mile from Killin, the "bridge"—an attractive, rambling, white-painted building—lies on the banks of the Lochay River, at the tip of Loch Tay. Frank W. Ogilvis, the owner, welcomes you to one of his 17 bedrooms, simply but comfortably furnished. Seven of these contain a private bath. The overnight charge is from £20 ($33) per person for a bed and a large Scottish breakfast. Guests can enjoy good drinks in one of two bars or sit in front of peat and log fires in the lounges. The cuisine is Scottish and continental. If you stay at least three nights, you'll be quoted a half-board tariff of £28 ($46.20) per person daily. The hotel is open from March to November.

Morenish Lodge Highland House, Killin, Perthshire FK21 8TX (tel. 05672/258), is a small Highland hotel, although formerly it was the shooting lodge of an earl, lying 200 feet above Loch Tay and less than 3 miles from Killin (on the A827 Aberfeldy road). The hotel, run by Graeme and Maureen Naylor, offers 13 double bedrooms, all with private baths. Furnishings are comfortable. Tariffs, which range from £30 ($49.50) to £34 ($56.10) per person daily, depending on the length of stay, includes B&B, a four-course dinner, and tax. All tariffs include VAT and a full breakfast. Many of the public rooms face the loch, and you can enjoy a good meal with wine in the Tay View room. Bar lunches are served only to residents. In the Laird's Bar, Scotch whisky, both blended and single malt, is served.

Dall Lodge Hotel, Main Street, Killin, Perthshire FK21 8TN (tel. 05672/217), is a 19th-century stone house overlooking the River Lochay a quarter of a mile north of Killin on the A827. The hotel specializes in serving many traditional Scottish foods, such as salmon, trout, venison, haggis, Aberdeen Angus beef, Scottish hill lamb, cloutie dumplings, and Scottish raspberry shortcake. A five-course dinner costs from £15 ($24.75). The hotel carries a wide range of fine wines and a comprehensive choice of malt Scotch whiskies. All eight bedrooms have hot and cold running water and hot beverage facilities, and they offer splendid views. Some units have private baths. The price for B&B is £25 ($41.25) per person daily. All tariffs include VAT.

---

2. The Grampian Region

Traveling north from the lochs—previewed in the prior section—heading toward Royal Deeside, you pass through Glen Shee and Glen Clunie, a most spectacular route that will give you your first taste of Highland scenery.

As you journey across uncrowded roads into Scotland's northeast, you'll review heather-covered moorland and peaty lochs, wood glens and salmon-filled rivers, granite-stone villages and fishing harbors, even North Sea beach resorts.

This is the Grampian region, with such centers as Aberdeen and Braemar, and such sights as Balmoral Castle and the Whisky Trail. Even the queen comes here for holidays.

BRAEMAR

This little Deeside resort is the site of the **Royal Highland Gathering,** which takes place there annually, either in late August or early September. It is usually attended by Queen Elizabeth. The "royal link" dates from the 1840s when Queen Victoria first attended the games.

The capital of the Deeside Highlands, Braemar is overrun with foreign visitors, as well as the British, during the gathering. Anyone thinking of attending would be wise to make application for accommodation anywhere within a 20-mile radius of Braemar not later than early April.

The gathering in Braemar is the most famous of the many Highland games. The spectacular occasion is held in the **Princess Royal and Duke of Fife Memorial Park.** Competitions include tossing the caber, throwing the hammer, sprinting, vaulting, a tug-o'-war, the long leap, Highland dancing, putting a 16-pound ball, sword dancing, relay races, and, naturally, a bagpiping contest. At a vast refreshment tent, Scottish lassies serve tea, coffee, buns, and other refreshments.

The romantic 17th-century **Braemar Castle** (tel. 03397/41213) lies half a mile northeast of Braemar on the A93. A fully furnished private residence of architectural grace, scenic charm, and historical interest, it is the seat of Capt. A. A. Farquharson of Invercauld. Opening onto the Dee River, it was built in 1628 by the Earl of Mar. John Farquharson of Inverey, the "Black Colonel," attacked and burned it in 1689. The castle is built in the shape of an L, with a spiral stairway and a circular main tower. Fully furnished, it has barrel-vaulted ceilings and an underground prison, and is known for its remarkable star-shaped defensive curtain wall. It can be visited from May 1 until the first Mon. in October daily from 10am to 6pm, costing £1.50 ($2.50) for adults, 75p ($1.25) for children. The castle has a gift shop, and a free car park.

Braemar lies 85 miles from Edinburgh and 58 miles from Aberdeen. Its summer only tourist information center is at Cluniebank Road (tel. 03397/600).

Where to Stay and Dine

Invercauld Arms Hotel, Braemar, Aberdeenshire AB3 5YR (tel. 03397/ 41605), is a lovely old granite building of which the original part dates back to the 18th century. In cool weather there's a roaring log fire on the hearth, and the staff offers you traditional Highland hospitality. You can go hill walking and see deer, golden eagles, and other wildlife. Fishing and, in winter, skiing are other pursuits in the nearby area. To spend a few days in this thoroughly pleasant hotel visiting fine old castles and whisky distilleries makes a perfect respite. In the pub close by you'll meet the "ghillies" and "stalkers" and then return to the Castleview Restaurant to sample a "Taste of Scotland" with fresh Dee salmon, Aberdeen Angus beef, venison, and grouse, together with the "dreaded haggis," on the extensive menu of local specialties. Of course, you'll find kippers and porridge with the full Scottish breakfast that is included in the room rates. A coffeeshop serves light meals, and the well-known Colonel's Bed bar offers entertainment on occasion. The hotel rents 68 well-furnished bedrooms, each with private bath, phone, and TV. B&B costs £52 ($85.80) per person daily in a single, rising to £75 ($123.75) in a double or twin.

Fife Arms Hotel, Mar Road, Braemar, Aberdeenshire AB3 5YN (tel. 03397/41644), near Braemar, was originally built in the 19th century as a holiday home for the duke of Fife, but was later converted into a stagecoach inn for passengers and horses. It boasts an elegant facade of intricately patterned gingerbread, multiple chimneys, gables, a Gothic portico, and a solid construction of pinkish sandstone. Inside, many modernizations have removed much of the 19th century, but it remains a comfortable and familiar place much favored by families. It's a quintessential Scottish provincial hotel, with a coffee buffet and a glass deli case in the lobby dispensing snacks. There are two bars on the premises, as well as a restaurant. In all, the hotel rents 87 centrally heated bedrooms, each pleasantly outfitted with functional pieces. Many contain private baths or showers. Half-board terms range from £26 ($42.90) to £32 ($52.80) per person daily, depending on the plumbing and the accommodation.

BALLATER

On the Dee River, with the Grampian mountains in the background, Ballater is a holiday resort center where visitors flock to view one of Scotland's most popular sightseeing attractions, Balmoral Castle (see below).

The town still centers around its **Station Square,** where the royal family used to be photographed as they arrived to spend holidays. The railway has since been closed.

From Ballater you can drive west to view the magnificent scenery of **Glen Muick** and **Lochnagar,** where you'll see herds of deer.

A summer-only tourist information center is at Station Square (tel. 03397/55306). Ballater lies 111 miles from Edinburgh and 41 miles from Aberdeen.

Where to Stay and Dine

Craigendarroch Hotel and Country Club, Braemar Road, Ballater, Aberdeenshire AB3 5XA (tel. 03397/55858), built in the Scottish baronial style, is set amid old trees on a 28-acre estate a few minutes' drive outside Ballater. The comfort of the 20th century has been added, but the owners have tried to maintain a 19th-century aura. The public rooms include a regal, oaken staircase and a large sitting room, but the feature is a leisure club, including a spa pool, two swimming pools, a sauna, and a solarium, along with various games and a beauty salon. Tennis courts are outside, and there is a dry ski slope. Views from the bedrooms open onto the village of Ballater and the River Dee.

There are 51 accommodations, each furnished in an individual style, but all with color TVs, direct-dial phones, radios, hairdryers, trouser presses, and private baths and showers. Rates are from £115 ($189.75) to £160 ($264) daily for two persons, with singles paying £25 ($41.25) less, tariffs including breakfast and VAT. The public facilities are luxurious, especially the study with oak paneling, a log fire, and book-lined shelves. In the Oaks Restaurant, guests enjoy such specialties as local game, Scottish beef, trout, and salmon. Fine crystal, fresh flowers, and bone china complement the menu. The French-style Café Jardin also serves light meals and drinks, and the Lochnagal Restaurant built above the club offers good views.

Tullich Lodge, Ballater, Aberdeenshire AB3 5SB (tel. 03397/55406), on the A93, 1½ miles east of Ballater, is a turreted country house built in the Scottish-baronial style, standing in 5 acres of its own gardens and woods above Royal Deeside and Ballater. The attractive hotel is tastefully decorated and furnished, often with antiques, its brass fittings and wood paneling providing the traditional touches.

Your pleasant hosts, Hector Macdonald and Neil Bannister, offer only 10 bedrooms, but they're of generous size and are beautifully furnished. All contain private baths or showers and phones. Half-board rates are £84 ($138.6) per person daily in a single or double. The lodge closes from December through March. Its dining room, commanding panoramic views of the "royal valley," serves some of the finest food along Royal Deeside. One of the chef's specialties is casseroles, although he does all the standard dishes with above-average flair, including locally caught trout and salmon, game and especially venison in season, as well as crab and lobster. A table d'hôte dinner, served from 7:30 to 9pm daily, goes for about £20 ($33). A bar luncheon is at 1pm with no fried foods. It's essential to make a reservation. In an amusing bar, you can order from a good selection of malt whiskies. To get the most out of the surrounding countryside, as well as this special hotel, I'd recommend whenever possible a stay of a minimum of two nights. It's a good place to unpack your luggage and settle in for a bit.

Balmoral Castle

"This dear paradise" is how Queen Victoria described this castle, rebuilt in the Scottish baronial style by her beloved Albert. It was completed in 1855. Today Balmoral, 8 miles west of Ballater, is still a private residence of the British sovereign. Albert, the prince consort, acquired the property in 1847, and the royal family first arrived there in 1848. As the little castle left by the Farquharsons proved too small, the present castle was rebuilt. Its principal feature is a 100-foot tower. On the grounds are many memorials to the royal family. The grounds can be visited in May, June, and July from 10am to 5pm Mon. to Sat. Visitors can also get a view of an exhibition of paintings and works of art in the castle ballroom. The remainder of the castle interior is never open to the public. In addition, there are country walks and pony trekking. Admission to the grounds and art exhibition is £1.50 ($2.50) for adults; children, free. For information, phone 03384/334.

BANCHORY

On lower Deeside, this resort is rich in woodland and river scenery. From this base, you can take excursions to two of the most popular castles in the Grampian region, Crathes and Craigievar.

Banchory lies 118 miles from Edinburgh and 17 miles from Aberdeen. It operates a summer-only tourist information center at the Dee Street Car Park (tel. 03302/2000).

Crathes Castle and Gardens (tel. 033044/525), 3 miles east of Banchory on A93, has royal historical associations dating from 1323, when the lands of Leys were granted to the Burnett family by King Robert the Bruce. The Horn of Leys, said to have been given by Bruce to symbolize the gift, is in the great hall. The castle's features include remarkable late-16th-century painted ceilings. The garden is a composite of eight separate gardens, which give a display all year. The great yew hedges date from 1702. The grounds are ideal for nature study, and there are five trails, including a long-distance layout, with ranger service. The complex includes a licensed restaurant, visitor center with permanent exhibitions, souvenir shop, wayfaring course, children's adventure playground, picnic area, and car park.

The grounds and gardens are open daily from 9:30am to sunset. The castle, visitor center, shop, and restaurant are open Easter weekend to October 28 daily from 11am to 6pm. A combined ticket to see everything costs £3 ($4.95) for adults, with children paying half price. Reductions are available for visitors wishing to visit the castle or the gardens only.

Structurally unchanged since its completion in 1626, **Craigievar Castle** (tel. 033983/83635) is an example of Scottish baronial architecture at its greatest height. The location is 6 miles south of Alford on A980 or 26 miles west of Aberdeen. Original molded plaster ceilings are to be seen in most rooms. The castle has been continually inhabited by the descendants of the builder, William Forbes, and is now preserved by the National Trust for Scotland. It is open May and June as well as the month of September daily from 2 to 6pm. Hours from July to the end of August are from 11am to 6pm (last tour at 5:15pm). The grounds are open all year from 9:30am to sunset daily. Admission is £2.40 ($3.95) for adults, £1.20 ($2) for children.

Where to Stay and Dine

The premier place to stay is **Invery House,** Bridge of Feugh, Banchory, Kincardineshire AB3 3NJ (tel. 03302/4782), a Georgian mansion of great charm, standing in its own gardens and wooded grounds. It's small, only 14 bedrooms, but its reputation is big as one of the leading hotels of Scotland. The proprietors, Sheila and Stewart Spence, have sensitively and painstakingly restored this mansion until today it is one of the grand addresses of the Grampian region. Invery House is that dream of what a Scottish country-house hotel should be (but all too often isn't). Antiques and oil paintings add the necessary charm, but all the modern necessities are here, too. The location is on 40 acres of gardens and woodland opening onto the banks of the River Feugh.

Mr. and Mrs. Spence have paid particular care to their beautifully furnished bedrooms, each one named after one of the novels of Sir Walter Scott, who worked on his romance *Marmion* here. Sometimes antiques grace the rooms, and everywhere you look to see the knowing touch of a decorator. Each bedroom has such amenities as a luxurious bathroom, phone, and TV. Rates range from £95 ($156.75) to £105 ($173.25) daily in a single, rising to £145 ($239.25) to £165 ($272.25) in a double including a five-course gourmet dinner. The hotel is also the outstanding dining choice in the area. Fresh produce goes into the imaginative dishes, which are handled skillfully in the kitchen and served with a certain formality. Dining hours are daily from 12:15 to 2:15pm and 7:15 to 9:45pm.

Raemoir House, Banchory, Kincardineshire AB3 4ED (tel. 03302/4884), is an 18th-century manor standing on 3,500 acres of grounds with such sporting attractions as shooting, fishing, and riding. It lies 2½ miles north of Banchory on A980. It is a journey into nostalgia, with its ballroom, antiques, fine tapestries, and log fires burning in the colder months. The rooms are handsomely decorated, most of them quite large, and all of the 28 bedchambers or suites contain private baths, phones, and TVs.

What is so lovely about Scotland is its curious mixtures—in this case, an 18th-century manor house with its own helipad. Meals are served in an attractive Georgian dining room, featuring a standard repertoire of familiar dishes, rather well done. Service is informal and prompt. The B&B rate ranges from £55 ($90.75) daily single, £85 ($140.25) in a double, and £105 ($173.25) for two in a suite. All prices include VAT and morning tea or coffee. The hotel is run just like a private house—no keys to bedrooms doors, but you can bolt yourself in for privacy. The adjoining Ha' Hoose with rentable rooms was once used by Mary Queen of Scots. Facilities include an all-weather tennis court and a nine-hole mini-golf course on the grounds.

Tor-Na-Coille, Inchmarlo Road, Banchory, Kincardineshire AB3 4AB (tel. 03302/2242), is a country-house hotel—really a Victorian mansion—standing on its own wooded grounds of about 6 acres. Public rooms are suitably spacious, most comfortable, and the whisky always tastes better in the modern bar. If you're on your way to see Balmoral Castle or to attend the Highland gathering at Braemar, you will be able to relax here, enjoying the gracious hospitality, as did Charlie Chaplin and his family, who once used the place as a retreat. The 25 bedrooms, many quite large, and restful and all of them have private baths, color TVs, phones, radios, and coffee makers. Singles cost from £44 ($72.60) to £70 ($115.50) daily, and doubles rent for £65 ($107.25) to £86 ($141.90), including a full breakfast and VAT. The hotel is interesting architecturally, and the room you may be assigned could have much character. Lunches are light meals in the bar, including smoked venison sausage blended with rum and red wine. Sunday lunch is a grander affair, when the main dishes include roast beef, turkey, and leg of pork. Food at night is by candlelight, and here might be your chance to try real Scottish salmon (the salmon leap at the Falls of Feugh nearby). Dinner is likely to feature the chef's special pheasant. The hotel has a high reputation for its food.

Banchory Lodge, Dee Street, Banchory, Kincardineshire AB3 3HS (tel. 03302/2625), built in 1738, was once the home of a well-known Deeside family. It is an 18th-century country house with much Georgian charm. On its own grounds, on the banks of the Dee, where it is joined by the Water of the Feugh, the lodge is open all year, accommodating guests in some 24 bedrooms, many of which over-look the river, all with private baths, phones, and TVs. The B&B rate is about £45 ($74.25) daily in a single, £80 ($132) in a double or twin. In the dining room, over-looking the river, furnishings and decor are in period style. Specialties include fresh Dee salmon and Aberdeen Angus roast beef. Guests can fish from the lawn or in one of the hotel's boats by arrangement.

ABERDEEN

The harbor in this seaport in the northeast of Scotland is one of the largest fish-ing ports in the country, filled with kipper and deep-sea trawlers. The **Fish Market** is well worth a visit, as it's the liveliest in Britain.

Bordered by fine sandy beaches (delightful if you're a polar bear), Scotland's third city, 130 miles from Edinburgh, is often called "the granite city," as its build-ings are constructed largely of granite, in pink or gray, hewn from the Rubislaw quarries.

Aberdeen is the capital of the oil workers who help harvest the riches from six North Sea oilfields. Their number has dwindled in recent years, however. The city lies on the banks of the salmon- and trout-filled Don and Dee rivers. Spanning the Don is the **Brig o' Balgownie,** a steep Gothic arch, begun in 1285.

In Castlegate is the **Mercat Cross,** a hexagonally shaped structure, built in 1686 and considered the handsomest of the old crosses in Scotland.

University of Aberdeen (tel. 0224/40241) is a fusion of two separate col-leges. King's College, the older, was founded under a papal bull issued in 1495. It contains the oldest school of medicine in Great Britain. The college's chapel is topped by a closed (imperial) crown that was erected about 1505 but was blown down in a storm and quickly replaced in 1633 by an exact copy. Marischal College, founded in 1593, is recognized as one of the finest granite buildings in the world. The two colleges were rival institutions until a royal ordinance enacted in 1860 united them both under the title of the present university.

The university is in old Aberdeen, as is the **Cathedral of St. Machar,** founded in 1131, although the present structure dates from the 15th century. Its splendid heraldic ceiling contains three rows of shields representing the kings and princes of Europe along with the Scottish ecclesiastical and aristocratic hierarchy. The modern stained-glass windows are magnificent, the work of Douglas Strachan. The cathedral is open daily from 9am to 5pm. Its phone number is 0224/485988, and that of the manse is 0224/483688.

Provost Skene's House, 45 Guestrow, is named for a rich merchant who was lord provost of Aberdeen from 1676 to 1685. Off Broad Street, it is now a museum with period rooms and artifacts of domestic life. Provost Skene's kitchen has been converted into a café serving tea, coffee, and light meals. Admission is free, and it can be visited from 10am to 5pm Mon. to Sat. For more information, telephone 0224/641086. There's parking available.

Where to Stay

Aberdeen, Scotland's Floral Capital, welcomes visitors all year. There's a wide choice of accommodation in the city: hotels, guesthouses, B&Bs, and self-catering units. Many hotels offer bargain rates at weekends. At the **tourist information cen-ter,** St. Nicholas House, Broad Street, Aberdeen, Aberdeenshire AB9 1DE (tel. 0224/632727), a helpful staff will book your accommodation and advise on the attractions of the area.

If you prefer to reserve in advance, I have some selections.

Caledonian Thistle Hotel, 10-14 Union Terrace, Aberdeen, Aberdeenshire AB9 1HE (tel. 0224/640233), sits in a grandly detailed, stone-fronted, 19th-century building in the center of Aberdeen. Recent restorations have added a veneer of Georgian-era gloss, which contributes to one of the most elegant series of public rooms in town. The lobby-level bar and Restaurant on the Terrace (recommended separately) are especially charming, and there is a café bar and restaurant on the ground floor. The hotel offers free parking in a walled-in lot on a street paralleling the hotel. The 77 rooms are at the top of a 19th-century stairwell, with Corinthian columns and a free-standing atrium. There is also elevator service. Each bedroom contains a TV, radio, mini-bar, private bath, and warmly upholstered furniture. Singles cost £68 ($112.20) daily; doubles or twins, £80 ($132) to £105 ($173.25).

Bucksburn Moat House Hotel, Oldmeldrum Road, Bucksburn, Aberdeen, Aberdeenshire AB2 9LN (tel. 0224/713911), is 4 miles north of Aberdeen by the A96 and just 2 miles from the airport. The hotel takes its name from the "burn" running underneath the hotel. Part of the building was converted from an original grain mill in the 1600s. The hotel is especially popular with business people, who enjoy the 98 large, well-equipped bedrooms, all with private baths, phones, TVs, mini-bars, trouser presses, and hairdryers. Singles rent for £75 ($123.75) daily and doubles go for £85 ($140.25). The Lairds Bar is busy serving bar lunches and bar-suppers, while up in the comfortable surroundings of the Mariner Restaurant, you can choose either table d'hôte or à la carte meals, later retiring to the Captains bar for a "wee nip o'whisky." This hotel is traditional but with modern conveniences.

Stakis Tree Tops Hotel, 161 Springfield Rd., Aberdeen, Aberdeenshire AB9 2QH (tel. 0224/33377), a 5-minute drive west of the center of Aberdeen, is a comfortable hotel built in the 1960s, with a sweeping white façade of traditional design. The windows of its more than 114 contemporary bedrooms look over landscaped grounds. Each contains a private, tile-lined bath, color TV, and phone, and many other extras for your comfort. Singles cost £60 ($99) to £102 ($168.30) daily, and doubles go for £90 ($148.50) to £120 ($198). The leather-covered chairs of the paneled main bar offer a cozy spot for conversation. You can dine in either the elegant Garden Room or in Rocco's Ristorante, the bistro-style Italian restaurant. The hotel invites guests to take advantage of the Leisure Club, with swimming pool, whirlpool, multi-gym, sauna, jogging machine, sunbeds, two all-weather tennis courts, and sports training.

Where to Dine

The leading choice for dining is **The Restaurant on the Terrace,** Caledonian Thistle Hotel, 10-14 Union Terrace (tel. 0224/640233). Both it and its adjacent bar were renovated into one of the most elegant Georgian restorations in Aberdeen. Beneath a high ceiling capped with elaborate re-creations of antique moldings and embellishments, you dine on such specialties as homemade seafood bisque topped with crème fraîche, suprême of River Dee salmon with watercress sauce, and medallions of Scottish lamb sautéed in walnut oil with a honey-and-rosemary sauce. Full meals costing from £16 ($26.40) are served daily from 12:30 to 2pm and 6:30 to 10pm. On Sun. night the last orders are at 9:30pm and no lunch is offered on Sat. At lunches, selections from a carving table are offered, costing from £10 ($16.50) for a complete meal with all the works, proving popular with the business community. Reservations at dinner are suggested.

Atlantis, 16 Bon Accord Crescent (tel. 0224/591403), is one of the best seafood restaurants in town. It's in a comfortably furnished basement near the center of town. You can enjoy several preparations of lobster, fish chowder, and an array of sole, scampi, and halibut. Some meat dishes are offered, as well as fresh vegetables, salads, and desserts. Full meals cost from £18 ($29.70) to £25 ($41.25) per person and are served from noon to 2pm and 7 to 10pm; closed Sat. lunch, all day Sun., some holidays, and for about 2 weeks at Christmas.

Silver Darling, Pocra Quay, Footdee (tel. 0224/576229), continues to win friends, drawn to its North Pier location for a "taste of the sea," as provided by chef and co-owner Didier Dejean. In the vicinity of a pilot roundhouse with a tower, the restaurant could only specialize in seafood and outstanding fish, and it does so exceedingly well. Fish is grilled in the style of Provence and seasoned with the classic *herbs de provence,* including garlic and basil. A set lunch is offered for £10.50

($17.35) and up, with an à la carte dinner averaging £25 ($41.25). Service is from noon to 2pm and 7 to 10pm; closed lunch Sat. and Sun. Reservations are necessary.

A Place in the Country

Pittodrie House Hotel, Pitcaple, near Inverurie, Aberdeenshire AB5 9HS (tel. 04676/444), 21 miles northwest of Aberdeen, was originally one of the castles in the area, built in 1490, but it was burned down by that avid Covenanter, the duke of Montrose. Rebuilt in 1675, it was a family home changed into a country-house hotel when Royal Deeside came into prominence through Queen Victoria's adoption of Balmoral as her holiday retreat. Twelve beautifully furnished bedrooms are offered, costing £44 ($72.60) daily for singles, £82 ($135.30) for doubles, tariffs including a full breakfast, service, and VAT. Rooms contain private baths or showers, phones, and TVs. Antiques and oil paintings decorate the public rooms, where open fires make the atmosphere cozy. The elegant restaurant serves such main dishes as venison, grouse, partridge, pheasant, or woodcock, depending on the season, and fresh fish, such as turbot, sea trout, and salmon. Dinners cost from £22 ($36.30) and are served daily from 7:30pm to last orders at 8:45pm. Bar lunches are served from 12:30 to 1:30pm Mon. to Sat. The location is 1¾ miles southwest of Pitcaple by the Chapel of Garioch Road.

Excursions in "Castle Country"

Aberdeen is the center of "castle country," as 40 inhabited castles lie within a 40-mile radius. Some of the most popular castle excursions are previewed below. For two others, refer to Banchory, above.

South of Aberdeen on the North Sea coast, set on a promontory with three sides protected by cliffs, **Dunnottar Castle** (tel. 0569/62173), about 2 miles south of Stonehaven (half a mile off the Montrose-Stonehaven road, the A92), was erected, beginning in the 14th century, as the home and fortress of the Keiths, the earls Marischal and Wardens of the Regalia for the Scottish kings. According to legend, an early Christian settlement on the site, more than 150 feet above the sea, was founded by St. Ninian in the 5th century. A short-lived stone house of worship erected in the 13th century caused the excommunication of Sir William Keith a century later because he started his castle keep on what were still consecrated grounds. The partially restored castle can be visited from 9am to 6pm Mon. to Fri. from 2 to 5pm Sun. Admission is £1.25 ($2.05) for adults, 50p (85¢) for children.

Dunnottar Castle was the last fortress to hold out against Cromwell in the Civil War. During this conflict, the Royal Regalia of Scotland, under the protection of the earl Marischal, was smuggled out of the castle and taken to **Kineff Old Church,** a mile closer to Stonehaven, where it was hidden under the floor from 1652 until the Restoration in 1660. The church of that day was replaced by the present structure. It is reached by taking the B967 off the A92 and following a little country road.

Muchalls Castle (no phone) was constructed by the Burnetts of Leys in 1619. Overlooking the sea, it is now owned by Mr. and Mrs. Maurice A. Simpson who allow the public to visit in June and July from 2:30 to 4:30pm Sun. and Tue. Any other time, it may be visited by written arrangement only. Admission is 60p ($1) for adults, 20p (35¢) for children under 12. The castle has intricate plaster ceilings and fireplaces as well as a secret staircase. The castle is inland from the village of Muchalls, 5 miles north of Stonehaven and 9 miles south of Aberdeen.

At **Drum Castle,** the handsome mansion (tel. 03308/204) was added in 1619, but the great square tower dates from the late 13th century, making it one of the three oldest tower houses in the country. Historic Drum lies 10 miles west of Aberdeen, off the A93. The castle is open May to September daily from 2 to 6pm, charging £2.40 ($3.95) for adults, £1.20 ($2) for children. The grounds are open all year from 9:30am to dusk, and admission is free or by donation.

Considered one of the most impressive of the fortresslike castles of Mar, **Castle Fraser** (tel. 03303/463) stands in a 25-acre parkland and woodsy setting. The sixth laird, Michael Fraser, launched the structure in 1575, and it was completed in 1636. The castle is full of interest and charm. Its great hall is spectacular, and you can wander around the grounds, including a walled garden. It is open from the first of May to the end of September daily 2 to 6pm, charging an admission of £2.40 ($3.95) for adults, £1.20 ($2) for children. The castle is off the B933, 3 miles south of Kemnay and 16 miles west of Aberdeen.

The ruins of the ancient seat of the earls of Mar, **Kildrummy Castle** (tel. 09755/71264), is on the A97 in the small village of Kildrummy, 35 miles from Aberdeen. It is the most extensive example of a 13th-century castle in Scotland. You can see the four round towers, the hall, and the chapel from the original structure. The great gatehouse and other remains date from the 16th century. The castle played a major role in Scottish history up to 1715, when it was dismantled. It is open to visitors April to September from 9:30am to 7pm Mon. to Sat., 2 to 7pm Sun. Hours from October to March are the same except for closing at 4pm. Admission is £1 ($1.65) for adults, 70p ($1.15) for children.

While you're in the area, you might want to stay at **Kildrummy Castle Hotel** (tel. 09755/71288), about 1½ miles south from the village on the A97, overlooking the ruined castle. This 19th-century graystone mansion, set in acres of landscaped gardens, contains 16 bedrooms, all with baths, color TVs, phones, hairdryers, and tea and coffee makers. The proprietor rents singles from £43 ($70.95) daily and doubles from £78 ($128.70), except in January and February when the hotel is closed. The public rooms have oak-paneled walls and ceilings, mullioned windows, and cushioned windowseats. The drawing room and bar open onto a flagstone terrace from which you can see the gardens of the castle. Traditional Scottish food is served in the handsome dining room, including such dishes as Cullen skink (smoked haddock soup), filet of sole stuffed with smoked Scottish salmon, and Aberdeen Angus steaks. Meals cost from £11 ($18.15) for lunch to £18.50 ($30.55) for dinner.

Near the village of Fyvie, on the Aberdeen-Banff road, **Fyvie Castle** (tel. 06516/266) was opened to the public (1986) by the National Trust for Scotland. The oldest part of the castle, dating from the 13th century, has been called the grandest existing example of Scottish baronial architecture. There are five towers, one each named after Fyvie's five families—the Prestons, Meldrums, Setons, Gordons, and Leiths—who lived there over 5 centuries. Originally built in a royal hunting forest, Fyvie means "deer hill" in Gaelic. The interior, reflecting the opulence of the Edwardian era, was created by the first Lord Leith of Fyvie, a steel magnate. His collections contain arms and armor, 16th-century tapestries, and artworks by Raeburn, Gainsborough, Romney, and Batoni. The castle, rich in ghosts, curses, and legends, is open in May daily from 2 to 6pm, June to August 11am to 6pm. Admission is £2.40 ($3.95) for adults and £1.20 ($2) for children. Fyvie Castles stands 8 miles southeast of Turriff off the A947 and 25 miles northwest of Aberdeen.

Haddo House (tel. 06515/440) was the creation of William Adam in 1731, having taken the place of an earlier structure. This Palladian house, now owned by the National Trust for Scotland, has been the home of the Gordons of Haddo for more than 5 centuries. It is inhabited by the marchioness of Aberdeen and Temair, who has turned it into the headquarters of the Haddo House Choral and Operatic Society. It is impressive in its way and also looks homelike enough for people actually to live here. The country park of some 180 acres surrounding the house is maintained by the Grampian Regional Council. The house is open from Easter weekend to October 31 from 2 to 6pm daily (last entrance at 5:15pm). Admission is £2.40 ($3.95) for adults, £1.20 ($2) for children. The park is open daily all year from 9:30am to dusk, and garden hours are 9:30am to 8pm daily. The house is off the B999 some 4 miles north of Pitmedden, 19 miles north of Aberdeen.

A Transport Museum at Alford

About 25 miles west of Aberdeen on the A944 at Alford is the **Grampian Transport Museum** (tel. 09755/62292), where exhibits and displays trace the development of transport in northeast Scotland. Some 100 vehicles of all types—bicycles, motorcycles, veteran and classic cars, steam vehicles, fire engines, agricultural vehicles, trucks, horse-drawn carriages, trams, and sledges—can be seen, several dating from before 1900. There are also photograph displays and reconstructions of a village wheelwright's shop and a 1930s garage workshop. An added, nonvehicular attraction is the Mortier dance organ, the largest in Scotland, built in 1923, whose music enhances the atmosphere of days gone by. The museum is open from the end of March to the end of September, as well as weekends in October, daily from 10:30am to 5pm. Admission is £1.50 ($2.50) for adults, 70p ($1.15) for children.

The ticket also admits visitors to the **Alford Valley Railway Museum,** housed in the reconstructed Alford village station of the Great North of Scotland Railway. On Sun. in season, trips are offered on the Alford Valley line's passenger trains, running on 2-foot-gauge tracks.

XXII

HIGHLANDS AND ISLANDS

1. SPEYSIDE

2. INVERNESS AND LOCH NESS

3. FORT WILLIAM AND LOCHABER

4. KYLE OF LOCHALSH AND SKYE

5. OBAN AND DISTRICT

6. THE INNER HEBRIDES

7. KINTYRE, ARRAN, AND ISLAY

From their romantic glens and their rugged mountainous landscapes, the Highlands suggest a timeless antiquity. Off the coast, mysterious islands, such as Skye with its jagged peaks, rise from the sea, inviting further exploration. These lands are sparsely inhabited even today, and much wildlife, such as the red deer, still flourishes.

As the unofficial capital of the Highlands, Inverness is the terminus of the rail journey from London, a distance of some 570 miles. Many visitors use it as a base for Highland adventures.

From Inverness, you can journey along Loch Ness (especially if you're a monster watcher) to Fort William, dominated by Ben Nevis, the highest mountain in Britain. Oban is the main resort on Scotland's West Highland coastline. It is also one of the major ports for journeying to the Hebridean islands.

If at all possible, try to explore some of these islands, the largest of which is Lewis, where the Standing Stones of Callanish, a prehistoric monument, evokes Stonehenge. Numerous inter-island air services allow you to go "island hopping."

Many pleasure trips are possible to the islands in the Firth of Clyde, Scotland's greatest yachting center. Dominated by the peak of Goat Fell, Arran is the largest of these Clyde islands.

1. Speyside

Aviemore is the winter sports capital of Britain, but it also enjoys mass popularity in summer. Aviemore Centre, previewed below, is Scotland's most modern holiday resort, an all-year, all-weather center, endowed with a multitude of outdoor pursuits, such as golfing, angling, skiing, or ice skating.

Those seeking a more traditional Scottish ambience will gravitate to one of the many Speyside villages, each with its own attractions and atmosphere. Ranking next to Aviemore, Grantown-on-Spey is another major center.

The Spey is the fastest-flowing river in the British Isles, famed not only for its scenery but also for its salmon and ski slopes.

Finally, on your way to Inverness, you might care to stop off at the old cathedral city of Elgin.

Our first stop up the Spey follows.

NEWTONMORE

This Highland resort on Speyside is a good center for the Grampian and Monadhliath Mountains, and it offers excellent fishing, golf, pony trekking, and hill walking. It lies 113 miles from Edinburgh and 43 miles from Inverness. Most motorists zip through it on the way to Aviemore, but sightseers may want to stop off and visit the **Clan MacPherson House and Museum,** Main Street (tel. 05403/332), at the south end of the village. Displayed are clan relics and memorials, including the Black Chanter and Green Banner as well as a "charmed sword," and the broken fiddle of the freebooter James MacPherson—a Scottish Robin Hood. Sentenced to death in 1700, he is said to have played the dirge "MacPherson's Rant" on his fiddle as he stood on the gallows at Banff. He then offered the instrument to anyone who would think well of him. There were no takers, so he smashed it. The museum is open from May to September daily from 10am to 5:30pm, Sun. from 2:30 to 5:30pm. Admission is free, but contributions toward the museum's upkeep are appreciated.

A track from the village climbs past the Calder River to Loch Dubh and the massive Carn Ban (3,087 feet), where eagles fly. Castle Cluny, ancient seat of the MacPherson chiefs, is 6 miles west of Newtonmore.

Where to Stay and Dine

Ard-Na-Coille, Kingussie Road, Newtonmore, Inverness-shire PH20 1AY (tel. 05403/214). Today the antiques that fill the interior of this elegant house evoke its earlier days as a hunting lodge. It was built in 1920 by the director of a Scottish oil company, who used it as a hunting seat only 6 weeks a year. Amid racks of antique porcelain, spacious and high-ceilinged bathrooms, which haven't been altered since they were built, and old English engravings, the owners rent seven rooms, all with private baths or showers. Each room is tastefully furnished. The cost for B&B is £28 ($46.20) to £35 ($57.75) per person daily. Clients who opt for a freshly prepared dinner pay another £17.50 ($28.90). Ard-Na-Coille translates from the Gaelic as "high in the woods."

KINGUSSIE

Your next stop along the Spey might be at this little summer holiday resort and winter ski center (it's pronounced King-youcie), the capital of Badenoch, a district known as "the drowned land" because the Spey can flood the valley when the snows of a severe winter melt in the spring. Kingussie lies 117 miles from Edinburgh and 41 miles from Inverness. You can visit the 6-acre **Highland Folk Museum,** on Duke Street, just off High Street (tel. 0540/661307), with its collection of artifacts, including weaponry, bagpipes, and fiddles, illustrating more than 2 centuries of Highland customs, plus the work of craftspeople. Naturally, there are tartans. A furnished cottage with a mill, and a farming shed that has been expanded to become a farming museum, stand on the grounds. It is open from 10am to 6pm Mon. to Sat. and from 2 to 6pm Sun. from April to October. The remainder of the year, it is open from 10am to 3pm Mon. to Fri. Admission is £1.50 ($2.50) for adults, 75p

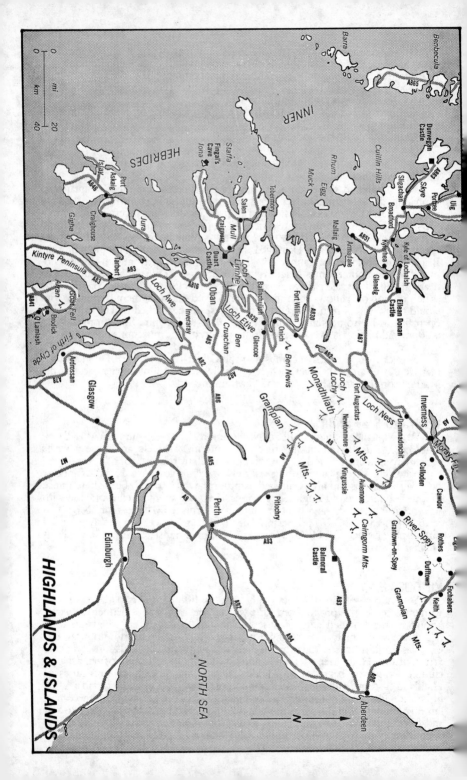

($1.15) for children. Live events and demonstrations, including piping, caber tossing, spinning, horseshoeing, and baking, are held most days, except Sun. in July and August, with a limited program in June and September.

In summer, it has a tourist information center at Caledonia Buildings, King Street (tel. 0540/661297).

The **Highland Wildlife Park,** at Kincraig, near Kingussie (tel. 05404/270), run by the Royal Zoological Society of Scotland, encloses a living showcase of Scottish animals, past and present. It has a large drive-through reserve, where red deer and European bison roam, plus a walk around area with a variety of mammals and birds, ranging from capercaillie to wolves. There is a visitor center with a café, shop, and toilets, and the park also has a lookout point for a view of the area and a place to have a picnic. It is open from late March to October from 10am to 4pm in spring and autumn and from 10am to 5pm in summer. Admission is £7 ($11.55) per car, regardless of the number of passengers. Kingcraig is a little village at a scenic spot at the northern end of Loch Insh, overlooking the Spey Valley to the west and the Cairngorm mountains to the east, lying 6 miles from Aviemore.

Where to Stay and Dine

If you'd like to stop here instead of at Aviemore, I'd recommend the following establishments:

Osprey Hotel, Ruthven Road, Kingussie, Inverness-shire PH21 1EN (tel. 0540/661510), is a convenient place to stay, with eight comfortable bedrooms, all with hot and cold running water and central heating. Four contain private baths. The proprietors charge from £22 ($36.30) to £40 ($49.50) per person for B&B. A dinner costs from £18 ($29.70). The place is known for its pure, fresh food, 100% homemade. Fresh, prime Scottish meats are served, including local venison, beef, lamb, pork, and free-range chickens. In summer, salmon and trout from local rivers, including the Spey, are offered either fresh or peat-smoked. The extensive wine list includes products from the majority of the wine-making sections of Europe. The hotel has a licensed bar, residents' lounge, and a TV lounge, and babysitter/listening service is provided. Laundry and ironing facilities are available. The staff will offer information and assistance in arranging for pony trekking or horseback riding. It's closed November and December.

For an elegant dining experience, try **The Cross,** 25-27 High Street, Kingussie, Inverness-shire PH21 1HX (tel. 05402/762). A visit here involves almost as much theater as it does fine food. Tony Hadley, the sensitive owner, personally explains the composition of each menu item. The establishment is in a stone-rimmed building fronted with Victorian plate-glass windows. In the 1800s, it was a grocery store. The focal point of the bar in the entrance area is a stone fireplace which, when I was last there, had an alderwood fire blazing merrily. Diners enjoy dishes prepared by Tony's wife, Ruth, whose specialties vary with the season, depending on the availability of produce in the local markets, and might include venison Francatelli, wild pigeon with grapes, or Highland lamb with sorrel. A selection from more than 300 wines rounds out any menu, and sorbets are served between courses. A seven-course gastronomic "extravaganza" is served on Sat. night, costing £25 ($41.25), including VAT. Dinner other nights is a four-course, fixed-price meal for £18.50 ($30.55), including VAT. Dinner is the only meal served, from 6:30pm to last orders at 9:30pm. It is advisable to reserve a table. The restaurant is closed Sun. and Mon. The Cross also rents three bedrooms, each a double or twin with private bath or shower. The half-board rate ranges from £42 ($69.30) to £48 ($79.20) per person.

AVIEMORE

At the foot of the historic rock of Craigellachie, the rallying place for Clan Grant, a little village has developed into a year-round holiday mecca since the 1960s. In winter, ski runs are available for both beginners and experts (four chair lifts and

13 T-bar tows). In summer, sailing, canoeing, pony trekking, hill walking, and mountain climbing, as well as golfing and fishing, are just some of the many activities.

The tourist information center is on Main Road (tel. 0479/810363).

Aviemore lies 129 miles from Edinburgh and 29 miles from Inverness.

In the heart of the resort, **Stakis Aviemore Centre** (tel. 0479/810624) is an all-purpose cultural, sports, and entertainment complex. Built nearly a quarter of a century ago within a loop road, it contains four hotels and their grounds. The center's activities are suitable for everyone and include ice skating, swimming, saunas, solarium, squash, table tennis, snooker, discos, putting, go-karting, and much more. Most sports facilities are open daily from 10am to 1pm, 2 to 5pm, and 6 to 9pm. Admission to the pool is £2 ($3.30) for adults, £1 ($1.65) for children. The Speyside Theatre, seating 720, changes its film programs weekly, and often is host to live shows and concerts. Also on the grounds is the Highland Craft Centre, a small shopping emporium.

Where to Stay

Stakis Coylumbridge Resort Hotel, Rothiemurchus, Aviemore, Inverness-shire PH22 1QN (tel. 0479/810661), christened by the duke of Edinburgh, stands in 65 acres of tree-studded grounds facing the slopes of the Cairngorms, and has extensive sports and leisure facilities. The 175 bedrooms are well appointed, each with private bath, TV, in-house films, hot beverage equipment, fresh fruit, phone, and daily newspaper. Singles cost from £60 ($99), and twins peak at £90 ($148.50), including a full Scottish breakfast and VAT. Meals are served all day in the Bistro Restaurant, and the Grant Room Restaurant offers a three-course buffet lunch and a table d'hôte dinner. In the hotel are two heated swimming pools, sauna, whirlpool, steambath, gym, hairdressing salon, gift shop, and games room. House entertainment is a regular feature during the evening, particularly on weekends. In winter, downhill and cross-country skiing equipment and training are available.

Stakis Four Seasons, Aviemore, Inverness-shire PH22 1PF (tel. 0479/810681), is an ideal holiday hotel offering excellent facilities for a comfortable, relaxed stay. The 88 bedrooms all have private baths, color TVs, radios, direct-dial phones, hot beverage facilities, trouser presses, hairdryers, baby-listening devices, and views of the surrounding hills and mountains. The tariff, including a full Scottish breakfast and VAT, is from £55 ($90.75) per person. The hotel has a first-class cocktail bar, a coffeehouse, and its own leisure complex with an indoor swimming pool, sauna, solarium, whirlpool spa, steamroom and gym.

Post House Hotel, Aviemore Centre, Aviemore, Inverness-shire PH22 1PJ (tel. 0479/810771), is a resort hotel, catering to winter and sports enthusiasts. Its beige-brick, two-story exterior rambles in a labyrinthine progression of wings, staircases, and long hallways, which funnel into the public rooms illuminated with big windows overlooking the countryside. In summer, doors open to reveal flagstone outdoor terraces ringed with viburnum and juniper. You can drink in the Illicit Still Bar, which has an antique whisky still and copper-topped tables. The main restaurant is capped with a soaring ceiling, trussed with beams. In the games room is a resident nanny—so if you have children, you're free to head for the slopes in winter without them. The 130 bedrooms are well furnished and each is equipped with a private bath, phone, and TV. Some family rooms are available. Singles cost from £52 ($85.80) and doubles or twins from £75 ($123.75).

Stakis Badenoch Hotel, Aviemore Centre, Aviemore, Inverness-shire PH22 1PF (tel. 0479/810261), overlooks the Craigellachie Nature Reserve and its much-photographed rock. The hotel is in the heart of Aviemore Centre. Summer and winter holiday makers face a choice of two standards of room: with modern facilities or economy bunk-bedded rooms with adjacent baths and showers. The hotel's facilities include a cocktail bar, a disco bar called Connexions, and a restaurant specializing in Scottish fare. Midweek ski packages, Christmas and New Year's packages, and special weekly tariffs are offered. Contact them for their "value for money rates." Otherwise, standard charges are £48 ($79.20) in singles, £80 ($132) in doubles. The hotel rents 72 rooms, each with private bath or shower, phone, and TV.

Where to Dine

Dalfaber Golf and Country Club (tel. 0479/811244) is part of a time-share project at the edge of the resort. The Country Club opens its restaurant, café, and bars to non-members. These facilities overlook the swimming pool of the clubhouse. For dinner, the leading choice is the Louisiana Restaurant, capped with a ceiling of pine, the kind of rustic woodsiness you would expect to find in Aspen. The restaurant's centerpiece is an open barbecue pit, the smoke from which is funneled upward through a copper and iron chimney. Comfortable wicker chairs offer a chance to listen to one of the entertainers during the evening. Sun. lunch is from the barbecue as is Mon. dinner. You get steak, chicken, or homemade burgers cooked in front of you, served with baked potatoes and as much salad as you can eat. The rest of the week, barbecued steaks are a specialty, as is Spey salmon. For an à la carte dinner, expect to pay about £12 ($19.80). There is also the table d'hôte menu for £9.50 ($15.70). Dinner is served from 7 to 10pm daily.

The Club Bar will serve you a homemade Scottish broth followed by such dishes as braised Scottish beef in a red wine sauce. Lunch is served daily from noon to 2:30pm and evening meals in the café are available from 6 to 9pm. The sizzle platter offered in the evening is a ribeye steak for only £5.85 ($9.80). The decor is a medley of knotty pine, large panoramic windows, and plants.

IN THE AVIEMORE ENVIRONS

The area surrounding Aviemore is rich in attractions. You can journey to the sky on the **Cairngorm Chair Lift,** whose lowest section lies 10 miles east of Aviemore. A round-trip passage on this longest chair lift in Scotland costs £3.50 ($5.80) per person during working hours, 9am to 4pm daily. In winter the uppermost reaches are closed during periods of high wind. The highest section is 4,084 feet above sea level. A midway stop is the Ptarmigan Restaurant, the loftiest (altitude-wise) eating spot in Britain at 3,600 feet. Hours are 9am to 4pm daily. The decor is rustic and woodsy, modern yet unpretentious, with meals costing £10 ($16.50). In summer, on a clear day you can see Ben Nevis in the west, and the vista of Strathspey from here is spectacular, from Loch Morlich set in the Rothiemurchus Forest to the Spey Valley.

Skiers are attracted to the area anytime after October, when snow can be expected. Ski equipment and clothing can be rented at the Day Lodge at the main Cairngorm car park. Weather patterns can change quickly in the Cairngorm massif, so for information about this and other aspects of the chair lift, phone 047986/261. To reach the place, take the A951 branching off from the A9 at Aviemore, then head for the car park near Loch Morlich.

North of Aviemore, the **Strathspey Railway** is billed as providing "a trip into nostalgia." The railway follows the valley of the River Spey between Boat of Garten and Aviemore, a distance of 5 miles. The train is drawn by a coal-burning steam locomotive. The newest locomotive used was made some 36 years ago, the oldest being of 1935 vintage. The round trip requires 17 minutes in each direction. Only two service designations—first class and third class in conformity with railroad tradition—are offered. Round-trip passage costs £4.25 ($7) in first class, £3 ($4.95) in third class. Schedules change frequently, but from June to the end of September, trains make five round-trip journeys daily. In spring and fall the trains run only on Sat. and Sun., making four round-trip journeys. The trains do not run in winter.

The backers of this railway, which takes you through scenes unchanged in a century, set out to re-create the total experience of travel on a Scottish steam railway that once carried wealthy Victorians toward their hunting lodges in "North Britain." The rail station at Boat of Garten where you can board the train has also been restored. To complete the experience, you can wine and dine aboard on Sat., when a single-seating dinner is served, costing £18.50 ($30.55), and at a single-seating lunch on Sun., when the price is £12.50 ($20.65). Reservations for the meals must be made. The dining car is a replica of a Pullman parlor car, the *Amethyst*. For reservations and hours of departure, call 0479/810725.

In the village of Inverdruie, 1½ miles of Aviemore on the ski road to Cairngorm, is the **Inverdruie Visitor Centre**. There, you'll find the **Cairngorm Whisky Centre & Museum** (tel. 0479/810574), open Mon. to Sat. from 10am to 6pm (later in high season) and Sun. from 12:30 to 2:30pm, April to September. In the museum are relics of whisky distilling in time past together with models of their modern equivalents. An audio-visual presentation is given on the history of whisky (Scotch, of course) and the industry. Despite the museum aspects, this is primarily a retail shop, stocking malt whiskies from 105 distilleries. In a tasting room—admission £3 ($4.95) per person—you can taste minute quantities of up to four different brands, then purchase your favorite in the shop if you wish.

Also at the Inverdruie center is the **Rothiemurchus Farm Visitor Centre,** with an audio-visual presentation. From here, guided walks and farm tours are organized by the ranger service. You can see red deer and Highland cattle as you tour.

Another opportunity at the Inverdruie center is to visit the **Old School Craft Shop** (tel. 0479/810005), where pottery, rugs, handknit articles, woodwork, and other fine traditional craftwork can be seen and purchased, as well as books and maps. You may want to visit the **Mostly Pine Tearoom,** with lots of antiques, and the **Ski-Road Skis Gift Shop,** featuring sports and fashion wear.

GRANTOWN-ON-SPEY

This holiday resort, with its gray granite buildings, stands in a wooded valley and commands views of the Cairngorm mountains. It is a key center for winter sports in Scotland. Fishermen are also attracted to its setting, because the Spey is renowned for its salmon. Lying 34 miles southeast of Inverness by road and 143 miles from Edinburgh, it was one of Scotland's many 18th-century planned towns, founded on a heather-covered moor in 1765 by Sir James Grant of Grant, becoming the seat of that ancient family. Grantown became famous in the 19th century as a Highland tourist center, enticing visitors with its planned concept, the beauty of surrounding pine forests, the Spey River, and the mountains around it. From a base here you can explore the valleys of the Don and Dee, the already-mentioned Cairngorms, and Culloden Moor, scene of the historic battle in 1746.

A tourist information center is at 54 High St. (tel. 0479/2773).

Where to Stay and Dine

Garth Hotel, the Square, Grantown-on-Spey, Morayshire PH26 3HN (tel. 0479/2836), on the narrowest edge of the historic square of town, is an elegant, comfortable hotel in what was built as a private home in the 17th century. There is a prosperous and wholesome air about it, enhanced by the well-polished brass hardware and the 4-acre garden extending toward the back, crisscrossed by footpaths. Guests enjoy the use of a spacious upstairs lounge, whose thick walls, high ceilings, wood-burning stove, and vine-covered veranda make it the perfect place for morning coffee or afternoon tea. There's an expansive bay window illuminating the plaid carpeting of the popular cocktail lounge. An array of sun parasols on the side lawn invites you to take advantage of the warm weather breezes. Gordon McLaughlan, owner of this attractive hotel, rents 14 individually furnished bedrooms, all with bath/showers, direct-dial phones, and color TVs. The charge is from £30 ($49.50) per person for B&B, plus another £16 ($26.40) per person if dinner is included. Extensive and selective meals are presented in the dining room. "Taste of Scotland" dishes are featured, with an emphasis on fresh local produce.

Tulchan Lodge, Advie, Grantown-on-Spey, Morayshire PH26 3PW (tel. 08075/200), built in 1906 to serve as the 22,000-acre Tulchan Estate's fishing and shooting lodge, is a place for both sports-oriented visitors and travelers who want to experience a place designed for the elegance required by King Edward VII, who came here for the sports, and other fastidious Edwardians. The lodge, with splendid views of the Spey Valley, has the added attraction of being in the heart of the Highland malt whisky country. Each of the 11 bedrooms is different in size and furnishings, and all have baths or showers and phones. Singles cost from £160 ($264) to £180 ($297) and doubles are priced from £250 ($412.80) to £280 ($462), each rate including half-board. The lodge has two elegant dining rooms, where Scottish and international dishes are served, with particular attention to Scottish beef, lamb, game, and fresh local seafood. The vegetables are grown in the lodge's garden. Tulchan Lodge is open from April to January. The hotel lies 9 miles northeast of Grantown on B9102.

THE WHISKY TRAIL

The major tourist attraction of the Moray District of Scotland, lying on the southern shore of Moray Firth and stretching in a triangular shape south from the coast to the wild heart of the Cairngorm Mountains near Aviemore, is the Whisky Trail, running through the glens of Speyside. Here distilleries, many of which can be visited, are known for their production of *uisge beatha* or "water of life." Whisky (note the spelling without the *e*) is its more familiar name.

Half of the malt distilleries in the country lie along the River Spey and its tributaries. Here peat smoke and Highland water are used to turn out single-malt (unblended) whisky. Several of the distilleries in Moray have opened their doors to visitors. If you're lucky, they'll give you a free sample. The Whisky Trail is 70 miles long. There are five malt distilleries in the area, including Glenlivet, Glenfiddich, Glenfarclas, Strathisla, and Tamdhu. Allow about an hour to visit each of them.

If you're traveling north on the A9 road from Perth and Pitlochry, your first stop might be at **Dalwhinnie,** which has the highest whisky distillery in the world at 1,888 feet. It is not in the Spey Valley but at the northeastern end of Loch Ericht, with views of lochs and forests.

Glenlivet

To reach your first distillery on the designated Whisky Trail, you leave Grantown-on-Spey and head east along the A95 until you come to the junction with the B9008. Go south along this route, and you can't miss it. The location of **The Glenlivet Reception Centre** is 10 miles north of the nearest town, Tomintoul. For information, call 08073/427. Near the River Livet, a Spey tributary, this distillery is one of the most famous in Scotland, and it's open to visitors from Easter until the end of October from 10am to 4pm Mon. to Sat.

Glenfarclas Distillery

Back on the A95, you can visit the Glenfarclas Distillery at Ballindalloch (tel. 08072/245), one of the few malt whisky distilleries that is still independent of the giants. Glenfarclas is managed by the fifth generation of the Grant family. Founded in 1836, it is open all year from 9am to 4:30pm Mon. to Fri., and also Sat. from June to the end of September, from 10am to 4pm. An exhibition center displays not only mementos of the Scotch whisky industry but also a genuine illicit still. There is a small craft shop, and each visitor is offered a dram of Glenfarclas Malt Whisky. There is no admission charge.

Dufftown

Dufftown is at the heart of the whisky-distilling country, with seven malt whisky distilleries in or around the town. The only distillery in Dufftown open to the public is **William Grant's Glenfiddich Distillery** (tel. 0340/20373). Glenfiddich pure malt Scotch whisky first ran from the stills on Christmas day, 1887, and the Grant family still owns and manages it. The distillery is open all year from 9:30am to 4:30pm Mon. to Fri. (excluding Christmas and New Year holidays), and, Easter to mid-October, from 9:30am to 4:30pm Sat. and from noon to 4:30pm Sun. Visitors are shown an audio-visual presentation, then taken on a tour of the distillery.

Glenfiddich is the only Highland distillery where malt whisky is bottled on the premises, so you can see the whole process from barley to bottle. Then try a complimentary dram. There is no charge for a tour of the distillery. On the premises is a gift shop where you can select from a wide range of items, including whisky, books, crystal, knitwear, and souvenirs.

Keith

Keith grew up because of its strategic location, where the main road and rail routes between Inverness and Aberdeen cross the River Isla. It has a long and ancient history, but it owes its present look to the "town planning" of the late 18th and early 19th centuries. Today it is a major stop along the Whisky Trail. The **Strathisla Distillery** on Seafield Avenue (tel. 05422/7471) is one of the oldest distilleries in Scotland. Established in 1786, it offers guided tours from early May to the end of September 9am to 4:30pm Mon. to Fri.

Rothes

A Speyside town with five distilleries, Rothes is just to the south of Glen of Rothes, 192 miles from Edinburgh and 49 miles from Inverness. It lies between Ben Aigan and Conerock Hill and was founded in 1766. The Glen Grant Distillery opened in the mid-19th century. It can be visited any time from mid-April to September, from 10am to 4pm Mon. to Fri. A visitor reception center offers guided tours. Call 03403/412 for information.

For food and lodging, **Rothes Glen Hotel,** Rothes, Morayshire IV33 7AH (tel. 03403/254), lies 3 miles north of Rothes on A941. The old turreted house, with many of its original pieces of furniture, stands back from the road, surrounded by about 40 acres of fields with grazing Highland cattle. This historic, castlelike building was designed by the architect who built Balmoral. Inside the house a warm fire greets you. The 16 bedrooms are well furnished with private baths or showers, phones, and TVs. The owners charge from £55 ($90.75) in a single, rising to £85 ($140.25) in a double. The dining room is paneled in wood, and good wholesome meals are served in true Scottish tradition. The bar lunches are popular, with a wide choice offered. A set four-course dinner with coffee and mints costs £19 ($31.35).

FOCHABERS

This village, on the Inverness-Aberdeen road, dates from 1776 and was created as one of the early planned towns by John Baxter, for the fourth duke of Gordon. Most of the buildings along High Street are protected and have not been changed much in 200 years. On the Spey, Fochabers is distinguished by its **Market Cross** and **Tower of Gordon Castle.**

Gordon Arms, 80 High St., Fochabers, Morayshire IV32 7DH (tel. 0343/820508), is a well-known, 18th-century coaching inn, run by Raul Suarez, who is justly proud of the hospitality he offers wayfarers. The 13 bedrooms are traditional in the old wing and modern in the new section. Singles with bath cost from £38 ($62.70) daily, and doubles also with bath run £52 ($85.80), including a full breakfast and VAT. Fishermen are fond of the place, as revealed by the "salmon house" for the storing of rods and tackle. The hotel is noted for serving some of the best food to be found along Speyside, including many national dishes. The Moray beef and salmon are hard to equal. Sometimes continental dishes appear on the menu. Meals, costing from £8 ($13.20) to £18 ($29.70), are served daily from noon to 2pm and 5 to 10pm. If you're here on a summer afternoon, you might have tea in the garden.

ELGIN

The center of local government in the Moray district, an ancient royal burgh, this cathedral city lies on the Lossie River, 38 miles from Inverness by road and 198 miles from Edinburgh. Once called the "lantern of the north," the **Cathedral of Moray** is now in ruins. It was founded in 1224 but extensively damaged in 1390 by the "wolf of Badenoch," the natural son of Robert II. After its destruction, the citizens of Elgin rebuilt their beloved cathedral, turning it into one of the most

THE WHISKY TRAIL

B9105

A941

B9103

Keith

Rothes
Glen Grant □

Strathisla □

A95

Craigellachie

Upper
Knockando   B9102   River Spey

River Fiddich

B9104

Tamdhu □

A95

Dufftown

Glenfarclas □

Glenfiddich □

Ballindalloch   Marypark

A95   B9008

B9009

The Glenlivet □

River Avon

B9008

A941

Grantown-
on-Spey

B9136   □

Tamnavulin   Livet Water

N

Knockandhu ●

miles   3

B9008   0   km   5

Tomintoul ●

attractive and graceful buildings in Scotland. The architect's plan was that of a Jerusalem cross. However, when the central tower fell in 1711, the cathedral fell into decay. But a faithful cobbler became its caretaker. By the time of his death in 1841 he had removed most of the debris. Today visitors wander among its ruins, snapping pictures. Best preserved is the 15th-century chapter house.

Samuel Johnson and James Boswell came this way on their Highland tour, reporting a "vile dinner" at the Red Lion Inn in 1773.

Where to Stay and Dine

I'm sure you'll fare better at **Eight Acres Hotel,** Sheriffmill, Elgin, Morayshire IV30 3UL (tel. 0343/543077), a modern, low-lying, motel-type unit, all 57 of its streamlined, functionally furnished rooms offering private baths or showers, phones, and TVs. Standing on spacious grounds, the hotel lies on the western approaches to Elgin on the main A96 Inverness road. The public rooms are generous, and the restaurant attracts a lot of motorists bound for Inverness. Rates in a single are £48 ($79.29), rising to £65 ($107.25) to £70 ($115.50) in a double, including breakfast. Guests can use the swimming pool, gym, and squash courts. The hotel offers quite a bit of entertainment at various times of the year, dinner-dancing to a live band, and occasional Scottish folk evenings. However, entertainment is not on a regular basis.

Mansion House Hotel, the Haugh, Elgin, Morayshire IV30 1AW (tel. 0343/ 548811), is a building enlarged by a local lawyer in 1883. Later it was acquired by a shipping family who offered it to the British government to house service personnel during both world wars. Today the property serves as an elegantly appointed hotel, where the baronial proportions of the original design still remain intact. Guests choose from an array of public rooms, including the Lantern Bar, a lounge bar, a residents' lounge, and a dining room. Each of the 18 bedrooms contains a private bath, TV, phone, radio, and hot beverage equipment. B&B rates are from £50 ($82.50) to £60 ($99) in a single, rising to £85 ($140.25) to £105 ($173.25) for two persons, the latter tariff for one of the four-poster accommodations. The establishment lies at the edge of the River Lossie, about a quarter of a mile from the center of Elgin. The hotel has a country club, with a swimming pool, Jacuzzi, sauna, Turkish bath, and gym. The Dip Inn, a multipurpose bistro bar, overlooks the pool.

---

2. Inverness and Loch Ness

After Glasgow, most motorists wanting to explore the Highlands head for Inverness, its ancient capital, lying 156 miles from Edinburgh. From its doorstep, one can explore a romantic land of hills, lochs, and lots of myths.

Of course, the most popular excursion is to Loch Ness, where one sets up an observation point to await the appearance of "Nessie," the Loch Ness monster. But even if the monster doesn't put in an appearance, the loch itself has splendid scenery. I have a scattering of recommendations around the loch for those wanting to base there. Finally, visitors going east may want to explore the old town of Nairn.

INVERNESS

The capital of the Highlands, Inverness is a royal burgh and seaport, at the north end of Great Glen, lying on both sides of the Ness River. It is considered the best base for touring the north. At the Highland Games, with their festive balls, the season in Inverness reaches its social peak. The tourist information center is at 23 Church St. (tel. 0463/234353).

What to See and Do

The city has a luxurious theater complex on the bank of the Ness, the **Eden Court Theatre,** Bishop's Road, which has a restaurant, bars, and an art gallery. Included in the repertoire are variety shows, drama, ballet, pop music, movies, opera, rock and folk concerts, and a summer-season traditional Scottish show with top stars. The theater, which opened in 1976, was constructed with an ingenious use of hexagonal shapes and has a horseshoe-shaped auditorium. Programs are advertised in most hotels and guesthouses. The box office is open from 10:30am to 8pm Mon. through Sat. (tel. 0463/221718).

Inverness is one of the oldest inhabited localities in Scotland. On **Craig Phadrig** are the remains of a vitrified fort, believed to date from the 4th century B.C., where the Pictish King Brude is said to have been visited by St. Columba in A.D. 565. The old castle of Inverness stood to the east of the present Castlehill, the site still retaining the name **Auld Castlehill.** Because of the somewhat shaky geography of Shakespeare in dramatizing Macbeth's murder of King Duncan, some scholars claim that the deed was done in the old castle of Inverness while others say it happened at Cawdor Castle, 4½ miles to the south where Macbeth held forth as thane of Cawdor.

King David built the first stone castle in Inverness around 1141. The **Clock Tower** is all that remains of a fort erected by Cromwell's army between 1652 and 1657. The 16th-century **Abertarff House** is now the headquarters of An Comunn Gaidhealach, the Highland association that preserves the Gaelic language and culture.

Inverness today has a castle, but it's a "modern" one—that is, dating from 1835. Crowning a low cliff of the east bank of the Ness, the **Castle of Inverness** occupies the site of an ancient fortress blown up by the Jacobites in 1746. The castle houses county offices and law courts. Mary Queen of Scots was denied admission to the castle in 1562, and she subsequently occupied a house on Bridge Street. From the window of this house, she witnessed the execution of her cousin, Sir John Gordon. For not gaining admission to the castle, she took reprisals, taking the fortress and hanging the governor.

Opposite the town hall is the **Old Mercat Cross,** with its **Stone of the Tubs,** an Inverness landmark said to be where women rested their washtubs as they ascended from the river. Known as "Clachnacudainn," the lozenge-shaped stone was the spot where the early kings were crowned.

Inverness Museum and Art Gallery, Castle Wynd (tel. 0463/237114), contains the display "The Hub of the Highlands," the story of the people, wildlife, environment, and culture of the Inverness district, as well as silver and changing exhibitions. It's open daily from 9am to 5pm Mon. to Sat. Admission is free. The museum has a coffeeshop open from 10am to 4pm.

West of the river rises the wooded hill of **Tomnahurich,** known as "the hill of the fairies." It is now a cemetery, and from here the views are magnificent.

In the Ness are wooded islands, linked to Inverness by suspension bridges and turned into parks.

From Inverness, you can visit **Culloden Battlefield,** 6 miles to the east, the spot where Bonnie Prince Charlie and the Jacobite army were finally crushed at the battle on April 16, 1746. A cairn marks the site on Drummossie Moor where the battle raged. **Leanach Cottage,** around which the battle took place, still stands and was inhabited until 1912. A path from the cottage leads through the Field of the English, where 76 men of the duke of Cumberland's forces who died during the battle are said to be buried. Features of interest include the **Graves of the Clans,** communal burial places with simple stones bearing individual clan names alongside the main road and through the woodland; the great memorial cairn, erected in 1881; the **Well of the Dead,** a single stone with the inscription "The English Were Buried Here"; and the huge **Cumberland Stone** from which the victorious "Butcher" Cumberland is said to have reviewed the scene. The battle lasted only 40 minutes: the prince's army lost some 1,200 men out of 5,000 and the king's army 310. A visitors' center and museum are open all year.

Between Inverness and Nairn, also about 6 miles to the east of Inverness, are the **Stones of Clava,** one of the most important prehistoric monuments in the north. These cairns and standing stones are from the Bronze Age.

Where to Stay

Culloden House, Culloden Moor, Inverness, Inverness-shire IV1 2NZ (tel. 0463/790461), 6 miles east from Inverness by A96 is a Georgian mansion with a much-photographed Adam facade. It includes part of the Renaissance castle in which Bonnie Prince Charlie slept the night before the last great battle on British soil, the Battle of Culloden. Superbly isolated, it is perfect for a relaxed Highland holiday, even if you stay within the extensive gardens and parkland. At the iron gates to the broad front lawn, a piper in full Highland garb plays at sundown, the skirl of the bagpipe accompanied by the barking of house dogs. Such notables as the prince of Wales and crown prince of Japan have stayed here, perfectly at home among the exquisite furnishings and handsome plaster friezes. Guests are welcome to spacious and comfortable public rooms, beautifully painted and furnished, and to the cozy bedrooms with sylvan views and history-laden atmosphere. All 21 of them contain a private bath and shower, phone, and TV. Singles pay from £85 ($140.25) and doubles from £115 ($189.75) to £155 ($255.75), with breakfast and VAT included. The hotel maintains traditional ideas of personal service. The food is served against a backdrop of refinement. Expect to pay about £28 ($46.20) per person for dinner.

Kingsmills Hotel, Culcabock Road, Inverness, Inverness-shire IV2 3LP (tel. 0483/237166), is an 18th-century house of much charm set in 4 acres of woodland garden only a mile from the center of Inverness. Once a private mansion, it stands adjacent to an 18-hole golf course, and the hotel has its own indoor pool and health spa, comprising sauna, steamroom, spa bath, fitness room, sunbed, hairdressing and beauty salon, and a three-hole mini-golf course. The owner maintains a country-house atmosphere with a small, informal, and hospitable Highland staff. Furnishings throughout the hotel are of a high quality, and all 68 rooms and suites have private baths, radios, color TVs, phones, and free in-house movies. Single rooms cost £62 ($102.30) to £85 ($140.25), and doubles go for £82 ($135.30) up to £180 ($297) for a suite. The rates include a full Highland breakfast. Dinner, offered nightly from 7 to 10pm, costs £16 ($26.40). All prices include VAT. The fish dishes are exceptional. Bar lunches and snack meals offer a wide choice, including Scottish fare. A notice in the lobby tells you that Robert Burns dined here in 1787, and the "Charles" who signed the guest register in 1982 was (you guessed it) the prince of Wales. His sister, Princess Anne, has also stayed here.

The Station Hotel, 16-18 Academy St., Inverness, Inverness-shire IV1 1LG (tel. 0463/231926), adjacent to the railway station, offers a high standard of first-class service, comfortable accommodations, and well-prepared food. The occupants of those baronial Highland mansions like to stop here when they're in Inverness on shopping or social expeditions, gathering for somewhat lively chats in the conservatory lounge. Grandly Victorian, the 67 bedrooms are tastefully decorated and welcoming, containing private bath, phone, and TV, costing from £58 ($95.70) daily in a single with bath or shower, from £85 ($140.25) in a double, including a full Scottish breakfast. The dining room is one of the finest in Inverness, serving good-quality Scottish dishes, plus some excellently cooked continental favorites. Lunch is served daily from noon to 2pm, and dinner from 7 to 9:30pm. A table d'hôte evening meal costs £16.50 ($27.25).

Dunain Park Hotel, Dunain Park, Inverness, Inverness-shire IV3 6JN (tel. 0464/230512), 2½ miles southwest of Inverness, stands in 6 acres of garden and woods, between Loch Ness and Inverness. This 18th-century house was opened as a hotel in 1974, and is furnished with fine antiques, china, and clocks, allowing it to retain its atmosphere of a private country house. Although Dunain Park has won its fame mainly as a restaurant, it does offer eight bedrooms, six with private bath or shower. The rates range from £75 ($123.75) in a single to £110 ($181.50) in a double or twin, including VAT and breakfast. A host of thoughtful details and pretty, soft furnishings have gone into the bedrooms, all of which have phone and TV. The breakfast served here is exceptional. You can order a simple lunch (in the garden, if you prefer). Snack meals are served from 12:30 to 2pm. But it is at dinner that the chef really delivers, offering a set meal for £21 ($34.65). Ann Nicholl, who enjoys an enviable reputation for her cooking, compiles her menus from the local venison, grouse, pheasant, pigeon, salmon, scallops, and lobster, as well as prime Scottish beef and lamb. Her dessert presentation is noteworthy. You'll definitely want to consider having a meal here, and you can do so daily from noon to 2pm and 7 to 9pm. The hotel also has an indoor, heated swimming pool and a sauna.

Bunchrew House Hotel and Restaurant, Bunchrew, Inverness, Inverness-shire IV3 6TA (tel. 0463/234917), 3 miles west of Inverness on the A862, is a fine Scottish mansion on the shores of Beauly Firth. The ancestral home of both the Fraser and the McKenzie clans, the house built by Simon Fraser, the eighth Lord Lovat, dates to 1621, the same year he married into the Stewart family. Set in 15 acres of landscaped gardens, the house has been restored as a country-house hotel. Guests get a glimpse of a bygone era when they relax in comfort in the paneled drawing room with roaring log fires in winter. Alan and Patsy Wilson and their staff welcome travelers to their six individually designed and decorated bedrooms, all with private baths with showers, color TVs, and phones. The Lovat Suite has a fully canopied four-poster bed, and the Wyvis Suite boasts a half-tester bed and Jacuzzi. The rooms, doubles only, range from £70 ($115.50) to £100 ($165) per night. You can dine in the candlelit restaurant on prime Scottish beef, fresh lobster and crayfish, local game and venison, and fresh vegetables.

Glen Mhor Hotel, 9-12 Ness Bank, Inverness, Inverness-shire IV1 4SG (tel. 0463/234308), looks out onto the River Ness. A house of gables and bay windows, it is a hospitable, family-run hotel with an endearing charm in spite of its creaky quality. The owners provide many thoughtful touches, such as a log fire blazing in the entrance lounge. From many of the individually styled bedrooms, you have views of the river, castle, and cathedral. Some of these are suitable for families, and children sharing a room with two adults are accommodated free. Amenities in the 30 rooms include private baths or shower rooms with toilets, color TVs, direct-dial phones, trouser presses, hairdryers, and baby-listening service. The B&B rate starts at about £22 ($36.30), rising to about £40 ($66) per person in a room where Prince Charles once dined. In a restaurant overlooking the river and specializing in Scottish dishes, you will enjoy such fine food as salmon caught in the river outside, shellfish, lamb, and beef. The wine list is considered one of the best in the country. In addition to the cozy cocktail lounge, there's a charming European Bistro bar called Nico's, which is open for food and drinks at lunch and in the evening. It's a popular nightspot, serving traditional Scottish meals and Italian pastas. Nicky Tams is called a "stable bar," serving a wide range of beer and ale. Ten of the hotel's bedrooms are in an annex called "The Cottage." These fully modernized rooms are small by American standards but comfortable and well equipped. Two of the ground floor rooms are suitable for disabled persons.

Where to Eat

Dickens International Restaurant, 77-79 Church St. (tel. 0463/71311), is reminiscent of a colonial bar in Singapore. Ionic columns combine with rattan furniture and potted palms to create an atmosphere that might have pleased W. Somerset Maugham. On a downtown street near the tourist office, the place offers a wide selection of European, Chinese, and international dishes, including many vegetarian specialties. There are eight kinds of beef and steak dishes. On the menu are Dickens's own steak, Peking duck, fresh local salmon, and chateaubriand, along with a wide range of appetizers and a good selection of seafood (several dishes are made with prawns). The widest choice of side dishes in Inverness is found here. Full meals average £10 ($16.50). Sun. lunch is also available, costing from £5.50 ($9.10). Meals are served daily from noon to 2pm and 5:30 to 11pm.

Stakis Steakhouse, Bank Street (tel. 0463/236577), a member of a chain, is one of the most attractive restaurants in the city center, lying on the banks of the river with a green, brown, and white garden-style decor, big windows, and padded banquettes. There's plenty of space for everyone, and the steaks and grilled meats are among the best in town. In the amber glow of polished brass lamps, guests enjoy bar lunches from noon to 2:30pm Mon. to Fri. Hot meals begin at £3.50 ($5.80). A full à la carte dinner will cost from £7.50 ($12.40) to £12 ($19.80). Specialties include chicken Kiev, roast chicken, and a full assortment of prime Angus steaks, some weighing in at your choice of 8 to 16 ounces. Dinner is served from 5 to 10:30pm Mon. to Fri., from 5 to 10:30pm Sun.

Brookes Wine Bar, 75 Castle St. (0463/225662), used to be a pram shop, lying on the street that runs beside the castle, behind a Victorian plateglass facade. Inside, the decor has a touch of France, an atmosphere enhanced by posters of vineyards. The ambience combines the elements of a Los Angeles bistro and a French garden. In many ways this is the most avant-garde place in town, certainly one of the most alluring, and it was the first wine bar to open in the Highlands. Wine is sold by the bottle or by the glass. You can even order a giant bottle of beer imported from Germany. There are 20 wines to choose from if you order by the glass.

As for food, you can choose what you want from a glass-fronted, refrigerated food case offering cold meats, fish, chicken, pâtés, mousse, a selection of salads, cheeses, and desserts. Hot dishes are also available, ordered from a menu written daily on the blackboard at the counter. The entire operation works on a counter-service basis, and hot dishes are brought to your table. You might order hot mushrooms gratinée, chicken Kiev, baked potato, or pan-fried filets of chicken breast with orange and ginger sauce served with buttered tagliatelle. For dessert, try the cream-filled ginger meringues or fresh red frangipani tart with cream. A full three-course meal costs from £8.50 ($14.05). The wine bar is open from 11:30am to 11pm Mon. to Wed., from 11:30am to 1am Thur. and Fri., and from 11:30am to 11:45pm Sat.; closed Sun.

NAIRN

A favorite family seaside resort on the sheltered Moray Firth, Nairn is a royal burgh, lying at the mouth of the Nairn River. Its fishing harbor was constructed in 1820, and golf has been played here since 1672, as it still is today. A large uncrowded beach, tennis, and angling draw a horde of vacationers in summer.

A summer-only tourist information center is at 62 King St. (tel. 0667/52753). Nairn lies 172 miles from Edinburgh and 16 miles from Inverness.

At **Cawdor Castle** (tel. 06677/615), south of Nairn, on B9090 between Inverness and Nairn, you encounter 600 years of Highland history. Since the early 14th century it's been the home of the thanes of Cawdor. The castle has all the architectural ingredients you associate with the medieval: a drawbridge, an ancient tower (this one built around a tree), and fortified walls. The severity is softened by the handsome gardens, flowers, trees, and rolling lawns. As I mentioned earlier, even the Scots can't agree as to where Macbeth, who actually was made Thane of Cawdor by King Duncan, committed his foul deed of murdering the king—at Cawdor or in the castle that once stood on Auld Castlehill in Inverness, if at all. The castle is open to the public from 10am to 5:30pm every day from May 1 to early October. Admission is £2.90 ($4.80) for adults, £1.50 ($2.50) for children. The castle has extensive nature trails, a snackbar, and a licensed restaurant.

Where to Stay and Dine

Newton, Inverness Road, Nairn, Nairnshire IV12 4RX (tel. 0667/53144), a castlelike hotel, stands just outside town in an attractive park of 35 acres, offering views across sweeping lawns and the golf course to the sea. Considered one of the finest of the "manor house" hotels of Scotland, it is spacious and sumptuous, drawing a clientele likely to include everybody from a prime minister to a Glasgow industrialist. A single rents for £50 ($82.50), and a double or twin goes for £80 ($132), including VAT and a full breakfast. The public rooms are furnished with taste, and the Moray Firth, viewed on a day when the sun is shining brightly, forms a spectacle of beauty from many of the Newton's windows. The 44 bedrooms have many fine appointments—sedate and comfortable. All of them contain private baths, phones, and TVs. There is a high standard of maintenance and personal service.

Clifton House, Viewfield Street, Nairn, Nairnshire IV12 4HW (tel. 0667/53119), reflects the dynamic personality of J. Gordon Macintyre, the owner of this honey-colored sandstone, vine-covered Victorian mansion. The Clifton has been owned by the same family probably longer than any other hotel in the north of Scotland. Fully licensed, it stands on the seafront, 3 minutes from the beach and golf links. Mr. Macintyre has spent a lot of time, trouble, and money in decorating the house, often with interesting prints, and in selecting the furnishings, as exemplified by the Clifton's old-fashioned parlor. The collection of pictures, paintings, prints, engravings, etchings, and drawings is unusual and extensive, not only in public rooms, the drawing room, the writing room, and the bar and restaurant, but also in the long corridor. The 16 bedrooms are pleasantly appointed. Singles rent for £42 ($69.30) to £50 ($82.50); doubles, from £80 ($132) to £90 ($148.50). All bedrooms have baths, except one that has a shower; some, however, do not have a toilet. Musical and theatrical performances are often staged in the hotel.

The Clifton also serves the best food in Nairn, a set dinner costing from £15 ($24.75). The cooking is often in the hearty Highland tradition—that is, game pie, pigeons in wine, lamb in a mustard sauce—although French specialties also tempt. Dinner hours are 7 to 9:30pm. Luncheon, from 12:30 to 1:30pm daily, is served in the Green Room, whose menu is based on what is available that day in the way of fish and shellfish, such as lobster, oysters, brill, and sole. The room is quite elegant, its china being Wedgwood Old and New. With only four tables, it is advisable to reserve your table by phoning early. Breakfast is special too.

DRUMNADROCHIT

This hamlet, lying about a mile from Loch Ness at the entrance to Glen Urquhart, has a big attraction, the official **Loch Ness Monster Exhibition** (tel. 04562/573), which opened in 1980 and has been packing 'em in ever since. You can follow the story from A.D. 565 to the present in a multi-media presentation as well as climbing aboard the sonar research vessel *John Murray*. The exhibition is the most visited place in the Highlands of Scotland, with more than 200,000 visitors annually. It is open daily from 9am to 9:30pm mid-June to the end of August, from 9:30am to 8:15pm in spring and fall. Because of fluctuating hours, telephone in advance if you're planning a winter visit. Admission is £2.75 ($4.55) for adults, £1.50 ($2.50) for children or £7.25 ($11.95) for a family ticket.

The ruined **Urquhart Castle**, on of Scotland's largest castles, is a mile and a half southeast of Drumnadrochit on a promontory overlooking Loch Ness. The chief of Clan Grant owned the castle in 1509, and most of the existing building dates from that period. In 1692 the castle was blown up by the Grants to prevent its becoming a Jacobite stronghold. It is here at Urquhart Castle that sightings of the Loch Ness monster are most often reported. It is open April to September from 9:30am to 7pm Mon. to Sat. and 2 to 4pm Sun. Winter hours are 9:30am to 4pm Mon. to Sat. and 2 to 4pm Sun. Admission charges are £1 ($1.65) for adults and 50p (85¢) for children.

Where to Stay and Dine in the Environs

Polmaily House Hotel, Drumnadrochit, Inverness-shire IV3 6XT (tel. 04562/343), graciously re-creates the pleasures of manorial country-house living, offering at the same time a contemporary style that reflects the sophistication of its owners. According to a packet of letters discovered by Nick and Alison Parsons, the house was probably built in 1776. The 18-acre estate lies 2 miles west of Drumnadrochit on the A831. You drive between stands of beechwood hedge, past stately trees, a pond, and an assortment of geese and ducklings before reaching the entrance. Inside, a series of plushly furnished rooms, each tastefully filled with antiques and vases of fresh flowers, creates a personalized kind of comfort. Nick worked as a foreign correspondent for Reuters in both Italy and Central America, which explains the positioning of foreign art with 18th-century Scottish furnishings. Nine spacious and elegant bedrooms contain high ceilings, leaded-glass windows, flowered wallpaper, and an antique charm. Seven rooms have private baths. Rates, with a Scottish breakfast included, are £40 ($66) in a bathless single and £45 ($74.25) per person in a double or twin with bath. The hotel has a tennis court, a swimming pool, and a croquet lawn flanked with garden statuary.

The restaurant attracts locals as well as hotel residents. Most dishes are prepared by Alison, using home-produced eggs and the best of fresh local ingredients. Specialties include flaked Arbroath smokie baked with cream and cheese, dill-cured and locally smoked wild salmon, and noisettes of spring lamb with fresh herbs and butter. A fixed price menu costs £16 ($26.40), and service is daily from 7:30 to 9:30pm.

FORT AUGUSTUS

This Highland touring center stands at the head (the southernmost end) of Loch Ness. The town took its name from a fort named for the duke of Cumberland. Built after the 1715 Rising, the present Benedictine abbey stands on its site. Fort Augustus lies 166 miles from Edinburgh and 36 miles from Inverness.

The **Caledonian Canal** bisects the village, and the locks are a popular attraction when boats are passing through. Running across the loftiest sections of Scotland, the canal was constructed between 1803 and 1822. Almost in a straight line, it makes its way from Inverness in the north to Corpach in the vicinity of Fort William. The canal is 60 miles long, 22 of which are artificial. The other part goes through natural lochs. In summer, you can take several pleasure craft along this canal, leaving from Fort Augustus.

Where to Stay and Dine

In accommodations, Fort Augustus offers the **Inchnacardoch Lodge,** Fort Augustus, Inverness-shire PH32 4BL (tel. 0320/6258), a family-run hotel in a beautiful setting overlooking Loch Ness, half a mile north of town. The house of many gables, a country residence of a 19th-century Lord Lovat of Lovat, chief of the Fraser Clan, offers 15 comfortable bedrooms, most with private bath. The charges are £30 ($49.50) to £40 ($66) daily in a single and £25 ($41.25) to £30 ($49.50) per person in a twin with private bath. All tariffs include a full breakfast and VAT. You can relax over coffee or drinks in the cocktail bar—but be careful. A wee dram of malt over your limit might cause you to see the Loch Ness monster. The hotel is open March to December.

SPEAN BRIDGE

This village is a busy intersection of the Fort William-Perth and Fort William-Inverness roads, as well as having daily train service to Fort William, Glasgow, and London, and bus service to Inverness and Fort William. Two miles outside the town, in Glen Spean, is the striking **Commando Memorial** by Scott Sutherland that the queen mother unveiled in 1952. In this area many commandos were trained during World War II. Numerous war movies have been filmed here.

Spean Bridge lies 133 miles from Edinburgh and 9½ miles from Fort William.

Where to Stay and Dine

Letterfinlay Lodge, Letterfinlay, Spean Bridge, Inverness-shire PH34 4DZ (tel. 039781/622), is a comfortable, well-appointed establishment on the A82 near Spean Bridge, about halfway between Fort Augustus and Fort William. Between the highway and Loch Lochy, against a backdrop of rugged scenery, it operates from March to November and is known both for its personal service and its level of cuisine, mostly plain Highland dishes that use high-quality ingredients, such as fresh salmon and sea trout, Aberdeen Angus beef, and Scottish hill lamb. Your bedroom window is likely to look out upon Loch Lochy. All 15 units, including some family rooms, are tastefully furnished, with private baths or showers. Charges are £18 ($29.70) to £28 ($46.20) per person, including a full Scottish breakfast. Dinner, including coffee, is £15 ($24.75). The hotel also offers a sun lounge and a cocktail bar. Trout fishing is available at the doorstep.

3. Fort William and Lochaber

Fort William, the capital of Lochaber, is the major touring center for the western Highlands. Wildly beautiful Lochaber, the area around Fort William, has been called "the land of bens, glens, and heroes."

Dominating the area is **Ben Nevis,** Britain's highest mountain, rising 4,418 feet. In summer when it's clear of snow, there's a safe path to the summit. Fort William stands on the site of a fort built by General Monk in 1655, which was pulled down to make way for the railroad. This district is the western end of what is known as Glen Mor—the Great Glen, geologically a fissure that divides the northwest of Scotland from the southeast and contains Loch Lochy, Loch Oich, and Loch Ness. The Caledonian Canal, opened in 1847, linked these lochs, the River Ness, and Moray Firth. It provided sailing boats a safe alternative to the stormy route around the north of Scotland. Larger steamships made the canal out of date commercially, but fishing boats and pleasure steamers still use it. Good roads run the length of the Great Glen, partly following the line of General Wade's military road. From Fort William you can take steamer trips to Staffa and Iona.

The ruins of **Old Inverlochy Castle,** scene of the famous battle in 1645, can be reached by driving on the A82 2 miles north of Fort William. At a point just one mile north of Fort William is **Glen Nevis,** one of the most beautiful in Scotland.

About 15 miles west of Fort William, on the A830 toward Mallaig, at Glenfinnan at the head of Loch Shiel, is the **Glenfinnan Monument,** which marks the spot where Bonnie Prince Charlie unfurled his proud red-and-white silk banner on August 19, 1745, in the ill-fated attempt to restore the Stuarts to the British throne. The monument is topped by the figure of a kilted Highlander. At a visitors' center one may learn of the prince's campaign from Glenfinnan to Derby and back to the final defeat at Culloden.

FORT WILLIAM

The name evokes redcoats billeted in rough barracks to keep the Highlanders of Lochaber under control. Fort William today is a busy tourist town on the shores of Loch Linnhe. Although it stands in the shadow of Ben Nevis, the mountain can't be seen from town. While the town is most often used as a touring center, in Fort William itself you can visit the **West Highland Museum,** Cameron Square (tel. 0397/ 2169), containing all aspects of local history, especially the 1745 Jacobite rising, plus sections on tartans and folk life. The museum is open from 9:30am to 5:30pm Mon. to Sat. in June and September, to 9pm in July and August, and 10am to 1pm and 2 to 5pm the remainder of the year. Admission is 60p ($1) for adults, 30p (50¢) for children.

Fort William lies 133 miles from Edinburgh, 104 miles from Glasgow, and 68 miles from Inverness. It has a tourist information center in the center of town (tel. 0397/3781).

Where to Stay

In Fort William, I'd recommend the following accommodations, beginning first with a deluxe suggestion:

Inverlochy Castle, Torlundy, Fort William, Inverness-shire PH33 6SN (tel. 0397/2177), 3 miles northeast on the A82, is another one of the places where Queen Victoria stayed. In her time it was newly built (completed in 1870), a Scottish mansion belonging to Baron Abinger. The monarch claimed in her diary, "I never saw a lovelier or more romantic spot." I do not wish to detract from that long-ago sentiment. Inverlochy Castle today is one of the premier places of Scotland for food and accommodations. The seventh baron of Abinger sold the estate while it was being used for commando training during World War II. The Hobbs family transformed it into a fine hotel in 1969, and Mrs. Grete Hobbs, who was born in Denmark, is a delightful hostess today, assisted by a staff of 54 persons. Against the scenic backdrop of Ben Nevis, the castle hotel, a *Relais & Chateaux,* has a mood inside of elegance and refinement, luxurious appointments and antiques, artwork and crystal, plus a profusion of flowers. Only 16 bedrooms, each with private bath, phone, and TV, are offered, all of them beautifully furnished. The prices reflect the opulence. Twins or doubles rent from £165 ($272.25) to £180 ($297), and suites for two cost £220 ($363) to £250 ($412.50), including breakfast and service.

The cuisine is one of the finest in Scotland, with the food cooked to order and served on silver platters. Sparkling crystal and fine china are placed on hand-carved polished tables where the guests enjoy such fare as salmon from the Spean or crayfish from Loch Linnhe, even produce from the hotel's own farm garden. Partridge and grouse are offered in season. Meals cost £35 ($57.75) and up, with VAT and service included. Men are required to wear jackets and ties, and no smoking is permitted in the dining room. Outsiders can dine here if there's room, but reservations are mandatory. Meals are served daily from 12:30pm to 1:45pm and 7:30 to 9pm. Closed mid-November to mid-March.

Alexandra, the Parade, Fort William, Inverness-shire PH33 6AZ (tel. 0397/

2241), is a familiar sight, a hotel with tall gables and formidable granite walls, so common in this part of the Highlands. But the hotel is no antiquated mansion—rather, it has been completely modernized, offering 72 double rooms and 19 singles that are pleasantly and attractively furnished, each with private bath, color TV, direct-dial phones, and tea and coffee makers. The rate in a double or twin is £72 ($118.80) daily, and a single costs £48 ($79.20) to £54 ($89.10). These tariffs include VAT, service, and a Scottish breakfast. Service and housekeeping standards are good. The chef makes excellent use of fresh fish, and the wine cellar is amply endowed. The vegetables are simply cooked with enjoyable results. A set dinner costs from £12 ($19.80).

The Croit Anna Hotel, Druimarbin, Fort William, Inverness-shire PH33 6RR (tel. 0397/2268), is on the A82 highway 2½ miles south of Fort William, overlooking Loch Linnhe and having fine views of the Ardgour Hills. Many of its 92 rooms have a private bathroom, and all have color TVs and tea and coffee makers. Singles rent for £32 ($52.80), with doubles or twins going for £31 ($51.15) per person, including VAT. In the hotel dining room, a four-course à la carte meal would be £15 ($24.75). Hotel facilities include a games room, panoramic lounge, gift shop, lounge bar, and guest launderette. It's open from April to October, and entertainment is provided on most evenings in season. The hotel is owned and managed by the same family who designed and built it on a traditional Highland croft that has been in their possession for more than 250 years.

Where to Dine

Factor's House, Torlundy, Fort William, Inverness-shire PH33 6SN (tel. 0397/5767), is a *restaurant avec chambres.* Outside of Inverlocky Castle, it serves the best food in Fort William and is also a desirable place at which to stay. Appealing to motorists, it lies 3½ miles northeast of Fort William on A82. Seven well-furnished bedrooms, each with bath or shower, phone, and TV, are rented at a cost of £42 ($69.30) daily in a single, rising to £72 ($118.80) in a double. But it is mainly as a restaurant that Factor's House is known. The owner, Peter Hobbs (likely to be wearing a kilt), is a gracious host. The cooking here is honest in that it doesn't trap itself in unnecessary adornments, and only good fresh British produce seems to be used. A set dinner is offered for £18.50 ($30.55), with most à la carte orders costing £22 ($36.30). Service is from 7 to 9:30pm Tue. to Sun. The staff takes a holiday from the middle of December to the middle of March.

ARDNAMURCHAN PENINSULA

One of the loveliest spots in the Western Highlands, this peninsula lies about an hour's drive west from Fort William. Much of it remains an unspoiled wilderness. The peninsula begins on the northern shore of Loch Sunart, and it faces the Isle of Mull.

Glenborrodale Castle, Glenborrodale, near Acharacle, Argyll PH36 4JP (tel. 09724/166). Here, in this tranquil setting, America's Cup yachtsman Peter de Savary has created one of the premier hotels of the Highlands. Set on 1,000 acres, Glenborrodale looks like one of those castles where you could easily imagine Sleeping Beauty slumbered for all these years. Overlooking the Loch, the turreted castle offers only 15 bedrooms and staterooms, each sumptuously furnished with private baths, often with four-posters. Of course, all the amenities are there, including direct-dial phone, color TV, and the like, but everywhere you look shows a respect for British country-house tradition and elegance. Comfort, in fact, seems to be the keynote around here.

From Easter until the end of October, guests are received on half-board terms costing from £100 ($165) per person nightly. Mr. de Savary restored, with the help of a few million pounds, a century-old Victorian castle that had been constructed by a mining tycoon. He filled it with antiques and period pieces and decorated it with objects of art and the finest of British furnishings. Vegetables come fresh from their gardens, and both traditional Scottish and modern British dishes are served in their elegantly appointed restaurant, including venison, fresh salmon, grouse, and pheasant. Many sporting activities are also available.

ARISAIG

This little village on the shores of Loch Nan Ceal looks out across the bay to the islands of Skye, Rhum, Eigg, and Muck. Its position is on the scenic highway known as the "Road to the Isles," since you pass through here en route to Mallaig, from which steamers sail to the Kyle of Lochalsh, the Outer Hebrides, and the lochs of the northwest coast. Private boats go to the isles directly from Arisaig. This was a haunt of Bonnie Prince Charlie during his travels in connection with the Jacobite Rebellion of 1745.

Arisaig lies 172 miles from Edinburgh and 88 miles from Oban.

Where to Stay and Dine

Arisaig Hotel, Arisaig, Inverness-shire PH39 4NH (tel. 06875/210), was an early Jacobite inn. The Stewarts (George, Janice, and Gordon) still reign here. On the shores of Loch Nan Ceal, in the heart of Bonnie Prince Charlie country, they run a topnotch inn. They offer 15 well-furnished bedrooms, six of which contain private baths. Amenities include direct-dial phone, TV, intercom, and beverage-making equipment. Some accommodations can sleep families of three or four. B&B ranges from £30 ($49.50) to £38 ($62.70) per person based on double occupancy. Single occupancy costs another £5 ($8.25) added to the rates quoted. In this warm, inviting, family atmosphere, you can enjoy some of the best food in the area, a real "Taste of Scotland" menu, including such dishes as roast pheasant, "Scotch beef olives" with haggis stuffing, and their own Gaelic pâté. Rates are substantially reduced from the end of October until the end of March.

ONICH

On the shores of Loch Linnhe, this charming little village lies to the north of the Ballachulish Bridge. It's a good center if you're taking the western route to Inverness, or going to Skye and Fort William. The location is 148 miles from Edinburgh and 79 miles from Inverness.

The Lodge on the Loch, Creag Dhu, Onich, Inverness-shire PH33 6RY (tel. 08553/238), may have changed its name, but to locals it will forever be known as the Creag Dhu Hotel, as it was once the country home of Lady McPherson, taking its former name from the rallying cry of her clan. Now a family-run hotel, it lies between Ben Nevis and Glencoe, with expansive lochside and mountain views. The loch views are of prawn-filled Linnhe and Leven. At this imposing country home with modern additions, the dinner, bed, and breakfast rate is £44 ($72.60) per person in the spring and autumn, rising to £65 ($107.25) per person in the summer (for a superior room). The 20 bedrooms have private baths or showers, color TVs, radios, phones, hairdryers, trouser presses, and tea and coffee makers. Under the supervision of the Young family, the hotel kitchen offers several traditional Scottish dishes among other fare. Ceilidhs, evenings of Scottish music and song, as well as talks and slide shows, are among the events held at the hotel. Special musical weekends take place in the spring and autumn, and there are courses in painting. Such activities as boating, sailing, waterskiing, and aqualung diving are offered, along with good sea and freshwater fishing, pony trekking, riding, golfing, swimming, and tennis. Receiving guests from April to the end of October, the hotel has an enthusiastic repeat clientele.

Onich Hotel, on A82, Onich, Inverness-shire PH33 6RY (tel. 08553/214), is perched on the shores of Loch Linnhe, commanding views of the Ardgour and Glencoe Mountains and the Firth of Lorne. Its gardens slope down to the water. Under family management, the hotel reflects a personal touch, both in its welcome of real Highland hospitality and in the appointments of its 26 bedrooms and lounges. The cuisine is backed up by a fine wine list. Dinners cost from £14 ($23.10). The bright, airy bedrooms have been modernized and have private baths,

TVs, phones, and tea and coffee makers. They rent for £34 ($56.10) per person nightly for B&B. Guests gather in either the Clan cocktail bar or the Deerstalker lounge bar, which is open all day for food and drinks. The hotel attracts the athletic-minded, as it's a center for walking, climbing, loch bathing, putting, fishing, sailing, windsurfing, and pony trekking.

BALLACHULISH

This small village enjoys a splendid scenic position on the shores of Loch Leven at the entrance to Glencoe. The Ballachulish Bridge links North and South Ballachulish.

A summer-only tourist information center (tel. 08552/296) is in the center of the village. Ballachulish lies 117 miles from Edinburgh and 80 miles from Inverness. The village is a good center for touring the western Highlands.

Ballachulish Hotel, Ballachulish, Argyll PA39 4JY (tel. 08552/606), stands right on the shores of Loch Leven, at the point where hills split Leven from Loch Linnhe. Built in the style of a Scottish manor house and extensively remodeled, it offers hospitality and warmth. The decor blends modern colors with old-style elegance. The 34 bedrooms have a high standard of comfort and convenience, but they vary considerably in style. All have private baths, color TVs, direct-dial phones, and tea and coffee makers. Depending on the season, singles go for £38 ($62.70) to £42 ($69.30) daily, and doubles cost £30 ($49.50) to £45 ($74.25) per person, the latter the charge for a suite with a four-poster bed and spa bath. All prices include a Scottish breakfast, VAT, and service. The hotel serves good food, attractively presented, made with fresh ingredients. A table d'hôte dinner is priced at £15.50 ($25.60). There are good snacks, too. The staff will arrange boat trips on the lochs or fishing expeditions.

GLENCOE

On the shores of Loch Leven, near where it joins Loch Linnhe, the Ballachulish Bridge now links the villages of North and South Ballachulish, at the entrance to Glencoe. The bridge saves a long drive to the head of the loch if you're coming from the north, but many visitors enjoy the scenic drive to Kinlochleven to come upon the wild and celebrated Glencoe from the east.

Glencoe runs from Rannoch Moor to Loch Leven between some magnificent mountains, including 3,766-foot Bidean nam Bian. Known as the "Glen of Weeping," Glencoe is where, on February 11, 1692, Campbells massacred MacDonalds —men, women, and children—who had been their hosts for 12 days. Although massacres were not uncommon in those times, this one shocked even the Highlanders because of the breach of hospitality. When the killing was done, the crime of "murder under trust" was regarded by law as an aggravated form of murder, and carried the same penalties as treason.

The glen, much of which now belongs to the National Trust for Scotland, is full of history and legend. A tiny lochan is known as "the pool of blood" because by its side some men are said to have quarreled over a piece of cheese, and all were killed.

This is an area of massive splendor, with towering peaks and mysterious glens where you can well imagine the fierce battle among the kilted Highlanders to the skirl of the pipes and the beat of the drums.

Glen Orchy, to the south, is well worth a visit too, for the wild river and mountain scenery is beautiful and photogenic. It was the birthplace of the Gaelic bard Duncan Ban MacIntyre, whose song, "In Praise of Ben Doran," is considered a masterpiece.

In the Glen

Almost where Glen Etive joins Glencoe, under the jagged peak of Buchaille Etive Mor dominating the road (A82), lies **King's House Hotel,** Glencoe, Argyll PA39 4HY (tel. 08556/259), 5 miles north of the village of Glencoe. A building has stood here since the late 14th century. During the Jacobite Rising of 1745, it was required to accommodate troops on their way south from Fort William. It is now a center for skiing and attracts thousands from far and near. Believed to be the oldest licensed inn in Scotland, the hotel has been enlarged and completely modernized. A total of 21 well-furnished, warm rooms, 11 with private baths, are provided, and also many have views of the majestic scenery. A single without bath costs £21.50 ($35.50) daily, with a bathless double or twin going for £42 ($69.30). With private bath, a twin or double rents for £46 ($75.90). The lounge, too, has views. The dining room relies on a lot of good fresh produce for its appetizing meals. There is a fine wine cellar, plus a bar. Such amenities as a drying room are provided for those who want to walk, fish, or go climbing. A set dinner is featured for £12 ($19.80).

Besides access from the Glasgow-Inverness highway, guests at the King's House Hotel can be met at the Bridge of Orchy railway station by arrangement.

A ski lift is almost opposite the hotel. The Buachaille Etive Mor guards Glencoe's eastern end. This mountain provides a challenge for climbers and was the training ground for Sir John Hunt and the party he took to the top of Everest in the coronation year. This is great climbing and walking country, and rescue techniques evolved and taught here have been widely used.

---

4. Kyle of Lochalsh and Skye

From the Kyle of Lochalsh you can take a ferry to the mystical Isle of Skye, off the northwest coast of Scotland. The island has inspired many of the best loved and best known of Scottish ballads such as "Over the Sea to Skye" and "Will Ye Not Come Back Again." On the 48-mile-long island, you can explore castle ruins, duns, and brochs, enjoying a Highland welcome. For the Scots, the island will forever evoke images of Flora Macdonald, who conducted Bonnie Prince Charlie to Skye. She disguised him as Betty Burke after the Culloden defeat.

From Skye, you can take a ferry service back to Kyle or to Mallaig from Armadale. The Armadale ferry transports cars, but the service is less frequent than the one to Kyle. If you're planning to take your car, reservations are recommended.

Caledonian MacBrayne, in the Ferry Terminal, Gourock, near Glasgow (tel. 0475/34531 for reservations, 0475/33755 for information), runs ferry services to Skye and to Mull plus 21 other islands. The company also offers inclusive tours for people and cars to island-hop, using their services between islands. This is an ideal opportunity to visit places well away from the beaten track. The information office at Gourock is most helpful, and someone there will assist you in planning a trip if you wish to make up your own journey.

The largest island of the Inner Hebrides, Skye is separated from the mainland by the Sound of Sleat on its southeastern side. At Kyleakin, on the eastern end, the channel is only a quarter of a mile wide and thus the ferry docks there. Dominating the land of summer seas, streams, woodland glens, mountain passes, cliffs, and waterfalls are the Cuillin Hills, a range of jagged black mountains. The Peninsula of Sleat, the island's southernmost arm, is known as "The Garden of Skye."

DORNIE

This small crofting village on the road to the Isle of Skye is the meeting place of three lochs—Duich, Long, and Alsh. On a rocky islet stands **Eilean Donan Castle** (tel. 059985/202), at Dornie, 8 miles east of Kyle of Lochalsh on the A87. This romantic castle was built in 1220 as a defense against the Danes. In 1719 it was shelled by the British frigate *Worcester*. In ruins for 200 years, it was restored by Colonel MacRae of Clan MacRae in 1932 and is now a clan war memorial and museum, containing Jacobite relics, mostly with clan connections. The castle is open from Good Friday until the last day of October, charging £1 ($1.65) for admission.

The village of Dornie lies 212 miles from Edinburgh and 74 miles from Inverness.

South of Dornie and Eilean Donan Castle is Shiel Bridge. From here, an "unclassified road" leads to **Glenelg,** after a twisting climb over Ratagan Pass with a fine

view of the mountain range known as the **Five Sisters of Kintail,** which is dominated by Sgurr Fhuaran, 3,505 feet high. In summer a car-ferry crosses the Sound of
Sleat to Skye. It was from Glenelg that Johnson and Boswell crossed to Skye in
1773. In Gleann Beag, 2 miles to the southeast, stand two of the best-preserved Iron
Age brochs on the Scottish mainland—**Dun Telve** and **Dun Troddan.** Brochs are
stone towers with double walls, probably built more than 2,000 years ago by the
Picts for protection against raiders. The walls of the two brochs are more than 30 feet
high.

Where to Stay and Dine

Just outside Dornie, across Loch Long and at the end of Loch Duich, **Loch
Duich Hotel,** 8-10 Francis St., Ardelve, Dornie, near Kyle of Lochalsh, Ross-shire
IV40 8DY (tel. 059985/213), overlooks one of the Highlands' most photogenic
castles, Eilean Donan. The 18-room hotel has a small lounge and bar where you can
wait for dinner, which will cost from £14.50 ($23.95). It's likely to be a magnificent
meal of fresh chowder or pâté, followed by local venison or perhaps a local fish. Bedrooms are simple, and many overlook Eilean Donan and the loch. Eight rooms
contain private baths. Including an enormous freshly cooked breakfast with porridge and eggs and bacon—you name it—the owners charge £24 ($39.60) per
person.

KYLE OF LOCHALSH

This popular center for touring the western Highlands is also a good jumping-
off point to the islands. A car-ferry leaves for Kyleakin on the Isle of Skye. There is no
need to book in advance. The journey is only 10 minutes. The ferry shuttles back and
forth all day, and you will have plenty of time to drive the length of Skye in a day,
returning to the mainland by night if you want to.

A summer-only tourist information center is in the center of town (tel. 0599/
4276).

The Kyle of Lochalsh lies 204 miles from Edinburgh and 125 miles from Oban.

Where to Stay and Dine

Lochalsh Hotel, Ferry Road, Kyle of Lochalsh, Ross-shire IV40 8AF (tel.
0599/4202). There's no way a visitor can talk about the Kyle of Lochalsh without
mentioning this landmark hotel. It was built as a luxury oasis when the British Railway finally extended its tracks in this direction. During World War II, it served as the
headquarters of a branch of the Royal Navy, which had mined the coastline. Today,
in memory of that period, a large (defused) mine sits near the flagpole on the seaside
lawn. The south shore of the Isle of Skye and the rock-studded inlet are visible
through crafted, small-paned windows, whose full-grain hardwood and brass fittings are similar to those on an ocean-going yacht. The 38 bedrooms have been
stylishly overhauled, each with private bath, phone, and TV. B&B is priced at £55
($90.75) daily in a single, £130 ($214.50) in a double. Evening meals cost from
£16 ($26.40) and include the best of Scottish cuisine and ingredients. The ground-
floor bar stocks a variety of malt whiskies, and the dining room has a panoramic
view.

On a hillside above the hotel, the Ferry Inn, run by the hotel, is one of the most
popular pubs in the area, attracting locals as well as visitors.

BALMACARA

Those planning to stay in the Kyle of Lochalsh district, taking the car and passenger ferry to Skye, may prefer a more peaceful oasis for a day or two. In the
Balmacara estate, now the property of the National Trust for Scotland, the
Balmacara Hotel, Balmacara, Ross-shire IV40 8DH (tel. 059986/283), is a good
choice. It stands on the shores of Loch Alsh, 3 miles from the Kyle of Lochalsh. Both
the contemporary design of the 29 bedrooms and the panoramic water view from
the hotel are similar to what visitors might discover in an isolated section of Scandi-
navia. Parts of the interior are covered with full-grain horizontal planks of varnished

pine, into which are set square windows presenting a sweeping view of forests, loch, and the far Cuillin Hills of the Isle of Skye rising in hues of red and blue. Owner Clive Williamson is happy to talk about the attractions of Wester Ross. Each of the comfortable bedrooms contains a private bath, TV, and phone. Singles cost from £35 ($57.75), with doubles or twins going for £55 ($90.75) to £68 ($112.20), including a full Scottish breakfast. A fixed-price evening meal goes for £14 ($23.10), while a lighter lunch averages around £6 ($9.90).

A hotel courtesy bus can be arranged to meet you at Kyle Railway Station when coming from Inverness, or at the Skye ferry terminal.

ISLE OF SKYE

Skye is the largest of the Inner Hebrides, 48 miles long and between 3 and 25 miles wide. It is separated from the mainland by the Sound of Sleat (pronounced "slate"). There are many stories as to the origin of the name, Skye. Some believe it is from the Norse "ski," meaning a cloud, while others say it's from the Gaelic word for winged. There are Norse names on the island, however, as the Norsemen held sway for 4 centuries before 1263. Overlooking the Kyle is the ruined Castle Maol, once the home of a Norwegian princess.

For those who want to overnight or spend a longer holiday on the island, I offer the following suggestions, scattered in the various hamlets. However, in summer be sure to reserve in advance, as accommodations are extremely limited.

There are coach tours three or four times a week in summer from Kyleakin where the ferry lands to Dunvegan Castle or to the north end of the island. They generally start at 10am, returning to Kyleakin around 6pm, so you need not take your car across with you. Telephone 0599/4328, **Clan Coaches,** for further information.

Sleat

Kinloch Lodge, Isle Ornsay, Sleat, Isle of Skye, Inverness-shire IV43 8QY (tel. 04713/333), lies 3½ miles north of Sleat by the A851. The white stone walls of this dignified manor house are visible from across the scrub- and pine-covered hillsides bordering the edges of this historic property. When it was built in 1680, it was a hunting lodge for the MacDonald estates. Today, after much rebuilding and expansion, the linden-flanked manor house is the private residence of Lord and Lady MacDonald, who welcome discriminating guests into the confines of their very elegant home. Portraits of the family's 18th-century forebears are the most striking details of the plushly decorated living rooms, where open fireplaces illuminate the burnished patina of scores of family antiques. Many of the bedrooms, nine in all, have been freshly papered and painted and contain private baths. From the windows of some of the bedrooms, guests sometimes catch glimpses of the sea, which washes up to the edge of the property's sloping gardens. Rates, with breakfast included, range from £70 ($115.50) to £75 ($123.75) per person, based on double occupancy. Singles pay a supplement of £16 ($26.40).

Every evening guests enjoy drinks in a peach-colored drawing room before consuming one of the well-prepared meals for which Lady MacDonald is justifiably famous. The author of eight bestselling cookbooks, she applies her techniques to imaginative recipes, for which the ingredients are usually shot, trapped, netted, or grown on the Isle of Skye. Dinner costs from £16 ($42.90) per person. The lodge is open from early March until mid-January.

Broadford

This town is the meeting point for the ports of Armadale, Kylerhea, and Kyleakin.

Broadford Hotel, Broadford, Isle of Skye, Inverness-shire IV49 9AB (tel. 04712/204), is a venerated inn dating from 1611, when it was established by Sir Lauchlin MacKinnon. It was here that a descendant of his first came up with the secret recipe for Drambuie liqueur, now a symbol throughout the world of Highland hospitality. The Broadford has seen a lot of changes since those days, and it's been completely modernized and brought up-to-date, both in its bedrooms and public facilities. The inn lies by the waters of Broadford River, and guests are allowed to fish for salmon and trout. The 19 bedrooms have baths, TVs, phones, and hot beverage facilities. For B&B, singles cost £31 ($51.15) daily, and doubles run from £52 ($85.80), with VAT included. The families who run the hotel offer good Scottish cooking, making fine use of the local produce. A dinner goes for £11 ($18.15). The inn lies 4 minutes from the Skye airfield, where there is direct daily service to Glasgow. Nearby are the ruins of the farmhouse where Samuel Johnson and his companion, James Boswell, spent a night on their tour of the Highlands.

Sligachan

Sligachan Hotel, Sligachan, Isle of Skye, Inverness-shire IV47 8SW (tel. 047852/204), nestles at the foot of the Cuillin Mountains at the head of a sea loch and is an ideal touring center from which to explore Skye. This family-run hotel, one of Skye's oldest coaching inns, has private baths in all 19 bedrooms. B&B costs £27 ($44.55) per person, and a four-course dinner goes for £12 ($19.80). The cuisine consists of local fare such as venison, lamb, salmon, oysters, and vegetarian dishes. The open fires and fine selection of malt whiskies will warm the cockles of your heart.

Portree

Skye's capital, Portree, is the port for steamers making trips around the island and linking Skye with the 15-mile-long island Raasay. Sligachan, 9 miles south, and Glenbrittle, 7 miles farther southwest, are centers for climbing the Cuillin (pronounced "coolin") Hills.

Royal Hotel, Bank Street, Portree, Isle of Skye, Inverness-shire IV51 9LU (tel. 0478/2525), stands on a hill facing the water and is said to have extended hospitality to Bonnie Prince Charlie during his flight in 1746. In less dramatic and rushed circumstances, you can book one of its 25 comfortable bedrooms, the preferred ones opening onto the sea. All the accommodations have showers or baths, toilets, TVs, tea and coffee makers, and central heating. B&B costs from £28 ($46.20) to £38 ($62.70) per person. A la carte meals and bar snacks are offered, a dinner in the restaurant averaging £13 ($21.45).

Rosedale Hotel, Beaumont Crescent, Portree, Isle of Skye, Inverness-shire IV51 9DB (tel. 0478/3131), in one of the more secluded parts of Portree, opens directly onto the sea. It was created from a row of fishermen's dwellings dating from the reign of William IV. Privately owned and managed by the second generation of the Andrew family, Rosedale is a warm and welcoming place, offering 23 bedrooms decorated in modern style. All have private baths, radios, color TV, and direct-dial phones. B&B goes for £26 ($42.90) to £32 ($52.80) per person daily, the tariff including a big Scottish breakfast. In the cocktail bar, you can be served a good range of Highland malt whiskies. The food is good, too. The hotel is open only from mid-May to the end of September.

Uig

This village is on Trotternish, the largest Skye peninsula, and ferry port for Harris and Uist in the Outer Hebrides. It is 15 miles north of Portree and 49 miles from Kyle of Lochalsh. **Monkstadt House,** a mile and a half north, is where Flora Macdonald brought Prince Charles, in the guise of a girl named Betty Burke, after their escape flight from Benbecula. In **Kilmuir** churchyard, five miles north, Flora was buried, wrapped in a sheet used by the prince. Her grave is marked by a Celtic cross.

Uig Hotel, Uig, Isle of Skye, Inverness-shire IV52 9YE (tel. 047042/205), an old coaching inn, has been furnished with warmth and imagination. In homelike comfort, guests are welcomed and shown to the lounge with its harmonious colors. The hotel stands on a hillside overlooking a small bay and a tiny fishing harbor. The food, excellently prepared Scottish fare, is served in a cheerful dining room with a view of the bay. The 18-room hotel comes equipped with private bath or shower in every unit. Rates range from £32 ($52.80) to £38 ($62.70) daily for singles, from

£64 ($105.60) to £76 ($125.40) for doubles, including a full Scottish breakfast and VAT. The hotel is open from May to early October.

Dunvegan

The village of Dunvegan grew up around **Dunvegan Castle** (tel. 047022/ 206), the principal man-made sight on the Isle of Skye, seat of the chiefs of Clan MacLeod who have lived there for 700 years. The castle, which stands on a rocky promontory, was once accessible only by boat, but now the moat is bridged and the castle open to the public. It holds many fascinating relics, including a "fairy flag." It is reputed to be the oldest inhabited castle in Britain. It is open from 10am to 5pm from Easter to the end of September and from 2 to 5pm during October. The castle is closed Sun., but the gardens, craft shop, and restaurant are open seven days a week. Admission to the castle is £3 ($4.95) for adults, £1.50 ($2.50) for children. To the gardens only, the entry fee is £1.50 ($2.50) for adults, 75p ($1.25) for children.

Boats leave the castle jetty at frequent intervals every day except Sun. from May to the end of September going to the **Seal Colony.** The seals in Loch Dunvegan, both brown and gray varieties, aren't bothered by the approach of people in boats and can be studied at close range. The 20-minute round trip costs £2.75 ($4.55) for adults, £1.75 ($2.90) for children.

At **Trumpan,** nine miles north of Dunvegan, are the remains of a church that was set afire in 1597 by MacDonald raiders while the congregation, all MacLeods, were inside at worship. Only one woman survived. The MacLeods of Dunvegan rushed to the defense, and only two MacDonalds escaped death.

Atholl House Hotel, Dunvegan, Isle of Skye, Inverness-shire IV51 8WA (tel. 047022/219), stands right in the village of Dunvegan, near Dunvegan Castle. Built in 1980 as a private home, it was converted to a guest house in 1923. The hotel, open year round, rents nine comfortable bedrooms, six of which have a private bath or shower. B&B costs from £23 ($37.95) daily in a single, rising to £46 ($75.90) to £52 ($85.80) in a double. Units contain facilities for making hot beverages. In the dining room, the owners place emphasis on good service and well-prepared local produce, including lamb, venison, salmon, and shellfish in season. Atholl house is a member of the "Taste of Scotland" program, with high standards of accommodation, Scottish hospitality, and Scottish cuisine. It has a residents' license. From the hotel, you have views over mountain moorland and Loch Dunvegan.

Skeabost Bridge

Eastward from Dunvegan is Skeabost Bridge, with an island cemetery of great antiquity. The graves of four Crusaders are here.

Nearby is the **Skeabost House Hotel,** Skeabost Bridge, Isle of Skye, Inverness-shire IV51 9NP (tel. 047032/202), one of the most comfortable, refreshing, and inviting country homes of Skye, receiving paying guests from April to mid-October. Modernized, it is interesting architecturally with its dormers, chimneys, tower, and gables. Inside the taste level is high, with wood paneling and carpets. Once a private estate, it has been converted into a lochside hotel, standing on grounds that in summer are studded with flowering bushes. The location is 35 miles from Kyle of Lochalsh and 5 miles from Portree. Sportslovers are attracted to the hotel, gathering in the firelit lounge for a whisky. The atmosphere is of hardy tweeds. The loch outside is well stocked with salmon and trout, and a short par-three golf course has been constructed. Of the 21 handsomely furnished rooms, all contain private bath or shower. Singles are accepted at a rate of £34 ($56.10) to £35 ($57.75) daily, depending on the plumbing, and doubles on a similar basis cost £68 ($112.20) to £72 ($118.80). All tariffs include a full Scottish breakfast. The Scottish fare, featuring smoked salmon, is served on fine china with elegant silver. A bar buffet lunch goes for £6.50 ($10.75), and a four-course dinner for £16 ($26.40).

THE SLEAT PENINSULA

A lot of Skye can look melancholy and forlorn, especially in misty weather. But for a change of landscape pace, head for the Peninsula of Sleat, the southeastern section of the island. It's long been known as the "Garden of Skye" because of the lushness of its vegetation. The reason for this is that its shores are washed by the waters of the Gulf Stream. Sleat also possesses several sightseeing attractions.

A ruined stronghold of the MacDonalds, **Knock Castle,** lies off the A851, 12 miles south of Broadford. It can be visited, admission-free, throughout the day. Another MacDonald stronghold, **Dunsgiath Castle,** has some well-preserved ruins open to view. They are found at Tokavaig on an unclassified road (a sign directs you) at a point 20 miles south and southwest of Broadford.

Clan Donald Centre

At Armadale, you don't have to have MacDonald as your last name to enjoy a visit to Skye's award-winning Clan Donald Centre (tel. 04714/305), with its historical exhibition, "The Headship of the Gael," woodland gardens, restaurant, and gift shop. You reach it from Broadford by traveling along a winding seaside road, eventually pulling into the well-kept grounds surrounding the sculptured ruins of Armadale Castle and the rebuilt baronial stables. A multimedia exhibition in part of the castle tells of the lost culture of the ancient Gaelic world under the MacDonalds, as Lords of the Isles. There is a countryside ranger service with a full summer program of guided walks and talks to introduce you to several miles of trails and the history and workings of the adjacent Highland estate. There is also a program of evening arts and theater events.

Admission is £2 ($3.30) for adults and £1.50 ($2.50) for children. The center is open daily from April to the end of October from 9:30am to 5:30pm. The licensed restaurant in the stables offers home-baking and good local food, from teas and coffees to a full meal. The drive from the ferryboat at Kyleakin is about 30 minutes, and the center is near the Armadale Mallaig ferry.

5. Oban and District

Oban (meaning "small bay") is the great port for the Western Isles and a center of Gaelic culture. It is the gateway to Mull, largest of the Inner Hebrides; to the island of Iona, the cradle of Scottish Christianity; and to Staffa, where Fingal's Cave inspired Mendelssohn to write his *Hebrides* Overture. There are cruises to Iona from early June to late September. For information about island ferry services to Mull, Iona, and the Outer Hebrides, get in touch with **MacBraynes Steamers** at their office in Oban (tel. 0631/62285).

OBAN

One of Scotland's leading coastal resorts, the bustling port town of Oban is set in a sheltered bay that is almost landlocked by the island of Kerrera. A yachting center and small burgh, it lies 50 miles south of Fort William and 123 miles from Edinburgh. A **Tourist Information Centre** is on Glencruitten Road (tel. 0631/62868).

From Pulpit Hill in Oban there is a fine view across the Firth of Lorn and the Sound of Mull. Overlooking the town is an unfinished replica of the Colosseum of Rome, **McCaig's Tower,** built by a banker, John Stuart McCaig, in 1897-1900 as a memorial to his family and to try to curb local unemployment during a slump. Its walls are two feet thick and from 37 to 40 feet high. The courtyard within is landscaped and the tower is floodlit at night. Outsiders have been heard to refer to the tower as "McCaig's Folly," but Obanites deplore this term, as they are proud of the structure.

On the island of Kerrera stands **Gylen Castle,** home of the MacDougalls, dating back to 1587.

Near the little granite **Cathedral of the Isles,** one mile north of the end of the bay, is the ruin of the 13th-century **Dunollie Castle,** seat of the Lords of Lorn, who once owned a third of Scotland.

You can visit **Dunstaffnage Castle,** 3½ miles to the north, which was believed to have been the royal seat of the Dalriadic monarchy in the 8th century. The present castle was probably built in 1263. It may have been the location of the Scots Court until the unification under Kenneth McAlpine and the transfer to Scone of the seat of Scottish government. The castle is open April to September from 9:30am to 7pm (Sun. from 2 to 7pm); October to March, from 9:30am to 4pm (Sun. from 2 to 4pm); closed Thur. and Fri. Admission is 75p ($1.25) for adults, 50p (85¢) for children.

Where to Stay

As a holiday resort, Oban has a number of good hotels and guesthouses within easy reach of the seafront and the piers from which cruises to the offshore islands can be booked.

Alexandra, Corran Esplanade, Oban, Argyll PA34 5AA (tel. 0631/62381), is a stone hotel with gables and a tower, plus a Regency front veranda, enjoying a sunny perch on the promenade. From its public rooms, you can look out onto Oban Bay. Two sun lounges overlook the seafront. The 55 bedrooms are substantial and pleasing, offering comfort and conveniences at £48 ($79.20) daily in a single, £78 ($128.70) in a double, including a full breakfast, service, and VAT. Bedrooms contain private baths or showers. The restaurant, serving good food, also opens onto the panorama. A complete dinner in the evening averages around £16 ($26.40). Dinner is sometimes accompanied by live music and dancing. The hotel is open from Easter to the end of October.

Great Western Hotel, Corran Esplanade, Oban, Argyll PA34 5PP (tel. 0631/63101), is a warmly old-fashioned hotel set directly on the waterfront across the street from the harborfront promenade. Each of its 84 well-furnished bedrooms contains a private bath and a sweeping view over the inter-island ferryboats and fishing vessels bobbing at anchor in the harbor. The hotel, which is owned by one of Britain's well-known chains, offers Scottish entertainment in one of its lounges and a well-appointed dining room and a spacious water-view lounge where drinks are served. Guests pay from £36 ($59.40) to £43 ($70.95) daily in a single, from £54 ($89.10) to £68 ($112.20) in a double.

Lancaster, Corran Esplanade, Oban, Argyll PA34 5AD (tel. 0631/62587), is distinguished by its attractive pseudo-Tudor facade. On the crescent of the bay, it commands views from its public rooms of the islands of Lismore and Kerrera, even the more distant peaks of Mull. Open all year, the hotel welcomes you to one of its 27 well-furnished bedrooms, charging from £28 ($46.20) to £33 ($54.45) daily in a single and £48 ($79.20) to £54 ($89.10) in a double, with breakfast included. Twenty-four rooms have private baths or showers. The fully licensed Lancaster is the only hotel in Oban featuring a heated indoor swimming pool, a sauna, a whirlpool, and a solarium.

Caledonian Hotel, Station Square, Oban, Argyll PA34 5RT (tel. 0631/63133), makes good on its promise of giving you a "taste for the Highlands." A fine example of Scottish 19th-century architecture, it occupies a landmark position, with a good view opening onto the harbor and Oban Bay looking toward the Mull of Kintyre. This convenient location puts you close to the rail, bus, and ferry terminals from which you can book passage to the Isles. The 70 bedrooms are up to date with private baths, phones, color TVs, and beverage-making equipment. Serviced by an elevator, the hotel offers singles for £48 ($79.20) nightly, with doubles climbing to £70 ($115.50). Good, reasonably priced Scottish fare is served in the dining room.

Knipoch Hotel, Kilniver, near Oban, Argyll PA34 4QT (tel. 08526/251), stands on its own grounds with views over Loch Feochan, lying 1½ miles north of Kilniver on A816 and 6 miles south of Oban. It is the premier place in the Oban district for both accommodations and food (see below). A much-altered and extended Georgian country-house hotel, it is family run by the Craigs, who have created a tasteful but simply decorated world of comfort. Guests relax in wood-paneled lounges before retiring to one of the 18 well-furnished bedrooms, each with private bath, shower, and TV. The single rate begins at £50 ($82.50) daily, rising to £100 ($165) in a double. Guests are received from mid-February to mid-November in this inviting place.

Where to Dine

Knipoch Hotel Restaurant, Kilniver (tel. 08526/251). At last Oban has a truly fine restaurant. Only trouble is, you have to drive 6 miles south to enjoy it (see previous recommendation). Jenny and Colin Craig, a mother-son team, offer a choice of three dining rooms and a daily-changing menu of five delectable courses. In their whitewashed Georgian house, the oldest part dating from the 16th century, they serve food daily from 12:30 to 1:30pm, when a set meal costs £13.50 ($22.30), and from 7:30 to 9pm, when a table d'hôte dinner is offered for £28 ($22.30). Salmon and halibut are smoked on the premises, and the menu relies heavily on Scottish produce, including fresh fish. Try the cock-a-leekie soup, followed by Sound of Luing scallops or saddle of Scottish lamb stuffed with herbs. The wine cellar is excellent, especially in its selection of bordeaux. Reservations are essential. The restaurant is closed from mid-November to mid-February.

McTavish's Kitchens, 34 George St. (tel. 0631/63064), is dedicated to preserving the local cuisine. Downstairs is a self-service restaurant, which is open in summer daily from 9am to 9pm, serving breakfast, main meals, shortbread, scones, strawberries, cakes, teas, and coffees. The two bars are the upstairs Lairds Bar and, around the corner from the self-service, the Mantrap Bar with a "real mantrap." The licensed second-floor restaurant has a more ambitious Scottish and continental menu with higher prices, but there are also budget lunches for around £5 ($8.25) for two courses, and high teas for £4.50 ($7.45). The table d'hôte menu includes an appetizer, a main course that might be fresh salmon, and a dessert such as strawberries or raspberries in season. The price is £9.50 ($15.70). The à la carte menu offers haggis, Loch Fyne kippers (oak-smoked herring), prime Scottish steaks, smoked salmon, venison, and local mussels.

In the Environs

Isle of Eriska Hotel, Ledaig, Connel, near Oban, Argyll PA37 1SD (tel. 063172/371), is a Victorian house that welcomes you at the end of a winding drive. In the Middle Ages, this forested island was considered a place of sanctuary, under the protection of the church. In the 19th century an industrialist purchased it, planted hundreds of beech trees, and built a bridge to the mainland. Today you can savor the splendors of a country life. From its pinnacle, you'll enjoy a panorama of the surrounding waterways, as well as views of a local colony of deer and the forest, which is still maintained as a private park. A magnificent front door leads to the entrance hall where a log fire blazes. A formal sitting room and a library/bar are pleasant, and a wide staircase leads to 16 well-furnished bedrooms, with modern baths, phones, and TVs. Bed and breakfast is £96 ($158.40) daily in a single, £120 ($198) in a double. Guests are charged £30 ($49.50) for dinner. The Isle of Eriska is owned by Mr. and Mrs. Robin Buchanan-Smith (he's a Protestant minister).

PORT APPIN

Twenty-four miles north of Oban lies a beautiful lochside district, including Lismore Island. Port Appin is a small village with stone cottages. On an islet nearby is a landmark, **Castle Stalker,** the ancient seat of the Stewarts of Appin, built in the 15th century by Duncan Stewart, son of the first chief of Appin. Dugald, the ninth chief, was forced to sell the estate in 1765, and the castle slowly fell into ruin. It was recently restored by Lt. Col. Stewart Allward and is once again inhabited. According to myth, there's a subterranean undersea passage at Port Appin where a piper supposedly entered with his dog. Only the dog returned, and he was hairless. It is open from March to September by appointment (tel. 088362/3944). The cost is £4 ($6.60) for adults, £2 ($3.30) for children, including the boat trip.

Where to Stay

The Airds Hotel, Port Appin, Argyll PA38 4DF (tel. 063173/236), is an old ferry inn dating from 1700, in one of the most beautiful spots in the historic district of Appin. Considered one of the outstanding hotels of Scotland, it is a *Relais & Chateaux,* midway between Oban and Fort William. The hotel overlooks not only Loch Linnhe, but the island of Lismore and the mountains of Morvern, an ideal center for touring this area of the country. You can take forest walks in many directions, or go pony trekking, sea angling, or trout fishing. Boats can be rented and trips arranged to see the seals and to visit the island of Lismore. The resident proprietors, Eric and Betty Allen, welcome you to one of their 14 comfortably furnished bedrooms from April to the end of November, charging £70 ($115.50) to £95 ($156.75) per person daily in a double or twin and £90 ($148.50) in a single. Everything is immaculately maintained and handsomely decorated, and the setting is tranquil. Each of the rooms has a private bath, phone, and TV.

It is the food that makes the Airds such an outstanding place to visit. Betty Allen is one of the great cooks of Scotland. In her repertoire of fine Scottish cuisine, home-baking is a specialty, and fresh produce is used in making up the menus. Specialties include Loch Fyne kippers, smoked-mackerel salad, and an exceptional kidney soup. Sole is often served stuffed with crab mousse, or perhaps you'll sample the roast haunch of venison with rowan jelly if featured. Desserts include such mouthwatering concoctions as baked lemon tart. A meal here will cost from £28 ($46.20). Reservations for dinner, served only at 8pm, are absolutely necessary. The hotel is closed November 5 to mid-March.

LOCH AWE

Twenty-two miles long and in most places only about a mile wide, Loch Awe for years acted as a natural moat protecting the Campbells of Inveraray from their enemies to the north. Along its banks and on its islands are many reminders of its fortified past. There is a ruined castle at Fincharn, at the southern end of the loch, and another on the island of Fraoch Eilean. The **Isle of Inishail** has an ancient chapel and burial ground, and at the northern end of the loch are the ruins of **Kilchurn Castle,** built by Sir Colin Campbell in 1440. The bulk of Ben Cruachan, 3,689 feet, dominates Loch Awe at its northern end and attracts climbers. On the ben is the world's second-largest hydroelectric power station, which pumps water from Loch Awe to a reservoir high up the mountain. Below the mountain are the **Falls of Cruachan** and the wild **Pass of Brander,** where Robert the Bruce routed the Clan MacDougall in 1308.

In this area, the Forestry Commission maintains the vast forests, and a road now makes it possible to travel around Loch Awe, so that it is more than ever a popular angling center. Sharp-eyed James Bond fans may even recognize some scenes that appeared in one of the films.

The Pass of Brander where Loch Awe narrows was the scene of many a fierce battle in bygone times, and something of that bloody past seems to brood over the narrow defile. Through it the waters of the Awe flow on their way to Loch Etive. This winding sealoch is 19 miles long, stretching from Dun Dunstaffnage Bay at Oban to Glen Etive, reaching into the Moor of Rannoch at the foot of the 3,000-foot Buachaille Etive (the Shepherd of Etive), into which Glencoe also reaches.

Where to Stay and Dine

Ardanaiseig, Kilchrenan by Taynuilt, Argyll PA35 1HE (tel. 08663/333). When one of the 19th-century Campbell family patriarchs erected this manorial seat in 1834, he designed its lines more along 18th-century styles. He planted some of the rarest trees in the British islands, many of them exotic conifers. Today, clusters of fruit trees within a walled garden, along with rhododendrons and azaleas, add to the arboreal interest of this elegant graystone property. The house stands between Loch Awe and the peaks of Cruachan, and a golf course is within a 40-minute drive. Rentable fishing vessels add another diversion. Until recently a private home, the hotel has formal sitting rooms graced with big chintzy chairs, fresh flowers, and polished tables. Upstairs, each of the 14 well-heated bedrooms contains a private bath, color TV, direct-dial phone, more chintz, and high ceilings. The price of a double room depends on its size, ranging from small to a master bedroom with a loch views at rates going from £150 ($247.50) to £205 ($338.25) daily, with singles renting for £92 ($151.80). The owners have employed an excellent chef, who makes use of fresh produce, game, and meats with skill and flair. To reach the property from Oban, take the A85 to Taynuilt, then follow a secondary road, the B845, to Kilchrenan. Follow the signs to Ardanaiseig. Guests are received from mid-April to mid-October.

THE CRINAN CANAL

The nine-mile-long canal, constructed between 1793 and 1801, was designed to provide water communication between the Firth of Clyde, Argyll, the western Highlands, and the islands. It runs roughly north from Ardrishaig and curves gradually to the west before reaching Loch Crinan on the Sound of Jura. Four miles north of **Cairnbaan**, on the canal, is the ruined hill-fort of **Dunadd**, once capital of Dalriada, kingdom of the Scots. There are numerous Bronze Age stone circles in the vicinity, and **Kilmartin churchyard**, five miles north of Cairnbaan, has a carved cross dating from the 16th century. **Carnasserie Castle**, also to the north of the canal, built in the late 16th century, was the home of John Carswell, the first post-Reformation bishop of the isles, whose translation of John Knox's liturgy into Gaelic was the first book to be published in that language.

Crinan, a yachting haven on the Sound of Jura, is overlooked by the early-11th-century **Duntrune Castle**, one of the oldest castles in Scotland, and still inhabited by the descendants of the original owners, the Clan Malcolm.

Where to Stay and Dine

Crinan is a charming little village and the address of my recommendation for a stopover in this area:

Crinan Hotel, Crinan, Argyll PA31 8SR (tel. 054683/261), off the B841, seven miles northwest of Lochgilphead, is an inn with a bright, attractive decor and modern comforts and conveniences. Because of its location on a canal and yacht basin, it is naturally a favorite with sailors, who book its 22 rooms with private bath in July and August, the peak sailing months. If you're reserving (and I highly recommend that you do), ask for one of the rooms with private balconies opening onto mountains and lochside sunsets. Bedrooms, which contain a phone and TV, rent for £40 ($66) daily in a single, from £85 ($140.25) in a double, including a breakfast that often features oatcakes and hot croissants.

The hotel's **Loch 16 Restaurant** is the finest in the area. Nick Ryan, co-owner of the hotel with his wife, Frances, is the guiding force behind the restaurant. Local fisherman bring their finest catches to him. The menu reflects that bountiful harvest from the sea, including lobster from Jura and large prawns (often cooked in a pan with tropical fruit). Try Nick's fish soup and go on to mussels from Loch Craignish prepared in a marinara style. The dessert list is always delectable. Everything tastes fresh at this rooftop location where you can watch the sun set over the loch. Lunch is served from 12:30 to 2pm and dinner at 8pm. Lunch costs £12 ($19.80); dinner is a set menu at £30 ($49.50), or you can order à la carte for about £35 ($57.75) per person. Closed Mon., Tues., and from the end of October until a week before Easter.

You can also order a set dinner for £25 ($41.25) in the **Telford Room**, nightly from 7 to 9pm. Again, the menu features fish, served only when freshly caught, and the "fruits" of the Scottish sea. When fish is not offered, guests settle for steaks and roasts. For dessert, try the lemon tart. Reservations are needed in both places.

INVERARAY

This small resort and royal burgh occupies a splendid Highland setting three-quarters of a mile northwest of Loch Fyne and 58 miles northwest of Glasgow. The hereditary seat of the Dukes of Argyll, **Inveraray Castle** (tel. 0499/2203) has been headquarters of the Clan Campbell since the early 15th century. In 1644 the original village was burned by the Royalist Marquess of Montrose, was rebuilt, and then the third duke of Argyll built a new castle between 1744 and 1788. The 11th duke opened the castle to the public and it is now presided over by the present laird, the 12th duke of Argyll and 26th MacCailein Mor, chief of the Clan Campbell. The castle is among the earliest examples of Gothic revival in Britain, and offers a fine collection of pictures and 18th-century French furniture, old English and continental porcelain, and a magnificent Armoury Hall, which alone contains 1,300 pieces. There is a castle shop for souvenirs and a tea room where tea, coffee, and snack meals are served. The castle is open from 10am to 1pm and 2 to 6pm in April, May, June, September, and October; closed Fri. In July and August, hours are 10am to 6pm; 1 to 6pm on Sun. Admission is £2.50 ($4.15) for adults, £1.50 ($2.50) for children. A family ticket is available for £7 ($11.55). The castle is closed on Fri. from the opening date until the end of June each year and in September and October.

At one end of the main street of the town is a Celtic burial cross from Iona. The parish church is divided by a wall enabling services to be held in Gaelic and English at the same time.

The **Bell Tower** of All Saints' Episcopal Church, set in pleasant grounds, contains Scotland's finest bells, the second-heaviest ring of ten in the world. An easy staircase leads to a safe pedestrian walkway on top of the tower to see the bells and fine views over the loch and glen. The tower is open from 10am to 1pm and 2 to 5pm Mon. to Sat., and 2 to 5pm on Sun. from May to the end of September. It costs adults 60p ($1) and children 30p (50¢), to ascend the tower, but the ground-floor exhibition is free. For more information, telephone 0499/2433.

The **Auchindrain Museum of Country Life** (tel. 04995/235), six miles southwest of Inveraray, is an open-air museum of traditional Highland farming life. It is a unique survivor of the past, whose origins are so far back as to be a subject for archeology. The farming township stands more or less as it was in the 1800s, but studies have revealed at least four centuries before that. At present, Auchindrain consists of 20-odd acres of "infield," about which stands 21 houses and barns of the 18th and 19th centuries. Some are furnished to their appropriate period, and others contain displays. There is also an exhibit center and a museum shop. Open daily from 10am to 5pm in summer, it charges £2 ($3.30) for adults, £1.20 ($2) for children over 8 years old. The museum is closed Sat. in April, May, and September. Auchindrain and mid-Argyll are in an area crammed with places of interest for historians, antiquarians, and archeologists.

A fine woodland garden may be visited at **Crarae Lodge,** four miles southwest of the village.

Where to Stay and Dine

The Great Inn, Inveraray, Argyll PA32 8XB (tel. 0499/2466), is part of the estates of the dukes of Argyll and is just a stone's throw from Inveraray Castle, home of the 12th duke and his family. The Great Inn was built in 1755, designed by the famous Scottish architect, John Adam. The inn specialties in traditional Scottish fare, including game, salmon, haggis, and fish from Loch Fyne. Food is served all day. Many visitors drop in for afternoon tea. All 25 rooms have been renovated, each with private bath or shower. B&B costs from £28 ($46.20) per person daily.

6. The Inner Hebrides

Geologists wandering through bog and bracken used to happen on painters and birdwatchers and stumble across an occasional sea angler or mountain climber. That era of solitude was some time ago, however. These special-interest individuals still frequent the islands of the Hebrides, but now you'll find more and more general tourists.

Nearly everybody has heard of Mull and Iona, but what about Rhum, Eigg, and Muck? (Sounds like a goblin Christmas recipe.) On these little islands of the Inner

Hebrides, visitors can meet crofters (small farmers) and fisher folk, even join in a real island *ceilidh* (singing party). Arran, Islay—that most southerly of the Hebridean islands—and the Isle of Jura, along with romantic Skye, are covered in other sections.

Mull, featured in Robert Louis Stevenson's *Kidnapped*, has wild scenery, golf courses, and a treasure trove of tradition. Iona played a major part in the spread of Christianity in Britain, and a trip there usually includes a visit to Staffa, a tiny, uninhabited volcanic island where Fingal's Cave inspired Mendelssohn.

This chain of islands lies just off the west coast of the Scottish mainland. To visit them, you'll be following a worthy tradition—in the footsteps of Dr. Samuel Johnson and his faithful Boswell.

Caledonian MacBrayne (tel. 0475/33755) provides the main link for boat transportation around the Inner Hebrides. Call them for information about departures.

MULL

The third largest island in the Hebrides, Mull is rich in legend and folklore, a land of ghosts, monsters, and the wee folk. Over open fires that burn on cold winter evenings, the talk is of myths and ancient times. The island is wild and mountainous, characterized by sea lochs and sandy bars.

Getting to Mull is easy, unlike travel to some of the other islands of the Inner Hebrides. It's best reached on a car-ferry from Oban, the trip taking 45 minutes. For times of departure, contact **Caledonian MacBrayne,** the Ferry Terminal, Oban (tel. 0631/62285). It's a roll-on, roll-off type of operation for your car.

The Mull Highland Games are held annually in July, filled with all the traditional events such as bagpiping, caber-tossing, and dancing. Another popular time to visit is in early October, when the Tour of Mull Rally is held. First run in 1969, it has been an attraction ever since. Motorsports lovers thrill to the idea of 120 miles of island roads, and twisting, tortuous ones they are.

If you come to Mull, be sure to bring a raincoat, as it is known as the wettest island in the Hebrides, a fact that upset Dr. Johnson, who visited here in 1773. Actually, Dr. Johnson was a latecomer to Mull, which has an ancient history. It was, in fact, known to the classical Greeks, and its prehistoric past is recalled in forts, duns, and stone circles.

Many visitors consider Mull more beautiful than Skye, a controversy I don't choose to get involved in, as both the islands are different, each with its many attractions. However, Mull is made additionally enticing in that it can be used as a launching pad from which to explore the famed islands of Iona and Staffa, coming up. Mull has a varied scenery, with many waterfalls. Its highest peak is **Ben More** at 3,169 feet, but it also has many flat areas. It is rich in wildlife, including roe deer, golden eagles, polecats, seabirds, and feral goats.

Guarding the bay (you'll see it as you cross on the ferry) is Duart Castle, restored just before World War I and once the seat of the fiery Macleans, who shed much blood in and around the castle during their battles with the Lords of the Isles. In the bay—somewhere—lies the *Florencia*, a Spanish galleon that went down laden with treasure. Many attempts have been made to bring it up, but so far all of them have failed.

To the southeast, near Salen, are the ruins of **Aros Castle,** once the stronghold of the Lords of the Isles, the MacDonalds. Its ruins date from the 14th century, and it was last occupied in the 17th century.

On the far south coast at Lochbuie, **Moy Castle** has a water-filled dungeon. The wild countryside of Mull was the scene of many of David Balfour's adventures in *Kidnapped* by Robert Louis Stevenson.

If you're driving along any of the single-track roads of Mull, remember to take your time and let the sheep and cattle have the right-of-way. Also, a car coming downhill toward you has preference, so seek a spot to pull off.

There are two nine-hole golf courses on the island. The Western Isles Golf Course at Tobermory, the island's capital, dates from the 1930s and is said to have possibly the best views of any course in the world. A newer course, flat and tight, opened in 1980 at Craignure. Sea fishing and river fishing are also popular on Mull, where anglers seek salmon and three kinds of trout: rainbow, sea, and brown. The trout is found in the fast-flowing rivers and hill lochs of the island. Some sportslovers take to the sea in pursuit of sharks and monster skate. Stalking, hiking, and hill walking are other activities for the fit.

At the end of the day, you might enjoy a dram of malt whisky from the **Tobermory Malt Whisky Distillery,** which has had a troubled history but is now back in business. Incidentally, visitors are welcome to visit the distillery in Tobermory, established in 1823. Call 0688/2119 for an appointment.

The Major Sights

Torosay Castle at Craignure (tel. 06802/421) is a Victorian mansion constructed in the mid-19th century by David Bryce, a famous Scottish architect. In his early years, Winston Churchill was a frequent visitor. The castle is set in gardens designed at the turn of the century by Sir Robert Lorimer. One writer said that a visit here is like returning to "the Edwardian age of leisure," and so it is. To the surprise of hundreds of visitors, the armchairs are labeled "Please sit down" instead of "Please keep off." This is very much a family place, home to four generations. It is the only castle and garden in private occupation in the West Highlands that is open daily to the public. The castle has family portraits by such famous artists as Sargent, along with wildlife pictures. It has numerous exhibits to intrigue visitors, including evidence for the Loch Ness monster. It's like browsing through a scrapbook of 100 years of family history to visit here. Later you can wander through 12 acres of Italian-style terraced gardens, which include a water garden with shrubs that grow in the Gulf Stream climate, along with a Japanese garden and life-size figures by Antonio Bonazza. You can enjoy extensive views of the Appin coastline from Ben Nevis to Ben Cruachan. The castle and gardens are open daily from 10:30am to 5:30pm from the first of May until mid-October. Admission is £2.50 ($4.15) for adults and £1 ($1.65) for children.

Duart Castle (mentioned above), off the A849 on the eastern point of Mull (tel. 06802/309), dates from the 13th century and was the home of the Maclean Clan. An imposing and majestic structure, it was sacked in 1691 by the Dukes of Argyll in retaliation for the Macleans' having supported the Stuarts in 1715 and 1745. It was allowed to fall into ruins. However, Sir Fitzroy Maclean, the 26th chief of the clan and the grandfather of the present occupant, began restoration in 1911, spending a considerable fortune in the process. It had been his ambition since he was a boy to see his ancestral home restored, a task he began at the age of 76. He lived until he was 102, so he had time to enjoy it. Many relics of clan history are found inside. Visitors can wander about, taking in such rooms as the Banqueting Hall, which is in the keep, the great tower that is the heart of the castle. Duart is open daily from May to September from 10:30am to 6pm, charging £2.50 ($4.15) for adults and £1.50 ($2.50) for children under 14.

The **Old Byre Heritage Centre,** near Dervaig (tel. 06884/229), houses an audio-visual museum with interchangeable slide shows covering the heritage of Mull. These include geological exhibits, along with artifacts from the island's history. In particular, six specially created taxidermic exhibits of wildlife found in Mull are shown in their native habitat. These shows take place every 30 minutes. The museum is open daily from 10:30am to 6:30pm from Palm Sunday to mid-October. Admission is £1.50 ($2.50) for adults and 75p ($1.25) for children. A gift and craft shop are on the premises, along with a licensed tearoom offering light meals and homemade baking.

Mull Railway

Even passengers who arrive on Mull with their car might want to take an excursion on the only passenger railway in the Hebrides. It was inaugurated in 1983, and its puffing engine and narrow-gauge tracks give the impression of a frontier-style excursion into the past. The tracks begin at the Old Pier in Craignure, running 1½ miles to Torosay Castle and its famous gardens. Some of the engines are powered by steam, others by diesel. Regardless of the mode of power, the view remains one of unspoiled mountains, glens, and seaside. Otters, eagles, and deer can sometimes be seen in the course of the 20-minute journey. Trains operate between late April and mid-October. The most frequent service occurs between June and mid-September when it begins Mon. to Fri. at 11:10am and on Sat. and Sun. at 11:15am. Most visitors use the train as an opportunity to spend a few hours to explore Torosay Castle before returning to the Oban ferryboat at Craignure. One-way fares are £1 ($1.65) for adults and 80p ($1.30) for children. A special round-trip ticket is available for families of two parents and two children, costing £4.10 ($6.75).

For more information, call the **Mull and West Highland Railway Co.** in Craignure (tel. 06802/494; 0680/300389 off-season).

Where to Stay and Dine

Always make a reservation if you're planning to spend the night on Mull. Here is a preview of a selection of hotels scattered across the island.

TOBERMORY   In a beautiful location above the harbor, looking out upon the bay, **Western Isles,** Tobermory, Isle of Mull, Argyll PA75 6PR (tel. 0688/2012), is a large graystone country inn on a bluff above Tobermory. It was constructed by the Sandeman sherry company in the late 1880s as a hunting and fishing lodge for their top-level staff and customers. It was owned for a number of years by the MacBrayne shipping company. The current owners welcome visitors to 24 rooms decorated in a mixture of styles, but they're homelike, spotless, and have electric heaters. Twenty have private baths or showers. B&B ranges in price from £33 ($54.45) to £38 ($62.70). You get good meals here, especially fish dishes. A four-course dinner goes for £12 ($19.80). The hotel is closed from mid-October to March.

The Tobermory Hotel, Tobermory, Isle of Mull, Argyll PA75 6NT (tel. 0688/2091), is in many ways the prestige hotel of Tobermory, occupying a prime position on the waterfront. With chimneys and gables, it is painted a pleasing pink. Reg and Jackie Gibbons welcome visitors all year in one of their 15 well-furnished bedrooms, seven of which contain private baths. Rates range from £21 ($34.65) to £27 ($44.55) per person nightly for B&B. Personal service is a hallmark of this little inn, and the place is known for its good Scottish food. You can order dinner at 7:30pm.

CRAIGNURE   A first-class hotel that opened in 1971, the **Isle of Mull,** Craignure, Isle of Mull, Argyll PA65 6BB (tel. 06802/351) stands near the ferry and the meeting point of the Sound of Mull and Loch Linnhe. From the picture windows of its public rooms you'll have panoramic vistas of mountains and the island of Lismore. Each of its 60 bedrooms, all handsomely furnished, comes equipped with private bath and shower, color TV, and tea/coffee-makers, B&B costs £43 ($70.95) daily in a single, £74 ($122.10) in a double, all prices including VAT. The food is good and served in the attractive dining room, which faces both sea and hills. The chef does both British and continental dishes. The sea trout is superb. Hopefully, you'll be there on a night when the specialty is roast haunch of venison with gooseberry sauce. A set dinner costs from £13 ($21.45). Other facilities include a cocktail bar and a resident's lounge. The hotel is open from mid-April to mid-October.

NEAR BUNESSAN   Three miles west of Bunessan by the A849 is **Ardfenaig House,** Bunessan, Isle of Mull, Argyll PA67 6DX (tel. 06817/210). You pass through two gates set into the bumpy access road, taking care not to let grazing sheep escape in the process. For a certain type of discriminating reader, a stay here can represent a perfect retreat in a cozily proportioned country house, where the thick stone walls and the blazing fireplace ward off the damp and chill of mists rising from the nearby Loch Caol. The house, two miles from the Iona Ferry, just off the main road from Craignure, is also the nearest licensed hotel to Iona. The slate-roofed house was originally built as a Georgian-era farmhouse by the Duke of Argyll as a residence for his chamberlain. In 1875 it was expanded into a hunting lodge. By 1971, after years of neglect, the house had degenerated into little more than a rotted and abandoned shell. At that time it was rescued and restored by I.C.A. Bowles who'd been a university librarian at Oxford before retreating to the Scottish Isles. The private library fills shelf after shelf of wall space. Many of the furnishings are heirlooms. The house is small enough, and the cubby-hole bar intimate enough, that the establishment can cater to only four guests. The owner accepts guests only between May and the end of September, charging from £65 ($107.25) per person daily for half board. The 15 acres connected to the house offer dozens of options for hiking. Reservations are absolutely necessary.

DERVAIG Two miles southeast by the B8073, the **Druimnacroish Country House Hotel,** Dervaig, Isle of Mull, Argyll PA75 6QW (tel. 06884/274), is small and exclusive. In Bellart Glen, this stone house owes its personality and charm to Wendy and Donald McLean. It is the only hotel built, owned, and run by a McLean on the island. Handsomely furnished and well appointed, the hotel occupies what was once listed as a "ruin" on an ordnance survey map. The McLeans attract an international coterie of guests to their six lovely rooms, which are available from May to October. Each has its private bath. As you enter your room, you'll find a welcoming bottle of Tobermory whisky (a miniature but a thoughtful gesture, nevertheless). Guests book in here on the half-board plan, costing from £62 ($102.30) per person per day. Wendy is a superb cook, and you get not only produce from their six-acre garden but also some of the finest lamb, Angus steak, venison, and salmon that Scotland has to offer. One reader wrote, "I could cover a page telling about the gourmet quality of the food so graciously served by Donald. Also this is the only hotel where I felt I could walk barefoot on clean carpets."

TIRORAN About a mile off the B8035 road, **Tiroran House,** Tiroran, Isle of Mull, PA69 6ES (tel. 06815/232) stands in wooded grounds sweeping down to Loch Scridain. Flowering shrubs abound and golden pheasants frequent the 12 acres that make up the property of the serenely remote country house. Guests in the house are made to feel at ease, as if they were personal friends of the owners. The nine bedrooms are individually decorated with charm and taste, each with private bath or shower. The charge is from £75 ($123.75) per person per day for half board. The house is decorated with fine art and antiques, and fresh flowers brighten the interior. Meals are served in the dining room, gleaming with polished wood, which has a vine-covered porch adjacent, also used for serving. Dinners may include such dishes as steak and kidney pie with oyster or mushroom sauce, crab mornay, or kidneys in wine with orange. The inn is open from mid-May to October. Although it is some distance from the nearest village, this is a good base for seeing the attractions of Mull.

IONA

Someone once said, "When Edinburgh was but a barren rock and Oxford but a swamp, Iona was famous." It has been known as a place of spiritual power and pilgrimage for centuries. It was the site of the first Christian settlement in Scotland. A remote, low-lying, and treeless island, Iona lies off the southwestern coast of Mull and is only a mile by 3½ miles in size. It is accessible only by passenger ferry from the Isle of Mull (cars must remain on Mull). The ferry to Iona is run by local fishermen, and it's quite informal in service, depending in large part on the weather. Service is generally from 8am to 7pm in summer and 9:30am to 4:30pm in winter.

From 1695 the island was owned by the dukes of Argyll, but the 12th duke was forced to sell to pay £1 million in real estate taxes owed since 1949. The island was purchased by Sir Hugh Fraser, the former owner of Harrods and other stores. He secured Iona's future and made it possible for money raised by the National Trust for Scotland to be turned over to the trustees of the restored abbey.

Iona is known for its **"Graves of the Kings."** A total of 48 Scottish kings, including Macbeth and his victim Duncan, were buried on Iona, as were four Irish kings and eight Norwegian kings.

Today the island attracts nearly 1,000 visitors a day in high season. Most of them come here mainly to see the **Abbey of Iona,** part of which dates back to the 11th century. But they also visit the site of the settlement founded there by St. Columba in 563, from which Celtic Christianity spread through Scotland.

Some visitors consider a visit to Iona the highlight of their trip to Scotland. Aside from viewing it as an unusual historical and archeological site, many persons come back with a renewed interest in both their faith and the power of religion. **The Iona Community,** Iona, PA76 6SN (tel. 06817/404) is an ecumenical religious group that maintains seminars and a communal lifestyle in the ancient abbey. They offer full board and accommodation to visitors who want to share in the community's daily lifestyle. The only ordained members of the group are its two "wardens," each of whom is a member of the Church of Scotland.

During the peak summer months between June and September, the community leads a series of discussion seminars, each of which lasts a week, stretching from Sat. to Sat. The cost of a week's full board during one of these seminars is £115 ($189.75) per person. Guests are expected to contribute a small portion of their day, about 30 minutes, to the execution of some kind of household chore. The daily schedule involves a wakeup call at 7:30am, communal breakfast at 8am, a morning religious service, and plenty of unscheduled time for conversation, study, and contemplation. Up to 50 guests can be accommodated at one time in bathless, bunk-bedded twin rooms. In addition to the abbey, there is the Iona Community's new center for reconciliation, the MacLeod Centre, purpose-built for youth, the disabled, and families. It also accommodates up to 50 guests.

For day visitors, the community leads tours through the rebuilt Benedictine abbey, maintains a gift and book shop, and runs a coffeeshop. Each is open daily from 10am to 4:30pm (the coffeeshop is closed on Sun.). The community is closed for 2 weeks at the end of October, for 2 weeks around New Year's, and in January and February.

There is much to do on Iona, but perhaps best of all, you can simply do nothing and absorb the kind of atmosphere that has drawn people on pilgrimages here for centuries.

One reader, Capt. Robert Haggart of Laguna, California, described his experience this way: "I was enchanted by the place. It really has a mystic atmosphere—one *feels* something ancient here, something spiritual, sacred, long struggles and wonderment about the strength of religion."

Most of the islanders live by crofting and fishing. In addition, they supplement their income by taking in paying guests in season, charging usually very low or at least fair prices. You can, of course, check into the hotel recommended below, but a stay here in a private home may be an altogether rewarding travel adventure. If you don't stay on Iona, you must catch one of the ferries back to Mull, and they stop running at 7pm in summer.

Where to Stay and Dine

St. Columba Hotel, Isle of Iona, Argyll PA76 6SL (tel. 06817/304), is one of only two hotels on the island. It lies just uphill from the village about a quarter of a mile from the jetty and within a 2-minute walk from the abbey. Built of clapboards and white stone, it welcomes guests from April to October. It rents 27 comfortable bedrooms, 9 of which contain private baths or showers. Depending on the season and the accommodation, singles range from £30 ($49.50) to £32 ($52.80) daily, with doubles costing from £54 ($89.10) to £66 ($108.90). These tariffs include VAT, dinner, bed, and breakfast. The food is good, especially the fish dishes, but remember, the last order is taken at 7pm. People turn in early on Iona. Try to get a room overlooking the sea, but know that it is virtually impossible to secure an accommodation here in season without a reservation made well in advance.

STAFFA

The attraction of this island is **Fingal's Cave,** a lure to visitors for more than 200 years and the inspiration for music, poetry, paintings, and prose. Its Gaelic name, An Uamh Ehinn, means "musical cave." The place is unique in that it is the only known such formation in the world with basalt columns. Over the centuries the sea has carved a huge cavern in the basalt, leaving massive hexagonal columns to create what Queen Victoria, after a visit in the 19th century, described in her journal: "The effect is splendid, like a great entrance into a vaulted hall. The sea is immensely deep in the cave. The rocks under water were all colors—pink, blue and green." The sound of the crashing waves and swirling waters caused Mendelssohn to write the *Fingal's Cave* Overture. Turner painted the cave on canvas, and Keats, Wordsworth, and Tennyson all praised it in their poetry.

The island of Staffa has not been inhabited for more than 160 years. Visitors can still explore the cave. Boat trips go there. If you're on Mull or if you've crossed to Iona, you can take boat trips costing £5.50 ($9.10) for adults and £3.50 ($5.50) for children to the rocky shores of Staffa. After docking, visitors are led along the basalt path and into Fingal's Cave. Inside, the noise of the pounding surf is deafening. Chances are you'll be taken over by an experienced Hebridean entrepreneur, seaman David R. Kirkpatrick. Weather permitting, he operates an open boat built in 1982 with canvas protection from the salt spray. The boat runs from Iona every day at 9:45am, stopping at Fionnphort, Mull, just across the channel, at 10am, then proceeding to Staffa for explorations of Fingal's Cave. Mr. Kirkpatrick leads passengers on foot to the cave. Time on Staffa is usually one hour and 15 minutes. Reservations are important: phone Mrs. Norah Kirkpatrick, Seaview Cottage (tel. 06817/373). Rubber-soled shoes and warm clothing are recommended for this excursion.

Another cave, **Clamshell Cave,** can also be visited, but only at low tide, and one appropriately named **Boat Cave** is accessible only by water.

---

7. Kintyre, Arran, and Islay

For many foreign visitors, the Atlantic seaboard of the old county of Argyll will represent a journey into the unknown. For those who want to sample a by gone age, this is one of the most rewarding trips off the coastline of western Scotland. My recommendations lie on islands, easily reached by ferries—except the Kintyre Peninsula, which is a virtual island in itself. You'll soon discover that the Gaelic traditions of the islands endure. Tranquility prevails.

ISLE OF ARRAN

At the mouth of the Firth of Clyde this island is often described as Scotland in miniature, because of its wild and varied scenery, containing an assortment of glens, moors, lochs, sandy bays, and rocky coasts for which the country is known. Ferry services, making the 50-minute crossing, operate from Ardrossan to Brodick, the major village of Arran, lying on the eastern shore. There are also ferry connections linking the northern part of Arran with the Kintyre Peninsula and the Highlands. Once on Arran, you'll find buses to take you to the various villages, each with its own character. A coast road, 60 miles long, runs around the island.

Arran contains some splendid mountain scenery, notably the conical peak of **Goatfell** in the north, reaching a height of 2,866 feet. It's called "the mountain of the winds."

Students of geology flock to Arran to study igneous rocks of the Tertiary Age. Cairns and standing stones at **Tormore** intrigue archeologists as well.

Arran is also filled with beautiful glens, especially **Glen Sannox** in the northeast and **Glen Rosa,** directly north of Brodick. In one day you can see a lot, as the island is only 25 miles long, 10 miles wide.

After the ferry docks at Brodick, you may want to head for Arran's major sight —**Brodick Castle,** 1½ miles north of the Brodick pierhead. The historic home of the dukes of Hamilton, the castle dates from the 13th century and contains superb silver, antiques, portraits, and objects d'art. The site, however has been occupied by a castle of some kind since about the 5th century, when the Dalriad Irish, a Celtic tribe, came here and founded their kingdom. The castle is the property of the National Trust for Scotland. It is open in April after Easter from 1 to 5pm on Mon., Wed., and Sat. From May 1 to September 30, hours are 1 to 5pm daily. The award-winning gardens and the country park are open all year, daily from 10am to 5pm. Admission to both the castle and gardens is £2.40 ($3.95) for adults, £1.20 ($2) for children. For information, telephone 0770/2202.

South from Brodick lies the village and holiday resort of **Lamlash,** opening onto Lamlash Bay. From here a ferry takes visitors over to **Holy Island,** with its 1,000-foot peak. A disciple of St. Columba founded a church on this island.

One of the best-known centers on the western coast is **Blackwater Foot,** which offers pony trekking and golfing.

Finally, in the north, **Lochranza** is a village with unique appeal. It opens onto a bay of pebbles and sand, and in the backdrop lie the ruins of a castle that reputedly was the hunting seat of Robert the Bruce.

Brodick

Douglas Hotel, Brodick, Isle of Arran, Bute KA27 8AW (tel. 0770/2155). Guests landing on Arran by ferryboat need walk only a few paces before reaching the symmetrical, red-sandstone facade of this country-comfortable hotel. In addition to serving as the best-known hotel in Brodick, it also doubles as a center for island social life. Families plan reunion dinners in the large dining room or else cluster in the basement bar amid nautical artifacts and scarlet trappings. The modernized interior contrasts sharply with the 1850s-era facade. The comfortable beds and the conservatively unpretentious furnishings contribute to low-key sojourns. Each of the 30 rooms has a phone, color TV, and tea and coffee maker. Fifteen of the rooms have private baths or showers. With breakfast included, the rate in a single is £30 ($49.50) daily, rising to £58 ($95.70) in a double.

Lamlash

Carraig Mhor, Lamlash, Isle of Arran KA37 8LS (tel. 07706/453), a pebbledash cottage, serves some of the finest food on the island, and its dinners are imaginatively prepared and beautifully presented (but you should always call ahead for a reservation). This modernized cottage stands in the center of the village overlooking the water. Peter and Penny Albrich welcome you to this place seven days a week, serving lunch 12:30 to 2pm from £7 ($11.55) and dinner 7 to 10pm from £15 ($24.75). The chef, who has had worldwide experience, makes extensive use of local produce—in particular, seafood and game. Lunches are mainly seafood. All bread and ice creams, among other offerings, are homemade on the premises. In the evening, there is an extensive à la carte menu available. In addition, the little restaurant offers one double, one twin, and one single room, with hot and cold running water, at a rate of £16 ($26.40) per person daily.

Kilmory

Lagg Hotel, Kilmory, Isle of Arran, Bute KA27 8PQ (tel. 077087/255). There has been some kind of inn in this sheltered hollow since 1791. The building you see today was last enlarged in 1964. The resident proprietors maintain the gardens, which stretch beside the rocky stream adjoining the 10-acre property. If the weather is sunny, you can enjoy tea on the lawn in the shade of palm trees, which thrive in this mild climate. In cooler weather, visitors are likely to be greeted by a log fire blazing in one of the two brick fireplaces around which before-dinner cocktails can be enjoyed in cozy nooks. A fixed-price evening meal in the carvery restaurant costs £14.50 ($23.95). Guests select from several roast joints, and you can also be served salmon or trout from the nearby river. The Sunday buffet lunch is a popular event on the island. The 15 well-furnished bedrooms, each with private bath or shower, cost from £28 ($46.20) per person nightly for B&B.

KINTYRE PENINSULA

The longest peninsula in Scotland, Kintyre is more than 60 miles in length, containing much beautiful scenery, sleepy villages, and miles of sandy beaches. It is one of the most unspoiled areas of Scotland, owing perhaps to its isolation. Former Beatle Paul McCartney, one of the richest men in the world, keeps a home here, drawn to Kintyre by its bucolic charm and individuality.

If you drive all the way to the tip of Kintyre, you'll be only 12 miles from Ireland. Kintyre is ancient Dalriada, the first kingdom of the Scots. It is joined to the mainland of Scotland by a narrow neck of land near the old port of Tarbert. The largest town on the peninsula is Campbeltown on the southeastern coast. In the evening, in some of the Kintyre village halls and hotels, you may hear the music of the *ceilidhs*.

The land mass has many attractions for the intrepid visitor willing to spend the time to seek them out. One beauty spot is the **Carradale House Gardens** (tel. 05833/234), lying off the B842, 12½ miles northeast of Campbeltown. From April to September daily from 10am to 5:30pm, you can visit this walled garden dating from 1870. Because of the outstanding azaleas and rhododendrons, it is best seen in late April, May, and June. You can also see the remains of a fort built on an island that you can reach by foot except at high tide. Admission to the gardens is 50p (85¢).

One of the major attractions of the peninsula is the ruin of **Skipness Castle and Chapel,** lying at Skipness, along the B8001, 10 miles south of Tarbert, opening onto Loch Fyne. The remains of the ancient chapel and the big 13th-century castle look out onto the Sound of Kilbrannan and the Sound of Bute. In its heyday, it could control shipping along Loch Fyne. A five-story tower remains.

TARBERT

A sheltered harbor protects this fishing port and yachting center that lies on a narrow neck of the northern tip of the Kintyre Peninsula, between West Loch Tarbert and the head of herring-filled Loch Fyne. Tarbert lies 93 miles from Glasgow and 135 miles from Edinburgh. Nearby is the finest accommodation on the Kintyre Peninsula.

Where to Stay and Dine

Stonefield Castle Hotel, Tarbert, Argyll PA39 6YJ (tel. 08802/836), occupying a commanding position, is a well-appointed hotel on 60 acres of wooded grounds and some of the most luxuriant gardens in Britain, lying on Loch Fyne, 2 miles outside Tarbert. The castle, with its turrets and steeply pitched roof, was built in the 19th century by the Campbells, whose laird did everything he could to collect the rarest plants found in every corner of the British Empire. The gardens today are believed to be one of the world's best repositories for more than 20 species of tree-size Himalayan rhododendrons, which in April offer a riot of color. The public rooms are decorated in part with antiques. Try to get one of the bedrooms in the main building, although you may be assigned an accommodation in the more modern wing. In all, there are 33 rooms, each with private bath, phone, and TV. Singles range from £45 ($74.25) daily, and doubles go for £80 ($132), including a full Scottish breakfast, service, and VAT. Meals utilize produce from the hotel's own garden. In the kitchen the staff does its own baking. Dinner ranges from £18 ($29.70). The hotel has many facilities, including a drawing room overlooking the loch, cocktail bar, tennis court, putting green, library, outdoor swimming pool, sauna, even yacht anchorage. It's imperative to book well in advance, as Stonefield has a large repeat clientele.

A mile outside the village on the road to Campbeltown, **West Loch Hotel,** Tarbert, Argyll PA29 6YF (tel. 08802/283), is an establishment built 200 years ago as a staging post for coaches heading for Campbeltown and for farmers driving their cattle to the markets at Stirling. Today the comfortably outfitted black-and-white hotel is one of the most attractive in the region, with two bars, one with an open fireplace and one with a woodburning stove, both with windows looking out to the West Loch. The hotel has a checkered history, having served over the years as a collection of apartments and even as a private house. It rents six attractively furnished but bathless bedrooms, costing from £20 ($33) per person daily with a continental breakfast included.

This "restaurant with rooms" specializes in local seafood and game, using only the best of fresh local produce. Vegetables and fruit are brought by carrier from the market in Glasgow, introducing fresh exotic produce to menus that change daily. Dinners, costing from £16 ($26.40), are served in the intimate dining room, and tempting pub meals can be consumed anywhere in the hotel. An excellent bar lunch goes for only £6 ($9.90). The specialties of the house include prime Aberdeen Angus steak *suibhne ma righ lochlann* (stuffed with locally grown oysters), wild Skipness Bay salmon in lime and pine-nut sauce, and Islay venison chops Auld Alliance (in whisky and cream).

CAMPBELTOWN

This is a fishing port and a resort, 176 miles from Edinburgh, with a shingle beach at the southern tip of the Kintyre peninsula. Popularly known as the "wee toon," Campbeltown has long been linked with fishermen.

Campbeltown Loch contains **Davaar Island,** which is accessible at low tide by those willing to cross the Dhorlin, a half-mile run of shingle-paved causeway. It's also possible to take boat trips there. Once on the island, you can visit a crucifixion cave painting, the work of Archibald MacKinnon, a local resident who painted it in 1887. It takes about 1½ hours to walk around this tidal island, with its natural rock gardens.

On the quayside in the heart of town is the **Campbeltown Cross,** which dates from the 14th century. This Celtic cross is considered the finest piece of carving from the Middle Ages left in Kintyre.

Where to Stay and Dine

Seafield, Kilkerran Road, Campbeltown, Kintyre Peninsula, Argyll PA28 6RY (tel. 0586/54385), is a homelike, comfortable guesthouse lying about half a mile from the center of town. The view from its front windows is over the waters of Campbeltown Loch. Between the main building and an annex, this little hotel offers nine bedrooms, each with private bath or shower, phone, and TV. Rooms are comfortably furnished and well maintained. Each of the cozy bedrooms has hot beverage facilities. B&B ranges from £28 ($46.20) per person daily. You can also order good-tasting dinners here for only £12.50 ($20.65).

ISLE OF GIGHA

One of the southern Hebrides, the 6-mile-long Isle of Gigha is often called "sacred" and "legendary." Little changed over the centuries, it lies off the Kintyre Peninsula's west coast. From Tayinloan, you can board a ferry for Gigha. Weather permitting, daily in-season sailings take about 20 minutes to reach the island, depositing you at Ardminish, the main hamlet on the island. For ferry times, phone 05835/254.

Gigha is visited mainly by those wishing to explore its famous gardens, arguably the finest in Scotland. **Achamore House Gardens** (tel. 05835/267) lie only a quarter of a mile from the ferry dock at Ardminish. These extensive gardens contain roses, hydrangeas, rhododendrons, camellias, and azaleas, among other flowering plants. They are open daily year round from 9am to dusk, charging adults an admission of £2 ($3.30) and children £1 ($1.65). Occupying a 50-acre site, the gardens were the creation of the late Sir James Horlick, who was considered one of the great gardeners of the world. The house is not open to the public.

Gigha has a rich Viking past, with cairns and ruins remaining on this bit of land where the marauders often stored their loot after plundering Scotland's west coast. King Haakon came here some 700 years ago and called the island "gud" or good, which was corrupted to Gigha (pronounced "ghee-a") by the Gaels.

Creag Bhan is the highest hill, rising more than 330 feet, and affording a view from the top of the islands of Islay and Jura (coming up) as well as Kintyre. On a clear day you can see Ireland, whence came many of the Celtic missionaries to convert the Hebridean islanders to Christianity. The Ogham Stone on Gigha is sought out by those interested in antiquity. It is one of only two standing stones in the Hebrides bearing Ogham inscriptions, a form of script used in the days of the Scots kingdom of Dalriada (early Irish-Celt settlers).

High on a ridge overlooking the village of Ardminish, you can see the ruins of the 13th-century Church of Kilchattan.

Gigha is the innermost island of the Hebrides, lying 3 miles off the Kintyre Peninsula. As there are virtually no roads on the island, it's best to leave your car on the mainland.

For food and lodging on Gigha, I recommend the **Gigha Hotel**, Isle of Gigha, Argyll PA41 7AD (tel. 05835/254), a small hostelry whose hospitable public bar is the major rendezvous point on the island. It feeds the day visitors who come over to see the Achamore Gardens, but it also shelters tranquility seekers who want to spend more time here. The hotel has nine handsomely furnished, well-maintained, twin-bedded rooms. From April to October, they accept guests, charging from £28 ($46.20) in a single, rising to £58 ($95.70) in a double. Even if you're only visiting for the day, you can enjoy the food served here, perhaps after a drink in one of the cozy lounges with open fireplaces. They specialize in traditional Scottish fare along with homebaked goods. Locally caught seafood, such as lobster, is served, and produce comes from the farms on the island, including dairy products. Game is featured in season. You might begin your meal with a well-flavored bowl of soup, ideal on a chilly day. Meals, costing £15 ($24.75), are offered daily from noon to 2pm and 7 to 8:30pm.

ISLE OF ISLAY

The southernmost island of the Inner Hebrides, Islay lies 16 miles west of the Kintyre Peninsula and less than a mile southwest of Jura, from which it is separated only by a narrow sound. At its maximum breadth, Islay is only 15 miles wide (25 miles long). Called "the Queen of the Hebrides," it is a peaceful, unspoiled island of moors, lochs, sandy bays, and wild rocky cliffs. Islay was the ancient seat of the Lords of the Isles, and today you'll see the ruins of two castles and several Celtic crosses.

Near Port Charlotte are the graves of the U.S. seamen and army troops who lost their lives in 1918 when their carriers, the *Tuscania* and *Otranto,* were torpedoed off the shores of Islay. There's a memorial tower on the Mull of Oa, 8 miles from Port Ellen.

The island is noted for its distilleries, producing single-malt Highland whiskies by the antiquated pot-still method.

MacBrayne Steamers operate a daily service to Islay—you leave West Tarbert on the Kintyre Peninsula, arriving at Port Askaig on Islay.

The island's capital is Bowmore, on the coast across from Port Askaig. There you can see a fascinating round church—no corners for the devil. But the most important town is Port Ellen, on the south coast, a holiday and golfing resort as well as Islay's principal port.

As accommodations are limited on Islay, always arrive with a reservation in your pocket.

Port Askaig

Port Askaig Hotel, Port Askaig, Isle of Islay, Argyll PA46 7RD (tel. 049684/245), is a genuine old island inn, dating from the 18th century, built on the site of an even-older inn. It stands on the Sound of Islay overlooking the pier where a Caledonian MacBrayne car-ferry berths daily. The hotel is charming, offering island hospitality and Scottish fare, including broiled trout, cock-a-leekie soup, roast pheasant, smoked Scottish salmon, and of course, haggis. The hotel is a major destination for anglers on Islay, and the bar at the inn is popular with local fishermen. All year the staff welcomes you to one of its nine well-appointed bedrooms, all with color TVs, radios, and hot beverage facilities, as well as central heating. Four of the rooms contain private baths. For a five-course dinner, bed, and a full Scottish breakfast, the charge is from £40 ($66) daily in a bathless single, from £45 ($74.25) in a single with a bath. Doubles, also on the half-board rate, cost from £35 ($58.60) per person in a bathless room, from £40 ($66) per person with bath. VAT and service are included in the rates. Your hosts are Mr. and Mrs. F. T. Spears.

Bridgend
Bridgend Hotel, Bridgend, Isle of Islay, Argyll PA44 7PF (tel. 049681/212), is striking, with Victorian spires capping the slate-covered roofs. The hotel forms part of a complex of buildings, which includes a roadside barn. One of the most beautiful flower and vegetable gardens on Islay is grown here, and the manager will identify the plants for you. The garden is sheltered by a combination of hillsides, stone walls, and windbreaks. This is one of the oldest hostelries on Islay, with somber charm and country pleasures. Guests enjoy drinks beside open fireplaces in both the Victorian cocktail lounge and the rustic pub where locals gather after a day in the surrounding fields. A table d'hôte dinner in the high-ceilinged dining room costs from £12.50 ($20.65). The 10 bedrooms are comfortable, each with private bath and TV. The charge is from £30 ($49.50) per person daily for B&B. The hotel is open all year.

ISLE OF JURA
This is the fourth-largest island in the Inner Hebrides. It perhaps takes its name from the Norse *Jura,* meaning "deer island." The red deer on Jura outnumber the people by about 20 to 1. At 4 feet high, the deer are the largest wild animals roaming Scotland. The hardy islanders number only about 250 brave souls, and most of them live along the east coast. The west coast is virtually uninhabited.

The capital, **Craighouse,** is hardly more than a hamlet. It is connected by steamer to West Loch Tarbert on the Kintyre Peninsula. If you're already on Islay, you can journey to Jura by taking a 5-minute ferry ride from Port Askaig, docking at the Feolin Ferry berth.

The breadth of Jura varies from 2 to 8 miles, and at its maximum length it is 27 miles long. The island's landscape is dominated by the **Paps of Jura,** reaching a peak of 2,571 feet at Beinn-an-Oir. An arm of the sea, **Loch Tarbert** nearly divides the island, cutting into it for nearly 6 miles.

As islands go, Jura is relatively little known or explored, although its mountains, soaring cliffs, snug coves, and moors make it an inviting paradise—nowhere is there overcrowding. The island has actually lost population drastically.

The square tower of **Claig Castle** is now in ruins, but once it was the stronghold of the MacDonalds until they were subdued by the Campbells in the 17th century.

Literary historians may be interested to know that George Orwell, in the bitter postwar winters of 1946 and 1947, lived at Jura. Even then a sick and dying man, he wrote his masterpiece, *1984,* a satire on modern politics. He almost lost his life on Jura when he and his adopted son ventured too close to the whirlpool in the Gulf of Corryvreckan. They were saved by local fishermen, and he went on to finish *1984,* only to die in London of tuberculosis in 1950. His life span hardly matched that of Gillouir MacCrain, said to have been 180 when he died on Jura in the days of Charles I.

In accommodations, the **Jura Hotel,** Craighouse, Isle of Jura, Argyll PA60 7XU (tel. 049682/243), the only hotel on the island, has so much lore connected to it that many guests return year after year, sometimes requesting the same table in the dining room, which offers panoramic views of the scattering of nearby islands, most of which are deserted. Jura-bred venison is the establishment's specialty. You'll find it in succulent forms, ranging from filet steaks to venison burgers served beside an open fireplace. A fixed-price dinner goes for £12.25 ($20.20). Only 5 of the 18 bedrooms have private baths, and rates for B&B range from £23 ($37.95) to £27 ($44.55) daily, depending on the plumbing. Its clientele includes many sailors and birdwatchers. The hotel is closed for 2 weeks at Christmas and New Year's.

INDEX

GENERAL INFORMATION

England

Accommodations: *see* Destinations *index*
Adventure/wilderness travel, 18–19
Air travel:
  to Britain, 6–8
  within Britain, 10
Alternative and special-interest travel, 15–21
  adventure/wilderness, 18–19
  with companion, 21
  educational, 19–20
  health and fitness facilities, 20
  inland waterways, 19
  international understanding, 17, 18
  opera tours, 20–1
  senior citizen vacations, 19
Architecture, 40–1
Art, 40

Babysitters, 21
Beverages, 42–3
Boat travel, 9–10
Britain: *see* Great Britain
Bus travel, 13–14

Cars and driving, 12–13
Children's attractions, London, 166–70
Climate, 21
Crime: *see* safety
Culture, 37–41
Currency, 21
Customs, 21–2

Dentists, 22
Doctors, 22
Documents for entry, 22
Drugstores, 22

Educational and study travel, 19–20
Electrical appliances, 22
Embassies, 22–3
Emergencies, 23
England
  culture of, 37–41
  history of, 34, 36–7
  map, 33
  orientation, 32–43
  where to go, 32, 35
  see also Great Britain
Etiquette, 23

Fast facts, 21–8
Film, 23
Food, 41–3

Government, 37
Great Britain:
  fast facts, 21–8
  getting around, 10–14
  getting to: by air, 6–8; by ship, 9–10
  government of, 37
  orientation, 1–3

Hairdressers, 23
Health and fitness facilities, 20
History of England, 34, 36–7
Hitchhiking, 23
Holidays, 23

Laundry and dry cleaning, 23
Libraries, 23
Liquor laws, 23–4
Literature, 24, 37–9
Lost property, 24

Medical services, 551
Mileage chart, 16
Music, 39

Newspapers, 24

Office hours, 24
Opera tours, 20–1

Pets, 24
Police, 24
Postal service, 24

Radio and television, 24
Religious services, 24
Restaurants: *see* Destinations Index
Rest rooms, 24–5

Safety, 25
Senior citizen vacations, 19
Senior discounts, 25
Shoe repairs, 25
Store hours, 25

Taxes, 25
Telephones, 25–6
Telex and fax, 26
Time, 26
Tipping, 26
Tourist information, 14–15, 26–7
Tours, 15
  see also Alternative and special-interest travel
Travel companions, 21

Waterways, inland, travel by, 19
Weather: *see* Climate

Weights and measures, 27–8

Scotland

Accommodations: *see* Destinations Index
Air travel to Scotland, 544–6
Ancestral roots, 544

Babysitters, 548
Banks, 548
Bar and pub hours, 548
Burns, Robert, places associated with, 559–64, 566–9

Cigarettes, 548–9
Climate and weather, 549, 553
Clothing sizes, 549
Currency, 549
Customs, 549

Dentists, 549
Doctors, 549
Drugstores, 550

Eisenhower, Dwight D., places associated with, 561–2
Electrical appliances, 550
Emergencies, 550
Etiquette, 550

Fast Facts, 548–53
Film, 550

Hairdressers, 550
History of Scotland, 540–1
Holidays, 550

Libraries, 550

Lost property, 550–1
Luggage storage, 551

Office hours, 548

Politics, 551
Postal service, 551

Religious services, 551
Rest rooms, 551
Ruskin, John, 503–4

Safety, 551–2
Scotland
    Fast Facts, 548–53
    getting around, 546–7
    getting to, 544–6
    history of, 540–1
    map of, 542–3
    people of, 541
    tourist information, 553
    where to go, 547–8
Scott, Sir Walter, places associated with, 555, 557, 558, 572, 634
Shoe repairs, 552
Shopping, 552
Store hours, 552

Tartans and kilts, 541, 544
Taxes, 552
Telephones, 552
Telex and fax, 552–3
Tipping, 553
Tourist information, 553

DESTINATIONS

England

ABBERLEY, 425
ALCESTER, 415–16
ALDEBURGH, 455–6
ALFRISTON, 269–71
accommodations:
    Deans Place (*B*), 270
    Star Inn (*M*), 270
    White Lodge Country House Hotel (*B*), 270
Drusilla's Zoo Park, 269
Moonrakers restaurant (*M*; fish/English), 271
ALNWICK, 534–5
ALUM BAY, 295
AMBLESIDE, 499–502
accommodations:

Kirkstone Foot (*B/MAP*), 500
Nanny Brow Hotel (*B/B&B/MAP*), 500
The Riverside Hotel (*B/MAP*), 500
Riverside Lodge Country House (*B/MAP*), 501–2
Rothay Manor (*M/B&B*), 500
Wateredge Hotel (*B/MAP*), 500–1
ARUNDEL, 277–9
Amberley Castle Hotel and restaurant (*M*), (*E*; French/English), 278–9
Norfolk Arms hotel and restaurant (*B/M*; English), 278
Pogey's (*M–B*; English/French), 278
sights and attractions, 277–8
ASCOT, 217–18

KEY TO ABBREVIATIONS: Accommodations *B* = Budget; *B&B* = Bed-and-Breakfast; *D* = Deluxe; *E* = Expensive; *M* = Moderately priced; *MAP* = Modified American Plan
Restaurants *B* = Budget; *E* = Expensive; *M* = Moderately expensive

ASHBOURNE, 472–3
ASHBY-DE-LA-ZOUCH, 468
AVON, 372–82
Bath, 372–9
Bristol, 379–81
Thornbury, 381–2
see also specific places
AYLESBURY, 235–6
accommodations:
The Bell (*M*), 235
The Bell Inn, Aston Clinton (*E*), 236
Hartwell House (*M*), 236
restaurants:
The Bell Inn, Aston Clinton (*E*; French), 236
Hartwell House (*M*; British/international), 236
Peebles (*M*; French), 235–6
Waddesdon Manor, 235

BAKEWELL, 473, 476
BAMBURGH, 532
BARNARD CASTLE, 526, 528
BASSENTHWAITE, 507
BATH, 372–9
accommodations:
Apsley House Hotel (*M*), 376–7
Bath Spa Hotel (*E*), 375
Dukes Hotel (*M*), 376
Fountain House (*E*), 375–6
Francis Hotel (*M*), 376
Homewood Park (*M*), 378
Hunstrete House, Chelwood, near Bristol (*M*), 378
Lansdown Grove Hotel (*M*), 376
Laura Place Hotel (*B*), 377
Number Ninety Three (*B*), 377
Pratt's Hotel (*M*), 376
The Priory Hotel (*E*), 375
Queensberry Hotel (*E*), 375
The Royal Crescent Hotel (*E*), 374–5
Ston Easton Park, near Farrington Gurney (*D*), 377–8
Sydney Gardens Hotel (*B*), 377
restaurants:
Hole in the Wall (*M*; Italian), 378–9
The Moon and Sixpence (*M*; meats/continental), 379
Popjoy's (*M*; meats/fish), 378
Tarts Restaurant (*E*; French), 379
Woods (*M*; meats/fish/vegetarian), 379
sights and attractions:
The American Museum, 374
Bath Abbey, 373
Bath International Festival, 373
A Georgia House, 374
Pump Room and Roman Baths, 373
Theatre Royal, 373–4
tours, 374
BATTLE, 268–9
Bateman's (Kipling's home, near Burwash), 269
Battle Abbey, 268
Blacksmith's Restaurant (*B*; English), 269
George Hotel (*B*), 268–9
Netherfield Place (*M*), 268
BEACONSFIELD, 238
BEAMISH, 528
BEDFORD, 239–40
BEDFORDSHIRE, 239–42
Bedford, 239–40
Whipsnade Wild Animal Park, 242

Woburn Abbey, 240–1
BIBURY, 391–2
BLANCHLAND, 528
BOLVENTOR, 354
BORROWDALE, 506
BOSTON, 480–1
BOURNEMOUTH, 300–3
accommodations:
Bournemouth Highcliff Hotel (*M*), 301
The Carlton Hotel (*M*), 300–1
Langtry Manor Hotel, 301–2
Mansion House, Poole (*M*), 302
Norfolk Royale Hotel (*M*), 301
Royal Bath Hotel (*M*), 301
Kingston Lacy, 302–3
restaurants:
Crust (*M*; seafood), 302
Bournemouth (*cont'd*)
Mansion House, Poole (*M*; English), 302
Sophisticats (*M*; fish/meats/Indonesian), 302
BOURTON-ON-THE-WATER, 396
BRAMPTON, 508
BRAY-ON-THAMES, 219–20
BRIDPORT, 305–6
BRIGHTON AND HOVE, 271–7
accommodations:
Alexandra Hotel, Hove (*M*), 276–7
Brighton Metropole (*E*), 274
Courtlands Hotel, Hove (*M*), 277
The Dudley, Hove (*M*), 276
The Grand (*D*), 273
Granville Hotel (*M*), 274
Hospitality Inn (*E*), 273–4
Old Ship Hotel (*M*), 274
Queens Hotel (*M*), 274
Regency Hotel (*B*), 275
Sackville Hotel, Hove (*M*), 277
Topps Hotel (*B*), 275
Twenty-One Hotel (*B*), 274–5
restaurants:
China Garden (*M*; Chinese/meats), 276
English's Oyster Bar and Seafood Restaurant (*M*; fish/seafood), 275
Langan's Bistro (*M*; French), 275
La Noblesse (*E*; French), 275–6
Old Ship Hotel Restaurant (*E*; seafood/French), 276
sights and attractions:
Engineerium, 272
The Lanes, 272
Royal Pavilion, 272–3
BRISTOL, 379–81
accommodations:
Bristol Hilton (*M*), 380–1
Grand Hotel (*M*), 380
Holiday Inn (*M*), 380
restaurants:
Harvey's Restaurant (*M*; French/meats), 381
Lettonie (*M*; French/game), 381
Michael's (*M*; French), 381
sights and attractions:
Bristol Cathedral, 380
St. Mary Redcliffe, 380
Theatre Royal, 380
BROADWAY, 400–2
accommodations:
Broadway Hotel (*B/B&B*), 401
Buckland Manor (*E*), 401
Collin House Hotel and Restaurant (*B/B&B*),

Broadway (*cont'd*)
401–2
Dormy House (*M/B&B*), 401
Lygon Arms (*M-E*), 400–1
Hunter's Lodge Restaurant (*M;* Swiss), 402
BROCKENHURST, 293
BUCKINGHAMSHIRE, 234–9
Aylesbury, 235–6
Cliveden, 236–7
Hughenden Manor, near High Wycombe,
238
Jordans Village, 237–8
Marlow, 237
Milton's Cottage, Chalfont St. Giles, 238
West Wycombe, 238–9
see also specific places
BURFORD, 392–3
BUXTON, 471–2

CAMBRIDGE, 436–44
accommodations:
Arundel House (*B*), 442
Cambridgeshire Moat House (*M*), 441–2
Garden House (*M*), 441
Gonville Hotel (*M/B&B*), 442
Post House Hotel (*M*), 442
Regent Hotel (*B*), 442
University Arms Hotel (*M*), 441
map, 439
nightlife, 443–4
orientation, 436
restaurants:
Charlie Chan (*M;* Chinese), 443
Midsummer House (*M;* French), 442–3
Restaurant Angeline, 443
Twenty Two (*M;* English/continental), 443
Upstairs (*M;* Moroccan), 443
sights and attractions:
bicycle rentals, 441
boat rentals, 440
Cambridge University, 437, 440
Emmanuel College, 438
Fitzwilliam Museum, 440
Great St. Mary's, 440
King's College Chapel, 437
Peterhouse, 437
Queens' College, 438
St. John's College, 438
Trinity College, 438
tours, 436–7, 440–1
CAMBRIDGESHIRE, 436–44
see also CAMBRIDGE; ELY
CANTERBURY, 250–4
accommodations:
Cathedral Gate Hotel (*B*), 253
Chaucer Hotel (*M*), 252
County Hotel (*M*), 251–2
Falstaff Hotel (*M*), 252
Howfield Manor (*M*), 252
Slatters (*B*), 252
Three Tuns (*B*), 252–3
restaurants:
George's Brasserie (*B;* French), 253
Sully's (*M;* English/continental), 253
Tuo e Mio (*M;* Italian/fish), 253–4
sights and attractions:
Canterbury Cathedral, 250–1
Pilgrim's Way, 251
tours, 251
CARMEL, 495–6

CASTLE COMBE, 363–4
Manor House (*M*), 363–4
CASTLE HOWARD (NORTH YORKSHIRE), 516
CHAGFORD, 320–2
accommodations:
Easton Court Hotel, Easton Cross (*B*), 321–2
Gidleigh Park Hotel, Chagford (*E:* French),
321
Great Tree Hotel, Sandy Park (*B*), 321
Castle Drogo, Drewsteignton, 320–1
CHALE, 296–7
CHALFONT ST. GILES, 238
CHARINGWORTH, 403
CHARMOUTH, 307
CHEDINGTON, 308–9
CHELTENHAM, 388–90
accommodations:
Greenway (*M*), 389–90
Hotel De la Bere and Country Club (*B*), 389
Queens Hotel (*M*), 389
restaurants:
La Champignon Sauvage (*M;* English/French),
390
Redmond's at Malvern View (*M;* eclectic), 390
Twelve Suffolk Parade (*M;* French), 390
sights and attractions:
Cheltenham Art Gallery and Museum, 388–9
Everyman Theatre, 389
Pittville Pump Room, 388
CHESHIRE, 487–95
Chester, 487–90
Liverpool, 491–5
Nantwich, 490–1
see also specific places
CHESTER, 487–90
accommodations:
Blossoms Hotel (*M/B&B*), 489
Chester Grosvenor Hotel (*E*), 488
Crabwall Manor (*E*), 488–9
Mollington Banastre (*M*), 489
Rowton Hall Hotel (*M/B&B*), 489
restaurants:
Abbey Green (*M;* vegetarian), 490
Arkie Restaurant (*E;* English/continental),
489–90
La Brasserie (*M;* French/continental), 490
sights and attractions:
Chester Cathedral, 487
Chester Zoo, 488
city wall, 488
Eastgate clock, 488
The Row, 487
CHICHESTER, 279–82
accommodations:
Chichester Resort Hotel (*B*), 280
Dolphin & Anchor (*M*), 279–80
Millstream Hotel (*B*), 281
Ship Hotel (*B-M*), 280
Spread Eagle Hotel, Midhurst (*M*), 281–2
restaurants:
Comme Ca (*M;* French), 280
White Horse (*M;* French/English/wine cel-
lar), 280
sights and attractions:
Chichester Festival Theatre, 279
Minerva Studio Theatre, 279
Old Bosham, 281
Roman Palace, Fishbourne, 281
Weald and Downland Open Air Museum,
280–1

CHIDEOCK, 306–7
CHIPPING CAMPDEN, 402–3
CHIPPING NORTON, 394–5
CIRENCESTER, 386–7
CLANFIELD, 392
CLARE, 451–2
CLIVEDEN, 236–7
CLOVELLY, 330–1
COLCHESTER, 446
CONISTON, 503–5
CORNHILL-ON-TWEED, 535–6
CORNWALL, 333–54
Bolventor, 354
Falmouth, 341–3
Fowey, 337–8
The Isles of Scilly, 345–8
Land's End, 349–40
Looe, 334–6
map, 287, 313
Mousehole, 348–9
Newlyn, 348
Penzance, 343–5
Polperro, 336–7
Port Isaac, 352–3
Portloe, 339–40
St. Ives, 350–2
St. Just-in-Penwith, 350
St. Mawes, 340–1
Tintagel, 353
Truro, 338–9
see also specific places
COTSWOLDS, THE, 383–403
Bibury, 391–2
Bourton-on-the-Water, 395–6
Broadway, 400–2
Burford, 392–3
Charingworth, 403
Cheltenham, 388–90
Chipping Campden, 402–3
Chipping Norton, 394–5
Cirencester, 386–7
Clanfield, 392
Kingham, 395–6
Lower Slaughter, 398–9
Lower Swell, 398
Malmesbury, 385–6
Minster Lovell, 393–4
Moreton-in-Marsh, 399–400
Northleach, 396–7
Painswick, 387–8
Shipton-under-Wychwood, 394
Stow-on-the-Wold, 396–8
Swindon, 387
Tetbury, 384–5
Upper Slaughter, 398–9
Winchcombe, 390–1
see also specific places
COVENTRY, 420–2
Ansty Hall (*M/B&B/M:* English), **422**
De Vere Hotel (*E*), 421–2
Hotel Leofric (*M:* English), **422**
sights and attractions:
Coventry Cathedral, 420–1
Ford's Hospital, 421
Museum of British Road Transport, 421
St. Mary's Guildhall, 421
COWES, 294–5

DARTMOOR, 318–20
accommodations, 319–20

The Castle Inn, Lydford, near Okehampton
(*B–M*), 319
Cherrybrook Hotel, Yelverton (*B*), 320
Holne Chase Hotel, Ashburton, near Newton
Abbot (*B*), 320
Manor House Hotel, Moretonhampstead
(*M*), 319
sights and attractions:
Cathedral of the Moor, 318
Moretonhampstead, 318
Museum of Darmoor Life, 319
Sir Francis Drake's House, Buckland Abbey,
Yelverton, 320
Widecombe-in-the-Moore, 318
DARTMOUTH, 325–7
accommodations:
Dart Marina Hotel (*M*), 326
Royal Castle House (*B*), 326
restaurants:
The Carved Angel (*E;* continental/fish), **326**
Horn of Plenty, Gulworthy (*E;* French/game),
327
Mansion House (*M;* French/seafood/
vegetarian), 326–7
DEDHAM, 448, 450
DERBYSHIRE, 470–6
Ashbourne, 472–3
Buxton, 471–2
Dovedale/Thorpe, 473
historic homes, 470–1
map, 474–5
National Tramway Museum, 471
Peak District Mining Museum, 471
Peak District National Park, 470
Royal Crown Derby, 471
see also specific places
DEVON, 311–32
Chagford, 320–2
Clovelly, 330–1
Dartmoor, 318–20
Dartmouth, 325–7
Exeter, 312–18
Lynton-Lynmouth, **331–2**
map, 287, 313
Milton Damerel, 329–30
Plymouth, 327–9
The Taw Valley, 332
Torquay, 322–4
Totnes, 324–5
see also specific places
DIDCOT, 230
DORCHESTER, 304–5
DORKING, 261–2
DORSET, 299–310
Bournemouth, 300–3
Bridport, 305–6
Charmouth, 307
Chedington, 308–9
Chideock, 306–7
Dorchester, 304–5
Lyme Regis, 307–8
map, 287
Shaftesbury, 303–4
Sherborne, 309–10
Wareham, 304
see also specific places
DOVEDALE/THORPE, 473
DOVER, 254–5
accommodations:
Dover Moat House (*M*), 255

Dover (cont'd)
  The White Cliffs (B), 255
restaurants:
  Brittania (M; English), 255
  Ristorante al Porto (B; Italian), 255
sights and attractions:
  Dover Castle, 254
  Roman Painted House, 254–5
DUNSTER, 366–7
Luttrell Arms (M), 366
sights and attractions:
  Coleridge Cottage, 367
  Combe Sydenham Hall, 367
  Dunster Castle, 366–7
DURHAM (COUNTY), 525–8
Barnard Castle, 526, 528
Beamish, 528
Blanchland, 528
Durham, 525–6
map, 527
see also specific places
DURHAM (TOWN), 525–6

EAST ANGLIA, 435–63
Aldeburg, 455–6
Cambridge, 436–44
Cambridgeshire, 436–44
Clare, 451–2
Colchester, 446
Dedham, 448, 450
East Bergholt, 456
Ely, 444–6
Essex, 446
Lavenham, 453–4
Long Melford, 452–3
map, 449
Norfolk, 456–63
North Norfolk, 460–3
Norwich, 456–60
Saffron Walden, 447, 448
Shipdham, 460
Suffolk, 450–6
Thaxted, 446–7
Woodbridge, 454–5
see also specific places
EAST BERGHOLT, 456
EAST MIDLANDS, 464–85
Ashbourne, 472–3
Ashby-de-la-Zouch, 468
Boston, 480–1
Buxton, 471–2
Derbyshire, 470–6
Dovedale/Thorpe, 473
Eastwood, 479–80
Grantham, 485
Leicester, 467–8
Lincoln, 481–4
Market Bosworth, 469
Melton Mowbray, 469–70
Newark-on-Trent, 479
Northampton, 465–6
Northamptonshire, 464–7
Nottingham, 476–8
Scrooby, 480
Sherwood Forest, 476, 479
Southwell, 478–9
Stamford, 484
Stoke Bruerne, 466–7
Sulgrave, 464–5
Vale of Belvoir, 468

Wansford-in-England, 484–5
Weedon, 467
see also specific places
EAST MOLESEY, 203–4
EASTWOOD, 479–80
EGHAM, 257–8
ELY, 444–6
Lamb Hotel (B), 445
Old Fire Engine House (M; English),
  445
sights and attractions in or near:
  aircraft museum, 445–6
  Ely Cathedral, 444
  Ely Museum, 444–5
  Grime's Graves, 445
ESSEX, 446–50
Dedham, 448–9
Saffron Walden, 447–8
Thaxted, 446–7
see also specific places
ETON, 215–16
ETTINGTON, 415
EVESHAM, 427–8
EXETER, 312–18
accommodations:
  Bickleigh Cottage Country Hotel, Bickleigh
    (B), 317
  Buckerell Lodge (M), 315
  Devon Motel (B), 315
  Oxenham Arms, South Zeal, Okehampton (B),
    317–18
  Rougemont Hotel (M), 315
  Royal Clarence Hotel (M), 315
  St. Olaves Court Hotel (B), 316
  Salston Hotel, Ottery St. Mary (B), 317
  White Hart Hotel (B), 315–16
restaurants:
  Coolings Wine Bar (B; English), 316–17
  Ship Inn (B; English), 316
  Tudor House (M; meats/vegetarian), 316
sights and attractions, 311
  Exeter Cathedral, 312, 314
  Exeter Guildhall, 314
  Exeter Maritime Museum, 314
  Powderham Castle, 314–15
  Rougemont House Museum, 314
  St. Nicholas Priory, 314
  Underground Passages, 314
EXMOOR NATIONAL PARK, 365–6
accommodations:
  Dragon House, Bilbrook (B), 365
  Periton Park, Middlecombe (B), 365
  Royal Oak Inn, Winsford (M), 365–6

FALMOUTH, 341–3
accommodations:
  Budock Vean Hotel, Golf and Country Club,
    Mawnan Smith, Falmouth (M), 342
  Falmouth Hotel (B), 341
  Greenbank Hotel (B), 341–2
  Penmore Manor Hotel (B), 342
Riverside restaurant, Helford, near Helston (E;
  French), 342
sights and attractions:
  Pendennis Castle, 341
  Poldark Mine and Heritage Complex, Wen-
    dron, 342–3
FARNE ISLANDS, 531
FOWEY, 337–8
FRESHWATER BAY, 295, 296

GERRARDS CROSS, 238
GLASTONBURY, 368–9
GRANTHAM, 485
GRASMERE, 501–3
accommodations:
Michael's Nook (M/MAP), 502
The Red Lion Hotel (B/B&B), 503
Swan Hotel (B), 503
White Moss House (B/MAP), 503
Wordsworth Hotel (B), 502–3
GREENWICH, 205–6
sights and attractions:
Cutty Sark, 205
Gipsy Moth IV, 205
National Maritime Museum, 206
Old Royal Observatory, 206
Royal Naval College, 205–6
Trafalgar Tavern (M; English), 206
GUILDFORD, 260–1
Angel Hotel (M), 261
Inn on the Lake, Godalming (B), 261
Loseley House, 260
Post House Hotel (M), 260–1

HADRIAN'S WALL, 495, 532–3
HAMPSHIRE, 284–99
Alum Bay, 295
Cowes, 294–5
Freshwater Bay, 295–6
Isle of Wight, 294–7
map, 287
The New Forest, 291–4
Newport, 295
Portsmouth and Southsea, 284–9
Ryde, 294, 295
Sandown, 295, 296
Shanklin, 295, 296
Southampton, 289–91
Totland Bay, 297
Winchester, 297–9
see also specific places
HAMPTON COURT, 203–4
HARROGATE, 517–19
accommodations:
Crown Hotel (M), 517–18
Fern Hotel (B/B&B), 518
Grant's Hotel (M/B&B), 518
Majestic Hotel (M), 517
The Old Swan Hotel (B–M), 517
restaurants:
Drum and Monkey (M; seafood), 518–19
Hodgson's Restaurant (M–E; English), 518
Millers (E; English), 518
HASLEMERE, 259–60
HASTINGS AND ST. LEONARDS, 266–8
accommodations:
Beauport Park Hotel (B), 267
Royal Victoria (M), 267
Roser's restaurant (M; French/seafood/game), 267–8
sights and attractions:
Hastings Castle, 266
The Hastings Embroidery, 266–7
St. Clements Caves, 267
HAWES, 522–3
HAWKSHEAD, 503–4
HAWORTH, 523–4
Old White Lion Hotel (B), 524
sights and attractions:
Brontë Parsonage Museum, 523

Ponden Hall, 523
Weaver's Restaurant (M; English), 524
HAYDON BRIDGE, 533
HEBDEN BRIDGE, 524–5
HELMSLEY, 519–20
HENLEY-ON-THAMES, 218–19
HEREFORD, 422–4
accommodations:
Green Dragon Hotel (M), 423
Hereford Moat House (B), 423–4
restaurants:
Effy's (M; English), 424
Fat Tulip (M; English), 424
sights and attractions:
Churchill Gardens Museum and Hatton Gallery, 423
The Cider Museum and King Offa Cider Brandy Distillery, 423
The Old House, 423
HEREFORDSHIRE, 422–8
HERTFORD, 232–3
HERTFORDSHIRE, 231–4
Fabdens Park hotel and restaurant, near Ware (M/E: English/French), 233
Hatfield House, 231–2
Hertford, 232–3
St. Albans, 233–4
see also specific places
HEXHAM, 533–4
accommodations near:
George Hotel, Humshaugh (M/B&B), 534
Hadrian Hotel, Wall (B), 533–
Langley Castle (M/B&B), 533
HIGH WYCOMBE, 238
HOLY ISLAND, 531–2
HOVE: see BRIGHTON AND HOVE

IRONBRIDGE, 429–30
ISLE OF WIGHT, 294–7
accommodations:
Bourne Hall Country Hotel, Shanklin (B), 296
The Clarendon Hotel and Wight Mouse Inn, Chale (B), 296–7
Country Garden, Totland Bay (B), 297
Farringford Hotel, Freshwater Bay (B), 296
Luccombe Chine House, Shanklin (B), 296
St. Catherine's Hotel, Sandown (B), 296
Biskra restaurant, Ryde (M; French), 295–6
bus trip, 294
Carlsbrooke Castle, 295
The Needles, 295
Osborne House, 295
sights and attractions, 294–5
ISLES OF SCILLY, THE, 345–8
accommodations:
Carnwethers Country Guest House, Pelistry Bay, St. Mary's (B), 347–8
Hotel Godolphin, St. Mary's (B), 347
Island Hotel, Tresco (M), 346
New Inn, Tresco (B), 346
Star Castle Hotel, St. Mary's (B), 347
sights and attractions:
Abbey Gardens, 345–6
Isles of Scilly Museum, St. Mary's, 347
Valhalla, 346

JORDANS VILLAGE, 237–8

KENDAL, 496, 498
Moon restaurant (*B*; English), 496, 498
sights and attractions:
　Abbot Hall Art Gallery, 496
　Kendal Museum of Archaeology and Natural
　　History, 496
　Museum of Lakeland Life and Industry, 496
Woolpack Hotel (*M/B&B*), 496
KENILWORTH, 419–20
KENT, 244–57
Canterbury, 250–4
country houses, castles, and gardens:
　Chilham Castle Gardens, 249–50
　Churchill's Home, 246
　Down House, 247
　Hever Castle, 247–8
　Ightham Note, 247
　Knole, 246–7
　Leeds Castle, 249
　Penshurst Place, 248
　Sissinghurst Castle Garden, 248–9
　Squerryes Court, 247
Dickens-related attractions:
　Bleak House, 244
　Charles Dickens Centre, 244
　Dickens Chalet, 244
　Dickens House Museum, 244
Dover, 254–5
map, 245
Quebec House, 244, 246
Romney, Hythe & Dymchurch Light Railway
　Co., 254
Tunbridge Wells, 255–7
see also specific places
KESWICK, 505–6
KEW, 204–5
KINGHAM, 395

LACOCK, 364
LAKE DISTRICT, 495–508
Ambleside, 499–501
Bassenthwaite, 507
Borrowdale, 506
Brampton, 508
Carmel, 495–6
Coniston, 503–5
Grasmere, 501–3
Hadrian's Wall, 495
Hawkshead, 503–4
Kendal, 496, 498
Keswick, 505–6
map, 497
Rydal, 501
Ullswater, 507–8
Windermere, 498–9
see also specific places
LAND'S END, 349–50
LAVENHAM, 453–4
LEDBURY, 427
LEICESTER, 467–8
LEICESTERSHIRE, 467–70
LEWES, 269–71
Kenwards restaurant (*E*; French), 271
Shelleys Hotel (*B*), 271
sights and attractions, 270
LICHFIELD, 433
LINCOLN, 481–4
accommodations:
　D'Isney Place Hotel (*B*), 483
　Eastgate Post House (*M*), 483

Grand Hotel (*B*), 483
White Hart Hotel (*M*), 482–3
restaurants:
　Harveys Cathedral Restaurant (*M*;
　　English/French), 483
　Whites of Lincoln (*M*; French), 483–4
sights and attractions:
　Greyfriars City and County Museum, 481
　Lincoln Cathedral, 482
　Museum of Lincolnshire Life, 481–2
　Newport Arch, 481
LINCOLNSHIRE, 480–5
Boston, 480–1
Lincoln, 481–4
Stamford, 484
Wansford-in-England, 484–5
Grantham, 485
see also specific places
LINTON, 524
LIVERPOOL, 491–5
accommodations:
　Atlantic Tower (*M*), 494
　Brittania Adelphi Hotel (*M*), 493–4
　Liverpool Moat House (*M*), 494
　Trials (*M*), 494
restaurants:
　Armadillo (*M*; English), 495
　Far East (*B*; Chinese), 494–5
　Jenny's Seafood Restaurant (*M*; seafood), 494
sights and attractions:
　Albert Dock, 492
　Beatles Shop, 493
　Beatles Story, 493
　Cathedral Church of Christ, 491–2
　Cavern Walks ("Beatleland"), 493
　Mersey Ferry, 493
　Merseyside Maritime Museum, 492
　Metropolitan Cathedral of Christ the King,
　　492
　Museum of Labour History, 493
　Tate Gallery, 492–3
　Walker Art Gallery, 493
　waterfront, 492–3
tours, 493
LONDON, 44–208
accommodations:
　Abbey Court, Notting Hill Gate (*M*), 86
　Academy Hotel, Bloomsbury (*B*), 93
　Alexander Hotel, South Kensington (*M*),
　　84–5
　Annandale House, Chelsea (*B*), 79
　Aster House, South Kensington (*B*), 86
　Aston's Budget Studios, South Kensington
　　(*B*), 85
　Aston's Designer Studios, South Kensington
　　(*B*), 85
　Aston's Luxury Apartments, South Kensing-
　　ton (*B*), 85
　Bailey's Hotel, South Kensington (*M*), 84
　Barkston Hotel, The, Earl's Court (*B*), 80
　Basil Hotel, Knightsbridge (*M*), 73, 76
　The Beaufort, Knightsbridge (*M*), 73
　Berkeley Hotel, Belgravia (*E*), 72
　Blair House Hotel, Chelsea (*B*), 79
　Blakes, South Kensington (*E*), 82, 84
　Blandford Hotel, St. Marylebone (*B*), 92
　Brown's Hotel, Mayfair (*E*), 61–2
　Bryanston Court Hotel, St. Marylebone (*B*),
　　90
　Cadogan Thistle Hotel, Chelsea (*E*), 78

London (cont'd)
  Cannizaro House, Wimbledon (E), 96
  The Capital, Knightsbridge (E), 73
  Cavendish Hotel, Piccadilly (E), 66
  Cisswood House Hotel, Gatwick (B), 97
  Claridge's, Mayfair (D), 59
  Claverley House Hotel, Knightsbridge (B), 76
  The Coburg Hotel, Paddington/Bayswater (M), 88–9
  Collin House, Victoria (B), 71
  Colonnade Hotel, Paddington/Bayswater (M), 89
  The Connaught, Mayfair (D), 60
  Diplomat Hotel, Belgravia (M), 72
  Dolphin Square, Westminster (M), 70
  The Dorchester, Mayfair (D), 59–60
  Dorset Square Hotel, St. Marylebone (E), 89
  Draycott, Chelsea (E), 78
  Drury Lane Moat House, Holborn (E), 69
  Dukes Hotel, St. James's (E), 63
  Durley House, Chelsea (D), 77–8
  Durrants Hotel, St. Marylebone (M), 90
  Ebury Court, Victoria (B), 70–1
  Eden Plaza, South Kensington (B), 85–6
  Edward Lear Hotel, St. Marylebone (B), 92
  Effingham Park Hotel, Gatwick (M), 97
  Elizabeth Hotel, Victoria (B), 71
  The Executive Hotel, Knightsbridge (B), 76
  Fenja, Chelsea (E), 78–9
  5 Sumner Place, South Kensington (B), 85
  Flemings Hotel, Mayfair (M), 62
  Gatwick Copthorne Hotel, Gatwick (M), 97–8
  Gatwick Hilton International, Gatwick (D), 96
  Gore Hotel, South Kensington (M), 84
  Goring Hotel, St. James's (M), 64
  Gravetye Manor, Gatwick (E), 96–7
  Green Park Hotel, Mayfair (M), 62
  Grosvenor House, Mayfair (D), 61
  Halcyon Hotel, Holland Park (E), 87
  Hallam Hotel, St. Marylebone (B), 90
  Hart House Hotel, St. Marylebone (B), 90
  Heathrow Penta Hotel, Heathrow (M), 98
  Hilton Kensington International, Kensington (E), 81
  Hotel Concorde, St. Marylebone (B), 92
  Hotel Conrad, Chelsea Harbour (D), 80
  Hotel La Place, St. Marylebone (B), 90
  Hotel Montcalm, St. Marylebone (E), 89–90
  Hotel 167 (B), 81
  Hotel Russell, Bloomsbury (M), 93
  Howard Hotel, Strand/Covent Garden (D), 68
  Hyatt Carlton Tower, Chelsea (D), 77
  Inn on the Park, Mayfair (D), 60
  Knightsbridge Green Hotel, Knightsbridge (B), 77
  Knightsbridge Hotel, Knightsbridge (B), 76–7
  Langshott Manor, Gatwick (M), 98
  Le Méridien, Piccadilly (D), 64–5
  Lewis House Hotel, Victoria (B), 71
  L'Hotel, Knightsbridge (M), 76
  The Londoner, Mayfair (M), 62
  London Hilton on Park Lane, Mayfair (E), 61
  London Marriott, Mayfair (E), 61
  Morgan Hotel, Bloomsbury (B), 93
  Mornington Hotel, Paddington/Bayswater (M), 89

Number Eight Hotel, South Kensington (B), 86
Number Sixteen, South Kensington (M), 85
Observatory House, Kensington (M), 81–2
One Cranley Place, South Kensington (M), 85
Parkes Hotel, Knightsbridge (M), 73
The Park Lane Hotel, Mayfair (D), 60–1
Pelham Hotel, South Kensington (E), 82
Pembridge Court Hotel, Notting Hill Gate (M), 86–7
Post House Hotel, Heathrow (M), 98
Prince Hotel, South Kensington (B), 85
The Regency Hotel, South Kensington (M), 84
Regent Palace Hotel, Piccadilly (M), 66
Ritz Hotel, St. James's (D), 63
Royal Garden Hotel, Kensington (E), 81
St. James Court Hotel, Westminster (E), 69
Sandringham (Igar) Hotel, Hampstead (B), 94
The Savoy, Strand/Covent Garden (D), 66, 68
Sheraton Park Tower, Knightsbridge (E), 72–3
Sheraton Skyline, Heathrow (M), 98
Stafford Hotel, St. James's (E), 63–4
Stakis St. Ermins Hotel, Westminster (E), 69–70
Strand Palace Hotel, Strand/Covent Garden (M), 68–9
Swiss Cottage Hotel, Swiss Cottage (M), 94
Swiss House Hotel, Earl's Court (B), 80–1
Tower Thistle Hotel, the Docks (E), 93–4
The Waldorf, Strand/Covent Garden (E), 68
Whites Hotel, Lancaster Gate (E), 88
Wilbraham Hotel, Chelsea (B), 79
The Willett, Chelsea (B), 79
airports, 50–1
American Express, 54
area codes, 54
babysitters, 54–5
banks, 55
church services, 55
dentists, 55
doctors, 55
drugstores, 55
emergencies, 55
evening entertainment:
  ballet, 192
  bars, 199–200
  cabaret river cruise, 194
  concerts, 192–3
  dancing to live music, 198
  discos, 197–8
  discount theater tickets, 189–90
  gambling, 202
  gay and lesbian nightlife, 200–2
  Gilbert and Sullivan, 193–4
  jazz, 199
  medieval "feestes," 196
  movies, 193
  music halls, 194
  nightclubs, 194–6
  open-air theater, 194
  opera, 192
  reservations, 189–90
  rock and soul music, 198–9
  strip shows, 196–7
  theater restaurant, 196
  theaters, 189–92
  theaters for kids, 167–8
eyeglasses, 55

London (cont'd)
fax, 57
geography of, 46–7, 50
hairdressers, 55
history of, 45–6
hospitals, 55–6
launderettes and dry cleaning, 56
lost property, 56
luggage, shipping, 56–7
maps, 48–9
  Bloomsbury and Russell Sq., 95
  Chelsea/Knightsbridge, 74–5
  City, The, 155
  Covent Garden, 67
  environs, 35
  Kensington, 83
  Piccadilly, 65
  Regents Park, 91
  Tottenham Court Road, 121
  underground, 53
  West End, the, 103
medical services, 57
one-day trips from:
  Greenwich, 205–6
  Hampton Court Palace, 203–4
  Kew, 204–5
  Runnymede, 206–7
  Syon Park, 207
  Thorpe Park, 207–8
orientation, 45–7, 50–2, 54–8
post offices, 57
pubs:
  The Anchor, Southwark, 135
  The Antelope, Belgravia, 132
  Boaters Wine Bar, Chelsea Harbour, 131
  Cittie of Yorke, Holborn, 134
  City Barge, Chiswick, 135
  The Clifton, St. John's Wood, 135–6
  Ferret & Firkin in the Balloon up the Creek, Chelsea Harbour, 131–2
  Front Page, Chelsea, 131
  Goose & Firkin, Elephant & Castle, 135
  The Grenadier, Belgravia, 132
  Jack Straw's Castle, Hampstead, 136
  King's Head and Eight Bells, Chelsea, 131
  Lamb & Flag, Covent Garden, 130
  Museum Tavern, Bloomsbury, 133
  Nag's Head, Covent Garden, 130
  Nag's Head, Knightsbridge, 133
  Old Coffee House, Soho, 130–1
  Prospect of Whitby, Docks, 134–5
  Red Lion, St. James's, 129–30
  Salisbury, Leicester Square, 130
  Shepherds Tavern, Mayfair, 133
  Sherlock Holmes, Leicester Square, 130
  Spaniards Inn, Hampstead, 136
  Star Tavern, Belgravia, 132–3
  Ye Olde Cock Tavern, The City, 133
  Ye Olde Watling, The City, 134
  Ye Old Mitre, Clerkenwell, 134
restaurants:
  Al Hamra, Mayfair (M; Lebanese), 102
  Au Jardin des Gourmets, Soho (M; French), 120, 122
  Bentley's, Mayfair (E; seafood/English), 101
  Bibendum, South Kensington (E; seafood/French regional), 114
  Bloom's, East End (B; kosher), 126–7
  Blue Elephant, (M; Thai), 117
  Bombay Brasserie, South Kensington (M; Indian/vegetarian), 115
  Boulestin, Covent Garden (E; French/seafood/meats), 109
  Boyd's Glass Garden, Kensington (M; English/light fare), 114
  Bracewell's, Mayfair (E; English), 101
  The Brasserie on The Park, Mayfair (B; seafood), 104
  Brinkley's, West Brompton (M; modern European), 116
  Burts, Soho (E; vegetarian/fish), 120
  Cavaliers, Battersea (B; English/meats), 125
  Chelsea Room, Chelsea (E; French), 105
  Cheshire Cheese, Fleet Street (B; English), 125
  Chez Nico, Fitzrovia (E; cuisine moderne), 122–3
  Chez Solange, Leicester Square (M; French bourgeois/pre-theater), 108
  Chuen Cheung Ku, Soho (B; Cantonese/Malaysian), 122
  Ciboure, Belgravia (M; French), 111
  Clarke's, Kensington (M; English/French), 113–14
  Coconut Grove, Mayfair (M; salads/seafood/vegetarian/American/Sunday brunch), 102, 104
  Compass Rose, Chelsea Harbour (E; international), 123
  Cut Above, The City (B; English/continental), 124
  Deals Restaurant and Diner, Chelsea Harbour (B; American/Asian), 123
  The Dickens Inn by the Tower, The Tower (B–M; English/seafood/meats/snacks), 127
  Drones, Belgravia (M; French/seafood/meats), 111
  Eatons Restaurant, Victoria (M; English/French), 106–7
  Eleven Park Walk, South Kensington (M; fish/northern Italian), 116
  English Garden, Chelsea (M; seafood/French), 105–6
  The English House, Chelsea (M; English), 105
  Frederick's Restaurant, Islington (M; French/desserts/cheese), 126
  Gavvers, Chelsea (M; French), 106
  Gay Hussar, Soho (M; Hungarian/Central European), 120
  Gaylord Mayfair, Mayfair (B; Indian/vegetarian), 104
  George & Vulture, The City (B; English), 125
  Harvey's at the Top, Knightsbridge (B; English), 113
  Hilaire, South Kensington (M; game/French), 115
  J. Sheekey Ltd., Leicester Square (M; seafood/English/pre-theater), 108
  Jamdani, Soho (M; Indian/Bangladesh), 122
  Joe Allen's Strand (M; American/international), 108
  Keats, Hampstead (M; French), 126
  Ken Lo's Memories of China, Chelsea Harbour (M; Chinese regional/seafood/dim sum), 123
  Ken Lo's Memories of China, Victoria (M; Chinese), 106
  Kingfisher, Holland Park (E; international), 119

London (cont'd)

La Croisette, West Brompton (M; French/seafood), 116–17

Langan's Bistro, St. Marylebone (M; French/meats/game), 118

Langan's Brasserie, Mayfair (M; English/French), 102

L'Artiste Assoiffe, Notting Hill Gate (M; French/cheeses), 119

La Tante Claire, Chelsea (E; French), 104–5

Launceston Place Restaurant, Kensington (E; British), 113

Le Cellier du Midi, Hampstead (M; French), 125–6

Le Gamin, The City (B–E; French/snack bar), 124

Le Gavroche, Mayfair (E; French), 100

Leiths, Notting Hill Gate (E; French/game/desserts/cheeses), 118–19

Le Poulbot, The City (B–E; French/pub fare/breakfast), 124

Les Trois Plats, Chelsea (M; British/French/Provençal), 106

The Lindsay House, Soho (E; 18th-century English/cuisine moderne/fish), 120

L'Ortolan, Shinfield, near Reading (E; French), 129

Mandarin Kitchen (B; Chinese/fish), 118

My Fair Lady, Camden Town (B; includes cruise; English), 127–8

The Oak Room, Mayfair (E; French), 100–1

Odin's, St. Marylebone (M; international), 117–18

Pavilion Restaurant, South Kensington (M; meats/vegetarian/"New Wave"), 115–16

Pelham Restaurant, South Kensington (E; French-modern), 114–15

Persepolis, Kensington (B; Iranian), 114

Phoenicia, South Kensington (M; Lebanese), 116

Pomegranates, Westminster (M; Asian/Indonesian/continental/Creole/Cajun), 110–11

Poons of Covent Garden, Convent Garden (M; Cantonese), 109

Porter's English Restaurant, Covent Garden (B; English), 110

R.S. Hispaniola, Charing Cross (M; meats/vegetarian), 128

Rib Room, Chelsea (M; seafood/meats), 105

RSJ, Waterloo (M; modern British), 126

Rules, Covent Garden (M; seafood/game/British), 109–10

St. Quentin, Knightsbridge (E; French/meats), 112

San Lorenzo, Knightsbridge (M; Italian), 112–13

Scotts, Mayfair (E; seafood), 101–2

Shezan, Knightsbridge (M; Indian/meats), 113

Simpson's-in-the-Strand, Strand (M; English/meats), 108

Spice Merchant, Bayswater (B; (Indian/meats/East African), 118

Suntory, St. James's (E; Japanese), 107

Tall Orders, West Brompton (M; Mediterranean/vegetarian), 117

The Tate Gallery Restaurant, Westminster (M; British), 111

Tiger Lee, West Brompton (M; Chinese/Hong Kong/fish), 117

Tower Thistle Hotel, The Tower (M; meats/English), 127

Turner's, Knightsbridge (E; international), 112

The Veeraswamy, Mayfair (M; Indian/vegetarian), 102

Very Simply Nico, Victoria (M; French), 107

Waltons of Walton Street, Knightsbridge (E; international/British/meats), 112

Waterside Cafeteria, The City (B; self-service), 124

Wiltons, St. James's (E; British/French/game), 107

Wine on Six, The City (B; wines/cold meats/fish/seafood), 124–5

Winstons Restaurant and Wine Bar, Bloomsbury (B; English), 110

see also pubs above; tea rooms below

shopping:
antiques markets, 177
art, 180
arts and crafts, 177–8
bargains, 172
Beauchamp Place, 174–5
Bond Street, 173
books, 178
brass rubbings, 178
British design, 179
Burberry, 184
Burlington Arcade, 175
Carnaby Street, 174
for children, 169–70
china, 179
chocolates, 179
clocks, 179–80
clothing, men's, 182–3
clothing (second hand), designer, 181
clothing, women's, 187–8
Covent Garden, 175–7
engravings, 182
Fortnum and Mason Ltd., 181–2
Harrods, 180
Irish wares, 182
jewelry, 182
Kensington High Street, 173–4
King's Road, 174
Knightsbridge, 173
Leather Lane, 187
Liberty & Company Limited (Liberty's), 180
maps, 182
Marks & Spencer, 180–1
miniatures, military, 183–4
New Caledonian market (Bermondsey Market), 186
notions, 184
Oxford Street, 173
Peter Jones, 181
Petticoat Lane, 186
philately, 184
Piccadilly, 173
Portobello Road market, 186
posters, 184
Princes Arcade, 175
purchase tax, 172–3
raincoats, 184
Regent Street, 173
Saint Christopher's Place, 174
Selfridges, 180
shoes, 184–5

London (cont'd)
  silver, 185
  Simpson's, 181
  souvenirs, 185
  sports goods, 185–6
  The Strand, 173
  street markets, 186
  travel center, 187
  woolens, 188
sights and attractions:
  Apsley House, 157
  Banqueting House, 153
  Battersea Park, 167
  Bethnal Green Museum of Childhood, 168–9
  boat trips, 171
  The British Library, 146
  The British Museum, 145–6
  Buckingham Palace, 151–2
  Burgh House, 162–3
  canal boat (Little Venice), 171
  Carlyle's (Thomas) House, 161
  Cenotaph, 152–3
  Central Criminal Court (Old Bailey), 154, 156
  Ceremony of the Keys, 142
  College Garden, 144
  Courtauld Institute Galleries, 160
  Dickens's (Charles) House, 161
  docklands, 166
  Exhibition Centre (Isle of Dogs), 166
  Fenton House, 162
  Freud Museum, 162
  Gray's Inn, 154
  Green Park, 163
  guildhall, 156
  H.M.S. Belfast, 165–6
  Hampstead Heath, 161, 169
  Hampstead Village, 161
  Harrods Sightseeing Bus, 171
  Hayward Gallery, 160
  Highgate Village, 163
  Holborn, 153–4
  Horse Guards Building, 153
  Houses of Parliament, 144–5
  Hyde Park, 163
  Imperial War Museum, 156
  Jewel House, 142
  Jewish Museum, 159
  John's (Samuel) House, 160–1
  Keats's (John) House, 161–2
  Kensington Gardens, 163
  Kensington Palace, 149–50
  Kenwood, 162
  Lincoln's Inn, 154
  Lincoln's Inn Fields, 154
  Linley Sambourne House, 158–9
  Little Angel Marionette Theatre, 167–8
  Lloyd's of London, 153
  London Design Museum, 159
  The London Dungeon, 166–7
  London Planetarium, 147
  The London Toy and Model Museum, 169
  London Transport Museum, 157–8
  London Zoo, 168
  Madame Tussaud's, 146–7
  Marble Arch, 163–4
  Museum of London, 157
  Museum of Mankind, 146
  National Army Museum, 156–7

  National Gallery, 148–9
  National Portrait Gallery, 159
  National Postal Museum, 158
  Natural History Museum, 168
  Old Bailey (Central Criminal Court), 154, 156
  Old Curiosity Shop, 154
  Queen's Gallery, The, 152
  Regent's Park, 163
  Rock Circus, 169
  Royal Academy of Arts, 160
  Royal Air Force Museum, 158
  Royal Courts of Justice, 154
  Royal Mews, 152
  St. Etheldreda's, 164
  St. James's Park, 163
  St. Martin-in-the-Fields, 164
  St. Paul's Cathedral, 150
  Science Museum, 158
  Sir John Soane's Museum, 156
  Speakers Corner, 164
  Staple Inn, 154
  Stock Exchange, 153
  Tate Gallery, 147–8
  The Temple, 154
  Thames Flood Barrier, 165
  tours, 170–2
  Tower Bridge, 164–5
  Tower of London, 141–3
  Unicorn Theater, 167
  Victoria and Albert Museum, 150–1
  walks, 171–2
  Wallace Collection, 159–60
  Westminster Abbey, 143–4
  Whitehall, 152
  Woburn House, 159
tea rooms:
  The Fountain Restaurant, Piccadilly, 129
  Oak Room Lounge, Le Méridien, Piccadilly, 128
  The Palm Court, Piccadilly, 128
  Palm Court Lounge, Piccadilly, 128
  Ritz Palm Court, Piccadilly, 128
telex, 57
tourist information, 56
transportation by:
  bicycle, 54
  bus, 52
  taxi, 52, 54
  underground, 51–3
weather, 57
wine bars:
  Bill Bentley's, Knightsbridge, 139–40
  Blushes Café, Chelsea, 140
  Bow Wine Vaults, The City (lunch), 137
  Bubbles, Mayfair, 138–9
  Cork and Bottle Wine Bar, Leicester Square, 138
  Daniel's Wine Bar, Piccadilly, 138
  Ebury Wine Bar, Victoria, 139
  Greens Restaurant and Oyster Bar, Piccadilly, 138
  Jamaica Wine House, The City (lunch), 137–8
  Le Métro Wine Bar, Knightsbridge, 139
  Methuselah's, Victoria, 139
  Olde Wine Shades, The City (lunch), 137
  Shampers, Mayfair, 139
LONGHORSLEY, 534
LONG MELFORD, 452–3

LOOE, 334–6
accommodations:
  Commonwealth Manor Hotel, East Looe (*B*), 335
  Fieldhead Hotel, Hannafore, West Looe (*B*), 334–5
  Hannafore Point Hotel, Hannafore, West Looe (*B*), 334
  Old Rectory Country House Hotel, St. Keyne, near Liskeard (*B*), 335
  Talland Bay Hotel, Talland-by-Looe (*B*), 335
  Well House, St. Keyne, Liskeard (*B/M:* continental/British), 335–6
LOWER BROADHEATH, 425
LOWER SLAUGHTER, 398–9
LOWER SWELL, 398
LUDLOW, 429
LYME REGIS, 307–8
LYNDHURST, 292–3
LYNTON-LYNMOUTH, 331–2

MALMESBURY, 385–6
MALVERN WELLS, 426–7
MARKET BOSWORTH, 469
MARLOW, 237
MATLOCK, 473
MELTON MOWBRAY, 469–70
MENDIP, CAVES OF, 371–2
MILTON DAMEREL, 329–30
MINSTER LOVELL, 393–4
MOORS AND DALES (NORTH YORKSHIRE), 519–23
MORETON-IN-MARCH, 399–400
MOUSEHOLE, 348–9

NANTWICH, 490–1
NEWARK-ON-TRENT, 479
NEWCASTLE UPON TYNE, 529–30
accommodations:
  County Thistle Hotel (*M*), 529–30
  Gosforth Park Thistle (*M*), 529
restaurants:
  Dragon House (*M;* Chinese), 530
  Fisherman's Lodge (*M–E;* seafood), 530
  21 Queen Street (*E;* English/French), 530
sights and attractions:
  Keep Museum, 529
  St. Nicholas Church of England Cathedral, 529
NEW FOREST, THE, 291–4
accommodations:
  Balmer Lawn Hotel, Brockenhurst (*M*), 293
  Carey's Manor, Brockenhurst (*M*), 293
  Chewton Glen Hotel, New Hilton (*E*), 292
  Crown Hotel, Lyndhurst (*B*), 292–3
  Lyndhurst Park Hotel, Lyndhurst (*B*), 292
  Master Builders House Hotel, Buckler's Hard (*B*), 294
  Montagu Arms, Beaulieu (*B*), 293–4
  New Park Manor, Brockenhurst (*B*), 293
  Le Poussin restaurant, Brockenhurst (*B–E;* French/game), 293
sights and attractions:
  Beaulieu Abbey and Palace House, 291
  Maritime Museum, Buckler's Hard, 291–2
  National Motor Museum, 291
NEWLYN, 348
NEWMARKET, 450–1
NEWPORT, 295
NORFOLK, 456–63

NORTHAMPTON, 465–6
NORTHAMPTONSHIRE, 464–7, 476–80
  Northampton, 465–6
  Nottingham, 476–8
  Sherwood Forest, 476, 479
  Stoke Bruerne, 466–7
  Sulgrave, 464–5
  Weedon, 467
  see also specific places
NORTHLEACH, 396
NORTH NORFOLK, 460–3
accommodations:
  Blakeney Hotel (*B–M/B&B*), 462
  Congham Hall (*M*), 462–3
  Elderton Lodge (*B/B&B*), 463
  Links Country Park Hotel and Golf Club (*M/MAP*), 463
  Maltings (*B/B&B*), 462
  Old Rectory (*B/B&B*), 463
sights and attractions near:
  Blickling Hall, 461
  Norfolk Lavender Ltd., 461
  North Norfolk Railway, 462
  Sandringham, 460–1
  Thursford Collection, 461–2
NORTHUMBERLAND, 530–6
  Alnwick, 534–5
  Bamburgh, 532
  Cornhill-on-Tweed, 535–6
  Farne Islands, 531
  Hadrian's Wall, 532–3
  Haydon Bridge, 533
  Hexham, 533–4
  Holy Island, 531–2
  Longhorsley, 534
  map, 527
  see also specific places
NORTHUMBRIA, 510, 525–36
  Alnwick, 534–5
  Bamburgh, 532
  Barnard Castle, 526, 528
  Beamish, 528
  Blanchland, 528
  Cornhill-on-Tweed, 535–6
  Durham (county), 525–8
  Durham (town), 525–6
  Farne Islands, 531
  Hadrian's Wall, 532–3
  Haydon Bridge, 533
  Hexham, 533–4
  Holy Island, 531–2
  Longhorsley, 534
  Newcastle upon Tyne, 529–30
  Northumberland, 530–6
  Tyne and Wear, 528–30
  see also specific places
NORTH YORKSHIRE, 516
  Castle Howard, 516
  Harrogate, 517–19
  Hawes, 522–3
  Helmsley, 519–20
  Moors and Dales, 519–23
  Ripon, 520–2
  Thirsk, 522
  York, 510–16
  see also specific places
NORWICH, 456–60
accommodations:
  Embassy Lansdowne Hotel (*B*), 459
  Hotel Nelson (*M*), 459

Norwich (cont'd)
  Maids Head Hotel (B–M/B&B), 458
  Post House Hotel (M), 458–9
  restaurants:
    Adlard's (E; English), 459
    Brasted's (E; English), 460
    Green's Seafood Restaurant (M; English), 459
    Marco's (M; Italian), 459–60
  sights and attractions:
    Mustard Shop, 458
    Norwich Castle, 457
    Norwich Cathedral, 457
    Sainsbury Centre for Visual Arts, 457–8
    U.S. Air Force Memorial, 458
NOTTINGHAM, 476–8
  accommodations:
    Albany Hotel (M), 478
    Nottingham Moat House (M), 478
    Strathdon Thistle Hotel (B), 478
  Shogun (M; Japanese), 478
  sights and attractions:
    Brewhouse Yard Museum, 477
    Museum of Costume and Textiles, 477
    Newstead Abbey, 477
    Nottingham Castle, 477
    Wollaton Hall, 477

OXFORD, 220–30
  accommodations:
    Bath Place Hotel (M), 228
    Cotswold Lodge Hotel (M), 225
    Dial House (B), 226
    Eastgate Hotel (M), 225
    Old Parsonage Hotel (B), 226
    Oxford Moat House (M), 225
    Randolph Hotel (M), 224–5
    Royal Oxford Hotel (M), 225–6
    Studley Priory Hotel, Horton-cum-Studley (M), 226–7
    Welcome Lodge (M), 225
    Weston Manor, Weston-on-the-Green (M), 226
  map, 221
  park and ride, 222
  pubs:
    Bear Inn, 229
    Trout Inn, 229
  restaurants:
    Cherwell Boathouse Restaurant (M; French), 228
    15 North Parade (M–E; French/continental), 228
    Gees (M; French), 228–9
    La Sorbonne (M–E; French/game), 228
    Le Manoir aux Quat' Saisons (E; French), 227
    Restaurant Elizabeth (E; French/continental), 227
    White Hart (M; English/game), 229–30
  shopping, 229
  sights and attractions:
    Addison's Walk, 223
    Carfax Tower, 222
    Christ Church, 223
    Didcot Railway Center, 230
    Magdalen College, 223
    Merton College, 223–4
    New College, 224
    Oxford Story, The, 222–3

Punt Station, 223
Salter's River Thames Services, 224
University College, 224
tours and tourist services, 222

PAINSWICK, 387–8
  The Country Elephant (M; English), 388
  Painswick Hotel (B/B&B), 387–8
  Thorne (M/MAP), 388
PENZANCE, 343–5
  accommodations:
    Abbey Hotel (B), 344
    Georgian House (B), 344
    The Queen's Hotel (B), 343–4
  restaurants:
    Berkeley (M; French), 344–5
    Harris's Restaurant (M; seafood/French), 344
  sights and attractions:
    Minack Theater, Porthcurno, 343
    St. Michael's Mount, 343
PITTVILLE, 388
PLYMOUTH, 327–9
  accommodations:
    Astor Hotel (B), 328
    Duke of Cornwall Hotel (B), 328
    Mayflower Post House (M), 328
    Novotel Plymouth (M), 328–9
    Plymouth Moat House Hotel (M), 328
  restaurants:
    Barbican Wine Lodge (M; fish), 329
    Chez Nous (E; French/fish), 329
    China Garden (B; Chinese), 329
  sights and attractions, 327–8
POLPERRO, 336–7
PORT ISAAC, 352–3
PORTLOE, 339–40
PORTSMOUTH AND SOUTHSEA, 284–9
  accommodations:
    Hospitality Inn (M), 288
    The Old House Hotel (M), 288–9
    The Pendragon (B), 288
  restaurants:
    Bistro Montparnasse (M; French), 288
    The Old House Hotel (M/M; French), 288–9
  sights and attractions:
    Broadlands, 289
    Charles Dickens's Birthplace Museum, 286
    D-Day Museum, 286
    H.M.S. Victory, 285
    Mary Rose, 285
    Portchester Castle, 286
    Royal Naval Museum, 285
    Royal Naval memorial, 286
    Royal Navy Submarine Museum, 286, 288
    Southsea Castle, 286
    Southsea Common, 286

RICHMOND, 258–9
  Kew Rendezvous (M; Chinese), 259
  The Petersham Hotel (M), 258–9
  sights and attractions:
    Ham House, 258
    Richmond Hill, 258
    Richmond Park, 258
    St. Anne's Church, 258
    St. Peter's Church, 258
RIPON, 520–2
  accommodations:
    Ripon Spa Hotel (B), 521–2
    Unicorn Hotel (B/B&B), 522

Ripon (cont'd)
sights and attractions in or near:
Fountains Abbey, 521
Newby Hall, 521
Ripon Cathedral, 520–1
Ripon Prison and Police Museum, 521
Studley Royal, 521
ROYAL TUNBRIDGE WELLS: *see* TUNBRIDGE
WELLS
RUNNYMEDE, 206–7
RYDAL, 501
RYDE, 294–5
RYE AND WINCHELSEA, 263–6
accommodations:
Durrant House Hotel (*B*), 265
The George (*B*), 264
Hope Anchor Hotel (*B*), 264–5
Mermaid Inn (*M*), 264
restaurants:
Flushing Inn (*M;* seafood/French), 265
Landgate Bistro (*M;* fish/game), 266
The Old Vicarage in East Street (*M;* English),
265
sights and attractions:
Lamb House, 264
Rye Museum, 263
St. Mary's Parish Church, 263
Smallhythe Place, 264

SAFFRON WALDEN, 447–8
ST. ALBANS, 233–4
accommodations:
St. Michael's Manor Hotel, St. Albans (*M*), 234
Sopwell House (*M*), 234
sights and attractions:
Cathedral of St. Albans, 233
clock tower, 233
Gorhambury, 233
Mosquito Aircraft Museum, 234
Shaw's Corner, Ayot St. Lawrence, 234
Verulamium Museum, 233
ST. IVES, 350–2
Barbara Hepworth Museum, 351
Garrack Hotel and restaurant (*B/M;* English/
seafood/French), 351–2
Pedn-Olva Hotel (*B*), 351
Porthminster Hotel (*B*), 351
Tregenna Castle Hotel (*B*), 351
ST. JUST-IN-PENWITH, 350
ST. LEONARDS: *see* HASTINGS AND ST.
LEONARDS
ST. MAWES, 340–1
SALISBURY, 356–63
accommodations:
Cathedral Hotel (*B*), 358
Grasmere (*B*), 357
King's Arms Hotel (*B*), 357–8
The New Inn (*B*), 358
Red Lion Hotel (*B*), 358
Rose and Crown (*M*), 357
White Hart (*M*), 357
map, 359
restaurants:
Crustaceans (*M;* seafood), 358
Harper's Restaurant (*B;* international), 360
Haunch of Venison (*M;* English/meats/
game), 360
Silver Plough, Pitton (near Salisbury) (*M;*
English/game/fish), 360
Stones Restaurant, Avebury (*B*), 363

side trips from, 360–1
sights and attractions:
Avebury Manor, 362–3
Avebury Museum, 363
The Great Barn Museum of Wiltshire Rural
Life, 363
Longleat House, 362
Mompesson House, 356
Old Sarum, 360–1
Regimental Museum of the Duke of
Edinburgh's Royal Regiment, 356–7
Salisbury Cathedral, 356–7
Stonehenge, 361–2
Stourhead, 362
tours, 357
Wilton House, Wilton, 361
SANDOWN, 295–6
SCROOBY, 480
SHAFTESBURY, 303–4
SHANKLIN, 295, 296
SHERBORNE, 309–10
SHERWOOD FOREST, 476, 479
SHIPTON-UNDER-WYCHWOOD, 394
SHREWSBURY, 428–9
accommodations:
Lion Hotel (*M*), 429
Prince Rupert Hotel (*B*), 429
sights and attractions:
Clive House Museum, 428
Rowley's House Museum, 428
Shrewsbury Castle, 428
SHROPSHIRE, 428–30
Ironbridge, 429–30
Ludlow, 429
Shrewsbury, 428–9
see also specific places
SOMERSET, 364–72
Caves of Mendip, 371–2
Dunster, 366–7
Exmoor National Park, 365–6
Glastonbury, 368–9
Taunton, 367–8
Wells, 369–71
SOUTHAMPTON, 289–91
accommodations:
Dolphin Hotel (*B*), 290
Polygon Hotel (*M*), 289–90
Post House (*M*), 290
Southampton Moat House (*M*), 290
restaurants:
Geddes (*M;* continental/seafood), 290
Kuti's (*B;* Indian/vegetarian/meats), 290–1
SOUTHSEA, 285
SOUTHWELL, 478–9
STAFFORD, 432–3
STAFFORDSHIRE, 430–4
Lichfield, 433
Stafford, 432–3
Stoke-on-Trent, 430–2
Tutbury, 433–4
see also specific places
STAMFORD, 484
STOKE BRUERNE, 466–7
STOKE-ON-TRENT, 430–2
accommodations and restaurants:
Crown Hotel (*B/B;* English), 432
Haydon House Hotel (*B/M;* English), 432
sights and attractions:
Chatterly Whitfield Mining Museum, 432
Gladstone Pottery Museum, 431

Stoke-onTrent (*cont'd*)
  John Beswick Studios, 431
  Minton Museum, 431–2
  Moorcroft Pottery, 431
  Royal Doulton, 431
  Spode, 431
  Stoke-on-Trent City Museum and Art Gallery, 431
  Wedgwood Visitor Center, 430–1
STOW-ON-THE-WOLD, 396–8
The Fosse Manor Hotel (*B/B&B*), 397–8
The Grapevine Hotel (*B/B&B/MAP/M*; English/French/Italian), 397
Stow Lodge Hotel (*M/B&B*), 397
Wyck Hill House (*E/E*: English), 397
STRATFORD-UPON-AVON, 404–16
accommodations:
  Alveston Manor Hotel (*M*), 411
  Arden Hotel (*M/B&B*), 412
  Dukes (*M*), 412
  Ettington Park Hotel (*M/B&B*), 410
  The Falcon (*M/B&B*), 411–12
  Grosvenor House Hotel (*B/B&B*), 412–13
  Moat House International (*M*), 411
  The Shakespeare (*M*), 410–11
  Stratheden Hotel (*B/B&B*), 413
  The Stratford House (*B/B&B*), 413
  The Swans Nest (*M*), 412
  Victoria Spa Lodge (*B/B&B*), 413
  Welcombe Hotel (*M/B&B*), 410
  White Swan (*M*), 411
getting to, 405
restaurants:
  Black Swan (*B*; pub style), 414
  Box Tree Restaurant (*M*; French/Italian/English), 413
  Da Giovanni (*M*; Italian), 414
  Hussain's (*M*; Indian), 414
  River Terrace Restaurant (*B*; afternoon tea), 413–14
  Shepherd's Garden Restaurant (*M*; English), 414
  Sir Toby's (*M*; vegetarian), 414
  White Swan (*B*; pub style), 415
sights and attractions, 405
  Anne Hathaway's Cottage, 406, 408
  Brass-Rubbing Center, 409
  Hall's Croft, 408
  Harvard House, 409
  Holy Trinity Church, 408
  Mary Arden's House and the Shakespeare Countryside Museum, 408
  New Place/Nash's House, 408
  Royal Shakespeare Company, 409
  Shakespeare's Birthplace, 406
  Stratford-upon-Avon Motor Museum, 409
  Swan Theatre, 409
tourist information, 405–6
tours, 405
see also specific places
STREATLEY-ON-THAMES, 220
SUFFOLK, 450–6
SULGRAVE, 464–5
SURREY, 257–62
  Dorking, 261–2
  Godalming, 261
  Guildford, 260–1
  Haslemere, 259–60
  map, 245
  Richmond, 258–9

Wisley Garden, 261
see also specific places
SUSSEX, 262–82
  Alfriston, 269–70
  Arundel, 277–9
  Battle, 268–9
  Brighton and Hove, 271–7
  Chichester, 279–82
  Hastings and St. Leonard's, 266–8
  Lewes, 269–71
  map, 245
  Rye and Winchelsea, 263–66
  Winchelsea, 263–66
see also specific places
SWINDON, 387

TAUNTON, 367–8
TAW VALLEY, THE, 332
TETBURY, 384–5
THAXTED, 446–7
THIRSK, 522
THORNBURY, 381–2
TINTAGEL, 353
TORQUAY, 322–4
accommodations:
  Homers (*B*), 323
  The Imperial (*M*), 322
  Orestone Manor, Maidencombe (*B*), 323
  Palace (*B*), 322–3
  Palm Court Hotel (*B*), 323
restaurants:
  Mulberry Room (*B*; meats/vegetarian), 323–4
  Remy's (*M*; French), 323
sights and attractions, 322
TOTLAND BAY, 297
TOTNES, 324–5
TRESCO: *see* ISLES OF SCILLY, THE
TRURO, 338–9
TUNBRIDGE WELLS, 255–7
accommodations:
  Calverley Hotel (*B*), 256
  Russell (*B*), 256–7
  Spa Hotel (*M*), 256
  Wellington Hotel (*M*), 256
restaurants:
  Downstairs at Thackeray's (*M*; French), 257
  Thackeray's House (*E*; French), 257
TUTBURY, 433–4
TYNE AND WEAR, 528–30
  Newcastle upon Tyne, 529–30

ULLSWATER, 507–8
UPPER SLAUGHTER, 398–9

VENTNOR, 295

WANSFORD-IN-ENGLAND, 484–5
WAREHAM, 304
WARWICK, 416–19
accommodations:
  Hilton National Hotel (*M*), 418
  Lord Leycester Hotel (*B/B&B*), 418–19
  The Westgate Arms (*B*), 419
Randolph's restaurant (*E*; English), 419
sights and attractions:
  Lord Leycester Hospital, 417–18
  St. John's House, 418
  St. Mary's Church, 417
  Warwick Castle, 416–17
  Warwick Doll Musuem, 418

Warwick (*cont'd*)
Warwickshire Museum, 418
WARWICKSHIRE, 404–22
Coventry, 420–2
Kenilworth, 419–20
Stratford-upon-Avon, 404–16
Warwick, 416–19
see also specific places
WEEDON, 467
WELLS, 369–71
accommodations:
Crown Hotel (*B*), 370
Red Lion Hotel (*B*), 370–1
Star Hotel (*B*), 370
Swan Hotel (*B*), 370
The Bishop's Kitchen (*M;* meats/fish), 371
WEST WYCOMBE, 238–9
WEST YORKSHIRE, 523–5
Haworth, 523–4
Hebden Bridge, 524–5
Linton, 524
see also specific places
WILMCOTE, 415
WILTSHIRE, 356–64
Castle Combe, 363–4
Lacock, 364
Salisbury, 356–9, 361–3
see also specific places
WINCHCOMBE, 390–1
WINCHELSEA: *see* Rye
WINCHESTER, 297–9
accommodations:
Lainston House (*M*), 298
Royal Hotel (*M*), 298–9
Stratton House (*B*), 299
Wessex Hotel (*M*), 298
restaurants:
Brann's (*M;* English), 299
Elizabethan Restaurant (*B–M;* English/French), 299
sights and attractions, 297–8
WINDERMERE, 498–9
WINDSOR, 210–17
accommodations:
Castle Hotel (*E*), 213
Oakley Court Hotel (*E*), 214
Royal Adelaide Hotel (*M*), 214
Sir Christopher Wren's House Hotel (*E*), 213
Ye Harte & Garter Hotel (*M*), 213–14
evening entertainment, 215
restaurants:
Antico (*E;* French/fish), 216
Eton Wine Bar (*M;* French), 216
House on the Bridge (*M;* British/international), 215–16
Montmorency Restaurant (*E;* English), 214–15
Oak Leaf Restaurant (*E;* French), 214
The Orangerie (*E;* French/English/game), 214
sights and attractions in or near:

Eton, 215–16
Eton College, 215
Mapledurham House, 217
Museum of Eton Life, 215
polo matches in
Windsor Great Park, 212
Queen Mary's Dollhouse, 210–11
Queen's Presents and Royal Carriages, exhibition of the, 211
St. George's Chapel, 211
Savill Garden, Windsor Great Park, 216
Stratfield Saye House, 216–17
tours, 212–13
town of Windsor, 212
Valley Gardens, Windsor Great Park, 216
Wellington Country Park, 217
Windsor and Eton Central Railway Station, exhibition at, 212
Windsor Castle, 210
Windsor Safari Park, 216
WOBURN, 240–1
WOODBRIDGE, 454–6
WOODSTOCK, 230–1
WORCESTER, 424–6
WYE VALLEY, 422

YORK, 510–16
accommodations:
Abbots Mews Hotel (*B*), 514
Beechwood Close Hotel (*B/B&B*), 514
Bilbrough Manor (*M/B&B*), 512–13
Cottage Hotel (*B*), 514
Dean Court Hotel (*B–M/B&B*), 513–14
Heworth Court (*B*), 514
Hudson's Hotel (*B/B&B*), 514
The Judges Lodging (*B/B&B*), 513
Middlethorpe Hall Hotel (*E*), 512
Mount Royale Hotel (*M/B&B*), 513
Viking Hotel (*M/B&B*), 513
pubs:
The Black Swan (*B;* pub style), 516
Kings Arms (*B;* pub style), 515
Ye Olde Starre Inne (*B;* pub style), 516
restaurants:
Kites (eclectic), 515
McCoy's at York (*M;* English/vegetarian), 515
19 Grape Lane (*M;* French), 514–15
Tony's Greek Restaurant (*B;* Greek), 515
sights and attractions:
Jorvik Viking Centre, 512
National Railway Museum, 511–12
Theatre Royal, 512
The Treasurer's House, 511
York Castle Museum, 511
York Minster, 510–11
tourist information, 510
YORKSHIRE: 509–25
map, 474–5
see also NORTH YORKSHIRE; WEST YORKSHIRE

Scotland

ABBOTSFORD (House of Sir Walter Scott),
558
ABERDEEN, 651–5
accommodations:
Bucksburn Moat House Hotel (*M*), 652

Caledonian Thistle Hotel (*M*), 651–2
Stakis Tree Tops Hotel (*M*), 652
restaurants:
Atlantis (*E;* seafood), 652
Pittodrie House Hotel, Inverurie (*M;* game/

Aberdeen (*cont'd*)
    seafood), 653
    The Restaurant on the Terrace (*B*; Scottish/
      salmon), 652
    Silver Darling (*E*; seafood), 652–3
sights and attractions in or near:
    Castle Fraser, 653
    Drum Castle, 653
    Dunnottar Castle, 653
    Fyvie Castle, 654
    Grampian Transport Museum, 654–5
    Haddo House, 654
    Kildrummy Castle, 654
    Kineff Old Church, 653
    Muchails Castle, 653
ABERFOYLE, 630
ACHRAY, LOCH, 629
ALFORD, 654–5
ALLOWAY, 561–2
accommodations near:
    Balgarth Hotel (*B&B*), 561–2
    Burns Monument Hotel (*B&B*), 561
sights and attractions:
    Burns Cottage and Museum, 561
    Burns Monument and Gardens, 561
    Land o' Burns Centre, 561
ANSTRUTHER, 610–11
ARBROATH, 641–2
ARDNAMURCHAN PENINSULA, 674–5
ARISAIG, 675
ARMADALE, 682
ARRAN, ISLE OF, 693–4
AVIEMORE, 659–62
accommodations:
    Post House Hotel (*B*), 660
    Stakis Badenoch Hotel (*B*), 660–1
    Stakis Coylumbridge Resort Hotel (*B&B*), 660
    Stakis Four Seasons Hotel (*B&B*), 660
Dalfaber Golf and Country Club restaurant (*B*; Scottish), 661
sights and attractions in or near:
    Cairngorm Chair Lift, 661
    Strathspey Railway, 661–2
AWE, LOCH, 685–6
AYR, 559–61
accommodations:
    Belleisle House Hotel (*B*), 560–1
    Caledonian Hotel (*B*), 560
    The Pickwick Hotel (*B*), 560
    Station Hotel (*B&B*), 560
sights and attractions, 559–60

BALLACHULISH, 676
BALLATER, 648–9
BALLINDALLOCH, 663
BALLOCH, 631
BALMACARA, 678–9
BANCHORY, 649–51
accommodations:
    Banchory Lodge (*B&B*), 651
    Invery House (*M/MAP*), 650
    Raemoir House (*B&B*), 650
    Tor-Na-Coille (*B&B*), 650–1
sights and attractions, 649–50
BEATTOCK, 566
BEN NEVIS (MOUNTAIN), 672–3
BLAIR ATHOLL, 645–6
BORDER COUNTRY, 554–9
    Abbotsford (house of Sir Walter Scott), 558

Dryburgh, 557
Jedburgh, 555
Kelso, 555–7
Melrose, 557–8
Peebles, 558–9
St. Boswells, 557
Traquair House, 558
see also specific places
BRAEMAR, 647–8
BRIDGEND, 698
BROADFORD, 679–80
BRODICK, 694
BUNESSAN, 690–1

CALLANDER, 629–30
CAMPBELTOWN, 696
CASTLE DOUGLAS, 570–1
COMRIE, 639–40
CONNEL, 684
CRAIGNURE, 690
CRAIL, 611–12
CRAMOND, 590
CRIEFF, 638–9
CRINAN, 685–6
CULROSS, 609
CULZEAN CASTLE AND COUNTRY PARK, 561–2

DALKEITH, 608
DERVAIG, 691
DIRLETON, 607–8
DORNIE, 677–8
DOUNE, 604–5
DRUMNADROCHIT, 671
DRYBURGH, 557
DUFFTOWN, 663–4
DUMFRIES, 566–70
accommodations:
    Cairndale Hotel (*B*), 567
    Station Hotel (*B*), 567
    Waverley Hotel (*B&B*), 567–8
restaurants:
    Bruno's (*B*; Italian), 568
    The Dining Room (*M*; Scottish), 568
    Globe Inn (*B*; Scottish), 568
sights and attractions in or near:
    Arbigland Gardens and Cottage, 569
    Burns Mausoleum, 566
    Caelaverock Castle, 569
    Drumlanrig Castle, 569
    Maxwelton House, 569–70
    Robert Burns House, 567
    Ruthwell, 569
    Shambellie House Museum of Costume, 569
    Sweetheart Abbey, 568
tourist information, 567
DUNBLANE, 603–4
DUNDEE, 640–1
DUNFERMLINE, 608–9
DUNKELD, 643–4
DUNVEGAN, 680–1

EDINBURGH, 578–601
accommodations:
    Barnton Thistle Hotel (*M*), 584
    Borthwick Castle, Gorebridge (*D*), 586
    Braid Hills Hotel (*M*), 584–5
    Bruntsfield Hotel (*B–M/B&B*), 584
    Caledonian Hotel (*M*), 581
    Carlton Highland Hotel (*M/B&B*), 582
    Clarendon (*B*), 585

Edinburgh (cont'd)
    Commodore Hotel (B), 584
    Crest Hotel (M), 583
    Dalhousie Castle (D), 585–6
    Dolphinton House Hotel, near West Linton
        (B–M/B&B), 586
    Donmaree Hotel, 583
    Edinburgh Sheraton (E), 581
    Ellersly House (M), 584
    George Hotel, 582
    Hilton National (E), 582–3
    Howard Hotel (M/B&B), 583–4
    Kinh James Thistle Hotel (M), 582
    Mount Royal Hotel (M), 583
    The Nova Hotel (B), 585
    Old Waverley Hotel (B/B&B), 583
    Roxburghe Hotel (M), 581–2
    Royal Terrace Hotel (M), 581
    Teviotdale House (B/B&B), 585
    Thrums Private Hotel (B/B&B), 585
American Express, 580
consulates, 580
dental care, 580
emergencies, 580
excursions from, 601–8
    Dalkeith, 608
    Dirleton, 607–8
    Doune, 604–5
    Dunblane, 603
    Gullane, 606–7
    Hopeton House, 605–6
    Linlithgow, 605
    North Berwick, 606
    Stirling, 601–3
fast facts, 580
festivals, 595–6
getting to and around, 578
hospital, 580
launderette, 580
lost property, 580
map, 579
medical care, 580
nightlife, 599–6
    bars, 599, 601
    films, 601
    pubs, 599–600
    theaters, 600–1
pharmacy, 580
post office, 580
restaurants:
    Alp Horn Restaurant (M; Swiss), 587–8
    Cosmo Ristorante (M–E; Italian), 588
    Cousteau's Bar and Seafood Restaurant (M;
        seafood), 588
    Cramond Inn, Cramond (B–M; Scottish), 590
    Dolphinton House Hotel, near West Linton
        (M; Scottish), 586
    Donmaree Hotel Restaurant (M; Scottish),
        587
    The Dragon's Castle (B–M; Chinese), 588
    Indian Cavalry Club (B; Indian), 589
    L'Auberge (M–E; French/game), 587
    Le Chambertin (M; French), 587
    Martins (M; Scottish), 587
    The Oyster Bar (M; Scottish/seafood), 588
    Pompadour Restaurant (E; Scottish/French),
        586–7
    Skipper's Bistro, Leith, (M; seafood), 589
    Szechuan House (B; continental), 589
    Verandah Tandoori (B; Indian), 588–9

    Vitner's Room, Leith (B–M; Scottish), 589
    Waterfront Wine Bar, Leith (M; salads), 589–9
    Whigman's Wine Cellars (M; seafood), 588
shopping, 596–9
sights and attractions:
    Edinburgh Castle, 590–1
    Lauriston Castle, 595
    National Gallery of Scotland, 593–4
    National Museums of Scotland, 594–5
    New Town, 593
    Palace of Holyroodhouse, 592–3
    Royal Mile, 591–2
    Scotch Whiskey Heritage Center, 595
    Scottish National Gallery of Modern Art, 594
    Scottish National Portrait Gallery, 594
tourist information, 580
tours, 596
ELGIN, 664–6
ELIE, 611
FALKLAND, 609–10
FIFE, 608–14
    Anstruther, 610–11
    Crail, 611–12
    Culross, 609
    Dumfermline, 608–9
    Elie, 611
    Falkland, 609–10
    May, Isle of, 610
    St. Andrew's, 612–14
    see also specific places
FOCHABERS, 664
FORT AUGUSTUS, 671–2
FORT WILLIAM, 672–4
accommodations:
    Alexandra (B), 673–4
    Croit Anna Hotel, The (B), 674
    Inverlochy Castle (D), 673
Factor's House restaurant (M; Scottish), 674
sights and attractions in or near, 672–4
FYVIE, 654

GATEHOUSE-OF-FLEET, 572–3
GIGHA, ISLE OF, 696–7
GLAMIS, 642–3
GLASGOW, 614–28
accommodations:
    The Albany (M), 618
    Babbity Bowster (B), 620–1
    Beacons Hotel (B), 620
    Central Hotel (B), 619–20
    Copthorne Hotel (M), 618–19
    Gleddoch House Hotel, Langbank (M), 621
    Holiday Inn (M), 618
    Hospitality Inn (M), 620
    Kelvin Park Lorne Hotel (B–M), 619
    One Devonshire Gardens (E), 618
    Stakis Grosvenor Hotel (M), 619
    Stakis Pond Hotel (M), 620
    White House Hotel (M), 619
American Express, 616
automobile repair, 616
banks, 616
emergencies, 616
fast facts, 616, 618
fax, 616
gay information, 616
map, 617
medical services, 616
nightlife, 627–8
orientation, 615–16

Glasgow (*cont'd*)
pharmacy, 616
post office, 618
pubs, 627–8
restaurants:
   The Belfry (*B;* pub style), 622–3
   The Buttery (*B–M;* Scottish/seafood), 622
   The Carvery (*B;* buffet), 622
   Colonial Restaurant (*E;* Scottish), 622
   Fountain (*M–E;* English/French), 621
   October, Bearsden (*E;* eclectic), 623
   One Devonshire Gardens (*E;* English), 621
   Rogano (*M;* Scottish/seafood/international),
      621–2
   Ubiquitous Chip (*M;* Scottish), 622
shopping, 626–7
sights and attractions:
   Burrell Collection, 624
   Cathedral of Glasgow, 623
   Glasgow Art Gallery and Museum, 623–4
   Glasgow Green, 624–5
   Haggs Castle, 624
   Hunterian Art Gallery, 625
   Hunterian Museum, 625
   Miss Towards's Tenement House, 625
   Museum of Transport, 625–6
   parks, 626
   People's Palace, 624
   Pollok House, 624
   Provland's Lordship, 624
   Royal Highland Fusiliers Museum, 625
telephones, 618
telex/telegrams, 618
transportation, 616
GLENCOE, 676–7
GLENEAGLES, 637–8
GRAMPIAN REGION, 647–55
Aberdeen, 651–5
Alford, 654–5
Ballater, 648–9
Banchory, 649–51
Braemar, 647–8
Fyvie, 654
Inverurie, 653
Kildrummy, 654
GRANTOWN-ON-SPEY, 662–3
GULLANE, 606–7

HIGHLANDS, 656
map, 658
see also specific places

INNER HEBRIDES, 687–93
Iona, 691–2
Islay, Isle of, 697–8
Jura, Isle of, 698
Mull, 688–91
Staffa, 692–3
see also specific islands
INVERARAY, 687
INVERBEG, 632
INVERNESS, 666–70
accommodations:
   Bunchrew House Hotel and Restaurant (*M*),
      668–9
   Culloden House (*M*), 667–8
   Dunain Park Hotel (*M/B&B*), 668
   Glen Mhor Hotel (*B/B&B*), 669
   Kingsmills Hotel (*M/B&B*), 668
   Station Hotel, The (*M/B&B*), 668

restaurants:
   Brookes Wine Bar (*B;* French), 669–70
   Dickens International Restaurant (*B;* Italian/
      continental/vegetarian), 669
   Stakis Steakhouse (*B;* Scottish), 669
sights and attractions in or near:
   Castle of Inverness, 667
   Craig Phadrig, 666
   Culloden Battlefield, 667
   Eden Court Theater, 666
   Inverness Museum and Art Gallery, 667
INVERURIE, 653
IONA, ISLE OF, 691–2
ISLANDS:
map, 658
see specific islands
ISLAY, ISLE OF, 697–8

JEDBURGH, 555
JURA, ISLE OF, 698

KATRINE, LOCH, 629
KEITH, 664
KELSO, 555–7
   Ednam House Hotel (*B/B&B*), 556
   Marlefield Country House Hotel restaurant (*M;*
      continental), 557
   sights and attractions in or near, 555–6
   Sunlaws House Hotel (*B*), 556–7
KERRERA ISLAND, 682
KILDRUMMY, 654
KILLIN, 646–7
KILMORY, 694
KINGUSSIE, 657, 659
KINTYRE PENINSULA, 695
KIRKCUDBRIGHT, 571–2
KIRRIEMUIR, 642
KYLE OF LOCHALSH, 677–8

LAMLASH, 694
LEITH, 589–9
LINLITHGOW, 605
LOCHABER, 672–4
LOCH LEVEN, 634
LOCKERBIE, 564–5
LOMOND, LOCH, 631–2
LUSS, 632

MAY, ISLE OF, 610
MELROSE, 557–8
MOFFAT, 565–6
MULL, ISLE OF, 688–91
Bunessan, 690–1
Craignure, 690
Dervaig, 690–1
sights and attractions:
   Duart Castle, 689
   Moy Castle, 688–9
   Mull Railway, 689–90
   Old Byre Heritage Centre, 689
   Tobermory Malt Whiskey Distillery, 689
   Torosay Castle, 689
Tiroran, 690–1
Tobermory, 690

NAIRN, 670–1
NESS, LOCH, 671
NEW ABBEY, 568–9
NEWTONMORE, 657

NEWTON STEWART, 573–4
NORTH BERWICK, 606

OBAN, 682–4
accommodations:
  Alexandra (B), 683
  Caledonian Hotel (B), 683
  Great Western Hotel (B), 683
  Isle of Eriska Hotel, Connel (M/B&B), 684
  Knipoch Hotel (B), 683–4
  Lancaster (B/B&B), 683
restaurants:
  Knippoch Hotel Restaurant (M; Scottish/seafood), 684
  McTavish's Kitchens (B; Scottish/continental), 684
sights and attractions in or near, 682
ONICH, 675–6

PEEBLES, 558–9
PERTH, 634–6
accommodations:
  Royal George (B), 635
  Station Hotel (B), 635
sights and attractions, 634–5
  Black Watch Regimental Museum, 634–5
  Branklyn Garden, 635
  Caithness Glass factory, 635
  Fair Maid's House, 635
  John Dewar & Sons, 635
  Kirk of St. John the Baptist, 634
Timothy's restaurant (B; Scottish), 635–6
PITLOCHRY, 644–5
PORT APPIN, 684–5
PORT ASKAIG, 697–8
PORTPATRICK, 574–5
PORTREE, 680
PRESTWICK, 563

RIVER CLYDE, 614–5
ROCKCLIFFE, 571
ROTHES, 664

ST. ANDREW'S, 612–14
accommodations:
  Grange Inn, 614
  The Peat Inn, Cupar (M), 614
  Rufflets Country House Hotel (B), 613–14
  The Rusack's (M), 613
  St. Andrew's Golf Hotel (B), 614
  St. Andrew's Old Course Hotel (D/B&B), 613
sights and attractions:
  Castle of St. Andrew's, 613
  Holy Trinity Church, 612–13
  Royal and Ancient (golf club), 612
  St. Andrew's Cathedral and Priory, 612
  University of St. Andrew's, 612
ST. BOSWELLS, 557
SCONE, 636–7
SKEABOST BRIDGE, 681
SKYE, ISLE OF, 677, 679–81
  Broadford, 679–80
  Dunvegan, 681

Portree, 680
Skeabost Bridge, 681
Sleat, 679
Sligachan, 680
Uig, 680–1
SLEAT, 679
SLEAT PENINSULA, 681–2
SLIGACHAN, 680
SPEAN BRIDGE, 672
SPEYSIDE (SPEY RIVER REGION), 656–66
  Aviemore, 659–62
  Ballindalloch, 663
  Dufftown, 663–4
  Elgin, 664–6
  Fochabers, 664
  Grantown-on-Spey, 662–3
  Keith, 664
  Kingussie, 657, 659
  Rothes, 664
  see also specific places
STAFFA, ISLE OF, 692–3
STIRLING, 601–3
  Park Lodge Hotel (B), 602–3
  The Heritage restaurant (B; French), 603
sights and attractions:
  Bannockburn Heritage Center, 602
  Museum of the Argyll and Sutherland Highlanders, 602
  Stirling Castle, 601–2
STRANRAER, 575–6

TARBART, 695–6
TARBET, 632
TAYSIDE (TAY RIVER REGION), 633–47
  Arbroath, 641–2
  Blair Atholl, 645–6
  Comrie, 639–40
  Crieff, 638–9
  Dundee, 640–1
  Dunkeld, 643–4
  Glamis, 642–3
  Gleneagles, 637–8
  Killin, 646–7
  Kirriemuir, 642
  Loch Leven, 634
  Perth, 634–6
  Scone, 636–7
  see also specific places
TIRORAN, 691
TOBERMORY, 690
TRAQUAIR HOUSE, 558
TROON, 563–4
TROSSACHS, THE, 629–31
TURNBERRY, 562–3

UIG, 680–1

VENNACHAR, LOCH, 629

WHISKEY TRAIL, 663–4
  map, 665
WHITHORN, 574

NOW, SAVE MONEY ON ALL YOUR TRAVELS!
Join Frommer's™ Dollarwise® Travel Club

Saving money while traveling is never a simple matter, which is why the **Dollarwise Travel Club** was formed 31 years ago. Developed in response to requests from Frommer's Travel Guide readers, the Club provides cost-cutting travel strategies, up-to-date travel information, and a sense of community for value-conscious travelers from all over the world.

In keeping with the money-saving concept, the annual membership fee is low —$18 for U.S. residents or $20 for residents of Canada, Mexico, and other countries—and is immediately exceeded by the value of your benefits, which include:

1. Any TWO books listed on the following pages.
2. Plus any ONE Frommer's City Guide.
3. A subscription to our quarterly newspaper, *The Dollarwise Traveler.*
4. A membership card that entitles you to purchase through the Club all Frommer's publications for 33% to 50% off their retail price.

The eight-page **Dollarwise Traveler** tells you about the latest developments in good-value travel worldwide and includes the following columns: **Hospitality Exchange** (for those offering and seeking hospitality in cities all over the world); **Share-a-Trip** (for those looking for travel companions to share costs); and **Readers Ask . . . Readers Reply** (for those with travel questions that other members can answer).

Aside from the Frommer's Guides and the Gault Millau Guides, you can also choose from our Special Editions. These include such titles as **California with Kids** (a compendium of the best of California's accommodations, restaurants, and sightseeing attractions appropriate for those traveling with toddlers through teens); **Candy Apple: New York with Kids** (a spirited guide to the Big Apple by a savvy New York grandmother that's perfect for both visitors and residents); **Caribbean Hideaways** (the 100 most romantic places to stay in the Islands, all rated on ambience, food, sports opportunities, and price); **Honeymoon Destinations** (a guide to planning and choosing just the right destination from hundreds of possibilities in the U.S., Mexico, and the Caribbean); **Marilyn Wood's Wonderful Weekends** (a selection of the best mini-vacations within a 200-mile radius of New York City, including descriptions of country inns and other accommodations, restaurants, picnic spots, sights, and activities); and **Paris Rendez-Vous** (a delightful guide to the best places to meet in Paris whether for power breakfasts or dancing till dawn).

To join this Club, simply send the appropriate membership fee with your name and address to: Frommer's Dollarwise Travel Club, 15 Columbus Circle, New York, NY 10023. Remember to specify which single city guide and which two other guides you wish to receive in your initial package of member's benefits. Or tear out the next page, check off your choices, and send the page to us with your membership fee.

FROMMER BOOKS
PRENTICE HALL PRESS
15 COLUMBUS CIRCLE
NEW YORK, NY 10023
212/373-8125

Date_____

Friends:
Please send me the books checked below.

FROMMER'S™ GUIDES

(Guides to sightseeing and tourist accommodations and facilities from budget to deluxe, with emphasis on the medium-priced.)

☐ Alaska	$14.95	☐ Germany	$14.95
☐ Australia	$14.95	☐ Italy	$14.95
☐ Austria & Hungary	$14.95	☐ Japan & Hong Kong	$14.95
☐ Belgium, Holland & Luxembourg	$14.95	☐ Mid-Atlantic States	$14.95
☐ Bermuda & The Bahamas	$14.95	☐ New England	$14.95
☐ Brazil	$14.95	☐ New York State	$14.95
☐ Canada	$14.95	☐ Northwest	$14.95
☐ Caribbean	$14.95	☐ Portugal, Madeira & the Azores	$14.95
☐ Cruises (incl. Alaska, Carib, Mex, Hawaii, Panama, Canada & US)	$14.95	☐ Skiing Europe	$14.95
☐ California & Las Vegas	$14.95	☐ South Pacific	$14.95
☐ Egypt	$14.95	☐ Southeast Asia	$14.95
☐ England & Scotland	$14.95	☐ Southern Atlantic States	$14.95
☐ Florida	$14.95	☐ Southwest	$14.95
☐ France	$14.95	☐ Switzerland & Liechtenstein	$14.95
		☐ USA	$15.95

FROMMER'S $-A-DAY® GUIDES

(In-depth guides to sightseeing and low-cost tourist accommodations and facilities.)

☐ Europe on $40 a Day	$15.95	☐ New York on $60 a Day	$13.95
☐ Australia on $40 a Day	$13.95	☐ New Zealand on $45 a Day	$13.95
☐ Eastern Europe on $25 a Day	$13.95	☐ Scandinavia on $60 a Day	$13.95
☐ England on $50 a Day	$13.95	☐ Scotland & Wales on $40 a Day	$13.95
☐ Greece on $35 a Day	$13.95	☐ South America on $35 a Day	$13.95
☐ Hawaii on $60 a Day	$13.95	☐ Spain & Morocco on $40 a Day	$13.95
☐ India on $25 a Day	$12.95	☐ Turkey on $30 a Day	$13.95
☐ Ireland on $35 a Day	$13.95	☐ Washington, D.C. & Historic Va. on $40 a Day	$13.95
☐ Israel on $40 a Day	$13.95		
☐ Mexico on $35 a Day	$13.95		

FROMMER'S TOURING GUIDES

(Color illustrated guides that include walking tours, cultural and historic sites, and other vital travel information.)

☐ Amsterdam	$10.95	☐ New York	$10.95
☐ Australia	$9.95	☐ Paris	$8.95
☐ Brazil	$10.95	☐ Rome	$10.95
☐ Egypt	$8.95	☐ Scotland	$9.95
☐ Florence	$8.95	☐ Thailand	$9.95
☐ Hong Kong	$10.95	☐ Turkey	$10.95
☐ London	$8.95	☐ Venice	$8.95

TURN PAGE FOR ADDITONAL BOOKS AND ORDER FORM

0690

FROMMER'S CITY GUIDES·

(Pocket-size guides to sightseeing and tourist accommodations and facilities in all price ranges.)

☐ Amsterdam/Holland	$8.95	☐ Montréal/Québec City	$8.95
☐ Athens	$8.95	☐ New Orleans	$8.95
☐ Atlanta	$8.95	☐ New York	$8.95
☐ Atlantic City/Cape May	$8.95	☐ Orlando	$8.95
☐ Barcelona	$7.95	☐ Paris	$8.95
☐ Belgium	$7.95	☐ Philadelphia	$8.95
☐ Boston	$8.95	☐ Rio	$8.95
☐ Cancún/Cozumel/Yucatán	$8.95	☐ Rome	$8.95
☐ Chicago	$8.95	☐ Salt Lake City	$8.95
☐ Denver/Boulder/Colorado Springs	$7.95	☐ San Diego	$8.95
☐ Dublin/Ireland	$8.95	☐ San Francisco	$8.95
☐ Hawaii	$8.95	☐ Santa Fe/Taos/Albuquerque	$8.95
☐ Hong Kong	$7.95	☐ Seattle/Portland	$7.95
☐ Las Vegas	$8.95	☐ Sydney	$8.95
☐ Lisbon/Madrid/Costa del Sol	$8.95	☐ Tampa/St. Petersburg	$8.95
☐ London	$8.95	☐ Tokyo	$7.95
☐ Los Angeles	$8.95	☐ Toronto	$8.95
☐ Mexico City/Acapulco	$8.95	☐ Vancouver/Victoria	$7.95
☐ Minneapolis/St. Paul	$8.95	☐ Washington, D.C.	$8.95

SPECIAL EDITIONS

☐ Beat the High Cost of Travel	$6.95	☐ Motorist's Phrase Book (Fr/Ger/Sp)	$4.95
☐ Bed & Breakfast—N. America	$11.95	☐ Paris Rendez-Vous	$10.95
☐ California with Kids	$14.95	☐ Swap and Go (Home Exchanging)	$10.95
☐ Caribbean Hideaways	$14.95	☐ The Candy Apple (NY with Kids)	$12.95
☐ Honeymoon Destinations (US, Mex &		☐ Travel Diary and Record Book	$5.95
Carib)	$14.95	☐ Where to Stay USA (From $3 to $30 a	
☐ Manhattan's Outdoor Sculpture	$15.95	night)	$10.95

☐ Marilyn Wood's Wonderful Weekends (CT, DE, MA, NH, NJ, NY, PA, RI, VT) $11.95
☐ The New World of Travel (Annual sourcebook by Arthur Frommer for savvy travelers) $16.95

GAULT MILLAU

(The only guides that distinguish the truly superlative from the merely overrated.)

☐ The Best of Chicago	$15.95	☐ The Best of Los Angeles	$16.95
☐ The Best of France	$16.95	☐ The Best of New England	$15.95
☐ The Best of Hong Kong	$16.95	☐ The Best of New York	$16.95
☐ The Best of Italy	$16.95	☐ The Best of Paris	$16.95
☐ The Best of London	$16.95	☐ The Best of San Francisco	$16.95

☐ The Best of Washington, D.C. $16.95

ORDER NOW!

In U.S. include $2 shipping UPS for 1st book; $1 ea. add'l book. Outside U.S. $3 and $1, respectively.
Allow four to six weeks for delivery in U.S., longer outside U.S.
Enclosed is my check or money order for $_____

NAME _____

ADDRESS _____

CITY _____ STATE _____ ZIP _____

0690